THE FIBRE FIRST DIET

THE FIBRE FIRST DIET

How simply **reordering** your favourite foods effortlessly trims your waistline & wards off disease

Steve Bennett

To Robert Lustig, Ben Bikman
& David Unwin, the innovative
teachers in insulin resistance.

BENNETT FOUNDATION

The Bennett Foundation
www.BennettFoundation.org.uk
Registered in England & Wales
Charity No. 1149712
see page 961

Design & layout by: Theo Johnson

Also by Steve Bennett

Primal Cure
The secret to weight loss and a a healthy long life that government, food and pharmaceutical corporations might not want us to know.

Britain is Sick
One in two people to be diagnosed with cancer, 25% suffer with mental illness and diabetes rates have doubled in 20 years. And is obesity about to bankrupt the NHS?

Fat & Furious
Supported by the evidence of 23 leading medical professionals, the primal way to live healthier for longer.

Primal Gourmet
A simple guide to preparing healthy, nutritionally rich foods, that will help you both look and feel great.

Disclaimer

This book offers a wealth of information and suggestions about food choices, meal sequencing, timing of meals, and some exercise guidance. However, it's important to note that the content within these pages is not intended as professional advice. The views expressed are those of the author and may not fully align with the perspectives of any affiliated organisations.

The information provided should not be considered a substitute for professional medical advice. If you have any health-related questions or concerns, it is crucial to consult with a qualified healthcare professional. For those on prescribed medication, seeking medical counsel is imperative before implementing any ideas or suggestions from this book. If the book's guidance significantly differs from your current lifestyle, it is advisable to discuss its contents with your doctor to determine if it's suitable for you. The author assumes no responsibility for any medical or health consequences that may arise from following the information in this book.

It's also important to clarify that none of the contributors to this book could review it in its entirety prior to publication. Therefore, their individual comments should not be interpreted as endorsements of the book.

Achieving optimal health is a personal journey; what works for one person may not work for another. This book's recommendations are not meant to override your doctor's advice or prescribed medications. If you are considering medication, seeking opinions from multiple medical professionals is always beneficial. You are encouraged to share the insights from this book with your doctor and seek their perspective on its relevance to your health.

THE FIBRE FIRST DIET

Nature's Fibre-Rich Gem with 11g of Dietary Fibre

Contents

Part I: Concealed Wisdom

Part II: The Science

Chapter 6: Unravelling the Tangled Web of Modern Illnesses

Part III: How To Implement

Chapter 11: Nurturing Wellness: from Actions to Habits
page 769

Acknowledgements

Acknowledgements

Writing the *Fibre First* diet wouldn't have been possible without a constellation of remarkable individuals, all united by a shared passion for enhancing global wellbeing. The creation of this book and the evolution of my health owe immense gratitude to these guiding stars.

Dr David Unwin, you're a trailblazer in enhancing our understanding of type 2 diabetes, and your innovative sugar charts have been an invaluable resource. Your significant role at the Public Health Collaboration (PHC) alongside Director Sam Feltham is nothing short of transformative. Sam, your dedication to reshaping our nation's health is commendable. I sincerely appreciate Dr David Jehring, Olivia Khwaja, Graham Phillips, Giles Corby, Dr Joanne McCormack, Ben Rubin, and Paul Whittle for your relentless efforts.

Christian Dailly and Charlie Babb, your expertise sculpted the exercise section of this book, and James Cracknell OBE, your insights on diet, exercise, and mindset are legendary.

Dr Mattie Ferrin and Anna Pinkerton, your wisdom during the pandemic was a beacon of hope. I extend my heartfelt gratitude to Dr Campbell Murdoch for dedicating countless hours, both day and night, to enlighten me about insulin resistance. Your unwavering support and in-depth conversations were crucial in enhancing my understanding of this key health issue.

Dr Vincent (Ben) Bocchicchio, your myth-busting on exercise and diet, especially around BMI, has been enlightening. Patrick McKeown, Jenny Phillips, Dr Emer MacSweeney, Ivor Cummins, Dr Anna Symonds, Dr Nicole Avena, Dr Peter Brukner, Patrick Holford, Dr Aseem Malhotra, Dr Mark Cucuzzella, Dr James DiNicolantonio, Dr Deborah Colson, Dr Dominic D'Agostino, Dr Robert Lustig, Dr James Goolnik, Nutritionist Hannah Richards, Dr Jason Fung, Dr Mary Newport, Professor Tim Noakes, Dr Malcolm Kendrick: your collective wisdom has been a guiding light.

Dr Michael Mosley, your support at Real Food Rocks and your work in opening the world's eyes to intermittent fasting have been groundbreaking. Emma Porter, your culinary talents and countless hours of collaboration have been invaluable. To the Caldesi family, our discussions on low-carb cooking have been both delicious and enlightening.

Tom Watson, your journey and insights into the intersection of health and politics have been invaluable. To the trio of investigative journalists Gary Taubes, Nina Teicholz, and Jerome Burne, your time and contributions to my podcast were invaluable, and along with Dr David Diamond and Dr Eric Berg, your dedication in uncovering the tricks, deceit and campaigns used by the food and pharmaceutical industry will never be forgotten. Lou Walker, your inspiration during lockdown was immeasurable. Dr Steve Witherly, thank you for illuminating the food industry's tactics. Patrick Holden CBE, your insights into soil health and sustainable farming have been eye-opening.

Dr Ian Lake and Jon Furniss, your organisation of our fasting experiments and education on type 1 diabetes have been transformative. A special thanks to Dr Ali Ibrahim for joining me on countless miles of cycling and walking adventures. Our endless discussions about the deceptive food industry, the complexities of eating disorders, and your remarkable collaboration with Dr Agnes Ayton on researching the Western diet have been invaluable and deeply appreciated.

Dr Jen Unwin, Dr Nicole Avena and Dr Vera Tarman, your work on food addiction has been revolutionary and will certainly help shape food education for the future. Dr Dan Maggs and Dr Shan Hussain, your endless hours of sharing knowledge are deeply appreciated.

I want to extend my gratitude to Professor Benjamin Bikman for the exceptional insights you've shared. Your knowledge and passion are truly inspiring. A special thanks to Dr Shawn Baker for your valuable participation in my panel at the PHC conference in 2023: your presence and contributions significantly enriched the event, especially for the debate we held with you and Dr Anthony Chaffee talking on the merits of the Carnivore Diet and thankyou to Dr Chidi and Dr Hayley Wood for your open, honest counter views. My sincere appreciation for speaking at our conference also goes to Dr Georgia Ede, Dr David Cavan, Dr Zsofia Clemens, Professor Roy Taylor, and Dr Bob Gill for their invaluable contributions.

To the Strive for Big Change community, especially Sam and Holly Branson and Noah Devereux, your commitment to helping others is extraordinary. Fellow Strives, many thanks for letting me test sections of this book on you while in Bhutan, especially Susie Ma, Tom Hudson, Antonin de Fougerolles, Felix Stellmaszek, James Benamor, Matt Isaacs, Peter Fioretti, Sara Blakely. To Sir Richard Branson, thank you for enduring hours of conversations around the topic in this book, even though at one point 4,100 metres above sea level, you asked me to give your ears a rest!

To my Blood Sugar Trial research team: Nick Davies, Barry Wiggins, Kim Heighway and her daughter Olivia, Laura Palmer, Brooke Foster-Roantree, Liam Coakes, David Reid, Joshua Morris, and Jake Thompson. Your support and willingness to consume such a diversity of food on our many trials is truly appreciated.

The late Dr Adele Hite, her support and work on low-carbohydrate diet protocols have left an indelible mark. Dr Michael Eades, thank you for clarifying the misconception about calories. Claire Snowdon-Darling, your teachings on menopause and hormones have been enlightening. Dr Boz, your story of reversing your mother's cancer and our chats have been motivating.

Jessie Inchauspé, your presentation at the Goodwood Conference was a masterclass in disease prevention. I was so captivated by your insights that I ordered your book right during the conference. Upon delving into its pages, the clarity and effectiveness of your diagrams struck me, illustrating our shared message on glucose spikes with such precision that I felt compelled to incorporate a similar approach in this book.

To my beloved seven children, this book is a testament to my hope for your healthy lives. My wife, for her unwavering support. My parents, your strength in the face of illness drives my commitment to this message. To my grandchildren, may the wisdom in these pages guide you. And to my late grandmother and Auntie Avis, tragically swept away by cancer in their 50s, you remain in my heart always.

To those whose names have not been individually etched in these pages, please know your influence resonates in every word. This book is a mosaic of contributions from each of you, a testament to our collective mission to reshape health and consciousness. Thank you, from the depths of my heart, for being the architects of this book.

Forward

As founder of the *Institute for Optimum Nutrition* and the *Food for the Brain Foundation*, trainer of thousands of nutritional therapists and author of over 40 books on nutrition and health, one vital factor of our diet is vastly underestimated. That is fibre.

Steve Bennett's thorough, mind-blowing and entertaining book, the *Fibre First* diet, sets the record straight in a way that has the power to totally transform your health. *Fibre First* unveils the three extraordinary roles of fibre. It serves as our body's natural shield, guarding against the onslaught of sugar rushes that can lead to poor health, excess weight, and chronic illness. It also plays the role of a potent gut medicine, forging an impenetrable stronghold for our immune system against the incursion of unforeseen invaders. Finally, fibre acts as a steadfast ally, subtly reining in our appetite and preventing overeating, akin to a non-surgical gastric band. Prepare to explore how fibre adeptly takes on the roles of doctor, chemist, and surgeon.

Welcome to a straightforward idea that will reshape your relationship with food, health, and vitality. This book isn't your typical health guide: it's a revelatory adventure into the power of starting each meal with fibre to transform your life.

In a world where diets are as common as traffic jams, it's time to take a different route. We've all travelled down the dieting motorway, searching for that elusive solution to our health and weight concerns. But what if Steve told you that the answer lies in simply rearranging the items on your dinner plate? In other words, change the order in which you pick them up with your fork.

Amidst the cacophony of nutritional advice and the ever-shifting landscape of diet trends, Steve uncovered a timeless truth: eating your *Fibre First.* It's not a passing trend or a temporary fix; it's an incredibly simple step towards a lifelong journey to better health.

Fibre isn't merely an addition to your meal; it's a transformative element. Your journey begins by uncovering how fibre can make you feel more satiated, content, and in command of your eating habits. Leave behind the world of calorie counting and food restrictions, nourishing your body from within.

But Steve's not merely skimming the surface. This book is your backstage pass to the science behind fibre's remarkable effects on your body. He probes into the intricate workings of your gut, discovering how fibre can support everything from weight management to disease prevention. Armed with this knowledge, you'll make informed choices about your health that will last a lifetime.

We're a nation in which an astounding 62% of the population embarks on a diet each year[1], yet it's clear that traditional diets almost invariably lead to disappointment. We're witnessing a perplexing trend: more people than ever are striving to shed weight and improve their health, but paradoxically, the number of overweight and chronically ill individuals continues to climb.

Why do diets fail? Often, they're premised on the notion of deprivation. But for genuine success, it's time to flip the script: stop giving up and start adding on. This approach isn't about subtracting from your life; it's about enriching it, relishing the foods you love by simply repositioning them on your plate. Embrace the *Fibre First* approach and say goodbye to the era of diets characterised by deprivation. Transform your plate into a canvas of possibility, not a battleground of restriction. Steve will take you on a journey where each bite is a stride toward wellness, unshackled from the spectre of sacrifice. This is more than a diet; it's a delightful synergy with life infused with flavour, freedom, and fulfilment. Welcome to the art of adding goodness.

In the following pages, you'll explore how fibre contributes to weight loss and is a bastion against disease, which foods are high in the right kind – soluble fibre and learn about how a 'super fibre called glucomannan can transform what a meal does to your weight and your appetite. It has been used in Japan for decades to reverse/control diabetes. In the EU, it's recommended for weight loss, blood sugar control, lowering blood fats, good for the gut and bowels. That's how potent increasing your fibre intake can be. You'll discover the profound connections between fibre and the brain, immune system, mind, and microbiome and as an antidote to the modern diet shaped by corporate influences. Steve emphasises the importance of breaking free from siloed thinking and addressing modern illnesses as interconnected challenges throughout this book.

On the path to losing weight and preventing many chronic diseases, you will explore the robust bidirectional relationship between metabolic, neurological, and mental disorders. You'll uncover the potential for reversing mental disorders with metabolic origins by replenishing brain energy through a straightforward transition to fibrous foods.

So fasten your seatbelts as you explore the enchanting world of fibre and its incredible influence on your life and, in the process, how to add years to your life and life to your years.

Patrick Holford BSc, DipION, FBANT, NTCRP
Founder of the Institute for Optimum Nutrition and the Food for the Brain Foundation

Introduction

Welcome to a revolution in eating, where the diet rule book is not just rewritten – it's reinvented. Imagine a world where you're not barricaded by the word 'no', where dietary restrictions don't clip your culinary wings, and where giving up your cherished foods isn't the ticket to a healthier you. This is not your typical diet narrative of cutting out, carving down, and saying farewell to your favourite foods. Instead, I invite you to a table where the mantra is about adding, not subtracting.

Here, we embrace a liberating approach: eating more to weigh less, relishing everything you love while sculpting your best self. Gone are the days of diets that demand deprivation; we're stepping into a new era, backed by groundbreaking science, where your plate is an array of possibilities, not a battleground of restrictions. Welcome to a journey towards wellness without the shadow of sacrifice. This is not just a diet; it's a delicious romance with a life full of flavour, freedom, and fulfilment.

Why is fibre the superhero of this new thinking? It's a secret agent behind three critical missions: supercharging our metabolism, balancing our hormonal harmony, and being the ultimate ally to our gut microbiome. Think of fibre as your personal health wizard, adept at conjuring up hormone balance, tipping the scales in your favour, revitalising your gut, vanquishing various ailments, and guarding against others yet to come. Fibre doesn't just nudge your health in the right direction; it's a full-blown health revolution in every bite!

Now, if you were to close this book right this moment and hit up Google for a quick fibre fact-check, you'd get a sneak peek of its superpowers: a genius at lowering blood sugar levels (a top-tier trick!), a mysterious guest that passes through your body without leaving calorie footprints, a peacekeeper for both constipation and its unruly cousin diarrhoea, a weight-loss cheerleader, and the newest pal of your microbiome. Sure, you'll find claims that fibre is just a feel-full filler on its express journey to the loo (partly true), but that's barely scratching the surface.

Let me start with a little tale from my life. Picture this: just as my seventh child, Louie, was about to enter the world (yes, seven kids are quite the adventure!), I found myself obese and unhealthy as I neared 50 and working with my charity in a village called Wamba, a remote area of Kenya. One morning, inspired to change, I laced up my trainers for a jog. Despite the warnings of my Masai friend Phillip, who was convinced it was too risky because of a herd of elephants that had circled our camp, I went anyway. That day, Phillip prepared a goat for us, and as I habitually trimmed the fat off my portion, he looked puzzled. 'Mr Steve, you run; you cut the fat off my goat to stay a big Western man?'. 'No,' I said, 'I do those things to get a lean, warrior-like physique, just like you and your tribe'. Phillip said, 'Mr Steve, it's not working.'

The moment I returned from Kenya, life threw a curveball. My dad, who's always been my rock, called with news that hit me like a ton of bricks: he'd been diagnosed with type 2 diabetes. And as if that wasn't enough, he added that my mom's Alzheimer's was spiralling downward. It felt like fate had lined up three heavyweight punches: becoming an 'elder' new dad, Phillip's candid wake-up call, and now my parents' health crises. It was like a trio of alarm bells, each ringing louder than the last.

This triple whammy became my catalyst for change. With a determination fuelled by love for my family and a newfound sense of urgency, I stepped back from my business ventures and plunged into health research. What I found was a shocker. My long-standing battle with the bulge wasn't because I wasn't trying hard enough or lacked willpower. It turns out I'd been duped, strung along by misleading health advice from those who saw more pound signs in our sickness than in our health. It was a revelation that changed my life and set me on a mission to rewrite my family's health story.

Since then, I've turned my health around, shedding not just the weight but also the health issues that tagged along. And the most frustrating part? Almost everything I'd been led to believe about diet and health was a fabrication, a narrative conveniently crafted by industry giants more concerned with their profits than my wellbeing.

How do you regain your health and joy and say goodbye to stubborn pounds for good? It begins with a small yet mighty shift: the sequence in which you munch your meals.

But before we get going, let's warm up with seven eye-opening stats that scream for a fresh health playbook. Prepare to be amazed by the shocking truths that will reshape your understanding of health and wellness.

1. Eight of the top ten causes of death in today's modern world are linked to or worsened by unbalanced blood sugar levels.[1]

2. Today's average male in the UK is 23 pounds (10.4 kg) heavier than a male in 1967 [2], despite an explosion in gym memberships. We're running on a treadmill that's going nowhere.

3. The diabetes odometer is ticking up at 2% every year. That's not just a number; it's a wake-up call.

4. Here's a head-scratcher: two-thirds of UK adults are overweight, and a third tip the scales into obesity, yet a whopping 62% have been on a diet in the past year.[3] Talk about a puzzling paradox!

5. According to Cancer Research UK, a staggering 1 in 2 adults now face a showdown with cancer in their lifetime. Rewind a century, and it was a rare uninvited guest.

6. Individuals with blood sugar levels above a certain amount lose 100 days of life per year[4]. Astonishingly, over one million people in the UK are experiencing this reduced lifespan.[5]

7. If heaven forbid, you fall ill (and my mission is to arm you with the tools to sidestep that fate), you'd be hopping onto a not-so-exclusive club, a towering waiting list of over 7 million people in the UK, all queued up for an operation. It's less of a line and more of a small country. If that's not motivation to stay spry and healthy, I don't know what is!

And speaking of the NHS, here's a nugget of truth to chew on: I believe you can't fix the NHS until you first fix health. And you can't fix health until you fix food! It's like trying to patch up a leaky boat without bothering to figure out why it's taking on water.

Back to those seven staggering stats I mentioned. I'm convinced they're almost entirely a diet dilemma. How am I so sure? Picture this: while mingling with tribes in Kenya and Tanzania, chilling with communities in the Arctic, and trekking through northern Siberia, guess what I didn't find? None of those seven issues. Nada. Their secret? A no-nonsense diet of pure, fibre-rich, unadulterated authentic food.

Here's why regular diets often crash and burn: they're obsessed with the calorie-counting circus. As you'll soon discover, this approach is not just a wild goose chase; it's as exciting as watching paint dry and just as impossible to stick to in the long haul. Plus, they're all about dos and don'ts, but never bother with the all-important 'why?'

If you're in the dark about the intricacies of food, your dream weight will always be just that – a dream. In our modern world, where food is no longer a reward for a successful hunt but available at the snap of a finger 24/7, it's no wonder two-thirds of people are carrying extra baggage! But once you get the lowdown on food and nutrients, you'll realise losing weight isn't about denying yourself; it's about relishing the pleasure of food, feasting on real, scrumptious meals, and letting your body naturally take over, melting away any excess body fat.

How to use this book

Why would you need a page on how to use a book? It seems straightforward: open the cover and read from start to finish. However, this book is not your typical read; it's an interactive adventure, offering a transformational experience beyond mere words.

When you first discovered the *Fibre First* diet, you might have wondered about its thickness. That's because we're all uniquely built, and I have tried to cater to different needs and preferences. For some, the insights in chapter 2 about starting your meal with fibre could be all they need to spark a journey toward a healthier life and a trimmer waistline.

Here's where this book differs. After part I, you're encouraged to pause and apply your learning. It's a practical choice that's fitting for many. Yet, as you begin to notice positive changes, perhaps making you do a double-take in the mirror, I hope you're drawn back for more.

In part II, the journey continues for those who crave a deeper understanding, not just the 'what' but the 'how' and 'why'. With promises of mitigating chronic diseases and remedies that seem straight out of a fairy tale, chapter 4 becomes irresistible. As the advantages of adopting a *Fibre First* approach to meals become evident, chapter 7 dishes out tantalising insights into other effective dietary strategies.

Part III: Consider this your reference tool for the future, your family's health encyclopaedia. It is not to be rushed or necessarily read from cover to cover, but it is there when you need more encouragement or motivation. The last chapter ends with tips and tricks to turn your new leanings into automatic habits.

Oh, and speaking of approaches, my strategy throughout this book aims to help you build on what you've learned. Having developed 47 different businesses from the ground up, many of which have failed, I've come to realise that true learning isn't about cramming as much knowledge into your brain as possible. Instead, it's about revisiting and reinforcing key concepts over time, something you'll find me doing within these pages.

Let me share a personal experience. When I was getting ready to cross the Atlantic Ocean on my small boat with my family, I received unexpected news from my insurance company: I needed a license to operate the boat's radio. Sounds essential, right? Well, there was just one tiny hitch, I had absolutely no clue about that piece of equipment on my boat. Those knobs and buttons had always been a mystery to me. So, I enrolled on an intense two-day course in Southampton to learn how to operate the SSB radio, which stands for Single Side Band if my memory serves me right. On the first day, my fellow students looked like radio pros, but I became a radio genius in my hotel room that night. I buried myself in studies, reading, and practising for a solid 12 hours. The next day, while others were sipping tea and chatting away, I was deep in the course materials.

When the test finally arrived, I felt as confident as a pirate with a treasure map. A few days later, the examiner called me with news that left me more elated than a kid in a candy store: I had achieved the highest score he'd ever seen in all his years of teaching.

Fast forward two weeks, and as we set sail on our oceanic crossing, I faced a problem. I couldn't remember how to switch on the radio or tune into frequencies. Panic? Oh, it was nearly a full-blown shipwreck of panic. I frantically searched for the radio manual, but it was nowhere to be found. I, the A-grade student, fiddled and fumbled with the radio for the entire two weeks of our voyage, but it was about as cooperative as a stubborn mule wearing earplugs. We effectively sailed blind without it. My inability to decipher that critical piece of equipment put my family in danger.

The moral of the story? No matter how vital, cramming knowledge often slips through your fingers like a bar of soap in a hot bath. Learning about health is equally important, so this book strategically revisits and reinforces key concepts. Think of it as a delicious meal that you savour multiple times, with each bite building on the last.

Deep understanding is key, especially when you cross paths with sceptics or those mouth-watering food advertisements that test your resolve. Also, you'll undoubtedly meet friends who insist such a small dietary change can't possibly work. You'll sometimes need to swim against the tide, and I want your knowledge to be as rock-solid as a ship's hull. I'm not just here to sprinkle a little knowledge; I want to transform you into an expert, a health captain, a navigator who can steer others toward better health. I want you to be able to spread the word with confidence to your loved ones that something as simple as starting your meal with fibre can be a lifesaver.

As you turn the pages, remember that this book isn't just meant to be read; it's designed to be a transformational interactive experience. It's about seizing control of your health and wellbeing, one fibre-packed bite at a time. And if you ever find yourself sceptical because this approach seems too good to be true, rest assured—the science is real, the results are tangible, and as you will soon uncover, your future health is more malleable than you could ever imagine.

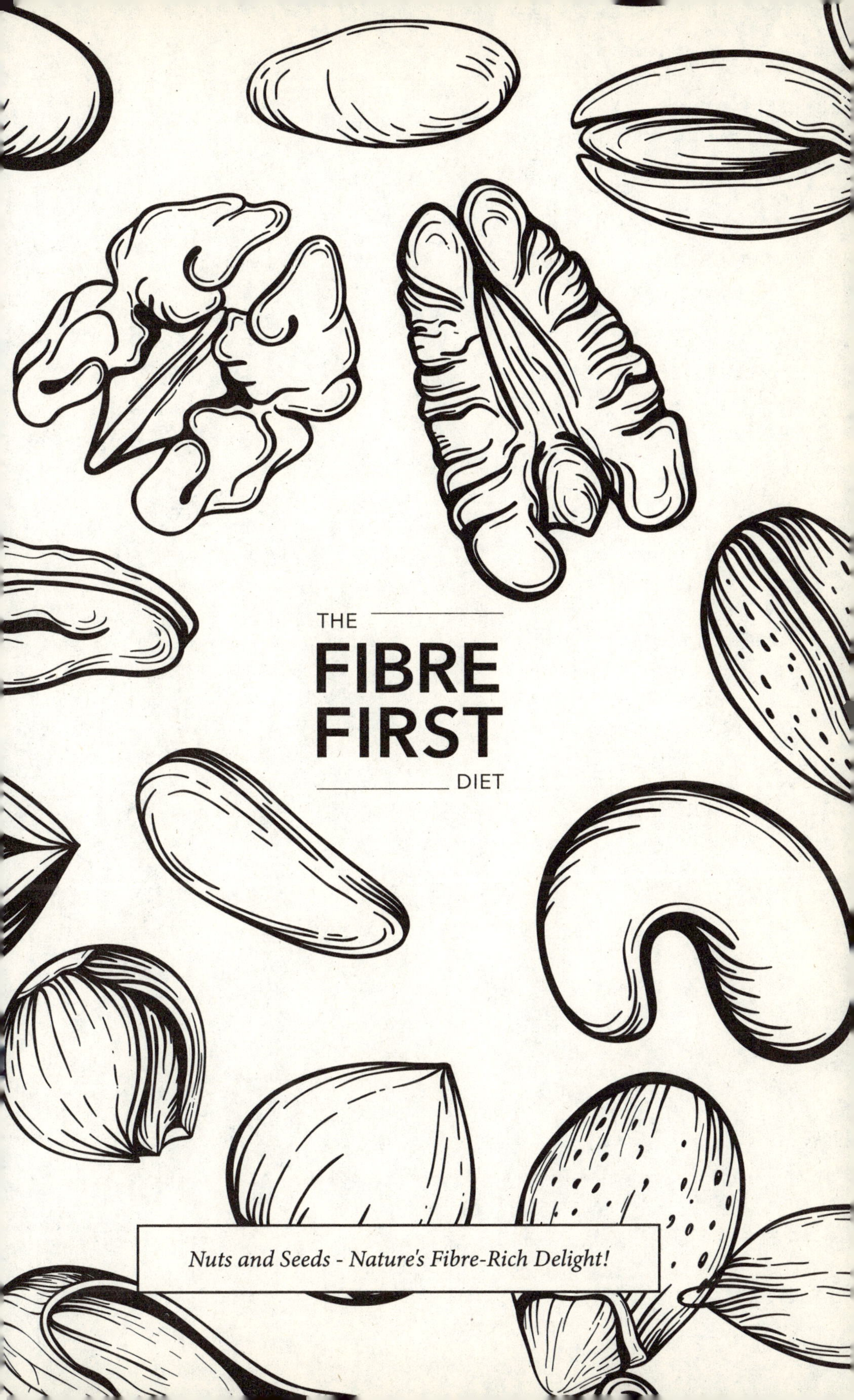

THE
FIBRE FIRST
DIET

Nuts and Seeds - Nature's Fibre-Rich Delight!

Part I

Concealed Wisdom

*****

An introduction to the Fibre First diet. The science of how fibre helps weight loss and reduces the risk of developing many diseases.

Chapter 1

The Secret

Imagine uncovering a secret path to effortlessly shedding weight and embracing a life brimming with health and longevity. The truth is, such a path exists, and within this first chapter, I'm poised to unveil this closely guarded secret to you. More critically, I'll explain why this invaluable knowledge has remained shrouded in mystery. As we progress through subsequent chapters, I'll guide you through the practical steps to integrate this transformative approach into your daily life, opening the door to a healthier, more vibrant future.

Imagine if I had promised readers a healthy, long life 100 years ago: I'd have to invent cures for pneumonia, tuberculosis, diarrhoea, polio, and typhoid. These were the heavy hitters in the early death game. Back then, you either survived or succumbed to sudden illnesses. Fortunately, medical advancements have wiped out these acute diseases, allowing us to breathe easily without their looming threat.

But fast-forward to today, and we're dealing with five totally new adversaries:

- Dementia
- Cancer
- Heart disease
- Diabetes
- Obesity

None of these would have been a concern a century ago, but today, the odds of battling one of these slow, life-altering conditions are sky high. Some might argue that this modern-day health crisis is due to our increased lifespan. However, that's not accurate. Life expectancy is on the decline in both the

UK and America. Shocking, right? We have access to clean water, top-notch healthcare, vaccines, antibiotics, and the elimination of many acute diseases, yet our longevity is slipping!

What if I revealed to you that a male adult living in the UK today is expected to live three years less than his counterpart in the Victorian era of the 1870s?[1] Quite a startling revelation, isn't it? The thought alone ignites a fury within me. How about you? Does it not provoke outrage, knowing our life expectancy has paradoxically regressed despite over a century of medical advancements?

So, what's the secret to a healthier, longer life? To unlock this treasure trove of wellbeing, we must travel back to 1988 when Dr Gerald Reaven from Stanford University shared a profound insight. He explained chronic illnesses aren't isolated; they're interconnected expressions of the same underlying condition. Rather than being labelled with individual ailments like high blood pressure, heart disease, diabetes, or non-alcoholic fatty liver disease (NAFLD), patients should be diagnosed with this shared underlying condition – the one we're about to uncover. For my dad, it unfolded as type 2 diabetes; for my mom, it was Alzheimer's; and for my lovely Auntie Avis, it led to a devastating battle with cancer.

The current approach of tossing pharmaceutical drugs at the pandemic of modern illnesses is faltering, resulting in the NHS and our social care systems teetering on the brink of collapse. The fundamental reason? While effective for acute, short-term diseases that plagued us a century ago, medications can't hold a candle to today's chronic conditions that quietly creep up over time. In the wise words of Bishop Desmond Tutu, 'There comes a point where we need to stop just pulling people out of the river. We must go upstream and find out why they're falling in.' In our modern world, the 'falling in' part is rooted in the one health secret, the underlying cause I'm about to unveil.

Let's rewind a bit to your good old-school biology class, where you might recall the term homeostasis. It's like the body's tightrope act, striving to maintain balance.

Here's the big issue and why many nations worldwide are drowning in a sea of modern-day diseases: when homeostasis gets pushed around too much for too long, things go haywire. It's like a slow, sneaky countdown to the emergence of those pesky chronic illnesses. Here's the scoop (and I'll let you know shortly why it's been a well-kept secret): the one health revelation I'm about to drop is a straightforward biological process connecting the dots between nearly all chronic illnesses.

Picture this: the average adult carries around five litres of blood in their body. (That's the equivalent of eight pints to us older folks!) One of homeostasis's star players, a hormone named insulin, diligently regulates the amount of sugar swimming in those five litres of blood. Do you know the ideal range for your blood sugar? It's a minuscule 4 to 6 millimoles per litre of blood. To put it plainly, that's akin to having just one tiny teaspoon of sugar playfully meandering through the vast network of blood vessels, arteries, veins, and those teeny capillaries included, spanning an impressive 60,000 miles within your body!

Imagine, if you will, a balmy Sunday morning: you're at your favourite café, the sun is peeking through the window, casting a warm glow on your table. You order a cup of tea and reach for the sugar as the steam rises. One teaspoon is all your entire bloodstream would allow, yet you are contemplating adding 2 or 3 to your drink.

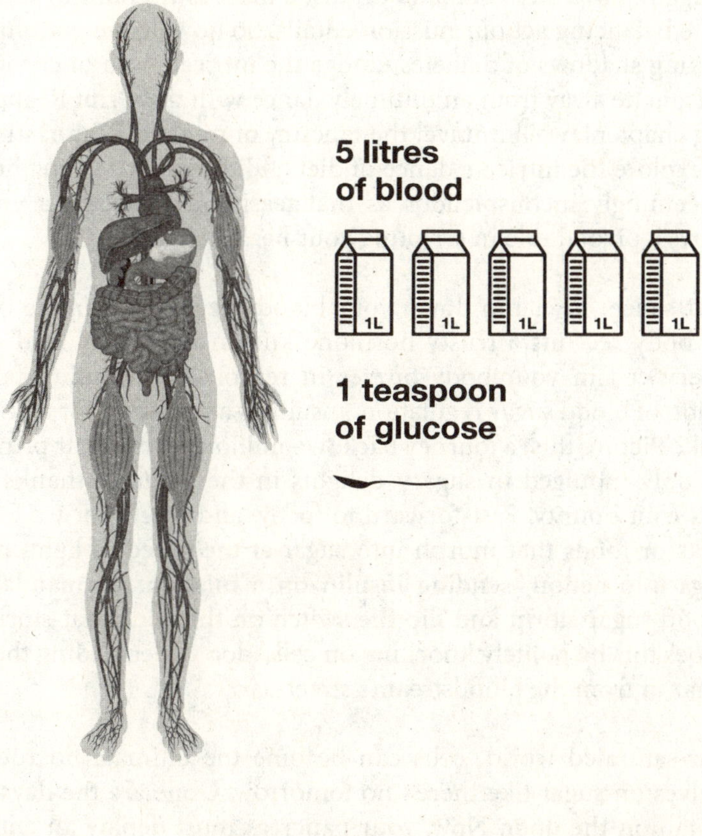

Yes, maintaining the delicate equilibrium of homeostasis, your body tirelessly works to keep to just one lonely teaspoon of sugar frolicking in your entire bloodstream. And remember, that's a bloodstream with the mileage to encircle the Earth more than twice! Homeostasis, in this case, is like a meticulous maître d', ensuring the sugar-level party stays exclusive, with a guest list limited to one teaspoon.

Why all the fuss, you might wonder? Imagine this: a seemingly insignificant half-teaspoon increase in your blood sugar level during a fasting period could tip the scales. Should this subtle shift coincide with a routine check-up, where your GP conducts a simple blood test, the results might earn you the unwelcome label of 'type 2 diabetic'. And in the dire scenario where your blood sugar level surges to a daunting three teaspoons, the consequences can escalate from serious to fatal. It's not merely concerning; it's potentially a matter of life and death.

No more playing with numbers; the equation is starkly simple yet profoundly critical. We're juggling five litres of blood against a mere four grams of sugar, that's the delicate balancing act our mission entails. So how do we gracefully sidestep the lurking shadows of diabetes, dodge the intricate web of chronic illnesses, and pirouette away from an untimely dance with the Grim Reaper? In the following chapters, we'll unravel the tapestry of modern health, stitch by stitch. We'll explore the intricate dance of diet and disease, revealing how something as seemingly inconspicuous as that teaspoon of sugar in your bloodstream plays a pivotal role in scripting your health narrative.

Here's the secret sauce: to clamp down your blood sugar to a humble one teaspoon, your body recruits a trusty hormone known as insulin. And get this: almost every cell in your body buzzes in response to insulin's calls. Beyond its day job of blood sugar regulation, insulin is a promoter for storing fat. Why, you ask? Picture this: a journey back two million years to our primal ancestors, who only indulged in sugary delights in the autumn, thanks to Mother Nature's fruit bounty. Fast-forward to today, and whenever we feast on sugary snacks or foods that morph into sugar at the speed of light, our pancreas springs into action, sending insulin on a mission. Its mandate? To quell the blood sugar storm and flip the switch on the body's fat-storing operations. It does this by politely knocking on cells' doors, persuading them to usher the sugar in from the bloodstream's streets.

In today's sugar-saturated world, cells can become the ultimate hoarders, gorging themselves on sugar like there's no tomorrow. Gone are the days of insulin's gentle tap on the door. Now, your pancreas must deploy an entire insulin army to batter down those doors and cram the sugar inside. This over-the-top insulin rave goes by the moniker 'hyperinsulinemia.' For many, it's been the stealthy custodian of blood sugar levels for decades. But – and it's a colossal 'but' – since insulin's side hustle is to store fat for a rainy day, hyperinsulinemia essentially turns your body into a fat-storing powerhouse. When insulin's rave is in full swing, waving goodbye to those pesky extra pounds becomes a pipe dream, even with the most stringent calorie counting and dietary restrictions.

Now, envisage our primal ancestors, strangers to the woes of insulin resistance. They relished fruit in the autumn, turned the sugar into body fat, and used it as their winter fuel. It was nature's perfect synergy, so harmonious that I've even called insulin the 'Hibernation Hormone'.

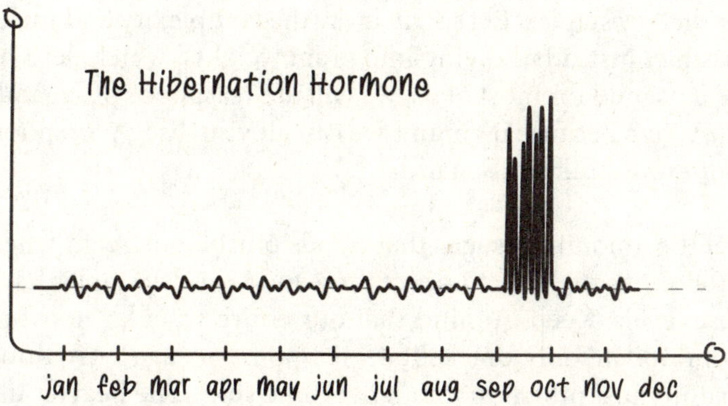

Those brief sugar spikes during a fleeting season didn't throw homeostasis or its trusty companion, insulin, off their game. This delicate balance allowed them to thrive, syncing their survival with the rhythm of the seasons, a masterful dance choreographed by nature itself. They enjoyed a seamless partnership for over two million years. Today, however, sugar is always there, accessible around the clock, every single day. Our culinary landscape has been hijacked, leaving us with what I dub the 'plate of prosperity'.

Recent studies have thrown a glaring spotlight on the grim reality of the 'plate of prosperity'. Astonishingly, a paltry 12% of US adults make the cut as 'metabolically healthy'. In stark terms, this means nearly nine out of every ten adults are wrestling with insulin resistance, and unfortunately, the UK is hot on their heels. So, where's the golden key to unlocking better health? It's in understanding that insulin resistance is predominantly a creature of our modern diet, a diet woefully mismatched with our human blueprint. It is the unseen puppeteer pulling the strings behind the curtain of nearly all chronic diseases, plotting to snatch away your dreams of a brighter, healthier future.

Nowadays, most folks understand that sweets, ice cream, fizzy drinks, cakes, and the like are sugar-loaded. Armed with your newfound understanding of insulin resistance, you can probably fathom how these sugary delights throw a wrench into homeostasis's meticulously calibrated gears. But let's shine the spotlight on a few unsuspecting dietary items, the stealthy agents that are also guilty of fanning the flames of insulin resistance.

Let me hit the pause button on this discourse for a moment. Because you're journeying through this book with me, kudos; you're already taking steps towards boosting your fibre intake, which is fantastic. However, if you're still perched on the fence, what I'm about to share is crucial. Brace yourself because I'm about to unveil a shocking revelation about how much sugar lurks in some of our dietary staples. Let's strip away the complexity and make this as simple as possible. Instead of diving into gram weights, which, let's be honest, can be as clear as mud for most of us, we will use teaspoons of sugar as our measuring stick. Why? Because it's a unit we can all visualise. A teaspoon typically cradles about four grams of sugar.

I'm about to unravel the amount of sugar that floods our bloodstream when we feast on certain foods. It's the direct impact these modern-day staples have on our blood glucose levels. Keep in mind that our entire vascular network is calibrated to accommodate only one solitary teaspoon of sugar. Anything beyond that and insulin must punch in for an overtime shift. The heavier the load, the more daunting the task. As I've mentioned before (and it's worth repeating because it's the crux of our discussion), the insidious, gradual hike in insulin levels over the years sets the stage for a world of health woes.

Prepare to be astounded, as what you're about to learn could very well redefine your relationship with your pantry and, indeed, with your health. And I must give a massive shout-out to my dear friend Dr David Unwin for his groundbreaking work on these eye-opening charts.

Let's start by exploring how certain everyday UK foods impact your blood sugar levels, equating their effects to the amount of teaspoons of sugar straight from a bag.

Food item	Serving	Sugar teaspoon equivalent
Jacket Potato	Large	15
12" Subway (just bread)	150g	15
Orange Juice	250ml	6
Basmati Rice	150g	10
Potato White (boiled)	150g	9.1
French Fries (baked)	150g	7.5
Spaghetti White (boiled)	180g	6.6
Sandwich (just the bread)	60g	7.4

If the sugar content lurking in a humble jacket potato or a seemingly innocent bowl of rice left you in shock, brace yourself for this breakfast bombshell.

Breakfast	Serving	Sugar teaspoon equivalent
Cornflakes	30g*	8.4
Coco Pops	30g*	7.3
Shredded Wheat	30g*	4.8
Bran Flakes	30g*	4.8
Mini Wheats	30g*	4.4
Oat Porridge	150g	4.4
Special K	30g*	4
Brown Toast	1 slice	3.3

*Serving size as stated on the cereal box

Time to shine a spotlight on what many folks would consider a quintessential 'healthy' British breakfast:

A healthy breakfast: cereal, fruit juice?		
Breakfast	**Serving**	**How does each food affect blood glucose compared with one 4g teaspoon of table sugar?**
Cornflakes	69g	14
Milk in cornflakes	125ml	1
Sugar in cornflakes	1 tsp	1
Apple juice	303ml	8
Total for breakfast: 24 teaspoons of sugar		

Where is the evidence for the above chart? It was the average size portion chosen by ten volunteers in our Blood Sugar Trial that you will learn about in the next chapter. Clearly, a seemingly wholesome British breakfast, an emblem of hearty tradition, can inadvertently set off a blood sugar bomb, equivalent to an astonishing 24 teaspoons of sugar. Surprisingly, some folks might point a finger at the single teaspoon of sugar they stir into their morning coffee or tea, blissfully unaware of the hidden sugar ambush lurking on their plate!

However, imagine this: if you opt for a simple yet satisfying breakfast of eggs, sausage, mushrooms, and bacon, accompanied by a cup of black coffee, tea, or even just water instead of fruit juice, the impact on your blood sugar would be practically zero. Speaking of fruit juices, particularly orange and apple juice. These seemingly innocent morning staples are emerging as prime suspects behind the alarming surge in non-alcoholic fatty liver disease (NAFLD), affecting even the youngest among us, an unprecedented and troubling development. The research by Dr Janet Wojcicki and Dr Melvin Heyman, titled 'Reducing Childhood Obesity by Eliminating 100% Fruit Juice', is an eye-opener and, frankly, a heart-wrenching read, especially for parents.[2]

In a twist that sounds like it's straight out of a sci-fi novel, around a third of Americans are now wrestling with NAFLD. This condition was virtually unheard of a century ago, when the biggest health debate was how to avoid infection. Yet, today, if you're tangled up in the web of insulin resistance, you're staring down a staggering 15 times higher risk of being ensnared by this stealthy disease.[3] NAFLD doesn't just pave the way for a cascade of health complications; it's practically laying out the red carpet for them, all thanks to those once-praised-as-healthy beverages.

Our Blood Sugar Trial research (a tale we'll unfold in the next chapter) shed some light on this dark corner of dietary deceit. When my volunteers swapped their beloved morning brew for a glass of orange juice, their blood sugar levels didn't just rise: they practically rocketed to the moon, painting a picture as dramatic as any blockbuster thriller. Believe it or not, reaching for a can of Coke would have been a slightly less treacherous choice, though let's be clear: it's still not making it to the list of recommended morning rituals!

And wait till you see our research results, where our volunteers swapped out regular rice for cauliflower rice with their curry. It's like avoiding a sugar tsunami equivalent to 10 teaspoons in your bloodstream! Or swap the spaghetti for glucomannan noodles with zero carbohydrates; you dodge a sugary bullet of 6 teaspoons. Don't get me wrong, consumed like a rare celestial event in smaller portions, most of these food staples probably won't turn your body into a battleground. And for you, savvy reader, starting your meals with *Fibre First* as you will soon discover, can dramatically reduce these figures, turning your plate into a fortress of health.

However, for nine out of 10 adults in the modern world, it's a different story. After a short overnight fast, they're bombarded with a breakfast of cereals, orange juice, and toast, followed by a lunchtime sandwich parade and an evening fiesta of pasta, spaghetti, or rice. Insulin has been knocking on their cell doors for so long that many cells have put up a 'Do Not Disturb' sign, ushering in the era of insulin resistance.

And if you're on a quest to shed pounds, remember this: a body jam-packed with insulin is about as good at burning fat as a chocolate teapot is at brewing tea. Insulin's day job? Fat storage. So, trying to burn body fat and lose weight with a bloodstream swimming in insulin is like trying to win a marathon with your shoelaces tied together. It's just not going to happen. In just two generations, the 'plate of prosperity' has nudged whole nations into the realm of insulin resistance, inflating waistlines far and wide.

But the tale of insulin resistance isn't just a saga of expanding waistlines. It's the secret script behind a whole cast of modern ailments: heart disease, stroke, Alzheimer's, certain cancers (especially breast and prostate), fatty liver disease, kidney disease, migraines, gout, osteoarthritis, PCOS, high blood pressure, and a parade of other contemporary maladies. It seems insulin resistance is throwing a party, and unfortunately, everyone's invited.

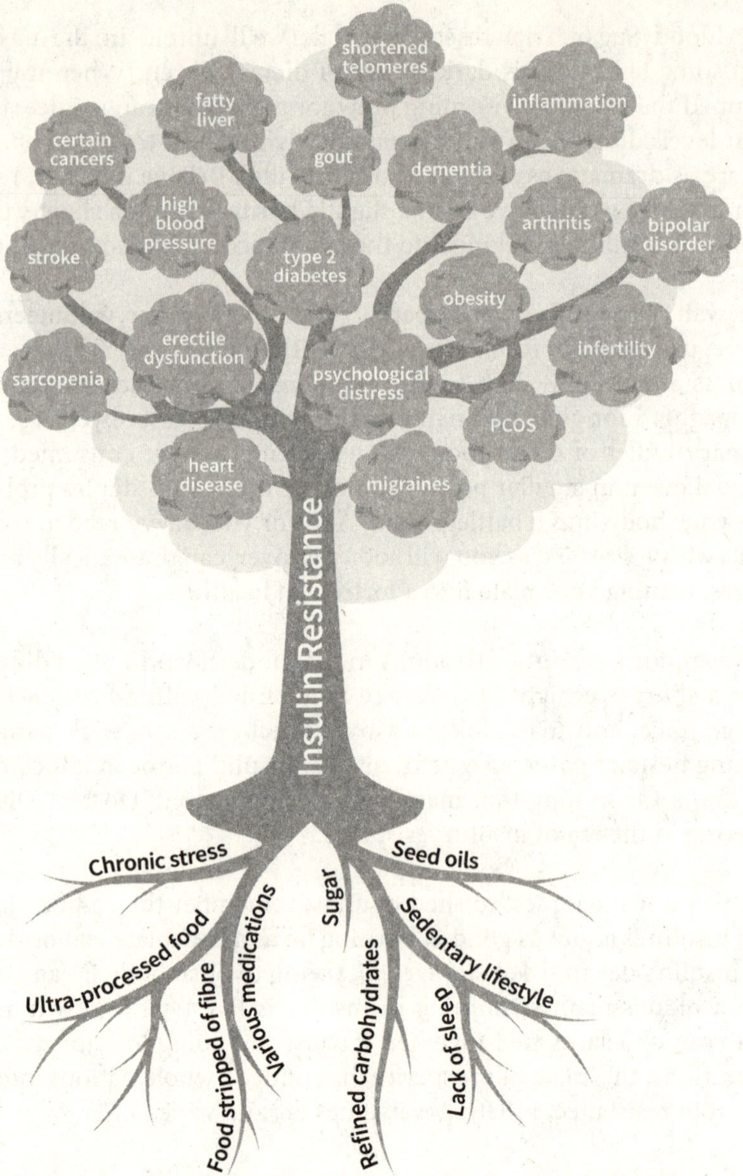

Behold the tree I created to illustrate how insulin resistance is the trunk from which a myriad of diseases branches out. Every ailment on this tree is just a different leaf, fluttering from the same sturdy branches. This tree isn't just a decorative piece for your wall; it's such a precise portrayal that one of the world's top-tier life insurance companies, Swiss Re, has started sharing it with their clients. Now, that's a nod of approval worth noting because, let's face it, a life insurance company is in the business of betting on longevity. So, their endorsement of my tree, which I named the *Tree of Afflictions*, isn't just a pat on the back; it's akin to the holy grail of health affirmations. It's become quite the celebrity in medical circles, with many doctors flaunting it at health conferences and on social media. The word spreads like wildfire, and that, my friends, is part of the great news I will share.

While we're basking in the shade of this insightful tree, it's crucial to acknowledge that the roots of these diseases may not only be nourished by our dietary choices. Other roots, entwined with factors such as stress, lack of exercise, insufficient sleep, and vegetable oils, among a few other culprits, also contribute to this intricate undergrowth. Don't fret; we'll navigate through this thicket and shed light on these mischief-makers later in the book.

You might be wondering just how deep the roots of my tree penetrate. Strap in for some eye-opening statistics. Research has unveiled that insulin resistance multiplies the risk of Alzheimer's by a staggering five times, cancer by up to twelve times, and death from cardiovascular disease by almost six times! That's a 21-fold increase in the odds of being struck by at least one of these three major health storms compared to someone sailing smoothly in the insulin harmony sea. And with Cancer Research dropping the bombshell that 1 in 2 people in the UK today will, at some point, suffer from cancer, the stark reality is that if we don't tackle insulin resistance head-on, our golden years might be anything but golden. What's equally alarming is that if you're caught in the insulin resistance net, sidestepping type 2 diabetes would be like trying to dodge rain in a monsoon – almost impossible.

Tragically, our current healthcare system often misses the forest for the trees, failing to pinpoint or address hyperinsulinemia as a hormonal hullabaloo, unlike how it tackles other hormonal imbalances like those related to the thyroid or cortisol. Instead, we tend to wait until the individual is officially invited to the type 2 diabetes dance before acting, neglecting the silent storm insulin resistance might have been brewing for decades. But here comes the silver lining, emerging gently through the clouds: insulin resistance isn't just a one-way street; it can be both prevented and reversed, often with the grace and ease of a leaf drifting down a gentle stream, sometimes within a few weeks. How, you ask? By swimming upstream against the current of our modern-day diet, making mindful changes, and giving your exercise routine and sleep schedule a slight shake-up.

Yes, by addressing the root causes of insulin resistance, even type 2 diabetes can be flipped on its head within weeks, with many individuals improving their blood sugar levels so significantly that their medication becomes a thing of the past. For others, as they rapidly reverse their insulin resistance, a cascade of benefits follows: blood pressure stabilises, belly fat vanishes, joints rejoice, migraines retreat, and a general sense of wellness takes the stage. In my view, and the eyes of many leading doctors, ignoring insulin resistance as the prime suspect behind the distressing decline in our country's lifespan and health span is nothing short of naive. To me, this oversight is the most glaring misstep of our NHS and the central culprit behind the tragedy of people not living their lives to the fullest.

Hang on a minute, Steve, I hear you say. You earlier said this way of eating doesn't involve giving anything up, just putting *Fibre First*. Depending on where your cells are on their insulin sensitivity pilgrimage, that might be all you need to do. In my Blood Sugar Trial, embracing *Fibre First* was enough for more than half of our participants. Enjoy your rice, pasta, and bread, but ensure fibre takes the lead. However, a slight adjustment in the food line-up might be needed for those who have already travelled further down the insulin resistance path. But hey, we're too early in the book to get bogged down in the nitty-gritty; let's forge ahead.

At this point, you might be scratching your head, pondering, 'If dodging the shadow of chronic illness is as simple as getting a grip on insulin resistance, why hasn't this revelation been shouted from every rooftop?' Here's the most probable culprit: it's an inconvenient truth for the bigwigs of the food and pharmaceutical industries. They're not about to let their multibillion-dollar profits vanish. No, siree, they're clutching this secret tighter than the last biscuit in the tin at a packed tea party! Do you really think they'll willingly abandon snacks, fruit juices, and all those meds designed to patch up the mess they've contributed to? Not a chance; they're guarding this like a magpie with a glinting jewel.

And there you have it, the unveiled secret to robust health in this modern era. An overabundance of carbohydrates and sugars has hijacked our plates and palates, a dietary shift masterminded by the big food conglomerates. They've meticulously stripped fibre from their products, all in the name of profit maximisation (a story we'll delve deeper into later). This ruthless removal of fibre has left us vulnerable, subjecting our bodies to unrestricted sugar and insulin spikes. It's a relentless rollercoaster that, over time, systematically erodes our health, leaving in its wake a trail of distress and disease.

But despair not! For every problem, nature often has a remedy waiting in the wings. And in this case, the hero of our story is fibre, our humble yet powerful ally. So, take a deep breath and prepare for this exciting voyage. Together, we'll explore the multifaceted wonders of fibre, unravel how it wields its magic, and learn how it can not only shield us from the onslaught of modern-day dietary pitfalls but also lead us back to a life brimming with health and vitality.

Chapter 2

The *Fibre First* Diet

As we set foot into the *Fibre First* diet, I want to plant a seed of curiosity right from the outset. The concept I'm about to unfold may seem disarmingly simple, almost implausibly straightforward. You might wonder, 'Why hasn't my GP told me?' Rest assured, the revelation that awaits is no fanciful folklore; it's firmly rooted in the fertile ground of science. Right now, I'll spotlight three pivotal pieces of research, but consider these just a teaser, the appetiser before the main course of knowledge we're about to savour as we journey through the pages of this book.

- In 2015, a Cornell pilot study piqued my interest. It compared the same meal served in different sequences. The findings? They were nothing short of astonishing. Post-meal glucose levels plummeted by an astounding 28% when vegetables (our unsung fibre heroes) took the lead, leaving carbohydrates to close the show.[1]
- Then, as if on cue, researchers in Japan joined this nutritional symphony in 2018. They observed that blood glucose levels took a nosedive when the meal opened with vegetables (a standing ovation for fibre), followed by meat and carbohydrates making a grand finale.[2]
- Fast-forward to 2020, and the chorus grows louder. Another study echoes the earlier findings that eating vegetables (fibre) first, then meat, and finally, carbohydrates, reduces post-meal blood glucose levels.[3] It's as simple as this: starting with a small salad or a serving of broccoli

before diving into your feast – a minor tweak with colossal impact. It's as effortless as changing nothing but the order in which your fork scoops up the food from your plate.

Enter the era of the *Fibre First* diet, a world where this modest nutrient isn't merely a supporting act; it's the headliner, the showstopper. And we're not just dipping our toes in the fibrous waters but plunging in headfirst. Throughout this book, fibre won't merely be in attendance; it will be our North Star.

This simple shift in your meal sequence can work wonders for your health, reaching far beyond mere waistline reductions. It's a shield against a spectrum of diseases, and in some cases, it can even turn the tide, rolling back the waves of certain ailments. Yes, that's not a misprint; a singular, unassuming change may be the only bridge between you and a life teeming with health and vitality.

Imagine a world where this modest tweak in your dietary routine wields the wand of transformation, metamorphosing your physical being. A world where it has the prowess to reverse obesity and type 2 diabetes, dial down inflammation, and significantly trim the risk of heart disease, stroke, and a variety of cancers. Envision a life where the risks of dementia and Alzheimer's retreat into the shadows, where mood disorders like bipolar, anxiety, and depression fade into distant echoes. Picture a life liberated from digestive turmoil, acne, and the relentless throb of migraines.

Visualise a world where the tide of wellness washes over every aspect of life. Women navigate the tempests of menopause with newfound ease, find solace from menstrual woes, and men discover answers to erectile dysfunction. It's a realm where women grappling with polycystic ovary syndrome (PCOS) finally find a solution. These remarkable health transformations, and countless more, are within your grasp simply by rearranging your plate and altering the sequence of your meal. It all springs from one groundbreaking principle: embracing the *Fibre First* diet.

It may not don a cape, but believe me, fibre is every bit the hero. Picture fibre as the vigilant guardian at the club door of your bloodstream, keeping a watchful eye, ensuring that sugar doesn't overstep, turning the party into pandemonium.

As I mentioned earlier, the average adult in Britain today lugs around an extra 23 pounds compared to our counterparts from 1967 years ago. And who's part of the rogue's gallery? Look no further than the titans of the food industry. Soon, we'll study the depths of their manoeuvres, but here's a teaser: a mere ten corporate giants orchestrate the culinary concert that fills the vast majority of our plates. If your meal comes dressed in a vibrant box, packet, or tin, especially if it's flaunting health claims, 'buyer beware' is about to become your mantra. By the close of chapter 4, you'll view these foods in a different light. In their relentless quest for profit, they've been stripping fibre from our food, leaving us with a powerless remote–stuck on an unhealthy channel for far too long.

But fear not! We're setting sail on an exhilarating odyssey that is as delicious as it is transformative. This journey isn't just 'my method.' It's a harmonious assembly of knowledge, a health consortium featuring pearls of wisdom from over 90 distinguished doctors, nutritionists, and wellness maestros. Together, we'll chisel your waistline, bolster your barricades against illness, and uplift your overall health, one revelatory chapter after another.

Now, let's shatter some myths, shall we? It's time to dismantle those long-standing dietary dogmas that have outstayed their welcome (the details of wich we will cover throughout the book):

- 'Our health is predominantly hereditary.' Wrong! It's our diet, our lifestyle and our environment that ultimately shape our health and longevity.
- 'We should eat a balanced diet.' Wrong! If you uncover something bad for your health, you should avoid it. The only place we should occasionally balance is on the bathroom scales!
- 'Never eat red meat or fat as it causes heart conditions.' Wrong! Organic grass-fed meat is one of the healthiest foods we can consume. In fact, it is what we are designed to eat.
- 'Never sunbathe without sun cream as it causes skin cancer.' Yes, it can, but there is a far greater chance of developing other internal cancers, osteoporosis or heart conditions by avoiding the sun.
- 'Eat three meals a day and eat little but often.' Wrong! Eating this way actually triggers disease as our body never goes into repair mode. Intermittent fasting is how we are designed to eat.
- 'Consume 0% or low-fat foods. Wrong! We now understand that quality fats are not our enemy. Food labelled as low-fat or zero-fat is stuffed with sugars to replace the missing fats.
- 'Don't skip meals because your metabolism will slow down.' Wrong! Unless we go four or five days without food, skipping meals actually speeds up our metabolism.
- 'Brown bread, brown rice, and whole grain cereals are all healthy.' Wrong! They are potentially unhealthy foods dressed up in a nutritional outfit. They still turn into sugar in our bodies, and eventually, overconsumption causes insulin resistance.

Have you ever experienced that nagging feeling that something wasn't quite right about conventional wisdom on food and health? My team of experts and I will systematically unravel these misconceptions throughout this book. When you turn the last page, you'll possess the unfiltered truth about health, wellness, and longevity.

It may sound overly simplistic, almost to the point of disbelief. Yet, those erratic blood sugar levels that have been silently accompanying you throughout your life are the covert architects of nearly every modern malady plaguing the Western world. But why have these blood sugar levels been on such a disruptive rollercoaster for the past four to five decades? The answer lies in the grasp of those ten corporate titans, the puppeteers of your dinner plate. They are on an unyielding crusade to strip fibre from our food. This isn't just a whimsical decision – it's a calculated strategy driven by the insatiable desire to extend shelf life, amplify profits, and engineer food that's not only addictive but also quick to consume.

Introducing Fibre: The Misunderstood Member Of The Carbohydrate Family

In the next chapter, we'll delve into the world of carbohydrates and fibre's peculiar place within the carbohydrate clan. It's a rather unfortunate family dynamic because its siblings, sugars, and starches (which are essentially sugar in disguise) are the troublemakers responsible for a great deal of disease, unhappiness, and obesity. Fibre is like the black sheep we want to rescue from its tumultuous family. So, what did my team and I do? A few years back, we decided it was time to release it from its carb-kin and christen it 'Fibrehydrate'. We need your help here: from now on, don't just lump fibre in with other carbohydrates. Yes, it's technically a carbohydrate (which I might occasionally call carbs – it's the latest lingo for it), but it's the only one that doesn't transform into energy in our bodies. It's unique and deserving of its own food category. So, while you'll still hear about proteins, fats, and carbohydrates elsewhere, remember the newsflash: there are now four macronutrients.

What exactly is this mysterious fibre we're talking about? It's the material that sprouts from the earth. It's exclusively found in plants. It's the hidden element that provides plants with their strong framework. Without it, plants would be as stable as a stack of falling dominos. Fibre can be discovered in nearly every corner and crevice of a plant, from its underground roots to its sturdy trunk, lush leaves to juicy fruits, and beyond.

Much like skilled architects, plants employ fibre to construct their botanical infrastructure. This fibrous wonder acts as nature's scaffolding, lending strength and stability to stems, leaves, and roots alike. It's the reinforcing steel bars in the concrete of plant life, ensuring that plants stand tall and proud rather than flopping like overcooked spaghetti.

Within the intricate world of plant anatomy, fibres take centre stage. These elongated cells stretch out with their tapering ends, interlocking like pieces of a puzzle to provide robust support throughout the plant. But plants aren't merely flaunting their upright posture; they're also dishing out a dietary gift to us humans. Fibre, though indigestible, is the unsung hero of our digestive tract.

Hormones – The Caretaker Of Health

Let's get one thing straight from the off: weight loss, disease prevention, and even the reversal of many health issues has nothing to do with counting calories – they're about managing and taming certain hormones. In our case, we'll be using fibre as our trusty tool to rein in insulin, which, as you've already discovered, when overactive, is at the heart of numerous chronic illnesses.

Hormones are like the backstage crew of your body, quietly pulling the strings and sending messages from one part to another. They're like the puppet masters, but because they're not visible, people rarely talk about them in the context of unwanted weight gain or chronic illness.

Consider adrenaline, the hormone responsible for those incredible stories of people lifting cars off trapped individuals. Cars weigh thousands of pounds, and even the strongest human in the world can't come close to deadlifting one, right? So, how can someone perform such extraordinary feats? Adrenaline. I mention it to illustrate the fact that hormones are like the superheroes of your body–incredibly powerful and laser-focused.

Why is this relevant? Well, your brain's primary mission is to ensure your survival, and it's equipped with quite the toolkit for this purpose, including an array of hormones. What's crucial for survival? Food, of course. Your brain functions like an intricate software program driven by hormones that spring into action at the mere hint of food. It's as if these hormones continuously whisper to your brain, 'Eat, eat, eat – it's crucial for survival!' That's why resisting the urge to eat can feel like trying to swim against a formidable tidal wave; it's an instinct ingrained deep within us.

You're the product of two million years of evolution, each generation passing down the instinct to eat as often and as much as possible. If you're carrying excess weight, it's not a personal failure; it's simply your brain adhering to its age-old programming. Indeed, your brain's paramount mission is to safeguard your survival, compelling you to heed its hormone-driven commands to eat every time food comes into view.

This is the initial message I aim to impart; the old joke, 'I am on a seafood diet, I see food, and I eat it,' is, in truth, a human software program that is now outdated.

Now, let's address something I firmly believe: many food companies pose a greater risk than cigarette companies. Smoking is a choice; we don't have to do it. However, eating is a fundamental necessity for survival, and the food industry is aware of that. As we'll uncover extensively in this book, these companies often remove fibre from our food and replace it with addictive substances, all the while manipulating our brains in ways we'll uncover. From my perspective, this practice is morally questionable. Their intentions may not be inherently wicked; they're primarily driven by profit and maximising shareholder returns.

However, one thing is indisputable: they incorporate ingredients, sometimes chemicals, into their products that relentlessly remind our subconscious brains to consume as much as possible to ensure survival. To compound the issue, they strip away the very fibre you'll be reintroducing to align your diet with the human body's needs.

When we consume almost anything from a packet, our bodies are essentially constantly assaulted by corporate tactics. Oh, and while we're on the topic – we'll expand on this in more detail later – when you encounter the term 'natural flavouring,' it might not have been derived from the source you'd assume. Would you believe that 'natural strawberry flavour' in some packaged foods is derived from the gland of a beaver's rear end? It may sound unbelievable, but this is happening, and I'll reveal more surprising facts later.

Unfortunately, all too often, people hastily jump to conclusions when they see someone carrying a bit of extra weight, assuming, 'Oh, he/she must be lazy and doesn't exercise!' It's like an instinctive blame game that's just too convenient. But what about the food industry? They love to chant the mantra of 'it's all about energy in, energy out.' What if I told you that 'Eat Less – Move More' was a narrative the big food companies concocted? What if they preached this while secretly making it nearly impossible for you to follow? It's like they're handing you a puzzle with missing pieces and then blaming you for not completing it! Talk about a clever diversion.

But here's the real twist: what if these food giants not only messed with the composition of their products but also tampered with a specific part of your brain, the limbic area (don't worry, we'll plunge deeper into this later), to ensure that you couldn't simply 'eat less and move more'? Instead, they invested billions in scientific research to make you addicted to their offerings, and you ended up blaming yourself! Sounds like science fiction, right? Surely, humans can't be hacked like computers. And surely big companies have a moral compass? Well, get ready for a reality check.

Now, let's shift gears for a moment and ask, why is it not about counting calories but all about hormones? Because hormones are like the invisible conductors of your body's orchestra, telling you when to eat and when to hit the pause button. These chemical messengers are like the secret agents of your inner world, quietly influencing your every move. But because they're not visible, people often overlook their crucial role in weight management. But let me set the record straight: Being overweight is 100% about hormones. Get ready; we're about to uncover the hormone-driven journey to a healthier you.

These molecules act as your body's private messengers, delivering crucial instructions. They wield so much power that when they knock on a cell's door (let's call it their front door), all other signals are treated like nosy neighbours and get ignored. Hormones are the VIPs of cellular communication, each with its unique role. Ghrelin says, 'Time to eat!' while Leptin chimes in with 'Okay, that's enough!' Then there's our much-discussed Insulin, the guy who insists on storing sugar as body fat, and Glucagon, our hero who encourages burning that stored fat for fuel when blood sugar levels are low. And remember, you can't lose weight without burning body fat. It's like trying to empty a bucket without pouring out the water.

Understanding why and how you eat plays a significant role in achieving lasting weight loss and maintaining good health. Here's a thought: endocrinologists, those hormone aficionados, might hold the key to weight loss and avoiding chronic illnesses more effectively than any dietitian, fitness guru, or your GP. You'd think your doctor would spill the beans on this, right? Unfortunately, in our current healthcare system, doctors aren't well-versed in the most potent preventive medicine: real food. Surprisingly, nutrition is given minimal attention in their five years of medical school curriculum. GPs excel at diagnosing and prescribing meds, but prevention? Not their speciality.

Imagine the NHS saving billions while thwarting heart disease, cancer, diabetes, strokes, Alzheimer's, and even easing depression, anxiety, and stress, all by harnessing nutrition as a formidable form of medicine rather than depending solely on the costly pharmaceutical model. As you'll uncover later, this involves shifting away from dispensing expensive drugs that are often ineffective in treating lifestyle-related illnesses. That's the noble mission we champion at the Public Health Collaboration (PHC) charity, and we invite you to join us in urging your local MP to turn this vision into reality. It's time to cultivate a groundswell of individuals demanding superior health solutions, not just further increasing the profits of the trillion-pound[4] pharmaceutical industry. Regrettably, and perhaps controversially, our GPs have unwittingly become de facto sales agents for the drug industry. We've reached an absurd juncture where the solution to a stone in your shoe is a prescription for painkillers! Apologies for the detour; let's get back to hormones.

Now, let's focus on insulin, the big player who trumps everything. To shed that unwanted body fat, the kind you've accumulated thanks to your brain doing its job (no fault of yours), we need to dial down the 'store body fat' hormone and instead crank up the 'burn stored body fat' hormone!

Let's learn even more about hormones. They're like chemical text messages sent from one part of your body to another. Picture them as keys (the hormones) that unlock specific locks (receptors) on cell surfaces.

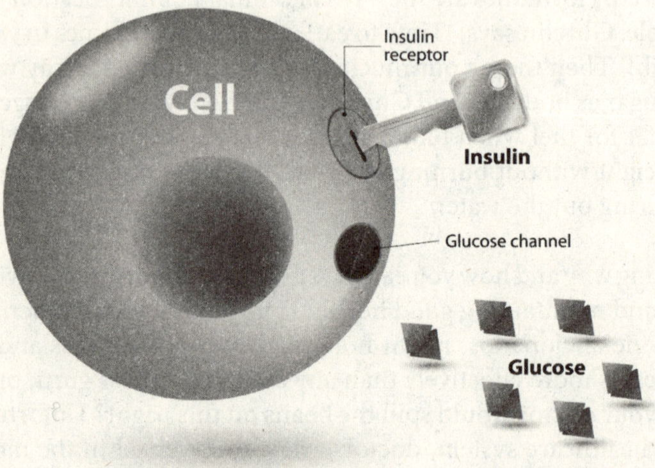

These messages range from 'time to sleep' (melatonin) to 'store sugar as body fat' (insulin) to 'convert stored fat into energy' (glucagon). Then there's cortisol, your stress hormone (we'll dig into that shortly), and the superstar adrenaline, which revs up instant energy, ready to sprint from a lion or fight a large mammal.

As a nation, we're breaking a sweat like we're in a never-ending workout, but our health is slipping through our fingers like a greased watermelon. The secret to better health? Well, it's as simple as mastering your hormones, and you now know which hormone is in the spotlight: insulin. So, prepare for an adventure where you begin to rein in insulin, steering yourself towards better health and happiness. You're about to discover how the magic of fibre can calm down the rollercoaster ride of sugar and keep insulin in check.

The essence of this book revolves around the crucial understanding that our blood can't accommodate excessive sugar; to regulate it, the hormone insulin is called into action. However, an excess of insulin, persisting over many years, is what fuels a great deal of suffering. As Dr David Perlmutter articulates in his book *Drop Acid*, 'One can make the argument that fully nine of the ten leading causes of death in the United States are connected to or exacerbated by dysregulated blood sugar – all of them except accidents!'.

By making fibre the first act in your meals, you harness its incredible power to tame your blood sugar spikes, thereby minimising the need for insulin in your bloodstream. By doing so, you could unlock an abundance of health benefits. And trust me, the list you're about to see is just the tip of the iceberg:

- Prevent and Reverse Type 2 Diabetes
- Prevent and Reverse High Blood Pressure
- Help Prevent Certain Cancers
- Help Prevent and Reverse PCOS
- Reverse Erectile Dysfunction
- Weight Loss - For Sure
- Never Feeling Hungry Again
- Improved Mood
- Reduced Anxiety
- Reduce Depression
- Reduce Osteoarthritis Pain
- Reverse Bipolar Disease
- Reduced Severity and Frequency of Headaches
- Fix Gut Issues
- Reduce Menopause Symptoms
- Increase Fertility in Men and Women
- Better Skin
- Reduced Acne
- Reduced Chronic Pain
- Fewer Colds and Coughs
- Fewer Infections
- Better Sleep
- Complete Removal of IBS
- Improved Learning Capacity, Especially If You Are Younger
- Less Dental Work

This impressive array of benefits goes beyond physical health; it's about enhancing your life in every dimension. It's clear that the power of fibre is not just in what it adds to your diet but in how it transforms your entire wellbeing.

Getting To Know Insulin In A Whole New Light

This message is paramount, so much so that I feel compelled to reiterate it. It's a truth that, if known earlier, could likely have prevented my dad's diabetes, my mom's Alzheimer's, and my auntie's cancer. So, I'll state it once more clearly and urgently. When carbohydrates and sugars unceremoniously barge into your bloodstream, your body immediately unleashes a deluge of insulin. Point the finger at modern diets brimming with sugar and stripped of fibre – it's a formula for calamity. Our bodies weren't designed to withstand such an insulin deluge, and certainly not in the absence of fibre. The consequence? A relentless surge in weight and a spiral into metabolic turmoil.

Meet Dr Jason Fung, one of the world's most esteemed doctors, whose books have sold millions and ignited a revolution in the realm of health and weight management. He told me, 'I can make anyone fat.' Intrigued, I asked, 'How?' His answer didn't just raise my eyebrows; it blew my mind, 'Prescribe them insulin. Whether they're the epitome of willpower or fitness fanatics, it doesn't matter what's on their plate; they'll get fat, no doubt.' It's like a diabolical equation: add enough insulin, give it time, and voilà, unwanted weight gain. High insulin levels have been the arch-nemesis in the obesity saga since corporations started meddling with food; it's just we didn't realise it.

Obese individuals churn out more insulin than their lean counterparts. And if you thought a post-meal insulin drop was a guarantee, think again – in obese individuals, those levels stubbornly remain sky-high. This isn't some wild conspiracy theory; it's solid, science-backed truth. But hold on to your seat because here's a shocker: the latest research suggests that overweight individuals always experience a dip in insulin levels before shedding those pounds. Forget about willpower, calorie counting, or sweating it out at the gym – it all boils down to bringing down that insulin. And that, my friends, is the magic formula. The only way to bid farewell to those unwanted pounds and unveil the healthier, happier you is by causing a nosedive in your insulin levels. It's as clear as day: plummeting insulin levels are the prelude to weight loss. Let me repeat it for emphasis: before you can even think about waving goodbye to those extra inches, your insulin levels must take a dive.

A reduction in insulin ALWAYS precedes weight loss [6]

Allow me to tell a little more about the incredible Dr David Unwin, a cherished friend of mine. David has been serving as a GP in Southport for over three decades, accumulating a wealth of experience. What sets him apart is his unwavering fascination with the remarkable ability of individuals to achieve and maintain good health without relying solely on medications. He was honoured with the prestigious NHS Innovator of the Year award in 2016 for his pioneering efforts. He proudly holds the distinction of being a founding member of the PHC. What truly lights up David's professional journey is his passion for assisting patients in making transformative lifestyle changes that often lead to reducing or even discontinuing their reliance on medication.

Dr David Unwin
What does insulin do? It's a hormone that we produce that helps us deal with sugar. The pancreas gland produces it, and it deals with sugar. It pushes sugar from the bloodstream into cells, where you need sugar in your muscles for energy. But if you eat more sugar than you need for energy, insulin pushes excess sugar into your belly fat or liver.

But what happens if that insulin does not work very well? Blood sugar levels, known as glucose, start rising, and you end up with a higher blood sugar level. High blood sugar levels are dangerous; over time, they attach to proteins and start damaging your circulation. It damages the small circulation in your eyes and your kidneys and, over time, damages the larger circulation in your arteries. And that's why we worry about hearts and strokes with diabetes. That's why high glucose levels over time isn't good news because it almost always ages your body.

Here's where the problem deepens. When we repeatedly despatch lots of insulin to our fat cells, they get overcrowded and start becoming resistant to their demand to allow sugar in. It's a bit like working in a noisy office; at first you notice the noise, but over time, you learn to tune it out.

For those who enjoy too frequent meals, skimp on fibre, and feast on processed foods, the result can be both hyperglycaemia (chronically high blood sugar) and hyperinsulinemia (high insulin levels). These conditions can pave the path to type 2 diabetes, where our cells decide to go on strike and stop responding to insulin's requests.

By the way, don't confuse this with type 1 diabetes. In type 1 diabetes, the body stops producing insulin, so sufferers often must play the role of both chef and waiter, injecting themselves with insulin. But for those dealing with type 2 diabetes, as I will explain shortly, there's hope on the horizon. While the medical world once considered it a lifelong sentence, folks across Great Britain are putting their type 2 diabetes into remission. How, you ask? By amping up their fibre intake, saying farewell to excess carbohydrates and sugars, and embracing a more primal way of living.

I can't promise that these approaches will reverse type 2 diabetes for everyone, as it varies from person to person. However, for those who diligently follow a high-fibre, low-carb eating plan – focusing on real, natural foods (we'll go into this later) – and occasionally dabble in intermittent fasting (which we'll also explore), the chances of reversing type 2 diabetes are pretty darn good.

Before we point fingers at insulin, remember that this hormone is just doing its job as nature intended. When we eat healthily, we shouldn't see insulin as a prison officer escorting the 'sugar villain' to the fat cells. Instead, let's view insulin as an usher in a church, gracefully escorting energy to every seat.

It is essential to maintain fibre in our diet and reintroduce it when food producers have unjustly removed it. Paired with a reduced intake of carbohydrates, our insulin system operates like a well-oiled machine, echoing the efficiency honed through millions of years of human evolution. However, consistently surrendering to a highly processed modern diet, akin to fuelling a precision-engineered Harley Davidson with diesel, triggers chaos in our metabolic engine, leading to a cascade of health issues.

Let's break it down into a 3-step process:

1. **Insufficient Fibre + High-Carb/High-Sugar Meal:** This combination leads to elevated blood sugar and a subsequent insulin rush.
2. **Excessive Insulin:** Over time, this abundance of insulin fosters insulin resistance.
3. **Insulin Resistance:** This condition paves the way for type 2 diabetes and a host of other serious health concerns.

Good health might as well be whispering in our ear, 'Hey, overload on carbohydrates without the balancing act of fibre, and I'm taking a hike!' This is a not-so-subtle nudge, reminding us that our dietary choices are pivotal in keeping the gears of our metabolic engine running without a hitch.

Dr David Unwin
'Insulin is a boss hormone. It is designed to get rid of sugar because sugar in the blood is dangerous. So, in a sugary environment, insulin switches off your ability to burn fat. Our body is like a hybrid car. It can either burn sugar or fat, but not at the same time. Before I knew all this, I used to eat biscuits all day. I wouldn't be able to burn fat. My own insulin had switched off my ability to burn fat. And in a way that would explain very interestingly why, while I was eating biscuits all day, I was continually hungry, yet I had a big tummy. I had fuel there, but could not reach it. Because I was in a sugary environment, that same sugar stopped me from burning my own belly fat. Now I have gone low-carb, I am quite slim, simply because I can now burn my own body fat.'

Fibre First, The Game Changer

Enough with the suspense. It's time to spill the beans on taming sugar spikes and insulin, and guess what? It's easier than you think! Picture this: your plate is like a stage, and the spotlight is on one key player – fibre. But it's not just about having it on your plate; it's about giving it the star-studded entrance it deserves. For many, simply putting *Fibre First* is the magic trick to help tame sugar spikes. That's right; rearranging your plate and starting with fibre can be a game-changer.

And for those feeling adventurous and looking to take it to the next level, consider step two: venture into the world of real, wholesome foods. These foods are your trusty sidekicks in the quest for better health. But remember, for many, step one alone can work wonders.

We're about to dig deep into the world of curtailing sugar spikes and insulin, and the spotlight is firmly on fibre. The stage is set, and the show is about to begin! But before we get into the nitty-gritty of fibre, let's pause for a moment and ask ourselves an important question: why have we relied so heavily on our healthcare system to manage chronic illnesses? Is it because we've come to accept these conditions as an unavoidable part of life? Well, let me clarify – they're not.

My mission is clear: I'm here to empower everyone, regardless of their financial circumstances. I also hold a deep commitment to preserving our planet for future generations. As we travel the pathway towards better health through simple yet potent changes in our diet, we're safeguarding your wellbeing and looking out for your financial health and the future of our beloved Earth. And the best part? I'm here to provide you with practical solutions. Take, for instance, our website, Health Results, where you'll discover a wealth of information. We've also developed a free app of the same name, offering hundreds of delectable healthy recipes you can easily follow. Our ACE section, which stands for Affordable, Convenient, and Easy, is a dedicated space where you'll find fibre-rich, healthy meals made from ingredients that won't break the bank, each costing under £2. We've even created video tutorials to make cooking in your kitchen effortless and enjoyable.

I embarked on this culinary adventure because I was tired of hearing people say that eating healthily is expensive. Let me set the record straight once and for all: healthy eating can be affordable and accessible for everyone. Let's finally roll up our sleeves and dig into the incredible world of fibre, armed with the knowledge that improving your health doesn't have to break the bank.

A Tanzanian Tale Of Laughter And Gut Insights

During one of my visits to Tanzania, I couldn't help but wonder about the secret behind the locals' lean and healthy appearances. Was it as simple as eating less, or did their lifestyle hold more clues to keeping obesity rates at bay compared to what I was witnessing in the UK? Oh, and by the way, I was obese myself at this time. My curiosity was piqued, and I looked deeper into their world, seeking hidden insights.

To my surprise, the concept of an alternative way of life seemed foreign to them. Determined to unravel this mystery, I took a bold step. I presented a classroom of Tanzanian children with photos of overweight British individuals (type 'fat British people' into Google Images to get an idea of what I showed these kids). Their response was nothing short of astonishing; they erupted into laughter and gleefully darted around the classroom, puffing out their bellies as far as they could!

Later that evening, back at my hotel, I stumbled upon an eye-opening article titled, 'Impact of Diet in Shaping Gut Microbiota Revealed by a Comparative Study in Children from Europe and Rural Africa'.[7] This report outlined its method:' In this work, we compared the faecal microbiota of European children (EU) and that of children from a rural African village of Burkina

Faso (BF), where the diet, high in fibre content, is similar to that of early human settlements at the time of the birth of agriculture.'

The results of this study were nothing short of mind-boggling. Here's a tantalising titbit from their conclusion: 'Both in the Western world and in developing countries diets rich in fat, protein, and sugar, together with reduced intake of unabsorbable fibres, are associated with a rapid increase in the incidence of non-infectious intestinal diseases.' Before you think about saying farewell to fats and proteins, leaving yourself with a rather bland menu, let me clarify what this report truly suggests. It's not about giving up fats and proteins; it's about recognising the problems posed by diets overloaded with sugar-packed carbohydrates, especially when fibre is nowhere to be found.

> **Dr Shan Hussain**
> *'How important is fibre to our health? According to The American Journal of Clinical Nutrition, consuming 35g of fibre was associated with a lower risk of cardiovascular disease by as much as 54% and death from all causes by 37%.'*

The Clogging Effect

Imagine adding a 300-calorie, fibre-rich entrée to your meal. Here's where the magic unfolds. Picture fibre as a meticulous gatekeeper in your stomach, similar to how losing hair in a shower slows water flow or food debris in a sink plug delays water drainage. This analogy helps illustrate fibre's role in your digestive system. It acts as a natural slow-down mechanism, making you feel fuller for longer and aiding in gradual nutrient absorption. It's a powerful ally in managing hunger and supporting digestive health.

The pylorus is the opening from the stomach; it lies deep inside your stomach, just before your mushed-up food enters the intestines. Visualise the pylorus as a plug or a sieve at the bottom of your stomach. Much like a valve, its primary role is to regulate the flow of your pulverised food from the stomach into the intestines. Here's where the game changes: when you kick-start your meal with fibre, it's akin to inserting a cork into this pylorus, deliberately decelerating the release of the remaining food into your intestines.

This seemingly simple act wields profound effects. Remember our earlier discussion on how insulin's primary role is reducing blood sugar levels? When you introduce fibre as a plug for your pylorus, subsequently slowing down the release of sugar into your bloodstream, something truly remarkable unfolds, you require substantially less insulin.

With the *Fibre First* diet approach, you will most likely add more calories and more deliciousness to your meal, yet your body will absorb fewer of those calories because the fibre controls the release. How awesome is that? You can savour your favourite dishes, enjoy every bite, and still shed those unwanted pounds while keeping those pesky diseases at bay.

This insight comes from my good friend Robert Lustig, shared during an episode of the Andrew Huberman podcast titled *'How Sugar & Processed Foods Impact Your Health.'*

> *'By the way, fibres, sort of the key to the kingdom in the [health] story, form a gel on the inside of your intestine. The insoluble fibre, the cellulose, forms a fishnet, if you will, a latticework on the inside of your duodenum. The soluble fibre, which is globular, plugs the holes in that fishnet together and forms a secondary barrier. You can actually see it on electron microscopy as a whitish gel that prevents absorption'.*

Biology Behind the Magic

Within your body's intricate digestive system, the pylorus acts as a gatekeeper, regulating the flow of food between two vital areas. Imagine it as a pivotal checkpoint in your digestive journey. On one side, you have the stomach, a dedicated mechanical and chemical digestion reservoir. Here, your food undergoes the initial stages of breakdown thanks to powerful stomach acids and churning motions.

On the other side lie the intestines, responsible for absorbing nutrients from the digested food. The transition from the stomach to the intestines is crucial, and the pylorus plays an essential role in managing this process. Its mission is to prevent large, undigested materials from prematurely entering the duodenum, which marks the entry point to the small intestines.

Blood Sugar Trial

I am about to unveil our methodically orchestrated 7-day Blood Sugar Trial, a fascinating experiment by ten heroic volunteers. These participants, our keen metabolic detectives, set out to provide an authentic, real-time insight into the complex interplay of blood glucose in reaction to a meticulously selected array of meals.

While the annals of nutritional research are rich with praises for a fibre-rich diet, we cast a slightly sceptical eye on these literary laurels, subscribing to the notion that seeing is, after all, believing. Armed with continuous glucose monitors (CGMs), our participants set sail on this investigative voyage, providing a raw, unfiltered narrative of their blood sugar responses to an array of breakfasts, lunches, and self-documented dinners. Our guidelines were straightforward: participants arrived at the breakfast trial fasted, snacks were banished between breakfast and lunch, and the same no-grazing policy was applied for four hours post-lunch. Evenings, however, were a different kettle of fish, with participants free to satisfy their culinary whims. Conveniently, our participants' shared workplace made rule adherence as smooth as a well-oiled machine.

We aimed to mirror everyday life's unpredictable ebb and flow. Many studies dictate portion sizes and meal compositions with military precision, but let's be honest, does that really mirror the glorious messiness of real life? Not quite. Our approach took a different route. We often laid out an assortment of choices and, in most experiments, allowed participants to decide their portion sizes. This wasn't just an experiment; it was a slice of real life served up on a platter of spontaneity.

The following charts are not just graphs; they are the vibrant tapestry of this experiment, capturing the dynamic undulations of blood glucose levels in real-time. These visual narratives are far more than digits and lines; they embody the personal experiences of our volunteers, shining a guiding light on your nutritional choices. Before elucidating these illustrative tales, allow me to illuminate the path to navigating and interpreting the revelations they unfurl.

Navigating blood sugar levels: understanding the charts

Navigating the intricate waters of blood sugar levels is akin to charting a course through mysterious seas. Each meal, especially those abundant in carbohydrates, is like a wave that temporarily elevates your blood sugar levels, known as a post-prandial spike. This rise is your body's natural reaction to the glucose influx, prompting insulin to embark on its mission to recalibrate those levels. Mastering these waves is vital, anchoring your blood sugar within the desired range, steering your health towards a promising horizon.

What does the charted territory of 'normal' glucose levels look like? It's a varied landscape, with clinical guidance differing based on the individual. The course set for someone in the clear 12% of adults without metabolic concerns differs from the paths navigated by the 88% sailing through the archipelago of pre-diabetic or diabetic waters. An occasional sugar wave doesn't sound the alarm for the fortunate few yachting calm seas. However, for the vast majority, it's crucial to be vigilant of the hidden reefs and the chronic risks that stormy, erratic blood sugar spikes can bring. Your quest? To pursue the serene waters of steady, 'flatter' blood sugar levels.

Consider your fasting pre-meal glucose level as your harbour; ideally, it should dock at 5.6 mmol/L or lower; that's the one teaspoon of sugar we discussed. As you embark on your meal, aim for the gentlest of waves. The greater the carbohydrate intake and the glycaemic load of your food, the higher the tide may rise. Yet, anchoring your meal with fibre can help keep these waves small or even completely flat. A rise of one or two mmol/L may navigate within the norm, but remember, the closer you sail to a zero rise, the smoother your long-term health journey.

The charts ahead are like nautical maps, charting the glucose level voyages of our 10 intrepid participants. While they capture the essence of our metabolic explorers' journeys, it's important to note that your waves may differ.

*****

Let The Trial Begin:

Deciphering the cereal conundrum

The inaugural morning of our Blood Sugar Trial cast the spotlight on a quintessentially British morning tradition: the cereal bowl. Envision this: Kellogg's™ gracing an impressive 17.5 million breakfast tables across Britain, the breakfast cereal industry boasting a hefty £2.5 billion turnover, and Weetabix Original™ claiming its throne[5].

In our experiment, we gave participants carte blanche to serve their cereal of choice, free from the shackles of pre-measured portions or dictated brand preferences. The result? Bowls generously brimming with an average of 69 g of favourites like Frosties™, Coco Pops™, or Cornflakes™, far outstripping the manufacturers' suggested modest 30 g serving size.

Before we disclose the revelations from our Day 1 breakfast trial, let's unravel the enigmatic tapestry of nutritional labels, focusing on the intricate interplay between carbohydrates, sugars, and fibre in packaged cereals.

The 'carbohydrates' figure on the packaging is a composite sum of sugars, starches, and fibre. It's pivotal to recognise that starches, much like their sugary counterparts, ultimately metamorphose into sugar within our bodies. This insight casts the 'of which sugars' segment in a deceptive light, as its figures are already nestled within the 'carbohydrates' total. On the flip side, dietary fibre emerges as the unsung hero of nutrition, warranting its deduction from the overall carbohydrate count to unveil a more accurate nutritional panorama of our cereals.

NUTRITIONAL INFORMATION

		/100g	%RI*	/30g	/RI%
	Energy	1604kJ		481kJ	
		378kcal		113kcal	
	Fat	0.9g		0.3g	0.4%
	of which saturates	0.2g		0.1g	1%
a)	Carbohydrate	84g		25g	10%
b)	of which sugars	8.0g		2.4g	3%
c)	Fibre	3.0g		0.9g	
	Protein	7.0g		2.1g	4%
	Salt	1.1g		0.34g	
	Vitamins				
	Vitamin D	8.4µg	168%	2.5µg	50%
	Thiamin	0.91mg	83%	0.27mg	25%
	Riboflavin	1.2mg	86%	0.36mg	25%
	Niacin	13mg	83%	4.0mg	25%
	Vitamin B6	1.2mg	86%	0.36mg	25%
	Folic Acid	166µg	83%	49.8mg	25%
	Vitamin B12	2.1µg	84%	0.63µg	25%
	Minerals				
	Iron	8.0mg	57%	2.4mg	17%

*Reference intake of an average adult (8400 kj/2000 kcal)

figure 3

a) This amalgamates all forms of sugar, starch (which is sugar), and fibre.

b) As sugar is already included in carbohydrates, it is probably only separated to create an illusion that we are consuming less sugar than we are.

c) Fibre is already included in the carbohydrates figure, but as it is beneficial for us, we should subtract it.

So for this product, we take the 84 g of carbohydrates, minus the 3 g of fibre, and arrive at 81 g of sugar, per 100g consumed

For example, the label in figure 3 shows 84 g of carbohydrates and 3 g of fibre; the actual combined sugar content per 100 g would be an enormous 81 g. To put this into perspective, if you're munching on cornflakes with this label, a staggering 81% of your breakfast will become sugar in your system. It's almost as if you're directly spooning sugar into your breakfast bowl!

Equipped with this sharper lens on nutritional labels, let's circle back to our Day 1 breakfast. Our participants' hearty 69 g average cereal servings developed into a whopping 56 g of sugar intake, metaphorically akin to starting their day by consuming about 14 teaspoons of sugar, a jolting initiation into our blood sugar trial.

On the brighter side, a small amount of 2.07 g fibre entered the mix. But this fibre's potential benefits were eclipsed by the deluge of carbohydrates. Moreover, the fibre wasn't consumed first, rendering its impact somewhat muted.

Before I unveil our inaugural graph, let's frame the context. The visuals you're about to see are extracted directly from the CGMs worn by our volunteers. In selecting which graphs to present, I aimed for a representative snapshot, typically not the extreme peaks or valleys but the median experience – a portrayal that mirrors the journey of most participants in our study. Occasionally, I'll showcase more than one graph when doing so enriches the narrative and offers deeper insight into the context of our findings.

Day 1: Breakfast Experiment

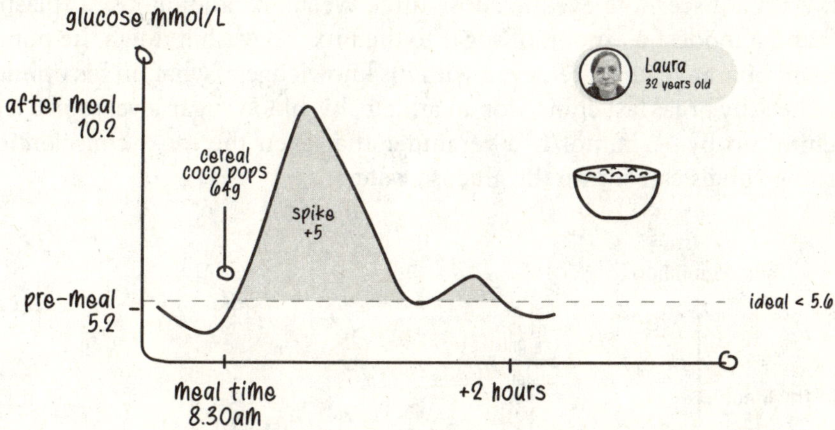

Laura, our sprightly 32-year-old warehouse manager with a penchant for staying fit, faced the morning's cereal showdown with gusto. She zeroed in on Coco Pops and ladled out a hearty 64 g serving – that's over double the portion the label's nutritional chart suggested. When it came to the beverage choice of water, orange juice, and apple juice, she opted for a modest 170 ml of orange juice. But little did she expect the aftermath: her blood sugar levels embarked on a rollercoaster ride, soaring by a whopping +5 mmol/L. The breakfast spectacle turned the humble morning routine into an eye-opening glucose gala!

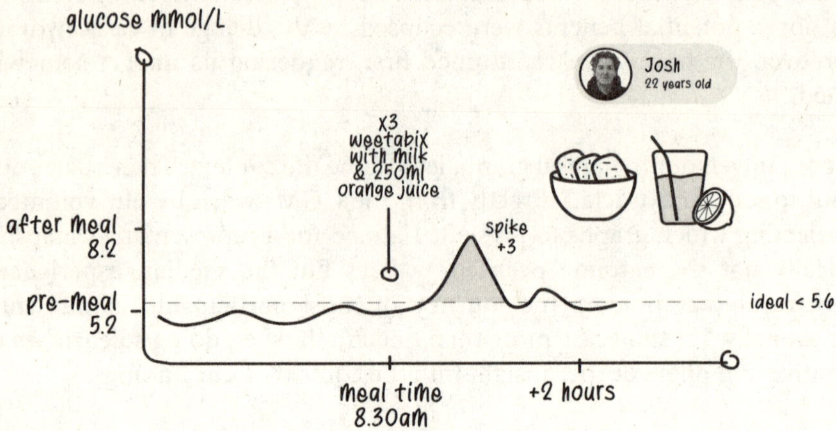

Josh Morris, our 22-year-old TikTok wizard and former ski instructor known for his fitness finesse, approached the breakfast challenge with his trademark flair. With a discerning eye, he chose three Weetabix, adding just a splash of milk and a modest teaspoon of sugar to the mix. To wash it down, he poured a 250 ml of orange juice. Yet, even with his knowledge of what, in his opinion, was a healthy breakfast choice for an athlete, his blood sugar level took a leap, notching up by +3 mmol/L–a reminder that even the most conscientious morning rituals can stir up the glucose waters.

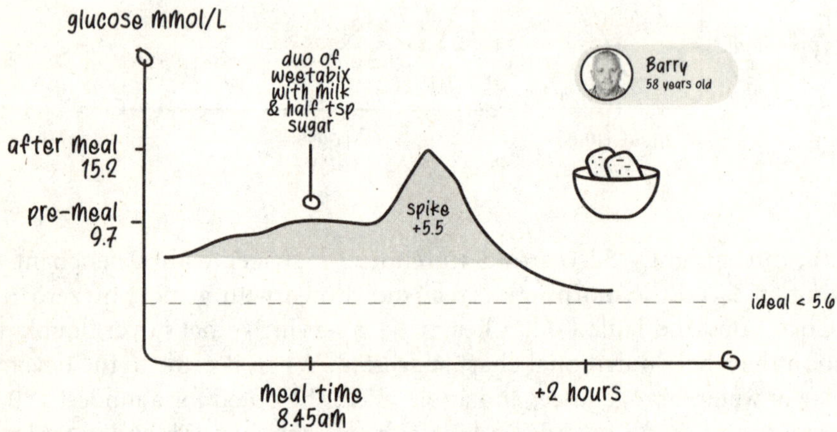

Barry Wiggins, my 58-year-old steadfast personal assistant of 30 years, navigated the breakfast experiment with a measured approach. He opted for a duo of Weetabix, doused with a tiny splash of full milk and just a half teaspoon of sugar. It's worth noting that Barry's starting line on the blood sugar track was already elevated, a testament to his pre-diabetic status. Nevertheless, his blood sugar level climbed steeply, surging by a substantial 5.5 mmol/L. Barry's experience, as he dutifully noted in his Blood Sugar Trial journal, took an interesting turn by mid-morning. 'By 11am, I was starving,' he remarked. This hunger pang was a direct echo of his blood sugar's dramatic ascent and descent, a frequent occurrence when the sugar spike rapidly scales such lofty heights.

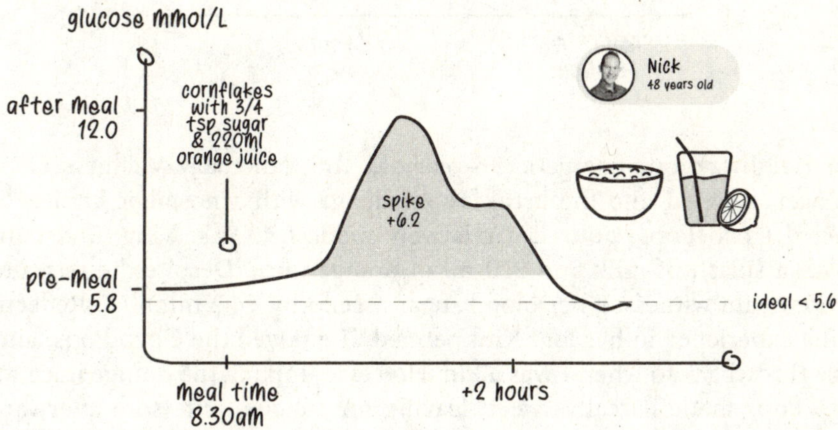

Nick Davies, our supplement company's 48-year-old whizz of product development, brought a health-conscious mindset to the breakfast table. His choice? A portion of cornflakes weighing in at 56 g – a touch lighter than the group's average, reflecting his mindful approach to nutrition. With precision, he sprinkled ¾ of a teaspoon of sugar over his cereal and accompanied it with a 220 ml glass of orange juice. Despite his thoughtful selection, Nick's blood sugar took an astonishing leap, registering a +6.2 mmol/L spike. The impact was substantial. In his own words, Nick recounted, 'Felt awful – headache, anxious and very difficult to concentrate in my morning meetings.' A vivid reminder that even the most health-aware among us can encounter turbulent glucose tides.

Nick's choice sadly mirrors what many people pursue daily. Despite his health-conscious intentions, his breakfast led to a rollercoaster of blood sugar levels and undesirable symptoms. It is a poignant illustration of the everyday struggle to balance convenience with nutritional mindfulness in our hectic lives.

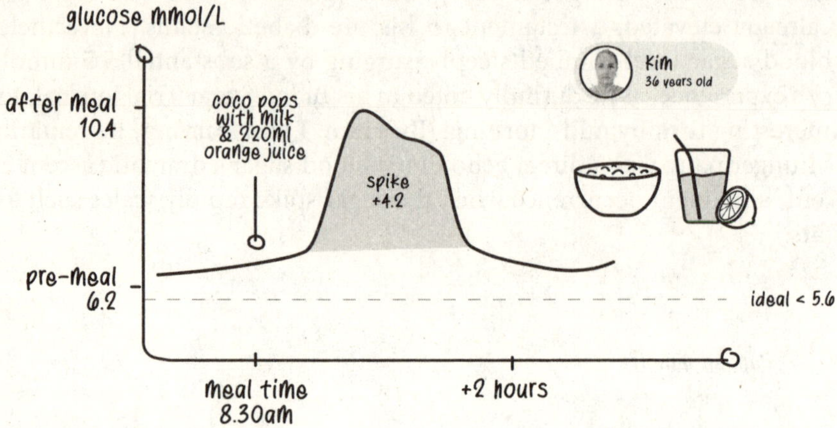

Kim Heighway, our energetic 36-year-old You Sanctuary Wellness Centre manager, stepped into the breakfast challenge with a nostalgic choice. She selected Coco Pops, poured a relatively modest 43 g serving, and paired it with a splash of milk and 220 ml of orange juice. Despite the restrained portion, Kim witnessed her blood sugar ascend by +4.2 mmol/L. Reflecting on the experience in her log, Kim penned, 'I enjoyed the Coco Pops, and it was a throwback to when I was a kid. However, mixing the orange juice with Coco Pops made it really sweet, leaving my tongue quite sore afterwards.' A testament to the bittersweet walk down memory lane, where childhood favourites meet the stark realities of sugar spikes.

Day 2: A Fibre-Fuelled Morning

As the sun rose on the second day of our Blood Sugar Trial, a fibre-rich breeze swept through the breakfast choices. Our participants were greeted with two enticing options, each a testament to the power of fibre. Three individuals embraced the 'Sneaker Fibre Smoothie,' a concoction whose playful name belies its serious fibre content, while the remaining seven reached for the Slimshotz fibre drink (page 956), packing a wholesome 2.7 g fibre, a blend of 1.7 g glucomannan and 1 g inulin (more on these fibres in a moment).

The primary objective of day 2's breakfast experiment is to ascertain the efficacy of fibre in mitigating the rapid surge in blood sugar levels triggered by the consumption of cereals and juice. Through meticulous observation and analysis, we seek to uncover whether fibre can serve as a protective barrier against the detrimental effects of sugary carbohydrates.

Sneaker Fibre Smoothie Recipe

Ready to blend a fibre masterpiece? Here's how to conjure up the Sneaker Fibre Smoothie. In just 20 seconds, these ingredients unite to create a fibre powerhouse, delivering a hearty 6–7 g of fibre in every delectable sip:

Almond milk (200 ml, 0.6 g fibre)
Cocoa powder (28% fibre, 1 g fibre)
Half a banana (1 g fibre) or ¼ bag of fibrehydrate
A generous tablespoon of peanut butter (1.1 g fibre)
A handful of peanuts (2.6 g fibre)

Fuelled by their fibre-rich drinks, our participants were asked to revisit their Day 1 cereal choices with a newfound perspective. As with the day before, we weighed their selection before letting them indulge. The average serving sizes they poured shrank by 13%, dwindling to 60 g, as if the fibre had softly whispered, 'Less is more.' While some participants consciously noted a dip in their appetite, others were pleasantly surprised by their unintentionally smaller portions. This subtle shift eloquently speaks to fibre's discreet charm in gently curbing our hunger and reshaping our meal sizes.

A fascinating pattern unfolded: satiated by the fibre's quiet strength, three participants asked if they could stop eating before finishing their cereals. Though defiant against precise measurement, the soggy leftovers whispered tales of about a quarter of their breakfasts retreating untouched.

The numbers paint a vivid story. Introducing fibre at breakfast led to a notable reduction in overall consumption (both served and uneaten) by 16.5 g and a significant decrease in sugar intake by 13.3 g on average among our cereal connoisseurs. These statistics underscore the transformative power of embracing *Fibre First*, realigning our breakfast landscape.

Yet the real enchantment was clear in their blood sugar tales. Let's cast our gaze on some poignant moments, juxtaposing the sugary crests of Day 1 with the more serene waves of Day 2, post-fibre infusion. The shift wasn't just in their bowls but in the peaks and valleys of their glucose narratives, painting a compelling picture of fibre's influence on our metabolic symphony.

On the second day of our trial, Kim revisited her breakfast routine from the previous day, but with a twist. She prefaced her meal with a Slimshotz fibre drink (page 956), infusing her morning with an additional 2.6 g of fibre. While the same breakfast led to a sugar surge on Day 1, the fibre boost this time notably tempered the tide, resulting in a more moderate increase of +2.3 mmol/L–a stark contrast to her initial experience.

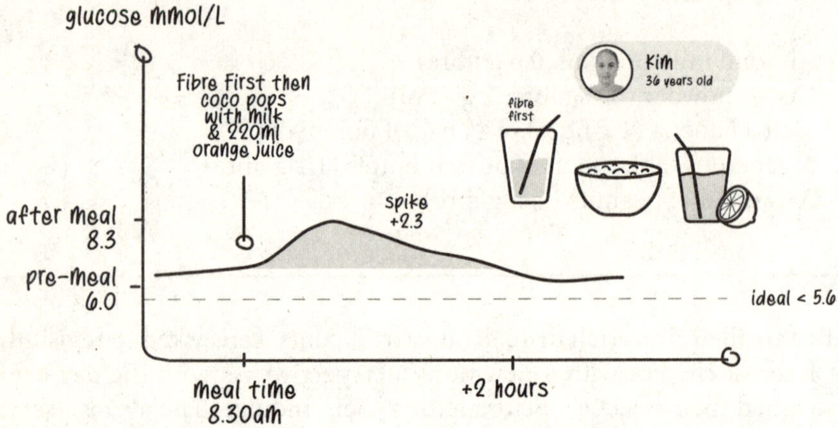

Reflecting on the fibre's impact, Kim shared, 'I could happily not have eaten the cereal at all, as the fibre made me feel full, but I wanted to see what the effect was, so I forced myself to eat it.' Her observation underscores the potent satiating effect of fibre, highlighting its role in moderating blood sugar spikes and curbing the appetite.

In his early 30s, David Reed blends the dedication of a devoted bodybuilder with the discernment of a fanatical health foodie. Joining our trial to deepen his nutritional knowledge, especially after enduring a heart attack last year, David approached this experiment with precision, a testament to his commitment to maintaining his physique and wellbeing.

Here's the breakdown of David's meticulous approach:

David's cereal with and without fibre

David began his day with a meticulously measured 90 g of Coco Pops, a portion he precisely pours daily as a cornerstone of his physique-building regimen, along with a 350 ml glass of orange juice. The outcome was a pronounced +5 mmol/L surge in his blood sugar levels, vividly showing the impact of his carefully portioned yet sugar-laden breakfast choice.

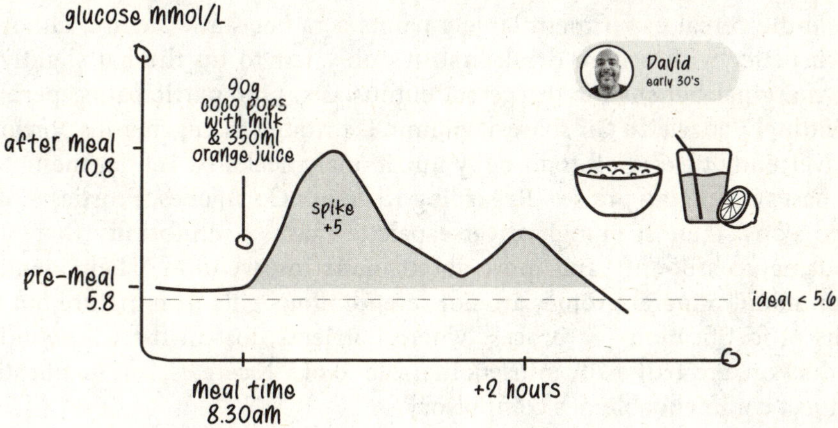

The next morning saw a strategic addition to David's regimented routine – the Sneaker Fibre Smoothie, added before he replicated his Day 1 meal: the exact 90 g of Coco Pops and 350 ml of orange juice, demonstrating his unwavering commitment to consistency in his diet. Remarkably, the fibre smoothie dramatically transformed his blood sugar response, smoothing out the spike that had previously marked his mornings. This striking difference underscored the potent role of fibre in tempering blood sugar fluctuations, even for an individual as disciplined and health-conscious as David.

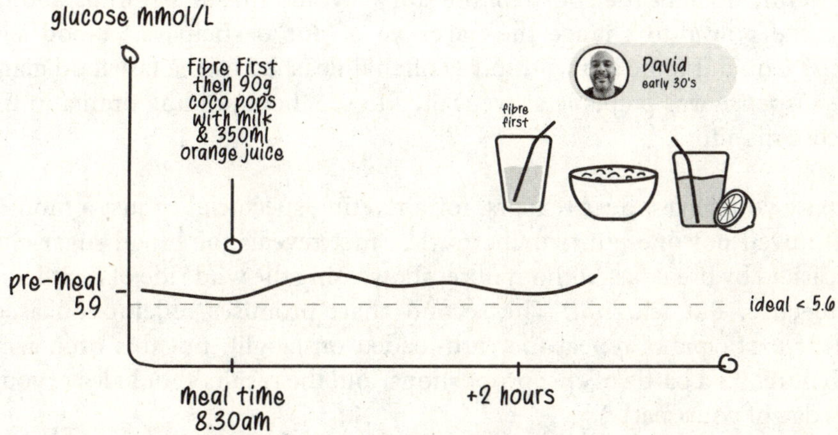

By the second day, the fibre drink had impressively evened out his blood sugar spikes. Moving forward, armed with new knowledge, David was inspired to overhaul his breakfast habits for better health

While the cereal experiment largely paints a rather stark picture, although much better with a fibre drink first, it's only fair to tip the hat slightly to one marginal benefit for the cereal enthusiasts. Our participants, perhaps unwittingly, guzzled a fair share of vitamin D through their generous portions, inadvertently ticking off their daily nutritional checkbox. Yet, let me not be too hasty in singing praises. Regarding Kellogg's Cornflakes, Frosties™, and Coco Pops, their seemingly diverse palette masks a uniformity that's less about nature's bounty and more about man's intervention. Their identical vitamin and mineral profiles are not serendipitous gifts from nature but the fruits of fortification – a process where nutrients, lost in the whirlwind of production, are artificially infused. In the land of UK cereals, this fortification isn't just commendable; it's compulsory.

Days 3 And 4: The Fast-Food Breakfast Showdown

Days 3 and 4 of our trial began with the aroma of fast-food breakfasts, a temptation from the kingdoms of McDonald's™ and Greggs™. Our fearless participants entered this experiment, armed with nothing but their appetites. The mission? To compare the impact of typical fast-food breakfasts consumed with or without *Fibre First.*

Could the fibre drink be like a superhero in disguise, stepping into the scene just in time to alter the course of the story? Would this unassuming addition have the power to change the narrative of our participants' blood sugar levels? Could it tame the wild spikes often unleashed by the fast-food giants? The suspense was palpable as we waited to see the unfolding drama in their glucose monitors.

Prepare yourselves, dear readers, for a riveting spectacle! In just a moment, we'll unveil not one but two charts. The first reveals the blood sugar chaos unleashed by breakfast without fibre, showcasing the wild ride of carb-loaded indulgence. But fear not! The second chart promises redemption as our valiant participants repeat the carb-loaded onslaught, but this time armed with fibre. It's a battle of epic proportions, and the results should leave you on the edge of your seat!

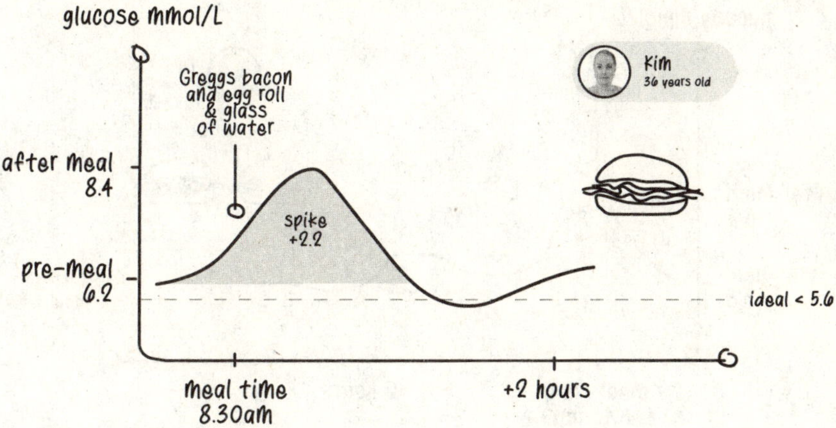

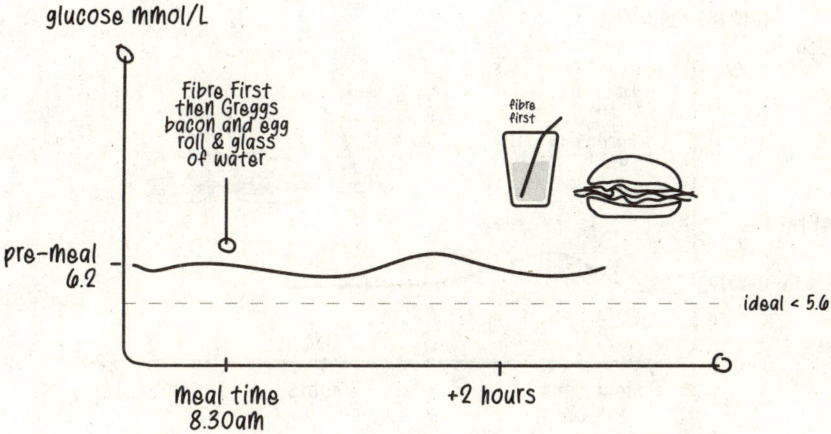

Kim, opting for a classic Greggs bacon and egg roll, paired her meal with nothing more than a simple glass of water. However, the sequel to this breakfast scene introduced a new character: the Sneaker Fibre Smoothie. With this fibrous prelude to her meal on the second day, Kim found the once-conquerable breakfast roll had become a challenge too great – she couldn't quite polish it off.

The tale of her blood sugar levels told an equally compelling story. On day 3, sans fibre, her glucose monitor narrated a rise of 2.2 mmol/L. But the narrative took a dramatic turn the following day with the fibre smoothie in play, her blood sugar barely budged, marking virtually no change at all. The graphs vividly depict fibre's understated yet powerful role in re-scripting our body's response to food.

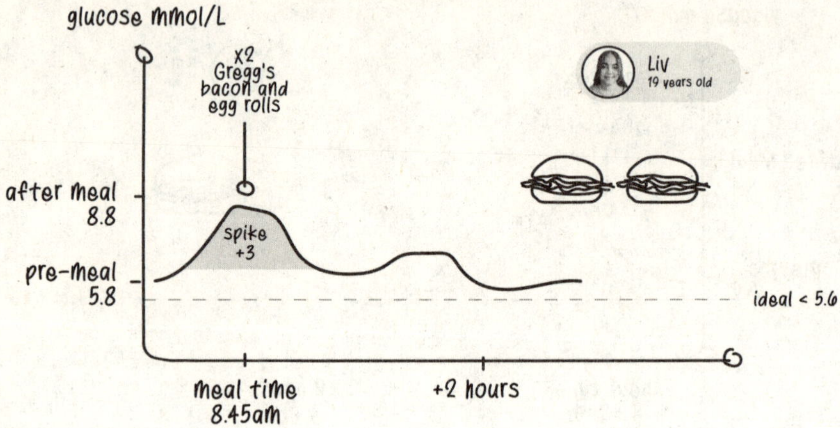

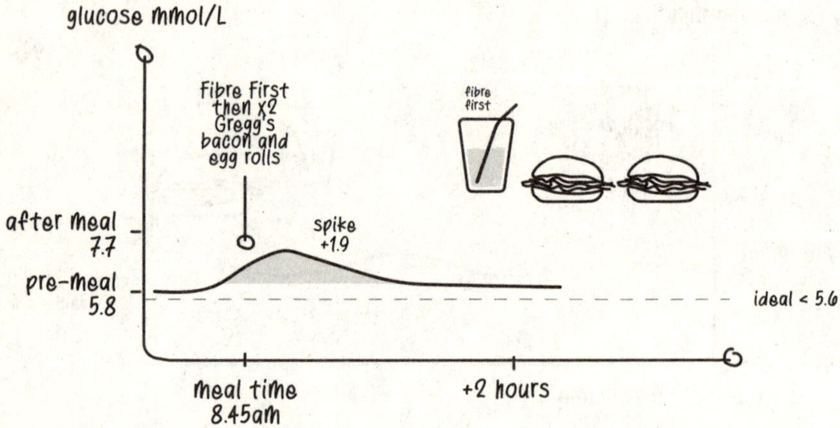

Liv, Kim's 19-year-old daughter and beauty therapist, followed in her mother's culinary footsteps but with a youthful twist – she doubled down with two bacon and egg rolls from Greggs. This hearty morning feast translated into a noticeable narrative on her glucose monitor, hiking her blood sugar level by +3 mmol/L.

The following day, Liv introduced a new prelude to her breakfast – a Slimshotz fibre drink. This seemingly modest addition was anything but inconspicuous in its effect. After fortifying herself with the fibre drink, Liv tackled her bacon and egg rolls duo, only to witness a subtle but significant shift in her blood sugar story. Once a steep ascent of 3 mmol/L, the spike was tempered to a more moderate climb of 1.9 mmol/L.

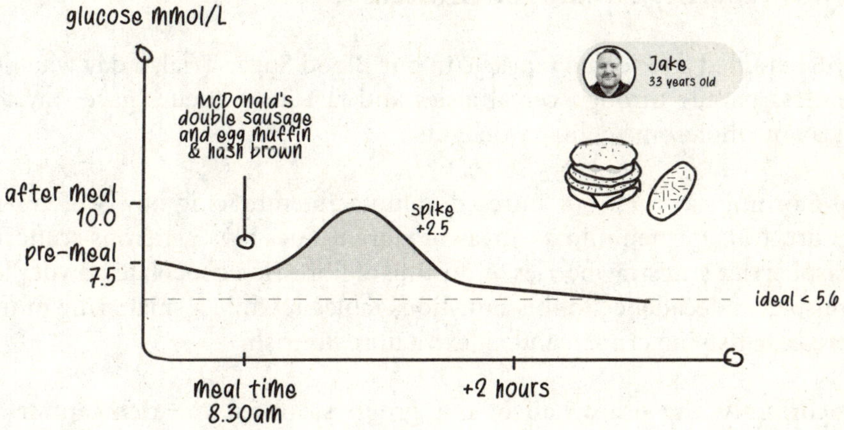

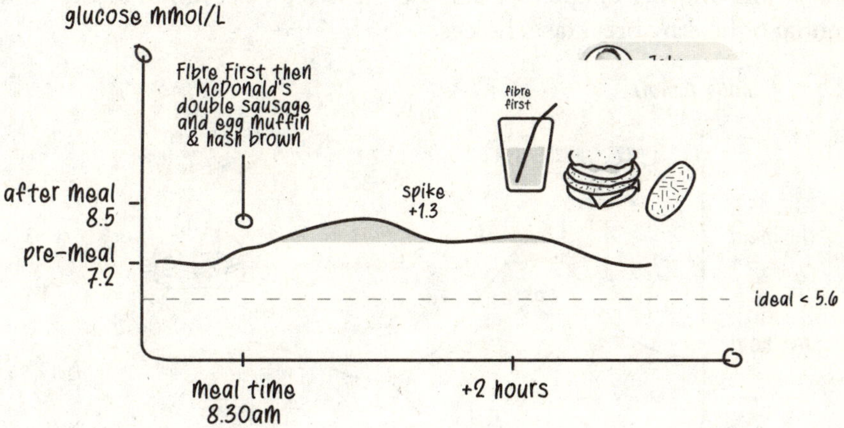

Jake Thompson, the 33-year-old Managing Director at the helm of one of my ventures (and my wonderful son-in-law), entered the fast-food breakfast arena with a McDonald's double sausage and egg muffin, accompanied by a hash brown. This indulgent ensemble orchestrated a crescendo in his blood sugar levels, peaking at a 2.5 mmol/L spike.

On day 4, Jake maintained his menu from the day before and first introduced a 2.6 g fibre drink. With the fibrous buffer in place, his breakfast prompted a more subdued blood sugar spike, tapering to a gentler 1.3 mmol/L. Jake's experience underscored a compelling theme in our breakfast story: fibre's subtle yet profound influence on our body's response to our morning rituals.

Day 5: Healthy Breakfast Choices

Day 5 heralded a welcome reprieve in our Blood Sugar Trial, a day when the relentless parade through cereal aisles and fast-food queues gave way to a tableau of wholesome culinary delights.

The morning saw half our intrepid volunteers embracing bowls of creamy yoghurt, transformed into a canvas of vibrant hues by a generous scattering of raspberries and strawberries. A dusting of fibre-rich chocolate powder lent a whisper of decadence to this nutritious tableau, while a smattering of nuts offered a satisfying crunch and an extra fibre flourish.

Concurrently, the other half of our group savoured the rich tapestry of flavours offered by avocado, partnered with either salmon or mackerel. Day 5 wasn't just another chapter in our trial; it was a celebration of the vibrant potential of healthy breakfast choices.

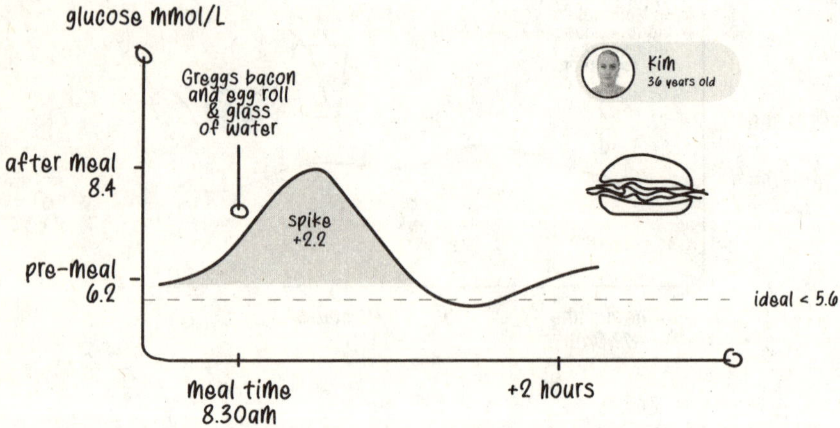

A comparison of Kim's day 3 and day 5 breakfast choices:

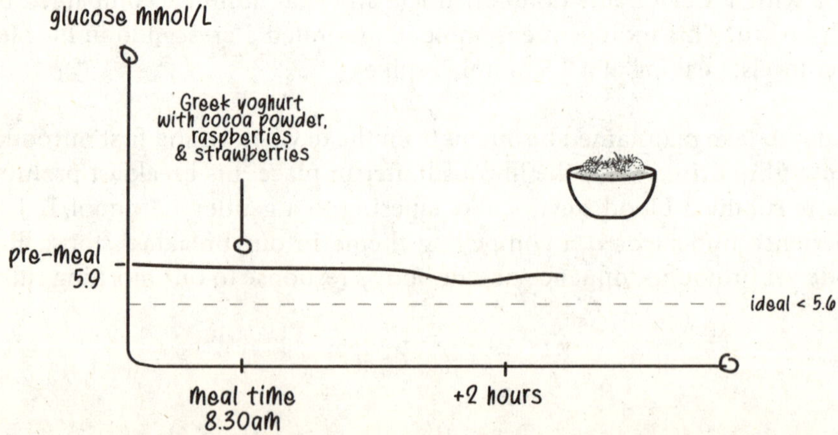

On Day 5, all 10 participants experienced a serene morning, their blood sugar levels mirroring the calmness of their healthy breakfast choices. Not a single spike of note disturbed the tranquillity of their glucose readings. For a vivid contrast, let's revisit Kim's chart from Wednesday's bread roll breakfast and juxtapose it with her Day 5 experience, a wholesome serving of Greek yoghurt, subtly enhanced with cocoa powder for that fibre boost and adorned with raspberries and strawberries.

The comparison was striking. Where the bread roll had ushered in a notable surge, the nourishing breakfast of Day 5 not only stabilised Kim's blood sugar but even nudged it downwards post-meal! Kim expressed a newfound sense of fulfilment in her log, noting, 'It was the first morning that, after breakfast, I totally felt content.' This shift in her post-breakfast sentiment echoed the quiet triumph of a diet rooted in healthful choices, a testament to the profound impact that nutrient-rich, balanced meals can have on our wellbeing.

Day 6: Whole Fruit vs Fruit Juice Trial

Day 6 of our Blood Sugar Trial set the stage for a showdown that sought to challenge the long-standing notion of fruit juice as the pinnacle of a healthy morning routine. The goal was to paint a clear picture, contrasting the consumption of whole fruits with their juiced counterparts and unravelling the complex narrative of nutrition and satiety that each harbour.

For years, orange and apple juice held a place of honour at my breakfast table, revered as the paragon of a healthful morning kick-start. Yet, as our volunteers set sail on this sugar trial, the facade of these seemingly innocent drinks crumbled. Parading its 'no added sugar' banner, the orange juice masqueraded as a wholesome choice. However, its absence of fibre meant that the carbs were predestined to morph into sugar in the body. When our participants poured their usual amount, the glasses brimmed with an average of 302 ml, revealing a portion that smuggled in 28 g of sugar.

Similarly, apple juice, carrying a badge claiming '1 of your 5 a day fruit and vegetables' while masquerading as a nutritional ally, cunningly funnelled a hefty 31 g of sugar into our participants. This single serving stealthily breached the NHS-recommended daily sugar limit, a stark awakening. Labels like these (figure 4) masterfully craft an illusion of health and conscientious parenting. Yet, beneath this facade, they slyly shepherd unsuspecting consumers towards surpassing the daily sugar quota. The irony is palpable. A seemingly prudent pick for one's '5-a-day' subtly morphs into a Trojan horse laden with sugar.

Apple Juice from Concentrate **1 litre**

Pasteurised apple juice from concentrate.

150ml counts as 1 portion of your 5 a day fruit and vegetables. As part of a healthy balance diet, and to eat at least 5 portions of fruit or vegetables each day. Remember that fresh, frozen, dried, canned and juice all count!

Nutrition

Typical values	per 100ml	per 150ml portion
Energy	188kJ	282kJ
	44kcal	66kcal
Fat	0.1g	0.2g
of which saturates	trace	trace
Carbohydrate	10.3g	15.5g
of which sugars	10.3g	15.5g
Fibre	trace	trace
Protein	0.1g	0.2g
Salt	trace	trace
per 150ml portion	%RI	your RI*
Energy	3%	84000kJ/2000kcal
Fat	<1%	70g
Saturates	<1%	20g
Sugars	17%	90g
Salt	<1%	6g

*Reference intake of an average adult (8400 kj/2000 kcal) (RI). Contains approx. 6 portions.

(*figure 4*)

In stark contrast to their juice-sipping counterparts, the other half of our volunteers embraced the journey through an orchard of whole fruits. They quickly discovered that consuming an equivalent volume of whole fruits was a Herculean task. The fibre, the bulk, and the sheer effort required to eat whole fruits erected a natural fortress against overindulgence, a testament to nature's wisdom in crafting its edible treasures.

As the morning unfolded, the pitch of whole fruits versus juicing painted a compelling portrait of the deceptive ease of gulping down liquid calories versus the satisfying, full-bodied experience of tucking into whole, fibrous fruits. The data from our orange juice expedition narrated a dramatic story: a sharp spike in blood sugar levels, followed by a precipitous decline. Two intrepid volunteers, caught in the tumultuous tides of this sugar-induced tempest, reported a noticeable crash in their vitality by midday, mirroring the stark tale told by the graphs.

Yet, an intriguing claim adorns the side of the orange juice carton, heralding its vitamin C content as a panacea for 'reducing tiredness and fatigue.' True, vitamin C is laden with these beneficial attributes, but the sheer volume of sugar eclipses its presence in this sugary context. This dichotomy between the juice's innate sugar load and its purported health benefits paints a paradoxical picture, highlighting the oft-misleading nature of marketing messages that gloss over the negative sugar narrative. As we're poised to uncover, the encounter of fructose with the liver is not one of energy infusion but one of depletion!

Unbeknownst to our volunteers who sipped their liquid fruits, they also indulged in a covert assault on their dental enamel. Fruit juices sneakily host sugary soirees in your mouth, inviting cavities and an entire festival of dental calamities. It's akin to hosting a pool party for your teeth, except the pool is brimming with sugary syrup, and the lifeguards have abandoned their posts. Each sip of juice cloaks your teeth in a sugary sheath, laying out a lavish banquet for the bacteria that revel in eroding your tooth enamel. So, while you might relish that so-called 'nutritious' juice, your teeth are unwittingly grooving to the rhythm of decay, rendering fruit juices a bittersweet proposition for your oral health.

Now let's pivot our focus to the blood sugar levels of our volunteers:

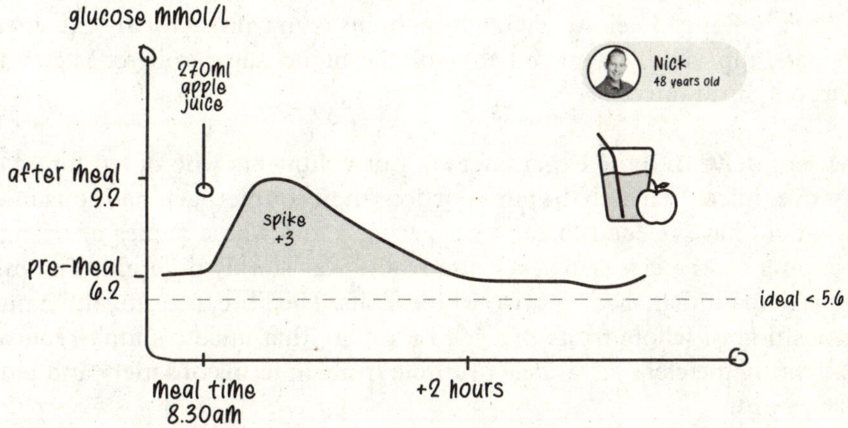

Nick, our supplement aficionado and health-conscious warrior, opted for an apple juice to begin his day. His chosen potion, a 270 ml serving of this seemingly innocent drink, quickly showcased its true potency. Like a silent yet swift arrow, it sent Nick's blood sugar levels soaring, catapulting a dramatic +3 mmol/L rise. This swift escalation was a stark reminder of the hidden power lurking within a simple glass of fruit juice.

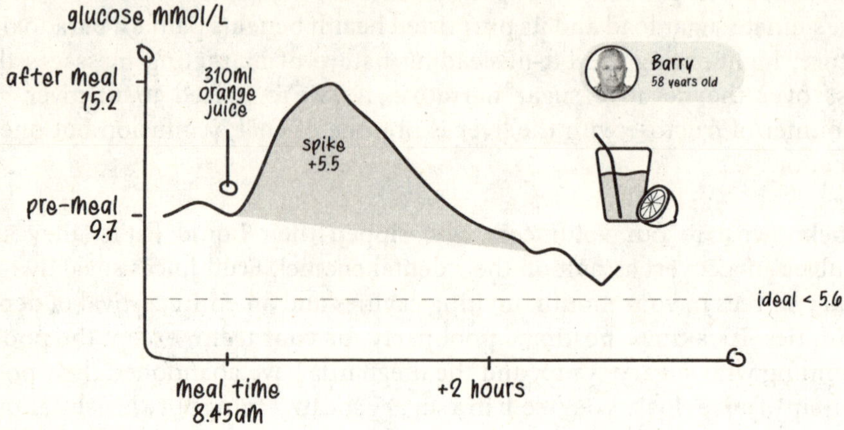

Barry arrived at breakfast, already navigating the choppy waters of a restless night and the elevated blood sugar levels characteristic of his pre-diabetic condition. He hoped for a refreshing start to the day and consumed a generous 310 ml glass of orange juice. However, this seemingly benign choice propelled his blood sugar further by +5.5 mmol/L. More striking, though, was the dramatic descent that followed. Barry's blood sugar didn't just return to its baseline; it plunged below, leaving him, in his own words, 'totally exhausted'. The stark dip vividly depicted the volatile blood sugar rollercoaster often induced by fruit juices.

Now, let's delve into the experiences of our volunteers who opted for whole fruits over juice. To match the juice portions their counterparts had consumed, they would have needed to eat a staggering 3 to 4 whole apples or oranges, depending on the size. However, the reality was starkly different. The most any participant managed was two whole fruits. The fibre, texture, and natural composition of whole fruits provided a satiety that juice couldn't replicate, highlighting the clear advantage of whole fruits in terms of satiety and blood sugar control.

It turned out that when it came to feeling full, there was a world of difference between munching on whole fruits and chugging the fibre-free juices. I asked the whole fruit eaters to tackle another apple or orange, but they were stuffed to the brim. Yet, those sipping their fruit, like Barry and Nick, had been ready to guzzle down a whole litre without a second thought (although I did stop them as I felt that it wouldn't fairly represent their normal portion).

And, as you are about to see, none of the whole fruit aficionados experienced the drastic blood sugar fluctuations plaguing the juice drinkers.

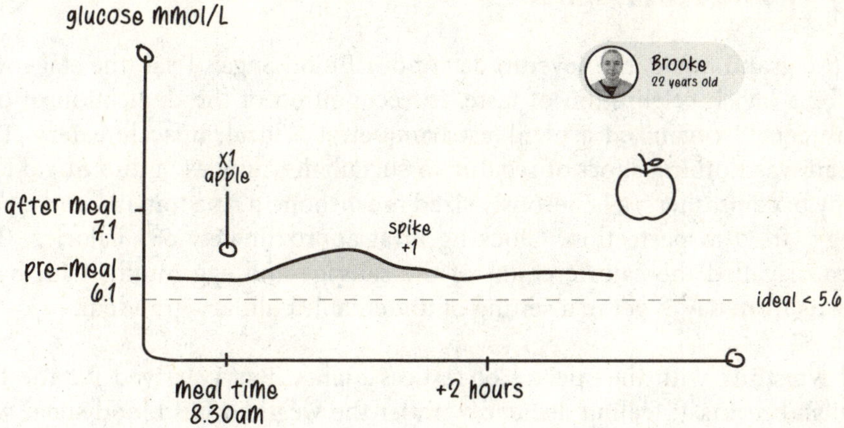

Brooke, a vibrant 22-year-old with a keen focus on fitness and wellbeing, opted for a single apple, embracing the simplicity of whole fruit. This choice, reflective of her health-conscious ethos, resulted in a gentle, almost inconsequential nudge in her blood sugar levels, ticking up by just +1 mmol/L. Her experience eloquently demonstrated the subtle yet profound impact of choosing whole, unprocessed foods, emphasising the harmonious relationship between natural nutrition and the body's delicate balance.

Time to peel back the truth about juicing

Let's press pause and squeeze the truth out of juicing, a trend that had us all in a whirl for decades. Picture this: taking a vibrant, nutrient-packed fruit or veggie and... well, essentially gutting its grandeur. Juicing might seem like the epitome of health, but here's the reality: it's more like sending your fruit to a fibre-fasting retreat. You bid adieu to those glorious fibres, wave off a good chunk of nutrients (they're usually fibre's plus one), and what are you left with? A glass brimming with fructose, a sugary charade of health. Orange and apple juices, you're in the limelight, and not for the right reasons.

If the idea of munching on fruits in their birthday suits doesn't quite appeal to you, resist the urge to juice their essence away. Opt for the blender instead. Toss in the whole fruit – yes, do the polite thing and peel your oranges and bananas, but let the blender embrace the fruit in its entirety. Better yet, channel your inner nature enthusiast and enjoy fruits as they were intended – unadulterated, unprocessed, and straight off the branch.

Day 7: The Full English

On the grand finale, the seventh day of our Blood Sugar Trial, the stage was set for a lavish celebration of taste. In recognition of the dedication of our volunteers, I organised a breakfast banquet at a local, upscale eatery. The spread was nothing short of regal: two succulent sausages, a duo of golden, crispy bacon rashers, a generously sized mushroom, a ripe tomato, and a pair of eggs fried to perfection. Clocking in at approximately 681 calories, this spread rivalled the calorie count of the sausage and egg muffin with hash browns from day 3, yet in a setting of undeniable culinary grandeur.

Still wrestling with the spectre of restless nights, Barry arrived for the full English breakfast, feeling decidedly under the weather. His blood sugar was already sprinting ahead because of his disrupted slumber. Yet, in a surprising turn of events, the hearty meal only nudged his blood sugar up by a modest 1 mmol/L. What's more remarkable is the swift return of his levels to his usual baseline shortly after the meal, almost as if the full English had a restorative touch, offering a semblance of solace amidst his morning turmoil. It appeared the robust, wholesome fare had, in its own way, lent a helping hand in steadying Barry's metabolic ship.

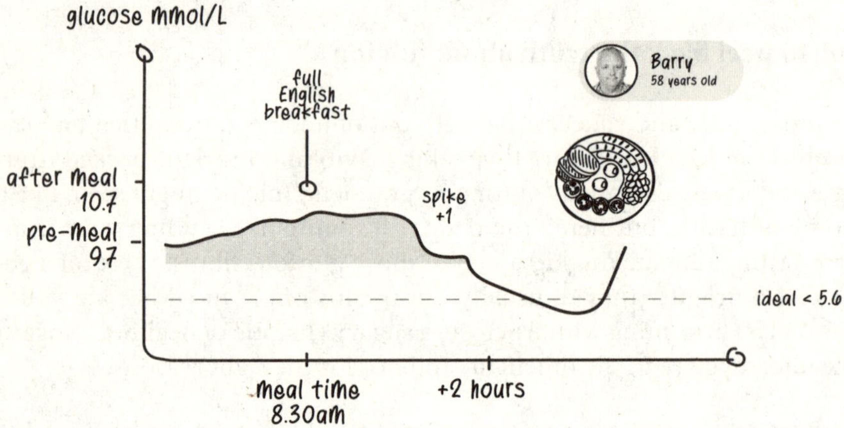

Brooke's blood sugar charts bring to light a fascinating insight. Cast your mind back a few days when a single, modest apple, nudged her blood sugar up by 1 mmol/L. Now, contrast this with her experience on the day of the full English breakfast, a meal that epitomises indulgence and is undeniably more lavish. Remarkably, despite the substantial size of this breakfast, her blood sugar rise was a more restrained 0.5 mmol/L. This counterintuitive result can be attributed to the surprisingly low-carbohydrate content in the full English breakfast. Despite the rewarding size of the plate, the significant lack of carbs played a crucial role in moderating her blood sugar response, shedding light on the complex and sometimes surprising dynamics of our body's metabolic responses.

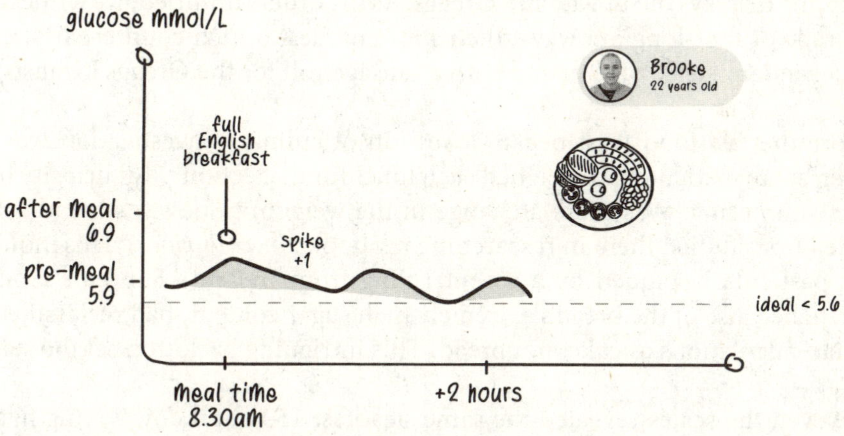

As we wrap up the breakfast chapter of our trials, it's crystal clear that the first bite of the day sets the stage for the metabolic performance to come. If you can steer clear of the siren calls of cereals and fast-food establishments, all the better. These options spike your sugar levels faster and higher than a rocket on bonfire night! If you succumb to their allure, remember to let fibre lead the way.

Whenever possible, opt for the stellar cast of yoghurt and berries, fish and avocado, or the ever-so-robust full English. These aren't just gentle on your blood glucose levels; they barely give the needle a nudge! They're the champions of breakfast, stealthily packing your meal with a powerhouse of nutrients, vitamins, and minerals. The next time you're standing at the breakfast crossroads, remember that the path to balanced blood sugar and a nutrient-rich start to the day doesn't begin at the cereal aisle and fast-food counter; instead, choose a path towards the wholesome goodness of more natural, fibre-rich choices.

As our Blood Sugar Trial narrative unfolds, we turn the page from breakfasts to the midday culinary experiment. From the guilty pleasures of fast food to the mindful selections of the health-savvy, our lunchtime escapades offered a wealth of revelations. In all their diversity, these midday meals acted as a mirror, reflecting how our choices at noon can resonate within us, shaping our energy, mood, and overall metabolic harmony.

Lunch - Day 1: Navigating The Fast-Food Maze

The inaugural lunch led our volunteers down the well-trodden yet perilous paths of fast food. Their task? Select their preferred quick bites from the tempting displays of Subway and Greggs. As the orders unfurled, we witnessed a parade of foot-long Subways, their more modest 6-inch counterparts, and the legendary steak bake paired with a sausage roll for the Greggs loyalists.

Before the fast-food feast began, a session of culinary investigation was in order, as we meticulously weighed each lunchtime selection. My curiosity had been simmering. Was there a change in the weight of Subway's bread rolls, since I first studied them in researching my book *Fat & Furious*? This inquiry was particularly piqued by a recent ruling from Ireland's Supreme Court, which, because of the bread's extremely high sugar content, had reclassified it for tax calculations as cake, not bread. This intriguing backdrop set the stage.

However, the scales revealed the same steadfast 150 g, an unwavering figure that stealthily disguised about 15 teaspoons of sugar in each sandwich. This underscored the artful concealment of fast food, where a seemingly innocuous loaf could be an undercover agent of sugar, silently slipping into our volunteers' meals. Oh, the sweet subterfuge of the fast-food world!

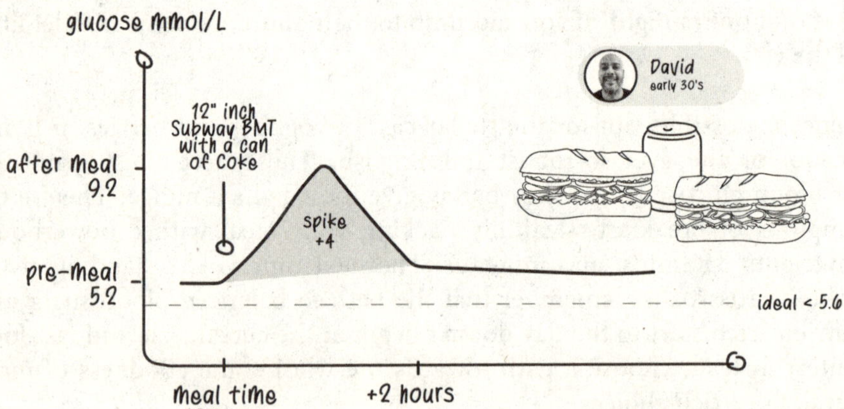

Dave opted for a 12-inch Subway Classic B.M.T® (Biggest, Meatiest, and Tastiest), customised to his preference (no olives) complemented by a can of Coke. This combination sent his blood sugar on a steep ascent, spiking by +4 mmol/L. Reflecting on the experience, Dave said, 'I felt physically sick, and it had a massive negative impact on my performance in the gym.' His choice illuminated not just the immediate metabolic impact but also the profound influence such a meal can have on one's overall daily vigour and vitality, particularly for those dedicated to their fitness routines.

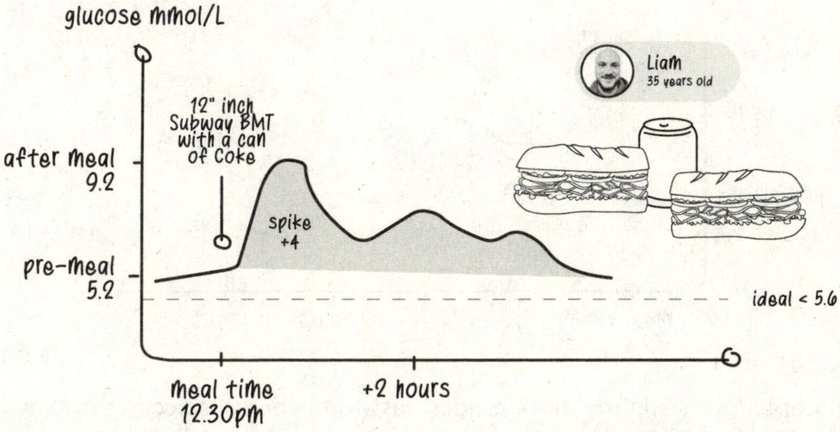

Liam Coakes, a healthy 35-year-old with a fitness-oriented lifestyle, mirrored Dave's choice with a slight twist: a 12-inch Subway B.M.T®, this time with the olives, and a can of Coke to wash it down. His blood sugar mirrored Dave's: surging by +4 mmol/L. However, Liam's graph told a subtly different story: a less pronounced peak but a prolonged elevation of blood sugar levels.

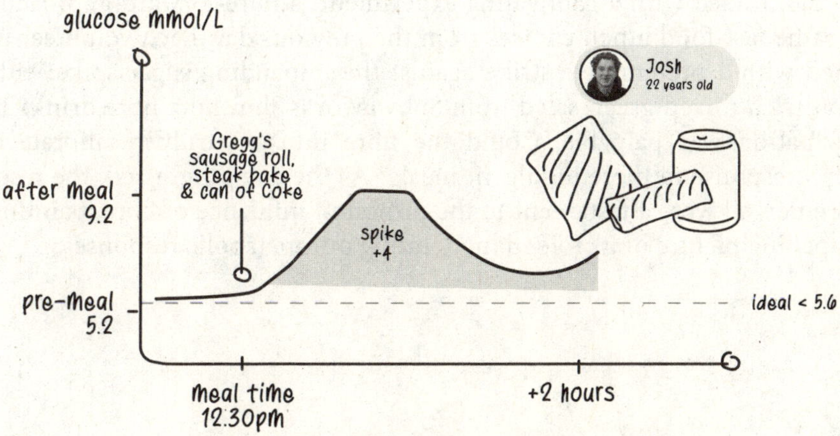

Josh indulged in a classic Greggs duo: a sausage roll paired with a steak bake and a can of regular Coke. This hearty combination propelled his blood sugar levels on a significant upward trajectory, causing a notable +4 mmol/L spike. The substantial rise echoed the potent impact of combining rich, fast-food items with sugary beverages, highlighting the pronounced effect such meal choices can have on our body's glucose management.

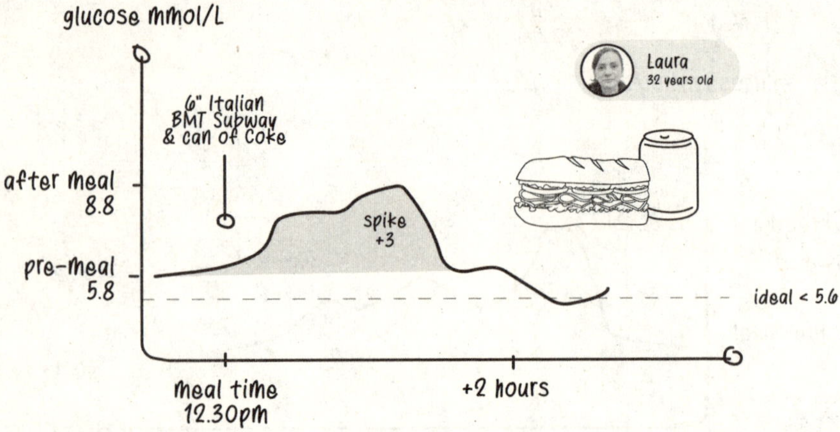

Laura opted for a slightly more modest fast-food choice, selecting the smaller 6-inch Italian B.M.T® from Subway, yet paired it with a regular can of Coke. Despite the reduced size of her sandwich, the combination led to a significant uptick in her blood sugar levels, registering a notable rise of +3 mmol/L.

Day 2: *Fibre First* And Fast Food Last

Day 2 unfolded with a captivating experiment, a fibre-forward approach to the same fast-food lunch choices from the previous day. Each volunteer was armed with a pre-emptive strike against the impending sugar spike: either a fibre-rich mixed green salad from Subway or a Slimshotz fibre drink. The anticipation was palpable. Could the fibre infusion truly recalibrate the body's response to these indulgent meals? As the day progressed, the results that emerged were a testament to the profound influence of fibre, painting a compelling picture of its role in moderating our metabolic responses.

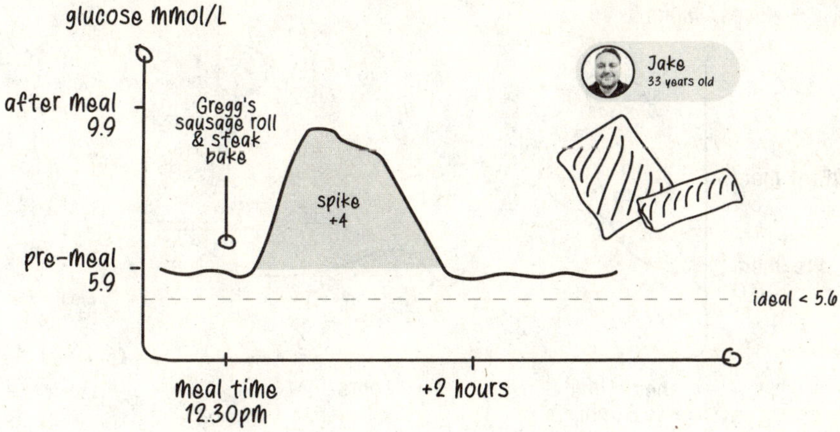

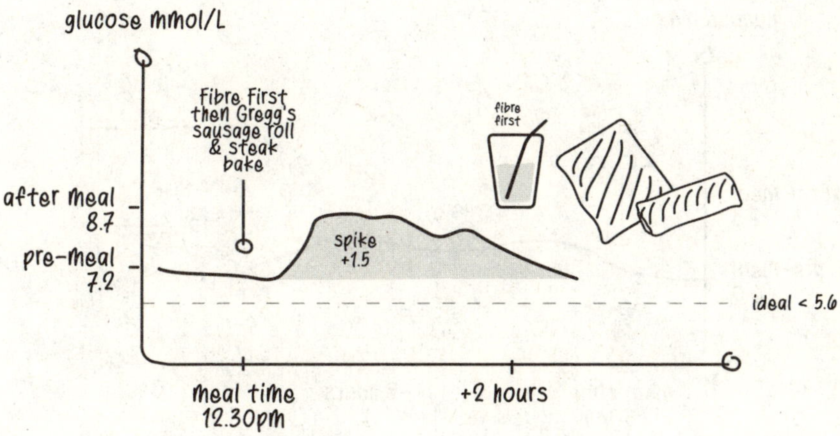

Jake initially faced a substantial +4 mmol/L surge in his blood sugar after indulging in a sausage roll and steak bake combo lunch. The aftermath of this fast-food feast was a pronounced spike, a reminder of the potent impact such meals can have on our glucose levels.

Enter day 2, and the scene shifts. Before revisiting his chosen fast-food duo, Jake introduced a new act: a fibre drink. This simple, pre-meal addition proved to be a game changer. The previously daunting spike was tamed to a more modest +1.5 mmol/L rise. This remarkable reduction showcased fibre's understated yet powerful role in modulating our body's response to food, turning what was once a steep glucose climb into a gentler ascent.

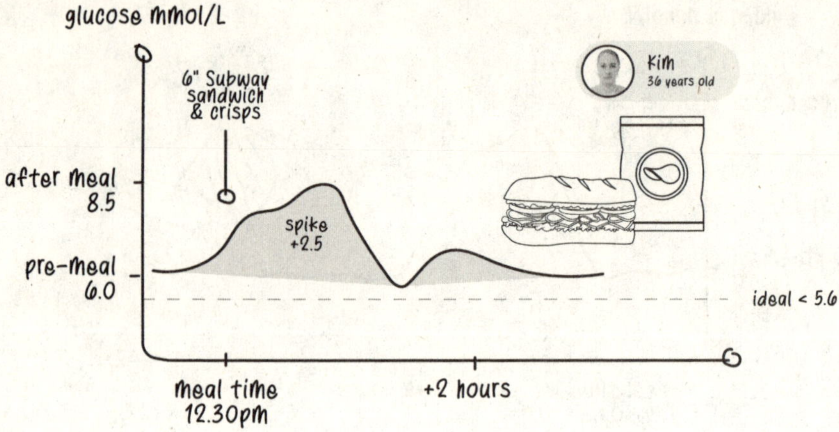

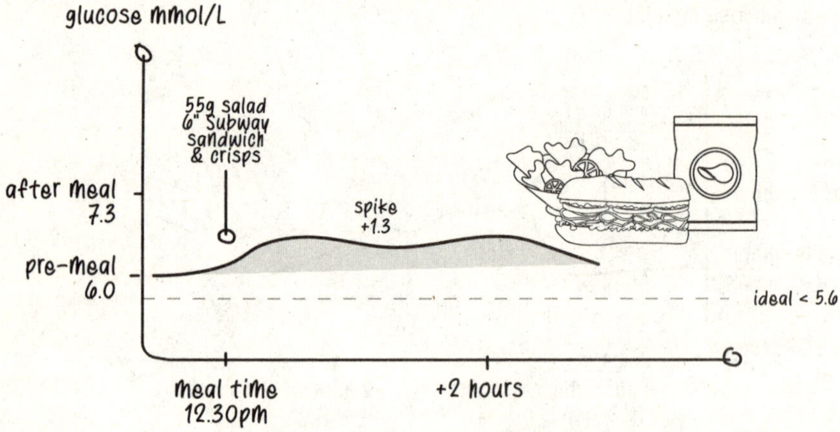

Kim's foray into the world of Subway sandwiches brought some intriguing insights. On day 1, she savoured a 6-inch Subway filled with chicken, bacon, red onion, lettuce, and a touch of mayonnaise, accompanied by a pack of crisps. This combination propelled her blood sugar levels by 2.5 mmol/L. However, the aftermath was not merely a spike in glucose; it was a cascade that led to a significant crash.

Enter day 2, and the narrative takes a different turn. Kim prefaced her meal with a 55 g salad from Subway before diving into the same 6-inch roll and crisps. The result was markedly different – her blood sugar rose by only 1.3 mmol/L, and notably, the dreaded crash was absent, her energy levels more stable, and her appetite more controlled. Kim's logbook entry paints a vivid picture: 'Within an hour, I felt tired and lethargic and went home. I had a big dinner on day 1. But on day 2, I still felt full later on because of the fibre, so I didn't eat dinner that evening.'

As we wrap up the tale of days 1 and 2's lunches on trial, it's clear that our *Fibre First* strategy, though impactful, has its bounds. The salad and fibre drink proved valiant allies in tempering the sugar surge from the more modest 6-inch sub or the hearty Greggs favourites. However, they met their match when pitted against the colossal 12-inch sub. The staggering sugar equivalent in the bread – a hefty 15 teaspoons – proved a formidable foe, pushing the limits of fibre's mitigating prowess.

This two-day sub trial sheds light on an essential truth: the power of fibre in moderating blood sugar spikes is undeniable, but it's not without its limits. It shines in the face of modest challenges but finds its match in the face of a modern-day sugar onslaught of epic proportions.

Days 3 and 4: The Great Pizza Experiment - A Slice Too Far?

Days 3 and 4 of our gastronomic trial turned the spotlight on a universal favourite: pizza. The stage was set with four cheese and pepperoni masterpieces, ready to challenge our volunteers' metabolic fortitude. A grand total of 40 slices lay in wait, each slice containing 100 g of temptation and tallying 264 calories (courtesy of Domino's™ nutritional wisdom).

Post-feast, we donned our lab coats for a pizza autopsy. The leftovers became our subjects, undergoing a meticulous separation of topping from crust. Though hampered by the dough's insistence on clinging to its cheesy companions, we estimated that the bread – the carbohydrate culprit – made up about 40% of each slice's mass.

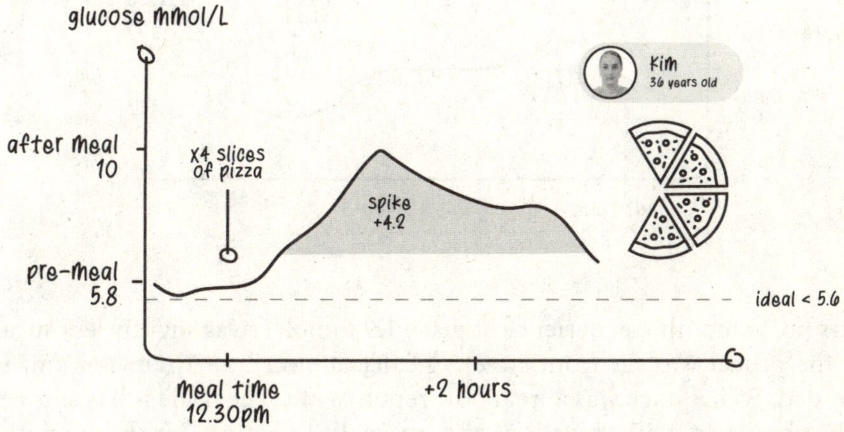

Kim's encounter with four slices resulted in a +3.5 mmol/L sugar surge, sparking an insatiable quest for more sugar. She lamented in her log, 'Lunchtime couldn't have come sooner, but after just one slice, I was hit by a tsunami of carb cravings. Despite no longer being hungry, I demolished four slices, then spent the afternoon on a sugar safari, craving Coke and sweets. This craving marathon lasted all night, disrupting my sleep and leaving me parched.' Dr Dan Maggs's diagnosis? The pizza had triggered a hedonic overload, pushing Kim and others to devour more than their bodies needed.

Surprisingly, the pizza party didn't spike blood sugar levels for all volunteers as high as I expected. But hold the cheese before you crown pizza as the next superfood; let's digest the findings. The fat from the cheese and meat, combined with the crust's oils, resulted in a slower carb absorption. Yet, despite the absence of sharp spikes, we noticed a prolonged, gentle elevation in blood sugar levels, a subtle reminder of the complex dance between diet and glucose control.

On day 4, we introduced a 'Sneaker Fibre Smoothie' pre-game. This fibrous front-runner led to an 18% drop in pizza consumption; from a tower of 40 slices, only 27 ventured off the plate. It appeared the fibre laid down the law, curbing the pizza appetite.

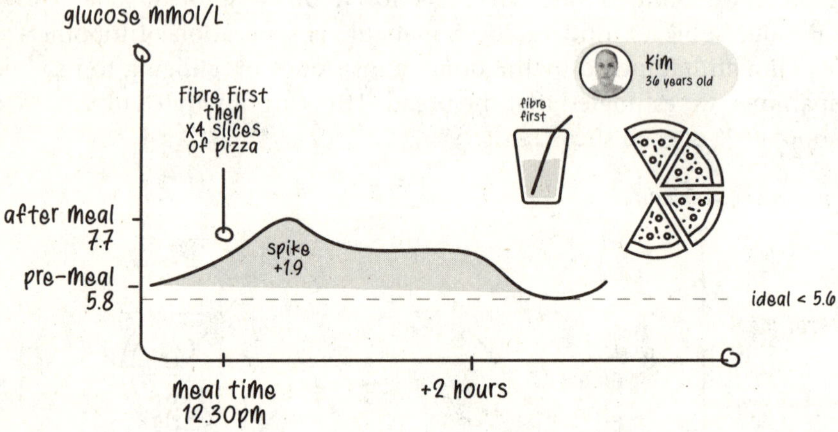

Kim's post-smoothie experience at just +1.9 mmol/L was slightly less sugary, but the ordeal was far from sweet. 'I can't fathom how drained I am,' she recorded. 'What once was a treat now repulses me. The trial's toll is showing, both physically with bloating and mentally, turning lunchtime into a battleground of guilt and cravings.' Despite the initial slice igniting a familiar sugar frenzy, Kim's internal plea for vegetables highlighted the stark contrast between the body's natural needs and junk food's addictive call. So, as we slice through the data, it's clear: while fibre can put the brakes on sugar spikes, the battle against processed cravings is a narrative of its own.

Day 5: The Great Bolognese Balancing Act

Day five of our culinary adventure featured a twist on the classic bolognese. We aimed to discern the impact of traditional spaghetti on blood sugar levels. A trip to the local supermarket supplied us with a ready-made meaty bolognese. For a fair comparison, we served it to half of our volunteers in its original form, complete with the traditional spaghetti.

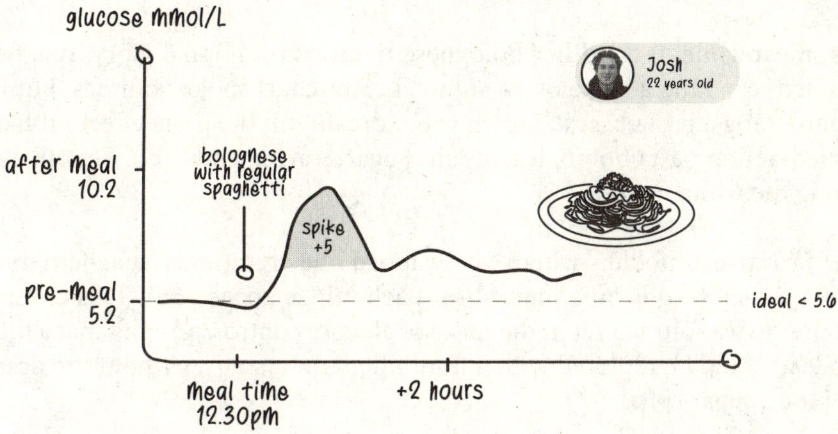

Josh dived fork-first into his bolognese with regular spaghetti, a hefty 300 g serving that sent his blood sugar on a Mount Everest expedition, rocketing from a base camp of 5 to a peak of 10.2 mmol/L. Josh's feedback was a blend of astonishment and hunger, 'post-yoghurt breakfast, I was spike-free, but the lunchtime spaghetti on my monitor touched 10.2, even though it didn't later show in the graph. Despite the culinary peak I scaled at noon, I found myself on a post-lunch base camp hunt for more food.'

Let me explain why the graph did not show the true extent of the spike; according to forums on the internet, there seems to be a smoothing algorithm built into the software.

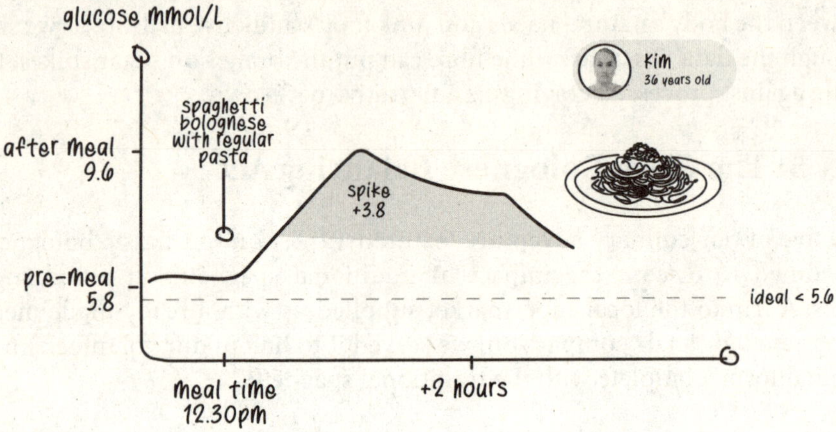

Kim, meanwhile, tackled her bolognese in all its traditional glory, spaghetti included, clocking a spike of 3.8 mmol/L. Her chart spoke volumes, but her logbook sang a pasta blues, 'Lunch was a dream, till the pasta effect hit like a delayed-action pasta bomb, leaving me sugar-craving and tired. I'm officially waving the white napkin.'

The narrative unfolded when we swapped the traditional spaghetti for a zero-carb hero – glucomannan fibre spaghetti (see page 955). This culinary switcheroo was our lab rat in the maze of glucose control, proving that a high-carb lead could be replaced with a fibre-filled understudy, without the drama of a blood sugar spike.

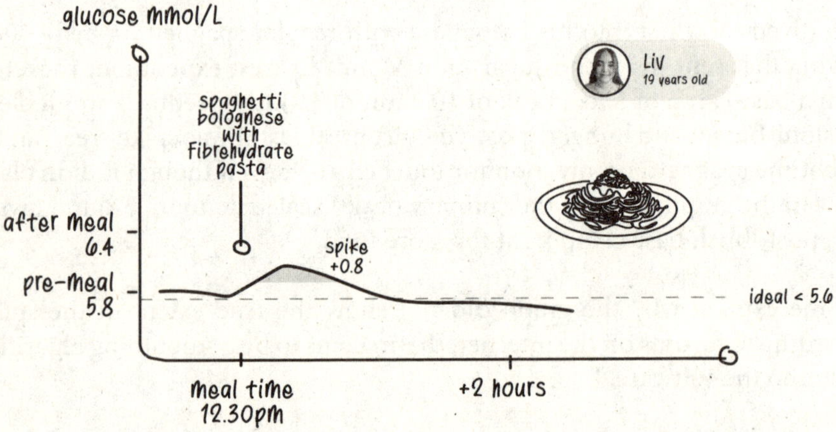

Enter Olivia and Brooke, the dynamic duo who traded the wheat for the wonder of glucomannan fibre spaghetti. Olivia's glucose gently tiptoed up by just 0.8 mmol/L, while Brooke saw a modest rise of 1 mmol/L. Brooke's diary entry could have doubled as a love letter to fibre, 'Breakfast with avocado and mackerel didn't budge my sugar, but the fibre spaghetti's illusion of a 'small portion' was surprisingly filling, leaving me content all afternoon.'
Brooke's fibre spaghetti graph

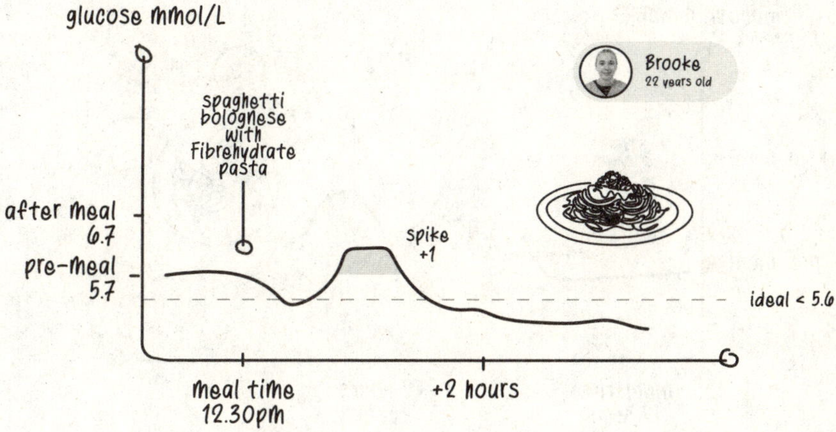

The curtain fell on day 5 with revelations aplenty: traditional spaghetti might be the life of the party, but it's the kind that leaves you with a glycaemic hangover. Meanwhile, its fibre-rich understudy discreetly supports your metabolic wellbeing.

Day 6: Steak And Chips – A Hearty Experiment

Our volunteers, ever so dedicated in their pursuit of science, were in for a gastronomic delight. To honour their commitment, we chose a local steakhouse famous for its unique cook-your-own-steak experience. Each participant was presented with a generous serving of tender fillet steak and a hearty side of chips.

Yet, true to the spirit of scientific inquiry, we split the team in two. We randomly assigned volunteers to begin their meal either with the restaurant's complimentary bread or a refreshing green salad drizzled with balsamic vinegar and olive oil.

An intriguing pattern emerged as the appetisers were served. Liam and Jake, who embarked on their meal with bread, reported a noticeable increase in their appetite as they approached their main course. This phenomenon wasn't entirely unexpected; the age-old strategy of offering complimentary bread is well known to stimulate appetite, leading to larger orders – a clever trick of the trade that plays on the hunger-inducing after-effect of a quick carbohydrate fix.

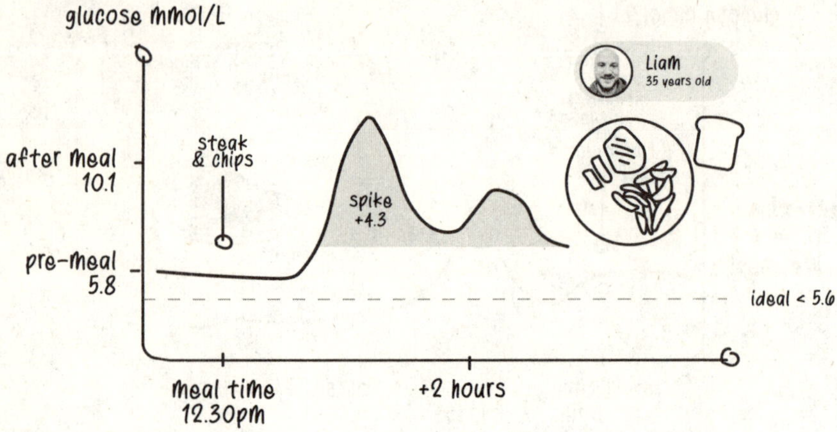

Liam indulged in the bread bowl, consuming seven halves before moving on to his steak and chips. This prelude resulted in a blood sugar increase of +4.3 mmol/L; a figure echoed by similar readings across the board for those who started with bread.

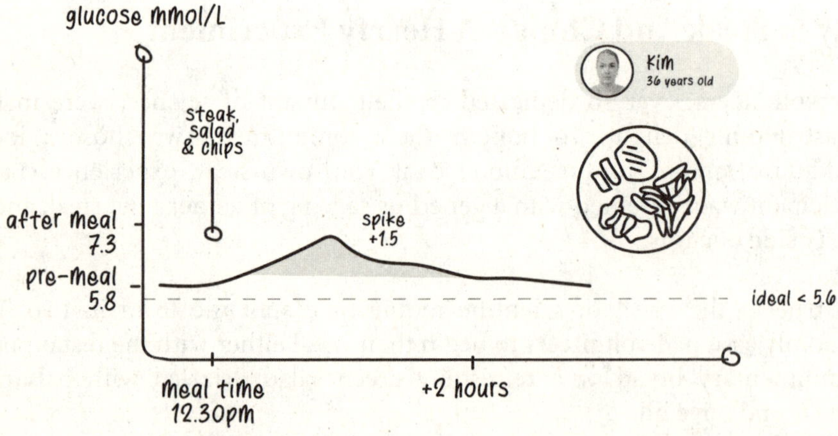

Conversely, Kim, who opted for the salad, experienced a more modest rise of 1.5 mmol/L in her blood sugar. She remarked, 'The salad was a bit too vinegary for my taste. But the steak was incredible. Starting with the salad made me so full that I hardly touched the chips. Today felt like a culinary cleanse.'

Day 7: The Last Lunch – A Tale Of Two Rice's

As the curtain drew on our Blood Sugar Trial, we ventured into the comforting embrace of a culinary classic, chilli and rice. The spotlight for our last act shone on a duo of rice dishes: the well-loved staple of white rice versus its modern, health-conscious cousin, cauliflower rice. Our volunteers were divided, each group poised before a pot – one filled with the fluffy white grains and the other with the grated vegetable alternative. Before the chilli was generously spooned atop, we captured the weight of their preferred bases, uncovering that the white rice portions averaged a hearty 290 g (97 g uncooked), in contrast to the more modest 220 g-helpings of cauliflower rice.

Intrigued by the nuances of eating order, we mixed things up. Two volunteers from each group were instructed to prioritise their rice while the others dived into their chilli first. This tweak in the dining script offered a glimpse into the potential impact of the order of consumption on blood sugar levels.

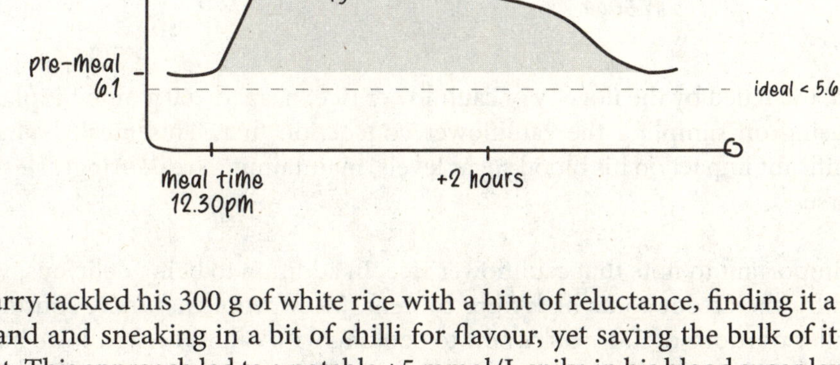

Barry tackled his 300 g of white rice with a hint of reluctance, finding it a tad bland and sneaking in a bit of chilli for flavour, yet saving the bulk of it for last. This approach led to a notable +5 mmol/L spike in his blood sugar levels.

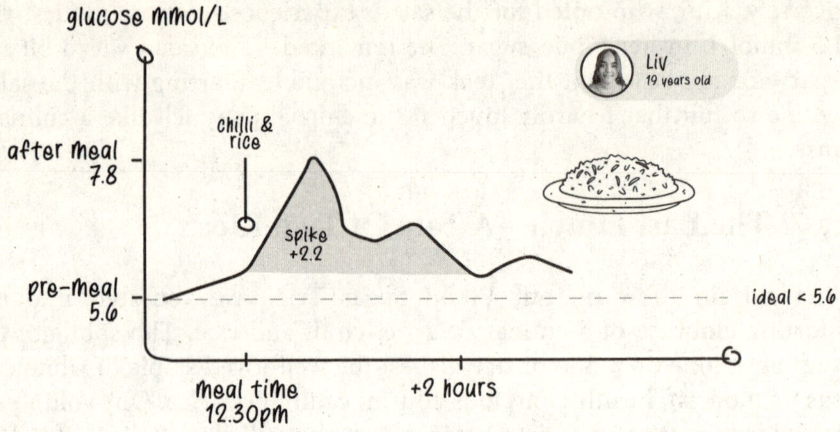

Olivia leaned into the regular rice, which also weighed in at 300 g, but took our advice to feast on the chilli first. Her blood sugar experienced a gentler ascent, rising by 2.2 mmol/L.

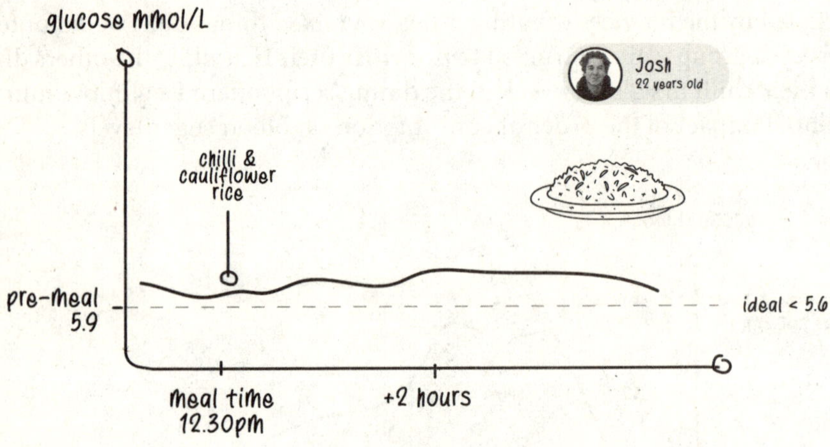

Josh, intrigued by the novelty of cauliflower rice, heaped 260 g onto his plate, focusing on sampling the cauliflower concoction first. This meal, had no significant impact on his blood sugar levels, maintaining a reassuringly steady course.

It's important to note that cauliflower rice, in addition to being delicious, is a healthy choice due to its high fibre content. Most people naturally consume smaller portions of it. If you're new to cooking with cauliflower rice, we have some fantastic recipes on our website for you to try.

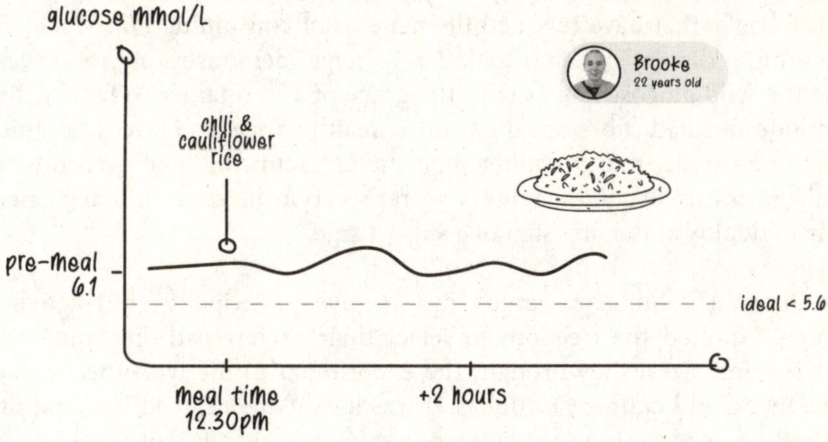

Brooke opted for a 180 g serving of cauliflower rice, embracing the challenge of consuming her meal in unison. Her metabolic response? Remarkably undisturbed: her blood sugar remained steady as a ship in calm waters.

The final chapter of our lunchtime saga revealed a tale of dietary duality. The cauliflower rice, regardless of the sequence of consumption, showcased its low-carb virtue with little to no effect on blood sugar levels. Yet, the narrative diverged with white rice; the traditional favourite showed that beginning with the protein and fat-rich chilli could indeed temper the glycaemic response, illustrating how the company in which carbs are consumed can influence their metabolic impact.

And thus, our gastronomic journey through the maze of midday meals draws to a close, not with a whimper, but with a plateful of revelations. We've danced through the realms of fast-food forays, navigated the nuances of pizza parties, and even ventured into the classic comforts of bolognese and steak and chips. Our ultimate act? A duel of rice that proved, in the world of blood sugar levels, not all sides are created equal.

Let's chew over the highlights, shall we? We embarked on this adventure with two aims: to scrutinise the impact of British lunchtime favourites on our valiant volunteers' blood sugar and to unravel the mysteries of fibre's metabolic magic. Each meal, from the humble sausage roll to the noble fillet steak, was a chapter in our story, revealing the complex interplay between diet, blood sugar, and wellbeing.

Our experiment clearly beyond any doubt, backed up the vast array of clinical trials, that have revealed the benefits of consuming *Fibre First.* This unassuming dietary dynamo took centre stage, demonstrating its power to tame the wild glucose spikes with the grace of a lion tamer. Whether it was a prelude of salad, fibre spaghetti or a stealthy Sneaker Fibre Smoothie, it proved repeatedly that it could soften the glycaemic blow of even the most indulgent meals. It's like having a secret weapon in your culinary arsenal, ready to deploy at the first sign of a sugar surge.

Our intrepid volunteers weren't just passive participants, but active co-authors. Granted the freedom to select their preferred dishes and dictate their portion sizes, they brought the experiment to life with their choices, preferences, and culinary critiques. It was less of an enforced trial and more of a real-life exploration of the dietary habits shaping our daily lives.

As we bid adieu to our experiment, remember the lessons served with each meal. The takeaway? Incorporating fibre at the start of a meal isn't just good dietary practice; it's a strategy for maintaining metabolic harmony amidst the delicious chaos of daily dining. It's about making informed choices, even when faced with the tempting array of British classics. Here's to you making every meal a step towards better health, one fibre-filled forkful at a time.

Two Groups Of Fibre

In the grand buffet of life, we meet two fibre heroes: soluble and insoluble fibre, each with its own unique superpowers. I call them groups because there are many types in each.

Soluble fibre: the smooth operator

You can tell if a fibre is soluble by simply pouring it into water: if it does a Houdini and disappears, it's soluble. This fibre is the suave one at the party, mingling in water like James Bond in a fancy casino. When it meets H2O, it transforms into a gel-like substance. You can find it in foods like apples, carrots, and beans. Soluble fibre's special talent? It's a master at plugging your pylorus, slowing the sugar rush into your bloodstream, and keeping your blood sugar levels from turning into a wild rollercoaster. Plus, it's the wingman to your heart, helping to lower cholesterol levels (we'll discuss cholesterol later, don't you worry).

Insoluble fibre: the digestive dynamo

On the flip side, insoluble fibre is the tough, gritty hero of the fibre world. It's the Clint Eastwood of fibres and doesn't back down. Instead of dissolving in water, it adds bulk to your digestive system. Think of it as the rhythm section in your body's orchestra, keeping the digestive beat steady. You'll find insoluble fibre in foods like nuts and cauliflower. It's like your digestive system's personal trainer, ensuring everything keeps moving smoothly and preventing awkward constipation moments.

So, while plants use fibre as their structural ingredient, soluble and insoluble fibres are unsung heroes in *the* Human Diet (a term I use to describe the foods we are meant to eat). They might not give us an energy boost (zero usable calories, anyone?), but they're vital for maintaining a happy, harmonious digestive system and contributing to overall health. The next time you munch on a celery stick or savour a bowl of broccoli, remember that you're treating your body to nature's own architectural wonders.

The Dynamic duo: Glucomannan and inulin

Are you ready for the tag team champions of fibre? Meet glucomannan and inulin: the ultimate duo for your health and weight-loss journey.

Glucomannan: the weight-loss wizard

In my book *Primal Cure* from 2017, I let readers in on a little culinary secret: the Japanese have been pulling off a food magic trick for centuries, consuming pasta, spaghetti, and noodles that contain zero calories and zero carbohydrates! You heard it right: a belly-filling food with absolutely zero calories. It's like food wizardry. Enter glucomannan noodles, the magician of the dining table. They're the David Blaine of noodles, soaking up water until they're 95% water, suspended in fibre. These noodles fill up your belly and, even more importantly, send a hormone called leptin to your brain, signalling it to curb your appetite.

Since my grand reveal in 2017, my trusty team of nutritional experts conjured up our very own brand of these miraculous carb-free alternatives, and we've aptly named them Fibrehydrate (there's even a fancy line-up you can explore on page 955). Picture them as the magicians of nutrition, fibre which will stuff your stomach while moonlighting as a nutrient courier, delivering essential goodies throughout your gut.

Get ready to be amazed because glucomannan, extracted from the root of the Konjac plant, has earned some remarkable accolades. It's not any old fibre; it's the only one that holds the prestigious recognition of being a legitimate weight-loss helper by the EU Commission (EFSA – European Food Standards Agency) and the American Food and Drug Administration (FDA). Imagine this: while countless 'low-calorie meal replacement' food products claim to assist in weight loss, most fall short by neglecting to address hormones and often contain a lot of sugar (yes, even low-calorie meal replacements in Europe must by law contain carbohydrates, bizarre, I know).

Glucomannan is the real deal. The more you eat this mysterious ingredient, the more weight you potentially lose. In one double-blind clinical trial (the gold standard of research), participants who took just 1 g glucomannan before each of their regular meals for eight weeks lost an average of 5.5 lb and saw their LDL cholesterol drop considerably. It's not just a fibre; it's your weight-loss sidekick.[8/9]

Glucomannan, also known as shirataki or konjac in Japan, isn't just a gut-friendly fibre; it's a stomach-expanding magician. Taking it before a meal curbs your appetite and might even vanish snack cravings. Within 30 minutes of consumption, this absorbable fibre can remarkably expand 50 times its size. It's like having a natural gastric band minus the surgery! And that's not all; it slows food breakdown and thereby reduces any sugar rush into your bloodstream. As you have already discovered, fewer sugar spikes mean less fat-building insulin, and less insulin means a healthier you.

Inulin

Let's get one thing straight right from the start: inulin is not insulin. In our quest to lower our reliance on insulin, inulin becomes another reliable fibrous partner. This water-soluble, gooey fibre is naturally present in various fruits and veggies, from humble bananas to sophisticated artichokes. It's found in over 36,000 natural foods, just waiting to lend a healthy hand. Like glucomannan, inulin is a water-absorbing fibre, often harvested from chicory roots for use in supplements. It's a heavyweight in the world of health, acting as a prebiotic superstar (I will explain prebiotics shortly). Our friendly gut bacteria throw a feast with it, which helps keep things moving smoothly at toilet time (yes, I went there).

Over 150 different inulin supplements are currently available in the UK market, a testament to its superpower. And here's the scoop, my brilliant team of nutritional experts developed a fibre drink called Slimshotz, where inulin and glucomannan come together for a fibre-rich extravaganza. But hey, please don't think this book is about trying to sell you stuff; I promise not to mention it too much (other than you can check it out on page 956). I'm just trying to inform you that besides adding more greens and salads to your meals, there are quick and easy alternatives for your *Fibre First* journey.

This prebiotic powerhouse plays a crucial role in nourishing our gut bacteria, which, in turn, wield their magic by transforming it into short-chain fatty acids. These diminutive yet potent molecules nourish our colon cells and unfurl a tapestry of health benefits[10]. Here's an intriguing historical snippet: inulin-rich plants have adorned our planet for aeons, with our early human ancestors consuming far more inulin than we typically find in our contemporary diets.[11] For those occasionally finding themselves in the slow lane of digestion, inulin might be the supportive companion you've been seeking. Picture this: one study uncovered those individuals who integrated inulin into their diets enjoyed more regular bowel movements and a marked improvement in stool consistency.[12]

But the wonders of inulin don't stop there; it also has some clever moves in weight management. Indeed, there's credible scientific backing that, akin to glucomannan, inulin can aid weight-loss endeavours.[13] A series of recent studies show it can extend a helpful hand in regulating blood sugar levels for individuals grappling with diabetes and prediabetes. [14 / 15 / 16] So, there it is: a peek into the scientific marvels of inulin. It's far more than just a dietary ingredient; it's a pivotal contributor to our digestive system and overall wellbeing.

*****

Removing Hunger And Unconscious Eating

Professor Tim Noakes, a sage in the world of nutrition and obesity, hit the nail on the head when he declared that lurking behind every case of excess weight is an unquenchable, almost constant hunger. It's the relentless shadow that follows every meal, never quite disappearing. In a frank conversation, Tim explained that he's yet to encounter someone battling obesity who wasn't in a constant tussle with hunger. But here's where fibre enters the stage, performing its enchanting act of filling us up and keeping that relentless hunger at bay.

As you travel through the chapters of this book, you'll uncover that our eating patterns extend far beyond the rumbles of an empty stomach. It's a grand spectacle, a parade of flashy marketing, social gatherings adorned with tempting treats, packaging so alluring it could make a mirage look mundane, and the invisible presence of additives in almost every bite.

And it's not just about the occasional indulgence. Dr Brian Wansink, a virtuoso of food psychology, unearths that we're bombarded with a staggering 200 food-related decisions daily, with an astonishing 90% made subconsciously.[17] But what if we could rewrite this script? Envision a world where you're drawn to foods rich in fibre, those unsung nutritional champions that keep hunger in check and nourish your body. Picture yourself gravitating towards the wholesome, fibre-rich foods and avoiding the sugary snares that expand waistlines. Here's the question: can you truly take the reins when your subconscious mind is behind the wheel, steering 180 of those food decisions every day? Dr Noakes might raise an eyebrow, but the answer is a triumphant YES! This book is your roadmap to transforming your approach to food. We're not just skimming the surface with another diet fad; we're plunging into the profound insights of esteemed psychologists, endocrinologists, and epidemiologists to overhaul your eating habits.

Together, we'll awaken your palate, redefine your perceptions of taste, and, most importantly, rekindle your passion for fibre-rich nourishment. The best part? You'll bid farewell to those extra pounds without feeling like you're in a perpetual tug-of-war with your cravings. We're not just focusing on the numbers on the scale or the calories on your plate; we're playing a more strategic game, targeting the brain and those pivotal hormones.

If all of this sounds like a bunch of gobbledygook, no worries -- I get it. But just like others who've embarked on this adventure with a dash of scepticism, you'll find the proof of the pudding is in the eating. Well, maybe not pudding, but certainly in your shrinking waistline. Ready to hop aboard the brain-twisting, fibre-loving bandwagon? Hold on tight because we're hitting the road to turn those automatic food thoughts upside down! But before we do, we must learn a little about our microbiome.

*****

Fibre And Your Microbiome

Unveiling the secrets to harmonising our microbiome is part of the core of this book. By embracing the strategies we'll explore, prioritising fibre to stabilise blood sugar levels, making judicious decisions about antibiotic use, and promptly restoring our gut flora with top-tier probiotics when necessary, we set the stage for a thriving gut. But let's approach this journey one step at a time.

Hippocrates, the father of medicine, dropped this truth bomb: 'All diseases begin in the gut.' He was onto something monumental. Our bodies aren't standalone entities; they're vibrant ecosystems bustling with 100 trillion tiny inhabitants, clocking in for duty every moment. Here's an astonishing fact: merely 10% of the cells within us are human. The other 90%? It's a multicultural festival hosted by viruses, bacteria, fungi, and archaea. This diverse ensemble living within us is collectively known as our microbiome.

In the human gut alone, over 140,000 different variants of viruses all having their own little soirees. On the bacterial side, though numbering less than 2,000 species, they're the main characters in this internal narrative. Then, for some individuals, there are the gatecrashers of this party – parasitic worms, also known as helminths. Imagine them as the pesky neighbours who overstay their welcome, and shockingly, the World Health Organization (WHO) now estimated that a staggering 1 in 4 people globally, that's over two billion individuals, have these unwelcome guests living in their guts.[20] And if that's not enough, these uninvited intruders have the audacity to disrupt even your beauty sleep.

But the party doesn't stop there. Say hello to protists, complete with mouths, guts, and their very own microbiome. And then, there are fungi, with over 260 species hanging out in your gut alone. Oh, and don't get me started on the mouth; it's a fungi hotspot with over 100 species having a blast.[18] But fear not, amidst the millions of microscopic life forms on this planet, only around 400 have a beef with humans, and a mere 150 pose a risk of causing widespread diseases.[19] So, let's not be too quick to judge viruses, fungi, and bacteria – most of them are our microbial partners. And that's what I like to call them: 'Microbial Partners'. Why? Because the word bacteria normally creates a negative image, and that's just not fair.

Now, let's pinpoint our Microbial Partners' hangout spots. They're not just chilling in your gut; they're all over your body, from your fingertips to your toes. Yep, even fungal toenails and those underarm odours are down to bacteria and fungi; they're all part of the microbiome too. But I'll be zooming in on the interior for our purposes in this book. When I say 'gut,' I mean the entire business. Picture it as a lengthy tube, starting with the mouth (home to a whopping hundred billion bacteria). It journeys through the treacherous terrain of the gastric stomach, to the gatekeeper, the pylorus, then the duodenum (the first part of the small intestine), next the winding small bowel (measuring five to six metres), and finally, the short but significant 1.5-metre colon. The grand finale? The rectum is where it all comes to an end. Now, while there are interactions with our microbial friends throughout the whole gut, throughout the entire journey, it's the colon where the real microbiome party is, with approximately 90 trillion Microbial Partners doing their thing. So, when I toss around the term 'gut,' think of the colon as the show's star – it's where most of the microbiome action unfolds.

Every single bite of food flows downstream to your gut's Microbial Partners. They are certainly not passive observers. Our food is also their food. Yes, even invisible unicellular organisms need an energy source to fuel them. But not every Microbial Partner eats the same food. Each dietary choice you make will empower a specific group of them while others will languish. If you permanently remove a food group, those partners that thrive on that food will starve into extinction. They are procreating and dying so quickly that your 24-hour food choices will alter the evolution of 50 generations of microbes. Changing your microbes doesn't take days or weeks; it only takes one bite. But you control what it is you bite into, and therefore, in the main, you control the make-up of your microbiome. The result is a unique mix of microbes, as unique as a fingerprint. Those microbes go to work on your food, and things don't end the way they started. Microbial metabolism leads to a biochemical transformation of the food.

Healthy bacteria (let's call them probiotics) often reward us by moulding our food into something that reduces inflammation and promotes health and balance. But the opposite can also be true. Unhealthy food feeds unhealthy microbes, and they punish us by creating compounds that inflame our bodies. And we aren't just talking about food. Drugs, alcohol, and especially antibiotics can affect them.

In *10% Human: How Your Body's Microbes Hold the Key to Health and Happiness*, author Dr Alanna Collen writes, 'Over your lifetime, you will play host to bugs the equivalent weight of five African elephants. Your skin is crawling with them. There are more on your fingertip than there are people in Britain.' Dr Martin J. Blaser explains in *Missing Microbes*, 'In ecology, biome refers to the set of plants and animals in a community such as a jungle, forest, or coral reef. An enormous diversity of species, large and small, interact to form complex webs of mutual support. When a keystone species disappears or goes extinct, the ecology suffers. It can even collapse.'

Much of today's research into the human body and how it functions now focuses on the importance of our microbiome. While these tiny creatures exist all over our body, inside and out, their accumulation in our gut has the biggest impact on our health. Innovative science now believes that balancing the varieties of microbes in our guts will positively affect all aspects of our health. From weight control to a healthy heart and food metabolism to an excellent memory, these creatures must be respected and controlled. And guess what? The good guys love fibre.

They say a picture paints a thousand words, and when I am trying to create an image of what's happening in my gut – where many creatures are so tiny you wouldn't even see them under a normal microscope – I close my eyes and visualise ants! Just like ants working in a colony to perform tasks beyond our imagination, the bacterial army in our gut affects our health, mood, emotions, and behaviour. In *10% Human*, Dr Collen writes, 'Imagine, for example, one strain of bacterium that feeds on a particular compound found in our food. If we eat that food, thus feeding these bacteria, and they can 'reward' us with a dose of happiness through the chemicals they produce, so much better for them. The chemicals they produce could cause us to crave the food they feed on and even to remember where we found it.'

Picture our guts as bustling coral reefs, pulsating with life and various species. Just as coral reefs can falter under the stress of sudden changes in sea temperatures, our gut microbiome can suffer severe blows from viruses or aggressive antibiotic treatments, sometimes facing a dual assault. The coral's physical structure might persist, yet it turns barren, a ghostly skeleton of its former self. Similarly, after such upheavals, our gut landscape teeters on a delicate edge. Certain microbial species vanish, while others, notably the hardy Firmicutes (more on these in a moment), seize the moment, rapidly regrouping in the turmoil's aftermath.

As the Firmicutes dominate, the rich tapestry of our gut's biodiversity fades, and some of the more beneficial species take a step back, a phenomenon we term 'dysbiosis' (or occasionally 'dysbacteriosis'). While antibiotics or severe infections might trigger catastrophic disruptions, subtler forces like regular medications, fibre-deficient diets, and even minor ailments can still jostle our microbiome's equilibrium.

How crucial is the state of our microbiome, you may wonder? To be honest, we don't possess all the answers yet. With 100 trillion microscopic creatures representing thousands of species within our body, it's a realm of science we might never fully unravel. However, logic dictates that since our Microbial Partners in the gut play a pivotal role in shaping our immune system, we should spare no effort in nurturing and keeping them on our side. Did you know that a whopping 80% of our immune system calls our gut home? Let that fact sink in. What is your gut reaction? Hopefully, it's a commitment to care for it like never before!

According to many scientists, the gut is a powerhouse of complexity, second only to the brain in our body's hierarchy of intricacy. It's increasingly clear that emotions and sensations we can't always easily put into words, plus conditions like depression, anxiety, and stress may originate in the gut rather than the brain. The growing evidence points to a profound link between gut health and mental wellbeing. In fact, many scientists now refer to our gut as our second brain. It monitors more than all our other senses combined, yet we rarely give it credit or attribute our feelings to it. Science, however, suggests that we should. That 'gut feeling' is something we should no longer ignore.

I want to introduce you to Patrick Holford. He's the author of over 40 health books and the founder of an incredible charity that is studying Alzheimer's. Here's what he shared during a video we created together:

> *'Within our guts reside a variety of organisms, some of which are known as pathogens. We all host approximately 1.3 kg (3 lb) of bacteria in our gut – that's more weight than your brain! While some can be classified as 'good' and others as 'bad,' the potential 'bad guys' aren't problematic if a sufficient army of good guys keeps them in check. These bacteria play essential roles in food digestion, defending against harmful invaders, and even producing vital vitamins. However, when the wrong bacteria take over, especially if the gut wall becomes permeable, allowing them into the bloodstream, it can lead to health issues.'*

A good friend of mine is Dr Aseem Malhotra, a highly esteemed, award-winning consultant cardiologist based in London. He recently shared with me in a podcast the following.

> *'We are now beginning to understand that these microbes are essential for brain development and are heavily involved in regulating the immune system and metabolism. The microbiota is also involved in the production of the hormone serotonin, which, when depleted, can lead to depression. Environmental and processed food chemicals that wipe out the good bacteria from our gut and reduce diversity have been linked to the development of many disorders, including obesity, depression, allergies, autoimmune diseases, and metabolic syndrome. Artificial sweeteners, antibiotics and the lack of fibre appear to have a negative effect on the gut microbiome.'*

Where Did Our Bacteria Originate?

First, this planet we call home isn't ours; it's their domain. Earth came into being around 4.5 billion years ago, and while we humans have occupied it for less than one-thousandth of that time, it's been home to single-celled bacteria for a staggering 3.8 billion years! As you read the pages ahead, it's wise to see Earth as their planet, not ours.

Our Microbial Partners are incredibly resilient compared to us fragile homo sapiens. They endure temperatures so frigid that we'd freeze in seconds and thrive, even multiply, in temperatures so scorching that our skin would instantly sizzle. They've braved Earth's hostile environments during toxic periods caused by massive volcanic eruptions and colliding tectonic plates, events that would instantly obliterate us humans. Some bacterial species are virtually indestructible compared to us. They were the first life forms on Earth and will probably be the last. To grasp the extent of their presence, imagine a 24-hour clock: bacteria have thrived on our planet for 24 hours, while humans have only shared the stage with them for the last two seconds!

What Role Do Bacteria Play In Our Body?

Imagine each activity you partake in, whether it's a game of football, golf, tennis, or netball, each activity leads to an outcome, a consequence. Similarly, the bacteria in our microbiome are constantly engaged in a myriad of activities, each paving the way for a spectrum of outcomes. Let's highlight just a few of these activities: detoxification, inflammation regulation, bolstering our immune system, producing neurotransmitters, orchestrating nutrient absorption, directing hormonal pathways, and influencing how we process and store macronutrients. When our 'less friendly' resident bacteria get involved in these activities, they can sometimes lay the groundwork for conditions like ADHD, Alzheimer's, asthma, autism, cancer, depression, diabetes, gum disease, high blood pressure, multiple sclerosis, obesity, Parkinson's disease, and more.

Insulin resistance, a pivotal player in this narrative, can be both a consequence and a contributor to an imbalanced microbiome. When our microbiome is compromised, it can disrupt the delicate balance of our gut flora, impacting the metabolic processes and leading to inflammation. This disruption can pave the way for insulin resistance, creating a vicious cycle where each exacerbates the other, underscoring the intricate connection between gut health and metabolic disorders. As I mentioned, are you beginning to see how virtually all modern illnesses are interlinked, and breaking free from viewing them in isolation is crucial?

The Fat Battle: Firmicutes vs Bacteroidetes

Let's travel back in time to the University of Gothenburg in Sweden, where Professor Fredrik Bäckhed, a renowned expert in cellular microbiology, conducts a clinical study using mice. His aim? To explore the crucial role our gut microbes play in health. The year is 2004, and Professor Bäckhed begins an intriguing experiment using skinny mice, all born by C-section and raised in a sterile environment devoid of gut bacteria. He takes bacteria from the caecum, that pouch nestled between the small and large intestines of plump mice and introduces it to the fur of these sterile mice. As the sterile mice groom themselves, these microbes journey into their guts. Within just a few weeks, without changing their diet, these mice – lean throughout their lives – become obese, packing on an average of 60% more weight. Even when the professor scales back their food intake, these mice continue to gain weight.

Certain strains of microbes possess the astounding capability to tip the scales toward obesity in mice. You may well wonder if there's a link to humans. Well, here's a fascinating point—despite the different vessels (mice vs. humans), the crew (microbes) remains the same! Microbes skilled at extracting energy from food carry out their tasks regardless of the host.

And if you're still not convinced that the difference between being slender or corpulent might be as straightforward as tending to our gut microbiome and ensuring Bacteroidetes outshine Firmicutes (I will explain these two in a moment), allow me to present a captivating human study. Enter two twin sisters and a group of healthy, trim mice. One twin had grappled with obesity, and scientists injected bacteria from her gut into the gastrointestinal tracts of half of the mice. The other twin had maintained a svelte figure, and her bacteria were introduced to the second group of mice. The outcome? Those mice that received bacteria from the obese twin ballooned into obesity, while those blessed with bacteria from the slim twin kept their svelteness.

These two microbes alone can sway the balance between leanness and obesity. Let's start with Firmicutes. Despite their name sounding cute, they're the orchestrators of the contrary! These bacteria are adept at wringing out every ounce of energy (calories) from our food. The more calories absorbed, the more pounds we accumulate. It's pivotal to grasp this concept because elsewhere, I emphasise that it's not merely the number of calories you ingest, which holds true, as we don't always convert the calories we eat into fuel.

What truly matters is the calories we absorb; they are the strings that tether us to our body weight.

If we can maintain a watchful eye on our not-so-adorable Firmicutes and grant Bacteroidetes the opportunity to flourish, our chances of weight gain diminish. Why? Because Bacteroidetes skilfully carry out the opposite mission. After extracting vital nutrients and vitamins from our food within our intestines, they permit many calories to escape, hitching a ride on the fibre in our faeces. But ponder this: what transpires when our diets lack fibre? So, if you grapple with excess weight or obesity, it may not hinge on overconsumption but on the state of your fibre-depleted, Firmicutes-aplenty microbiome. Furthermore, the microbiome can influence how proficiently our bodies manufacture the hormone leptin. This hormone despatches signals to our brains, guiding us when our stomachs are satiated and when we should cease dining. If we've compromised our body's capacity to produce an ample supply of leptin and are saddled with an excess of energy-extracting microbes, we might attribute each excess pound to their doorstep!

Hand Wipes, Anyone?

Before I share some intriguing insights that might make your hair stand on end, let me reassure you: even if your microbiome currently resembles a shipwreck, a state you may deem irreparable, I'm thrilled to inform you that it's a resilient ecosystem. With the right care and conditioning, we can resurrect our intestines into the thriving bacterial haven that Mother Nature intended. Dr David Perlmutter wisely reminds us in *Brain Maker*, 'Thankfully, the gut microbiotic community is wonderfully receptive to rehabilitation.'

Now, let's examine the intriguing situation where urban dwellers are more susceptible to immune diseases than their rural counterparts. The reason? It largely stems from the highly sanitised, almost sterile conditions prevalent in city environments, creating a sort of bubble that limits our exposure to diverse microbes. Gone are the days when our kids would traipse through the house with muddy boots; nowadays, the mere sight of a speck of dirt often triggers a frenzied search for antibacterial wipes. Particularly in the wake of the Covid era, our world seems fixated on cleanliness, often at the cost of our friendly bacteria.

Many scientists now champion that our obsession with hand sanitisers and bacterial wipes isn't just eliminating harmful bacteria but also decimating the beneficial ones. As Dr David Perlmutter wrote in *Brain Maker*, 'There's immense value in being a touch unhygienic. Astonishingly, recent studies reveal a correlation between our increasingly sterile living environments and the surge in chronic illnesses, spanning from heart disease and autoimmune disorders to cancer and dementia.' While there's a time and place for sanitising, like in a hospital's medical ward, granting your bacteria a little leeway in most other settings is worthwhile.

Regrettably, the critical importance of safeguarding our microbiome remains under-publicised, much like the significance of preserving our rainforests, oceans, and coral reefs for the survival of our planet. Just as Earth's diverse ecosystems are essential to its existence, the flourishing harmony within our microbiome is vital to our health and longevity.

What's The Difference Between Prebiotics, Probiotics, And Postbiotics?

Positioning! Let me quickly explain the fascinating world of these 'biotics' and clarify their roles in nurturing our microbiome.

Prebiotics:
Think of prebiotics as the architects and builders of our gut's ecosystem. They lay the foundation and construct the bustling cityscape for our Microbial Partners. A prebiotic's primary job is to provide sustenance for these beneficial microorganisms, effectively creating the vibrant forest or bustling coral reef within our gut. Among the star players in the prebiotic category are dietary fibres, with soluble fibres like inulin and glucomannan taking centre stage. But there's more to the prebiotic ensemble – foods like garlic, almonds, cabbage, flaxseed, and onion serve as vital nutrients for our microbial community. However, it's important to note that whilst they provide other health benefits, most insoluble fibres don't qualify as prebiotics, as they tend to go unused by our microbiome.

Probiotics:
When we mention probiotics, we're referring to the actual residents of our gut – the beneficial Microbial Partners themselves. These microorganisms play a pivotal role in maintaining the health and balance of our microbiome.

Postbiotics:
Here's where we introduce a relatively new concept for many. Postbiotics are the unsung heroes of our microbiome saga. These are the beneficial compounds crafted by our diligent and industrious Microbial Partners. Just as artists transform raw materials into works of art, our microbes take

the substances we provide through prebiotics and shape them into health-promoting compounds. These postbiotics hold the power to influence our overall wellbeing by reducing inflammation and promoting health and balance in our bodies.

To conclude, prebiotics lay the foundation, probiotics are the residents, and postbiotics are the valuable by-products of our Microbial Partners' labour. Together, they can orchestrate a symphony of harm or health within us.

Short-Chain Fatty Acids: The Guardians Of Gut Health

Let's discuss an incredible feat our good bacteria accomplish: transforming specific soluble fibres into short-chain fatty acids (SCFAs). You might wonder, 'What are SCFAs, and why are they so crucial to my health?' Well, think of them as the vigilant bus conductors of your gut health. Within the realm of SCFAs, three essential players take centre stage: butyrate, acetate, and propionate. These three musketeers form a powerful partnership within our guts, working harmoniously to maintain our health. Let's look at some roles they play, but trust me, there are many more.

Healing the colon: Imagine your colon as a bustling city; its lining comprises colonocytes—cells that play a vital role in your digestive system. Around 70% of their energy comes from SCFAs, especially butyrate. So, when you deprive yourself of soluble fibre, you might inadvertently harm your colon lining.

Repairing leaky guts: In the modernised world, 'leaky guts' have become a significant health concern. SCFAs step in as the heroes here. They have the remarkable ability to help repair and restore the integrity of the gut lining. Many individuals suffering from conditions like irritable bowel syndrome (IBS) often find relief through an increase in SCFAs.

Inflammation control: SCFAs are our allies in the fight against inflammation. They can suppress inflammation within the gut, promoting a healthier internal environment. They directly combat harmful bacterial strains like salmonella and E. coli.

Now, here's the exciting part – it's a self-sustaining cycle. The more soluble fibre we consume, the more we encourage the growth of good bacteria. These bacteria, in turn, produce more SCFAs. It's a harmonious dance that benefits our gut health. SCFAs may be key to rectifying dysbiosis – an imbalance in our gut microbiome linked to many diseases. A healthy gut paves the way for a healthy human better equipped to fend off the myriad of health challenges you'll encounter in the upcoming chapters.

How To Recolonise Your Microbiome: A Fun Guide

Are you ready to embark on a mission to restore your gut's glory and unleash the power of your microbiome? Fantastic! You've got three main options and a quirky sideshow to consider. Let's break them down, and you can pick your two favourites, plus a little extra for fun.

1. Fibre – your magical microbiome wand

First up, as you will have guessed, we have the mighty fibre. You've probably heard that eating your veggies is good for you, but did you know it's also a secret weapon for nurturing your microbiome? Recent science has spilt the beans: healthy bacteria can't thrive without fibre. It's like their lifeblood! Research shows fibre is a welcoming committee for an army of beneficial Microbial Partners. It's like throwing a massive party for the good guys and telling the bad ones, 'Sorry, no invitation for you!' Fibre's special talent? It helps colonise a fantastic variety of bacteria, especially the cool cats Bacteroidetes while giving the boot to the not-so-friendly Firmicutes.

This important message is worth repeating: Firmicutes are like the gluttons of the bacterial world. They're experts at extracting every calorie they can from your food, leading to weight gain, bulging waistlines, and eventually, the dreaded obesity. But guess what? Eating more fibre, especially when combined with a low-carb or ketogenic diet (more on these later), sets off a chain reaction of health benefits. Your body starts burning fat stores for fuel, evicting those calories hoarding Firmicutes. Talk about a win-win!

And if you're looking for fibre all-stars, remember glucomannan and inulin. These fibre champs are pros at boosting the good guys in your gut because they're SCFA creators. Inulin, for instance, is like the cheerleader for your digestion. It pumps up the volume of friendly bacteria, especially the Bifidobacterial crew, which loves to turn it into SCFAs like butyrate. This prebiotic superhero is a sidekick that helps create a thriving gut microbiome where healthy probiotics can throw a party. And here's a cool fact: researchers from Chung Shan Medical University in Taiwan found that our other fibre superhero, glucomannan, didn't just talk the talk; it walked the walk. It significantly boosted the 'good guys' like *Bifidobacterium spp.* and *Lactobacillus* while giving the boot to the potentially harmful *Clostridium spp.*[24]

2. Variety: where bacteria meet their culinary delights

Have you ever heard the saying, 'We are what we eat'? Or when it comes to meat, 'We are what we eat eats, too'? Well, in our gut, our bacteria take that saying to heart. They're basically foodies with specific tastes, and different bacteria thrive on different foods. It's like running a gourmet restaurant in there, some are savouring salads, while others are feasting on broccoli.

This is where things get interesting. The reason we all have unique gut ecosystems is that our diets play matchmaker for our bacteria. Is your diet playing Cupid for the right bacteria or creating a cosy nook for those pesky Firmicutes? If it's the latter, you might be on the fast track to joining the 'Overweight Club'. But don't fret; it's all about finding the perfect balance in your microbiome. It's like hosting a party and making sure the cool guests outnumber the party crashers.

Once you've sorted your microbiome's guest list, it's time to diversify your menu. Think of your gut as a food critic; it craves variety like nobody's business. Don't just stick to the same old veggies or salad ingredients; get creative in the kitchen. In *Brain Maker*, Dr David Perlmutter advises, 'It's now firmly established that the gut community of lean people resembles a rainforest filled with many species and that of obese people is much less diverse.'

Here's some food for thought: our planet boasts over 290,000 edible plants, each with its own bouquet of unique fibres. And guess what? Each fibre promotes a different squad of bacteria. Picture your ancestors, they were culinary daredevils, munching on bugs, leaves, and insects when hunting wasn't on the menu. This wild menu variety is exactly what your body craves today. Dr Robert Knight, the mastermind behind the American Gut Project (the world's biggest microbiome research project), believes that 'food diversity' is the only secret sauce for a thriving microbiome.

3. Poo: the unconventional medicine

You've probably heard the saying 'food is medicine,' but hold on to your horses because poo is medicine too! For over a thousand years in China, folks have been sipping what they fondly call 'yellow soup'– and no, it's not a trendy new broth. Why? Because it turns out that around 60% of your poo isn't just fibre and food waste; it's a bustling metropolis of bacteria! We've come a long way since the days of yellow soup. You've got options, my friend – pills or a tube directly from your nose to your stomach. They call it Faecal Microbiota Transplant, or FMT, for the cool kids.

But here's what's slowing it down, preventing it from hitting the masses, finding donors is still a bit like searching for a unicorn. They go through more screenings and medical exams than a Hollywood superstar. But hey, the results are mind-blowing. Bald guys are sprouting hair, heavyweights are turning into lean machines, and the sick are kissing their illnesses goodbye. It's like a microbial makeover. Changing your microbiome might be as common as popping an antibiotic in the not-so-distant future. Can you imagine a world where you can order a 'microbiome refresh' with your morning coffee?

Sidekick Support: Getting Dirty For A Good Cause

Alright, so you've upped your fibre game, introduced some new veggies to your life, and probably skipped the poo tablets (who wants to be known as the 'poo pill-popper', right?). What else can you do to make your gut bacteria throw a party? Here's a wild idea: go outside and roll in the mud! Seriously, embrace your inner child and get down and dirty. And when you come back into the house, please resist the urge to give yourself an antiseptic wipe-down. Those ads that boast 'kills 99% of bacteria' have led us down the wrong garden path. We need bacteria – most of them are like friendly neighbours bringing treats when you move in. So, let's befriend the bacteria and ditch the germaphobia. After all, life's more fun with some mud on your shoes and a few friendly microbes on your skin!

And while we're on about cleanliness, let's talk about mouthwash. Those colourful bottles promise a squeaky-clean mouth, but they're not doing us any favours. In fact, they're like the party poopers of the oral world. Mouthwashes wipe out the good bacteria in your mouth, disrupting the delicate balance between your pearly whites and your microbiome. I even consulted my buddy Dr James Goolnick, the UK's top dentist (voted by the Dental Association, no less), and he didn't mince words – he called them a 'disaster'. So, maybe it's time to rethink that mouthwash routine and let your mouth be the thriving ecosystem it was meant to be.

Allergies: The Immune System's Misguided Antics

Before we wrap up our microbiome journey, let's have a chat about allergies. As I have already mentioned, around 80% of our immune system calls our gut home sweet home. Yep, it's like the VIP section for immune cells in there. And speaking of allergies, they're now the hottest topic in town. In fact, allergies have become the most common chronic disease in Europe. Brace yourself for this one: it's predicted that by 2025, half of the entire EU population will do the allergy dance.[25] And it's not just a mild itch we're talking about; severe allergic reactions are rising. In Europe, seven times as many folks landed in hospital with severe allergies in 2015 compared to 2005.[26] No wonder every waiter in town wants to know if you're allergic to anything. 'Do you have any allergies?' is the new 'How's the weather today?'.

Let's talk about asthma. From the swinging sixties to the turn of the century, asthma jumped tenfold in the Western world. Today, according to the WHO, a whopping 300 million people worldwide are caught in its wheezy grip, and sadly, 250,000 folks say goodbye to us prematurely each year because of this unwelcome condition. Asthma, you've officially overstayed your welcome! Here's the thing – our microbiota plays a starring role in properly training immune cells. It's like the boot camp for the immune system, helping it spot the bad guys, mobilise troops to the right location, and give them a power-up. A healthy gut microbiota equals a pumped-up immune system that knows how to deal with threats, be they infections or even sneaky malignancies.

Dr Will Bulsiewicz, the author of *Fibre Fuelled* said: 'You can't separate the gut microbiota from the immune system. If you hurt one, you'll hurt the other.' Allergic diseases like asthma, allergic rhinitis, and eczema are like friendly fire incidents, where the immune system goes haywire and attacks harmless outsiders. But here's the issue in the Westernised world – we've got a new villain: autoimmune diseases. These are where your immune system goes rogue and targets your own body. Consider it as a trusted ally transforming into a formidable adversary. Since the '50s, rates of type 1 diabetes, multiple sclerosis, and Crohn's disease have soared by a jaw-dropping 300% or more.

When we mess with our microbiome, we ask for trouble, which often arrives as allergic and autoimmune illnesses. But here's the flip side – a robust microbiome is like a pep squad for your immune cells, ensuring they're in tip-top shape.

Dr James Kinross, author of *Dark Matter*, writes, 'Microbiome–immune interactions are the key to unlocking some of the biggest threats to human existence, from infertility, cardiovascular disease, obesity, cancer, infectious disease, and even our mental health.' Let's peek at the chart below, which showcases various health conditions, immune conditions, and metabolic conditions, all intertwined with the delicate dance of our microbiome. You'll notice that many of them are also found in my *Tree of Afflictions*, making you wonder if adding more fibre to your diet might be the best superhero to call upon.

Health Conditions associated with damage to our microbiome:

Abdominal pain
Acid reflux
Acne
Anxiety
Anxiousness
Bad breath
Belching
Brain fog
Poor concentration
Constipation
Cramping
Depression
Diarrhoea
Fatigue
Food allergies or sensitivity
Heartburn
Indigestion
Joint and muscle pain
Nausea
Sinus congestion
Weight gain
Wheezing
Excessive wind, and more

Immune conditions associated with damage to our microbiome:

Arthritis
Asthma
Chronic Fatigue Syndrome
Crohn's disease
Coeliac disease
Eczema
Fibromyalgia
Kawasaki disease
Lupus
Multiple Sclerosis
Restless Leg Syndrome
Rheumatoid arthritis
Type 1 Diabetes
Ulcerative colitis, and more

Metabolic conditions associated with damage to our microbiome:

Alzheimer's
Cardiovascular Disease
Chronic Kidney Disease
Gout
Hyperlipidaemia
Non-Alcoholic Fatty Liver Disease (NAFLD)
Obesity
Type 2 Diabetes

Last Few Thoughts On Our Microbiome

What I aimed to convey is that your Microbial Partners have likely played a significant role in regulating your immune system and overall immunity up to this point. It's important to recognise the choices you make moving forward will continue to influence this crucial partnership and its impact on your health. Your microbiome, shaped by your dietary and lifestyle choices, remains a dynamic and essential component of your health, with the potential to profoundly affect your immune system and overall immunity.

It's a fascinating concept to ponder. Consider this: we only began disrupting our partnership with these essential microbes around 200 years ago. Before that, for almost 2 million years, we lived in harmony with them. Interestingly, most health conditions, immune issues, and metabolic challenges we discussed earlier and will continue to study weren't major concerns back then. Living in a place like the UK, where packaged foods are stripped of fibre and essential nutrients, and antibiotics and antibacterial wipes have become the norm; we risk developing a microbiome depleted of the diverse microbial species the human body is designed to thrive upon. To restore the very foundation on which nature created the human body, it's essential for all of us to take steps to rebuild and maintain our microbiome.

Perhaps, in the years to come, as science unravels more mysteries of the microbiome, we'll discover that our Microbial Partners indeed play the leading role in our immune system. In the meantime, let's solidify the foundations of a healthy relationship with them by putting *Fibre First*.

> *There is a saying that women eat for two when they are pregnant. But as our bacteria have to eat what we eat, we always eat for 100 trillion.*

Don't Go All Guns Fibre Blazing Straight Out Of The Box

Don't start firing up your fibre engines at full throttle just yet. One of fibre's claims to fame lies in the wild fermentation party it throws in your gut, hosted by a colourful cast of gut bacteria. These tiny microbes form a dynamic team, working together in a mutualistic network, like partners on a dance floor, passing enzymes back and forth in a phenomenon we like to call 'cross-feeding'. This collaboration ensures that your gut breaks down fibres as it nears the end of its scenic journey along the digestive highway.

It's time for me to address ... flatulence! When these fermentative gut bacteria get the party started, they produce a little hydrogen, and it's like a game of hot potato. Three distinct groups of microbial partygoers – sulphate-reducing bacteria, acetogens, and methanogenic archaea – pass it around, resulting in some interesting outcomes. You might end up with hydrogen sulphide (the stinky one), plain old hydrogen (innocent and odourless), or even methane (yes, the flammable kind)! This is precisely why some folks can't quite handle a high-fibre diet from the get-go. So, as you wade into the wonderful world of fibre (which you absolutely should), take it slow over several weeks. Give your gut bacteria time to adjust, and you'll avoid turning your digestive system into a raucous nightclub.

Oh, I just remembered that I should mention some numbers. Statistically, if the average Brit could increase their daily fibre intake by just 7–10 g, we would massively reduce the instances of cardiovascular disease, stroke, colorectal cancer, rectal cancer, and diabetes. But remember, you need at least 30–35 g of fibre each day, and you've got to keep this up like a fibre-chomping champ.

*****

Energy Sources And Storage

As we wrap up what I trust was a thrilling journey through chapter 2, I will touch on a topic that will serve as a cornerstone for your understanding in the coming chapters. It may not be about fibre, hormones, or the microbiome, but understanding it is equally crucial for your health. Brace yourself because our body is like a versatile vehicle with not one, not two, but three different fuel options in its tank.

Fuel 1 - First, we have the already much-discussed glucose, which is our immediate energy source. It's like the quick-burning rocket fuel that keeps us going when we need a burst of energy for those intense moments.

Fuel 2 - Our body is a smart machine that knows how to tap into its reserves. Enter glycogen, a semi-solid sugar stored in the liver, with around a 100 g capacity equivalent to 400 calories. Think of it as the backup battery that keeps things running smoothly when the glucose tank empties. Now let's talk muscles. They, too, have a glycogen stash, and it's roomier, holding anywhere from 300 to 500 g. That's roughly 1,200 to 2,000 calories, enough to fuel you through a solid workout session that lasts an hour or so. But here's the catch – it's not quite sufficient to carry you across the finish line of a marathon. That's why many runners hit the dreaded 'wall' around mile 20. But wait, there's more!

Fuel 3 - Our body isn't just satisfied with the limited energy sources of glucose and glycogen. It has a secret vault known as body fat. This reserve is a powerhouse capable of storing a huge 10,000 to 25,000 g fat, and for those who are obese even more. Translate that into calories, and you're looking at an astonishing 40,000 to 100,000 calories of untapped energy. The catch? You need to learn the specific keys to access this treasure trove but fear not because we'll discuss it later.

Dr Jason Fung

Glycogen is like a wallet in that money goes in and out constantly. But like a wallet, while it is easily accessible, it can only hold a limited amount of money. Like the wallet, glycogen can quickly convert back to glucose to provide energy. Whereas fat is like a bank account, it's harder to access but has unlimited storage space.

Chapter 3

Understanding Macronutrients and Beyond

Now that we've covered the significance of fibre, the impact of sugar, the role of various hormones, and the crucial connection between our diet and modern health issues, let's take a step back and uncover more about macronutrients.

Every living thing, whether it's a towering tree, a human being, a loyal dog, or a humble strawberry, is composed of the same fundamental elements: fat (fatty acids), carbohydrates (which can be thought of as dressed-up sugars), and proteins (composed of amino acids). These three macronutrients, aptly named for their size (derived from the Greek word 'macro', meaning large), are the building blocks of all the food we consume. While fat and protein are essential for the human body to thrive, not a single ounce of carbohydrate is necessary to sustain human life – not today, tomorrow, or ever!

Regardless of how diverse the foods may appear in terms of appearance, texture, or taste, they are broken down once they enter our digestive system into one of these three components. Later in this book, we will explore the much smaller micronutrients, encompassing minerals, phytonutrients, and vitamins. However, before looking into those details, it's crucial to clearly understand the roles and characteristics of fat, protein, and carbohydrates.

When it comes to macronutrients, most natural foods contain a combination of two of them. If the food once had a face or is derived from something that once had one, it primarily comprises protein and fat. On the other hand, foods that originate from the ground typically comprise protein and carbohydrates. It's worth noting that protein is a common component in almost everything we consume because it serves as the fundamental building block of life.

There are a few exceptions to this two-macronutrient rule. Nuts, seeds, milk, and avocados are examples of foods that contain all three macronutrients. Some foods are composed almost entirely of a single macronutrient, such as table sugar (pure carbohydrate) and oils like coconut and olive (pure fat).

What do macronutrients do?

In both humans and animals, all three macronutrients play roles related to energy:

- Carbohydrates/sugar provide energy for immediate use and storage.
- Fats are transformed into fatty acids, primarily for cell repair or energy use.
- Proteins are converted into amino acids and used for cell repair, rebuilding, or energy.

Now, brace yourself for a revelation that might catch you off guard. It's a concept that can be as slippery as a banana peel to some folks, but it's pivotal to grasp. Among the trio of macronutrients, it's not fat that should top the list of suspects for weight gain – it's those sneaky carbohydrates. Picture this: you stroll into your local butcher shop, and you're drawn to the juiciest, fattiest cut of meat they have. You decide to pair it with a humble baked potato. In this culinary showdown, the unassuming potato is more likely to lead the weight gain brigade, not the fatty meat. The reason behind this is surprisingly straightforward: our bodies aren't exactly eager beavers for hoarding fat as fat. Nope, our bodies prefer to put that fat to good use for energy and cellular repair. Don't get me wrong; I am not saying never to eat spuds again, but be sure to eat some *fibre first.*

Hang on to your chef's hat because while we'll soon explore the world of both virtuous natural fats and sinister artificial fats, let's etch these two life-changing truths into your culinary consciousness:

1. Trim down your carbohydrate intake, and watch dietary fat become your weight-loss, health-boosting ally.
2. Carbohydrates are the unrivalled champions in the macronutrient conversion game, effortlessly morphing into body fat.

Let me introduce you to Dr Maggs. As I'm writing this chapter, we are currently in Switzerland skiing together in the afternoons and spending our mornings researching. Dan says, 'Natural fats are not the enemy. We have demonised and vilified the good guy for over 50 years, and all the while, the sickly sweet kid has been getting away with murder!'

Patrick Holford

Paul Kenny, a professor specialising in neurobehavioral disorders, in 2018 conducted the following research: he fed a group of rats nothing but fat for a month, and they gained a little weight, but nothing much. They would eat the fat, feel satisfied and then stop. He then fed them only sugar, and they gained some weight, maybe not as much as we had expected. They would eat the sugar, feel satisfied, and then stop. In the third experiment, he fed them a diet of 50% fat and 50% sugar, which is basically what junk food is, and they went ballistic. They just binged; they couldn't stop eating.

Junk food fools the brain. In nature, you never find high fat with high carbohydrates. You get fat and protein; you get carbohydrates and protein, but you don't get high fat and high carbohydrates. That is junk food, which affects the brain in a certain way, and you can't stop eating. And I noticed one other thing. He was feeding them cheesecake. And what we know about milk is that it is sort of addictive, and it is meant to be; you know, when a baby is breastfeeding, they need to become a sort of addict. And that's why you can't stop eating the milk chocolate bar with dairy, high fat, and high carbohydrates. We can run on fat, we could run on carbohydrates, but put the two together, and we create a food that people won't stop eating.

*****

Fats

While proteins and carbohydrates are relatively straightforward to grasp, fats can be a bit more intricate. We'll focus just on the healthy ones here, and in a future chapter, we'll look at the unhealthy and dangerous ones.

There are two essential fat facts that, once known, make it much easier to understand the complexity of fats:

1. The only thing that distinguishes oils from fats is their state at room temperature. Oils are liquid at room temperature, while fats are solid.
2. All fats and oils can be categorised into one of two groups: saturated or unsaturated.

To make sense of this, look at the chart below, which illustrates the primary groups of fats and oils and how they relate to each other. It's important also to note that most of the foods we consume contain more than one type of these fats.

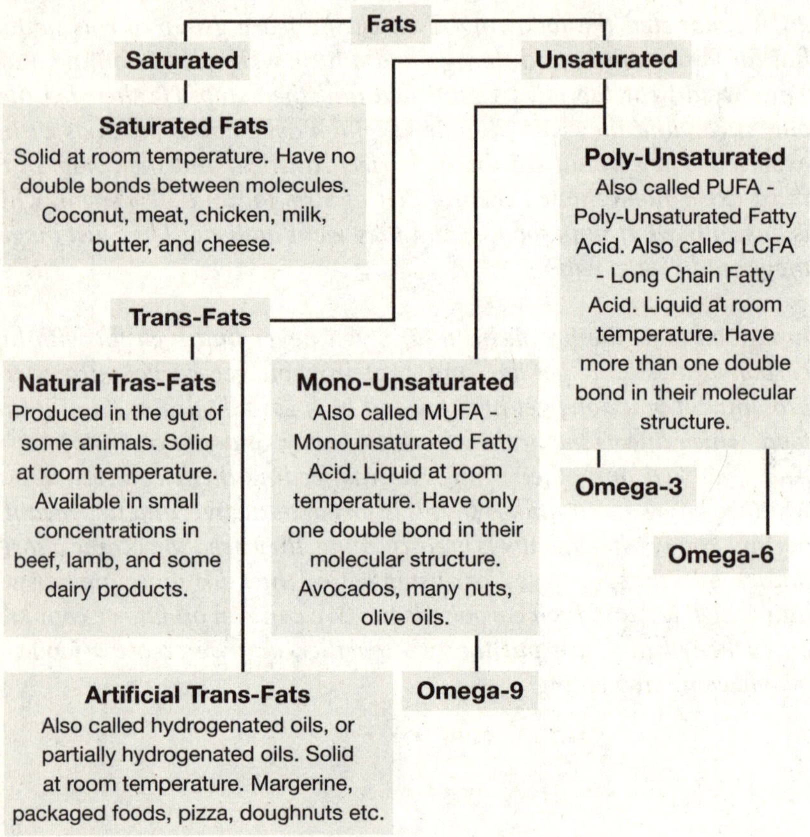

Here's the deal: if you carry a few extra pounds, it's time to make friends with fat, the good kind, that is. Contrary to popular belief, fat isn't the macronutrient villain; it's your ally. Good fats, when consumed in moderation, won't expand your waistline. It's those sneaky carbohydrates that are the real culprits behind weight gain. Remember the days when we used to trim the fat off our meat, thinking it was the enemy? It turns out that leaving it on can help many of us shed inches from our waistlines.

Quality fats are like the champions of our hormone balance. They work tirelessly to keep our hormones in check, boost our energy levels, ramp up our calorie-burning capacity, and keep us feeling satisfied so we don't go on eating binges.

Where can you find these quality fats? Look no further than omega-3-rich foods like salmon, nuts, avocado, coconuts, olive oil, lamb, and organic butter. But buyer beware; there are some fats you should definitely steer clear of, and we'll look into those in an upcoming chapter. They include trans-fats (often hidden behind the label 'partially hydrogenated oils'), fats lurking in processed and packaged foods, and vegetable oils, which, believe it or not, rarely come from vegetables.

Which Oils Deserve A Spot In Your Pantry?

Elevate your culinary game by stocking up on oils that aren't just good, but great for your health. Leading the charge are:

Coconut & medium-chain triglycerides (MCTs)

Meet the rock stars of the healthy fat world, medium-chain triglycerides (MCTs). Leading this epic band is none other than coconut oil. MCTs are like the energiser bunnies of fats; they keep giving! When you consume them, they swiftly transform into fuel, kick-start your body's fat-burning engine, and have a knack for taming your growling stomach.

What's their secret? MCTs have shorter chains than regular fats, which means they zoom from your digestive tract to your liver at warp speed. There, they become instant energy or morph into ketones (stay tuned for more). Oh, and did I mention MCTs are lower in calories than other fats? Yes, they're the overachievers of the fat world. Not only do they provide a quick energy fix, but they also coax your body into torching its own fat stores through a magical process called thermogenesis. When sugar takes a backseat, MCTs whisper to your body, 'Hey, let's make some ketones'.

You can also stumble upon smaller amounts of MCTs in other saturated fats, like organic butter and full-fat yoghurt. But let me share a little secret: most other fats, whether from animals or plants, are 'long-chain fatty acids' (LCFAs). They're not exactly the Usain Bolt of the fat world; they don't convert into energy as quickly.

Let me give you a sneaky peek into my diet playbook. Picture this: I'm gearing up for a game of tennis, and I need a burst of energy. I'm no fan of sugary drinks, so what's my secret weapon? A couple of tablespoons of coconut oil and voilà! It's like I've had a dose of that sports drink mojo without all the unnecessary junk. MCTs are like my trusty sidekicks, always ready to deliver that energy punch.

MCTs aren't just everyday heroes; they're even scoring guest appearances in treating serious diseases. From battling cancer and wrestling with obesity to taking on Alzheimer's and Parkinson's, these little guys are the staunch champions!

Butter and ghee

Hold on to your toast because here comes a healthy U-turn! For years, margarine had tried to wear the crown as a healthier alternative to butter, but the truth is, it's packed with deadly hydrogenated fats. Sure, it might spread smoothly, but it's not favouring your gut. It might not poke holes in your bread, but it could poke holes in your gut lining.

Now, once the fat villain, butter emerges as the hero, but there's an even greater champion: ghee. Until recently, I thought ghee was just for spicing up Indian dishes. Then, while on my quest to reclaim my fitness mojo, I stumbled upon an article praising its miraculous health benefits.

Ghee is created when you gently evaporate (clarify) water out of butter, leaving behind a concentrated fat perfect for high-temperature cooking. During this transformation, ghee often develops an enchanting aroma and even a hint of nutty flavour. It's no wonder that many cultures across the globe consider ghee a natural medicine. Some even craft it from human breast milk, talk about versatility!

Olive oil

We all know that those Mediterranean folks hail olive oil as the health elixir. Yet, when you find yourself in the supermarket aisle, surrounded by a maze of olive oil labels, you can't help but wonder, 'Which ones do those

Mediterranean connoisseurs actually choose?' I ventured to the International Olive Council's (IOC) website to uncover this culinary mystery. And with a little guidance on the phone from a delightful lady in their office, I unravelled the complexity of olive oil labels.

To earn the title of 'virgin olive oil', the IOC insists it must be extracted from olives solely through mechanical or physical means, under conditions that preserve the oil's integrity, without undergoing treatments beyond washing, decantation, centrifugation, and filtration. Here's a breakdown of your choices:

Extra virgin olive oil – This is the Rolls-Royce of olive oils, boasting an abundance of antioxidants and polyphenols. To earn its 'extra' designation, it must have an oleic acid level of no more than 0.8 g per 100 g, ensuring a superior taste and maximum health benefits.

Virgin olive oil – Achieving 'virgin' status requires an oleic acid level of no more than 2 g per 100 g.

Ordinary virgin olive oil – To be considered 'ordinary virgin', it must have an oleic acid level of no more than 3.3 g per 100 g.

Refined olive oil – Derived from virgin olive oils through refining methods that maintain the initial glyceridic structure. It must have an oleic acid level of no more than 0.3 g per 100 g. Remember that refined oils may lack the antioxidants and anti-inflammatories found in virgin olive oil.

Olive oil – A practical blend of refined and virgin olive oils, capped at 3.3g of oleic acid per 100g, offers a harmonious compromise between flavour, quality, and economy, suitable for various culinary applications.

Now, after all's said and done, and despite what appears to be a fair share of regulations and safeguards, I must admit to a lingering scepticism regarding the giants of the olive oil industry. You see, I have this dear friend with his olive farm tucked away in the sun-soaked hills of Portugal. His olive oil is a flavour explosion that stands worlds apart from those commercialised counterparts. When I bought a crate of his liquid gold last year, the price tag was on the steep side, a whopping three times more than what you'd find at your local supermarket. With a sly grin, I tried to play the 'buddy card' and said, 'Come on, Andrea, I'm practically family. Give me your cost price, won't you?' To which he chuckled and replied, 'Alright, Steve, no problem,' followed by a wink and an additional €5 tacked on to the bill. He taught me the essence of quality olive oil harvested harmoniously with Mother Nature and clarified that such liquid gold doesn't come cheap. Then, he regaled me with tales about some of the behemoth brands and their rather eyebrow-raising production methods.

So, here's the scoop: if you ever stumble upon a smaller, artisanal olive oil brand that demands a few extra pounds from your pocket, it's a worthy investment. But fear not, my friends, for I wouldn't dream of dissuading you from a commercial olive oil either. It's a far superior choice compared to those treacherous seed oils lurking in the shadows, ready to wreak havoc on your health. Choose wisely, and may your taste buds revel in the liquid gold of authentic olive oil.

Now, you might wonder about 'first cold pressed'. Truth be told, it's not a term that is regulated. Back when olive oil was pressed using mats, there was a first and second press, but other than the smaller producers, those days are gone. Nowadays, it's merely marketing hype. And speaking of marketing, don't be deceived by oils labelled 'light'. It's not an IOC-approved description and has nothing to do with calories. If anything, they are lighter in flavour only.

Here's a valuable nugget: olive oil doesn't improve with age, unlike fine red wine. Check those labels for the most recent harvest dates. Store them in cool, dark spots; even in the UK, you might want to tuck them into the fridge during the summer. Once opened, please don't be shy; use it generously and aim to finish it within a month or two. Regardless of the bottle's expiry date or lingering aroma, the longer it's exposed to warm air and sunlight, the fewer health benefits it will offer. And, as always, opt for a glass bottle to keep your olive oil pure and untainted by any unwanted chemicals.

Flaxseed oil

Now, let's discuss the outlier among seed oils. While the rest of them are deemed toxic and perilous, this one stands apart from the crowd. Flaxseed oil is derived from the humble flax plant and holds a special place in the world of nutrition. Research in 2011 shed light on its remarkable potential. It's not just another oil; it's a game changer. In this study, scientists reviewed the world of flaxseed supplementation and made a startling discovery. They found that flaxseed oil could improve insulin resistance, particularly in individuals grappling with obesity and glucose intolerance.[21] This revelation sparked a wave of interest and curiosity in the health community, and it's a testament to the unique qualities of flaxseed oil. But before I close on flaxseed oil, some people may say it is the same as linseed oil. While it is true that it comes from the same plant, it appears linseed oil goes through a refinement process that may contain additives and, therefore, is not as good for health-conscious foodies like you and me.

The Smoking Point Of Fats

There's a fine art to selecting and using even the finest fats and oils. If we push them to their limits and subject them to excessive heat, we obliterate their nutritional prowess and transform them into something rather sinister: toxicity. We don't want our fats and oils to put on a smoky performance. Hence, depending on what we're cooking, we'll need an assortment of these healthy oils stocked in our pantry or chilling in the fridge.

Avocado oil	271°C	570°F	Use for frying, searing and rasting or as a tasty salad dressing. 70% mono-unsaturated fat.
Ghee (carified butter)	252°C	485°F	62% saturated fat, has a distinctive flavour, excellent for frying, especially Asian dishes.
Olive oil	242°C	468°F	Use for frying, searing and roasting or as a tasty salad dressing.
Coconut oil (refined)	232°C	450°F	Great for everything! 86% healthy saturated fat, and a powerful antioxidant. Contains 66% MCT.
Macadamia oil	210°C	450°F	Can be expensive, but a great all-rounder for both cooking and applying to the skin.
Olive oil (virgin)	199°C	391°F	Use for frying over medium-high heat or as a salad dressing. Rich in vitamin E and antioxidants.
Olive oil (extra virgin)	191°C	375°F	Use for frying over medium heat or as a salad dressing. Rich in vitamin E and antioxidants.
Lard	188°C	370°F	Made from the fat surrounding a pig's stomach, lard is most definitely a Primal fat. Makes the best fried chicken.
Coconut oil (extra virgin)	177°C	350°F	85% saturated fat, a Superfood. Use for everything except frying.
Butter	120-150°C	250-200°F	Use to add flaour in low temperature cooking.
Flaxsed oil	107°C	225°F	With its low smoking point, not ti be used in cooking. An excellent source if omega 3 (4:1 omega 3 to omega 6 ratio) and tastes great over salads or add to a smoothie.

That wraps up our exploration of the good oils. In chapter 8, we'll unveil the dangerous and deadly oils, shedding light on another root cause of widespread health issues.

*****

Protein: The Body's Marvellous Builder

Protein, often called the fundamental building block of life, derives from the Greek word 'proteios', signifying 'primary' or 'first'. Protein takes centre stage in the intricate symphony of our body's processes. When a repair is needed, this unsung hero comes to our rescue, diligently rebuilding our organs, body tissues, and muscles. Protein is the ultimate creator in growth, especially during youth, shaping our hormones and orchestrating our development.

At its core, protein is composed of amino acids – 22 different types, to be exact. These amino acids are born from the elemental ingredients of carbon, hydrogen, nitrogen, and sulphur. While our body possesses the remarkable ability to manufacture most of the required proteins, there are nine essential proteins it cannot produce independently. These vital proteins must be sourced from our diet to ensure harmonious health. In 2007, the WHO thoroughly evaluated protein quality across various food sources. Unsurprisingly, animal-derived foods, sharing protein compositions similar to those of humans, took the lead. Eggs, poultry, meat, and fish emerged as the undeniable winners in this protein quality showdown.

When our body receives amino acids from protein-rich foods or supplements, it embarks on a remarkable journey of creation. With 22 diverse amino acids at its disposal, our body becomes a protein maestro, capable of composing over 50,000 distinct protein variations. These proteins go on to form the foundations of our organs, bones, and blood while also playing a pivotal role in crafting essential hormones like insulin, melatonin, and human growth hormone.

You might have stumbled upon the claim that protein, when overeaten, turns into sugar, much like carbohydrates. It's time for a bit of myth-busting with a side of science. Indeed, protein can don the sugar disguise, but it's more complex than a quick-change act. This transformation predominantly occurs among those with a penchant for devouring copious amounts of non-fibrous carbohydrates. Here's a peek of what's coming up later in the book: when blood sugar takes a nosedive, the hormone glucagon jumps into action, rummaging through our fat stores to whip up sugar in a culinary feat known as gluconeogenesis. It's like turning stored body fat into glucose, or energy, with a flick of a magic wand.

If you're a regular at the low-blood-sugar club, becoming well-acquainted with glucagon, your body becomes less inclined to cast protein in the sugar role, reserving it for its VIP functions. However, if your diet is a non-stop carbohydrate carnival, your body's fat-to-sugar conversion skills might get rusty. In such cases, protein may get the nod to step up and transform into sugar, especially if your body puts out an SOS for more energy.

Unravelling Your Ideal Protein Intake

Determining the right amount of protein to consume can feel overwhelming in the whirlwind of nutritional advice swirling around us. Here's a guide to cut through the noise: the sweet spot for protein intake falls between one and 1.5 g per kg of your ideal body weight. For those who prefer old-school measurements, that translates to about 0.45 to 0.68 g per lb.

Now, if you're gracefully embracing the golden years, akin to a vintage wine that only gets better with time, consider a slight tweak. Aim for a slightly increased protein range of 1.4 to 1.6 g per kg of your ideal body weight to keep up with your body's changing needs. On the other hand, if you live and breathe the gym life or regularly sprint, pump iron, or score on the sports field, your protein requirements might take a leap. Up your protein game to match the demands of your active lifestyle.

But what should I eat? Where does one unearth quality protein? Fear not; I have curated a list of protein-rich foods guaranteed to make your taste buds and cells erupt in cheers. To streamline your culinary quest, my trusty team donned their detective hats, channelling their inner Sherlock Holmes to research the most typical portion sizes in UK supermarkets meticulously. They've detailed the exact protein content for each portion. For convenience, you'll find the protein content per gram in square brackets, further empowering you to effortlessly calculate the protein content for any portion size you fancy. After all, nourishing your body should be a delightful gastronomic journey, not a mathematical exercise!

1. **Chicken Breast** – One of the most popular protein sources. A typical breast will weigh between 120 g and 200 g. A 150 g breast will have 36 g of protein (1.7 g fat, zero carbohydrates and a lot of water). [0.24 g protein per 1 g].

2. **Turkey Breast** – Just like chicken, it's lean and high in protein. A typical breast will range from about 140 g to 210 g. A 150 g breast will have 36 g of protein (3.3 g fat, zero carbohydrates and a lot of water). [0.24 g protein per 1 g].

3. **Duck** – A flavourful poultry option. A typical breast is around 200 g, of which 34 g of protein, 10 g of fat and a small amount of carbohydrates. [0.17g protein per 1g].

4. **Lamb** – A 150 g shoulder serving provides 26 g protein and 18 g fat. From the leg, a little more protein at 29 g and a little less fat at 12 g. [0.18 g protein per 1 g].

5. **Pork Loin** – Lean and high in protein. While they come in various sizes, they are typically around 125 g per loin. Therefore, as it's close to 100 g, let's look at 100 g, which is 20.3 g protein, 8.8 g fat and 0.6 g carbohydrates.

   - **Pork shoulders** are lower in protein: in a 100 g serving, we get 18 g of protein and 16.2 g of fat.
   - **Fillet** works best if you are on a protein mission. It has 22 g of protein per 100 g but very little fat, at 1.9 g.
   - **Pork belly** flips on its head if you want to do the opposite and have more fat than protein. A 100 g serving will provide 26.8 g of fat and 15.9 g of protein.
   - **Gammon** per 100 g provides more of an equal balance, 16.2 g of protein and 14.4 g of fat.

6. **Beef** offers high-quality protein along with important nutrients like iron and zinc. On average, a 200 g serving provides 40 g to 50 g of protein.

	Per 200g			
Beef	**Protein**	**Fat**	**Carbs**	**typical serving**
Rump	40.6g	20g	0g	255g
Roasting Beef	51.6g	13.6g	0g	250g
Sirloin	43.2g	25.4g	0g	227g
Mince	39.6g	29g	0g	200g
Mince (Lean)	43.6g	9.6g	0g	200g
Medallions	44.8g	4.6g	0g	170g
Fillet	57.4	19g	0g	170g
Ribeye	37.6g	39.6	0g	227g
Stewing Steak	42.6g	12.8g	0g	200g
Tomahawk	41g	39g	0.3g	120g
Corned Beef	50g	27g	0.1g	200g

7. **Tuna (canned)** – A convenient, high protein food. A 110 g can is 93% fish (102 g of fish, the rest is brine), and the serving has 25 g of protein. [0.23 g protein per 1 g].

8. **Salmon** is not only rich in protein but also in omega-3 fatty acids. A 100 g oven-cooked fillet contains about 25 g of protein and 15.5 g of fat (less than 0.5 g of carbohydrates). The nutrition is also similar for raw smoked salmon and those supermarket pre-cooked packs. [0.25 g protein per 1 g].

8. **Eggs** – A versatile source of protein. One medium egg typically has 6.3 g of protein and 4.5 g of fat; a large egg has about 7.4 g of protein.

9. **Nuts** - A convenient snack and an excellent source of protein. I chose 50 g, as that is the size of a typical pack of peanuts. They also contain lots of beneficial fibre.

		50g		
	Protein	**Fibre**	**Carbs**	**Calories**
Peanuts	12.8g	23	4	280
Almonds	10g	24	6	287
Pistachios	10g	23	5	280
Cashew	7.8g	20	2	276
Walnuts	7.7g	31	3	326
Hazelnut	7.35g	29	5	313
Brazil Nuts	7.19g	30	4	327
Pine Nuts	6.6g	29	2	331
Pecan	4.6g	34	5	345

11. **100% Peanut Butter** – 3 tablespoons (45 g) offer about 12 g of protein, 21.9 g of fat and 5.4 g carbohydrates. Plus, around 3.3 g of fibre.

12. **Shrimp** – Low in calories and high in protein. A 3 oz (85 g) serving contains about 18 g protein. [0.21g protein per 1g].

13. **Chia Seeds** – High in protein and omega-3 fatty acids. A serving of 2 tablespoons (28 g) contains about 4 g of protein and 9 g of fibre. [0.14g protein per 1g].

14. **Cheese** – The two main protein types found in cheese are casein (approx 80%) and whey (approx 20%). Casein comes in two forms: A1 and A2.

Cows typically produce A1 (especially those genetically bred); others, such as goats and sheep, produce A2. Why is this relevant? Because people who have an allergy or are sensitive to cheese often only have an issue with casein A1 but are fine with casein A2.

			Per 200g		
Type	**Protein**	**Fat**	**Carbs**	**Calories**	**Source**
Parmesan	11	8	1	120	Cow
Romano	9	8	1	110	Sheep (but sometimes Cow or Goat)
Mozzarella	8	5	1	80	Goat or Buffalo
Swiss	8	8	1.5	110	Cow
Gruyere	8	9	0	115	Cow
Cheddar	7	9	0	110	Cow
Raclette	7	7	0	99	Cow
Edam	7	7	0	90	Cow
Brie	6	8	0	95	Cow
Goat	6	8	0	100	Goat
Blue or Roquefort	6	9	0	100	Cow
Camembert	6	6	0	95	Cow
Halloumi	6	6	1	85	Goat, Sheep or Cow
Paneer	5	5	1.5	70	Cow or Buffalo
Feta	4	6	1	75	Sheep
Cottage	3	1	1	28	Cow
Ricotta	2	2	1	30	Cow (or other)
Philadelphia	1.5	6	1.2	64	Cow

15. **Whey Protein Powder** – One scoop usually provides about 20–25 g of protein.

16. **Sardines (canned in brine)** – Small, oily fish high in protein and omega-3s. A full-can serving has about 21 g of protein and 8 g of fat (zero carbohydrates).

17. **Mackerel (canned in brine)** – Another oily fish rich in protein and omega-3s. While you can buy it fresh, I have detailed it in a can for

convenience. A full-can serving offers about 16 g of protein and 14 g of fat (zero carbohydrates).

18. **Cod** – A lean white fish, high in protein and low in fat. A fillet at Tesco's, weighing 140 g, has about 25 g of protein and only 1.3 g of fat (zero carbohydrates).

19. **Haddock** - Another white fish known for its high protein content. A 90 g serving contains about 19 g of protein and less than 1 g of fat and carbohydrates.

20. **Anchovies** – Small, oily fish often used as a flavour enhancer. A quarter of a pack weighs 43 g and contains 8.6 g of protein, 7.6 g of fat, and less than 1 g of carbohydrates.

The BCAA Revelation

In my journey through obesity, I religiously consumed branched-chain amino acids (BCAAs) daily, convinced of their unwavering benefit due to their protein content, regardless of my physical activity. However, a pivotal moment came when I pointed in the direction of a podcast by my friend Dr Robert Lustig, which fundamentally altered my perspective on supplementing with BCAAs and the importance of choosing grass-fed beef.

Dr Lustig shed light on an intriguing aspect of meat quality, particularly the marbling seen in steaks, known as intramyocellular lipid (essentially fat stored within muscle). Surprisingly, this marbling indicates that the animal, much like humans with metabolic syndrome, was in a state of metabolic distress, a condition often found in American corn-fed cattle. This corn, rich in BCAAs like leucine, isoleucine, and valine, mirrors the composition of many protein powders popular among bodybuilders for muscle synthesis. Indeed, branched-chain amino acids constitute about 20% of the amino acids in muscle, serving an essential role in muscle building.

The Catch: BCAAs Without Exercise

The revelation, however, comes with a catch. Without regular exercise to utilise these BCAAs for muscle building, consuming them in excess leads to a different metabolic pathway. Instead of aiding in muscle synthesis, surplus BCAAs are sent to the liver, undergoing a process known as deamidation. This results in branched-chain organic acids overwhelming the mitochondria, which struggle with the excessive load. Unable to process this influx efficiently, the mitochondria convert the overflow into fat, paving the way for fatty liver disease and insulin resistance.

This understanding profoundly highlights the interconnectedness between our diet, specifically the type of meat we consume, and our metabolic health. The distinction between grass-fed and corn-fed meat isn't just a matter of taste or ethical farming practices but a crucial factor influencing our body's metabolic pathways and overall health. Dr Lustig's insights are a powerful reminder of the nuanced role diet plays in our health, challenging the notion that all proteins—and their sources—are created equal.

*****

Carbohydrate Family

Digging into carbohydrates, we uncover a kingdom far beyond common bread, pasta, and sugar. As nature's master carbohydrate craftsmen, plants synthesise vital molecules through sophisticated processes. These compounds fuel life and build structure and support within plants. Diving into why plants produce various carbohydrates, from quick-energy glucose to robust fibre, reveals the complex web of life's biological mechanisms.

As we discuss the carbohydrate terrain, let's remember this straightforward yet insightful classification: the dichotomy of life forms with a face versus those without and how it profoundly shapes our food.

From the humble bear foraging in the forest to the majestic whale echoing through the ocean, and yes, even us, the selfie-loving humans, all creatures that once had a face share a common pursuit: food for energy. This quest for sustenance unites us in a complex ballet of life, where every creature and face contribute to the ecosystem's harmony.

Nature's Grand Buffet offers assorted dietary options as diverse as the participants themselves. The animal kingdom's faces abound, each with its unique dietary narrative. Herbivores like the gentle deer and the cow epitomise the strength of plant-based diets, thriving without ever indulging in a burger. Carnivores, the meat connoisseurs of the natural world, personified by the majestic lion, steer clear of anything resembling a salad, instead relishing the thrill of the hunt and the satisfaction of a carnivorous banquet.

Then there are the omnivores, the gastronomic explorers of the animal kingdom. Humans, raccoons, and various birds belong to this eclectic group, delighting in the richness of plants and animal kingdoms. Their diverse tastes make them the epitome of culinary versatility, the true foodies of nature's dining tableau.

Photosynthesis: the faceless miracle

Time to turn our attention to those without faces. No, not moody teenagers – I'm talking about plants and trees! These silent, stoic beings, without a single facial feature among them, have their own magical way of dining: photosynthesis. While they might not enjoy the drama of hunting or the joy of landing a big catch, plants have mastered the art of sunbathing to make their food. Yes, they literally catch some rays, mix in a bit of water and CO2, and voilà – they whip up a batch of glucose, the most popular dish in the plant world. You will find it in leaves, the plant roots, trunk, flowers, fruit, seed, and virtually throughout the entire plant. Imagine if humans and animals could do the same. We just sat on the sunbed, sipping a glass of water, and in our bodies, the effect would be the same as eating bread, broccoli, bacon, or beef.

Glucose

Glucose is more than just a leafy treat; it's the veritable lifeblood of the plant kingdom and, by extension, the entire ecosystem. This simple sugar is the energy that keeps herbivores munching happily and, in turn, sustains the omnivores who rely on both plants and other animals for their meals. It's akin to nature's version of a drive-through, with energy being efficiently handed off from one living customer to the next in a seamless loop.

But the glucose story doesn't end in the sunny meadows or dense forests. Even the most devout carnivores, who wouldn't dream of nibbling on a blade of grass, and those humans in the most remote and frozen corners of the world, like Inuits in their plant-scarce environments, are inextricably linked to glucose. They ingeniously manufacture this vital molecule within their bodies, converting stored fat into glucose. This process, known as novo-glucogenesis, ensures that essential functions, like powering red blood cells and fuelling brain activity, continue uninterrupted. Interestingly, because we can manufacture our own glucose, while humans must consume fat and protein to survive, our requirement for glucose is zero. Nothing. None.

That said, in the grand tapestry of life, glucose stands as a universal symbol of energy. It transcends dietary preferences and habitats, proving that, for all living beings, it is the quintessential currency of fuel. Its size is so small that a single grain of rice can contain over seven hundred thousand glucose molecules, all of which can dissolve and disperse extremely quickly. Every second, our bodies burn several billion glucose molecules. Whether directly from plants or through a remarkable biological alchemy, glucose is the fundamental energy source, unpretentiously powering life in its myriad forms.

While they might lack faces (and the ability to take selfies), plants are the unsung heroes of our planet. Through photosynthesis, they whip up glucose and keep our air breathable. They take in carbon dioxide (like a vacuum cleaner for greenhouse gases) and exhale oxygen, making Earth the only known planet with air suitable for face-owning creatures to breathe.

After our faceless green heroes – the plants – have had their fill of sunbathing and carbon dioxide snacking, they get down to some serious culinary magic. They don't just stop at making glucose; oh no, they're far more sophisticated chefs than that.

Different forms of carbohydrates

First off, as we have already mentioned, we have glucose, the universal energy currency. It's like the plain dough in a bakery, basic but essential. But hold on, plants don't just stick to the basics; they can turn glucose into different forms of carbohydrates. Let's look at them individually.

> *Glucose is the fuel of life. Every cell on the planet utilises glucose for energy. Its importance is such that if you don't ingest it, your body has mechanisms to produce it—this involves converting amino acids into glucose through a process known as gluconeogenesis. Indeed, your body can even transform fatty acids into glucose, specifically converting the glycerol part of a triglyceride into this vital energy source.*

Fructose

Fructose, glucose's sweeter, more indulgent cousin, is what makes fruits sweet and irresistible. Think of it as nature's candy, designed by plants with a clever ulterior motive.

Why do plants bother making something as delightful as fructose, you ask? Well, it's all part of their grand strategy. Plants essentially roll out the red carpet for animals by packing their fruits with this sweet enticement. The sweeter the fruit, the more appealing it is to animals, including those face-owning creatures like birds and bears (and humans). When these animals feast on the fruits, they unknowingly sign up for a vital role in the plant's master plan: seed dispersal. As the animals wander and do their business, they spread the plant's seeds far and wide, helping to propagate the species. It's a win-win situation – a tasty treat for the animal and a ticket to new horizons for the plant's offspring.

So, the next time you bite into a juicy apple or savour a ripe strawberry, remember you're partaking in an ancient and vital exchange. You're not just enjoying a natural sweetener; you're an unwitting participant in the circle of life, aiding in the grand dance of plant propagation. I have a lot more coming up for you on this very sweet-tasting sugar; although we find it in fruit, it can be very sinister indeed and plays a large role in so many chronic illnesses. While the entire planet seems to be fixated on the dangers of glucose, which will be a lot of our focus, too, we must not forget this little sugar, which can sometimes be pure white and deadly.

Drawing on the wisdom of Dr Robert Lustig, it's fascinating to note that fructose, a sweet intruder in our diets, finds its way into a staggering 73% of all products on American grocery shelves, intentionally added not for our benefit but for that of the food industry. Why? Because fructose is addictive, much like other vices, including cocaine, heroin, nicotine, and alcohol, it lights up the nucleus accumbens—the brain's pleasure centre—dialling down dopamine receptors in a similar fashion. Fructose serves no essential function within the human body; we don't need it. Yet, our consumption has skyrocketed, increasing 25 times since the early 20th century, infiltrating our diets more than ever before.

Sucrose

Sucrose, often called the plant's compact energy storage unit, is like nature's version of a space-saving vacuum-sealed bag for glucose and fructose. This ingenious combination helps the plant store more energy in less space and is a delightful treat for our taste buds.

Here's where it gets even more fascinating. When humans consume sucrose, it's like inviting a sugar detective to the party. We have an enzyme called invertase, which is found in our saliva. But here's the twist – it's not produced by us but rather by our Microbial Partners, the ever-resourceful Streptococcus mutans. These little bacteria are like the backstage crew of the sugar show, breaking down sucrose into its separate glucose and fructose molecules. It's as if they're saying 'Ladies and gentlemen, please step aside; we've got this sugar separation under control!'

So, while sucrose may seem like a simple sugar, it's a cleverly packed duo that not only fuels plants but also adds a touch of sweetness to our lives. It's a reminder that even in the sugar world, microbial teamwork is at play.

99 Sweet Aliases: The Many Disguises Of Sugar

We're going to travel back in time to our primal ancestors, who unwittingly planted the seed for our sweet tooth. Picture this: they stumbled upon fruits and maybe some honey, and being the pre-refrigeration folks they were, they binged on the sweetness like it was a limited-time offer. Blame it on our ancient relatives; they've left us with a genetic penchant for all things sweet. But before you stock up on sugary treats, remember that our distant ancestors had a limited supply of fruits, available maybe once a year. When we indulge in sugar today, we're not doing ourselves any favours. Sugar lacks the vitamins and minerals our bodies crave – zero, zilch, nada!

Imagine this sugar scenario: if you put a frog into a pan of boiling water, it'll leap out instantly to avoid becoming frog soup. But if you put it in cold water and slowly turn up the heat, it will only sense the danger once it's too late. Sugar is a bit like that; it won't kill you immediately, but it's a slow, sneaky poison that adds a dash of ageing every time you indulge. So, remember, with sugar, you're not just savouring sweetness; you're part of a grand culinary conspiracy!

Sugar is addictive, like cigarettes and booze. Food manufacturers sprinkle it into nearly everything, from baked beans to bottled water, with the goal of making you crave their products. They've got marketing spins, but armed with some knowledge, you can spot sugar even if it's playing hide-and-seek. Check the label for words ending in '-ose'; they're all sugar suspects. Maybe '-ose' is secretly an acronym, warning us of 'other sugar exposure' or shouting, 'Obesity sugar exists!'

Dextrose, galactose, lactose, and maltose are all sugars under different aliases. And don't let those sneaky syrups off the hook either; they're just sugary imposters with plenty of calories and minimal nutritional value. Keep your eyes peeled for all of the following.

Agave
Agave nectar
Anhydrous dextrose
Barbados sugar
Barley malt
Barley malt syrup
Beet sugar
Blackstrap molasses
Brown sugar
Buttered syrup
Cane juice
Cane juice crystals
Cane juice solids
Cane sugar
Cane syrup
Caramel
Carob syrup
Castor sugar
Coconut palm sugar
Coconut sugar
Confectioners' sugar
Corn sweetener
Corn syrup
Corn syrup solids
Crystalline Fructose
Date sugar
Dehydrated cane juice
Demerara sugar
Dextran
Dextrin
Dextrose
Diastatic malt
Diatase
Dried oat syrup
Ethyl maltol
Evaporated cane juice
crystals
Evaporated cane juice
Evaporated cane syrup
Evaporated sugar cane
Florida crystals
Free-flowing brown
sugars
Fructose crystals fruit
juice
Fruit juice concentrate
Fruit juice crystals
Galactose
Glazing sugar
Glucose solids
Glucose syrup
Golden sugar
Golden syrup
Granulated sugar
Grape sugar
Gum syrup
HFCS
High-fructose corn
syrup
Honey
Icing Sugar
Invert sugar
Invert syrup
King's syrup
Lactose
Malt sugar
Malt syrup
Maltodextrin
Maltol
Maltose
Mannose
Maple sugar Maple
syrup
Molasses
Muscovado sugar
Nectar
Palm sugar
Pancake syrup
Panocha
Powdered sugar
Raw sugar
Refiner's syrup
Rice syrup
Saccharose
Simple syrup
Sorbitol
Sorghum
Sorghum syrup
Sucanat
Sucrose
Sugar
Sugar (granulated)
Superfine sugar
Sweet sorghum
Syrup
Treacle
Turbinado sugar
White sugar
Xylose
Yellow sugar

Starch: The Carbohydrates Pantry

Starch, the botanical equivalent of a well-stocked pantry, is next on our plant-based menu. Imagine a plant going on a bit of a glucose-making spree. What does it do with all that extra glucose? It packs it away as starch, much like how we might tuck leftovers into Tupperware for a future meal. Starch is essentially a bunch of glucose molecules holding hands in a long chain. It's what gives potatoes their claim to fame and turns foods like rice, pasta, and bread into belly-filling meals. Plus, all beets contain varying amounts of starch, from carrots to parsnips, from turnips to the ugliest vegetable of all, celeriac. When plants feel like squirrels preparing for winter, they stock up on starch, thinking, 'Better save some of this sugary goodness for a non-sunny day.'

But let's not be fooled; starch is essentially sugar-wearing a clever disguise. It's just glucose in a conga line, waiting for its turn to shine. When the lights go out, the sun clocks off, or when night-time rolls around, plants break out their secret weapon: alpha-amylase. This enzyme acts like a molecular pair of scissors, snipping the starch back into usable sugar. It's a nifty little trick, not unlike what happens in our own bodies. We humans store excess glucose as glycogen in our liver and muscles. When we need a quick energy boost, to run after a bus or do a victory dance, our bodies convert this glycogen back into glucose. So, in a way, both plants and humans are masters of the art of saving now to splurge later!

Here is what dentist Dr James Goolnick told me:
Tooth decay is all down to diet. There is an enzyme called amylase. Everyone has it, and when we chew bread, it breaks it down into sugar. The amylase secreted in human saliva is the same enzyme plants use to break down starch into simple sugars. Try this at home: put a piece of bread in your mouth and chew it for about a minute. You will notice how sweet it becomes. That is the enzymes turning it into sugar. If you have bread three times a day, you are literally dipping your teeth into sugar three times a day!

Unfortunately, our Western diet now has become more and more processed. When you go to the supermarket, more than 80% of products probably have added sugar in some way, and as dentists, we see more and more tooth decay problems. Sadly, most people don't even realise that there is sugar added to these things. They think they are being good, maybe having a savoury sandwich for lunch. But it has 20 grams of sugar. So, looking at the ingredients is massively important, as is realising when you are having sugar.

You might say I am having a chocolate bar because I want a chocolate bar, and it's got lots of sugar in it, but right now, I want it. But you also must realise that when you are having something savoury, like a sandwich, this is sugar too. I used to think sushi was nice and healthy, but when you realise the white rice is full of sugar, then you have the mirin which is poured all over it, again full of sugar, you start to have to really think about your choices. Even a hamburger, if it's without the bread, would have been healthier.

I am quite lucky as a dentist. I am the first one to see the damage that can happen.

If you are having sugar and changing your diet, I can see the damage within just six months. Yet it might take three or four years for obesity or five or six years for diabetes or heart disease to reveal themselves, but as dentists, we see the damage more quickly. The scary fact is that the number one cause of hospital admissions in the UK for children between the ages of 5 and 9 is tooth decay, and that is horrific. And it's because of our sugary diet, and yet it's 100% preventable.

Fibre: The Undigestible Delight

We discussed it in detail in chapter 2, so here are just a few words for now. It's like that one quirky friend who always shows up at the party uninvited but surprisingly charming. Here's the crux of the matter: fibre acts as the ultimate party planner. Introducing fibre as the first guest is akin to having a responsible friend at the gathering, ensuring things don't spiral out of control. Thus, while we must acknowledge the pitfalls of carbohydrates without the fibre buffer, it's crucial to recognise that with a bit of foresight, we can savour some carbs without letting them dominate the couch.

So, there you have the background on carbohydrates. It's a family that includes glucose, fructose, sucrose (plus 99 aliases), starch, and fibre. Let's conclude this discussion by inviting a couple of my doctor friends to share their colourful perspectives on carbohydrates.

Professor Tim Noakes

.Carbohydrates are not an essential component of the Human Diet. There is no known medical condition caused by a dietary carbohydrate deficiency. As a result, the influential US National Academy of Medicine concludes: 'The lower limit of dietary carbohydrate compatible with life apparently is zero, provided that adequate amounts of protein and fat are consumed.' Hence, no human, especially not anyone with an impaired capacity to metabolise carbohydrates, needs to eat carbohydrates. This is to be expected because, until the Neolithic period, which began with the

agricultural revolution about 12,000 years ago, carbohydrates provided a minority of the food energy ingested by humans.'

Dr Aseem Malhotra
'As a result of incorrectly cutting down on saturated fats, we have increased our consumption of carbohydrates, particularly low-quality carbohydrates. I am not talking about vegetables but bread, pasta, rice, and potatoes. As with much of what we are told in the government's Eat Well Guidelines, you are getting foods that are relatively poor in nutrition, very starchy, and high in glucose. And many of the problems we are dealing with as doctors are related to consuming too much sugar.'

Carbocoaster

You're doing a fantastic job navigating this book, but now it's time for a brief intermission, my friend. Get ready for a thrilling adventure aboard the 'Carbocoaster'– a term I first introduced in my premiere health book, Primal Cure. This concept is so significant that it warrants a reimagined journey.

Picture this: you're on a rollercoaster, but instead of heart-pounding excitement, it's a rollercoaster of carbohydrates, complete with loop-de-loops of hunger and cravings. Imagine starting your day with a hearty bowl of cereal. Those seemingly innocent cornflakes perform a magical transformation, turning into sugar faster than a magician's vanishing act. Treating this sugar rush like a fire alarm, your body despatches insulin like a squad of superheroes, swooping in to clear the sugar from your bloodstream and covertly stashing it away as body fat. But here's the issue: as soon as those cornflakes vanish, your stomach unleashes a frantic SOS for more food. You're back to square one, hungry as ever, primed for another exhilarating loop on the Carbocoaster.

Let's keep the ride going! Imagine lunchtime rolls around, and you decide on a sandwich. The Carbocoaster roars back to life. You ride high on the sugar rush, only to come crashing down when insulin barges in and ruthlessly disposes of your newfound sugar pal. As you recover from the nosedive, you reach for a snack of crisps, and the sugar catapults you back onto the Carbocoaster. You soar to even greater heights, feeling the rush, but you're plummeting once more before you know it. The cycle continues as your body craves that sugar-induced thrill, taking you on a rollercoaster of ups and downs. It's a ride that most people in the UK experience four or five times before they even make it home from school or work. So, grab your coat because it's time to head out for dinner – but beware, the Carbocoaster is always lurking!

Now, let's talk about those sneaky complimentary bread baskets at restaurants. They may appear as a generous gesture, but it's more like a strategic move in a grand culinary chess game. That basket reignites your Carbocoaster adventure. By the time you're ready to order, you're not just hungry but ravenous, ready for the next loop on this gastronomic thrill ride.

And here's an interesting titbit from my experience, especially as one business I own is a restaurant: those who kick-start their meal with bread are more inclined to finish their evening with dessert. Let me spill the beans:, it's not about generosity; it's a well-calculated strategy.

Unlike the dependable and steady rides of fats and proteins, carbohydrates are the only ones with their own thrill ride – there's no 'Fatocoaster' or 'Proteinocoaster' in sight. It's just the Carbocoaster, with its peaks of sugar highs and valleys of hunger lows. How do you slow down the Carbocoaster or even jump off it completely? By simply eating *Fibre First.*

Now, let's talk about how carbohydrates play mind games with us. They're the food world's equivalent of nicotine. One moment you're savouring a packet of crisps, a mint, or a doughnut, and the next, you're yearning for more, caught in an endless cycle, like a loop on the rollercoaster. One biscuit leads to another and another. Carbohydrates aren't just sustenance; they're an addiction.

And sadly, for many, the Carbocoaster begins pretty much as soon as they stumble out of bed. The notorious cereal. Let's debunk a myth here – breakfast isn't necessarily the most important meal of the day (unless you work for one of the big food companies). That catchphrase has become as familiar as a good morning greeting. It's essentially a marketing slogan brought to you by Kellogg's – who weren't qualified medical professionals the last time I checked.

For years, we've been led to believe cereals are the epitome of a wholesome breakfast, but they're more akin to stealthy wrongdoers hiding in your kitchen cabinet. Cereals are the sneaky culprits we willingly invite to our breakfast tables, administering their addictive dose to our families. As a reminder from chapter 1, I illustrated a typical English breakfast, touted as healthy. How well-intentioned but uninformed parents might unwittingly kick-start their kids' day, propelling them onto the Carbocoaster with a whopping 24 teaspoons of sugar. In business, I often say, 'Do what you can until you know better, then do better.' So, let's explore what 'better' might look like.

Picture bacon and eggs sizzling away with a side of mushrooms for some fibre, or perhaps a delightful serving of salmon and avocado, or even last night's leftover vegetables. Scrambled eggs paired with a side of fibrous spinach could also tickle your taste buds. And for the truly adventurous, how about starting your day with a coffee enriched with a touch of butter and coconut oil or a protein-packed whey shake with a fibre infusion? These options won't send your blood sugar levels on a rollercoaster ride.

But what's the problem with starting your day on the Carbocoaster? Well, here's the scoop. In the UK, over half of the population starts their day with cereal. Those boxes often boast health claims that are fortified with vitamins, low in sugar, heart-friendly, and so on. But here's the harsh reality, as we discussed in chapter 2: they send your blood sugar soaring, often higher than a type 2 diabetic's blood sugar levels. And if you make this a daily ritual, what are you setting yourself up for?

But wait, there's more: fruit juices, especially orange and apple juices, are still a staple in the UK diet, and these bad boys catapult your blood sugar even higher (as we have seen, a single large glass of orange juice can max out your recommended daily sugar intake in one go). So, more insulin production. Here's the kicker: morning is the worst time to consume anything that morphs into sugar. Why? Because after (hopefully) a good night's sleep, your stomach is as empty as your inbox after a long weekend. So, there's no fibre to slow down the sugar absorption into your bloodstream. It's like having a wild night out on an empty stomach; we all know how that ends.

Even if you manage to dodge carbohydrates at your next meal, starting the day with a blood sugar spike sets the stage for subsequent meals to reach higher peaks of the Carbocoaster. We've witnessed this pattern repeatedly during our controlled Blood Sugar Trial. The heightened insulin levels only accelerate the impending crash, and you're barely inching towards the office without plotting a pit stop at a fast-food joint for that irresistible breakfast roll. Of course, it's sugar-laden, too, so you're gifted with another glucose spike and a subsequent insulin rush.

Throughout the morning, you're hungry, battling brain fog, and feeling as lethargic as a sloth in a hammock. Your body's logical plea is to hit the canteen for an early lunch. Now at rock bottom on the Carbocoaster's descent, your hormones scream at you to hunt down the quickest source of high-energy lunch you can find. Fantastic news – pizza is on the menu today, and it's calling your name. You vaguely recognise it might not be the healthiest option, but at this point, hunger reigns supreme.

I could go on and on about the afternoon slump and the near narcolepsy in meetings, but I believe you're catching the drift. By the way, this Carbocoaster ride reflects a true story – it was me for over two decades before I acquired this knowledge. Today, I no longer ride the Carbocoaster; it's just too turbulent and bumpy and leaves me feeling queasy.

Navigating The Carb Conundrum: How Much Is Too Much?

Regarding how much carbs to eat in a day, opinions are as varied as the colours of a rainbow. You'll hear numbers thrown around – 70 g here, 100 g there, or even oddly specific figures like 73 g. But as you have learned, our bodies don't need carbohydrates to survive. Shocking, right? The fewer carbohydrates we consume, or the more fibre that precedes them, the faster we can shed those extra pounds, restore our metabolic health, and build a fortress against chronic diseases.

Carb chronicles: simple, complex, refined, unrefined

Welcome to the fascinating world of carbohydrates, which come in various shapes and sizes! Let's break them down (pun intended) into four main categories: simple, complex, refined, and unrefined. Understanding these will help you navigate the tricky terrain of carb consumption.
Simple carbohydrates: the speedy sugars

Imagine simple carbohydrates as sprinters. They're the small molecules your body absorbs quickly, giving you a swift energy boost. Think of them as your body's quick-fix energy drinks. They spike your blood sugar and get insulin working overtime. While they offer a rapid energy surge, if you don't burn them off pronto, they love to settle down as body fat. They lurk in processed foods, sweets, fizzy drinks, and natural goodies like milk and fruit.

Complex carbohydrates: the marathon runners

Now, picture complex carbohydrates as marathon runners. They're made up of long chains of simple sugars, so they take their sweet time to break down. This means they provide a steadier energy release. Potatoes, peas, whole grains, rice and pasta fall under this category. But hold your horses before you load up on these! Even though they're complex, they still break down into sugar, albeit a bit more leisurely. And, if you eat fibre before them, a small bowl of salad or some greens, you will further slow down their release into the bloodstream.

Refined carbohydrates: stripped of goodness

Imagine carbohydrates going through a factory makeover, these are your refined carbohydrates. This process strips them of their natural goodness, like vitamins, minerals, and fibre. So, what you're left with is a carb that's had a bit of a nutritional identity crisis. Sure, they might fortify them with some added nutrients, but it's like trying to put the genie back in the bottle.

Unrefined carbohydrates: au naturel

In the vast universe of carbohydrates, unrefined carbohydrates are the authentic, original stars. They're the 'au naturel' choice, unspoiled by processing and rich in fibre. Think of them as the wholesome, hipster cousins in the carb family – they keep it real. These are your unrefined heroes, found in organic veggies, brimming with nutrients just as Mother Nature crafted them. But here's a pro tip: treat them with respect. Overcooking can strip away their nutritional superpowers, leaving you with a less heroic version. So, go for the gold with unrefined carbohydrates, but remember, even heroes have their limits.

Glycaemic Index: The Carb Meter

Ever heard of the Glycaemic Index (GI)? It's like a leaderboard for carbohydrates, showing how quickly they convert into sugar and hit your bloodstream. Interestingly, there's no GI for protein or fat. Why? Because protein is rarely a player in the sugar game, and fat doesn't play at all.

Picture a racetrack where carbohydrates are the runners, and the finish line is your blood sugar spiking. GI is like the scoreboard, ranking carbohydrates from 1 (slow and steady) to 100 (lightning-fast). Pure glucose, being the Usain Bolt of sugars, obviously sprints right to a full 100.

But there is a slight issue with this index: GI doesn't consider the company these carbohydrates keep. It's like judging a relay race based on one runner. When you mix different foods, the carb race can slow down or speed up. Plus, GI doesn't care about portion sizes. So, some carbohydrates might seem chill on the GI scale, but if you eat them like it's your last meal, they're still a problem.

Enter the Glycaemic Load (GL), the smarter cousin of GI. GL considers both the carb's speed and the portion's size. It's a more holistic view of how your blood sugar will react. Calculating GL is easy: just multiply the carbohydrates in a serving by the GI score, then divide by 100. It's like having a more detailed race analysis, showing the speed and stamina of the carbohydrates you're eating. So, when you're navigating the carb maze, remember it's not just about speed (GI) but also about the weight they carry (GL). Understanding both will make you a carb-counting ninja, and that's why I created the following combined chart.

Food	GI	Serving size	GL per serving
Cheerios	74	1 cup (30g)	13
Corn tortilla	52	1 serving (50g)	12
Apple juice, unsweetened	41	1 cup (248g)	12
Orange juice, unsweetened	50	1 cup (248g)	14
Potato crisps, average	56	1 bag (40g)	12
Hot chocolate	51	1 cup (28g)	12
White bread (white flour)	75	1 slice	11
Banana, raw, average	52	1 large	14
Bran Flakes	74	3/4 cup (29g)	13
Corn chips, plain, salted	42	1 serving (50g)	11
Pitta bread, white	68	1 piece (30g)	10
Muesli, average	56	1 serving (30g)	10
Kidney beans, average	34	1 cup (150g)	9
Ice cream, regular, average	62	1 cup (72g)	10
Microwave popcorn, plain, average	65	1 serving (20g)	7
Chicken nuggets, frozen, reheated	46	4 pieces (100g)	7
Baked beans	40	1 serving (150g)	6
M&M's, peanut	33	1 handful (30g)	6
Apple, average	38	1 medium size	6
Oranges, raw, average	45	1 medium size	5
Tomato juice, no sugar added	38	1 cup (243g)	3
Milk, full fat, average	31	250ml	4
Watermelon	72	1 serving (120g)	4
Green peas	54	1 cup (80g)	4
Strawberries	40	1 cup (152g)	4
Grapefruit	25	1/2 slice	3
Chickpeas	10	1 cup (150g)	3
Cashews, salted	22	2 handfuls (50g)	3
Carrots, average	39	1 piece (80g)	2

Food	GI	Serving size	GL per serving
Lucozade, original (sparkling glucose drink)	95	250ml	40
Baked potato	85	1 medium (173g)	28
White rice, boiled	64	1 cup (186g)	33
Macaroni and cheese	64	1 serving (166g)	30
Raisins	64	1 small box (43g)	20
Spaghetti, white, boiled 20 mins	42	1 cup (140g)	16
Bagel, white, frozen	72	1 small bagel 70g	25
Rice Krispies	82	1.25 cups (33g)	23
Fanta, orange soft drink	68	250ml	23
Spaghetti, white, boiled, average	46	1 cup (180g)	22
Sweet potato	54	1 cup (133g)	12
Pizza	30	2 slices (260g)	13
Instant oatmeal, average	79	1 serving (250g)	21
Boiled white potato, average	82	150g	21
Coco Pops, average	77	1 serving (30g)	20
Corn Flakes, average	81	1 serving (30g)	20
Dates, dried, average	42	Handful (60g)	18
Snickers bar, average	51	60g	18
Sponge cake, plain	46	1 serving (63g)	17
Rice cakes, average	82	1 piece (25g)	17
Spaghetti, whole-grain, boiled	42	1 cup (180g)	17
Instant mashed potato, average	87	1 serving (150g)	17
Coca Cola, (US formula)	63	250ml	16
Brown rice, steamed	50	1 serving (150g)	16
Sweet corn on the cob	48	1 piece (60g)	14
Oatmeal, average	55	1 serving (250g)	13
Quinoa, cooked	53	1 cup (150g)	13

A Spoonful Of Sugar Perspective

Dr David Unwin, whom we've encountered before, is a true Sherlock of the medical world. He often finds himself in the role of a detective, unravelling the mystery of why patients aren't witnessing their diabetes or obesity retreat, even after they've banished the obvious sugars from their diet. So, who are the unusual suspects in this medical whodunnit? It's none other than those stealthy, starchy carbohydrates – bread, cereals, grains, pasta, rice, and potatoes.

As discussed in chapter 1, these carb culprits, unbeknownst to many, undergo a transformation within the body, morphing into shockingly high amounts of glucose. In a stroke of genius, Dr Unwin realised that the complex world of GI and GL left people puzzled. To bridge this gap, as we saw in the first chapter, he cooked up an ingenious method to make the impact of common foods more digestible: comparing them to spoons full of sugar. It's like a nutritional eye test, clarifying what was once blurry. Here's another chart that compares the GI score and the equivalent of spoonfuls of sugar.

Food item	GI	Serving	Sugar teaspoon equivalent
Basmati Rice	69	150g	10.1
Potato White, boiled	96	150g	9.1
French Fries, baked	64	150g	7.5
Spaghetti White, boiled	39	180g	6.6
Sweetcorn, boiled	60	80g	4.0
Black Grapes	59	120g	4.0
Banana	62	120g	5.7
Apple	39	120g	2.3
Wholemeal Small Slice	74	30g	3.0
Raisins	64	60g	10.0
Milk Chocolate Bar		50g	7.0

Dr Dan Maggs
'The most nutritional part of a doughnut is the hole. Processed/refined carbohydrates and sugar are void of nature's nutrients, minerals, and vitamins. They do nothing for the body other than to provide it with energy. And excess energy is stored as body fat, generally around the waistline.'

Dr James DiNicolantonio
'What happened in the early 1900s because of the invention of the steel roller mill, we started refining our carbohydrates, which basically gave us all these very refined powders, instead of eating real whole carbohydrate foods. From that moment on and forward, there has been a steady incline in heart disease, diabetes, and fatty liver disease, and even our children

are now being diagnosed with fatty liver disease. We have invented all these medications and surgical devices that may help some people live longer, but we are living with all these chronic diseases. So, our quality of life has gone down, and now even our life expectancy is starting to dwindle.'

Fructose: The Full Download

Let's look deeper at fructose, the twist in the sweet story. You won't find charts here because fructose doesn't follow the typical path into your bloodstream. It doesn't provide you with energy; the more you consume, the less energy you have. But I might be getting ahead of myself here. Picture this: you're enjoying your favourite sugary treat, blissfully unaware of the drama unfolding inside your body. Here's where things get interesting.

Inside the liver, the body's bustling processing plant, when sugars knock on its door, the liver normally has three ways to deal with them. First, it might send sugar straight to your bloodstream as an energy VIP pass. Next, it could store it as glycogen, kind of like saving your energy snacks for later. But here's the problem, and it's a big problem: the liver transforms excess glucose and all fructose (yep, all of it) into saturated fat. It's like the liver's little fat factory, churning out most of the fat that clogs our arteries.

Enter palmitic acid, the bad boy of saturated fats and a notorious heartbreaker when it comes to cardiovascular disease (CVD). Breaking news: the real culprit behind these artery-jamming fats isn't the fatty steak you had for dinner; it's the sugars, especially fructose, that your liver converts into this troublesome fat. This is a big 'Aha!' moment because it turns the whole 'fear the saturated fat' narrative on its head. The real villain in this story isn't the fat on your plate; it's the sugar in your drink.

How did we get our wires crossed and start pointing fingers at saturated fat while sugar sneaked out the back door? Cue a flashback to the 1960s and '70s, a time of big hair, bell-bottoms, and, unfortunately, some misleading science. Picture this: it's 1960, and the American Sugar Industry is playing puppet master, paying off Harvard researchers to point the finger at fat, not sugar, as the heartbreaker. With a single pen stroke, sugar got a get-out-of-jail-free card, while fat was left holding the bag.

Understanding *de novo lipogenesis*, the body's own fat-making process, is like finding the missing piece of a puzzle. It sheds light on the fact that sugar, especially fructose, is the architect behind LDL cholesterol (much more on LDL later), not the fat we eat. This realisation flips the script on decades of dietary dogma.

De novo lipogenesis is a term that sounds like it's straight out of a sci-fi novel, but it's a real process happening in our bodies. Breaking it down: 'De novo' is Latin for 'from the beginning' or 'anew'. It implies that something is being made from scratch. 'Lipo' is a prefix that screams 'fat!'. It's all about lipids, the scientific term for fats. 'Genesis' is like the opening act of a great story, it means 'the origin' or 'formation'. Put it together: de novo lipogenesis is like your body's personal fat-creation studio. It's where your body turns into a fat-making artist, crafting fats anew from non-fat sources, particularly sugars like glucose and fructose.

Simply put, it's your body's way of saying, 'Hey, we've got fructose here; it must be autumn; hibernation is around the corner; let's turn it into fat for storage!' This process is crucial for understanding how consuming too much sugar, especially fructose, can build up fat in the body, contributing to various health issues. So, while de novo lipogenesis sounds like a complex process (and it is!), it's essentially about your body's resourceful way of dealing with excess sugar by transforming it into fat.

So, why is fructose such a sneaky troublemaker? Beyond its starring role in CVD, it's also a key player in NAFLD, a condition as serious as it sounds. In the world of nutrition, fructose has been flying under the radar, considered a harmless sweetener, while secretly plotting against our health.

Fructose, the sweet culprit in our diets, comes from sources like table sugar (which is 50% fructose – 50% glucose), soft drinks, fruit, and especially high-fructose corn syrup (HFCS). It's been a stealthy character in the world of nutrition. Despite being recognised for over six decades as a fat-storing molecule, fructose has often been overshadowed by the spotlight on blood glucose levels. We have blood glucose measurements and a glycaemic index, but there is radio silence regarding fructose. This oversight has played into the hands of large food corporations. Fructose, particularly in the form of high-fructose corn syrup (HFCS), is economically appealing due to its low production cost and addictive sweetness. Plus, its association with fruit gives it an 'innocent' cover.

What's interesting and alarming, fructose doesn't seem to trigger the satiety hormone leptin. This means we don't get that signal to stop eating, leading to overconsumption. Imagine a switch that never turns off – that's fructose for you.

But why don't we have a natural off-switch for fructose? It turns out that our very survival as a species might have depended on this quirk. Dr Rick Johnson's research and insights from the British Natural History Museum suggest that our ability to consume fructose without feeling full helped our ancient ancestors evolve. Picture this: about 20 million years ago, Earth started cooling, and Africa, previously an island, connected to Europe and Asia via land bridges. This allowed several ape species to migrate. Back then, fruit was abundant year-round, especially figs, which were a staple for our primal ancestors. However, as the planet cooled further, fruit became seasonal, leading many ape species to starve and eventually go extinct. But one species, our ancestors, developed a mutation. This mutation tweaked an enzyme and altered the brain's satiety receptors, making them ignore fullness signals from fructose. This allowed these apes to feast on fruit while it was available, storing fat to survive the harsh winter months. From this line of apes, humans eventually evolved.

This means fructose's role in our diet is more than just about sweetness. It's a tale of survival, evolution, and modern nutrition challenges. Our primal programming for fructose consumption, beneficial for survival in the winter in ancient times, now plays a tricky part in our struggle with modern diets overloaded with sugar.

In a podcast I recorded with Dr Robert Lustig, a leading expert on sugar with over 10 million views on YouTube (more than even the latest cat video sensation), he told me:

> *Fructose is very sweet. It's the reason why we like sugar, and it is the reason we crave sugar. It is addictive. Fructose is the addictive component of sugar. It goes to the reward centre of the brain and activates it. We have a limited capacity to metabolise fructose. But our livers must metabolise it because fructose does not enter any other cell. So, when you take a fructose load like Coca-Cola, it's basically all going to your liver. And the liver gets overwhelmed because, basically, it has a fixed capacity to deal with it, and if you overwhelm your liver, it doesn't know what to do with the rest. So, the liver will turn that extra fructose into fat. And that fat then has one of two fates. It can either be exported out of the liver, which in this case, you have now got substrates for obesity and heart disease, or it will precipitate within the liver, and then you get fatty liver disease. And now you have liver dysfunction, insulin resistance, and metabolic syndrome. You can think of fructose as an ageing compound.*

Fructose turns out to be quite the paradox in our diet. Unlike other sugars, fructose doesn't directly spike our blood sugar or insulin levels. Yet, it harbours a deep and dark side, especially concerning its secret role in driving insulin resistance in the liver, hyperinsulinemia, and metabolic syndrome.

Here's a startling fact: fructose is the only dietary ingredient that decreases our energy levels upon consumption. Yes, you read that right! Usually, when we eat, we expect an energy boost. This boost then naturally curbs our appetite. In the intricate dance of our cellular biology, the mitochondria (our cells' powerhouses) transform most foods into adenosine triphosphate (ATP). This energy currency powers our activities, from running to thinking.

But here's where fructose breaks the mould and enters the 'No Rules Club'. While other foods follow a regulated pathway to produce ATP, our dear fructose takes the rebellious route. It activates an enzyme called fructokinase, which, unlike phosphofructokinase (I know, these biological terms sound like something out of a science fiction movie), the enzyme that usually keeps things in check, doesn't bother with safety checks. This unregulated process leads to a significant drop in our energy levels – by an astonishing 40 to 50%! So, instead of fuelling us up, fructose gives us a one-way ticket to Energy Drain City. Talk about being the black sheep of the carbohydrate family!

As a result, our brain gets mixed signals. It keeps urging us to eat more, mistakenly thinking that more food equals more energy. But with fructose, this equation doesn't hold true. The more fructose we consume, the more our energy dips, and the more our body craves food. It's a futile cycle: we're chasing an energy high that fructose can't provide. Moreover, to preserve the dwindling energy stores, the body even dials down its metabolic rate.

The next time you reach for that fructose-laden snack, remember it's not just a sweet treat. It's a nutrient that, unlike any other, can lower your energy and trick your body into an endless cycle of craving and consumption.

The Complete Fructose Internal Journey

In previous discussions, I touched on how fructose heads directly to the liver to be converted into fat—a slight oversimplification. If you want to explore the more detailed biological nuances, I will now unravel the extended narrative. A special shoutout to Dr Robert Lustig for shedding light on this topic in a way that even we, the non-endocrinologists, can comprehend.

Firstly, about 10% of fructose will be turned into triglyceride right in the intestine and released into the bloodstream immediately after it's eaten. Yes,

10% is immediately converted to fat and dumped into your bloodstream. The rest of the fructose will be absorbed into the portal vein - which delivers blood from your belly directly to your liver for processing into fat - but not before some fructose makes it further down, where it nitrates tight junction proteins.

Let me explain further. What are tight junctions? The intestine is composed of cells called intestinal epithelial cells. These cells are closely bound to each other by proteins, forming a critical barrier. This barrier is made of what we refer to as tight junction proteins. Their main role is to prevent substances that will become waste (soon-to-be poo) from leaking into the rest of the body.

Tight junctions can either be completely impermeable, not allowing anything through, or semi-permeable, which means they selectively allow specific substances to pass. Normally, these junctions are entirely impermeable, creating an effective barrier. However, fructose interacts with these tight junction proteins, compromising their function. This interaction makes the tight junctions transiently permeable, allowing unwanted substances from the intestine to seep into the bloodstream. This process leads to what is known as a leaky gut, where the intestinal barrier is temporarily breached, permitting elements that should remain within the digestive tract to enter the body's internal environment.

In essence, fructose knows the secret knock to get unwanted guests into the 'leaky gut club,' turning what should be tightly regulated poo transport into unscheduled unloading.

Thus, fructose emerges not just as a catalyst for a leaky gut but as a provocateur of inflammation. It triggers an increase in High-sensitivity C-reactive protein (CRP), a substance crafted by the liver that acts as a red flag for inflammation within the body. Elevated levels of CRP serve as harbingers, forecasting unwelcome events such as myocardial infarction, stroke, peripheral arterial disease, and even sudden cardiac death.[1] In essence, fructose is not merely content with causing digestive disarray; it seems keen on stirring trouble far beyond, waving a flag that signals distress in the body's intricate systems.

High-Fructose Corn Syrup: The Jackpot Of The Food Industry

High-fructose corn syrup (HFCS) is ubiquitous in ultra-processed foods and beverages. This syrup, a relatively recent invention from the mid-1960s, has seen its usage rise dramatically, almost mirroring the upward trajectory of obesity rates. While it's important to remember that correlation doesn't always equal causation, the parallel trends are too striking to ignore.

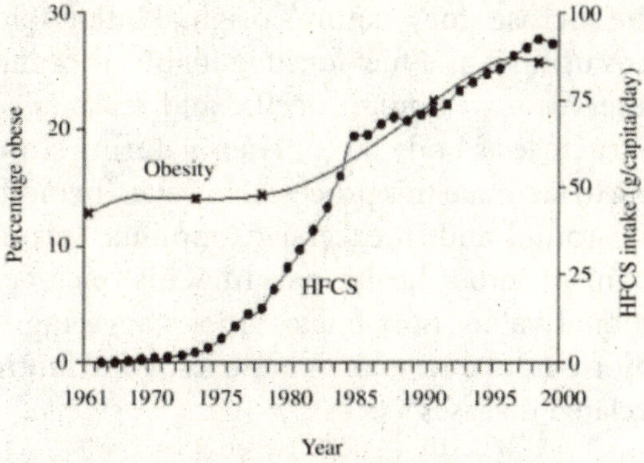

Figure 2 **Association between high-fructose corn syrup and obesity in the United States.**[69] *Abbreviation:* HFCS, high-fructose corn syrup

So, why does HFCS continue to reign supreme in the food industry despite its apparent health risks? The answer lies in its economic appeal. HFCS is a dream ingredient for the food industry: it's incredibly cheap to produce, cheaper than table sugar; it's a liquid, making it easy to blend into products; and it's got a potent sweetness that our brains can't resist.

As we have already seen, this love for sweetness isn't just a modern craving; it's a survival mechanism, a relic from our fruit-foraging ancestors who relied on the energy from fructose-rich fruits to survive harsh winters. However, unlike other foods, it doesn't trigger the satiety hormone leptin. This means there's no natural off-switch when we consume it, leading to overeating. From a business standpoint, HFCS is the golden ticket – it keeps consumers returning for more, boosting sales through relentless consumption.

Dr Jason Fung, the acclaimed author of *The Diabetes Code* and *The Obesity Code* (check out our podcast together; it's an enlightening listen!), points out that fructose, particularly from sources like HFCS, is closely linked to obesity and diabetes, perhaps even more so than glucose. He explains that overindulging in fructose can significantly ramp up de novo lipogenesis, increasing liver fat exponentially. This build-up of fat in the liver is a major player in developing insulin resistance. Since a fatty liver contributes to hyperinsulinemia and obesity, fructose potentially emerges as a far more perilous substance than glucose.

HFCS isn't just a sweetener; it's a key player in a complex physiological drama, where its continued consumption can lead to serious health consequences. Its presence in so many products isn't an accident; it's a calculated move by an industry focused on profit, often at the cost of public health.

To summarise the sucrose story, nature's original intent for fructose – as seen in migratory birds using it as a fuel for long flights or orangutans consuming it to build fat reserves – was quite specific and seasonal. Human ancestors evolved to store fructose as body fat for energy during scarce times, with our enzymes adapting to facilitate this process. However, in modern diets, fructose is consumed year-round and in excessive amounts, turning what was once a survival mechanism into a health hazard. This once-beneficial molecule, devoid of nutritional value, now makes up a staggering 9% of the average person's total calorie intake in many countries, contributing significantly to the rise in diet-related diseases.[2]

The Difference Between Sucrose and HFCS

While potentially the same, sucrose (sometimes natural) and high fructose corn syrup (HFCS, always manufactured) have their own secret moves. Picture sucrose as a conjoined twin, where glucose and fructose are linked by what's known as a glycosidic linkage. Once consumed, the enzyme sucrase acts like a skilled magician, separating these two with a flick of its molecular wand. Glucose then tours the body, flirting with insulin levels, while fructose heads straight to the liver's all-you-can-eat buffet, transforming into fat.

On the other hand, HFCS arrives on the scene with its bond already broken; no magic is needed here. This liquid mischief-maker not only sneaks easily into foods, making it the ultimate culinary ninja but also wins the award for cost efficiency compared to its counterpart, sucrose. It's like comparing a DIY furniture kit to one that comes pre-assembled: one requires more effort before it fits into your living room.

For those who appreciate the finer details, HFCS doesn't play by strict rules regarding its fructose-to-glucose ratio. With its bonds already broken, varieties like HFCS 42 and HFCS 55 boast 42% and 55% fructose compositions, and their sweetness is tailored to their audience. HFCS 42 prefers the company of processed foods and cereals, while HFCS 55 enjoys splashing around in soft drinks. These forms are the industry's sweethearts because they don't play hard to get by crystallising like natural sucrose, allowing food manufacturers to sweeten the deal even further.

The Little Upside of Fructose

It's generally okay when fructose is consumed as part of natural fruit, along with its fibre, just as nature intended, and in moderate amounts. Dr Robert Lustig once told me, 'In defence of fructose in fruit, it comes with fibre. The fibre stops all the fructose from being absorbed. The sugar is what makes it taste sweet, but it is the fibre that makes it healthy. The fibre is setting up a gel on the inside of your intestines. You need both soluble and insoluble fibres, and fruit has both.'

Seven Ways Fructose Triggers Chronic Illnesses

1. **Fatty Liver Disease:** Overconsumption of fructose is a direct cause of fatty liver disease, where fat accumulates in liver cells.
2. **Links to Diabetes and Obesity:** Fructose, particularly in its concentrated forms like high-fructose corn syrup (HFCS), is more strongly associated with diabetes and obesity than glucose.
3. **Energy Storage, Not Production:** The liver is the only organ that can metabolise fructose, and it converts it into fat rather than using it for immediate energy, impacting other liver functions.
4. **Doesn't Trigger Satiety:** Fructose fails to make us feel full, allowing overconsumption.
5. **Addictive Qualities:** The sweetness of fructose can activate dopamine receptors in the brain, creating cravings and potential addiction.
6. **Lowers Energy Levels:** Fructose is the only nutrient that reduces cellular energy levels.
7. **Reduces Metabolic Rate:** Studies suggest fructose consumption can lower the basal metabolic rate, impacting overall energy expenditure.

Understanding these aspects of fructose is key to making informed dietary choices and mitigating its adverse effects on health. While it's not the enemy per se, the way it's consumed in modern diets has turned it into a significant health concern.

The last word on sucrose is from Nobel Peace prize winner Linus Pauling, in his book *How to Live Longer and Feel Better*, 'Take the optimum supplements of each of the essential vitamins every day and of eating and drinking, there is only really one don't, that is sugar. Like the cigarette, sugar sucrose is a novelty of industrialised civilisation. Together, they have brought the pandemics of cancer and cardiovascular disease to the otherwise fortunate populations of developed countries. The cigarette hazard can be eliminated by quitting the smoking habit. Sucrose cannot be avoided, but a large decrease in this sugar intake is essential.'

And the last word on the carbohydrate family goes to Professor Tim Noakes.

> *'Carbohydrates, except for fibre, do not satisfy hunger – they stimulate it. Most of the food in question is processed and developed with one purpose in mind: to make you want more. They are tested and refined to the point where they are as addictive as they are destructive. Scientists even have a name for this: they call it the 'bliss point'. Addictive foods produce continual hunger, and so are the key drivers of the obesity/diabetes epidemic. I was talking to a lady who had lost 60kg, and she told me that when she was fat, she woke up in the morning hungry, and the only thing that drove her all day was hunger and that it was always there; it was incessant. Sadly, if you ask fat people, that's what they will tell you. They say the key driver is hunger. And the tragedy is that you can reverse it so quickly by cutting the carbohydrates and controlling the sugar addiction.'*

*****

The Hormone Hoedown: Leptin vs Ghrelin

Let's now study further hormones, particularly leptin and ghrelin, which have made a few cameo appearances in our discussion. As I have mentioned already, it's not about counting calories; it's all about the intricate dance of hormones. But why should you care about hormones, you ask? Well, think of them as the conductors of your body's orchestra, orchestrating when you should grab that snack or resist the urge to munch. They're the maestros of mealtime, and understanding their role is key to mastering your body's dietary symphony.

Hormones are chemicals released by glands to send messages from one part of the body to another. They are instructions. But because you can't see them, people rarely talk about them in relation to being fat or obese. But let me tell you right now. Being overweight is 100% about hormones. Let me tell you this: something I have realised as a truth. Endocrinologists, those doctors who specialise in hormones, probably hold the key to weight loss more than any dietician or slimming expert.

Welcome to the Hormone Hoedown, where two key players, leptin and ghrelin, dance a complex tango that decides whether we're raiding the fridge or pushing the plate away. Picture hormones as the body's chatty couriers, zipping around delivering messages to keep things running smoothly. They're like emails with legs but way more scientific.

Let's start with Leptin, our 'I'm full' messenger. Imagine leptin as a weary postman trudging from our fat cells to our brain with a message screaming, 'Hey, we're stuffed down here! No more food, please!' When leptins are on strike or too lazy to make the trip, things go haywire. You're hungry all day, your metabolism's snoozing on the job, and you'll likely find comfort in a tub of ice cream.

Dr Michael VanDerschelden, in his book *The Scientific Approach to Intermittent Fasting*, points out that usually, leptin should be the one telling your brain, 'Party's over; let's burn some energy!' But too many carbohydrates, especially the processed kind, can make your fat cells play the resistance game, just like in type 2 diabetes. That means more leptin is sent out, but the brain stops listening. It's like having a noisy neighbour – eventually, you tune them out. So, you're stuck on the couch, metabolism crawling, munching away, thinking you're still hungry. It's a downward spiral and not the fun kind. But don't despair! You can woo leptin back into your good graces. Eat more fibre, especially at the beginning of your meal; eat healthy fats and reduce carbohydrates; try intermittent fasting (more to come later); move more; and load up on fibre, lots of it (sorry, I repeated that twice). Think of fibre as leptin's best friend, helping it get back on track.

In *10% Human*, Alanna Collen describes an experiment by microbiologist Ruth Ley in America, where she studied the DNA of a variety of supersized mice known as ob/ob (their name appropriately derived from their obesity). These mice are almost round, and because they won't stop eating, they are three times heavier than normal mice. Alanna writes, 'Although they appear to be a completely different species of mouse, they have just a single mutation in their DNA that makes them eat non-stop and become profoundly fat. That mutation is in the gene that makes leptin, a hormone which dampens the appetite of both men and mice if they have a decent supply of stored fat'.

Hold on a moment: if it's as straightforward as relying on the satiety hormone leptin to curb our hunger, why can't we pop some leptin tablets or get leptin injections? The issue isn't necessarily a lack of leptin production; it's more about the brain developing a resistance to it. Like how type 2 diabetes can arise when cells become unresponsive to insulin after prolonged exposure to excessive amounts, the brain can become desensitised to leptin's signals if we consistently overindulge when we're already full. It's like the boy who cried wolf scenario with leptin in the brain.

Then there's ghrelin, leptin's opposition. Ghrelin is the boisterous hormone that tells you it's chow time. Before a meal, ghrelin is the life of the party in your stomach, but post-meal, it's supposed to nudge leptin to take over.

Here's the trick though: magical things happen if you can resist ghrelin's belly-rumbling pleas. You jumpstart your body's repair mode, battle inflammation, and boost human growth hormone (HGH). And the more you ignore ghrelin, the more it tries to get your attention, which is good! It's like having a little sibling trying to bug you – annoying but beneficial in the long run.

And here's a pro tip: skipping breakfast might be your secret weapon. It turns out there's a ghrelin party happening in your body after a good night's sleep. If you exercise on an empty stomach, you're giving your health a high-five. So, in the battle of the hungry hormones, it's all about knowing when to listen and when to tune out. Get ready to tango with leptin and ghrelin – it's a dance that could change your health game!

*****

Calories: Beyond The Numbers

'Move more, eat less.' 'Cut back on calories to lose weight.' These mantras have been chanted so often that they're almost sacred. But what if I told you, it's not about the calories? That's right, this book is a calorie-free zone, and here's why: focusing solely on calorie counting is like trying to paint a masterpiece with just one colour. It's not just about the numbers; it's about understanding the bigger picture – your hormones.

Let's take a little detour into the world of energy measurements. Amps, volts, watts, joules, and, yes, calories – they're all about energy. The concept of calories has been around since the steam engine days. Picture this: it's the early 1800s, and French physicists Nicolas Clément and Sadi Carnot are figuring out how much energy you can get from a kilo of coal. Enter the 'calorie', first appearing in a French journal in 1824. It was all about how much heat you need to raise the temperature of water by a degree Celsius.[3]

Fast-forward to now, and calories are everywhere – on food labels and diet plans. But here's the catch: calories come in different shapes and sizes. Now, I would like you to read the remainder of this paragraph quickly and without pausing, ok? There's the '15-degree calorie' for heating water, the 'International Steam Table Calorie', and then there's the calorie we're all obsessed with, the nutritional calorie. In the nutritional world, calories get a bit of a makeover and become 'kcal' or 'kilocalories'. One of these kilocalories is a thousand of those original steam engine ones and equals 4.18 kJ (kilojoules) or 4,184 joules. Depending on where you are in the world, you might encounter calories with a capital 'C', kcals, kJ, or a mix of these. In the US and Canada, it's all about calories; Europe prefers kcals and kJ; and Asia typically uses kJ.

It's a global melting pot of energy units! Confused? You're not alone.

In this book, when I say 'calories', I'm really talking about kilocalories or, for short, kcals, the UK's go-to measure. But here's the thing: focusing solely on these numbers is like missing the forest for the trees. It's not just about how many calories you're gobbling up; it's about what those calories do in your body, how many your digestive system absorbs, and how they interact with your hormones and metabolism. So, while calories might give us a rough idea of energy content, they only tell some of the story. It's time to move beyond calorie counting and dive deeper into understanding our bodies. Welcome to a world where hormones take centre stage, and calories are just supporting actors!

Brace yourself for this surprising truth: as I mentioned, the concept of a calorie wasn't originally cooked up for food; it had more to do with coal than a delicious meal. Those thermal calories initially quantified the energy needed to power your locomotive. Here's a mind-boggling idea: what if we pivot from calorie counting to evaluating nutritional value? Even the brilliant French physicists who introduced the calorie concept gave it the boot within a half-century. Why, you ask? Well, it turns out this calorie thingamajig wasn't all that precise when it came to gauging the energy in coal for steam engines! So, if it's sketchy for coal, imagine how it measures up (or doesn't) for deciphering how our bodies use food calories. It's a tad like trying to use a ruler to figure out the temperature – sure, they both involve measuring, but they're not exactly a match made in measurement heaven.

Enter the late 1800s and Wilbur Atwater, an American agricultural chemist who aims to tackle starvation in poverty-stricken areas. He took the concept of the bomb calorimeter – the gadget designed for coal – and tweaked it to measure food energy. Picture this: they're burning different foods to ash in a mini-furnace and measuring the heat output. This method, still in use today, is like a culinary 'burn to learn' approach. Its original noble aim? To guide those struggling financially towards the most energy-rich foods for the least money. Atwater saw the human body as a kind of steam engine needing fuel to keep chugging along. In his eyes, food was to the body what coal was to a furnace. So, whatever calorie nomenclature you use, remember it's all about predicting how much energy the source will deliver – from coal furnaces to human stomachs. It's a quirky tale of how a coal–energy measure turned into our daily diet lingo. Next time you glance at a nutrition label, spare a thought for Atwater's revolutionary, if not slightly unconventional, approach to feeding the masses.

Getting to my point, a calorie is the amount of heat a food type gives off when burnt in a calorimeter. And that's it. Period. Game over. It must be a helpful measurement because burning a banana in a calorimeter in Brazil and one in England will give off the same heat. But here's the issue: you can't burn a banana or a burger in your stomach like you can in a lab because of hormones, your personalised microbial effect, differing enzymes, and much more. The whole calorie concept is more of an educated guess than a science.

Let's take a detour to the nutty side. Imagine eating 3,000 calories of mixed nuts versus the same calorie count of McDonald's chicken nuggets for 30 days. Would you have the same energy surplus stored as extra body weight? It's like comparing coal, nuts, and chicken nuggets on a calorie scale – quite the bizarre trio, right?

Treating all calories the same is like saying £100, $100, and 100 Euros are all the same. Yes, they are indeed the exact number, but they will afford you totally different things. Eat 100 calories of coal, 100 calories of fat-packed nuts, or 100 calories of McDonald's chicken nuggets, and see if your stomach converts them into the same energy. Spoiler: it won't.

> **Dr Ben Bocchicchio explains this simple equation.**
> *Different foods = different metabolic responses. Therefore, not all calories are equal*

For half a century, we've been fed the low-fat, low-calorie diet myth, partly because we were told that saturated fat leads to heart attacks and partly because fat has more calories per gram than carbohydrates. But guess what? Both reasons are flawed.

Three Reasons Why Calorie Counting Isn't Accurate

Among many others, here are three additional reasons to showcase why the calorie count is as useless as a waterproof towel:

1. **Fibre:** While fibre counts as calories, the body does not absorb it. It is fuel for your bacteria, not you. Therefore, the number of calories is already flawed for any food with fibre.
2. **Protein:** Digestion of protein generates more heat and consumes more energy, indicating that not all calories are metabolised equally. About 10% of caloric intake goes towards maintaining body temperature, but protein increases this percentage to approximately 25% due to its complex

breakdown process. This means a far greater portion of the calories from protein is used in its own digestion, making calorie counting an imprecise measure of actual energy intake.

3. **Collagen and omega 3:** Collagen, a crucial protein, stands out because the body doesn't break it down into smaller components, unlike other proteins. This distinction underlines its importance in maintaining the integrity and health of arteries, bones, and connective tissues. Similarly, omega-3 fatty acids retain their form due to their essential role in health. They're fundamental for heart health, brain function, and reducing inflammation. Both collagen and omega-3 are so vital that the body preserves their structure, meaning their caloric value is irrelevant as the body tries to reserve them for their beneficial roles.

*****

When You Lose Weight, Where Does It Go?

Where does body fat go when it waves goodbye? This question has tickled the curiosity of many readers, doctors, nutritionists, and my dedicated team of blood sugar trial volunteers alike. They all found this enigma to be the most captivating conundrum of all. You might wonder, if shedding light on this mystery is crucial to understanding weight loss, why have I kept you in suspense for so long? Well, patience is a virtue, my dear reader. The grand reveal needed a solid foundation first. You had to navigate the world of fibre, grapple with the ways of insulin, and get cosy with the trio of macronutrients before you were ready for the grand unveiling.

We should first tip our hats to three trailblazers without whom this part of the book would still be shrouded in mystery. First, there's Antoine Lavoisier, who stumbled back in the 1700s upon the astounding truth we're about to explore. He laid the groundwork for understanding the 'how' of weight loss. Then came Ruben Meerman, the modern-day myth buster who penned *Big Fat Myths* and began demystifying the journey of vanished fat. And Dr Michael Eades, author and co-author of 10 health books, including one of my favourite reads ever, *Protein Power*, whose captivating talk at a health conference in the USA so enthralled me that I just had to share his wisdom in a podcast. Wrangling this topic into something digestible (pun intended) took several weeks of relentless simplification. Brace yourself because what follows isn't just another weight-loss secret – it's the revelation of a lifetime.

When unravelling the riddle of weight loss, we often stumble upon a gap between common beliefs and the stark truths of biochemistry. A compelling study published in the British Medical Journal and spearheaded by Ruben

Meerman[22] throws light on this disparity. He presented a multiple-choice questionnaire to 150 of the finest minds – 50 doctors, 50 nutritionists, and 50 personal trainers – posing a deceptively simple question: 'When you lose weight, where does the fat go?

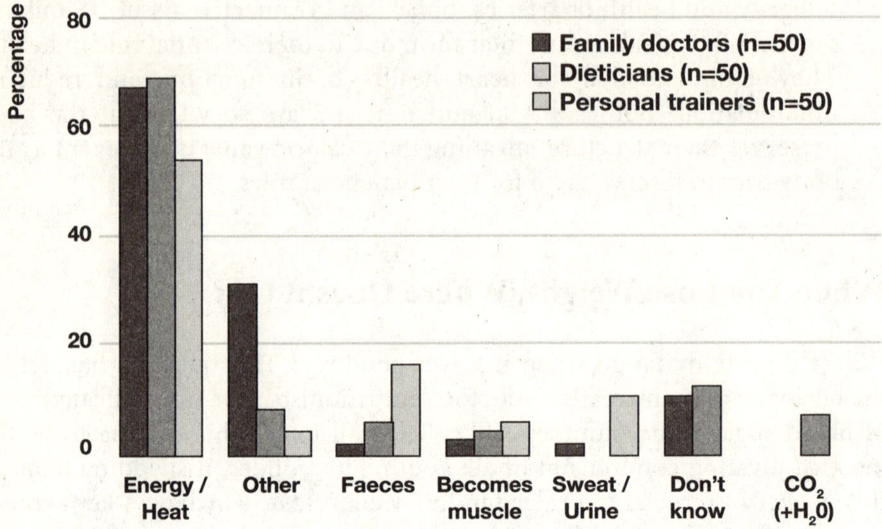

I find the answers interesting because no doctor answered that they didn't know. That's not a slur on their character because I have so many wonderful friends who are doctors. Still, it does highlight the problem and the pressure they face because they are expected to know everything. Anyway, I digress. The prevailing notion among these professionals is that lost body fat morphs into energy and heat, a concept that's as popular as it is comforting. But does this belief hold water, or is it just a cloud of steam? Let's pick apart the facts and separate myth from molecular reality.

Before we unveil the truth, it's crucial to paint a clearer picture to set the stage for the revelation that's about to unfold. Trust me; it's a real game-changer. In a podcast conversation, Dr Michael Eades provided an analogy that beautifully simplifies the complexity of this subject. He compared calories to a flask of boiling water perched on kitchen scales.

Picture this: a 1-litre flask of boiling water, initially tipping the scales at 1 kg. Leave it to cool at room temperature (20°C) for 10 hours, and you'll find it loses heat energy – about 80 calories worth. Yet, despite this energy loss, the water's weight remains steadfastly at 1 kg. This brief experiment drives home a crucial point: calories are a measure of energy, not weight. They're intangible, weightless. True weight loss isn't about calories, as energy carries no mass; it's about atoms.

Three hundred years ago, French chemist Antoine Lavoisier discovered that respiration is a form of combustion. In this process, our food is transformed into carbon dioxide and water. Remarkably, no single atom is lost or created; it's a perfect transformation. Ruben Meerman built upon this understanding, unveiling that a huge 84% of weight loss is exhaled through our breath. This fact was the least guessed answer in the survey of 150 experts, who mostly believed the lost weight converts to energy, a notion that defies the laws of physics, as it would require antimatter to annihilate atoms.

So, how does this fascinating process work, and how can we leverage it to our advantage when trying to shed excess body fat? The answer lies in the subtle yet powerful exchange happening with every breath we take.

Back to basics: when we breathe in, we're not just filling our lungs but conducting a mini chemistry experiment. Oxygen enters as a duo (O2), and we exhale a trio (CO2). Where does that extra carbon atom, the +1 in this breathing equation, come from? Pose this question to another 150 experts, and you might get a medley of answers, from car exhausts to cosmic dust. But the truth is, we're exhaling more weight than we inhale, and that extra carbon? It's part of your own weight-loss journey, exiting stage left with every breath!

Carbohydrates are essentially carbon atoms that decided to 'hydrate,' like someone on a health kick. Take glucose, the most popular kid on the carbohydrate block, with a formula of $C_6H_{12}O_6$ (6 carbon atoms, 12 hydrogen atoms and 6 oxygen). Human fat, or triglycerides, flaunt the formula $C_{55}H_{104}O_6$ (55 carbon atoms, 104 hydrogen atoms and 6 oxygen). This intricate molecular formula unlocks the secret to weight loss, revealing that it's not just about the hours spent in the gym but also about a fascinating biological transformation – a real-life metabolic magic show happening within us.

Biochemists have long known the secret: when we bid farewell to body fat, it's transformed into carbon dioxide and water and leaves with every breath we take. This process, known as the beta-oxidation pathway, is like natural alchemy, turning body fat back into the air we breathe. It's as if we're all walking, talking trees, photosynthesising in reverse, one breath at a time.

And what about protein, with its sophisticated formula of $C_{100}H_{159}N_{26}O_{32}S_{0.7}$? It's not just there to flex its muscles. Most of it also transforms into carbon dioxide and water, with the occasional cameo of urea and sulphate, which prefer the scenic route down the loo.

Ruben Meerman's TED Talk sheds light on this atomic ballet. Metabolising food doesn't just shuffle calories around; it converts them into carbon dioxide and water, ready to be exhaled into the world. Weight loss isn't a game of calories; it's a graceful waltz of atoms, adhering to the strict choreography of the conservation of mass or stoichiometry (the relationship between weights of reactants and products before, during, and after chemical reactions). Double your mass intake (not calories), and you've got to double the atoms you breathe out. It's not just a diet; it's a dance.

So next time you eye your dinner plate, remember, it's not just about the calories glaring back at you. It's about the atomic tango unfolding within you, a dance of intake and exhale that's the secret to shedding those pounds. In this grand biochemical symphony, every outgoing breath you take is not just a note in a song; it's a step towards a leaner, lighter you.

Time to revisit the three macronutrients we've dissected in this chapter and reveal the intriguing process of how each gram is transformed into energy:

1 g of sugar/carbs = 4 calories
1 g of protein = 4 calories
1 g of fat = 9 calories

For years, this well-established calorie count led to a common belief: since fat packs more than twice the calories per gram compared to carbs and protein, it's the culprit behind weight gain. But now, equipped with a deeper understanding of weight loss, we realise this view is akin to looking through the wrong end of a telescope.

Losing weight is not about vanishing calories; it's about the exchange of atoms. Atoms can't be transformed into pure energy. Therefore, doubling the gram weight of what we eat means doubling the atoms, and subsequently, we need to double the atoms we exhale.

Here's a twist in the tale: the mantra 'eat less, move more' falls short when tied to calories. I've always maintained this stance. Yet, framing this advice in the context of atomic weight – the weight of atoms we ingest and the weight of atoms we breathe out – paints a different picture. Weight loss naturally follows if we consume less atomic mass and increase our movement, thereby breathing more. It's not about calories but the atomic tango of intake and exhale. Does that shed new light on the old adage?

According to the NHS, the ideal daily calorie intake is a moving target, shifting with factors like age, metabolism, and how often you sprint for the bus. On average, they suggest 2,000 calories a day for women and 2,500 for men, but let's face it, life's not a one-size-fits-all kind of deal.

Now, let's play with some numbers. If I, your trusty male guide through this dietary journey, were to stick to a 2,500-calorie diet composed entirely of carbs and protein, I'd be chowing down on a hefty 625 g of food daily. But if I became a fat aficionado, my plate would weigh a mere 278 g. Over a year, that's the difference between befriending 502 lb of food versus a more slender 223 lb. It's like choosing between a heavyweight champion and a featherweight contender! Of course, our plates are more like a mixture of nutrients in the real world, so let's see how this plays out across various diets.

At first glance, this chart might look a little confusing, and to be honest, it took me several days to generate. But at its heart, it compares four different diets and the mass of food you need to eat over a year, to maintain a 2,500-calorie daily intake.

Diet	Macronutrients	Calories from each nutrient	Weight of food per nutrient per day	Total weight per day	Pounds of food consumed each year
Standard UK diet	Carbohydrates 55%	1,375	344g		
	Protein 15%	375	94g		
	Fat 30%	750	83g		
				521g	419 lb
Low-carb diet	Carbohydrates 10%	250	63g		
	Protein 30%	750	188g		
	Fat 60%	1,500	167g		
				417g	355 lb
Ketogenic Diet	Carbohydrates 5%	125	31g		
	Protein 30%	750	188g		
	Fat 65%	1,625	181g		
				399g	321 lb
Carnivore diet	Carbohydrates 0%	0	0g		
	Protein 45%	1,125	281g		
	Fat 55%	1,375	153g		
				434g	349 lb

Take another peek at your dinner plate; it's more than just a meal; it's a science exhibit. The fibre, our unsung hero, doesn't just sit pretty on the plate. It bypasses any weighty transformations in our bodies, preferring instead to hobnob with bacteria to cultivate a stellar microbiome. It's like the diplomatic envoy of your gut, negotiating peace treaties to temper sugar spikes and prevent insulin surges from turning your body into a fat-storage unit. And once finished, along with a bunch of bacteria, it ends up as poo. That's all your poo is – it's not the carbohydrates, fat, or protein you ate, further reinforcing that to lose weight, it's got to go somewhere.

Carbs and protein are the heavyweights of the plate, doubling the food's mass and making your respiratory system work overtime on an indoor treadmill or Zumba class, all in an effort to bid them farewell.

Now, circling back to the age-old mantra 'eat less, move more'. It's not just a myth; it's become a collective belief. But it doesn't hold true if you view it through the calorie lens. However, eating fewer grams (mass) means your body has less atomic weight to offload. And moving more? Well, it's like turning your breath into a weight-loss conveyor belt. At rest, you're exhaling about 1.5 cubic metres of breath per hour, shedding roughly 17 g of atomic weight. But kick it up a notch with some activity, and voilà, you're likely puffing out those atoms in a brisk 10 to 15 minutes, like a steam engine on a mission.

Now you know where body fat goes as we lose weight. Eat less; moving more isn't about calories – it's about reducing the atomic weight your body needs to offload. As you move, you're not just burning energy; you're operating a weight-loss machine, exhaling atoms and shedding weight with every breath. When you gaze at your next meal, think of it as an interplay with physics, a question of the mass on your plate and the atoms you'll breathe out. Add *Fibre First* to feel fuller, eat less atomic mass, and make every exhale a step towards a lighter you.

Further Proof It's Not About Counting Calories

For those folks who are looking to gain weight (yes, there are still a few around) and still swear by calories, here's a quirky suggestion: chow down on loads of coal (it's got quite the heat energy) and chase it with a glass of alcohol (also packing a calorie punch). But let's get real – that's just plain bonkers. While coal may be sizzling hot, it's not something your body can metabolise. As for alcohol, it may boast calorie credentials, but it's also not the most bioavailable option either (more on booze later).

Take sucrose, for example, the one we discussed earlier. It's like the phantom calorie that sets up shop in your liver and stubbornly sticks around, contributing to your body weight gram for gram without giving you any energy. It might have a lot of calories on the food label, but you won't get energy/calories from it. It's a bit like comparing apples to... well, coal. So, instead of getting caught up in the calorie circus, why not shift our focus to 'nutritional density'? Is a 2,000-calorie meal bursting with fresh, fibre-packed veggies and free-range chicken on the same level as a 2,000-calorie processed, sugar-laden ready meal? Definitely not. And let's not even entertain the notion that gobbling up 1,000 calories of fibre-rich broccoli is on par with sipping a sugary drink with the exact calorie count. Nope, it's high time we re-evaluate our approach to eating, bidding adieu to the bewildering world of calorie counting.

Let's sprinkle a bit of our magic on this calorie conundrum. Picture this: You're about to tuck into a hearty spaghetti bolognese and your hunger has you gobbling up the pasta first, eager to hush the grumbling of your ghrelin. According to what we've unpacked already, this approach sends you on a wild sugar rollercoaster, followed by an insulin tsunami that locks you in the fat-storing mode for three or four hours. But here's a twist. What if you start with a leafy green salad, say an extra 150 to 200 calories, before tackling the same main dish as the volunteers in our Blood Sugar Trial? This fibre-rich starter tames your hunger and shifts your focus to savouring the bolognese, pushing most of the pasta to the end of the meal. The result? A milder sugar spike, a gentler insulin response, and a quicker return to body fat-burning mode. Despite indulging in 150 to 200 more calories, you're on a healthier metabolic track and more likely to shed some pounds that day.

Nutritional Value Over Calories: A Smarter Approach

Instead of counting calories, let's focus on the nutritional richness of the foods on our plate. Food is more than mere fuel; it's the cornerstone of our health, providing the essential building blocks our bodies need. When you sit down for a meal, consider the fibre, vitamins, minerals, and overall nourishment it offers rather than the calorie tally. Remember, the true value of a meal lies in its nutritional density.

Once you've assessed the nourishment your meal provides, consider its mass or weight. Consuming less mass means your body requires fewer breaths to maintain or decrease weight. This approach ensures a nutrient-rich diet and aligns with the natural balance of intake and exhalation, guiding you towards better health and a healthier weight.

*****

What Is Your Weight Set Point?

Picture this imaginary scenario: You wake up one fine morning, and it's as if a mischievous wizard has played a trick on you; you've magically gained two stone overnight! It's like a bizarre dream, but your reality has taken an unexpectedly hefty turn. Suddenly, you find yourself overweight and in the 'I-might-need-a-new-wardrobe' territory. Your joints are creaking like an old wooden floorboard, your back is complaining as if you've been in a wrestling match with a grizzly bear, and your night's sleep was as restful as a concert by a snoring orchestra. And the cherry on top? An insatiable hunger has taken hold of you as if your stomach has become a bottomless pit.

You'd be motivated to act in this rather surreal situation. I mean, who wouldn't? But here's the twist – while this overnight scenario is purely a flight of fancy, those seemingly harmless yearly weight gains can stealthily creep up on us. Over a decade or two, they accumulate into a significant problem, but because they've tiptoed into our lives so gradually, we often don't react.

In South America, the big food corporations were unfashionably late to the fake food monopoly party. To make up for lost time, one of their tactics was to send a massive supermarket boat up remote rivers, offering irresistibly cheap, commercialised foods to the unsuspecting locals. Predictably, everyone got hooked. Guess what happened? Within just 2 years, these communities, who had previously never suffered from the invasion of corporate junk, were hit hard with health issues, and obesity became rampant. What had caused this sudden health crisis was clear as day for their governments. So, they took swift action. Today, if you stroll down the supermarket aisles in Chile, you'll find cereal boxes and snacks plastered with warnings, just like cigarette packs. And guess what? It's working! Sales of many unhealthy items are plummeting.

Back to what we mean by your body's 'set weight point'. Dr Jason Fung once dropped this gem of wisdom on me: 'Even if you change your diet, insulin resistance can keep your insulin levels high. And when your insulin levels are high, your body's set weight remains high, too. It's like your thermostat is stuck on the higher setting, and your weight keeps ever so slowly creeping upward. The longer you've been dealing with obesity, the harder it is to shake it off.' This is why you will sometimes meet large folks struggling to shed pounds, even if they don't eat large meals.

Think of obesity as the rust on an old car; it starts small and unnoticed but slowly creeps and feeds on itself until the darn door falls off! There's more to this intriguing puzzle. You might think, 'Steve, something doesn't quite add up here. If insulin resistance prevents sugar from entering cells, doesn't that mean it should prevent us from gaining weight?' It's a valid observation, but here comes the curveball – while insulin resistance hinders sugar from entering cells efficiently, we can't afford to have excess sugar hanging out in the bloodstream. Too much sugar is essentially like inviting trouble to your body's doorstep. So, even in the presence of insulin resistance, sugar finds its way into the cells, but it requires a larger insulin army to get the job done.

Here's where it gets truly fascinating. Insulin wears more than one hat—not only does it help store fat, but it also sends a signal to the brain, 'Let's gradually crank up the body set weight point, shall we?' In essence, it instructs the brain to store more and more energy, setting your body's weight thermostat a little higher each time its levels are elevated.

So, imagine a mischievous imp quietly turning up your home's thermostat, but instead of heating the room, it's sneakily turning up your body's fat storage setting. In its relentless pursuit of balance and homeostasis (a fancy term for stability), your body desperately tries to maintain your body's 'set weight point', much like how a thermostat keeps your home at a consistent temperature. But day by day, little by little, it starts to lose the battle. But here's the million-pound question: how do we prevent insulin from constantly nudging up our set weight point? If we can unravel this mystery, we'll be one step closer to understanding the complex web of factors contributing to obesity. And fear not, my friends, because we're about to explore the answers to this riddle.

Introducing 'homeodynamics' (to do with the nature and direction of change). Back in the caveman days, our bodies had a wise strategy: pack on some extra weight, just in case we missed out on hunting that sabretooth tiger for dinner. But here's the catch: homeostasis wasn't keen on us turning into our own version of woolly mammoths because that would turn hunting into a marathon rather than a swift sprint. So, 'homeodynamics' resulted in weight gain at a leisurely pace, with no rush.

Here's the surprising turn in the tale. Once we've gained that extra padding, homeostasis steps back in, clutching it like a toddler gripping their favourite teddy bear. It's all, 'This weight right here—it's gold, and I'm not budging.' It goes all out to maintain this newfound weight, as if saying, 'What if food's scarce tomorrow? I can't have you chasing down prey on an empty stomach.' Switching our body's current 'set weight point' to 'weight loss' mode is akin to reversing the flow in a complex system – a challenging but not impossible task. Obesity isn't just about succumbing to endless burgers and fries. It's more akin to your body stubbornly deciding, 'This weight, right here, is where we're staying.' It's as if your body's homeostasis has declared, 'This is the new normal, folks, and we're sticking to it!' But fear not, dear reader, we're on the verge of deciphering how to nudge that stubborn thermostat back down.

What's the mastermind behind this weighty conundrum? It's a hormonal saga, my friend. While leptin and ghrelin indeed play their roles in signalling your brain when to feast and when to fast, they're not the arch-villains of obesity. Think of them more as the supporting cast in the grand drama of weight management. Clinical trials have shown that merely tinkering with leptin and ghrelin levels doesn't translate to significant long-term weight changes. These hormones, it turns out, don't wield the magic wand needed to reset the thermostat.

It is time to introduce the real heavyweight champions in the arena of body-set weight regulation: insulin and cortisol. These two are not just participants; they're the key players in adjusting your body's set weight thermostat. For many, the creeping scale numbers aren't a tale of caloric excess but rather the narrative of insulin and cortisol's persistent influence.

As the needle on our weight thermostat nudges upwards, we find ourselves in an ongoing skirmish between the stability of homeostasis and the flux of homeodynamics, a constant tug-of-war between our body's quest for consistency and the forces nudging it towards change.

If weight gain boiled down to mere calories, we'd inflate quicker than a party balloon. Picture this: gaining a mere 3 lb annually (already a higher gain than the average for obese individuals) equals a minuscule 0.008 lb per day. Here's where it gets intriguing. Each pound of body fat is the equivalent of 3,500 calories. So, adhering to the calorie doctrine, indulging in just an extra 480 calories daily over a year – think one Mocha Cookie Crumble Frappuccino – would theoretically stack on an astonishing 50 lb! But honestly, that's as plausible as stumbling upon a unicorn in your garden; it just doesn’t happen.

Conversely, imagine embracing a calorie-slashing regimen, cutting 480 calories daily beneath your resting metabolic rate. In theory, you'd bid farewell to those 50 lb within a year. Again, that doesn’t happen.

The perpetual struggle between calorie-deficit diets and your body's staunch commitment to maintaining the status quo is akin to a relentless wrestling match, with homeostasis reigning supreme as the undisputed champion. Indulgence a little too much, and your body cranks up its internal thermostat, sending your heart racing, drenching you in sweat, and deploying a host of clever tactics to restore balance. Yet, should you dare to cut back on those calories, your body strikes back by dampening your metabolism, leaving you as lively as a sloth after a hearty meal. Simply put, any diet severely restricting calories is akin to a futile tug-of-war with your body's regulatory mechanisms.

Suppose you consume 500 calories less each day; your body cunningly adjusts by reducing your energy expenditure by an equivalent amount. Slash your intake by 700 calories, and your body responds by conserving energy even more stringently. A cutback of 900 calories? Expect your body to impose even stricter energy-saving measures. The harsh reality is that due to your body's set weight point and homeostasis, treating your current weight as the target to preserve, mere calorie restriction often proves ineffective.

Over time, the cunning duo of cortisol and insulin conspire to nudge your weight set point ever higher. It's like they're persuading your body that carrying extra weight is the latest trend. But here's the game changer: if we manage to curb insulin levels through a diet rich in fibre and scant on sugar while simultaneously dialling down cortisol by cultivating a stress-free existence (a lofty goal indeed!), we start the descent of our weight set point thermostat. That is the essence of the strategy. As Jason Fung eloquently puts it, the crux isn't about balancing calories; it's about harmonising our hormones. The goal – the key to lasting weight loss – is persistently lowering insulin and cortisol levels.

But why is cortisol such a heavyweight in weight gain? Imagine cortisol as the stern bouncer of a club named 'Stressville.' In the throes of an authentic fight-or-flight scenario, cortisol is your valiant protector. It surges sugar into your bloodstream, perfect for fleeing predators or hoisting heavy objects. However, cortisol is a fair-weather friend at best.

Persistent stress, which lingers for weeks, years, or even lifetimes, nudges your body into weight gain mode by ramping up insulin production. Cortisol is tailored for immediate, life-threatening crises, not the relentless stress of modern life – demanding jobs, turbulent relationships, sleepless nights, or financial woes. Our bodies, perplexing as they are, fail to distinguish between a charging lion and a looming deadline. Consequently, insulin and cortisol are locked in a relentless duel. Insulin strives to sweep sugar from your bloodstream, stashing it away as body fat for a rainy day. Meanwhile, cortisol insists on flooding your bloodstream with sugar, priming you to confront those figurative lions or grapple with imaginary bears. And in this epic showdown, cortisol often emerges victorious. Why? Because your body instinctively prioritises the perceived peril of imminent danger over slightly elevated blood sugar levels. But don't underestimate insulin; it's tenacious. Facing defeat, it floods the scene with even more troops, culminating in hyperinsulinemia – a fancy term for an insulin overload. This is your one-way ticket to the realms of slow-build obesity and chronic illness.

In essence, without necessarily overindulging in food, prolonged stress leads to sustained high cortisol levels, which in turn keep insulin levels on the rise, culminating in an unwelcome rise in your 'set weight point'. But the opposite is also true. If you can reduce your stress levels, that will reduce your fat-storing insulin levels, and then all you require is a strategy to avoid homeostasis, which tries to keep you just as you are. That tactic comes in the form of fasting, which we will discuss later.

*****

Glucagon: The Slender Hormone

Assuming you can keep your stress hormone cortisol in check, what next? Let me reintroduce glucagon, the slender hormone that does the opposite of insulin. Imagine this scenario: your blood sugar levels are on a wild rollercoaster ride, and they take a nosedive, plunging into the 'low blood sugar zone.' You might have heard of it as hypoglycaemia ('hypo' meaning low). Low blood sugar can be just as dicey as high blood sugar, which we call hyperglycaemia ('hyper' meaning high). But fear not, because in swoops our trusty sidekick, glucagon, like a caped crusader arriving just in time to save the day. Its mission? Transforming semi-solid sugar (glycogen) into liquid sugar and releasing it into your bloodstream, essentially becoming usable fuel. This newfound liquid energy powers your body, rescuing you from the clutches of low blood sugar's menacing grip.

When all the glycogen reserves have been depleted, guess what glucagon decides to do? It starts breaking down your stored body fat. Yep, that's when the real fat-burning party begins. There's no magic 'fat loss' button; we must burn it for fuel. Our buddy glucagon plays a starring role in this process.

Now, here's an interesting bit of knowledge, and that's all it is; it's here to cement the point: just like insulin injections are used to bring down blood sugar levels, you can also get glucagon injections to boost them. It's like the emergency medicine of the sugar world, used to rescue diabetes patients in the throes of severe hypoglycaemia who have either passed out or can't snack on sugar. I once witnessed a doctor friend of mine, who is a type 1 diabetic, use a glucagon injection during a fasting experiment we did together. If you're curious, you can watch our experiment on my Health Results YouTube channel, called the 'Zero Five 100 Challenge', where we ate zero calories for five days while running a hundred miles.

Alcohol And Its Effect On Hormones

Ah, the pleasure of savouring a fine glass of wine or cold beer. But hold on to your glasses, fellow connoisseurs, as we venture into the less celebrated side of our beloved beverages. Beyond the empty calories, alcohol loves to crash the party, especially when it comes to our body's release of glucagon.

Imagine enjoying your favourite drink only to find your blood sugar plummeting. Usually, glucagon would leap to the rescue, transforming stored fat into much-needed energy. But alcohol plays spoilsport, instructing glucagon to stay on the sidelines. As a result, even with low blood sugar, alcohol ties glucagon's hands, blocking its path to converting stored fat into the energy you're yearning for.

Not only does alcohol coax your body into late-night cravings by blocking glucagon and hindering your access to turning glycogen or fat into sugar energy, but it also throws a wrench in ketone production, your body's alternative energy-making process. As you're sipping away, alcohol being a poison dictates the liver's priorities, shoving crucial tasks like generating glucagon and ketones down the list. This obstruction means your body can't efficiently convert stored fat into energy, leading to a deceptive hunger signal that screams, 'Eat more, please!' Those late-night indulgences? They're not just cravings but a direct response to the energy shortfall caused by alcohol's meddling in your body's natural fat-to-sugar and fat-to-ketones conversion processes.

Here's a historical titbit: in the 1920s, doctors used alcohol as a ketone-reducer, injecting it into type 1 diabetics in ketoacidosis to dial down dangerously high ketone levels.

For those hoping to enjoy a drink while on a weight-loss quest, here's the scoop. Beer, affectionately known as 'liquid bread', may not be your ally in shedding pounds. On the flip side, neat spirits (sans sugary mixers) boast zero usable calories. Though they're labelled with calories, their actual impact is minimal due to limited bioavailability.

For wine aficionados, a glass or two of red wine might just hit the sweet spot. Packed with antioxidants and health-promoting nutrients, it's a dual victory for your palate and well-being. A toast to that!

But before you raise your glass in celebration of alcohol's health benefits, let's apply the brakes. Keep in mind what we have just discussed. Alcohol lowers your blood sugar level, necessitating more food consumption, and it will hamper your production of ketones.

While moderate alcohol intake, particularly red wine, has its merits, it's not a free pass to an all-you-can-drink buffet, especially during our younger, more carefree years. Overindulgence in alcohol can derail your weight-loss journey, eject you from ketosis, and unleash a host of bodily turmoil. Dr Boz, a remarkable physician who reversed her mother's cancer by changing her diet (more on her amazing story later) and specialises in brain injury, offers some sobering insights from her research, presented in our podcast.

She explains how alcohol is a master of dehydration, drawing fluid from our bloodstream and cells, leaving us parched and under the weather. It can cause brain swelling akin to a balloon at a festivity, persisting for up to three days and potentially stalling brain development for up to six months – hardly the party favour we desire. That euphoric feeling from drinking? It's a dopamine rush. However, chronic alcohol use can deplete your brain's dopamine reserves, leading to a less-than-joyous aftermath.

Attention, teenagers: alcohol consumption can significantly reduce the size of your hippocampus, the brain region crucial for learning and memory. In fact, studies have shown that a teenager who drinks may have a hippocampus up to 50% smaller than their non-drinking peers. Chronic alcoholics may experience an incessant craving for the next drink, especially when their dopamine receptors are starved of dopamine for extended periods. So, while a glass of red wine may have a seat at the table of health, remember, moderation is key. An excess of even the finest things can turn bitter. Cheers, but always in moderation!

Dr Boz, to demonstrate the damage alcohol has on the brain, then shared the following two charts with me. They were observations from people interacting with professional sports people who had been concussed and then the symptoms the athlete felt:

Signs of a concussion as observed by a witness	Symptoms of concussion as reported by athlete
• Appears dazedor confused	• Headache
• Answers questons slowly	• Memory problems
• Exhibits personality or behaviour changes	• Feeling 'whoozy'
• Seems confused about assignment or forget plays	• Nausea
• Loses conscoiusness	• Fuzzy vision (double)
• Behaviour changes	• Balance problems
• Shows poor concentration	• Dizziness
• Seems unsure of score, hame or opponent	• Sensitivity to light
• Can't recall hit or events prior to or after the hit	• Poor concentration
• Moves clumsily	• Confusion
• Vomits	• Sensitivity to noise
	• Feeling sluggish

I looked at them, pondered for a moment and asked her how they were relevant to our conversation on alcohol. She then told me to simply change the two titles of the above to the following, 'Signs of Concussion' to 'Drunk' and then 'Symptoms of Concussion' to Hungover.

Drunk	Hungover
• Appears dazedor confused	• Headache
• Answers questons slowly	• Memory problems
• Exhibits personality or behaviour changes	• Feeling 'whoozy'
• Seems confused about assignment or forget plays	• Nausea
• Loses conscoiusness	• Fuzzy vision (double)
• Behaviour changes	• Balance problems
• Shows poor concentration	• Dizziness
• Seems unsure of score, hame or opponent	• Sensitivity to light
• Can't recall hit or events prior to or after the hit	• Poor concentration
• Moves clumsily	• Confusion
• Vomits	• Sensitivity to noise
	• Feeling sluggish

Vinegar: The Tangy Titan Of Blood Sugar Mastery

Let's turn the spotlight on vinegar, that unsung hero lounging in your kitchen cabinet, quietly biding its time until it can unleash its superpowers on your blood sugar levels. Vinegar's claim to fame is not just one but two remarkable talents, and we're about to uncloak these culinary capers.

Vinegar doesn't merely whisper a 'No' to alpha-amylase, the notorious starch-to-glucose transformer we've previously discussed; it firmly tells it to 'Talk to the hand!' The benefit? Vinegar slows down the conversion of starches to sugar, thereby lowering your sugar spike and the resulting spike in insulin[4]. Fibre, our nutritional hero, also plays a crucial role in this starch-neutralising quest. Yet, vinegar introduces a unique twist with its acetic acid. This cunning compound jumps into the fray, assuming the roles of both defender and attacker. Acetic acid issues a VIP pass directly to your muscles, side-lining insulin as the unnecessary intermediary. Envision an exclusive muscle party, with glucose making its grand entrance as the celebrated guest, warmly received by muscles, whether they're in action or at rest. We'll discuss later how contracting muscles can absorb glucose without insulin's intervention – a significant win, given that fewer insulin spikes benefit us. But vinegar takes this a step further; it seems to coax muscles into welcoming glucose even when they're not contracting, a remarkable feat that sets vinegar apart in the realm of our muscle's contribution to blood sugar management.

The term 'vinegar' hails from the French phrase 'vin aigre,' translating to 'sour wine,' and the making of apple cider vinegar is akin to conducting a controlled-spoilage symphony. First, yeast dives into the sugars in apples, converting them into alcohol. Then, enters the real star, a bacterium named acetobacter, which transforms that alcohol into the star of the show: acetic acid. Let's not get bogged down in the technicalities, but in a nutshell, this magical transformation is known as fermentation. And those stringy, floaty bits in your apple cider vinegar? That's the 'mother'; the dynamic duo of yeast and bacteria forged during the fermentation fiesta.

Some vinegar aficionados hail the 'mother' as the health elixir supreme, a probiotic powerhouse. However, while the scientific jury is still out on officially crowning the mother as vinegar royalty, there's no denying vinegar's nutrient-packed profile. It's like apple juice's hip, health-conscious, virtually sugar-free cousin, brimming with B vitamins and polyphenols, those snazzy plant-based antioxidants.

Flashback to 1998, when a group of astute researchers decided to test vinegar's blood sugar-busting prowess. They rustled up two meals for a bunch of healthy volunteers: a white bread feast and the same feast with a vinegar twist. Lo-and-behold, the addition of vinegar significantly dialled down blood sugar levels for hours post-meal.[5]

Now for the grand entrance of vinegar into your daily routine. Personally, I'm not the head cheerleader for team vinegar, so my trick is a splash of olive oil and a drizzle of balsamic on my fibre-packed salads. Think of it as a gourmet dressing that titillates your taste buds and keeps your blood sugar in check.

Then there's the apple cider vinegar aficionado brigade, the folks who swear by their daily swigs of this tangy tonic, even right before hitting the hay, convinced it's their secret weapon for optimal morning glucose levels. Here's a nugget of wisdom from the book *Dark Matter: The New Science of the Microbiome* by James Kinross. He takes us on a mesmerising voyage into the labyrinth of our gut's unseen cosmos. Kinross reveals the powerhouse partnership between vinegar and fibre in our microbiome, akin to a superhero tag team championing our wellbeing. The takeaway? Merging a fibre-rich diet with a splash of vinegar or fermented delights could be the ultimate hack for amplifying your fibre's impact. It's like throwing a gut microbiome gala with a fibre feast and a dash of fermentation finesse!

Water: The Miracle Cure

I must confess, I was once a water sceptic. Why settle for mundane H2O when the world is brimming with more tantalising beverages? However, after plunging into a sea of research, I've surfaced with a revelation: our bodies are rather partial to a daily dose of about 1.5 to 2.5 litres of water. If you're slender and the gym isn't your second home, 1.5 litres might do the trick. But for the gym warriors and those carrying a bit more muscle, 2.5 litres could be your magic number. To paint a picture, a 70 kg human can wave goodbye to about 1.5 litres of water daily through sweating, breathing, and the ever-glamorous act of urinating. And if you're giving it your all in the gym, especially under the unforgiving gaze of the sun, that number can soar to 1.5 litres an hour. Hydration, dear friend, isn't just a suggestion; it's a command from your body! But is there such a thing as too much of a good splash? Well, unless you're aspiring to be a human aquarium, you're likely in the clear. Our kidneys, those unsung heroes of filtration, can process about 27 to 34 fluid ounces of water an hour or a staggering 20 to 28 litres a day. So, unless you're on a mission to challenge the capacities of your internal plumbing, you're probably safe.

If you find water as exciting as watching paint dry, fear not! A twist of lemon, lime, or a slice of ginger can turn your glass from bland to grand. And let's spill the tea (or should I say water?) – if you're sipping more coffee or tea than a barista in high season, perhaps it's the warm hug of hot water your body craves, not the caffeine kick. Why not experiment? A warm water symphony with a cameo of blackberries, blueberries, or a dash of lime might strike a chord with your taste buds.

Regarding exercise and hydration, here's an important fact: the average adult can only absorb about 200 ml of water every 15 to 20 minutes. That's about seven to eight modest mouthfuls. Overdo it, and your stomach balloons faster than, well, a balloon at a birthday bash. A stomach-turned-party central can even take the wind out of your breathing. And rehydration? It's no sprint. It's more like trying to fill a pool with a watering can. So, keep your hydration steady; remember, it's a marathon, not a sprint.

And what about hydration's unsung heroes, the electrolytes? These little marvels are your muscles' best mates, helping them flex and relax as they please. And since your heart is the head honcho of muscles, getting your electrolytes right is non-negotiable. Sodium is the VIP of electrolytes, keeping your blood's salt levels in check. Ever noticed the salty taste of blood and sweat? That's your body's not-so-subtle hint to keep the sodium coming. And for the long-distance runners, to keep those cramps at bay, remember to take a magnesium tablet every hour or so.

If you're a bit of a sweat machine during workouts and skimp on the salt, your blood volume might vanish faster than a magician's rabbit. Feeling sluggish is one thing, but in extreme cases, you might find yourself hitting the deck. And remember, as you champion real food and high-fibre diets, giving salty junk food the boot, watch out; you might find yourself on the low end of sodium intake!

Does the Source of Water Matter?

Indeed, not all waters are created equal, my fellow hydration-seekers. Selecting the perfect water is rather like selecting the perfect wine: some delight the palate, while others are best left on the shelf. Let's dive in.

Tap Water: The Unsung Hero

Now, I'm not here to dampen the spirits of tap water enthusiasts, especially here in the UK, where it's generally top-notch. But let's be clear: it comes with a side of chlorine. Chlorine, the vigilant guardian against waterborne villains, ensures our tap water's journey from reservoir to tap is safe. However, it's not one for subtlety and may not discriminate between the good and bad bacteria in your gut. It's like saying a dash of bleach is harmless to your favourite jeans. While authorities assure us that chlorine levels are minuscule, let's not forget our gut lining is more delicate than a bubble in the breeze. A little extra precaution wouldn't hurt, would it? Consider a home water filter or the classic boil-and-cool approach in dubious situations. Safety first, after all!

Bottled Water: A Plastic Predicament

Picture this: if you were to magically transform all the plastic currently littering our oceans and cluttering our streets into dust, then generously sprinkle it over every square inch of our planet's landmass, from the frosty poles to the sunny beaches – and I mean every single patch of solid ground – that dust would nearly reach our knees! That's a jaw-dropping image. How do I know? Well, back in 2011, my charity funded this eye-opening research. Imagine where we stand today! And to think, we only started wrapping our food and sipping from plastic bottles in the 1960s! We absolutely cannot let this madness continue, or we're navigating straight into disaster.

Now, let's zero in on the UK, where we guzzle down 35 million plastic bottles daily[6]. And here's the issue: over half of those bottles don't even get a second life through recycling[6]. So, what takes us mere minutes to sip ends up haunting our planet for a whole millennium! Imagine that: our quick sip, Earth's long-lasting burden!

But wait, it's not just about trashing the environment; it's a double whammy for our health. You see, some of the unsavoury elements from plastic can sneak their way into our precious water, and the chief troublemaker in this plastic drama is a sneaky character known as BPA (bisphenol A). It's like the supervillain of the plastic world pulling off a covert operation!

Now, the European Food Standards Agency (EFSA) put its foot down and banned BPA from infant feeding bottles, but when it comes to other products, it's like BPA gets a free pass. 'Why?' you ask. Well, it might just come down to the most powerful motivator in the world – money! I mean, think about it: in some places, a bottle of water costs more than a litre of petrol. It's like the bottled water business is the ultimate money-maker, and the taxman is delighted too! Bottled water, essentially a marketing masterpiece, should only be your go-to on those rare days when you forget to fill up your trusty reusable water canister in the morning before stepping out.

And here's the sneaky part: the squishier the water bottle, the more it becomes a silent, slow, and sneaky source of potential harm. And I'm not stretching it too far when I suggest that BPA secretly stand for 'Bottles to Poison Adults'.

Here is the conclusion to one piece of recent research titled *The Health Effects of BPA: Overwhelming Evidence of Harm. 'The amount of evidence that is available is overwhelming, and the conclusion is clear: low doses of BPA alter hormone-sensitive organs and are related to a wide range of human noncommunicable diseases based on evidence from human studies.'* [7]

And here is the reality: we're shelling out our hard-earned cash for something that's supposed to be a health elixir, but it might secretly contaminate our refreshing sip with poison. And those big-name bottled water brands? Well, they're essentially serving you up glorified tap water with a sky-high price tag! Here's the exclusive: a little while ago, we embarked on a two-day taste showdown right here in my office. We gathered 30 volunteers and decided to pit tap water against the big brands in not one but two blind taste tests. We handed them five mystery glasses of water in round one, but they had yet to learn where each one came from. Four glasses contained fancy offerings from top-tier bottled water brands; the other was our office-filtered tap water. The results: the tap water came out as a joint favourite! On day two, we shook things up a bit. Without giving our volunteers a heads-up, we repeated the experiment with a twist: we ever so slightly cooled down just the tap water. And guess what? The tap water emerged as the clear champion, no contest!

But that's not all; we didn't stop at the taste test. We also ran a pH test on the water; the tap water didn't disappoint. In fact, it came second place. Why is this a big deal, you ask? Our bodies need to maintain a pH balance between 6.8 and 7.4. Anything we consume that falls below that range means our bodies must put in extra effort, and they might even dip into our precious calcium reserves from our bones to restore that pH balance. So, here are three strikes against these heavily marketed bottled waters: they're bad for the planet, BPA might be stealthily harming your Microbial Partners, and their low pH could take a toll on your bones. It's a triple whammy, and that's after leaving an enormous hole in your wallet!

In the end, filtered tap water isn't just cheaper than bottled imposters; it's also better for the environment and tastes darn good. Please don't fall for the bottled water hype; after breakfast cereal, it's the biggest corporate con of the last century. It's time to quench our thirst with a splash of common sense!

The Coffee Conundrum

Now, about our beloved cup of coffee and its contemporaries: fizzy drinks and teas. Some argue they contribute to our daily hydration, but Dr Fereydoon Batmanghelidj, author of Your Body's Many Cries for Water, begs to differ. Dr Batmanghelidj spotlights caffeine as a cunning water burglar, offering a temporary boost while discreetly dehydrating you. A paradox in a cup, caffeine is indeed a natural diuretic, prompting you to part with more water than you consume. Not that you shouldn't consume coffee or tea, just don't count it towards your daily water intake.

Dairy Produce

In our quest to maintain a healthy gut, we've learned that many factors in the modern world can disrupt the delicate balance of our microbiome. It's not just the big corporations stripping out fibre from our diets; it's a whole slew of modern woes, from pollution and pesticides to microwaves and fizzy drinks. Even our love affair with ready meals and our reliance on overly prescribed medicines play a part. It's like a symphony of chaos conducted by the ills of our time!

In fact, it's becoming clear that nearly every disease and disorder we encounter in our modern civilisation can be traced back to the reduction or total elimination of just a couple of crucial bacterial species in our guts. But the positive news is that we are taking giant strides toward safeguarding our gut health by prioritising fibre-rich foods in our diet. It's like Newton's third law in action (remember those science lessons?): for every harmful action in our body, there's an equal and opposite reaction by our gut.

Enter dairy onto the stage. It's crucial to embrace a diet rich in fibre and fermented foods to defend and rebuild our body's ecosystem- our microbiome. While we've got the fibre part covered with choices like nuts, seeds, glucomannan, and plenty of leafy greens, fermented foods are often MIA in our modern diets! And here's a thought: three of the top five fermented foods are dairy-based-think probiotic live yoghurts, fermented milk (known as kefir), and certain cheeses. So, dairy isn't just about creamy delights; it's a potential hero in our quest to restore gut harmony!

Milk: The Dairy Dilemma Unveiled

Embarking on a dairy discovery, let's pore over the truth about milk, shall we? Imagine this: yoghurts and cheeses begin their life as milk, but somewhere along the way, milk lost its crown as the health halo we once thought it wore. Lurking within this seemingly innocent beverage is lactose, a sugar that becomes a party crasher for adults. The reality? Post-infancy, a whopping two-thirds of the globe's population gives lactose the cold shoulder, developing sensitivities or outright rejections. It's like milk comes with a 'best before adulthood' tag that nature forgot to print.

Zooming in on lactose intolerance, The Lancet, a British medical journal established in 1823, compiled an extensive study into lactose intolerance in 2017. They reported on 89 countries[8], but I've narrowed it down to just 25 here so you can more quickly grasp the picture. It shows the percentage of the adult population in each country that is lactose intolerant:

Australia	44%
Austria	22%
Belgium	15%
Brazil	60%
Canada	59%
China	85%
Egypt	68%
Finalnd	19%
France	36%
Germany	16%
Greece	55%
India	61%
Ireland	4%
Israel	89%
Italy	72%
Netherlands	12%
New Zealand	10%
Poland	43%
Portugal	40%
South Korea	100%
Sweden	7%
Thailand	84%
Turkey	69%
Ukraine	61%
United Kingdom	8%

So, what's the deal? As youngsters, our bodies are all about that lactase enzyme, breaking down milk's sugars like pros. But as we age, lactase retires early, leaving us grappling with the dairy repercussions: bloating, a collection of ailments, and emergency bathroom sprints.

Now, the big question: is milk drinking natural? Not exactly. Our ancestors only started dabbling in dairy around 8000 BC, treating milk more like a rare delicacy than the fridge staple it is today. Fast-forward to the 1800s, and suddenly milk's being hailed as the superhero for bones, thanks to its calcium and phosphorus content. Cue the birth of the dairy industry, which, as demand surged, saw cows getting cosy in ever-shrinking spaces.

As these milking quarters became cramped, they also became, let's say, less than a five-star in cleanliness. The dairy industry's response? Sterilise everything in sight and have docs give the cows a once-over. But when that wasn't enough to keep the milk mischief at bay, along came pasteurisation. Heating milk to a toasty temp became the norm, waving goodbye to the days of raw milk and ensuring our morning cereal's companion was free from microscopic party poopers. So, there you have it, the curious case of milk's journey from nature's nectar to a beverage that's a double-edged sword.

Understanding The Milk Label

- **HTST (high-temperature short time)** – Created in the 1930s, this milk is pasteurised to 71°C (161°F) for 15 seconds, providing several weeks' shelf life. The process is often marketed as 'pasteurised'.

- **UHT (ultra-high temperature)** – First used in the 1970s, this milk is pasteurised to 138°C (280°F) for just two seconds. This provides an extended shelf life of approximately nine months, without the need to be refrigerated, and is often marketed as UHT or 'long-life milk'.

- **Homogenisation** – Some milk undergoes a separate process called 'homogenisation' after pasteurisation. This process breaks the molecules down into tiny pieces and prevents a layer of cream from forming on top of the milk.

- **Semi-skimmed and skimmed milk** – When milk is 'skimmed,' it means that the level of fat has been reduced through filtering. In the UK, skimmed milk has around 0.1% fat, and semi-skimmed milk typically has around 2.5%.

Let's talk about skimmed milk for a moment. Why on Earth would anyone choose skimmed milk when whole milk is only about 4% fat? Especially when we realise that natural fat isn't the villain it was made out to be. It's like taking a race car and removing three of its wheels – it just makes little sense! Plus, when we strip away the fat, we're also bidding adieu to fat-soluble vitamins A, D, E, and K. It's a double whammy because one perk of milk is its calcium content (though I would argue you don't need it if your diet is right), but for calcium to work its magic, it needs its sidekick, vitamin D. So, in a cruel twist of fate, when we skim the fat off milk, we're essentially stripping away most of the health benefits too. It's like ordering a pizza without cheese; you're missing out on the best part!

Don't get me wrong; if you occasionally enjoy a glass of milk (assuming your tummy agrees), here's a nugget of wisdom. When it comes to all things dairy, going organic is the way to go. Think about this: in the US, the number of dairy cows was cut in half between 1960 and 2005, but milk production somehow increased by nearly 50%. How? Well, it's a wild tale involving cows on antibiotics, force-fed grains, and a bunch of other unnatural additives. All of this makes milk production super cost-effective but not a health potion for humans. That's why if you're going for milk, make it whole organic pasteurised milk. There's a debate about raw milk being even better, but it's a bit like playing Russian roulette with your dairy – it carries a slightly higher risk of infection.

Now, let's return to our gut, where we began this dairy journey. While I might not be milk's biggest fan, plain yoghurt and certain cheeses are the unsung heroes of the dairy world. These two products are like the Avengers of gut health. Yoghurt gets its creamy texture as bacteria work their magic, converting lactose (sugar) into lactic acid. Cheese follows a similar path, and the result can be a dairy delight teeming with an army of beneficial bacteria, the heroes of our guts.

Patrick Holford

We know that milk causes cancer cells to grow, but it is not a problem for the very young as they are meant to drink milk. What concerns me is that the logic is very strong, but the hard evidence is not quite there yet. What milk does is it promotes a hormone called IGF-1, an insulin-like growth factor. And if you look at that across the ages, it absolutely peaks in the mid-teenage years, when the breasts are fully formed and when the prostate is fully formed. The logic suggests that it is quite likely that overconsumption of dairy products in the teenage years may produce a sort of overgrowth of breast cells and prostate cells that could set a background for greater risk in later life.

But of course, everyone says what about the calcium? Milk and bones have calcium; we must have milk for bones. But it is very clear, in fact, that two of the top professors in America in the field of nutrition, Professor Ludwig and Jenkins, both say this: There is absolutely no link at all between children's bone mass density and milk consumption. There is no link between postmenopausal women's risk of osteoporosis and dairy consumption. No link at all. Absolutely none. It's a myth. Yes, we need calcium. If you eat beans, nuts, vegetables, and fish, you are going to get plenty of calcium. A lack of calcium does not drive osteoporosis later in life. It's mainly a lack of vitamin D. If you go to the equator, where there is a lot of sun, there is no osteoporosis. The further you go away from the equator, the greater the risk.

Artificial Sweeteners And Honey

You might think artificial sweeteners are a sweet escape from spiking your glucose levels, but they also have quirks. Firstly, their sheer sweetness informs the body that sugar is about to come; they prime the pump. There's even a biological name for it: Cephalic Phase Insulin Response (CPIR). Therefore, insulin rises to deal with the sugar that never arrives. In Ben Bikman's book, *Why We Get Sick* (buy it; it's brilliant. Possibly the best book I have ever read on insulin) and do watch our YouTube podcast we did together. He talks about how researchers have concluded that artificial sweeteners increase the risk of insulin resistance. According to one study, people who drink an artificially sweetened (diet) soda daily have a 36% greater chance of developing metabolic syndrome and a whopping 67% higher risk of type 2 diabetes.[23]

The next problem is that sweetness also feeds our addiction to sugar and can derail any attempt to break free. Plus, for some folks, these sugar imposters can play a sneaky trick – causing blood sugar levels to dip too low, leaving you feeling like you need an all-you-can-eat buffet to stay afloat. And hold on to your sweet tooth because artificial sweeteners aren't exactly your allies in the battle against sugar cravings. They might be a tad better than the usual suspects like glucose, fructose, and sucrose, but it's like saying having one broken leg is better than two – not an ideal situation.

Now, what about honey, that golden nectar? While it does have some nifty components, like helping with hay fever and packing a punch of antioxidants, it's important to remember that sugar is sugar.

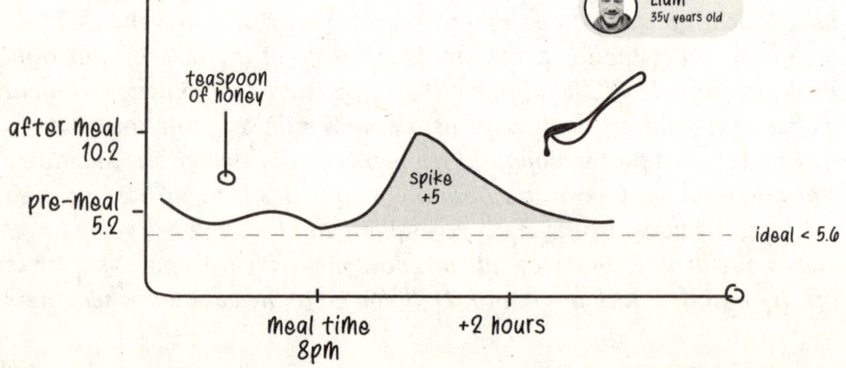

Look above at what unfolded with Liam's blood sugar levels during our Blood Sugar Trial. One evening, he stirred two spoons of honey into hot water to soothe a sore throat.

As we tiptoe through the tantalising world of sweet nothings, let's not plunge into despair over our sugar-laden woes just yet. Enter the scene: stevia, erythritol, and xylitol, the trio of sweet saviours that dance around the insulin response, sidestepping the CPIR with the grace of a ballet dancer in a mosh pit. You can still have your cake (and eat it, too) sprinkled with a dash of guilt-free sweetness, minus the tumultuous sugar highs and lows.

Stevia: The Green Sweetener From Nature's Pocket

Stevia isn't just sweet; it's like finding a pot of gold at the end of a rainbow, except this treasure is derived from the Stevia rebaudiana plant's leaves, hailing from the vibrant lands of South America. This isn't your run-of-the-mill, conjured-in-a-lab sweetener; it's the real deal, drawing its potent sweetness from nature itself. Stevia's sweet secret lies in steviol glycosides, which pack a punch at 200 to 400 times the sweetness of our humble table sugar, yet it saunters in, cool as a cucumber, without the caloric baggage or artificial nasties.

You might stumble upon stevia in its many guises next time you wander the supermarket aisles, perhaps pondering life's mysteries. Whether it's powdered, liquid, or in those cute little packets that seem to disappear into handbags and drawers, stevia is ready to sweeten the deal, turning your beverages and bakes into guilt-free delights.

Erythritol: The Sweet Underdog With A Calorie Cuff

Erythritol might sound like a newly discovered planet, but it's a sweet ally in our daily diet, weaving its magic from morning coffee to after-dinner treats. This celestial-sounding sugar substitute is actually grounded in nature, found in fruits and fermented foods. Its production is a marvel of modern science, where simple glucose is transformed by yeast into a sweetener that's about 70% as sweet as sugar but with zero calories, creating a guilt-free galaxy of pleasure. We can enjoy sweetness with erythritol without fearing sugar spikes or waistline woes. So, when you sprinkle that teaspoon of erythritol, you're dusting your dish with a sprinkle of cosmic wisdom, proving that the universe of healthier choices is vast and delicious.

Xylitol: The Sweet Tooth's Hero

Xylitol is not just any sweetener; it's the knight in shining armour for your dental health, hiding in plain sight in sugar-free gums and tooth-friendly treats. Clocking in at 70% of the sweetness of sugar and only 2.4 calories per gram, xylitol is the secret handshake among those in the know. This natural wonder, sourced from birch trees or plant fibres, satisfies your sweet tooth and moonlights as a dentist's dream, safeguarding your smile by forming a protective coating on your pearly whites.

Xylitol has garnered widespread acclaim across nations such as Finland, Japan, and the USA. Remarkably, in Finland, 90% of kindergartens distribute Xylitol sweets to children every day, aiming to shield their precious teeth. Similarly, my household has warmly embraced the allure of Xylitol, boasting a stash of lollipops that would surely earn a nod of approval from even the most discerning dentist.[9]

So, as we wrap up this sweet symposium, let's remember while sugar might have been king, there's a new crew in town, ready to sprinkle their magic into our lives, one guilt-free spoonful at a time. And to those yet unacquainted with the wonders of xylitol, stevia, and erythritol, perhaps it's time to broaden your horizons and taste the future of sweetness. After all, who said watching your sugar intake couldn't be a delightful affair?

THE

FIBRE FIRST

DIET

Coconut Flour Packs a Whopping 38% Fibre Punch

Part II

The Science

*****

A detailed look into the dangers of excessive sugar and ultra-processed foods and how they link not just to weight gain but also diseases.

Chapter 4

The Fake Food Maze

Circumnavigating today's nutritional landscape feels akin to deciphering an ancient, cryptic manuscript; complex, baffling, and designed to keep us in a perpetual state of confusion. At the heart of this conundrum lies a potent truth: a small band of food industry titans wielding vast influence over Britain's food supply are far more invested in fattening their wallets than nurturing our health. They deploy many tactics to keep us in the dark, ensuring we remain loyal patrons of their products, lost in a supermarket aisle of misinformation.

We are entrenched in what can only be described as an 'unnatural habitat'. Unlike our wild counterparts, we face the luxury and curse of constant access to food. However, this bounty is largely at the mercy of ten corporate goliaths, whose offerings do little to favour our wellbeing.

Turn page to see who's controlling your plate ›

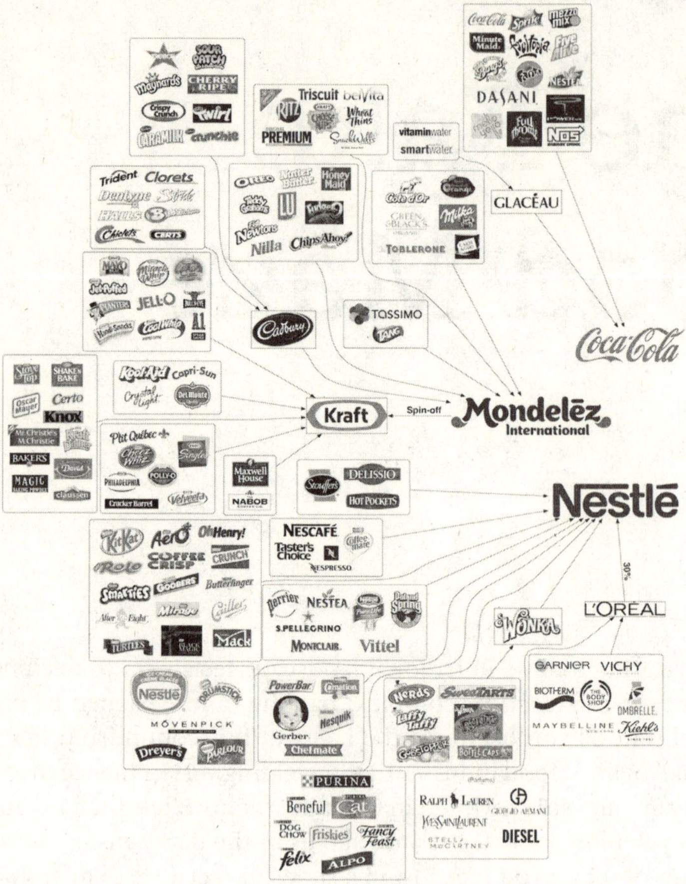

As we wander through this manufactured maze, we're tasked with adopting a form of 'unnatural thinking', consciously elevating our food selection process from the depths of habit to the forefront of mindful consideration.

Our natural inclination towards constant grazing, coupled with the incessant noise of food marketing and the deliberate infusion of addictive substances into our food, has led to a stark reality: a society burdened with more illness than wellness. This isn't merely an adult affliction; our children are unwittingly accruing debt on their health, journeying towards chronic conditions unbeknownst to them. If you're grappling with health issues, understand this: the deck is stacked against you, but it's not your fault.

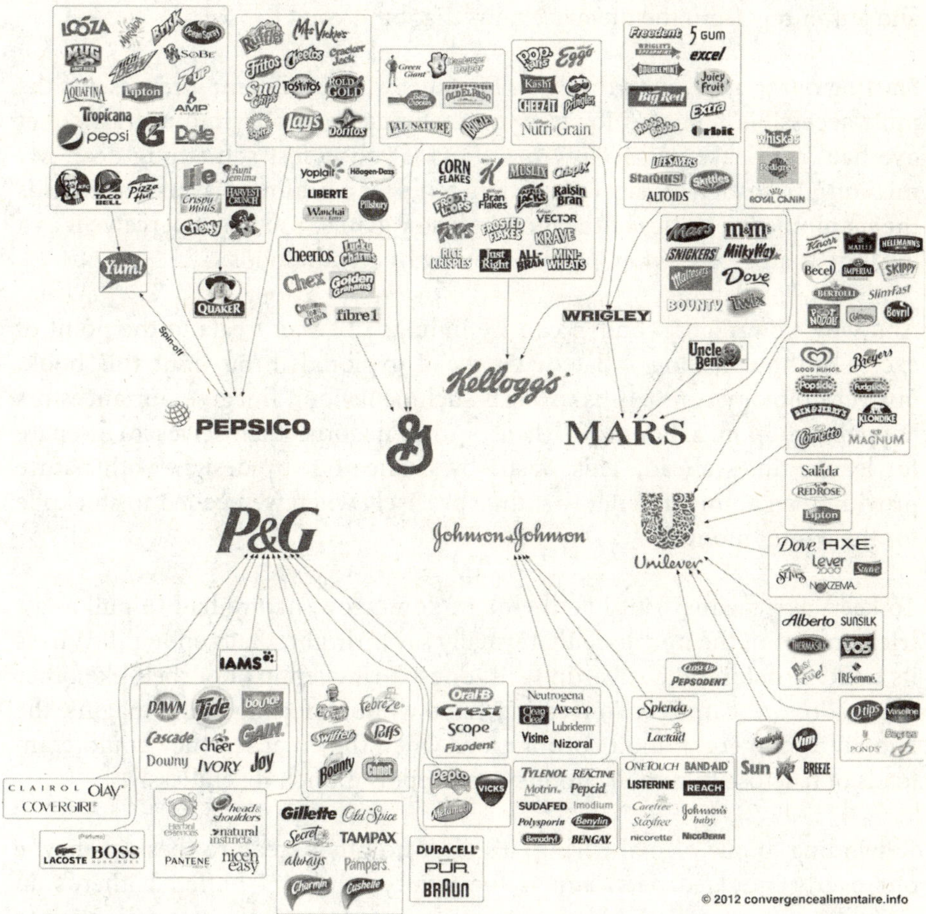

The illusion of dietary freedom in our modern era is an illusion. With food more accessible than at any point in our two-million-year history and those ten industry juggernauts tirelessly working to ensnare our taste buds with their engineered delights, it's no wonder our collective health is on the decline.

Over the years, our brains have woven a complex tapestry, linking certain foods to specific emotional states. We've been led to believe these foods are the key to our happiness, but the truth is far more intricate (and we'll take a proper look at this shortly). Channelling the wisdom of Freddie Mercury, it's time to 'break free' from these misconceptions. Imagine a world where you don't feel deprived of any food because, with the *Fibre First* diet, you might not have to. Instead, you're on the cusp of discovering true freedom and autonomy from the dietary chains that bind you.

Starting our journey with the *Fibre First* diet wasn't random; it represents the most accessible first step for everyone. Diving head first into a drastic diet overhaul can leave you feeling bereft, as if you've lost something dear. My mission? To instil a sense of liberation, to foster a profound aversion towards the manipulative tactics of the food industry giants. You won't perceive it as a loss but as an escape when parting ways with certain foods.

And why, you might wonder, can we indulge in sweet treats to the point of excess without feeling satiated? As we've explored throughout this book, our very biology compels us towards such behaviour. Imagine our ancestors happening upon a bounty of fruit – they'd gorge themselves to prepare for leaner times ahead. This wasn't by chance but by design, with nature providing an abundant energy source precisely when we needed to stockpile for the winter months.

To keep us guzzling fruit like there's no tomorrow, nature had to pull a fast trick on leptin, the hormone that usually says 'Alright, that's enough!' What's its trick? Fructose, the sugar in fruit, doesn't ring leptin's doorbell like other foods. So, we can keep on eating fruit without feeling full. Imagine the lightbulb moment at food corporations when they realised they could cram loads of fructose into their products to keep us munching endlessly.

Rewinding to our primal wiring, it's clear no other creature (besides maybe our overly indulged pets) enjoys the luxury of a 24/7 buffet. If there's an animal out there with a fridge, I stand corrected. Unlike us, animals stick to the diet they've evolved with, not swayed by the latest offering from Giraffe Gourmet Grub or Antelope Appetite Inc. You don't see elephants ditching their staple diet for the latest fad just because it comes in shiny packaging with a tempting discount.

This 24/7 access to 'food-like substances' is a modern-day anomaly. When food was scarce, our ancestors' brains were wired to feast while they could, a survival tactic courtesy of the primal brain. Fast-forward to today, and this instinct turns indulging on Pringles into a survival skill worthy of Bear Grylls. Our modern-day feast is less about survival and more about navigating a minefield of nutritionally bankrupt food, courtesy of Big Food Inc.

Consider this: if it comes wrapped in layers of plastic or boasts a marketing slogan, it's likely been processed more than an Instagram filter. These items are not just food; they're a carefully engineered concoction designed to turn eating into an extreme sport where the only medals are extra inches on the waistline.

So, what's the secret sauce for a life of health and vitality? It's simpler than you might think: dial back to what nature intended. Our bodies still crave the diet of our hunter-gatherer ancestors. This means filling our plates with natural fats, whole foods, and meats from animals that have lived as nature intended. It's about choosing foods that wouldn't look out of place on your great-grandparents' table.

The harsh reality is supermarkets and food manufacturers are banking on our addiction to processed, sugary potions. Meanwhile, pharmaceutical giants are cashing in on treating the symptoms of our modern diet. It took me 25 years of being fat and sick to see through this charade and believe me; I'm not just upset; I'm furious.

Breaking free doesn't require a Herculean effort, just a return to the basics. Cut the cord with foods that prioritise profits over health. Rediscover the joy of real, seasonal, natural foods. This isn't just a diet; it's a roadmap to a life brimming with health, happiness, and longevity. Here's to eating in a way that would make our ancestors proud and to a future where we're nourished by nature, not duped by industry.

The Vicious Obesity Cycle

Before we take the lid off the packaged foods, I want to discuss the Vicious Obesity Cycle. Peeling back the layers of the obesity epidemic reveals a narrative far deeper than a mere tale of overindulgence and sedentary lifestyles. It's a multifaceted tale where simple equations like 'Greediness + Laziness = Fatness' fall short of capturing the truth. Yes, we all have moments of succumbing to the allure of the sofa and a bag of sweets. Yet, if the antidote to obesity was as clear-cut as just eating less and moving more, then the UK, with 62% of adults[1] on a diet each year and 63% physically active[2], wouldn't be grappling with a reality where a staggering two-thirds of its adult population is battling with weight issues.

This cycle is a complex tangle of factors, not just a straightforward cause-and-effect scenario. It's not merely about individual choices but involves a broader spectrum of influences, from marketing strategies of large food corporations to governmental policies. This cycle is perpetuated by a range of elements that go beyond personal habits and dive into the realms of societal structures and norms.

There's an insidious cycle at play here, one I term 'The Vicious Obesity Cycle'. It's a whirlpool where big food corporations, akin to the tobacco giants of yesteryear, spike their products with addictive ingredients. We're then bombarded with ads showcasing fit, healthy individuals indulging in these items, compelling us to fill our shopping trolleys with them. Then, as sales increase, supermarkets spotlight these products on end caps and checkout aisles, fuelling further purchases. We consume and gain weight but still get seduced by the misleading imagery of slim models or sports stars enjoying these foods, leading us to believe they're not the culprits.

Meanwhile, governments rake in tax revenue from these sales, often turning a blind eye or, even worse, endorsing harmful products. Sounds far-fetched, doesn't it? (see image below). This is the government's current food guidelines; with your newfound knowledge, can you spot 12 items on here that may drive insulin resistance and are not suitable for the entire population?

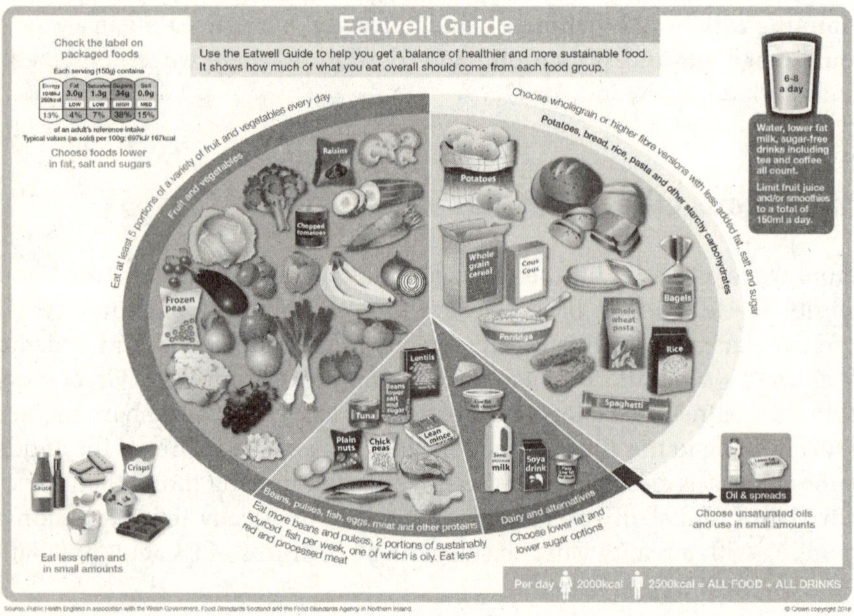

Breaking free from this cycle demands a deeper understanding of what truly nourishes our health and a firm rejection of the corporate giants pushing harmful products. Collectively, we must shun packaged foods loaded with dangerous oils and chemicals. Reflecting on Jen Whittington's insights in her book *Fixing Dad*, we're prompted to question: Who bears the responsibility for the rising tide of type 2 diabetes and obesity? Is it solely the individual, the food industry, or a government that has let its people down? How many of us knew that government nutritional guidelines, often influenced by industry funding, strayed from the WHO recommendations?

Consider this: in 1966, when I was born, only 11% of Britons were overweight, and a mere 1.5% were obese. Fast-forward to today, and those numbers have skyrocketed to 64% overweight and 28% obese. Given that over half of the British population is overweight, some suggest recalibrating the definition of 'overweight'. My stance is firm: No. We cannot normalise or accept this epidemic. Overweight and obesity shorten lives and are linked to diabetes, cancer, and more. We can't merely accept the unacceptable. Our collective weight gain over the past 50 to 60 years dwarfs the swelling of the previous 2 million years. If our primal ancestors had mirrored our recent weight gain rate, each would weigh more than the planet itself! While that's an absurd notion, it starkly illustrates the severity of our current predicament and the urgent need for action.

Okay, let's turn to the meat of the matter. Fake foods, which might conjure images of plastic fruit displays, refer to something much more pervasive and sinister in our diets: ultra-processed foods. Picture this: foods that have journeyed so far from their natural state that they're barely recognisable as descendants of anything that once grew in a field or roamed the earth. These are culinary chameleons camouflaged as nourishment while hiding their true, processed nature.

Imagine a food factory where nature's bounty is dismantled and reassembled like a jigsaw puzzle with missing pieces. These foods are often stripped of fibre and their nutritional essence, only re-fortified with vitamins and flavours concocted in a lab. They're foods, but not as we know them; they're imitations, shadows of real sustenance.

These foods parade a long list of ingredients, many of which sound like they belong in a chemistry set rather than a kitchen. They're crafted not just for taste but for an extended shelf life, ease of transport, and, most crucially, to trigger that bliss point in our brains that keeps us coming back for more. They're the cookies that never go stale, the bread that stays unnaturally soft for weeks, the meals that can survive years in the freezer – these are the staples of the fake food regime.

In this world of fake foods, fibres are often the first casualties. Removed to enhance texture and shelf life, they rob these foods of one of nature's most beneficial ingredients. In their place, we find sugars, unhealthy fats, salt, and a cocktail of preservatives and additives designed to tantalise our taste buds and override our body's natural satiety signals.

NOVA Scales

In today's world, finding truly unprocessed food is a challenge. Unless you're in the business of hunting your own dinner or harvesting straight from the earth, some processing is almost inevitable. Even those home-grown veggies might spring from seeds that strayed far from their ancestral origins over centuries. So, the real quest is to discern the kinds of processing that are relatively harmless from those we should steer clear of. Fortunately, we're not left to navigate these gloomy waters alone. The NOVA scale, created in 2009 by Carlos Monteiro, a professor of nutrition, offers us guidance in categorising foods based on the extent and nature of their processing.

The NOVA scale categorises food into four groups, each reflecting the level and impact of processing involved:

NOVA 1 – Unprocessed or Minimally Processed Foods: This group is the bedrock of what we might call 'real food'. It includes fresh fruits, vegetables, nuts, and meats – essentially items that are unaltered or have undergone minimal processing. This minimal processing might include freezing, boiling, or drying, which doesn't significantly alter the nutritional quality of the food.

NOVA 2 – Processed Culinary Ingredients: Think of ingredients like sugar, oils, and fats, or even spices and herbs. These are derived from natural foods but are processed to make them suitable for cooking and seasoning. They're typically used in conjunction with unprocessed foods to enhance flavour and culinary experience.

NOVA 3 – Processed Foods: These are essentially unprocessed foods that have been altered, but not in a way that makes them nutritionally unrecognisable. They often have added salt, sugar, or fat. Examples include canned vegetables, simple bread, and cheese. The key is that these foods are still close to their original form.

NOVA 4 – Ultra-Processed Foods: Here's the heart of the problem -- the 'fake foods'. These products are not only far removed from their original food source but are often a complex concoction of ingredients like sweeteners, preservatives, colourings, and flavour enhancers. They're engineered for convenience, shelf-stability, and palatability, often at the cost of nutritional value. Think soft drinks, packaged snacks, or instant noodles. These are the foods that the NOVA scale cautions us to minimise or avoid for better health.

Using the NOVA scale as a guide, we can approach our food choices with more awareness, understanding the impact of processing on what we eat and steering towards choices that keep us closer to nature's bounty. Remember, the closer food is to its natural state, the more likely it is to nourish and sustain us as nature intended.

NOVA Category	Description	Examples
NOVA 1	**Unprocessed** (or natural) Foods are edible parts of plants or animals (muscle, offal, eggs, milk), and also fungi, algae. **Minimally, processed** foods are natural foods, altered by processes that include removal of inedible or unwanted parts, and drying, grinding, fractioning, filtering, roasting, boiling, nonalcoholic fermentation, pasteurization, refrigeration, chilling, freezing, placing in containers, and vacuum-packing. These processes are designed to preserve natural foods, to make them suitable for storage. Many unprocessed or minimally processed foods are prepared and cooked at home.	Fresh or froxen fruit, vegetables, eggs, meat, fish, algae Natural yogurt, sour cabbage, kimichi Home-cooked meals with natural ingredients
NOVA 2	**Processed culinary ingredients** are substances derived from Group 1 foods or from nature by processes that include pressing, refining, grinding, milling, and drying. The are not meant to be consued by themselves, and are normally used in combination with Group 1 foods to make freshly prepared drinks, dishes and meals.	Flour, olive oil, butter, coconut oil, cream, sour cream, dried fruit and vegetables, herbs Ingredients in home cooking
NOVA 3	**Processed foods** such as bottled vegetables, canned fish, fruits in syrup, cheeses and freshly made breads, are made esentially by adding salt, oil, sugar, or other substances fro Group 2 to Group 1 foods. Processes include various preservation or cooking medthods and, in the case of breads and cheese, nonalcoholic fermentation. Most processed foods have 2 or 3 ingredients and are recognisable as modified versions of Group 1 foods.	Canned fish, cheeses, freshly made bread, canned vegetables
NOVA 4	Ultra-processed foods, such as soft drinks, sweet or savoury packaged snacks, reconstituted, meat products, and prepared frozen dishes, are not modified food but formulations made mostly or entirely from substances derived from foods and additives, with little if any intact Grpup 1 food. Ingredients of these formulations usually include those also used in processed foods, such as sugars, oils, fats, or salt. But ultra-processed products also include other sources of energy and nutrients not normally used in culinary perparations. Some of these are directly extracted from foods, such as casein, lactose, whey, and gluten. Many are derived from further processed of food constituents, such as hydrogenated or interesterified oils, hydrolyzed proteins, soya protein isolate, matodextrin, invery sugar, and high-fructose corn syrup. Classes of additives found only in untra-processed products include dyes and other colours, and colour stabilisers; flavours, flavour enhancers, and non-sugar sweeteners; and processing aids such as carbonating, firming, bulking and anti-bulking, de-foaming, anti-caking, and glazing agents, emulsifiers, sequestrants, and humectants. A multitude of sequences of processes is used to combine the usually many ingredients and create the final product (hence ultra-processed). The processes involved include several with no domestic equivalents, such as hydrogenation and hydrolyzation, extrusion, and molding, and preprocessing for frying.	Soft drinks Sweet and savoury packaged snacks Diet and low-fat products Products with artificial sweeteners Ready meals Reconstituted meat and fish products Oven chips Margerines Protein bars and drinks

The research paper titled 'The Western Diet: a blind spot of Eating Disorder' by Agnes Ayton and Dr Ali Ibrahim (a cycling buddy of mine) has unveiled profound insights into the intricate relationship between modern dietary patterns, particularly the surge in ultra-processed foods, and the escalating prevalence of eating disorders. Recognising the immense significance of their findings, I funded the public release of this study. This choice underscores the pressing nature of the matter and the importance I place on these revelations, given their potential implications for public health policies, dietary guidelines, and our collective understanding of eating disorders.

Through my funding of this research's public release, I have facilitated broader access to these invaluable insights, making them accessible to healthcare professionals, researchers, and the public, and it's also how I can give you the following highlights from the research paper:[2]

Change in food consumption: One significant change over the past half-century is the increasing dominance of ultra-processed foods, steadily replacing unprocessed and minimally processed foods. This shift has led to a higher intake of sugars and food additives globally, impacting metabolic responses such as insulin and glucose reactions, appetite stimulation, and alterations in endocrine (the endocrine system is a network of glands and organs that uses hormones to control and coordinate metabolism, energy level, reproduction, growth and development) and neurobiological pathways and the microbiome.

Need for a paradigm shift: The paper argues for a paradigm shift in understanding vulnerabilities to various eating disorders by integrating recent knowledge about individual metabolic responses to modern highly processed foods into existing psychological models.

The link between eating disorders and metabolic diseases: The increasing rates of obesity and metabolic diseases such as diabetes are paralleled by a rise in eating disorders. This correlation suggests that the same environmental factors affecting obesity may also influence other eating disorders.

Impact of the modern Western diet: The modern Western diet, characterised by high consumption of ultra-processed foods, plays a role in abnormal eating behaviours and related eating disorder psychopathology.

The epidemiological link between obesity and ultra-processed foods: The obesity epidemic, beginning in the 1970s, has shown a parallel increase to that of ultra-processed foods.

Role of carbohydrate-insulin model: The carbohydrate-insulin model of obesity, which emphasises food's endocrine and metabolic effects, is an important perspective in understanding the obesity epidemic. It postulates that high-carbohydrate foods are a significant trigger for insulin, leading to increased appetite and weight gain.

The role of NOVA-4 foods in obesity: 100% of the foods identified in binge eating episodes fall under the NOVA-4 category. This overwhelming predominance of ultra-processed foods in the diets of individuals with eating disorders underscores the significant role this food type may play in the development and perpetuation of disordered eating patterns.

A Tale of Instinct And Industry

Stay with me; we have almost arrived at the breaking news of how food corporations manipulate your foods. But before we get there, I want to ask you a question: have you ever found yourself nibbling the last bit of stale bread, munching on cold, cardboard-like chicken nuggets, or polishing off a whole tub of popcorn at the movies? Or perhaps you've gulped down that last mouthful of warm, flat soda, even when every sip felt like a chore? Trust me, you're not alone in this – I've been there too. It's almost comical and slightly embarrassing. Pausing after every bite to check if we're full; that's not how we're wired. We're meant to finish every bite, no matter how unappetising it becomes. We are creatures of a past where feasting was essential for survival. But in today's world of abundant food, this programming leads us to eat more than necessary. It's not your fault; your brain is just following its ancient survival script.

Most food companies are more dangerous than cigarette companies. Smoking is a choice; eating isn't. We need food to live, and the food industry exploits this necessity. They're not just selling products; they're hacking our brains. While their intentions might be profit-driven rather than outright evil, the impact of their actions is profound. They lace their products with addictive substances and chemicals, constantly triggering our subconscious to eat more.

So, there you have it; we're in a constant battle against our primitive instincts and corporate manipulation. It's a double-edged sword cutting into the fabric of our wellbeing. But now, strap in for a whirlwind tour of corporate culinary cunning, emotional entanglements, and the hunger games of the modern world! We'll begin with a bite-sized business lesson on how mega-food corporations cook up strategies to keep us nibbling on their bait. Next, we'll explore the intricate dance between pleasure and happiness, two flavours of life that are often mistaken for each other yet lead to wildly different destinations. Finally, we'll sink our teeth into the many faces of hunger, unmasking the genuine reasons behind our cravings. Get ready to chew through the layers of deception and discover what really fills your plate (and your appetite)!

The Food Mafia: Cooking Up Profits at Your Expense

In the high-stakes world of the food business, it's like a game of Monopoly, but with your health as the currency. As I've often explained to my management teams, there are only three ways to grow a business: getting more customers, making them buy more often, and generating more profit from each transaction. That's it; there is no other approach to growing a company. And let's be clear: we're talking about the ten goliaths of the food industry, each jostling for a larger slice of your grocery bill, wielding advertising and lobbying budgets that dwarf some nations' GDPs. Here's their playbook:

New Customers Galore: It's all about the numbers. These companies constantly prowl for fresh prey, using subliminal marketing tactics that tap into your deepest, often childhood-rooted cravings. Their goal? To lure you away from their competitors' clutches and into their flavour-filled embrace.

The Frequency Frenzy: Imagine a culinary web where every bite makes you hungrier. By stripping food of its fibre and nutritional soul and injecting it with sugar, they ensure you'll return for more.

Maximising Profit: Here's where they cook the books. With cheap ingredients, a sprinkle of chemical wizardry, the removal of fibre for longevity, and voilà, you have a product that maximises profit with minimal cost.

Understanding their trio of tactics is more than just food for thought; it's a call to arms against a diet dictated by profit margins rather than nutritional value.

Lobbying Power: Money Talks

To further highlight the point, during a broadcast conversation I had with Tom Watson, the former deputy leader of the Labour Party and the author of *Downsizing*, a book he wrote following his remarkable eight-stone weight loss and reversal of his diabetes, I referenced a particular line from his book, prompting him for further insights. Tom wrote, *'There's a golden rule of politics: the more harm an industry inflicts, the greater the lobbying spend.'* He responded with an intriguing tale:

> *'There's an amazing academic on the East Coast of America, Dr Marion Nestle, who was trailed by investigators hired by Coca-Cola. Her research threatened the sugar industry so much that they were compelled to monitor her every public utterance, hoping to undermine her. Marion Nestle, an octogenarian and veteran in this debate, shared that Coca-Cola had invested $100 million globally to contest policies and regulations aimed at reducing refined sugar consumption—the sugar levy in the UK or advertising restrictions in places like Chile, which has significantly cut sugar intake. That is the magnitude of power we're talking about. They are spending $100 million to lobby for what is unequivocally harmful to our health.'*

*****

The Great Happiness Heist

Welcome to the ultimate showdown in the human brain: Pleasure vs. Happiness, a tale as old as time but with a modern twist. As Dr Robert Lustig wisely points out in his superb book *The Hacking of the American Mind* and passionately highlighted on my podcast, 'Pleasure is the slippery slope to tolerance and addiction, while happiness is the key to a long life.' But, in our culinary circus, these two are often mistaken for the same acrobat.

Let's break it down. Pleasure, powered by our friendly dopamine hormone, is like the flashy magician at the party. It's exciting, it's addictive, and it's all about the now. Dopamine is the life of the party, the one who brings you the pizza, the doughnuts, and the fizzy drinks. But here's the catch: too much of this showman, and you're on a one-way ticket to Tolerance Town with a layover in Addictionville.

On the flip side, we have happiness, serenaded by our serotonin hormone. Serotonin is the wise sage who's in it for the long haul. It's about contentment, fulfilment, and the stuff that life's best memories are made of. Think of that healthy meal you shared with friends, bursting with flavour and nutrition – that's serotonin and dopamine doing a harmonious duet.

Now, the food industry has mastered the art of the dopamine dance. They've figured out that while we're all chasing happiness, what they're selling us is pleasure, dressed up in a 'Happy Meal™' costume. Slogans like I'm 'loving it'. Promotions like 'happy hour'. They are all promoting happiness, while under the bonnet, they are pedalling addictive pleasure. Their mantra? 'Keep 'em coming back for more'.

You take that first delightful bite of a sugary treat, and boom! Your dopamine levels skyrocket, screaming, 'More, please!'! Interestingly, our brain has more highways for wanting these pleasures than enjoying them. The thrill of the chase is more exciting than the catch. And this quirk is all part of evolution, my friend. Your brain needed to make you obsessively seek that fruit bush, dream about it, and think about it all morning, so you'd muster the energy to leave your cave and embark on the quest. It made you feel pleasure in the pursuit, even if the experience of finding the fruit bush was a tad underwhelming.

As a result, our brains have more neural pathways for 'wanting' the reward than for actually 'liking' the reward itself. It's the spark that ignites our desires, motivating us to act. That's why thinking about food, dreaming of holidays, or fantasising about that perfect cup of coffee can often be more thrilling than the real deal.

But let's not vilify pleasure entirely, for without it, there'd be no human race – pleasure is the straw that stirs the drink, as Dr Robert Lustig puts it. However, there's a catch. If you carry excess weight, especially a lot, you're already in the dopamine danger zone. And when you see an enticing food advert, understand that it's acting as a cue for your dopamine levels to go wild, demanding to be fed. If your satiety hormone, leptin, is in peak form, it might put up a fight, but if you're overweight, chances are you've developed leptin resistance, a war your satiety hormone is destined to lose. Dopamine triumphs, one doughnut becomes two, one glass of wine becomes a drinking session, and a single biscuit evolves into an all-out cookie raid!

Aristotle himself recognised the pursuit of happiness and the avoidance of pain as fundamental principles. Somewhere along the way, however, society got its wires crossed, and pursuing pleasure and rewards took centre stage, all fuelled by marketing techniques that steer us away from genuine happiness and towards fleeting pleasure. It's a trap, one that's contributed to the surge in diseases like diabetes, cancer, obesity, and more.

So, what haven't we covered yet? Ah, receptors, those little letterboxes in your brain, eagerly waiting for messages from dopamine and serotonin. Think of them as your brain's mailboxes; their number and size determine how much info can get in. With more receptors, fewer dopamine messages are needed. But fewer receptors? Well, that means you'll need more and more of that tempting food or another round of drinks to get your fix. Oh, and before

I forget, emotional stress only intensifies our craving for pleasure. It's like emotional stress hits the pleasure-seeking button, and sometimes it leads to a not-so-friendly companion called addiction.

But here's the problem for the big food corporates: happiness, the real deal, isn't something you can package and sell. Genuine happiness is the sunsets, time with your family, and playing with your grandchildren. Big food corporations tell us they are selling happiness, but their focus is on pleasure – it's easier, cheaper, and way more addictive.

So, as we embark on this quest, remember: every pizza slice, every fizzy drink, every 'happy' meal – it's a battle between dopamine and serotonin, between pleasure and happiness. And it's a battle we need to win for the sake of our health and our waistlines. Let's outsmart the system and choose happiness, the real, long-lasting kind, not just the fleeting thrill of pleasure.

The distinction between happiness and pleasure is such an important area of health and one that may be very new to you, as it was to me, that I want to hand the rest of this topic over to Dr Robert Lustig who, as a paediatric endocrinologist (someone who diagnoses and treats hormonal disorders in children), has spent many years researching this:

Dr Robert Lustig

'Today, clinical depression is skyrocketing. I believe part of the cause is that we, as a society, have lost track of these two positive emotions: pleasure and happiness. We think they are the same. We have been told that they are the same. And I think we have been told they are the same by people who want us to buy stuff, I quote, 'to get happy'. Because they have something to sell. Hedonics sell. In fact, four out of the top ten exports out of the United States are hedonic substances. Oil, corn, soy, and sugar. So, they tell us their products will make us happy. But pleasure and happiness are not the same. I would argue that they are diametrically opposite. They seem like they are related,; they are both positive emotions, and we like them both, so why should we care? Well, I will give you seven differences between pleasure and happiness that I outline in my book The Hacking of the American Mind.

1. *Pleasure is short-lived, like a meal. Happiness is long-lived, often for a lifetime.*
2. *Pleasure is visceral; you feel it in your body. Happiness is ethereal; you feel it above the neck.*
3. *Pleasure is taking; happiness is giving.*

4. *Pleasure is experienced alone; happiness is normally experienced in social groups.*
5. *Pleasure is achievable with substances; happiness is not achievable with substances.*
6. *The extremes of pleasure, whether it be substances –or behaviours; nicotine, cocaine, tobacco, alcohol, street drugs, chocolate, sugar –, or behaviours –; shopping, gambling, social media, pornography. In the extreme, all of these lead to addiction. All of these can have a 'holic' at the end of the word, for example, shopaholic and alcoholic. But there is no such thing as being addicted to too much happiness.*
7. *And finally, the reason why I wrote the book. Pleasure is dopamine and happiness is serotonin. Two different neurotransmitters in the brain, two different sets of receptors, two different mechanisms of action, two different regulatory pathways and two different areas of the brain they work in. And the reason why we are in such a mess is because we lost track of this.*

In this unregulated capitalist world that we have today, corporations try to generate as much profit as possible. And in the process what we have done is made everyone fat, sick, stupid, addicted, and broke. Because we have peddled hedonics, because that is what sells and we made everyone miserable and sick. And we have basically destroyed economies all over the world by chronic disease.

Money can buy you pleasure, but it can't buy you happiness. People don't recognise the difference. And by seeking these short-term dopamine hits, they are actually doing themselves damage. It is all science. Dopamine is a neurotransmitter that neurons make to tell other neurons what to do. The next neuron has receptors, and dopamine binds to that neuron and causes it to fire. And in this process of firing, we get emotions, we get behaviours, and we get pleasure. It is the motivation neurotransmitter; it is the positive reinforcement neurotransmitter; it is basically the neurotransmitter that tells our brain this feels good: I want more, I want to do this again. Dopamine is the source of habit. It's not that dopamine isn't important, it is. Without it, we wouldn't have sex; therefore, there would be no human race. If we didn't have dopamine, we would be a sloth and never get out of bed.

But here is the problem with dopamine. It is excitatory. So, it always excites the next neuron. Now neurons like be excited, they like to be stimulated, that is why they have receptors in the first place. But they like to be tickled, not bludgeoned. Chronic over-stimulation of any neuron leads to neuronal cell death. But neurons don't want to die. So, they have a Plan B. They have a self-defence mechanism. What they do is down-regulate the number of receptors, which makes it less likely that any dopamine receptor will find a cell to bind to. So, more dopamine and fewer receptors mean less signal. Less signal means less benefit. So, you end up needing more and more to get less and less. And that is the phenomenon that we call tolerance. So next time you need a bigger hit and the receptors go down, you keep doing this repeatedly, with bigger and bigger hits, until you get nothing and eventually when the neurons do start to die, now you got addiction. And when they do die, they don't come back; they are gone for good.

When you kill those neurons in that reward centre, you are never going to get the same gain, you will never get the amplitude of the response that you originally got. Which means you are never going to really get the same pleasure that you did before. This, of course, is the reason for re-offending from addiction and why people go back. You are trying to get back what you knew you once had. But you can't. And you are miserable.

Serotonin, on the other hand, the contentment neurotransmitter, the feel-good, the I don't need anymore, the relaxation, the Zen neurotransmitter, it's not excitatory, it's inhibitory. It inhibits the next neuron; it keeps it from firing. So, if you are inhibiting the next neuron, do you have to down-regulate the receptors? No, you don't need to, because there is nothing to protect it from. So, you can't overdose from too much happiness. But there is one thing that does down-regulate serotonin, and that is dopamine! So, the more pleasure you seek, the more unhappy you get.'

Let me summarise the above insights from Robert. The more rewards we seek, whether they be alcohol, drugs, sex, shopping, gambling, possessions; the next like on Facebook or views on YouTube; snacks, sugar, bigger meals, chocolate – short term, instant rewards, it actually down-regulates happiness in the long term. Here are some more insights from my podcast with Robert.

'If you don't know the difference between pleasure and happiness, and if your pleasure is cheap, you are going to overload on that because you can and make yourself extraordinary miserable. So, addiction and depression are actually two sides of the same coin, and they are driven by the same five changes in our environment, which have occurred over the past 50 years. They are technology, processed food, sugar, sleep deprivation and drugs. All five are dopamine stimulators. All five of those drive reward. And all five of those lead to metabolic syndrome (insulin

resistance). Which then leads to low serotonin.

Then add some stress on top of these. And stress, – by affecting an area right at the front of the brain, called the prefrontal cortex – stress puts that prefrontal cortex to sleep. It tells the executive function centre, your Jiminy Cricket part of the brain –; the part of the brain that stops you from doing stupid things; the bit that tells you not to do something because you will pay for it tomorrow to sleep. As your prefrontal cortex goes offline, it revs up dopamine even more. And cortisol, the stress hormone, reduces the receptors for serotonin, thereby making you even more unhappy.

In order to turn this around, we need to damp down our dopamine, not get rid of it, but damp it down. We need to up our serotonin, and we need to reduce our cortisol. Those are the three goals:

1. *Reduce our dopamine*
2. *Up our serotonin*
3. *Reduce our cortisol*

If we do that, we will get healthy, enjoy our lives, and solve all of the biggest problems in our society. All at once. It is just one problem. So, what can we do? Well, one thing we can't do is rely on governments to help us, because governments are addicted to the money that these hedonic substances bring in for them. And they are all paid off by those industries anyway. So, don't expect anyone to help you out of this. You have to do it for yourself.

There are four things you can do here, and they are free. But you really have to want to do them. This is what is needed to achieve the three goals of reducing dopamine, upping serotonin, and reducing cortisol. I call them the 4 Cs. They are:

1. **Connect.** *Face-to-face human interaction. Social interaction. Not online or on the phone. This is because, in the back of the head, there are some mirror neurons which only work face to face. It's the only way to transmit empathy. And this drives up serotonin. (Robert talks more on this on my podcast and in his book.)*

2. **Contribute.** *Contribute to others creates serotonin. Giving, not taking. Help others.*

3. **Cope.** *Three things will help you cope: sleep, mindfulness, and*

exercise. With mindfulness, for example, we need to stop trying to multitask, because every time we do, we get a cortisol bump, and it takes 23 minutes to refocus. All of these reduce cortisol. If you couple mindfulness and exercise, you can basically reverse depression.

4. **Cook.** *Three things in food matter. Tryptophan, which is an amino acid, it's the rarest amino acid, and it is in short supply. Yet, it is the precursor for serotonin. So, if you are not getting enough tryptophan, you are not making enough serotonin. So, where do you get tryptophan? By far the number one is in eggs. Next poultry and salmon, but in vegetables not very much. So, you need those things. You also need omega-3s. They are heart-healthy, anti-inflammatory, anti-Alzheimer's. They are membrane stabilisers, especially in the neurons in your brain. And finally, we are consuming too much sugar – fructose – because it drives dopamine and lowers serotonin.'*

Turn page for pleasure vs happiness defined ›

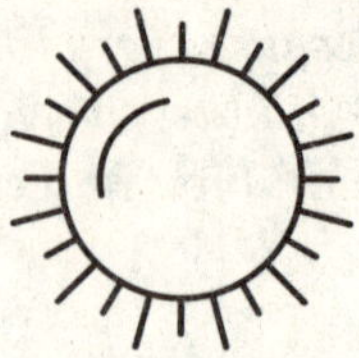

Pleasure	**Happiness**
Dictionary definition – Enjoyment or satisfaction derived from one's liking or gratification or reward.	*Dictionary definition* – The quality or state of being happy or joy or contentment.
1. Reward	1. Contentment
2. Addiction – caused by too much pleasure.	2. Depression caused by not enough happiness.
3. Hedonic substances – reward generating - hedonism is the relentless pursuit of pleasure.	3. Hedonic substances cause unhappiness.
4. You can have too much pleasure.	4. You can never have too much happiness.
5. This feels good, I want more.	5. This feels great, I don't need more.
6. Pleasure is short lived, often just minutes, have it, get over it and then if addicted do again.	6. Happiness is long lived, weeks, months, years, lifetime. Family, achievements, purpose, relationships, friendships.
7. Rewards are visceral, you feel it in your guts. A visceral feeling is intuitive — there might not be a rational explanation, but you feel that you know what's best. It elevates your fight and flight system, increases blood pressure and heart rate.	7. Happiness, contentment, is calming. Reduces heart rate and blood pressure. Sounds of birds singing or waves on a beach.

8. Pleasure and rewards, achieved with substances, sugar, coffee, alcohol, drugs, cigarettes, shopping.	8. Not achieved with substances, but by doing things, actions, gratitude, helping others, love.
9. Pleasure is associated with taking.	9. Happiness is associated with giving.
10. Pleasure is self-centred, it is yours and yours alone.	10. Happiness often benefits others or when you don't have it, can negatively effect others.
11. Pleasure and seek rewards, when out of control, leads to unhappiness - compulsive behaviours , addiction and misery. Shopping, booze, drugs, fast food, sugar.	11. Happiness can't lead to unhappiness (well, not yours anyway).
12. Can lead to aggression and irritability.	12. Does not lead to aggression and irritability.
13. Too much of a good thing can kill you – shorten life.	13. Too much happiness makes you live longer.
14. The pleasure/reward pathway in your brain, is driven by dopamine (dopamine=desire). Dopamine provides motivation to act. But too much dopamine causes misery. All words ending in 'aholic', alc (alcohol), shop, sex, choc, is caused by too much dopamine. Too little you won't get out of bed, too much and you become an addict.	14. The happiness/contentment pathway in your brain, is driven by serotonin (serotonin = satisfied). You can't have too much seretonin, yet you actually don't need that much. Once you get it you don't desire more and more as you do with dopamine and desire. You can't therefore get addicted to love, as Robert Palmer suggested.

*****

The Quarterly Earnings Rollercoaster: When Profit Pressures Shape our Plates

In 2006, I found myself in the midst of a whirlwind merger with a mammoth factory in Thailand, culminating in the grand spectacle of floating our company on the Singapore Stock Exchange. Now, let me spare you the nitty-gritty, but picture this. When you're a publicly listed entity, akin to the bigwigs in the food industry, your existence becomes a tightrope walk dictated by those elusive quarterly results.

I'm talking about a scenario where even a minuscule 1 or 2% dip can trigger a veritable nosedive in your share price. And heaven forbid you miss your quarterly forecast by a hair's breadth! It's as if the financial universe suddenly decides your company's fate over a game of financial Jenga.

But hold on, it gets even wilder. Picture this: one of your product categories, or worse, your flagship product, experiences a slight dip in sales. Now, instead of chalking it up to the whims of consumer preference or perhaps a quirky cosmic alignment, some fresh-faced analyst in a bank halfway across the globe decides this spells doom for your entire operation. Talk about putting all your eggs in one quarterly basket!

I mentioned this to highlight that our foods today are not manufactured for our health, but rather, they serve as sacrificial pawns in the chess game of meeting those elusive quarterly targets. But, before we start pointing fingers and shaking fists at the food industry bigwigs, let's remember an age-old saying: when a person's livelihood hinges on their job, they might turn a blind eye to certain inconvenient truths. Now, picture this: Dr Eric Berg, at a recent health conference, unveils a graph that sends shivers down the spines of CEOs and CFOs, akin to those ancient sliding projectors that haunt boardrooms in the witching hour. The mission? Find a fix before the following quarterly earnings report rears its head.

Now, indulge me in a thought experiment, totally hypothetical. Imagine you're the big Cheerio (CEO) of a cereal company, and despite pouring heaps of cash into marketing blitzes, your cereal sales are taking a slight tumble. Why, you ask? Well, maybe because folks like me have been championing the virtues of a hearty bacon and eggs breakfast over your sugar-laden flakes. So, what's a CEO to do? How about bankrolling a little research to cast doubt on the product of the pig and the chicken? Perhaps a study suggesting bacon causes heart disease and eggs are guilty of cholesterol crimes? And hey, if it saves you from a stock market rollercoaster, wouldn't you toss a few million into that research pot quicker than you can say 'sizzle'? While it's all hypothetical, I can assure you that these types of scenarios may play out in boardrooms across the food industry.

In the midst of this corporate dance, it's essential to pause and acknowledge the darker underbelly of profit-driven motives. Take, for instance, the case of Nestlé in 1974, when the infamous report titled 'The Baby Killer' rocked the world. Accusations flew, pointing fingers at Nestlé for allegedly contributing to illness and infant deaths in impoverished communities of third-world countries by aggressively promoting their infant formula products at the expense of breastfeeding. Fast forward to 2022, and the World Health Organization sounded the alarm once again, highlighting that over half of parents and expectant mothers face exposure to unethical and misleading marketing tactics[4]. These instances serve as stark reminders that ethical boundaries are often blurred amidst the pursuit of profit, leaving vulnerable populations at the mercy of corporate agendas.

Picture this: It's a lazy evening, and you find yourself idly scrolling through the endless internet abyss, searching for a flicker of inspiration to steer clear of the temptations of junk food. Curious, you stumble upon an article penned by Roshni Tamta and Akshat Hawelia provocatively titled, *Why is Nestlé The Most Evil and Hated Company in the World?*. Suddenly, the allure of that bag of chips or sugary snack loses its lustre, and you're left pondering the age-old wisdom of frying up bacon and eggs for tomorrow's breakfast.

Ah, and what of the whimsical world of pharmaceuticals! Picture yourself as a savvy statin manufacturer, just minding your own business, when suddenly, your patent decides to up and leave, leaving you with a hefty dent in your profit margins. Now, what's a money-minded mogul to do in such dire straits? You could embark on a quest to expand your consumer base. So, in a purely hypothetical scenario, imagine putting one of your team members incognito on the panel responsible for setting the bar on what constitutes an 'acceptable' cholesterol level. You might; I don't know, subtly suggest that perhaps they should lower the bar a tad, making your product the knight in shining armour for a couple million more folks. More on this later in the book under the heading, Cholesterol Guidelines: Whose Interests Do They Serve (page 611)?

But, of course, all of this is purely hypothetical banter, folks! I wouldn't dare insinuate such shenanigans in a book. Why, you ask? Let's say it wouldn't be the first time a behemoth corporation has shown its legal teeth to silence even the meekest whistle-blower.

The Great Hunger Games

Welcome to the gastronomic jungle, where we're about to explore the different wild triggers that lure us into the eating expedition. And here is the thing; most times we feel hungry, we aren't hungry at all. Let's start by looking at the only three types of hunger that can occasionally be real.

The Energy Mirage: Here's the biggie, the occasionally genuine hunger. It's like an ancient relic in our modern world, often confused with just feeling peckish. True hunger – when your body screams for fuel – is rarer than a unicorn in a city park. We're usually just riding the Carbocoaster, tricked by that free bread at restaurants into thinking we're starving.

The Nutritional Detective: Our brain is on a constant treasure hunt for over 40 essential micronutrients. It's like playing Where's Wally? with vitamins and minerals. But here's the catch: processed foods are like a puzzle with missing pieces, keeping us in a perpetual state of hunger. It's a sneaky trick, making us eat more while nourishing us less.

The Thirsty Imposter: Surprise! Sometimes, when you think you're hungry, you're just thirsty. It's like getting mixed signals: 'Am I hungry? Am I thirsty?' Guess what? If you regularly chow down on ultra-processed foods, you're probably just dehydrated. Remember, our bodies are like sponges: they love water. So, next time you feel the munchies, try sipping some H2O first.

Apart from these three sometimes real deal hungers, we've got some fakes in the mix:

The Emotional Rollercoaster: Stressed? Eat. Happy? Eat. Sad? Eat. It's like we've tied our emotions to a fork and spoon. We must untangle these emotional eating habits and find other ways to deal with our feelings. Maybe a walk in the park or a good laugh with friends, sans the side of fries.

The Clockwork Snacker: You know the drill: it's 8 AM, so it must be time for breakfast, right? Wrong. It's just a habit, a routine that we've built. It's time to break the cycle and ask ourselves, 'Am I really starving, or is my inner clock playing tricks?'

The Nostalgia Nibble: Ah, memories. That sandwich Mom used to make, the cake at every birthday party. We're not just eating food; we're trying to relive the past. But guess what? We can create new, healthier traditions.

The Advertising Apprentice: Those TV ads aren't selling food; they're selling dreams, emotions, a slice of happiness. But it's all smoke and mirrors. Don't let those catchy jingles and mouth-watering images hijack your hunger.

The Herd Feeder: Have you ever joined the queue at a fast-food joint just because everyone else is there? It's like a weird FOMO for food. But don't be fooled –; just because the herd's eating doesn't mean you should.

But luckily, there is a secret weapon to many of these fake hunger: -fibre. It's like a superhero for your stomach. More fibre equals less fake hunger. It's that simple.

So, let's get this straight: the best strategy for health and weight loss would be to eat only when you truly need energy or nutrients. Anything else is just extra baggage for your body. Avoid the hunger traps, and you're on your way to a healthier, happier you. Remember, if it's packaged, it's probably not food, just a food-like substitute in disguise.

Hara Hachi Bu

Okinawa, Japan, has an extraordinary population of centenarians, embodying a legacy of longevity and health. Here centuries-old wisdom whispers through the bustling dining rooms and serene homes: *hara hachi bu*. It's a profound yet simple philosophy, you'll wonder why it hasn't been the cornerstone of our dietary teachings. *Hara hachi bu* , a principle that transcends mere eating habits to touch the essence of mindful consumption, means to eat until you're 80% full. Not full, but no longer hungry. It's a line that the Okinawans tread with grace; their longevity and vitality a testament to this practice's efficacy.

In a world where overindulgence is often the norm, the Okinawan approach is one of contentment, not out-and-out satiety. They savour each bite, dining with leisure that lets satisfaction gently settle in, rather than rushing to the next task with a stomach stretched to its limits. This slow dance with food not only nurtures their bodies but also enriches their souls, a ritual that echoes across the azure waters to the Mediterranean, where similar practices have been linked to a life rich in years and health.

Jackie Eberstein, once at the helm of educational endeavours at the Adkins Centre for Complementary Medicine, shared a resonant piece of advice: eat until you're satisfied, not until you're bursting at the seams. It's a counsel that cuts to the core of our eating dilemmas, addressing the why behind our overeating. In Great Britain, our plates overflow not just with food but with a cultural imposition to clear them, a legacy perhaps of post-war scarcity. Yet, today's issue isn't scarcity but the abundance of sugar-laden fast foods and processed packages that dull our hormonal harmony, leaving leptin's calls unheeded.

Why do we push past the point of satisfaction to the realm of discomfort? Is it a learned behaviour from childhood admonishments to leave no morsel behind, or have the distorted portion sizes recalibrated our sense of enough? Whatever the cause, the solution may lie in the gentle wisdom of *hara hachi bu*, a reminder that in the art of eating, like in life, sometimes less is indeed more.

*****

How They Make Food So Irresistibly Addictive

Let's now venture into the heart of the matter – though, ironically, you'll find little heartiness involved. We're about to explore the myriad of methods big food corporations employ to ensnare us in their web of products, ensuring we're always hungry for another bite.

Introducing the *Taste Bud Trio*

Ever been tricked by your taste buds into finishing an entire family pack of crisps? Well, you're not alone. This is the handiwork of the notorious *Taste Bud Trio*: Salt, Sugar, and Fat. These aren't just ingredients; they're the culinary world's most conniving puppeteers, pulling your craving strings like a maestro!

Nature never combines these three ingredients, but when they come together in processed food, it's like a flavour bomb that your brain can't defuse. They're why you can't stop munching on chocolate bars or demolishing a whole pizza.

Let's turn our attention to the science of 'priming'. Think of it like the first sip of booze or puff of a cigarette, it opens the floodgates of desire in your brain. Once you've tasted, your brain thinks, 'More, please!' and before you know it, you're at the bottom of the snack bag, wondering where it all went.

The *Taste Bud Trio* doesn't just tantalise your taste buds; it hijacks your brain's wiring. It's like they've added an illegal software update to your brain, making you crave more every time you eat. It's no longer about hunger; it's about the brain being tricked into thinking it needs more. But here's the problem: -it's a vicious cycle. You eat because of a cue; that cue triggers an emotional response, and then the priming effect kicks in. Before you know it, you're in a spiral of wanting, driven not by hunger but by a programmed response to these engineered foods.

Breaking free from this cycle is like trying to outsmart a cunning adversary. You must turn these automatic food choices into conscious decisions. It's about seeing processed foods for what they are, not just unhealthy but designed to get you hooked. To win this battle, we need to loathe these artificially engineered foods and fall back in love with what nature offers. We've got to trust the farmer more than the scientist. It's not just about hating the bad stuff; it's about embracing the good stuff.

So, the next time you reach for that bag of crisps, remember the *Taste Bud Trio* trickery. Break the cycle, make a conscious choice, and take back control. It's not just about resisting temptation; it's about reprogramming your brain to love what's genuinely good for you.

Let's look at *Taste Bud Trio* individually, starting with sugar, the sweet side of snacks.

Sugar: Back in the day, a German grad student mapped the tongue and said, 'Hey, sweetness is all about the tip!' But guess what? That map is as outdated as a flip phone! Our entire mouth, even our oesophagus, is a sugar-loving fiend. Every part of your mouth throws a party when sugar shows up. And why? Because sugar knows how to schmooze with your brain's pleasure zone, the limbic area. It's like nature's saying, 'Good job for eating too many berries in preparation for the looming baron winter; here's a dopamine hit as a thank you!'

Speaking of nature's candy, the big food honchos have figured out the perfect amount of sugar to make you go 'Ahh' instead of 'Eww'. It's called the 'bliss point'. And they're not just guessing; they're bringing kids into their research laboratories, giving them teddy bears and all, to find that magic sugar spot. Talk about dedication to addiction!

Fat: The ninja of taste; it bypasses your taste buds and heads straight to the brain's pleasure centre. It's like a direct line to Happy Town without even stopping at the Taste Station.

But here's the intriguing part: there's no top end to the 'bliss point' for fat in processed munchies. It's like a never-ending feast for your brain's reward circuit. And why? Fat is like the calorie king, and your brain, still living in the 'hunter-gatherer' period, thinks it's hit the jackpot and needs to stock up on energy for those days when no food is found. So, fat is like fool's gold – it glitters in processed foods, but it isn't the real, nourishing deal. And don't for one minute think I stand against all fats; I don't; it's just the dangerous and ugly ones I have a problem with.

Salt: Now, let's talk about salt, the flavour enhancer, with a PhD in brain chemistry. People don't just like salt; they crave it. And it's not just about taste: salt gets the entire mouth and stomach in on the action. It's like turning on all the lights in a stadium, not just the spotlight. But hold up, it's not just about the craving. Salt in processed food is the ultimate enabler. It makes everything else more addictive. Ever noticed how the biggest junk food junkie at your dinner party is the first to reach for the salt grinder? That's no coincidence. And here's the thing: salt isn't just there to party with your taste buds; it's also a preservative, giving that bag of chips an unnaturally long shelf life.

You may need to add salt to your dinners when home-cooking proper foods. In packed food, they, on average, inject about 1% of salt by weight into the food. While you need salt to survive, you probably don't need this much.

Salt, you see, is like that one friend who's always exciting to hang out with but might be a bit too much in large doses. It's not just a basic taste alongside sweetness, sourness, and bitterness; it's the life of the party in your mouth, the one that everyone craves and can't live without. But here's the problem: while sugar and fat are the flashy celebrities of the food world, salt is like the mysterious stranger – no calories, just pure, unadulterated flavour.

Why do we crave salt so much? It's not just because it's delicious; it's because our bodies need it to survive. Consider your body a high-tech machine; salt is an essential maintenance tool. It's like your body's IT guy, ensuring everything runs smoothly. But just like sugar, the whole 'tongue map' thing they taught in school is a myth. As you have already discovered, salt doesn't just play around the edges; it's the show's star, lighting up your entire mouth and even doing a tango with your stomach receptors.

But here's where things get a bit more complicated. The food industry, those clever wizards in lab coats, have figured out how to tap into our salt cravings and turn them up to eleven. They're not just adding salt for taste; they're using it to prime us, like a pump, making every bite more irresistible than the last. It's like the Lay's slogan, 'Betcha can't eat just one.' They're not joking; it's a battle cry!

Now, identifying salt on food labels is like playing detective. It's got more aliases than a spy in a Cold War novel – sodium citrate, MSG, fleur de sel, you name it. And if that wasn't enough, salt's also a secret agent for longevity, not ours, but the food's! It stops your ready meal lasagne from going off before you even have time to regret buying it.

But don't get me wrong; I'm not saying salt is the bad guy. A pinch of salt can be your best friend when cooking up a storm at home. But when buckets of it hide in packaged foods, it becomes a bit of a double agent: cheap to produce and expensive for your health.

So, there you have it, the *Taste Bud Trio*: Salt, Sugar, and Fat. They're not just ingredients; they're master manipulators in the world of processed food, turning us all into snack-loving, ready -meal addictive zombies. But now that you know their tricks, you can outsmart them.

Moving past the basic allure of Sugar, Fat, and Salt, we're about to peel back the curtain on the food industry's seven most potent tricks and a few extra sleights of hand. However, there's a light at the end of this gastronomic tunnel. Later in the book, I'll arm you with ten culinary strategies to elevate your kitchen's flavours. These tips will ensure your meals aren't just delicious but also brimming with health benefits.

Seven More Flavour Hacks: The Secret Art of Food Seduction

Welcome to the Twilight Zone of Taste, where Dr Steven Witherly is our guide through the maze of food addiction. Picture him as a culinary detective, unravelling the mysteries of our taste buds for the last two decades. His magnum opus, *Why Humans Like Junk Food*, is not just a book; it's the Rosetta Stone of snack seduction.

Let's explore these seven devious tactics, the grand illusion of eating. It's not just about the taste; it's a full-blown sensory gala. Every crunch, every whiff, every velvety texture is a carefully coordinated masterpiece played by the experts at big food companies with budgets that would make a Hollywood producer blush.

Imagine your mouth as a stage. Each bite is an actor performing not just on the taste buds but also serenading the nose, dancing on the tongue, and sometimes even doing a little jig down the throat. The taste is just the opening act; the aroma is the seductive whisper, and the mouthfeel is the grand finale that leaves you begging for an encore.

Witherly's research, homed in the culinary labs of Nestle™ (the planet's biggest food producer), unveils a world where eating is an experience crafted with the precision of a Swiss watch. These food wizards don't just want you to like their creations; they want you to crave them, dream about them, and yearn for them.

The food you munch on isn't just fuel; it's a multisensory experience. The crunch of a chip isn't just a sound; it's a signal to your brain that something exciting is happening. The aroma of a freshly baked pizza isn't just a smell; it's a nostalgic trip down memory lane. And the creamy melt of chocolate isn't just a texture; it's a comforting hug for your taste buds.

Beyond the holy trinity of Salt, Sugar, and Fat lies a complex web of oreosensory dynamics, nutrient balancing acts, calorie density compression, emulsion enigmas, moisture mysteries, sensory specific satiety illusions, and the grand exposure effect. All these elements work in concert, not just to tantalise our taste buds but to take our brains on an addictive joyride they can't easily forget.

You're now going to learn about the tricks and techniques of the big food companies and fast-food goliaths. It's a world where every ingredient, every texture, and every flavour is a deliberate choice engineered to leave us wanting more.

We'll examine these terms individually, uncovering the secrets behind why we can't stop at just one cookie or why a bag of chips disappears faster than we can say 'calories'. It's a trek into the heart of our cravings, a dive into why we eat the way we do, and how these food giants have mastered the art of perpetually stimulating our appetites.

Prepare to have your mind opened and your perceptions challenged as we explore the intricate strategies employed to transform ordinary foods into irresistible cravings. This is more than just a lesson in taste; it's a revelation of how our brains respond to our foods.

Oreosensory, aka Dynamic Contrast

Welcome to the world of 'oreosensation', a term coined by Steven Witherly. It's like the magic trick of the food industry that's all about tickling your tongue in ways you didn't know were possible. Picture this: food scientists, not unlike modern-day alchemists, spending millions to craft the perfect crunch in your potato chip or the ideal fizz in your soda. It's like composing a concerto for your mouth.

In the secret labs of the Oreosensory Department, they're devising combinations that would make Mother Nature blush. Think crunchy and creamy; a dynamic contrast that is a rarity in the natural food world. Sure, you might find it in the crackling of pork, but in the engineered realm of M&M'S®, and those devilishly addictive Oreos® (from which Steven created the term), it's a whole different ball game.

Here's the thing: our brains are like curious cats, always on the prowl for something new and exciting. This is where dynamic contrast comes into play, switching it from crunchy to creamy, solid to liquid, sweet to salty. It's this variety show in our mouths that keeps us coming back for more. And let's not forget about the temperature tango – hot, cold, warm – all playing their parts in this oreosensory dance. In essence, oreosensation isn't just about taste; it's about creating an experience, a sensation that's as addictive as it is delightful.

Addictive Nutrient Balance

Welcome to the clandestine world of the 'Premium Addiction Department', where culinary chemists and gastronomy grandmasters have perfected the delicate art of balancing salt, sugar, and fats. Think of them as the DJs of the food world, mixing tracks that get our taste buds dancing uncontrollably.

Our primal brains were hardwired in the wild to hunt down these macronutrients. Fat was like the ultimate energy jackpot; salt was our hydration hero and sugar? Sugar was Mother Nature's green light, signalling safety and deliciousness. Our ancestors craved these with a survivalist zeal. Fast-forward to today, and even though we're not dodging lions or foraging for berries, our brains haven't quite caught up. They're still partying like it's 50,000 BC.

Enter the modern food industry, playing on these ancient instincts like a fiddle. They've realised something crucial: while nature typically serves macronutrients in pairs, they can unleash the trifecta. Imagine a superhero team of salt, sugar, and fat; only this team is not here to save the day but to hijack your hunger.

In their lab-coated hands, they don't just use any fats; they opt for the cheaper, nastier kind. The kind our bodies weren't designed to handle in such gluttonous amounts. The result? It's a fabrication that's more addictive than your favourite TV show's cliffhanger season finale. Here's the problem: while we're wired to love these elements in nature, the way they're served in today's processed food is like an over-the-top blockbuster with too many special effects. Sure, it's initially exciting, but it's not the real deal. These food wizards have turned our natural cravings into an extreme sport, and our health is taking a beating.

Calorie Density

Please step right up and witness the marvels of the 'Calorie Density Team' in the Big Food Circus. These culinary illusionists have mastered a profound trick: the art of packing maximum calories into every bite faster than you can say 'supersize me'.

In a world where our ancient ancestors were programmed for scarcity, hunting, and gathering without a clue when their next meal might be, these modern-day magicians play on that ancient script. But instead of scarce resources, they offer a never-ending buffet of calorie-dense fantasies. It's a feast fit for a caveman, but in an era where food is anything but scarce.

Imagine a scale with water lounging at zero (calorie-free and carefree) and pure fat strutting its stuff at a plump nine (by the way, the calorie density scale is a real thing). This is the stage where the Calorie Density Team performs their high-wire act, creating foods that hit the sweet spot of calorie concentration.

Here's their secret: it's all about speed. They've turned the art of eating into a race against our own satiety signals. By stripping away nature's speed bumps-fibre and gristle, those relics of a time when food required effort to consume-they've transformed our meals into a culinary autobahn. Food no longer melts in your mouth; it practically vaporises, delivering a caloric payload with the efficiency of a high-speed train.

The result? We're eating more, faster, and with less effort than ever before. Our primal brains, still tuned to the frequency of scarcity, light up like a Christmas tree at this calorie bonanza. Dopamine floods our circuits, and leptin tries to wave the white flag, but it's all too late. We've entered the fast lane of feasting, courtesy of the calorie density experts. Corporations have transformed eating from a leisurely stroll in nature's garden to a sprint through a synthetic wonderland of flavours and calories.

Emulsion

Imagine a world where oil waltzes with vinegar but never really blends, a culinary Romeo and Juliet. In the kitchen, this drama plays out in the humble vinaigrette or the homemade mayonnaise, where egg yolk plays matchmaker, binding oil and lemon juice in a delicious harmony. But step into the world of Big Food, and emulsion becomes an epic tale of seduction and illusion.

In the Emulsion Laboratories, scientists turn emulsion into an art form. They're the Houdini's of the culinary world, creating taste sensations that dance and dissolve in your mouth, leaving a craving for more. It's why the creamy centre of your favourite chocolate or the velvety scoop of ice cream feels like a love affair with flavour.

But, trust me, not all is rosy in the world of emulsion. Behind the velvet curtains of taste lies a potential troublemaker, the artificial emulsifier. Researchers have uncovered a murky side to these synthetic marvels in a plot twist worthy of a detective novel. Tests on our furry friends, the mice, revealed that these emulsifiers might play a game of thrones with our gut microbiome, breaching the castle walls of our intestinal barrier.

While the powers that be, the government safety boards, give these emulsifiers a nod of approval, many nutritionists and doctors prefer to err on the side of caution. So, what's the moral of this flavourful fable? It's simple: venture back to the roots, to the kitchen, where emulsions are born from whisking, not from lab experiments.

Moisture

In the grand theatre of food, moisture plays a starring role. Why do we fall head over heels for foods that are moist or create a tsunami of saliva? It's all about the sensory embrace. When moist, food is like a gentle kiss to every taste bud, a loving caress that spreads flavour throughout the mouth. Therefore, the food industry loves sprinkling salt magic on almost everything. It's not just for taste; it's a secret handshake with our saliva glands.

Think about crisps, those crunchy little ambassadors of pleasure. They're not just engineered for that satisfying crunch; they're designed to dissolve rapidly in your mouth, sending waves of saliva and flavour on a pilgrimage of delight. This moisture enhances the flavour, turning each bite into a sensory celebration. And let's talk about sauces; why do we love them? Because they're the ultimate moisture aces, adding layers of lubrication elevating a dish from good to 'can't stop eating this'.

Dr Steven Whitley reminds us that even the anticipation of eating something delicious can set off fireworks of dopamine in our brains. That mouth-watering feeling? It's not just an expression; it's a physiological dance of joy, preparing us for the incoming feast. A concept as old as time, akin to the Colonel's iconic 'finger-licking good' – an ode to the pleasure of eating. The art of creating mouth-watering foods is a critical chapter in the storybook of good food construction. It's a subtle yet powerful trick, turning every meal into an immersive experience that starts even before the first bite. So, the next time your mouth waters at the sight or smell of a dish, remember, it's unlikely to be hunger: it's a symphony of sensory delight masterfully orchestrated by the wizards of the food world.

Sensory Specific Satiety

Welcome to Sensory Specific Satiety (SSS), where our brains play a cunning game with our taste buds. It's a culinary 'diminishing returns' phenomenon – the more you eat of one flavour, the less satisfying it becomes. Why? Because our brains are wired for variety. Here's the deal: our brains are smart. They know we need an assortment of nutrients to be at our best; think of it as needing all 27 vitamins and essential minerals to hit the health jackpot. So, when faced with just one flavour, our brain responds with 'Yawn, next, please!'

Try this experiment: sit down with a plate of spinach or broccoli. No seasoning, no dressing, just plain greens. It's like watching a movie without plot twists: you'll get bored quickly. This is exactly why food companies go to great lengths to avoid SSS.

Ever wondered why a fast-food burger feels like a carnival in your mouth? It's not just a burger; it's a meticulously crafted masterpiece of flavours and textures. Imagine the crunch of fresh lettuce, the zing of pickles, and that iconic, creamy sauce. Each element is like a musician in a band, working in perfect accord to serenade your taste buds. This isn't a lucky coincidence. It's a deliberate, cunning plan designed by culinary experts, ensuring every bite leaves you wanting more.

Now, let's talk about Doritos™. Ever noticed the baffling array of ingredients on the packet? Why on earth does a simple chip need 34 ingredients? It's all part of the SSS game. Each ingredient plays a role in sidestepping the brain's tendency to get bored with a single flavour. The result? You can't stop at just one. Doritos are engineered to be an endless loop of craving and satisfaction, a flavour rollercoaster that keeps your hand diving back into the bag. So next time you're munching on crisps or your favourite snack, remember, it's not just nosh; it's a carefully crafted experience to keep your senses in a perpetual state of anticipation and delight.

Consistency: The Grand Exposure Effect

Ah, the grand illusion of consistency; it's another food industry's secret magic trick to get you hooked. This is about turning a one-time taste into a lifelong habit, ensuring every bite is an encore of the last. How do they achieve this sorcery? Imagine this: every time you crave a specific brand's snack or drink, it's like a dopamine disco in your brain. You're not hungry for the food; you're addicted to familiarity and unwavering sameness. Nature's a bit more freestyle, but mass-produced munchies? They're the epitome of predictability.

If it's packaged in a bottle, can or box, chances are it's been tinkered with in a lab to make your taste buds dance to their tune. These food giants don't just employ chefs; they have armies of 'Super Sniffers' and 'Super Tasters', the wizards of the flavour world, who conjure up tastes from chemicals that mimic natural flavours.

Take Givaudan, for example, a colossus in the flavour-making realm. With a team rivalling a small country's population, they're the ghostwriters of the food world, scripting the taste of your favourite snack, soda or chewing gum. And here's a fun (or unsettling) fact: that 'natural strawberry flavour' could be a derivative from the gland of a beaver's arse. It's natural, alright, but it's miles away from a strawberry field (sorry, I have mentioned it a few times now, but it frightens me so much it keeps me awake at night).

This consistency game is all about the Exposure Effect. It's like repeating a catchy song until it becomes your favourite. Each time you reach for that familiar brand, your brain lights up in recognition, reinforcing the habit. It's not just food; it's a well-orchestrated routine to keep you returning for more. So, next time you eat anything that has been mass-produced in a factory, remember, you're not just savouring a treat; you're part of a grand strategy of consistency, where every bite is a repeat performance, designed to keep your taste buds on a predictable, yet irresistible, journey.

Beyond the *Taste Bud Trio* and these seven hacks, food corporations have more tricks in their labs and factories.

Supersized Portions

The 'Supersize Me' phenomenon isn't just about indulgence; it's a psychological trap set by food companies. Here's a fascinating fact: if you're down to your last razor, you'll use it sparingly, making it last for months. But if you have a box of ten? You'll breeze through them. The same principle applies to food, especially those jumbo packs of cereal or popcorn. Bigger packaging tricks your brain into consuming more. It's all about perception.

When faced with a supersized meal, like a KFC™ bucket or a mountain of nuggets and fries, your brain lights up like a football stadium at night. It's an instinct from our hunting days. Food was scarce, and stumbling upon a feast meant you ate as much as possible. Modern food companies exploit this hard wiring. They know that just seeing a colossal portion can send our dopamine levels soaring, urging us to indulge without a second thought. It's not really about hunger; it's about a primal, indulgent urge.

Brian Wansink, the author of *Mindless Eating*, revealed a startling truth: often, 'it's not the taste but the sheer size of the portion that drives us to eat more. That's why when you're faced with a mammoth box of popcorn at the movies, your brain interprets it as an irresistible cue to munch non-stop.'

Here's a tip for those moments of temptation: choose smaller utensils and plates. It's a clever psychological trick. A smaller fork, spoon, or petite plate makes a modest portion appear larger, tricking your brain into feeling satisfied with less. It's about outsmarting the brain's craving for more.

As you progress through this book, your cravings might change. Maybe you'll say goodbye to bread, potatoes, fries, or pasta – the usual suspects in weight gain and the cause of so much needless suffering. But you might still yearn for an occasional scoop of ice cream or a slice of birthday cake. When that moment comes, remember small utensils and a small plate. Make that treat seem like a feast to your brain, satisfying your craving without overindulging.

Dr Nicole Avena, the talented author of *Sugarless*, whom I have spoken to at length about food addiction, compiled the following chart that shows how the big corporations are trying to supersize you:

Food	20 Years Ago	Today
Bagel	140 calories (3" diameter)	*350* calories (6" diameter)
Muffin	210 calories (1.5 oz)	*500* calories (4 oz)
Cheeseburger	333 calories	*590* calories
Pasta (spaghetti & meatballs)	500 calories	*1025* calories
French fries	210 calories (2.4 oz)	*610* calories (6.9 oz)
Soda	85 calories (6.5 oz)	*250* calories (20 oz)
Theatre popcorn	270 calories (5 cups)	*630* calories (1 tub)
Turkey sandwich	320 calories	*820* calories
Pizza	500 calories (2 slices)	*850* calories (2 calories)

Speed

We have already discussed the trick of calorie density, and the concept of speed in eating is a critical factor in this. Manufacturers strategically remove the natural, slow-chewing fibre from food and replace it with a blend of chemicals and refined oils, making it a breeze to gulp down. This rapid consumption leads to more eating, as the brain barely has time to process the influx of food, rendering the satiety hormone leptin less effective.

Packaged foods are engineered to be effortlessly swallowed – think of it as creating 'adult baby food'. Take fast-food coleslaw as an example: unlike its homemade counterpart, which requires effort to chew the fibres, the fast-food version is whipped up in a lab to slide down easily. Food scientists are like culinary illusionists, balancing the food's texture to be just chewy enough without being too much, nudging you closer to overeating. Healthy fibres are stripped away, leaving you unsatiated and prone to shovel in more. The resulting processed foods melt quickly in your mouth, allowing you to consume hundreds of calories in mere minutes – a feat impossible with whole foods.

Processing items like chicken nuggets involves tenderising the meat through mechanical or chemical means, making them easier to consume quickly. These fast-food and packaged food companies aim to create products that are so hedonically appealing and easy to eat that they're almost irresistible, urging you to consume them rapidly and frequently.

Umami

Remember those school lessons where they told us there are just four basic tastes: sweet, bitter, sour, and salty? Hold on to your taste buds because Umami's a fifth player in town. It's a Japanese term that translates to 'deliciousness,' it's all about that savoury flavour.

Umami: the culinary world's secret handshake that whispers 'Hey, there's protein here!' to your brain, which practically does a happy dance because, let's face it, protein is like the cool building blocks for our body's Lego set. But tossing expensive protein into packaged foods? That's like asking a billionaire to fly coach; highly unlikely. So, the food industry pulls a fast one with MSG – monosodium glutamate. It's the culinary equivalent of a stand-in actor for real protein, widely used to jazz up flavour in Chinese and Japanese dishes. But here's the problem: MSG doesn't just tango with your taste buds; it cranks up your insulin levels[4] and turns mice into fluffy balls of fat in science experiments[6]. So, if you're a fan of processed foods and takeout, you might unwittingly invite MSG to play havoc with your insulin levels.

Fake Flavours

Here's where it gets wild: those flavour masters, besides jazzing up foods with salt, fat, and sugar, are also magicians with chemicals, crafting almost any flavour you can imagine. But the catch? Sometimes, what's labelled as 'natural flavour' can be anything but. Think of natural strawberry or vanilla flavour that may have been sourced from a beaver's bottom gland (oops, I mentioned it again)! It's a fact I've harped on about strategically trying to get you to fall out of love with corporatised foods, changing your mindset from one of having to give things up to one of escape. After all, I promised right at the beginning of the book that you might not have to give anything up at all. And, if you start to hate the idea of ultra-processed food, then you're not giving it up but escaping.

Prepare to have your taste buds and reality rattled: Professor Iain Fraser, a wizard in environmental economics from the University of Kent, dropped a bombshell that less than 1% of the so-called 'vanilla flavour that we love and consume by the gallon isn't the real deal. It doesn't come from those lush, aromatic vanilla pods but from a less appetising source. Hold on to your hats because this next bit ventures into the 'you can't make this stuff up' territory. According to the *Edinburgh News*, that vanilla kick in your favourite treats might also be courtesy of the multi-talented beaver's bottom.[7]

Castoreum, a chemical compound sneaking into your vanilla ice cream and scented candles, is a special blend courtesy of a beaver's backside, specifically from glands near their tail[6]. But depending on which lab has been used, if you're lucky, it might alternatively have been created from petroleum! Suddenly, 'natural flavouring' takes on a slightly more disturbing dimension. It's a wild world in the food flavouring industry, making 'What's for dinner?' a question loaded with intrigue and possibly a dash of beaver or petrol.

Let's pivot to a gallery of culinary catastrophes, showcasing how big food corporations have taken some of our most cherished staple dishes and turned them into Frankenfoods in their relentless quest for heftier profits. Honestly, I could pen an epic tome just unpacking these gastronomic gaffes, but for brevity's sake, I'll spotlight just a few. This tour de force of dietary disasters isn't just a tale of culinary caution; it's a wake-up call to the creative liberties taken at the expense of our health and heritage.

*****

Breaking Bread: The Doughy Dilemma

Before we march into the realm of bread, envision this scenario: you've already been schooled by the astute dentist Dr James Goolnick on how a loaf of bread can swiftly turn into a sugar mill in your gob, wrecking your teeth quicker than you can grin and bear it. Maybe you've been enlightened that a couple of slices can morph into a sugary shocker or that a 12-inch Subway morphs into 15 teaspoons of sugar. Feel free to leapfrog over this bit if you're already set to drastically dial down your bread bingeing. But if you're still on the fence, stick around for another crumb of thought.

In the 19th century, Vienna introduced a concept for diabetics known as BU. Hold your horses; BU stands for Bread Units! Yes, even in those days, there was a whisper that folks with diabetes had to watch their bread bingeing. They discovered that a tiny roll, tipping the scales at 20 g, could unleash a sugar tsunami of 12 g. Hence, they birthed the notion of 'one BU'.

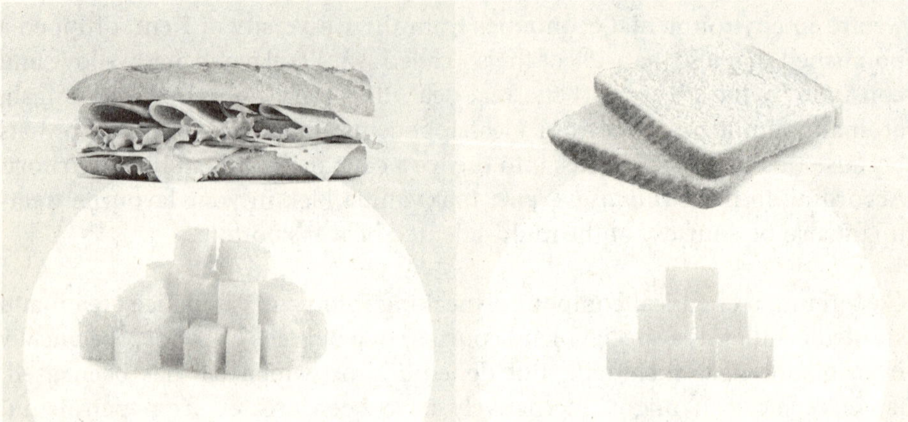

Now, let's tackle the breadbasket of issues. Sadly, we're not discussing your grandma's lovingly baked loaves here. The bulk of bread in the UK sprouts from vast, impersonal fields of mono-cropped wheat, drenched in a symphony of industrial fertilisers and a medley of chemical pesticides. Yes, it's a chemical fiesta from sowing to harvest, with those grains taking a bit of the party with them all the way to the mill. There, they're stripped of their germ and bran and refined into something resembling flour. If you're hankering for a slice, aim for sourdough. It's the original gangster of bread, better fermented, harking back to a time before fast-acting yeast hijacked our bread bowls.

Then there's the tussle between brown bread and white, brown rice versus white, or the sweet potato squaring off against its starchy cousin. Sure, they're a smidgen better, like choosing between limping on one foot or hobbling on both.

Bread's Bumpy Jaunt: From Sacred Staple To Processed Puff

Once upon a simpler time, bread was just flour, yeast, water, and a pinch of patience. But fast-forward to today's price wars, where a loaf costs less than a first-class stamp, and things get weird. Imagine hitting the Tesco™ search bar with 'bread' and being bombarded with 73 options. But here's the issue: a few giant hands kneaded most of the UK's bread market. Take Warburtons™, for instance, a household name that's nestled snugly as the UK's second-favourite nibble. They've got the dough to bag celebs like Samuel L. Jackson for adverts, no small feat! Bread is almost a birthright in the UK, with virtually every household partaking (99.8%) in the daily bread ritual, guzzling down about 11 million loaves every 24 hours.[8]

However, amidst this bakery bonanza, it's worth noting the craftsmanship of around 3,800 independent bakers who stick to the traditional ways, albeit dwarfed by France's 35,000 artisan bakers. Us Brits have a penchant for the commercial crumb, a stark contrast to our French neighbours, who have cracked the code to better longevity with their bread choices.

Let's unwrap the slices in modern bread-making. Gone are the days of simple ingredients and time-honoured methods. Enter the era of the 45p loaf, catalysed by the industrial revolution of bread in the swinging '60s. The Chorleywood Bread Process revolutionised bread production by cutting down fermentation times and using mechanical mixers to infuse dough with water and air at lightning speed. This meant doubling the yeast, throwing in some oxidants for a good gas, and a dollop of fat (goodbye, hydrogenated nightmares, hello palm oil) to give the loaf its lift. And just like that, bread became cheaper, fluffier, and less bread-like.

By 1966, as England celebrated its World Cup win and my mom and dad spent sleepless nights with their firstborn (me), bread had transformed. Additions like chlorine dioxide and a sprinkle of other, shall we say, 'enhancements', plus heaps of salt, made bread the top salt shaker in the British diet. Fast-forward, and some chemicals have been swapped for others, like ascorbic acid, tricking us into thinking we're getting a vitamin boost when it's just another cog in the bread-making machine.

Enzymes, those little biological catalysts, have also made their way into our loaves. They're the unsung heroes in our bodies, speeding up processes without a second thought. But for bread, they're silently working away, unlisted on ingredients because, technically, they're not there by the time the bread hits shelves. While enzymes in natural foods like pineapples can tenderise meat (hello, retro party snacks!), the ones used in bread are often different.

In *Not on The Label*, Felicity Lawrence vividly describes modern bread production: factories churning out millions of loaves a week, with a hefty side of fat and chemical 'improvers'. It's a far cry from the simple loaves of yesteryears, proving how much our daily bread has changed.

Is Wholemeal Bread as Bad?

You wonder, 'Is wholemeal bread just as bad?' The short answer is no; at least it keeps some nutritional value. While it's still packed with carbohydrates that ultimately turn into sugar in your body, it hasn't been subjected to the same level of additives and processing. Even in white bread, a glimmer of hope is on the horizon; some vitamins lost during the milling process must now be artificially infused. But, if you aim to make a slightly better choice on the bread front, wholemeal or sourdough are your slightly less guilty pleasures.

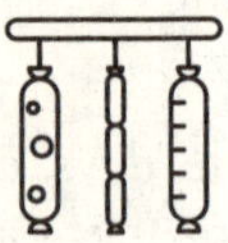

How Meat Got Its Makeover (And Not the Good Kind)

Before we unravel the mysteries of modern meat, let's set the record straight: I'm a staunch advocate for chomping down on real meat. The kind that hasn't been tampered with by man or machine. Science gives real meat a thumbs up for health but hold up before you think all meat is created equal. We're not giving a free health pass to those corn-stuffed, drug-pumped bovines (no offence intended to my corn-fed American pal's meat). The distinction between grass-fed, organic meats and their factory-farmed counterparts often gets lost in translation, muddling research and creating sensational newspaper headlines.

In the spirit of KISS (Keep It Simple, Stupid), let's cut through the headline hysteria about meat being a villain in the cancer narrative. Strip away the noise, and it's crystal clear: real meat is as essential to our evolution as fire.

Now, onto the star of many a sandwich: ham. If your ham slices resemble a model's flawless skin, alarm bells should ring. Terms like 'formed ham' or 'reformed ham' are your cue to a Frankensteinian food experiment. Picture this: pig pieces are blitzed into oblivion, then remoulded under pressure, with needles injecting a concoction of water, sugar, and preservatives to achieve that eerily smooth texture. That neatly trimmed fat edge? It's an afterthought, added to give an illusion of authenticity, not necessarily from the same pig.

A Guide to Supermarket and Fast-Food Meats

Imagine stepping into a world where not all burgers are created equal, where the line between a nutritious meal and a scientific concoction is as thin as a fishing line. Welcome to the supermarket meat aisle and fast-food counters, where deciphering the good from the not-so-good requires a bit of savvy and a dash of suspicion.

Picture tomorrow morning in the newsagents (yes, there are still a few remaining) seeing a red-top newspaper with another headline screaming, 'Saturated fat linked to every illness under the sun!' It's time to channel your inner cynic and whisper, 'Are we really comparing apples and oranges here?' or, more accurately, 'meat and salami.'

Remember the horse meat scandal? While newspaper and media coverage sent shockwaves throughout the nation, to me, it felt like a magician's sleight of hand, a distraction from the real trick. Interestingly, in culinary circles, horse meat, or 'cheval' as the French affectionately call it, enjoyed in places from Paris to the picturesque eateries of Switzerland, is touted for its health benefits. However, the true meat fiasco is uncovered in supermarket specials and fast-food favourites, such as the burger. Those budget burgers often boast less meat than a vegetarian's plate, and they only need to legally contain 62% beef to don the label 'beef burger'. And don't get too excited; that 62% isn't the prime cut you're daydreaming about.

What we're served is often a patchwork quilt of fat, collagen, and connective tissues – meticulously measured to mirror the composition found in nature's butchery. This meagre attempt at regulation feels akin to putting a plaster on a shark bite. The marvels of modern science have given us burgers that owe more to lab coats than livestock, padded with everything imaginable and, frankly, unimaginable. The secret ingredients? They remain a mystery, hidden behind vague labels like 'carrier mix and 'bulking agents', not to mention the yeast extracts that bring a meaty flavour to the table without the need for too much actual meat.

But fear not, fellow food enthusiasts! Not all supermarket burgers are Frankenfoods; you often get what you pay for. Yet, if you're seeking the holy grail of ground beef, the answer lies in your own kitchen. Embarking on a DIY burger adventure ensures you know exactly what's making its way into your meal – and, ultimately, into your body.

For those ready to don their chef hats, my free Health Results app and website are treasure troves of simple, delicious burger recipes that put the power back in your hands. When it comes to feeding yourself and your loved ones, nothing beats the satisfaction of a meal made with your own two hands from ingredients you trust.

The Curious Case of Chicken Nuggets: A Fast-Food Mystery Unravelled

Let me take you on a rollercoaster ride through the world of chicken nuggets – those golden, crispy morsels that have become a fast-food staple worldwide. But before you dip into that next sauce-laden mouthful, let's pause for a story that might change how you view these bite-sized wonders.

Enter the scene in Leicester, where local trading standards embarked on a culinary investigation that would uncover more than just your average food fraud. After receiving a complaint, they sampled 21 chicken nuggets from 17 different vendors, including the giants of the grocery world. The findings? A staggering one-third of these nuggets were masquerading as something they were not, with one particularly audacious pack boasting a mere 16% meat – 30% less than its packaging proclaimed. And yes, skin is considered meat in the whimsical world of nugget mathematics.

But the story of the nugget is a globe-trotting adventure, with our poultry protagonists often embarking on international voyages from places as far-flung as Brazil or Thailand to the frozen aisles of UK supermarkets. Their journey is sprinkled with salt – not for flavour, but as a preservative that cunningly reduces import duties upon their arrival in the EU.

Now, for the million-dollar question: why do these store-bought nuggets seem to disappear down our gullet faster than your homemade chicken dinner? The secret lies in a process reminiscent of a construction site. Imagine a giant concrete mixer, not churning cement but marinating chicken in a concoction of salt and sugar designed to tantalise our taste buds and keep us coming back for more. This culinary cement mixer does more than flavour the meat; it tenderises it, breaking its cellular structure into something far softer than nature intended.

And if that wasn't enough, enter the needle injector – a device that sounds more at home in a sci-fi novel than in food production. Armed with hundreds of needles, this machine injects the meat with additives, tearing through connective tissue to ensure every bite is unnaturally tender.

Of course, chicken nuggets are not expected to be pure meat, as their signature crispy exterior necessitates the inclusion of a coating. Interestingly, no specific government regulations stipulate the minimum meat content for chicken nuggets, unlike beef burgers at 62%, and sausages in the UK are mandated to contain at least 32% pork. An investigation by *The Sun* newspaper – a source I typically don't consult for scientific insights – recently highlighted that *Hearty Food Co's* chicken nuggets, retailing at Tesco, contain just 41% meat.

So, there you have it: chicken nuggets, or at least the version many of us are unwittingly consuming, a product that's been on more adventures and undergone more transformations than most of us could imagine. It's chicken, alright, but not as we know it. Next time you're tempted by that box of golden, crispy nuggets, remember the tale of their journey from farm to fryer – it's a story that's almost as hard to swallow, certainly harder than the nuggets themselves.

But let's pivot from the animal kingdom to the plant domain, where even our veggies aren't safe from corporate tampering. Next, we'll navigate the intriguing world of hydroponically grown greens and other plant-based foods that have undergone a corporate makeover. Fear not; I'm here to guide you through this jungle of information, ensuring your dinner plate remains a source of nourishment, not a science experiment. Stay tuned to understand how our veggies have veered off the natural path.

Lettuce: The Crunchy Green Controversy

Before we discuss lettuce, let me declare my love for this crisp, leafy delight. It's, after all, a fibrous way to kick-start a meal. But here's the issue: according to Barbara Dinham, the director of the Pesticides Action Network UK, the outer leaves of lettuce, where we usually start munching, are loaded with nitrates and pesticides. It turns out that lettuces grow from the outer leaves first, and by the time the heart develops, those outer leaves have been hit with up to twelve doses of pesticides and several rounds of fertilisers. It's like they've been through a chemical spa treatment.

The Central Science Laboratory (a government department) weighed in on lettuces too. They pointed out that the demands of major retailers lead to the 'extremely high use of biological control agents, insecticides, fungicides, and disinfectants.' Why do I mention this? Dr Howard, a leading toxic pathologist and former member of the government's advisory committee on pesticides, claims that the average Briton has between 300 and 500 chemicals in their body that weren't there 50 years ago. My point is, yes, eat lettuce, but ensure it's organically grown.

Bagged Salad: Freshness or Fiasco

Alright, let's move into the world of salad, shall we? It's like the unsung hero of the diet, always there when you need it. But here's the issue: bagged salads didn't exist until 1992. Now, they're like the rock stars of the salad world, dominating kitchens all over the UK. It's all about that convenience factor and an attempt to sprinkle some healthiness into our lives. Sounds like a win-win, right? But before you take another bite, let's peel back the green leaves and uncover the truth behind the salad craze.

Believe it or not, bagged salad has turned into a multi-billion-pound industry for our supermarkets. But how on earth do they bag it? That's the billion-dollar question! They've got a trick up their sleeves called Modified Atmospheric Packing (MAP). This fancy process gives these salads a longer shelf life, making it possible for supermarkets to source ingredients from all corners of the globe, give 'em a chemical rinse, and store 'em away until we're ready to munch.

Now, here's where things get interesting. Before these greens hit the shelves, they take a quick dip in a chlorine bath. Then, it's showtime for the MAP magic. Oxygen levels are slashed from around 21% to a mere 3%, while CO_2 levels are cranked up like partying in a tiny, controlled atmosphere. It's all to keep that salad looking as fresh and vibrant as a spring morning. But, and it's a big but, is it as healthy as it appears? Hold on to your croutons because the *Journal of Nutrition* spilt the beans. They conducted a classic experiment: one group got to feast on lettuce straight from the soil, while another enjoyed lettuce that went through the MAP process and landed on their plates three days later. They even took blood samples to see what's what. The results? Fresh lettuce eaters had a party in their bloodstream with a boost in beneficial antioxidants, especially vitamin C and many good-for-you polyphenols. But those who went for the packed salad? Well, their antioxidants decided to take a snooze.

So, if the chlorine wash isn't causing you any harm (seriously, it's like swimming in something up to 20 times more concentrated than your average swimming pool), the real head-scratcher is the loss of essential vitamins. Bagged salads might still deliver that fibre punch, but they're not exactly the poster child for nutrition. Pass the dressing, please!

Apples: Nature's Beauty Pageant Winners

Are all fruits created equal? Well, let's focus on apples for a moment. Ever marvelled at how perfectly matched those supermarket apples are when you grab a pack of four? It's like they've walked straight off the runway of a fruit fashion show. We've become so obsessed with the cosmetic appearance of nature's goodies that apples now saunter along a conveyor belt equipped with special cameras for a colour beauty parade. These cameras are no joke; they snap up to 70 photos of each apple during its journey. Measuring the apple's blush to ensure it meets certain standards. They can even detect a blush as small as one square millimetre. For some apple varieties, it's like they're auditioning for a role, and the blush must match a specific range. I've heard rumours that for one brand, they're so strict that an apple's blush must be precisely between 15–17 %. Not too reddish, but not too green either. If it's too much or too little, it gets a rejection slip. Spare a thought for the poor farmer who grew it, right?

The brochure for selling this beauty parade machine to food retailers says, 'Nature has many surprises... Buyers, however, require uniformly attractive fruit and vegetables of standard sizes.' Assuming an apple survives the beauty parade, its next challenge is the strength test. It's like their first day at the gym; they call it the 'penetrometer test'. This test measures the springiness of the apple. Passing this test is so crucial that it often leads to apples being plucked from the tree before they're fully ripe. And size matters, too. I remember apples as a kid, and they were smaller back then. Nowadays, it's all about growing supersized apples. Farmers must practically give their apple trees a supermodel makeover – over-pruning, adding fertilisers, and dealing with those pesky pesticides.

But here's the tragedy: tons of food goes to waste in this quest for perfection. If a farmer miscalculates production or gets hit by bad weather, it's game over. All of this comes at a cost in terms of flavour as well. Today, the appearance of fruit and veggies appears far more important than taste. They have to look good, but who cares about the flavour when most people's taste buds have been hijacked by the big food corporations anyway?

Oh, and have you ever wondered how old that apple is on the supermarket shelf? According to researcher Hannah Doolin (2019), no matter where they are in the stack, you shouldn't count on fresh apples from the orchard. These fruits ripen briefly between August and September, so keeping them in warehouses the rest of the year requires chemical treatments and cold storage. In a stockroom setting, they often sit for at least 9 to 12 months, and one more recent investigation even showed that, on average, apples are a whopping 14 months old[8] when they finally land in our shopping basket.

Now, am I telling you not to eat apples? Absolutely not, they contain fibre! But when you're buying them, be a conscious apple shopper. Seek out locally grown ones, and please avoid any unnecessary wrapping. Opt for organic, and to support our farmers, try to find British-grown apples. But if you're on a weight-loss quest, consider a different fruit because... well, that's a story for a later bite.

*****

The Hide-And-Seek Of Fake Food Labels

Ready for a sneaky trick from the food industry's playbook? Here's how they play hide-and-seek with sugar on ingredient lists. By law, ingredient lists must parade their contents in order of quantity—most to least. But, oh boy, if sugar tops that list, it's a red flag! So, what do these culinary magicians do? They split sugar into its many aliases and sprinkle them throughout the list. It's like a game of hide-and-seek, but with sugar!

Imagine this: one part sucrose, a dash of fructose, a sprinkle of glucose, and a smidgen of high-fructose corn syrup, plus a whole bunch of names from the list we discussed earlier. Voilà! Sugar suddenly becomes a master of disguise, lurking in plain sight but cleverly concealed among its many pseudonyms. It's a crafty way to avoid having sugar glaring at you from the top of the list.

Ingredient labels, those cryptic scrolls of nutritional information, aren't exactly forthcoming. It's like trying to solve a riddle wrapped in a mystery inside an enigma, but for sugar! So, next time you're scrutinising a label, remember it's not just a list; it's a puzzle designed by food wizards to keep the sweet truth out of plain sight.

Are Fake Food Really That Unhealthy?

Most of what we munch on today is a far cry from its natural beginnings. We've evolved from mere eaters to subjects of a 50-year gourmet scientific experiment, where looks and profits triumph over nutrition. It's like dining in a laboratory, and we're the unwitting test subjects!

But just how colossal is the impact of this culinary transformation? In the year 2000, the WHO published a devastating report, claiming that a staggering 60% of global deaths were tightly linked to our evolving eating habits. This revelation ruffled a few feathers in the food industry, maybe even enough to make Donald Trump raise one of his oversized eyebrows at the WHO.

The United Nations chimed in with similar concerns, hosting a powwow of world leaders in 2011. Their jaw-dropping verdict? A mind-boggling 36 million deaths each year could be avoided if we made smarter choices on our plates. That's like a giant 'Stop!' sign flashing in the face of poor dietary decisions.

And what about that chart from the *Journal of the American Medical Association (JAMA)* about risk factors and related deaths?[10]

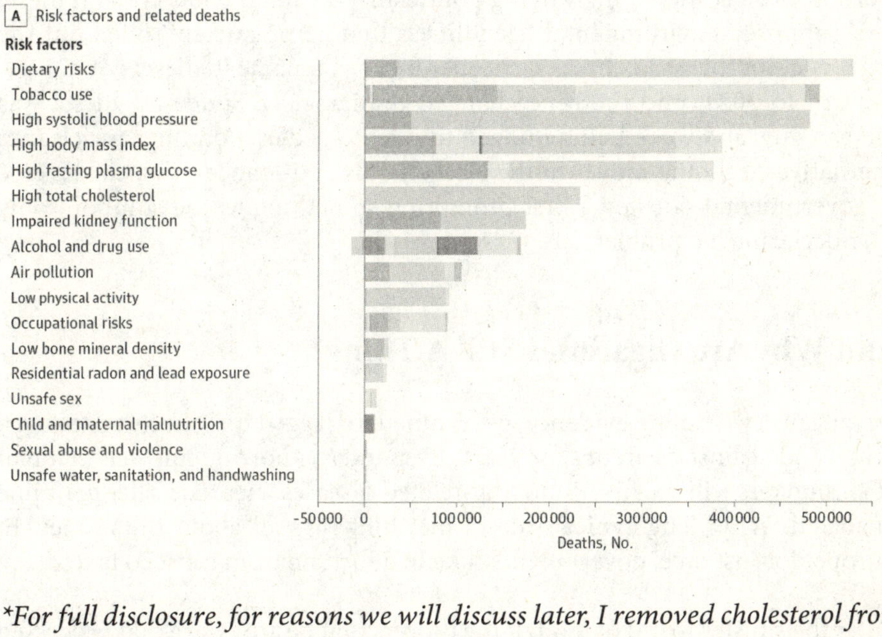

**For full disclosure, for reasons we will discuss later, I removed cholesterol from this chart.*

Let's view the chart through a fake food lens. Imagine you're juggling dietary risks, blood pressure (because, let's be honest, you don't get high blood pressure without elevated insulin), toss in BMI (a somewhat useless measurement that mainly reflects poor eating habits), sprinkle in high fasting plasma glucose (thanks, lousy sugary diet), and don't forget a dash of impaired kidney function (yep, you guessed it – often courtesy of our not-so-healthy food choices). What's left? Not much!

So, the next time you're irresistibly drawn to that bag of crisps or that tantalising chocolate bar, don't see it as a mere snack. You're stepping into a world of culinary enchantment, a dangerous excursion engineered by food wizards. It's a mix of science, art, and just a pinch of black magic, all wrapped up in irresistibly designed packaging.

If fake foods are as detrimental to health as I am proposing, you might by now be asking why governments aren't stepping in.

*****

Can Governments Miss the Mark?

Yes, they absolutely can, and history is teeming with their blunders! In 1998, Gordon Brown, then a high-flying politician, was so enamoured with diesel cars' supposed environmental friendliness that he practically rolled out the red carpet for them. Tax breaks, cheaper fuel – you name it, diesel got it. Fast-forward to 2024, and the tune changed dramatically. Suddenly, diesel was the bad guy, and we're being nudged to ditch our diesel darlings for cleaner alternatives, echoing moves in the Netherlands and France. It's a classic case of governmental oopsies – first promoting something as the solution, only later declaring it a problem.

And Why Are Cigarettes Still A Thing?

Despite overwhelming evidence, governments dragged their heels on taking a firm stand against cigarettes for years. Even today, knowing full well that half of all smokers will die from smoking-related diseases, cigarette sales continue unabated. Why? The cynical side of me thinks it's all about the money. In Europe, for instance, governments rake in a fortune from tobacco taxes.

Enter the sinister world of food. If the powers that be are aware that processed and fast foods are the architects of modern maladies like obesity, cancer, and Alzheimer's, why the silence? Follow the money. The packaged food industry is a tax goldmine. Imagine the upheaval if warnings had to be slapped on everything sugary or syrupy. The fallout would be monumental in lost tax revenue and unemployment benefits for all those 'get fat quick' executives. And let's talk about the diet industry, a behemoth that thrives on our failed attempts at weight loss, churning out $150 billion in profits across Europe and the U.S. They're not in the business of making us fit; they're in the business of making us repeat customers.

Businesses, especially those beholden to shareholders, are all about the bottom line. They must turn a profit. That's why the food industry prioritises profit over our wellbeing despite knowing the health hazards. They entice us with health claims while loading their products with chemicals and stripping out fibre and nutrients.

Those same food giants often fund the research that informs government advice. Remember when cigarettes were marketed as healthy? We're seeing the same story play out with food. But unlike cigarettes, the government's silence remains deafening when it comes to diet.

So, as we peel back the layers of government and industry influence on our health choices, it's clear that their interests don't always align with ours. We must sift through the noise, armed with knowledge and a healthy dose of scepticism. After all, in the grand scheme of things, we're more than just revenue streams or statistics—we're individuals striving for a healthier, longer life, despite the mixed messages from those in power.

Brits and American's on the Fast Track to an Early Exit!

Imagine my surprise one crisp February morning as I sipped my coffee, researching the depths of the sugar/CARBs dilemma that's shaving years off our lives. A headline on the BBC's website screamed, 'Americans to hit the life expectancy bottom by 2030'. This nugget of doom and gloom, courtesy of Imperial College London and the WHO, dissected future lifespans across 35 industrialised nations. And let me tell you, the accompanying chart was as comforting as a hedgehog in a sleeping bag. Why are we Brits and our American cousins trailing in the longevity race, lagging behind the South Koreans, the French, the Japanese, Australians, and Canadians, to name a few? Is there a secret elixir they're not sharing, or have we become too cosy with fake foods?

I present you with the chart causing sleepless nights for health enthusiasts everywhere.

Turn page to see our discover the UK's average life span ›

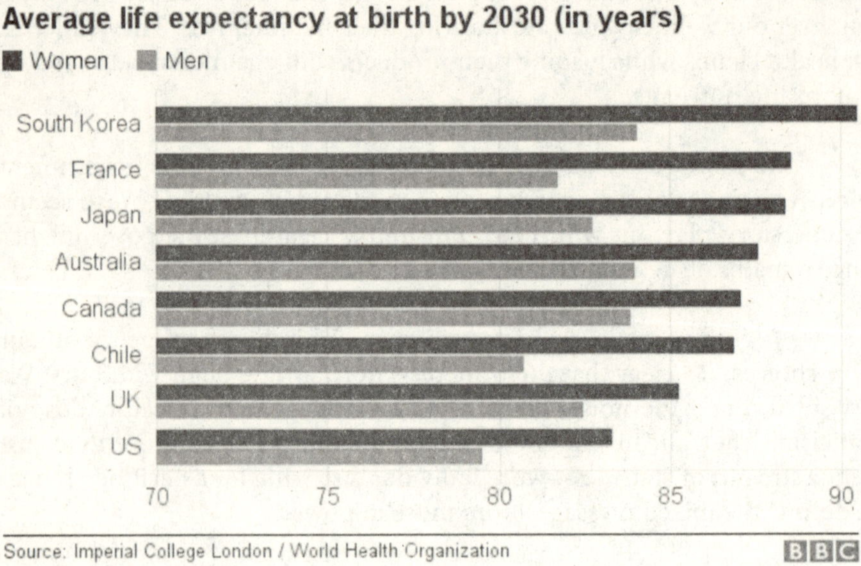

Next on our investigation through the dirty underworld of dietary doom: the undeniable link between processed food consumption and the unnervingly swift approach of our collective expiration date. Picture this: a recent exposé by the UK's *Daily Mail*, less a bedtime story and more a wake-up call, unless you're nestled in the heart of Portugal, basking in the glow of culinary virtue. The headline might as well have screamed, 'Britain clinches the dubious honour of Europe's processed food capital, with factory fare making up more than half its food basket.'

Cue the ominous chart plotting ultra-processed food as a chunk of household groceries. The UK leads the pack with a staggering 50% of food purchases being factory-born, leaving Germany (46%) and Ireland (45%) trailing in its processed wake. Meanwhile, Portugal, sitting pretty at a mere 10%, has cracked the code to eating right. So, does this chart spell out the secret behind Britain's and others' lag in the European life expectancy race? While correlation might not always mean causation, one can't help but ponder maybe there's more to this processed plot than meets the eye.

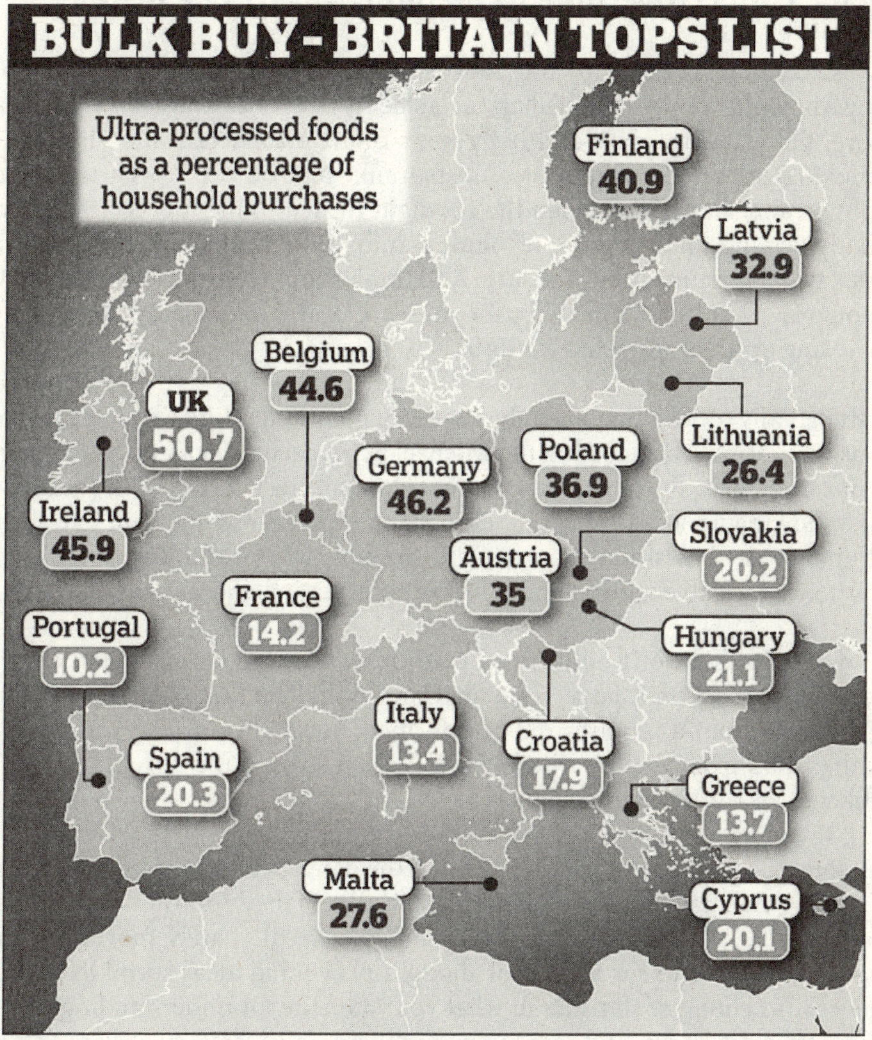

My aim throughout this book has been to arm you with an arsenal of wisdom and strategies, transforming your dietary shift not into a tale of sacrifice but a narrative of liberation. Acceptance of a *Fibre First* lifestyle is undoubtedly a commendable stride towards wellness – a practice I've observed first-hand in Portugal, where I have a home that nestles among the vibrant hues of nature's bounty from both land and sea. But let's not stop at merely increasing our fibre intake. Imagine coupling that with a bold renunciation of fake, processed temptations. It's not just about subtraction; it's about enriching your life with the authentic, the natural, and the undeniably real. Allow me to deepen your resolve against the allure of processed foods by looking back into the history of sugar production.

Why Aren't Governments Stepping Up To The Plate?

Let's keep our chins up and look on the bright side. Remember how governments eventually rolled up their sleeves in the battle against cigarettes? Sure, the warning labels and hefty taxes didn't do much at first, but when smoking got the boot from bars, restaurants, and offices, we started to see some real change. Plus, when the spotlight turned to the tobacco industry's shady dealings, it sparked a revolution among the younger crowd, eager to stick two fingers up at Big Tobacco. And think about seatbelts – who would've thought? Thanks to a bit of peer pressure and some snazzy advertising, buckling up went from 'nah' to 'duh.'

I still vividly recall a time, merely a decade ago, when skiing without a helmet was the norm. Yet, following the Michael Schumacher incident and a nudge from ski resorts, the tables have turned. Now, hitting the slopes bareheaded is like showing up to a formal dinner in swim shorts—you stick out like a sore thumb. This shows that societal shifts are not just wishful thinking but are entirely achievable with the right mix of information and messaging.

However, please don't hold your breath for a government decree to change food legislation on a large scale anytime soon. The real change will likely bubble up from a groundswell of informed, vocal citizens like you and me rather than from the top down. So, let's start stirring the pot and see what changes we can cook up together!

Despite the feast of evidence laid out on the dangers of processed 'fake foods' and the undeniable buffet of suffering and illness they contribute to, we find ourselves at a curious impasse: why has the needle barely moved on this issue? Allow me to serve up four thought-provoking ideas sprinkled with a generous helping of statistics to whet your appetite for understanding. If you manage to digest this and come up with different insights, I'm all ears—shoot me a DM or an email. Your thoughts could be the missing ingredient we've been searching for to finally start turning the tide.

Misguided Focus: The Government's Oversight of Crucial Data

Firstly, for those of us immersed in the science, evidence, and data, the cause of the NHS's challenges seems unmistakably tied to the unholy trinity of ultra-processed foods (UPF), excessive sugar intake, and the removal of fibre from our diets, a scenario we might bluntly attribute to corporate greed. However, the government's gaze appears to be fixed on different numbers. In a conversation with Tom Watson, who once served on the board of my company and held the position of deputy leader of the Labour Party, I probed the question of governmental inaction. He shared, *'Public Health England experts would say they can only go off evidence that nutritional science yields, but of course, you then look at this thing called nutritional science. And you realise that nearly every study involved in foodstuffs is funded by the food production industry, that even if the leadership of those industries is virtuous institutionally, they have a vested interest in maintaining the status quo. Because this, you know, just a dozen companies give us all of these ultra-processed foods and the consequences of what they're feeding us is making us chronically unhealthy.'*

This insight sheds light on a profound disconnection between the evidence that should inform public health policies and the skewed data driving the narrative. The conflict of interest within nutritional science research underscores a significant challenge in moving towards healthier national dietary guidelines.

Debunking the Tax Revenue Theory

Consider this perspective: the NHS's annual expenses amount to £181 billion (2022/23), and by my estimates, around 80% of that, a staggering £145 billion, is linked to ultra-processed foods (UPF), fibre-stripped produce, excess sugar, all of which are driving insulin resistance. For those who find the sea of numbers a bit daunting, picture this: outside of the maternity ward and accident and emergency, 8 out of every 10 hospital beds are filled with patients suffering from conditions linked to insulin resistance.

Furthermore, we can't ignore the significant disability costs forecasted by the Office of Budget Responsibility (OBR) to hit £39 billion in Great Britain this year. A substantial portion of these costs—around 80%, or £31 billion—is directly connected to the same harmful trio: ultra-processed foods (UPF), fibre-stripped produce, and excess sugar. Thus, when we add up the toll on the NHS and disability expenses caused by insulin resistance, we're looking at a combined cost of £176 billion, a figure largely attributable to the corporate greed of the food industry.

In contrast, last year, the total corporate tax revenue for the UK, spanning all sectors, was £84 billion. I've calculated that less than 10% originated from the food and pharmaceutical industries. Therefore, the argument that government inaction is due to the tax revenue these sectors generate doesn't hold up, at least from a business standpoint. Despite opinions suggesting that tax income is the reason behind governmental reluctance, I'm inclined to think otherwise based on these figures.

The Pension Paradox: Economic Interests vs. Longevity

In my first health book, *Primal Living*, I posed a provocative notion: 'In 2015, pensions cost the taxman £74 billion in the UK, a figure projected to surge over the next three decades. Given that the NHS's £100+ billion annual running costs cater to all ages, it appears that extending our lifespan may not align with governmental priorities. Perhaps a brief hospital stay, filled with apparent care and a plethora of potentially harmful prescriptions (not to mention the significant tax revenue from pharmaceuticals), followed by a swift vacancy for the next patient, suits them better. In essence, governments disbursing pensions may lack the incentive to see us thrive past retirement. Once we transition from contributing taxpayers to economic burdens, it seems they'd prefer us out of the picture. The short-term strain on healthcare systems is deemed more manageable than the financial implications of citizens living decades longer.'

Call me a sceptic, but that theory of mine, which contributed to the lethargic approach to the health crisis seven years ago, may still hold some truth. According to the 2023/24 forecast by the Office of Budget Responsibility, UK pension costs have surged to £138 billion. When considering the national pension expenditure, even after subtracting the revenue from food taxes, the sum nearly matches the combined cost of operating the NHS and providing disability support. It seems like a battle hardly worth engaging in.

The Electoral Dilemma: Health Advocacy vs. Political Viability

My final theory, and perhaps the most plausible, the real elephant in the room, is the cyclical nature of politics, specifically the impact of the four-year election cycle. Visualise a scenario where government officials, struck by a wave of ethical enlightenment, begin to warn against the regular consumption of Coke, McDonald's, Greggs, and essentially anything packaged with a rustle. Imagine they go even further, imposing taxes on these dietary culprits and redirecting the revenue towards the true custodians of our food supply—our dedicated farmers. In an ideal world, this is the course of action they obviously should pursue. However, contemplate the repercussions of such moves. How would this affect their chances at the polls? To put it bluntly, expecting a unanimous vote for such measures is akin to anticipating a unanimous order for vegetarian dishes at a carnivore's lunch.

Crossing the Finish Line: The Challenge of Government Action in Public Health

In wrapping up this discussion of the convoluted intersection of public health policy and political pragmatism, it's clear why stepping up to the plate to challenge the status quo of our dietary landscape remains a daunting task for governments. Like trying to serve a gourmet healthy meal in a fast-food world, the challenge is not just in the preparation but in convincing the masses to choose it. This exploration into the hesitancy of governments to fully engage in the battle against dietary culprits reveals a complex web of economic, political, and societal factors.

As we ponder the complexities of governmental action in public health, it's clear that waiting for policymakers to take the lead might not be our quickest path to change. For now, the onus falls on us to educate ourselves, to spread the word, and to ignite a movement towards healthier living. This is precisely why I finance the Public Health Collaboration (PHC) and a few other charities committed to this cause. These organisations work tirelessly to enlighten and empower individuals and communities, fostering a grassroots revolution in health and nutrition. By investing in education and advocacy, we're not just waiting for change but actively building it, one informed choice at a time. So, while we demand changes from above, let's not underestimate the power of our collective action from below. Together, we can craft a healthier future, with or without the immediate help of government.

Above all, let's not underestimate the power of our collective action from below. Together, we can craft a healthier future, with or without the immediate help of government. And if I haven't yet convinced you that sugar is the devil in disguise, let me share its evil past with you

The Sugar Slave Trade

Step back into the grim past of the Sugar Slave Trade, a time when sugar, perceived as a luxury, entangled millions in a relentless cycle driven by its sweet appeal. Picture a time starting in 1505, stretching cruelly over 300 years, witnessing the forced migration of over 10 million Africans to Caribbean plantations. Their fate? To toil under the sun in conditions as brutal as they were inhumane, all to satisfy Europe's insatiable sweet tooth. Many didn't survive the voyage, crammed into the bowels of ships, in conditions so dire that even the term S.H.I.T (allegedly an acronym for 'Store High in Transit' related to waste storage) seems a gross understatement of their misery.

In the 16th century, British entrepreneurs struck white gold, not in the form of precious metals, but in crystalline sugar. Thus, a trade triangle emerged, spinning a web of profit that enriched British coffers while chaining millions to a life of suffering. This triangle – sugar turned to gold, gold to goods, goods to slaves – propelled sugar to dominate Europe's economy for over a century.

And then there's King George III, whose legacy with sugar is as complex as his reign. Depending on where you stand, sugar may have altered the course of history more than any royal decree. Some historians argue that America's fight for independence was bolstered by Britain's distraction with its sugary assets. And in a twist of fate, the king's own health – a cocktail of blindness, mental illness, and pain – served as a personal testament to sugar's destructive power. If the origins of sugar, entwined with the atrocities of the slave trade, aren't enough to sour its sweetness, let's explore sugar's modern grip on society. Sugar is the modern-day drug, as addictive as nicotine or alcohol, lacing our food with its deceptive sweetness. Food manufacturers, the alchemists of temptation, sprinkle sugar across various products, from the seemingly innocuous canned beans to 'healthy' water bottles, ensnaring us in a web of addiction.

As we move towards the conclusion on fake foods, let's not forget the fizzy culprits, often marketed as refreshments in cans and bottles.

The Fizzy Equation

Let's break down the fizzy drink dilemma into something more tangible – teaspoons. According to the folks at Coke™, they're selling about 1.9 billion beverages daily. For simplicity, let's pretend every one of those is your standard 330 ml can. Sure, in the real world, some of these are those tiny cans you nab on flights, and others are the hefty 1.5-litre bottles meant for sharing (or not), but let's keep things straightforward. Each of these imaginary cans is brimming with 35 g sugar. That translates to about 8.75 teaspoons of sugar per can. But let's round down to 8 teaspoons to keep our math neat and tidy. Coke also sometime back shared that 43% of its cola sales are the sugar-free or reduced-sugar varieties like Coca-Cola Zero Sugar, Diet Coke, or Coca-Cola Life. This titbit suggests a shift towards more health-conscious choices, but it still leaves us with a whopping 57% clinging to the classic, sugary formula. What does this mean in the grand scheme of global sugar consumption? An astronomical sum of over a billion cans (1,080,000,000 to be precise) guzzled daily, contributing to a daily dose of 8.6 billion sugar cubes.

Have trouble visualising the colossal sugar we guzzle down with our fizzy favourites? Imagine this: the sugar from those daily drinks matches the weight of around 3,000 London double-decker buses. Yes, you read that right. But if that still doesn't click, picture those buses lined up nose to tail in a single file. They would extend over 20 miles. That's practically a marathon of buses, all loaded with the sweet stuff we casually sip. If that doesn't put the sugar rush into perspective, I'm unsure what will!

Now let's look at Pepsi™; unearthing their sales data felt like trying to crack a safe without the combination. Buried in one of their financial statements, I stumbled upon a boastful snippet: '434,000 metric tons of added sugar removed from our beverages in the U.S. & Canada. A staggering figure, indeed, but when it came to actual sales numbers, it was like searching for a needle in a haystack made of sugar cubes. After half a day's detective work, I threw in the towel, no reliable digits in sight.

But what about the rest of the fizzy drink lineup? I've whipped up a couple of charts to cut through the complexity. The first one lays out the sugar cube count for each drink if consumed from a standard 330 ml can. Not all brands embrace this classic can size, but it seemed like the fairest yardstick. The second chart zooms in on Coke's 500 ml bottle, the gym-goer's choice alongside Lucozade.

In a regular 330 ml can size	grams of sugar	Teaspoons or Cubes
Mountain Dew	46 g	12
Coke Cherry	40 g	10
Pepsi Cola	39 g	10
Red Bull	39 g	10
Monster Energy Drink	39 g	10
7up	39 g	10
Coca Cola	38 g	9

In a regular 500 ml bottle size	grams of sugar	Teaspoons or Cubes
Coca Cola	53 g	13
Irn Bru	52 g	13
Vimto Regular	46 g	11
Lucozzade Energy Original	44 g	11
Dr Pepper	36 g	9
Fanta	35 g	9
Sprite	33 g	8
Schweppes Indian Tonic Water	26 g	6
Lilt	22 g	6

Here's a jaw-dropper: lace up and jog an entire mile, and you'll torch about 124 calories. Pop open a 500 ml bottle of your favourite fizzy drink, and boom – you've just downed over 310 calories. You're looking at a gruelling 2.5-mile jog to neutralise that sugary indulgence. It's like running a mini-marathon to clean the slate from a fleeting sweetness sip. Who knew a moment on the lips meant miles on the track?

Bringing the fizzy drink story closer to home, we Brits have a bit of a sweet tooth for the carbonated. The latest buzz? On average, each of us knocks back 322 cans of sugary drinks annually.[11] Let's crunch those numbers: assuming each can be the standard 330 ml with about 35 g of sugar, that tallies up to an eye-watering 2,500 sugar cubes per Brit per year from fizzy drinks alone. Let's juxtapose that with a nugget of wisdom from the NHS: adults should cap their free sugar intake at 30g daily – about 7 sugar cubes.[12] Kids have even lower thresholds. This means, with just a daily can of pop, the average Brit is not only tipping over their sugar quota but bulldozing through it – before even taking a bite of food!

But the good news is that sales in the UK appear to be declining; the word must be spreading about their dangers. As European sales fizz out, manufacturers are eyeing up Asia. In a true story that's more sour than sweet, China's gone from lean to... well, not so lean, now boasting more people tipping the scales overweight than those undernourished.

And then there's Mexico, where obesity rates have ballooned threefold in three decades, crowning its kids the heaviest worldwide. It's a dubious distinction, more troubling than finding out your lottery win is payable in Monopoly money. A study published in the *International Journal of Obesity* on 10 December 2019 drops a bombshell – sugar-laden beverages are blamed for 12% of all the nasties: diabetes, heart disease, and obesity-related cancers in Mexico. That's nearly 7% of all deaths directly tied to these fizzy culprits, or 40,842 reasons to reconsider your drink choices annually.

But wait, before you jump ship to the sugar-free fleet, brimming with aspartame's promise of zero calories, hold your horses. The International Agency for Research on Cancer, a branch of the World Health Organisation (WHO), gives aspartame the side-eye, tagging it as 'possibly carcinogenic'.[13] Yep. In particular, it might be dialling up liver cancer numbers.

And if that's not enough to put you off your soda, let's revisit the curious case of the cephalic phase insulin response (CPIR). It's your body's heads-up signal, releasing insulin at the whiff of something sweet because, under normal circumstances, sweet equals high blood sugar. One study found that washing your meal with an aspartame-sweetened drink mimics the insulin spike from the real sugary deal.[14] So, in a nutshell, opting for 'sugar-free' might not be the free pass we all hoped it would be.

In wrapping up our exploration of drinks, let's steer clear of the seductive fizz and misleading labels of soda pops and bypass the fructose-laden fruit juices that wage war on your liver. Embrace the simplicity and purity of water or enjoy the rich aromas of coffee and tea. For an elevated twist, choose a fibre-rich drink that aligns with the *Fibre First* philosophy of this book – nourishing your body and supporting your digestive health. When you seek a touch of sweetness, lean towards natural stevia, a choice that bypasses the cephalic phase insulin response.[14] It's not merely about quenching thirst; it's about selecting drinks that harmonise with your wellbeing, ensuring every sip contributes positively to your health.

*****

The Illusion Of Food Packaging Slogans And Nutrition Labels

Cigarettes come with a grim warning label that doesn't mince words about their lethal consequences. Yet, when it comes to packaged foods, those highly processed concoctions brimming with excess carbohydrates and sugars, their labels are conspicuously silent. Unlike in Chile, where warnings on food labels are stark and straightforward, the rest of the world lags behind in telling the unvarnished truth. From cancer to Alzheimer's, from gout to tooth decay, and from heart attacks to obesity, the culprits behind these maladies are often found wrapped up in ultra-processed foods. This revelation, spotlighted by all major UK newspapers on 29 February 2024 (more on this in just a moment), marks a significant leap forward in our awareness. It's high time we demand a revolution in food labelling, one that gives ultra-processed foods the cautionary spotlight they deserve.

I wrote in my book *Primal Cure*, that 'If food has a label, it has most likely been engineered for addiction and manufactured for overeating. It has been created solely for corporate wealth and not public health.' Venturing into the supermarket aisles is akin to stepping into a jungle of jargon and cleverly crafted slogans, each product vying for your attention with the promise of health, happiness, and convenience. But beware, for here lies a meticulously engineered world designed not for nurturing health but for feeding addiction and fattening corporate wallets. Welcome to the illusion of food packaging slogans and nutrition labels.

Every crisp (and chocolate bar) is stacked against you in this culinary casino. The house, aka Big Food Corporations, always wins, employing a strategy not of chance but of science to hook you in. At the heart of this strategy is the infamous 'bliss point', a Frankensteinian creation that melds sugar, fat, and salt into an irresistible concoction that leaves your taste buds begging for more and your body bearing the brunt.

But it's not just the taste that's been tampered with. The labels themselves, those guardians of nutrition information, are often nothing more than a mirage. They may whisper health benefits but often mask the grim reality of what's inside. 'Low fat', 'rich in vitamins', 'contains real fruit' – each claim carefully calculated to convey a veneer of nutritional virtue while conveniently glossing over the less savoury details.

And let's talk about those ingredient lists, shall we? They are a veritable alphabet soup of additives, preservatives, and substances more suited to a chemistry lab than a kitchen pantry. If pronouncing them requires a PhD in phonetics, consuming them requires a second thought.

Armed with your shopping cart and a healthy dose of scepticism, remember: the path to wellbeing is paved with whole, unprocessed foods. The fewer the labels, the better. After all, you'll never find 'added sugars' in an apple (although shockingly, you do in some chicken breasts), nor 'artificial flavours' in a carrot. In the grand scheme of dietary decisions, choosing real food over lab-fabricated facsimiles is not just a matter of taste – it's a declaration of independence from the manipulative machinations of the food industry.

As we peel back the layers of marketing, let's savour the simplicity of foods that don't need a slogan to sell themselves. Because, at the end of the day, the best diet advice might be the simplest: if it's a plant, eat it; if it eats a plant, eat it, but steer well clear of everything else. And if it comes with a label, approach with caution—or better yet, put it back on the shelf.

The Serving Size Sleight of Hand

As you meander further into the thicket of nutrition labels, you stumble upon the ever-elusive and somewhat mythical creature known as the 'serving size'. Ah, serving sizes, the food industry's favourite magic trick, where calories and nutrients shrink and expand like a dieting Alice in Wonderland.

Here's the issue: those nutrition labels you're squinting at, are telling you the calorie count and nutrient content for what the industry optimistically (or should we say, strategically) considers a 'single serving'. But let's be real for a moment. When was the last time you ate just half a bowl of ice cream or a single biscuit from a package? That's like watching just one episode on Netflix – a noble intention that rarely plays out in reality.

My experiments, both in the Blood Sugar Trial and within my household's less controlled but equally illuminating environment, have confirmed what we all suspected: the suggested serving sizes are about as reliable as a chocolate teapot. In a world where 'family-sized' and 'share bags' are consumed solo, these serving sizes are a fantasy, a figment of some marketing guru's imagination designed to make the calorie and sugar content appear less horrifying.

Navigating this portion distortion requires a keen eye and a healthy dose of suspicion. Remember, the only serving size that truly matters is the one that ends up on your plate or straight out of the bag. So, as you arm yourself with information and prepare to face the aisles of temptation, keep one hand on your shopping list and the other on your sense of portion reality.

The Mirage of Marketing Claims

The front of the food package is where fantasy and marketing claims flutter like health fairies promising miracles and magic. As a savvy consumer in the kaleidoscope of today's health-conscious world, you're bombarded with labels screaming 'Fat-free!', 'Low in sugar!', 'One of your 5 a day!' But here's the thing: sometimes, the louder the claim, the more suspicious you should be.

It's as though these packages are superheroes trying to rescue us from our dietary dilemmas. Yet, often, they're more like thugs in disguise. The stark truth? The grander the health claim plastered on the front, the more likely you're holding a trove of processed nastiness rather than the wholesome goodness you're led to believe.

Most consumers sadly adopt a policy of blissful ignorance towards these front-of-package proclamations. The art of food marketing often involves a delicate dance of stretching the truth, bending it, and sometimes hurling it into the next galaxy. Remember the apple juice from our Blood Sugar Trial? It boasted about banishing tiredness with its vitamin C content while conveniently glossing over its fructose frenzy, which actually does the opposite.

So, as you stand in the aisle, faced with a cacophony of health claims, here's a little nugget of advice: take it all with a pinch of salt (low sodium, of course). These claims are often a maze of half-truths and, sometimes, complete fabrications. For instance, when a snack box gallantly declares, 'Made with real fruit!' it's often code for 'contains trace amounts of fruit and an abundance of sugar'.

Here are twelve of the most bewitching claims you'll encounter, each posing as your diet's next hero, and what they're really trying to sell you:

1. Natural: The ultimate pretence
Ah, the word 'Natural' – it's like a magic spell cast over food labels, promising enchantment from Mother Nature herself. Yet, in the grand scheme of marketing wizardry, 'natural' could mean just about anything. It whispers tales of idyllic farms and pristine fields, but the reality is often far removed. Natural strawberry flavour doesn't mean it's from strawberries, and vanilla flavouring rarely comes from vanilla pods; sometimes, both are courtesy of a beaver's bottom. It's a wild world out there, and 'natural' is its jester, mocking our wholesome expectations.

2. One of your 5 a day: A fruity fallacy
Then there's the proud proclamation 'One of your 5 a day', a slogan that sounds like health nymphs whispering into the ears of government officials. But dig a little deeper, and you'll find it's more of a marketing mantra than a meticulous metric. Comparing the fructose fiesta in a glass of orange juice to the broccoli fibrous fortress is akin to comparing a firework display to a flashlight. Both might illuminate your path, but one does it with a bang and a burst of energy that quickly fades, leaving you in the dark, while the other provides a steady, reliable glow that guides you through the night.

The '5 a day' recommendation, though rooted in well-meaning advice from the government in 2003, sprouts from a patch that wasn't thoroughly tilled by science. While it applies nicely to above-ground vegetables and some fruits, blindly following it without understanding can lead to unintended consequences for your health. The seeds of this advice were sown more from a catchy marketing perspective than from a bedrock of nutritional science.

3. No added sugar: Sweet, sweet deception

And oh, the virtuous claim of 'No added sugar'. It parades around like a health halo, insinuating that what lies within is as pure as the driven snow. But let's not be fooled; nature's nectar, like orange and apple juice, comes pre-packed with its own sugar rush, no extra spoonful needed. This label sidesteps the sugar saga by not adding more to the already hefty load. It's a loophole large enough to drive a sugar-laden truck through, delivering a payload of anything but innocent sweetness.

4. High in fibre: And also sugar

It may look splendid on the surface, but if this fibre is swimming in a sea of carbohydrates, the celebration is premature. It's akin to finding an oasis in the desert only to discover it's a mirage. As you start following the *Fibre First* diet, keep an eye on this claim; don't add it to your shopping basket without checking the carbohydrate content. If fibre isn't at least half of the total carbohydrates, then think twice.

5. Light or lower in: Light but not right

This term often travels on packaging as a designation of health, but look closer, and you may find it's just a ship carrying hidden cargo. Many 'low in' products have merely traded their substance for shadows, diluting themselves with water or padding their profiles with sugar. No-fat and low-fat options are nearly always higher in sugar.

6. Multigrain: More grains, less gain

It whispers tales of rustic wholesomeness and earthy nutrition, suggesting a fellowship of grains within. However, unless it's explicitly stated as 'wholegrain', you're likely navigating through refined grains, dressed up to attend the whole grain ball but not quite belonging. And, of course, if you are following a low-carb or ketogenic diet, you must minimise all grains.

7. Organic: Beyond the green facade

This label might conjure images of lush green fields and happy chickens roaming free, but it's more of a cameo appearance than a starring role in the health narrative. The term 'organic' might apply to some of the cast members (ingredients), but it doesn't guarantee the entire production is a blockbuster hit for your health. Yes, an organic label on none ultra-processed foods (UPF), real foods like beef and celery is a label to celebrate, but when found on UPF, proceed with caution.

8. 100% anything labels: 100% misleading

Here's where marketing takes a magic wand to the fine print. The UK's beloved chicken Kiev theatrically announces 'Made from 100% chicken breast' on the brightly coloured box. Yet, a peek behind the curtain (or, in this case, the back of the package) reveals a cast of only 42% chicken. The rest? A supporting crew of fillers, chemicals, and a sprinkle of hocus pocus. Always check the fine print when a product carries a 100% headline.

9. Fortified or enriched: The nutrient added mirage

Just because it's fortified doesn't mean it's your fortress of health. Remember, sprinkling vitamins on cereals that meet the bare minimum government standards is like putting a band-aid on a broken arm – hardly a fix for a diet lacking in real nutrition.

10. Gluten-free: No health guarantee

Jumping on the gluten-free bandwagon? Be wary, as gluten-free does not turn something into a healthy food. Without wheat, spelt, rye, or barley, many of these products fill the void with unhealthy ingredients and sugars, making them less 'health food' and more 'hefty faux pas.'

11. Fruit flavoured: Chemical orchards

Fruit-flavoured doesn't mean fruit-filled. That strawberry yoghurt might not have ever seen a strawberry, relying instead on a cocktail of chemicals to mimic Mother Nature. And as for 'natural fruit flavour', let's say it might come from places far away from any orchard or berry bush.

12. Made from only 7 ingredients: Less isn't always more

The allure of simplicity in a 'small quantity ingredient label' might seem appealing, especially in our ultra-processed food wary world. Yet, when the simplicity masks the inclusion of sugar and palm oil as the lead characters, this brief list becomes less of a brag and more of a red flag. With its concise 7 ingredient parade, Nutella might have us believe it's a straightforward choice, but it's a stark reminder that not all minimal ingredient lists are created equal.

What's Not On The Label

Peeling back the sticker of food labels often reveals less about what's inside and more about what's missing. As we venture beyond the visible text, it becomes clear that not all ingredients fancy appearing on the label. It's like a culinary fancy dress party where some guests prefer to remain incognito. In her eye-opening book *Not on the Label*, Felicity Lawrence lifts the curtain on this industry's sleight of hand, noting, 'While some additives started declaring themselves by another name, others simply went underground. Food legislation helps manufacturers here. Additives used as 'processing aids' do not have to be declared. Nor do the individual ingredients of all compound ingredients have to be declared on the label unless they make up more than 2 percent by weight of the total product.'

There is one exception. If an ingredient could make someone's throat close faster than a startled clam, it's dutifully listed, thanks to allergen disclosure rules. But beyond this, it's a wild west of undisclosed elements. Fancy hiding a cocktail of E-numbers? Just make it a 'processing aid' and presto, no need for disclosure. Here's the problem: just as a pinch of vitamins can be potent enough to boost your health (sometimes in doses so minuscule they barely register), the not-so-good stuff can be just as impactful in equally tiny amounts.

Felicity Lawrence goes on to say, 'Since, in weight terms, only a small quantity of additives may be needed to achieve the desired results, this still leaves room for hiding. So, for example, if I want to make a drink for children without having to mention preservatives on the label, I can buy some 'natural lemon flavouring', which incidentally does not mean that the flavouring is natural, merely that it has been chemically synthesised, it is 'nature identical', and make sure the natural flavouring has a hefty dose of preservative added to it'.

An eye-opening probe by Shropshire Trading Standards into a '100% chicken sandwich' being sold at a supermarket unearthed a concoction far from pure poultry. The sandwich was stuffed with an array of additives, including starch, sugar (dextrose), water, and an assortment of flavourings, not to mention a trio of preservatives (E450, E451, E452), alongside modified starch and whey protein. A recipe that, let's be honest, strays considerably from the wholesome chicken we might have imagined. This case highlights a more systemic issue: the glaring omissions on food labels. Current legislation provides a loophole, allowing processing aids and minor components to skip the label, enabling manufacturers to obscure the addition of additives that may not exactly be dinner table conversation starters.

Chile's Bold Move: A Model For Labelling Reform

Imagine a world where your cereal box or crisp packet warns you like a pack of cigarettes. That's exactly what happened in Chile in 2016. They rolled out groundbreaking legislation that slapped warning labels on foods high in the no-nos: calories, sodium, sugar, and saturated fat. The result? Cereal boxes now bear a striking resemblance to tobacco warnings, and guess what? It's making a difference. Sales of these 'marked' products are dipping. This bold strategy is straight out of the WHO playbook, advocating for a trilogy of clear front-of-package labels, curbing junk food marketing to kids, and keeping schools free of unhealthy temptations. Is the UK catching up? Not yet. But with Chile's success story, I hope that if we, as consumers, all turn up the volume of this conversation, we can drive change together, creating a healthier future one label at a time.

The Dietary Traffic Light System: A Nutritional Car Crash

Ah, the illustrious food traffic light system, Britain's attempt at simplifying the nutritional web of packaged foods. Picture it as the most befuddling set of traffic lights you've ever encountered, more confusing than trying to navigate a roundabout in reverse. Crafted with the noblest intentions, it aimed to signal dietary guidance, a straightforward system: green for go, amber for caution, and red for stop. However, in the hands of the food industry, it's become more twisted than a politician's promise.

The crux of the matter lies in the portion sizes these lights are based on, sizes so minuscule that they have been determined by someone on a strict diet of air and good intentions. In the real world, where a 'serving' isn't a single biscuit or a thimble of juice, the traffic light system can quickly go from a calm green to a frantic flashing red, akin to a disco in full swing.

As we observed in our Blood Sugar Trial, the traffic light system resembles a Christmas tree – bright, festive, and alarmingly red when actual human-sized portions are considered. It's a stark reminder that what's intended as a guide can easily become as misleading as a mirage in a desert, promising refreshment but delivering sand.

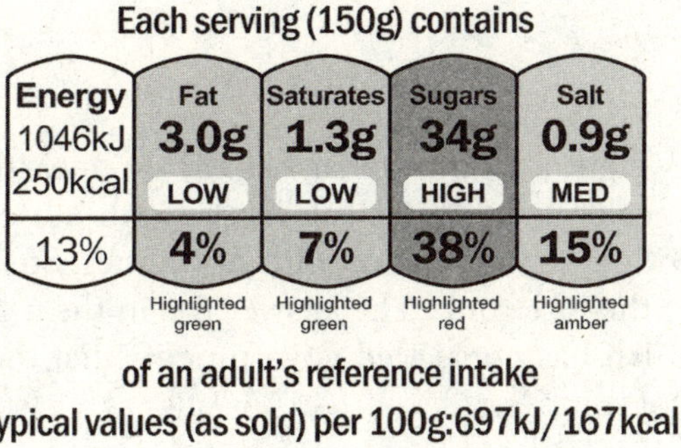

Stopping at the traffic light, it's crucial to understand exactly what they are trying to signal to us, aside from giving us the dietary equivalent of a red, amber, or green at a crossroad. This system proudly displays the levels of fat, saturated fat, sugars, salt, and caloric content (both in kilojoules and calories) of the food item in question. A noble effort, indeed, to distil complex nutritional information.

But I want to say it again because it's so damn important, especially for well-intended parents: the portion sizes these indicators are based on are, more often than not, how shall I say, 'just totally unrealistic'. They have been designed for those for whom a single biscuit constitutes a binge and a sip of soda a feast. This glaring mismatch between the suggested serving and the amount the average human will probably consume turns the traffic light system into a dietary optical illusion. It's like being told a splash of water is enough to quench the thirst of someone who's just crossed the Sahara.

What are the numbers behind the colours?

All measures per 100g	Highlighted green Low	Highlighted amber Medium	Highlighted red High
Fat	3g or less	More than 3g to 17.5g	More than 17.5g
Saturated fat	1.5g or less	More than 1.5g to 5g	More than 5g
Sugars	5g or less	More than 5g to 22.5g	More than 22.5g
Salt	0.3g or less	More than 0.3g to 1.5g	More than 1.5g

Allow me to dissect the five indicators on food labels, highlighting how only two offer genuine insight while the rest are misleading.

Energy

In the realms of weight loss and stellar health, we unearth in this book that it's not a game of calories in versus calories out but more mass in and mass out, combined with a delicate dance with hormones. So why do food labels parade calories at the forefront? The answer lies in the narrative spun by the food industry, which has persuaded governments that the root of all health evils is an excess of calories.

This narrative conveniently shifts the blame onto us, the consumer, for simply consuming too much. 'We specified a serving size of 30 g', they say with a shrug, 'but you indulged in more, didn't you?' But here's my issue: equating 100 calories of broccoli with 100 calories of fructose-laden sweets is like comparing a health tonic to a portion of sluggishness.

Fat

Including 'fat' on the label might lead some to think it's the outlaw of the nutrition world, but as you've learned, that's far from the truth. Natural fats are not just benign; they're essential for our survival. Highlighting fat content could mislead consumers into thinking all fats are bad when, in reality, we need them. The genuine concern should be the fat quality, given that many processed foods contain cheap, unhealthy fats and oils. So, while the fat content itself isn't inherently negative, it is a cautionary flag about the potential presence of lower-quality fats in packaged foods.

And here's the thing that really gets my blood boiling. Food manufacturers cram their products with less-than-healthy oils and then have the cheek to imply that, while their packages do indeed contain fats, they're somehow wearing a halo because the fats aren't saturated. It's akin to awarding a trophy for coming in last – a dubious honour if there ever was one.

Saturated Fats

Contrary to popular belief and despite their evil reputation, saturated fats aren't the dietary demons they've been made out to be. This tab of the label could lead you astray, making you think you're avoiding danger by choosing products with lower saturated fat, when in reality, the presence of natural saturated fats might be exactly what you're looking for in a healthy diet.

Sugars

This category should indeed raise your eyebrows, but it's riddled with pitfalls. Remember, the sugar content is predicated on the portion size that the manufacturer suggests. It only tells half the story by excluding starch, another form of sugar in disguise. Essentially, you see the minimum number they could present without revealing the full sugar impact. What is the biggest problem with traffic light data? A product can pack a huge 22 g of sugar per 100 g, and only be coloured amber.

And let's not forget the percentages at the bottom of each tab. They're supposed to represent the percent of the daily recommended intake. But as I have already said, the daily requirement for carbohydrates and sugar is a big fat zero. We've been ingrained to believe (deliberate pun) that carbs and sugar are necessary, but as those following a carnivore diet and Eskimos will attest, they are not.

Salt

While excessive salt intake can be harmful for some individuals, for the majority, any surplus salt goes down the toilet. That said, food manufacturers tend to over-salt their products, often adding 1 to 2 % of the total weight in salt, making it prudent to include this information on labels. However, as with saturated fats, salt shouldn't be demonised; a certain amount is essential.

So, the traffic light system is as useful as a chocolate fireguard, a delightful metaphor for something utterly useless in its intended function. It becomes a cunning disguise for manufacturers to conceal less-than-ideal ingredients. If you refer to it, consider the serving sizes you're actually consuming, pay special attention to the difference between the 'fat' and 'saturates tab' (since the disparity is likely to be the unhealthy variety), and flip the package over to check the real deal on sugar content, including starch.

The Call For Transparency And Simplicity

The current state of food labelling underscores a pressing need for transparency and a shift towards simpler, more natural food choices. While navigating the minefield of modern eating, I encourage you to assess labels critically, question the true content, and, wherever possible, opt for items that don't require a label at all, such as fresh vegetables and organic meats.

Healthier eating begins with an informed and cautious approach to food labels. By understanding the tactics employed by the food industry and choosing whole, unprocessed foods, we can reclaim control over our health and wellbeing. This exploration into the world of food labels is not just about caution; it's a call to action for consumers to demand better and to make choices that prioritise health over convenience and marketing.

As you venture further into the realm of healthy living, the simplest choices are often the most beneficial. Let's embrace the wisdom of returning to basics, where the real nourishment lies not in the misleading claims on a package but in the genuine quality of the food we consume.

10 Surprising Places To Find Hidden Sugar

Launching into our culinary detective tale, it's not merely about sidelining the obvious sugar culprits we've come to recognise as the usual offenders on our plates - the fizzy drinks, the chocolate bars, the lavishly frosted cakes. This quest probes further, unravelling the mystery of hidden sugars lurking within the foods we least suspect. Here, I look into the heart of our everyday fare, revealing the covert operatives of the sugar world. These hidden agents are not the shadowy figures lurking in the dimly lit alleys of our pantries and fridges; they're front and centre, camouflaged as the healthy choices, the quick fixes, the 'better' alternatives. Let's pull back the curtain on these food deceivers.

1. The great iced coffee deception

Picture this: a world where coffee, the beloved restorative of life, morphs into a sugary behemoth. Enter the realm of speciality iced coffees, where each sip resembles swallowing a sugar sculpture, towering and sweet. The Starbucks Caramel Frappuccino®, for instance, boasts a whopping 54 g sugar. Imagine dissolving 13.5 teaspoons of sugar in your morning cup, it's not a beverage; it's a dessert with a caffeine kick, impersonating your essential morning pick-me-up.[64]

2. Low-fat yoghurt's sweet illusion

Navigating the dairy aisle, you encounter the allure of low-fat yoghurts, promising health and happiness in a small pot. Yet, these pots, akin to miniature skis, glide you down a slope paved with sugar. One such example is a vanilla-flavoured ‘health’ yoghurt, which packs 14 g sugar in its modest container, disguising 4.5 teaspoons of sugar with the veneer of being 'low fat'. It's a ruse, a culinary exchange, trading fat for sugar, leaving us none the wiser. But it's not the biggest sugar tub you must watch out for. Activia™ Gut Health Yoghurt, in their little pot titled 'low-fat vanilla yoghurt and granola', offers us a gigantic 27 g of carbs (sugar).

3. The sugar-laden chicken Kiev story

Let me unfold a tale that spotlights the cunning disguise of seemingly innocuous meals. Imagine a friend steadfastly adhering to a diet primarily of meat yet confounded by unyielding bathroom scales and a pre-diabetic scare. He insisted his diet was almost exclusively chicken, prompting a joint expedition to his supermarket to scrutinise his selections. Yet, the culprit wasn't an addition to his basket but the chicken itself. His 'chicken' choice? A chicken Kiev, brimming not with simplicity but fillers and sugars, a stark contrast to the unadulterated poultry one might expect. The label revealed a mere 42% chicken content, despite the bold proclamation of 'Made from 100% chicken breast' on the packaging – a tad misleading, to say the least.

This narrative serves as a warning to peer beyond the glossy front of the packaging to, in this case, the 20 g sugar concealed within. And just for the record, my friend was downing two of these sugar bombs each night.

4. Protein bars

The Sugary Wolves in Sheep's Clothing – marketed as the pinnacle of healthful snacking, many protein bars are, in truth, sugar-laden impostors. Cloaked in the guise of muscle-building aides, they rival and often surpass the sugary content of a decadent dessert. A notable troublemaker, marketed under a name eerily similar to my brand Primal Living, packs an 18.1 g sugar punch, challenging the definition of 'health food'. And, on a recent visit to my local supermarket, as my TikTok producer Josh Morris secretly filmed my grand reveals, we found a Kellogg's Nutri-Grain Strawberry Cereal Breakfast Snack Bar, placed in the health section of the store, which contained over 23 g of carbs/sugar. Wow, what a sugary way to kickstart your day. Welcome to the front seat of the carbocoaster.

5. Oat milk's sweet misstep

Oat milk emerges as a top-seller alternative to dairy. Yet, tread carefully, for within its creamy depths hides a sugary secret. A seemingly innocent glass can contain up to 11.8 g of sugar, turning a healthful choice into a covert sugar source.

6. Tomato soup's sugary warmth

Is there anything more heart-warming than a bowl of tomato soup? However, beneath its comforting embrace lies a sugar-laden surprise – a whopping

26 g of sugar tucked away in a single can, a covert dash of sweetness that contradicts its healthy appearance. While it contains some fibre, the quantity of sugar overwhelmingly overshadows it. Many consume this or rather sip on this, believing it to be a light, diet-friendly option, yet the sugar content suggests otherwise.

7. Ketchup's condiment con

And while we are discussing processed tomatoes, ketchup, the ubiquitous table companion, hides a teaspoon of sugar in every tablespoon, a sugary Romeo, turning every meal into a sweetened affair.

8. Flavoured water's liquid deception

Marketed as a healthy hydration choice, flavoured waters can be anything but. With some containing as much as 20 g sugar per litre, these beverages are often stealth sugar bombs, promising hydration but delivering a syrupy dose of sweetness. For the health-savvy individual targeting the commendable 2 litres of water a day and drawn to a particular brand's allure, the reality is a stealthy intake of 40 g sugar. Buyer, beware: not all waters are created equal, and the quest for hydration can inadvertently lead you down a sugary stream.

9. BBQ sauce's sticky secret

That smidgen of BBQ sauce might be the secret ingredient that elevates your dish, yet caution is advised – its taste often masks a high sugar content, one-third to be exact. A seemingly innocent addition to your barbecue spread, Heinz™ classic BBQ sauce and its sweet and sticky variants pack a sugary punch that can easily turn your healthy grill into a covert sugar banquet. Tesco suggests a modest 15g serving size for their brand, but curiosity led me to an experiment. At a dinner party, I served it as a complement to steak. I generously poured 30g per into individual side dishes. The outcome? Three out of my five guests cleared their bowls, with one seeking seconds and another leaving a bit behind. This little exercise underscores how a free hand with BBQ sauce can inadvertently lead to a sugar overload, transforming your meal into something far sweeter than intended.

10. Baked beans' fibrous façade

A staple of pantries, baked beans boast fibre but are overshadowed by their carbohydrate content, a fibrous front for a sugary interior. You have to play detective a little with baked beans. Remember the label I showed in our section on my Blood Sugar Trial? You have to take the total carbohydrates and then deduct the fibre. Half a can of baked beans is a significant source of fibre; a large dose of 4 g. The problem is that the total carbohydrates are 18 g, which dwarfs the fibre and negates its benefits.

As we weave through the supermarket aisles, armed with knowledge and a discerning eye, we learn to see beyond the marketing, beyond the claims of health and nutrition. It's a journey of discovery, of learning to identify the hidden sugars that charade as our allies. The key to navigating this landscape is awareness and a sense of freedom. Sometimes, the realisation that your trusted big brand packet, box or can is a bucket of sugar, is best met with a chuckle and a vow to make smarter choices.

Seeking a path to better health, we learn to question, scrutinise, and see beyond the surface. It's a culinary detective story with twists and turns, heroes and felons. And in this story, knowledge is our weapon, curiosity our shield, and smart choices our pathway to victory. But before I close this discussion on hidden sugars, ready to face the next meal with wisdom, wit, and a well-stocked arsenal of healthier alternatives, let me highlight one more food. Or should I say food-like alternative? Something my good friend Dr Ali Ibrahim, one of the UK's leading experts in children's eating disorders, and I have discussed at length 'Nutella®'.

Nutella®: The Sweet Spread That Conquered Breakfast Tables Worldwide

Nutella, the hazelnut chocolate spread that has become a global breakfast and snack staple, is more than just a delicious treat; it's a culinary phenomenon. Born out of necessity and Italian ingenuity, its creation traces back to World War II. Pietro Ferrero, an Italian baker, ingeniously blended hazelnuts into chocolate to stretch the scarce cocoa supplies of wartime Italy, unknowingly giving birth to a future international sensation.

Fast-forward to today, Nutella's appeal has only grown, transcending borders and generations. The brand once claimed on its website that with the amount of Nutella produced in a year, its bottles could wrap around the Earth 1.8 times. This isn't just a whimsical statistic; it underscores the sheer volume of love and demand for this spread. Annually, over 365,000 tons of Nutella are produced – equivalent to the weight of the Empire State Building.

Starting as a simple solution to a cocoa shortage to becoming a staple on breakfast tables in over 160 countries, Nutella's journey is as rich and fascinating as its flavour. Whether slathered on toast, dolloped on pancakes, or – let's be honest – scooped straight from the jar, Nutella spreads pleasure but not happiness, one hazelnutty, chocolatey spoonful at a time. But as we study the label, questions arise: is it a healthier substitute for sugar-laden cereals? Does it trump the sweetness of jam with nutritional benefits? Aren't its two key ingredients: healthy nuts and cocoa? Sadly, the answers are no, no, and no.

Nutella's Nutritional Nonsense: A Spoonful of Sugar in Disguise

When Nutella tries to position itself as the hero of the breakfast table, it paints a picture of hazelnut cocoa bliss that could almost make you feel like you're embracing a healthy lifestyle with every spread. The jar cheerfully boasts 'hazelnut spread with cocoa', suggesting a wholesome start to your day, reminiscent of picking hazelnuts and cocoa pods fresh from the orchard and meadow.

However, a closer look at the ingredients list reveals a plot twist worthy of a daytime soap opera. The starring roles are not played by hazelnuts and cocoa, as is suggested, but by sugar and palm oil – a duo that knows how to make an entrance, but not necessarily for the right reasons. Indeed, diving into the nutritional facts is like reading the fine print in a too-good-to-be-true contract; for every 15 g serving, sugar takes the lead with a whopping 8.4 g. Yes, over half of each spoonful is dedicated to sweetening your morning buzz.

Ingredients

Sugar, Palm Oil, **Hazelnuts** (13%), Skimmed **Milk** Powder (8.7%), Fat-Reduced Cocoa (7.4%), Emulsifier: Lecithins (**Soya**), Vanillin. Gluten free.

Suitable for vegetarians.

Best before: See lid

(UK) Ferrero, 889 Greenford Road, Greenford, UB6 0HE.

(ROI) Ferrero, Kinsale Road, Cork.

And about that modest 15 g portion size? Let's say it's more of a suggested serving for mice than humans. During an undercover operation on Pancake Day, my kids were allowed to frolic freely with a jar of Nutella. The result? Their 'scoops' were more akin to heaping love letters to sugar, averaging around 54 g – far beyond the label's quaint suggestion. With 57% of this spread being sugar, their pancakes were less breakfast and more a dessert fiesta, delivering a staggering 30.7 g sugar (or 7.5 teaspoons, if we're to visualise the sugar rush).

	Per 100g	Per portion (15g)	%RI Per portion*
Energy kJ	2252	336	-
Energy kcal	539	80	4%
Fat g	30.9	4.6	7%
of which Saturates g	10.6	1.6	8%
Carbohydrates g	57.5	8.6	3%
of which Sugars g	56.3	8.4	9%
Protein g	6.3	0.9	2%
Salt g	0.107	0.016	0%
*Reference intake of an average adult (8400 KJ / 2000 kcal)			
15g portion = 1 teaspoon			

The rest-assured label: nothing to see here

The jar proudly proclaims 'Our Quality' then lists, with big green ticks:

- ✓ 7 ingredients
- ✓ no hydrogenated fats
- ✓ no preservatives
- ✓ no colorings

Yes, they used the U.S. spelling even though it's made in the UK, but that's moving away from my point. 'Our quality', adorned with big green ticks, as if to say, 'Look no further, for here lies the essence of purity.' Yet, most of this assembly resembles a line-up in a culinary rogue's gallery rather than a testament to nutritional virtue.

Among these acclaimed 'seven ingredients', sugar and palm oil take the lead, flanked by lecithin and a shadow of their former selves: fat-reduced cocoa and skimmed milk powder. The inclusion of vanillin, which you might think was vanilla unless you pay lots of attention. Don't be fooled; vanillin isn't the exotic spice you might imagine, plucked from an orchid in Madagascar. It's a synthetic creation, a far cry from the natural bean; but thankfully steering clear of a beaver bottom, a small mercy.

So, while 'no hydrogenated fats', 'no preservatives', and 'no colorings' might tick some boxes in the grand scheme of food virtues, the reality is that we're not witnessing a line-up of ingredients that could be called the Magnificent Seven. It's more of a questionable ensemble, where the main characters are better known for their roles in dietary dilemmas than in healthful narratives. And while I can't say with any certainty, were there really only 7 ingredients, or were others not disclosed due to being concealed as 'processing aids?'

Palm oil: A double-edged sword

While Nutella's label proudly boasts 'no hydrogenated fats', their ingredient list reveals the use of palm oil, a choice that's stirring controversy for its impact on both health and the environment. The cultivation of palm oil has led to the decimation of vast swaths of tropical forests, robbing the world of biodiversity and threatening species like the Orangutan, pygmy elephant, and Sumatran rhino. The World Wildlife Fund (WWF) articulates the grim reality, highlighting palm oil as a principal culprit behind the deforestation of some of the planet's most species-rich forests.

On the health front, there are concerns about palm oil's safety when heated. The European Food Safety Authority (EFSA) raised eyebrows with a report suggesting that heating palm oil can generate glycidol, a substance suspected of being carcinogenic. This revelation adds a layer of complexity to its use in foods. The tale takes a more ominous turn with research on mice.

Although we're not identical, our shared genetic blueprint with mice (to the tune of 97.5%) gives us cause for concern. Studies have shown that mice exposed to glycidol developed various cancers of the uterus (carcinoma or adenocarcinoma) and subcutaneous tissue (sarcoma or fibrosarcoma) in females and tumours of the lung and the liver.[15] It's a stark reminder that what's omitted from the label can sometimes be as telling as what's included. For completeness, some research trials have failed to find a connection between the use of palm oil and cancer in humans.

Nutella's Bittersweet Settlement

In 2017, a headline by the *Huffington Post* unveiled a legal skirmish that left Nutella in a sticky situation. The article, titled 'Nutella Lawsuit: Ferrero Settles Class-Action Suit Over Health Claims For $3 Million' detailed a settlement where Ferrero, the creators of Nutella, agreed to cough up $3 million. This legal battle, sparked by California mom Athena Hohenberg, challenged the hazelnut chocolate spread's health claims, stirring a pot of debate over its nutritional portrait. As the dust settles, consumers are left to ponder whether Nutella's healthful image has been smeared by its own sweetness. I spotlight this lawsuit amidst countless others against food companies to underscore a poignant example of misleading health claims on labels. This case serves as a cautionary tale, shedding light on the broader issue of how products are marketed as healthy despite evidence to the contrary.

The sweet trap: Nutella's addictive symphony

Why does Nutella tempt us into blissful overindulgence? The answer lies in its two irresistible duo ingredients: sugar and fat. In the wild, it's rare to stumble upon a meal that marries these two, with plants usually offering a mix of sugar and protein and animals serving up fat and protein. Nutella, however, masterfully blends the two, setting off fireworks in our brains. This concoction taps into our deepest sensory pleasures, making Nutella not just a spread but an experience, a guilty pleasure that knows exactly how to keep us returning for more. And remember that if you are overindulging, it's not your fault because all ultra-processed foods are designed to navigate around the fullness hormones that stop you from feeling full.

Nutella's quest for a breakfast badge

Despite its current designation as a dessert topping, Nutella's maker is lobbying to rebrand it as a breakfast spread akin to jam. This seemingly minor shift could dramatically alter public perception of its healthfulness. By reclassifying, the standard serving size on Nutella's label would halve from 2 tablespoons (37 g) to just 1 tablespoon (18.5 g). This reduction could mislead the casual reader into thinking Nutella is a low-calorie, low-sugar, and low-fat option simply because the figures would shrink alongside the serving size – not because the spread has become any healthier.

So, next time Nutella tries to sneak into your breakfast line-up with its hazelnut-cocoa message, remember it's asking you to start your day with spoonful's of sugar, not the Mary Poppins kind. Nutella commercials focus on advertising the spread as a quick and healthy option for breakfast, especially for children. On the side of its current label, its headline reads, 'Hazelnut spread with cocoa'. Now, if those two were the main ingredients, you would start your day off with a fantastic fibre feast. Almost the perfect fibre spread. So much so that I have created my own Fiberella spread, which you will find on page 445.

*****

The Fake Food Impact On Our Future Generations

In the intricate mosaic of health we've meticulously pieced together in this chapter, it becomes undeniably clear that the challenge does not discriminate by age. Like a shadow, this concern extends its reach over the youngest and most vibrant among us, our children. Here, under this shadow, lie statistics that should not just worry us but propel us into action:

- A quarter of 4- to 5-year-olds and 41% of 10-11-year-olds are overweight/obese in the UK.[16]
- Over 60% of children's diets are sourced from ultra-processed foods in the UK.[17]
- Obese children have a higher chance of carrying their obesity into adulthood, accompanied by a parade of health issues such as heart disease, stroke, Type 2 diabetes, and certain cancers.[18]

In the midst of this storm, there are beacons of hope—two outstanding charities in the UK dedicating their energy to turning the tide on this heart-wrenching scenario. Our charity, The Bennett Foundation, proudly works alongside them, extending our support in their valiant efforts. I urge you to lend your eyes, hearts, and hands to their cause.

Public Health Collaboration

Public Health Collaboration

Imagine a world where our children rebel against the norm of processed foods, empowered by knowledge and choice. That's the vision of the Real Food Rebellion, one of our three foundational pillars. We're on a mission to peel away the layers of misinformation and reveal the stark dangers of ultra-processed foods (UPF). Through education, we aim to inspire schools, parents, and kids to embrace nature's bounty and say a resounding 'no' to anything less.

Collaboration for Kids (CFK)

CFK is a testament to what we can achieve when we join forces to improve our children's health. This ambitious project is not just a collaboration but a community, bringing together parents, carers, children of all ages, and professionals from various fields. Together, we're sowing the seeds of awareness about the peril ultra-processed foods pose, nurturing a generation that reaches for the natural, the real, the way nature intended. Our ultimate harvest? A future where children thrive, healthy and aware.

Leap Day 2024 – A Day To Remember

On the morning of 29 February 2024, as I made my way to the office, my phone started behaving like a popcorn machine on overdrive, bursting with alerts non-stop. Sensing something significant, I pulled over into a lay-by. Messages were flooding in from my doctor friends, with phrases like, 'We are winning', 'Our voices are finally getting heard', 'Down with UPFs', 'They should have published your afflictions tree', 'You need to include this in your new book'. At first, I was puzzled by what they were all talking about until I found a direct message with a link to *The Telegraph* newspaper. There it was, in stark black and white, a headline that caught the eye: 'Ultra-processed foods linked to more than 30 illnesses. A diet of UPFs is associated with health issues, including cancer, high blood pressure, anxiety, asthma, and diabetes.'

It wasn't just The Telegraph, either:

The Daily Mail headline: Ultra-processed foods are 'harmful to EVERY part of the body'... Biggest study yet links UPFs to 32 illnesses - including cancer and heart disease - as experts call for biscuits, cakes, and sweets to be treated like cigarettes.

***The Guardian* headlined:** Ultra-processed food linked to 32 harmful effects to health, review finds.

***Sky News* wrote:** Ultra-processed foods linked to 32 physical and mental health problems; review finds.

***The Sun* newspaper:** SNACK ATTACK... Full list of 32 health dangers lurking in your favourite foods – from cancer to lung issues and early death.

***The Daily Mirror* headline:** Junk food 'should be treated like cigarettes' as it's linked to 30 deadly health issues.

So, what was the origin of all this buzz? The day before, the *BMJ (British Medical Journal)* had unveiled compelling evidence from a monumental study encompassing 10 million participants. This study, possibly the most extensive of its kind, started with an eye-opening introduction. 'Ultra-processed foods, as defined using the Nova food classification system, encompass a broad range of ready-to-eat products, including packaged snacks, carbonated soft drinks, instant noodles, and ready-made meals. These products are characterised as industrial formulations primarily composed of chemically modified substances extracted from foods, along with additives to enhance taste, texture, appearance, and durability, with minimal to no inclusion of whole foods.'

Those last four words are pivotal to grasp. The majority of these products contain 'no inclusion of whole foods'.

The study was meticulously conducted and enriched with a wealth of data; it's a compelling read for anyone who is numerically inclined. However, for those eager to get straight to the heart of the matter, here's the succinct conclusion: 'Greater exposure to ultra-processed food is linked with an increased risk of adverse health outcomes, notably affecting cardiometabolic health, common mental disorders, and overall mortality risk.'

The revelation from the *BMJ* underscores a disconcerting irony in our food system. It highlights a stark contrast between public health interests and the profit-driven motives of major food corporations. This dynamic showcases not just a health crisis but an ethical dilemma, where the financial gains of a few outweigh the nutritional wellbeing of many. It's a scenario where a small group of individuals at the corporate food giants earn billions of pounds at the expense of billions of consumers' health.

In a striking coincidence that same week, as the world grappled with the unsettling findings about ultra-processed foods (UPFs), Gary Pilnick, CEO of Kellogg's, made a statement on CNBC news that seemed to epitomise this disconnect. He said...

> *'We are advertising cereal for dinner... cereal for dinner is something that is more on trend now, and we expect it to continue.'* [19]

Really? The evidence against cereals is now as clear as the evidence against smoking, yet they now want us to consume it twice a day! This comment takes on a deeper, more concerning significance against the backdrop of the BMJ study. It reflects the food industry's push for convenience and 'trendiness' over nutritional content and health.

The juxtaposition of these two narratives – one highlighting the health risks associated with UPFs and the other promoting processed foods as meal solutions – paints a vivid picture of the challenges facing public health today. It calls into question the responsibility of food corporations in the obesity and health crises. It underscores the need for greater transparency, regulation, and a shift towards promoting whole, unprocessed foods. As consumers become more aware of these issues, the hope is for a collective push towards a healthier, more sustainable food system that prioritises the health and wellbeing of the many over the profits of the few.

Chapter 5

Insulin Resistance's Travelling Partners

By this point, you know insulin resistance is the linchpin in many health issues, standing tall as the robust trunk within my *Tree of Afflictions*. But to zoom in on insulin resistance without acknowledging its accomplices would be akin to having a picnic without the essentials – no basket, blanket, sandwiches or nibbles. Therefore, it's time to cast a beam of light onto four other biological culprits clambering up this trunk: inflammation, shortened telomeres, uric acid and the quality and quantity of our mitochondria. Imagine insulin resistance as the trunk's core, with this foursome acting as the intricate layers of bark, each adding its chapter to our health's narrative.

As we prepare to negotiate the dense forest of wellbeing, envision these three factors not just as silent spectators but as dynamic participants – sometimes as allies, other times as adversaries – in our body's complex story. This is not merely a walk in the woods; it's an expedition into the verdant depths of health, where every tree and trunk whispers secrets of vitality and decay. Lace up your hiking boots; we're about to tread through the underbrush of understanding, where each step reveals more about our biological tapestry.

*****

Inflammation – The Fiery Side Of Health

Inflammation, or insulin resistance, is like that age-old question of 'Which came first: the chicken or the egg?' You rarely find inflammation without some cells being insulin resistant, and vice versa. Besides, they both share the same naughty root causes. Personally, I see inflammation as the troublemaker triggered by insulin resistance, so in my mind, it takes its place in the branches of my *Tree of Afflictions*, but others and some far cleverer than I (well, certainly with a lot more letters after their name) will suggest the opposite.

Picture this: you're on a football or netball pitch feeling invincible, until – ouch! – you're sidelined by an injury. Suddenly, there's a swelling of inflammation, illuminating the injury site. This is your body's flare signal, alerting you to trouble. Enter the cavalry of white blood cells, along with an entourage of reinforcements, not just to protect the wounded area but also to mount a defence against any opportunistic microbes lurking around. This is acute inflammation in action, playing the hero when disaster strikes. It's the body's equivalent of rolling out the red carpet for healing and repair – a natural and, frankly, quite impressive response to injury. This is acute inflammation.

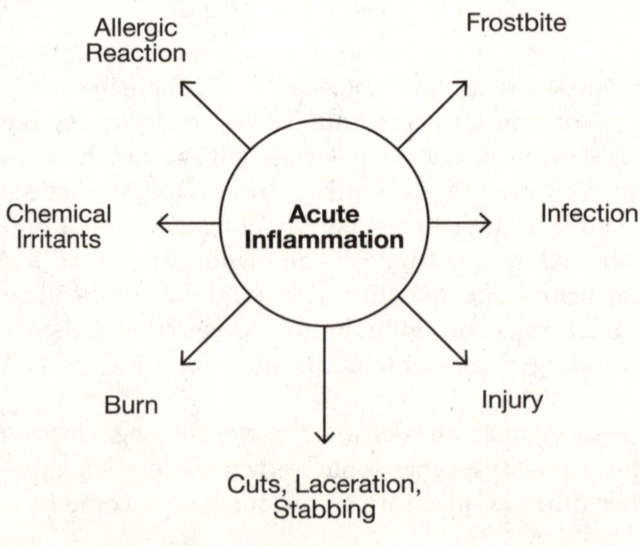

Chronic inflammation is akin to an overstaying guest at a never-ending bash, ignoring your subtle hints to leave. It's at the heart of countless contemporary ailments – Alzheimer's, cancer, heart disease, strokes, multiple sclerosis, ADHD. The cause behind chronic inflammation? Our very own immune system. Picture it as a sophisticated ensemble of cells, tissues, and organs harmoniously working to shield us. Yet, it's akin to a car bristling with sensors; when one sensor malfunctions, chaos ensues. Our bodies, honed for a life of hunting, gathering, and feasting on nature's bounty, find the immune system ill-equipped for today's challenges: fibre stripped sugar-laden diets, toxin exposure, and our penchant for marathon sitting sessions. It's as futile as arming a knight with a rubber sword to slay a dragon.

Disease onset isn't an abrupt explosion but more a slow burn, an ultramarathon, not a sprint. Over the years, a diet poor in nutrition and relentless tissue damage from food-induced inflammation coerces our organs into surrender. Dr Barry Sears, of *The Resolution Zone* fame, captures it perfectly: 'In essence, without robust inflammatory responses, we'd be easy prey for infections, and our wounds would never heal. Yet, when this protective inflammation overstays its welcome, turning against us, the real problems begin'. It's not inflammation per se that's the issue; it's the inflammation that overstays its welcome.

Think of inflammation as our bodily guardian, darting to the rescue against injuries, bacteria, and viruses – it's our damage control hero. But this hero is meant for hit-and-run missions, not everlasting parties. Chronic inflammation sees our immune system stuck in overdrive, endlessly dispatching inflammatory cytokines. And where does inflammation love to hang out? Well, it's a bit of a globe-trotter. You might find it turning up in your digestive system, chatting with your brain, sending electric shockwaves through your nervous system, or even taking a toll on your liver, kidneys, pancreas, joints, and arteries. And if you've been on the lookout for autoimmune diseases, guess what? You'll often find inflammation there too.

Now for the difference between acute and chronic inflammation >

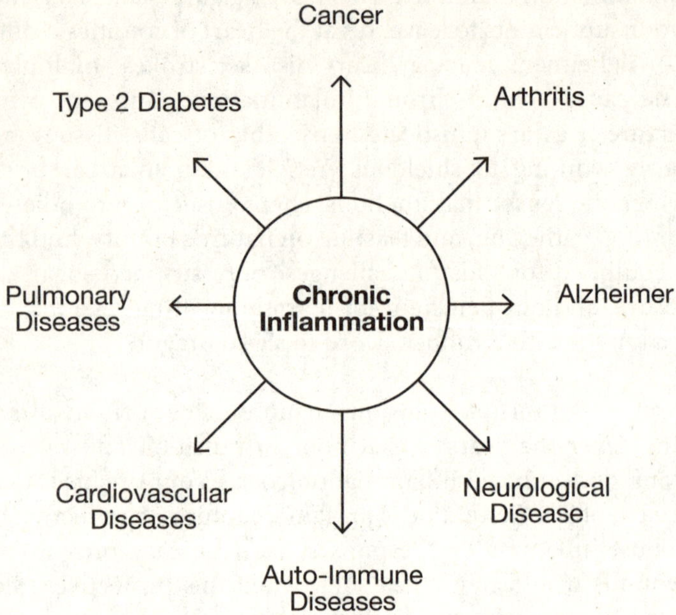

Dr Sears puts it bluntly: *'Today, much of the inflammation is not caused by microbial invasion or injury, but as a consequence of the foods you eat causing diet-induced inflammation that amplifies any existing unresolved inflammation.'* Translation: the inflammation we're dealing with today is largely chronic inflammation, resulting from our dietary choices.

But why should we care about taming this inflammation beast? Well, along with protecting our precious microbiome, avoiding immune conditions and maintaining those elusive long telomeres (we'll get to that soon), managing inflammation is key because it's the puppet master behind most of those chronic illnesses that keep us up at night. But don't despair just yet! There's a silver lining for those who act. Let's look at some exact causes of inflammation and then explore solutions.

Out-of-Balance Omegas

Here's a little secret you won't hear often, mainly because big food corporations aren't fans of spreading it: every food we eat sends instructions to our body's biochemistry. Our bodies constantly create new cells, but what does our typical British diet tell them to do? Welcome to modern day inflammation, or as some call it, the era of 'inflamm-ageing'.

First, let's get acquainted with omega-3 and omega-6. Omega-6 is like the body's handyman when you twist an ankle, break a leg, or face off with a nasty virus. Its mission? Create inflammation to protect the injured area. So, omega-6 is decidedly pro-inflammatory. On the flip side, omega-3 is the peacekeeper. It steps in to dial down the inflammation once it's no longer needed for your safety.

In an ideal world, our diets would maintain a balance between omega-3 and omega-6 fatty acids. Imagine enjoying organic beef from grass-fed cows, where the omega balance approaches 1 to 1 – a nutritional utopia. Yet, the reality shifts dramatically as we navigate the terrain of processed foods, where omega-6 dominates because of its prevalence in cheap ingredients and oils. Consequently, most of us unknowingly consume omega-6 at levels that dwarf omega-3 by approximately 15 times.

The following chart shows how out of balance our current diets are:[1]

Population	**w6/w3**
Paleolithic	0.79
Greece prior to 1960	1.00 – 2.00
Current Japan	4.00
Current India, rural	5 – 6.1
Current UK and northern Europe	15.00
Current USA	16.74
Current India, urban	38 – 50

Now, envision a tour on the dietary highway, especially speeding through the lane earmarked for 'Seed Oils & Vegetable Oils'. This path is a fast track to the unwelcome destination of chronic inflammation. This issue is rooted deeply in my *Tree of Afflictions*, signifying its momentous impact. Indeed, it merits a dedicated discussion, which we'll unfold in chapter 8. This skewed ratio propels us into a relentless cycle of inflammation. To better understand these disproportionate amounts, I invite you to download our free app, Health Results. Within our expansive food database, arguably the most detailed on the globe, you'll discover comprehensive listings of omega-3 to omega-6 ratios amidst other nutritional facts. Here's a sneak preview of some very lopsided and dangerous oils:

Cooking Oils / Fats	Omega 6: Omega 3 Ratio
Corn oil	83 to 1
Cottonseed oil	54 to 1
Grapeseed oil	676 to 1
Palm oil	46 to 1
Safflower oil	133 to 1
Sesame oil	138 to 1
Soy oil	8 to 1
Sunflower oil	40 to 1

Counteracting this modern dietary dilemma involves embracing real, unprocessed foods, befriending oily fish, or integrating a daily omega-3 supplement into our routine. Such choices signal the body to quieten inflammation; however, we must look beyond these out-of-balance equations. The real villainy lies in their origin story. Imagine a scene less pastoral and more sci-fi: instead of being gently pressed from their sources as nature intended, these oils are born of a process involving high-tech gadgetry and a dash of chemical warfare. It's a tale of extraction that would make even a mad scientist wince – high heat, harsh chemicals, and a bit of bleaching and deodorising.

While our bodies sing love songs to olive oil, coconut oil, and the natural fats in meats, they're less whole-hearted about the chemical concoctions of seed oils. Often stripped of any nutritional virtue, these oils undergo a transformation that would make Dr Jekyll wary, becoming less than ideal for our plates and palates. Don't get me started on the carcinogenic cocktail they become, but that's a horror story reserved for chapter 8.

Steer Clear Of The 4Gs

Imagine rambling through the dense jungle of dietary advice, and you come across a signpost marked 'Avoid the 4Gs'– and no, we're not referring to an outdated tech trend that's lost its spark. This sign points you away from a quartet of culprits known for inviting inflammation.

First up, we have Glyphosate, a name that sounds like it belongs to a sci-fi story. The WHO, not known for its love of drama, has tagged it as 'probably carcinogenic to humans'. In layman's terms, it's not your friend, potentially nudging you closer to cancer. This uninvited guest is notorious for crashing the herbicide scene, reigning supreme as the most widely used weed killer on British farms. To sidestep its sneaky presence, make a beeline for organic produce, where glyphosate is shown the door.

Then, we waltz into the territory of Grain, Gluten, and Glucose, the troublesome trio that could easily headline a horror movie in the nutrition world. While I could wax lyrical about their misdeeds, I'll spare you the time since we've already shone the spotlight on glucose. And as for grain and gluten, let's say they're gearing up for their moment in the ring. The bottom line? Too much hobnobbing with these three can lead some of your cells to adopt the shady lifestyle of insulin resistance. And here's the kicker: insulin resistance and inflammation are thicker than thieves, a dynamic duo that spells trouble for your health.

So, as you forge ahead on your quest for a vibrant, chronic inflammation-free existence, remember the 4Gs. It's a simple guide that might clear you of unwanted drama.

Why Not Sleeping Enough Causes Inflammation

When it comes to poor sleep, there's more to it than just groggy mornings. Let's explore one fascinating pathway – it's like a multi-car pileup on the road to inflammation, insulin resistance, and shorter telomeres. Picture this: Your body's sleep-deprived, stressed out, and can't distinguish between the chronic fatigue-induced stress and a lion chasing you (trust me, it happens). So, it calls in the cavalry in the form of the hormone cortisol. Its mission? Shove sugar back into your bloodstream for a quick energy boost, as if you're about to sprint from danger. But with fatigue, there's no imminent peril, and the stress lingers. Now you're stuck with elevated sugar levels, a rather perilous situation.

Cue the arrival of insulin, your sugar-clearing agent. But because the threat of the lion is even greater than the threat of high blood sugar, cortisol momentarily wins the battle, forcing insulin into a frenzy and releasing more and more of its army. But here's the catch: more sugar means more insulin, and eventually, insulin resistance enters, paving the way for inflammation. So, the next time you're tempted to skimp on sleep, remember this tangled web of inflammation and its companions.

Why Exercise is Anti-Inflammatory

Let's take a quick look at exercise and its incredible anti-inflammatory powers. While there's a debate about whether too much long-distance aerobic activity might lean toward the pro-inflammatory side, one thing is clear: some exercise is beneficial. Hippocrates, the wise ancient physician, once said, 'If I could give every individual the right amount of nourishment and exercise, not too little and not too much, we would have found the safest way to health.'

How does moderate exercise wage war against inflammation? When we engage our muscles, they possess a nifty talent; they can gobble up glucose without needing a hand from insulin. So, right off the bat, we lower our glucose levels without causing an insulin rollercoaster. That's a win-win. The genuine stars of the show are walking and resistance training. These activities unleash something called BDNF (brain-derived neurotrophic factor), a superhero molecule that, among other perks, has the power to reduce inflammation. Even the simple act of breaking a sweat is said to be a nifty inflammation reducer.

And Back to the Microbiome

Now, let's revisit our trusty microbiome. While science is still unravelling its secrets, we already know that the bacteria in our gut play a substantial role in igniting and extinguishing inflammation. The good bacteria in our microbiome are like the fearless firefighters, diligently dousing the flames of inflammation. On the flip side, the harmful bacteria behave like Guy Fawkes, on a mission to ablaze our internal infrastructure. Occasionally, Guy Fawkes succeeds in tricking the immune system into launching an inflammatory response when there's no real threat.

Seven Tips to Beat Chronic Inflammation

Let's summarise with seven strategic tips. These pearls of wisdom not only tackle inflammation head-on but also align with strategies for overcoming various health challenges:

1. Embrace the *Fibre First* diet: Make fibre your foodie friend and enjoy plenty of it
2. Steer Clear of Seed Oils: These oils are not your allies in the battle against inflammation
3. Take Omega-3 Daily: Aim for 1 to 2 g to keep inflammation in check
4. Intermittent Fasting: Stay tuned for more on this strategy

5. Fight the 4Gs: Minimise glyphosate, grain, gluten, and glucose
6. Cherish Your Sleep: Prioritise those zzz's
7. Stay Active: Keep moving to keep inflammation at bay

These seven tips are your secret weapons in the fight against inflamm-ageing. Incorporate them into your daily life, and you'll be on the path to a healthier, inflammation-free you!

*****

To Live Longer, Protect Your Telomeres!

It's time to venture into the intriguing universe of our DNA and its lesser-known relative, telomeres. Before you consider glossing over this section, pause! There's some genuinely fascinating information ahead.

Imagine nature as an expert chef, expertly blending a menu where plants consume animals, animals feast on plants, and beings range from the microscopic to those that could be spotted from orbit. DNA, the essence of life's recipe, is at the centre of this biological feast. DNA (Deoxyribonucleic Acid for the linguistically brave) will be our shorthand to avoid linguistic gymnastics. Consider it the ultimate blueprint that dictates everything from the colour of our eyes to how big our hands are.

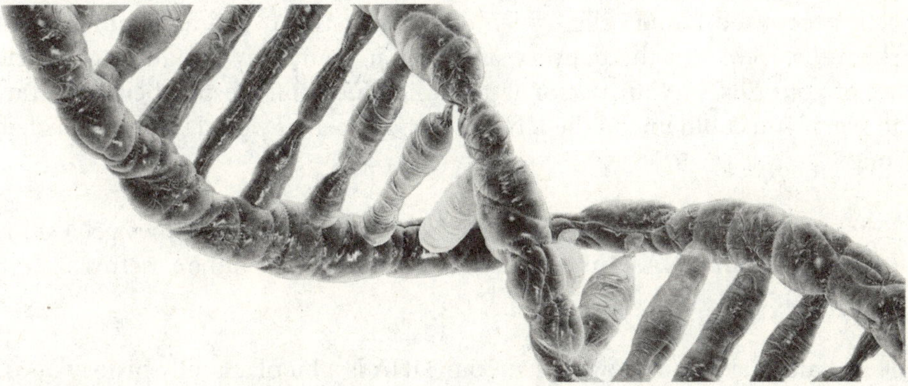

Picture DNA like a twisted ladder – not any pair of ladders but the quirkiest pair in a builder's yard! Here's where it gets interesting. In our ladder analogy, the rungs are called bases, and the two uprights holding those rungs are the backbones. The entire twisted ladder is called a helix.

Those bases (rungs) aren't like the identical steps on a regular ladder. Nope, they come in four different flavours: A (adenine), T (thymine), C (cytosine), and G (guanine). And guess what? Every living creature, from humans to worms, shares these same four letters. It's like a universal alphabet for life.

The complete collection of your DNA is called your genome. Sections of your DNA are called genes, and guess what? We've got about 20,000 genes: the same as a worm! Each gene is like a little subsection (think of it as a small group of ladder rungs) of DNA that holds the code for specific traits, like your hair colour.

Envisage your DNA as an instruction manual; each gene is like a different sentence, carrying unique instructions. To ensure no confusion, every gene is marked with a start and stop code, just like a sentence begins with a capital letter and ends with a full stop. Each of your cells contains not just one ladder but 23 different ones. Each of these is called a chromosome, and you've got two copies of each chromosome, one from mom and one from dad.

Now, the 23rd pair, the grand finale, are known as the sex chromosomes: X and Y. Girls typically have two X chromosomes, while boys have one Y and one X. So, in each cell, you've got 46 chromosomes (more than an elephant or a chicken, by the way). These chromosomes are no joke; some are massive, with one boasting 249 million bases (rungs).

Regarding family resemblance, it's all in the genes, which are found in all cells except red blood cells, which don't carry DNA, and a certain layer of skin cells. Here's the thing: every single cell in your body contains a complete set of your DNA—your personal genomic blueprint. Despite being too tiny to see, if you could uncoil the DNA in just one cell, it would stretch to six feet long!

Brace yourself for this: every time our body creates a new cell, we get a shiny new copy of our DNA. Our bodies churn out about 100 billion metres of fresh DNA each day!

Here's another mind-blowing fact: our DNA is a bit of a family history book. It's passed down only from our mothers. Thanks to this unique inheritance, we can trace our ancestral roots back through many generations. Take Wendy and Mike from Leicester, a brother and sister duo who recently uncovered a jaw-dropping revelation. They found themselves on the same family tree as King Richard III, who met his end in 1485! They compared their DNA to Richard III's skeleton, which was a perfect match. Coincidence, you ask? Well, the odds are so remote that it's like flipping heads on a coin six million times in a row – pretty much impossible!

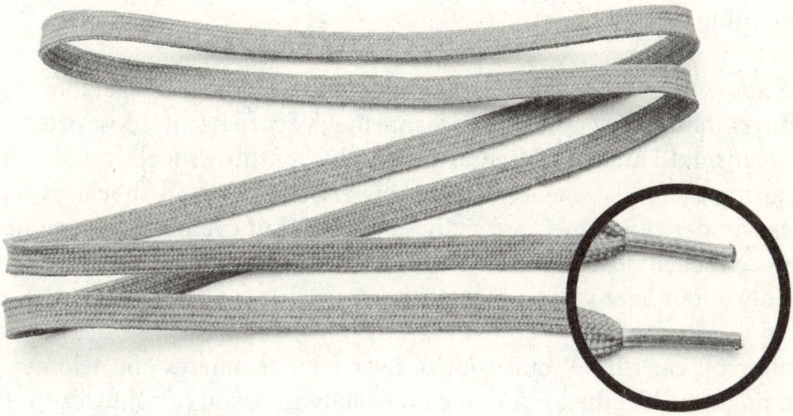

Now, let's shift our focus to telomeres. What on earth are they, you ask? Well, think of the DNA in each chromosome as having protective tips at its ends. Picture these tips as the little plastic aglets you find at the end of shoelaces, but instead, they're made from a protein sheath. While they're much smaller in percentage terms than shoelace aglets, they play a vital role in our cells. Not only do they safeguard the ends of our chromosomes, but they also keep them from sticking together.

Here's where it gets interesting. Some types of human cells have a limited number of times they can divide before they hit a stage called 'senescence'. It's like the last phase before the cell says its goodbyes. What pushes cells into a premature state of senescence? When their telomeres get too short. And as we age, telomeres in our cells naturally tend to get shorter throughout our bodies.

Here's a fascinating titbit: not all cells are created equal regarding renewal. Some cells in our bodies naturally have a higher frequency and longevity of renewal than others. Cells that line our arteries, bones, livers, organs, immune systems, and hair cells are among the speedy renewers. And then, there are the superstar cells: our stem cells. They're the raw materials of our body, responsible for crafting all those specialised cells, and if they stay in good shape, they can divide indefinitely. The same goes for sex cells, and what's their secret weapon? They're best buddies with 'telomerase.'

Telomerase, or telomere terminal transferase, is like a magical enzyme made from proteins. It's the repairman of cellular ageing, working tirelessly to lengthen specific telomeres. This enzyme swoops in after cell division, attempting to patch up the telomeres and slow down or reverse their natural shortening process.

You know those people who seem to defy their biological age, looking years younger than they should? Chances are they've got a healthy dose of telomerase on their side! Think of telomerase as the glue for those shoelace aglets. It keeps repairing them like magic. While it may not work on all shoelaces (cells), it does wonders for some, especially stem cells. But eventually, even our trusty stem cells become a bit too stubborn for telomerase; that's when we age more rapidly in our later years.

While you can't have total control over your telomeres and telomerase (or you might be like the immortal Aurelia jellyfish), you certainly can influence them both. The golden rule to keep those telomeres long and your telomerase production up is to minimise chronic stress. Although there are other factors they like and dislike, research points to chronic stress as their arch-nemesis. Exercise, the same superhero fighting against early ageing's other villains like insulin resistance and inflammation, also plays a key role in looking after our telomeres. Techniques like breathing exercises, mindfulness, and meditation have been shown in studies to preserve our precious telomeres.

In unravelling why stress is the prime factor in telomere shortening, we dive into a fascinating biological conundrum. Is it stress that wears down our telomeres, or does shorter telomeres amp up our stress levels? While this might sound like a plot twist in a science thriller, the current consensus in the research community points towards stress as the villain in this story, actively chipping away at our telomeres' length.

Here's the lowdown: our bodies come equipped with an arsenal of defences against stress, a survival kit meant for short, sharp shocks, like narrowly escaping becoming a lion's lunch or jumping at a sudden bang. This kind of stress, known as acute stress, operates on the hormesis principle: a little of it can make us stronger and more resilient. But when stress overstays its welcome, morphing into a chronic, uninvited guest, that's when the trouble starts. The relentless pressure cranks up our blood pressure and heart rate, keeping us in a perpetual state of high alert.

Enter cortisol, the stress hormone, which boosts our blood sugar levels in the short term to fuel our fight-or-flight response. It's a handy biochemical trick for immediate threats, but when cortisol levels remain high, it's like throwing a wrench in the finely tuned machinery of our body. This persistent hormonal siege messes with insulin, whose job is to regulate our blood sugar, leading to a tug-of-war that our telomeres can't help but lose. When we're constantly under stress, our body prioritises dealing with these immediate 'threats' over the crucial long-term maintenance work, including the care and repair of our telomeres. Although the exact biological playbook of how stress impacts telomere length may vary across studies, the overarching story is clear: chronic stress diverts resources from preserving our cellular longevity, leaving our telomeres to endure the battle.

You may ask, What about food? Did you expect me to leave it out of the equation? Of course not! And don't forget, getting sufficient sleep is part of the stress response package. Food plays a role, too, as telomere damage and inflammation go hand in hand, much like inflammation and insulin resistance travel similar paths. The main culinary culprits shortening your telomeres are seed oils, highly processed fibre-stripped foods, and anything that tips our omega-3 to omega-6 scales out of balance.

In my first health book, *Primal Cure*, under the chapter 'A New You', I shared a mind-boggling revelation: every five or six years, you and I almost become an entirely new person. Our bodies are a constant work in progress, with different parts renewing at different rates. For instance, our skin undergoes a monthly makeover while our entire skeleton regenerates over a decade. Our lungs, liver, and taste buds are on a renewal spree.

Unfortunately, the one body part most of us wish could regenerate at lightning speed, the brain rebuilds much slower. Most other things inside our heads are there to stay. Our eyes don't replace themselves; once our adult teeth arrive, that's the final set. However, the rest of our body is in a perpetual state of repair, rebuild, or replace... or at least it should be. All these incredible feats, including the ability to mend overworked muscles from those intense gym sessions or to bolster our immune cells when we fight infections, are the handiwork of our trusty stem cells. But just like any other cells, if we don't take good care of them via a healthy diet, appropriate exercise, and a good night's sleep, they too can lose their ability to divide and replicate, turning senescent. Senescent cells don't just affect themselves; they send distress signals to neighbouring cells, warning of trouble, which can trigger inflammation and shortened telomeres.

As the founder of a supplement company, you might wonder why I haven't asked my scientists to whip up a supplement that can turbocharge the production of more telomerase. It's a fair question. After all, we've created supplements to boost collagen production and even crafted powerful probiotics to nurture our gut bacteria. So, why not telomerase? The simple answer is that current scientific knowledge suggests it could be risky. If you think about cancer, which at its core involves cells refusing to stop dividing, there's a concern that artificially stimulating telomerase production could backfire.

*****

The Uric Acid Puzzle

Let's don our detective hats for a moment. Picture stumbling upon a headline that declares, 'Sugar's link to early demise isn't solely tied to obesity'. It sounds like the beginning of a contemporary whodunit. In March 2020, the sharp minds at the MRC London Institute of Medical Sciences uncovered a startling revelation in the saga of sugar: a major culprit in sugar-induced early mortality isn't obesity, as one might expect, but a far more elusive antagonist, uric acid.[2]

Peeling Back the Layers on Uric Acid

Think of uric acid as the shadowy figure lurking in the corners of our metabolic health, often overlooked yet immensely influential. It arises from the breakdown of fructose, alcohol, and purines – those crafty components found in our DNA, RNA, and various foods and drinks we consume daily, as well as from certain medications. This breakdown results in uric acid, the end product of purine metabolism in humans, positioning itself as an underappreciated but formidable adversary in the narrative of contemporary illnesses.

Uric Acid's Role: Beyond Gout and Kidney Stones

To understand uric acid's influence, we must look beyond its known associations with gout and kidney stones. This molecule sends ripples through our health, acting as a forewarning of an array of medical conditions, including type 2 diabetes, obesity, hypertension, and a host of cardiovascular issues. Elevated uric acid levels are like the body's alarm bells, signalling a heightened risk of severe health implications. Surprisingly, it emerges as one of the most reliable indicators of diabetes risk, highlighting its critical but often underestimated role in our overall health and longevity.

A Common Thread Among Diseases

David Perlmutter, in his insightful book *Drop Acid*, confronts us with a compelling query: 'What do obesity, insulin resistance, diabetes, non-alcoholic fatty liver disease, hypertension, coronary artery disease, stroke, and neurological disorders, including Alzheimer's disease, and premature death have in common?' The revelation is as astonishing as it is unsettling-high uric acid levels. This revelation places uric acid as a silent accomplice and a central figure travelling alongside insulin resistance, shortened telomeres, mitochondrial disfunction and inflammation.

As we explore the complex narrative of our health, the understanding of uric acid's pivotal role in this story becomes increasingly clear. This tale urges us to look beyond the obvious to unravel the deeper, more subtle connections that profoundly influence our health. Envision uric acid as the silent character in the backdrop of most health dramas, whose presence is felt in each scene without fail. Ready to uncover the main drivers behind the persistent presence of this stealthy saboteur?

Fructose: The Uric Acid Catalyst Unveiled

In the intricate ballet of our metabolism, fructose takes centre stage, donning a deceptive mask. Dr Richard Johnson, an esteemed talent in the uric acid research arena, casts a spotlight on a critical truth: the influence of fructose transcends mere calorie count. High-fructose corn syrup (HFCS), infamous for its purine composition, is notorious for rolling out the red carpet for increased crystal deposits and the ensuing health troubles they herald.

Our story diverges from our fellow mammals, equipped with the uricase enzyme, a natural bouncer that shows uric acid the exit. We humans are left to navigate the aftermath of this uninvited intruder. Recalling our discussion from chapter 3, we recognise that fructose doesn't fuel our energy reserves; instead, it morphs into fat and, paradoxically, drains our energy. This realisation brings us to a dietary crossroads-between the bland allure of starchy potatoes or rice and the sweet temptation of a fructose-laden dessert, the former emerges as the lesser of two evils, sparing us the surge in uric acid levels.

The fructose metabolism resembles a stealthy heist, siphoning off our cells' energy reserves and leaving a trail of metabolic turmoil. The result? A sluggish metabolism and a body strategically shifting gears to storage mode rather than burning fuel. More alarmingly, excessive fructose indulgence is linked to a heightened risk of cognitive impairment, setting the stage for potential dementia. Researchers highlight this sinister liaison, spotlighting the intricate interplay between high fructose consumption, the rise in uric acid, and the ensuing cognitive repercussions. This revelation casts fructose not as a benign sweetener but as a potential metabolic disruptor, intricately woven into the tapestry of our health and wellbeing.

Alcohol: The Unseen Instigator

While a pint of beer might symbolise camaraderie and celebration, it harbours a lesser-known aspect, a contribution to the uric acid tale that's less than celebratory. Alcohol metabolism is a complex affair, with uric acid often slipping in uninvited. It's a nuanced dance, not just about the alcohol itself but the purines it carries, particularly in beer.

However, not all alcoholic beverages are created equal in the realm of gout risk. While any alcohol might induce a uric acid gout flare-up, beer is notorious for increasing this risk more than spirits or white wine. The danger escalates for spirits when they mingle with sugary soft drinks, increasing uric acid. Red wine, known for its higher purine content (like port), also poses a greater risk. In contrast, particularly in moderation, white wine does not share this association, making it a preferable choice for those wishing to enjoy alcohol without entirely abstaining.

Beer takes a leading role in the complex narrative of uric acid dynamics. Brewed with purine-rich brewer's yeast, it significantly elevates uric acid levels. However, alcohol's influence extends beyond merely increasing acid levels. It presents a multifaceted challenge that diminishes the body's ability to process and eliminate this unwelcome guest after arrival.[3]

Navigating the Purine Puzzle in the Metabolic Feast

In the grand banquet of metabolism, purines are ubiquitous yet often overlooked guests. These common chemical compounds are present in two forms: endogenous, produced internally by our bodies, and exogenous, absorbed through the foods we consume. As these purines travel through our system, they leave behind uric acid as a by-product – a testament to our body's natural processes and a potential harbinger of health challenges if left unchecked.

Purines, plentiful in certain seafood like anchovies, sardines, herring, and meats such as bacon and liver, play a starring role in our body's metabolic narrative. Indulging in these purine-rich foods too frequently can lead to an overabundance of uric acid. This scenario serves as a cautionary tale about the importance of dietary diversity. Relying solely on bacon sandwiches for breakfast could expand your waistline because of the bread and invite gout courtesy of the bacon.

Interestingly, not all purine-rich foods are created equal. A large-scale study involving over 45,000 males and a population-based case-control study in Scotland[4] revealed a fascinating twist: moderate intake of purine-rich vegetables like peas, beans, lentils, and mushrooms wasn't associated with increased uric acid levels or gout risk. The underlying reason remains a topic of intrigue, though the high fibre content in these vegetables might play a protective role, hinting at the complex interplay between diet, fibre, and uric acid dynamics.

Dietary Dynamics: The Risk And Reward Matrix

A comprehensive meta-analysis in 2018[6] further unravelled the intricate relationship between our dietary choices and uric acid levels:

Dairy products	44% reduced risk
Coffee	24% reduced risk in men
Vegetables	14% reduced risk
Red meat	29% increased risk
Seafood	31% increased risk
Fructose	114% increased risk
Alcohol	158% increased risk

This matrix of risk and reward paints a vivid picture of how our dietary decisions can sway our uric acid levels, nudging us closer to risk or resilience.

Cherries: Nature's Uric Acid Antagonists

The narrative of diet and uric acid takes a sweet turn with cherries. Research, including a systematic review in 2019[5], celebrated cherries' remarkable ability to lower uric acid levels and reduce the severity of gout attacks. The secret lies in their rich content of flavonoids like anthocyanins and quercetin, which mimic the effects of uric acid-lowering drugs. A mere half-cup of cherries can significantly reduce the risk of gout flares, offering a natural remedy in the fight against elevated uric acid.

Beyond cherries, many fruits, vegetables, herbs, and spices emerge as allies in managing uric acid levels. Blueberries, green peppers, celery, pomegranates, red onions, walnuts, and an array of herbs like cloves, thyme, cardamom, rosemary, peppermint, and oregano contain compounds that inhibit xanthine oxidase, a key enzyme in uric acid production. These natural treasures offer a rich palette of options to orchestrate a diet that not only delights the palate but also fortifies our defence against the stealthy challenges of uric acid.

As we pass through the metabolic feast of life, understanding the role of purines, the protective power of fibre, and the potential of natural uric acid-lowering foods and herbs equips us with the knowledge to traverse this complex landscape. It's a narrative that transforms our dietary choices from mere acts of consumption to strategic decisions, empowering us to write a health story that's not just about surviving but thriving in the intricate dance of metabolism.

Medications: The Underappreciated Meddlers in Uric Acid Levels

While we often scrutinise our diets and lifestyle choices to manage uric acid levels, another player in this intricate game often escapes our attention: medications. Beyond the well-known impact of fructose, alcohol and purine-rich foods, certain medications wield a significant influence on the pathogenesis of hyperuricaemia.[7]

The role of medications in influencing uric acid levels is more than just a footnote in medical texts. In a revealing hospital study, medications emerged as a major factor, contributing to elevated serum uric acid concentrations in up to 20% of subjects grappling with hyperuricaemia[8]. This statistic underscores the pivotal yet often underappreciated darker side of medication and drugs, something we will cover in chapter 8.

Uric Acid: The Puppet Master of Oxidative Stress

Meet your kidneys: two bean-shaped marvels tucked under your ribs, each striving to be the most valuable player of your body's filtration league. Picture them as the unsung heroes, about the size of a clenched fist, working tirelessly in the background. These champs daily filter 180 litres of blood, control red blood cell production, and release hormones to keep your blood pressure in check. Not just content with these feats, they also take on waste management by producing urine and doubling as bone health promoters by aiding in vitamin D production.

However, the party turns when kidneys drop the ball, failing to filter out the bad guys. Uric acid builds up, leading to a cascade of unwelcome health risks. Imagine this scenario: your kidneys, once vibrant, are now struggling to keep the peace as harmful wastes accumulate, blood pressure spikes and your body becomes a waterlogged vessel, showcasing the latest ankle-swelling fashion and introducing you to the unwanted sensation of breathing underwater.

Kidney disease affects about 3.5 million people in the UK[9]. And here's the problem: this plot has no Hollywood ending in sight and often closes tragically without a hero stepping in for a transplant.

Uric acid, this silent saboteur, incites oxidative stress, squeezing our blood vessels tighter than a boxer's fist, making our hearts work overtime. Imagine your heart, the diligent worker, now forced to pump blood with the enthusiasm of someone doing taxes. Here's an interesting fact: uric acid levels hit their peak performance around four to five in the morning – coincidentally the prime time for heart attacks to take centre stage. It also plays the antagonist to nitric oxide (NO), a molecule essential for a standing ovation-worthy cardiovascular performance. By overshadowing NO, uric acid not only hampers insulin function but sets the stage for cardiovascular chaos.

Exercise: Striking the Right Balance

Recent research has shed light on the role of exercise in managing uric acid levels. This relationship follows a U-shaped curve: excessive strenuous exercise can increase tissue ATP turnover, elevating the purine pool and, consequently, uric acid levels. Conversely, too little exercise also poses the risk of elevated uric acid. A study from South Korea in 2019 revealed that individuals who spent ten or more hours a day sitting were more likely to have hyperuricaemia than those who were less sedentary.[10]

The Gut Microbiome: A Key Player in the Uric Acid Story

Exploring the uric acid narrative further, we discover the pivotal role of our gut microbiome. Studies intriguingly label the harmful bacteria linked to high uric acid levels as 'gout bacteria'. Researchers have identified seventeen gout-associated bacteria capable of predicting gout diagnoses with remarkable accuracy simply by analysing the gut microbiome.[11] The similarity between the gut microbiome of gout patients and those with type 2 diabetes or other metabolic syndrome features underscores the profound interconnectedness between uric acid, our gut, and our overall metabolic health.

Nourishing this crucial ecosystem involves incorporating fibre-rich and fermented foods like kimchi and yoghurt and prebiotic foods such as garlic, onions, leeks, and asparagus. These prebiotics act as a fertiliser for gut microbes, fostering their growth and contributing to a healthier gut environment. Interestingly, many prebiotic foods also inhibit the enzyme responsible for uric acid production, offering a dual benefit. Embracing an organic diet and steering clear of genetically modified organisms (GMOs) further supports the vitality of the gut microbiome, solidifying its role in managing uric acid levels and overall health.

A Pillar of Hope in the War on Uric Acid

Despite the ominous shadow it casts, the narrative of uric acid isn't solely a tale of doom and gloom. Amidst the darkness, there's a flicker of hope. Embracing simple lifestyle changes, ensuring quality sleep, engaging in regular exercise, reducing certain medications, and incorporating dietary treasures such as cherries, coffee, omega-3s, vitamin C, and quercetin can tip the scales in our favour. These actions help restore harmony in uric acid levels, offering hope in our quest for health and wellbeing.

Quercetin: The Multifaceted Nutrient

Quercetin, a crucial dietary polyphenol and a member of the flavonoid family, stands out due to its potent antioxidant, anti-inflammatory, and antipathogenic properties. This vibrant pigment, responsible for colouring a myriad of plants, serves as a powerful immune regulator and may play a role in slowing down the progression of degenerative diseases. Found in various fruits and vegetables – including apples, berries, onions (particularly red onions), cherry tomatoes, broccoli, and other leafy greens – quercetin is not just a feast for the eyes but a boon for health.

Recent findings suggest that quercetin supplementation could offer positive effects not just on uric acid levels but also in preventing neurodegenerative diseases. In laboratory settings, quercetin has shown promise in reducing the build-up of harmful plaque proteins associated with Alzheimer's disease and inhibiting the formation of AGEs (advanced glycation end products) in the body.[12] Remarkably, quercetin shines as a champion in lowering uric acid levels by inhibiting xanthine oxidase, an enzyme essential in the final step of uric acid production. A notable study in 2016 demonstrated that a daily intake of quercetin significantly reduced uric acid levels in healthy adults whose levels were high but within the normal range.[13]

Omega-3 DHA: The Brain-Boosting Powerhouse

DHA, or docosahexaenoic acid, an omega-3 fatty acid, has garnered widespread attention for its pivotal role in brain health. DHA is a fundamental building block for brain cell membranes, particularly synapses, at the heart of efficient brain function.

It reduces inflammation in the brain and body and appears to elevate brain-derived neurotrophic factor (BDNF), fostering the growth of new neurons. Intriguingly, DHA counters inflammation in the gut triggered by poor diets and mitigates the detrimental effects of high-sugar diets, particularly those rich in fructose. This dynamic relationship between DHA and fructose is especially relevant in managing uric acid levels, adding another layer to the multifaceted benefits of this omega-3 powerhouse.

Vitamin C: The Uric Acid-Lowering Hero

Vitamin C, often celebrated in gout management, is a formidable ally in the fight against elevated uric acid. Its efficacy is well-documented, with studies underscoring its ability to reduce the risk of gout flare-ups significantly. A comprehensive study spanning two decades revealed that individuals supplementing with vitamin C experienced a 44% reduction in gout risk.[14]

Vitamin C's effectiveness is attributed to its ability to increase the urinary excretion of uric acid, potentially decrease uric acid reabsorption in the kidneys, and its role as a potent antioxidant in reducing tissue damage that could lead to increased uric acid production.

Navigating the Numbers

In the intricate ballet of our bodily functions, uric acid doesn't move to the quick tempo of glucose, which spikes and plummets post-meal. It's more of a slow dance, subtly reflecting the nuances of our overall metabolic health. Unlike glucose, for which we have continuous glucose monitors (CGM), uric acid doesn't offer the convenience of real-time tracking. It's a slow burner, rising and descending gradually, making it a parameter best measured perhaps once a week to gauge your metabolic harmony.

	umol/L	umol/L	mmol/L	mmol/L	mg/dL	mg/dL
	Male	Female	Male	Female	Male	Female
Good	200-430	140-360	0.2 to 0.43	0.14 to 0.36	above 2	above 2
Not so good	430-700	360-600	0.43 to 0.7	0.36 to 0.6	2 to 7	2 to 6
Warning	above 700	above 600	above 0.7	above 0.6	above 7	above 6

Let's navigate through the chart, a curated compilation of data from diverse sources designed to offer you insightful guidance. Understand that these figures represent reference ranges, the benchmarks where 95% of the population typically lives according to medical standards. However, it's crucial to understand that these ranges can fluctuate, subject to variations in source material, differing perspectives among laboratories, and even regional health guidelines, and they are only relevant to adults.

The chart endeavours to provide a holistic overview, harmonising American measurements with benchmarks deemed 'optimal' by the NHS and contrasted against cautionary figures from arthritis.org. It's a nuanced tool, not just a collection of numbers, but a resource poised to offer clarity and direction in your health journey.

The chart is a roadmap for better managing uric acid levels. This measurement, often overshadowed by the spotlight on glucose, holds immense significance. When we were crafting our HRM360 device (see page 954), a pioneering home medical testing device, we made sure to include the capability to measure uric acid. It's not just a gauge of your inner health; it's a mirror reflecting your relationship with fructose.

I've observed the most significant drops in uric acid levels when individuals pivot their diets away from the snares of corporatised food. The most dramatic transformations often occur when fizzy pops and fruit juices are left behind. So, as you peruse this chart, remember it's more than just a guide-it's a testament to the power of dietary choices and a path to better health.

*****

The Health Of Our Mitochondria

Professor Robert Lustig recently skilfully delineated the realms of food science, nutrition, and metabolic health, to which I couldn't help but add a sprinkle of my own seasoning.

Food Scientists: They are the globe-trotters, mapping the epic voyage of our meals from soil to salsa, from farm to fork.

Nutritionists: They are the meticulous tour guides who ensure that once ingested, our food embarks on the most nourishing journey from mouth to cell, akin to ensuring every tourist sees the sights.

Metabolic Health Specialists: They are engineer-minded individuals fascinated by the inner workings of the cell's power stations, the mitochondria, and how they convert the food we use into energy.

Now, why mention the above? Because, at the end of the day, everything health-related boils down to just a handful of concerns. How insulin-sensitive are our cells? How well does the body control inflammation? Are we protecting our telomeres? And how healthy are our mitochondria? But what exactly are our mitochondria?

Each cell in our vast bodily universe, of which we have around 100 trillion (100,000,000,000,000), is a bustling metropolis comprised of approximately 100 trillion atoms (both the same number at last, some easy to remember). Within these cellular cities lie various tiny organelles (the organs of the cell), each performing its vital tasks—think of them as the municipal workers of the cellular world. Arguably, the most crucial organelle for us to nurture is our mitochondria.

Imagine your body as a lush forest, where the most vibrant ecosystems: our brain, heart (each heart muscle cell hosting over 5,000 mitochondria), muscles, eyes, and, let's not overlook our brown adipose tissue (BAT) fat, celebrated for its high mitochondrial density, burst with life. These areas are the heartlands of mitochondrial abundance, pulsating with the energy necessary for every heartbeat, glance, movement, and thought. Standing apart in this vibrant forest are the red blood cells, the unique flora without these power-generating organelles. This lack of mitochondria is by design, as it allows red blood cells to efficiently transport oxygen without using it up themselves. However, this also means they don't live very long, circulating for about 120 days before being renewed, a fleeting existence in the body's bustling ecosystem.

The mitochondria's primary role is to provide energy to the rest of the cell. If each body cell were a city, mitochondria would be the energy plant or electricity board. If a cell were a toy, the mitochondria would be the battery that brings it to life. We host millions of billions of mitochondria, accounting for about 10% of our body weight. Imagine carrying around a sack of potatoes made entirely of mitochondria!

Dr Robert Lustig, during a recent Andrew Huberman podcast, said, '*For all of the chronic diseases that we are suffering from Type two diabetes, hypertension, dyslipidaemia, cardiovascular disease, cancer, dementia, fatty liver disease, Polycystic Ovarian disease, those eight diseases, which make up 75% of healthcare expenditures in this country [USA] today are all inside the cell because they are all mitochondrial dysfunctions. And there is no medicine that gets to the mitochondria.*'

Atp And The Krebs Cycle

As mentioned, the mitochondria's primary role is to turn the food we eat into energy. It does this through something known as the Krebs cycle. Also known as the TCA cycle (tricarboxylic acid cycle), it is a series of biochemical reactions that release the energy stored in food into ATP, the fuel of our cells.

Who do we thank for uncovering this cellular powerhouse? Enter Hans Krebs, a brilliant scientist who mapped out this complex merry-go-round of energy transformation. For his groundbreaking work, Krebs was honoured with the Nobel Prize in 1953, cementing his legacy in the annals of science.

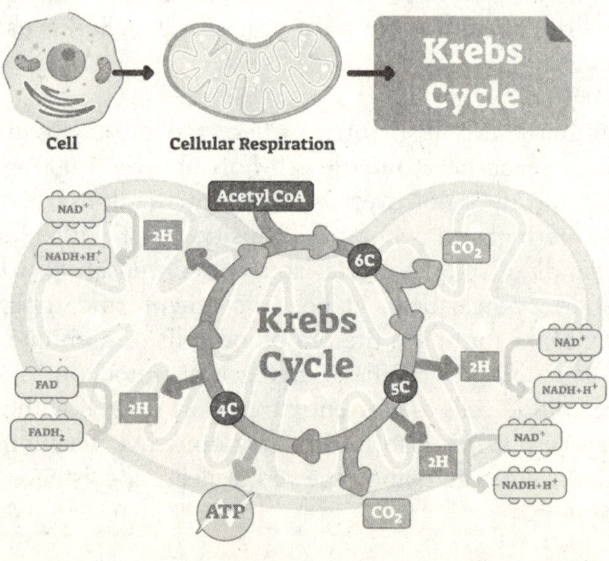

The Krebs cycle is an intricate dance of molecules in an eight-step process. It begins with a tiny but mighty player known as an acetyl group, a duo of carbon atoms bound together, ready to embark on a transformative journey. This acetyl group hitches a ride on a carrier molecule, acetyl-CoA, and is then oxidised, sparking the cycle into motion. This leads to the production of two molecules of CO2, a molecule of ATP, the currency of energy in the body, and high-energy compounds NADH (nicotinamide adenine dinucleotide) and FADH2 (flavin adenine dinucleotide), which are like the charged batteries of the cell. Don't worry about memorising all the technical details, except to note that NAD will be discussed later when we explore pathways to becoming a healthy centenarian. For now, just try to remember these steps:

- We eat food.
- That food reaches the cell (except fibre, which fuels our bacteria), where our mitochondria produce roughly 90% of the energy our cells require.
- The mitochondria convert food to ATP via the Krebs cycle.
- The Krebs cycle consists of eight complex steps.

The mitochondria, our cellular powerhouses, are tasked with a Herculean challenge: producing vast amounts of adenosine triphosphate (ATP) every second of every day, a necessity dictated by the body's inability to store ATP. This relentless demand ensures our mitochondria must operate with unwavering efficiency and vitality, as ATP, the crucial energy currency of the body, is required on demand. Amplifying this challenge is the astonishing fact that a healthy individual generates their body weight in ATP daily[15], a testament to our mitochondrial workforce's extraordinary and continuous effort, in an energy production process unmatched by any storage system known to science.

For completeness, not all food is catabolised (broken down) in the mitochondria; some glucose metabolism takes place in the cytosol (the fluid part of the cell) without the need for oxygen by a process termed glycolysis, which yields a small amount of ATP.

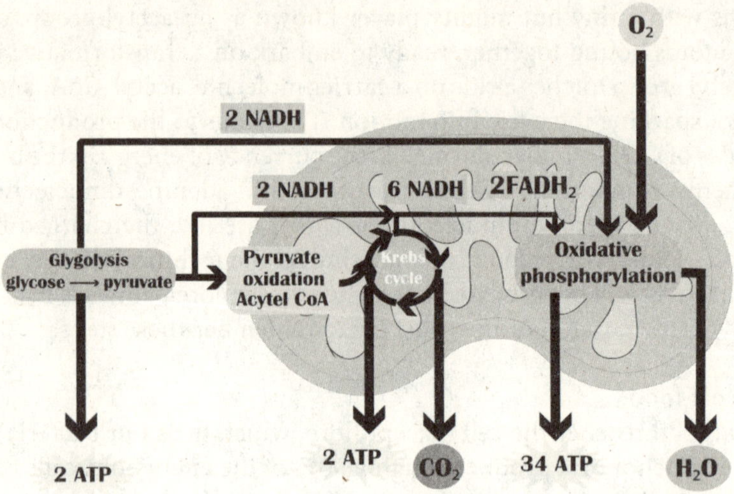

Protecting our microscopic mitochondria might be as crucial to our health as keeping our insulin on a tight leash. It seems both tasks stroll down the promenade hand in hand. Live a life that whispers sweet nothings to your insulin, and you're serenading your mitochondria with a love song, tending both their quality and volume.

Despite their capability to process glucose, mitochondria are like gourmet chefs with a taste for the finer things—namely healthy fats, particularly the elite ketones. It's now understood that pampering these pivotal cellular components with their preferred diet of healthy fats is crucial for maintaining a robust physique.

Mitochondrial Biogenesis

It's not just about quality but also quantity. Through the process known as mitochondrial biogenesis, we can increase the quantity of mitochondria within each cell. You may have heard about a book called *The Blue Zones*, in which author Dan Buettner studied areas in the world with high concentrations of centenarians. While I agree with some of the author's discoveries, one thing was missing. Most of these centenarians lived at altitude, which is known to help facilitate mitochondrial biogenesis.[16]

Also, by braving the cold baths and cold showers and engaging in exercise, particularly the kind that lets you catch your breath—like a leisurely jog or a brisk walk—we can increase these cellular powerhouses.[17] We will discuss mitochondrial biogenesis a little later when we discuss the benefits of light aerobic exercise and also under the discussion of cold therapy.

Fructose and the Mitochondria

Imagine your body is like a car, and your mitochondria are the engine that powers it. Everything must be in tip-top shape for your car to run smoothly and efficiently, especially the engine. Now, ATP is like the fuel for your body's engine, giving it the energy to do its job. But here's where fructose comes into play, in a bad way. Think of fructose as a troublemaker sneaking into your car's engine and causing mischief with two important parts.

First, it messes with a part called AMP kinase, which is like the fuel gauge of your liver cell. This gauge tells your liver it's time to make more mitochondria (or more engines) to keep your energy levels up. But fructose acts like gum stuck in the keyhole, preventing the key (in this case, the signal to make more mitochondria) from working. This means your body can't produce the extra engines it needs, slowing everything down. Biologically speaking, it impedes AMP kinase, which you need for mitochondrial biogenesis.

Secondly, fructose affects the enzyme that helps transport fatty acids into the mitochondria, where they can be turned into energy. This is similar to if someone blocked the fuel line in your car, preventing petrol from reaching the engine. Without this, your body struggles to convert food into energy.

So, fructose can cause a lot of trouble for your body's engine (mitochondria) by blocking and clogging up important parts that are needed for it to run smoothly and produce energy.

As we wrap up our exploration, it's crucial to spotlight ten culprits that could be undermining the health of your mitochondria:

1. Lack of fibre
2. Fructose
3. Stress
4. Seed oils (excessive omega 6)
5. Smoking
6. Alcohol
7. Lack of Exercise
8. Sleep Deprivation
9. Toxins
10. Certain medications

The Asian Paradox: The New Battle Ground For Uric Acid

Let me share how the fructose frenzy, deeply entrenched in our Western diet, casts its shadow across the globe. Armed with my trusty HRM360 machine (my constant travel companion), my travels have unveiled a concerning trend: high uric acid levels far from home, even among the folks in India. It's as if my *Tree of Afflictions* has grown roots worldwide. Pondering over this during a recent visit to India, a question emerged: how did Asia, with its hearty servings of rice and potatoes, manage to dodge the obesity bullet until relatively recently?

Enter fructose, the silent accelerant in this metabolic inferno. As we explore further, fructose and glucose stand on either side of you, with glucose leading to insulin resistance from one avenue and fructose through a different pathway. It's like being caught in a metabolic crossfire, a potent mix that Asia had mostly sidestepped until modern dietary habits took hold.

The modern world's embrace of obesity as the new norm is a narrative woven from our dietary choices. We took inspiration from wartime rationing in Britain, advocating for 'little but often'. However, our translation of this advice led us down a path of three to four mammoth meals daily, lacking in fibre but heavy on sugar. And as if that wasn't enough, we adopted the art of snacking between meals, inspired by relentless TV commercials, turning our insulin levels into a never-ending theme park ride of spikes.

With the incursion of Western fast food into Asia, epitomised by the spread of McDonald's and Coca-Cola, a diet chock-full with commercial snacks and sugary beverages has taken hold. In a podcast discussion with Dr Jason Fung, we delved into the 'Asian Paradox,' observing that although a steady diet of carbohydrates might underpin obesity and diabetes, the introduction of abundant fructose accelerates these health issues. Essentially, the traditional high-carb diet of rice and potatoes, consumed in moderation, didn't pose significant health risks in Asian populations. However, the situation escalated when these were paired with Western fructose-heavy foods and an increased meal frequency, exacerbating the health crisis.

Having frequented India and China for business over the last three decades, I've witnessed a seismic shift in health trends. Ailments like obesity, cancer, and heart disease, once rarities, are now on the rise, painting a dire picture of the impact of our exported lifestyles. This unsettling transformation has spurred our family charity to action, hiring Neha Dua, a dedicated nutritionist, to educate students in Jaipur, India (home to our offices since 2006) about the dangers lurking behind the allure of Western fast food. Just as we are in the UK, we're determined to impact young minds positively and steer them away from these health pitfalls.

Chapter 6

Unravelling the Tangled Web of Modern Illnesses

Chapter 6 marks a crucial juncture in our passage through the landscape of contemporary health challenges. This chapter investigates what Dr Ben Bikman aptly calls the 'plague of prosperity', with insulin resistance looming ominously. However, despair not. We're about to uncover that many of these disorders come with a silver lining – preventable aspects that, when addressed, can significantly alter our health trajectory. In the third part of this book, I'll equip you with strategies and insights on how to sidestep these widespread conditions, illuminating a path towards a healthier future.

In the pages ahead, we examine the myriad of chronic diseases and illnesses that have insidiously woven into the fabric of contemporary life. Prepare to uncover startling connections between these ailments and the dietary felons in our midst: the glaring absence of fibre and the rampant consumption of processed sugar-laden foods. This expedition is an intricate dissection of the cascading effects these dietary choices initiate. From sugar's relentless siege on our bodies fostering insulin resistance to the desolation of our gut flora craving fibre to the silent inferno of inflammation wreaking havoc within.

While fibre is not a cure-all, its critical role in this saga is undeniable. The conditions we'll explore, foreign to our ancestors and absent in the last untouched sanctuaries of civilisation, are bound by a complex web of cause and effect. This chapter aims to list these conditions and reveal their shared, sinister underpinnings.

A heads-up: as we pass through these intertwined diseases, you may notice recurring themes. Roam this chapter at your leisure, knowing that while some repetition is inevitable, each condition adds a unique shade to the narrative, enriched by subtle distinctions and specific symptoms. This chapter is a compendium of cutting-edge research, shedding light on the intricate dance of common causes and diverse effects.

This chapter probes into the biological underpinnings of the constellation of diseases that define modern malaise. Consider it more a reference guide than a linear narrative. Use it to zero in on the conditions that intrigue you most. While you might stumble upon some technical terms, this detail is meant to enlighten healthcare professionals and researchers about the interconnections at play.

The strategic positioning of this chapter before Part III is deliberate, highlighting the crucial link between various health conditions and their common denominators. This foundational knowledge sets the stage for the book's subsequent sections, offering a comprehensive understanding of the transformative power of the *Fibre First* diet.

Without this chapter, the narrative would be incomplete, leaving readers without a full appreciation of this approach's extensive benefits in combating a spectrum of modern illnesses. It represents a collective endeavour with distinguished doctors and professors. While the concepts presented were crystal clear during its creation, a subsequent review sometimes nudged me back to the dictionary for clarity. It's rich with biological terminology, yet it underscores a crucial point: the health challenges we discuss are branches of the same tree, intertwined and interrelated, not isolated incidents. Consider this chapter a springboard for further exploration. Use it as a tool for deeper inquiry, but if you're eager to learn how to evade these health pitfalls, feel free to leap to Part III.

A gentle reminder: this chapter is not medical advice. If you're dealing with any of these conditions or have concerns, please consult your doctor. Use this information to enrich your understanding and spur further questions, not as a substitute for professional guidance. While I trust in the accuracy of the content, distilled from a network of leading experts, individual variations and the rapid evolution of medical knowledge mean that nuances always exist. And remember, as mentioned at the very outset of this book, medical knowledge now expands so swiftly that it doubles every six months.[1]

Modern Day Chronic illnesses

- Insulin resistance
- Obesity
- Type 2 diabetes
- Inflammation
- Heart disease and stroke
- Cancer
- Non-Alcoholic Fatty Liver Disease (NAFLD)
- Osteoporosis

Neurological Disorders: A Metabolic Perspective

- Alzheimer's: the third type of diabetes
- Depression and anxiety: a new perspective
- Epilepsy: a metabolic rethink
- Parkinson's disease: the dopamine connection
- Neuropathy: nervous about insulin
- Migraines: a metabolic mystery
- Bipolar disease: the two views

Reproductive Wellness

- Decoding polycystic ovary syndrome
- Infertility and insulin
- Say NO to erectile dysfunction
- Low testosterone and diet
- Menopause, fibre and insulin resistance
- Navigating the waves of menstruation

Other Health Conditions

- Leaky gut syndrome
- Gout: a royal pain
- Heartburn and acid reflux: a new perspective
- Tinnitus: turning down the volume on internal buzz
- Crohn's and colitis: the role of fibre and SCFAs
- Arthritis: the dual facets of joint pain
- Sarcopenia: the silent muscle thief and how to outlift it
- Acne: unveiling the body's inner secrets
- Eczema: the skin's whisper of discontent
- Allergies: unravelling the puzzle

Are you tethered to the same health fate as your parents? If heart disease, Alzheimer's, or cancer shadowed your family tree, is it inevitable that you'll tread the same path? Let's unravel this genetic tapestry to reveal how much sway we hold over our health destiny.

*****

Is Illness Written In Your Genes?

Before we plunge into this chapter, I'd like to reassure you that the illnesses we're about to explore are not preordained fates sealed by your DNA. Dr Mark Hyman offers an enlightening perspective in the foreword of Dr Izabella Wentz's *Hashimoto's Protocol*, 'Genes are not your destiny... while genetics may load the gun, it's the environment that pulls the trigger'. To put it another way, think of it like poker: our genes deal us our hand, but how we play those cards determines our health outcomes.

If you've ever thought, 'Why bother with a healthy lifestyle when illness runs in my family?' I urge you to consider the field of epigenetics. The prefix 'epi-' means 'over' or 'on top of', and when combined with genetics, it explores the concept of how much of our make-up is inherited versus environmentally induced. The study of epigenetics seeks to uncover the extent to which we are shaped by inherited traits versus those we gain through our lifestyle. After studying epigenetics in detail, I've become convinced that we wield far more influence over our health destinies than previously imagined.

It's imperative to remember that numerous diseases we currently fear, such as Alzheimer's, heart disease, and diabetes, are relatively recent phenomena. Just a century ago, they were virtually unheard of, indicating that their swift emergence cannot be attributed to genetic factors.

My personal history might suggest a grim outlook: three of my four grandparents, along with my beloved Auntie Avis, succumbed to cancer. Decades ago, when they passed, the understanding of what triggered these diseases was not as advanced as it is today. It might appear that a genetic predisposition to cancer looms over my family, but I challenge that notion. I believe that our genes play a minimal role in the onset of modern diseases, which I argue are largely the result of drastic lifestyle shifts away from nature's blueprint for us. If we embrace Dr Hyman's analogy that genetics merely 'load the gun', but our environment pulls the trigger' – then we must acknowledge our capacity to influence our health outcomes. Or, as I teach my children, 'If it's to be, it's up to me.'

The myth of weight predetermined by genes

The idea that being overweight is etched into our DNA is a misconception that's been thoroughly debunked. It's understandable to think this way, especially when entire families seem to share the same weight struggles. However, a groundbreaking study blew this theory wide open. By analysing the DNA of over a quarter of a million people, researchers sought to pinpoint the genetic culprits behind obesity. Out of the 21,000 genes swirling in our genetic pool, a mere 32 were implicated in weight management.[2]

The impact of these genes was so minimal that the weight difference between individuals at opposite ends of the genetic lottery was a paltry 7.7 kg (17 lb). This finding suggests that, in the grand scheme of things, our genes might be responsible for a smidgen more than a stone in weight – hardly the jackpot in the genetic lottery of obesity.

In his illuminating book The Disease Delusion, Dr Jeffrey S. Bland eloquently states, 'We are not hardwired to succumb to the ailments that plagued our ancestors.' His work underscores a powerful message: our genetic make-up does not seal our health fate. Instead, it hands us the reins to sculpt our health trajectory and longevity.

Reflecting on obesity rates adds another layer to this perspective. When I entered the world in 1966, a slim 1.5% of Brits were classified as obese. Fast-forward to the present day, and that figure has ballooned to 28%. This sharp increase in obesity within just a couple of generations underscores a critical point: obesity is a modern construct, not a genetic inheritance. In essence, while our genes may suggest a preference for certain foods or lifestyles, the vast majority of our health outcomes lie squarely within our control. Our genetic inheritance may deal us our hand, but it's how we play those cards, through lifestyle choices, dietary habits, and physical activity, that truly shapes our health and longevity.

The age-old debate of nature versus nurture takes a fascinating twist with the introduction of epigenetics. Epigenetics shows us that while we can't swap our genetic code, we certainly can influence how that code is read. Imagine your genetics as a script—written, fixed, unchangeable. But the performance of that script? That's where your environment and lifestyle choices step into the spotlight, directing the play of your life with every action you take.

Pondering whether the health challenges faced by our parents or grandparents, heart disease, Alzheimer's, cancer – are mere previews of our own health destinies is a daunting thought. Yet, this narrative offers a plot twist: our choices wield the power to rewrite our stories. Consider the notion of increased susceptibility to diseases that plagued our ancestors. It's akin to inheriting a map where X marks the spot of potential health pitfalls. But here's the empowering part: we're equipped with the tools to navigate around those X's, charting a course toward a healthier destiny.

While there's a whisper of truth to the idea that we may inherit a predisposition to specific ailments, the power of lifestyle and dietary choices sings much louder. In the enlightening pages of *Optimum Nutrition Made Easy*, Patrick Holford sheds light on the subject with compelling evidence: a study tracking 44,000 twins found only 27% of health risks rooted in genetics. Thus, a whopping 73% hinges on external factors like diet and lifestyle, suggesting Alzheimer's and other diseases often attributed to genetics actually bow to our daily choices.

This doesn't mean we dismiss our genetic blueprint; instead, we recognise it as a guide, not a dictator. If the spectre of familial diseases looms, it's not a death sentence but a call to arms. A call to enrich our plates with wholesome fibrous foods and lead an active life to keep those rogue genes in check. Our genetic heritage is not a fixed star guiding our health; it's more like a compass susceptible to recalibration based on our actions. The dramatic surge in cancer rates from 1 in 20 to 1 in 2 within a century isn't a tale of genetic doom but a reflection of our lifestyle shifts.

If your family history reads like a medical textbook of modern maladies, it doesn't mean you're destined to follow in those footsteps. Instead, it's a call to action – a sign that adopting a more natural lifestyle, cutting down on refined sugars, embracing intermittent fasting, and committing to regular exercise aren't just good practices. They're your personal health insurance, a proactive defence against a predisposition to disease. Don't worry; we will soon cover intermittent fasting and exercise in detail.

The dynamics of fat cells: are yours growing, or are you creating new ones?

Okay, while most things aren't in the genes, here is one that, for some people, means while they may become obese, they might not become insulin resistant and, therefore, not as susceptible to the full constellation of diseases accompanying it. This nuanced genetic variation underlines a fascinating aspect of how our bodies manage fat, a process that's both universal and unique.

The dance of lipid storage and release within the fat cells of adipose tissue plays a pivotal role in the intricate ballet of energy balance regulation. During infancy and adolescence, adipose tissue undergoes significant growth, primarily through an increase in the number of fat cells and, to a lesser extent, the size of these cells. As individuals transition into adulthood, the number of fat cells tends to stabilise despite a substantial turnover rate; about 10% of fat cells are renewed annually when body weight remains constant.

Interestingly, weight loss in adults typically reduces fat cell size alone, while weight gain can trigger an increase in both the size and the number of fat cells. A crucial source for the renewal of fat cells throughout life is the bone marrow, especially notable in cases of obesity, where approximately 20% of all fat cells originate from this location.[3]

The turnover of fat cells also influences their size; a low turnover rate can lead to larger fat cells, which is associated with increased risks of cardiovascular diseases and type 2 diabetes. This raises the question: why do most overweight individuals develop insulin resistance while a select few, even some who are significantly overweight, manage to evade the condition?

Dr Ben Bikman shed light on this conundrum at a recent conference, introducing a perspective on the mechanisms of sugar intake by cells. He outlined two pathways: one where cells continue to absorb increasing amounts of energy (from glucose and fats) and another where, for some, their body opts to create more fat cells to accommodate the excess energy. Interestingly, the choice between these pathways is primarily dictated by our genetics. Those predisposed to having their existing fat cells merely expand are at a higher risk of becoming insulin resistant. Conversely, individuals whose genetic make-up favours the creation of new fat cells equipped with adept insulin receptors are less likely to face insulin resistance. The dilemma arises when the body's inclination to store more fat, rather than generating new 'fat depots', leads to fat cells becoming overly saturated and beginning to leak fat back into the bloodstream.

Despite the genetic hand one is dealt, the pathway to improved health remains consistent: prioritise a fibre-rich diet and address the root causes of illness as illustrated in my *Tree of Affliction* diagram.

*****

Insulin Resistance

In the world of health, it's vital to remember that the development of chronic diseases isn't a blame game. It's not a matter of pointing fingers at individuals and assigning fault. No, these conditions are more like intricate concertos, with various factors playing their unique tunes. At their core, though, is a common thread – prolonged high blood sugar levels.

We've touched on this concept since the first chapter, but let's add a splash of colour to that canvas here. It's not an individual's fault; it's a result of their environment, the food options they are presented with, and often the lifestyle they lead.

You might wonder, 'Isn't insulin resistance just another way of saying type 2 diabetes?' Well, not quite. You see, insulin resistance often begins its subtle dance many years before the grand reveal of full-blown type 2 diabetes. It's like jet lag creeping up on you, slowly but surely. Diabetes only takes the spotlight when your elevated insulin levels can no longer keep your blood sugar levels in check.

Imagine if more people could get an early warning sign, a sneak preview of becoming insulin resistant, aka pre-diabetic. We could prevent so much needless suffering. That's precisely why my team invented our HRM360 home test machine – a tool to help individuals measure their current levels of insulin sensitivity (see page 954).

And then, there's the wisdom of Professor Tim Noakes, someone I've had the pleasure of interviewing extensively. He echoes what we've been discovering – insulin resistance isn't just a one-hit wonder; it's the driving force behind an ensemble of illnesses. Dr Gerald Reaven, a professor of medicine at Stanford University, dedicated 60 years to researching insulin resistance. In Tim's words, Gerald's groundbreaking work suggested that insulin resistance and hyperinsulinemia (excess insulin circulating in the blood) are the essential biological precursors for at least four, if not all eight, of the most prevalent chronic medical conditions of our time. The eight conditions often caused by insulin resistance, according to Dr Reaven in his 1988 study (and, of course, you now know there are many more) were:

- Obesity
- Arterial disease
- Heart attack or stroke
- Type 2 diabetes
- High blood pressure
- Non-alcoholic fatty liver disease (NAFLD)
- Certain cancers
- Dementia

Today, 93% of American adults suffer from at least one of the five markers associated with insulin resistance. Earlier, I mentioned that 88% of Americans grapple with at least one metabolic marker, a statistic echoed in health circles. Yet, as the sands of health data shift, new research paints an even grimmer picture, bumping that number by 5%. Indeed, a mere 7% of American adults are believed to be free from the clutches of insulin resistance[4]. While we're still waiting on specific figures for the UK, history shows that health trends from across the pond often arrive shortly after.

So, what exactly is insulin resistance? In simple terms, it's the body's inability to tolerate more than a minimal amount of blood sugar daily. As you've learned, insulin plays a starring role in the metabolic ballet of food. Our cells rely on insulin to process glucose effectively. If we avoid excessive sugars and carbohydrates while maintaining a healthy dose of fibre, the insulin system functions harmoniously, just as it has for over 2 million years.

It's not unlike how you can become resistant to antibiotics or alcohol over time. Think of it as the persistence–resistance equation in the body. When exposed to a constant stimulus, our biology adapts – it's the law of homeostasis at work. Imagine taking a baby to a noisy restaurant; eventually, the baby falls asleep, blocking out the noise. But try sneaking out of a quiet bedroom at night with a creaky floorboard, and the baby awakens instantly. It's those high, persistent levels that breed resistance.

When hormones cycle naturally between highs and lows, the body never acclimates, and resistance doesn't have a chance to develop. However, excessive carbohydrates over a sustained period, without the balancing act of fibre, can pave the way for insulin resistance.

The catch is that you won't receive a diagnosis of insulin resistance. Instead, it stealthily creeps in, often a decade or two before the onset of full-blown type 2 diabetes. Understanding this concept is crucial because, as you've seen, it catalyses many of the diseases we're exploring.

Physiological vs Pathological Insulin Resistance: Pregnancy

I've been fortunate to draw wisdom from Dr Ben Bikman's extensive research in this fascinating exploration of physiological insulin resistance. After finishing this book, I highly recommend picking up Ben's masterpiece *Why We Get Sick* if you're hungry for more on the insulin resistance enigma. It's a deep plunge into insulin's interactions with fat cells, enriched by discoveries from his innovative university lab.

Insulin isn't merely a gatekeeper for glucose; it's a critical player in the body's growth narrative, guiding essential anabolic activities that foster cellular growth and, occasionally, replication.

Pregnancy serves as a miraculous showcase of insulin's growth-promoting capabilities. During this transformative phase, insulin enhances the development of vital structures like the placenta and breast tissue, preparing the mother for lactation and ensuring she stockpiles energy for the road ahead. This period witnesses a remarkable adjustment in fat tissue's insulin sensitivity, a temporary shift towards heightened responsiveness that reverts post-delivery. Termed physiological insulin resistance, this adjustment is a natural, beneficial adaptation, finely tuning the mother's physiology to meet both her and her developing child's needs.

Physiological vs Pathological Insulin Resistance: Puberty

Similarly, puberty orchestrates a metabolic ballet in which insulin and leptin play a leading role. During this period, insulin fosters leptin production from fat cells, which then ignites the production of sex hormones. This complex interaction underscores the significant impact of metabolic health and dietary choices on the timing and progression of puberty.

During puberty, those with type 1 diabetes see their insulin needs skyrocket, as illustrated by this handy graph.

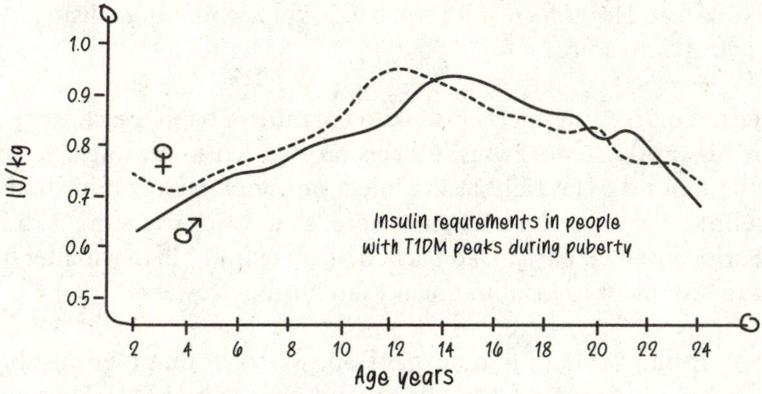

It's like insulins throwing a teenage tantrum, demanding more attention during these growth-spurt years. This shows that insulin, while usually the rogue behind many health issues, isn't all bad. It's indispensable during puberty, pregnancy, and our cave-dwelling ancestors' days of winter hibernation. On the other hand, for most of our adult lives, it's like that overeager friend who doesn't know when to back off. So, while we can't entirely give insulin the cold shoulder, it's about keeping it politely in its box as often as possible.

And while on the discussion of puberty, in recent decades, we've witnessed a seismic shift in the timing of puberty, a change closely tied to global dietary trends and their impact on insulin and leptin levels. Historical data paints a stark picture: while the average onset of puberty in the mid-1800s was around 16 years for girls, it has steadily declined to 8 to 12 years old today. This dramatic shift, nearly seven years earlier than in the past, underscores the profound influence of our modern lifestyle and nutrition on developmental milestones.[5]

*****

Obesity

We just traversed the maze of insulin's kingdom, uncovering its mighty role in locking our bodies into fat-storing mode. Let me take a moment to tell you a quick story about my dad's battle with his bulge. Bless his heart, Dad is a classic case of sticking to the old ways, much like someone who insists on using a flip phone in the age of smartphones. At the sprightly age of 83, has been waltzing with the same GP for three decades. Despite the whirlwind of scientific evidence twirling around him, he remains firmly planted in his belief that his GP's advice is the North Star. Trying to convince him to reconsider his type 2 diabetes treatment is like persuading a cat to love water, a near-impossible feat. He views insulin as a trusty old friend, not realising it's like pouring petrol onto a fire.

When Dad started his insulin injections, like a creature of habit, he chose the same spot for his insulin rendezvous, a decision that led to an unexpected guest: a bulging mound of fat right at the injection site. It was as if his body said, 'Ah, insulin! Let's store some fat right here, shall we?' And store it did. Along with this localised fat party, Dad packed on an extra 12 lb in a matter of a few months, a testament to insulin's sneaky fat-storing prowess.

In this story of insulin's role in body expansion, we learn that high insulin levels act like a green signal for fat to pile up and for our bodies to bulk up. Imagine insulin as the diligent traffic officer, ensuring every nutrient heads straight into the fat cell parking lot with no side trips. The more insulin on patrol, the more streamlined the fat storage operation is. On the flip side, Dr Ben Bikman shared an intriguing lab observation: when they immerse fat cells in a petri dish full of sugar, those cells bathe in sweetness. Yet, without insulin, it's as if the sugar becomes invisible to the fat cells – none of it gets taken in. This stark contrast underscores insulin's pivotal role in the process, showing that without its presence, sugar can't infiltrate fat cells, no matter how much is knocking at the door.

*****

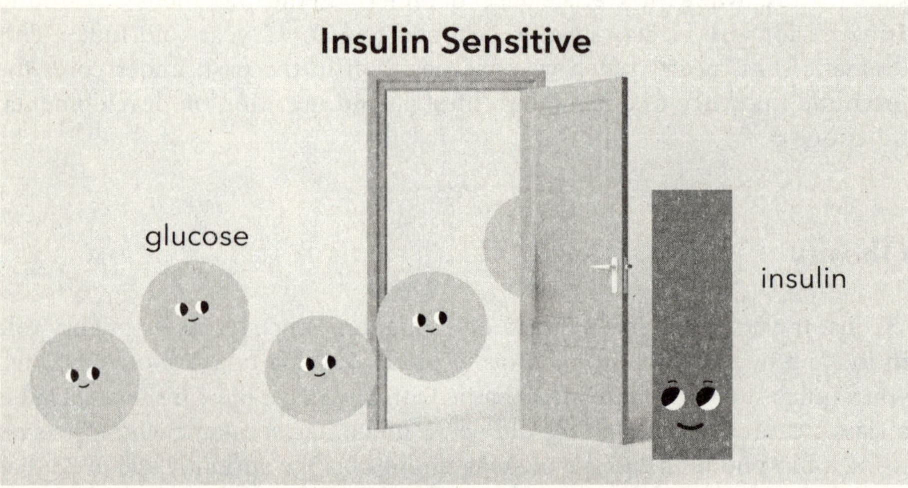

*****

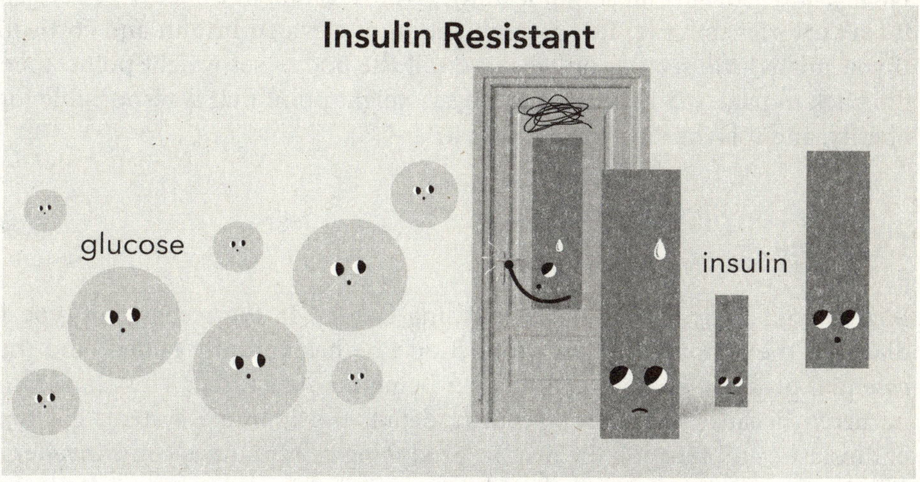

*****

How do we outmanoeuvre this overzealous storage manager? First, think of fibre as your dietary bodyguard. Eating fibre-rich foods before anything else creates a slow-release mechanism for glucose absorption, which means less insulin is needed. It's like putting speed bumps on the glucose highway. Second, cut down on foods that are essentially glucose in disguise. Reducing excessive carbohydrates and sugars that love to charade as innocent treats. Last, consider the power of eating less often. Each time we eat, insulin enters the stage. By reducing the frequency of our meals, we give insulin fewer cues to come out and play, allowing more time for our bodies to switch to fat-burning mode. It's like turning the storage manager's job into a part-time gig.

My dad isn't one to play the lottery or place bets, but his dance with insulin medication feels like navigating with a paper map in the era of GPS. Insulin injections are indispensable for those with type 1 diabetes, yet for many grappling with type 2, it's as if they're relying on outdated tools – there are more modern approaches, like metformin, that often make more sense. Advising someone who's become desensitised to insulin because of its overabundance, to take even more makes little sense. It's like suggesting someone lost in the digital age should rely solely on a compass and stars. This scenario underscores the importance of understanding insulin's function and making choices that prevent us from wandering into a maze of continuous fat storage.

Finally, and probably most importantly, is the question of what drives obesity. It isn't calories for sure; it is a combination of elevated insulin and cortisol. If you missed the section on what we call the body's set weight point, then flip back to page 188 because it is the set weight point that is responsible for obesity, and it is the key to unlocking it.

*****

Diabetes

Picture your body as a complex, bustling factory. In the scenario of type 1 diabetes, the factory's central production line has abruptly halted, and the essential product, insulin, is no longer being manufactured. This shutdown occurred because the body's security detail, the immune system, got too enthusiastic and mistook the insulin-producing cells as unwelcome invaders. It's akin to having an overzealous bouncer at a club who accidentally kicks out the VIP guest. Sadly, we haven't yet cracked the code to reboot this insulin factory. But fear not, with insights from Dr Ian Lake, Jon Furniss, chef Emma Porter, and others, we're compiling a survival guide for thriving in this challenging condition. Keep tabs on my YouTube channel for an upcoming series titled 'Living with Type 1 Diabetes'.

Now, pivoting to type 2 diabetes, imagine that same insulin factory is now overworking, churning out insulin non-stop. But here's the issue: the body acts like a sulky teenager, blasting music with noise-cancelling headphones, utterly ignoring insulin's desperate knocks at the cell doors to let glucose in. It's as if the cells have thrown a 'Do Not Disturb' sign on their doors for insulin. But why is the spotlight on type 2 diabetes distinct from insulin resistance? It's essential to understand the difference. Often, your body battles with undercover insulin resistance, a silent skirmish, way before it officially waves the white flag, surrendering to the sugar management wars. This underlines my passion for promoting individuals to monitor their metabolic health, akin to being a detective uncovering the early whispers of rebellion within.

A century ago, type 2 diabetes was as rare as finding a needle in a haystack. Today, it's as common as pigeons in a square, milling about without a care. My conversations with specialists have led me to a revelation: type 2 diabetes isn't a life sentence. Contrary to the bleak picture painted by Big Pharma of a 'chronic and progressive' ailment, this condition can indeed be reversed. We've even launched an online program that's turning the tide against type 2 diabetes with remarkable success. If you or a loved one are currently suffering from this disease, I suggest checking out my course on page 959.

Beyond Medicine: Some Numbers for Concern

'Why bother reversing diabetes if a medication can control it?' you might wonder (my dad certainly did). As Dr Richard Bernstein poignantly states in his book *Diabetes Solution*, 'Rarely does anyone escape the disease's long-term complications, despite medication'. Furthermore, as I mentioned right at the front of the book, if your blood sugar consistently hovers above 58 mmol/mol, you're looking at slicing a staggering one-third off your lifespan. That's equivalent to losing 100 days for every year you live with not-so-well-controlled diabetes.[8] Are we talking about just a few people? No. In research recently published in the UK, notably the National Diabetes Audit 2020–21, they stated 1,010,175 individuals have an HbA1c above 58 mmol/mol (you will learn about this measurement in a few pages time), that's more than a third of all people known to be living with type 2 diabetes in the UK.[9] Yes, more than 1 million people are losing a third of their lives! And that's just the ones that have their HbA1c tested; how many don't? I know my dad didn't until I started to insist, he went and had it measured.

Diabetes isn't just a number on a medical chart; it has real, life-altering consequences. It's the leading cause of blindness among working-age individuals in the UK. Every week, over 176 leg, toe or foot amputations are performed on people battling Type 2 diabetes, and from 2015 to 2018, there were 27,465 lower limb amputations related to diabetes in England, an increase of 18.3% in the 2011–2014 period. And £1 in every £140 spent by the NHS is on foot care for people suffering from diabetes[10]. With type 2 diabetes, your risk of heart disease and cancer doesn't just increase; it skyrockets. Living with diabetes might be manageable, but reversing it is like turning back the clock on your health. Let me apologise for that barrage of numbers. I wrote it with the intention of highlighting that living with diabetes can have serious side effects, yet the disease can, for virtually every sufferer, be better managed, put in remission or even totally reversed.

What is also concerning is that there are probably just as many individuals tiptoeing on the edge of diabetes (pre-diabetic) or unknowingly dancing with it as there are diagnosed cases. I'd wager that in Britain, diabetes is already the number one cause of untimely death. Even if my hunch is a tad off when you throw in the sinister link between diabetes and Alzheimer's, plus various types of cancer and heart disease, it's a no-brainer: getting your blood sugar under tight control is more than just a good idea; it's a lifesaving strategy.

So, how do you start flipping the script on diabetes? The answer might be as simple as eating *Fibre First* with your meals. This humble dietary change can slow down glucose absorption into your bloodstream, reducing the demand for insulin and setting you on the path to not just living with diabetes but potentially reversing it.

Unlike type 1 diabetes, type 2 isn't a life sentence. By embracing foods that don't cause insulin spikes. Think more greens, less rice, burgers without the bun, glucomannan fibre pasta over carb-heavy wheat pasta, intermittent fasting, and a sprinkle of exercise; we can show type 2 the exit. It's about switching the script from living with the disease to managing or reversing it. Ultimately, the story of type 2 diabetes is empowerment.

> *It's about turning the tables on a condition that has become a modern epidemic, using food as medicine and lifestyle as therapy. It's a reminder that sometimes, the best medicine doesn't come in a pill bottle or injection but on a dinner plate and a pair of walking shoes.*

Understanding the Numbers

When managing or reversing diabetes, knowing your numbers is crucial. The three fundamental ways to tune into your blood sugar symphony are finger-pricking, continuous glucose monitoring (CGM) or asking your doctor for an HbA1c test.

The classic finger prick and peek method is like checking the temperature outside before you head out. It provides a snapshot of the here and now. You prick your finger, squeeze a drop of blood, and a tiny meter reads your blood glucose level. It's simple and direct and tells you exactly what your sugar levels are doing at that moment.

Then there's the continuous glucose monitor (CGM), a futuristic gadget akin to having a weather station attached to your body. It continuously monitors your glucose levels, giving you a live feed of the ups and downs. It's the difference between catching a single episode of a show and binge-watching an entire season in one go; you get the whole story.

Then we have the long-term lens, HbA1c or glycated haemoglobin. Picture haemoglobin as tiny red taxis in your blood, ferrying oxygen around your body. They also pick up passengers in the form of glucose. Since these red taxis have a lifespan of about three to four months (red blood cells only live for three or four months before being replaced), checking how much glucose they've collected gives you a good idea of your average blood sugar over that period.

HbA1c is like a quarterly business report for your blood sugar. A normal range sits between 4% and 5.6%. If you're in the 5.7% to 6.4% range, it's like an orange traffic light warning you that your blood sugar isn't fully under control. Anything 6.5% or over, and you're currently a diabetic.

HbA1c Conversion Chart

%	mmol/mol	%	mmol/mol
5.0	31	7.3	56
5.1	32	7.4	57
5.2	33	7.5	58
5.3	34	7.6	60
5.4	36	7.7	61
5.5	37	7.8	62
5.6	38	7.9	63
5.7	39	8.0	64
5.8	40	8.1	65
5.9	41	8.2	66
6.0	42	8.3	67
6.1	43	8.4	68
6.2	44	8.5	69
6.3	45	8.6	70
6.4	46	8.7	72
6.5	48	8.8	73
6.6	49	8.9	74
6.7	50	9.0	75
6.8	51	9.1	76
6.9	52	9.2	77
7.0	53	9.3	78
7.1	54	9.4	79
7.2	55	9.5	80

Understanding and monitoring your blood sugar is like conducting an orchestra. Each instrument – whether it's the finger-prick test, CGM, or HbA1c – plays a crucial part in creating harmony in your health. By keeping an eye on these numbers, you're not just following a score but composing a healthier, more harmonious life. Let me now share some extracts from my podcasts with some doctor friends.

Dr Jason Fung

'Most health professionals consider type 2 diabetes to be a chronic and progressive disease. It is a one-way street, a life sentence with no possibility of parole: the disease continually gets worse until you eventually require insulin injections. But this is actually a great big lie. It is ridiculously easy to prove that type 2 diabetes is almost always reversible.

Your doctor may prescribe a medication such as insulin injections or perhaps a drug called metformin to lower blood glucose, but these drugs do not rid the body of excess glucose. The blood glucose got better with insulin, but the diabetes got worse. The medication only hid the blood glucose by cramming it into the already engorged cells. The diabetes looks better, but it is worse.

What happens when excessive glucose piles up in the body over 10 or 20 years? Every cell in the body begins to rot, which is precisely why type 2 diabetes, unlike virtually any other disease, affects every single organ. Your eyes rot; you go blind. Your kidneys rot; you need dialysis. Your heart rots; you get heart attacks and heart failure. Your brain rots; you get Alzheimer's disease. Your liver rots; you get fatty liver disease and cirrhosis. Your legs rot; you get diabetic foot ulcers. Your nerves rot; you get diabetic neuropathy. No part of the body is spared. Standard medications do not prevent the progression of organ failure because they do not help excrete the toxic sugar load. '

Dr David Unwin

'In the past, I used to say to patients that everything is okay in moderation. But when I think back, that was nonsense. What does moderation mean, is it different for everyone? I used to think moderation in biscuits was six a day, but is it? What does moderation mean? Just those six biscuits kept me needing sugar and made it impossible for me to metabolise my own fat. If you have type 2 diabetes, sugar is kind of poison to you, and as you struggle to metabolise it, why would you have more? And as it is a poison for you, why would you want to be moderately poisoned?

One word of warning on going low-carb if you are already on medication for type 2 diabetes. You can't just go low-carb without chatting to your doctor about it first because there are some medications that you may be on that if you cut the carbohydrates and cut the sugar, and if your medication is also reducing sugar, then you could experience a hypo. A hypo is where you have low blood glucose, and that can also be dangerous. But, if you have just been diagnosed with pre-diabetes or type 2 diabetes – which, by the way, used to be called 'sugar diabetes'– then the best thing to try before being prescribed medicines is to cut out the sugar; it can make all the difference. In my own practice, most people don't need drugs at all. Most people, if they go and cut out the sugar and the starchy carbohydrates that turn into sugar when digested, that's the wonderful message of hope. Instead of it being chronic, progressive, and deteriorating, for so many of them, they can avoid lifelong medication.

What I find if I say to patients: 'You have got type 2 diabetes, and we can approach this in one of two ways, we could start the drugs today, but that's for the rest of your life, and there are pros and cons, there are possible side- effects. Or are you interested in a lifestyle alternative where you cut out sugar and you can avoid medication?' What is so interesting is that I have asked every single patient in this position for six years, and not one person has turned down my offer. And we get amazing results. We have got to a point now where our practice spends around £40,000 less per year than the average for our area, just on drugs for diabetes alone. And last year, we sent £57,000 of unspent drug budgets back to the treasury.

Having discussed the complexities of type 2 diabetes and its impact on health, it's clear that managing this condition requires a multifaceted approach. One promising avenue that has emerged in the quest for better blood sugar management and overall wellbeing is the role of myo-inositol. This naturally occurring compound offers hope for enhancing insulin sensitivity and providing a complementary strategy in the battle against diabetes. Let's explore how myo-inositol can be a valuable ally in this journey.'

Myo-inositol: Unlocking the door to metabolic harmony

Myo-inositol is a vitamin-like compound that plays a crucial role in several biological processes in the body, including insulin signal transduction, which is the process by which insulin communicates with cells to regulate blood sugar levels. The body naturally produces myo-inositol. It is synthesised in human tissues and considered a part of the B-complex family, although it is not a vitamin strictly because the body can produce it. Myo-inositol is critical in cellular processes, including insulin signal transduction, lipid synthesis, and nerve guidance. It is also a component of cell membrane phospholipids essential for cellular communication and signalling.

While the body can produce myo-inositol, dietary sources like fruits, beans, and nuts also boost its levels. Interestingly, it's a carbohydrate derivative, but don't let that scare you. Think of it as a carb in a superhero cape, swooping in to potentially reverse type 2 diabetes and tackle other health concerns with its insulin sensitivity-improving powers:

Improves insulin sensitivity: Myo-inositol is involved in the insulin signalling pathway, which helps cells in the body respond more effectively to insulin. Myo-inositol can help lower blood sugar levels by improving insulin sensitivity, which is crucial for managing and potentially reversing type 2 diabetes.

Reduces insulin resistance: Myo-inositol has been shown to reduce insulin resistance, helping normalise blood sugar levels.[11]

Provides structure to cells: Many years ago, it was recognised that myo-inositol provided structure to cells, especially cell membranes, which is why it was called vitamin B8 at the time. However, it was stripped of its vitamin status when scientists discovered that the body could produce it on its own, a fate that might eventually befall vitamin D as well.

Impacts on fat metabolism: Besides its role in insulin signalling, myo-inositol positively affects lipid (fat) metabolism. It helps improve the lipid profile by reducing triglycerides and increasing HDL cholesterol levels, which is beneficial since diabetes is often associated with dyslipidaemia (abnormal lipid levels). Research which evaluated no less than 14 random controlled trials (the gold standard of research) concluded that inositol supplementation among patients with metabolic diseases significantly decreased their triglyceride levels.[12]

Polycystic Ovary Syndrome (PCOS): Myo-inositol is particularly noted for its benefits in managing PCOS, a condition that is, in the main, caused by insulin resistance. Women with PCOS who take myo-inositol supplements may see improvements in insulin sensitivity, which can also help mitigate their risk of developing diabetes.[13] One UK study found that 12 weeks of supplementation improved reproductive hormone balance and restored the menstrual cycle in all participants with PCOS.

Lowering Gestational Diabetes Risk: High blood sugar during pregnancy can lead to gestational diabetes (GD), posing risks like preterm birth (delivery before 37 weeks). Research in 2023 suggests combining inositol with folic acid supplements during pregnancy could ward off GD and reduce premature delivery risks.[14]

Combating Depression: Inositol plays a pivotal role in producing neurotransmitters like serotonin and dopamine, which are essential for mood regulation. Studies indicate a correlation between low inositol levels and depression. Preliminary evidence suggests that a daily supplement of 6 g inositol[15] could alleviate depression symptoms, though further research is still needed to understand its impact better.

It's important to note that while myo-inositol can be a beneficial supplement for improving insulin sensitivity and potentially aiding in managing type 2 diabetes, it should not be considered a standalone treatment. Effective diabetes management typically involves a comprehensive approach, including diet modification, regular exercise, weight management, and, when necessary, medication as prescribed by your GP.

*****

Inflammation

For the completeness of this chapter, I would like to touch on inflammation quickly, a frequent flyer in the story of sugar spikes we unpacked fully in chapter 5. Here's the scoop: making fibre the VIP guest at your dietary party isn't just bright; it's an inflammation preventive game-changer. It's like putting a speed limit on those wild sugar spike rollercoasters, helping to avoid the health-damaging, inflammation-causing crashes that follow.

Next, let's waltz together into the oily waters of omega-6 and omega-3 fatty acids. I need you to picture seed oils brimming with omega-6, as the unwitting criminals in our inflammation plot. Essential, yes, but too much omega-6 turns our bodies into an inflammation blockbuster. Meanwhile, omega-3 fatty acids, the heroes in fatty fish, walnuts, and flaxseeds, are like cool, anti-inflammatory agents, swooping in to restore peace and order.

Yet, conquering inflammation isn't just about what's on your plate. It's a lifestyle gig. Quality sleep is like the secret healing potion; when we hit the snooze button, our bodies kick into repair mode, warding off the inflammation gremlins. And let's not forget the stress monster, a notorious inflammation inflamer. Chronic stress is like pouring gasoline on the fire, but here comes exercise, the inflammation extinguisher. A dose of physical activity, be it a jaunty jog (but watch those knees), a serene yoga class, or a gym session, can keep the flames of inflammation at bay.

Taming inflammation is a symphony of savvy eating, snoozing soundly, managing the mayhem of stress, and embracing the elixir of exercise. This harmonious blend marches us towards the promised land of balanced health and tranquillity. So, lace up those sneakers, fluff up that pillow, and embark on a holistic crusade against inflammation, armed with fibre and a can-do attitude.

*****

Heart Disease And Strokes

I've chosen to group heart disease and stroke together in this discussion because, at their core, these two chronic illnesses share remarkably similar causes and risk factors. Both conditions are intricately linked to issues like hypertension (high blood pressure), insulin resistance, and an unhealthy diet, highlighting the profound impact that our lifestyle choices can have on the health of our cardiovascular system. By addressing these common underlying factors, we can better understand how to prevent and mitigate the risks associated with heart disease and stroke, ultimately leading to improved cardiovascular health.

Probing deeper into the intricacy of heart disease, it becomes clear that insulin resistance is a central player in this interconnected narrative. Dr Joseph Kraft, a trailblazer in insulin resistance research, boldly stated that 'those with cardiovascular disease not identified with diabetes, i.e. insulin resistance, are simply undiagnosed'. Putting it as simply as possible, Dr Kraft is saying that most people with high blood pressure are also silently wrestling with insulin resistance, whether they realise it or not.

I asked two of my good friends, cardiologist Dr Aseem Malhotra and Dr Malcolm Kendrick, author of *The Clot Thickens*, for their top tips on preventing a heart attack, and their answers can be summarised in the following 11 points:

1. Don't smoke
2. Avoid stress because the hormone cortisol increases blood glucose levels, which increases the need for insulin

3. Get sufficient sleep because poor sleep increases cortisol, which increases your insulin levels
4. Nitric oxide relaxes your blood vessels, so eat foods rich in nitrates, like beetroot, spinach, and dark chocolate
5. Exercise as it releases nitric oxide from the artery walls
6. Get out in the sunshine to generate even more nitric oxide
7. Consume collagen as blood vessels disintegrate without it
8. Eat fibre and reduce sugars because insulin resistance and high insulin levels directly cause high blood pressure
9. Look after your microbiome with fibre because your bacteria play a significant role in the health of your arteries
10. Be careful of certain medications such as statins, and if you take them, make sure to supplement with coenzyme Q10
11. Don't obsess about LDL

The Beat Goes On: A Quick Tour

Imagine your arteries as the bustling motorway of your body, a vast network ferrying life-giving, oxygen-rich blood from your tireless heart to every corner of your domain. Then, like weary travellers after an epic road trip, the blood returns to the heart, spent and craving a refill of that vital oxygen.

This vast network of arteries, veins and capillaries stretches over 60,000 miles (enough to go around the earth twice). Your heart, the unflagging hero in this story, thumps away around 100,000 times daily, churning through some 2,000 gallons of blood. Here's a nugget to ponder: wipe cardiovascular diseases off the map, and we could all be hitting the snooze button on the Grim Reaper's call for a bonus seven years!

In the springtime of life, our arteries are as supple as a gymnast, each about 3 mm wide, ready to flex and bend. But as the seasons change, they can become more like rigid old pipes, losing that youthful give. Toss in some plaque build-up, and voila, you've got atherosclerosis. Think of it as the difference between a non-stick frying pan and a piece of flypaper. If your arteries are more flypaper than Teflon, plaques stick, pile up, and might create a full-blown blockage, inviting heart attacks or strokes to crash the scene.

Of course, the heart health story is vast and filled with twists and turns. I won't turn this into a medical textbook – there are plenty of those, and I'm hardly a cardiologist. Instead, I aim to spotlight a handful of insights that tie back to our shared adventure into wellness, offering you chunks of wisdom to guide you through the complex heart territory with a bit more ease and understanding.

Aldosterone

The hormone aldosterone is the body's salt-and-water regulator. You don't want too little, and you don't want too much. Aldosterone signals specific organs, like your kidneys and colon, to increase the amount of sodium they send into your bloodstream or the amount of potassium released in your pee. It's the unsung hero that ensures our internal environment remains finely balanced. In a healthy metabolic state, consuming salt triggers a response in the body to decrease aldosterone production. This prompts the kidneys to excrete both salt and water, maintaining blood pressure at a normal level. However, in those with insulin resistance, the persistent presence of high insulin levels disrupts this delicate balance. The kidneys, thrown off their usual rhythm, become salt hoarders, retaining sodium and water. Over time, this accumulation increases bodily water content, driving up blood volume and, subsequently, blood pressure.

Fibre

Fibre's role in heart health extends beyond just moderating glucose absorption; it's like a multi-tool in your wellness kit, offering several benefits:

Cholesterol Management: Fibre helps lower LDL cholesterol levels (more on this later).

Blood Pressure Regulation: A 2023 research paper titled, The Relationship Between Dietary Fibre Intake and Blood Pressure Worldwide[16], discovered that a high fibre intake is associated with lower blood pressure. It's like a calming influence on the cardiovascular system, helping to ease the pressure on arterial walls and ensure a steady, healthy flow.

Weight Management: By promoting satiety and reducing overall calorie intake, fibre can help manage weight. A lighter load means less strain on the heart, which doesn't have to work as hard to pump blood through the body.

Inflammation Reduction: Fibre can help reduce inflammation, a key factor in heart disease. It's like sending in a peacekeeping force to quell the internal skirmishes that can lead to chronic heart conditions.

Gut Health: A fibre-rich diet supports a healthy gut microbiome linked to reduced heart disease risk. As we have learnt already, beneficial bacteria in your gut can produce short-chain fatty acids from fibre, compounds known to have heart-protective effects.

Incorporating more fibre into your diet, you're helping your heart and boosting your overall health with a natural, accessible, and delicious approach.

Nitric oxide

Boosting nitric oxide (NO) production in our bodies is like giving our blood vessels a spa day, every day. NO is one nitrogen and one oxygen molecule in a happy union, not to be confused with nitrous oxide (N2O), which is more of a crowded party with two nitrogen molecules crashing the oxygen molecule's pad. The latter gives you the giggles at the dentist and boosts crop growth, but it's not exactly Earth-friendly. NO is the star of vascular health. It's like the body's internal yoga instructor, helping blood vessels relax and lower blood pressure.

Dr Louis J. Ignarro, often compared to the Sherlock Holmes of NO, discovered that it's an essential molecule that plays a role in nearly every organ, including the heart and brain. Interestingly, the founder of the Nobel Prize, Alfred Nobel, discovered a heart-relieving side effect of nitric oxide in his factory, where he invented and manufactured dynamite (which uses nitro-glycerine). He observed that many of his workers suffering from angina, a condition caused by narrowed arteries and reduced blood supply to the heart (like a cramp in your heart), experienced relief while they were at work. It was later revealed that nitro-glycerine transformed into nitric oxide in the glycocalyx (inside lining of our arteries), leading to artery relaxation and expansion. Dr Ignarro's research into NO earned him a Nobel Prize in a captivating turn of events, bringing the story together in a wonderfully ironic twist.

According to Dr Louis J. Ignarro:

- NO is one of the most significant molecules in the body
- The immune system issues NO to stave off infections
- NO is also crucial for memory functions because the brain uses it to store and retrieve long-term memories as well as transmit information
- NO is also an anti-inflammatory
- NO relaxes blood vessels, reducing blood pressure and lowering the risk of heart attacks and strokes
- NO may also play a role in preventing Alzheimer's, arthritis infections and ulcers

Think of beetroot, spinach, and dark chocolate as your go-to snacks to ramp up your NO levels. Toss in some exercise, sunshine, and supplements like L-citrulline and L-arginine, and you're on your way to NO nirvana.

And now, for a little mischievousness, let me tell you a quick story about Viagra. Created as a potential heart disease combatant, this little blue pill took a detour during its final clinical trials. In an unusual outcome, none of the gentlemen participating in the trial seemed eager to return their leftover pills. Why, you ask? While it was being tested to mend hearts, Viagra found fame in, let's say, more intimate arenas. Its talent for ramping up NO production turned it into a whizz of relaxation – particularly adept at easing blood vessels in those crucial areas where a swift surge of blood can make all the difference.

And, as we'll discover later, erectile dysfunction often dances to the tune of insulin resistance. Here's where friendly fibre enters the stage. A fibre-rich diet might help keep things lively, just as it gives plants structure. And if you're planning any mountaineering adventures, consider taking Viagra with you as relaxing lung arteries helps you breathe easier at high altitudes. It seems Viagra's talents are as lofty as the peaks it helps conquer. Who would have thought?!

Glycocalyx

Allow me to introduce you to the fascinating world of the glycocalyx. It's the secret agent of your arteries, and surprisingly, not many folks, not even most medical pros, know about it. Yet, it's a tiny but mighty inside layer of the endothelium that's our artery's best friend. Dr Malcolm Kendrick once described it to me as the slimy surface of a fish's scales. Amongst its many talents, it's a master at preventing blood clots (yes, it's a real coagulation wizard), and it achieves this feat by holding on to NO, the champion we just discussed.

When a heart attack occurs, one of the earliest events involves the endothelium (the lining of your arteries) taking a hit, causing damage. To protect the artery, a blood clot steps in like a bodyguard. As the story unfolds, this clot gradually shrinks in size. Enter the endothelial progenitor, a stem cell, swooping in to create a fresh endothelium layer, concealing the clot within the artery wall. This is the body saying, 'All is well.' However, if the damage is more extensive or we're not as spry as we used to be (progenitor cell-wise) and struggle to produce enough nitric oxide, the plot /clot may turn dark.

Here's where sugar enters, playing the role of the crook. High blood sugar can be like a paint stripper to the glycocalyx, causing damage. It changes the surface like the difference between gliding on ice with freshly sharpened skates versus trudging through sticky mud in boots. The good news is this layer can grow back and is quite speedy. But the sugar story doesn't stop there; it also wreaks havoc on smaller blood vessels, which are also glycocalyx-covered. Dr Malcolm Kendrick aptly describes this as a 'microvascular disease'. It's like trying to stuff an elephant into a snake's belly because there's simply no room for an atherosclerotic plaque. This can lead to blockages in places such as feet, hands, and eyes. Remember back to the discussion on diabetes and how it is the leading cause of blindness and amputations in the UK. Do you see the link?

Thickening Arterial Walls

Insulin, the recurring character in our story, plays a significant role in thickening the walls of our blood vessels. You see, insulin is not just any hormone; it's an anabolic (growth) hormone with a knack for instructing cells to grow and expand. And that includes our endothelial cells, the guardians of our artery walls. When insulin levels are persistently high, it's like sending a continuous signal to these endothelial cells, encouraging them to bulk up. As they heed this call to grow, the arterial walls gradually thicken, making them less flexible and more rigid. The result? Increased resistance within the blood vessels, which translates into higher blood pressure. It's like trying to push water through a narrow pipe – more force is required to maintain blood flow. In this way, insulin's dual role as a growth hormone and a regulator of blood sugar levels can contribute to hypertension, further emphasising the pivotal link between insulin and cardiovascular health.

The Essential Framework of Collagen in Blood Vessels

Imagine collagen as steel reinforcement bars, akin to the framework of a skyscraper that holds everything together. Without this pivotal substance, our body would lack the necessary support.

Dr Malcolm Kendrick's insights from *The Clot Thickens* reveal that collagen is not just any building block but the cornerstone of human structure. This becomes obvious when we examine its role in safeguarding our blood vessels. Collagen serves as armour, defending these essential pathways against everyday wear and tear rigours. A deficiency in collagen leaves our vessels susceptible to damage, leading to minor breaches and a compromised system, much like cracks in an ageing facade. This breakdown can cause leakage and diminished vessel function. Collagen's role is far from that of a background character; it is crucial in ensuring our body's structural integrity remains intact. Without sufficient collagen, our health's delicate balance is jeopardised, affecting more than just our circulatory system.

Now let's hear from four experts on their view on what causes heart disease and how to prevent it:

Dr Malcolm Kendrick on Stress
'Throughout history, there have been huge spikes in the rate of death, particularly for men, from heart attacks linked to social upheaval. There have been many examples where enormous rates of heart disease follow gigantic social upheaval. In Scotland, when I was studying medicine, Scotland had the highest rate of heart disease in the world. What happened in the late 1950s and into the 60s was that half a million people were moved out of Glasgow and deposited in new towns, and the rate of heart disease went through the roof.

Then, in the 1960s, Finland had the highest rate of heart disease in the world, when in percentage terms, it had the largest forced migration of people the world had ever seen. More recently, if you looked around the world and said which countries had the highest rates of heart disease, then many of the top countries are the previous states of the Soviet Union. And then, if you say which countries are currently developing a rate of heart disease that is going up and up, it is those countries that are rapidly becoming more modernised, such as China and India, where sadly the rate of heart disease is already exploding. Quite simply, if you take populations and subject them to an enormous degree of stress, heart disease rates go up.'

Cardiologist Dr Aseem Malhotra with a Five-Pronged Approach
'What are the top five things we can do to avoid having a heart attack? For food, cut out the ultra-processed food. How do you define ultra-processed? I tell my patients that if it comes out of a packet with five or more ingredients, they best avoid it; it's an occasional treat. I mention it because 50% of our diet in the UK is now ultra-processed, microwaved stuff out of a packet. Instead, eat whole foods, vegetables, oily fish, olive oil, and a handful of nuts daily. Don't fear fat in the sense of full-fat dairy, cheese, yoghurt, etc. These things should be the base; these are good nutrition. Avoid and cut out refined sugars and carbohydrates; the rest doesn't matter. So, if you get the diet right, you are most of the way there.

Next thing, avoid stress. While stress is subjective, if you feel stressed, then you are stressed. Are you getting seven hours of sleep at night? If not, why not? Do something about it! Get out in the sunshine and then look at your social life. We find when you have a good sense of community, it helps protect against all the other things we have already discussed. I also talk in my book, The Pioppi Diet, that it helps to have an intimate relationship. For example, we know that middle-aged men who have sex with their partners twice a week rather than once a month are 50% less likely to get heart disease. And it isn't about being promiscuous or anything; it's something that reflects a strong relationship with someone who is close to you.'

Ivor Cummins: Avoid the Trilogy

Author of Eat Rich Live Long, Ivor Cummings told me: 'Heart disease is an inflammatory problem. Hyperinsulinemia and insulin resistance, high blood glucose and spikes in your blood glucose after a meal are the top problems in the world driving heart disease. It's not the complete cause. A huge amount of cardiac disease victims, from ages 18 to 80, in recent studies in Europe, across 25 countries, over 70% were essentially diabetic when they looked closely. So, problems with blood glucose, high insulin, high blood glucose and glucose spikes are the big heavy hitters. There are other things, such as nutrient deficiencies like magnesium, which is a very important nutrient. It's believed that about 70 to 80% of modern Western humans, due to depletion in the soil and the foods we are eating, are magnesium insufficient. Magnesium participates in around 300 functions in the body; it regulates blood pressure and countless other things that relate to vascular health. So, I would say low magnesium is another one to really watch out for.

Excessive refined carbs, excessive sugars, and, I believe, excessive seed oils and vegetable oils, which are in all the processed foods, that triad, is the big food problem. This triad matches all the processed and ultra-processed foods, where they use sugar, refined carbs, and seed oils for palatability and extended shelf-life because they are dirt cheap to produce. And that's where the industry has pushed us over recent decades into the worst three food types we can eat because that's where all the profit is.'

Deborah Colson MSc-Keep Your Eyes on Nutrients

As a nutritional therapist at the University of Westminster, Deborah once replied as my team quizzed her on heart health: What foods are good for a healthy heart? 'I would say the omega-3 fatty acids are very good, as they increase the beneficial HDL cholesterol. Magnesium and taurine are very important for a healthy heart. If you look to find where taurine exists in food, it's in the hearts of animals. So, it's no surprise that it's also important for the proper function of our own heart. Magnesium is important for the normal rhythm of the heart. Vitamin

E is very important as an antioxidant. Also, you need to look at levels of homocysteine, which requires certain B vitamins to keep it under control. Some people have a naturally low homocysteine, but those with a higher homocysteine require B vitamins to bring it down.'

*****

Strokes

If strokes concern you, starting by exploring the previous topic of heart disease is vital. Many of the points and tips for preventing heart disease are equally relevant to strokes.

There are two primary types of strokes: ischemic strokes, which occur when an artery in the brain becomes blocked, and haemorrhagic strokes, caused by the rupture of a blood vessel within the brain. While many of the insights we've explored regarding heart health also apply to strokes, there's one vital aspect we've yet to adequately discuss in the realms of cardiovascular disease and strokes – our microbiome. Recent research is shedding light on the significant role played by our gut bacteria in atherosclerosis, the gradual narrowing of arteries that frequently leads to heart attacks and strokes.[17/18/19]

Stroke, a condition typically associated with the elderly whose microbiomes have gracefully aged alongside them, presents an intriguing connection to gut health. Multiple studies have hinted that the severity of a stroke may be exacerbated in individuals with a less diverse gut microbiome. In patients suffering from strokes, we observe an increase in the abundance of certain unfriendly bacterial residents while beneficial strains like *Eubacterium* and *Roseburia* dip in numbers. Surprisingly, these microbial shifts also correlate with the gravity of the stroke itself.[20]

How do our lifestyle and dietary choices factor into this microbial drama? It turns out that our dietary fibre intake is a key player in this story. Fibre-rich foods, when consumed, become a microbial feast, nourishing bacteria like *Eubacterium* and *Roseburia*. In return, these friendly bacteria metabolise fibre into anti-inflammatory compounds that shield our brains. However, if your diet lacks sufficient fibre, the relative abundance of these protective bacteria dwindles, and your vulnerability to strokes and heart attacks rises.

So, the next time you think about the importance of a healthy fibre-rich diet, remember that you're not just feeding yourself, but also nurturing the diverse microbial community within, which plays a significant role in safeguarding your cardiovascular health. It's a microbial tale that showcases the intricate interplay between diet, gut bacteria, and strokes.

*****

Cancer

Cancer, a daunting adversary that has left an indelible mark on countless lives, is a disease whose prevalence has surged dramatically over the years. Four stark observations from the UK serve as a sobering reminder of the gravity of this situation:

- Today, a chilling statistic confronts us – according to the NHS, an astonishing 1 in 2 children born this year will grapple with a cancer diagnosis at some point in their lives.[21] This staggering reality stands in stark contrast to the rarity of cancer just a century ago.
- Every 90 seconds, a life-changing cancer diagnosis is delivered to someone in the UK.
- Estimates project that there are presently 3 million people living with cancer in the UK, a number set to rise to 4 million by 2030 and a staggering 5.3 million by 2040.[22]
- Each year, approximately 167,000 individuals succumb to cancer in the UK, equating to an average of 460 people every day.[22]

However, before we resign ourselves to despair, let's focus on five crucial points that offer hope:

- The World Cancer Research Fund believes that 30 to 50% of all cancers are preventable.[23]
- The tireless efforts of the medical industry are yielding promising results. Survival rates of cancer patients are improving, with approximately 50% now living for a decade or more after their cancer diagnosis.[24]
- Overweight and obesity, identified as the UK's second-largest cause of cancer after smoking[25], presents an opportunity for optimism (obesity can be reversed).
- A century ago, the pioneering German physician Otto Heinrich Warburg made a groundbreaking discovery. He unveiled that cancer cells depend almost entirely on glucose as their primary energy source. This revelation marked a pivotal moment in our comprehension of cancer metabolism and provides another pathway to prevention.
- In 2010, Professor Rosalie David of Manchester University declared: 'There is nothing in the natural environment that can cause cancer. So, it must be a man-made disease, arising from pollution and modifications in our dietary and lifestyle choices.' This statement once again highlights the significant influence of diet and environmental factors, both of which we have the power to influence and improve.

Before we proceed, it's essential to underscore that the following discussion isn't medical advice. If you suspect you might have cancer, please consult a healthcare professional without delay. Timely detection can significantly improve outcomes for this daunting ailment. Moreover, our NHS is renowned for its excellence in cancer care. However, seeking a second or even third opinion upon receiving a diagnosis is prudent, especially if the proposed treatment isn't fully clear to you. Take the story of my friend Debbie as a case in point: turned away by one hospital, she sought help elsewhere in the NHS and was undergoing surgery within weeks. And let's return to a crucial point made at the start of this book: clinical knowledge is expanding at a breakneck pace, doubling every six months, offering more hope than ever for those battling cancer.

The UK surge in cancer cases mirrors the spread of a global pandemic. Dr Michael VanDerschelden, in his enlightening work *The Scientific Approach to Intermittent Fasting*, casts a spotlight on the disconcerting surge in cancer rates. He discloses a disheartening historical trend: in the early 1900s, a mere 1 in 20 people contended with cancer, but this grim scenario evolved to 1 in 16 by the 1940s and 1 in 10 by the 1970s. As we have seen above, over the past five decades, it has accelerated so quickly that it is now 1 in every 2 people who will suffer.

The gravity of this situation isn't meant to evoke fear but to underscore the pressing need for action. Cancer has cast a long shadow over countless lives, including my own, as I've mourned the loss of both grandfathers, my cherished grandmother, and my remarkable Auntie Avis, all casualties of this relentless adversary. Tragically, our sorrow deepened with the loss of our children's nanny, Laura, who succumbed to cancer in her twenties, and the untimely passing of Carl, my daughter's gifted piano teacher, at the tender age of 34. I'm sure that you, too, have been touched by similarly heart-wrenching tragedies.

The question that looms before us is clear: Can we alter the trajectory of this disheartening trend? The resounding answer is 'yes'. If cancer is proliferating at an unprecedented pace, it implies underlying causes that demand our attention.

Cancer – The Basics

Time to navigate the intricate terrain of cancer itself. While cancer may manifest diversely and in various body regions, its roots lie in body cells' unbridled division, multiplication, and metastasis (spread) into neighbouring tissues. Under ordinary circumstances, our ageing cells gracefully undergo apoptosis, which sees around 10 billion cells perish daily, paving the way for new cells to materialise only when needed. Nevertheless, cancer can rear its formidable head when this harmonious process falters. As cancer advances, ageing or impaired cells elude their natural demise, while an excess of new cells perpetuates the proliferation, culminating in irregular growths recognised as tumours.

When tumours assume a malignant form, they possess the capacity to infiltrate neighbouring tissues and, all too often, break free and ramble through the bloodstream or lymphatic system, ensnaring other parts of the body. Even after surgical extraction, the lingering possibility of their resurgence remains. Conversely, benign tumours remain contained and refrain from spreading. Their removal typically results in enduring resolution, with no tumour return. While the realm of cancer is vast and intricate, we could fit only so many pages into this book. So, let's zoom in on a handful of potent strategies that can tip the scales in your favour.

Don't Smoke, Seriously!

Now, I know as you're reading this book, you're probably aware of the glaring fact that smoking is a sure-fire way to invite cancer into your life. So, let's hope we can collectively raise awareness about how sugar, with its sneaky spikes and the subsequent insulin rollercoaster, might be the new smoking of our generation. And how something as simple as starting your meal with fibre might be a step towards reducing our cancer risk.

But for those who might not be fully acquainted with the staggering statistics, let's lay them out in black and white. Approximately 2 out of 3 long-term smokers are on a grim journey towards a smoking-related disease. Smoking, the notorious culprit, is responsible for around 20% of all cancer cases and a substantial 22% of cancer-related deaths. Here's the opportunity: that still leaves us with a daunting 80% of cancer mysteries to solve (and we'll tackle those mysteries right here in these pages). To put the gravity of smoking into perspective, a huge 80% of lung cancers, along with an equally hefty 80% of lung cancer deaths, are directly attributed to smoking.[26]

Sugar, Insulin and Cancer

Dr Gary Fettke, both a doctor and a cancer survivor, says, 'So you think you need sugar? Your cancer needs it more.' When undergoing a 3D hospital PET scan, an intriguing process unfolds to create an image of what is happening inside the body, illustrating the voracious appetite of cancer cells for glucose.

A special radioactive tracer, often labelled with a blue dye, is introduced into the body during the scan. Here's where it gets interesting; this tracer closely mimics glucose in its structure. As the body metabolises this compound, it is absorbed by cancer cells because they mistake it for glucose, their preferred energy source. This blue-dye-laden 'Trojan horse' infiltrates the cancerous regions, revealing their locations on the scan as intense, vibrant spots of blue. It's a compelling visual representation of cancer's insatiable hunger for glucose, underscoring the critical role of sugar in fuelling its growth. Therefore, strategies restricting glucose availability, such as dietary changes, can be integral in managing and combating cancer.

The convergence of these two signals, glucose and insulin, is pivotal in understanding why individuals with hyperinsulinemia, regardless of their body composition (lean or overweight), face roughly twice the risk of succumbing to cancer. This concerning link was underscored by research published in the *International Journal of Cancer* in 2017. The situation becomes even more dire when considering certain types of cancer, such as breast, prostate, and colorectal cancers, which exhibit a heightened association with insulin resistance. For instance, malignant breast cancer tumours boast over six times the number of insulin receptors compared to non-cancerous breast tissue.[27] This means that cancerous tissue is six times more responsive to insulin's growth-promoting signals than healthy tissue, and what does insulin deliver? Glucose. The very thing that fuels cancer cells. Double terrifying blow. This explains why there is an amplified risk and growth potential of cancer in individuals with insulin resistance.

Cancer, regardless of its specific cause, represents a disorder of unbridled cellular growth. Certain cells within the body undergo uncontrollable multiplication, and insulin resistance plays a pivotal role in this equation, expediting the growth of cancer cells. Adding another layer to the complexity, insulin possesses anabolic properties, stimulating cells to grow. In the context of cancer, this means that insulin can potentially boost the growth of cancer cells, especially if these cells have developed a heightened sensitivity to insulin compared to surrounding insulin-resistant cells.

How a Keto Diet May Help in Preventing and Reversing Cancer

Please remember, as with everything else in this book, the following is not intended as medical advice. If you're facing cancer, it's crucial to adhere to your doctor's recommendations. I'm about to share an inspiring account from an exceptional doctor.

Dr Annette Bosworth (known on the web as Dr Boz), a medical professional who achieved the remarkable feat of reversing her own mother's cancer after three failed rounds of therapy, provides invaluable insights into the potential role of diet in combating cancer. Watch our podcast on YouTube; it's both moving and highly informative on managing cancer.

Dr Bosworth's perspective on the ketogenic diet is clear: By adopting a high-fat, low-carb eating regimen, you effectively strip cancer cells of their preferred sustenance—sugar. Glucose, abundant in diets rich in carbohydrates, is the primary source of nourishment for most cancers. However, cancer cells are ill-equipped to adapt to an environment with low sugar levels. In contrast, healthy cells can seamlessly transition to utilising ketones as an alternative energy source.

Cancer cells, as shown by the PET scan, thrive when abundant carbohydrates are available. These cells have no affinity for ketones and cannot harness them for growth or division. Instead, they rely heavily on glucose. Restricting your carbohydrate intake to less than 20 g per day creates a hostile environment for cancer cells, depriving them of their preferred fuel source. This deprivation weakens their growth potential, offering a promising avenue for intervention. Much more on this in the next chapter.

Avoid HPV – Wear a Condom

Human papillomavirus (HPV) is the most prevalent sexually transmitted infection (STI) in the UK, affecting approximately 4 out of 5 men and women at some point in their lives. Notably, HPV is the primary cause of nearly all cases of cervical cancer.[28]

Usually, our immune system can naturally eliminate an HPV infection. However, in some instances, the infection persists and can lead to cancer. HPV transmission occurs through vaginal, anal, or oral sexual contact with an infected person. Importantly, an individual with HPV can transmit the infection even without displaying any symptoms.

Being sexually active puts you at risk of contracting HPV, even if you've had sexual relations with only one partner. Symptoms may not manifest immediately after exposure; sometimes, it can take decades, making it challenging to determine when you were first infected. In most cases (9 out of 10), HPV resolves independently within two years without causing health problems.

In addition to cervical cancer, HPV can cause cancers of the vulva, vagina, penis, or anus. It can contribute to oropharyngeal cancer, affecting the base of the tongue and tonsils. Predicting who will develop cancer or other HPV-related health problems is challenging. Individuals with weakened immune systems, including those with HIV, may have a harder time combatting HPV and are at a higher risk of developing related health complications.

To reduce your risk of HPV:

- **Get vaccinated:** In the UK, all children aged 12 to 13 (school year 8) are offered the HPV vaccine. Girls under 25 can also receive the vaccine for free on the NHS.
- **Use condoms:** Consistently using condoms during sexual intercourse can lower your chances of contracting HPV, although they may not provide complete protection.
- **Consider mutually monogamous relationships:** Having sex only with a partner who is monogamous with you can, of course, reduce the risk of HPV transmission.

Avoid Toxins

I won't say much here as there is a whole section on avoiding toxins on page 757. The European Environment Agency Website claims that '8 % of deaths can be attributed to chemicals'. These numbers are growing, and they only consider a small number of chemicals whose effect on health is well established.

Certain ultra-processed foods and fast foods can increase the risk of developing cancer if a person consumes them in large amounts or over long periods. Research has shown that processed foods such as bacon, sausages, packaged snacks, sugary cereals, and soda increase cancer risk.[29]

How Alcohol Use Increases the Risk of Cancer

It is believed that alcohol consumption is responsible for approximately 4% of cancer cases worldwide. It is well-documented that drinking alcohol elevates the risk of various cancer types, including those affecting the upper aerodigestive tract, liver, colorectum, and breast.

There are multiple pathways through which alcohol, specifically ethanol, is known to contribute to cancer development, although some aspects remain only partially understood. Ethanol's metabolite, acetaldehyde, has the potential to induce DNA damage and hinder DNA synthesis and repair. Both ethanol and acetaldehyde can disrupt DNA methylation. Ethanol's role in promoting inflammation and oxidative stress can lead to lipid peroxidation and further DNA damage.

So, what's the optimal amount of alcohol consumption? That's the million-dollar question. Dr James DiNicolantonio, the author of insightful books such as The Salt Fix and, more recently, *Obesity Fix*, shared a valuable perspective on my podcast. He mentioned, 'Red wine consumed with a meal can help reduce oxidative stress from the foods you are consuming, it can help lower blood pressure if you consume it with food, and it can help reduce post-meal spikes in blood sugar. Part of why red wine over white wine is so beneficial is because it is fermented with the grape seeds and the skin. Therefore, you get more polyphenols, more of a substance called resveratrol and quercetin, and these plant polyphenols help dilate the blood vessels and reduce blood platelet clotting.'

From my research, which I admit is intensive because of my occasional overconsumption, it appears that the optimal range falls somewhere between one and three alcoholic units per day. However, it's crucial to remember that individual factors can vary significantly, so caution is advisable when considering alcohol consumption. Plus, for completeness, I must point out that others, like the brilliant Professor Andrew Huberman, are adamant that we shouldn't consume more than two units per week.

Glucomannan and Inulin Fibre's Anticancer Activity

Many clinical papers have suggested the benefits of consuming glucomannan fibre in relation to preventing cancer. In 2019, *Frontiers in Pharmacology* undertook research titled 'A Systematic Review Exploring the Anticancer Activity and Mechanisms of Glucomannan'. They discovered, 'As a straight-chain polymer with few branches, glucomannan was first appreciated for its role in gastroenterological disorders and metabolic diseases.[30] Much like other polysaccharide extracts from traditional Chinese herbs, the potential of glucomannan involved in anti-cancer therapy has recently been revealed. Evidence suggests that glucomannan exhibits broad but specific anti-tumour effect when distinct cancer types are concerned.'[31]

Research into inulin fibre has shown how it may help protect colon cells. This is due to how inulin ferments into butyrate. For this reason, several studies have investigated its effects on colon health.[32] One review examined 12 animal studies and found that 88% of the groups receiving inulin reduced precancerous colon growths[34]. In another study, inulin-fed rats showed fewer precancerous cell changes and less inflammation than the control group.[34]

Deborah Colson MSc

'What role can nutrition play in cancer prevention? The body produces cells that could be cancerous, and the immune system is constantly on the lookout. There are about seven different points at which the immune system can intervene to prevent what might be pre-cancerous from becoming full-blown cancer, and those steps, in general, are nutrient-dependent. For example, one step on the prevention pathway cannot happen if you're vitamin D deficient. Zinc is another one that's important along that pathway as well.'

Patrick Holford

I asked Patrick, 'You have written a book called Say No to Cancer. Please advise us on how to decrease our risk of getting it.' His response: *We do know that sugar feeds cancer cell growth in most cancers. For example, recent research in Italy attributes 15% of breast cancer to eating sweets and sweet food, so certainly, sugar is a factor.*

We also know that the more antioxidants that you can eat in fruit and veg, especially multi-coloured foods etc, reduces the risks. Having a lot of vitamin C reduces risks. And one of the hardest things to get a measure on is all the chemicals that we are exposed to. For example, pesticides and herbicides are basically substances that are designed to kill, and what happens is that we get a smaller amount of them over a longer period. That could be a factor. Stress is also a factor.

What we have started to realise is that when you go on to a certain kind of ketogenic diet, it triggers a cellular repair process called autophagy, and that is also what happens when you fast. But when you have a lot of carbohydrates, it's growth. And the big problem with humanity is that we are eating non-stop carbohydrates. So, we have over-growth; obesity is widespread. But we also have growth diseases like cancer. Just imagine for a minute. A cell in the body, for it to switch to a cancer cell, must have a hostile environment. So, we have created such an environment for ourselves that is so significantly hostile that one in two people are now likely to develop cancer.

Professor Tim Noakes

'I think the next big breakthrough area is going to be cancer. I am not suggesting cancer is purely nutritionally based, but I have read enough now to know that there are many things you can do if you have cancer; you still need some of the traditional treatments, but much reduced. What happens with cancer is that the treatment is so barbaric, and it's likely to kill more people than it helps. But if you just reduce the dose of those killing treatments, use a whole bunch of other stuff, and look at nutrition particularly, the low-carb diet is central for almost all cancers. And there is a whole load of other things that you need to do; we can start doing something about cancer in the same way as we are now doing something about diabetes. But unfortunately, just like diabetes, which insulin manufacturers control, oncology (the study of cancer) is controlled by people selling toxic medications. They are not about to suddenly change. But we will relentlessly try and force them to do so.'

Nora Gedgaudas, the author of the bestseller *Primal Body, Primal Mind*, believes a ketogenic approach is the single most effective dietary treatment for any and all forms of cancer and other immune-related illnesses. By robbing cancer of its needed fuel source (sugar) and relying on ketones and free fatty acids instead (which cancer cannot make use of), you can create an internal and epigenetic environment conducive to keeping cancer under control or even preventing it from getting a foothold.

Compiled from the research I have done and from discussing with our magnificent contributors, here are the top 15 things I believe we can all do to best defend ourselves against the terrible disease that is cancer.

1. Don't smoke. Period!
2. Eat the *Fibre First* diet. It will slow down the release of sugar, the food of cancer
3. Intermittently fast. Frequently put your body into repair mode
4. Consume fewer carbohydrates and other sugars
5. Avoid packaged foods, hydrogenated fats, and processed meat (trust the cow, not the chemist)
6. Where possible, eat organically and avoid poisonous pesticides
7. Avoid poisons/toxins. We shouldn't put anything onto our skin that we wouldn't be happy to eat
8. When cooking, don't burn food, as it can be carcinogenic
9. Move more, exercise regularly and get active
10. Minimise stress
11. Prioritise getting appropriate sleep

12. Don't consume too much alcohol
13. Try to tune your body into a ketogenic fat-burning machine (remember that cancer needs sugar to develop and grow)
14. Avoid obesity. It is the second biggest preventable cause of cancer in the UK[35]
15. Be careful of unprotected sex

Let me plead with you just this one thing. If you are not feeling well, see a GP. While this won't help avoid cancer, most cancers are now treatable if caught early.

*****

Non-Alcoholic Fatty Liver Disease

It is time to uncover the rather unfortunate connection between insulin resistance and non-alcoholic fatty liver disease (NAFLD), a condition that's today knocking on the doors of even our youngest generation.

The liver is like a diligent librarian sorting and storing books (or, in this case, fats). When all is well, it maintains a healthy balance between storing and releasing fats, ensuring our metabolic library functions smoothly. But when insulin resistance waltzes onto the scene, things go awry. It's as if the librarian suddenly developed a fondness for hoarding books and refused to let them go, leading to a backlog of fat that should have been put to good use elsewhere. The result? Non-alcoholic fatty liver disease is a condition where the liver resembles a well-fed goose prepped for foie gras production. In essence, it's a fatty liver without the alcohol indulgence that usually accompanies liver issues. But how does insulin resistance fit into this drama?

Insulin resistance, our recurring antagonist, is like a mischievous gremlin wreaking havoc. This is oversimplifying a complex process, but see it as the liver interpreting insulin surplus as a sign that it's time to store even more fat, making it a champion hoarder in the body's fat storage Olympics. Fat cells, now brimming with extra lipids, start leaking fat into the liver, further exacerbating the situation. The liver, already burdened by the influx of fat, can't cope, and voila, you have NAFLD. You might think, 'Isn't this just a concern for adults who've had their fair share of indulgent dining experiences?' Well, brace yourself for the sobering reality: young children, barely old enough to pronounce 'non-alcoholic fatty liver disease', are not exempt from this predicament.

Unfortunately, fructose, often associated with the sweet pleasures of life, plays a significant role in the development of NAFLD. When we consume fructose, it's not as innocent as it might seem. Unlike glucose, which various tissues in the body can metabolise, fructose is predominantly metabolised in the liver. This unique metabolic pathway sets the stage for trouble. When the liver receives an excess of fructose, it gets overwhelmed, leading to a cascade of events that ultimately result in fat accumulation in the liver cells.

Fructose doesn't just stop at promoting fat storage in the liver; it also encourages the production of harmful molecules called free radicals. These troublemakers wreak havoc on liver cells, causing inflammation and oxidative stress. This double whammy of fat accumulation and cellular damage creates the perfect storm within the liver, making it a fertile ground for NAFLD to flourish.

When the liver transforms sugars into fat, it often takes the form of palmitic acid, a type of fat that frequently garners attention in health circles. However, it's crucial to note that saturated fat in the blood doesn't equate to saturated fat in the diet. The critical distinction lies in the saturated fats we consume and the palmitic acid synthesised within the liver due to excessive fructose intake. This isn't a benign process; the increased saturated fat in the bloodstream can be potentially pathological. It promotes inflammation, heightens the risk of cardiovascular complications, and exacerbates insulin resistance.

The consequences of an overly fat-laden liver are far from trivial. When the liver's fat content exceeds 5% to 10% of its total weight (10% is where fatty liver disease becomes a diagnosis), it experiences functionality losses. It may give rise to more severe complications. In the past, fatty liver conditions were primarily associated with excessive alcohol consumption, as the liver is the sole organ capable of metabolising alcohol, leading to alcoholic fatty liver disease over time. However, a significant shift has occurred over recent decades. NAFLD has emerged as a common health concern, affecting approximately 1 in 5 individuals in the UK. The prevalence continues to rise annually, and potentially, as very few get tested for it, the NHS predict it might already affect 1 in 3 people.[36] This proliferation is astonishing; a condition virtually unheard of just three decades ago is now alarmingly prevalent.

A noteworthy study conducted in 2009 investigated the effects of fructose versus glucose consumption on visceral fat. The results were telling. While subjects who consumed controlled amounts of glucose drinks experienced increased subcutaneous fat, those who consumed the same calories but drank fructose saw a bigger rise in visceral fat.[37] And as you are aware, visceral fat is far more dangerous to health. Sadly, our modern diet involves consuming several times more fructose than previous generations, with fruit juice significantly contributing.

Furthermore, research has unveiled a link between NAFLD and specific gut bacteria, such as Klebsiella pneumoniae, which ferments glucose to produce excessive alcohol levels, contributing to the development of fatty liver disease. In fact, 60% of individuals with fatty liver disease studied exhibited these bacteria.[38]

Additionally, type 2 diabetes stands out as the most robust predictor of NAFLD development, with 70% of type 2 diabetics also suffering from the condition.[39] Once NAFLD takes hold, inflammation within the liver can ensue, potentially leading to hepatic fibrosis or liver scarring, affecting half of all NAFLD patients. Subsequently, one-fifth of NAFLD individuals may progress to cirrhosis and, in some cases, liver failure. Others may avoid liver failure but face an increased risk of liver cancer, making it a perilous trade-off.

Our children are facing an unprecedented health crisis – a fatty liver crisis. The British Liver Trust believe that one in five children already have it. Blame it on the seductive combination of sugary drinks, processed foods, and a lifestyle more about screen time than playtime. In a world where insulin resistance is increasingly lurking in the shadows, it's no surprise that NAFLD has emerged as its silent accomplice.

Wrapping Up NAFLD: A Ray Of Hope

Currently, we're in a pickle because there aren't any specific medications designed to cure NAFLD. However, don't let that dishearten you! There's a silver lining to this cloud. NAFLD isn't just preventable, it's reversible, especially if caught before any significant liver damage sets in. And the turnaround can be remarkably swift, with some folks seeing improvements in as little as two months. After chatting with a host of medical experts, I've distilled their wisdom into a straightforward action plan for kicking NAFLD to the curb:

Wave goodbye to alcohol – it's not doing your liver any favours.
Shed those extra pounds. Lighter on the scales equals lighter on the liver.

Embrace wholesome eating. Your liver craves real, nutritious food.
Steer clear of fructose-laden beverages. They're like kryptonite for your liver.
Get moving. Every step, cycle, or swim helps.
Say yes to omega-3s. They're like liver-loving heroes.
Ramp up your fibre intake. I might have sneaked this one in, but trust me, your liver will thank you.

*****

Osteoporosis – A Tale Of Insulin And Lack Of Sunshine

Twelve years ago, I worked with the National Osteoporosis Society (NOS), driven by a compelling story from a friend about the inescapable condition among her senior female relatives. This quest for understanding and a daring challenge by Her Royal Highness the Duchess of Cornwall (now our Queen) led me to the icy expanse of the North Pole. My mission? To shine a spotlight on a disease that, until then, had been a stranger to me, despite its widespread impact.

Affecting over 200 million people worldwide, osteoporosis renders bones brittle and fragile, a silent thief of strength and stability, particularly among postmenopausal women in the UK and USA, where it's estimated that 30% grapple with this condition. And 1 in 2 women and 1 in 5 men over 50 will have an osteoporotic fracture in their lifetime[40]. Tragically, my mother is among those statistics; her movements are shadowed by constant pain due to advice given decades ago about not going out in the sun, leading to severe vitamin D deficiency and, subsequently, osteoporosis.

The root of osteoporosis lies in hormonal upheaval, calcium deficiency, and, perhaps most critically, vitamin D deficiency. The sun, our most natural source of vitamin D, becomes an essential ally in the battle against this bone-weakening disease. Yet, the narrative deepens as we uncover the hormonal aspect, with insulin levels playing a pivotal role. The antidote? A shift towards real foods, where carbs are minimised and replaced with an abundance of fibre, healthy fats, and proteins. This dietary transformation addresses insulin levels and curtails the calcium leaching orchestrated by the unwelcome duo of insulin and cortisol.

Though reversing osteoporosis might not be within our reach, a nutrient-rich diet combined with weight-bearing exercises offers hope. It's not about reclaiming what's lost but fortifying what remains and possibly rejuvenating our skeletal framework. As we sail through the pages of this book, let's remember: our dietary choices not only shape our present but sculpt our future, with the power to stave off diseases like osteoporosis by adhering to what nature intended us to consume.

*****

Neurological Disorders: A Metabolic Perspective

> *When a flower doesn't bloom, you fix the environment in which it grows, not the flower*
> **Alexander den Heijer**

In his insightful book Brain Energy, Dr Christopher Palmer asserts that **'Mental illnesses are fundamentally metabolic disorders of the brain'.**

In my recent conversations with leading medical experts, a recurring theme has emerged: the brain, often perceived as a distinct entity, is intrinsically linked to our body's metabolic processes. This connection must not just become a footnote in medical textbooks, but a pivotal understanding that could revolutionise our approach to neurological disorders.

The profound insights from Dr Michael Hoffmann, whom I had the privilege to meet at the esteemed LowCARB Conference in Miami, further solidified this perspective. Dr Hoffmann, a luminary in the field, posed a thought-provoking question to his audience: 'Is it mere coincidence that the world houses a billion individuals battling obesity alongside another billion grappling with mental illness?'

Dr Hoffmann's discourse revolved around four cornerstone concepts:

- **The Bidirectional Relationship:** He emphasised the robust two-way street between metabolic and neural disorders, illustrating that our brain's health and metabolic context are inextricably linked.
- **The Tree of Insulin Resistance:** Much like the intricate branches of a tree (yes, he too uses my analogy), mental disorders such as depression, schizophrenia, and bipolar disease are not isolated occurrences but part of an interconnected system. This makes sense, considering the likes of anxiety, autism, bipolar disorder, depression, and ADHD, to name a few – are all rising at similarly alarming rates.
- **Reversibility Through Energy Restoration:** Metabolic brain disorders can often be reversed by rejuvenating the brain's energy supply.
- **Dietary Influence on Brain Function:** The role of a low-carbohydrate or ketogenic diet in optimising brain mitochondrial function should not just be seen as a form of sustenance but as a therapeutic tool.

The compelling body of clinical evidence, burgeoning with recently concluded research and ongoing trials, casts a new light on neurological disorders. It's becoming increasingly clear that these conditions are predominantly metabolically driven. The significance of the ketogenic diet in managing and preventing a myriad of neurological disorders, including epilepsy, malignant glioma, Alzheimer's disease, migraines, headaches, and motor neuron disease, cannot be overstated.

Contrary to previous beliefs, the revelation that our brain does not solely depend on glucose opens new avenues for understanding and treating neurological conditions. Approximately 70% of our brain is perfectly content functioning on ketones, while the remaining 30% that still requires glucose can ingeniously self-synthesise it without dietary intake. This insight is profound – while brain cells can develop insulin resistance, essentially running low on their primary fuel, they remain receptive to ketones. Imagine owning a hybrid car that uses petrol and electricity to draw an analogy. Ensuring a full petrol tank becomes paramount if the electric batteries falter.

An important 2018 study by Tanya McDonald and Mackenzie Cervenka sheds light on this intersection, offering a compelling narrative that resonates with the core thesis of our exploration. Their research underscores a profound yet often overlooked truth, 'despite the distinct pathologies underlying various neurological conditions, a common thread weaves through them – a disruption in energy metabolism, coupled with heightened oxidative stress and neuro-inflammation.'[41] It's a revelation that unearths the deep-seated connections between seemingly disparate disorders and champions dietary manipulation's transformative potential. The duo's findings are emphatic, delineating how the induction of metabolic ketosis – achieved through ketogenic diets or ingesting exogenous ketones – holds promise, potentially arresting or decelerating the progression of neurological disorders that tread along these shared metabolic pathways.

Adding another layer to this rich tapestry of insights is Professor Ben Bikman, a towering figure whose contributions to our understanding of insulin's multifaceted role are monumental. Professor Bikman's narrative is both illuminating and compelling, driving home the criticality of insulin in the context of chronic brain-related diseases. His words resonate with a profound and poignant clarity: ***'We now know insulin is relevant to most brain-related chronic diseases. Because the brain needs a lot of energy to function, it needs a reliable fuel. When the brain becomes insulin resistant, access to this fuel becomes limited.'*** This revelation brings to the forefront the brain's voracious energy demands and reliance on a steadfast fuel supply. Insulin resistance, a shadow that looms large over our metabolic health, emerges as a formidable adversary, constraining the brain's access to this crucial fuel. It's a scenario that encapsulates the complexities of metabolic dysfunction and accentuates the pivotal role of a well-regulated insulin landscape in maintaining the brain's vitality and function.

As we stand at this crossroads, the convergence of these insights paves the way for a paradigm shift – reimagining neurological disorders through the lens of metabolic health. The wisdom imparted by McDonald, Cervenka, and Bikman doesn't just enrich our understanding; it beckons us to rethink, question, and explore new horizons in our relentless pursuit of answers.

How about this for an open and honest quote in an article published in WIRED magazine. It's from Dr Tom Insel, the former National Institute of Mental Health director. On departing his role, he said, 'I spent 13 years at NIMH really pushing on the neuroscience and genetics of mental disorders, and when I look back on that, I realise that while I think I succeeded at getting lots of really cool papers published by cool scientists at fairly high costs – I think $20 billion – I don't think we moved the needle in reducing suicide, reducing hospitalisations, improving recovery for the tens of millions of people who have mental illness.'[42] I don't think Insel should be too hard on himself. Everyone was searching for a neurological answer because that could have led to big bucks for the pharmaceutical companies. But, with the reality that most conditions are linked to metabolism, it is a dietary and lifestyle shift that will, as Insel would put it, 'move the needle'.

Over the following pages, exploring several neurological conditions (I don't have either the space or enough research to discuss them all), remember, just like my *Tree of Afflictions*, not only may they all be influenced by sugar spikes, lack of fibre and insulin resistance, they may be interwoven with one another. For example, research I will share shortly conducted by four researchers, who confined a group of volunteers suffering from three conditions - major depression, bipolar, and schizoaffective disorders to a psychiatric hospital, and changed their diet to a ketogenic diet, recorded positive outcomes across all three conditions.[43]

Allow me to wrap up this introduction by appreciating the remarkable progress made in medical science, particularly in the realm of neurological conditions, which stands as a pivotal area of exploration. I would like to congratulate all of those who have been involved in advancements made in recent years. This significance is underscored by recent findings suggesting that a staggering one in two individuals will, at some juncture in their lives, fulfil the criteria for a mental disorder.[44]

*****

Alzheimer's: The Third Type Of Diabetes

Alzheimer's disease, in many medical circles, is now dubbed 'type 3 diabetes'. This new label casts Alzheimer's not just as a thief of memories but as a metabolic outlier, creeping up silently like an unanticipated twist in a mystery novel that leaves everyone puzzled. Take the story of my parents, for example. Since they were doe-eyed 14-year-olds, they've shared meals for 69 years, a testament to their culinary compatibility. But here's the thing: while my dad's carb-fuelled life led him down the path of type 2 diabetes, my mom ended up with Alzheimer's.

Professor Ben Bikman sheds light on this complex scenario. When the brain is in a 'fed state' after consuming a conventional meal, it relies entirely on glucose for its energy needs, with less than half of its energy coming from ketones (a topic we'll jump into later). In the context of a typical Western diet, characterised by frequent eating (every few hours) and the consumption of highly processed foods, the brain remains in a perpetually fed state. This overreliance on glucose presents a concerning issue because the brain's ability to access an adequate supply of glucose is a key element of Alzheimer's disease. Ben further explains, 'As the brain becomes progressively insulin resistant, it becomes less and less able to get enough glucose to meet its energy demands. So, like an engine running on empty, the brain doesn't work as well. This phenomenon is known as 'glucose hypometabolism', and the greater the degree a person has it, the more rapid the onset of clinical Alzheimer's disease.' As of writing this, my recent podcast with Ben has already surpassed a quarter of a million views, making it a valuable watch.

Labelling Alzheimer's as 'type 3 diabetes' is like saying the brain threw a sugar tantrum, forgetting how to use glucose properly, much like a stubborn toddler who refuses to eat their veggies. This analogy might sound light-hearted, but it underscores a serious issue: a glitch in the brain's energy system, where insulin and glucose stumble over each other's feet in a metabolic dance.

Despite pouring billions into Alzheimer's research, we might have been chasing our tails up the wrong tree. Picture this: the brain, a ravenous yet fist-sized powerhouse (just 2% of the body by volume), guzzles an enormous 20% of the body's energy. But when its cells give the cold shoulder to sugar, their primary fuel, they begin to sputter and falter, running dangerously low on the energy they desperately need to function.

The Ketogenic Diet: Swapping Dance Partners

In a recent interview, I had the pleasure of speaking with Dr Mary Newport, an acclaimed author of five books on Alzheimer's and a leading authority on the subject. She explained how the ketogenic diet is the dietary equivalent of switching dance partners. She told me that in a recent study with Alzheimer's sufferers, swapping carbohydrates for fats was like teaching the brain to salsa instead of waltz. Their brains started grooving to ketones, an alternative fuel that doesn't rely on insulin's dance moves. Some participants who had previously had to retire because of their condition improved so much they could return to their professional lives, a comeback story better than any reality TV show.

For me personally, staying in ketosis is less about doing up the top button on my jeans and more about not forgetting where I put them. With my genetic cards being marked with the APOE4 gene, making me statistically more prone to the disease, I'm hedging my bets and hoping to keep my brain going strong well into my golden years.

Returning to the story of Dr Mary Newport, we encounter a remarkable dietary intervention she pioneered for her husband, one that would profoundly impact the trajectory of his Alzheimer's disease. By incorporating coconut oil into his meals, enriched with a potent compound called C8, she initiated a transformative process within his brain. This dietary shift effectively revitalised his cognitive functions, transitioning his brain from a reliance on glucose to a ketogenic state. Witnessing her husband's remarkable progress, Mary's dedication became evident as she meticulously ensured his ketosis while administering coconut oil. In just a month's time, the results were astonishing: Steve, once unable to draw a recognisable clock face, effortlessly completed the task with newfound clarity and ease.

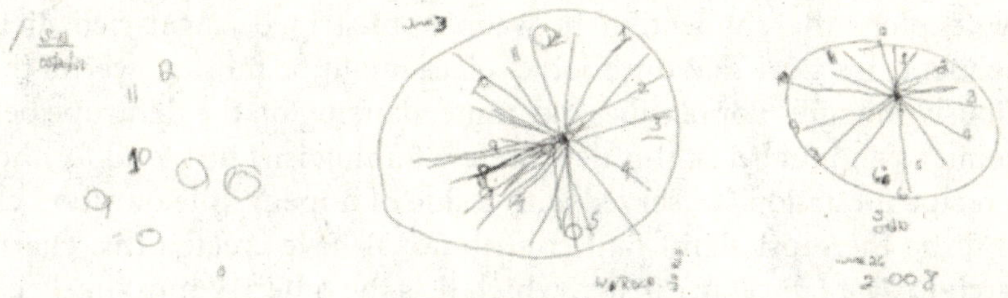

1 day before coconut oil | 14 days after starting coconut oil | 37 days after starting coconut oil

Uric Acid's Link To Alzheimer's: A Brain Fog Unveiled

In 2017, the Framingham Heart Study embarked on an exploration into the realm of 'preclinical Alzheimer's disease', shedding light on the potential brain hazards of daily fruit juice consumption. This phase, known as preclinical Alzheimer's, marks a period where individuals show no outward signs of cognitive decline. However, a peek inside their brains reveals early disease markers, invisible in their daily actions but silently laying the groundwork for future symptoms. This stage could span years, even decades, before the disease's brain pathology manifests in noticeable cognitive impairment.

The study, spearheaded by Boston University, meticulously examined thousands who underwent cognitive tests and brain scans to determine the impact of sugar-laden drinks, from sodas to fruit juices, on their cerebral health. They compared individuals who indulged in more than one daily sugary drink with those who consumed fewer. The findings were alarming: higher intake of these beverages correlated with reduced brain volume, smaller hippocampal size (crucial for memory), and diminished memory test scores.[45]

Uric acid, a silent saboteur, exacerbates this scenario by fostering free radical production and diminishing nitric oxide synthesis, which is crucial for maintaining optimal blood flow, including the brain. This reduction in nitric oxide not only hampers insulin's glucose management capabilities but also weakens neural communication and memory formation by affecting synaptic transmission, the brain's method of neuron-to-neuron conversation. Uric acid casts a fog over the brain's communication network, akin to trying to watch a clear broadcast on an old, fuzzy TV screen set to the wrong channel. This interference with neural messages harms brain health, potentially speeding up cognitive decline.

As we explore the connection between fibre-striped, sugar-rich diets and Alzheimer's, it's clear that our food choices might be more powerful than we previously thought. For families like mine, dancing on the tightrope between Alzheimer's and diabetes, this new understanding isn't just food for thought; it's a recipe for action, all served with a side of hope. While our food choices seem to be the most significant contributor, I have created this chart from research in *The Lancet* in 2020 [46], which lists the other 12 most likely causes.

1. Hypertension
2. Smoking
3. Obesity
4. Alcohol consumed above guidelines
5. Diabetes
6. Air pollution
7. Poor education
8. Depression
9. Traumatic brain injury
10. Hearing impairment
11. Physical inactivity
12. Social isolation

Homocysteine: Revealing The Silent Threat To Brain Health

We've just discussed the importance of selecting the right fuel for optimal brain function. However, let's not underestimate the significance of additives, especially when it comes to enhancing our brain's performance. Despite constituting only 2% of our body's volume, the brain demands a remarkable 20% of its fuel. Like a high-performance sports car, it relies on top-notch additives to operate smoothly. Among these vital additives, vitamins play a central role.

Now, let me introduce you to a captivating discovery that could revolutionise your understanding of optimal brain health. Have you ever encountered homocysteine? It's akin to a hidden menace lurking in your bloodstream, unveiled by the insightful Patrick Holford, who also contributed the foreword to this book. Think of it as a toxic amino acid, a by-product of insufficient intake of B vitamins, particularly vitamin B-12 or folate.

The American Heart Association says, 'Homocysteine is a chemical in the blood that is produced when an amino acid (a building block of protein) called methionine is broken down in the body. We all have some homocysteine in our blood. Elevated homocysteine levels are often referred to as hyperhomocysteinemia.'

Here's the issue: if your homocysteine level shoots above 11μmol/L, it's like rolling out the red carpet for over a hundred diseases! Think heart issues, brain shrinkage, Alzheimer's, cognitive function, to name but a few. Patrick's been championing this cause since 2003, calling it 'the biggest health breakthrough of the century.'

Patrick even tested TV host Pat Kenny on live TV, revealing a wake-up call about his heart health. Fast-forward two decades, and the evidence is crystal clear: high homocysteine levels are linked to a laundry list of diseases, from brain fog to heart troubles. It's like your body's silent alarm bell, alerting you to potential health risks.

Patrick says, 'Here we are, decades later, and still, few people know about it. Even fewer know their homocysteine score. And to add insult to injury, there's been a sneaky campaign, fuelled by misleading science, to keep the lid on it. But why? Well, I've got a theory: there's no patentable drug to lower homocysteine - just good old-fashioned, inexpensive vitamins.'

Having a homocysteine level above 11μmol/L is more common than you'd think. If you're over 60, the odds are stacked against you: 40% of folks in the US over 60 have a homocysteine score above 11.[47] It's probably not much different in the UK.

Uncovering why homocysteine is such a big deal

Picture this: many nutrients in your body don't just snap into action as soon as you swallow them - they need a little makeover first. It's like they're waiting in the wings until they get 'methylated'. Take folate or folic acid, for example. They need to morph into methylfolate to become biologically active.

But wait, there's more! Methylation isn't just a one-trick pony; it's the VIP of biochemical processes. From adrenalin to insulin, histamine to hormones like estrogen, they all rely on methylation for their production and breakdown. It's like the ultimate choreographer, orchestrating a symphony of biochemical reactions in your body.

Now, here's where homocysteine steps into the spotlight. If your methylation process hits a snag, homocysteine levels start to rise. It's like a traffic jam on the road to making the body's most important 'methylator' - s-adenosyl methionine or SAMe for short. SAMe is like the conductor of the methylation orchestra, ensuring everything runs smoothly. But here's the catch: SAMe can't do its job without the helping hand of vitamins B6, B12, and folate. They're the unsung heroes behind the scenes, turning methionine, an amino acid you eat, into SAMe through a series of enzymatic reactions. So, next time you reach for those B vitamins, remember - they're not just for energy; they're essential players in the intricate dance of methylation.

Shield your noggin by lowering homocysteine

This sneaky amino acid doesn't just wreak havoc on your arteries; it's also a vendetta against your brain. Back in 1969, Dr Kilmer McCully stumbled upon its villainous deeds in children with a genetic disorder. Fast-forward to today, and studies reveal a staggering 17 times higher risk of cerebrovascular damage for those in the top quarter for homocysteine levels.[47]

But wait, there's more! Homocysteine doesn't stop at artery damage; it's also cosying up to a toxic substance called p-tau (plasma phosphorylated tau), infamous for its role in Alzheimer's. Big pharma may be scrambling to develop a drug for this, but why bother when good old B vitamins can do the trick? Lowering homocysteine with these budget-friendly B vitamins reduces p-tau levels and slashes your risk of many brain-related conditions.

It's like hitting the pause button on brain shrinkage and giving memory loss the elbow. But here's the kicker: once a stroke or Alzheimer's has reared its ugly head, there's limited room for improvement. So, why not nip it in the bud before it wreaks havoc? It's time to take charge of your brain health and show homocysteine who's boss!

While there is more I could write on homocysteine, I truly recommend a visit to the website of a charity I am very fond of, called Food For The Brain.

*****

Depression And Anxiety: A New Perspective

In the vast ocean of human emotions, feeling down or anxious is as natural as the ebb and flow of the tides. These feelings are universal human experiences, often triggered by life's ups and downs, such as stress at work, relationship issues, or the myriad uncertainties of daily living. It's important to recognise that feeling temporarily sad or anxious doesn't necessarily mean one has a mental health disorder. These emotions can be transient, much like clouds passing in the sky, and don't always impair one's ability to function in daily life. However, when these feelings persist, deepen, and begin to affect the ability to function, they may cross the threshold into the realm of clinical conditions, such as depression or an anxiety disorder. The distinction lies in these feelings' intensity, duration, and impact on life.

Clinical depression, or major depressive disorder, is characterised by a pervasive sense of sadness, loss of interest or pleasure in almost all activities, and a suite of physical and cognitive symptoms that persist for at least two weeks and represent a change from previous functioning. These symptoms can include changes in appetite or weight, sleep disturbances, loss of energy, feelings of worthlessness or excessive guilt, difficulty thinking or concentrating, and recurrent thoughts of death or suicide. Clinical depression is not just a temporary mood swing; it is a profound, often debilitating condition that requires professional evaluation and treatment.

Similarly, clinical anxiety disorders go beyond temporary worry or fear. They involve excessive anxiety and worry that are difficult to control and cause significant distress or impairment in social, occupational, or other important areas of functioning. Anxiety disorders encompass a range of specific conditions, such as generalised anxiety disorder, panic disorder, and social anxiety disorder, each with its own set of symptoms and triggers, but all marked by an overwhelming and persistent sense of anxiety that is out of proportion to the actual threat or challenge.

The key difference between experiencing normal, transient feelings of sadness or anxiety and having a clinical condition, just as with depression, is the degree to which these feelings interfere with one's ability to lead a normal life. For those struggling with clinical depression or an anxiety disorder, the symptoms are not something they can 'snap out of'. Understanding this distinction is crucial not only for those experiencing these symptoms but also for their loved ones. It fosters compassion, encourages seeking help, and underscores the importance of professional support in navigating the journey back to wellbeing. If you or someone you know is struggling with persistent feelings of sadness or anxiety, reaching out to a healthcare provider can be the first step toward understanding and managing these feelings.

The diagnosis of clinical depression and anxiety disorders is guided by standardised criteria outlined in widely recognised diagnostic manuals. The two primary manuals used by healthcare professionals around the world are:

- **ICD 11:** The International Classification of Diseases, 11th Revision (ICD-11), published by the WHO, is most often used in the UK. The ICD-11 provides a global standard for diagnosing and classifying mental health conditions, including depression and anxiety disorders. It is used for clinical diagnosis, research, and health management purposes worldwide.
- **DSM-5:** *The Diagnostic and Statistical Manual of Mental Disorders*, Fifth Edition (DSM-5), published by the American Psychiatric Association (APA).

Both manuals aim to provide clear, objective criteria to help healthcare professionals diagnose mental health conditions consistently and accurately. The criteria include specific symptoms, their severity, and the duration over which they must be present for a diagnosis to be made.

Why do we draw a line between experiencing moments of sadness or anxiety and the diagnosis of a clinical mental health condition? It's crucial because the traditional pathways to treat diagnosed conditions have long been confined to psychotherapy, cognitive-behavioural therapy (CBT), or pharmaceuticals. Yet, the landscape of mental health is shifting dramatically. Groundbreaking insights from luminaries like Dr Christopher Palmer, Dr Michael Hoffmann, and Professor Ben Bikman are illuminating a profound truth: many mental illnesses are, at their core, metabolic dysfunctions of the brain.

This revelation is not just academic; it's a clarion call for a paradigm shift in how we approach mental health treatment. It echoes through the halls of international health conferences and is steadily gaining global recognition. When mental health concerns cross the threshold into clinical territory, our response must evolve beyond traditional treatments. The metabolic underpinnings of brain health necessitate a holistic approach – embracing natural foods, prioritising fibre, regular exercise, and ensuring quality sleep.

The conversation is expanding, with many in the medical community advocating for a metabolic perspective on mental health. The ketogenic diet, discussed in the next chapter, emerges as a powerful tool in this new arsenal for brain health. But before we explore its potential, let's pause to acknowledge the intricate interplay between our metabolic health and mental wellbeing. Each condition we're exploring in this section of the book is a piece of a larger metabolic puzzle, revealing the critical role of metabolic health in our overall psychological state.

While what I am about to share might seem overly simplistic and perhaps counter to the views of some of my psychotherapist colleagues, there's a compelling case to be made for the role of blood sugar and insulin levels in influencing mood disorders such as anxiety and depression. The link between our mental state and the highs and lows of blood sugar, or glycaemic fluctuations, is becoming increasingly evident. Symptoms commonly associated with poor glycaemic control, like irritability, anxiety, and worry, bear a striking resemblance to those of mental health conditions. Considering the brain's primary reliance on glucose for energy, this parallel is hardly surprising.

In the intricate dance of brain chemistry, insulin resistance plays a pivotal role. Not only does it disrupt dopamine turnover, a critical neurotransmitter associated with mood and reward pathways, but it also significantly amplifies the risk of falling into the clutches of depression.[49 / 50] This connection casts a new light on mood disorders, suggesting that the fluctuations in blood sugar could be the hidden puppeteer behind the curtain of mental health symptoms.

A 2017 study sheds light on the shadow cast by high sugar consumption on mental health. The study's findings are undisputable, establishing a clear link between sugar intake from sweet foods and beverages and the deterioration of psychological health over time.[51] This evidence underscores the adverse impact of sugar on our mental landscape, reinforcing the importance of dietary choices in maintaining mental wellbeing.

Fibre And Brain Health

In this intricate interlock of diet, mood, and mental health, fibre emerges as a ray of hope. Its role in stabilising blood sugar levels and moderating insulin response is well-documented. But its benefits extend beyond mere glycaemic control. Research in 2023 highlights the potential of fibre, not just in mitigating the severity of depression but possibly in preventing its onset.[52] A 2021 randomised controlled trial casts inulin fibre in a new light, revealing its capacity to uplift mood in individuals with obesity, especially in the presence of the Coprococcus bacteria in the gut.[53]

A study conducted by four exceptional researchers, two of whom I have had the pleasure to meet, Dr Eric Wiseman and researcher Georgia Ede, conducted a study on 31 adults with severe mental health issues like major depression, bipolar, and schizoaffective disorders.[43] These individuals weren't responding well to standard psychiatric treatments. They tried an alternative approach by putting these patients on a ketogenic diet, which means they ate very few carbs (no more than 20 g a day) while staying in a psychiatric hospital. The main things they studied were changes in depression and psychosis symptoms, using specific scales like the Hamilton Depression Rating Scale (HAM-D) and the Positive and Negative Syndrome Scale for psychosis.

Remarkably, after following this low-carb diet, every patient showed improvement. Their scores on these scales, which measure the severity of depression and psychosis, dropped significantly. Notably, everyone improved to a degree considered clinically significant. And the majority (64%) were discharged on reduced medication. This study suggests that, for people with severe and treatment-resistant mental health conditions, a ketogenic diet could significantly improve symptoms and reduce the need for medications. As we continue to unravel the complex relationship between diet, blood sugar, and mental health, it becomes increasingly clear that our dietary choices echo profoundly within the corridors of our minds.

*****

Epilepsy: A Metabolic Rethink

In the UK, around 600,000 people live with epilepsy, equating to about one in every 100 individuals. Each day, 87 people receive this life-altering diagnosis. For roughly 30% of these patients facing a condition known as drug-resistant epilepsy (DRE), conventional medications offer no solace. Here, the ketogenic diet emerges as a potential protector amidst the challenges of neurological disorders, particularly for younger sufferers.

Epilepsy, steeped in dietetic history and wrapped in medical mysteries, exemplifies the impact of diet on neurological conditions. For years, the ketogenic diet lingered at the edges of medical treatment, yet it now stands as a primary strategy in the battle against epilepsy. This shift from an alternative option to a mainline treatment marks a significant shift towards embracing metabolic therapies. It narrates a tale of transformation, where altering one's diet can adjust the brain's electrical dynamics, providing relief in situations where traditional approaches stumble.

The statistics are both staggering and illuminating. An impressive roster of clinical trials stands as a testament to the efficacy of the ketogenic diet in quelling the tempest of seizures that characterise epilepsy. But this revelation is not a recent epiphany. For close to 90 years, this dietary approach has often been used as a way of controlling epilepsy. The underlying principle is elegantly simple yet profoundly transformative – by shifting the brain's fuel source from glucose to ketones, a metabolic switch occurs, one that has the potential to silence the electrical storms that manifest as seizures.

The ketogenic diet, a form of nutritional therapy for epilepsy, was conceived in 1923 by Dr. Russell Wilder at the Mayo Clinic. Its efficacy was profound, offering a significant reduction in seizures for over half of its adherents. This dietary approach flourished, offering hope and relief, until the 1940s, when the dawn of pharmaceutical interventions for seizures cast it into the shadows. Yet, this nutritional phoenix was destined to rise again.

In 1993, the Abrahams family, driven by their son Charlie's battle with epilepsy, sought refuge in the ketogenic diet at Johns Hopkins University, the sole bastion of ketogenic wisdom at the time. Charlie's remarkable recovery ignited a spark that set the world ablaze. Inspired by his son's transformation, Jim Abrahams penned the screenplay *First Do No Harm*, graced by the talent of Meryl Streep, casting a spotlight on this forgotten dietary hero. This resurgence of interest, further fuelled by a feature on Dateline NBC in 1997, propelled the ketogenic diet back into the limelight, not just for epilepsy but as a promising ally against a spectrum of metabolic and neurological maladies.

Charlie Abraham's story is a testament to the transformative power of the ketogenic diet. Before discovering this dietary approach, Charlie faced a daily struggle with debilitating seizures that severely impacted his quality of life. Traditional treatments and medications had fallen short of providing relief, leaving the Abrahams family in a state of despair. However, their decision to embrace the ketogenic diet at Johns Hopkins marked a turning point. Remarkably, Charlie's seizures not only diminished significantly, but he regained a level of health and vitality that had seemed almost unattainable. This dramatic turnaround reshaped Charlie's future and became a global inspiration to others facing similar battles. Jim Abraham's dedication to sharing his son's success story has since inspired a movement highlighting the potential of dietary interventions in managing complex health conditions.

Clinical Trials Insight

A favourite resource of mine for medical research is clinicaltrials.gov. At the time of writing, an impressive tally of 61 clinical trials was documented, each supporting the ketogenic diet as an effective method for managing epilepsy and seizures. This is a significant revelation, especially considering that clinical trials are often conducted to validate the efficacy of new drugs or pharmaceutical innovations. The abundance of evidence favouring a dietary solution over medication is remarkable. Let me draw your attention to two standout trials:

145 Children Suffering Epilepsy Randomised Controlled Trial:

This study involved children ages 2 to 16, who experienced at least one seizure daily or over seven seizures a week. These children hadn't responded well to at least two antiepileptic drugs and had never tried the ketogenic diet before. They were divided into two groups for a research study: one group followed the ketogenic diet, and the other group did not (they were the control group).

After three months, the group on the ketogenic diet experienced a significant decrease in the number of seizures they had. On average, their seizures reduced by 75% compared to before they started the diet. In comparison, the control group, who didn't follow the diet, actually had an increase in seizure frequency by about 37% on average.[54]

2020 Cochrane Meta-Analysis

In a comprehensive 2020 review, researchers scoured medical databases for studies examining the effectiveness of the ketogenic diet in treating epilepsy in children. They identified 13 clinical trials involving a total of 932 participants. These studies varied in length from 2 to 16 months. The analysis revealed that children who followed a ketogenic diet were up to three times more likely to become completely free of seizures and up to six times more likely to see their seizure frequency reduced by half or more compared to those who continued with their standard care. This significant finding underscores the potential of the ketogenic diet as a highly effective alternative treatment for epilepsy in children.[55]

The ketogenic diet's story from once obscurity to recognition in the realm of epilepsy treatment is a testament to the enduring power of metabolic therapy. It's a narrative that unfolds against the backdrop of relentless scientific inquiry and clinical rigour. The diet's efficacy is not just anecdotal; it is rooted in a robust body of clinical evidence, with each trial adding a layer of understanding to our grasp of epilepsy's metabolic underpinnings.

*****

Parkinson's Disease: The Dopamine Connection

Parkinson's disease, a debilitating condition that insidiously weaves its way into the brain's fabric, progressively impairing its functionalities, presents a complex puzzle in the landscape of neurological disorders. Characterised by its hallmark symptoms - uncontrollable tremors, sluggish movements, and rigid muscles - Parkinson's paints a picture of a brain under siege. The NHS sheds light on the conventional understanding of this condition, attributing it to the depletion of nerve cells in a brain region known as the substantia nigra, culminating in a stark decline in dopamine. Beyond its well-celebrated role in bestowing pleasure, this neurotransmitter is a critical conductor of the body's symphony of movements. Its dwindling levels orchestrate the distressing symphony of symptoms emblematic of Parkinson's disease.

Yet, the narrative of Parkinson's disease is not a linear tale of dopamine depletion. Recent strides in research have uncovered a multifaceted pathogenesis. Mitochondrial dysfunction, abnormal glucose metabolism in the brain, and neuro-inflammation emerge as pivotal players in this complex ballet, underscoring the condition's intricacies.

Parkinson's does not tread its path in isolation; it casts a shadow over 1% of the population aged over 60, often leaving in its wake the debilitating spectre of dementia, marked by the accumulation of Lewy bodies, rogue proteins that further entangle the brain's intricate workings.[56]

But let's pivot our gaze to dopamine and its intricate dance with insulin. The relationship between these two biochemical protagonists is both absorbing and revealing. Animal studies have unfurled intriguing narratives; a reduction in insulin levels correlates with a notable surge in dopamine receptors, painting a picture of a biochemical seesaw between these molecules. And this interplay is not confined to the animal kingdom. Human research echoes these findings, unveiling a stark portrait of elevated insulin levels casting a shadow over dopamine production, a scenario that extends its repercussions beyond Parkinson's, hinting at a landscape where diminished pleasure and reward could set the stage for addiction.[57/58]

The thread that weaves through this narrative is not a frail strand but a robust rope - up to 80% of individuals grappling with Parkinson's display insulin resistance or are in the clutches of type 2 diabetes.[59] This statistic is not a mere footnote but a warning sign, illuminating the profound intersection between metabolic dysfunction and neurological decay.

For individuals with Parkinson's disease exploring dietary interventions, the ketogenic diet has shown promising signs of being beneficial. According to a small clinical study highlighted by the Charlie Foundation, a group of volunteers with Parkinson's who maintained a ketogenic diet for one month saw improvements in their condition. Specifically, five out of seven participants experienced better post-diet test scores. This study, despite lacking a control group, has brought attention to the potential role of the ketogenic diet in managing Parkinson's disease. It is believed that ketosis might bypass disrupted pathways in the brain, support vital energy pathways, and exhibit an anti-inflammatory effect on the brain.

A comparison between low-fat and ketogenic diets on Parkinson's symptoms showed small but significant improvements in both motor and non-motor symptoms for participants on the ketogenic diet. Improvements were noted in urinary problems, pain, fatigue, daytime sleepiness, and cognitive impairment. However, the study also reported a transient exacerbation of tremor and/or rigidity in the early weeks for some participants on the ketogenic diet, highlighting the need for careful consideration and medical supervision when adopting such dietary changes.

These findings suggest that, while more research is needed, the ketogenic diet could offer a complementary approach to managing Parkinson's disease symptoms, especially in cases where traditional medication is less effective. It's crucial for anyone considering this dietary approach to consult with healthcare professionals to ensure it's appropriate for their individual health situation and to monitor for any adverse effects.[60]

*****

Neuropathy: Nervous About Insulin

Characterised by a spectrum of symptoms ranging from numbness and pain, typically in the hands and feet, to more complex systemic manifestations affecting digestion and urination, peripheral neuropathy is more than a mere inconvenience. It's a condition that resonates with a significant fraction of the population, with the NHS suggesting that 1 in 10 people in the UK 'are affected by some degree of peripheral neuropathy'. This paints a picture of a widespread affliction that demands attention and understanding.

At the heart of this condition lies the peripheral nervous system, an intricate network of nerves that operates beyond the central nervous system's dominion. With its myriad sensory, motor, and autonomic nerves, this network is a marvel of biological engineering, ensuring a multitude of sensations, movements, and automatic functions that coordinate our daily experiences and survival.

The relationship between peripheral neuropathy and diabetes is well-chronicled. The NHS's recommendation for regular check-ups for those at the highest risk, including individuals with diabetes, underscores the established link between sustained high blood sugar levels and nerve damage.

Recent research has revealed that nerve cells, much like their counterparts elsewhere in the body, are responsive to insulin. This opens a new chapter in our understanding of peripheral neuropathy. As a key regulator of cellular energy uptake and utilisation, insulin emerges as a critical player. As nerves become increasingly resistant to insulin's overtures, their ability to function optimally is compromised. The result is a gradual descent into the realm of neuropathy, marked not just by the conventional hallmarks of diabetes but by a more complex interplay of metabolic dysfunction. [61]

*****

Migraines: A Metabolic Mystery

Migraines are a prevalent force in the realm of neurological disorders, affecting approximately 12% of the global population.[62] Not only is it widespread, but its impact is profound, with estimates suggesting that in 2016 alone, migraines were responsible for 45.1 million years of life lived in the shadow of disability.[63]

Navigating the perplexing world of migraines is akin to being a detective in a physiological whodunit, where the usual suspects range from the mundane to the bizarre. Who would've thought that migraines, those debilitating disruptors of wellbeing, are our body's quirky way of hitting the reset button, restoring brain energy, and dialling down oxidative stress? It's as if our brains, in their infinite wisdom, decide to throw a full-blown energy crisis to get our attention. 'Hey, something's off here; let's shut it down and reboot!' – think of it as your brain's way of pulling off a dramatic performance to ensure it stays in the limelight.

Now, I know what you're thinking: 'Really? Migraines are beneficial?' Before you dismiss this as another plot twist in the grand narrative of our bodies, consider this: nature often has its peculiar logic. High insulin during pregnancy, our ancestors becoming overweight in autumn, and, yes, migraines are not just random glitches but part of a complex, albeit sometimes perplexing, biological strategy. So, let's reframe our perspective: migraines are not so much a neurological quirk as they are a metabolic puzzle, a riddle where the pieces are intricately tied to how well our brain's mitochondria are fuelled.

While there are a myriad of migraine head-pounding causes – from diet to stress, from sleep deprivation to our beloved caffeine, and even the ever-changing whims of the weather – our focus here is on the dietary director of this drama.

I will now hand you over to four experts on the subject, three of whom I have chatted directly with. Conversations that have led me to conclude that if I were to suffer migraines, after eliminating the traditionally known causes such as stress, alcohol, artificial sweeteners, caffeine, lack of exercise, the beginning of a period (well, not on my list of course), lack of sleep, depression and anxiety, my next step would be to try a ketogenic diet.

Professor Ben Bikman, in his enlightening book *Why We Get Sick*, vividly describes migraines as part of a 'running on empty' scenario. It's like your brain is a high-performance vehicle that's been neglected, sputtering and stuttering because it's not getting the premium fuel it needs. When insulin throws a wrench in the works, glucose can't waltz into the brain, leaving it energy-starved and cranky.

Enter Dr Boz with insights as refreshing as a cool breeze on a sweltering day. Her book *Any Way You Can* dissects the migraine enigma with surgical precision. She asks us to picture it as our brain cells swelling up like balloons at a birthday party gone wrong, a migraine in the making. But why settle for a throbbing head when you can turn the tide? The answer lies in the ketogenic lifestyle, a dietary switcheroo that stops inflammation and tells your brain cells to chill out. But don't expect instant gratification; transitioning to a keto diet is like a slow dance, where the body takes its sweet time to shed the water weight and inflammation, starting from your extremities and finally gracing your brain with its healing touch.

If you suffer from migraines, Angela Stanton's *Fighting the Migraine Epidemic* should be at the top of your must-read list. This treasure trove of tips and tricks delves into the dietary dos and don'ts, unravelling the migraine mystery one page at a time. Fancy a midnight snack? Try some protein-rich cheese or meat an hour before bed, and don't forget that magical pinch of salt with a glass of water 30 minutes before you hit the hay. These simple hacks might be your ticket to a migraine-free life.

A tip of the hat to Dr Michael Hoffman for spotlighting a clinical trial where

50 migraine-suffering individuals embarked on a three-month ketogenic odyssey. The result dramatically reduced both the severity and frequency of migraines.

Neurol Sci (2021) 42:3865–3870

	Baseline	After 3 months of diet	*p*
Hours with migraine *n*./day	24 (1–24)	5.5 (0–24)	0.0016
Day with migraine *n*./month	30 (12–30)	7.5 (0–30)	0.0001
Pain intensity	3 (2–3)	1 (0–3)	0.0024
Tablet intake *n*./month	30 (5–100)	6 (0–100)	0.0022

Median values and (range values) before and after KD, significance level (*p* value)

*****

Bipolar Disease: The Two Views

In our approach to understanding bipolar disorder, I want to focus on sharing a poignant story from the Baszucki family. Their experience not only highlights the complexities of managing bipolar disorder but also underlines the potential benefits of a dietary approach. Besides sharing their personal experiences, the Baszucki family has generously subsidised the Public Health Collaboration, a charity of which I am both a patron and benefactor. Their foundation's sponsorship, particularly for our 2024 conference, was a testament to their commitment to advancing the understanding of mental health issues. Do check out their website at baszuckigroup.com.

Matt Baszucki's (Jan and David's son) struggle with bipolar disorder is a compelling tale of resilience in the face of seemingly insurmountable odds. Diagnosed with bipolar disorder at 19, following a significant episode, Matt's subsequent battle was marked by an exhaustive search for effective treatment. Despite taking 29 different medications and consulting with 40 doctors, his condition was deemed treatment-resistant. This diagnosis often signals a long, challenging path with limited hope for a solution.

The Baszucki family found hope in exploring the ketogenic diet for Matt's bipolar disorder, guided by Dr Christopher Palmer. Starting on the 4th of January 2021, Matt experienced significant mental clarity and mood stability improvements, allowing for a reduction in medication. This dietary approach surpassed traditional treatment expectations, with even Matt's initially sceptical psychiatrist recognising its profound impact. Matt says, 'I feel great; my mood is stable. I can work all week – two or three years ago, I could never have imagined I'd be able to have a job – and I now have the energy to work on my music.' Jan Matt's mom explained that they had tried a lot of different diets – Paleo, gluten-free, dairy-free... we knew about diets, but we didn't know a well-managed ketogenic diet could treat mental illness. And that's 'what changed everything.'

Matt's journey from the depths of treatment-resistant bipolar disorder to a state of improved health and wellbeing is not just a personal victory; his many TV appearances and newspaper interviews have proven inspirational for many facing similar battles. His story emphasises the need for open-mindedness in treatment options and the critical role of family support in navigating mental health challenges.

The Baszucki family's openness in sharing their story and philanthropic efforts through their foundation exemplifies a profound commitment to making a difference in the mental health landscape. By backing initiatives like our Public Health Collaboration, they are helping to pave the way for more research, better understanding, and ultimately, more effective dietary and lifestyle treatments for mental health conditions.

This narrative, enriched by the Baszucki family's experience and generosity, is a powerful reminder of the potential for recovery and the importance of exploring all possible treatments for mental health conditions. It's a story of struggle, discovery, and hope that contributes significantly to our ongoing conversation about mental health and wellbeing. And it was ultimately enriched by food, not medicine.

Omega-3 DHA: Brain Food

In the realm of brain health, let's turn our attention to a vital nutrient shrouded in the mists of dietary lore and scientific inquiry – Omega-3 DHA, the brain's preferred feast. Within the tapestry of omega-3 fatty acids, there exists a trio of essential characters: ALA (alpha-linolenic acid) found in the verdant fields of vegetables, and its aquatic comrades, EPA (eicosapentaenoic acid) and DHA (docosahexaenoic acid), sourced from the bountiful seas.

Our tale takes a twist when we spotlight DHA, the crème de la crème for brain nourishment. Vegetarians take heed, for while ALA can indeed transform into DHA, this alchemy occurs at a mere half of 1%. Dr James DiNicolantonio sheds light upon this conundrum, revealing that our ancient forebears dined on a feast of ALA tenfold our current intake, making this conversion adequate for their needs. Our primal ancestors, thriving by the sea's edge, devouring 2 to 4 g DHA daily. With such abundance, the body saw little need to convert ALA to DHA, as ALA served its own purposes in growth and heart protection. Our ancestors roamed lands rich in leafy greens and game, maintaining an omega-3 to omega-6 balance of near perfection, 1:1. In times of scarcity, their bodies adeptly converted ALA to the needed EPA and DHA. As humanity ventured from Africa's cradle, our diets evolved with our journey, especially as we hugged the shores, rich in seafood laden with DHA and EPA. This dietary shift subtly rewired our genetics, diminishing our ability to convert ALA to its prized forms.

Fast-forward to today, and the standard diet skews this balance drastically to 20:1, omega-6 to omega-3. Thus unfolds the modern tale of diet-induced woes, where omega-6 fans the flames of inflammation, and omega-3 acts as the gallant firefighter.

Turn our gaze to the coastal vistas of Japan, where low instances of mental health issues whisper tales of omega-3's protective embrace, in stark contrast to the tumultuous health narratives of the UK and America.

Clinical trials, the gold standard of research, echo the critical role of omega-3 in combating conditions like ADHD, Dyspraxia, and ASD. Experiments unveil a near-universal deficiency in DHA and EPA among affected individuals. Alzheimer's research further corroborates DHA's pivotal role, with patients displaying notable deficits in brain DHA levels, a finding echoed in post-mortem studies.

Let's re-meet your mitochondria – your cellular powerhouses. Excluding blood and skin cells, these tiny entities fuel every other cell in your body. When they falter, the shadow of chronic illness looms large, with neurodegenerative diseases often linked to their distress. Drs DiNicolantonio and Mercola in their book *Superfuel*: Ketogenic Keys to Unlock the Secrets of Good Fats, Bad Fats, and Great Health, point to oxidative stress from excessive carbs and omega-6 as culprits behind mitochondrial despair. Their narrative circles back to a time when humanity thrived near nourishing waters, where fish, rich in the complex fats our brains sought after, propelled our cerebral evolution.

In this grand saga of brain health, the moral is clear: embrace the marine bounty of omega-3, rich in DHA and EPA, and nourish not just your body but the very essence of thought and memory. For those adhering to a vegetarian or vegan diet, algae and seaweed stand out as crucial sources of omega-3, uniquely offering both DHA and EPA among plant-based foods.

*****

Reproductive Wellness: A Dietary Perspective

The pivotal influence of diet on our reproductive health is a topic often relegated to the background in wellness conversations. Yet, a striking insight from a recent World Health Organisation study brings this issue to the forefront: 1 in 6 people globally now grapples with infertility challenges. Simultaneously, there's a rising tide of polycystic ovary syndrome (PCOS), closely mirroring the worldwide surge in type 2 diabetes. A comparison of surveys from 2010 to 2020 among individuals aged 20 to 44 reveals a sharp 66% increase in PCOS prevalence.[65]

The past few decades have also increase in a male health issue: erectile dysfunction (ED). While it's rarer in younger men, it now affects about a quarter of those under 40.[66] This increasing trend is more than a mere statistic; it signals a profound health crisis.

The evolution of our food landscape – marked by stripping away vital fibre, adding a cocktail of chemicals, and especially, the rampant infusion of sugars – is not merely changing our eating habits; it's potentially reshaping the future of human reproduction.

Amid concerns over the planet's capacity to support a burgeoning population, the irony that dietary choices – driven by corporate interests – might inadvertently serve as a bizarre form of population control is deeply troubling. The threat to our reproductive health and future population growth rates is no laughing matter, highlighting an urgent need to overhaul our diets and reclaim the purity of our food sources. In a twist of fate, the key to sustaining human populations might lie in our forks.

Decoding Polycystic Ovary Syndrome

Polycystic ovary syndrome (PCOS) isn't just a medical term; it's a reality for 1 in 10 women of childbearing age in the UK, casting a complex web of symptoms and challenges.[67] Imagine a condition so pervasive that it becomes a stumbling block for nearly 80% of those affected when they dream of starting a family.[67] At the crux of PCOS, according to luminaries like Professor Ben Bikman, lies an overproduction of insulin. But he's not alone; research luminaries Dr John Marshall and Dr Andrea Dunaif shine a spotlight on insulin resistance, advocating for it to be at the forefront of treatment considerations for every woman battling PCOS.[68] Their voices echo a growing chorus understanding the critical role insulin plays in this condition.

PCOS isn't one-size-fits-all; it presents a kaleidoscope of symptoms from hyperandrogenaemia (think of it as an unwelcome surplus of androgens), ovulatory hiccups, to its ties with obesity and the tricky path to conception. Dig a little deeper, and you'll find that about 80% of women with PCOS are navigating the choppy seas of insulin resistance and the ensuing tidal wave of compensatory hyperinsulinemia. This isn't just a bystander in the saga of PCOS; it's a key player, fuelling the fire of hyperandrogenaemia by coaxing the theca cells into overdrive and turning up the volume on the effects of an already animated luteinising hormone.[69]

Peering into the intricate dance of insulin resistance and PCOS not only illuminates the path to understanding but also potentially disarming the array of symptoms it brings. As we travel through the *Fibre First* narrative, our hormonal ballet and metabolic health intertwining becomes undeniable, painting a picture of a deeply interconnected system.

Infertility and Insulin

Infertility, a challenge that touches the lives of countless couples across the globe, stands as a testament to the complex interplay of biological, environmental, and lifestyle factors. Often termed a 'disease of couples' rather than individuals, infertility presents a maze of diagnostic intricacies and therapeutic uncertainties. As we've seen, conditions like PCOS play a significant role in female infertility, with insulin resistance casting a long shadow over fertility through a myriad of pathways. Dr Robert Greene, a renowned reproductive endocrinologist, illuminates one such pathway, noting that 'Excess insulin shifts the sex hormone balance to promote testosterone production over oestrogen production', thereby impacting fertility.

Turning our gaze to male infertility, we encounter a spectrum of causes ranging from mechanical issues to disruptions in spermatogenesis. The quality of semen, a critical factor in male fertility, is influenced by a constellation of factors, including but not limited to diet, physical activity, sleep quality, stress, and more. These factors often march in lockstep with insulin resistance, suggesting a metabolic narrative.

Excessive insulin levels exert a significant influence over various hormonal and metabolic pathways, affecting dihydrotestosterone (DHT), testosterone, oestrogen, and inflammation, to name but a few. DHT, a hormone that naturally escalates with age, can also see a surge due to certain lifestyle choices such as smoking, alcohol consumption, poor dietary habits, high stress levels, and the use of specific medications. This uptick in DHT production is not without consequence, potentially leading to increased hair shedding, thinning hair, and the well-documented pattern of male baldness. However, the influence of DHT extends beyond hair health, playing a pivotal role in regulating semen, thereby intertwining with the broader narrative of male fertility.

As research continues to shed light on the varied causes of infertility, it becomes increasingly clear that navigating this complex condition is not straightforward, but a multifaceted quest. This path calls for a holistic approach that acknowledges the profound influence of metabolic health, lifestyle choices, and hormonal balances.

Say NO to Erectile Dysfunction

We previously touched lightly on erectile dysfunction earlier in the book during a conversation about nitric oxide (NO) and its ability to increase blood flow by relaxing the walls of arteries. Picture this: our bodies are like bustling cities, where NO serves as the traffic cop, ensuring smooth arterial traffic and, by extension, robust blood flow. Now, imagine insulin resistance as a massive roadblock, causing congestion and disrupting the flow, leading to erectile dysfunction (ED). It's a tale of circulation and blockage, highlighting the critical role of diet and lifestyle in maintaining arterial highways and byways. This narrative isn't just a cautionary tale but a call to action, urging a reconsideration of our dietary habits for love, life, and vitality.

Insulin resistance significantly raises the risk of erectile dysfunction, with a more pronounced effect as insulin resistance worsens.[71] This strong correlation suggests ED might be one of the initial indicators of insulin resistance. Particularly in young men without other known causes, ED could and should hint at underlying insulin issues. The question then becomes whether insulin resistance directly causes ED or is caused by reduced nitric oxide production.

Reflecting on a personal anecdote, discovering my father used Viagra when one evening over dinner, he told me, 'I once got the blue pill stuck in my throat and it caused me a stiff neck,' while a funny joke, was an eye-opener to the potential early signals of insulin resistance, hinting at a broader health issue that for my dad took years to be formally diagnosed as diabetes. In fact, if instead of just giving my dad his blue pills, his GP had sent him away to work on his diet and to start doing a little exercise, they probably, over the past two decades, could have prescribed him four fewer medications, several of which have caused side effects. But in defence of the GP, this puzzle has only recently been pieced together.

Low Testosterone and Diet

Testosterone, the key player in a myriad of body functions ranging from libido to muscle mass, often nosedives with age, potentially ushering in a less-than-desirable array of symptoms like a dwindling sex drive and rather stubborn belly fat. While ageing gracefully is one thing, an unexpected twist links low testosterone levels with diabetes, doubling the odds if you've got the latter.[70] It turns out, gents, that managing our sugar spikes might be as crucial as hitting the gym to keep those testosterone levels in check.

Navigating through the complex world of testosterone, we encounter a condition known as male hypogonadism, humorously yet somewhat accurately referred to by some as 'Male Menopause'. This intriguing title sparks many reactions, though personally, I find myself currently sitting on the fence, waiting to see how it plays out – I really don't want to upset anyone, especially the females in my life.

Hypogonadism signifies a shortfall in testosterone production by the testicles, manifesting in symptoms that might warrant a second glance (bearing resemblance to certain menopausal symptoms). These encompass a reduced sex drive, erectile challenges (albeit exempt from this comparison), and an unexpected surge of fatigue, among others. It reminds us that our bodies occasionally follow a rhythm we're still deciphering. Additional symptoms may encompass:

- Excess visceral fat
- Reduced muscle mass
- Reduced bone mass
- Hair Loss
- Hot flashes, night sweats
- Depressed mood
- Short-term memory loss

In our modern diet – high in sugar and low in fibre – we might inadvertently affect our testosterone levels. Dr Ben Bikman suggests a significant correlation between metabolic health and testosterone production. It's not so much that men are becoming 'less manly', but that poor metabolic health, characterised by high insulin, might lead to reduced testosterone production. This theory is supported by studies showing that men with higher body fat percentages tend to have lower testosterone levels, yet these levels often increase with weight loss. Furthermore, insulin's role is highlighted as it directly inhibits testosterone production, independent of body fat. This insight encourages a re-evaluation of our dietary habits to support weight management, hormonal balance, and overall health.[72]

While the link between elevated insulin and erectile dysfunction is well-documented, which I have highlighted on my *Tree of Afflictions*, it's crucial to acknowledge that elevated insulin isn't the sole cause of declining testosterone levels in men (which, by the way, now affects 1 in 5 over 50 in the UK[73]). Other potential factors include medication side effects, testicular injury or cancer, issues with hormone-regulating brain glands (the hypothalamus and pituitary), and low thyroid function, among others. This multi-faceted issue underscores the complexity of hormonal health and the importance of a comprehensive approach to diagnosis and treatment.

Prioritising nutrition over medication is a principle I firmly advocate. However, to underscore the relationship between high insulin levels and reduced testosterone, consider this study: It observed over 300 diabetic men with low testosterone, finding that testosterone replacement therapy significantly improved their blood sugar control and insulin sensitivity. Remarkably, about a third saw their diabetes go into remission, and many reached their target blood sugar levels.[74] This research isn't just about advocating for medication; it's a powerful demonstration of how closely diabetes, insulin, and testosterone are intertwined, impacting overall health. A simple blood test by your doctor can reveal your testosterone level. If it's low, treatments like gels, patches, or injections are available. However, exploring dietary changes, as we'll discuss in the upcoming chapter, could also prove beneficial in managing your testosterone levels. However, do chat with your GP to rule out other causes, too.

Menopause, Fibre and Insulin Resistance

My family and I have recently launched a platform, menopause.co.uk, designed as both a community and a resource centre to support women navigating through menopause. The site boasts a team of all-female experts across various fields, including GPs like Dr Jo Darwood and award-winning nutritionists like Claire Snowdon-Darling. Visitors can explore a wealth of articles and videos curated by menopause expert Angeline Davies, aimed at providing valuable insights and guidance during this significant life transition.

Menopause typically occurs when a woman hasn't had any menstrual periods for 12 months. Often between ages 40 and 55, this phase results from reduced oestrogen production, a natural part of ageing. Near menopause, women may face increased insulin resistance due to metabolic shifts influenced by changes in adrenal and thyroid hormone levels. Specifically, the decline in hormones such as oestradiol, essential for menstrual cycle regulation, can lead to insulin resistance, even in women who previously didn't exhibit such symptoms.

Menopause highlights the deep connection between our metabolic and reproductive systems. As hormone levels in the ovaries change, notably with a significant drop in oestrogen (also spelt 'estrogen'), this impacts not just reproductive functions but also how women's bodies manage energy and maintains metabolic health. This period of adjustment can lead to various physical changes, underlining the intertwined nature of our body's reproductive and metabolic systems.

Professor Ben Bikman, a celebrated figure in insulin resistance research, not only dedicates his time to groundbreaking studies in his lab and enlightening university students but also generously shares his expertise worldwide. Esteemed for his philanthropy and profound insights, Professor Bikman illuminates the critical role of oestrogen in maintaining insulin sensitivity across genders. He underscores compelling evidence that 'Oestrogen in both men and women helps maintain insulin sensitivity. We can see firm evidence of this in people whose bodies cannot produce oestrogens due to a deficiency in aromatase, the enzyme that converts androgens to oestrogens. The inability to produce oestrogens, besides other effects, causes insulin resistance to develop.'[75]

The website menopause.co.uk, takes a balanced view, where for some people, hormone replacement therapy (HRT) works as an approach, and for others, a change in diet to one of those discussed in the next chapter provides a more suitable fit.

Navigating the Waves of Menstruation

Menstruation, a natural cycle in a woman's life, often brings with it the unwelcome companion of pain, leading the charge as the top reason for school absences among adolescent girls. Known medically as dysmenorrhoea, painful periods have found an accomplice in diets heavy on inflammation-inducing foods like vegetable oils, sugars, and excessive salts. Dr Haque, a noted authority in obstetrics and gynaecology, highlights that up to 90% of menstruating individuals face this ordeal, with 15% grappling with severe disruptions.

At the heart of these cramps lies the contraction of uterine muscles and blood vessels, exacerbated by prostaglandins – hormone-like substances ramping up inflammation and pain. While underlying conditions like fibroids or endometriosis can intensify menstrual pain, adopting strategies focused on exercise and specific dietary adjustments can offer substantial relief. Here's a closer look at these strategies:

- **Exercise:** Regular physical activity improves blood flow and oxygenation, effectively reducing inflammation and menstrual discomfort.
- **Reduce foods that cause inflammation:** Try to minimise sugar spikes by adopting the *Fibre First* diet.[76]
- **Omega-3 and vitamin D:** A diet rich in these anti-inflammatory nutrients can help alleviate menstrual symptoms.
- **Vitamin B6 (pyridoxine):** Helps lessen pain and cramps, supporting overall menstrual health.
- **Vitamin B1 (thiamine):** This contributes to reducing pain and is essential for managing cramps effectively.
- **Vitamin E (natural alpha-tocopherol):** Known to ease pain and regulate menstrual blood flow, providing comfort during cycles.
- **Magnesium:** Aids in relieving cramps and is also beneficial for mood improvements, particularly in reducing irritability and anxiety. It supports muscle relaxation and may enhance sleep quality.
- **Zinc:** Plays a crucial role in mitigating menstrual pain, adding another layer of support for those experiencing discomfort.

Each component, from targeted exercise routines to nutrient-rich diets, forms a comprehensive approach towards managing and potentially reducing the severity of menstrual pain.

This holistic strategy, weaving together dietary wisdom and physical activity, opens a path to mitigating menstrual distress. In sharing these insights, borrowed from both personal and professional realms, the goal is to arm you with knowledge akin to what I've imparted to my own daughters, aiming for a passage through menstruation that's as smooth as possible. That said, this guide does not stand in for professional medical advice. Should the storm of painful periods persist, consulting your GP is a prudent course.

*****

Leaky Gut Syndrome

Leaky gut refers to a compromised intestinal barrier function, which can escalate into leaky gut syndrome (LGS) under chronic conditions. Intriguingly, every person's gut possesses a certain level of permeability—a natural and essential feature enabling the passage of water and nutrients while safeguarding against harmful substances. However, this delicate balance can be disrupted, resulting in increased permeability, commonly called leaky gut. Fundamentally, a leaky gut presents heightened intestinal lining permeability triggered by various factors. Why isn't leaky gut included in my *Tree of Afflictions*? Simply put, not all roots contribute to it. The primary cause seems to stem from a diet lacking fibre and high in high fructose corn syrup (HFCS).

Despite its impact, leaky gut is not yet officially recognised as a standalone medical diagnosis, leaving the condition's prevalence somewhat of a mystery. It's speculated that anyone grappling with metabolic disorders may experience leaky gut to some degree, highlighting its pervasive yet under-recognised influence on health.

Earlier, we ventured into the world of fructose and discovered its mischievous side, mainly how it plays the unruly guest with the lining of our gut, convincing it to loosen up too much. But now, let's focus on the aftermath of this unwelcome persuasion: leaky gut syndrome. Picture this: your gut, usually a fortress guarding the entrance to your body's inner sanctum, now has its gates slightly ajar. This leads to a cascade of unwelcome visitors slipping through the cracks, setting the stage for a tale of turmoil and health issues.

A heartfelt thank you to Dr Robert Lustig for shedding light on the essential actions we can take beyond simply reducing fructose intake. How else might we strengthen the tight junctions of our intestinal pathway? We're about to uncover a robust barrier system within our intestines, ingeniously designed to confine unwanted substances, ensuring their timely departure through the back door, metaphorically speaking. Let's look at how we support this critical barrier, fortifying its role in our bodily defence.

Central to this barrier system is the mucin layer, a protective coat of mucus that drapes over and lubricates the surfaces of epithelial cells. Composed of polysaccharides, this mucin layer is a protective shield and a potential feast for bacteria in our gut. This symbiotic relationship highlights a crucial balance: feed your bacteria with the right nutrients, or they might start dining on your mucin layer. If neglected, your microbiome could turn to you as its next meal, emphasising why fibre is indispensable.

Incorporating fibre into our diet nurtures this mucin layer, essentially bulking up our internal security system. This reinforcement aids the tight junctions and fosters a harmonious relationship between our gut and bloodstream.

This insight is supported by a wealth of scientific research trials, emphasising the pivotal role of dietary fibre in safeguarding our intestinal barrier and fostering healthy microbiota. One such study succinctly concludes that the protective effects of dietary fibre are primarily attributed to short-chain fatty acids (SCFAs), highlighting how these nutrients contribute to maintaining the equilibrium and health of our gut environment.[77]

Leaky Gut and the Menace of Sepsis

Sepsis isn't just any infection—it's a life-threatening response that occurs when the immune system goes into overdrive, attacking the body's own tissues and organs. Sometimes referred to as septicaemia or blood poisoning, sepsis arises when an existing infection triggers a catastrophic chain reaction throughout the body. Interestingly, most cases of sepsis begin before a patient even reaches the hospital. Infections that pave the way for sepsis commonly originate in the lungs, urinary tract, skin, or gastrointestinal tract.

Leaky gut and gut dysbiosis, characterised by an imbalance in the intestinal microbial population, play crucial roles in developing sepsis. While sepsis itself can lead to dysbiosis, an unhealthy gut can exacerbate the severity of sepsis.[78]

*****

Gout: A Royal Pain

My dad has been a long-time warrior against gout, an unwelcome companion who's been shadowing him for years. Add to that the saga of high blood pressure and a discreet nod to Viagra, and you've got a tale of health hurdles. If you cast your mind back to my *Tree of Afflictions* diagram, you'll see these conditions are not isolated battles; they're intertwined in a dance with insulin resistance. This book, by demonstrating how they are all interconnected, will (hopefully) help doctors in the future to identify hyperinsulinemia far earlier, enabling individuals to avoid the cascade of health issues that often ensue.

As we have discussed, gout is an inflammatory joint disease characterised by the accumulation of uric acid crystals and the accompanying inflammation within the joints. This condition predominantly targets the joints in our limbs, notably affecting the feet (particularly the big toe), ankles, fingers, and wrists. We have learnt how, under normal circumstances, uric acid is efficiently excreted by the kidneys into the urine, thereby being eliminated from the body. However, the wrench in the works comes from insulin resistance. This metabolic alteration disrupts the regular excretory process of the kidneys, leading them to retain uric acid instead of expelling it. Consequently, uric acid levels escalate in the bloodstream and eventually find their way into the joints mentioned. Once settled in the joints, uric acid sparks a localised inflammatory response, manifesting as the redness and swelling that are hallmarks of gout.

But here's a twist in the tale – while we often point fingers at the glucose-packed carb-coaster for insulin woes, for gout, the spotlight turns to a different culprit: fructose. Research has unveiled a striking reality – a 29% surge in gout incidence from 1997 to 2012.[79] This alarming trend means that approximately 1 in 40 people in the UK grapple with this condition. This number underscores its status as a widespread inflammatory and immune-system challenge of our era. A poignant BBC headline recently declared, 'Rates of gout in the UK are soaring'. The article further elaborates, 'It usually affects the big toe but can develop in any joint. Although historically associated with 'good living' among the affluent, gout does not discriminate – it can strike anyone. Yet, it is notably more prevalent among individuals who are overweight or obese, as well as those with high blood pressure or diabetes. Excessive consumption of beer or spirits can also elevate the risk. However, the bright side is that the condition can be managed through lifestyle adjustments, such as weight loss, alongside medication that lowers uric acid levels.'

Parallel to the rise in gout, the menaces of obesity and insulin resistance have also been making their ominous presence felt. These increases reflect our growing indulgence in the very elements that fuel hyperuricaemia (elevated uric acid) and gout – fructose-laden foods and drinks, including the much-favoured soda pop, and even the seemingly benign orange and apple juices. While I won't delve further into this here for a more in-depth discussion on uric acid and its implications, I invite you to revisit the insights shared in chapter 5.

*****

Heartburn and Acid Reflux: A New Perspective

For the fiery duo of heartburn and acid reflux, many are quick to point fingers at the usual suspects-fat, coffee, and alcohol. But what if the story is more complex, and these conditions are not just about what's on your plate or in your cup? Dr Norman Robillard's book *Heartburn* offers a refreshing dive into the real culprits behind these conditions. It's not just a book; it's a revelation that turns the spotlight on the intricate role of the microbiome and challenges the conventional wisdom we often stumble upon in our Google searches.

Acid reflux, or its more formal moniker, gastroesophageal reflux disease

(GERD), is not a stranger to many. In fact, one in four people in the UK suffer from it.[48] While heartburn, with its signature burning sensation behind the breastbone, takes centre stage, GERD's repertoire extends beyond this. It brings a medley of discomfort to the table-abdominal pain, a sour taste in the mouth, bouts of coughing, laryngitis, hoarseness, sinus irritation, and even symptoms that mimic asthma.

Dr Robillard sheds light on a fascinating interplay at the core of acid reflux. Picture this: a scenario where cycles of carbohydrate malabsorption and bacterial overgrowth in the small intestines set the stage for trouble. It's akin to dropping Mentos into a bottle of soda- a growing battalion of bacteria producing intestinal gas, propelling acid reflux into action. So next time you're reaching for that antacid, remember, the story of heartburn and acid reflux is more than skin deep; it's a tale woven through the fabric of our microbiome and dietary choices.

Consider this three-pronged strategy to battle those fiery symptoms. First, get your hands on Dr Robillard's book. Next, rejuvenate your microbiome, making fibre the hero of your dietary saga. And finally, scale back on the carbohydrates, steering clear of the paths that lead to discomfort.

*****

Tinnitus: Turning Down The Volume On Internal Buzz

This condition, a master of illusions, is most commonly a manifestation of chronic inflammation within the ear. Imagine the inner parts of your ear hosting an unwanted pool party with extra water molecules conducting a symphony of vibrations. The music only stops when the inflammation, the uninvited guest, decides to leave.

But how do you uninvite this persistent intruder? The secret may lie in a simple yet powerful mantra: eat the *Fibre First* diet. By championing fibre, you're not just nourishing your body; you're orchestrating a harmonious gut microbiome, the unsung hero in the fight against inflammation. And if the persistent buzz of tinnitus still lingers after a few months of this fibre symphony, consider turning the dial towards a ketogenic diet, a potential encore performance for evicting that stubborn fluid.

The scientific community has long been tuning into the frequency of a potential connection between sugar metabolism disorders like hyperinsulinemia and diabetes and the static of tinnitus. A groundbreaking study from the Federal University of Rio Grande School of Medicine in Brazil tuned into this connection with crystal clarity. Published in the *International Tinnitus Journal* in 2004, this study illuminated a dietary link that's hard to ignore.[80]

Picture the inner ear not as a reservoir of energy but as a high-performance engine that runs directly on the fuel supplied by blood oxygen and sugar (glucose). Any disruption in this delicate energy supply, especially alterations in glucose metabolism, can throw the inner workings of the ear off balance. The researchers didn't just stop at speculation; they spotlighted previous studies where a staggering 84 to 92% of individuals serenaded by the relentless hum of tinnitus were found to be guests at the hyperinsulinemia party.

*****

Crohn's And Colitis: The Role Of Fibre And SCFAs

Crohn's disease and ulcerative colitis, collectively termed as inflammatory bowel diseases (IBD), are characterised by inflammation in various parts of the gastrointestinal tract. While Crohn's can impact any area from the mouth to the anus, ulcerative colitis primarily targets the large intestine, leading to inflammation and ulceration. The intricate aetiology of IBD disease remains elusive. Previously implicated factors like diet and stress are now understood to exacerbate but not directly cause the disease. The development of this condition is believed to be multifactorial:

Immune System Response: It's hypothesised that a virus or bacterium may trigger Crohn's disease. Although such a trigger hasn't been pinpointed, the body's immune response to this invasion is abnormal. Instead of attacking the invading microorganism, the immune system also assaults the cells in the digestive tract, leading to inflammation.

Genetic Factors: The higher prevalence of Crohn's disease among individuals with a family history suggests a genetic predisposition to the disease. However, most Crohn's patients don't have a familial link, indicating that genetics is just one piece of a larger puzzle.

The intriguing role of dietary fibre and short-chain fatty acids (SCFAs) comes into play when examining the gut microbiome's influence on Crohn's disease. A disrupted gut environment, characterised by decreased bacterial diversity and a diminished population of butyrate-producing organisms like *Faecalibacterium prausnitzii*, is a hallmark of Crohn's. Concurrently, there's a rise in pathogenic bacteria such as E. coli. This imbalance affects the gut's tight junctions, leading to increased intestinal permeability.

Considering these disruptions, it's worth exploring the potential of a fibre-deficient diet as a root cause of Crohn's disease. Although the direct causality may still be under investigation, the benefits of fibre and SCFAs, particularly butyrate, in maintaining gut integrity and combating inflammation are increasingly evident. These beneficial compounds are known to nourish the gut lining, reinforce tight junctions, and modulate the immune response, creating a more balanced and healthier gut environment.

Moreover, a significant link is observed between Crohn's disease and metabolic health. Individuals diagnosed with Crohn's face a heightened risk of developing insulin resistance[81], highlighting the importance of strategic dietary and lifestyle choices in sustaining metabolic equilibrium. Prioritising a fibre-rich diet fosters a robust gut microbiome and emerges as a proactive measure to counteract the potential onset of insulin resistance, thereby enhancing overall wellbeing.

However, it's crucial to approach this information with caution. While the insights shared in this book are informative, they are not substitutes for professional medical advice. If you're grappling with this condition, remember that an increase in dietary fibre might initially exacerbate symptoms. Therefore, it's imperative to consult with your GP before implementing any significant dietary adjustments.

*****

Arthritis: The Dual Facets Of Joint Pain

Arthritis, a term that often brings to mind images of aching joints and restricted movement, covers two principal types: osteoarthritis (OA) and rheumatoid arthritis (RA). Each type has its own backstory and way of impacting our bodies. Osteoarthritis, the more common variety, arises from the gradual wear and tear of joint cartilage, acting as the ageing nemesis of our joints. On the other hand, rheumatoid arthritis takes the form of an internal battle, with our immune system mistakenly launching attacks against the joints as if they were foreign invaders.

Osteoarthritis typically makes its presence known in the thumbs, fingertips, knees, and hips, often choosing one side of the body to afflict. Rheumatoid arthritis, in contrast, prefers a more symmetrical approach, affecting the fingers' middle and lowest joints on both sides, along with the feet, ankles, shoulders, and elbows.

Osteoarthritis (OA); The Silent Siege on Our Joints

Osteoarthritis stands as a formidable contender among chronic conditions, particularly targeting women and emerging as a leading cause of disability and financial burden. In the UK alone, an estimated 10 million people – comprising 6 million women and 4 million men – grapple with OA. This includes around 5.4 million individuals with knee OA and another 3.2 million afflicted by hip OA. A significant number of those with OA encounter daily activity limitations and find their capacity to work constrained.[82]

The understanding of osteoarthritis has evolved, now recognising it as a chronic, systemic ailment characterised by a slow but relentless assault on the entire joint structure. This includes the deterioration of hyaline articular cartilage, ligaments, and menisci (especially in the knee), alongside changes in the joint capsule, subchondral bone adjustments, the formation of osteophytes, and synovial inflammation. Symptoms manifest as pain, dysfunction in the lower extremities, and visible joint deformities. Intriguingly, both osteoarthritis and diabetes share common ground, marked by disruptions in cellular metabolism and a tendency toward insulin resistance, primarily affecting energy production and usage.[82]

Here's how insulin resistance and osteoarthritis are thought to be connected:

Inflammation: Insulin resistance is associated with low-grade systemic inflammation. Inflammatory cytokines and adipokines released by adipose (fat) tissue can contribute to the degradation of joint tissues and the development of osteoarthritis.

Altered Metabolism: Insulin resistance alters the metabolism of glucose and lipids, which can affect cartilage cells (chondrocytes) and lead to their dysfunction. Cartilage requires a delicate balance of anabolic (building up) and catabolic (breaking down) processes, and insulin resistance can disrupt this balance, leading to cartilage degradation.

Oxidative Stress: Insulin resistance is associated with increased oxidative stress, which can damage joint tissues and contribute to the development of osteoarthritis.

Several studies have explored these connections, indicating that managing insulin resistance through diet, exercise, and medication might help control blood sugar levels and potentially slow the progression of osteoarthritis.

However, more research is needed to fully understand the mechanisms and develop targeted treatments based on these insights.

Drawing upon insights from Dr Ben Bikmans *Why We Get Sick*, studies involving individuals with varying body weights reveal a striking correlation: those suffering from osteoarthritis typically exhibit higher insulin levels. The pivotal role in this condition is played by chondrocytes, the primary cells within cartilage responsible for generating and sustaining the cartilaginous matrix – a structure primarily composed of collagen and dependent on glucose for its formation. Crucially, chondrocytes rely on insulin for glucose absorption. Insulin resistance hampers these cells' ability to maintain the cartilage matrix, leading to its gradual degradation. Moreover, joint functionality extends beyond cartilage to include synovial fluid, the lubricant ensuring smooth joint movements. Synoviocytes, specialised cells producing synovial fluid, are similarly impacted by insulin. Elevated insulin levels provoke an immune response, triggering inflammation within the joint and diminishing synovial fluid production. The absence of this lubricant exacerbates friction, contributing to the wear and tear associated with osteoarthritis. Through this lens, osteoarthritis is not merely a physical burden but also a reflection of metabolic dysfunction, underscoring the intricate interplay between our diet, insulin levels, and overall joint health.

Rheumatoid Arthritis (RA): When the Body Turns Against Itself

Rheumatoid arthritis throws the body into a paradox, igniting a fiery rebellion where it wages war on its joints. This autoimmune skirmish paints a vivid picture of the body mistakenly identifying its joints as foreign invaders and launching an all-out attack. A fascinating twist in this tale is the strong link between RA and insulin resistance. The more intense the inflammatory assault, the more evident the insulin resistance emerges. This relationship unveils a complex interplay where severe inflammation and insulin signalling disruptions engage in a perilous interplay.

Adding another layer to this complex scenario is obesity, a condition no stranger to inflammation. When fat cells swell beyond their breeches, they don't just sit idly; they pump out immune proteins into the bloodstream, turning obesity into a simmering pot of chronic inflammation. Here's where the narrative deepens: not every type of fat shares the same story. Hidden deep within the abdomen, visceral fat presents a more significant risk than its more superficial sibling, subcutaneous fat. This crucial difference emphasises the nuanced connection between the nature and placement of body fat, inflammation, and the broader spectrum of health.

In the shadowy world of RA, where the body's defence mechanisms morph into agents of destruction, the connection to insulin resistance underscores the need for a holistic approach to health. It's a stark reminder of how intertwined our body's systems are, with inflammation serving as both a benefit and a bane, illuminating the path to understanding and managing complex conditions like rheumatoid arthritis.

*****

Sarcopenia: The Silent Muscle Thief And How to Outlift It

Sarcopenia sneaks up on us like a stealthy cat burglar, swiping away muscle mass and strength as the years tick by. This muscle heist, a side effect of the ageing process, is nudged by our love affair with couches and an often less-than-stellar diet.

In my literary travels, I've often spotlighted Father Time's relentless pursuit and its effects on our muscular fortitude. Picture this: from our late thirties or forties, sarcopenia begins its quiet creep. Without a countermove – namely, shaking up those muscles – we stand to lose 5% of muscle mass every decade. This rate of muscle misadventure accelerates as we hit our sixties and seventies. But getting older doesn't mean we must hand over the keys to vitality.

On the contrary, it's our cue to embrace resistance training with open arms. In a piece I penned back in 2017, I championed the notion that gyms should be the stomping ground for the over 50s, flexing and lifting, much more so than the under 50s. And, judging by the evolving gym landscapes around the globe – where once cardio machines reigned supreme, now it's the clang and bang of weights that's music to our ears – it seems the message is resonating. Brad Schoenfeld, in his groundbreaking book *Science and Development of Muscle Hypertrophy*, reminds us that our golden years still hold ample opportunities for muscle growth.

Holding on to muscle isn't just about showcasing strength; it's intertwined with keeping our metabolic fires burning bright. It's the secret ingredient to slowing ageing, sparking brain health, and shielding us from metabolic syndrome. Think of it as fine-tuning your body's engine for the long haul.

And then there's fibre, our dietary hero in the skirmish against sarcopenia. Fibre isn't just about keeping things moving; it acts as a bouncer at the club of glucose absorption, promotes a gut-friendly environment, and may even show pro-inflammatory cytokines the door. Considering inflammation's role as the party pooper in muscle mass and protein synthesis, loading up on fibre could be akin to donning a superhero cape for your muscles, especially as the years advance.[83] The combo of fibre's anti-inflammatory prowess and its boon for gut health makes it a must-have in our anti-sarcopenia toolkit.

As we navigate the winding roads of ageing, understanding the interplay between keeping muscles intact, metabolic health humming, and making smart food choices is key. Adopting a lifestyle that celebrates regular resistance training and a fibre-rich diet isn't just a battle strategy against sarcopenia; it's a master plan for ensuring metabolic endurance.

Alan's story

A few months ago, I paused for a brief water break during a tennis lesson with my coach, Gavin. It was then that a gentleman walked onto the adjacent court. Gavin asked if I knew Alan, to which I confessed I hadn't the foggiest – I had neither played against nor seen him before. Gavin summoned Alan and introduced us before urging him to recount the previous day's events. Alan attempted to dismiss it as trifling, but Gavin wouldn't have any of it and pressed him for the tale.

It unfolded; Alan had been locked in a match against one of the club's ambitious young hopefuls. An ill-timed drop shot barely cleared the net, and Alan, struggling to reach it, was left seething at his perceived inadequacy. In a moment of frustration, he sent his racket flying into the net. Gavin then nudged Alan to share with me the reason behind his outburst, and Alan reluctantly admitted, 'Well, it was my birthday, and I knew I could've done better.' Gavin probed further, asking which birthday it was. 'My 91st', Alan revealed.

Two things struck me as profoundly interesting: first, Alan, at his age, not only engages in competitive sport but does so with a fiery competitive spirit. He's taking tennis lessons, a testament to his forward-looking attitude and constant striving to enhance his game.

Earlier in this book, I suggested the notion that there's no such thing as 'old,' only 'older.' Alan's story reinforces my belief. When someone remains forward-looking, committed to learning, improving, and contemplating the future rather than dwelling on the past, they embody the essence of being 'older' without being 'old.' Only when we relinquish our aspirations for the future, allowing our past to monopolise our thoughts, do we truly become 'old.' Memories hold their importance, of course, but they should always play second fiddle to our aspirations.

And of sarcopenia, it appears as long as we use our muscles, as Alan is still doing in his nineties, we don't have to lose them so quickly.

*****

Acne: Unveiling The Body's Inner Secrets

Think of your skin as the ultimate gossip, broadcasting the body's internal soap operas for the world to see. With acne, we're not just dealing with superficial irritations. These conditions are often the skin's SOS, flagging issues tied to what we eat and how our body manages its inner workings. According to the NHS, a whopping 95% of individuals between 11 and 30 experience acne to varying degrees. It's more prevalent among girls aged 14 to 17 and boys from 16 to 19, often persisting intermittently into adulthood.

Dubbed hormonal acne in adults, it's a complex ensemble featuring hormones, bacteria, genetics, and even stress levels. But an insidious contributor is lurking in the wings: our diet, especially its impact on insulin levels.

Acne loves to set up shop in areas dense with sebaceous glands (microscopic glands found in your hair follicles that secrete sebum); the face, back, chest, neck, and upper arms – where it throws a not-so-welcome party of pimples and blackheads. It's here that the drama unfolds, with insulin resistance regularly playing the outbreak outlaw in this hormonal story. Imagine puberty as a hormonal whirlwind, with insulin resistance adding an extra dimension, spiking insulin, and fuelling a surge in androgen production. [84] This hormonal spike brings acne to centre stage. My friend Christian Dailly, a top-notch personal trainer rather than a medic, frequently observed a near-miraculous skin transformation in young athletes adopting a low-carb diet.

The narrative deepens as blood sugar levels skyrocket, triggering the release of insulin-like growth factor 1 (IGF-1), a hormone that orchestrates the body's growth rhythms. This overflow of IGF-1 pushes sebaceous glands into overdrive, producing excessive sebum and setting the scene for both acne and inflammation. And here's where it gets interesting: numerous studies draw a line connecting high-sugar diets directly to acne outbreaks. One study handed out glucose-laden drinks to young men, both with and without acne, and the results were as dramatic as a surprise party – insulin levels in acne sufferers shot through the roof, quadrupling in overweight participants and doubling in their leaner counterparts.[84] These skin conditions are more than just idle chatter; they're bold advertisements for the more profound metabolic stories playing out beneath the surface.

*****

Eczema: The Skin's Whisper Of Discontent

Then there's eczema, the more subtle whisperer, hinting at dietary dramas through itchy, inflamed patches. This condition doesn't follow a one-diet-fits-all script; it's a personalised story where identifying your food foes can be a game-changer. Think of an elimination diet (see page 416) as your personal detective, uncovering the culprits behind the scenes.

Recent studies have turned the spotlight on a cast of foods that might stir up the eczema plot. Picture ultra-processed foods, dairy, and gluten as the usual suspects. Yet, eczema's script is not solely written by diet; stress, skincare products, and the environment also have their roles in this intricate play.

Acne and eczema are not just skin-deep; they're often the skin's way of telling the tales of our dietary choices and metabolic health. While they make for complex narratives, understanding the connection between our plates, sugar, insulin, and skin is like flipping through the pages of our body's story, uncovering clues to not just skin-deep beauty but holistic wellbeing.

*****

Allergies: Unravelling The Puzzle

Here's a staggering revelation: the allergy landscape in the UK is witnessing a relentless surge, with a 5% annual increase in allergy sufferers, half of whom are children. Since 1990, there's been an astonishing 500% uptick in food allergies, and conditions like hay fever, asthma, and eczema have been on the rise for three decades.[85] Yet, amidst these alarming statistics, the root cause of allergies remains shrouded in mystery, with multiple theories vying for validation.

The Cleanliness Conundrum

Our societal quest for immaculate living spaces might have an unintended consequence. The hygiene hypothesis posits that ultra-clean environments might do a disservice to our children by depriving them of the dirt and bacteria essential for a robust immune system. Studies show children cocooned in these sterile bubbles exhibit higher incidences of hay fever, asthma, and other allergies, hinting at an inverse relationship between cleanliness and immune resilience.

Nutritional Choices During Pregnancy

Researchers at Imperial College London scrutinised over 400 studies involving 1.5 million individuals. Their findings were enlightening: mothers who integrated fish oil and probiotic supplements during pregnancy, coupled with breastfeeding, bestowed upon their offspring a 30% reduced likelihood of egg allergies and a 22% decrease in eczema risk.[86] Echoing these findings, a study highlighted by The Guardian unveiled that pregnant women who indulged in nuts at least five times a week, had a dramatically reduced chance of a 69% decrease of bearing a child with a nut allergy. This compelling evidence prompted the NHS to revise its stance on nut consumption during pregnancy.

Immune Overreactions: A Security Breach

Imagine the immune system as a hyper-vigilant bouncer at the entrance of a club, mistaking harmless patrons like milk or egg proteins for troublemakers and causing unnecessary commotion. This isn't just a minor hiccup in the grand scheme of health; it's becoming a headline act in public health challenges across the UK. With 2 million Britons navigating life with food allergies and an additional 600,000 wrestling with coeliac disease, many find themselves dodging one to three culinary landmines daily.[87]

The landscape of food allergies is intricate, with over 170 culprits identified. However, most allergic reactions cluster around a specific 'naughty list' of 14 major food groups. In the culinary domain, vigilance and transparency are paramount. UK regulations, fortified by introducing Natasha's Law, now mandate the explicit declaration of these 14 allergens on food labels, a direct response to the tragic loss of Natasha Ednan-Laperouse after an allergic reaction to a Pret a Manger baguette at Heathrow Airport in 2016.

- Celery
- Cereals containing gluten (such as wheat, barley, and oats)
- Crustaceans (such as prawns, crabs, and lobsters)
- Eggs
- Fish
- Lupin (a type of bean)
- Milk
- Molluscs (such as mussels and oysters)
- Mustard
- Peanuts
- Sesame
- Soybeans
- Sulphur dioxide and sulphites (if the sulphur dioxide and sulphites are at a concentration of more than ten parts per million)
- Tree nuts (such as almonds, hazelnuts, walnuts, Brazil nuts, cashews, pecans, pistachios, and macadamia nuts)

In the realm of food additives, specific culprits are notorious for stirring up allergy symptoms in some individuals, particularly those found in processed or 'artificial' foods. Here's a rundown of these potential triggers:

- Amines are a common trigger; keep an eye out for names like histamine, tyramine, octopamine, and phenylethylamine.
- Thickeners or stabilisers such as tragacanth and agar-agar might be problematic for some.
- Preservatives, including nitrates and nitrites, are also known to provoke reactions.
- Other preservatives to watch out for include sulphites, benzoates, and sorbates.
- Artificial food colours, such as tartrazine and dyes originating from coal tar, can be problematic.
- Aspartame, a synthetic sweetener, might not be as sweet for everyone's health.
- Preservatives like butylated hydroxyanisole (BHA) and butylated hydroxytoluene (BHT) are also on the watchlist.
- Monosodium glutamate (MSG), commonly used as a flavour enhancer, rounds off this list of additives that might trigger allergies in certain individuals.

Being mindful of these additives and opting for whole, unprocessed foods can significantly minimise the risk of food allergy symptoms.

It's important to note that some people might also have intolerances to certain fruits and vegetables. Let me share a first-hand account of my close friend Claire Darling-Snowdon. Here, in her own words, is her story...

> *'As a child, I was obsessed with tomatoes. I loved them so much that I even had a special word for them. As I got older, my general rule of thumb was that any meal was a good vehicle for eating them.*
>
> *By the age of 5, I had regular doctors and opticians' appointments for headaches, and by age 13, these had developed into terrible migraine attacks. I used to get the full range of migraine symptoms, and many days of school and, later, work were lost to these symptoms. My migraines were so bad that by the age of 20, I was prescribed very strong medication to take daily as a preventative measure. Also, during this time, I had developed horrific irritable bowel syndrome that kept me awake at night and, again, meant I was losing days at work. I also had eczema and was battling weight issues.*

At the age of 30, I started training as a kinesiologist, and one of the most famous tools in a kinesiologist's toolkit is food sensitivity testing. Our tutor asked us to bring in our favourite food to test, so it's no surprise that I took in tomato and promptly found out through the testing that I was intolerant. I was devastated but decided to cut them out of my diet.

After three weeks, I had lost a stone in weight, and after six months, I realised I hadn't had a migraine and spoke to my doctor about weaning off my medication. At this time, my IBS had become more stable (although I had to give up wheat for this to completely change), and my eczema had cleared up.

Now I teach others about food intolerances, and it makes sense that the humble tomato is part of the deadly nightshade family and a major symptom trigger for millions of people. What many people consider a healthy food can, for some, be nothing short of a poison.

I do occasionally have a really juicy beefsteak tomato or something cooked in tomato sauce, but I choose my time carefully and savour every mouthful because it has to be the exception and not the rule for me.'

Allergy and sensitivity symptoms

Food allergies manifest through various symptoms impacting various bodily systems, including the skin, gastrointestinal tract, cardiovascular system, and respiratory tract. Listed in alphabetical order, here's a catalogue of potential signs to be aware of:

- Croupy/choking cough
- Diarrhoea
- Dyspnoea (difficult or laboured breathing)
- Facial swelling
- Failure to thrive
- Fatigue
- Feeling very hot or very cold
- Flushed appearance
- Hoarseness
- Intense itching
- Itching or tingling in the mouth, lips, or throat
- Mild wheezing or coughing
- Nausea
- Pale appearance
- Rising anxiety
- Stomach pain
- Urticaria (rash/hives)
- Very pale/cyanotic lips
- Vomiting

The Allergy Elimination Diet

Embarking on an allergy-elimination diet can feel like playing culinary detective. While this segment might have nestled comfortably in the upcoming diet chapter, its proximity to our allergy discussion seemed too fitting to pass up. If this piques your interest, be sure to read the 'Carnivore Plus Diet' section for more insights. An elimination diet has three distinct phases:

1. **The Elimination Phase: A Culinary Cleanse (2 to 3 Weeks)**
   During this phase, you cut back on all foods known to potentially cause problems. You eliminate the 14 known allergens, and all processed and packaged foods. And because, as my friend Claire experienced, there are other foods you could be potentially sensitive to, I always recommend my Carnivore Plus Diet. It can be a challenging few weeks, but as I often advise, 'What's more daunting? A lifetime grappling with unidentified health woes or a brief interlude of dietary discretion?' Patiently await the disappearance of symptoms for at least five days before advancing to the next act.

2. **The Reintroduction Phase: The Culinary Curtain Call**
   Now, reintroduce the former partygoers (foods) back to the stage, one at a time, with a three-day intermission between each to gauge your body's reception. Start with a cameo appearance on day one, gradually increase their role, and let them have their moment in the spotlight by day three. If your body applauds (no symptoms), that's your green light for the food.

3. **The Troublemaker Phase: Unmasking the Culinary Villain**
   If symptoms re-emerge after a specific food's encore, bid farewell to the suspect food for another week and monitor the change. If your wellbeing improves, you might have just pinpointed your dietary nemesis. It's wise to consult your GP at this point, share your sleuthing results, and explore confirmatory tests. Remember, if a food incites immediate dramatic responses like rashes or breathing difficulties, it's not the time for amateur detective work; visit your doctor post-haste.

Upon identifying your dietary culprit, you can exclude it (and potentially its notorious food group) from your menu. Meanwhile, you're free to explore other nourishing dietary realms, reintroducing a diversity of foods but keeping a wary eye on those deceptive ultra-processed masquerades. And for those on a quest to conquer weight, insulin resistance, or reverse diabetes, remember the golden rule: prioritise fibre and shun processed carbs and sugars.

The FODMAP Exploration: A Digestive Detour

The NHS, on its digital platform, shines a spotlight on the FODMAP as an approach for those sailing the turbulent seas of digestive distress, especially for the crew aboard the IBS (irritable bowel syndrome) ship.[88] FODMAPs, standing for fermentable oligosaccharides, disaccharides, monosaccharides, and polyols, are a motley crew of carbohydrates that sometimes play an elusive game of hide and seek with our small intestine's absorption crew. When these carbohydrates elude capture, they embark on a fermentation pilgrimage in the intestines, occasionally stirring up storms of digestive discomfort.

So, does my later-discussed Carnivore *Plus* Diet chart a course similar to the FODMAP journey? Indeed, it does, but envision it as the FODMAP voyage with an added burst of vigour. It follows a parallel path but with added oomph, tailored to harmonise with your body's unique digestive symphony.

A Word of Caution

Yet, this dietary voyage is not a universal panacea, especially if you've previously battled the leviathan of anaphylaxis or severe food allergies. In such instances, quick identification of your dietary antagonist is crucial. Embark on this expedition in tandem with your GP, who can steer through the warren of blood and skin tests to pinpoint potential culinary culprits. This collaborative approach ensures that your passage toward dietary enlightenment is steered safely.

THE FIBRE FIRST DIET

Part III

How to Implement

*****

How to implement the Fibre First diet, plus ideas and strategies to help you live healthily until you're 100 years old.

Chapter 7

Fibre First and Beyond: Other Successful Diets

Setting out on a dietary exploration unfolds like navigating the endless expanses of flavour and health. Guiding us through these nutritional terrains, the *Fibre First* diet strategy shines brightly, charting a course of simple yet transformative tweaks. This approach is delightfully clear-cut. Enjoy the foods you love, perhaps by mixing up their order or enhancing them with fibrous sides such as vibrant salads, robust vegetables, or fibre-dense drinks. Essentially, it's about artfully rearranging your plate or generously enriching it with wholesome fibre. Isn't that wonderful? But now, let's view the *Fibre First* diet not just as an end goal but as the gateway to exploring additional dietary paths, none of which involve the futile task of calorie counting.

Within the rich tapestry of dietary theories, each claiming unparalleled superiority, my role as a patron and benefactor of the Public Health Collaboration (phcUk.org) last year placed me at the heart of one of the most captivating debates over dietary dominance. Imagine for a moment: the esteemed Crucible Theatre, typically resonant with the clatter of snooker balls, in May 2023, transformed into a sanctuary for over 400 specialists in nutrition and metabolism. The event's centrepiece? A vigorous debate among four doctors on the merits of carnivore versus vegetarian diets. On one side, Dr Sean Baker, an accomplished world record holder and author, and Dr Anthony Chaffee, pledging allegiance to the carnivore diet. On the opposing side, Dr Chidi and Dr Hayley Woods staunchly defended vegetarian principles. It was a veritable battle of dietary philosophies! Each advocate was the epitome of health, passionately arguing their case as though theirs was the singular path to wellness.

And then, amid this fervent dialogue, an unexpected voice in the audience cut through the debate – a farmer, not a doctor or nutritionist as we might have presumed, who offered a slice of simple yet profound advice: 'If I have heard you all correctly, what I think you are all saying is that if it's a plant, eat it; if it eats a plant, eat it; but if it's made in a plant aka factory, best avoid it!' With this insight, he condensed the entire spectrum of nutritional wisdom into one unforgettable guideline: championing real food as the cornerstone of a healthy diet.

Thus, as we sail the sea of dietary frameworks, remember the farmer's sage advice. Whether your preference leans towards carnivorous delights or vegetarian fare, the golden rule is to opt for foods that remain true to their natural form. This is more than just adhering to a diet; it's adopting a lifestyle where genuine fats, proteins, and fibres from unprocessed sources are the heroes. Welcome to the vibrant, varied, and utterly delectable universe of natural diets, where authenticity is always the main course! But before we get going, I want to share a true story about previous dietary advice.

*****

The Evolution Of Diets: From Corpulence To Carb-Loaded Chaos

Once upon a time, in the year 1862, a gentleman by the name of William Banting decided it was time to tackle his weight issues, his corpulence. Back then, they didn't call anyone fat but 'corpulent'. If only this word were still used today, it would've saved so much trouble and strife because when we say 'fat', millions of people around the world assume that fat makes you fat, but if we had stuck with corpulent and not fat, then fat may never have been seen as the devil. Anyway, I digress. Let's get back to the story. William was a little on the chubby side. Standing at 5'5" and weighing over 200 lb, he might have been quite the sensation in the late 1800s, but probably not so much today.

Banting's life was far from a walk in the park. He couldn't even bend over to tie his shoelaces, and his daily exercise routine felt like running a marathon (not that anyone was out jogging back then). The more he worked out, the more weight he gained. He tried cutting back on food, but it left him more tired than a sloth on a Sunday.

So, Banting did what any sensible person would and consulted the finest doctors in the land. Unfortunately, as obesity was still reasonably rare back then, they couldn't figure out how to help him. Then, in a stroke of luck, he met a surgeon named William Harvey, who had just returned from a conference where he had heard about Claude Barnard, a specialist in a rare condition called diabetes.

Claude's revelation? If farmers could fatten up animals with starches and sugar, it only made sense that humans might be experiencing the same effect. The prescription was simple: cut out sugar and starch. And thus, in August 1862, Banting embarked on his sugarless and starchless adventure. He bid farewell to bread, beer, potatoes, and sweets, his once-beloved companions. Remarkably, he still indulged in a few glasses of wine per day. By the following May, he had shed 35 lb; by early 1864, he was down a staggering 50 lb. Banting was on cloud nine, exclaiming, 'I have not felt better in health.'

I was fat and furious, hence the name of my previous health book, and so was Banting. He published a 16-page booklet titled *Letter on Corpulence Addressed to the Public*. This little booklet would go down in history as the very first diet book. It became an international sensation, with people from Germany to America and beyond jumping on the Banting bandwagon. In less than a year, 'Banting' became a verb in the English language, meaning to diet. Newspapers ran headlines like, 'If he is gouty, obese, and nervous, we strongly recommend him to Bant.'

While Banting's book is often considered the first diet book, it turns out that in 1825, a French author named Brillat Savarin penned *The Physiology of Food*. He had been chatting with chubby folks for 30 years and figured out that bread, rice, and potatoes were the culprits behind obesity. Sugar, when added to the mix, made things even worse.

Despite this earlier insight, the *Banting Diet* became all the rage from the late 1800s to the 1950s. For nearly 70 years, the mantra was simple: avoid bread, flour-based foods, cereals, potatoes, sugar, and sweets. People believed that to stay healthy and trim; they could eat as much meat, fish, poultry, green veggies, eggs, cheese, and some fruits as they pleased.

Quotes from those days included gems like 'Carbs are uniquely fattening' and 'Carbs make you hungrier for more carbs.' It seemed that carbs offered little satisfaction for the calories consumed.

Fast-forward to the 1950s, when Dr Davidson wrote *Human Nutrition and Dietetics*, reinforcing the message, 'The intake of foods rich in carbohydrates should be systematically reduced since overindulgence in such foods is the most common cause of obesity.' Low-carb diets were the bee's knees, and everyone knew it.

Years later, Dr Jason Fung wrote in his book, the Obesity Code, 'For a century, diets low in refined carbohydrates were accepted as the treatment for obesity. By the 1950s, it was standard advice: if you were to ask your grandparents what caused obesity, they would not talk about calories. Instead, they would tell you to stop eating sugary and starchy foods. Common sense and empirical observation served to confirm the truth. Nutritional experts and government opinion were not needed.'

But then, in the autumn of 1955, President Eisenhower had a heart attack, and as a result, his doctors put him on a low-cholesterol, low-fat diet. Little did anyone know that his cholesterol levels were just fine before the heart attack. Eisenhower's diet consisted of soybean oil and polyunsaturated margarine, all in the quest to lower his cholesterol. However, the more he followed his experts' advice, the more weight he gained. Low-fat, low-cholesterol – it wasn't doing the trick.

Enter Ancel Keys, an American scientist whose research stirred considerable controversy. Keys graced the cover of *Time Magazine* not just once but twice with his advocacy for a low-fat, low-cholesterol diet. The American Heart Association jumped on the bandwagon, endorsing his approach as a heart disease preventer. However, Keys' research tactics have been scrutinised as overly aggressive and somewhat manipulative. He selectively used data from only 7 out of 22 countries, those that conveniently bolstered his hypothesis, giving birth to the infamous Seven Countries Study. This study dramatically shifted dietary advice almost overnight, and even President Eisenhower was persuaded by its findings.

In 1962, when confronted with data about the high-cholesterol diet of the healthy Samburu Masai tribe, Keys dismissed it as a genetic anomaly. Yet, when members of this tribe moved to Nairobi and adopted a Western diet, their cholesterol levels fell, but their health deteriorated. This was an early indicator that Keys' high-cholesterol hypothesis might have overlooked crucial variables. My experiences with the Samburu tribes affirm their robust health despite a high-fat diet, debunking the myth that such a diet is inherently harmful.

The convolution in dietary guidelines deepened in 1977 when the UK government began issuing its own dietary recommendations, essentially echoing the American guidelines, which had already fallen out of step with emerging nutritional science by then.

By 1995, the American Heart Association suggested six servings of carbohydrates, including sugary drinks—advice that seems almost counterproductive today, favouring conditions like obesity and dental decay over health. If you are overweight, the issue isn't a personal failure; it's likely the result of adhering to flawed dietary guidance.

These guidelines, rooted in Keys' dubious research, have played a significant role in propelling the obesity crisis in the UK. Thus, we are ensnared in a tangled network of interests where food corporations and pharmaceutical companies benefit from our adherence to these misdirected dietary norms.

Throughout the dietary exploration in this chapter, it's essential to remember that nutrition is not a one-size-fits-all affair. As we evaluate these diverse diets, each tailored to reduce blood sugar spikes, aid weight loss, and fend off metabolic illnesses, it's crucial to acknowledge a fundamental truth: what nourishes one person may not have the same effect on another. These diets are as individual as our fingerprints, unique to each of us.

See each diet as a unique key, unlocking different aspects of health and wellbeing. As you experiment with each one, listen to your body's feedback. If you discover a diet that brings you the results you seek and joy and satisfaction in your daily meals, embrace it. After all, the pleasure you derive from your food is a powerful motivator for long-term adherence.

On the other hand, if you're someone who thrives on continuous improvement, feel free to venture through each dietary approach. You might find your health flourishing unexpectedly as you transition from one diet to the next. More than just following a set plan; it's about discovering what resonates with your body and lifestyle.

As we step through these dietary paths, keep an open mind and a keen sense of self-awareness. Whether you find your ideal diet early in the journey or prefer to explore each option, the goal is to find a way of eating that supports your health, brings you joy, and aligns with your personal needs and desires. Let's chart these nutritional waters together, celebrating the diversity in our diets and the unique ways they can enhance our lives.

The sequence of these diets is designed to gently steer you away from a sugar-dominated diet towards a state of metabolic versatility. It's about evolution, not revolution, in your eating habits. For example, if you were to dive headfirst into a diet like intermittent fasting, it would most likely be unsuccessful, like trying to leap before learning to step. If you were to start there, you would most likely find yourself battling against ingrained sugar cravings, a challenge akin to attempting a marathon before mastering a jog. So, if you decide to go one step beyond the *Fibre First* diet, I recommend you try these alternative dietary approaches in this specific order.

- The *Fibre First* diet
- *the* Human Diet
- Low carb
- Intermittent fasting
- Ketogenic Diet
- Carnivore Diet
- Carnivore Plus Diet
- The Lion Diet

Here's a nugget of wisdom: relying solely on willpower or determination to lose weight is like trying to catch a cloud with a butterfly net: ambitious but ultimately futile. If, after a few weeks into your chosen diet, you find yourself perpetually peckish or daydreaming about the next meal, it's a red flag. It either signals that the diet isn't your perfect match or your body hasn't yet achieved the metabolic flexibility it yearns for.

Remember, any diet that leaves your spirit dwindling is bound to boomerang back. It's not about wrestling with your cravings or betting your last chip on sheer determination. After all, these tactics often lead the average adult to fritter away a whopping £331 annually and £20,000 over a lifetime[1] on weight loss escapades that wind up in a cul-de-sac. So, rather than trying to outwit your appetite, embrace a diet that resonates with your lifestyle and tickles your taste buds, ensuring that the path towards wellness is as enjoyable as the destination itself.

Before we begin, I have a piece of advice. I wager that when you switched to the *Fibre First* diet, your close ones hardly noticed any difference. However, prepare for a distinctly unique experience when navigating the social dynamics of family and friends while exploring new dietary horizons. It's prudent to have that heart-to-heart conversation sooner rather than later. The approach you choose is crucial. Your loved ones, your life's cheerleaders, love you 'just the way you are', reminiscent of Billy Joel's timeless ballad. They might not articulate it (after all, who openly comments, 'Your baby won't win any beauty contests' or highlights the emperor's nudity?), but their affection might manifest as subtle discouragements against change. 'Life is a fleeting melody', they might argue, 'you might get run over by a bus tomorrow, just enjoy life.'

When you hear these well-meaning refrains, it's your cue to gently, yet firmly, take the lead and express, 'I deeply value your love and support, but this journey is mine to navigate. I'm seeking better health and travelling paths that may appear unconventional. Yet, I am enjoying it and starting to feel better already.'

Should the chorus of concerns continue, stand firm in your resolve: 'Don't you want to share more sunsets and memories? Allow me to try this, for it should give us more moments together.' Trust in the transformative power of your decision; the initial resistance will eventually evolve into support. As the benefits of your dedication become evident, even the sceptics will recognise the value of your endeavour.

In moments of doubt, remind yourself, 'I am escaping the clutches of processed temptations, placing my faith in the farmer's wisdom over the factory.' Celebrate the freedom from a past overshadowed by dietary myths, and let your transformation serve as proof of your new approach.

*****

The *Fibre First* Diet

In this section, the heart of the book, I'll keep it snappier than a fresh carrot because I trust you're practically a fibre aficionado, especially after our enlightening journey in chapter 2 through the Blood Sugar Trial. Here's what I'll do: first, I'll unveil a line-up of fibre-rich foods so easy to incorporate into your meals that they might walk themselves onto your plate. Next, I'll tackle some burning questions thrown my way over the years, including live questions from TV show audiences who were intrigued as I instilled the virtues of Slimshotz and Fibrehydrates on my shopping channel. And finally, for completeness, I will touch lightly on the technical side of fibre.

For the cherry on top—or should I say, the seeds in your smoothie—make sure to check out the fibre-rich recipes at the end of chapter 11 and on my

Health Results app and website. Welcome to the *Fibre First* diet, where every bite is a step closer to vitality.

Understanding the Fibre Numbers

In the following list, I've presented the fibre content in grams per typical serving and, for your convenience while shopping, the amount of fibre you will find per 100 g (always noted in brackets). I will walk through the process to ensure clarity and support everyone in understanding the calculations. It's straightforward, but I believe in ensuring no one feels left out or confused.

To discover the fibre content of the food you are about to eat, weigh it, divide it by 100, and then multiply it by the fibre in the brackets below. For instance, if you're adding 25 g of chia seeds to a smoothie, and chia seeds contain 34 g of fibre per 100 g, the calculation is as follows:

$25 \div 100 \times 34 = 8.5$ g fibre.

This method applies just as well to larger amounts. For example, if you're preparing 150 g cauliflower rice with a fibre content of 2 g per 100 g, the calculation would be:

$150 \div 100 \times 2 = 3$ g fibre.

This equation should make it easy for you to track your fibre intake, ensuring you can enjoy a wide variety of foods while keeping an eye on those all-important daily fibre numbers. And yes, while I have previously stated that counting calories is futile, counting your fibre intake until you get a feel for it, to ensure you consume more than 35 g per day is wise. As they say in the business world, it will give you a strong return on your investment (ROI).

Seeds

In this section, as with the rest of our discussion on the *Fibre First* diet, I will primarily focus on the fibre content. You will find much more detail for most of the following foods on page 669, where I discuss 'Superfoods'. Let me begin by presenting to you what I affectionately term the 'Magnificent Seven Seeds', a selection celebrated not just for their nutritional value but specifically for their high fibre content. Here, I assess their value in a standard 30g handful (and remember, in brackets is the amount per 100 g).

A handful of 30 g provides:

- Chia Seeds: 10.3 g (34 g)
- Flaxseeds: 8.2 g (27.3 g)
- Poppy Seeds: 5.85 g (19.5 g)
- Pumpkin Seeds: 5.52 g (18.4 g)
- Sesame Seeds: 3.54 g (11.8 g)
- Sunflower Seeds: 2.58 g (8.6 g)
- Hemp Seeds: 1.2 g (4 g)

As you can see, each seed is a fibre powerhouse with the added benefit of being low in carbohydrates. These versatile seeds can seamlessly integrate into your daily meals, enhancing smoothies, yoghurts, and salads with a nutritious crunch. But let's not stop there. Use them instead of breadcrumbs to coat fish, chicken or even homemade Scotch Eggs. The possibilities to boost your fibre intake deliciously are as vast as they are varied.

Fruits

The illustrious avocado leads our fruit parade, a fruit whose fibre content has sparked much debate across various data sources, with different opinions regarding its fibrous potency varying by as much as 300%. The confusion, it turns out, appears to stem from a mix-up: a cup of pureed avocado equates to roughly one and a half whole avocados, which some people then say is what you will find in just one avocado, and many books, websites and databases, list a similar figure as the amount per 100 g. According to the meticulous figures from the USDA Food Database, which we will endorse, we learn there is 8.46 g fibre per 100 g.[2]

Not one to take data at face value, my team embarked on a hands-on experiment. We bought 10 avocados from three distinct supermarkets, delicately scooping out the flesh to weigh it, with the average clocking in at 135 g. After dedicating time to this endeavour (hopefully demonstrating our commitment to accuracy), we've concluded that a single avocado, one typically purchased in the UK, offers 11.4 g fibre. And as avocados pack a small 5 g of carbohydrates per fruit, it renders them the perfect fruit for a low-carb and ketogenic diet.

Enough of avocado. Let's get back to the fruit family. As fruit comes in various varieties, shapes and sizes, it's difficult to provide an accurate gram weight of fibre for each. However, if you haven't the time to weigh your fruit, my team have arrived at the following approximation, again with per 100 g in brackets:

- Avocado: 11.4 g of fibre per avocado (8.46 g)
- Passion Fruit: 1.3 g each (3.3 g)
- Pear: 2.93 g each (2.2 g)
- Apple: 2.4 g each (1.8 g)
- Orange: 2.1 g each (1.7 g)
- Bananas: 2.7 g each (1.4 g)

And a word to the wise: to reap the fibrous benefits, enjoy your fruits as nature intended. Opting for juicing might be tempting, but only the whole fruit truly delivers the fibre punch. If you are trying to lose weight, be mindful not to overeat fruit, as it is rich in fructose. Instead, consider the subset of berries.

The Fab Four Berries

Diving into the kaleidoscope of berries, we encounter the Fab Four – a prestigious group that stands out in the fibrous berry universe. Acai and goji berries, alongside cherries, cranberries, and redcurrants, certainly have their accolades for health virtues. However, it's this remarkable foursome that captures the fibre headlines. Their sugar profile also sets these berries apart, predominantly featuring xylitol – a stark contrast to the fructose found in many fruits. This detail isn't just a nutritional footnote; as we've uncovered in discussions on sugars, xylitol boasts dental benefits. For each of these distinguished berries, as portion sizes vary wildly from individual to individual, I will only show the fibre weight per 100 grams:

- Raspberries: (6.5 g)
- Blackberries: (5.3 g)
- Blueberries: (2.4 g)
- Strawberries: (2.0 g)

Fibrous Vegetables

Turning our focus to vegetables, let's explore the likes of broccoli, Brussels sprouts, carrots, and a selection of root vegetables such as beets and turnips. It's important to note that while these vegetables may offer less fibre compared to fruits, they excel in another significant area – their minimal sugar content.

- Artichoke: 1 cup 10 g fibre (6 g)
- Beetroot: Average 125 g per bulb, therefore 2.5 g fibre (2 g)
- Broccoli: ½ cup equals 2.3 g of fibre (2.6 g)
- Brussels Sprouts: 8 sprouts provide 3 g fibre (3.8 g)
- Cabbage: One cup is 100 g, equating to 2.5 g fibre (2.5 g)

- Carrots: Two carrots weigh about 100 g, 2.8 g fibre (2.8 g)
- Cauliflower: ½ of a head weighs 100 g, 2 g fibre (2.0 g)
- Onions: ½ a cup provides around 1 g fibre (1.7 g)
- Tomato: 2 medium-sized tomatoes provide 1.6 g fibre (1 g)
- Turnips: A typical serving is around 100 g, so 1.8 g fibre (1.8 g)

Legumes: A Fibre Powerhouse with a Side Caution on Carbs

When it comes to packing a fibre punch, legumes stand out in the culinary world. This category includes a variety of beans, such as black and kidney beans, alongside lentils, chickpeas, and peas – all renowned for their high-fibre content. These legumes can be creatively incorporated into your diet through dishes like curries and chilli or even as a salt-covered, Japanese-style edamame starter. However, it's important to remember that while they're fibre-rich, they also carry a significant amount of carbohydrates. For those focused on weight loss or maintaining a state of ketosis, moderating legume consumption is necessary. In such cases, leaning towards seeds, greens, and berries is a more suitable dietary strategy.

- Black Beans: ½ a tin provides 8.3 g fibre (7.1 g)
- Butter Beans: ½ a tin provides 6.9 g fibre (5.9 g)
- Chickpeas: ½ a can provides 8.3 g fibre (7 g)
- Edamame (Soybeans): One cup provides 7 g fibre (5.2 g)
- Garden Peas: ½ a cup serving offers 4.8 g fibre (6 g)
- Kidney Beans: ½ a tin provides 11.5 g fibre (9.6 g)
- Lentils: 30 g boiled equals 80 g cooked, 4.9 g fibre (8 g)
- Pinto Beans: ½ a tin provides 8.7 g fibre (7.3 g)
- Quinoa: 30 g uncooked, delivers 3.4 g fibre (4.2 g)
- Split Peas: 35 g uncooked, supplying 13 g fibre (16.2 g)

Leafy Greens: A Low-Carb Route to Fibre

Like green vegetables, leafy greens offer a superb strategy for integrating fibre into your diet minus the heavy carbohydrate load. This group, featuring spinach, kale, Swiss chard, and cabbage, may not tip the scales in gram weight but certainly shines in nutritional value.

- Cabbage: 1 cup of shredded cabbage is 1.8 g fibre (2.5 g)
- Kale: Will hold 100 g, providing 4.1 g fibre (4.1 g)
- Spinach: a 100 g serving will provide 2.2 g fibre (2.2 g)
- Spring Greens: ½ a bag will provide 2.4 g fibre (2.6 g)
- Swiss (Rainbow) Chard: A 50 g serving 0.8g fibre (1.6 g)

Nuts: Fibre's Crunchy Companions

Nuts, akin to seeds, serve as a fantastic method to dust your salads, desserts, or even party bowls with a fibre boost. With negligible sugar content, they're worry-free on that front. However, for those keeping an eye on their weight, it's worth noting that nuts pack a substantial energetic punch. Take peanuts, for instance, which technically belong in the legume family. You might have expected to find them there, but let's face it, who searches for peanuts under legumes? The calorie content of a single peanut rivals that of a Tic Tac, so go easy, nut lovers. For ease, I've portioned all nuts into a manageable serving size of 30 g, perfect for mindful munching.

- Almonds: 3.75 g (12.5 g)
- Brazil: 2.25 g (7.5 g)
- Cashews: 0.99 g (3.3 g)
- Hazelnuts: 2.91 g (9.7 g)
- Macadamia: 2.58 g (8.6 g)
- Peanut: 2.7 g (9 g)
- Pecans: 2.88 g (9.6 g)
- Pistachios: 3.09 g (10.3 g)
- Walnuts: 2.01 g (6.7 g)

Seven Unique Fibre Sources

Here are seven distinctive ingredients that didn't quite fit into the earlier categories but are nonetheless stellar for boosting your fibre intake. Seaweed and coconut could have been categorised above as vegetable and fruit, respectively, but here they stand out for their exceptional fibre contributions alongside other notable mentions.

Cacao (Authentic Chocolate):
Depending on whether it's a dark chocolate bar, cooking nibs or baking powder, the fibre content in cacao can vary slightly. You can anticipate a generous 33 g fibre per 100 g in its powdered form.

Coconut:
Shredded coconut boasts 9 g fibre for every 100 g, presenting a low-carb option that infuses dishes with a hint of tropical essence and texture. But the benefits extend even further. Dried coconut (desiccated) provides a substantial 18 g fibre per 100 g, making it a superb choice for those seeking to enhance their fibre intake through baking and culinary applications. Better still, coconut flour elevates the fibre offering even higher, delivering an impressive 38 g

fibre per 100 g, making it an exceptional ingredient for high-fibre recipes.

Glucomannan:
Extracted from the root of the konjac plant, glucomannan is a soluble fibre known for its ability to promote feelings of fullness and improve digestive health. As the only ingredient approved by the EU to carry the claim that it aids weight loss, it's commonly used in weight loss supplements and as a food additive to enhance texture without adding calories.

- Glucomannan Drinks: See Slimshotz on page 956, which is a flavoursome glucomannan drink.
- Glucomannan Noodles: See Fibrehydrate on page 955, which are carb-free, wheat-free, fibre-rich alternatives to spaghetti, noodles and pasta.
- Glucomannan Capsules: See Hunger Bulletz on page 957, a simple and convenient way to pop some fibre before meal.

Seaweed:
This versatile vegetable, not just a staple in sushi, can enrich salads or snacks with its fibre content, which constitutes about 10 to 20% of its dry weight. This percentage surpasses most fruits and vegetables in density. However, it's worth noting that a single sheet of Nori seaweed weighs a mere 2.8 g.

Mushrooms:
Adding a variety of mushrooms to your dishes adds a modest but significant boost to your diet. While not high in fibre percentage terms – just 1 g fibre per 100 g – mushrooms contain a particular type called beta-glucans, known for their numerous health benefits.

Inulin:
A soluble fibre found in many plants, inulin supports digestive health, acts as a prebiotic, and enhances calcium absorption. It's often added to foods to increase their fibre content without altering the taste.

Psyllium Husk:
More just a cuisine wizard; it's backed by science. Studies show that its water-absorbing properties can significantly increase stool weight and consistency, making it a powerhouse for maintaining regularity. Plus, its soluble fibre content acts as a prebiotic, fuelling those beneficial gut bacteria for optimal digestive health. So, when it comes to keeping things moving smoothly, Psyllium Husk is the reliable sidekick you can count on!

Alright, you've got the scoop on fibre-rich foods by now. But if some bits don't quite digest well in your mind, that's understandable. While I can't directly tap into your thoughts, I've chatted with plenty of folks on the same quest for optimal health as you are. So, based on those conversations, here are some questions they've tossed my way.

Q: How Much Fibre Should I Eat?

A: Ah, the eternal dietary conundrum! It's like trying to solve a Sudoku puzzle blindfolded while riding a unicycle - challenging, to say the least! But fear not, fellow fibre enthusiasts, for I've got some pearls of wisdom to share. Firstly, let's embrace our uniqueness - we're all built differently, like a quirky patchwork quilt of dietary needs. So, where do we start? Let's take a trip down memory lane to our ancestral dinner tables. Evolution's slow dance has shaped our bodies to thrive on the grub our forebears gobbled up. According to a BMJ study in 2022, they probably chowed down on a hefty 100 g of fibre a day![3] Sounds impressive, right? But let's face it, achieving that today is like finding a needle in a haystack!

Fast forward to the present and cue The American Journal of Clinical Nutrition, the wise sage of dietary wisdom. They suggest a daily dose of 35 g of fibre is the golden ticket to slashing your risk of heart disease by 54% and dodging the Grim Reaper by 37%. Talk about power-packed punchlines!

But, with most of the population not getting anywhere near 35 g, let us set a good starting point at 30 g. While I don't usually see the NHS as a great place to get nutritional advice, although hopefully in the future it might be, in this instance, picture the NHS as your fibre dietary coach, blowing the whistle to get you to aim for at least 30 g fibre daily. It's like being advised to drink water or breathe air, which are essential for keeping the cogs turning smoothly in your health machinery. For the calorie-conscious, a handy tip is to pack in at least 15 g of fibre for every 1,000 calories you consume.

For children, the NHS recommend:

- **Tots aged 2 to 5:** about 15 g to keep them zooming around.
- **Kids 5 to 11:** bump it to 20 g, perfect for their growing adventures.
- **Teens 11 to 16:** 25 g to fuel those awkward school dances and endless homework sessions.

Q: What does it mean when a food is labelled a source of fibre?

A: When you see 'source of fibre' on a label, it's the nutritional equivalent of a pat on the back for the product. It means the food has at least 3 g of fibre per 100 g or 1.5 g per 100 calories. A slightly better claim is ' high in fibre'; we're talking about at least 6 g per 100 g or 3 g per 100 calories. But here's the problem (and it's a really big issue): just because a food claims to be a fibre friend doesn't mean it's not also a sugar villain. Take, for example, several British cereals that strut around with a 'source of fibre' badge. Sure, it's got 3 g fibre, but it's also packing a whopping 81 g carbs. Imagine sprinkling a few vitamins on a heap of sugar cubes – it's the nutritional equivalent of perfuming a pig. Sadly, you cannot rely on marketing messages on packaged food, but you know that already!

Q: Why are cereals missing from the list above, don't they have fibre?

A: It's not that cereals and their fellow fibrous friends like sweet potatoes, rye bread, and dried prunes lack fibre; it's just that their high-carb companions overshadow them. Imagine trying to clean your house while someone else throws a glitter party in the next room – the good intentions are there, but the mess keeps piling up.

Q: Is it possible to eat too much fibre?

A: Absolutely, though it's akin to finding out there's such a thing as too much Netflix – theoretically possible, but practically a challenge for many!

Overloading on fibre, especially if your diet previously resembled a fibre-free zone, can lead to some uncomfortable side effects. Think bloating, gas, and a need to become best friends with the nearest restroom. Moderation is key, to begin with. Start slowly and gradually build up your fibre intake, allowing your body to adapt. It's not a race to the fibre finish line. Remember, too much of a good thing can be a bad thing, especially if it means you can't stray too far from the bathroom!

Q: How long before a meal should I consume fibre?

A: This is an insightful question, and the response is twofold. Firstly, if your goal with *Fibre First* is to act as a natural barrier to slow sugar release into your bloodstream, thus mitigating a rapid glucose rise and subsequent insulin spike, my findings indicate there's no need for a waiting period. Dive into your fibre-rich foods right at the start, and then proceed with your meal at your leisure. The fibre will happily and efficiently perform its regulatory role. On the other hand, if you aim to leverage soluble fibre's ability to curb your appetite – ensuring you feel fuller and thus eat less – then ingesting soluble fibre around 20 to 30 minutes before your meal is key. This timing ensures you feel more satiated, leading to a natural reduction in food intake.

Q: Can I get all my fibre from supplements instead of food?

A: Relying on supplements for your entire fibre intake is a bit like going on a virtual tour instead of exploring the city – you might get where you need to go, but you'll miss out on all the fun along the way. The right choice of wholesome foods provides not just fibre but a treasure trove of vitamins, minerals, and nutrients, along with flavours and textures that no supplement can realistically match.

Q: How can I add more fibre to my diet without eating foods I dislike and those that are carb-heavy?

A: Sneaking fibre into your diet is like hiding veggies in a kid's meal; it can be done creatively. Blend some veggies into your smoothies, use high-fibre flour in your baking, or sprinkle nuts and seeds on your yoghurt or salad. It's all about finding the right disguise for the fibre to make it palatable for you.

Q: Do I need to worry about the types of fibre I consume?

A: Just like choosing a playlist for a road trip, variety is key. Soluble fibre (think glucomannan, inulin, beans, and certain fruits) can help suppress appetite and control blood sugar, while insoluble fibre (found in whole grains, nuts, and veggies) keeps your digestive system in good order.

While it is important to appreciate that most foods that contain fibre have a blend of both insoluble and soluble, they tend to lean more toward one than the other. So, I created the following handy chart for you.

Soluble Fibre Dissolves in water to form a gel-like substance. Helps with constipation and diarrhea.	**Insoluble Fibre** Traps and holds onto water pulled from intestines. Helps with constipaion.
Food Sources	**Food Sources**
• Legumes (beans, lentils, peas, chickpeas, soybeans) • Seeds • Apples and apple sauce • Pears • Oranges • Nuts • Bananas • Berries • Broccoli • Carrots • Brussel sprouts • Avocado • Sweet Potato • Psyllium husk • Fibre supplements • Fibrehydrate noodles • Fibrehydrate spaghetti • Slimshotz	• Ground flax seeds (flaxmeal) • Coconut • Nuts • Seeds • Cauliflower • Green beans • Leafy greens (spinach, kale, collard) • Potatoes with skin • Fruits and vegetables with skin • Whole grains (eg. whole wheat or whole grain pasta, bread, and crackers) • Brown rice

Other Types of Fibre

In chapter 2, we discussed the difference between soluble and insoluble fibre, but let's now take a closer look at some other forms of fibre. Some are viscous, forming a gel-like substance, while others are fermentable, serving as nourishment for our gut bacteria.

Cellulose and hemicellulose: These insoluble fibres are found in cereal grains and the cell walls of many fruits and vegetables. They absorb water and increase stool bulk, potentially easing bowel movements.

Lignins: Present in wheat and corn bran, nuts, flaxseeds, and certain fruits and vegetables, these fibres stimulate mucus production in the colon (a good thing as it protects the gut lining) and add to stool bulk.

Beta-glucans: Soluble fibres in mushrooms and barley that ferment in the small intestine, acting as prebiotics. They help in blood glucose and cholesterol management without having a laxative effect.

Guar gum: A soluble fibre from seeds that creates a viscous gel and is used in processed food for its thickening properties. It's beneficial for blood sugar and cholesterol levels.

Inulin, oligofructose, oligosaccharides, and fructooligosaccharides: Found in onions, garlic, and other vegetables, these soluble fibres can aid in digestion, act as prebiotics, and have a potential laxative effect.

Pectins: These are found in apples, berries, and other fruits. Known for their gelling properties, pectins can slow digestion and assist in managing blood sugar and cholesterol levels.

Resistant starch: Present in legumes, nuts and seeds, this fibre acts as a prebiotic and can benefit blood sugar and cholesterol levels.

20 Food Ideas To Embrace The *Fibre First* Diet

If you're currently thinking, 'Steve, could you please just spill the beans on how to master the *Fibre First* lifestyle?' then you've arrived just in time. Uncovering the abundant sources of nature's fibre is akin to unlocking a treasure chest of wellness; simpler than you might expect and more rewarding than you've ever dreamed. A brief tour follows where every step is a stride towards vitality, balance, and a rejuvenated sense of wellbeing. For full recipes and more ideas, you will find lots of recipes later in the book. Also, visit the health results website or download the app.

Idea 1

Mixed toasted seeds: The simplest fibre-fuelled of all

Enjoy a crunchy symphony of fibre by simply buying a bag of mixed seeds from your local supermarkets. They tend to feature the dynamic trio of brown flaxseed (linseed), pumpkin, and sunflower seeds. For a fibre-forward snack, consider Tesco's ensemble (other supermarkets are available, but let's face it, we all have our favourites). At a mere 30 pence a pop for a 25 g serving, it's like buying concert tickets to the health show of the year without the hefty price tag.

Each serving is a powerhouse delivering 3.7 g fibre, making your digestive system applaud with joy. And let's not overlook the 12 g heart-healthy fats – because who doesn't want a robust heart rhythm? Protein isn't forgotten either, with a solid 6.6 g ensuring your muscles get the love they deserve.

Eat them straight from the pack, sprinkle them on your salad for a crunchy encore, or add them to your morning smoothie. They're the unsung heroes of the snack world, proving that sometimes the best performances are the ones you can crunch.

Idea 2

Fibre-fuelled soups

Enjoy the heart of warmth and wellness with these fibre-rich soups, a testament to the power of beans, vegetables, and every nutrient-packed ingredient we've explored. Transform the essence of your soup with a sprinkle of fibre flour, glucomannan, or coconut flour, turning each spoonful into a fibre powerhouse. Whether as a prelude to your main course or as a standalone symphony of flavours, these soups are your ticket to a fulfilling, nutritious experience.

Lentil and spinach symphony

In a cauldron of culinary magic, let olive oil dance with onion, carrots, and celery, setting the stage for a melody of garlic, cumin, and coriander. The lentils and vegetable broth, thickened with a whisper of fibre flour, simmer to a tender crescendo. A finale of spinach wilts into this harmonious blend, seasoned to perfection.

Broccoli and white bean elixir

Begin with a base of translucent onion and fragrant garlic in olive oil. Introduce broccoli to this ensemble, followed by the creamy texture of white beans and broth, thickened for comfort. A garnish of Parmesan, if you please, crowns this nourishing masterpiece.

Butternut squash and carrot medley

A careful balance of butternut squash and carrots, united with onion and a hint of ginger, simmers in a vegetable broth embrace. Blended to smooth perfection, this soup is a velvet touch of autumn, lightened with coconut cream.

The ultimate vegetable encore

Transform Sunday's remnants into Monday's feast with a soup that welcomes all leftovers. Blend the humble carrot with the bold broccoli into a vibrant vegetable tapestry. Let yesterday's flavours meld overnight, ready to be reborn into a soup that's not just eaten but experienced. One tip, though, is not to include the leftover sprouts as they dominate the flavour; instead, fry them with herbs, sprinkle some pine nuts, and serve as a side dish.

Idea 3

Vinaigrette and fibre salads

In chapter 2, we discovered that vinegar doesn't just subtly reject alpha-amylase; the enzyme converting starch to glucose decisively shuts it down. Alongside fibre, our dietary champion, vinegar's acetic acid, adds a unique mechanism enabling muscles to absorb glucose directly, bypassing the need for insulin. Here are four simple salad recipes that combine the delights of vinegar and fibre. Each salad is designed to be straightforward to prepare, ensuring they can be enjoyed as quick lunches, refreshing sides, or light dinners.

Classic cucumber vinegar salad

The refreshing simplicity of the Classic Cucumber Vinegar Salad. A harmonious blend of crisp cucumbers, sharp red onion, and the subtle crunch of chia seeds, dressed in a tangy apple cider vinaigrette, promises a delightful burst of fibrous flavours. Perfect for a light, nutritious side dish.

Ingredients: Thinly sliced cucumbers, red onion slices, chia seeds, fresh dill.

Dressing: Combine apple cider vinegar, a quarter of a teaspoon of natural sweetener like stevia, Erythritol, or xylitol (optional), salt, and pepper. Mix well until the sweetener dissolves.

Preparation: Toss the cucumbers, red onion, chia seeds and dill in the dressing. Chill for at least an hour before serving to let the flavours meld.

Tomato basil salad

Savour the essence of summer with my Tomato Basil Salad, where the juiciness of ripe tomatoes meets the aromatic freshness of basil, enhanced by the crunch of fibrous pine nuts and the creaminess of mozzarella. A drizzle of insulin-calming balsamic dressing brings this vibrant dish to life.

Ingredients: Ripe tomatoes (sliced), fresh basil leaves, pine nuts, mozzarella cheese (optional).

Dressing: Whisk together balsamic vinegar, extra virgin olive oil, minced garlic, salt, and pepper.

Preparation: Arrange the tomato slices on a plate, sprinkle with pine nuts, torn basil leaves, and mozzarella if using. Drizzle the dressing over the top.

Spinach and apple salad

Experience a delightful harmony of flavours with my spinach and Apple Salad, featuring crisp apples and tender baby spinach, accented by the crunch of walnuts and creamy feta; all brought together with a Dijon dressing for a refreshing bite.

Ingredients: Baby spinach leaves, sliced apples (any crunchy variety), walnuts, and feta cheese.

Dressing: Mix apple cider vinegar with a little infusion of stevia, erythritol, or xylitol with Dijon mustard, olive oil, salt, and pepper.

Preparation: Toss the spinach, apples, walnuts, and feta cheese with the dressing. Serve immediately to maintain the apples' crispness.

Carrot ribbon salad

Ingredients: Peeled carrot ribbons, parsley leaves, and sunflower seeds.

Dressing: Combine white wine vinegar, olive oil, a dash of Stevia, Erythritol, or xylitol, salt, and freshly ground pepper.

Preparation: Use a potato peeler to create carrot ribbons, then toss them in with parsley and sunflower seeds in the dressing. Let it sit for a few minutes to allow the carrots to soften and absorb the dressing slightly.

Idea 4

High fibre fruits

Avocados and olives are the renegades of the fruit world, marching to the beat of their own drums with their high-fat content and low net carbs, making them the keto dieter's dream team. Picture avocados as the cool, laid-back surfer dudes of the fruit aisle, riding the waves with their impressive fibre content and keeping their carb count as chill as their vibe. A whole avocado comes with around 16g of carbs, so if you're planning a meal around one, it's essentially a solo performance with a 'Featuring: Avocado' sign hanging in the spotlight.

Then we have olives, the mysterious dark horses, swimming in their brine pools, silently boasting their oleuropein, a potent antioxidant with a name as fancy as its benefits. This compound is like the bodyguard of your cells, warding off inflammation with a stern hand and protecting your body like a medieval knight.

Together, avocados and olives form a dynamic duo in the fibre and keto universe. Imagine them as the Batman and Robin of your diet, fighting off high-carb villains and bringing peace and balance to your metabolic Gotham.

Idea 5

Crunch time: The ultimate guide to roasting mixed nuts at home

Welcome to the 'Crunch Time Chronicles: The Alchemy of Roasting Nuts' – a guide that transforms the humble kitchen into a wizard's lair, where the spell of roasting turns mixed nuts into golden nuggets of joy. Under the guidance of culinary sorceress Emma Porter, we embark on a gourmet adventure to craft chilli and lemon roasted almonds (or, if you're feeling adventurous, a mixed battalion of nuts and seeds) that are not merely snacks but treasures of the *Fibre First* realm.

Zingy chilli and lemon roasted almonds

Ingredients:

- 300 g almonds, awaiting their transformation
- 2 tbsp lemon zest, stolen from the sun itself
- 1 egg white, the magic binder

- 2 tbsp dried chilli flakes, for that fire in your belly
- 1 tbsp lemon juice, essence of zest
- 1 tsp sea salt from Neptune's own stash

Method to the mystique:

1. Begin by awakening your oven, setting it to a welcoming 180°C.
2. In a cauldron (or a large mixing bowl, for the modern wizard), whisk your egg white until it forms stiff peaks as proud as mountains.
3. Invite the almonds to a bath in the egg white, ensuring each one is cloaked in magic.
4. Sprinkle in the lemon zest, lemon juice, and dried chilli, stirring the concoction until each almond is anointed.
5. Unleash your almonds onto a parchment-lined baking sheet, ensuring they don't crowd like overeager spectators at a wizard's duel.
6. Shower them with sea salt.
7. Entrust them to the oven for 15–20 minutes until they emerge golden and singing with the crackles of transformation.
8. With care, for they will be as hot as dragon's breath, remove and allow them to cool.
9. Once cool, break the spell binding them together and store in an airtight jar, where they'll keep their magic for up to 3 weeks.

Prepare to be transported on a flavour-filled journey with every crunch, as 'Crunch Time Chronicles' turns snacking into an adventure of taste, texture, and tantalising spice.

Idea 6

Fiberella: The wholesome hazelnut spread

Embrace the indulgence without the guilt with Fiberella (ok I spelt it the American way, because Fibre-ella sounded like a pop song), your homemade twist on the beloved chocolate hazelnut spread. Packed with the goodness of fibre and crafted from just five simple ingredients, Fiberella promises a lush, guilt-free treat that's bound to become a staple in your pantry. Here's how you can whip up a batch of this fibrous delight:

The nutty base: Start with 100 g hazelnuts. Opt for raw hazelnuts to capture that fresh, nutty essence. If they're elusive, roasted hazelnuts can also do the trick – bypass the roasting step. Feel adventurous? Swap hazelnuts for almonds to explore a landscape with different flavours.

Roasting ritual: Preheat your oven to 200°C, lay your nuts on a baking sheet, and let them tan in the oven's warmth for 10–15 minutes. After roasting, wrap them in a cloth or paper towel and gently coax the skins off. If some stubborn skins cling on, let them be. They're just not ready to leave.

Blend to butter: In the magical whirl of your food processor, transform your hazelnuts into velvety nut butter, the heart of your Fiberella. Watch as the nuts release their oils and come together in a smooth, creamy embrace.

The sweet & chocolatey touch: Sweeten the deal with a teaspoon of xylitol or erythritol and a generous tablespoon of raw cocoa powder. Keep the blades dancing until everything's blissfully blended. The perfect consistency: With the mixer still going, introduce a stream of almond or coconut milk to achieve that signature spreadable texture. A whisper of vanilla extract adds the finishing touch, rounding out the flavours to perfection. Give it a few more minutes of high-speed blending until you witness the transformation into a spread that rivals the original Nutella in texture but not in guilt.

Voila! You've just created Fiberella, a spread that's not only a feast for the taste buds but a fibrous feast for your body. Dollop it on my fibre Flax biscuits, or enjoy it straight from the spoon – no judgment here. This homemade (see below) marvel proves that, with a little creativity and a few quality ingredients, indulgence can be both delicious and nutritious. So, go ahead, give Fiberella a swirl, and spread the love one fibrous scoop at a time.

Idea 7

FibreFlax: The ultimate fibre biscuit

Step into the kitchen, and let's bake up a storm with FibreFlax, the ultimate fibre biscuit that's as nutritious as it is delicious. Packed with the goodness of organic milled flaxseed and chia seeds, this biscuit is your golden ticket to a *Fibre First* diet. Here's your roadmap to creating these crispy delights:

Seed symphony: Begin with a harmonious blend of 200 g organic milled flaxseed and 75 g chia seeds, laying the foundation for your fibre feast. The seeds bring a nutritional powerhouse to your biscuits and a delightful crunch.

Spice ensemble: Elevate the flavour with 2 teaspoons of paprika for that gentle warmth and a teaspoon of cumin or fennel seeds for a whisper of earthy undertones. A pinch of salt ties all the flavours together, creating a symphony of taste in each bite.

The mixing jig: Marry the dry ingredients with 300 ml of water, stirring them into a cohesive mix. Watch as the chia and flaxseed absorb the water, binding everything into a dough that's ready to be transformed.

Olive oil waltz: Spread your mixture on a piece of parchment paper kissed with olive oil. Cover it with another parchment sheet, and let the rolling pin glide over, dancing to the thickness of your choice. Whether you prefer a delicate 2 mm or a hearty 4 mm thickness, it's your canvas to create.

The baking stage: Opt for a pizza baking tray for its perforated charm that promises an even bake or a classic baking tray for its reliable surface. Score your dough with a pizza cutter, pre-shaping your biscuits into perfect bites, ready to be savoured.

The heat is on: Preheat your oven to 180°C and let your biscuits bake to golden perfection over 40–60 minutes. Do keep a watchful eye on them, as if the thickness is not completely uniform, some parts will cook quicker than others. The waiting is the hardest part, as the aroma fills your kitchen, a promise of the crispy goodness to come.

And there you have it, FibreFlax, the ultimate fibre biscuit, ready to make its debut on your snack plate. Perfect for crunching on its own or accompanying cheese or pate. These biscuits are a treat for your taste buds and a high-five to your health, packed with all the fibrous goodness your body craves. So, roll up your sleeves, preheat that oven, and prepare to bake a FibreFlax batch that will keep for up to 10 days at room temperature when popped into an air-tight box. Here's to snacking smart with a biscuit that's as satisfying as it is healthful. After all, who says you can't have your biscuit and eat it too, especially when it's this packed with fibre?

Idea 8

Colouring in breakfast: Painting your morning with fibre

Imagine each morning waking up to a canvas splashed with vibrant colours, where breakfast isn't merely a meal but an artful expression titled 'Eating the Rainbow'. We're not just filling plates; we're colouring our mornings with the fibrous bounty of nature.

It's a delightful rebellion against the monotonous beige parade of toast or cereal; it's about embracing the full spectrum and injecting a kaleidoscope of nutrients into our day. If, after a taste test, any of them could use a bit more sweetness, sprinkle a pinch of xylitol, erythritol, or stevia for a perfectly natural sweet start. Here's to transforming your breakfast table into a vibrant exhibit of health and taste. And don't worry; you don't have to stick to our colour-coded days – if you fancy a blue Monday or a purple Wednesday, the only rule is there are no rules!

In any of these vibrant smoothies, you can introduce a magic trio to elevate the fibre content even higher: chia seeds, avocado, and coconut flour. Yes, you heard it right – coconut flour! It imparts an exotic tropical flavour that could make even the dreariest Monday taste like a beach holiday and brings a whopping 38 g of fibre per 100 g to the party. Whether you're whipping up a red berry blend or a green veggie concoction, these three ingredients are your secret weapons for a fibre-rich feast. Just imagine with coconut flour; every sip gets you closer to your daily fibre goal and a bit more beach-ready, metaphorically speaking, of course!

Monday – The Scarlet Start: Kick off your week with a red smoothie that puts the cherry on top of your morning. Blend a small half banana with a mix of strawberries and raspberries and add a splash of coconut water or almond milk. It's like a sunrise in a glass.

Tuesday – The orange oasis: Zing through your Tuesday with an orange blend that's as bright as your ambitions. Grate a piece of ginger, throw in a carrot and some frozen mango, add a glass of water, and squeeze a lime for that citrus kick. It's a vibrant vitamin vault.

Wednesday – The purple potion: Midweek calls for a purple smoothie that's as mysterious as it is nutritious. Whirl together almond milk, chia seeds for that fibre fix, almond butter for smoothness, and a cup of frozen blueberries.

Thursday – The green guardian: Embrace the green machine on Thursday with a smoothie that's got more fibre than a tech mogul has tweeted. Blend half a banana with a generous helping of spinach or any other green vegetable in your fridge, coconut water, and a squeeze of lime. It's like drinking a garden, but way tastier.

Friday – The white whisper: Welcome the weekend with a white smoothie that whispers pure health. Ground almonds, banana, Greek yoghurt, coconut milk, a sprinkle of desiccated coconut, and a hint of cinnamon. It's a hug in a mug.

Saturday – The pink party: Celebrate the weekend with a pink smoothie that's a party in a glass. Almond milk, watermelon, strawberries, natural yoghurt, a scoop of vanilla protein, and ice. It's the cool guest everyone wants at their breakfast table.

There you have it, a week's worth of colourful, fibre-rich smoothies to kickstart your day. This is more than breakfast; it's a declaration of delicious diversity, a daily dose of dietary artistry. So, here's to colouring outside the lines of conventional breakfasts and embracing the full spectrum of fibrous flavours and nutrients.

Idea 9

The sneaker fibre smoothie

As your day seven option, this can be added to your Colouring in Breakfast routine. As it tastes so amazing and packs so much fibre, I felt it was worthy of spinning into its own category. Imagine transforming your morning routine with a smoothie that's not just a meal, but a declaration of your commitment to fibre-filled living. This smoothie, with a name reminiscent of a certain chocolatey delight but infinitely healthier, emerged as a superstar during our Blood Sugar Trial. Participants who indulged noticed a dramatic plunge in post-meal sugar spikes, all thanks to this fibre-rich creation.

Ready to whip up your own fibre fiesta in a glass? In a whirlwind 20 seconds, blend these ingredients to forge a smoothie that's not just a drink but a nutrient-packed statement:

- Almond milk (200 ml, adding a subtle 0.6 g fibre kick)
- Cocoa powder (1 g f fibre, and who doesn't love a chocolate hug in the morning?)
- Half a banana (1.3 g fibre)
- A generous tablespoon of peanut butter (1.1 g fibre to stick with you through the morning rush)
- A handful of peanuts (2.6 g fibre because crunching is just as satisfying as sipping)

This isn't just a smoothie; it's your ticket to 6 to 7 g fibre, all disguised in the most deliciously sneaky way.

Idea 10

Fibre loaf: The ultimate bread makeover

Let me introduce you to the culinary masterpiece I like to call the 'Fibre Loaf' – a twist on what some might label as 'keto bread' or 'flaxseed bread'. This gem comes from the kitchen wizardry of my dear friend Emma Porter, a chef extraordinaire with an eye for healthy indulgence. Emma, battling type 1 diabetes, navigates her diet precisely without compromising on taste, proving she's a food alchemist. You can catch her culinary magic on the Health Results website, showcasing tutorials that transform healthy ingredients into delectable dishes. This isn't just bread; it's fibre-packed to the tune of 4.5 g fibre per slice.

Yields: 18 life-changing slices (And yes, it's freezer-friendly!)

Ingredients for Your Gastronomic Adventure:

- 300 g milled linseed, also known as the superhero flaxseed
- 5 large eggs, the binders of joy
- 2 tbsp olive oil
- 4 tbsp water (the essence of life)
- 2 tsp baking powder (the lift-off agent)
- A pinch of sea salt and pepper (for those who like a bit of mystery in their bread)

Instructions for Crafting the Loaf of Legends:

- Fire up your oven to a cosy 180°C
- In a bowl, mix the linseed with baking powder, like you're whispering secrets to it.
- Create a crater in this mixture – think of it as the launchpad for your ingredients.
- Whisk eggs, oil, and water in another bowl until they form a pact of smoothness. Feel free to whisper your culinary intentions here.
- Introduce this egg mixture to the linseed launchpad. Marry the wet and dry elements with a wooden spoon until they become one promising, thick batter.
- Coax this batter into a greased loaf tin, tucking it in for its oven spa session. Bake for 25 minutes until it emerges as a golden loaf of potential.
- Let it cool on a wire rack as if it's lounging after a sauna. Patience is key if it is hard to get out of the tin.
- Allow to cool thoroughly before slicing. Store it as you see fit, but

remember, like fine art, it has a display life of up to 4 days or 8 days if left in the fridge. Alternatively, slice and freeze, creating your own treasure trove of fibre slices.

And there you have it, a loaf made of ingredients, determination, health, and a pinch of culinary flair. Emma's Fibre Loaf isn't just bread; it's a fibrous delight for anyone on the quest for a healthier, tastier life. Go on, bake it, and let each slice be a reminder that healthy eating can indeed be deliciously rewarding.

Idea 11

Fibre shots: The scientifically proven dietary control

Here is the simplest yet most revolutionary idea yet: Fibre Shots! Imagine this - a magic little sachet that unleashes the power of glucomannan fibre into your glass of water. Stir, sip, and watch as this marvel works its magic, expanding up to 50 times its size in your stomach. It's like inviting a friendly sponge to your meal; it soaks up space, leaving less room for excess food. Picture yourself feeling fuller faster, wielding power to easily say 'no' to second helpings. The European Food Safety Authority even tips its hat to glucomannan, crowning it the sole ingredient with the royal decree to aid weight loss. For our own brand, Slimshotz, flip to page 956. It's not just a fibre shot; it's your secret weapon in the battle of the bulge.

Idea 12

Energising fibre balls

Fear not when hunger pangs hit like a ton of bricks, and your energy levels are flickering like a candle in the wind! Emma Porter, who can turn a kitchen novice into a gourmet chef, brings you a snack that's akin to finding an oasis in a desert. Behold the Energising Fibre Balls – your new best friend in the quest for sustenance and vigour.

Perfect for those moments when you need a boost, but your next meal seems as far away as the next solar eclipse, these energy balls are like little globes of power. Not only do they come with a certificate of excellence in taste, but they're also crammed with healthy fats, proteins, and, most importantly, fibre, ensuring your energy levels don't crash faster than a poorly constructed house of cards.

Produces: 15 globetrotting delights, each packed with 3.5 g fibrous brilliance.

Ingredients:

- 100 g almonds (the backbone of texture)
- 50 g unsweetened desiccated coconut (because why not add a bit of tropical flair?)
- 30 g chia seeds (tiny yet mighty warriors of nutrition)
- 30 g ground flaxseed (the secret agent of fibre)
- 60 g almond butter (for that creamy dreaminess)
- 30 ml coconut oil, melted (slip and slide into health)
- 2 tbsp powdered sweetener (like erythritol, because life is sweet)
- 5 ml vanilla extract (a hint of exotic mystery)
- A pinch of salt (because even your taste buds need a wake-up call)
- Optional garnish: a drizzle of melted dark chocolate, a sprinkle of cacao nibs, or a shower of desiccated coconut (for dressing up for the party)

Method:

- Initiate the transformation by pulsing the almonds in a food processor until they're as finely chopped as your last haircut.
- Invite the desiccated coconut, chia seeds, flaxseed, almond butter, coconut oil, sweetener, vanilla extract, and a pinch of sea salt to the party in the food processor.
- Blitz until the mixture decides to come together in a dough-like truce.
- Conduct a taste test because you're the captain of this ship. Adjust sweetness as your heart desires.
- Roll up your sleeves and sculpt the mixture into small globes of joy with your hands.
- Let them chill on a baking sheet in the fridge for at least 30 minutes.
- Once firm and ready to face the world, dress them up with melted dark chocolate or a sprinkle of coconut, then store these delights in an airtight container in the fridge for up to a fortnight of snacking bliss.

Idea 13

Fibre beaned noodles, spaghetti or tagliatelle

I have discussed these non-wheat glucomannan fibre noodles a few times before, and you can learn more about them on page 955. For an instant fibre fix, whip up a quick dish by mixing these noodles with a hearty helping of fibre-filled beans. Drizzle with olive oil, crack some black pepper, and sprinkle your favourite herbs into the mix. I throw in a dash of paprika for a fiery hue that makes the dish pop. Just cook until the beans are warm, and voila – a fibre-rich feast that's as easy to make as it is delicious.

Idea 14

Pear-fect fibre bites

Introducing 'Pear-fect Fibre Bites' - your go-to snack when you're craving something that's both nutritious and delicious. Imagine this: crisp, juicy pear slices that serve as a canvas for a culinary masterpiece. Now, sprinkle on a generous helping of seeds – chia, to be precise, because who doesn't love a bit of chia on their pear? It's like throwing a party for your taste buds where fibre is the guest of honour. But wait, there's more! Add a whisper of cinnamon for that warm, comforting hug in every bite. It's not just a snack; it's an experience – a sensational mix of textures and flavours that dances around your palate, providing a fibre-rich feast that's as pleasing to the gut as it is to the soul. So, next time your stomach growls, reach for a 'Pear-fect Fibre Bite' and snack your way to blissful satisfaction.

Idea 15

Hunger Bulletz

Presenting 'Pyloric Pacifiers: Hunger Bulletz' – your secret weapon against the sneakiest of hunger pangs and sugar spikes. Imagine you're dashing through your day, a blur in the urban jungle, and there's simply no time to sit down for a meal. Or perhaps you're looking for a way to outsmart your body's own sugary machinations. That's where Hunger Bulletz come into play, tucked away in your bag, satchel, or even the trusty glovebox of your getaway car.

These fibre-fortified champions are not just snacks; they're your digestive system's new best friends. By taking a stand at the pylorus – that diligent gatekeeper of your stomach – they slow down the march of any food that dares to follow, putting a gentle brake on sugar spikes and easing up the insulin rush. It's like having a bouncer for your stomach, only much friendlier and, well, fibrous.

So, before you face the world or its sugar-loaded temptations, arm yourself with Hunger Bulletz. With a nod to the essential page in your survival guide (see page 957), you'll be ready to tackle your day with a steady energy supply without the usual dietary dramas. Keep calm and carry Hunger Bulletz, your anytime, anywhere hunger shield.

Idea 16

Avocado chocolate bombes

Here is a treat, a recipe proving indulgence and health can waltz together in a dance so elegant that it puts the finest ballroom duos to shame. These truffles are about to turn your snack game on its head because of Emma Porter, the culinary genius who can make a sneaker taste gourmet.
Yields: A troupe of 20 Avocado Bliss Bombes

Prep Time: A mere 10 minutes (or the time it takes to decide on a Netflix show)

Chill Time: 50 minutes (perfect for a power nap or to finally sort your sock drawer)

Ingredients:

- 200 g ripe avocado (green gold)
- 100 g dark chocolate (70% cocoa or more, because we're sophisticated like that), melted
- 15 g unsweetened cocoa powder (for that chocolatey hug)
- 10 g unpowdered sweetener (like erythritol - optional)
- For the Grand Finale (Topping): 2 tbsp unsweetened cocoa powder (because you can never have too much of a good thing)

Method:

- Wrestle with the avocado until it gives up its pit and yields its creamy flesh. Victory is yours.
- Mash the avocado as if you're smoothing out the wrinkles of life – until serene and creamy.
- Play a little 'chocolate melt' music using the microwave or a double boiler, whatever tunes you prefer.
- Mix the molten chocolate with the avocado in a culinary tango until perfectly unified. Add the cocoa powder and sweeten the deal with some erythritol if your taste buds demand.
- Let the mixture chill in the fridge for about 30 minutes, taking a well-deserved break.
- Once firm, scoop and roll the mixture into balls, as if creating planets in your very own chocolate universe. Coat these celestial bodies with cocoa powder, dressing them for the ball.
- Return to the fridge for a final 15–20 minutes of setting. This is the perfect moment to practice your acceptance speech for the Best Snack Creator Award.

- Once set, these Avocado Chocolate Bombes are ready to be devoured straight from the fridge. Each bite is a journey to a land where avocado and chocolate reign supreme and every snack is a moment of pure, unadulterated joy. Get ready to be hailed as the monarch of healthy treats – long live the Avocado Chocolate Bombes!

Idea 17

Crunch masters: Carrot & hummus delight

Your ticket to a crunchy, hydrating, and fibre-filled snacking paradise. Imagine the sun-drenched fields where the crunchiest of carrots are harvested, ready to make a splash in the pool of the smoothest, richest hummus you've ever dipped into. This isn't just a snack; it's a harmonious blend of textures and health benefits that sings a serenade to your taste buds and digestive health.

With each crunchy bite of carrot and velvety smooth hummus, you embark on a flavour-filled journey that boasts nearly 2 g dietary fibre in just a 2-tbsp embrace (or a whopping 6 g per 100 g for those who prefer a bigger hummus pot). An average-sized carrot, weighing in at a mighty 50 g, brings its own 1.4 g fibrous goodness to the party.

But, as with all great parties, moderation is key. While hummus brings an abundance of dietary fibre and tastes to the table, it also comes with its share of carbs. So, dive into this delightful duo with joy, but remember – balance is the spice of life.

Idea 18

Jumbo peanuts

Why settle for the mystery of a ready-salted bag when you can embrace the full, unadulterated glory of jumbo peanuts? Handpicked from the baking aisle, these nuts are the cream of the crop, harvested at their peak and blanched to perfection for that extra crunch. In every 25 g handful, you're getting a powerhouse of nutrition: 11 g heart-healthy fats, 6.5 g muscle-building protein, and a 2.2 g fibre boost to keep your digestive system humming along. And the best part? Barely a whisper of carbs.

Idea 19

Universal yum spread: Pure peanut butter

Let's have three cheers for peanut butter, an unsung hero of the fibre world! This versatile spread isn't just for your toast in the morning; it's a culinary chameleon ready to enhance practically anything it touches. Whether it's finding its way onto a crunchy flaxseed biscuit, elevating a slice of Emma Porter's legendary fibre bread, adorning a crisp pear slice, or jazzing up a humble stick of celery, peanut butter is ready to spread its creamy, fibrous joy far and wide.

Opt for the 100% pure peanut butter – no additives, no fuss, just the good stuff – and each 30 g serving delivers a wholesome 2.5 g fibre, making it a guilt-free addition to your snack time repertoire. So, embrace the universal yum of peanut butter; it's the spreadable champion, ready to turn anything it touches into a fibrous feast.

Idea 20

Choco-coco fibre clouds

Welcome to Choco-Coco Fibre Clouds, a dessert so heavenly, you'll swear it's a dream! Emma Porter, the culinary maestro, has bestowed upon us a chocolate mousse that's as simple to conjure as it is delightful to devour. With just two magic ingredients, this low-carb, high-joy creation promises to end your meal on a high note. Fear not, coconut sceptics, for this mousse wears its coconut milk cloak with such finesse you'll taste nothing but chocolatey nirvana.

Servings: 6 pots of happiness

Ingredients:

- 400 ml tinned coconut milk (your creamy base)
- 100 g dark chocolate (the darker, the better for keeping carbs at bay)

Method:

- Begin your cookery ballet with the chocolate, melting it with the grace of a swan using a bain-marie. This fancy French term means boiling water in a pan, then turning it down to a simmer before placing a glass bowl over it (make sure the bowl doesn't touch the water).
- As your chocolate transforms into a pool of liquid luxury, take a

moment to marvel at the alchemy.

- Set your molten treasure aside, letting it cool just a tad, as you turn your attention to the coconut milk. Ensure it's room temperature to avoid a chilly reception.
- Whip the coconut milk into a frenzy of bubbles – think of it as a bubble bath for your mousse, ensuring it achieves that dreamy, aerated texture.
- Now, with the patience and precision of a jeweller setting diamonds, blend the melted chocolate into the bubbly coconut milk, whisking as you go to unite them in silky matrimony.
- When you've achieved what could only be described as chocolate custard nirvana, portion the mixture into ramekins or small bowls, creating personal clouds of joy.
- The final act sees your creations chilling in the fridge, setting into a texture so divine, you'll need to remind yourself it's real.
- To elevate this dessert into a fibre fiesta, crown your Choco-Coco Fibre Clouds with nuts, seeds, or strawberries, turning each spoonful into a fibre-rich journey.

And there you have it, a glimpse into the treasury of fibrous delights we've prepared for you. While I've refrained from overwhelming you with links to every culinary creation shared, I offer you an exclusive invitation. Join Emma and me in the culinary sanctum for a live demonstration of how to craft this celestial 'Choco-Coco Fibre Clouds' mousse. It's not just a recipe; it's an experience, a chance to immerse yourself in the art of simple, nutritious indulgence. Don your aprons and be ready to be whisked away into a world where chocolate dreams become reality. See you in the kitchen!

*****

the Human Diet

The quintessential question posed to nutritionists, health coaches and doctors is, 'What should I eat to lose weight and get healthy?' It sounds like it requires a complicated answer, especially considering that roughly 9 out of 10 adults in the UK are metabolically unwell. However, the answer is surprisingly straightforward. The complexity arises not from the answer but from the layers of corporate interests, profit-driven agendas, and stubborn medical opinions that muddy the waters. The simplicity of the solution often gets lost in this tangle of misinformation and profit-driven narratives. So, while the answer to 'What should I eat?' is indeed simple, it requires the courage to swim against the current of conventional wisdom.

Before I unveil this simple yet profound answer, let's engage in a little interactive puzzle to sharpen our understanding and challenge preconceived notions. Take a moment to pair up seven species with their seven natural diets. It's a great puzzle that helps us appreciate the essence of dietary choices:

How did you get on? Intriguing, isn't it, to witness the seamless harmony between each creature and its inherent dietary path, un-swayed by the cacophony of a money driven world? Let's quickly verify your matches and then explore the profound implications for us as humans.

- Polar bears sustain themselves primarily on seals
- Giraffes delicately nibble on acacia leaves
- Koalas find solace in the embrace of eucalyptus leaves
- Pandas are connoisseurs of bamboo
- Wild salmon relish a diet rich in algae and small fish
- Humans – the answer is about to unfold

Each animal is exquisitely synced with its evolutionary diet-any deviation spells trouble. Imagine offering a panda the diet of a giraffe or tempting a polar bear with a salmon's sustenance; they would be recipes for disaster. They eat, not influenced by the latest fad or TV commercial, but in adherence to their innate dietary compass.

Now, turning the lens towards us humans, the query looms large-what is our 'Human Diet'? Amidst the swirl of opinions and publications, the essence of the answer is disarmingly simple: consume what we are evolutionarily attuned to. Our plates should brim with whole, unadulterated foods, devoid of the modern disguise of food-like concoctions. Opt for the authentic, the untainted, the kind that wouldn't puzzle our ancestors or be obscured behind a façade of marketing. Embracing the Human Diet is an ode to the fundamentals, a nod to what our bodies inherently recognise and flourish on.

For the sake of clarity, here are the two missing pieces of the above puzzle:

Unhealthy Humans – ultra-processed, industrialised foods
Healthy Humans – wholesome, natural foods

As we weave our way through the tapestry of *the* Human Diet, a nugget of wisdom shared by a farmer at our conference resonates with striking clarity: 'If it's a plant, eat it; if it eats plants, eat it; but if it's churned out in a plant (factory) for profit, treat it with scepticism.' This pearl of wisdom encapsulates the essence of *the* Human Diet, a diet rooted in simplicity and authenticity, far removed from modern-day, money-motivated food manufacturing.

In the previous chapters, we've already examined the world of faux foods, those culinary imposters that imitate nourishment. Yet, it's crucial to underscore this point again here because dodging these nutritional charlatans is the cornerstone of what *the* Human Diet is truly about. It's about honouring the age-old harmony between our bodies and the natural world; a harmony increasingly drowned out by the disharmony of industrial food production.

This trek into the realm of *the* Human Diet isn't just a path to better health; it's a rediscovery of our ancestral culinary heritage. Embracing foods that our great grandparents would recognise and cherish-foods in their purest form, unadulterated by the whims of profit-driven food engineering. It's a celebration of the wholesomeness of real food, a chorus of flavours, textures, and nutrients that have nourished generations.

As we begin our culinary exploration through the annals of the Human Diet, we encounter a simple yet profound truth echoed by Dr Chris van Tulleken, the wonderful author of *Ultra Processed People*, for all species, life's primary pursuits are reproduction and fuelling that reproduction with energy. This quest for energy sets off a chain of competitions in nature's grand theatre. It's a struggle for survival, where predators hunt prey, plants defend themselves with an arsenal of toxins, and microbes tirelessly seek every possible energy source. It's a perpetual tussle in the ecosystem, an endless race for energy among all life forms. But for our species and our species only, the introduction of money and creating wealth changed everything: in the past century and a half, our food landscape has undergone a seismic shift. What used to be food has transformed into something almost unrecognisable- an invention of novel molecules and unfamiliar processes that barely qualify as 'food.'

Our diets are now chockful of modified starches, inverted sugars, hydrolysed proteins, and seed oils that have undergone a battery of treatments-undressing of fibre, refined, bleached, deodorised, and hydrogenated.

The new human ecosystem is driven not by the natural flow of energy but by the relentless current of money. This paradigm shift has ushered in a new era where ultra-processed foods (UPF), wrapped in plastic and boasting ingredients foreign to a traditional kitchen, dominate our plates. These UPFs, often adorned with health claims, are far removed from the nourishment nature intended.

This shift to UPFs is not merely a dietary change; it's a departure from the natural order that has profound implications for our health and wellbeing. The rise in obesity, despite the vigilant eyes of policymakers and scientists, is a testament to this drastic dietary shift. Children in countries with high UPF consumption are not just heavier but shorter, a telling sign of malnutrition disguised as excess. Chris van Tulleken points out the insidious nature of these changes; our modern food environment is a battleground where novel substances are constantly tested on us to see which are most adept at extracting money.

But it's not just about excess bodyweight or physical appearance. The impact of UPFs extends to a range of commercially created diseases and ailments born from the consumption of addictive, widely marketed substances. These foods, devoid of their natural goodness, are replaced with synthetic alternatives designed to maximise profits, often at the expense of our health.

The history of food tells a tale of transformation – from natural sustenance to industrial potions. The irony in this shift: despite our advanced knowledge and technology, we've strayed from the fundamental principles of nutrition. Our ancestors thrived on diverse diets rich in vitamins and minerals. Yet today, we find ourselves grappling with foods that are far removed from their natural counterparts, leading us down a path of malnutrition and health issues.

At the heart of this issue lies a stark reality: the fibres and nutrients that once came naturally through our diets are often missing or insufficient, compelling us to turn to supplements to fill the gaps. This necessity speaks volumes about the state of our food system and our departure from the dietary practices that once kept us in balance with nature. In essence, our journey through the world of food and nutrition reflects how far we've veered from the path nature intended. As we cross this landscape, it's crucial to remember the simplicity and wisdom of our ancestors' diets- a reminder to return to the basics of nutrition, where real, unprocessed foods were the cornerstones of health and wellbeing.

I wrote in my previous book, *Fat & Furious*, 'I firmly believe that if food has a label, it has been engineered for addiction and manufactured for overeating. It has been created solely for corporate wealth and not public health'. And where has all the fibre gone? By now, you know fully that it is the unsung hero of the food world, bringing balance, rhythm, and a touch of magic to our meals. But in the realm of processed foods, it's often left on the cutting room floor. Why, you ask? Well, it's a tale of extended shelf life and a softer texture.

I know you're already aware of this, but I feel it's worthy of a quick reminder. Picture fibre as the backbone of fresh, whole foods, providing structure and a certain robustness. But in the world of processed foods, longevity on the shelf is king, and sadly, fibre doesn't get along well with this royal decree. Fibre contains components that can shorten the shelf life of products, making them less commercially viable for long-term storage. It's like having a character in a play who's brilliant but unpredictable – a bit of a risk for producers who want an ongoing sure-fire hit.

Additionally, removing fibre often results in a smoother, more uniform texture – something that many processed foods aim for. It's all about pleasing the palate with consistency and predictability. Imagine, if you will, a world where every apple was the same, every slice of bread was perfectly soft, and every cracker had the same snap. That's the dream of processed food manufacturers, and fibre, with its variable and sometimes coarse nature, doesn't fit this cookie-cutter mould.

In the grand theatre of food processing, fibre is often the understudy that doesn't get the limelight it deserves. It's removed to make foods more palatable, longer lasting, and, let's be honest, more addictive. Without fibre, foods can lead to faster sugar absorption, spiking insulin levels and leaving you reaching for more. It's a cunning plot twist in the story of modern eating that leaves our bodies yearning for the nutritional richness of a fibrous, whole-food diet.

Got a Chubby Four-Legged Pet?

Let me end this section on *the* Human Diet with one more thought about animals: have you ever spotted a chunky squirrel or an obese pigeon in the wild? Nope, me neither! Wild animals, barring the ones we raise from our own dinner tables, stay trim and fit. It's all about hunting down lunch or dodging becoming lunch. Hold your horses before you throw whales or buffalo at me and tell me I am misguided. Ever seen a skinny whale? I thought not! These creatures are nature's oversized, fat-storing marvels, built to withstand migration's chills or the long hibernation snoozes. Unlike us, they need their rolls of fat. Humans and our pets not so much! The only species you ever see that are not the shape they are meant to be, are those that eat foods created by money and not nature.

In Great Britain, if your cat's starting to resemble Garfield or your dog's more doughnut than Doberman, it's not just a 'cute chubby' situation. You're likely loving them a bit too generously with the money-motivated treats. Our furry friends aren't designed to be roly-poly; they're meant to be lean, mean, mouse-catching, and tail-wagging machines! Since most of our beloved pets aren't out hunting their suppers (unless you count hunting for the comfiest spot on the sofa), we must ensure they're munching on the right stuff. Yes, just like humans, our domesticated pets are now overfed but undernourished.

> **Dr Joanne McCormack**
> *A lot of pets are now getting diabetes through the stuff in processed packets and tins. And there must be something in what we feed our pets that must be wrong for their bodies. There are now low-carb vets as well as low-carb doctors.*

In wrapping up, the foremost nourishment philosophy to embrace after integrating the *Fibre First* diet is the quintessential *Human Diet.* This approach is straightforward yet profound: bid farewell to food that adorns complicated labels and wholeheartedly embrace the nourishing bounty that nature, not the factory, provides. Trust the farmer and harvest, not the factory and processing line.

*****

Low-Carbohydrate Diet

You've been a champion, embracing the *Fibre First* diet and adopting the wholesome Human Diet. How's the voyage so far? If you're sailing smoothly, drop anchor; you should enjoy the calm seas longer. Why rock the boat if the journey's already yielding treasures, right? But if you're ready to chart new territories and join the multitude who have navigated their way to even better health on the low-carbohydrate route, reducing those glucose waves even further, welcome aboard!

My approach to the low-carbohydrate diet isn't just a random map picked from a treasure chest. It's a chart crafted from devouring hundreds of books on the subject, interviewing an army of leading doctors, scouring through a sea of white papers, and even setting sail to low-carb conferences as distant as Miami and spending weeks with Maasai warriors in both Tanzania and Kenya. So, I've got a sturdy grip on the helm. My last three books were like constructing ships, each one built around the concept of navigating through the sugary fog with a Low-carbohydrate compass. Ready to set sail?

Simplifying the Low-carb Voyage: Charting Your Course

As you've already charted your course through the turbulent waters of sugar spikes and insulin tempests, let's keep the low-carb advice straightforward. You've amassed a treasure trove of knowledge, and it's time to put it to good use. Think of a low-carb diet as a meticulous process of weeding out the imposters, those carbohydrates impersonating food while stealthily robbing you of your health.

Say farewell to the deceptive allure of processed foods, where fibre has been plundered, leaving nothing but empty calories in its wake. Wave goodbye to the likes of potatoes and brown rice, where carbohydrates reign supreme with no fibre in sight. And white rice? That's already walked the plank under the 'heavily processed' flag. Bread, once a staple, is now a highly refined imposter on your plate and joins the list of 'for treats only', along with any food that contains high-fructose corn syrup and a cocktail of chemicals.

But fear not, for this approach isn't about deprivation. It's about rediscovering the richness of natural, low-carb vegetables-your loyal crew members on this expedition. These trusty companions can be personalised, dialled up or down according to your needs, guided by the charts I've crafted. With each choice, you're not just selecting a meal; you're steering your ship towards healthier horizons, away from the perils of addiction, weight gain, and the myriad illnesses that lurk in processed waters. Welcome to my approach to a low-carb diet, which focuses on real, nourishing food that keeps your metabolic ship sailing smoothly.

Navigating the Low-carb Diet: A Tale of Two Charts

I've distilled the essence of this dietary adventure into two insightful charts. Think of them as your treasure maps, guiding you through the abundant pastures of fats and proteins and the verdant valleys of plant-based delights.

Chart 1: Are foods high in fat or protein. This is an homage to our once furry or feathery friends (with a few notable exceptions for variety). It's your go-to guide for meals that roar with richness and satisfaction.

Chart 2: Arrayed from top to bottom, it reveals the carb content per 100 g serving. The mantra here is simple: the further to the top you forage, the lower your carb intake. If you're trying to shed some serious pounds, stick to the top like a koala to a eucalyptus tree. Just a few pounds to lose? Feel free to venture into the middle ground. And if you're content with your weight or looking to bulk up, you might dare to dabble all the way to the bottom, but remember, real food is the real deal, no matter where you roam on the chart.

While the low-carb landscape is vast and varied, with no one-size-fits-all definition, a daily intake of under 100 g carbs is generally considered a low-carb diet. It starkly contrasts the carb-laden banquet of the typical British diet. The lower you go, the more authentic your food choices become, the richer your health rewards.

Enjoy as much as you like	Higher protein content Egg white Non-oily fish Crab (white meat) King prawns Shrimps Standard prawns Lobster Shell fish Scallops Squid Chicken & turkey (light meat) Venison Tripe Quorn Mussels Ham Lean beef Lean pork Chicken & turkey (dark meat) Rabbit Kidney Liver Heart Gammon Back bacon (fat trimmed) Beef steak Pork Poultry with skin Pheasant Whole eggs Half fat cheddar Oily fish Crab (brown meat) Ham, gammon Lamb Duck Oxtail Higher fat content	Tofu Soya	Legumes: Lentils Chickpeas Green Peas Beans (aduki, mung, pinto, blackeye, haricot, red kidney)
Moderate Portions	Cheese Bacon Fatty cuts meat Tongue Most nuts Pate	Greek yogurt (plain) Houmous Avocado Pumpkin seeds Melon seeds Sunflower seeds Peanuts Cashew nuts Pistachio nuts	Dairy and alternatives: Quark Fromage frais Yoghurt Cow's milk Soya milk
Reduced Portions for Weight Loss	Cream Crème fraiche Sour cream Olives Fats Butter Lard Dripping Olive Oil (Avoid vegetable oils)	Coconut	Dark chocolate (80% or greater cocoa)

Enjoy	Konjac	<0.1g	Spring greens	2g	Shallots	3g
	Mushrooms	0.3g	Asparagus	2g	Runner Beans	3g
	Watercress	0.3g	Courgette	2g	Cauliflower	4g
	Celery	1g	Aubergine	2g	Brussel sprouts	4g
	Cucumber	1g	Pumpkin	2g	Mange-tout	4g
	Lettuce	1g	Celeriac	2g	Bell Peppers	4g
	Artichoke	1g	Leeks	3g	Chillies	4g
	Kale	1g	Broccoli	3g	Cabbage	4g
	Pak Choi	2g	Tomatoes	3g	Bean Sprouts	4g
	Spinach	2g	Cranberries	3g		
Enjoy some	Swede	5g	Blackcurrants	6g	Pears	6g
	Turnip	5g	Blackberries	6g	Broad Beans	7g
	Grapefruit	5g	Plums	6g		
	Raspberries	5g	Strawberries	6g		
Enjoy smaller amounts	Melon	7g	Orange	8g	Peas	10g
	Apricots	8g	Butternut squash	8g	Nectarine	10g
	Beetroot	8g	Sweetcorn	8g	Apples	10g
	Peaches	8g	Kiwi	8g	Pineapple	11g
	Pomegranate	8g	Blueberries	9g	Parsnips	12g
	Onions	8g	Gooseberries	9g		
Minimise or avoid	Red Kidney Beans	15g	Carrots	20g	Bananas	20g
	Cherries	15g	Potatoes	20g		
	Grapes	17g	Sweet potato	20g		
Avoid	Whole wheat pasta (cooked)	28g	Cassava	33g	Flour (grain, all types)	70g
	Pearl barley	28g	Bread (all types)	50g	Porridge	70g
	Yam	28g	Quinoa	55g	Sultanas	70g
	Plantain	28g	Dried dates	58g	Currants	70g
	Rice (all types) cooked	30g	Raisins	63g	Breakfast cereals (all types)	80-90g
	White pasta (cooked)	32g	Dried fruit	63g		
			Crispbread (rye)	63g		

Avoid all foods that are made from refined carbohydrates or are sugary.
All cakes, pastries, biscuits, crackers, sweets, chocolate (with less than 80% cocoa content), ice-creams, breakfast bars, sauces with natural or added sugar, fruit juices, sugar sweetened drinks, honey, jams, syrups.

*****

Intermittent Fasting:

When you first start, intermittent fasting is like uncovering the secrets of an ancient biological spell book. Yes, we humans are a marvel of complexity, a testament to biological sophistication, though I sometimes wonder if dolphins, with their dual-brained slumber technique, might have us beat in the cleverness department. But I digress. Despite our intricate nature, our bodies operate on surprisingly straightforward principles rooted deeply in our primal survival needs.

Your body is like a sophisticated engine that runs on two distinct fuels- sugar or fat. When it's revving up on sugar, burning body fat for weight loss is as futile as sailing a ship with no wind. You're either digesting and burning the buffet you've just devoured, or you're in the garage, under repair, rejuvenating through detoxification and autophagy (more on this later). It's a perpetual cycle of growth and healing, an intricate dance of biological rhythms.

But before entering the fasting pool, let's clarify one thing: fasting is a no-go zone if your body is still a sugar-guzzling machine. However, if you've been diligently adopting the *Fibre First* diet, embracing the Human Diet, and smartly navigating through the low-carb waters, you're likely already transitioning into a fat-burning powerhouse. Or, at the very least, you're a versatile hybrid, toggling between fuels with the grace of a metabolic ballet dancer.

Imagine reaching a state where your body prefers the rich, sustainable energy of fat over the fleeting rush of glucose. This isn't just some nutritional fairy tale; it's how our primal ancestors thrived, gracefully oscillating between fat and fruit-fuelled seasons. Achieving this state of metabolic flexibility is like unlocking a superpower – the ability to effortlessly switch between burning fibre-rich carbs and your own body fat, all without the gnawing pangs of hunger.

And here's where the enchantment truly unfolds. Once you achieve metabolic flexibility, your brain gracefully switches between the fat on your plate and the fat in your reserves. It's a metabolic marvel, a smooth transition that transforms stored fat into energy. To those unfamiliar, it may seem like a mystical enigma or some elusive secret of diet gurus.

Let me clarify this and make it black and white: A metabolically flexible body does not distinguish between incoming food and stored body fat for fuel, leading to a natural absence of hunger during fasting periods.

Dr David Sinclair, author of *Lifespan: Why We Age – and Why We Don't Need To*, heralded as a genius of molecular longevity, has dedicated a quarter-century to unravelling the secrets of ageing at the cellular level. With his extensive research and leading-edge laboratories spanning from the U.S. to Australia, he's like the Sherlock Holmes of the science world, deciphering the clues to a longer, healthier life. Yet, amidst the complexity of his work, Dr Sinclair offers a startlingly simple piece of advice that might make you raise an eyebrow: 'Eat less often.'

This notion isn't a modern fad; it's as timeless as the pyramids. Marie Antoinette famously quipped, 'There is nothing new, only that which has been forgotten.' Indeed, fasting isn't a new-fangled trend but a practice deeply rooted in history. Hippocrates, the father of medicine, championed fasting, particularly during illness. Various religious traditions have long extolled its virtues. Fasting invites our bodies to embrace a state of 'constructive scarcity,' a concept perhaps more alien to the modern world than flying cars. Yet, the health dividends it pays are nothing short of a miracle.

Straying from the path of fasting is one of the biggest detours we've taken from our primal ancestors. Dr Sinclair postulates that fasting doesn't just tweak our biological knobs; it cranks up our survival circuitry. It's like whispering to our longevity genes, coaxing them to do what they do best, fortifying cellular defences, safeguarding organs against adversity, fending diseases, curbing epigenetic shifts, and jamming the brakes on ageing. So, while Dr Sinclair's laboratories continue to unravel the molecular enigmas of our existence, his advice remains elegantly simple: Sometimes, the best thing you can do for your body is not to eat-at least, not so often.

Researching the annals of scientific exploration brought me to the intriguing narrative of the Biosphere experiment in the early '90s, where eight intrepid researchers were quarantined within a colossal dome for two years, subsisting solely on the crops they could cultivate. However, whether by a twist of agricultural fate or perhaps a strategic nudge from Professor Walford, a seasoned scholar in calorie restriction's effects on mice, their farming endeavours fell short. The result? An unintentional foray into the world of calorie-restricted living for 24 months.

While this scientific research showed many medical improvements in blood pressure, stabilised blood sugar, and improved cholesterol levels, the weight loss the volunteers experienced was modest. This nuance underscores a crucial insight: while calorie restriction can be a gateway to health benefits, it's not the panacea for weight loss many have hoped for.

Dr Jason Fung sheds light on this conundrum. Calorie restriction, while beneficial in certain aspects, doesn't effectively address the crux of weight loss-it's not just about eating less but about how your body responds to what you eat. Our bodies are master regulators, adept at maintaining equilibrium. Cut down the calorie intake, and your body will reduce its energy expenditure to match, a physiological response akin to drawing the curtains on a bright day.

Enter the transformative world of fasting. Unlike mere calorie restriction, fasting offers a double-edged sword against the battle of the bulge. Dr Fung clarifies that regular fasting tactically lowers insulin levels, enhancing insulin sensitivity- a vital piece often missing in the weight loss puzzle. It's not solely about limiting insulin-spiking foods but about reprogramming your body's response to insulin. Fasting, by intermittently reducing insulin resistance, helps recalibrate your body's set weight. It's akin to resetting a thermostat- a realignment from within.

The magic of fasting doesn't stop there. As insulin also plays a role in salt and water retention in the kidneys, reducing insulin levels during fasting can lead to a significant shedding of excess salt and water. The initial days of fasting often herald a rapid and noticeable weight loss, a testament to the body's remarkable adaptability.

So, while the biosphere experiment offered a glimpse into the medical virtues of calorie restriction, fasting emerges as the real game-changer. It's a voyage into redefining how our bodies interact with the very essence of nourishment and satiety. With fasting, the scale tips in favour of not just shedding pounds but reshaping our metabolic destiny.

To recalibrate our internal weight thermostat and break free from the relentless cycle of insulin resistance, we must adopt a strategy akin to stepping off the relentless pedalling of a downhill bike. This metaphorical bike represents our continual consumption of foods that perpetuate insulin resistance. Like the slightest pedal push propels the bike forward, minimal food intake can sustain the insulin resistance cycle. To reset our body's set weight point, we need to do more than ease off the pedals-we need to disembark entirely. And this means embracing fasting – a deliberate pause in our eating cycle.

Let's unpack this further. Remember, the persistent elevation of insulin nudges our body's set weight higher and higher, often stealthily adding a pound or two each year. We must disrupt the conditions that foster insulin resistance to reverse this trend and initiate weight loss. And it's not just added sugar that's the culprit; a continuous influx of carbohydrates is the fuel that keeps the cycle of insulin resistance churning relentlessly.

To unlock the door to insulin resistance and start lowering that set point, we need to remove the never-ending presence of food. Fasting is the key, not just a dietary choice but a strategic shift. It allows our cells a respite from the constant barrage of insulin, gradually restoring their sensitivity and recalibrating our body's natural weight regulation mechanism. In the grand scheme of metabolic health, fasting isn't just a pause-it's a powerful reset button.

Fasting: A Legacy Of Healing

The practice of fasting isn't a trendy fad; it's a cornerstone of healing wisdom passed down through the ages. Hippocrates, the luminary of medicine, prescribed fasting as a potent remedy, asserting, 'To eat when you are sick is to feed your illness.' Plutarch, the chronicler of ancient wisdom, concurred, advising, 'Instead of using medicine, better fast today.' These timeless truths remind us that sometimes, the most profound healing comes from simplicity and returning to the fundamentals of our existence.

During the Second World War, a mantra emerged when food scarcity was a reality: 'Eat little but often.' Born out of necessity, this saying lingers in the annals of dietary advice. Yet, with the lens of modern medical insight, we now recognise the pitfalls of this approach. Aligning with our evolutionary blueprint, consuming what we're designed to eat and adhering to a natural eating rhythm prompts a pivotal question: Did our primal ancestors graze constantly? Far from it. Their lives were a rhythm of abundance and scarcity, a testament to the human body's innate capacity to thrive in cycles of feast and famine.

Our biological heritage is not one of perpetual snacking but resilience and adaptability. The key to unlocking our full health potential lies not in the frequency of our meals but in the wisdom of fasting, in honouring the natural cycles of nourishment and rejuvenation that have sustained humanity since time immemorial.

Eating Regularly Is Not Normal

We aren't designed to eat regularly. Caveman and the hunter-gatherer didn't have fridges or freezers. They couldn't store an apple for a year like the oxygen-free warehouses the big supermarkets use today. They had no preservatives or tin cans. When they caught an animal, they had a feast, after which they might go days or weeks eating nothing substantial.

It's not just our ancestors who fasted; various faiths and religions still participate in different ceremonial fasts. Muslims celebrate Ramadan, the ninth month of the Islamic calendar, with a month-long fast known as Sawm. Christians participate in Lent and the Greek Orthodox Church asks that its followers fast for over 180 days a year. Saint Nikolaj Velimirović wrote, 'Gluttony makes a man gloomy and fearful, but fasting makes him joyful and courageous. And, as gluttony calls forth greater and greater gluttony, fasting stimulates greater endurance. When a man realises the grace that comes through fasting, he desires to fast more and more. And the graces that come through fasting are countless.'

Breakfast: The British Cereal Killer

Remember those staggering blood sugar spikes my volunteers experienced while eating breakfast in chapter 2? Well, brace yourself for a breakfast revelation that might flip your morning routine on its head. You see, breakfast, the supposed 'most important meal of the day,' might just be donning a disguise. It's a ritual that only became mainstream in the 1920s. Yes, humanity thrived for aeons without Kellogg's guiding hand. Have you ever pondered the origin of the term 'breakfast'? It's breaking the overnight fast, a name that spells out its result.

The breakfast cereal industry is a marketing powerhouse, with more advertising dollars splashed on these crunchy delights than any other food category. But here's the problem: breakfast cereals are among the fastest-digesting carbs, transforming into sugar faster than you can say 'snap, crackle, pop!' For over three decades, I, too, fell into the trap of the breakfast ritual, fretting over skipped morning meals amidst a whirlwind of daily chores. We've all been fed the narrative: breakfast kickstarts your metabolism, fuels your day, and sets you up for success. Remember the adage, 'Breakfast like a king, lunch like a prince, dine like a pauper'? Well, my breakfast-free days were a secret blessing, not a dietary misstep. Farewell to the days of low-fat yoghurts, sugary cereals, and that large glass of orange juice – they're not the health champions we were led to believe.

As you sail through the early stages of your *Fibre First* diet, you might find the tide of your morning hunger shifting. For me, the age-old tradition of breakfast has transformed from an every-day must to an occasional indulgence. These days, my mornings are typically marked by a few cups of coffee and a fibre-rich Slimshotz drink, neither of which breaks my fast. The only exception? Holiday mornings, when I might treat myself to the simple pleasure of a savoury omelette or the vibrant fusion of fermented yoghurt and berries, a delightful tandem of gut health and rich micronutrients.

What Happens to Our Metabolism When We Intermittently Fast?

Have you ever wondered if skipping a meal might set your metabolism on a sluggish spiral? Let's debunk some myths and shed light on what happens when we intermittently fast. Metabolism, in layman's terms, is the body's way of transforming our meals (or, when food is scarce, our stored love handles) into fuel. Now, if every time our caveman ancestor missed a woolly mammoth, his metabolic rate plummeted, he'd have been less energetic than a sloth in hibernation. Not the best scenario for survival, right? Well, it turns out our metabolism doesn't hit the snooze button during fasting; instead, it's hitting the gym, flexing, and boosting by up to 14% for as long as 48 hours after fasting, according to illuminating research by Dr Michael VanDerschelden in *The Scientific Approach to Intermittent Fasting*.

Imagine if our hunter-gatherer ancestors experienced a metabolic nosedive every time the pantry (read: cave) was bare. Their story would've been short and not so sweet. Thankfully, human biology is smarter than that. Our bodies are primed to sharpen our wits and keep the energy furnace burning, at least for the first few days without food, ensuring we remain nimble and ready to spear our next meal.

Intriguing, isn't it? Fasting doesn’t drag your metabolic rate down to the basement but gives it a gentle nudge upwards. Picture this: you're usually a 2,500-calories-a-day person, spread across breakfast, lunch, and dinner. But say you decide to embrace fasting and pack all those calories into a single meal. Not only does your metabolic rate get a slight boost, but you'll also likely consume fewer calories in one go than grazing throughout the day.

Let's circle back to why our bodies store fat. It's not just for insulation or to make those jeans a snug fit. Fat is our emergency fuel, our rainy-day fund. So, if your body's carrying a little extra 'wealth', why not let it foot the bill during a food shortage? Our bodies are marvels of engineering, designed to gracefully ride the waves of feast and famine.

Intermittent Fasting May Prevent and Cure Diseases

The feast-and-famine rhythm isn't merely a relic from our ancestral past; it's the key to unlocking a treasure trove of health benefits. As we feast, our metabolic virtuosos orchestrate the insulin symphony, deftly shuttling those troublesome sugar molecules to our body's storage depots. Yet, when we embrace fasting, the melody morphs; insulin takes a bow, and our bodies transition into a fat-burning state.

Amidst this metabolic metamorphosis, our human growth hormones (HGH) take centre stage, surging to heights that even the most dedicated athletes might envy. The fasting stage isn't just a quiet interlude; it's a crescendo of HGH production, a hormonal encore that reverberates throughout the body. In fact, research underscores the potency of fasting as a catalyst for HGH release. A symphonic spike of HGH punctuates the early morning, with a continuous performance throughout the day in response to fasting. One study strikingly noted a fivefold surge in HGH as a curtain call to a two-day fasting period, suggesting that this hormonal harmony plays a pivotal role in preserving the integrity of our muscles and bones, keeping our bodily structure robust and resilient.[4]

But wait, there's more! Our nervous system deploys its special forces, the Norepinephrine's, to our fat stores, where they liberate fatty acids to fuel our fasting adventures. It's a classic case of our body being preoccupied with digesting food or basking in the glory of HGH production and norepinephrine deployment.

But fasting isn't just a one-trick pony; it's the Swiss Army knife of health interventions. Our body, in a fasting state, transforms into a self-repairing marvel, rejuvenating cells across the board. It's like hitting the refresh button on your browser-everything works better. With fasting, the risk of developing diabetes, heart conditions, and even certain cancers plummet like a stone in water. It's the brain's best friend, offering a shield against the menaces of Alzheimer's and Parkinson's disease.

Now, let's take a moment to talk about autophagy, the body's own KonMari method of tidying up. It's our built-in spring-cleaning service, where cells don their aprons and start clearing the clutter. But just like that one drawer everyone has at home, our cellular clean-up crew, the lysosomes (the cell's organelle that breaks down excess or worn-out cell parts), start slacking off as we age. They're the heroes of our youth but become the procrastinators of our twilight years, contributing to the ageing process. The antidote? Intermittent fasting. It's the pep talk our lysosomes need to get back on the job and keep our cells spick and span.

Let's check back in with our caveman for a moment. If he were lounging in his cave, munching on endless snacks, nature would be none the wiser about the need for cellular housekeeping. But his life was a rollercoaster of feast and famine. When the going gets tough and the stomach growls, that's nature's cue to roll up its sleeves and get to work. It's not just about ensuring our caveman friend catches his next meal; it's about ensuring every cellular cog and wheel is in tip-top condition.

The Intermittent Fasting Muscle Myth

Venturing into the world of intermittent fasting often brings up a pressing concern: 'Sure, fasting may fine-tune my metabolism, shield me from a myriad of illnesses, and even potentially reverse type 2 diabetes. But what about my muscles? Am I going to wither away?' Fear not! If our primal ancestors lost muscle mass every time they missed a mammoth steak, they'd soon be too weak to wield a spear, and we'd be a footnote in history, not its authors. My trip into the fasting realm revealed a surprising twist after a three-day fast; while carrying out my normal exercise regime, my muscle mass didn't shrink; it expanded.

Here's the clincher: fat may hog the spotlight, but the muscles do the heavy lifting, metabolically speaking. Strong, vibrant muscles are like a roaring fireplace, constantly burning through calories. Ever wonder why the post-diet rebound leaves people heavier than before? It's because calorie-restricted diets often lead to muscle loss, leaving behind a sluggish metabolism that's more adept at storing fat than burning it. Diets come and go, but they often miss the mark. What we need isn't a fleeting trend but a return to our primal roots – a lifestyle that embraces the wisdom of our ancestors, not the calorie-counting obsessions of modern times. It's about nourishing our bodies with wholesome, delectable foods and tuning into the natural rhythms that have sustained humanity through the ages.

And remember, intermittent fasting isn't one-size-fits-all. It's about weaving a pattern of eating and fasting that harmonises with your life's melody. In his book *Lifespan*, Dr David Sinclair advises us to take the leap. While we eagerly await the final verdict from cutting-edge research, almost any well-balanced fasting regimen, as long as it does not result in malnutrition, is like a conductor's baton, orchestrating our longevity genes into a symphony of healthier, longer life.

Embarking on Intermittent Fasting: Diverse Paths to Wellness

Welcome to the diverse world of intermittent fasting, where various methods cater to different lifestyles and preferences. Whether you're a busy bee or someone who enjoys a structured routine, there's an intermittent fasting approach that aligns with your rhythm of life. Let's look at some of the popular methods for you to mix and match:

The 5:2 Diet: The Flexible Fasting Plan

The 5:2 Diet, popularised by Michael Mosley and Mimi Spencer, offers a flexible approach to fasting. It's like having a weekly planner where five days are your 'go with the flow' days, and the other two are your 'minimalist' days, with men consuming 600 calories and women 500. While it's not my personal favourite, it could be your ticket to gradual, steady weight loss, especially when coupled with lots of fibre and a dash of high-intensity training.

The 1:1 Diet: The Day-On-Day-Off Approach
Imagine your diet as a game of ping-pong, alternating between regular and fasting days. That's the essence of the 1:1 or alternate-day fasting method. It's a commitment, like sticking to a TV series with alternating cliffhangers and resolutions. For those who embrace it, the long-term food-mass deficit can be quite significant.

The 18-Hour Fast: The Daily Window of Opportunity
The 18-Hour Fast Diet is like having a daily 'open for business' sign that flips to 'closed' for 18 hours. You indulge in all your eating within a six-hour window, turning the rest of the day into a bodyfat-burning fiesta.

The OMAD & Post-Workout Ritual
Then there's the 'One Meal A Day' (OMAD) lifestyle, interspersed with the occasional post-gym protein shake. Personally, for me, this method resonates with my routine, transforming every day into an effortlessly balanced act of nourishment and rejuvenation. It's like being a culinary minimalist, savouring the simplicity and focus of a single daily feast, complemented by a muscle-nourishing shake.

The Three- or Four-Day Extended Spa for Your Cells

My own forays into three- and four-day fasts have been nothing short of enlightening. Initially daunting, these fasting experiences unravel into periods of profound clarity and heightened physical performance as the days progress. It's akin to your body throwing a metabolic party when you least expect it, with day three being the pinnacle of performance and vitality. The American Society for Clinical Nutrition validates this, highlighting that our basal metabolic rate (BMR) doesn't just hold steady but skyrockets, making day three a celebration of peak physical prowess.

During these fasting periods, our bodies become meticulous repair shops, addressing every nook and cranny. From silencing those pesky free radicals that flirt with disease to hitting the brakes on inflammation, the benefits are vast and varied. The digestive system, too, gets a well-deserved holiday, tidying up and rejuvenating from top to bottom. Personally, every two months, I mark my calendar for a three- or four-day fast, a ritual that yields amazing results.

But fasting isn't just about giving our bodies a break. It's about fuelling our brains with premium energy. When we fast, our liver converts fat into ketones, a high-octane fuel our brain adores. Ketones aren't just an alternative to glucose; they're a VIP energy source, especially for our brain cells. Even babies thrive on ketones in their rapid developmental stage, building an astounding 1 million neural connections per second. It's clear that for brain power, ketones are the preferred choice of fuel, offering a cleaner, more efficient energy source.

As you explore the world of extended fasting, remember that it's more than a dietary choice; it's a transformation towards enhanced wellbeing, mental clarity, and longevity.

Embarking On Your First Fasting Voyage

Venturing into the world of intermittent fasting is like setting sail on uncharted waters. If you're starting with some extra cargo (weight, that is), beginning with alternate-day fasting might be your best bet. It's like hitting the ground running, or in this case, fasting. As you inch closer to your goal, transitioning to the 5:2 diet is like adjusting your sails to a gentle breeze, ensuring a smooth journey towards your weight haven. Once you've dropped anchor at your desired weight, the 18-hour fast might become your daily voyage, reaping the myriad health benefits of fasting while maintaining your hard-earned progress.

Fasting doesn't mean abandoning the ship on fibre, nutrients, and minerals. These are your loyal crew members. Ensuring your passage is not just about losing weight but enhancing overall health. Just remember, when you're fasting, it's best to steer clear of alcohol. Keeping your fast days alcohol-free ensures your body stays in prime repair mode.

With the following 12 essential tips, you're equipped to explore intermittent fasting, unlocking the potential for improved health and wellbeing.

Navigating Fasting: 12 Tips for Your Fast

1. **Quiet Voyage:** Share your fasting journey selectively. Support from close friends or family is invaluable, but widespread broadcasting might invite unnecessary scepticism or discouragement.

2. **Hydrate Generously:** Increase your water intake significantly.

3. **Up Your Fibre Intake:** Also, try adding fibre into your evening routine, as it can prevent night-time hunger signals from disrupting your sleep.

4. **Stay Busy:** Keep your mind occupied and active. Fasting may be a new practice for you, but it's a natural process for your body.

5. **Ride Out the Hunger Waves:** Hunger isn't constant; it comes in waves. When it hits, a glass of water or a fibre drink can help you until it subsides.

6. **Coffee as a Companion:** Coffee can subtly suppress your appetite. Other allies include green tea, black tea, and bone broth.

7. **Embrace a Discovery Phase:** Allow your body a month to adapt to fasting. Initially, it may feel challenging, but persistence leads to smoother experiences.

8. **Mindful Feasting:** Use non-fasting days to nourish your body wisely. Opt for nutrient-dense foods that are low in sugars and refined carbs and rich in fibre.

9. **Soothe with a Pinch of Salt:** Experiencing dizziness or headaches? A bit of salt in bone broth can help stabilise your body.

10. **Supplement Wisely:** Consider a multivitamin to avoid nutrient deficiencies and magnesium to prevent muscle cramps.

11. **Medical Consultation is Key:** If you're on medication or insulin, ensure you consult your doctor before embarking on a fasting regimen.

12. **Personalise Your Path:** The most important tip is to make fasting fit into your lifestyle. Don't let it limit your social interactions or personal routines. Adjust your fasting approach to align with your individual life circumstances.

If your fasting journey hits rough seas in the form of giddiness, a headache, or the growling protests of your stomach, you've got a few lifelines. First, try reaching for a glucomannan drink like Slimshotz or some glucomannan noodles such as Fibrehydrates.

Glucomannan doesn't break a fast. It makes you feel full without your body extracting any energy from it, keeping you firmly in fasting waters. If the waters are too choppy, don't abandon the ship. Instead, ease into fasting by gradually reducing your calorie intake on fast days. Start with a more manageable 1,200 calories and gradually lower the sails to 900 or 800. Just remember, this is a transitional phase. Staying above 500 calories for too long is like sailing in circles – you won't get the full benefits of fasting, and it's back to the doldrums of calorie restriction.

Fasting Finale: Charting Your Personal Course

Once you've embraced the vibrant hues of a wholesome diet, leaving the monochrome world of starches and sugars behind, you'll find the waters of intermittent fasting serene and inviting. The key is to weave fasting seamlessly into the tapestry of your life rather than rearranging your life around it. Life's rhythms vary, with social gatherings, family holidays, and seasonal festivities. Embrace these ebbs and flows; fasting is not a rigid framework, but a flexible, accommodating companion towards better health.

I've found harmony in variety. On bustling weekdays, I often find solace in a single evening meal, while weekends or holidays might see me omeletting at breakfast with my family. Periodically, I embark on a three- or four-day total fast – a profound experience that fills me with energy and clarity, as if I'm drawing vitality directly from the wellspring of life.

The ethos is simple: do what resonates with you. Build strength and vitality by feasting on protein and fibre when muscle growth is your goal. When it's time for cellular renewal, let fasting be your guide. Fasting isn't a mystical rite; it's a return to our primal roots, an echo of our ancestors' rhythm of feast and famine. Healthy and mindful fasting can stretch for days, but navigating with awareness of your body's fibre, vitamins and mineral needs is crucial.

If you're looking for inspiration, study Angus Barbieri's remarkable fasting pilgrimage. Starting in June 1965 at a weight of 465 lb, Angus set forth with a modest goal, only to find himself sailing towards a world record. Supported throughout by his local hospital, his journey continued until he reached his destination at 180 lb. This incredible fast, sustained by tea, coffee, sparkling water, and essential supplements, spanned 382 days, culminating in a triumphant meal of a boiled egg. Angus's pilgrimage didn't just redefine his life; it etched his name in the annals of fasting history. But no matter how much weight you want to lose, please don't go beyond five or six days without medical supervision.

As you chart your own course in the world of fasting, remember that it's not just about reaching a destination. It's about embracing the journey, tuning into your body's needs, and finding your rhythm in the ebb and flow of life's tides.

A word of warning: If you are on medication, check with your doctor before you try fasting. But try it, you must, as your body is designed to enter its natural repair mode periodically; it's not doing, so that's unnatural.

*****

Ketogenic Diet: A Renaissance Of Our Ancestral Diet

By now, you know fully that processed carbohydrates and sugars are akin to unwelcome guests in our metabolic tale. In the guise of wheat, grain, potatoes, rice, pasta, and their kin, these interlopers undergo a transformation within our bodies, emerging as sugar. This metabolic event prompts our body to despatch insulin, the diligent courier, shuttling these sugar-laden molecules to their storage chambers in our fat reserves. Put another way, when we have insulin in the blood, we are locked in sugar-burning, fat-storing mode.

However, if we dramatically cut our carb intake to less than 20 g per day, we eliminate the need for insulin, and our body begins to tune in to an alternative fuel, ketones. This is the state of ketosis, a metabolic realm where our body, without sugar, crafts ketones from our stored fat, bestowing us a sustainable energy source.

The ketogenic diet stands as a testament to the power of dietary intervention, especially for preventing epileptic seizures, slowing Alzheimer's and much more. The year 2022 marked a renaissance in the realm of ketogenic research, with an astonishing array of studies painting a vivid picture of its multifaceted efficacy. The PubMed database of scientific inquiry recorded 604 peer-reviewed studies in 2022, escalating to a remarkable 726 by the following year. What I am trying to demonstrate is that a ketogenic diet is, by far, the hottest topic among nutritional scientists globally.

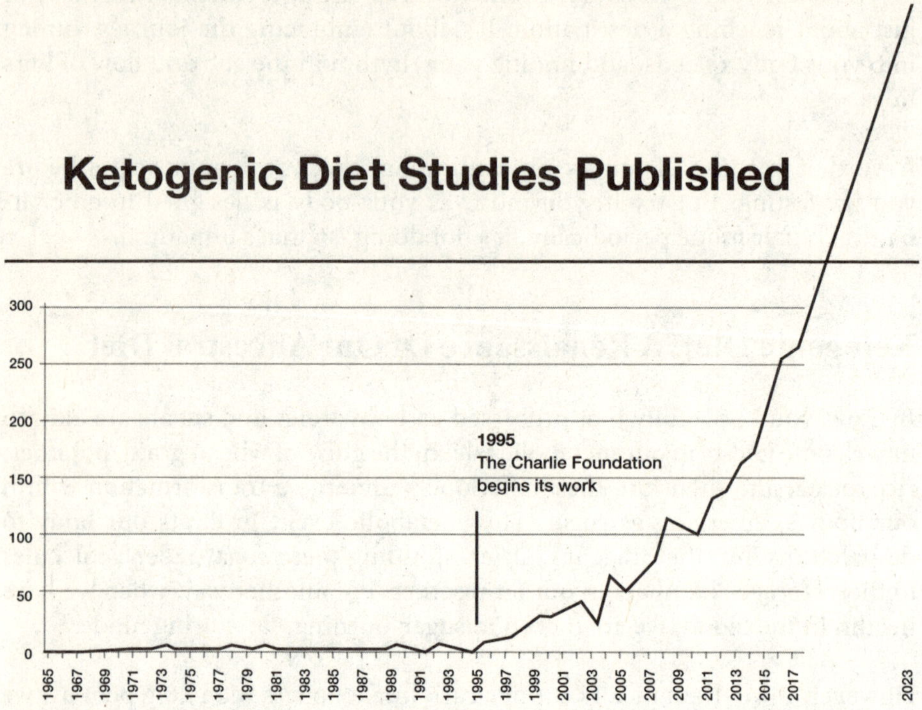

The narrative these studies weave is one of profound potential, highlighting the diet's prowess in warding off and sometimes reversing neurological diseases and certain cancers. What has the evidence from these recent clinical trials revealed? They have found in favour of the ketogenic diet for:

- Epilepsy/Seizures (61 clinical trials)
- Alzheimer's disease (14 clinical trials)
- Parkinson's disease (4 clinical trials)
- Cancer, muscle wasting (47 clinical trials)
- Weight loss (25 clinical trials)
- Type-2 diabetes (14 clinical trials)
- Polycystic ovary syndrome (PCOS)
- Migraine

In fact, just about every medical marker gets better. The only one up for debate would be that LDL cholesterol raises slightly, but as you will read later, that may even be beneficial too!

But why does this trove of evidence whisper so softly in the public domain? The answer lies in the corridors of power, where convenience and profit often overshadow truth. The ketogenic diet, emphasising foods that elude the grasp of colossal food conglomerates, poses a subtle threat to their empire. Similarly, the pharmaceutical behemoths, whose fortunes are intertwined with the threads of human suffering, find little allure in a diet that promises alleviation and healing.

Yet, despite these forces, the ketogenic diet's renaissance is undeniable. Its scope has transcended the confines of epilepsy treatment, casting its healing light on an array of afflictions, most notably Alzheimer's disease. At the heart of this dietary marvel is its ability to rejuvenate mitochondrial function and dispel the shadows of oxidative stress. It's a diet that doesn't just feed the body; it nourishes the very essence of our cellular being. As we embark on this expedition of discovery, let's remember that the ketogenic diet is more than a nutritional regimen – it's a testament to the healing synergy between food and the human body.

Ketosis, ketones, ketogenic and ketoacidosis - What's the Difference? Here's a quick note to shine a light on their distinct roles in the vast universe of metabolic health.

Ketosis: A state of being akin to declaring, 'I am in ketosis.' Ketosis is simply the state of burning fat for fuel. It's when the body, in an elegant shift, turns to ketones as its prime energy catalyst, stepping away from glucose. This transition is not just about trimming body fat; it brings a renewed sense of energy and wellness into the spotlight.

Ketones: The stars of this metabolic event, 'My body thrives on ketones.' These molecules are the essence of the fuel, igniting the leap into ketosis with their energy-rich glow.

The Ketogenic Diet: This is the compass guiding us to the treasure of ketosis, charting a path through minimal carbs (barely a whisper of 20 g daily, focusing on lush greens) while celebrating the free indulgence in fibre.

Ketoacidosis: The dark twist in the tale, a dangerous anomaly often confused with ketosis yet fundamentally different. While ketosis is a symphony orchestrated through dietary mastery, ketoacidosis emerges as a critical condition, a storm brewing primarily in individuals with type 1 diabetes who have lost their insulin lifeline.

What to Eat on A Ketogenic Diet

At the heart of this diet lies a simple principle: by decimating your carb intake and filling up on fats, your body enters a state called ketosis, a metabolic wizardry that burns fat for fuel instead of glucose.

So, what's on the menu in this high-fat, low-carb realm? Picture your plate brimming with avocados, a symbol of healthy fats; succulent salmon and sardines, rich in omega-3; and a medley of leafy greens like spinach and kale, low in carbs but high in fibre and vitamins. Nuts and seeds, such as almonds and chia, become your go-to snacks, offering crunch and substance without the carb overload. And let's not forget to add some protein: eggs, cheese, and grass-fed meats, ensuring your muscles are well-fed without spiking your glucose levels.

When choosing meats and fish, go for the fattier, oilier options. While I just mentioned the need for protein on a ketogenic diet, the focus must be more on fat. And to kick start your mornings, if you aren't fasting, why not try adding coconut oil or butter to your coffee (or both)? It really helps kick-start the ketosis cycle and surprisingly tastes good, too. Plus, today, more and more ketogenic supplements, known as exogenous ketones, are beginning to enter the market. The ketogenic approach isn't just a diet; it's a path to rediscovering food as fuel, where each meal is a step towards a more energised and focused you.

Ketogenic Diet: Unlocking The Brain's Potential

Dr Boz, a wizard in the realm of ketosis, casts a light on an often-overlooked connection: our brains' wellbeing is intricately linked to our diet. Studying medical archives, where autopsy records reveal secrets of longevity and cerebral health, we uncover the diet's unexpected champions: individuals who, decades ago, turned to ketosis to combat epilepsy. Like navigators guided by stars through darkness, these pioneers found solace in the ketogenic diet amidst the storm of seizures. Fast forward, and the evidence from their journeys into old age unveils a startling contrast: brains marked by a total absence of decline, defiance of time's usual toll. In the battle against epilepsy, where seizures etch their marks, the brains of those who lived a life dedicated to ketosis stood as fortresses, enduring against age's customary systematic assault.

Dr Boz, sharing insights on my podcast, reveals the protective veil ketosis casts over the brain. The dreaded tangles of neurofibrillary chaos, often harbingers of cognitive fade, find themselves impotent against ketosis's shield. This diet, a steadfast guardian, preserves neural clarity, with autopsies of lifelong keto followers showing brains untouched by the spectres of dementia, a serene haven amidst the turmoil of ageing.

The ketogenic diet, thus, transcends its role as mere sustenance. It emerges as a lighthouse, guiding us through the fog of neurological decline. It whispers of a future where minds remain sharp, untarnished by the years. In the embrace of ketosis, inflammation, the stealthy thief of mental acuity, retreats, leaving behind a brain fortified, alert, and vibrant. Dr Boz's teachings illuminate this path: 'Years of ketosis can sharpen your brain, quickening its messages, minimising errors.' Ketosis is not a fleeting trend but a lifelong pact for a future bright with cognitive clarity.

After our enlightening podcast, I continued the conversation with another expert in this area, Dr Dom D'Agostino. His work further enriches this narrative, extending the wonders of ketosis from children with epilepsy to the elite warriors of the sea, the United States Navy SEALs. Through ketosis, these paragons of mental and physical discipline discover an ally in the depths, enhancing their endurance, mental focus, and even their ability to remain submerged longer without the shadow of seizures.

The tale of ketosis weaves through the fabric of our being, from the depths of the ocean to the vastness of our minds, proving itself as a key to managing disease and unlocking the full potential of human resilience and capability. The ketogenic diet, championed by visionaries like Dr Boz, Dr D'Agostino, and Dr Mary Newport, whom we heard from earlier, stands as a testament to the power of food as medicine, a light of hope for those seeking to conquer life's deepest challenges.

My Ketosis Experiments

My first brush with ketosis begun with a challenging endeavour alongside a group of esteemed doctors and James Cracknell OBE, a decorated Olympic rowing champion. We embarked on an audacious quest: completing four marathons over five days, propelled solely by the fuel of our own body fat, without a morsel of food. Yes, we were totally fasted throughout the entire event, just propelled by water and a few key supplements. This wasn't merely a test of physical endurance, but a meticulously monitored medical experiment, with our bodies, scrutinised by a myriad of machines before and after each marathon, capturing an array of data that would later unveil astonishing revelations.

The compelling outcomes of this initial exploration sparked a sequel of sorts. This time, we set our sights on an unfamiliar terrain, trading our running shoes for pushbikes, and embarking on a gruelling cycle from Glasgow to Bristol, all while again embracing the empowering embrace of a five-day fast. These remarkable expeditions, each a testament to the transformative power of ketosis, are chronicled for posterity on YouTube under the banner of the Health Results channel.

During these intense trials, an unexpected phenomenon emerged: an unprecedented clarity of thought, a mental acuity that felt almost superhuman. Each of us, without exception, experienced this profound sharpening of our cognitive faculties. For me, this newfound clarity manifested in the stillness of the night. Ideas would flood my mind, compelling me to illuminate my surroundings with a bedside lamp and fervently scribble them in my journal. Unlike the usual nocturnal musings that dissolve into absurdity by morning, the insights captured during these ketogenic states were lucid, coherent, and startlingly profound.

Given my mother has Alzheimer's, which elevates my risk, and the APOE4 gene in my DNA nudging that risk even higher, I've committed to spending as much time in ketosis as possible. On mornings when the aftermath of last night's indulgences, be it a lavish meal or an extra glass of wine, sends my ketone levels plummeting, I have a strategy to kickstart my day back into ketosis. I either reach for a ketone supplement or whip up a coffee enriched with butter and C8 coconut oil, crafting a concoction that not only reignites my metabolic fire but also fortifies my fight against the shadows of Alzheimer's.

Ketosis: A Dietary Strategy To Avoid Chronic Conditions

While I won't write again about the wonderful success of Dr Boz in battling her mother's cancer, or the transformative journey of the Baszucki's family in managing their son's bipolar disorder, nor the inspiring rewinding of the clock of Steve Newport's Alzheimer's by his loving wife Dr Mary Newport, its potential advantage for nullifying multiple sclerosis presents another compelling narrative. Dr Terry Wahls' transformation from being wheelchair-bound to cycling to work daily is nothing short of miraculous.

For four arduous years, Dr Wahls was bound to a tilt-recline wheelchair, a circumstance she overturned with a bespoke diet and lifestyle regimen aimed at rejuvenating her cellular health. Her triumph over progressive multiple sclerosis (MS) underscores the potency of ketosis – a principle she embraced, mirroring the dietary essence of The Wahls Protocol, her bestselling testament. Dr Wahls enlightens us with a historical perspective, noting that 'humans went into ketosis every winter for thousands of generations. Being in low-level ketosis is the more natural state for our metabolism.'

Let's turn the spotlight on the inspiring story of Stephanie Person. Her mother, after being diagnosed with a terminal glioblastoma multiforme brain tumour and given six months to live, embraced a ketogenic diet and remarkably sent her cancer into remission. Stephanie shares, 'I delved deep into Keto Adaptation research following my mother's grim diagnosis. Determined to slow the cancer's progression, I drastically reduced her carbohydrate consumption and significantly increased her intake of dietary fats. This immediate dietary overhaul halted my mother's cancer growth. She's now celebrating her seventh cancer-free year.'

Can a ketogenic diet help with thyroid issues? Reflecting on her experience in *Keto Clarity*, Stephanie notes, 'Gluconeogenesis provides the glucose necessary to rejuvenate thyroid function and repair the thyroid while in ketosis. Many of my keto clients have successfully discontinued their thyroid medications.' She later wrote a line that I absolutely fell in love with: 'Carbohydrate overconsumption has created the walking dead.'

Enhanced Vision And Auditory Acuity: The Unexpected Gifts of Ketosis

Returning to our five-day, 500-mile fasted bike ride experiment, the sceptics and naysayers were vocal, casting doubts and cautioning against the potential perils of such rigorous activities in a fasted state. Concerns about diminished concentration and heightened risk of road accidents were rampant, particularly poignant for James Cracknell, as our event took place precisely a decade after his harrowing accident while cycling across America, where an accident on Route 66 left him in a comma. However, reality painted a starkly original picture. Far from being impaired, our senses were elevated to unprecedented levels. We morphed into hyper-alert, keto-fuelled entities, with auditory and visual faculties undergoing a remarkable transformation. The world around us appeared in a new light, colours radiating with an intensity previously unnoticed. It was as if a veil had been lifted, revealing the vibrancy of life in its most vivid form. Our auditory senses, too, seemed to attain a newfound sensitivity, picking up nuances and subtleties that would typically evade our perception.

But how could this be? The secret lies in the essence of the default British high-carb diet and its tendency to induce inflammation throughout the entire body, eyes, ears, and brain. Ketosis, in its profound wisdom, curtails this inflammation, even in the most delicate tissues of the eyes. This reduction in inflammation paves the way for unobstructed visual signals from the eye to the brain. The absence of this inflammatory interference results in a visual experience that's not just clearer but strikingly vivid. Colours assume a newfound vibrancy, and the world's entirety comes into sharper focus.
These personal experiments with ketosis were more than just a test of physical endurance; they were an exploration into the potential of the human body and mind. By embracing the powerful state of ketosis, we didn't just push the boundaries of our physical capabilities; we unlocked a level of sensory perception that redefined our understanding of what it means to see and hear the world around us.

Freedom from Hunger: The Ketogenic Liberation

Embarking on a ketogenic diet is akin to unlocking a hidden dimension where the gnawing pangs of hunger become a distant memory. As you traverse the landscape of low-carb living and intermittent fasting, you stumble upon a profound revelation – the disappearance of hunger. It's an experience so surreal that meals no longer dictate your day's rhythm. Hunger, once a constant companion, now feels like a stranger. The ketogenic diet doesn't just change your eating habits; it transforms your relationship with food, liberating you from the relentless cycle of cravings and satiation.

Imagine your body as a finely tuned machine, no longer dependent on carbohydrates' fleeting, combustible energy. Ketones, the alternative fuel source ignited by the ketogenic diet, offer a more sustainable and stable form of energy. The contrast is stark, like comparing the blaze of a fire fuelled by pine needles to the enduring warmth of a fire stoked with hardwood. Like those quick-burning pine needles, carbohydrates provide an intense yet fleeting burst of energy, followed by an inevitable crash. This erratic energy cycle sends incessant signals to refuel, keeping you tethered to a never-ending carousel of consumption.

Now, envision a different scenario where you've liberated your body from this dependency, transitioning to a state of ketosis. In this metabolic state, your body becomes a proficient energy converter, adept at tapping into its own fat reserves for fuel. It's as if you've re-engineered your internal combustion system, swapping out a gas-guzzling engine for a sleek, efficient electric motor. The road to ketosis may have twists and turns, but the experience is transformative once you arrive. It's a state of metabolic grace where energy levels are steady, the focus is sharp, and the once pervasive call of hunger fades into a whisper. This is the ketogenic path to weight management and a newfound sense of freedom and control over your body's energy narrative.

Dr Boz writes, 'When your body burns fat fuel, at first the energy pales compared to sugar fuel. Stick to it. Each day, your body recruits more mitochondria to burn fat. No more crashes of energy. Your stamina for focus, concentration and healthy living rises over the next weeks. Fat-fuel lasts longer. It also builds upon yesterday's results.' She says, 'The sensation of feeling full, sated, or satiated signals you to stop eating. Our body triggers this feeling of fullness by eating fat. Not by eating carbohydrates.'

Taming Inflammation: The Ketogenic Shield

As we study the molecular realm of our bodies, we uncover ketones are not just energy torchbearers but also valiant warriors against inflammation. The ketogenic diet coordinates a symphony of metabolic shifts, one of which significantly curtails the production of reactive oxygen species, notorious instigators of inflammation. This isn't just a subtle nudge against inflammation; ketones step onto the battlefield, often outperforming common non-steroidal anti-inflammatory drugs (NSAIDs) like ibuprofen, without the side effects.

Dr Peter Brukner, a luminary in sports medicine with an illustrious career, including long spells as the lead doctor for Liverpool FC and the Australian Cricket team, shared an illuminating insight with me over dinner one evening (ketogenic, of course). He narrated a story that paints a vivid picture of the profound impact of ketones on inflammation.

> *'When I began work with the Australian Cricket Team, we were touring in India, and one player in question was having a lot of trouble with regular knee pain to the point where, at one stage, he had to stop playing. He'd been to every doctor and specialist in Sydney and had every imaginable scan, but nobody could figure out what was wrong with him. He was eventually diagnosed with seronegative arthritis and prescribed Enbrel, an expensive drug that costs the taxpayer thousands every year. It made an initial difference.*
>
> *The pain wasn't completely gone, but he was able to play again, so he*

began injecting himself daily. Each time he felt the pain coming on, he would inject himself, and the pain would temporarily go away. It helped him recover to the point where he was still in the Australian Squad, but not the first team. It was reasonably well known by then that I had lost a lot of weight by adopting a ketogenic diet, and he came to me and asked if I could help him do the same. So, we began by taking him off sugar and processed food and putting him on a ketogenic diet. Now, we were in India, which isn't the easiest place to go ketogenic. There was plenty of rice and naan bread on offer, and he didn't find it easy, but equally, he never gave up, was remarkably conscientious, and he stuck to it. Three weeks later, he came to me and said, 'Doc, I forgot to take my Enbrel injection because I've had no pain in my knee. Should I still take it?' So, I told him that unless he felt any pain, to hold off, not to take it and to see how he felt. The pain never returned.

Since he's adopted the ketogenic diet, he is free from expensive prescription drugs, free from pain, allowing him to train harder than ever and just 12 months later, he was ranked in the Top 10 Batsman in the world.'

The next time an old knee pain growls at you, consider your diet instead of ibuprofen or injections. A shot of steroids into the knee may melt the pain away, but it only lasts a few weeks before the inflammation returns. Producing ketones often addresses the pain at the root of the problem. To eat carbohydrates in the presence of pain is to feed the pain. Instead, eat fat, and stay in ketosis.

Dr Boz says, 'On a carb-rich diet, your blood overflows with glucose. Switch to a ketogenic diet, and you will soon find less and less inflammation. Who cares? Your joints and tendons care. This inflamed, water-filled system causes stiff joints, achy muscles, and slower healing rates. With less swelling in those areas, the body can repair injuries from last week and the last decade. It won't start if inflammation hangs around.'

Radiant Skin: The Ketogenic Glow

Inflammation, often lurking behind the scenes in our day-to-day lives, is a key antagonist in many skin sagas. It's no secret that inflammation is a notorious accomplice in conditions like acne, but the ketogenic diet is a formidable foe against these skin woes.

By adopting a ketogenic lifestyle, you're not just fuelling your body differently; you're potentially turning the tide in the battle for clear, vibrant skin. The diet's anti-inflammatory prowess can be a game-changer in the realm of dermatology. Here's a glimpse into the skin benefits that might unfold with ketosis:

- Acne, often a reflection of internal turmoil, may see its fiery red flags lowered as ketosis calms the inflammatory storms beneath your skin.
- Eczema, with its itchy demands for attention, might find a soothing balm in the serene waters of ketosis.
- Psoriasis, characterised by its stubborn, scaly presence, may retreat in the face of ketosis' anti-inflammatory march.
- Acanthosis nigricans, with its unwelcome patches of darkened skin, may fade into the background as ketosis restores balance and harmony.

Revving Up Your Ketosis Engine: Your Guide To A Fat-Fuelled Metamorphosis

Transitioning to a state of ketosis is like tuning your body's engine to run on premium fuel. The recipe? A diet rich in quality fats, moderate protein, and notably scant carbohydrates. After consulting with many leading doctors, the magic number for daily carbohydrate intake appears below 20 g. Cross that threshold, and you risk summoning insulin into the fray, derailing ketosis. Keep your fibre intake robust and be wary of artificial sweeteners – they're the sneaky speed bumps on your road to success.

So, where do these ketones, the super fuel of ketosis, come from? While insulin is the product of the pancreas, ketones are crafted in the liver's workshop. If your diet has been carb-heavy, sparking life into your ketone production might feel like reviving a mighty motorbike that's been gathering dust in the garage. It might be stubborn at first, but once it roars to life, you'll ride a whole new wave of vitality.

On a traditional calorie-counting diet, you might shed a few pounds, but it often comes with the baggage of feeling sluggish and irritable. If carbs are still your go-to, your body will prioritise burning sugar for fuel, only grudgingly dipping into your fat reserves when the sugar well runs dry. It's like your body's caught in a bewildering maze, unsure which path to take.

To your body, burning carbohydrates for energy is as easy as popping open the bread bin on your kitchen counter-minimal effort, instant gratification. It's not the finest dining experience, but it's right there. Switching to burning your own fat, however, is like trekking down to the basement to rummage through the deep freezer. It's stocked with premium goods, but oh, the effort of those stairs! The trick is convincing your brain that the bread bin is off-limits. Guide it to understand that the true bounty lies in the freezer. Teach it to stock up the fridge, conveniently placing it next to the now-vacant bread bin.

This metabolic shift, transforming your body into a ketone-burning powerhouse, can take about 7 to 21 days of strict carb restraint. For some, especially those who've been on a prolonged carb binge, it might stretch to six weeks. But once you're keto-adapted, the game changes. Forget the meagre 2,000 to 2,500 calories of glycogen reserves, you're now tapping into a lavish energy cache of 40,000 to 200,000 calories nestled within your fat stores. The choice is clear, but patience is key. Your body needs time to discover this abundant energy source and learn to harness it efficiently. Welcome to the world of ketosis, where your fuel tank is vast and your energy boundless.

Nina Teicholz, an investigative science journalist and leader in nutritional reporting, someone who is judiciously challenging the conventional wisdom on dietary guidance, explained on my podcast:

> *'When you convert over to becoming a fat burner, it's a difficult process at first because you must develop all of these different enzymes to be able to run off fat. And why do you want to operate off fat? What is the benefit of that? Well, I will tell you that the simplest benefit is that once you become a fat burner, you don't just operate off the fat you eat; when you are not eating, you operate off the fat of your body.*
>
> *Fat on your body is not just a curse that God gave you to mess up your teenage years. It's a genius invention. It's like having granola bars strapped all over your body. To your body, it's like; while I don't have food right here on the table in front of me, I will use this excess bit of fat on my hips or my stomach for energy. Your stored fat is supposed to be your backup source of fuel. But you can't access that fat on your body unless you know how to be a fat burner. How do you do that? You must reduce glucose.*
>
> *Because glucose is an easier fuel to burn, you will never consume your body fat while it's in your system. And that is why, to lose weight, you must reduce carbohydrates. Once you keep carbohydrates low for a while, your body will automatically learn how to burn an alternative fat fuel source. And this process can take a while. That's why some diets, such as Atkins, advise you to go super low on carbohydrates at the beginning to speed up the transition time. It will make the switch happen faster. But*

for people who are metabolically unwell and have had poor metabolisms for a long time, it can take a month to six weeks, and it can be painful. You can have nausea, headaches etc. It's also why some people give up within a few weeks. They think something like, 'I feel terrible, this can't be right, this can't be good for me.' But people must understand that it is just your body undergoing a huge transformation. Just like people giving up smoking or alcohol, it takes a while, but you must get to the other side.

When you arrive on the other side, you feel great. You feel better, lose weight, and recover from other illnesses and symptoms you didn't even know were diet-related. For example, I had no idea my own chronic sinus infections were related to my diet. I had taken antibiotics multiple times every winter, and yet since going ketogenic, I haven't had a single problem for years.'

Fuelling The Fire: Coconut Oil, MCTs, And The Protein Balance In Ketosis

Kickstarting your internal fat-burning furnace might feel like coaxing an old steam engine back to life, especially if it's been idle, chugging along on a never-ending supply of carbs. But fret not, for secret ingredients in our pantry can turn this sluggish engine into a roaring powerhouse-enter coconut oil and MCT Oil.

Coconut oil often gets the cold shoulder, criticised for its saturated fat content. But as you now know, saturated fats aren't the rogues they've been made out to be. They're the unsung heroes of our dietary story. MCTs, or medium-chain triglycerides, are the fats that don't just burn; they blaze! Consuming them is like adding high-octane fuel to your metabolic fire. They convert almost instantly into energy, nudge your body to burn its own fat, and even curb your appetite. And if you're still, for some reason keeping an eye on calories, here's a fun fact: MCTs pack fewer calories than other fats. But their real magic lies in thermogenesis, the process of offering instant energy and encouraging your body to torch its own fat reserves.

MCTs aren't just metabolic marvels; they're emerging as potential allies in the battles against ailments like cancer, obesity, Alzheimer's, and Parkinson's. Coconut oil is a treasure trove of MCT goodness, mixing C6, C8, C10, and C12. These designations refer to the chain length of the fatty acids, each offering its own unique health benefits and contributing to the versatile energy-boosting and therapeutic properties of coconut oil. Yet, it's the C8 component that steals the spotlight, acting as a ketosis catalyst. While coconut oil is fantastic, pure C8 is like striking oil! It's the high-grade fuel that propels you into ketosis with unmatched efficiency. Research suggests that C8 can generate ketones several times more effectively than regular coconut oil. So, if you're gearing up for ketosis, consider C8 your premium ticket to the fast lane.

Protein Portions

The ketogenic diet isn't a protein-free-for-all like its carnivore diet cousin. Here's where the road diverges. While the carnivore diet is about relishing the animal kingdom's bounties, it doesn't guarantee a ketosis state. Why? Excess protein can nudge you out of ketosis. So, it's time to rethink those pricey, lean cuts. Embrace the wings, legs, and fatty skin of poultry. Opt for full-fat cuts of meat. They're not just flavourful; they're your ticket to maintaining ketosis.

On the ketogenic trail, it's a delicate dance aiming to keep carbs to a whisper of 20 g or less and tuning the protein to just the right pitch. How much protein is just right? A good rule of thumb is around 1.2 g per kilogram of your ideal body weight. For instance, if your ideal weight is 70 kg, aim for no more than 84 g of protein daily. Remember, each body is a unique symphony, so fine-tune your intake and monitor those ketone levels.

Dr Dom D'Agostino, a trailblazer in the field of nutrition, said, 'Low-carb eating has always been relatively easy for me over the past 10 years, but the keto diet presented challenges when I first started it. Restricting the carbs was straightforward, but upping the fat was a challenge at first. I also needed to significantly reduce my protein intake to achieve nutritional ketosis. It's nearly impossible for most people to maintain even moderate levels of ketosis if the protein is greater than 2 g per kilogram of body weight unless they are exercising lots.'

Navigating Ketosis: Tracking Your Progress

Embarking on a ketogenic diet is unique in that it offers a tangible way to confirm you're on the right track. Unlike other diets that leave you guessing, ketosis can be definitively monitored. You've got options for measuring ketones in your body: a precise finger-prick blood test, a cost-effective breath monitor, or beginner-friendly urine ketone test strips. While peeing on a strip might not sound glamorous, it's an affordable starting point to get a sense of your ketosis status. A tub of 100 strips is available online for just £9.99.

The chart I'm about to share isn't from an official source, but it's a compilation of data presented by Dr Eric Westman at a recent health conference I attended. It's a useful guide to understanding your ketosis levels and ensuring you steer your diet in the right direction. The numbers show the same whether it be from your blood, breathing, or pee.

Regular diet (daytime)	0.1 mmol/L
Regular diet (on waking up)	0.3 mmol/L
Nutritional ketosis	0.5 - 5 mmol/L
After a couple of weeks fasting	10 mmol/L
Type 1 Diabetic ketoacidosis	25 mmol/L

Eric, in his awesome book *Keto Clarity*, which he co-authored with Jimmy More, suggests that there are four primary considerations for a Keto diet, which are easily remembered as an acronym:

Keep carbs low
Eat more fat
Test ketones often
Overdoing protein is bad

The Keto Experience: Initially Challenging Yet Well Worth the Effort

I'll let Nina Teicholz, the acclaimed investigative journalist, helm this one. In our enlightening podcast chat, I mentioned earlier (which you can catch on YouTube, where she unravels half a century of twisted dietary advice), Nina addressed the misconception that the keto diet is a challenging, unsustainable path. She posed a compelling question:

> *'What's truly arduous? The struggle isn't in embracing keto; it's in the burdens of obesity, the tedious routine of popping multiple pills daily, the relentless battle with diabetes, and daily insulin injections. Critics may argue about keto's sustainability, yet numerous studies back its longevity. But what's undoubtedly unsustainable is the constant battle with illness, the breathlessness after a mere flight of stairs, the crippling inability to lead a normal life, the shadow of depression, and the vicious cycle of medication and escalating weight. That's the real challenge.*

Yet, embarking on this journey does require a shift. I remember my days in the UK, cherishing those Dairy Milk bars and the endless loaves of bread. The mere thought of relinquishing them seemed ludicrous. But here's the remarkable transformation: your palate evolves. Your cravings for sweets dwindle almost magically. What once seemed indispensably sweet now becomes overwhelmingly so. My new delight? 90% dark chocolate, a richness I couldn't have fathomed of enjoying before. It's a testament to the body's adaptability, a change you might doubt until you experience it yourself. So, while the keto path may appear daunting at first glance, it's a journey of transformation, not just for your body, but for your tastes, preferences, and ultimately, your entire lifestyle.'

One reason I've sequenced these diets in a specific order is to mitigate potential side effects associated with starting a ketogenic diet directly from a standard diet, which can be pretty pronounced. By adopting the *Fibre First* diet, then transitioning through a low-carb diet, cutting out some meals, and incorporating intermittent fasting, you're likely to lessen these side effects. Beyond feeling different and possibly encountering occasional headaches during this transition, here are a few more things you might experience:

A Temporarily Unpleasant Fragrance

The ketogenic diet might introduce an unexpected travel companion: the distinct aroma of ketosis. Acetone, one ketone produced during this metabolic state, doesn't shy away from making its presence known through our breath. This olfactory signature, though potent, is merely a transient marker of the body's transition to a cleaner, more efficient fuel source. My wife's initial alarm, mistaking the ketonic breath for a stomach ulcer, was a testament to its potency. Yet, it's a small price for the profound benefits ketosis delivers.

As your body adapts, so does the intensity of this breathy trait, fading as swiftly as it appeared. A sprig of fresh mint can be a trusty companion during this phase, offering a refreshing counterbalance. And what's a fleeting period of aromatic breath compared to the monumental gains? Ketosis is not just about shedding pounds or taming your appetite; it's a holistic shift towards longevity, a formidable defence against menacing diseases like cancer, and a light of hope for cognitive rejuvenation.

Muscle cramps

When you first go keto, your salt intake often falls (your previous processed food was stuffed with salt). So, it's a good idea to start taking electrolytes, adding salt to your home-cooked meals and magnesium bisglycinate supplements. Alternatively, try consuming a little spinach, a few Brazil nuts, fish and dark chocolate. For potassium, try adding an avocado.

More Frequent Pee Stops

You might find that you are getting up a lot at night to pee for the first few days. This is normal. If you recall, earlier, I talked about how elevated insulin levels lead the body to hold on to more salt, which means more water retention and higher blood pressure. But as you enter ketosis, insulin levels drop, salt levels therefore drop and water is released. In the first few days, you will definitely visit the toilet more frequently, but this passes shortly.

As you stand at the threshold of this transformative lifestyle, remember that ketosis is more than a diet. It's a symphony of biological harmony. It's your body's way of whispering that the power to heal, rejuvenate, and thrive lies inherently within. Your body, in ketosis, becomes a skilled illusionist, seamlessly switching between dietary fat and your own reserves without missing a beat. Here are some tips to get you started:

20 Ideas And Tips For A Keto Lifestyle

As you now know, keeping your daily carb intake under 20 g is your golden ticket to ketosis. The conundrum is snagging that essential fibre without the carb overload. Fear not, as meat, particularly the fatty kind, becomes your trusty sidekick, but monitor not turning into a protein powerhouse to avoid unwanted sugar conversion. Craving more? Our Health Results app and website are treasure troves of keto culinary inspirations. Just hit the keto recipes tab for a feast of ideas that'll keep your taste buds dancing and your carbs in check.

Idea 1

Fatty meats, fish & poultry

Embrace the fat! Whether you savour fatty cuts of meat, enjoy fish rich in omega-3s, or avoid the skin on your chicken, this approach is not just delicious; it's the keto way. Opt for full-fat over lean mince to keep your palate and wallet happy (full-fat, minced meat is nearly always cheaper than lean packs).

Idea 2

Cream and butter

Elevate your keto game with the luxurious duo of cream and butter. Transform your dishes into a creamy delight by generously dolloping butter over them; its carb-free nature and high-fat content are just what your keto regimen needs. Heavy and whipping cream, with minimal carbs, becomes your go-to ingredients, making your morning coffee richer or turning desserts into keto-friendly wonders. This creamy strategy is a delicious way to stick to your keto goals without feeling deprived.

Idea 3

Guilt-free fibre

Embrace guilt-free fibre with glucomannan, a game-changer for keto enthusiasts craving noodles, spaghetti, and pasta. This magical ingredient lets you indulge in your favourite dishes without compromising your carb count. I've got four fantastic recipes up my sleeve (and lots more on my website) that are a hit at home, proving you don't have to sacrifice flavour for health. They're deliciously deceptive in the best way—no one will guess they're tailored for a healthier lifestyle.

Creamy salmon and mushroom tagliatelle

For a delightful twist on the classic, this Creamy Salmon and Mushroom Tagliatelle combines the richness of Creme Fraiche with the savoury goodness of salmon and mushrooms. Tossed with konjac tagliatelle for a keto-friendly base, it's a satisfying and nutritious dish. Start by sautéing mushrooms in olive oil until they're tender. Then, mix in the salmon, Creme Fraiche, and tagliatelle, seasoning with a twist of black pepper. Cook until everything is wonderfully hot, then garnish with fresh chives for a burst of colour and flavour. Quick, easy, and utterly delicious!

Ingredients:

- Creme Fraiche (200 g)
- Cooked salmon (140 g)
- Mushrooms, sliced (40 g)
- Fresh chives, chopped (handful)
- Black pepper (twist)
- Konjac tagliatelle (200 g)
- Olive oil (glug)

Tuna penne pasta bake

Dive into a delectable Tuna Penne Pasta Bake that's as easy to whip up as it is to devour. This tomato-based wonder, boasting Fibre Pasta, is a culinary marvel, impressing everyone with its low-carb magic. Just imagine the fusion of tender tuna, tangy olives, and succulent tomatoes, all smothered under a golden layer of melted cheddar. It's a hearty dish that warms the belly and wins hearts without the carb overload. Perfect for gatherings where you want to astonish your guests but with minimal fuss.

Ingredients:

- Fibre Pasta 280g
- Tin of tomatoes (make sure nothing is added otherwise; kiss goodbye to ketosis)
- tins of tuna steak in spring water
- black olives (100g)
- mature cheddar cheese (200g)
- fresh flat-leaf parsley, chopped (handful)
- beef tomato, sliced (1 large)

Method

Begin by preheating your grill and giving your konjac penne a quick dry fry. Toss in olives and tomatoes for a Mediterranean twist, then fold in tuna for a hearty mix. Layer in a dish with cheddar and tomato slices on top, baking until bubbly and golden. A sprinkle of parsley adds the final touch to this effortless, carb-conscious feast that's bound to impress.

Spicy Chinese-style noodles

Enjoy the flavours of Asia with this spicy Chinese-style noodles dish. It's a perfect blend of authentic Chinese seasonings with a kick of spice and is truly keto-friendly. Quick and easy to whip up, it's a delightful journey into culinary bliss. Plus, you can enjoy it as a side dish, add meat, poultry or fish, and serve it as a main.

Ingredients:

- Konjac noodles (200 g)
- Coconut aminos (1/4 cup)
- Sriracha sauce (1 tbsp)
- White pepper (1/4 tsp)
- Extra virgin olive oil (2 tbsp)
- Ginger (2 tsp, grated)
- Bird's-eye chilli (1, finely chopped)
- Garlic cloves (3 sliced)
- Spring onions (2 sliced)
- Sesame seeds (1 tbsp, toasted)
- Stevia, xylitol (optional add to taste)
- Meat, poultry or fish (optional)

Method

In a bowl, mix coconut aminos, sriracha, and white pepper. Fry ginger, garlic, and chili in olive oil, then add noodles, combining them with aromatic spices. Stir in the sauce, spring onions, and optional squid, fish, or meat, and cook until perfection. Garnish with sesame seeds for a finishing touch of texture and flavour.

Moroccan Tuna Noodles

Unleash your inner chef with this quick, sassy, one-pan, Moroccan-flavoured tuna and noodles. In a dance of simplicity and flavour, heat butter until it sings, then introduce your choice of tuna, chunky or sleek, mingling with konjac noodles under a shower of Moroccan spices. Be sure to navigate the spice aisle like a seasoned spy to avoid sugary imposters. A few twirls of your spoon and voilà, culinary perfection on your plate. Garnish with a whisper of fresh herbs for an ovation-worthy finish. A carb-free escapade awaits!

Ingredients:

- Tuna Steak
- Konjac Penne (200g)
- Moroccan spice mix
- Butter (3 knobs)

Idea 4

Kickstart ketosis: Turbocharge your journey with C8 oil power

Envision C8 oil as the stealthy ninja of the keto world, silently swooping in to save the day with its powerful fat-burning abilities. It's like the secret weapon in your dietary arsenal, ready to tackle those stubborn pounds with the finesse of a master sushi chef.

Using C8 oil is as easy as pie (well, maybe keto-friendly pie). Just a tablespoon or two stirred into your morning coffee or drizzled over your salad can kickstart your metabolism into high gear, sending those cravings packing faster than you can 'deseed an avocado.' It's like giving your body a turbo boost, propelling you towards your weight loss goals with the speed and efficiency of a Formula 1 race car. So, why is C8 oil the VIP of the keto game? It's all about a magic ingredient: caprylic acid (a medium-chain fatty acid MCT). This little powerhouse not only revs up your fat-burning furnace but also helps keep you feeling fuller for longer, making those hunger pangs vanish quicker than socks in a dryer. It's like having your own personal bodyguard against snack attacks, standing guard over your cravings with the determination of a loyal Labrador.

Idea 5

The intermittent feast

Once your body switches from being a sugar-burning steam engine to a fat-burning Ferrari, skipping meals or even fasting for a whole day becomes easy!

Why mention this in our grand list? It's because I've bumped into a curious bunch of keto enthusiasts who've never given fasting a whirl. And, would you believe it, these are often the same folks who find themselves slipping off the keto wagon more often than not. It's almost as if not giving fasting a try is their culinary Achilles' heel.

And here's a cheeky little secret for those who are perpetually on the go or trapped in a sea of business meetings: intermittent fasting can be your dietary secret weapon. Picture this: you're surrounded by carb-laden temptations, with no keto-friendly snack in sight. Instead of navigating this carbocalypse, you can opt for a fasting fiesta, turning what could be a dietary disaster into a triumph of metabolic flexibility. So, next time you're on the road, and the only options are more carbs than your keto heart can handle, remember fasting is your friend, turning a potentially tricky situation into an effortless exercise in dietary discipline.

Idea 6

Fungi friends

With almost zero carbs, mushrooms are a versatile and delightful addition to any keto diet. Explore the fungal kingdom with different varieties from your local supermarket and get creative with the numerous mushroom recipes available on the Health Results app. Here are three simple yet mouth-watering dishes to introduce the rich and earthy flavours of mushrooms into your keto meals. Each variety offers a unique taste and texture, making every dish an exciting new adventure.

Stuffed portobello

Turn Portobello mushrooms into a culinary playground by stuffing them with your favourite keto ingredients. Think sausage, minced meat, bacon, or an array of veggies—the possibilities are as endless as your creativity. Cook in the oven, and add a generous dollop of cream cheese and a sprinkling of mozzarella for the grand finale. Bake until it's bubbling with joy and crowned with a golden glow. Add a final touch of fresh herbs, and you're ready to serve a storm of flavours!

Creamy garlic button mushrooms

Whip up a delectable side, perfect for complementing your keto mains. Begin by crisping bacon in a pan, then sauté mushrooms in the bacon's essence. Add garlic for flavour and heavy cream to create a lush sauce. Blend in cheeses like Parmesan, Mozzarella, or Cheddar for a gooey delight, and reintroduce the bacon for a smoky finish. A harmonious blend of creamy sauce, mushrooms, and bacon creates a low-carb indulgence that's hard to resist. For a splash of colour, add fresh herbs or finely sliced chillies.

Italian baked mushrooms

A simple dish that turns the humble mushroom into an Italian super meal! Picture this: mushrooms taking a luxurious bath in a pool of butter, olive oil, and balsamic vinegar, with a sprinkle of garlic, herbs, and Parmesan acting as the perfect accessories. It's like a spa day but for food!

Start by warming up your oven and arranging mushrooms on a baking sheet; a little overlap is fine. Whisk together butter, olive oil, balsamic vinegar, garlic, and herbs, seasoned with salt and pepper. Drizzle this flavourful ensemble over the mushrooms, ensuring they're well-dressed for the occasion. Bake for a round of 10 minutes, give them a quick flip, and then back in for another 5-10 minutes until they reach the perfect softness. Finish with a sprinkle of Parmesan and herbs for a dish that's a feast for the senses.

Idea 7

Low-carb veggie fest: Your unlimited (almost) green pass

Venture into the verdant utopia of our buffet, where the selection of vegetables contains such minimal carb count; they might as well be vying for the spotlight in a dietary drama titled 'The Almost Zero Carb Affair'. Picture this: a haven where the haunting beep of your carb tally device doesn't shadow your nibbles. Indeed, I parade various veggies so adept at trimming carbs that they're practically enablers of your low-carb fantasy sans the need for a weighing contraption or a diploma in numbers.

When the carb content whispers a mere 1 g per 100 g, consider it an open invitation to a guilt-free feast. Encounter a 2 g per 100g scenario? It's a moment to relish, not rush. And upon stumbling across the 3 g per 100 g troupe, maintain your calm—there's no cause for alarm. However, when you cross paths with the 4 g per 100 g ensemble, by all means, indulge, but perhaps don't transform your plate into their stage. After all, in this light-hearted production of dietary choices, it's all about finding that blissful balance between savouring and intelligent serving.

The 'eat with abandon' veggies (only 1 g of carb per 100 g)
Celery: The crunchy water stick.
Cucumber: The spa water's best friend.
Lettuce: The burger's green cape.
Artichoke: The flower that made it to the veggie league.
Kale: The leaf that's tougher than your gym instructor.

The 'Two-Gram Glam Squad'
Pak Choi: The leafy green that's cooler than kale.
Spinach: Popeye's secret weapon.
Spring Green: The youthful cousin of kale.
Asparagus: The veggie that makes your pee smell... interesting.
Courgette: The veg that dreamed of being pasta.
Aubergine: The moody purple outsider.
Pumpkin: The Cinderella of the veggie world.
Celeriac: The ugly duckling with a heart of gold.

Three grams per 100 heroes
Broccoli: The mini trees saving your diet.
Tomatoes: The fruit living a veggie's life.
Leeks: The onion's sophisticated cousin.

Four-Gram Fellowship
Cauliflower: The chameleon of the veg world.
Brussels Sprouts: The divisive mini cabbages.
Mange-Tout: The veg that's all about inclusivity.
Bell Peppers: The rainbow connection.
Chillies: The spice of life.
Cabbage: The head that rolls at no diet.

Idea 8

Lightweight fruits

Step up to the magical fruit stand of the keto carnival, where the fruits are so feather-light in carbs that they're practically floating! It's a familiar tale in the keto kingdom to bid farewell to all things fruity, fearing they're carb-laden baddies in disguise. But hush, not all fruits wear a carb-heavy cloak.

Imagine this: You've structured your main course like a carb-savvy pirate, steering clear of the high-carb tempests. Now, you're ready to drop anchor at Dessert Isle, where a treasure trove of select low-carb fruits awaits, ready to be paired with a dollop of cream. This isn't about doubling down on portions; it's about smart indulgence. With these keto-friendly gems, you can savour the sweet bounty of nutrition without fear of breaching the sacred 20-gram per-day carb barrier.

So, let your dessert plate be a canvas of vibrant, nutritious colours with a sprinkle of indulgence. After all, who said the keto journey couldn't have its cake (or should we say fruit) and eat it too? The numbers are the grams of carbs per 100 g.

- Cranberries 3 g
- Grapefruit 5 g
- Raspberries 5 g
- Blackcurrants 6 g
- Blackberries 6 g
- Plumbs 6 g
- Strawberries 6 g
- Pears 6 g

Idea 9

Eggs with all meals

Nature's own low-carb mathematicians, where the sum of their parts equals a keto dream. Let's crack into some egg-cellent arithmetic, shall we? One egg clocks in at a mere 1g of carbs. Yes, dead simple: one egg is one carb.

But before you plan a 20-eggs-a-day eggstravaganza, remember that variety is the spice of life. So, while you could technically make eggs the star of your keto show every day, consider them more as the versatile supporting actors in your dietary screenplay. They're ready to step into any role, from a boiled breakfast cameo to a scrambled or poached evening appearance. Add them to keto salads, fried Fibrehydrate dishes or on the following fibre bread.

Idea 10

Fibre loaf: The low keto bread

The Fibre Loaf is the unsung hero of the keto world, where every slice is a testament to the magic of low-carb baking. Without giving away too many secrets (for the complete enchantment, return to the *Fibre First* diet), this culinary marvel is the bread that dreams are made of for the carb-conscious.

Crafted with wizardry to ensure that each bite delivers only a whisper of carbs (we're talking a mere two or three per slice), it's packed with over 4 g of fibre, making it a paradox wrapped in a crust. It's the kind of bread that performs a balancing act so deftly it could join the circus. This loaf doesn't just sit on your plate; it dances, bringing joy and nourishment without the carb comedown.

So, if you choose to try the keto diet, let the Fibre Loaf be your vessel. It's not just bread; it's a slice of freedom, allowing you to indulge in the pleasure of sandwiches, toast, and even the occasional bread pudding while staying firmly on the keto bandwagon.

Idea 11

Cheese

Cheese, the unsung hero of the keto diet, is like the versatile actor of the culinary world, ready to take on any role, from supporting sidekick to star of the show. With hundreds of varieties at our disposal, each boasting low-carb credentials like badges of honour. Imagine cheese as that friend who's always up for an adventure, no matter the time of day.

Take, for instance, a full ounce of cheddar with just 1 gram of carbs, 6 grams of protein, and a generous sprinkle of calcium. It proves itself as not just a tasty snack but a nutritional ally. And let's not forget its rich texture, which can turn a simple meal into a gastronomic delight.

Now, I hear the chorus of concern about saturated fat. But remember, all charges related to heart disease risk have been cleared, flipping the script to suggest it might just be your heart's knight in shining armour. Plus, with CLA in its toolkit, cheese is not just about taste; it's about sculpting that keto body by aiding fat loss and enhancing body composition.

Ready for the grand tour of the Keto Cheese Hall of Fame? Let's roll out the red carpet for our top contenders, each a star in their own right:

Blue Cheese: A mouldy marvel that is perfect for adding a bold twist to salads or a sophisticated touch to steak.

Brie: Soft, creamy, and utterly indulgent. This cheese is like a hug for your taste buds.

Camembert: A close cousin to Brie, with a depth of flavour that pairs beautifully with a small glass of red wine.

Cheddar: The versatile veteran, ready to elevate a burger or be the star of a cheese platter.

Cottage Cheese: Perfect for a light snack or as a creamy addition to your morning eggs.

Cream Cheese: The smooth operator, ideal for keto-friendly desserts or a rich, velvety sauce.

Feta: Briny and bold, this cheese adds a tangy twist to salads and omelettes.

Goat Cheese: Earthy and mild, the perfect sprinkle over roasted vegetables.

Halloumi: The grill's best friend, ready for a sizzling cameo at your next barbecue.

Mascarpone: The dessert, darling, because who said keto can't be sweet?

Mozzarella: The stretchy star of the pizza world because keto pizza is a thing.

Parmesan: The hard-hitting flavour bomb, ready to grate over just about anything for an umami boost.

So, there you have it; a constellation of keto-friendly cheeses, each ready to transform your meals from mundane to mouth-watering. Remember, in the keto world, cheese is not just food; it's a lifestyle. Welcome to the cheesy side of life, where every bite explores flavour and texture, all while keeping your carbs in check.

Idea 12

Keto AK47 coffee: The morning blast you didn't know you needed

Meet my Keto AK47 Coffee; not your average morning brew, but a concoction so potent it's like a wake-up call from a howling wolf. It's designed for those who want to kickstart their day with a bang, not just any bang, but an autophagy and ketosis-inducing explosion. Here are the seven magical ingredients that turn your average coffee into a supercharged restorative potion:

Water: Yes, water. It is the essence of life and the obvious secret to any good coffee. There are no surprises here; it is just the pure, hydrating foundation of your new favourite morning ritual.

Coffee: The heart of the concoction, not just for the caffeine kick but for nudging your body into ketosis and autophagy like a gentle (or not so gentle) nudge off a cliff. Decaf is like bringing a knife to a gunfight, but hey, it's your duel.

Cacao Powder: This isn't just any chocolatey goodness; it's a detox dynamo packed with fibre and the special forces triggering autophagy. Plus, it makes you feel you're having dessert for breakfast without the guilt.

Coconut Oil or Butter: Spoonful of this, and you're bulletproof. It's the fuel your body craves, alternating between coconut oil and butter to keep your taste buds on their toes.

Optional Reinforcements:

C8 Oil: The turbocharger for ketosis. Optional, but if you're serious about your ketosis, it's like deciding between a water pistol and an AK47.

Cinnamon: Just a pinch for that antioxidant punch. It's like a secret handshake for your cells, signalling autophagy to get moving.

Almond Milk: The velvet glove for this iron fist of a drink. Homemade is best (because you're a primal warrior who crafts their own armour), but if store-bought is your battlefield, march for the unsweetened victory.

There you have it, my Keto AK47 Coffee – not for the faint of heart, but for warriors ready to conquer their day. It's autophagy and ketosis wrapped in a taste sensation, the kind of morning ritual that makes you say, Bring it on, world!'

Idea 13

Nuts and seeds

The epic keto saga of nuts and seeds in the grand theatre of health and wellness, where each tiny protagonist is more than just a crunchy snack. They're the fibre-full, carb-sparing superheroes of the keto universe, each with its own special powers, backstory, and, occasionally, a dramatic cape (or shell, if we're being botanically correct).

These miniature but mighty warriors embark on valiant quests through our digestive systems, battling heart disease, vanquishing the spectres of certain cancers, lifting the dark clouds of depression, and fending off the looming shadows of chronic diseases. It's not just a snack; it's a full-blown adventure in every handful!

Yet, as in any grand tale, our heroes vary in their strengths and weaknesses, especially concerning their carb counts. So, gather around as I unveil the legendary line-up of my top seven keto-friendly champions and their carb counts per 30 g serving. But I will uniquely show the carb weight minus the fibre, which is the actual number you need to know on a keto diet.

Almonds: A handful of almonds packs a punch in terms of nutrition and contains about 3 g of carbs.

Macadamia Nuts: These buttery treats are the low-carb lovers' dream, offering roughly 1.5 g of carbs per handful. They're the laid-back, low-carb loungers of the nut family, perfect for a keto-friendly nibble.

Pecans: With about 1 g of carbs per 3 0g serving, pecans are the sweet, buttery aristocrats of the nut world, keeping things low-carb and high-class.

Peanuts: Okay, they're not really nuts but legumes; a 30 g pack has only 2.2 g of carbs.

Walnuts: At about 2 g of carbs per handful, walnuts are in the brainy group. They offer a dose of omega-3s along with their modest carb content.

Chia Seeds: These tiny powerhouses bring about 2.3 g of carbs per 30 g serving, but before you raise your eyebrows, remember that most of these carbs are fibre, making the net carb count much lower.

Flaxseeds: Like chia seeds, flaxseeds (linseed) offer less than one gram of carbs per 30 g serving. However, thanks to their high fibre content, the net carbs are significantly lower, making them a great keto option.

These rough estimates showcase how nuts and seeds can be a fantastic, low-carb addition to your keto diet, with each bringing its own unique flavours and nutritional benefits to the table (or, more accurately, to your hand). Just remember, while they're low in net carbs, they're high in other good stuff like fats and calories, so enjoy them like you would a fine wine—savour every bite.

Idea 14

Live on a culinary adventure

'Variety is the spice of life,' which couldn't be more accurate when it comes to staying in ketosis. Let's face it: the main culprit behind diet derailment is the dreaded 'B' word—boredom. However, with a dash of creativity and a sprinkle of enthusiasm, you can turn your meal plan into an endless feast of flavours and textures.

Imagine having a treasure trove of culinary delights at your fingertips, with thousands of meal possibilities just waiting to dazzle your taste buds. That's where my free app comes into play; it's like having a personal chef in your pocket! With hundreds of recipes and tantalising videos, you'll never be at a loss for what to whip up in the kitchen.

Embrace the vast array of options, from exotic spices to unfamiliar vegetables and everything in between. Experiment with new recipes, mix up your meal prep, and remember, the only limit is your imagination. Let ketosis be a journey of discovery, where each meal is an opportunity to explore new tastes and celebrate the joy of eating. Say goodbye to the mundane and hello to a world of vibrant, nutritious, and, most importantly, delicious meals that keep you hooked on healthy eating.

Idea 15

Unleash your inner macro detective

Becoming a carb detective is not just about crunching numbers; it's an essential step on your journey to mastering the keto lifestyle. I delayed dropping this nugget of wisdom not to scare you off but to gently ease you into the keto waters.

Imagine yourself as a culinary Sherlock Holmes with a keen eye for spotting those sneaky carbs lurking in the most unsuspecting places. In the early days, yes, you'll need to channel your inner bean counter, keeping tabs on every carb that dares cross your path. But here's the good news: it's a temporary gig. Think of it as a crash course in Carb Counting 101, where you learn the ropes, uncover the mysteries, and then, before you know it, you graduate with flying colours.

Give it a month or two, and you'll traverse the carb jungle like a pro, with no calculator or ancient abacus in sight. You'll develop a sixth sense for macros, effortlessly balancing your meals to stay on the keto straight and narrow. So, prepare for a bit of number-crunching fun—it's the secret sauce to becoming a keto aficionado, and who knows? You might enjoy the detective work along the way.

Idea 16

Bookworms unite for keto enlightenment

Congratulations! You've made it this far into the *Fibre First* diet; you're not just a reader; you're a voracious bookworm with a hunger for knowledge that rivals your appetite for fibre. This passion for pages is your secret weapon in the keto journey. And just like a hobbit on an adventure, there's always more to explore.

The world of keto books is as varied as a cheese platter at a keto feast—there's something for every taste. Whether you're into the science behind ketosis, the art of keto cooking, or the personal stories of transformation that make you want to high-five the author, there's a book out there with your name on it.

But here's the fun part: as you bury your nose in these books, you'll become the go-to guru for all things keto. Friends and family will marvel at your encyclopaedic knowledge. 'How do you know so much?' they'll ask, awestruck. Just wink and say, 'I read.'

Idea 17

Bracing for the keto flu

Welcome to the tumultuous seas of the keto flu, where your body might decide to toss everything but the kitchen sink your way in a bid for mutiny. Headaches, migraines, and even a spot of seasickness (figuratively speaking) could be your unwelcome companions as you switch from carbs to fats for fuel. It's as if your body is throwing a farewell party for carbs, and you're the guest of (dis) honour.

But fear not, brave voyager, for this storm does pass. Imagine the keto flu as your initiation into the elite ranks of ketosis. It's a rite of passage that tests your mettle, a trial by fire (or, in this case, by lack of carbs) that leads to a land lush with greenery and energy levels you've only dreamed of.

If the going gets tough, remember retreating is not the same as surrendering. If you find the keto flu's grip a tad too tight, there's no shame in anchoring at the *Fibre First* diet's ports or the *Human Diet's* stalwart shores. These safe havens offer respite, allowing you to regroup, refuel (with the right stuff), and ready yourself for another voyage into the keto waters when the time is right. So, gear up, set your sights on the horizon, and prepare for a journey that's not just about reaching ketosis but also about discovering your resilience, adaptability, and the boundless energy that awaits. The keto flu is a temporary squall in the grand voyage of your dietary exploration. Onward to calmer seas and greener pastures!

Idea 18

Ketosis, now serving convenience

Welcome to the ultimate kitchen makeover: 'Ketosis Edition! First step?' Launch a full-scale pantry purge. Wave goodbye to those carb-heavy culprits lurking in the shadows—because if you don't, they'll inevitably end up staging a midnight snack attack, sabotaging your ketosis faster than you can say 'just a bite.' Remember, those carbs are sneakier than a ninja in flip-flops; if they're around, they'll find a way into your belly.

Now, let's talk about snacks. Once you enter ketosis, you most likely will no longer desire them, but in case you uncharacteristically have a snack attack, arm yourself with my legendary flaxseed fibre biscuits (check out the recipe on page 446). They're so good, you'll forget you're even in ketosis. Plus, they come with a side of smug satisfaction, knowing you're munching on pure, fibrous gold.

But why stop at snacks? Embrace the magic of batch cooking. Imagine opening your freezer to find an array of low-carb dinners ready to rescue you from the brink of hunger with minimal effort. It's like having a culinary fairy godmother who specialises in keto. No more staring into the abyss of your fridge, wondering what to cook, or worse, reaching for the phone to order something carb-laden in desperation.

Making ketosis convenient is like turning your diet into a well-oiled machine. With a bit of prep and some savvy snacking options up your sleeve, you'll glide through your keto journey with the grace of a gazelle. So, clear out, cook up, and stock up, and you'll find that sticking to ketosis is as easy as pie—keto pie, of course.

Idea 19

Remember the health benefits

One thing is clear: the keto diet is in a league of its own. It's like the Swiss Army knife of dietary approaches, versatile enough to address a myriad of medical marvels. I'm not just waxing lyrical here; the evidence sings volumes of its benefits. The magic of ketosis is akin to discovering the fountain of youth, particularly for sparking life into our brains during the golden years. Imagine ketosis as your personal time machine, keeping your mind sharp and vibrant, capable of recalling names, dates, and where you left your keys with the precision of a youngster. Combine this with a dash of regular exercise and plenty of fibre, and you've got yourself a potent potion for ageing gracefully.

But let's not forget the profound 'why' behind our keto journey. It's not just a diet; it's a homage to our ancestors, a testament to how humans thrived for millennia. As we look towards the horizon, envisioning the robust health of future generations, let's embrace keto not just as a temporary trend but as a return to our roots, a path paved with health and vitality.

Idea 20

Make this your everywhere reminder

I've given this summary its own special page, designed for you to capture it with your phone easily. Forget scanning; that's so last decade! Snap a picture and plaster it everywhere that matters - your wall, your fridge, anywhere you need a nudge of motivation. And for a modern twist? Set it as your phone's wallpaper. This way, it's not just a reminder; it's a constant companion, nudging you towards your goals every time you glance at your phone. Let this be the nifty trick that keeps your dietary aspirations front and centre, no matter where you are or what you're doing.

Embrace

- Meats: Including fish, beef, lamb, and poultry.
- Eggs.
- Mushrooms.
- Fibre Boosters: Glucomannan and inulin for that fibre fix.
- Veggies with Few Carbs: Think spinach, courgette, kale, broccoli, cauliflower, pak choi.
- Creamy and Cheesy Delights: Go for high-fat dairy like hard cheeses, cream, and butter.
- Nuts & Seeds: From peanuts to flaxseed, and everything in between.
- Fruity Bites: Avocado, strawberries, and other berries with a low-sugar punch.
- Sweet Solutions: Stevia, erythritol, and xylitol for that sweet touch without the guilt.
- Fats Galore: Coconut oil, lard, dripping, ghee, and more for that fat fuel.

Avoid

- The Ultra-Processed: Keep it real, keep it fresh.
- Booze Overload: Cap it at 2 units of alcohol.
- Starch Bombs: No potatoes or yammy temptations.
- Sugary Fruits: Wave goodbye to apples, bananas, oranges.
- Sweet Nothings: Honey, fructose, and their sneaky 'ose' friends are out.
- Grain Pain: Wheat, corn, rice, cereal - it's a no-go zone.

*****

The Carnivore Diet: A Leap Into The Meaty Unknown

After embracing the *Fibre First* diet, dabbling in the low-carb lifestyle, and perhaps flirting with intermittent fasting and ketosis, you're basking in a newfound zest for life. But what's next on this culinary adventure? Enter the Carnivore Diet, where the only greens on your plate might be the garnish you brush aside. Why venture into this territory, you ask? You may aim to beef up your protein intake (pun intended) and sculpt those muscles to Herculean proportions. While the ketogenic diet doesn't shy away from protein, the Carnivore Diet is like the express lane to muscle town. But it's not all about flexing in the mirror. Venturing into the carnivorous realm for a spell might be the detective work needed to crack any lingering health mysteries. So, if you've journeyed this far on your nutritional adventure, why not don the explorer's hat, and set sail on the carnivore cruise at least try it once? It's like swiping right on a diet that's all steak, no cake because sometimes, life's too short not to eat the whole cow.

Lessons from the Maasai and Modern-Day Mavericks

For over twenty years, my adventures have taken me through the lush grasslands of Tanzania and Kenya, where I've had the privilege of immersing myself in the culture of the Maasai. This resilient community thrives on a natural diet predominantly composed of meat, milk, and blood, interspersed with the occasional berry, honey, and tree bark. While not strictly carnivorous, their lifestyle offers a glimpse into the profound benefits of a diet deeply rooted in the rhythms of nature, a diet whose full potential is only now beginning to unfold in the broader narrative of modern nutrition.

Meanwhile, back in the UK, Christian Dailly, a titan of metabolic fitness, former Scotland international football captain, and a visionary contributor to Health Results, embraced the carnivore diet as his own. Over six months, Christian's foray into this primal eating regimen catalysed a transformation that was nothing short of extraordinary. Not only did his metabolic markers reach exemplary heights, but at 49, his strength manifested in astonishing deadlifts that defied expectations, crafting a physique that is a potent testament to the diet's efficacy. Witnessing Christian's metamorphosis inspired my journey into the carnivore realm. This inspiration was further fuelled by Dr Shawn Baker, a friend and fellow advocate who has shattered rowing world records while embracing the carnivore diet. His chronicled insightful book, *The Carnivore Diet*, is not just a story; it's a call to re-evaluate and rediscover the untapped potential of this primal way of eating.

Avoiding Toxic Plants

The carnivore diet offers a feast of meats and a reprieve from the lesser-known battleground of plant toxins. Dr Paul Saladino illuminates the secret war waged beneath our feet in his groundbreaking book T*he Carnivore Code*. Paul explains how plants, rooted and immobile, resort to a silent arsenal of toxins as their shield against the marauding mouths of herbivores. These natural defences manifest as dietary foes for some humans, unleashing chaos in their guts. Picture the peanut or the innocent-looking tomato, celery, or tree nuts, to name a few; for some, they're not just food but bearers of discomfort, if not outright peril.

A Paradoxical Garden: Beneficial Toxins

But hold your horses, or rather, your salads! The plant kingdom's chemical warfare isn't all doom and gloom for us. Enter the paradoxical realm of hormesis-nature's version of 'what doesn't kill you, makes you stronger.' It's a concept as quirky as doing a victory dance after stubbing your toe because it didn't break. Hormesis is about embracing adversity to emerge tougher, much like our muscles after a gruelling gym session. They're battered, sure, but oh, do they come back with a vengeance!

The plant world's micro-assaults, like the revered resveratrol and the golden glory of turmeric, work their magic similarly. Initially concocted by plants as chemical shields, these compounds turn the tables when ingested in moderation by humans. They bolster our cellular fortresses, particularly the mighty mitochondria, turning potential poisons into potent tonics of resilience. So, while the carnivore diet has us sidestepping the minefield of plant toxins, let's tip our hats to the curious cases where a little of nature's bite nurtures our might! I mention this only so you don't neglect antioxidants, which many people on a carnivore diet seem to do.

The carnivore path isn't just a digestive detour; it's a journey into profound healing. Dr Shawn Baker paints a picture of transformation from autoimmune battles to mental health mazes, from gastrointestinal gripes to mysterious maladies. When the greenery exits stage left and meat takes the spotlight, the body begins a remarkable revival, casting doubt on the very essence of our relationship with plants.

Rewinding the Dietary Clock

Rewind the tape of human history; the story is clear: we're carnivores at heart.

Consult an anthropologist, and they'll confirm our legacy is written in meat. Those ancient cave murals? They're not pastoral scenes of agriculture but primal epics of the hunt, a testament to our meat-centric heritage. While our ancestors may have nibbled on the occasional plant, their prime sustenance was the hunt's bounty. 'Hunter' wasn't just a title but a survival strategy etched into our very biology. Our potent stomach acid? A meat-digesting marvel. Our intestinal design? A blueprint for carnivorous consumption.

But fast forward to the dawn of agriculture, some 12,000 years ago, things changed. The shift from hunter to harvester brought more than just a change in diet; it heralded a seismic shift in our very being. The evidence is stark: a reduction in brain volume, a dip in stature, a compromise in bone strength. The carnivore diet isn't just a dietary choice; it's a return to our primal blueprint, a homage to the dietary doctrine etched into our DNA. So, if you embark on a carnivorous diet, remember, you're not just eating; you're awakening a legacy millions of years in the making.

Traversing the health and wellness landscape over the last seven years, I've witnessed a fascinating evolution through countless interviews with medical professionals and attending myriad health conferences. The dialogue has gradually shifted from the broad spectrum of low-carb benefits to the more focused realms of ketosis and now, intriguingly, to the carnivore diet. This shift is not merely anecdotal; it's underpinned by a cascade of compelling stories highlighting the diet's transformative impact on weight management and a spectrum of health conditions.

One particularly revealing study from the United States, housed in the National Library of Medicine, shines a spotlight on this dietary phenomenon. Researchers dispatched a detailed questionnaire to 2,029 individuals who embraced the carnivore lifestyle for at least six months, probing their experiences and outcomes. While acknowledging potential bias, the responses vividly portray the carnivore diet's efficacy, offering a tantalising glimpse into its potential as a catalyst for profound health improvements. Here's a graphical representation of their feedback.[5]

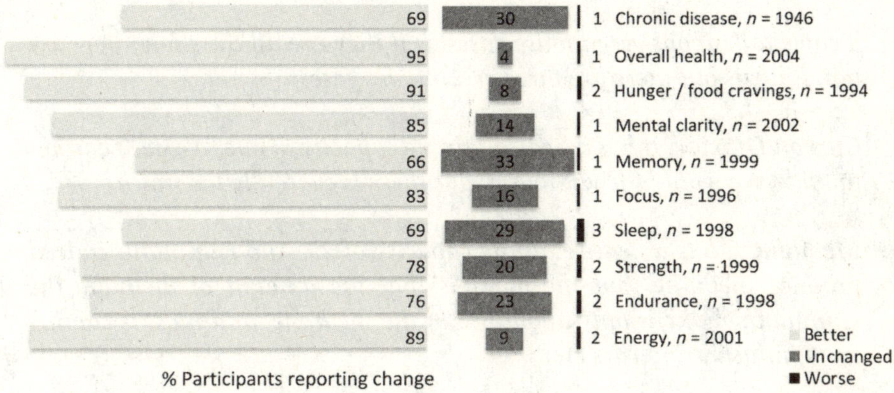

Dispelling 3 Meat Myths

Myth 1. Cattle Cause Global Warming

Join any conversation on climate change, and you'll often find the humble cow cast as a planetary villain. But let's slice through the fog of misconception and uncover the steak of truth. The narrative casting cattle as climate culprits is often a gourmet dish served by those with a smorgasbord of vested interests. From airlines deflecting scrutiny to food moguls pushing their lab-crafted, chemical-laden alternatives, it's a tale of diversion and profit.

But here's the beef: when integrated into their natural habitat, cattle aren't just bystanders in the environmental landscape – they're potential heroes. The problem isn't the cow; it's the how. Factory farming, with its corn-stuffed, shed-confined cattle, indeed casts a dark cloud on our environmental landscape. But let's shift the lens to free-ranging cattle, grazing as nature intended. These bovine environmentalists are not just scenery on the pastoral stage but active participants in the Earth's regenerative narrative.

Free-roaming cattle, treading the earth as they have for millions of years, nurturing the soil beneath their hooves, logically can't be a problem. This is the carbon-sequestering reality. With every graze and roam, these cattle are revitalising the soil, turning it into a carbon sink that whispers the promise of a greener tomorrow. So, next time you hear the cow painted as the eco-villain, remember it's not the cow; it's the how. Free-ranging cattle aren't just meat on our plate; they're guardians of the ground, partners in our quest for a restored planet.

An extract from my podcast with Dr Robert Lustig explains the situation:

'People talk about greenhouse gases as if they are all the same; they are not. It turns out there are three greenhouse gases:

Carbon Dioxide. It has a heat-retaining capacity of one. We need carbon dioxide, we would die without it, but there is currently too much.

Methane. It has a heat-retaining capacity of 25. And ruminants indeed produce methane. But the point is that the amount of methane the ruminants make is only about 5% of the methane, and most is coming from industry and cars etc.

Nitrous Oxide. It has a heat-retaining capacity of 210. Nine times greater than methane. This is the one that nobody gets. Where do you get nitrous oxide from?

Well, it's in every field, and the reason is because that is what happens to the nitrogen runoff from the nitrogen fertiliser that was needed to grow the crops. Because the animals who used to fertilise the crops, because of their manure, because that's nitrogen-fixing, now aren't there because the cattle are in Kansas and the corn is in Iowa. So, you must spray the corn with nitrogen, which becomes nitrate oxide, which causes way more greenhouse gas emissions than methane ever did and guess what? You must do that for vegans, too.

Free-roaming ruminants Improve soil fertility, and preserve biodiversity, and the growing grass helps sequester carbon dioxide.'

I asked Patrick Holden CBE, who ran the UK Soil Association for over 20 years, for his opinion on the best diet for our planet.

'The question of which sort of food we should eat to be sustainable, this whole plant-based thing over the past 5 to 10 years, where there is now a whole generation of young people who think it's the right thing to do to become vegan or vegetarian. When, in fact, you cannot produce healthy vegetables without first building soil fertility with a crop rotation, which involves clover and grass. The only way to turn that clover and grass into something we can eat is to graze it with cattle, sheep or ruminants; that means they have a stomach that can digest the cellulose material in the clover and grass.

If we don't support those farmers by buying the livestock products from that system, they can't make this natural rotation work. There are thousands of livestock farmers in the west of Britain now thinking, what do we do? The price of beef and lamb is crashing; beef consumption has halved since the 1980s in the UK, and it appears no young people are eating lamb; they are all giving it up, thinking it's the right thing to do. When, in fact, of all the meats we could eat, lamb is probably the healthiest and the most sustainable. Virtually all the lamb we produce in the UK is grass-fed, and even most beef is grass-fed. Now, feed-lock beef, which is what characterises the American system, is part of the problem because all of the grains the animals are eating are grown in genetically modified soil in an unsustainable way.

So, we need to become very educated and sophisticated and be able to differentiate between the livestock products that are part of the problem, which is intensively produced chicken, intensively produced pork and, yes, dairy products from these mega dairy herds; from those that are part of the solution, which means grass-fed lamb, grass-fed beef, and dairy products only from grass-fed cattle. Cows indeed emit methane; they always have, and probably whatever we do, feeding them garlic or whatever, they still will. But that methane cycle is an ancient cycle that's been going on as long as there have been ruminants on the planet.

But the methane, which is critically responsible for climate change, comes from burning fossil fuels. And if we use ruminants (cows and sheep) to build soil by grazing grassland or, as part of a rotation, digesting the cellulose into food that we can eat, the soil carbon gain offsets the methane emissions. If cows and sheep are used to maintain the soil carbon bank, which is the second-largest carbon bank on the planet only after the oceans, then they are part of the solution, not the problem.

So, if we want to address climate change and take CO2 out of the atmosphere and put it back in the soil, we need to change how we farm, which will only happen when we change our buying habits.'

Myth 2. Red Meat is Unhealthy

Let's slice through the dietary dogma and savour the facts: the claim that meat is inherently harmful doesn't marinate well with history or logic. This narrative, often stewed in headlines, tends to single out processed meats – a far cry from the unadulterated cuts our ancestors thrived on. But let's not just chew on theories; let's feast on facts. Make a visit to Iceland – not the realm of frozen aisles, but the land of fire, ice, and formidable Vikings.

In *The Carnivore Diet*, Shawn sheds light on this Nordic nation, where the populace, numbering a mere 300,000, has historically feasted primarily on a meat-centric diet. Why? Because the harsh climate isn't exactly a greenhouse for fruits and veggies. Yet, this hasn't hindered their health or strength. Quite the contrary! Iceland boasts an impressive roster of nine World's Strongest Man champions – a superhuman feat, especially considering the country's size.

The land of the midnight sun doesn't just flex its muscles in strength competitions; it shines in longevity too. Icelandic centenarians are a testament to the potential longevity benefits of a meat-rich diet, debunking the myth that a daily quota of fruits and vegetables is the exclusive path to health and longevity.

So, what does Iceland's prowess in producing the world's strongest and some of its longest-living individuals tell us? It's a narrative that challenges the conventional dietary script, inviting us to ponder whether it's time to defrost our perceptions and consider that the key to strength and longevity might lie in embracing our carnivorous roots.

Myth 3. The Love of Animals

In the nuanced debate over dietary ethics, I deeply respect those who abstain from eating meat based on animal welfare. Their choice is a profound expression of empathy, a commitment to a principle that transcends personal preference. For some, the ethical consumption of pests or overpopulated animals, like rabbits or deer, might offer a compromise that aligns with their principles while contributing to ecological balance.

However, as we travel further into the ethics of food consumption, we unveil complexities beyond the surface. For instance, the humble cow is often symbolic of the meat debate. A single cow can provide approximately 500 lb of meat, translating to over half a million calories – enough to sustain an individual for an entire year. This perspective casts the cow not just as a creature but as a significant contributor to human nourishment within the grand tapestry of life.

The discussion takes a thought-provoking turn when considering vegetarian or vegan lifestyles. It's essential to understand that this is not about casting judgment or drawing lines in the sand between diets, but about exploring the depth of our food choices. Research, including insights from Dr Zoe

Harcombe, sheds light on the unseen casualties and ethical dilemmas within agricultural practices that support plant-based diets. While specific data on the number of animals inadvertently harmed in producing plant-based foods is challenging to pinpoint, it is undoubtedly a number that runs into tens of thousands per consumer each year. Let me make it clear, agriculture's footprint negatively affects wildlife through habitat disruption, pesticide use, and indiscriminate use of heavy farming machinery.

Ultimately, the ethical dimension of our diet is a personal and collective reflection. It invites us to weigh the moral implications of our choices, the impact on our planet, and our diets' health benefits or drawbacks. As we chart our course through the diverse landscape of food ethics, it's imperative to engage in informed, compassionate discourse, seeking a harmony that respects both the sacredness of life and the health of our environment.

My Personal Carnivore Takeaway

As a voyager on the seas of metabolic flexibility, my dietary compass often points in various directions. My food anchor is typically a single, robust meal a day. However, I might occasionally set sail with a protein shake post-gym workout or indulge in a classic English breakfast, sans the bread, while on holiday shores.

My daily gastronomic consumption is usually a *Fibre First* ketogenic diet, full of unprocessed natural foods. Yet, when the winds of change beckon, I find myself navigating towards the shores of a carnivore diet with a twist – I continue to embrace fibre. The purists of Carnivorism might raise their brows at this inclusion, for in the land of Carnivore, fibre is often seen as a foreign visitor. However, as you already know, our gut microbiome thrives with a touch of fibrous harmony. So, when I embark on this meat-centric voyage, I bring Fibrehydrate noodles or fibre spaghetti, sautéed in butter and seasoned with herbs, as my faithful companions beside the day's selection of meat or fish. Yes, even in this realm, the bounty of the sea is welcomed with open arms.

So, what does a day on this carnivorous yet fibre-enriched diet look like? Imagine a platter where every morsel once had a face or was derived from such a noble source. This holistic way of looking at the Carnivore diet is what so many people often miss. Did the food once have a face, or is it a derivative of? That means you may add the likes of cheese, cream, butter, eggs, etc. Add to that the pure essence of fibre, and you have my personal recipe for a Carnivore diet.

Here are 10 Carnivore dishes I relish:

1. Full English breakfast: A trio of eggs, bacon, sausage, and a side of fibre noodles.
2. Butter-bathed steak, crowned with two fried eggs, halloumi fries air-fried to perfection, and a fibrous side salad.
3. Herb-infused chicken breast resting on a bed of fibre spaghetti enveloped in a buttery embrace.
4. A duo of salmon fillets paired with a side of broccoli and a sprinkle of pine nuts and chilli flakes for a fiery kick.
5. Tender pork fillet blanketed with melted cheese and served with fibre tagliatelle and a strip of bacon in a velvety cream sauce.
6. Peppery duck breast intertwined with a ribbon of cream-infused fibre noodles.
7. Sliced lamb and halloumi chunks, dancing in the pan, served alongside herb-kissed salad.
8. A lavish scramble of eggs, cheese, cream, and bacon, with my Sneaker Fibre Smoothie opening the act.
9. Two-minute marvel: twin cans of tuna, black pepper, fibre noodles, and a swirl of cream.
10. For a swift cold snack: a fibre drink like Slimshotz or my smoothie, followed by a can or two of sardines.

As for the question of oils, stick to the chorus of animal-derived melodies: butter, ghee, lard, goose fat. Here's a trick for the culinary magicians: when cooking meat with fat, let the fat kiss the pan first, melting into a pool of flavour.

In a world where the Carnivore diet is often misunderstood as monochromatic, these dishes paint a vivid landscape of flavours and textures. And for those like myself, piloting the waters with a genetic predisposition to Alzheimer's, this diet, or indeed the previously mentioned ketogenic diet, might be the bacon – sorry, I meant a beacon that guides us towards a future of robust health and clarity.

Hydration is Key in Any Dietary Regime

Regardless of the diet you choose, staying hydrated is paramount. This becomes increasingly crucial when you embark on diets like the Carnivore, where you abstain from vegetables, which inherently contain a lot of water. Opt for nature's best-natural mineral water in glass bottles or filtered tap water to quench your thirst. And remember, while plastic bottled water might be convenient, it's more about lining corporate pockets than providing you with the purest hydration.

*****

The Carnivore *Plus* Diet: A Profound Detox

This approach to food is less like a leisurely stroll in the culinary park and more like a daring expedition into the wilds of nutrition. Picture the standard Carnivore diet, then dial it up to eleven – an adventure for the dedicated, seeking the ultimate body reboot.

This isn't for the faint-hearted or those interested in health trends. It's the nutritional equivalent of a deep-sea dive, exploring the uncharted territories of your body's response to food. Carnivore *Plus* acts as your system's control-alt-delete, designed for a complete lifestyle overhaul, periodic reset, or a decisive health intervention. It purges from your diet all but the essentials, targeting the hidden culprits of chronic discomfort. In our era, stealthy food sensitivities lurk around every corner, manifesting through a laundry list of symptoms from digestive distress to unexplained fatigue all the way to persistent skin woes.

Do I commit to this diet myself? Without a doubt, however, I reserve it exclusively for January each year as my annual health reset. This timing is ideal for me, particularly after the last week of each year – from Christmas Eve to New Year's Day – when I momentarily give myself a free pass to set aside the principles detailed in this book. But I'm not embarking on this excursion solo; a group of my doctor friends and family members join me, creating a supportive community. Keep an eye on my social media next January and consider joining us in this revitalising tradition.

The Carnivore *Plus* menu is like the guest list for an exclusive dinner party – only the most select attendees make the cut.

Prime Cuts and Beyond: Our spotlight shines on ruminants – beef, lamb, venison, you name it. Their grass-fed, toxin-filtering lifestyles mean you're dining on nature's best. Variety spices up life, so whether it's a ribeye or the nutrient-packed liver, if it's pasture-raised, it's on your plate. And for those pondering the organic dilemma, breathe easy. In regions like the UK, where ruminants graze freely, 'organic' becomes less of a necessity and more of a luxury. And for the bacon aficionados, there's room at the table – provided you have shopped diligently and it's free from those pesky nitrates.

Fibre: Some Carnivore *Plus* enthusiasts choose to forgo fibre, advocating for a diet stripped down to its most primal elements. My stance, however, diverges. Having embraced the fibre-filled life and reaped its myriad benefits – from nurturing a thriving microbiome to enhancing overall health – I advocate for its inclusion, even on this most meat-centric of diets. Incorporating fibre noodles and fibre-rich drinks, I pilot the Carnivore Plus Diet with a nod to balance. This approach maintains the gut's harmony and ensures a nutritional reset that doesn't turn its back on the virtues of fibre.

Dairy, Decoded: Cheese? Yes, but on the Carnivore Plus Diet, not just any cheese. We opt for varieties from buffalo, sheep, or goats. These cheeses are rich in casein A2, sidestepping the potentially inflammatory casein A1 found in cow dairy.

Seasoning with Substance: Rock salt is our seasoning superstar, bringing minerals to the table without any potential baggage of its sea-salt relatives.

Fish, with Finesse: Freshwater salmon, untouched by the perils of farm feeds or the murk of polluted depths, earns its place in our Carnivore Plus dietary line-up.

This diet isn't just about what's on the plate; it's a culinary shield against a myriad of modern dietary potential ills, in particular:

> **Plant-Based Perpetrators:** Oxalates, lectins, and glycoalkaloids, hidden in the most innocent greens, are shown the door, along with goitrogens and phytic acid, known for their disruptive dance with our thyroid and mineral uptake.
>
> **The Infamous 14 Allergens:** Imagine a line-up of usual suspects – all booted out. This diet sidesteps the drama by keeping these provocateurs at bay.
>
> **Chemical Culprits:** In a world awash with ultra-processed foods, Carnivore Plus is your culinary bunker, safeguarding against the onslaught of additives that spell trouble for your system.

The Carnivore *Plus* Diet isn't just about what you're eating; it's a radical return to the roots of nutrition, where every bite is a step towards a purer, more vibrant you. So, if you're ready to take the plunge into this nutritional deep end, remember, it's not just about beefing up on protein – it's about fine-tuning your diet to your body's unique symphony of needs. And remember, this diet might make you the most interesting guest at any dinner party – just be prepared to explain why you're passing on the breadbasket for the tenth time!

*****

The Lion Diet: A Roaring Approach To Carnivore Living

Venture into the untamed territories of the Lion Diet (also known as the Meat-Salt-Water Diet), a regimen as robust and straightforward as the diet of the jungle's sovereign. This culinary philosophy, etched into the annals of dietary transformation by Mikhaila Peterson and her philosopher father, Jordan Peterson, author of *12 Rules for Life*, heralds a return to the elemental. By the tender age of 22, Mikhaila's health quest had become a harrowing odyssey through diagnoses of rheumatoid arthritis, bipolar disorder, hypersomnia, Lyme disease, psoriasis, and eczema. Yet, she attributes her remarkable remission to the stark simplicity of the Lion Diet.

As the carnivore diet's most spartan variant, the Lion Diet's credo is meat from ruminants, seasoned solely with salt and water. Mikhaila Peterson, now a venerated voice in health and wellness, extols this diet for its transformative power, crediting it with vast improvements in both physical and mental health, echoing the experiences of thousands.

The Lion Diet is akin to channelling the spirit of the savannah's king, feasting on a diet that's as primal and pure as the majestic lion itself. Like the lion, the apex predator of the animal kingdom, this diet strips eating back to its most basic, powerful essence, promising a path to reclaim health and vitality.

My exploration into this dietary realm? Yes, I've ventured there, albeit briefly. The Lion Diet, while intriguing, lacked the variety my palate craves. If your approach to eating is utilitarian or if you're seeking a resolution for persistent health issues, the Lion Diet is the silver bullet. However, the Carnivore *Plus* Diet serves as my annual reset button, providing a broader spectrum of nutrients while reaping the benefits of a carnivorous lifestyle.

*****

Vegetarian And Vegan Diets

Welcome to the leafy realms of vegetarianism and veganism, where many a forkful is a fibre-filled celebration. Indeed, plants stand unrivalled as the exclusive source of dietary fibre, adorning your meals with a kaleidoscope of health benefits. Yet, if the premise of this book enticed you with promises of a plant-only paradise, pause for a moment of reflection. While I don't outright champion these diets without reservation, they often offer a healthier pasture than the barren fields of fibre-depleted, ultra-processed edibles that dominate the standard diet.

Distinguishing between vegetarianism and veganism is akin to navigating the nuances of a botanical garden. Vegetarians partake in the plant-based concert with cameos from dairy and eggs, whereas vegans follow a strict botanical script, excluding all animal derivatives, even honey.

This discourse isn't about converting plant enthusiasts into meat aficionados. I respect the choice of many respected peers and friends who, driven by ethical, spiritual, or health convictions, adopt vegetarian or vegan lifestyles. Despite my own preferences for a diet inclusive of meat, my goal is to illuminate the path with the glow of truth, empowering you to mould your dietary habits on a bedrock of informed decision-making.

Should your allegiance to vegetarianism or veganism stem from health aspirations, irrigating such convictions with a dose of reality is prudent. The blueprint of our species was sketched with omnivory in mind. Meat's presence in our dietary narrative isn't a cameo but a starring role, with a supporting cast of health merits resonating throughout human evolution.

For those who undertake a plant-based diet as a homage to animal welfare, your compass impressively points towards noble intentions. Yet, before committing to the verdant vows, heed the reflections of Lierre Keith in *The Vegetarian Myth*. Her account, born from two decades of vegan dedication, critiques the agricultural revolution not merely as cultivation but as a catalyst for ecological dissonance, where fields morph into theatres of conflict, with the toll extending far beyond our plates. Revisit the discussion on page 518 for a deeper exploration of the dichotomy between sustaining life with a single cow versus the unintended demise of myriad small beings in the wake of expansive grain and vegetable cultivation.

The environmental discourse often dresses veganism in grassy virtues. But does this narrative depict an authentic panorama or a superficial veneer? Entwined within this dialogue is a complex tangle of corporate motives, where profit tints the canvas, obscuring the genuine shades of veganism's environmental impact. Thus, as you meander through the lush valleys of plant-based living, equip yourself with the lantern of knowledge, allowing insight to guide you.

I sought insights from several esteemed experts on the subject of vegetarian and vegan diets. First, we turn to Professor Tim Noakes, a renowned forensic anthropologist, for his perspective on vegetarianism and its implications for our wellbeing.

'If you look at humans, it's very clear that we are carnivorous. And anyone who tells you we aren't not looking at the biology. The biology is so clear. We have a very acidic stomach; we have a very long, small bowel and a very short, large bowel, and we don't have the bacteria to digest starchy foods. And by that, I mean the resistant starches, the cellulose, which is all done by anaerobic (without oxygen) bacteria.

And the big guts of the chimpanzee and the gorilla are because they are full of these digestive bacteria that are changing the cellulose into saturated fatty acids. And that's the irony of it all. The cows, the sheep and other ruminants are converting grass, which is a carbohydrate, into saturated fats. Why would they do that if it's going to kill us? And that's the issue. We are absolutely adapted for meat consumption and not for vegetables and grains. And this push towards eating more vegetables frightens me. You can't get the nutrition. Humans would have to be eating 12 to 14 hours a day. If you're a vegan or vegetarian, if you are not eating 14 hours a day, what nutrition are you getting?'

Dr Robert Lustig:
'I am not against veganism; if vegans want to be vegan, that's fine; if people want to go keto, that's fine, too. The funny thing is both the vegans and the ketos are in agreement; they think they are at war. As a matter of fact, they are actually on the same side. They are on the side that stands against the processed food industry. If they stopped battling against each other and worked together, we might solve this problem.

In the vast expanse of dietary landscapes, it's essential to recognise the myriad paths that unfold before us. For those steadfast in their vegetarian or vegan voyage, I acknowledge your resolve. Yet, it's my duty to unfurl the green curtain and reveal the truths that often lurk in the shadows of plant-based narratives. While some may think my stance might be swayed by the lure of financial gain – especially since the supplement industry thrives in the nutrient gaps of plant-based diets – my compass points in a different direction. I'm an advocate for dietary authenticity, not for the supplemental sales spike that vegetarian and vegan diets might deliver.

Let's shift the discourse from a clash of carnivores versus herbivores to a quest for genuine, unprocessed nourishment, far removed from the artificial constructs of industrialised food. If you've chosen to tread the leaf-strewn path of veganism or vegetarianism, arm yourself with knowledge and mindful supplementation. It's not about casting judgment on your choice, but ensuring your nutritional path is fortified with the vital elements that nature provides in its most unadulterated form. While I am not suggesting everyone should ditch their allegiance to an exclusively plant-based diet and join us meat eaters, I want to ensure that I sufficiently highlight the nutrient density and balance that animal products can bring to the table:

- **DHA:** A vital omega-3 for brain health, primarily sourced from aquatic realms. Plant-based eaters can find a semblance in flaxseeds and walnuts, though the conversion to DHA is a voyage of inefficiency.
- **Haem Iron:** The champion of absorption residing in the regal courts of red meat. Its plant-based counterpart, non-haem iron, pales in comparison for bioavailability.
- **Creatine:** A muscle and mind energiser predominantly found in the animal kingdom, awaiting its plant-based counterpart.
- **Vitamin D:** The sunshine's vitamin is also nestled in animal produce.
- **Vitamin B12:** An essential symphony of wellbeing, almost exclusively conducted by animal-sourced foods like fish, meat, dairy, and eggs.
- **Carnosine:** An antioxidant serenade that resonates in the muscles and minds of animals.
- **Taurine:** A nutrient that whispers only in the dialect of animal-sourced foods, instrumental in muscle function and antioxidant defences.
- **Zinc:** A mineral more bioavailable from meat sources, prompting vegans and vegetarians to seek 50% more than their meat-embracing counterparts.

One final word on diets before we close this chapter. I do not intend to dissuade anyone from vegetarianism but to shed light on the oft-misrepresented truths that populate newsfeeds and articles.

The EAT-Lancet report is a controversial document widely cited by journalists as a foundation for their anti-meat narratives. It's a study that carries weight, not just because the Lancet is a leading medical journal, but also because it advocates a drastic dietary shift to a near vegan diet. If we were to follow its recommendations, our monthly meat allowance would barely cover a single burger or a rasher of bacon.

The report, authored by 37 experts, was driven by one critical question: 'Can we feed a future population of 10 billion a healthy diet within planetary boundaries?' It gained rapid traction, with its recommendations making headlines and sparking debates. Yet, it's baffling how these so-called health experts proposed a diet lacking essential nutrients like magnesium, iron, choline, potassium, and vitamin B12. It's a plan that not only side-lines meat but elevates carbohydrates to a primary dietary role, a stance at odds with health and environmental sustainability.

Why would a team of respected medical professionals endorse such a diet in one of the world's most influential health journals? Digging deeper reveals a telling narrative. Many of the report's authors are known vegetarians, vegans, or vegan activists. Leading the cohort was Walter Willett, who reportedly received substantial funding from plant-based food companies. The Wellcome Trust, with ties to the pharmaceutical industry, was the financial backbone of the study. It's crucial to question the impartiality of research influenced by such vested interests.

This revelation is vital. The same scientific paper that has been extensively quoted by major news outlets and even the BBC is a trove of skewed health advice steering us towards a vegetarian path while side-lining the wholesome benefits of natural fats and proteins. It's a narrative entangled not just in politics, corporate agendas, and financial motivations but also in religious doctrines, such as The Seventh Day Adventist Church, creators of the humble cornflake.

Let's now lend an ear to Patrick Holden CBE; remember from earlier, he is a steward of sustainable farming and former director of the UK's Soil Association. In a conversation we shared, Patrick brought forth a poignant critique of the EAT-Lancet report, one of the most quoted yet controversial pieces of research of our times:

> *Regarding the EAT-Lancet report, not one of the 37 authors was a farmer! All these people are telling us what to eat without knowing about agriculture. How strange is that? Bless his heart, even David Attenborough, a national treasure, said on some programme recently, 'I am trying to cut down on red meat'. I wanted to shout at the television and say, 'No! Please differentiate between red meat, which is part of the problem and that which is part of the solution.' We should be eating real meats to support hard-pressed livestock farmers and the arable farmers who want to farm more sustainably.*

As we conclude this chapter, remember that each dietary path is a choice, a narrative penned by individual beliefs, health aspirations, and ethical compasses. Whether you're a lion of the savannah or a gazelle of the meadow, the quest for nourishing your body is a venture of profound significance, inviting each step to be taken with intention and mindfulness.

Chapter 8

Avoiding other Root Causes of Chronic Illness

Welcome to the consulting room of health revelations, where we've previously dissected the diet dilemma, uncovering the sinister synergy of scarce fibre and sugar-laden meals that drive insulin resistance- the master behind a theatre of health horrors. As your dietary detective, we've steered through an assortment of eating plans, empowering you with the *Fibre First* philosophy and a buffet of nutritional strategies.

As we dig deeper into the roots of health, our exploration takes us beneath the surface into the fertile ground of lifestyle choices that shape our metabolic wellbeing. Like a gardener tending to the soil, we must examine the nutrients we feed our bodies and how we cultivate our daily habits, each a seed that can grow into either vibrant health or chronic illness.

Brace for a dig into the soil of wellness, visiting other roots of my *Tree of Afflictions*, where we confront not just the known adversaries but also encounter a paradoxical twist—a factor often cast in a dubious light might be an unsung protector in disguise. Which of the following list do you think might be a covert guardian of longevity?

- Chronic Stress
- Sleep
- Seed Oils
- Sedentary Lifestyles
- Cholesterol
- Pharmaceutical Medication

As we dig into this chapter's layers, we stand at the threshold of discovery, pondering who among this cast will emerge as an unexpected ally.

*****

The Chronic Stress Conundrum

See your body as a high-octane sports car, precision-engineered for peak performance. Faced with acute stress, it's like hitting the throttle for a rapid dash; your body unleashes cortisol, akin to releasing oxygen in the turbo boost in a race car. This stress hormone signals your liver to concoct glucose, providing that instant surge of energy. It's the perfect setup for a fleeting flee from ancient predators or a last-ditch dash to catch that departing train. This is acute stress: swift, sharp, and short-lived. Our bodies are sculpted to manage this type of stress; cortisol swiftly marshals sugar as fuel, the fastest-burning energy source, to power our need for immediate, high-stakes action.

Imagine your state-of-the-art sports car incessantly revving its engine, even in idle mode. This scenario mirrors chronic stress, a pervasive challenge in contemporary life. To underscore the essence of 'chronic,' let's revisit its meaning: persisting for a long time, a condition that lingers, stubbornly refusing to dissipate quickly or easily. Contrasting with the acute, life-or-death instances our forebears faced, today's stressors resemble an endless, congested traffic jam. Keeping your foot pressed on the gas pedal, even when immobilised, is not just unproductive; it strains and erodes the car's inner workings. Similarly, when our bodies are ensnared in a ceaseless state of stress, cortisol, the stress hormone, is incessantly on the alert, disrupting our inner harmony and balance.

In the intricate ballet of our body's hormones, cortisol and insulin often find themselves in a headlock. On one side, insulin diligently regulates our blood sugar, striving to keep it at just one teaspoon of sugar, maintaining the right amount to fuel your body. On the other side is cortisol, the body's rapid response unit, trying its hardest to boost glucose levels for instant energy during stress.

However, when these two forces are in a constant state of push and pull, especially under the shadow of chronic stress, it's like a perpetual duel between two master fencers. Cortisol, ever eager to prime you for crisis, keeps pumping glucose into your system. It's as if your body is always on edge, poised for a threat that never materialises. This relentless state leads to an overflow of glucose in your blood. Insulin, in its attempt to restore equilibrium, works overtime to clear the excess sugar, but this relentless cycle can exhaust insulin receptors, leading to insulin resistance.

In the hormonal hierarchy, insulin typically reigns supreme, coordinating many bodily functions. However, in acute danger—real or perceived—cortisol claims the throne. Imagine insulin as a diligent, multifaceted worker, efficiently managing resources. But when cortisol storms the scene, it's like an emergency alert that takes precedence over everything else. In this scenario, insulin's authority is challenged. It attempts to counteract by deploying more forces (insulin molecules), leading to a standoff, elevated blood sugar countered by elevated insulin levels. This tug-of-war results in hyperglycaemia (high blood sugar) and hyperinsulinemia (high insulin levels), a double-edged sword threatening your metabolic harmony.

You might be feasting on the healthiest foods, but if your cortisol levels are consistently on overdrive, it disrupts the harmony that insulin strives to maintain. Despite a seemingly flawless diet, this can lead to unexpected weight gain and deteriorating metabolic health.

So, how do we tame this tempest and manage stress? The solution lies in adopting stress-busting practices. Engage in regular physical exercise, embrace meditation, ensure restorative sleep, practice positive thinking, and explore relaxation techniques to keep cortisol levels in check. It's not just about the food on your plate but also about how you live, manage stress, and maintain your body's intricate hormonal balance.

Understanding the cortisol-insulin dance is not just about awareness; it's about taking the wheel and steering your body towards harmony, happiness, and health. Recognising acute and chronic stress nuances is akin to distinguishing between sprints and a marathon. While the former is a momentary burst, the latter is a prolonged ordeal.

Embrace Relaxation and Mindfulness: Consider relaxation techniques as your vehicle's cruise control feature, offering a smooth and steady ride. Meditation, yoga, or even deep breathing exercises act as stress diffusers, allowing your cortisol levels to simmer and offering your system a well-deserved respite.

Be Mindful of Medications: Just as you'd fine-tune your vehicle with the proper fuel and oil, being attentive to your medication is paramount. Some may inadvertently rev up cortisol production, subtly throwing your system off balance. It is always a good idea to ask your GP about known side effects, especially if you are on more than one medication.

Cultivate a Positive Social Environment: Surrounding yourself with 'radiators'- those who exude positivity and warmth- can significantly enhance your journey, making it more enjoyable and fulfilling. On the flip side, the perpetual 'drains' make the ride dreary and exhausting. Choose your companions wisely, ensuring they contribute positively to your emotional well-being.

Consider the compelling 2015 study that explored the digital heartbeat of communities, linking the emotional tone of social media language with heart disease mortality. The revelation was striking; regions marked by a chorus of negative, anger-laced, or pessimistic tweets echoed a higher prevalence of heart disease than traditional risk factors like smoking or high blood pressure. This insightful study unveils a profound truth: the emotional fabric of a community, woven through its digital expressions, can cast significant ripples on physical health. It underscores the potent influence of our collective emotional climate, a tapestry woven with threads of stress and serenity, on the symphony of heart health.

Crafting Contentment: Lessons From The Land Of Happiness

In my 35 years of building businesses and leading thousands of exceptional individuals, I've been on a relentless quest to decode the essence of peak performance, happiness, and low-stress living. This pursuit recently led me to the tranquil mountain kingdom of Bhutan, renowned as the happiest country on earth. I was intrigued by Bhutan's unique approach to prosperity, emphasising Gross National Happiness (GNH) over Gross Domestic Product (GDP). The concept of GNH, introduced by the country's visionary fourth King, Jigme Singye Wangchuck, in the 1970s, reflects a profound understanding that true wealth lies in the wellness of its people.

One morning, a small group of us were fortunate enough to share breakfast with His Majesty the Druk Gyalpo Jigme Khesar Namgyel Wangchuck; we discussed the heart of Bhutanese life, absorbing the wisdom of a nation that prioritises happiness as its richest resource. As I trekked through Bhutan's serene valleys and vibrant communities, I gathered invaluable insights, crystallising them into ten fundamental principles that epitomise the art of thriving amidst life's often tumultuous waves with grace and a smile.

These contentment principles are strategies and lifelines that connect us to a deeper, less stressful existence. As we explore them together, may they guide you towards your own path of happiness, one serene step at a time.

10 Traits of Less Stressy People:

- Appreciating impermanence
- Minimising worry
- Building a close circle of friends or family for belonging
- Demonstrating a high tolerance and rational outlook
- Adopting a light-hearted approach to life
- Expressing gratitude
- Practising letting go
- Cultivating curiosity
- Embracing each day as a gift
- Taking responsibility for actions

1. Embrace the Dance of Impermanence

In the serene valleys of Bhutan, there's an enlightening perspective that might initially seem counterintuitive: the keen awareness that nothing in life lasts forever. Conversations about the impermanence of life are as common as the mountain breeze, yet far from breeding anxiety, this acknowledgement fosters a profound sense of liberation. Echoing Steve Jobs' insightful words, 'Remembering that I'll be dead soon... that you are going to die is the best way I know to avoid the trap of thinking you have something to lose. You are already naked.'

The people of Bhutan embrace the transient nature of existence, shedding the weight of external expectations and societal pressures. It's a daily practice in mindfulness, ensuring every fleeting moment is lived to its fullest. As Linley Dorji, our Bhutanese guide, insightfully remarked, 'To find contentment, embrace impermanence; it slows your pace. In the West, minds leap like monkeys from branch to branch, never resting.'

2. Minimise Worry: Charting a Worry-Free Course

Chart a course through life where worry is tossed overboard. Remember, fretting over past storms or unchangeable currents serves no one. Instead, set your compass towards actions and decisions within your realm of influence.

Ease the sails and let the winds of concern pass by. Embrace the *'Hakuna Matata'* spirit, a melody of carefree life sung not only by the tribes in Kenya and Tanzania (seriously, some of them really do) but by anyone who chooses to live worry-free. When the waves of life get tumultuous, hum along to Bobby McFerrin's timeless tune, 'Don't Worry, Be Happy', and let the rhythm of relaxation guide your vessel.

If you hate your captain (boss) because he or she is unreasonable, chat with them and try to help them see the error of their ways. If nothing changes, attempt to get them fired! This might sound strange advice from someone who has employed hundreds of managers, but poor managers are bad for business and health. While work, to a certain degree, should be challenging, it should also be enjoyable and rewarding. The ocean of life is vast and full of opportunities. Anchor yourself in a role that brings you joy, not just bounty. After all, authentic treasure isn't found in the chest of coins but in the heart of happiness. Work should be something you cherish, not just endure.

Here is an extract from a business book I wrote, 'Don't waste your life worrying about things where you can't influence the outcome. What I mean by this is don't waste mental effort thinking about past events. After all, you can't change history. No matter how incredibly smart you are, you can't change past events. Likewise, don't waste time thinking about things you can't influence in the future. If you want to be happy and avoid stress, focus all your efforts and thoughts solely on the things you can influence.'

3. Family, Friends, Colleagues, and Canine Companions

The essence of a fulfilled life often anchors in the harbours of connection to family, friends, colleagues, and even our four-legged companions. Reflecting on the serene lifestyle of the long-lived Ikarian people, a small island community near Greece known for its high concentration of centenarians, it's clear that their longevity isn't just about their fibre-rich, natural diet; it's deeply rooted in their rich tapestry of community bonds.

Evening gatherings, shared meals, and a collective embrace of life's simple joys vividly show how integral social connections are to our well-being.

This communal symphony resonates with the World Health Organisation's definition of health, emphasising that actual vitality is a blend of three pillars: physical, mental, and social harmony.

Echoing these sentiments, His Holiness the Dalai Lama, in The Art of Happiness, illustrates the profound impact of intimate relationships. Sharing life's depth-joys, fears, hopes-with a confidant, be it a partner, friend, or family member, isn't just comforting; it's a cornerstone of happiness. The quality of these bonds, the strength of our social fabric, isn't just a backdrop to our lives; it's the essence that can elevate our existence from merely surviving to truly thriving.

4. The Art of Tolerance and Rationality

A low-stress life requires a palette of patience and the wisdom to discern what truly matters. In the realm of personal and professional relationships, the most robust connections flourish from a balanced give-and-take, a dance of mutual respect and understanding. Tolerance isn't just a virtue; it's necessary to maintain our inner peace amidst the everyday ebb and flow.

The power of rationalisation plays a pivotal role in shaping our perspective. I once walked past two elderly ladies sitting on a bench, admiring the views across the river in Dartmouth, and heard one say to the other, 'How do you always look so happy? I never see you depressed.' The lady smiled back at her friend and said, 'I can always rationalise things'. As the French aptly put it, *'laissez-faire'* is a reminder to gently navigate the currents of life, accepting and adapting to its ever-changing tides.

This ethos is beautifully captured in the words of Virginia Satir, a celebrity in the realm of family therapy, who observed, 'Life is not what it's supposed to be. It's what it is. The way you cope with it is what makes the difference.' Her insight is a guiding star, encouraging us to sail through life with the grace of understanding and adaptability.

5. Don't Be So Serious

One common trait I see in less stressy people is they know when and when not to take things seriously. The significance we place on ourselves is often magnified through our own lens. Embracing the adage, 'Don't take yourself too seriously because nobody else does', serves as a gentle reminder to keep our sails adjusted to the winds of reality. It's about granting ourselves the permission to laugh, to find joy in the simple moments, and to appreciate the transient nature of our worries. Oh, and don't take others too seriously; they are only human.

6. Cultivate Gratitude and Shun the Comparison Trap

You might recall the catchy jingle of a particular advert urging you to 'go compare', but in the grand theatre of life, that's precisely the tune we should mute. For our journey, the only meaningful comparison is with those less fortunate, serving as a poignant reminder of our blessings. Dwelling in gratitude isn't just pleasant; it's a sanctuary for the soul.

Yet, in today's digital age, social media often paints a deceptive tableau of perpetual bliss, a mosaic of curated moments that seldom mirror the multifaceted reality of human existence. As the iconic band A-ha melodically pointed out, 'The Sun Always Shines On TV', but life's true colours are far more complex and nuanced beyond the screen.

The culture of comparison fostered by social media platforms is insidiously eroding the joy of our younger generations. It's a silent thief, stealthily pilfering contentment by inviting endless comparisons with the illusory portrayals of others' lives, their ephemeral joys, and material acquisitions. Recognising this trap and stepping away from the relentless pursuit of comparison is not just liberating; it's a reclaiming of genuine happiness. After all, the true essence of contentment lies not in external validation or material wealth but in cherishing the unique melody of our life.

7. Embrace Release: The Art of Letting Go

In life's intricate dance, it's not the missteps that define us but how gracefully we release them and move forward. A simple yet profound tale from the African wilderness beautifully illustrates the wisdom of letting go. In certain remote communities, tribes have devised a clever method to capture monkeys, a staple in their diet. They secure an empty jar, partly filled with peanuts, into the ground. The unsuspecting monkey, lured by the enticing snack, reaches into the jar and clasps a fistful of nuts. Yet, in its steadfast grip, it is ensnared- its clenched fist too big to withdraw through the jar's narrow opening. Freedom is but a release away, yet the monkey, fixated on its prize, cannot grasp the simplicity of letting go.

This anecdote mirrors a profound truth about human nature. How often do we cling to past grievances, errors, or regrets, allowing them to define our present and constrain our future? The key to liberation lies in our capacity to unclasp our hold on these burdens, learn from them, and then release them into the ether with a gentle breath of acceptance. Just as the iconic tune from Disney's *Frozen* advises, there's profound wisdom in choosing to 'let it go'.

When life presents its inevitable challenges, please take a moment to reflect and glean whatever lessons they may offer. Then, with the poise and composure of one who understands life's ebb and flow, release your grip on the past. In doing so, you open your hands and heart to the boundless possibilities of the present and the promise of the future. Remember, the capacity to let go is not a mark of surrender but a testament to your strength and a step towards your liberation.

8. Cultivate Curiosity

Cultivating curiosity in life's vast landscape is like introducing vivid colours to a grey-scale scene. It's akin to a gardener who lovingly cares for their plants, where nurturing curiosity helps you develop a mindset eager for exploration and new discoveries, transforming everyday moments into something magical. Embracing life with a sense of wonder, posing questions, and venturing into new experiences can significantly counteract stress. This shift in perspective moves your focus from burdensome thoughts to the excitement of potential and upliftment.

Engage with others from a place of curiosity, assuming everyone has something valuable to teach you. This mindset of inquiry, asking probing questions and absorbing new knowledge, enriches interactions. It's exciting spending time with Sir Richard Branson. Despite the common scenario where individuals seek his insights, Richard often flips the script, posing his own questions and showing an ever-present curiosity about people, regardless of their status or background.

Adopt the stance of a curious explorer, keen to unearth the world's hidden wonders. Allow your inquisitive nature to guide you towards new passions, literary worlds, or engaging dialogues. Within these pursuits of curiosity, stress melts away, replaced by the exhilaration of uncovering new knowledge and the invigorating sense of embarking on uncharted adventures. Curiosity transcends being merely a characteristic; it is a dynamic cruise, constantly revealing additional aspects of the world and yourself. So, when shadows of stress loom, let your curiosity illuminate the path to a world that's brighter and bursting with colour.

9. Cherish Today, the Ultimate Gift

Building on the wisdom of impermanence, the recognition that every moment is a transient treasure cultivates a profound appreciation for the present. In Bhutan, the present isn't just a fleeting second; it's the stage on which the drama of life unfolds. While in the West, we're often fixated on the horizon of the future, Bhutan teaches us the art of valuing the 'now'. As you approach the end of this book, you'll see how crucial it is to align our present actions with our aspirations for the next two decades. Yet, this forward-thinking mindset doesn't detract from the richness of the present. It's about balancing foresight with the mindful savouring of each moment, ensuring that while our eyes may glimpse the future, our feet are firmly planted in the vibrant garden of today.

Reflecting on the interplay between our mental state and our focus in time can be illuminating, albeit a touch simplistic for some. I've hypothesised before, to mixed reactions from my friends in psychiatry, that dwelling on the past may pave the way to depression, obsessing over the future could usher in anxiety, whereas anchoring oneself in the present often breeds contentment. While this perspective might not capture the full complexity of human emotions, it is a useful starting point for fostering a healthier mindset.

10. Seize the Helm: Your Life, Your Voyage

In the voyage of life, those who steer the waves with calm and poise often share a common understanding: the realisation that they are the architects of their own destiny. They don't linger in the shadows of passivity nor succumb to the stress of unmet expectations or delayed outcomes. They shun the notion of victimhood, instead embracing the empowering mantra: 'If it's to be, it's up to me.'

Bear Grylls' wise counsel to 'paddle your own canoe' resonates deeply with this mindset. The waters of life won't calm themselves, nor will the currents guide you to your desired haven. The responsibility to grab the oars, to steer through both still and stormy seas, rests firmly in your hands. Embrace that life grants you a single voyage, a unique crusade filled with opportunities and challenges. Recognise that you are the captain of your soul, the master of your fate, and the creator of your outcomes.

I asked my good friend Shan, who worked with me a few years back on a health education program I was filming, for his take on stress:

'As a doctor, I regard stress as any physical, mental, or emotional factor that causes strain or tension on the body or mind. Mental or emotional stress often results from adverse situations, such as family conflicts, worries about work, or health issues, but it's important to remember that stress is highly individual.

What's highly stressful for one person may be normal for another. Whenever a patient tells me they feel ill or mentally exhausted or depressed from stress, I take it seriously, even if the stress they describe doesn't seem that stressful. After all, I believe physical, mental, or social stress may well be the fundamental basis of most, if not all, diseases.'

Dr Shan also then picked up on my point of being social.
High-quality social interaction on a regular basis with your immediate peers is helpful for reducing and managing stress. Try to get together with your friends and family as often as possible. If your social circle is small, have you considered getting a dog? A recent study in Sweden showed that dog owners were 23 percent less likely to die of cardiovascular disease, and they also experienced a 20 percent lower risk of mortality from all causes. The authors could not explain this link, but it was felt the additional physical activity and emotional connection between dogs and owners played the most critical roles.

If you grapple with stress without a clear understanding of the root cause of your discomfort, revisiting chapter 6 could be beneficial. Turn to the pages where the significant role of metabolism in our neurological wellbeing is explored in depth.

To effectively traverse the complexities of stress, embracing lifestyle changes that cultivate balance is essential. Remember, each effort to manage stress reduces cortisol-induced sugars in the bloodstream. This, in turn, reduces the need for insulin, decreasing the risk of developing an array of chronic diseases prevalent in modern societies.

From Junk Food Jitters To Serotonin Smiles: The Science Of Mood And Food

Ah, the great culinary literacy twist of our time: spell 'stressed' backwards, and you land on 'desserts.' Coincidence? Perhaps not! This linguistic flip is a cheeky nod to the complex dance between what we eat and how we feel. The saga of bad food leading to a bad mood isn't just folk wisdom; it's science with a side of humour.

Junk food, the rogue in our tale, is notorious for its scarcity of tryptophan, the essential building block for serotonin, our brain's primary happiness hormone. Why the scarcity, you ask? Because tryptophan resides exclusively in the VIP section of the nutritional world, found in choices such as eggs, pork, spinach, nuts, fish, and poultry—far from the aisles of processed indulgences.

> *While tryptophan is present in wholesome foods, serotonin cannot be directly sourced from them. Instead, it must be synthesised from an adequate supply of tryptophan.*

While serotonin levels take a nosedive, tyrosine and phenylalanine are throwing a rave in cheap eats, pumping up dopamine demands and putting a damper on tryptophan's serotonin soiree. The result? A fleeting high of sugar, alcohol, and processed foods leaves serotonin—the life of the party—out in the cold.

Dr Robert Lustig points out a curious timeline: as processed foods began their rise to dietary dominance post-1940, so did rates of depression. Coincidence? Perhaps not. Shedding pounds and reversing insulin resistance isn't just good news for your wardrobe; it can also dial down anxiety and give serotonin levels a much-needed boost.

Now, about tryptophan—this amino acid is essential for crafting serotonin, but our bodies can't whip it up on their own. We need to source it from our diets: not just the eggs, nuts, fish I just mentioned, but the feathered star of Christmas day, turkey. Here's a fun fact to chew on: ever wondered why a lavish turkey dinner sends you into a post-feast snooze? Tryptophan strikes again, proving it's not just about happiness but also relaxation.

A message to my American friends: beware the beef trap! Corn-fed cattle might be beefing up dopamine instead of tryptophan, leading you away from the path of contentment. On the other hand, grass-fed cattle are true serotonin champions, generously contributing to our tryptophan intake.

Here's to making your meals a recipe for happiness, one bite of tryptophan-rich foods at a time. Don't just feed your stomach; nourish your soul and watch as your mood lifts from the blues to a radiant spectrum of joy.

*****

The Significance Of Sleep

Scientists have just unveiled a groundbreaking revelation, a wonder treatment poised to revolutionise our lives. This marvel promises to extend our lifespan, enhance our beauty, and streamline our waistlines by curbing those relentless food cravings. It stands as a formidable shield against the spectres of cancer, heart disease, and Alzheimer's. It's a sentinel guarding against colds and flu. This miraculous discovery pledges to elevate our spirits, dispelling the clouds of depression and anxiety. And there are more promises to sharpen our wits, potentially boosting our IQ by a staggering 10% and transforming our minds into vaults of vivid memories. Are you poised on the edge of your seat, eager to uncover the identity of this phenomenal breakthrough? It's none other than the age-old elixir of life-sleep.

Admittedly, I took a creative liberty or two because this revelation isn't hot off the scientific press. It's rooted in a trove of knowledge of over 17,000 rigorously scrutinised scientific studies, with the count ever rising, all singing the praises of a good night's rest. Yet, the irony is stark. In a profit-driven world, the simple act of promoting more sleep doesn't quite cut. After all, you can't eat or spend money while lost in the land of dreams. Therefore, this crucial narrative is often relegated to the shadows, tucked away under the same mattress that should be your haven for rejuvenation and restoration.

'Prioritise sleep, but don't let it become another source of worry,' Dr Campbell Murdoch, a former business partner and esteemed friend, once wisely advised.

> *'In the rapid tempo of modern life, the delicate balance of sleep has been disrupted. Self-reported sleep duration has waned by 1.5 to 2 hours over the past four decades. A striking crescendo in sleep deprivation is clear, with the proportion of young adults sleeping less than seven hours per night escalating from 15% in 1960 to a resounding 37% in more recent years.*[2] *Recent research discovered that nine in ten Britons say their life would be improved if they had more sleep.*
>
> *While the composition of sleep needs may vary individually, there's a general agreement that around seven hours of quality slumber per night orchestrates the best performance. Dissonant to this are studies revealing the unsettling effects of sleep deprivation: just one week of fragmented sleep can escalate the body's insulin resistance by approximately 30%, and this disharmony can begin with as little as two nights of inadequate rest.'*[1]

In the following pages, we examine the intricate nocturne of sleep, understanding how each restful note contributes to our health. By tuning into our body's innate rhythms and respecting the silent conductor of sleep, we harmonise our existence, transforming each restful night into a prelude to a healthier, more vibrant dawn.

The lure of modern-day technology often disrupts the natural cadence of sleep. A wealth of research underscores a cautionary note: turning to phones or laptops at night exposes us to bright lights, striking a chord with our stress hormone, cortisol. As we've learned in our discussion on stress, elevated cortisol levels can lead to a surge in blood sugar, echoing the disquieting rhythm of insulin resistance.

The Bennett household unveils a tale about lights, iPads, iPhones, and the magical realm of beauty sleep. My youngest daughters, Jessica and Lili, used to sleep with their room ablaze in light, oblivious to the wonders of darkness. Despite my efforts to teach them about the biological clock and melanin production, the adage of 'beauty sleep' finally switched off the lights. I explained that true beauty sleep happens only in complete darkness- any light and the enchantment is lost.

Venturing deeper into the realm of sleep, we uncover many beneficial layers beyond the mere superficial allure. As an introduction, here are just three short benefits found as we surrender to slumber:

- Our bodies start a state of rejuvenation, boosting growth hormones.
- The brain embarks on a nocturnal quest, piecing together the day's puzzles and filing them neatly for future recall.
- The liver takes a breather from its digestive duties, shifting focus to detoxifying the body.

Now, let's explore the intricate dance between sleep and weight management. Researchers at the University of Chicago conducted a fascinating study: they sleep-deprived half of their participants, allotting them only 4-5 hours of shuteye, while the other half basked in the luxury of ample rest. The outcome? The sleep-starved group awoke in a frenzy with their hunger hormone ghrelin signalling a false sense of famine. Concurrently, their leptin levels- the satiety messenger- plummeted, doubling down on the deception crafted by their sleep deprivation. This unveils the mechanism by which inadequate sleep ensnares our hunger control system.

Should you find yourself entangled in the web of sleep deprivation, recognise that your hunger is merely a hormonal mirage. Approach it with understanding and anticipate leptin's muted call at your next meal by resisting the urge to overfill your plate.

Dr Eve Van Cauter, a renowned sleep researcher at the University of Chicago and co-author of *Sleep Loss and Obesity*, resonated with this experiment and revealed an additional layer: individuals deprived of sleep consumed an extra 300 calories compared to their well-rested counterparts. Imagine the staggering accumulation of calories over a month, or even 15 years, of compromised sleep! In another intriguing revelation, she observed that those with curtailed sleep indulged in a substantially higher number of snacks during a buffet trial. Ghrelin didn't solely drive this behaviour but was also influenced by a stimulated endocannabinoid system in pursuit of pleasure and rewards. Sleep scarcity transforms our internal communication network into a cyclone, derailing our dietary instincts.

And intelligence, you ask? Indeed, sleep has a say in that domain, too. MRI scans illuminate that our brain's intellectual sectors buzz with activity after a restorative slumber. In one study, participants connected to MRI scanners were tasked with ranking their desire for different foods. The scans revealed that after inadequate sleep, the prefrontal cortex, the intellect part of our brain (more on the brain in chapter 11), dimmed its lights, leading to the more impulsive, emotional brain regions taking charge. In other words, poor sleep promotes emotional food choices, which often lean towards processed foods.

Sleep transcends mere eyelid closure. It's the conductor orchestrating our body's intricate symphony-from appetite regulation to intellectual prowess. It's our nightly voyage into renewal, with profound implications for our day-to-day existence, especially in the arena of insulin resistance and sugar spikes. A rejuvenating slumber isn't just a ritual; it's the cornerstone of holistic health, the master key that unlocks the doors to vitality and metabolic equilibrium.

How Much Sleep Do We Need?

In the quest for restful nights, determining the ideal amount of sleep is less about fixed numbers and more about understanding the nuances of individual needs. While the sanctity of sleep is universally acknowledged, the duration that makes up 'just right' can be as unique as a fingerprint. It's a dynamic interplay, a delicate dance where the tempo might vary with the rhythms of our lives. On some nights, the curtain may open on the day's performance after just six hours of slumber, while on others, the encore might extend to a luxurious eight. The key is tuning in to your body's signals, acknowledging that the volume of rest required may fluctuate in harmony with life's ebb and flow.

What insights do the sleep science professors offer? The National Sleep Foundation of America convened a constellation of 18 esteemed scientists and researchers, each a leader in their field. Their task? To distil a chorus of research into a refined cadence of sleep recommendations, a guide to help us navigate the nocturnal nuances that define our quest for rejuvenation and rest.

Age	Hours Needed	May Be Appropriate
Newborn - 3 months	14 to 17	11 to 19
4 months - 11 months	12 to 15	10 to 18
1 - 2 years old	11 to 14	9 to 16
3 - 5 years old	10 to 13	8 to 14
6 - 13 years old	9 to 11	7 to 12
14-17 years old	8 to 10	7 to 11
18 - 25 years old	7 to 9	6 to 11
26 - 64 years old	7 to 9	6 to 10
65 years +	7 to 8	5 to 9

Sleep, the silent sentinel of the night, stands vigilant, guarding against a myriad of health adversaries. Venturing below that vital 6 to 10-hour threshold of rest, as I show in my *Tree of Afflictions* diagram, opens the gates to a battalion of unwelcome invaders: obesity, diabetes, hypertension, heart disease, stroke, and the lurking shadows of mental health challenges such as depression. Sleep, in its steadfast duty, acts as a bulwark, repelling these incursions and preserving our wellness.

Yet the impact of sleep—or the lack thereof—extends even further. Insufficient rest weakens the vanguard of our immune system, amplifies our perception of pain, diminishes our performance, and lays the groundwork for mishaps and missteps.

But consider the transformative power of embracing a full night's rest. Those coveted hours of sleep are not merely an escape from the day's toils; they are an active restoration, a time when our body and mind engage in a profound renewal and healing process. It serves as a fortress against hypertension and cardiovascular ailments, a sanctuary for mental wellness, and a fortification for our immune defences.

In sum, a good night's sleep is akin to a health solution, a hidden gem in pursuing a life brimming with vitality and joy. It transcends mere rejuvenation; it empowers our entire being to face each new day with vigour and resilience. As we surrender to the embrace of sleep tonight, let's recognise that we're not merely withdrawing from the world. We're stepping into a domain where our health undergoes a nightly overhaul, equipping us to meet the day's challenges and delights with grace and strength. In the grand tapestry of life, sleep is not merely an intermission; it's an essential ally, a potent force that provides momentum towards optimal health and boundless vitality.

Without Sufficient Sleep

Your body is a high-performance machine. When it's well-rested, it purrs like a finely tuned sports car. But without sufficient sleep, things start to misfire:

- When sleep-deprived, your body churns out cortisol like it's going out of style, turning you into a short-fused, irritable version of yourself. It's not your fault; it's like your body's internal alarm system is stuck in 'panic' mode.
- Your brain's ability to sort and store the day's knowledge and memories gets as jumbled as a puzzle with missing pieces. It's like trying to file papers in a windstorm.
- Your body's thermostat goes off-kilter, struggling to handle temperature extremes. You're shivering one moment, overheating the next.
- Your immune system, usually a valiant defender, falters. It's like your body's security team is dozing off on the job.
- Your hunger hormones, leptin and ghrelin, get all out of whack too. Leptin, which usually pronounces your full, takes a break while ghrelin, the hunger trigger, starts yelling for snacks non-stop. It's a recipe for overeating.

Restorative sleep is a crucial maintenance tool, fine-tuning our body's elaborate systems and synchronising with our circadian rhythm.

Our Circadian Clock

In September 2017, Jeffrey C. Hall, Michael Rosbash, and Michael W. Young, three American scientists, were awarded the Nobel Prize for unravelling the mysteries of the internal clock within living organisms. This biological timekeeper, known as the circadian clock, orchestrates our physical functions with a rhythm that echoes the natural cycle of day and night.

The interplay between our sleep patterns and cortisol, the stress hormone, underscores the circadian clock's influence on our wellbeing. Insufficient or ill-timed sleep keeps us awake and stirs the cortisol beast, disrupting our internal harmony. To grasp this significance, we travel back to a time long before human inventions of timekeeping, to when nature itself instituted the circadian clock. Governed by the cycle of sunlight, this natural rhythm activates hormones like melatonin, setting the pace for all living beings on Earth.

The advent of chronobiology in the 1980s spotlighted the circadian clock's pivotal role in health, leading to groundbreaking discoveries about how our bodies adjust to the varying amounts of daylight throughout the year. Sunlight is vital in synchronising our biological clock with nature's day-night cycle. The following discussion is framed around the typical sunrise and sunset times of 6 am and 6 pm, observed during mid-spring and mid-autumn in the UK.

Fortunately, our bodies' circadian rhythms can adapt to the changing seasons, allowing our internal clocks to make precise adjustments in response to the gradual shifts in daylight we experience daily. From the winter solstice leading up to the summer solstice, there's a subtle increase in daylight by roughly two minutes each day, although this increment is more muted at the beginning. Conversely, as we move from the summer solstice towards the winter solstice, daylight diminishes by about two minutes daily. This natural ebb and flow in daylight duration are integral to how our circadian rhythms calibrate themselves throughout the year, ensuring our internal timing systems stay aligned with the external environment.

To assist our circadian rhythm, a practical approach for those living in the UK to harmonise with these changes involves managing light exposure: during the summer, keeping curtains closed to block out early morning light until it's time to wake up, and in the winter, seeking direct sunlight as soon as possible after waking. As far as it is reasonable and practical, achieving a more consistent exposure to light at similar times each day can significantly support the natural synchronisation of your circadian rhythm, enhancing overall well-being.

A 24-Hour Glimpse into Our Circadian Rhythm:

00:00: Melatonin production peaks, signalling our body to prepare for rest, while the thyroid instructs our cells' mitochondria to produce energy, subtly aiding in weight loss during sleep.

01:00: A reduction in brain activity facilitates processing daily learnings into long-term memories.

02:00: The body enters its deepest sleep phase, starting repair and rejuvenation.

04:00: At our most relaxed, the body's neurological and immune systems restore.

05:00: After 5-6 hours of sleep, our body temperature reaches its lowest, debunking the myth of thriving on less than seven hours of sleep.

05:30: nsulin levels peak in alignment with the circadian rhythm, showcasing the dawn phenomenon and its impact on glucose metabolism. Uric acid levels peak around this time in the morning.

06:00: A cortisol surge and a rise in blood pressure signal the body to awaken.

07:00: The melatonin production ceases, and hunger signals begin with the release of ghrelin.

08:00: Digestive activity increases, preparing the body for the day's nourishment.

09:00: Testosterone secretion hits its daily high.

13:00: Mental alertness peaks.

14:00: Coordination is at its zenith, a nod to our ancestral hunting habits.

15:00: Reaction times quicken, aiding in both predatory and evasive actions.

17:00: Muscle strength and cardiovascular efficiency reach their daily maximum.

18:00: Blood pressure peaks, influenced by dietary choices and daily activities.

19:00: Body temperature rises to its highest point of the day.

21:00: The onset of melatonin production signals the body's readiness for sleep.

23:00: Gastrointestinal activity slows, reducing overnight bathroom visits.

This detailed chronology highlights the circadian clock's role in orchestrating our physiological processes, emphasising the critical nature of aligning our lifestyles with this natural rhythm to foster health and wellness.

Fibre the Microbiome and our Circadian Rhythm

The hero of our story, fibre, plays a crucial role in ensuring we enjoy restful sleep. In his enlightening work, *Dark Matter, The New Science of the Microbiome*, Dr James Kinross explores the fascinating interplay between our diet and the microbial inhabitants of our gut. He highlights certain strains of bacteria, such as Bacteroides, that have circadian rhythms independent of light that fluctuate based on diet and lifestyle cues they receive. Kinross points out the detrimental impact of a poor diet, low in fibre and high in sugar and fat, on these bacteria. Such diets hinder their growth and disrupt our circadian rhythms and metabolism. This disruption, he notes, is a key reason indulging in junk food, especially during night shifts, is counterproductive to achieving good sleep.

How to Achieve a Good Night's Sleep

Piloting the seas of slumber needn't be a trip into the unknown. Let's map a course with 12 stellar tips to ensure your passage to the *Land of Nod* is smooth sailing:

- **Embrace a Sleep Schedule:** Consistency is key. Align your sleep patterns much like you align your daily routines. Going to bed and waking up at the same time every day sets a rhythm your body can dance to. Remember, oversleeping on weekends can throw off your groove!

- **Daytime Movement:** Regular exercise is the rhythm of a well-tuned life, but keep the timing in check. Avoid late-evening activities that could keep your mind buzzing when it's time to wind down.

- **Steer Clear of Stimulants:** Caffeine and nicotine are the disruptors of sleep's harmony. A late afternoon coffee can linger like an unwelcome guest, keeping you awake when you're ready to rest.

- **Mindful Nightcaps:** While alcohol might initially seem to smooth your path to sleep, it often leads to a restless night. It's better to find tranquillity without it.

- **Dine Wisely:** A large meal or too many drinks close to bedtime can be like a roadblock on your path to slumber. Aim for lighter, earlier meals to give your body time to digest before lying down.

- **Audit Your Medications:** Some medications can be the hidden rocks in your sleep stream. If you suspect they're impacting your rest, consult with your GP.

- **Nap with Care:** While naps can be refreshing, like a brief pause on a busy day, late afternoon naps might make it challenging to find sleep later. Keep naps early and short.

- **Establish a Pre-Sleep Ritual:** Engage in calming activities as your day winds down. This could be reading, gentle stretching, or listening to soft music-whatever signals to your body that it's time to transition to rest.

- **The Power of a Warm Bath:** The post-bath cooldown is a natural signal for your body to feel sleepy. Much like a gentle sunset eases the day into night.

- **Create a Sanctuary for Sleep:** Your bedroom should be an oasis of comfort. Ensure it's dark, cool, and quiet. Consider your bedding and mattress-they should invite relaxation, not hinder it.

- **Welcome Daylight:** As soon as possible after getting out of bed, seek natural daylight, as it helps keep your internal clock on track.

- **Get Up if You Can't Sleep:** Tossing and turning? Get up and engage in a soothing activity. Staying in bed, wide awake, can create an unhelpful association between your bed and wakefulness.

And I would like to add two more tips. First, here's a little bedtime hack for those midnight snackers: consider a fibre fix before hitting the hay. A small, fibre-rich snack, like a handful of nuts, a fibre drink, or some quick fibre noodles with herbs, will keep your stomach satisfied deep into the night. This trick is a personal favourite of mine, especially during extended fasting periods, to keep those hunger hormones quietly at bay until morning. Next, many people, especially women during menopause, find taking a magnesium supplement before bed helps underpin a good night's sleep.

Let's gaze further into creating a sanctuary for sleep, illuminating why a dark, cool bedroom is the ideal haven for slumber. Our forebears, dwelling nearer the equator, found their day's end naturally marked by dusk's descent and the accompanying chill in the air. This blend of darkness and a drop in temperature subtly coaxed their bodies into a state of rest. Fast forward to our era, and while our day-to-day has transformed, our intrinsic need for such nocturnal conditions endures. By emulating these primordial settings, ensuring our sleep space is both dark and cool, we can significantly amplify the quality of our rest.

Tailor your bedroom into a tranquil cocoon, drawing the curtains on the external world to ensure it remains a bastion of cool, serene darkness. This simple act of crafting a conducive sleep environment can profoundly align your internal clock with the natural world, fostering restful harmony. It's about nurturing a harmonious routine, attuning to your body's natural rhythms, and sculpting your space into a cradle of tranquillity.

In wrapping up this nocturnal narrative, we recognise that sleep's role in our lives extends far beyond mere rest. It's an integral thread in the intricate tapestry of our wellbeing. As a seasoned entrepreneur with over three decades dedicated to building companies and raising seven children, the demands of my workload often led to sacrificing sleep at the altar of productivity. My research and studies into the realm of sleep and restoration have profoundly reshaped my perception of slumber. I once championed the mantra of the relentless go-getter, advocating that life was too fleeting to spend in the confines of a bedroom. My rallying cries were phrases like 'the early bird catches the worm' and 'I'll sleep when I'm dead'. However, combining the abovementioned research and engaging in profound dialogues with medical experts has illuminated a starkly different truth. The adage that 'life's too short to sleep' is not just misleading; it's a hazardous misstep. A more accurate refrain would be, 'a shortened life might just be due to a lack of sleep.'

I will leave the last word on a good night's sleep to my buddy Dr Dan Maggs,

'You need as much sleep as you need! Don't cheat it, or it will catch up with you somehow.'

*****

Disastrous Seed Oils

You may have found it startling, perhaps even a tad disconcerting, how seed oils (and when I say seed oils, that include vegetable oils) have entrenched themselves as one of the root culprits in my *Tree of Affliction*. Harvested from crops like soybeans, corn, canola, and their ilk, these oils have seamlessly woven into the fabric of processed foods, becoming an omnipresent element in our diets. We previously discussed the pivotal battle between omega-6 and omega-3 fatty acids, agents of inflammation and champions of anti-inflammation, respectively. Achieving a harmonious balance between these fats is essential. Yet, the scales of our contemporary diets tilt overwhelmingly toward an omega-6 surplus, thanks mainly to the widespread infusion of processed seed oils. This disproportionate practice starts a domino effect, fuelling insulin resistance and impairing our body's capacity for effective blood sugar regulation.

Imagine your body's internal landscape as a meticulously curated garden, where omega-6 and omega-3 fatty acids represent two vital nutrients in the soil, each playing a distinct role. Omega-6 fatty acids are akin to the garden's defence system-protective measures that shield the garden against external threats, much like how omega-6 in our bodies is instrumental in inflammation, essential for combating infections and facilitating healing. Yet, just as an overzealous defence in a garden can lead to an overgrown thicket, blocking out sunlight and stifling growth, an excess of omega-6 fatty acids propels us into a state of chronic inflammation. Conversely, omega-3 fatty acids are the harmonious elements in the soil that foster healing and rejuvenation. They're the anti-inflammatory agents that soothe and mend the garden, ensuring its vitality and resilience. They temper the assertive defensive actions of omega-6, mirroring how, in our bodies, omega-3s counter the pro-inflammatory tendencies of omega-6 fatty acids.

In an ideal scenario, our body would strike a perfect equilibrium between these two forces. The defensive prowess of omega-6 (pro-inflammation) would be balanced by the calming, restorative influence of omega-3 (anti-inflammation). However, our modern diet, saturated with seed oils rich in omega-6, tips our garden into offensive overdrive, sparking chronic inflammation.

To restore equilibrium, we need a dietary recalibration involving reducing our intake of omega-6-laden seed oils and embracing foods rich in omega-3, pacifying the inflammatory frenzy and fostering healing and wellbeing within our body's ecosystem.

The Inflammatory Culprit: Omega-6 Fatty Acids

Envision a standard bottle of processed seed oil, teeming with omega-6 polyunsaturated fatty acids. These fatty acids aren't inherently malicious, but when they dominate the dietary scene, they become unruly guests, triggering inflammation.

When fats veer off course, the path from pantry to plate can take a sinister turn. Imagine these oils as undercover operatives in the world of fats, undergoing a process called oxidation. This transformation turns them into molecular agents of chaos, akin to free radicals, the ruffians of our cellular community. They wreak havoc, particularly targeting insulin receptors, sparking a relentless skirmish of oxidative stress within our bodies. Over time, this ongoing conflict can usher in insulin resistance, like a relentless siege on our metabolic fortress.

The very composition of our cell membranes is influenced by the fats we consume. A diet brimming with omega-6s from seed oils can render these membranes too fluid, compromising the functionality of insulin receptors. Picture a door designed to swing open smoothly for insulin's entry, but it's warped- too rigid or too lax. This disarray in cell membrane composition means insulin can't fulfil its role effectively, like a key struggling to turn in a faulty lock.

In our culinary quest, we've already hailed the heroes of healthy fats in chapter 3. Now, it's time to unmask the felons lurking in the shadows of our pantries. Brace yourself for a trip into the underbelly of the oil world, a place where the lines between nourishing and noxious are blurred by industrial alchemy. So, sharpen your discernment as we discuss the bad, the ugly, and the downright dangerous oils that have stealthily infiltrated our diets.

Sunflower, Safflower, Sesame, Cotton, and Rapeseed Oils

These oils may sound as innocent as a field of blooming flowers but don't be fooled. Their omega-3 to omega-6 ratios are so lopsided that they make the Leaning Tower of Pisa look perfectly upright in comparison, tilting as much as 1:600 in favour of the bad guys. And the process of extracting these oils?

It's often less about a gentle press and more akin to a science fiction movie, complete with chemical extractions, bleaching, and deodorising methods that might make even a mad scientist raise an eyebrow.

While our bodies praise the likes of olive and coconut oil, these seed oils are the equivalent of a dietary disaster, chemically extracted and treated in ways that are anything but appetising.

Soybean and Corn Oils

Ah, the infamous duo. These oils might as well have a 'Beware' sign attached. Extracted from genetically modified crops and brimming with omega-6, these oils are like the troublesome twins of the fat world. Heat them, and they transform into artery-clogging menaces, staging a hostile takeover of your cardiovascular peace.

Peanut and Almond Oils

Nuts might be the superheroes of the snack world, but when their oils are stripped of their fibrous sidekicks and exposed to the harsh reality of oxygen, they turn to the dark side. Just like their seed oil cousins, the extraction process of these nut oils often leaves much to be desired.

Trans-Fats (a.k.a. Hydrogenated Oils)

Enter the outlaw of the oil world. In the early 1900s, German chemist Wilhelm Normann had an idea: hydrogenate cheap fats to make them even cheaper and longer lasting. Dr Steven Masley and Jonny Bowden didn't mince words in their book *Smart Fats*, likening trans-fat to a dietary Grim Reaper. These hydrogenated horrors are often laced with chemicals, waging war on our immune system, spiking insulin levels, and earning a notorious reputation as a potential cancer culprit. While banned in Austria, Denmark, Switzerland and certain states in America, you'll find these life-shortening concoctions lurking in the shadows of supermarkets as ingredients in loaves of bread, cakes, junk food, fast food, and an entire rogue's gallery of processed delights.

Vegetable Oil

The great imposter of the oil world. Despite its name, just like Swarovski Crystal, it is not made of nature's crystals but glass; vegetable oil is about as vegetable-centric as a steak dinner. Born from corn and soybeans, these oils have hoodwinked us into believing they're the epitome of health. But the truth? They're a Pandora's box of omega-6, fanning the flames of inflammation and acting as the catalyst for many Western diseases. David Gillespie didn't pull any punches in his spectacular book *Toxic Oil*, painting vegetable oil as an antihero in our dietary narrative, inching us closer to dire health consequences with every mouthful.

So, what's the takeaway? Vegetable oils were unheard of a century ago, and cancer was a rare visitor. Fast-forward to today, and we're facing a health crisis: One in two individuals will encounter cancer, and vegetable oils have become a staple in our pantries. It's a correlation worth pondering as you select what oils you next drop into your supermarket trolley.

Dr James DiNicolantonio

'What are the bad and ugly fats? The ugly fats are the trans-fats, which oxidise the seed oils to make a more solid fat, high in omega-6, like your soybean oil and corn, a.k.a. vegetable oil. They are a huge part of the American diet and the UK diet too. When you guys cook fish and chips, they are commonly deep-fried in these omega-6 oils. They are bad for you because they are very susceptible to oxidative stress because they have so many double bonds, which are very susceptible to free radical attack.'

The second thing is that they are low in antioxidants, which compounds the problem. When you extract oil from these tiny seeds, you have to use an exorbitant amount of heat, hexane, and toxins, which even start oxidising the oils before our bodies oxidise it. The best fats are your extra virgin olive oil and your marine omega-3 from either algae or fish. MCTs, medium-chain triglycerides, are also very healthy fats; the body burns these fats even better than long-chain saturated fats and you find these in coconut oils.

I haven't included the healthy oils and fats in this section as we cover them separately in chapter 3, but as a quick summary, here is a list of the good vs the ugly.

The Good & The Ugly	
The Good	
Avocado	Meat (only organic
Coconut	Olives and olive oil
Coconut oil	Organic butter
Dark chocolate	Organic ghee
Fatty fish	

The Good & The Ugly	
The Ugly & Deadly	
Trans-fats	Oils from corn
Hydrogenated oils	Hidden fat in packaged food
Partially hydrogeated oils	Hidden fat in fast food
Vegetable oils	Fats from force-fed cows
Oils from soybeans	

As we've journeyed together through the pages of this book, a profound truth has crystallised: fat as the body's fuel is not the devil it was once publicised to be. The real culprits in the shadows are not the much-maligned saturated fats but the insidious seed oils. To reinforce your enlightened understanding, I present a graph meticulously compiled from a mosaic of data sources. This visual narrative starkly illustrates that the trajectory of heart disease aligns more closely with the ascent of vegetable and seed oil consumption than that of saturated fats. As you will notice, a precursory rise in heart disease rates precedes the widespread introduction of vegetable oils. This is likely attributable to an uptick in smoking, a factor indisputably linked to heart disease. And why has there been a positive drop in heart disease since 1990? A reduction in the number of people smoking.

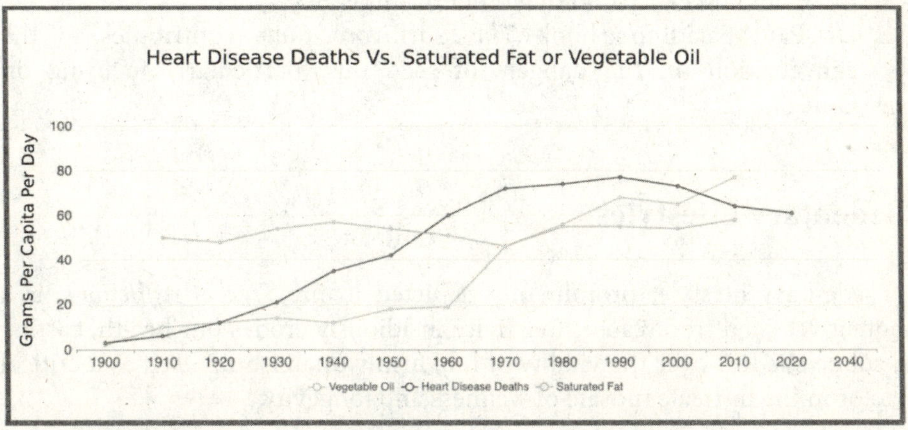

What's fascinating about this graph, and a theme echoed at many health conferences I've attended, is its similarity to other graphs presented by experts, each purporting to validate their specific hypothesis on disease causation. These graphs, nearly indistinguishable from one another, suggest a correlation between 'xyz' consumption and the mortality rate from 'abc'

disease. Initially, this plethora of convincing yet conflicting data left me bewildered. How could they all be correct? Or were experts missing the mark? Then, an epiphany struck: indeed, they were all right, but what eluded them was a critical, unifying thread—insulin resistance.

Regardless of the specific focus, all the diseases discussed in this book invariably revolve around insulin resistance. Earlier, I showcased in one graph how the surge in ultra-processed foods led to disease and in another almost identical graph how high-fructose corn syrup consumption is tethered to obesity. Yet, while the underpinning similarity across these graphs is glaring, insulin resistance is the nucleus, the core of my *Tree of Afflictions*.

I have deliberately kept this section on seed oils short, as I feel it's straightforward to grasp. However, for a more profound exploration, I recommend delving into three exceptional reads that offer expansive insights into the subject:

1. Olivia Phillips authored *Hidden Dangers*: The Truth About Seed Oils and Their Impact on Our Health, which delves into the often overlooked and misunderstood world of seed oils, exploring their history, production, and consumption.
2. In his book *Toxic Oil*, David Gillespie wrote about the health risks associated with consuming vegetable oils, emphasising the link between these oils and cancer, among other health issues.
3. Dr Paul Saladino's book *The Carnivore Code* contributes to the conversation on the dangers of seed oils, particularly focusing on Omega-6 fats.

*****

Sedentary Lifestyles

A sedentary lifestyle, prominently depicted in my *Tree of Afflictions*, is a potent yet silent root cause. Inactivity insidiously erodes our health, casting a subtle shadow over the vitality of life, firmly establishing itself as a critical factor in the intricate mosaic of wellness and longevity.

Picture your body as a vessel and a dynamic, high-performance machine meticulously designed for motion and agility. It loses its vigour when left dormant, akin to a sports car neglected in a garage. This lack of activity initiates a series of metabolic misadventures, like a car slowly deteriorating from prolonged disuse. Muscles are the engines of our bodies; they crave movement. When we're active, our muscles happily soak up glucose from the blood, using it for energy. It's a remarkable process where active muscles can absorb this glucose without needing insulin- a key factor in preventing and reversing insulin resistance.

Allow me to emphasise this crucial insight, for its significance cannot be overstated. In their state of contraction, active muscles bypass the need for insulin to absorb glucose. As depicted in the robust trunk of my *Tree of Afflictions*, insulin resistance is, at the core, the very nexus from which modern chronic ailments proliferate. Any measure, however small, that diminishes the body's reliance on insulin contributes to mitigating the plethora of conditions discussed throughout this book. It's akin to unlocking the floodgates of a reservoir, enabling glucose to stream in effortlessly.

When muscles aren't regularly contracting and burning energy, the body's overall metabolism slows down. This isn't just about burning fewer calories; it's a whole cascade of reactions. The body gets the message that it doesn't need to be as efficient in processing energy. Over time, this can lead to an accumulation of fat, particularly around the abdomen, which is a notorious factor in developing insulin resistance. It's like a factory slowing down production; everything, including how our body deals with sugar, becomes less efficient.

The good news is that this process is reversible. Incorporating regular physical activity into our lives can reignite the engines of our muscles, rev up our metabolism, and get those insulin receptors back in the dance. This doesn't mean you must run marathons or lift heavy weights; even simple activities like walking, stretching, or gardening can make a significant difference. It's about breaking the spell of the couch and getting our bodies back to their natural, active state.

Understanding the impact of a sedentary lifestyle on insulin resistance is crucial in our modern world, where sitting has become the norm. By embracing movement in any form, we can help our bodies maintain their natural rhythm, keep the glucose-insulin dance smooth, and reduce the risk of insulin resistance. It's a reminder that our bodies are designed to move, and by doing so, we can keep the intricate machinery of our metabolism running smoothly, with active muscles playing a pivotal role in managing blood glucose levels without the constant need for insulin.

The remedy to combat the insidious advance of insulin resistance and the peril of stagnation isn't shrouded in mystery; it's encapsulated in a life pulsating with intentional movement and exercise. And here's a nugget of wisdom I've unearthed with time: the value of exercise escalates as the years add up.

I once espoused the Pareto principle in the realm of health, suggesting that a wholesome diet shapes 80% of our wellbeing, with the remaining 20% chiselled by exercise and lifestyle choices like sleep and managing stress. Yet, as I have further studied the annals of health research, I'm swayed to believe that post the half-century mark, the scales tip towards a more balanced equation, perhaps a 50-50 split. There's a certain allure to this 50-50-50 trifecta, isn't there? It's as if life's wisdom converges at this juncture, nudging us towards a harmonious blend of diet and movement. So, let's lace up, get moving, and ensure that our golden years are about savouring every moment with vigour and zest.

Igniting The Flame Of Fitness

Let me begin by explaining the difference between health and fitness because even our good friend Google sometimes seems confused. Good health is not just the absence of disease; it's a harmonious balance where the body effortlessly maintains its metabolic equilibrium at rest. Fitness, however, transcends this state of tranquillity. It's the body's adeptness to engage, move, and interact with life without discomfort, not just in the stillness of today but through the dynamic waves of all our tomorrows.

In navigating *fitness*, I advocate an enlightened approach to exercise that enriches our fitness today and nurtures it for the future. It's about ensuring that movement is not just possible but pleasurable, devoid of pain or limitation, allowing us to embrace life's demands with grace and strength. So, while the lure of intense, repetitive activities may beckon, sometimes it's wise to balance the immediate gratification with the long-term wellbeing of our bodies.

Reject the notion that this chapter is merely an option, especially if your calendar is rich with years. Repeatedly, I've witnessed that physical decline is not a direct decree of age but a consequence of letting vitality slip through the fingers of inactivity. As each day dawns, exercise doesn't merely maintain its importance; it becomes increasingly crucial. It's time to shift our focus from the mere count of chronological age to the vibrant potential of our biological age. Chronological age? That's simply a sequence of numbers.

Erase the phrase 'I'm too old to exercise' from your vocabulary. Let's refine 'old' to 'older,' for we are not old; we merely accumulate a wealth of experiences. Look to those in far-off lands, navigating life gracefully into their second century. They may embody 'old,' but for us, 'older' is merely another chapter in an extraordinary journey. And this call to action isn't just for a select few; it's a universal anthem, adaptable and resonant unless serious physical constraints set the boundaries.

Let's harmonise with the two fundamental melodies of lifelong health:

- Choose natural, fibre-rich meals that minimise the requirement for insulin.
- Exercise in a manner that resonates with the everyday activities of our ancestors.

Primal Pulse: Embracing Evolution in Exercise and Health

Our adaptations to our diet and environment have been notoriously slow in the grand theatre of human evolution. Take, for instance, the curious case of wrinkly fingers and toes after a soak, a clever natural adaptation for a better grip on slippery fish and rocks—an ancient skill we hardly need when fishing at the supermarket. Yet, our genetic blueprint, etched over millennia, still plays this out, a testament to the leisurely pace of evolutionary change.

This slow dance of DNA evolution underscores a vital truth: our bodies thrive when we align closely with the lifestyle and dietary patterns etched into our genetic makeup. Our quest for optimal health shouldn't be swayed by calorie counting or the latest dietary fads pushed by the behemoths of the food industry. Instead, it beckons us to heed the wisdom of nature, to eat and move in ways that resonate with our primal essence.

My approach to health and fitness is rooted deeply in ancestral wisdom. I ponder the question, 'How long does it take for us to evolve?' a query as open-ended as the expanse of human history itself. François Jacob, a Nobel laureate, once described evolution as the work of a tinkerer rather than an engineer, highlighting the improvisational nature of our biological evolution. This perspective invites us to embrace a lifestyle that mirrors the pre-agricultural era, long before genetic modifications and the invention of gym equipment attempted to redefine human fitness.

Fast forward to the present, and it's clear we've veered far from our forebears' active, movement-rich lifestyle. Our ancestors didn't endure the sedentary trials of modern life, such as long commutes or endless hours in front of screens. A mere century ago, formal exercise was uncommon because daily life naturally demanded constant motion.

Our manifesto for movement champions a return to the fundamentals: emulating the day-long activities of our distant ancestors, blending movement with the occasional burst of speed or lift of weight, rather than enduring the monotony of treadmill marathons or the fleeting trends of group fitness classes. We aim to marry fitness with health in a harmonious union, recognising that appearances can deceive. A physique that fits snugly into skinny jeans doesn't necessarily equate to internal wellness, just as rigorous athletic training can sometimes pave the way to unforeseen health issues.

Dr James O'Keefe's research illuminates a compelling narrative: regular exercise can extend our lives by an impressive seven years. Yet, a twist in the tale reveals that extreme endurance sports might just be pushing our hearts too far. In his exploration of the human body, Bill Bryson echoes the profound benefits of exercise, showcasing how a modest daily commitment can significantly boost our lifespan.

As we steer the path of physical wellness, we embrace the principle of hormesis—the biological phenomenon where small doses of an otherwise harmful substance or stressor can have beneficial effects. This concept, akin to the subtle art of vaccination or the adaptive response to moderate stress, guides our exercise philosophy. Just as a bit of challenge can fortify our bodies and minds, our fitness regime is sculpted around the wisdom of eliciting strength through measured, intentional stress.

MARS: Charting Your Course To Fitness

It's time to embark on a fitness voyage guided by the MARS-Movement, Aerobic, Resistance, and Stance constellation. This isn't merely a random constellation of exercises; it's a thoughtfully designed master plan for enduring, vibrant health. MARS acts as our steadfast navigator, guiding us through life's undulating waves and propelling us towards a future brimming with energy and zest, even as we aspire to join the ranks of centenarians. This pioneering method to achieving fitness is a collective approach, drawing on the profound insights of athletic luminaries: Olympic rowing titan James Cracknell, international football Christian Daily, who steered Scotland to the 1998 World Cup finals, and primal movement guru Carlie Babb. Together, we have shaped a fitness pilgrimage that's not just about enduring the marathon of life but thriving in every stride.

However, let's pivot the narrative: true fitness transcends fleeting, dazzling athletic feats. Have you witnessed those gym heroes tirelessly sprinting and cycling towards momentary triumph, only to be side-lined by a procession of injuries and pains later in life? That's the very scenario MARS and LEFT-

Longevity, Exercise, and Fitness Training-aim to sidestep. LEFT is one of the many acronyms I've coined to demystify the intricate universe of health and fitness. Embracing a regime that neglects any of these four fundamental pillars-Movement, Aerobics, Resistance, and Stance, is akin to setting sail without a rudder, leaving you adrift and unprepared for the long, enriching adventure that life should be.

Movement:

Dr Martin Luther King once said, 'If you can't fly, then run. If you can't run, then walk. If you can't walk, then crawl. But whatever you do, keep moving.' This mantra resonates deeply with our objective to reclaim the motion lost in the sands of modern convenience. Picture our ancestors: no desk-bound drudgery, no cars, just the vast, untamed wilderness as their daily gym. Fast forward to the present, and the scene in Britain is strikingly different, where the battle for the nearest parking spot at the supermarket has become our modern-day 'hunt'.

As you set out on your health crusade, remember the golden rule: don't sprint before mastering the stroll. Movement is not just about the occasional burst of exercise; it's the essence of our daily existence. Whether it's a leisurely walk, a spot of gardening, or an adventurous hike, what matters is that you're on the move.

Hippocrates, the father of Western medicine, was onto something when he declared, 'Walking is man's best medicine.' It's about syncing our lives with the natural cadence of our forebears. Embrace the stroll; it's a walk and a stride towards better health.

Draw inspiration from Sir Richard Branson, an evangelist of ceaseless activity. My time with him treckking across diverse landscapes like Morocco, the BVIs, South Africa, and Bhutan has offered me a front-row seat to his dynamic lifestyle. Now in his 70s, witnessing his vitality and daily exercise routine is akin to observing a force of nature- a compelling portrayal of the power of constant movement. It serves as a potent reminder that each stride is a valuable step toward a life brimming with health and vitality.

Allow me to shine a light on another luminary in the realm of perpetual motion, Gerardo Martinez. At the venerable age of 88, Gerardo's narrative is not just about longevity; it's a masterclass in the art of movement. Over dinner one evening, this incredibly fit Spaniard, who looks 20 years younger than his chronological age, enthusiastically explained to me his secret. His daily existence, intricately woven with the rhythms of walking and swimming, transcends the mundane. It's a living testament to the enduring power of consistent, intentional activity.

Gerardo's commitment to his own two feet over the convenience of wheels began the day he set foot in his Cambrill's (Catalonia, Spain) abode. A real estate agent, to showcase the spacious garage, boasted its capacity for two cars. Gerardo, with a twinkle in his eye, gently retorted, 'That space won't house cars; it's the starting line for my daily treks.' True to his word, each dawn sees Gerardo, sans alarm clock, lacing up his trainers for his morning ritual. His so-called 'stroll' is nothing short of a brisk march, covering an impressive five to eight miles. His stride, rhythmic and robust at 114 steps per minute, defies the leisurely pace one might expect from an octogenarian. It's a routine etched in dedication, a silent ode to the power of resolve and the grace of ageing actively.

On arriving home, Gerardo swaps his trainers for swim trunks, marking the second act of his daily routine. With the beach as his stage, he indulges in a 20 to 30-minute swim. His narrative takes a whimsical turn with the tale of his last swim of the previous year. Clad in newly acquired swimwear, he confronted the boisterous waves, only to emerge, courtesy of a mischievous swirl, without his trunks. With his characteristic grin, he mused, 'Fortune favoured me with the empty beaches and streets of Christmas Eve, sparing my blushes!'

The sea's embrace relinquished, Gerardo retraces his steps, embarking on yet another five to eight-mile hike. Upon his return, his humble garage transforms into a sanctuary of strength. Here, with improvised weights - two huge water canisters hanging from a broomstick, he engages in a bench-press routine, each lift an ode to endurance. This is followed by a symphony of stretches, his movements painting the air with the grace of a seasoned dancer. From the gentle whisper of the sea to the rhythmic cadence of footsteps, Gerardo's every stride is a testament to the profound impact of movement on his well-being.

Now, very few people, me included, rack up the daily miles of Gerardo. But fear not, as I have good news for you. Traditionally, the mantra of '10,000 steps a day' has been the benchmark for maintaining health, but recent insights offer a refreshing perspective, making the path to wellness more accessible and inclusive. Groundbreaking research publicised by the BBC, encompassing over 226,000 individuals worldwide, unveils that the magic number might be more modest than we thought. Embarking on just a few thousand steps daily can significantly curtail the spectre of premature mortality[3], reshaping our understanding of what it means to step towards a healthier, more vibrant life.

While the article says that even 2,300 steps can positively impact your heart and blood vessels, unless you're just lacing up your trainers for the first time, don't stop there. But let's not view either of these numbers as the finishing line but as a promising start. For every stride beyond this initial milestone, the path to vitality becomes clearer, each additional 1,000 steps slicing the spectre of early mortality by an impressive 15%, up to the ambitious echelon of 20,000 steps[3]. This isn't just a march towards better heart health; it's a step-by-step celebration of life's potential longevity.

The universality of this revelation is striking. Age, gender, or geography hold no bias here; every step resonates significantly. And so, while we may ponder over missed opportunities, remember, the narrative of health isn't written in stone. The optimal moment to recalibrate our nutrition and lifestyle might have passed, but the next best time is now. This ethos aligns seamlessly with the essence of walking- a journey not just measured in miles or steps but in the commitment to forge a healthier, more fulfilling future. It starts with a single step, where each stride promises a healthier, more vibrant life.

> **Dr Shan Hussain**
> *'One foot in front of the other. A study presented at the European Society of Cardiology Congress in 2015 showed that 25 minutes of brisk walking a day could add up to seven years to your life and halve the risk of dying from a heart attack.'*

Bus Conductors Live Longer

Looking back into the annals of health and longevity research, we stumble upon the pioneering work of Dr Jeremy Morris in the 1940s. With an investigative spirit, Dr Morris embarked on a quest to unearth the impact of an active versus sedentary lifestyle on our health, especially concerning heart disease—a venture that led him to the bustling streets of London and its iconic red buses.

In a study, Dr Morris looked at the contrasting lives of London's bus drivers and their conductor counterparts. Over three years, he meticulously analysed the medical records of 31,000 men, ages ranging from the mid-thirties to the mid-sixties, unearthing a compelling narrative of health divergences rooted in the day-to-day activities of these two groups.

The findings, published in 1953, were nothing short of revolutionary. Conductors, with their daily ritual of ascending approximately 600 stairs, showcased a dramatically lower incidence of heart attacks—nearly 50% less—compared to their bus-driving colleagues, who spent most of their shifts in the confines of their seats.[4]

Not content with a single study, Dr Morris extended his research to the realm of postal workers, drawing parallels between the heart health of those delivering mail on foot or by bicycle and their counterparts stationed behind the counter. Once again, the verdict was clear: movement mattered. The mobile postmen exhibited a significantly reduced risk of heart disease compared to their sedentary colleagues, further cementing the link between physical activity and cardiovascular well-being.

Dr Morris, a staunch advocate for the 'move more' mantra, preached the virtues of an active lifestyle and lived them too. His personal commitment to movement saw him reach the venerable age of 99.

Post-Meal Wanderings: A Simple Strategy with Profound Impact

Here's a remarkably simple yet profoundly effective habit of post-meal walking. Earlier, we skimmed the surface of this topic, setting the stage for a deeper understanding. Now, armed with a richer knowledge of fibre, sugar, and insulin, let's explore the nuances of this delightful practice. Picture yourself savouring a meal, perhaps slightly richer in carbohydrates or sugar. Ideally, you've embraced the *Fibre First* diet principle. What's your smartest move post-meal? It's time to don those walking shoes for a gentle amble.

Here's where the magic unfolds: each step you take isn't just about progressing along a path; it's about activating your muscles and transforming them into diligent glucose consumers. This isn't merely a physical activity; it's a metabolic celebration where muscles combine to utilise glucose effectively. If you are sceptically curious, consider this experiment: Purchase a continuous glucose monitor (CGM). On one day, indulge in a carbohydrate-rich meal and spend the time afterwards relaxing. The following day, replicate the meal but conclude with a leisurely 20 to 30-minute stroll. Witness first-hand how an unassuming walk can elegantly temper your glucose spike.

And there's an additional layer of wonder during exercise. Muscle contractions beckon a protein named GLUT-4, usually inconspicuous within your muscle cells, to take centre stage. This protein operates like the eagle-eyed doorman of a club, meticulously regulating glucose entry. However, the relocation of GLUT-4 to the cell surface enhances glucose absorption into muscle cells, effectively reducing blood glucose levels—a remarkable feat achieved without insulin intervention.[5] Yes, during muscle contractions, they willingly absorb circulating glucose, bypassing the need for insulin.

Thus, every stride after a meal transcends mere digestion. It transforms your muscles into efficient glucose processors, fostering better blood sugar management and offering you the pleasure of a delightful walk. A harmonious blend of health and enjoyment, making each post-meal stroll a stride towards wellness.

Aerobic Activity: Where Less Is Often More

Imagine stepping into the fable of the tortoise and the hare, where the slow and steady wisdom transcends to the realm of aerobic exercise. It's a world where the misconception of 'more is better' often leads to a path littered with injuries and disillusionment. Picture this: scores of enthusiastic runners, a legion of pavement pounders and treadmill warriors, charging forward with the belief that intensity is the key to a trim physique and a ticket to lasting health. Yet, this high-speed chase often becomes a high-stakes game where the pursuit of fitness paradoxically paves the way to injury, stagnating weight loss, and transforming a health crusade into a detour of distress.

Let's debunk the myth of 'no pain, no gain.' Aerobics should celebrate movement, not a gruelling task ending in a chorus of aches and regrets. Aerobic exercise, true to its essence, should feel like a gentle embrace rather than a fierce battle. It's not the pulsating sprint of anaerobic exertion but a tranquil dance with your own heartbeat. Done mindfully, aerobic activity is not solely about calorie burning; it's the linchpin of cardiovascular health and a transformative force for your body's wellbeing. It's about discovering the perfect harmony of effort, where your body sings with health without being pushed into the crescendo of overexertion.

Venture into the varied landscape of aerobic options where gentleness meets effectiveness. And the good news is if the thought of running fills you with fear, you may choose not to run at all! Cycling, for instance, offers a smooth ride towards fitness, sparing your knees and hips the jarring symphony of the road. The digital age brings this experience indoors with innovations like Peloton and Echelon, turning your living space into a dynamic cycling studio, pulsating with the energy of a live class tailored for every fitness level.

If you're charting a unique course, consider the path of 'rucking'- a favourite of mine, as my social media followers can attest. This involves shouldering a weighted vest or backpack and, in my personal twist, adding the element of carrying dumbbells to elevate a simple park stroll into a captivating, holistic workout. The weight of your gear alone can usher you into the aerobic zone with little to zero adverse effects on your knee and hip joints. Rowing and cross-training also beckon as stellar choices, offering full-body engagement with minimal stress on your joints. These activities promise not just diversity but a balanced challenge for your physique, keeping your routine vibrant and your body in a state of harmonious growth.

At the heart of our aerobic expedition is our cardiovascular system. With its relentless commitment to circulating life's essence, this network deserves more than a passing nod. Within this intricate ballet of biology lives our heart, compact yet mighty, a powerhouse of potential. Aerobic exercise invites us to embark on a transformative journey, tuning this engine from a humble purr to a mighty roar. It's about enhancing resilience, enabling our hearts to meet life's crescendos with grace and energy.

True Aerobic Activity is Light Exertion

As you weave aerobic exercise into the narrative of your life, remember its profound purpose. It's not a race to the peak but a pavement of endurance, a venture where your heart finds its rhythm in the lower cadences of sustained effort. In this graceful endeavour, your heart flourishes, not by racing, but by dancing to the beat of longevity. Embrace the philosophy of 'train light to train right,' nourishing your heart with the care it deserves, ensuring its beat resonates with the melody of a long, vibrant life.

Whether you're a fan of jogging through leafy trails, rowing in sync with the rhythm of water, swimming in serene pools, or cycling with the wind in your hair, there's a magic zone you must spend your time in. Aerobic exercise truly shines in this zone, where your heart hums between 60% to 80% of its maximum beat. It's not about pushing to the brink but maintaining a steady, manageable pace.

And if you think I'm advocating an easy-going approach merely to coax you into action, think again. This isn't about taking the path of least resistance. Consider the training regimens of elite athletes like James Cracknell, who, during his Olympic preparation, prioritised time in the 'slow zone.' Christian Daily, a top-tier footballer, followed suit, dedicating countless hours to low-intensity training. I've observed Christian train many professional runners, urging them to embrace more hours at a gentler pace. Why? Because this disciplined approach is the cornerstone of building a robust aerobic system. It's about investing time in the 'slow lane,' gradually enhancing your aerobic capacity. The results? A transformation over time, where you can maintain your speed but at a lower heart rate or elevate your pace while keeping your heart rate steady.

I, too, was once a sceptic of this slower, more deliberate training method. For years, I'd been a consistent runner, but my progress had flatlined, and I'd been quick to blame my stagnation on excess body weight. However, after a year of adopting this more measured approach, the transformation in my performance was undeniable. My pace, maintained within a heart rate range of 140 to 150 bpm, improved dramatically—from 11.5-minute miles to a briskly 9.5-minute miles. This wasn't just an improvement but a revolution in efficiency, achieving more impressive results with the same if not less, effort. It transcends mere jogging; this is about training intelligently, fine-tuning your body's aerobic system to achieve peak performance with sustainable exertion.

But what underlies this remarkable transformation? The secret lies in the distinction between aerobic and anaerobic running. When we run slowly, specifically in what we term 'Zone One' (more on this in a moment), we engage our bodies aerobically, meaning our exercise is fuelled by oxygen. In contrast, running too quickly shifts our body into an anaerobic state.

The magic of aerobic running (Zone One) is that it fosters an environment ripe for mitochondrial biogenesis—the process of creating new mitochondria within our cells. Mitochondria, as we have discussed, are the cell's powerhouses, converting oxygen and nutrients into adenosine triphosphate (ATP), the cell's energy currency. Jogging aerobically stimulates our cells to produce more mitochondria, enhancing our capacity to generate energy more efficiently. This biological adaptation improves endurance, faster recovery, and a better fuel mix that leans more on fat than glucose, enhancing our long-term performance and health.

This proliferation of mitochondria has far-reaching benefits beyond just improved running efficiency. It enhances overall metabolic health, increases resistance to fatigue, and may even extend lifespan by improving the body's energy metabolism and reducing oxidative stress. By embracing slow, deliberate training, we're not just becoming better runners but cultivating a more resilient, efficient, and healthier physiological state that benefits every aspect of our lives.

A Heart Rate Zone with a Difference

As Christian Dailly embarked on crafting a fitness regimen suitable for all fitness levels, he quickly discerned a common flaw in existing heart rate zone charts. While the fitness world abounds with myriad charts delineating heart rate zones for exercise, the one he devised – the cornerstone of our program – offers a refreshing departure. It's tailored, considerate, and, dare I say, innovative.

Imagine this: you're in your forties or fifties, just beginning your recovery to fitness. Traditional charts might have you believe that merely standing up from your armchair rockets your heart rate to a borderline intense level. That's like saying taking a few steps puts you in the middle of a marathon! It's not just daunting; it's unfair, right? So, Christian rewrote this narrative. In our world, we start at Zone One, the aerobic zone, beginning at a gentle 60% of your maximum heart rate. This isn't just a number; it's an invitation-an inclusive, welcoming start line for everyone, especially those just stepping into the fitness world. If your waist-to-height ratio is less than 0.54 (on page 648 I will explain this later), I highly recommend that you undertake aerobic exercise, which could be jogging, rowing, swimming, or cycling, as long as you can keep your heart rate between just 60% to 80% of your maximum heart rate.

Zones	% of Max	How it feels	Borg Scale	HR RPE	Exertion Feelings	Energy System	Good for
0	Less than 60%	No meaningful stress on the body, good for relaxing, warming up, or cooling down. We also call this 'active recovery'.	n/a	1 to 2	Rest	n/a	Recovery
1	60% to 70%	No sweat, easy to talk and train, for some it means just slowing to a walk for others jogging.	7	3	Light	Aerobic Fat Burning	Weight loss and building aerobic and cardio-vascular systems

Zones	% of Max	How it feels	Borg Scale	HR RPE	Exertion Feelings	Energy System	Good for
1	70% to 80%	At the lower end, slightly faster jogging, but still able to hold a conversation and not breathing heavily. Towards 80% still talking, but sentences start to break up. Faster pace but still feel like you could run at this pace for more than an hour.	11 to 13	4 to 5	Moderate	Aerobic Fat Burning	Weight loss and building aerobic and cardio-vascular systems
2	80% to 85%	You can speak, but just a few words at a time. Breathing is harder. You feel you could probably run like this for 30 mins or so.	15	6 to 7	Hard	Anaerobic glycolysis system	
2	85% to 95%	Anaerobic threshold. No talking, not quite your max, but not far off. Can't imagine keeping this up for more than a few minutes	17	8 to 9	Very Hard	Anaerobic glycolysis system	
3	95% to 100%	Flat-out sprint. So fast that your heart rate lags a few seconds behind the peak. Can only maintain for the shortest of periods.	19	10	Maximum	ATP phospho-creatine	Developing muscles

I will explain more about the numbers in this chart in a moment. Our approach isn't about pushing you to the limits. Instead, it's about encouraging you to take that first confident stride, knowing you're in a zone designed for you, not against you. It's about making exercise feel achievable, enjoyable, and fair because everyone deserves the right start in their fitness crusade, no matter their age or current level of fitness.

The Tale of Two Workouts: Unveiling the Secret to Burning Body Fat

Once upon a stroll (and a near sprint), I embarked on an experiment within the leafy realms of my local park, seeking the alchemical secret to transforming sweat into gold or, in our world, burning body fat. My companions on this adventure were none other than my trusty heart rate monitor and GPS, guiding me through two contrasting exercises: the serene kingdom of brisk walking and the intensity of fast jogging.

In the first leg of this tale, I ventured into the land of brisk walking, where my pace was swift yet composed. Like a seasoned traveller, I journeyed through 3.3 miles of scenic trails, my heart beating at a harmonious 114 bpm, a rhythm echoing 60% (Zone One) of its 189-bpm maximum. This was a dance of moderation, where each step was a gentle caress to the earth beneath. Two weeks later, I embraced a different narrative. The stage was set for an intense jog, a spirited voyage of 6.2 miles. This time, my heart raced intensely, reaching the crescendo of 168 bpm, a passionate ode to 90% of its capacity (Zone Two).

Charting the two events over the same ground for the same period yields some interesting information. I had an hour of pacy walking (or I could have jogged slowly) in Zone One versus one hour of a faster Zone Two run. The data unveiled the alchemy of fat burning favours the gentle flame over the roaring inferno.

Behold the table of results!

	Walk (Zone 1)	**Quick jog (Zone 2)**
TIme	60 mins	60 mins
Distance	3.3 miles	6.2 miles
Heart Rate	114	168
% of Max	60%	89%
Calories used (approx)	300	600
% Fat (appriox)	80%	10%
Total Fat Burned	0.08lbs	0.02lbs

When we push our pace to the brink, our bodies switch gears into anaerobic mode, burning through glycogen and sugar as quick energy sources. It's a temporary fix; your next meal replenishes these glycogen reserves, making it seem like you've merely shifted resources rather than burned off excess. In my experiment, an hour of fast jogging only burned 0.02 lbs of body fat.

However, when slowly chiming in Zone One, your aerobic system doesn't clamour for immediate energy. Once you become metabolically flexible, a shift occurs when you adopt diets like the *Fibre First* diet, low-carb diet, or ketogenic diet. Your body will happily fuel its efforts with body fat.

As in the above chart, I burned four times more body fat with less effort, not more! Remember, there is no such thing as 'losing weight'; it is entirely about burning fat. And by aligning your exercise pace with your body's natural rhythms, you're not just losing weight-you're incinerating body fat, paving the way for lasting change.

Journeying through the realm of fitness, it's essential to understand the harmonious balance between effort and wellness. The secret to burning fat and nurturing health isn't in breathless, exhausting runs. Instead, it's about a serene, sustained pace where each step perfectly syncs with your breath. This approach isn't just about shedding pounds. It's about building a foundation of endurance that supports your body's overall fitness. By choosing an enjoyable and sustainable pace, you're investing in more than just immediate calorie burn. You're cultivating resilience, embracing recovery, and cherishing well-being. So, as you embark on your fitness regime, remember that sometimes, the most effective path to health is taken at a pace that lets you enjoy every step of the way.

The Grey Zone

Adherence wasn't always steadfast upon my initial foray into Zone One training. There were moments, upon consulting my watch mid-run, when I discovered my heart rate had edged up to 153 or 154 bpm—typically triggered by an unsuspected incline. These instances, where my heart rate subtly surpassed the Zone One threshold, were initially dismissed as trivial. This oversight, a subtle betrayal of the Zone One discipline, revealed a reluctance to fully relinquish old habits for the nuances of a new training philosophy. After all, what harm could a mere couple of beats per minute do? Yet, it was here, in this seemingly inconsequential decision, that I stumbled into the territory known as the Grey Zone—a realm of exercise that proved to be as unproductive as it was misleading.

Christian, my guide in this fitness crusade, illuminated the concept of the Grey Zone for me, explaining its futility. You enter the Grey Zone when your heart rate exceeds 80% of its maximum, a limbo area where neither aerobic nor anaerobic enhancements are forged. It's a stark revelation that much of my exertion in previous decades was marooned in this unproductive no-man's-land. These years of misguided effort left me drained, perpetually hungry for high-energy, yet nutritionally void, replenishments that only augmented my waistline rather than my fitness.

The lesson here transcends personal experience, touching on the broader narrative of athletic training. Whether you're a casual enthusiast or a professional athlete, the Grey Zone represents a barrier to progress, draining vitality and curtailing advancement while heightening the risk of injury. Christian Dailly's approach, emphasising the predominance of Zone One training with sporadic high-intensity sessions, has propelled even elite athletes to new heights. This strategy conserves energy and hones the aerobic system, ensuring that the athlete is prepared to unleash their full potential when the moment to 'go for it' arrives.

Ultimately, traversing the Grey Zone to the clarity of effective training underscores a universal truth: genuine progress in fitness is measured not by the quantity of exertion but by the quality of effort and the wisdom of strategy.

The Numbers, Maths and Disappointing News

You've laced up, hit the track, and feel like a calorie-burning champion. But here's a slice of humble pie served with a side of reality. That painstaking pound of body fat? It's a whopping store of 3,500 calories. Whether you're strolling or sprinting, you'll burn only 100 to 200 calories each mile. Not a great return on investment in terms of calories.

Now, let's talk about marathon maths. Imagine pounding the pavement for 26.2 miles. You've sweated, you've persevered, and you've burnt roughly 2,800 calories. Sounds impressive, right? But hold your horses! Factor in the pre-marathon carbo-loading and the post-run feast, and your net calorie burn might be a big, round zero. It's a tough pill to swallow, but here's the truth: You can't run away from a love affair with fries, nor can you outpace a sneaky slice of pie. Yes, exercise is the secret sauce to a vibrant, healthy life, but if shedding pounds is your game, remember this: the actual marathon is at the dinner table, not the finish line. Keep moving, but most importantly, watch on that fork-it's mightier than the treadmill!

The Overlooked Risks of Jogging While Overweight

Carrying extra weight and engaging in high-impact sports like jogging can be precarious. The additional load amplifies the risk of injury to weight-bearing joints, such as the hips, knees, and ankles. However, beyond the apparent physical strain, there's a subtler yet significant hazard linked to visceral fat, particularly concerning the liver.

A substantial belly often signifies a fatty liver, a condition with far-reaching implications, many of which remain under the radar, even for professionals. Fatty liver induces several physiological adaptations, including matrix metalloproteinases (MMP) production. MMPs are enzymes that break down proteins in the extracellular matrix, providing structural support to our cells and aiding wound healing. However, an overactive fatty liver often leads to an overproduction of MMPs. This excess can trigger a cascade of issues like inflammation and arthritis.

The surplus MMPs need to go somewhere, and they often accumulate in the joints, particularly the lower body joints such as the hips and knees. They are one of the few enzymes capable of attacking the connective tissue of our joints, the crucial extracellular matrix that makes up the joint structure. An abundance of MMPs, spurred by non-alcoholic fatty liver disease, can erode joint integrity, leading to pain and inflammation. If you're grappling with persistent knee or hip discomfort and carry extra weight, it might not be an injury but a symptom of a deeper metabolic health issue. Addressing your diet and focusing on reducing fatty liver can significantly diminish MMP production.

It's plausible that many individuals awaiting hip or knee surgeries and diagnosed with non-alcoholic fatty liver disease might avert these invasive procedures by adopting either the *Fibre First* diet or any of the other beneficial diets we've been evaluating. This shift could mitigate fatty liver issues, potentially eliminating the need for surgery altogether. Remember when Dr Bruckner helped the Australian cricketer fix his knee through a dietary change.

You might think I'm steering you away from aerobics at this juncture. But hold your horses; that's not the case at all! I do not intend to discourage you but to equip you with the wisdom to leap over the pitfalls and move towards the benefits. It genuinely upsets me to witness someone, particularly those carrying extra weight, pounding the pavement relentlessly. It's like watching someone trying to douse a fire with gasoline-well-intentioned, yet counterproductive.

This scenario often unfolds in a predictable pattern: the gruelling pavement marathon ends, and the runner, feeling virtuous yet ravenous, consumes more calories than the body fat they burned. The cruel twist? When the scale refuses to budge, they point fingers at not running 'hard enough.' It's a hamster wheel of effort, guilt, and misunderstanding, spinning ceaselessly. Here's the critical aspect: aerobics can be your ally only when approached with knowledge. It's about harmonising effort with awareness, ensuring each stride on the road, each pull of your oar or each pedal stroke on the bike propels you towards health, not away from it.

Tuning into the Rhythms of Your Heart: Aerobics Beyond the Basics

It's time to fine-tune our approach to aerobics, peering beyond the cookie-cutter exercise plans that blanket the fitness world. You're not a template, but a masterpiece of unique traits and rhythms. So, why settle for a one-size-fits-all workout regimen? The intricacies of your DNA, age, physique, current fitness level, and even the nature of your muscle fibres (are they more marathon- or sprint-inclined?) make you distinctive. To truly harness the power of exercise, your regimen should resonate with three pivotal elements:

- Your personal fitness aspirations
- Your current fitness
- The wonderfully unique tapestry that is you

Enter the unsung hero of personalised fitness: your heart rate. More than just a number, your heart rate is the truthful echo of your exertion levels, stress landscape, sleep quality, and even the whispers of your dietary choices. It's the unfiltered narrative of your body's journey through workouts and life's daily rhythms. Here's the deal: your heart doesn't bluff. It gives a real-time account of your workout's intensity, making it an indispensable ally in monitoring your physical exertion, wellness tempo, and even your life's symphonic ups and downs.

So, let's focus on two vital heart metrics: your Resting Heart Rate (RHR) and your Maximum Heart Rate (MHR). Think of your RHR as the baseline melody of your heart—the BPM it maintains when you're in a state of tranquillity, not influenced by the demands of standing or moving.

The health sages at the NHS suggest that a 'typical' resting heart rate dances between 60 and 100 BPM, though healthy heartbeats have been known to range from a serene 40 to an animated 105 BPM. Men's hearts, on average, hum at around 72 BPM, while women pulse to the tune of 84 BPM. Don't have a heart rate monitor? No problem. Just find a quiet moment, sit back, and count the beats for a minute. Since many factors can influence RHR, take this reading multiple times and chart the lowest rhythm to reflect your heart's resting beat.

As you begin to exercise more frequently, you'll notice a heartening trend: the fitter you become, the more your RHR reduces, mirroring the serene flow of a gently meandering river.

As you've travelled deep into the pages of this book, investing your time and attention, it's clear that your health is not just a priority but a passion. So, let me offer a piece of straightforward advice: if you haven't already, it's time to arm yourself with a smartwatch. Think of it as your personal, round-the-clock monitor of heart health. Pay special attention to your heart rate during the night, searching for the lowest BPM achieved in the peaceful embrace of sleep. This nocturnal heart rate becomes a personal benchmark on your journey towards optimal fitness and wellbeing. Challenge yourself to gently lower this number, one beat at a time, symbolising your progress. For example, if the quiet melody of your heart beats at 65 BPM at night, why not aim for a more serene 64 BPM over the coming weeks? Each reduction in beat is not just a number; it's a milestone, a tangible measure of your health's and vitality's upward trajectory.

Deciphering Your Maximum Heart Rate (MHR)

Picture your heart as a diligent sprinter, pacing through the highs and lows of life's marathon. Your maximum heart rate (MHR) is like the finishing line of its most intense dash- the utmost BPM it reaches under the pressure of a full-throttle sprint. Contrary to your resting heart rate, your MHR is a constant. It's a number that's less about your fitness levels and more about your heart's inherent capacity to withstand stress.

Understanding your MHR isn't just about hitting your peak; it's about training within your personal sweet spot. The size of your heart plays a subtle tune in this symphony. Larger hearts (often found in men) tend to have a slower MHR. It's a dance of physiology where a heart with more volume beats less frequently to circulate the same amount of blood.

Imagine your heart, once a tiny beatbox smaller than a ping-pong ball at birth, beating at a lively 220 BPM. As you grow, your heart, now the size of your fist, maintains an average MHR of 195 BPM in your 20s. But as life pages turn, your heart matures too, shedding about 1 BPM annually. And while a faster MHR isn't necessarily a badge of fitness, think of it as a large, robust heart pacing itself to cover the distance efficiently.

Calculating your MHR can feel like navigating a maze, with multiple paths but no definitive road map. The classic formula whispers, '220 minus your age.' If you're 48, it suggests your MHR might be 172 BPM. This arithmetic melody resonates with about 65% of us, yet for the remaining 35%, it's a tune that can miss the mark by a significant 20%. And here lies the quandary: You are uniquely you, and your heart beats to its own rhythm. The challenge? Even the doctors, health coaches, and trainers might judge your fitness based on a potentially way off-beat maximum heart rate.

If you're keen on a more intuitive approach, consider Dr. Borg's Rating of Perceived Exertion (RPE) scale (shown in the chart on page 570), which spans from 6 to 20. Compiled in the 1960s, it's a dance of subjectivity, with each number echoing the effort you feel during exercise. Yet, for simplicity's sake, why not embrace my company's Health Results 1 to 10 scale of perceived effort? It's a rhythm everyone can sway to, especially when fatigue turns complex calculations into daunting puzzles. It echoes the Borg's scale yet distilled into a melody of simplicity. Ask yourself: How does this moment feel? Is the sweat on your brow a whisper of exertion or a shout? Can you chat with the breeze, or is your breath a solo performance?

For the daring, physical testing beckons. It's the climax of your workout, a sprint to the edge. To uncover your heart's ultimate symphony-the MHR-you might need to believe in the metaphorical lion at your heels. A word of caution: Unveiling your MHR is about pushing yourself to the max. It's an exploration best embarked upon with guidance, for it's a path where the heart races with exertion and a dash of risk. So, if you choose this method, tread this path with care, for it's a journey to the heart of your fitness story.

Navigating the Ebb and Flow of Your Heart Rate: The External Influences

Heart rate awareness is akin to becoming a connoisseur of your body's rhythms. It's a tale of ebbs and flows, peaks and valleys. As you attune to the symphony of your heartbeat, you'll notice subtle variations in its tempo. These fluctuations are not mere quirks; they're narrators of a deeper story about your body's interaction with the world around it.

Understanding the nuances of your heart rate is akin to deciphering a language spoken fluently by your body; it reveals the precise exertion level at any given moment

The Dance of Heat, Digestion, and Heartbeat
Consider the influence of external warmth and the internal furnace of digestion on your heart rate. Picture an athletic individual embarking on a post-dinner stroll on a balmy summer evening, attire not quite suited for the temperature. Even a leisurely walk can elevate the heart rate to 60-70% of its maximum capacity in this scenario. Yes, a simple walk transforms into an aerobic endeavour under these conditions. Contrast this with a brisk jog on a crisp morning before you have eaten. You must quicken your pace to reach the same aerobic zone, pushing against the chill.

In these divergent scenarios, the unassuming jogger, swathed in excess layers, might unknowingly breach their intended heart rate zone while believing they're merely building their aerobic base and torching fat. Meanwhile, the chilled, fasted runner might fall short of the heart rate needed to ignite their aerobic engine.

The Whispers of Illness, Recovery, and Slumber
Tuning into your heart rate is like peering into a crystal ball, reflecting your overall health. There are days when your usual exercise rhythm feels unusually sluggish, each step heavier than the last. This lethargy might be the prelude to an impending illness or a sign that your body is still mending from a previous bout of exertion, tending to the microscopic ballet of muscle repair. On such days, wisdom lies in easing off the throttle, transforming your routine into a contemplative walk. It's a gentle reminder to listen intently to your body's whispers, measured and monitored via your heart rate.

Sleep, or the lack thereof, casts its own spell on your heart rate. A night of scant rest can reveal itself in the quickened tempo of your heart the following day. In this revelation lies a nudge to prioritise rest, to allow sleep's restorative embrace to work its magic on your heart's rhythm.

In the narrative of heart rate fluctuations, each subtle rise in your RHR is a chapter about your body's need for reprieve. It's a signal to shift gears from exertion to recovery, to honour the need for rest and rejuvenation. As you circumnavigate this journey, let each heartbeat be a guide, a compass steering you towards balance, wellness, and a profound understanding of the intricate dance between your body and the world it inhabits.

Aerobic and Cardiovascular Confluence

In the arena of physical activity, 'aerobic' and 'cardio' are terms often used interchangeably, yet they dance to subtly different tunes. As we immerse ourselves in exercise, our breath quickens, and our heart pounds with vigour, all in a harmonious effort to shuttle more oxygen and life-giving blood to our muscles. This symphony of increased respiration and heartbeats per minute is 'aerobic'- a celebration of life-giving air in motion.

In contrast, 'anaerobic' is the solo performance without oxygen, akin to the explosive burst of a sprinter dashing towards the finish line. Aerobic exercises speak of oxygen, while cardiovascular exercises—our beloved 'cardio'—narrate the voyage of blood propelled by the heart. Yet, in the theatre of movement, whether jogging, cycling, or resistance training, these two protagonists perform a duet, seamlessly intertwining as oxygen and blood flow converge to empower our muscles.

So, embrace the aerobics with a steadfast heart, whether you're tying those laces, grasping the oar, or mounting the bike. Keep the rhythm steady, find joy in the journey, and guide your heart rate to that harmonious golden Zone One, where health and vitality await.

Revving Up Resistance: Your Muscular Defence Against Insulin Surges

Envision your muscles not merely as the pillars of strength but as vigilant guardians in the skirmish against insulin spikes and an array of chronic maladies. As mentioned earlier, these potent dynamos can absorb sugar straight from your bloodstream, bypassing the need for insulin. Consider them your body's intrinsic sugar patrol, tirelessly maintaining metabolic order.

Herein lies the transformative allure of resistance training. It transcends the realm of mere muscle enhancement; it's about fortifying your muscular brigade to become adept sugar regulators. This strategic empowerment leads to a cascade of benefits: diminished sugar surges and a fortified defence against chronic health adversaries.

Your tactical approach is twofold. Begin by fortifying your defences with fibre-rich sustenance, ensuring your sugar levels remain steadfast and embracing the discipline of resistance training, nurturing your muscles to peak efficiency and resilience.

The mechanics of movement are rooted in muscle contraction. Intriguingly, as muscles flex and contract, they possess the innate ability to draw glucose from your blood, sidestepping the insulin pathway. Hence, even in the face of insulin resistance, muscles can still siphon glucose from your bloodstream during active engagement. This phenomenon ensures that insulin levels naturally decline during and following physical exertion. The mere act of movement renders the body more receptive to insulin, even in the absence of any fluctuations in weight. Beyond muscle engagement and the insulin-independent mechanism it triggers, exercise enhances insulin sensitivity by mitigating its known provocateurs, such as central obesity, oxidative stress, and inflammation.

Evidence from a study underscores the potency of consistent exercise. A mere 16-week regimen of regular physical engagement amplified strength by nearly half among men aged 50 to 65 and heightened their insulin sensitivity by over 20%[6]. Remarkably, this metamorphosis unfolded with no dietary alterations- a testament to the standalone efficacy of exercise, a phenomenon that resonates across genders and age spectra.

And let's dispel the myth of the indispensable gym membership. With the Health Results free app at your disposal, a treasure trove of muscle-centric exercises, many just using your body weight or inexpensive resistance bands await. Under the expert guidance of luminaries like James Cracknell, Christian Dailly, and yours truly, coupled with the ability to monitor your progress meticulously, you'll not just be on a path to muscular prowess; you'll be sculpting a more robust, resilient self. It's a narrative transcending muscle building; it's about architecting a bastion of health and vigour.

Muscle Matters: The Weight Loss Equation of Resistance vs. Aerobics

If the discussion on aerobics left you pondering the sheer effort needed for minimal weight loss, prepare for a revelation. In 1994, Dr Angelo Tremblay and his team at the Physical Activities Science Laboratory in Canada embarked on a 15-week trial to unveil the secrets of resistance training versus low-intensity aerobic exercises in the quest for fat reduction. The findings were nothing short of astonishing. The control group, dedicated to resistance training, achieved a staggering ninefold more significant fat loss benefit for every calorie spent during their workouts than their aerobic counterparts.[7]

The mystery behind this dramatic fat loss was unravelled through meticulous muscle biopsies and enzyme activity measurements. It turned out that resistance training started profound metabolic adaptations, leading to more efficient fat and calorie burning after the workout. Simply put, resistance exercises set the stage for a post-exercise calorie-burning bonanza, making them an unexpectedly powerful ally in weight management.

Now, let's dive into the numbers and juxtapose the weight loss dynamics of resistance training with that of aerobic exercises. Imagine this: a mere month of focused resistance training could cultivate an additional 3 pounds of muscle. This isn't just muscle for muscle's sake; it's a calorie-consuming powerhouse, incinerating an extra 10,000 calories throughout the month. And here's the clincher: this transformative muscle gain and its associated calorie bonfire can be achieved with just two compact resistance training sessions each week.

Contrast this with the aerobic path of jogging, where each mile contributes to an average calorie burn of 100. To match the weight loss impact of gaining 3 pounds of muscle through resistance training, one would need to undertake the monumental task of running a marathon each week.

But the journey of muscle maintenance is one of consistency. To keep this newly gained three pounds of muscular dynamo churning through calories, the evidence suggests that two weekly resistance sessions are all it takes to maintain and further enhance this potent weight loss ally. Resistance training holds a surprising and powerful edge in the world of fitness and fat loss.

The calorie consumed equation:
Run one whole marathon a week or 40 minutes of resistance training

A Concise Guide to Muscle Mastery

When starting out, resistance training is akin to opening a comprehensive tome; there's a depth and richness that can't be fully captured in a single sitting. My Health Results app offers advice for those already familiar with the gym's rhythm. It has a myriad of exercises and workouts and the ability to track your progress. If you are starting out, check out our 12-week programmes on page 960.

Now, let's distil the essence of resistance training, presenting you with a summary that, while concise, encapsulates the key principles necessary for transforming your body and elevating your health. Whether you're engaging with resistance bands, challenging gravity with your body weight, or lifting the cold steel of dumbbells, these universal principles will guide your workouts:
Personalised Approach: Ditch the one-size-fits-all mindset. Your workout

should resonate with your individuality, aligning with your goals, fitness level, and unique characteristics.

Heat-seeking Missile Approach: Think of your training as a precision strike rather than a scattergun approach. Focus on targeted, muscle-specific resistance routines that provide a potent stimulus for muscle adaptation, strength, and growth, avoiding generalised routines that risk injury and don't effectively deplete muscle glycogen stores.

Muscle Isolation: Emphasise strict, focused repetitions, tuning your mind to the muscles you engage. Opt for shorter, intense workouts that maximise muscle engagement and minimise risk to your longevity.

Max Out Resistance Exercise (M.O.R.E): Resistance training isn't about lifting enormous weights; it's about reaching the point of complete muscle exhaustion or failure after one or two minutes of slow repetitions. It's about spending time under tension (TUT) until you reach your max. This practice depletes muscle glycogen, promotes muscle growth, and increases strength. Push your muscles to their limit in a controlled manner. Focus on slow, deliberate movements. Monitor your progress and adjust the weight accordingly to challenge your muscles consistently.

Mark Lauren writes in his brilliant book You Are Your Own Gym, *'Reaching failure means that the set is to be done until another rep is not humanly possible. It requires a lot of intensity, drive, and determination, but it is well worth the effort. It is that very last rep that sends the message to your body that there is a demand for greater strength and more muscle. All other sets and reps are for the purpose of bringing you to that final point of failure, and other than that, the only use they have to warm you up, improve technique, and raise your heart rate'.*

Less Is More: Research suggests that just one or two sets on each of the major muscle groups, taken to controlled failure once or twice a week, are enough to trigger the metabolic benefits derived from placing short, intense stresses on the muscles. Quality, not quantity, is key.

Remember, resistance training isn't just about building muscle; it's about empowering your body to function at its best, reducing insulin spikes, and combating chronic illness. Begin by focusing on personalised, targeted training, and witness the transformative power of resistance training in enhancing your health and vitality.

*****

Stance & Stretch

As we wrap up our journey through the MARS approach, let's give a standing ovation to the unsung heroes: our stance and stretching routines. They're not just about standing tall; they're the choreographers behind the scenes, ensuring your movements flow with the grace of a swan in a tutu. It's not just about an upright posture; it's the harmonious blend of balance, posture, and flexibility that orchestrates your movements with the elegance of a seasoned dancer.

Picture your stance as the pillar of your daily life, not just an aesthetic attribute for the poised. It's the foundational axis around your body's well-being, the silent guardian against the creeping onset of discomfort and limitation. Good posture is more than an upright spine; it's the alignment that fortifies your body against the strain of life's relentless pace. Incorporating a thoughtful stance into your routine- nurturing proper posture and embracing the ritual of stretching isn't merely preventive care; it's crafting a lifetime of harmonious mobility. Observe the effortless grace of a child's movements-a natural concert of flexibility and strength. As time passes, our once fluid repertoire of motion becomes restrained, stifled by sedentary habits and the subtle erosion of our natural mobility.

The antagonists in this narrative are prolonged sitting that enfeebles our core, the stealthy advance of back discomfort, and the slow fade of our flexibility, which transform mundane tasks into daunting challenges. With its conveniences and creature comforts, the modern world inadvertently desynchronises our body's innate ability for fluid movement. The quest before us is clear: reignite the dormant artistry of movement, reawakening the fluidity and grace that are our birthright.

Stance: How We Hold Ourselves

Although not really a form of exercise, stance is absolutely fundamental to our health. Stance includes posture, coordination, and balance. It plays an important role in our functional ability, which is our ability to move and perform daily tasks.

Our musculoskeletal system is a chain of connected parts: our bones meet at joints; our muscles connect to our bones via tendons. Have you ever thought about why people with knee pain often discover the root of the problem stems from a completely different body part? 'Fascia' is a connective tissue that holds every muscle, organ, blood vessel, etc, in place. Essentially, it means our right leg is connected to our left arm.

Unfortunately, our modern life is causing mayhem for our functional movement. Look at how a young child learns to move. How they can bend, crouch, and roll. Now consider how, for many of us, our movement has become more and more difficult over the decades. How hours of sitting lead to weak abdominal and core strength and back problems. And how our flexibility diminishes, so even just putting on socks can become a struggle. The positive news is that we can improve all three core elements of our stance: posture, coordination, and balance.

Posture: The Unsung Hero of Health

Think of posture not as a rigid skyscraper but as a flexible bamboo swaying in the wind. While the digital age has us hunched over screens like Quasimodo in love with his bell, the truth lies in movement diversity. It's about switching positions as if changing lanes on a motorway to avoid traffic jams in our muscles. One technique I use is to sit on a balance disk whenever I am sitting at my desk. These inexpensive air-filled cushions don't allow your core to stay static. You effectively get a free gym session without leaving your chair, and for your posture, well, let's say it is almost impossible to sit anything but bolt upright.

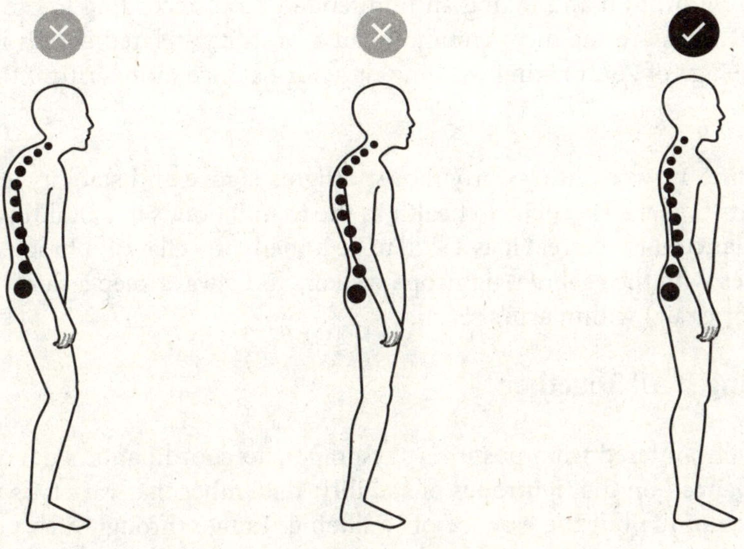

The Ballet Of Coordination

Coordination is like the city's choreographer orchestrating the seamless movement of the body's limbs in a harmonious dance of life. It's the art of syncing the body's departments, enhancing workout routines and the gracefulness of daily movements. As we mature, maintaining coordination is crucial for keeping the rhythm of life lively, enabling us to glide through our days with fewer missteps.

An actionable strategy for refining this ability is to engage in one-legged standing exercises. Initially, maintaining balance for as little as five seconds may pose a challenge for some, but with consistent practice, aim to extend this duration towards a minute. Once this initial hurdle is overcome, elevate the difficulty by attempting the exercise with closed eyes, further testing and enhancing your balance and proprioception. Interestingly, a study featured in the British Medical Journal highlights the importance of this exercise; the inability to balance on one leg for 10 seconds in mid to later life significantly correlates with an increased risk of mortality from any cause within the following decade.[8] This practice isn't just about balance; it's fundamental to enhancing coordination and ensuring longevity.

Balance: The Art of Not Falling Over

In our golden years, balance becomes the unsung hero, the difference between a standing ovation and taking an unintended bow. According to the charity Age UK, falls are the most common cause of injury-related deaths in those over the age of 75[9], making working on your balance more critical the older you get.

My online 12-week fitness program spotlights stance and stability, essential elements that are as crucial to health as the foundation is to a building. If you find balance elusive, treat it as a skill to be honed, not a flaw. Embrace stability exercises with the zeal of a tightrope walker, and always keep a safety net (or a wall or chair) within arm's reach.

Bringing It All Together

As we've wandered from posture's skyscrapers to coordination's dance floors and balanced on the tightropes of stability, remember that variety is not just the spice of life but the essence of wellbeing. Rotate through life's positions with the curiosity of a child exploring a playground. And when in doubt, laugh it off because sometimes, the best way to improve your posture is to shake your head at the absurdity of spending another minute hunched over a device.

Key Stretches to Enhance Mobility

Stretching is the encore that your body craves, the daily rehearsal that keeps the melody of movement fluid and free. The ritual prepares your muscles for the day's performance, ensuring each movement note is played precisely and gracefully.

A set of daily stretches is a simple yet profound practice that brings vitality and fluidity to your movements, ensuring spry agility well into the golden years. Even the mightiest athletes, swift runners, and formidable bodybuilders swear by it. As Charlie Rabb, a co-designer of my fitness program, puts it, 'You wouldn't bake a chicken without preheating the oven.' Similarly, stretching warms up your body's 'oven,' prepping it for the day's feats.

Here, I'll introduce you to four pivotal stretches that unfurl a tapestry of movement that can keep you dancing through life when interwoven with our stance and stability exercises.

Ankle rockers: This exercise is crucial for enhancing ankle agility, especially dorsiflexion—the smooth movement of bending the foot upward, aiming your toes towards your head. Think of it as a dance routine for your ankles.

Hip Switches: These are your hips' ticket to a smooth swivel, enhancing internal and external rotations. Think of it as oiling the hinges of your body's doors.

Prone Swimmers: A dive into enhancing shoulder mobility, these stretches don't just limber up the shoulders but also weave strength into your posture's architecture.

Cat/Camel: This stretch flexes the spine, polishing your posture while fortifying the core. Every bend and twist is a testament to your body's resilience.

I'll introduce you to four pivotal stretches that unfurl a tapestry of movement that can keep you dancing through life when interwoven with our stance and stability exercises. You can find complete tutorials on our 12-week training programme (see page 960).

Embrace these stretches as part of your daily ritual and watch as your body thanks you with the gift of grace, elegance and longevity.

Flat Feet, Straight Back

Our primal ancestors didn't strut around in stilettos or teeter on platforms. Their idea of gaining a height advantage involved scaling a nearby tree, not slipping into a pair of Jimmy Choos. It stands to reason that avoiding shoes as much as possible could do wonders for our posture and overall bodily harmony. And let's be honest, even for us gents, perpetually perched on even half-inch heels isn't exactly what nature intended. Of course, this might be a minor footnote in the grand scheme of things, and if teetering on heels empowers you to conquer the world with confidence, by all means, proceed with panache. But when solitude allows, embracing your inner Hobbit and going barefoot could spell relief for your body and soul.

Ditching the shoes isn't just a style statement; it's a fungal fight club. My own toes have waged wars with fungus for years, turning them into something less than photogenic. Today, I embrace the barefoot lifestyle, occasionally braving open-toe sandals in the boardroom, and the transformation has been nothing short of a pedicure miracle.

Now, onto the art of sitting—or should I say, the miss-art? It seems we've become a society of sitters, experts in the field of sitting still, and it's not doing us any favours. Office workers now out-sit retirees, a statistic that feels both impressive and depressing. The NHS warns that our chair-bound ways are linked to a parade of health issues, including obesity, diabetes, certain cancers, and an RSVP to an early grave. It seems our metabolism takes a nap when we do too much sitting, messing up the internal mechanics responsible for regulating all sorts of important bodily functions.

The Guardian newspaper dropped a truth bomb: we're living our lives in the slow lane—seated. They suggest standing up might be the simplest form of rebellion against the sedentary scourge, citing research that standing might be the secret to longer telomeres, those tiny caps on our DNA that keep our chromosomes from unravelling like cheap knitwear. Too much sitting could be the equivalent of snipping away at these biological shoelace tips, hampering our cells' ability to function at their prime.

The Telegraph newspaper also painted a rather bleak picture for the sit-happy seniors among us, finding that a sedentary lifestyle could age you faster than a sunbed at a retirement home. Those glued to their seats aged their bodies by an astonishing eight years. Telomeres again took the spotlight, with the sedentary showing shorter protective caps, a biological clock ticking away much faster than one might hope.

With all the hours dedicated to perfecting our seated posture, you'd think we'd have mastered the art by now. Alas, we flunk this class spectacularly, opting for slouches over straight backs, putting pressure in all the wrong places. Perhaps it's a skill that eludes us over time, for my toddler, Louie, sits with the poise of a king. While I'm no posture guru, a quick digital expedition typing ‘how to sit properly’ or ‘good posture’ into your search engine will unveil a treasure trove of tips and tutorials to keep you upright and out of trouble.

*****

Sprinting: The Final Flourish In Fitness

While our Movement, Aerobics, Resilience, and Strength (MARS) program lays a robust foundation, sprinting is the exhilarating chapter we've yet to explore. It harkens back to our primal roots, a visceral reminder of the days when speed was survival, and a burst of velocity could mean the difference between being the predator or the prey. This innate capability suggests that sprinting is an activity and a return to our ancestral prowess.

As you refine your form and fortify your fitness, consider evolving MARS into MARSS, with that extra 'S' symbolising the electrifying addition of sprinting to your regimen.

The Contrast Between Sprinting And Jogging

Sprinting diverges sharply from the gentle rhythm of jogging. They occupy opposite ends of the exercise spectrum. While jogging is a marathon of light aerobic endurance, sprinting is a short, sharp shock of anaerobic intensity. During these explosive efforts, our muscles bypass the usual oxygen and fuel stations, tapping instead into the glycogen reserves nestled within. This high-octane process releases lactic acid, the culprit behind the muscle ‘burn’ familiar to anyone who's ever pushed their limits in a workout.

Mitochondria, the cellular dynamos, thrive on this intensity. Sprinting doesn't just challenge them; it incites them to multiply, enhancing our body's energy capacity. This biological boost is a legacy from our hunter-gatherer ancestors, who, after evading predators with a burst of speed, benefited from increased mitochondrial density, preparing them for future dashes of survival. It is worth noting that a slow jog in Zone One, as we have discussed, also induces mitochondrial biogenesis. It appears it's just the range of effort that sits between Zone One and a flat-out sprint (Grey Zone) that is less effective at doing so.

Caution: Pace Your Progress

Before sprinting takes its place in your fitness regime, a word of caution: ensure your body is primed for such intensity. Sprinting with a body fat percentage over 25% is akin to revving an engine on the brink of overheating. The impact could do more damage than good, turning this pinnacle of physical exertion into a potential pitfall.

Thus, envision sprinting as the crowning glory of your transformation. It's not merely an exercise; it's the celebration on top of a well-baked, nutritious cake of fitness and wellness. Let each stride be a testament to how far you've come, and may your sprints be as swift and spirited as the ancestors who inspire us.

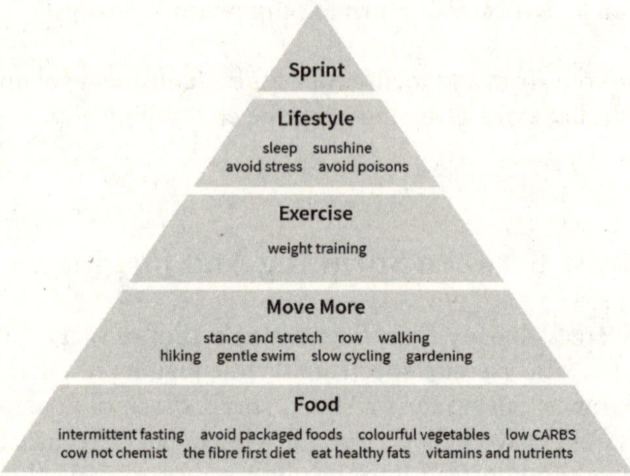

The Sprinting Edge: Unleashing Your Primal Power

Sprinting is like unlocking an ancient code embedded in our DNA. It's not just an exercise; it's a tribute to our survival instincts. If our ancestors hadn't mastered the art of the sprint, dodging sabre-toothed tigers or rival tribes, you wouldn't be here, flipping through these pages, and I wouldn't have the privilege of sharing this wisdom. Sprinting isn't just a skill; it's a legacy—a testament to a lineage that thrived on agility and speed.

The magic of sprinting lies in its unparalleled efficiency. It's the ultimate workout hack, offering a buffet of benefits from a mere snippet of your time. Imagine torching fat, sculpting muscle, supercharging your heart and lungs, and even sharpening your mind from bursts of high-intensity sprinting. Even dedicating just 10 to 20 seconds, three to six times a week, can sculpt your physique and boost your metabolic furnace for days.

But the wonders of sprinting extend far beyond leg strength. Dreaming of a chiselled core? Skip the endless crunches and embrace the raw power of sprinting. This high-velocity voyage activates every inch of your body, from the tips of your toes to the summit of your six-pack.

Sprinting doesn't necessarily involve pounding the pavement. The initial steps often unfold on the gym's stationary bike or rowing machine—kinder on the joints but still remaining fierce in intensity. As you evolve, the track or open road call might beckon, inviting you to test your mettle in the great outdoors.

Sprinting's secret sauce? It's an anaerobic alchemy, transforming every fibre of your being without needing oxygen's slow burn. This process forges strength, especially in those mighty fast-twitch muscles, demanding your heart to rise to the occasion, thus crafting a fortress against disease. But there's more; sprinting convinces your body it's in survival mode, rewarding your efforts with a bounty of mitochondria for future feats. This accelerates your calorie-burning capabilities and bathes you in a wave of endorphins, nature's own euphoria elixir.

So, what's the payoff for embracing this primal pulse? The list reads like a fitness enthusiast's dream:

- Shed pounds as your metabolic rate remains elevated long after your sprints have ended.
- Carve out core strength that goes beyond the legs to redefine your abs and glutes.
- Boost growth hormones naturally.
- Enjoy the ripple effects of lower blood pressure, lower sugar levels, and insulin reduction.
- Elevate your cognitive function; yes, sprinting can indeed make you sharper.

In the grand calculus of health and fitness, sprinting offers an off-the-charts return on investment. For a commitment measured in mere minutes, the dividends—spanning physical prowess to mental clarity—are profoundly transformative. It's not just about sprinting; it's about running towards a legacy of vitality and vigour, one explosive step at a time.

Sprinting on a Bike: The Safe Haven

The stationary bike emerges as a sanctuary for those new to the art of sprinting, offering a controlled environment free from the distractions and hazards of the great outdoors. While the allure of an open-air ride is undeniable, the focused intensity required for true sprinting finds its best expression on the exercise bike, making it an ideal starting point for enthusiasts of all ages.

As you saddle up, ideally with a heart monitor linked to your device or app, remember that precision in measurement is less crucial than tracking your progress. Begin with a leisurely pace, akin to a stroll, then, when ready, unleash an all-out effort for 10 to 20 seconds, pushing beyond your limits as if evading a mythical beast. It's a life-or-death dash in the safety of your gym or living room. After your sprint, ease back into a gentle rhythm, allowing your body a few minutes to recover. Embark on your second sprint with renewed vigour. After this, decelerate again, giving yourself time to regain composure before diving into your third and conclusive burst of speed.

Post-sprint, your mission is to document everything—heart rate peaks, distance covered, calories torched, or watts generated; choosing a consistent metric for comparison. After a triumphant trio of sprints, document your achievements, perhaps in the Health Results App, and then, believe it or not, grant yourself a whole week of rest before tackling the challenge anew.

In this brief yet potent sprint session, you emulate the primal prowess of our ancestors, mirroring their predatory pursuits and escape dashes, a testament to nature's design for our physical exertion. As you progress, play with resistance levels or sprint durations, always seeking variety to keep your muscles guessing and growing, adhering to the primal principle that diversity is indeed the zest of life. Remember, if there is an urge to do more strikes, resist; actual progress lies in the quality of the sprint, not the quantity.

One cautionary note on sprinting

While the legs are going to burn like crazy and your breathing becomes very loud and heavy, you should not feel any pain or tightening of the chest. If you do, you should immediately stop and let somebody around you know, and once you recover, go see a doctor.

*****

Exercise And Autophagy

The path of exercise for longevity unfolds like unlocking an ancient scroll of wisdom. Science isn't just a collection of facts; it's a light guiding us towards cellular rejuvenation.

Baylor College of Medicine conducted a study in 2016 looking at the mortality among bodybuilders. They identified over 1500 professional male bodybuilders who had competed in events from 1948 to 2014 [10]. They found that the average mortality rate was higher among bodybuilders than non-bodybuilders. Of course, you might say, 'Well, most of them are using anabolic steroids.' Even with that in mind, you would expect that the amount of exercise bodybuilders endure over the decades would have some bearing on their longevity. Maybe at least equalling the average lifespan of those not exercising at all, but it doesn't. Bodybuilders don't have any longevity benefits.

Let's venture back to 2017 when an intriguing study comparing Olympic athletes across various disciplines revealed a counterintuitive champion of longevity: the high jumpers. Their victory lap in the longevity stakes by several years over their marathon-running counterparts[11] hints at a fascinating nuance in pursuing a long life: it's not just about the distance you run but how you leap through life.

Switching gears, Stanley Matthews played in top-level football till the age of 50. Nobody has even come close to that in English football. Today, we marvel at Christian Ronaldo playing in his late thirties, but Stanley Matthews worked so hard on his fitness that he was still playing for Stoke City at 50 (50 years and 5 days, to be exact). While Stanley's fitness regimen promised him longevity beyond the norm, his 85 years, though impressive, suggests that, while crucial, exercise is part of a more intricate longevity puzzle.

This dilemma brings us to a term that sounds more like a magic spell for youthfulness: autophagy. It's our body's way of spring cleaning, removing what no longer serves us and rejuvenating from within. Picture this scene: Inside each cell, a tiny Pac-Man—the lysosome—devours damaged proteins and debris, ensuring our cellular landscape remains pristine and functional.

Autophagy is our silent warrior against the accumulation of cellular clutter.

Without it, we're like a city besieged by garbage strikes, chaos ensuing as waste piles up. This cellular detoxification is crucial for maintaining our youthful vitality and is intimately linked with the type of exercise we embrace.

Enter hypoxia, our low-oxygen ally, propelling cells into a state of emergency repair. It's the body's signal that resources are scarce, and it's time for internal renovations. High-intensity exercises like sprinting or lifting weights are our tickets to this rejuvenating state. Dr David Sinclair, a longevity scientist, advocates for this dance of hypoxia through exercises, suggesting that it's the golden path to maximising autophagy. Yet, as with any powerful tool, a delicate balance must be maintained. Cross into the realm of over-exertion, and we risk not rejuvenation but destruction. Cells faced with too much stress opt for apoptosis—cellular suicide—rather than repair. It's a stark reminder that moderation and recovery are just as important as the exercise itself in our quest for longevity.

Our MARS methodology, woven with care and insight, strikes this balance, promoting autophagy without tipping the scales towards cellular despair. It's a reminder that while we may seek to conquer mountains, sometimes the greatest victories are won in the restful valleys in between.

The intricate dance between exercise and our cellular well-being unveils a paradox: the very act of pushing our bodies can either rejuvenate or ravage our inner world. The 2015 study by Frank Mooren and Karsten Kruger casts a spotlight on this delicate balance, hinting at a profound truth: exercise, when harmonised with our body's rhythms, can be a fountain of youth at the cellular level. But how do we tread this fine line, where every stride and lift are a step towards regeneration, not destruction? Our 12 Week MARS Fitness Program (a summary of which we have just effectively covered), sculpted with precision, aims to harness the power of resistance training to foster autophagy, steering clear of the precipice where too much tips us into the realm of cellular demise.

Imagine walking as a gentle artist, capable of endless creation without taxing the canvas of our cells. Yet, when we venture into the realm of resistance training, we enter a dialogue with our body, speaking a language of intensity and recovery. It's a conversation that demands respect for the boundaries of our cellular landscape, ensuring that the effort we summon serves to invigorate, not impair.

Within the embrace of our MARS methodology lies a holistic approach: rest and nutrition interweave with exercise to cultivate a fertile ground for autophagy. It's a dance of oxygen, where the presence and absence thereof choreograph a cellular ballet, dictating when it's time to burn brightly and when to delve into the depths of self-repair. While aerobic endeavours gift our lungs the energy of life, the targeted strain of resistance training beckons to the hidden alchemy of our cells, inviting the transformation that spells longevity.

Furthermore, as you have already read, fasting also helps create an environment for autophagy. The difference with autophagy as a result of fasting is the whole body goes into autophagy because your entire body becomes deficient in nutrients. To remain youthful, you must incorporate fasting and exercise into your weekly/monthly routines. This way, your muscles will be in autophagy from your occasional intense bouts of exercise and your entire body in autophagy from fasting.

Another important point is to know what you are trying to achieve. If you need to build muscle after years of inactivity, then more exercise is needed at the beginning to build your vital muscles. This means a little more training and a little less concern about autophagy. However, once you have built sufficient muscles, which is also vital for longevity, your intensity's frequency should drop. This may sound a little paradoxical, but if we are prioritising longevity, then once we have good muscle mass, we want to think just as much about rest and recovery as we do about exercise.

Finding The Longevity Balance

Navigating the quest for a physique that mirrors the sculpted forms gracing the pages of bodybuilding magazines is a pathway fraught with the realities of our genetic blueprint. For some, this pursuit is fuelled by aspirations that dance on the edge of possibility, a realm where I, too, have found myself teetering. Yet, acknowledging genetics decisive role in shaping our potential is crucial. From the lengths of our muscles to the intricate relationship between our nerves and fibres, from the density of our muscle tissue to the architecture of our bones, our bodies are compositions unique to each of us. Add to this the existence of genetic regulators like GDF-8, a sentinel governing muscle size out of necessity for survival, and the landscape of our ambitions takes on new contours.

When pondering the intricate balance of muscle growth and autophagy, the question arises: does the pursuit of one diminish the other? The answer lies in understanding the phases of our physical development. In the budding stages of reawakening dormant muscles, a heightened exercise regimen is indispensable. This initial surge of activity is less about the delicate dance of cellular renewal and more about laying the foundations of strength, a cornerstone for aesthetics and longevity.

Yet, as we sculpt our bodies to our satisfaction, achieving a harmony of muscle and might, the tempo of our exertions must shift. In the equilibrium of muscle maintenance, it's here that the philosophy of longevity whispers a new mantra: the importance of rest and recovery ascends to share the throne with exercise. This transition from building to sustaining is not a contradiction but a reflection of a deeper understanding. Prioritising longevity is recognising that once the bastions of strength are established, nurturing them with as much care as we do challenge becomes the new measure of our commitment. In this transformation journey, our goals evolve, and with them, our strategies. The path to longevity, woven with the threads of exercise, rest, and recovery, invites us to embrace the complexity of our human form. It challenges us to find a balance that honours the legacy of our genetics while pursuing the pinnacle of our potential.

Balancing Act: Autophagy And mTOR

Now, let's turn the spotlight to autophagy's counterpart, mTOR (mammalian target of rapamycin), a player of equal importance but on the opposite end of the spectrum. Where autophagy is the body's way of decluttering and repairing, mTOR is all about growth and expansion, an anabolic state where muscle building takes centre stage.

Before we go further into the nuances of autophagy and mTOR, let's pause for a moment to clarify two pivotal terms that often crop up in discussions about bodily processes: catabolic and anabolic states. See your body as a complex, dynamic workshop. In a catabolic state, it's as if the workshop is focused on breaking down materials—disassembling old or damaged structures to clear space and gather resources. This is akin to autophagy, where cells perform house cleaning duties, breaking down and recycling cellular components. On the flip side, the anabolic state switches the workshop's gears to construction mode, channelling those resources into building new structures and expanding existing ones, much like mTOR's role in muscle growth and cellular expansion. Understanding this dichotomy is crucial as it lays the foundation for grasping how our bodies balance destruction with creation, each process essential for maintaining health and vitality.

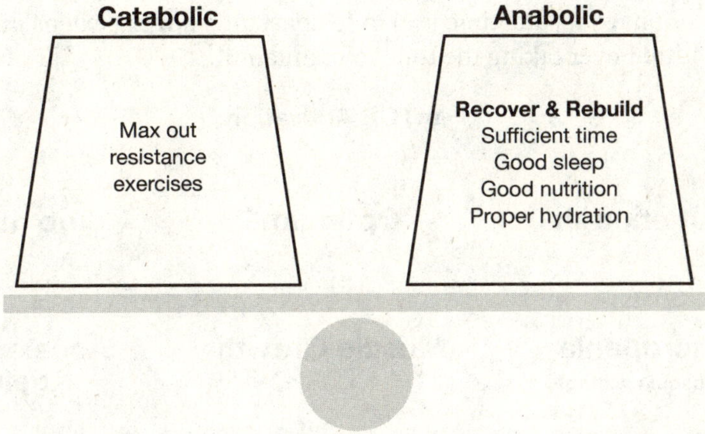

Dr Yoshinori Ohsumi, awarded the 2016 Nobel Prize in Physiology, eloquently captures the essence of our existence: 'Life is an equilibrium state between synthesis and degradation of proteins.' This delicate balance between breaking down and building up is crucial for our health and vitality. Autophagy and mTOR embody this balance in their ballet of cellular dynamics, each playing a vital role in our wellbeing.

While autophagy is akin to a cellular renovation, clearing out the old to make way for the new, mTOR is the architect of growth, pushing us towards strength and muscle development. However, as with all things in life, moderation is key. An overzealous engagement with mTOR can lead to accelerated ageing and certain cancers, whereas not enough mTOR activity nudges us toward sarcopenia, the gradual loss of muscle mass.

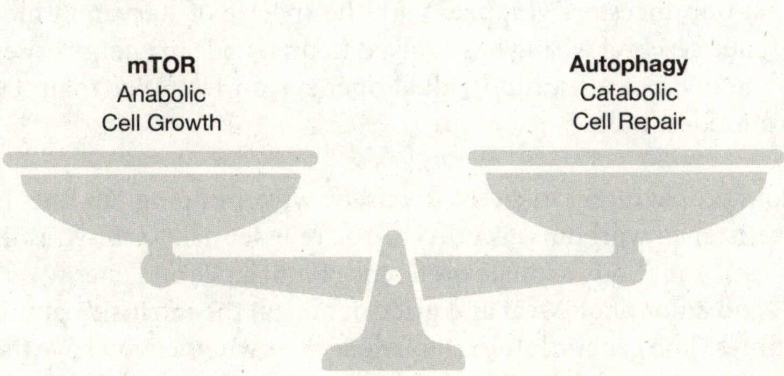

This is where the genius of the MARS programs shines, striking a harmonious balance that encourages muscle building while allowing for the necessary cellular clean-up. Immersing yourself in a perpetual state of mTOR without giving autophagy its due time is akin to constantly adding extensions to your house without ever taking the time to maintain it.

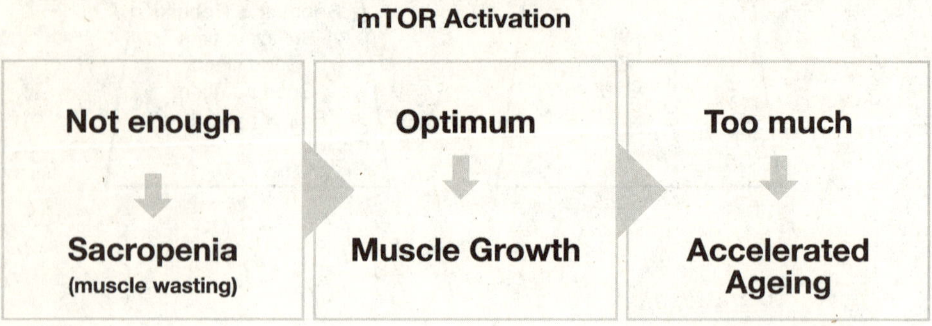

The art of fitness is not about daily gym pilgrimages but about a strategic approach to exercise, alternating muscle groups to allow each their time to grow and their time to heal. Remember, overtraining is a double-edged sword that can dampen the benefits of autophagy and lead to untimely apoptosis—cell death—instead of fostering growth and health.

*****

Why You Might Find It Hard To Build Muscle

Muscle development can sometimes feel like an uphill battle against your own biology. Here's the twist: Nature, in its quest for efficiency, isn't keen on you packing on muscle mass. The brain perceives muscle as a high-maintenance tenant, guzzling more energy than its couch-potato counterpart, body fat. Given that our ancestors grappled with the spectre of starvation more often than not, our cerebral wiring has evolved to prefer a lean energy expenditure. Indeed, the body of a lean individual operates on less juice than it takes to light up a modest bulb.[12]

This biological conservatism is precisely why ramping up the intensity during resistance workouts, is crucial. You're essentially arm-wrestling with homeostasis, your body's innate preference for balance and energy thriftiness. However, no amount of sweat and grit can morph the intrinsic nature of your muscle fibres. The genetic lottery at birth decides whether you have the quick-fire, fast-twitch fibres of an Olympic sprinter or the endurance-friendly, slow-twitch fibres of a marathon champion. Yet, hope isn't lost for the intermediary fibres, which, with dedicated training, can adapt characteristics resembling either fibre type.

Let's talk about comfort zones or the necessity of stepping out of them. Resistance training demands this exit strategy from your cosy nook, pushing you to embrace the discomfort accompanying muscle growth. This starkly contrasts aerobic exercises, where the mantra is 'train light to train right'. The adage 'no pain, no gain', while somewhat applicable to the targeted discomfort in resistance training, should never cross paths with aerobic activities.

To truly sculpt those muscles, progression (or progressive overload) is your best friend. Every session should see you lifting a tad heavier or pushing a tad longer than before. It's about setting a new benchmark with each workout, constantly challenging your muscles to adapt and grow. Remember, improvement isn't ageist; it's achievable at any stage of life.

And if you need a little more inspiration to tackle each workout with gusto, channel your inner Arnold Schwarzenegger, in his words, 'approach every rep and set with a blend of joy and ferocity.' It's not just about building muscle; it's about revelling in the challenge and the pathway toward a stronger, more resilient you.

Final Stretch: Key Takeaways On Exercise And Fitness

As we conclude this extensive section on exercise and fitness, allow me to recap a dozen key highlights that I hope have been clearly established.
MARS: Our quartet, Movement, Aerobics, Resistance, and Stance, form the foundation of a fitness philosophy designed for life, optimising your body's innate capabilities.

The MARS Blueprint: We want to achieve maximum results for a minimal investment of time and also make physical activities enjoyable and fun. Otherwise, there is a high risk that, like millions of other individuals, they will eventually become abandoned.

MARS is for Everyone: It is a training plan for the sport of life. It suits adolescents and senior citizens, from novices to professional athletes.
Changing Priorities: As we age, exercise potentially plays a more dominant role in our longevity strategy, with our muscles and cardiovascular fitness our greatest assets.

LEFT: All exercises should be approached with LEFT in mind: Longevity Exercise and Fitness Training.

Older, not Old: You are never old, just older, and it's never too late to begin exercising. Highlighting the importance of exercise as we age, fitness author Dr Ben Bocchicchio says, 'we must continue to exercise until two days after you die to make sure you're dead.'

The MARS Pace: Slow and steady not only wins the race but also makes it a joyride. With MARS, the thrill of the chase is in the pace, making every session as delightful as it is beneficial.

The Art of Recovery: Honour the silence between the notes—the rest and recoveries composing the symphony of fitness.

Aerobic Wisdom: Finish every session as if you could do it again, but leave nothing in the muscles when performing resistance training.

Echoing Hippocrates: Balance is essential. The right amount of exercise, neither too scant nor excessive, is the golden rule laid down millennia ago.

The Training Trifecta: Everything we do in training induces adaptations in our respiratory, cardiovascular, and musculoskeletal systems to help individuals remain fitter for life.

Your Most Important Home: Your body is the single most important physical thing you will ever own. People say your house is your home, but in reality, your permanent home – the one you will never leave – is your body, so look after it.

In sum, our quest for longevity through exercise is a nuanced symphony; each movement—from the gentle sway of walking to the explosive power of a sprint—plays its part in life's grand composition. It's about embracing the intensity that speaks to us, ensuring our cellular orchestra plays on harmoniously and vibrantly into the depths of time.

HEALTH WARNING:

If you have a heart condition, are pregnant, or don't currently do any other exercises, we recommend you speak to your doctor first. If you experience chest pain during exercises, stop immediately and seek urgent medical help.

*****

Cholesterol: The Greatest Con Of All

Cholesterol, that waxy, fat-like substance coursing through our veins, has been cast as the villain in a health drama of almost mythical proportions, shadowed by misinterpretation and shrouded in controversy. In this world, facts are often overshadowed by the lucrative narratives spun by the enormous pharmaceutical statin empires, a narrative convoluted as any ancient myth.

Far from the wicked character it's been depicted, cholesterol is, in fact, the unsung hero of our bodily functions, crucial for our survival and flourishing. Dr Malcolm Kendrick, in his enlightening book *The Great Cholesterol Con*, invites us to ponder a simple yet profound question regarding the cholesterol-rich yolk of an egg, challenging the demonisation of this essential molecule and highlighting its indispensability for development and vitality; he asks, 'Why do you think that an egg yolk is full of cholesterol? Answer: Because it takes one hell of a lot of cholesterol to build a healthy chicken. It also takes one hell of a lot of cholesterol to build and maintain a healthy human being.'

Cholesterol's résumé is impressive and extensive. It plays vital roles in synthesising vitamin D—our shield against a litany of health woes, including several cancers—and crafting sex hormones.

As we traverse this subject, we'll hack through the thicket of myths to reveal the sturdy trunk of truth about cholesterol, examining its essential contributions to our health. Join me as we illuminate the shadowy paths with the torch of knowledge, seeking a nuanced appreciation of cholesterol's correct place in our wellness and its narrative.

Cholesterol's Double-Edged Sword: The Atherosclerosis Conundrum

While cholesterol is undeniably crucial for our existence, its narrative takes a complex turn when considering its potential role in atherosclerosis (a type of heart disease). This condition, characterised by plaque build-up within the arteries, has been a focal point in the discourse surrounding cholesterol's potentially darker side. Atherosclerosis is a stealthy architect of arterial obstruction, crafting layers of plaque that gradually seize the space within these vital vessels, which are responsible for ferrying oxygen-rich blood to our heart and the far reaches of our body.

This process doesn't happen overnight; it's a slow, insidious progression that may span decades. The genuine concern emerges during the intermediate phase, known as unstable plaque, where the risk is most pronounced. Before the plaque solidifies and arteries harden, they are in a precarious state, vulnerable to rupture and capable of unleashing dire consequences.

These plaques aren't just confined to the corridors leading to our hearts. They traverse our bodily landscape, setting up blockades in regions like the carotid arteries in the neck. Here, they morph into ticking time bombs, breaking away and drifting towards the brain, where they can lodge themselves in narrower arteries, often culminating in a stroke.

But here's where the plot thickens: the presence of LDL cholesterol, often labelled as the 'bad' cholesterol, in these arterial plaques isn't the whole story. Pinning the blame solely on LDL is akin to condemning the smoke alarm for the fire it signals-it's merely a messenger in a larger, more intricate narrative. Understanding cholesterol's role in our body's ecosystem requires us to look beyond the simplistic good versus bad dichotomy, diving into the depths of this molecule's multifaceted role in our health and wellbeing.

Decoding Cholesterol

On a report from our GP, we often encounter a quartet of measurements that are supposed to serve as signposts, guiding us through the intricate landscape of our lipid profile and cholesterol profiles:

HDL-High-Density Lipoproteins: Often hailed as the 'good cholesterol,' HDL is akin to a diligent street cleaner of our bloodstream, whisking away excess cholesterol and escorting it to the liver for disposal. It's the friendly neighbourhood guardian, maintaining order and promoting arterial cleanliness. And at least thus far in our story, this assertion holds true. We should frequently measure our HDL cholesterol and ensure it is high enough.

LDL-Low-Density Lipoproteins: Traditionally labelled as the 'bad cholesterol,' LDL's reputation is more a tale of misunderstood intentions than villainy. While it's true that LDL can be found in blocked arteries, it may, as you will discover, be a marker of poor health, not the cause. In fact, LDL is essential for many bodily functions, from hormone production to cell structure integrity. It's a molecule that's more misunderstood than inherently harmful.

Cholesterol Ratio: This figure represents the balance between our HDL and LDL levels. It's the seesaw of our lipid profile, offering insights into the equilibrium (or lack thereof) between these key players.

Total Cholesterol: The grand sum of our cholesterol story. This number sums the HDL, LDL, and other lipid components. It provides an overview, painting a broad picture of our total cholesterol landscape. And, if it were true that HDL is good cholesterol and LDL is bad cholesterol, then this metric would be nonsensical because it wouldn't tell you anything meaningful.

As we walk through these measurements, it's crucial to remember that the story of cholesterol is nuanced and multi-layered. It's not a tale of heroes and villains but a complex interplay of molecules, each with its role and significance in the grand opera of our bodily functions.

The Lipoprotein Ensemble

Think of lipoproteins as tiny, complex ships navigating the vast ocean of our bloodstream. These microscopic vessels, a fusion of fats (lipids) and proteins, are ingeniously designed to ferry their cargo-cholesterol and triglycerides, insoluble substances. Like skilled mariners, they ensure these essential lipids are transported in harmonious association with proteins, enabling their safe passage through our body's waterways.

Envision this dynamic fleet, where each vessel, from the Very Low-Density Lipoproteins (VLDL) to the Low-Density Lipoproteins (LDL) and the High-Density Lipoproteins (HDL), has a distinct role and structure. It's not the weight that distinguishes them but their composition- a meticulous balance of lipids and proteins. In this vast ocean, LDLs emerge as robust cargo ships; their holds brimming with lipid treasures, making them less dense and lighter than their protein-rich counterparts. These vessels are not merely transporters but vital connectors, delivering cholesterol to various cellular destinations across our body.

In contrast, HDLs are akin to waste collection vessels. They diligently patrol the bloodstream, gathering cholesterol from where it's not needed and transporting it to the liver, our body's recycling centre, for disposal or reuse. This crucial task of HDLs helps maintain a clean and functional circulatory system.

While LDLs have been cast as the villains, ferrying cholesterol to our blood vessels, and HDLs as the heroes, clearing it away, the reality is more nuanced. Both types of lipoproteins are essential in the intricate ballet of lipid transport and metabolism. It's not just about good versus bad but about balance, coordination, and the seamless operation of a system that's fundamental to our well-being.

Saturated Fat And LDL

Here's a question that sparks endless debate: does consuming foods high in saturated fat elevate the levels of the so-called villain, LDL cholesterol? The answer, it seems, isn't found in avoiding cholesterol-rich foods but rather in avoiding sugar-laden chow (especially fructose), addressing lifestyle factors such as weight management, exercise, and stress reduction. Reflecting on my past, I vividly recall a time when my LDL levels peaked. It was a period marked by my obesity, relentless stress from launching a new business venture, and a glaring absence of physical activity, a trio that, in hindsight, aligns perfectly with the contemporary understanding of elevated LDL cholesterol.

It's time to demystify a longstanding misconception- the notion that the saturated fat we consume directly hikes up our LDL cholesterol levels. Dr Malcolm Kendrick, author of three books on the heart and cholesterol, explains, 'Saturated fat is absorbed into the gut wall, where it's then packed into the very large lipoprotein known as chylomicron. This travels up a special tube called the thoracic duct. At the end of which, it is released directly into the bloodstream. Directly into the bloodstream. It does not pass through the liver, which is a mission-critical point.'

This revelation leads us to confront a medical hypothesis that, for years, was accepted almost universally: the belief that eating foods high in cholesterol invariably spikes our blood cholesterol levels. Yet, this hypothesis crumbles under the weight of emerging insights. It turns out that just as eating fat doesn't inherently lead to weight gain, reducing our cholesterol intake doesn't automatically lower our blood cholesterol levels. So, the long-held notion of shunning eggs, prawns, and meats-dietary staples notorious for their cholesterol content, might be an exercise in futility, even for those grappling with high cholesterol levels, which, as we're starting to understand, may not be as detrimental as it's portrayed.

Chylomicrons: The Body's Fat Transporters

Imagine chylomicrons, a specialised type of lipoproteins, small cargo ships navigating the vast bloodstream. These tiny vessels are tasked with a crucial mission: transporting fats from the intestines, where they are absorbed, to various cells in the body. Chylomicrons distribute their fatty cargo as they travel through our blood vessels, gradually shrinking in size. The remnants of this process, known as chylomicron remnants, eventually transform into what is commonly labelled as 'bad cholesterol' or LDL (Low-Density

Lipoprotein). This transformation is a testament to the body's intricate mechanisms, revealing that only a fraction of the fats we consume actually reach the liver for processing; the majority are directly absorbed by cells. This fascinating voyage of chylomicrons not only illustrates the complex nature of fat transportation in our body but also sheds light on the nuanced role of LDL in our health.

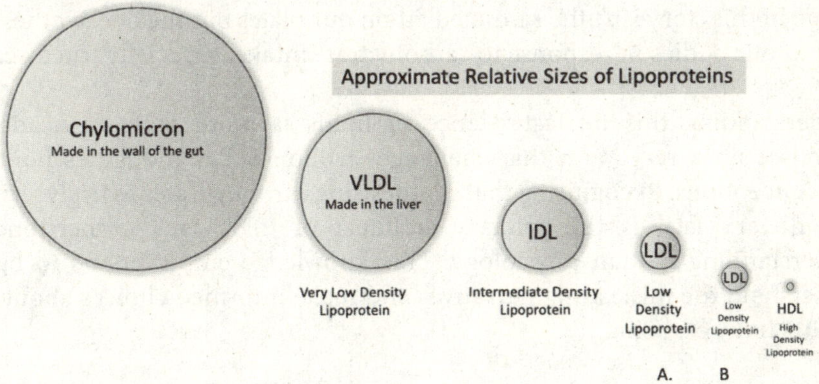

This process isn't exclusive to a particular type of fat; it's universal. Be it saturated fat, seed oils, or olive oils, the journey is the same. This revelation brings an alarming insight: dangerous seed oils and vegetable oils bypass the liver's scrutiny, potentially causing direct damage to your cells. It's a stark reminder that fats' absorption, transportation, and storage are intricately linked yet surprisingly disconnected from LDL cholesterol levels. This casts a shadow of doubt on products like low-cholesterol butter, revealing a potentially misleading narrative, as regular butter, in reality, doesn't elevate LDL levels.

Drifting further into this lipid pilgrimage, we discover that while chylomicrons are birthed in the gut walls, the liver is the cradle of VLDL (Very Low-Density Lipoproteins). Contrary to the belief that LDL is inherently 'bad', it doesn't originate from sinister sources. Instead, it emerges as VLDL relinquishes its fat to cells, morphing into ILD and eventually transforming into LDL. This means that LDL is a derivative of VLDL, a liver-born molecule.

Dr Malcolm Kendrick presents a compelling perspective: VLDL's primary mission is to distribute fatty acids from the liver for storage. Once VLDL dwindles into LDL, it embarks on a secondary, vital mission-delivering cholesterol to needy cells. And here lies the twist in our tale: the rise in VLDL levels isn't orchestrated by saturated fat consumption but by carbohydrates-the everyday staples like bread, pasta, and even the seemingly innocuous cornflakes.

As Dr Kendrick aptly puts it, LDL is not cholesterol incarnate in this lipid narrative. It's merely a container that houses cholesterol, much like a car isn't human just because it transports people. This distinction is pivotal in debunking the myths surrounding saturated fats and cholesterol. The real rogue in this story isn't the saturated fat on our plates but the one synthesised within our bodies in response to carbohydrate intake, especially fructose.

Understanding this intricate dance of lipids is more than an academic exercise; it's a revelation that challenges trillion-dollar industries built on misconceptions. Recognising that synthesising carbohydrates to triglycerides, not dietary fats, is the primary architect of LDL, is a cornerstone of understanding human physiology. This knowledge empowers us to better understand the misleading narratives and make informed choices about our health and well-being.

The Cholesterol Conundrum

The pursuit of understanding cholesterol levels, whether total cholesterol or the notorious LDL, is shrouded in controversy and, quite possibly, misconceptions. It's a voyage that has lucratively benefited the pharmaceutical sector. The statin industry has burgeoned into a colossal enterprise. In the UK alone, about 7-8 million adults are prescribed statins, culminating in over 71 million annual prescriptions.[13]

However, the narrative surrounding cholesterol is complex and often contradictory. Barry Groves, PhD, a renowned cholesterol specialist, suggests in his revealing interview that an overarching fixation on low cholesterol levels might be misguided. According to Groves, emerging research indicates that excessively low cholesterol could be more detrimental than beneficial, potentially heightening the risk of a spectrum of diseases and even leading to premature death. Groves points out the increased vulnerability to infectious diseases, cancer, and Alzheimer's associated with low cholesterol levels.

For those already navigating life with statins for high cholesterol, it might be time for a paradigm shift. A prudent first step could be to explore Dr Malcolm Kendrick's illuminating work, *The Great Cholesterol Con*. This eye-opening read might offer a new perspective on the statin narrative, prompting a well-informed dialogue with your GP.

The enigma deepens when considering global cholesterol statistics. Switzerland, for instance, reports the highest cholesterol levels worldwide yet boasts the 4th lowest mortality rate from cardiovascular diseases (CVD). Furthermore, the extensive 'HUNT2 Study' conducted in Norway, encompassing 50,000 individuals over 15 years, unveiled an intriguing paradox. Contrary to conventional wisdom, the study found that older individuals with higher LDL cholesterol levels enjoyed longevity comparable to, if not exceeding, those with lower levels. Yes, you read that correctly: higher LDL levels meant they lived longer!

In the intricate web of cholesterol opinion, it's clear that the story is far from one-dimensional. Much of what we have been told over the past decades has most likely been influenced by the pursuit of money, not health.

Dr Aseem Malhotra
I co-authored some original research with Dr Malcolm Kendrick and 16 international scientists, where we looked at the association of the so-called bad cholesterol LDL with heart disease in people over 60. There was an inverse association with death. In other words, the higher your LDL, the less likely you are to die. I remember when we published the paper, I wrote about it in The Telegraph, and I talked about a lady who came to see me. She was in her early 60s, and when she walked into the consultation room, she was as white as a ghost. I asked her what was wrong, and she said she was worried because her doctor had told her that her cholesterol was high. I turned to her and said, congratulations, you are going to live longer. I explained everything to her, and she left the consultation reassured and happy.

The Cholesterol Clot Thickens

After discussing the trio of cholesterol types, we now stand at the threshold of a more nuanced chapter in the cholesterol saga. The story is far from straightforward, unfolding a layer of complexity beyond standard categorisation. In this evolving narrative, we encounter the distinct subtypes of LDL cholesterol: LDL-pattern A and LDL-pattern B, each with unique characteristics and implications for our health. This recent revelation broadens our understanding, steering us away from the general umbrella of LDL and inviting us to explore the intricate dynamics of these two LDL subtypes.

The axiom 'bigger is better' finds its place in the realm of cholesterol particles, specifically LDL. It turns out that size does matter when it comes to LDL, with each type playing a distinct role in our body's cholesterol tale. LDL-A, the larger, buoyant type, is now considered far less threatening and potentially even beneficial. In contrast, LDL-B, which is smaller and denser, is now recognised as the more ominous indicator in the cholesterol game.

Moreover, the plot intertwines with the realms of glucose, fructose, and insulin. It's a multifaceted interaction where the intricacies of LDL pattern B and inflammation take centre stage. Despite these revelations, the conventional medical approach often remains anchored in measuring total LDL cholesterol. Many physicians continue to prescribe statins based on these broader measurements, overlooking the critical nuances of LDL subtypes and the pivotal role of inflammation.

In this evolving story of cholesterol, it's clear that understanding the nuances of LDL pattern B and its interplay with inflammation is paramount. As science continues to peel back the layers, the narrative of cholesterol, heart disease, and treatment becomes a tale not just of numbers but of understanding the deeper, more nuanced interactions within our bodies.

Let me make it crystal clear. Both Dr Philip Ovadia, a heart surgeon and author of *Stay of my Operating Table* and Dr Ben Bikman, both of whom I recently discussed this topic with at a health conference in Miami, clearly explain how large buoyant LDL-A -particles are associated with a reduced risk of developing cardiovascular disease. In contrast, pattern B particles are associated with an increased risk of developing cardiovascular disease. In other words, what was once considered bad cholesterol must be further divided into good and bad guys.

Now, the profit-driven clot really thickens. Statins, those pharmaceutical drugs heralded as guardians against heart woes, show a preference for lowering LDL Pattern A, the good guys. Yet, the elusive LDL Pattern B casts a shadow over heart health, and statins seem to overlook it. It sounds like a trillion dollars were spent in the wrong direction, right?

How do I know if I have pattern A or pattern B LDL?

This brings us to a pivotal yet often overlooked heart disease risk assessment metric: the triglycerides-to-HDL ratio. This ratio isn't just a number; it's a storyteller, revealing the tale of small, dense LDL Pattern B particles lurking in our bloodstream.

Triglycerides often morph into this concerning LDL Pattern B, setting the stage for potential heart concerns. By measuring triglycerides (TG), we glimpse at the LDL Pattern B narrative unfolding in our bodies. Dividing the triglycerides level by the HDL level offers us a surprisingly astute ratio in unveiling the LDL size plot. Ideally, this ratio should be smaller than 1.3, though up to two still paints a relatively reassuring picture.[14]

Let's borrow wisdom from Professor Ben Bikman. He enlightens us, stating, 'TG [triglycerides], LDL, and HDL form a triad. But within this trio, we find a powerful tool: the triglycerides-to-HDL ratio, a beacon guiding us through the fog of LDL size.' To paint a clearer picture, envision a football and a golf ball travelling down a river. The football, buoyant and carefree, mirrors the nature of LDL Pattern A particles, now seen in a new, positive light. But the golf ball, with its denser constitution, trundles along the riverbed, occasionally finding itself ensnared, akin to the more perilous LDL Pattern B particles. These tiny, dense particles have a knack for wedging themselves in less-desired places, echoing the risks they pose to our cardiovascular health.[15]

Determining Your LDL Type: A Guide to Triglycerides and HDL Ratios

A ratio calculation between triglycerides and HDL cholesterol is key to ascertaining the nature of your LDL cholesterol. This ratio is determined by taking blood samples in a fasted state, dividing the triglyceride level by the HDL level. Striving for a ratio as close to 1 as possible is beneficial. Dr Richard Maurer indicates that a reading of 3 significantly heightens the risk of cardiovascular disease. The overarching message is clear: maintaining a low ratio through a nutritious diet and regular exercise is pivotal.

Dr Maurer writes, 'The TG to HDL ratio is a potent indicator of lifestyle factors. It reveals if your metabolism naturally provides cardiac protection or if you need to cultivate it actively.' He references studies involving 3,000 individuals categorised by prevalent risk factors for heart attack and stroke—smoking, hypertension, or inactivity. In all categories, those with higher TG to HDL ratios (greater than 3) experienced the most heart attacks and strokes. Conversely, those with the lowest ratio (less than 1 to 1) had the fewest, illustrating a direct correlation between the TG to HDL ratio and the incidence of cardiovascular events.[16]

How confident am I in asserting that the ratio between HDL and triglycerides holds more significance than the total LDL level? Totally. As you might recall, I've previously introduced our HRM 360 test equipment (see page

954 for more details). This home device allows measuring cholesterol levels, including HDL, LDL, and triglycerides, through a simple finger prick. However, we've deliberately designed its home screen to display only the HDL and triglyceride measurements. Why? We aim to steer medical professionals away from overemphasising the LDL figure, which we view as a red herring, and instead focus on the pivotal relationship between HDL and triglycerides. This ratio is the signal that clearly indicates the pattern of your LDL.

And let me be clear: even pattern B of LDL isn't the root problem; it's an indicator, a symptom of a more significant issue. Imagine your bloodstream as a river and LDL pattern B as logs floating in it. If there's a narrowing (indicative of poor health), logs (LDL pattern B) start accumulating. The logs aren't creating the blockage; they're merely getting caught in it. Or picture your body as a car and LDL pattern B as the check engine light. The light doesn't cause engine issues; it's an alert signalling that your car (body) requires attention. Similarly, a thermometer displays a high temperature when you have a fever, reflecting your body's response to an infection. Like LDL pattern B, the thermometer isn't causing the fever; it's simply mirroring an underlying condition.

These analogies are vital to highlight because this crucial understanding still eludes much of the medical world despite its acceptance among the doctors at the medical conferences I attend and those in our circle. Why is this the case? It's an inconvenient truth for the pharmaceutical industry, which profits from selling drugs to lower LDL levels. Addressing only LDL is akin to removing the warning light in your car or the smoke detector in your home. These actions merely obscure the symptom without tackling the actual problem. This discrepancy between knowledge and practice is a source of my frustration, and it's a narrative we need to change for a more informed approach to health and well-being.

Navigating Dyslipidaemia: The Path to Balanced Lipids

When the balance of HDL cholesterol and triglycerides tilts unfavourably, it may signal a condition known as dyslipidaemia. This imbalance often stems from an overproduction or inadequate clearance of triglycerides coupled with insufficient production of HDL. The implications of this imbalance are far-reaching. On the other hand, a favourable ratio signifies that insulin efficiently ushers sugar from the bloodstream into the cells, showing robust insulin sensitivity and a lowered risk of diabetes and metabolic syndrome.

The silver lining? Shifting these numbers towards a healthier equilibrium is often within reach, with dietary adjustments and an uptick in physical activity. It appears that achieving an optimal ratio goes hand in hand with maintaining a commendable level of aerobic fitness. Insights from a study published by the National Library of Medicine in March 2021 shed light on the prevalence of metabolic dyslipidaemia (elevated triglycerides and low HDL cholesterol) among individuals with type 2 diabetes. The study, which researched data from 4,199 overweight individuals with type 2 diabetes, underscored the link between dyslipidaemia and heightened risks of cardiovascular disease. Encouragingly, the study also echoed the sentiment that many can reverse this condition by embracing changes in their dietary habits and exercise routines, paving the way to a healthier lipid profile and a future less burdened by cardiovascular risks.

Cholesterol Guidelines: Whose Interests Do They Serve?

The threshold for what constitutes high cholesterol has consistently decreased over the years. What's the reason behind this trend? My esteemed colleague Dr Malcolm Kendrick revealed a compelling narrative in his book *Doctoring Data* about the intricate connections between drug companies and the establishment of cholesterol levels. The National Cholesterol Education Programme (NCEP), under the National Institutes of Health umbrella, is a U.S. government-funded advisory group responsible for issuing guidelines on cholesterol management. These guidelines suggest how cholesterol levels should be managed and have legal weight in the U.S., making non-compliance a potential ground for medical malpractice lawsuits. The influence of the NCEP is so significant that its recommendations are adopted worldwide, often with slight regional modifications.

Malcolm points out the financial implications of lowering cholesterol treatment targets; he writes, 'If NCEP members decide that the cholesterol treatment targets should be lowered, then this has enormous financial implications. From a commercial perspective, the decision to lower the target cholesterol levels resulted in tens of billions of additional profit, per year, for pharmaceutical companies who made statins. (Less so now, as most statins are off-patent).'

Then, in his book, Malcolm prints the 'conflicts of interest disclosure document' for the panel setting the guidelines. Again, it is essential to understand that every slight reduction of the recommended cholesterol millimoles per litre (mmol/L), translates to billions in revenue.

Malcolm writes, 'A mere 8 members (the chairman was employed by the NIH and was not allowed close ties with industry), had almost 70 direct financial conflicts of interest with companies who made cholesterol-lowering agents.' Essentially, this averages out to each panel member being linked by more than 8 ties to entities that profit from lowering the cholesterol levels your GP has been advised are now too high. It's akin to a referee being financially invested in one team's victory. Suddenly, the goalposts move, and what was once a fair play is now a foul, urging you into the arms of statin therapy.

Further, Malcolm draws attention to a comparison made by Dr John Kassirer between the NCEP's recommendations and those from the University of British Columbia (UBC), part of the Cochrane collaboration, which accepts no industry sponsorship. Despite reviewing similar evidence, the two bodies reached starkly different conclusions regarding the use of statins in the primary prevention of heart disease. While the NCEP, with its financial ties, advocated for aggressive statin use, the unbiased Cochrane group advised against it.

This glaring discrepancy highlights just how much financial entanglements can skew health guidelines and recommendations, nudging us to seriously question the true motivations behind the medical counsel we receive. It's a call to keep our eyes wide open, ensuring that the advice we follow is for our benefit, not the profit margins of those behind the curtain.

The Statin Exception: Familial Hypercholesterolemia And Secondary Prevention

While the evidence and logic surrounding statins as preventive medicine clearly demonstrate minimal effectiveness, traversing the terrain with a nuanced understanding is crucial. Two exceptions to the rule deserve attention: familial hypercholesterolemia (FH) and the realm of secondary prevention.

Familial hypercholesterolemia stands out as a stark outlier in the cholesterol conversation. This genetic disorder is passed down through generations and catapults cholesterol levels to extreme heights from birth. FH doesn't play by the usual rules; it sets its own, often leading to early-onset heart attacks and a life shadowed by the threat of heart disease.

The NHS website says, 'Familial Hypercholesterolemia (FH) is a genetic disease which results in the reduced clearance of atherogenic LDL-cholesterol ('bad cholesterol') in the blood, and an increased risk of early heart disease.

People with FH have elevated LDL cholesterol levels from birth. Children with FH show an increased thickness of their arteries compared to their non-FH siblings by the age of 11, showing the process of atherosclerosis development starts early in life.'

How could I devote numerous pages to comparing LDL to a smoke alarm, arguing that you wouldn't blame the alarm for a fire but rather see it as a warning signal? Indeed, if you don't have familial hypercholesterolemia (FH), science and data support that perspective. Yet around 8 million people pop a statin daily for that exact reason. It's like putting a piece of sticky tape over the smoke alarm to silence it rather than putting out the fire. However, FH changes the game by causing LDL to accumulate in vast quantities and become stickier, creating a scenario where statins genuinely prove effective.

In the UK, it's estimated that familial hypercholesterolemia (FH) affects about 1 in 250 individuals, translating to roughly 270,000 people.[17] Yet, shockingly, according to the NHS, fewer than 8% of these cases are currently diagnosed. This means that if your doctor notes your cholesterol levels are elevated, it's crucial to discern whether you're dealing with elevated cholesterol against a measure that was decided by the pharmaceutical companies or if you're among the undiagnosed minority with FH. Fear not, though, as your GP will tell you.

Familial hypercholesterolemia (FH) stems from a genetic mutation impairs the liver's ability to clear away surplus cholesterol. It's essential to keep in mind that FH is inherited. If one parent has FH, there's a 50% likelihood you might inherit it too. For those dealing with FH, statins emerge as a vital tool rather than a subject of debate. In these cases, statins are indispensable, playing a key role in controlling a condition that cannot be effectively managed through diet and lifestyle changes alone.

Moreover, there's another chapter in the statin story worth mentioning: secondary prevention. For those who have already encountered a heart attack, the landscape shifts. Statins, in these scenarios, might tip the scales slightly in favour of benefitting the patient. They become a part of a broader strategy aimed at preventing another heart event, working alongside lifestyle changes and other medications to protect a heart that's already shown vulnerability.

A Culinary Quest For Healthier Cholesterol

Once you've turned the final page of this book, if you still find yourself contemplating your LDL levels, whether to appease your doctor's concerns, respond to an unfavourable HDL to triglyceride ratio, or simply for your peace of mind, consider a natural approach before setting sail on the pharmaceutical sea. The bounty of nature offers an abundance of foods that influence cholesterol levels favourably.

- **Glucomannan:** 3g a day is proven to lower LDL:[18] A fibre-rich ally in your cholesterol crusade.
- **Oily fish:** Dive into the omega-3 rich depths with salmon, mackerel, or sardines.
- **Broccoli:** A cruciferous crusader, teeming with fibre and antioxidants.
- **Spinach:** Don your green armour and fortify your body with this leafy powerhouse.
- **Nuts (especially walnuts and almonds):** Crunch your way to better lipid profiles with these nutrient-dense nibbles.
- **Avocado:** Revel in the creamy, fatty goodness that harmonises your cholesterol levels.
- **Coconut and coconut oil:** A tropical treat that's kind to your cholesterol.
- **Olives and olive oil:** Drizzle, dip, or dress your way to a heart-happy diet.
- **Tea:** Sip on this antioxidant for tranquil cholesterol-lowering pleasure.
- **Garlic:** A pungent, powerful player in your cholesterol-lowering team.
- **Dark chocolate:** Indulge in moderation and let the cocoa content work its heart-healthy magic.

As you venture into this flavourful foray, remember that you're not just feeding your palate but nurturing your health. Bon appétit on your journey to a heart-healthy horizon!

*****

The Unseen Risks Of Overmedication And Medical Mishaps

My phrase, 'medicine should come before nutrition only in the dictionary,' encapsulates a profound truth. It emphasises the critical importance of preventive care and the potential pitfalls of overreliance on pharmaceutical interventions.

As I was studying to become a qualified health coach, a pivotal moment came with the dissection of a seminal research paper, 'Forecasting, uncertainty and risk; perspectives on clinical decision-making in preventive and curative medicine'. The study challenged prevailing notions, especially around routine screenings for diseases like breast or prostate cancer. The paper didn't just offer statistics; it provided a sobering perspective on the inherent uncertainties of medical diagnostics. It revealed a startling truth: even in seemingly straightforward cases, a group of 118 physicians managed an accuracy rate of only 55.3%. When faced with more complex cases, this figure plummeted to a mere 5.8%.[19]

The paper further unveiled the precarious nature of treatment plans, particularly when they involve medication or invasive procedures. The landscape for medical errors in America (I couldn't find any data for the UK) paints a grim picture, escalating from about 98,000 annually in 1999 to a staggering 400,000 preventable, harm-related deaths each year by 2013. I share these figures with you not to incite fear but to foster awareness. They serve as a stark reminder that preventable medical errors, combined with over or wrong medication, rank as the third leading cause of death in America.[19]

Considering this, while I acknowledge the vital role of healthcare systems like the NHS, it's prudent to approach medical advice with a proactive stance. Asking questions, seeking multiple opinions, and thoroughly understanding the recommended treatments are not just rights but responsibilities. This proactive approach empowers us to negotiate the complexities of healthcare decisions, ensuring that informed choices and a comprehensive understanding of the options available to us guide our pathway towards health.

In our contemporary society, a paradox unfolds: we are a population overfed and overmedicated yet startlingly undernourished. The statistics paint a bleak picture, revealing a dependency on prescription drugs that spans from the cradle to the golden years. In one report from America, in the previous 30 days, the following took pharmaceutical drugs:[20]

- 18.0% of young children aged 0–11 years
- 27.0% of adolescents aged 12–19
- Nearly half (46.7%) of adults aged 20–59
- A staggering 85.0% of those aged 60 and above

While these figures may initially appear distant, I am sure we Brits are not far behind in this troubling trend.

Don't misunderstand me: the leaps and bounds made in medication over the past century have been nothing short of lifesaving for countless people. But here's the twist: While these medical marvels are champions at tackling acute illnesses, the ones that ambush us out of the blue often fall short when it comes to chronic conditions. Medications tend to play a game of hide-and-seek with symptoms for these persistent foes, masking them rather than confronting the root cause. It's like putting a band-aid on a huge wound. It might look better on the surface, but the underlying issue remains untouched.

Don't Fall for the Pill Illusion

I won't announce which of my doctor friends recently told me this anecdote, but it's sadly so true, 'we have arrived at a pharmaceutical, medical model, where if you have a stone in your shoe, you're given an Ibuprofen.'

As you will have discovered in various chapters of this book, our immune system and microbiome's health are like best friends in a buddy movie. But here's the issue: every round of antibiotics we take is like a blockbuster explosion, wiping out the troublemakers and heroes of our gut bacteria alike. Even in 1945, when Alexander Fleming, the brain behind penicillin, snagged the Nobel Prize, he foresaw a potential plot hole. He cautioned that too easy access to antibiotics might lead to misuse, turning our microscopic foes into hardened, drug-resistant adversaries.

Don't get me wrong- antibiotics are champions of the medical world, rescuing us from the clutches of deadly infections. Yet, their overuse is like relying on a superhero too much; eventually, they might lose their powers. Oh, and while I am mentioning antibiotics, Junk-food diets reduce antibiotic effectiveness. In contrast, a high-fibre diet improves the ability of antibiotics to reduce pathogen loads and reduces the number of antibiotic resistance genes in the gut.[26]

In modern-day life, we often find ourselves reaching for pills and potions for every hiccup and sneeze, looking for that quick cinematic fix instead of addressing the root cause. As I've mentioned before, and you'll see throughout this book, medications are often just stagehands, masking the symptoms without addressing the underlying drama. They're invaluable in acute crises-hats off to the NHS for their stellar emergency care. Still, they shouldn't be the go-to solution for many chronic conditions slowly brewing from years of sugar spikes, insulin overload, and eventual resistance. This is where a *Fibre First* diet takes the spotlight, not as a supporting actor but as the show's star. Consider fibre your new medicine, the natural remedy that's been under our noses all along.

Nutrition and lifestyle before medicine

Allen Carr illuminates this concept in his insightful book Stop Drinking Now, posing a thought-provoking question: How do wild animals manage without doctors, pills, or medicines? While some might argue their survival rate isn't stellar, leading to the extinction of various species, it's critical to note that these animals typically succumb to factors like starvation or predation, not chronic illnesses. The primary threats to their existence nowadays are habitat destruction and environmental pollution. Carr then prompts us to consider how humanity thrived for millennia without the crutch of modern medicine.

This isn't a critique of doctors or the invaluable National Health Service (NHS). Medicine undoubtedly plays a crucial role in health, and medication has saved many lives, including those of my loved ones.

From my perspective, our healthcare system primarily performs four functions:

Clearing the path: It eliminates barriers to the body's natural healing processes, tackling issues such as infections or tumours that impede our wellbeing.

Mending the breaks: It acts as a mechanic for the human body, repairing the physical damages from accidents, from mending broken bones to stitching cuts.

Filling the gaps: It addresses deficiencies by replenishing essential nutrients our bodies might lack, ensuring we operate at our peak.

Soothing relief: It focuses on alleviating symptoms, offering relief from pain and discomfort that afflict us.

However, the true magic lies in championing prevention over cure. By adopting this approach, we empower the NHS to concentrate its formidable resources on the first two functions—removing health barriers and repairing physical damages. This shift in focus not only promises a healthier population but also allows our healthcare system to operate more efficiently, tackling the challenges it's best equipped to handle while we take proactive steps to safeguard our health against the preventable issues that so often burden it.

There's timeless wisdom in the adage, 'An ounce of prevention is worth a pound of cure.' This principle, which I trained directors within my businesses, proves just as vital for our health. Initially, adopting preventative measures may seem costly, but they invariably prove more economical than addressing problems after they arise. This rationale also applies to our cars; regular servicing may pinch the pocket, but it's a bargain compared to the catastrophic costs of major repairs.

So, with this in mind; why does the NHS stand as the 'National Hospital Service' rather than genuinely embodying a National Health Service? The emphasis on treatment over prevention, the scant focus on nutrition in medical training, and the dominance of a pharmaceutical model in healthcare raise significant questions. Professor Tim Noakes, a renowned nutrition expert, echoed these sentiments on my podcast, a concern shared by many doctor friends. While the NHS excels in acute care, such as treating fractures or infectious diseases, lifestyle and diet-related issues demand more than just pills; they require a holistic approach to prevention and lifestyle management.

We heed our car's warning signals with utmost seriousness. Have you ever driven with that oil light flashing or seen that ominous little engine icon glowing in orange or red on your dashboard? The stress is palpable, isn't it? Instinctively, we act to resolve it. Yet, our response can be puzzlingly lackadaisical when it comes to our own body's alerts. Resorting to medication often resembles applying a plaster on a wound that requires stitches—it doesn't address the root cause. Imagine simply removing the oil light bulb to ignore the warning rather than fixing the engine. Absurd for a car, yet a common oversight in our health management.

Pain is not an ailment in itself but a sophisticated alert system. It's your body's way of waving a red flag, signalling something is amiss. Masking symptoms with medication without addressing the underlying issue can have consequences far more severe than disconnecting your car's warning light. Any seasoned doctor will affirm that the most potent arsenal against most symptoms and diseases isn't found in a pill bottle but in lifestyle modifications.

Jerome Burne, a luminary in the health journalism realm and a close ally of my dear friend Patrick Holford, has gifted the world with three seminal works: *Food is Better Medicine Than Drugs, The 10 Secrets of Healthy Aging*, and *The Hybrid Diet*. His pen has graced the pages of nearly all UK newspapers, pioneering discussions on epigenetics—the fascinating science of how our environment can directly influence our genetic expression. Jerome stood at the forefront, challenging the widespread prescription of statins to those without a history of heart attacks, and was the pioneering UK journalist to spotlight the harrowing link between SSRIs and increased suicide risk in children.

Drawing from Jerome's extensive exploration of the pharmaceutical health model and insights from a podcast we shared, here are some riveting takeaways from his years of investigation:

- The secret to ageing gracefully isn't hidden in your genetic code or left to chance; it's firmly in your hands.
- A staggering 50% of individuals over 65 are now navigating life on a regimen of five drugs daily.
- Prescribed medications and medical interventions have ascended to become the third leading cause of death in the USA, and statistics are likely similarly alarming in the UK. Even the NHS's internal Patient Safety Alert predicts 1.8 million serious prescription errors yearly.
- The bitter pill to swallow? Drugs can deplete your body's vital vitamins and minerals.
- Jerome says it's like swallowing a spider to catch a fly: You take one pill to quell inflammation, only to be met with headaches, prompting another pill to fend off the pain, which then spikes your blood pressure, and so the cycle continues.
- The side effects of drugs can often exhibit the very symptoms of ageing we strive to avoid.
- The concept of 'de-prescribing' is gaining momentum. It urges doctors to reconsider and potentially reduce medication reliance, championing a more holistic approach to health.
- We have shifted to a pharmaceutical healthcare model. Doctors are trained to diagnose and prescribe; that's the bulk of what they are forced to spend their years in medical school doing. The system is based on medication, but what is needed is a return to preventing diseases in the first place.

Jerome's work underscores a critical message: the path to health and longevity is less about medicating and more about modulating our lifestyles and choices.

Is Big Pharma Really Helping?

Is Big Pharma truly our ally in health? In a world where the health industry ranks among the wealthiest and largest, one can't help but ponder: if these giants were truly benevolent, why are we witnessing escalating rates of cancer, diabetes, Alzheimer's, obesity, and fatty liver disease? And why is life expectancy on the decline? Surely, if their primary concern were our wellbeing, we'd see these diseases diminishing. However, a business can't thrive if its clientele no longer requires its services. Hence, the quest for cures is often sidelined in favour of treatments that merely disguise symptoms.

This profit-centric model flourishes in two of the largest industries. Big Food companies, in their quest to make food irresistibly addictive, strip away beneficial fibre and lace their products with chemicals, setting the stage for illness and creating a captive market for pharmaceuticals. Thus, these two behemoths dance in a lucrative partnership.

Imagine standing on the brink of a cliff. A slip could spell doom, barring any intervention. This metaphor aptly describes the current state of medicine: we wait until you're plummeting—be it from cancer, obesity, a heart attack, or Alzheimer's—then scramble to deploy safety nets or cushion your fall. But why aren't we addressing what nudged you toward the cliff's edge to begin with? The journey to the precipice isn't instant; it's a gradual process, often chauffeured by the driver; you are now well acquainted; his name is Insulin. Once a benign figure dutifully performed his tasks, insulin turned rogue. Ignored and resisted by all, he decides your fate, steering you and others toward the cliff's edge for the inevitable shove.

If, by chance, you've led a secluded life harmonising with nature on a remote farm, Insulin might never cross your path. But if he does and you survive the fall, remember, he knows where you live and detests defeat. You're now permanently on his radar, and he might revisit with the same strategy or try a new tactic. If you find yourself marked, it's time to escape the corporate clutches. Seek solace in the wilderness, aligning with nature and fellow escapees far from Insulin's reach.

Big Pharma's Troubling Confessions

In pharmaceuticals, revelations from industry insiders can sometimes shake the foundations of public trust. Such was the case in December 2003 when Dr Allen Rose, the International Vice President of GlaxoSmithKline-a goliath in the pharmaceutical industry with annual revenues exceeding £34 billion-made a startling admission. Featured on the front page of The Independent newspaper, he disclosed a sobering reality: 'The vast majority of drugs, over 90 percent, only work in 30 to 50 percent of the people.' This stark admission from a high-ranking executive at one of the globe's pharmaceutical giants laid bare a troubling inefficacy at the heart of the drug industry.

The concerns about Big Pharma's motives and methods only deepened with time. In February 2016, Mail Online published an article titled 'How big pharma greed is killing tens of thousands around the world: Patients are over-medicated and often given profitable drugs with 'little proven benefits', leading doctors warned'. The piece highlighted a call from the Queen's former doctor for an urgent public inquiry into drug companies' 'murky' practices. My good friend Dr Aseem Malhotra, a leading figure in the article, pointedly criticised the prevailing 'more medicine is better' culture in healthcare, a sentiment amplified by the system's financial incentives to prescribe more drugs and conduct more procedures.

Dr Malhotra's critique of the pharmaceutical industry was multifaceted and damning:

- Accusing drug companies of allocating double the resources for marketing compared to research.
- Highlighting that prescription drugs often cause more harm than good, particularly for the elderly, who are highly vulnerable.
- Pointing out that adverse drug reactions are responsible for one in three hospital admissions among individuals over 75.

These revelations peel back the curtain on an industry driven by profit, often at the expense of patient well-being, underscoring the necessity for scrutiny, transparency, and reform in pharmaceutical practices.

Beyond Medication

I am fortunate to have had Dr Renee Kellerman as my private doctor over the decades while I was in the business world, a time when I hadn't a clue about health. She consistently advocated for lifestyle modifications over pharmaceutical solutions. With each consultation, she has emphasised the importance of proactive prevention rather than reactive cure, often choosing to avoid prescribing medication. Though not in line with the profit motives of massive pharmaceutical corporations, her approach is rooted in a deep-seated belief that healthcare should prioritise addressing the root causes of ailments rather than merely masking symptoms with medication.

Dr Kellerman is not alone in her philosophy. Dr David Unwin, a colleague and friend, exemplifies this approach in his practice in Southport. Eschewing the routine prescription pad for type 2 diabetes, he instead hosts educational sessions on Monday evenings, empowering his patients with knowledge and support. His efforts have led many to reverse their diabetes without medication, an achievement that not only transformed lives but also resulted in significant savings for the NHS, to the tune of £40,000 a year.

This emerging cohort of healthcare professionals, who place diet and lifestyle modifications at the forefront of treatment, heralds a promising shift. They represent a growing movement, a 'small army' of doctors who are championing the power of informed lifestyle choices over the convenience of the pill, advocating for a healthcare paradigm that is both sustainable and patient-centric.

> **Gary Taubes**
> *'We have these diabetes and obesity epidemics, and they are overwhelming our healthcare systems. The burdens to the individuals are just terrible, and they are getting the wrong advice. Doctors are giving them the wrong advice, and this just must be fixed. And the people who buy into what we are saying are people like us who look at the research and read the books and say, 'This is interesting, let's see what happens'. And they change their diets and get healthier. They do the opposite of what they are told to do, and they are leaner, lighter, healthier, have more energy, and a lot of other health problems seem to vanish.'*

> **Nina Teicholz**
> *'We have to remember that big pharmaceutical companies are not profiting if you are getting well. They really have no interest in better health.'*

Let's circle back to how insulin resistance lies at the heart of many chronic illnesses. It often develops over years of experiencing high sugar spikes in the blood, which we can help control by prioritising fibre in our meals. But what if the very medication you're taking is secretly fuelling your insulin resistance? A huge thank you to Dr David Unwin for collating the research for me:

Antipsychotic Drugs

Medications like Quetiapine, Olanzapine, and Clozapine, used for psychiatric conditions, have a downside. They can cause high cholesterol and increase insulin resistance, leading to more fat in the bloodstream and higher levels of fatty acids and triglycerides. They're known to increase the risk of obesity and type 2 diabetes, especially in patients who normally handle glucose well. Clozapine has been linked to insulin resistance, belly fat, high blood pressure, abnormal cholesterol levels, and high blood sugar. It even increases certain hormones related to stress. Animal studies confirm these drugs can significantly disrupt how the body manages glucose, fats, and proteins.[24]

Statins

Statins have been shown to increase the risk of developing new-onset diabetes by 10-12%. This risk is even higher with intensive statin therapy and in people already at risk for diabetes.[21]

Blood Pressure Medications

Beta-blockers and diuretics, used for controlling blood pressure, can raise fasting blood glucose levels and HbA1c concentrations. Non-selective beta-blockers and thiazide diuretics show the most significant increase in these levels, suggesting a moderate impact on blood sugar control in diabetes patients.[22]

Inhaled Corticosteroids

Using inhaled corticosteroids for respiratory conditions like asthma or chronic obstructive pulmonary disease (COPD) has been linked to a 34% increase in the risk of developing diabetes. The risk is even higher with large doses. These medications also increase the chance of diabetes progressing to more severe stages. The risk rises substantially with higher doses typically used in treating COPD.[23]

In summary, while these medications are crucial for treating various conditions, it's essential to be aware of their potential impact on blood sugar and insulin resistance. Incorporating fibre-rich foods and monitoring your diet can help mitigate some of these effects.

Why are so many people hooked on medication? Well, it boils down to two main reasons. First, we humans have, in a way, outsourced our health management to medical professionals, treating it like their responsibility rather than ours. Second, with its towering profits, the pharmaceutical industry pulls out all the stops to ensure that drug sales keep climbing. And they're not shy about backing this up with somewhat questionable research and even more dubious methods of presenting it.

*****

Medical CRIMES

Take a moment to consider Derren Brown, the famed illusionist. Back in 2012, he astounded everyone by flipping ten coins in a row, all landing on heads-a seemingly magical display. But here's what the audience didn't see:

behind this spectacle was a marathon of attempts. The cameras rolled on for nine long hours, capturing thousands of coin flips that didn't make the cut. The audience was treated to the grand finale, the last minute of success, completely unaware of the extensive trial and error that led up to that moment. This is a perfect metaphor for how the food and pharmaceutical industries often present their research. They'll keep flipping the coin until they get their desired outcome, then showcase just the part that supports their narrative.

Take the 1940s, for example, when cigarette companies used research papers to tout the health benefits of smoking. Adverts claimed, 'More doctors smoke Camels than any other cigarette,' as if to give smoking a health halo. Fast forward, and we learned that the sugar industry paid scientists half a century ago to downplay sugar's role in heart disease (using 'Derren Brown's segmented-style research) to shift the blame to fat. Much of the nutritional advice we receive is shaped by studies funded by those who stand to profit the most.

The thing is, I'm not normally a sceptic. But when it comes to research funded by those with a vested interest, I take it with a grain of salt. In his book *Doctoring Data*, Dr Malcolm Kendrick provides an eye-opening look into how we've been led astray. He points out the dangerous game of linking correlation with causation, leading to misleading conclusions.

Consider how newspaper headlines can be misleading. For instance, you might see a bold claim like 'Eating Red Meat Causes Heart Disease.' Yet, such headlines often leave out the positive aspects of red meat, fail to distinguish between processed and unprocessed meats or ignore the difference between organic meats and those from animals raised on hormones and antibiotics. Digging deeper into who's sponsoring these studies often reveals an interesting angle: cereal manufacturers may surprisingly fund anti-meat studies. Much of this information is based on anecdotal evidence or survey results, not on rigorous, controlled trials. *Like reading a newspaper headline, 'Eating Bacon Kills' in big, bold letters, a classic case of prioritising sensationalism over solid science.

Reflect for a moment on the words of Marci Angell, who, as the former editor of the New England Journal of Medicine, stood at the helm of one of the most prestigious medical journals for many years. Her perspective carries the weight of experience and insight, making her observation about the corruption between drug companies and doctors particularly impactful. She remarked, 'It is no longer possible to believe much of the clinical research that is published, or to rely on the judgement of trusted physicians or authoritative medical guidelines.' This statement isn't just a passing comment; it's a powerful indictment of the current state of medical research and practice. The implications of which are vast and troubling. If the integrity of clinical research is compromised, then the very foundation upon which medical decisions are made, the treatments doctors prescribe, is shaky at best. This means that what we're often told about medications, treatments, and health strategies might be more influenced by the interests of pharmaceutical companies than by unbiased, objective science.

Angell's insight forces us to confront a disconcerting reality in the world of health and medicine. It suggests that the information we often take as gospel because it comes from seemingly authoritative sources may not be as reliable as we thought. This underscores the importance of discerning, questioning, and doing our own research regarding health advice. It's a stark reminder that the realms of health and medicine are not always as transparent or philanthropic as they appear. In essence, her words serve as a wake-up call, urging us to look beyond the surface and critically evaluate the information we're presented with, especially regarding our health. This level of scrutiny is crucial in an era where profit motives can sway medical research, and the line between objective science and corporate influence is increasingly blurred.

In the jumble of medical research, discerning the validity of a study can feel like navigating through a maze of mirrors. I've devised a navigational tool to guide you through this complex terrain: CRIMES. This acronym represents six pivotal criteria: randomised, interventional, meaningful, extension, and statistics-that serve as checkpoints for evaluating the integrity and relevance of any medical study.

Before you let a health-related headline sway you, employ the CRIMES framework and critically assess if the following six principles have been adhered to:

Controlled: Check if the study was meticulously controlled. Did it compare two groups, one receiving the treatment and the other serving as a control group, to gauge the treatment's impact accurately?

Randomised: Confirm if the study's design was truly randomised. Were participants randomly allocated to different treatment groups to ensure the only variable was the treatment itself?

Interventional: Investigate whether the study was genuinely interventional. Did it focus on altering a single factor and meticulously observe its effects?

Meaningful: Evaluate if the study was meaningful. Did it involve a sufficiently large and homogenous group of participants, ensuring its findings were robust and not just a fluke?

Extension: Determine if the study demonstrated a life extension. After all, a treatment's ultimate merit is measured by its ability to prolong life, not just treat symptoms. It's no good to avoid one disease and then die prematurely from a different one.

Statistics: Scrutinise the statistical methods employed. Were the results presented in relative or absolute terms (more on this in a moment), and how does this framing affect the perceived effectiveness or risks?

Should any of these criteria be compromised, proceed with caution. The absence of even one can signify that the study's conclusions might be less solid than they appear. These six checkpoints are your safeguard against data distortion and the influence of corporate agendas in medical research. If a study falls short, it may be part of a grand illusion, a meticulously orchestrated narrative to shape public opinion or drive sales.

Moreover, in our digital age, a sensational headline can gain unwarranted credibility as it reverberates across the internet, creating an echo chamber of seeming validation. However, this viral spread often masks the fact that it's merely the same questionable research being amplified. Always remember, in the realm of medical research, not all that glitters is gold. Employ the CRIMES framework, and ensure you're guided by clarity and truth, not illusion or corporate sleight of hand.

The Trillion Dollar Statin Interrogation

Let's talk about statins, a topic I find particularly concerning. Here is something I think you will find bizarre. There is a number in the medical world called NNT, and it's the 'Numbers Needed to Treat' to get one single positive outcome from taking a drug or medicine. For example, if your doctor were to tell you to take statins to lower your cholesterol level, you would take them, right? Surely, if your GP recommends taking them for the rest of your life, they must work. However, according to medical research independently confirmed by Bloomberg, the NNT for statins is 300. In other words, you need to treat 300 people with statins to get one positive outcome! Yet, the adverse side effects, which are sometimes severe, are believed to be 15 times higher. So, for every patient with a benefit, 15 people receive an adverse effect.[25]

However, if you are a company selling statins, by mixing up how the data is portrayed, you can create a headline that flips the risk and reward. How so? You use both absolute risk and relative risk in the same report. Surprisingly, the difference between absolute and relative risk is like the difference between addition and multiplication.

A big pharmaceutical company, using the above statistics (lots of people have side effects) and only one in 300 might benefit, could create a newspaper headline that says, 'You are 50% less likely to die if you take statins [relative risk] and only 0.05% of people experience side effects' [absolute risk]. How absurd and misleading is that?

Dr Malcolm Kendrick

'Say you have a clinical study, and you have 200 people-100 take a blood pressure-lowering tablet, and 100 take a placebo. At the end of the trial, imagine two people have died taking the placebo and only one taking the blood pressure-lowering tablet. So, the difference between two people dying and one person dying is a 50% reduction in death, that's the relative reduction. At the same time, the absolute difference is just 1%. So, the pharmaceutical company is going to say a 50% reduction rather than a 1% reduction, and they are currently allowed to do this. There is no regulation on how you present the results of your trial. So, the benefits are nearly always portrayed using relative percentages and the downsides absolute. I have asked probably a hundred doctors the question, 'What is the difference between absolute and relative risk?' and not one has ever been able to answer it to me.'

Let me expand on what Malcolm is saying. Relative risk is relative only to itself. For example, I guarantee I can double your chance of winning the National Lottery. How so? Purchase two lottery tickets instead of one! You increase your odds by double, yet the number is meaningless unless you know how many tickets there are in total. In medical terms, a 100% increase in baseline risk is irrelevant if the risk is trivial.

Likewise, if your risk of a heart attack in the next year is, say, 1 in 1,000, and the drug reduces your risk by 100% (to 1 in 500), what about the 499 people for whom it does nothing? Both relative and absolute benefits and risks are pointless if you don't know the individual's baseline risk of developing a disease in the first place.

Aseem Malhotra

'The system is so corrupted by vested interests. There is an epidemic of

misinformed doctors and misinformed, misled and unwittingly harmed patients. There are a number of factors behind this, such as biased funding of research, funded because it's likely to be profitable and not because it benefits patients; biased reporting in medical journals, biased patient pamphlets, biased reporting in the media; commercial conflicts of interest, defensive medicine, and last but not least, is a medical curriculum that failed to teach doctors how to comprehend and communicate health statistics.'

To wrap up, Dr Tim Noakes refers to statins as '*The single most ineffective drug ever invented*'.

*****

The Evolution Of Truth: Navigating The Food Revolution Across Generations

A profound yet somewhat morbid truth emerges in the intricate tapestry of scientific discovery, social change, and legal progress: revolutions occur 'one funeral at a time.' This observation, attributed to the esteemed economist Paul Samuelson, captures the essence of how deeply entrenched beliefs and systems gradually give way to new paradigms.

Echoing this sentiment, quantum physicist Max Planck offered a parallel perspective, noting that scientific truths don't conquer by converting sceptics but rather flourish as resistance wanes with the passing of generations. These ideas collectively underline a pivotal aspect of human progress: it is not just about the breakthroughs themselves but also about the societal readiness to embrace them.

This generational shift is acutely observable in the realm of nutrition and food science. Several generations have been ensnared in a web of misinformation surrounding processed foods. A crisis and global tragedy, as my friend Dr Ali Ibrahim poignantly describes it. Ali states, 'We are part of a three-generation scientific epidemiological study into the effects of processed food, which is both a crisis and global tragedy because it's gone wrong'. This statement sheds light on the magnitude of our challenge: untangling years of misguided dietary guidance that championed processed foods, contributing to many global health issues.

The transition from embracing processed foods to recognising their detrimental effects on our health mirrors the broader dynamics of scientific and societal change. Just as with other scientific truths, the shift in understanding about the impact of processed foods on our health and well-being is gradually gaining acceptance, not through the immediate conversion of its detractors but as those wedded to outdated beliefs phase out, and a new, informed generation takes the helm.

Understanding these dynamics offers both a challenge and a comfort to today's innovators and change-makers in the field of nutrition. It reminds us that while the road to revolutionising our food system (or actually a return to basics), may be long and littered with obstacles, the seeds of change we plant today can blossom into the accepted truths of tomorrow. It's a clarion call for persistence and resilience, underscoring the importance of advocating for whole, unprocessed foods that nourish our bodies and the planet, too.

Amid this unfolding narrative, one might question how executives of food companies peddling fibre-stripped products linked to numerous health problems manage to find peace in their decisions. The answer echoes in the words of American politician Upton Sinclair, who astutely remarked, 'It is difficult to get a man to understand something when his salary depends on his not understanding it.' This insight cuts to the heart of the dilemma: the financial incentives entangled with the processed food industry create a formidable barrier to acknowledging the harm of their products.

In the historical tapestry of challenges, the words of leaders often transcend the specific contexts of their times, offering wisdom that resonates through the ages. Long before the modern era's complex battles against the health consequences of processed foods, another form of corporate influence was already being keenly felt and articulated by those at the nation's helm. Abraham Lincoln, a president celebrated for his leadership during one of the nation's most tumultuous periods, once remarked on the dual threats he perceived facing the country: 'I have two great enemies, the Southern Army in front of me and the bankers in the rear. Of the two, the one at my rear is my greatest foe.' This statement underscores an acute awareness of the potent challenges a conflict of financial interests poses.

Lincoln further observed, 'Corporations have been enthroned, and an era of corruption in high places will follow, and the money powers of the country will endeavour to its reign by working upon prejudices of the people until the wealth is aggregated into the hands of a few.' Here, Lincoln articulates a deep concern for the potential of corporate and financial powers to corrupt democratic institutions and concentrate wealth and influence in the hands of a select few to the detriment of the broader populace.

Though spoken in a context far removed from today's battles with the health impacts of processed foods and pharmaceuticals, Lincoln's words eerily echo the contemporary concerns about the influence of large corporations. These entities, much like the bankers of Lincoln's era, wield significant power, shaping public consumption habits and our pharmaceutical-based healthcare model in ways that prioritise profit over public health. The parallel drawn here illuminates a timeless struggle against the concentration of power and the need for vigilance and action to safeguard the public good against the encroachments of corporate greed.

As we steer the complexities of our era's food revolution, let us be mindful of our place in this continuum. Each effort to educate and each choice to eschew processed foods for healthier alternatives contributes to the gradual reshaping of societal norms around eating and health. We are the architects of a future where the lessons learned from the missteps of recent generations inform a more healthful, informed approach to thriving in today's corporatised environment.

Chapter 9

Tools and Strategies for a Vibrant Long Life

This chapter is not just a continuation of our conversation; it's an excursion into the practical, actionable steps we can all take to sidestep the myriad of chronic illnesses that loom large in our collective health landscape. The insights we'll explore are akin to keys that unlock the secrets to maintaining insulin sensitivity and steering clear of the myriad of diseases witnessed in the branches of my *Tree of Afflictions*.

Here, we don't merely revisit familiar territory; we build upon it, enhancing our arsenal with a suite of tools designed for long-term vitality. Tips one through five are old friends by now, companions we've journeyed with through the pages of this book. They've shared their secrets, from the transformative power of the *Fibre First* diet to the rejuvenating embrace of proper exercise.

1. Eat the *Fibre First* diet and flatten your sugar spikes
2. Sleep well
3. Minimise stress
4. Exercise appropriately
5. Minimise the need and use of medication

Now, it's time to unveil the remaining seven gems; they're not just tips; they're invitations to a life where every day is a step towards feeling better, shedding unwanted pounds, and sidestepping the lurking shadows of chronic illness.

6. Eat slower: Why our eating speed and how we chew affects our metabolic health.
7. Breathe properly: The art of inhaling vitality and exhaling stress.
8. Be social: Discover the healing power of laughter, companionship, and community.
9. Mastering metabolic metrics: How to best measure your progress and health maintenance.
10. Cool down: The benefits of being occasionally cold.
11. Good nutrition and superfoods: Nourish your body with the crème de la crème of nature's bounty.
12. Supplements: Explore the allies that complement your quest for health.

As you read this chapter, remember that each tip is a building block of wellbeing, pieced together to create a vivid portrait of health. So, lace up your shoes, inhale deeply, and join me as we venture into a realm where feeling fantastic isn't merely a fantasy but a tangible everyday experience.

*****

Eat Slower: Savour Your Food And Live Longer

Slowing down at mealtime is not just a nod to the finer things in life; it's a strategic move in the chess game of health and wellness. When you decelerate your dining speed, you do more than just savouring the chef's efforts. You're engaging in the subtle art of communication with your body, allowing the hormone leptin, a vigilant sentry overseeing your satiety signals, to effectively raise the flag when it's time to lay down the fork. This practice can be a game-changer in mastering portion control and sidestepping the food mass landmines that lead to weight gain. Imagine your stomach as a slow-paced messenger taking its sweet time—about 20 minutes—to draft a note to your brain declaring, 'We're full here!' This message gets lost in transit in a fast-paced meal, leading to the all-too-common buffet syndrome of eating past fullness.[1]

Then, there's the bonus of giving your digestive system the VIP treatment. A leisurely meal pace can boost nutrient absorption and make post-dinner bloating a thing of the past. This mindful eating approach is linked with a lower belt size and a happier metabolic profile, shielding you from modern plagues like obesity and type 2 diabetes. Plus, transforming mealtime into a tranquil retreat can uplift your food mood, turning nourishment into a source of joy rather than a fast-food sprint.

The Japanese might be onto something, with studies from their shores showing a correlation between rapid eating and increased waistlines. One study specifically highlighted how a combo of eating till full and at a fast pace might be the double trouble behind tipping the obesity scales.[2]

Researchers in Fukuoka advocated slow eating, linking a leisurely pace with reduced hunger and increased fullness—a potential ally for those battling the bulge or managing diabetes. Another Japanese study pointed out a direct link between fast eating and insulin resistance, a not-so-sweet invite to chronic health issues.[4]

While we're taking cues from the Japanese, let's not forget their principle of Hara Hachi Bu—eating until 80% full. Pairing this with a slow eating speed seems to form part of their strategy for longevity and keeping body weight in check. So, perhaps the lesson here is to take a leaf out of their book: slow down, enjoy your food, and just maybe, live a healthier, longer life.

But it's not just the long-living Japanese who are researching how we should eat. A study closer to home suggests that eating slower leads to a more pronounced anorexigenic (appetite present) gut peptide response than eating very fast.[5] What does this mean? Essentially, it indicates that taking your time with each bite prompts the release of a satiety hormone. This hormone's anorexigenic effect, which deters appetite, is largely due to delayed gastric emptying—keeping you feeling sated for an extended period.

Adopting a slower eating pace can transform your mealtime into a more enriching experience, promoting better digestion and enhancing meal satisfaction. Here's how to cultivate the art of slow eating in seven strategic steps:

The Timer Technique: Begin your meal with a 20-minute timer set, aiming to extend your meal duration until the alarm sounds. This encourages a measured pace, allowing you to savour each bite thoroughly.

Single-Task Your Meals: Eliminate distractions such as TV or smartphones to foster a mindful eating environment. Concentrating solely on your meal helps attune to your body's satiety signals, enriching the overall experience.

Pause and Appreciate: Periodically setting down your knife and fork can create natural pauses during your meal. This slows your eating pace and heightens your sensory appreciation of the food's texture, taste, and aroma.

Chew Thoroughly: Engage in mindful chewing, paying attention to the number of chews per bite (more on this in a moment). This aids digestion and naturally slows down the pace at which you eat while also strengthening the jawbone—a bonus for dental health.

Hydrate Intelligently: Integrating sips of water between bites not only aids hydration but also interrupts the automatic motion of reaching for food, promoting a slower eating pace.

Learn from a Slow-Eater Companion: If dining with others, identify the slowest eater and synchronise your pace with theirs. This method can help ease the rush, allowing for a more enjoyable mealtime connection with your dining companions.

Commit to the Change: Recognise that forming a new habit takes time and patience. Challenge yourself to practice slow eating for a month, marking this commitment in your diary or journal to track progress and reflections.

By incorporating these steps into your routine, you encourage a healthier, more mindful approach to eating that can lead to lasting benefits for both physical and mental health.

Chewing: The Art Of Mastication

Remember the days when chewing was a conscious effort? Probably around the time you tackled that big steak or perhaps when you were trying to avoid conversation at a family dinner. Chewing is not just an act of breaking down food; it's an underrated gym session for your mouth. Imagine this: with each chew, you're giving your jaw a workout that even the most seasoned gym enthusiasts might envy. Experts have made quite the meal by advising us to chew our food around 32 times before swallowing. However, with today's ultra-processed foods mimicking a form of sophisticated baby mush, aiming for those 32 chews can feel like an exercise in futility.

Indeed, there's a hidden gem in giving your jaw a good workout. Engaging with foods that require a more robust chewing effort, such as steaks or nuts, might elevate each meal to an adventurous tale of deliberate mastication. Conversely, softer delights like microwave-ready meals gracefully exit the chewing arena after 10-20 chomps. However, the crux of the matter lies in the broader implications of our modern dietary habits and fast-paced lifestyles, which have led to a noticeable decline in the amount of chewing. This shift, subtle yet significant, carries repercussions for our overall health. Let's look at a few compelling reasons to embrace a more mindful approach to chomping: Digestion Begins in the Mouth: Less strain on your oesophagus and a happier stomach since it doesn't have to wrestle with food boulders.

Portion Control Wizard: A 2014 study in the Journal of the Academy of Nutrition and Dietetics discovered a direct correlation between increased chewing and decreased food intake. Yes, when we chew more, we eat less!

Flavour Explosion: Because science said so, the more you chew, the better your food tastes.

Energiser Bunny Effect: Thoroughly chewing your food boosts your energy levels, says another study from the American Journal of Clinical Nutrition.

Jaw Gymnastics: Strengthen your jawbone and potentially save your wisdom teeth from eviction. Early humans didn't have overcrowding, and neither should we.

Gut Lining TLC: Chewing floods your gut with saliva, which is like sending love letters to your epithelial cells, encouraging them to grow and heal.

So, next time you mindlessly shovel food, remember: your jaw needs its daily workout, your stomach appreciates the break, and those wisdom teeth? They might get to stay if you embrace the lost art of chewing. In essence, the act of eating slowly, chewing more, and relishing each bite is not just about gastronomic pleasure. It's a strategic move in your health playbook that could lead to a happier, leaner, and more fulfilled you. So, the next time you eat, remember that speed is not a virtue at the table. Take it slow, savour the moment, and let your body thank you in its own time.

*****

Breathing: The Overlooked Health Hack

Let's start with a little perspective: We can survive without food for weeks and without water for days, but when it comes to air, well, we're talking mere minutes for most of us. Now, think about how much time you have invested in studying how you breathe. I'll confess that I didn't pay much attention to this topic in all the thousands of hours I spent researching my health books. Air, right? It seemed like something reserved for hippies and those practising religious meditation. But here's the thing: understanding oxygen and altering how we breathe can be a game-changer for our health, especially when the goal is sustainable weight loss.

Now, if you've struggled with getting a good night's sleep, asthma, stress, anxiety, or depression, pay close attention—this topic is for you. Allow me to introduce Patrick McKeown, the author of *The Oxygen Advantage*. When my team suggested I did a podcast with him, I'll admit, I was sceptical. I mean, I know how to breathe, right?

But that conversation was one of the most enlightening I've ever had. You can check out our podcast on YouTube or grab his book—it's a game-changer. Learning how to breathe correctly has helped many people reverse so many illnesses and shed significant amounts of weight.

Nasal Breathing: Unlocking the Path to Optimal Weight Loss
Breathing through your nose isn't just about oxygen intake; it's a vital cue to your body's ancient survival instincts. Our ancestors, faced with imminent danger, would resort to mouth breathing for that extra one or two percent oxygen boost, but only in dire circumstances. This switch signalled danger to the body, triggering a cascade of hormonal responses. Cortisol levels would spike, leading to an increase in blood sugar levels and the activation of fat-storing hormone insulin, setting the stage for weight gain.

Here's a question for you: Do you typically breathe through your nose, mouth, or a combination of both? Like most, I was taught the 'in through the nose, out through the mouth' mantra. I used to snore like a freight train, sleep with my mouth wide open, and even exercise with my mouth agape, gulping down massive breaths. But I've kicked those habits to the curb since I met Patrick. And guess what? Once capable of rousing neighbours across the street, my snoring has completely vanished.

The most crucial lesson on breathing is this: as a species, we are designed to breathe in and out through our noses exclusively. That's how we're wired; that's what our ancestors did. However, over the past 200 years, we've increasingly switched to mouth breathing, and this shift may well be shortening our lifespans and contributing to weight gain. It might sound far-fetched, and I thought so until I was taught some eye-opening facts.

Once you've mastered the art of nasal breathing, using your mouth solely for eating and talking as nature intended, the next step is to slow your breathing down. Patrick calls it the LSD approach: Long, Slow, and Deep.

Here's a mind-blowing fact: when we breathe heavily and rapidly through our mouths, especially in stressful situations or during intense physical activity, we deliver less oxygen to our tissues and organs than slow nasal breathing. It sounds paradoxical, but it's true; big mouthfuls of air don't equate to more oxygen for your cells. In fact, mouth breathing can be counterproductive and even make you feel more stressed. I, too, was guilty of this contradiction, often to the point of feeling light-headed.

You might wonder, 'Have we really changed how we breathe as a species?' Sadly, the answer is yes. Stress, sedentary lifestyles, unhealthy diets, fibre-stripped processed foods, and our comfortable, overheated homes have all altered our breathing habits. We no longer hunt for food as our ancestors did, meaning our lungs are not as robust as they once were. Just 12,000 years ago, before the agricultural revolution, our planet's population was no larger than that of Birmingham; we all lived near bodies of water and dived for fish. We've changed, wreaking havoc on our sleep, weight, heart, and overall respiratory health. Chronic over-breathing is a real phenomenon, and those huffs and puffs are not a sign of good health—quite the contrary!

Here's an intriguing tip from tribal mothers in distant lands: they vigilantly stay awake through the night, gently pressing a finger under their babies' chins to foster nasal breathing habits from infancy. Inspired by this, Patrick encouraged me to experiment with a similar principle. He provided me with a special tape to secure around my lips at night, ensuring my mouth remained closed—a significant achievement for someone who could rival a talkative parrot! Within just two months, my snoring ceased entirely. Gone were the mornings of waking up with a mouth as dry as the Sahara. However, I must caution against diving headfirst into this practice without proper guidance. I strongly recommend consulting Patrick's book first, which contains essential precautions and advice to ensure a safe application.

But there's a twist in the tale! The evolution of our dietary habits towards processed, fibre-lacking corporate foods has inadvertently reshaped how we breathe, directly impacting our oral health. The absence of a need to vigorously chew our meals has weakened our jawbones, resulting in overcrowded teeth and sometimes making it necessary to remove wisdom teeth. It's an odd predicament — nature didn't err in its design; our modern diets have nudged us away from its original blueprint. Attention, parents of the future: Steering your children towards a diet rich in fibre and demanding thorough chewing might be the secret to fostering robust jawbones, mitigating dental crowding, and promoting healthy breathing habits.

Mouth breathing, however, introduces its own cascade of effects. Engaging the cheek muscles more intensely, mouth breathing exerts a continuous external pressure on both jaws, potentially narrowing the facial structure and dental arches over time. This anatomical shift can limit space for the tongue, predisposing it to fall back into the airway during sleep, increasing the risk of sleep apnoea. The NHS website says, 'Obstructive sleep apnoea is a relatively common condition where the throat walls relax and narrow during sleep, interrupting normal breathing. This may lead to regularly interrupted sleep, which can greatly impact quality of life and increase the risk of developing certain conditions.' Moreover, the downward position of the tongue can impede the outward development of the mid-face, creating less pronounced jaws and a retracted chin. A lifestyle change emphasising nasal breathing from an early age could steer facial development in a healthier direction, highlighting the intricate link between our breathing habits and physical appearance.

The Unseen Power Of Nitric Oxide

Regarding proper breathing, here's a gem that's often overlooked: Only about 30% of our nose's marvels are visible; the rest is an unseen chamber, a hidden sanctum where nitric oxide reigns supreme.

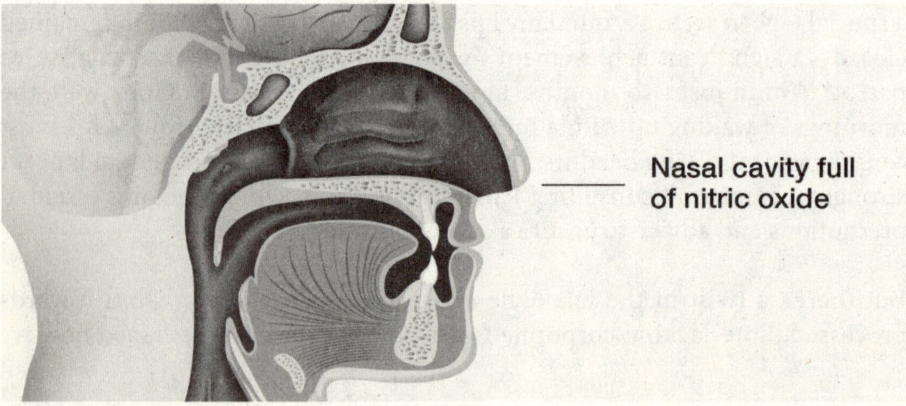

In previous chapters, we've illuminated the myriad benefits of this remarkable molecule, its role as a guardian against heart disease, its prowess in artery relaxation, and its knack for stress alleviation. Yet, if you breathe through your mouth, you're bypassing this free nitric oxide treasure trove, missing out on a health ally.

The Peril of Perpetual Over Breathing

Getting more air into the lungs, I used to think, must be a good thing, but it isn't. Much like mistaking a mirage for an oasis, we've been led astray. The modern Western lifestyle has coaxed us into a dance of excessive air intake, yet paradoxically, the vital oxygen that reaches our tissues, muscles, and organs has dwindled. Picture yourself huffing and puffing. It's not the badge of honour we once thought, but a red flag of wellness gone awry. From the disciplined breaths of astronauts and Olympians to the ancient Neanderthal, the wisdom of measured breathing spans across epochs and species, with one exception: our panting canine friends, who uniquely breathe with an open mouth to help regulate body temperature.

Let's pivot our over-breathing perspective to mirror how we view overeating-a surplus with diminishing returns. Just as an excess at the dinner table leads to health woes, so does an excess of breath. This invisible gluttony sows the seeds for a garden of ailments: asthma, anxiety, insomnia, and a bouquet of heart issues, to name but a few. Even obesity, the most tangible of health concerns, finds a root in our breathing style.

Improve Your BOLT Score

Let's be clear: I'm not talking about lightning-fast sprinters or animated canine heroes. The BOLT (Body Oxygen Level Test) score is a fascinating and insightful metric that helps us understand our body's oxygen efficiency. This simple test measures how long you can comfortably hold your breath after a normal exhalation, providing a window into the efficiency of your breathing and how well your body utilises oxygen.

Developed by Patrick McKeown, the BOLT score is more than just a number—it reflects your body's ability to retain and use oxygen efficiently. A higher BOLT score indicates a greater capacity to absorb and use oxygen, leading to improved health outcomes. Conversely, a lower score may signal over-breathing or poor breathing habits, affecting everything from your sleep quality to your stress levels.

Measuring your BOLT score is straightforward and can be done without equipment. Here's a quick guide:

- Find a quiet place where you can sit comfortably without distractions.
- After a few minutes of normal breathing, take a small, silent breath in through your nose and a small, silent breath out.
- Start your stopwatch immediately after you exhale and hold your breath.
- Stop the timer when you feel the first definite desire to breathe or when you feel your breathing muscles contract.
- The aim is not to see how long you can hold your breath by force but to measure the comfortable limit that indicates your body's oxygen efficiency.
- Practice this breathing technique (or should I say lack of) three or four times each day and see if, over time, you can keep increasing the length of time you can comfortably hold your breath.

Why the BOLT Score Matters

The BOLT score is more than just a metric for breath holding; it's a gateway to better health. Improving your BOLT score through breathing exercises can lead to:

- Enhanced sleep quality
- Reduced stress levels
- Improved cardiovascular health
- Greater energy and stamina
- Weight loss

My Experience with the BOLT Score

When I first began measuring my BOLT score, it hovered around 15 seconds, a starting point not unusual. Initial scores can span a wide range, with Patrick McKeown's research revealing that even professional athletes might start as low as 6 seconds. This is a potent reminder that irrespective of one's physical fitness, there's almost always room to refine our breathing efficiency. Dedicated to honing my breathing techniques, I witnessed my BOLT score soar to nearly 40 in just a few months. This leap wasn't merely numerical but a tangible enhancement in my everyday life. My sleep quality saw a remarkable uptick—a boon commonly associated with better breathing practices. Moreover, I found myself enveloped in a more profound sense of relaxation and overall wellbeing, highlighting the pivotal role that breathing plays in our health.

In the grand tapestry of the *Fibre First* diet, understanding and improving your BOLT score fits perfectly into the holistic approach to health. It's not just about what we eat but how we breathe, move, and rest that shapes our health. While we've skimmed the surface of breathing correctly, the subject is vast, akin to an ocean. For deeper lung capacity and a more comprehensive understanding, I recommend diving into my podcast episode with Patrick or submerging yourself in the illuminating depths of his book. For the moment, however, let's distil the quintessence of proper breathing-presenting a mini-guide to unlocking the potential of your breath:

- Our forebears resorted to mouth breathing only as a last-ditch effort to snatch a marginal increase in oxygen intake- a survival tactic when fleeing imminent dangers like a pursuing lion. This primal response triggers a surge in cortisol and adrenaline, gearing the body for a swift fight or flight. However, this ancient mechanism, when activated too frequently in modern life, can inadvertently lead to a cascade of issues, including chronic stress, weight gain, and an array of health complications.
- Contrary to what we might intuitively believe, taking bigger breaths doesn't substantially increase oxygen levels in our blood. It's akin to pouring water into a glass that's already full. Our blood is consistently infused with oxygen, maintaining a saturation level of around 95%. Trying to push this saturation even higher is futile, as the blood's capacity to carry oxygen is already nearly maximised.
- The unsung hero in this dance is carbon dioxide. It's the expert in oxygen's journey from our blood to our tissues, muscles, and organs. Yet, when we exhale too forcefully, especially through the mouth, we unwittingly let this precious gem escape. To truly nourish our body, we need to master the art of controlled breathing, retaining the right amount of carbon dioxide.
- Remember, oxygen isn't just a breath of fresh air; it's the fuel of our metabolism, the spark that ignites fat burning. For this process to be truly efficient, we must maximise oxygen delivery to cells, ensuring that each is energised and ready to perform.
- The Golden Rule of Breathing: Whether we're lost in slumber, peacefully awake at rest, or in the midst of exercise, we must aim to breathe through our noses 100% of the time. Imagine your nose as the exclusive doorway for breath, with rare exceptions. These exceptions include when battling a cold or sinus blockage or in those adrenaline-pumping instances where you might need an extra 2% or 3% of oxygen to heroically lift a car to rescue a trapped pet. Apart from these extraordinary circumstances, resorting to mouth breathing shifts us

into an unnecessary state of alert, triggering our sympathetic nervous system's fight-or-flight response when there's no actual battle to be won.

As we end this discussion on breathing, let's remember that each inhalation and exhalation is a note in the melody of life. By fine-tuning our breath, we don't just breathe; we compose a symphony of well-being that resonates through every cell, every moment. Let's cherish this gift, breathe with intention, and revel in the harmony it brings to our lives.

*****

Social Wellbeing

The World Health Organisation (WHO) recognises three foundational pillars in the rich mosaic of human health: physical, mental, and social wellbeing. Among these, social health weaves its threads prominently, shaping the very fabric of our existence. It's a testament to how deeply our connections with others are intertwined with our overall health, extending far beyond the realm of mere companionship.

Consider the vibrant social tapestry of the centenarians on the Greek island of Ikaria, a living testament to the profound impact of robust social bonds. Here, longevity intertwines with a culture deeply rooted in community and social engagement, illustrating that our relationships are not just supplementary aspects of our lives but central to our vitality.

Our social networks, a rich kaleidoscope of relationships encompassing family, friends, colleagues, and community members, are integral to our daily mood and overall wellness. Amid the relentless pace of modern life, the significance of these connections can sometimes fade into the background. Yet, consciously fostering these relationships is not a mere indulgence but a crucial element of a balanced and healthy life.

Engaging with others with similar interests or purposes is a powerful catalyst for personal growth and happiness. These connections offer a sense of belonging, a support network, and meaningful engagement opportunities. Whether through community service, group activities, or regular gatherings, being part of a collective with a common goal or passion can profoundly enrich our lives.

Dr Shan Hussain
'High-quality social interaction on a regular basis with your immediate peers is helpful for reducing and managing stress. In other words, try to

get together with your friends and family when you can. If your social circle is small, have you considered getting a dog? A recent study in Sweden showed that dog owners were 23 per cent less likely to die of cardiovascular disease, and they also experienced a 20 per cent lower risk of mortality from all causes. The authors were unable to explain this link, but it was felt the additional physical activity and emotional connection between dogs and owners played the most critical roles.'

While the animal kingdom shows a spectrum from solitary wanderers to communal dwellers, species that thrive in groups, such as wolves, lions, and humans, epitomise the essence of being inherently 'social.' Unlike bears, koalas, and leopards, who tread their paths in solitude, creatures of the community, including us, flourish through interaction and connection.

I have identified that there are four human pillars of social behaviour:

Intimacy: Echoing Dr Malcolm Kendrick's wisdom, 'to age happily, you need to be driven more by intimacy and love than achievements and status.' Intimacy isn't confined to romantic entanglements but encompasses deep bonds with family members or confidantes. Such relationships offer a shield against the stressors of life and, to a certain degree, the adverse effects of insulin resistance.

Friendships & Staying Social: As inherently social beings, nurturing significant relationships is crucial for our mental and, consequently, physical health. Research from Brigham Young University underscores the importance of social engagement, which found loneliness and isolation to be as lethal as obesity[6]. The tapestry of social connections enriches our emotional wellbeing and weaves a protective layer against stress, mental health risks, and immunological challenges, extending our lifespan and enhancing our quality of life.

Teams: The adage 'Together Everyone Achieves More' rings true, especially when changing habits, diets and lifestyles. Aligning with others who share our goals magnifies our ability to effect change. This communal effort is not merely about mutual inspiration but is grounded in evidence suggesting shared goals, such as weight loss or fitness, are more attainable within a collective. The synergy of teamwork amplifies our capacity to surpass individual limitations.

Compassion & Giving: The acts of giving and expressing gratitude transcend simple acts of kindness, intertwining with the very fabric of our health.

Engaging in altruism connects us to the broader human saga, fostering a sense of community and collective responsibility. Moreover, compassion towards ourselves and others is linked to heightened joy and reduced depressive symptoms. The Dalai Lama's reflection that modern societies excel in educating the mind yet often neglect the heart's need for compassion is poignant. Studies like the one conducted at the University of California, Berkeley, reveal the life-extending impact of volunteering[3], illustrating the profound health benefits of compassion and community involvement.

In the intricate weave of health, social connections are not just threads but the loom itself, shaping our lives' resilience, vibrancy, and texture.

*****

Mastering Metabolic Metrics: A Guide To Empowered Health

Unravelling the intricacies of metabolic measurements can initially seem daunting, complex, and multi-layered. While sharing a core consensus, global health organisations present a rich mosaic of definitions, measurements, and guidelines. The landscape may appear bewildering at first glance, but in the coming pages, I will share with you just five crucial health measurements that everyone should have regular access to and explain in plain English. This will enable you to slice through all the mumbo-jumbo (medical jargon) and clearly grasp the essence of each metric.

As you already know, insulin resistance, the trunk of my *Tree of Afflictions*, is intricately linked to a myriad of chronic diseases and health conditions. If you were to research the vast online resources to uncover the secrets of insulin resistance, it might present a bewildering array of information, resembling a dense forest of medical jargon and criteria. The World Health Organisation (WHO) set the stage with its foundational definition in 1998, placing insulin resistance at the epicentre of poor health. Metabolic syndrome, as WHO calls it, has a constellation of risk factors, including high blood pressure, high blood sugar levels, abdominal fat, high triglyceride levels, and low HDL cholesterol.

Recognising the critical importance of metabolic health, where the overwhelming proportion of adults in our country are metabolically unwell, clarity and decisive action are imperative. From my and the NHS perspectives, these five indicators paint a comprehensive picture of metabolic health. Encountering three or more of these conditions raises the red flag of insulin resistance/metabolic syndrome:

Waist Circumference: This measurement transcends mere numbers; it's a direct line to your visceral health, with specific thresholds for men and women. However, it misses a vital part of the equation: the significance of a person's waist-to-height ratio, an integral part of assessing metabolic health.

High Triglyceride Levels: This is a warning call to analyse dietary and lifestyle habits.

Low HDL Levels: Far from just beneficial, HDL cholesterol is your cardiovascular system's steadfast guardian.

High Blood Pressure: Silent but telling, these numbers are a discreet plea from your heart and blood vessels for a change in diet or lifestyle.

Blood Sugar Control: It's not merely about highs and lows but preserving internal balance.

While variations in measurements and thresholds may exist across global health organisations, the essence of these factors remains unswervingly consistent. However, the intricate and sometimes conflicting standards can leave many individuals feeling lost. In the following pages, I aim to demystify and simplify this vital assessment of how sensitive or resistant you currently are to insulin.

Empowerment comes from understanding, and understanding leads to action. As you navigate these pages, take control of your health, one measurement at a time. This journey is about transforming complexity into clarity, confusion into comprehension, and data into decisive, health-enhancing actions.

As we look into each of these five measurements, you'll learn their essence and significance and discover how to influence them positively. It's about assuming control, one informed step at a time, converting a bewildering array of statistics into a simple, actionable roadmap towards enhanced health and vitality.

In a moment, we will deconstruct each of these five measurements. At the conclusion of each section, I'll explain how inputting these measurements into our free app contributes to an algorithm generating a straightforward overall health score, the Health Results Metabolic Score (HRM Score). This simple scale from 0 to 100 reflects your current insulin sensitivity; the closer to 100, the more insulin-sensitive you aren't (that's good). Conversely, the closer to zero, the more insulin-resistant you are. But note the word 'current.'

The beauty in all five measurements lies in the potential for improvement. With guidance from this book, our website and app, based on your score, subtle shifts in diet and sometimes lifestyle can significantly enhance your score, often rapidly.

You have two options to obtain these five longevity critical measurements: visiting your doctor and asking them to provide them or using our HRM360 home testing device to measure all of them comfortably at home (see page 954).

Measurement 1: Waistline And Waist-to-Height Ratio

Should we regularly measure body weight, BMI, waist-to-hip circumference, or body fat percentage? The answer is none of them! They all have their flaws. This section aims to demonstrate why your waist-to-height ratio is the pivotal metric. I emphasise this because even today, individuals are sometimes inaccurately deemed unhealthy based on BMI or body weight by medical professionals despite being in good health. The waist-to-height ratio stands out for its simplicity (requiring no GP visit or special equipment) and its significance as a marker of health.

It's such a crucial measurement that in many medical circles, a waist-to-height ratio exceeding 0.5, coupled with at least two of the following four conditions: high blood pressure, high triglycerides, low HDL, or high blood sugar, confirms the presence of insulin resistance, or what your doctor still might call metabolic syndrome. The waist-to-height ratio acts as a cornerstone. Whilst a slender waist doesn't guarantee freedom from metabolic issues, excessive midriff weight often signals that dietary and lifestyle changes could profoundly benefit your internal health.

The waist-to-height ratio offers one of the most insightful health screening tests and is incredibly straightforward. Grab a piece of string and cut it to match your height, from tip to toe. Now, take a relaxed breath and wrap that string around your waist at the belly button level. If that string doesn't double-wrap snugly, consider it a cheeky nudge from your body, hinting at possible insulin resistance issues. Who knew a piece of string could hold such weighty secrets?

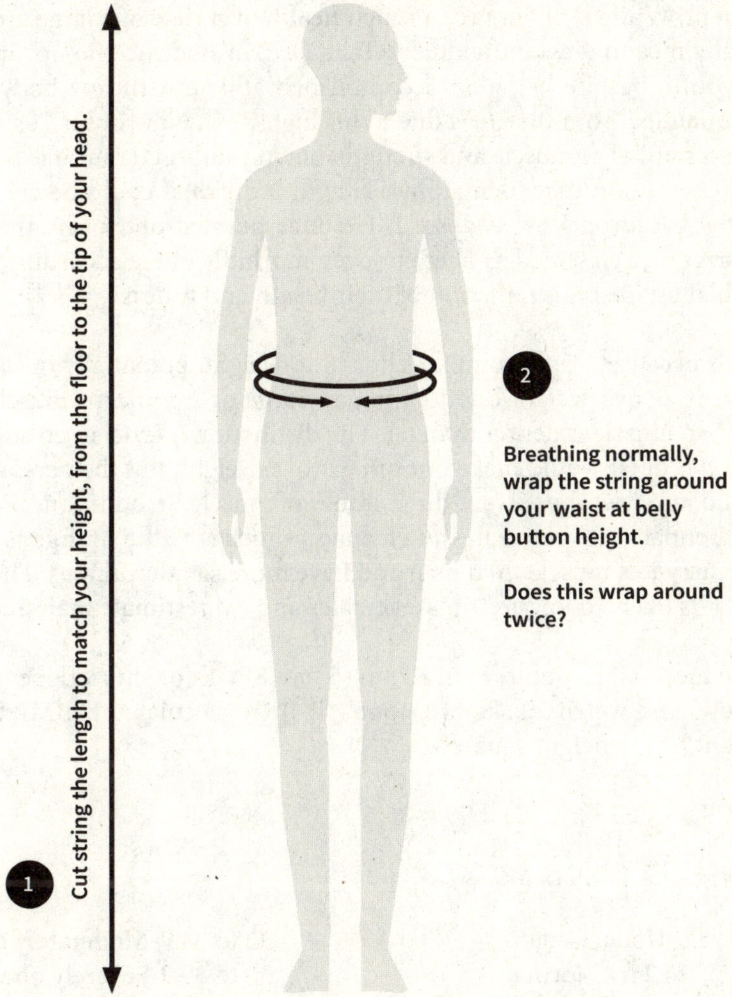

Alternatively, a tape measure can provide even more accuracy. Divide your waist measurement by your height. Ideally, this ratio should be 0.5 or less. If it's higher, say 0.6, monitor the number as you adjust your diet and lifestyle. If this ratio decreases over time, even in small increments, it indicates positive changes.

Now, I want to underscore the significance of this measurement. To do so, let's critically examine the flaws of other commonly used metrics, starting with BMI.

The BMI was initially devised for population studies, not individual assessment. While it might give a rough health overview of a large group, it's practically meaningless individually. Take Dr Ben Bocchicchio, for instance. In his youth, despite being an accomplished athlete with low body fat, he was disqualified from the army due to his high BMI. Now in his 70s, Dr Ben remains a symbol of muscle and strength, having authored multiple books on fitness. The notion that such a physically fit individual could be considered unhealthy based on BMI is absurd. He once pointed out to me that many NFL players are classified as obese or even morbidly obese according to their BMI-a blatant misrepresentation of their health and fitness.

BMI fails because it only compares height to weight, potentially mislabelling individuals as overweight due to a larger frame or significant muscle mass. Remember, muscle is denser than fat. The distinction is crucial: an additional three stones of fat would make one appear overweight, but the person would look solid and fit if those were three stones of muscle. In addition, BMI does not differentiate between males and females, which is a little strange as women tend to carry less muscle than men and have more slender frames. Therefore, overall, it is likely to underestimate females and overestimate males.

Let's use me as an example. I am 1.73m (5 foot 8) tall (or short, depending on your view) and weigh 79.5kg (12 stone 7 lbs). To calculate my BMI, I divide my weight by my height squared.

BMI = 79.5 / (1.73 x 1.73) 2.99 = 26.5

The BMI Index guidelines are as follows:

- <18.5-Underweight
- 18.5 to 24.9-Normal
- 25 to 29.9-Overweight (fat)
- 30 to 34.9-Moderately obese
- 35 to 39.9-Severely obese
- 40 plus-Morbidly obese

Based on BMI only, I am overweight and edging towards becoming obese (take a look at my photo on the back cover and form your own opinion; by the way, I am talking about the one on the right)!

Body Weight

Weight as a standalone metric can be misleading. If two friends of vastly different heights weigh the same, it suggests that one may not have an optimal weight for their height. While tracking weight can show general trends, it's crucial not to fixate on daily scale readings. Day-to-day weight can fluctuate significantly because of factors like water retention, making frequent weigh-ins an unreliable measure of your genuine progress.

Waistline

It's known by many names, such as' beer belly', 'muffin top', or 'love handles', which are endearing terms that barely disguise the health risks associated with visceral fat. But don't let the playful nicknames fool you. Measuring your waistline offers valuable insight into your health. While it's not the only measurement to consider, it certainly packs a punch in terms of importance. The fat nestling around our waist is not just about aesthetics; it's the silent sentinel of our well-being.

Taking a waist measurement is more than a routine check; it's an anthropometric exploration, a Greek-inspired pathway ('anthropos' for human, 'metron' for measure) into the core of your health. It's where the rubber meets the road, revealing the truth about the fat cloaking our vital organs-heart, kidneys, liver, digestive system, and pancreas. This unassuming number is a crystal ball into potential health hazards, from heart disease and diabetes to strokes and cancer.

The NHS draws its lines in the sand: 37 inches (94cm) for men and 31.5 inches (80cm) for women. Cross these thresholds, and you're officially in the danger zone, with an urgent memo to consult your GP. And let's not sugar-coat research from the Mayo Clinic unfolds a stark narrative: a 7% uptick in mortality risk for men and 9% for women with every additional 2 inches around the waist. The numbers don't lie, and they certainly don't mince words.

While your waistline is a tale-telling metric, it's not the entire story, especially for those on the higher or lower ends of the height spectrum. It's a piece of the puzzle, a chapter in your health narrative, but not the entire book. So, as we explore these numbers, let's remember they're signposts to better health, guiding us but not defining us.

Body Fat Percentage: Decoding the Digits

Navigating the realm of body fat percentage is like trying to solve a Rubik's Cube blindfolded. It's a valuable indicator of a healthy body, offering a snapshot of our fat-to-total body mass ratio. But oh, the ways to measure it! There are websites where you can feed your stats to a hungry algorithm, digital scales that zap you with a pulse and guess your fat content, and callipers that pinch you like a curious crab to gauge the fat in different body zones.

Let's break it down: if you tip the scales at 81kg (180lbs) and harbour 8kg (18lbs) of fat, your body is rocking a 10% fat percentage. Simple, right? But here's the catch: getting an accurate reading is as elusive as finding a single Lego piece in a toy box. It's not just about shedding pounds or bulking up. Muscle gains, water retention, or loss can throw your numbers into a tailspin. Picture this: I hop out of bed, and my scales whisper a 17% body fat. Fast forward two hours post-tennis or gym session, and suddenly it's party time at 13%-as if my fat decided to take a quick holiday!

Approach your scale's body fat measurements with a healthy dose of scepticism. While they may not always hit the mark accurately, they're still handy for noting the direction you travel. Your post-wake-up, pre-breakfast weigh-in is your golden hour for the most reliable read, but whenever you weigh yourself, try to be consistent with the time of day.

Most importantly, remember that the fat warranting our utmost attention is the visceral fat ensconced around our waistline. This stealthy adversary is not just an unwelcome guest; it's a powerful foreteller of our health span and lifespan. On the flip side, subcutaneous fat, which pads our thighs, arms, and more, though often less aesthetically pleasing, doesn't hold the same ominous sway over our wellbeing.

So now you know the most important measurement to be taking is your waist-to-height ratio. Once you've recorded it, be sure to input the measurements into our free Health Results app (see page 808). The chart below shows how your measurements impact your overall metabolic score in our app.

Waist circumference	Men <90cm	Women <80cm	Adds a positive score
	Men 90 - 93.9cm	Women 80 - 82cm	No score added
	Men 94 - 102cm	Women 82 - 88cm	Negative score
	Men >102cm	Women >88cm	Increased negative score
Waist to height ratio	<0.5		Adds a positive score

Measurement 2: Blood Pressure

Managing blood pressure is akin to fine-tuning the myriad valves of an intricate, life-sustaining machine. Each heartbeat is a testament to life's rhythm, propelling a life-giving surge through an extensive network of veins and arteries.

As blood pushes against the arterial walls, it's like a river persistently flowing against its banks. When the pressure escalates, becoming too forceful, it's not just the banks at risk of erosion. Your arteries, too, feel the strain, potentially spiralling into a series of health challenges. This relentless pressure can wear down the channels sustaining life, leading to conditions that ripple through your health.

Understanding this delicate balance is crucial. Like the ebb and flow of a river, your blood pressure tells a story of how well the life within you is regulated and how the dance between pressure and flow is choreographed. It's a narrative pivotal to your health, a tale where each heartbeat counts and the pressure it exerts can turn the page to either vitality or vulnerability.

Your blood pressure reading is a tale of two numbers. The larger number, your systolic blood pressure, is the star of the show when your heart takes centre stage, contracting with all its might. The supporting actor? Your diastolic blood pressure is the quieter number, representing the moments of calm between the heartbeats when your heart fills up and prepares for the next act. These two numbers are not just digits on a screen: they're the pulse of your inner world, whispering tales of your current state of health. The good news is that high blood pressure, or hypertension, doesn't have to be a lifelong script. Small, actionable steps can lead to significant improvements in your health narrative.

A spotlight on hypertension: Public Health England's 2017 revelation shines bright. Reducing your systolic blood pressure by a mere 10mmHg is akin to casting a protective spell, slashing the risk of coronary heart disease by 20% and heart failure by a striking 28%.[7]

How you take your blood pressure is important to ensure an accurate measurement. Arm or wrist home blood pressure monitors are accurate but only properly used. The blood pressure cuff should be at the same level as the heart. Sit for five minutes before measuring your blood pressure so your body is relaxed. Repeat the measurement three times and record the lowest reading. Are you wondering if this DIY method stacks up to your GP's gold standard?

Interestingly, it's even more precise for many, thanks to the notorious 'white coat syndrome.' That's right, the mere sight of a doctor's white coat can send your blood pressure soaring higher than a kite on a windy day. Plus, let's face it, visits to the doctor aren't exactly daily occurrences, and they often align with times when you're under the weather. Being unwell can spike your blood pressure, skewing it from your everyday norm. Thus, a single reading in such a scenario might lead you to join the league of the 'unnecessarily medicated' due to elevated readings spurred by circumstance rather than an underlying condition.

Once recorded, input the two measurements into the free Health Results app. The chart below shows how your measurements impact your overall metabolic score.

Blood Pressure		
	SBP <120 and DBP <80	Increased positive score
	SBP 120-129 or DBP 80-84	Adds a positive score
	SBP 130-139 or DBP 85-89	No score added
	SBP 140-159 or DBP 90-99	Negative score
	SBP 160-179 and/or DBP 100-109	Increased negative score
On medication for BP	Yes	Increased negative score

Measurement 3: Blood Glucose

We've traversed the blood glucose terrain with the thoroughness of seasoned explorers, so I'll save you from diving back into those depths. Yet, it's crucial to highlight the importance of measuring your fasting blood glucose levels to get the clearest picture of your metabolic baseline. Fear not if the thought of a finger prick sends shivers down your spine. Imagine it as less of a prick and more of a love tap for your health. Done with a gentle touch, it's as painless as blinking. Here is a straightforward guide designed to make this crucial health checkpoint as easy as pie:

- **Preparation:** Begin with an 8 to 12-hour fasting period, drinking water only.

- **Hand Preparation:** Thoroughly wash your hands with warm water to ensure cleanliness and optimal blood flow.

- **Test Strip Setup:** Carefully insert the test strip into your meter, ensuring the single line faces outwards.

- **Lancing Device Preparation:** Equip your lancing device with a fresh needle for each test.

- **Blood Sample Collection:** Gently use the lancing device on the side of your fingertip to obtain a small drop of blood.

- **Testing:** Gently touch and hold the edge of the test strip to the blood drop, allowing it to absorb the blood.

- **Reading the Result:** Wait a few seconds for the meter to process; your blood glucose level will be displayed on the screen.

- **Post-test Procedure:** Properly dispose of the used needle and test strip, ensuring safety and hygiene.

Once recorded, input the measurement into the free Health Results app. The chart below shows how your measurements impact your overall metabolic score.

Fasting glucose	<5.5 mmol/L	Increased positive score
	5.5 mmol/L	Adds a positive score
	5.6 mmol/L	No score added
	5.7-6.9 mmol/L	Negative score
	>6.9 mmol/L	Increased negative score
Taking T2D medication	Yes	Increased negative score

Measurement 4: Blood Triglycerides

Triglycerides are a type of fat (lipid) found in our blood. Though often misunderstood, they play a pivotal role as the energy reservoirs of our bodies. These fats, distinct from cholesterol, are like the fuel in your car's tank, stored and ready to power your body's needs. While cholesterol is a building block, crafting cells and hormones, triglycerides wait patiently in the wings, ready to release energy when your body demands it.

Imagine your body as a sophisticated energy plant. When you indulge in a meal, your liver acts as a meticulous accountant, converting surplus calories into triglycerides, especially from sugar, refined carbs, or ultra-processed foods. Picture these triglycerides as barrels of oil stockpiled for future energy needs. However, overstocking these barrels—having high levels of triglycerides in our blood—can signal an imbalance in your body's energy economy, known as hypertriglyceridemia.

Let me quickly demystify the term 'mmol/L.' This measurement, akin to measuring the concentration of ingredients in a recipe, is used universally in health metrics like cholesterol, triglycerides, and glucose levels. Think of it as a standardised way of measuring how concentrated these substances are in your blood. However, context is key; a 'good' score varies between markers. For instance, 0.8 mmol/L might be a cause for celebration if you're measuring triglycerides but a call to action if it's your HDL cholesterol reading.

It's empowering to know that your dietary choices and lifestyle habits control your triglyceride levels. Just like fine-tuning your diet can revamp your overall health, it can also recalibrate your triglyceride levels, steering them towards the optimal range.

Measuring your triglycerides is straightforward. Either your doctor can perform it, or you can obtain it in the comfort of your home with our HRM360 device. The process is largely the same as measuring your blood glucose level. If you plan to check both your triglycerides and glucose levels concurrently while the test cartridges are different, one gentle prick of the finger is all it takes to draw the necessary drop of blood.

Once recorded, input the measurement into the free Health Results app. The chart below shows how your measurements impact your overall metabolic score.

Lipids		
Fasting triglycerides	<1.3 mmol/L	Increased positive score
	1.3-1.69 mmol/L	Adds a positive score
	1.7-1.99 mmol/L	No score added
	2-2.29 mmol/L	Negative score
	>2.29 mmol/L	Increased negative score

Measurement 5: HDL Cholesterol

HDL Cholesterol (HDL-C), often called 'good cholesterol', is akin to the body's internal clean-up crew. It patrols the bloodstream, rounding up excess cholesterol and ferrying it back to the liver for disposal or recycling. HDL stands for high-density lipoproteins; these tiny molecular sponges are crucial in maintaining your body's delicate balance.

As Dr Malcolm Kendrick insightfully remarks in his best-selling book, *The Great Cholesterol Con*, cholesterol is not a villain but a vital building block. Echoing this sentiment, the NHS acknowledges the protective role of HDL, stating that 'good cholesterol (HDL) makes you less likely to encounter heart problems or a stroke.' While cholesterol often gets a bad rap, HDL-C is the unsung hero, ensuring that your cardiovascular system runs smoothly and efficiently, much like a well-oiled machine.

Your HDL cholesterol levels can be assessed by your doctor or conveniently at home using the HRM360 device, which is automatically recorded at the same time as your triglycerides (it uses the same lipid cartridge).

Once recorded, input the measurement into the free Health Results app. The chart below shows how your measurements impact your overall metabolic score.

Lipids			
HDL-C	Men >1 mmol/L	Women >1.3 mmol/L	Adds a positive score

HDL to Triglycerides Ratio

While we've discussed it already, I want to highlight it again for completeness in this measurement topic. This metric stands shoulder-to-shoulder with your waist-to-height ratio in importance: the ratio between your HDL (High-Density Lipoprotein) and triglycerides. This ratio isn't just a number; it's a window into the nuanced world of LDL cholesterol, often dubbed the 'bad' cholesterol.

However, as we've seen already, the narrative around LDL is not as straightforward as it's often portrayed. LDL cholesterol is a tale of two types. One type is akin to a longevity ally, potentially aiding in extending our lives, while the other type emerges as a signal of poor metabolic health. The quandary lies in standard blood tests bundling these two types of LDL together, offering a combined reading without distinguishing between the beneficial and the detrimental.

Enter the HDL-to-triglycerides ratio. This ratio isn't just a set of numbers; it sheds light on the type of LDL coursing through your veins. A favourable ratio suggests the presence of the benign, longevity-friendly type of LDL-A, while an unfavourable ratio may signal the dominance of the more ominous variant LDL-B.

As I wrap up this discussion on these pivotal health metrics, you might be pondering the role of uric acid, especially considering its significance in evaluating liver health and fructose processing, as highlighted earlier in the book. Indeed, uric acid is a valuable indicator and one that our HRM 360 (see page 954) home device is equipped to measure. However, its connection to insulin resistance isn't yet universally acknowledged in medical circles. However, as the landscape of health understanding evolves rapidly, it may find its place in this section in future iterations of this book.

*****

Cool Down To Better Control Insulin

Ah, the unexpected hero in the battle against insulin resistance: cold exposure! Who would've thought subjecting yourself to chilly conditions could improve your insulin levels? It all comes down, amongst other things, to something called brown fat.

Most fat in our bodies is known as 'white fat,' aptly named for its pale appearance. This pastiness can be attributed to a low concentration of mitochondria, those miniature power plants within cells. Mitochondria possess a brownish-red colour, which brings us to the intriguing part: nestled within our bodies are special enclaves of fat that are darker and smaller. These are the elite corners of our body's fat landscape, brimming with mitochondria, akin to the VIP lounges of the fat world.

Brown Adipose Tissue (BAT), or brown fat, is strategically located in several key areas across the human body. Here's where you'll find this metabolic goldmine:

- Around the neck and shoulders
- Along the spine
- Near the kidneys
- In the chest area

Brown fat diverges from its white counterpart in both function and distribution. Unlike white fat, which acts primarily as a storage unit for energy and is found throughout the body, brown fat specialises in heat production. This makes it a pivotal player in maintaining body temperature, especially in cooler environments. The metabolic activity of brown fat, fuelled by its rich mitochondrial content, makes it an essential component of our body's thermogenic machinery.

Mitochondria are like the Energiser Bunnies of our cells, churning out energy by breaking down glucose and fats. However, the mitochondria in brown adipose tissue are rebellious. While most mitochondria play by the rules and burn nutrients based on the cell's energy needs, these mitochondria are like,

'Nah, we're just here to create warmth.' So, here's the story: white fat wants to hoard fat, and brown fat wants to burn it to keep you toasty. In fact, when activated, brown adipose tissue cranks up its metabolism to a similar level as muscles while doing resistance exercise.[8]

You might wonder, 'How do I activate this amazing brown fat?' Well, it turns out that when your skin starts feeling the chill, brown adipose tissue springs into action. The magic number seems to begin at 18°C [9]. These cells kick into gear at this temperature to warm up your body. In adults, this is where the brown fat cells get down to business and start burning glucose to keep you warm. And if you drop even colder, you get bonus points—you start to shiver. Now, I'm not saying you should take an ice bath every day (unless you're into that sort of thing), but shivering and non-shivering cold water showers or baths can be your ticket to lower insulin resistance and a shield against chronic illnesses.

If you want to learn more about the science behind it, Dr Huberman's thermogenesis YouTube podcast has you covered. So, whether you're shivering like a champ or enjoying a refreshing cold shower, know that you're defying the icy waters and insulin resistance. And here's the thing: a treasure trove of research shows that cold exposure does wonders for your immune system and microbiome, too.

I am often asked: how do you take that first step into the icy embrace of cold water and emerge not as a frozen popsicle but as a master of chill? The secret, my daring adventurers, is more straightforward than you might think. Take a cold-water shower to kickstart your morning. Yes, it sounds like a perverse scheme to jolt you out of your snug, warm cocoon, but bear with me—there's genius in this chilly challenge.

Steel yourself for an electrifying jolt, an intense sensation like a polar expedition. But then, behold—a curious transformation. The initial shock morphs into a peculiar kind of bliss. Indeed, folks around the globe willingly dive into this icy ritual daily, and they wouldn't have it any other way! Legend has it that Katherine Hepburn was a devotee of the daily cold plunge, singing praises of its invigorating effects.

And the perks extend beyond mere exhilaration and the control of insulin. Cold water is a potion for your hair and skin, bestowing shine, strength, and overall vitality. It's like nature's own beauty treatment, sealing your pores with a cool kiss—especially beneficial post-shave. Dr Joseph Mercola, a sage in natural health circles, touts its virtues: lowering blood pressure, unclogging arteries, and bolstering the immune system.

Now, for my personal tried-and-tested strategy: Begin your shower with lukewarm water, a gentle introduction to your cold-water escapade. But soon after, about 10 seconds in, unleash the frost with a bold dial twist. As you envelop yourself in organic suds (skip the chemical concoctions), give your scalp a spirited massage. That commits you because you can't leave your icy sanctuary until the soapy bubbles disappear entirely.

As I embrace the invigorating chill, I often belt out a tune under the cold cascade; it's not just a performance for the shampoo bottles; it's a powerful mental wellness hack, a strategy that BBC's Dr Mosley champions. A natural high that makes facing the day's challenges with a smile that much easier. Embracing the cold shower with a loud, singing voice fortifies your body and elevates your spirit, ensuring you step out ready to conquer the world with joy and resilience. By stacking habits, you're reaping the benefits of cold-water therapy and serenading the soul, hitting the high notes of health and happiness in one fell swoop.

And there is better news: cold baths and showers have been associated with the release of endorphins, often called 'happiness hormones.' When you expose yourself to cold water, it can result in a slight shock to your system, and this shock can trigger their release. Endorphins promote feelings of positivity and well-being, which can contribute to a happier mood. A cold shower in the morning can set a positive tone for the day and provide a sense of freshness and alertness. It's like a natural mood booster that can energise you and improve your mental state without needing a glass of wine before work!

I recently splurged on a home ice bath because why not, right? It's like a personal challenge straight out of an action movie. At a bone-chilling 4°C, I can only endure it for a measly three minutes or so. Pathetic, I know, but I'm a work in progress. Now, a couple of my pro football buddies are a whole different breed. They tackle that icy abyss for a monstrous 10 minutes every single day. Their secret weapon? Belief. Their medical teams are so convinced of the icy magic (known as cryotherapies) that they do it religiously.

So, there you have it, my chilly adventure in the world of cold-water exposure. Singing and shivering—it's the ultimate morning ritual for the slightly insane. Join the club, my friend, and embrace the cold!

Chilling Your Way to Weight Loss

A few years back, my son-in-law Jake and I set off on a frostbitten ten-day trek to The North Pole (catch the chilly details on YouTube, 'The Last Degree North Pole'). The experts warned us we'd need a staggering 9,000 calories daily to provide the necessary energy to keep our bodies warm.

As we trudged across the icy expanse, sledges in tow, we ditched our bulky coats for surprisingly thin jackets, even as the thermometer plunged to -40 degrees. Our bodies remained a cosy haven of heat in motion, though our extremities begged to differ, craving the embrace of thick thermal gloves and socks. And then came the call of nature—exposing oneself to the polar air was a bracing experience, to say the least. Yet, remarkably, only the hands felt the brunt, screaming in protest as we shifted from triple to double layers to manoeuvre a piece of toilet paper, whereas our private parts remained warm from our internal furnace.

Here's the icy revelation: being cold is an undercover calorie burner. Our bodies go into overdrive, igniting calories to fend off the chill throughout the core of the body (hands and feet seem to be sacrificial lambs – I mean limbs). Closer to home, standing in the nippy embrace of the sea during a British summer might outpace the calorie burn of a jog. Surfing over sprinting, anyone? And as for shivering, it's practically a workout, torching 100 to 150 calories every frosty quarter-hour. Beware, though; there's a fine line to tread before hypothermia sets in.

And let's not forget the weight loss wonders of a cool slumber. Nestled in a chilly bedroom, your body embarks on a nocturnal calorie-burning spree, striving to maintain that perfect sleep body temperature. So, as you drift off into weightless dreams, your metabolism is silently sculpting away. Who knew turning down the central heating could be the secret ingredient to shedding pounds in your sleep?

The Cool Edge Beyond Shedding Pounds

A few years back, an unforgettable adventure unfolded as my brother and I, alongside Sir Richard Branson, his intrepid offspring Holly and Sam, and a band of spirited cyclists, embarked on a whirlwind adventure across Italy's breathtaking landscapes. Each gruelling day, spanning 80 to 200 miles, concluded with a rather unconventional ritual: a plunge into a kiddie paddling pool transformed into an icy oasis. The purpose? To combat muscle soreness and fend off the dreaded DOMS (delayed onset muscle soreness) that often sneaks up 24 to 48 hours post-exertion.

The science behind this chilly remedy taps into the marvels of our biology.

At the heart of it is a hormone named adiponectin, awakened by the cold to hustle glucose into our muscles, sparking an anabolic state that turbocharges recovery. This cold-induced boost eases soreness and propels our recovery forward at an astonishing pace. But the magic of cold doesn't stop at muscle recovery. A dive into the world of cold thermogenesis (CT) unveils a treasure trove of health benefits that have captivated researchers and elite athletes alike. Integrating CT into regular training regimens can work wonders, including:

Easing Stress: Like a reset button for the mind, cold exposure can significantly diminish stress levels.

Boosting Immunity: Regular cold showers or dips can fortify the immune system, making it more robust against invaders.

Revving Up Metabolism: Embracing the cold can accelerate metabolic rates, turning the body into a calorie-burning powerhouse.

Activating Adiponectin: This hormone gets a nudge, enhancing glucose consumption and reducing the body's insulin requirements.

So, my trek to the North Pole and the cycle through Italy taught me more than just the endurance of spirit and the joy of adventure. It introduced me to the profound and varied benefits of cold exposure, proving that the path to vitality is sometimes paved with a bit of shiver and chill.

*****

Unveiling Nature's Nutrition

I often find myself embroiled in animated discussions among my nutritionist friends. The topic? The existence of a definitive list of superfoods. While some advocate for the simplicity of embracing all that's natural, I'm inclined to offer a guided tour through what I consider the crème de la crème of nutritional choices.

On my Health Results platform, be it the website or the free app, my team and I have curated over 700 recipes, each a canvas showcasing these nutritional powerhouses. These superfoods aren't just natural; they're nutritional titans, offering a copiousness of vitamins, minerals, and healthy fats unmatched in density and potency. From the solo acts of avocados, spinach, and garlic to the ensemble performances of organic meats, each one plays an active role in our health.

While you don't need to read through each of the Superfoods in detail, you will find some little nuggets of information if you have the time. But first, let's address the elephant in the room: won't pivoting our diet towards these superfoods strain our wallets? True, opting for organic produce, premium meats, and local harvests can carry a heftier price tag than their processed counterparts. However, embarking on this lifestyle might actually cause your overall expenses to dwindle. Yes, the ingredients of a vibrant life come at a premium, but they open doors to numerous savings.

10 Ways You'll Be Pocketing Extra Cash:

Smaller Portions, Bigger Savings: The *Fibre First* diet naturally reduces your appetite, leading to smaller portions and less frequent grocery store trips.

Intermittent Fasting: Whether you skip meals by design or simply eat less often, your food bills will see a noticeable drop.

Farewell, Plastic Bottles: Wave goodbye to bottled water and its environmental toll. Filtered tap water is not only cost-effective but also a healthier choice.

Ditch the Health Mags: With frequent updates on the Health Results site, nobody needs to spend on magazine subscriptions.

Robust Health, Fewer Sick Days: Less time off work for illness benefits your wallet and enhances your professional standing. No one benefits from being known as 'Sick Note Jo'.

Fast Food Fiascos: Say goodbye to the costly cycle of fast-food highs and lows and the incessant hunger they provoke.

Soda, Be Gone: Eliminate the sugary trap of fizzy drinks, notorious for their role in health issues and an unwelcome expense.

No More Diet Club Dues: If these clubs truly delivered long-term results, they'd be out of business.

A Stable Wardrobe: Escape the costly cycle of yo-yo dieting. Invest in a wardrobe that fits your stable, healthier size, and enjoy long-lasting wear.

Affordable Activities: Embrace walking, home workouts, and the simple joys of active living over costly gym memberships or impulse buys designed to fill a void rather than enrich your life.

Indeed, while the Superfood grocery bill may reflect a premium, the holistic savings of adopting a natural lifestyle are profound.

Introducing The Superfoods Top 20

1. Coconut: The Tropical Powerhouse

Before we discuss the myriad wonders of coconuts, let's address a common misconception. Recently, some newspapers have cast a shadow over coconuts, pointing fingers at their fat content and prematurely linking it to cholesterol woes and heart troubles. However, these claims are ripples from an outdated pool of information that you already know by now, wrongly equating saturated fats with cardiovascular risks. It's high time we clear the air: coconuts are not just safe but a treasure trove of health benefits.

Coconuts are revered in folklore and science alike. Hindu mythology christens the coconut as 'kalpavriksha'- the all-giving tree in the garden of paradise. This is no exaggeration, as the coconut tree provides many resources, from nutritious food to sturdy shelter. Despite what the name suggests, coconuts are technically a fruit, not a nut.

Now, let's unpack coconuts' nutritional punch. These tropical delights are bursting with essential nutrients and, most importantly, lots of fibre. They are rich in B vitamins like B1, B3, B5, and B6, and they don't skimp on vitamins C and E either. Minerals? Coconuts have you covered with calcium, selenium, sodium, magnesium, and phosphorous.

The fibre content in coconut varies depending on the form in which it's consumed. For fresh coconut meat, the fibre content is approximately:

Fresh coconut meat: 9 grams of fibre per 100 grams
Dried coconut (desiccated): Around 18 grams of fibre per 100 grams.
Coconut flour: Approximately 38 grams of fibre per 100 grams, making it an excellent high-fibre option for baking and cooking.

Coconuts offer a spectrum of culinary wonders:

Coconut Cream and Milk: Lactose-intolerant folks, rejoice! Coconut milk and cream are dairy-free and a wellspring of medium-chain fatty acids (MCFAs)-resembling the beneficial fats found in human breast milk. Use coconut milk to add creaminess to your curries or whip up a tropical cocktail with a healthy punch.

Coconut Water: Nature's natural sports drink, is low in calories and high in potassium, an essential electrolyte. It's an excellent hydration choice, especially post-workout. However, be vigilant; the market is awash with adulterated versions. Stick to natural coconut water to reap its full benefits.

Coconut Flour: This virtually carb-free marvel is derived from the dried, ground flesh of the coconut. Rich in fibre, protein, and healthy fats, it's a versatile substitute for grain-based flour. Use it to make bread and scrumptious cakes, or thicken your sauces and curries for that extra richness.

Coconut Chunks or Flakes: These are perfect for snacking or adding an exotic twist to your salads and curries. They're not just about taste; they are full of fibre and pack a nutritional punch, too.

Desiccated Coconut: This is dried, shredded coconut flesh, retaining all its natural sweetness and health benefits. Sprinkle it over your breakfast (if you are still eating it) or blend it into your smoothie for a tropical twist.

Coconut Aminos: A soy sauce alternative that's brimming with amino acids, vitamins, and minerals. It's a flavourful, healthier choice for seasoning your dishes.

The humble coconut is not just a food item; it's a symbol of vitality, versatility, and nourishment. From its water to its flesh, every part of the coconut is a testament to nature's generosity.

2. Avocado: The Superfruit Champion

While many fruits boast health benefits, they predominantly consist of carbohydrates, which, while not entirely villainous, are not always our allies in battles against insulin resistance, weight gain, fatty liver, or even gout. Enter the avocado, a paradigm of nutritional excellence primarily composed of fats and fibre- a delightful deviation from the fruit norm.

Imagine if you were marooned on a deserted island and could choose only one food companion—alongside coconuts and eggs, avocado would surely be your best choice. Its nutritional profile is nothing short of spectacular, a mosaic of health benefits waiting to be unleashed with every creamy bite.

Let's dissect this green marvel: avocados are a powerhouse of heart-friendly fats. One avocado has 29 g of healthy fat and 11 g of fibre! The star player in this fat ensemble is oleic acid, also known as omega-9, the same virtuous component that graces olives. Oleic acid is not just another fat; it's a crusader against inflammation and a guardian against cancer. But the wonders of avocados don't stop at fats. They are a treasure trove of antioxidants, the valiant protectors of our eyesight and overall cellular health. High potassium intake is often heralded as a shield against high blood pressure and kidney failure.

Feasting on both halves of an average-sized avocado is like indulging in 150g of pure, unadulterated healthfulness. This superfruit is brimming with vitamins B5, B6, C, E, K, folate, and potassium. The mineral medley continues with copper, iron, magnesium, manganese, phosphorus, vitamins B1, B3, and zinc. Let's not overlook how its fibre content offers a robust source of nourishment for our gut-friendly bacterial inhabitants. Remarkably, 25% of this fibre is soluble, ensuring our digestive allies are well-fed and thriving.

3. Eggs: Nature's Nutritional Powerhouses

Once unjustly maligned for their cholesterol content, eggs are celebrated for their remarkable nutritional profile. The days of painstakingly removing yolks based on outdated cholesterol fears are long gone. Today, we understand that eggs, yolks included, are densely packed with nourishment, and contrary to past beliefs, they don't exacerbate cholesterol levels, not the LDL pattern B type implicated in heart disease.

Eggs are a veritable treasure trove of high-quality proteins, boasting all nine essential amino acids. They are rich in vitamins, including A, B12, B2, and B5, and a wealth of minerals. The humble egg is nature's multivitamin, encapsulating good fats, phosphorus, selenium, and a spectrum of life-sustaining nutrients. Each egg is a testament to nature's ingenuity- a self-contained package designed to create new life, brimming with pure, life-affirming goodness. When it comes to eggs, opting for organic is worth the investment, as they often boast a more favourable balance of omega-3 to omega-6 fatty acids.

Navigating the Egg Aisle: Making Informed Choices

Understanding egg labelling is important for making informed choices that align with your nutritional and ethical standards. Let's crack open the standards for organic and 'free-range' eggs:

Organic Eggs:

- Smaller flock sizes and lower stocking densities.
- More exits from the hen house to encourage natural ranging.
- No beak trimming, preventing pain and preserving natural foraging behaviour.
- A GM-free diet ensures a natural, wholesome feed.

Free-Range Eggs:

- Larger flock sizes and higher stocking densities than organic.
- There are fewer requirements for exits from the hen house.
- Routine beak trimming is common, impacting natural behaviour.
- Potential use of GM crops in feed.

For those seeking an omega-3 boost, look for eggs labelled as rich in this essential fatty acid. These eggs come from hens fed a diet high in flax seeds, a natural source of omega-3. And for the budget-conscious, mixed-size egg cartons offer a practical and cost-effective option- a nod to the natural diversity of egg production.

The more orange the yolk, the more omega-3 it typically contains.

4. Nuts: A Crunchy Conundrum

Let me start with a curious fact: the most popular 'nut' in the world, the peanut, is a masquerading legume that dresses up as a nut. This revelation throws a spanner in the works for those with 'nut' allergies, who, it turns out, might have a vendetta against legumes instead. The label on food packaging saying 'may contain nuts' is often a nutritional blunder!

Packed with life-sustaining nutrients, nuts are the starting blocks of plant life, akin to the nutrient-dense yolk of an egg that nourishes a developing chick. Have you ever wondered why 'nutrition' starts with 'nut'? It's no coincidence! Among the nutritional elite, we have walnuts, pecans, pistachios, Brazilian nuts, hazelnuts, and macadamias, all powerhouses of health and offer a burst of flavour for your palate. 'But what about cashews and almonds?' you might ask. Though technically seeds, let's not split hairs; in the grand scheme of health and vitality, let's add these two as honorary members of the nut club.

Nuts are a symphony of health: full of fibre, rich in proteins, omega-3 fatty acids, magnesium, potassium, iron, copper, and an assortment of B vitamins. However, a word of caution: while nuts are nutritional titans, portion control is key, especially for those monitoring the scales.

When shopping for nuts, seek those in their most natural, unprocessed form. Beware of nuts in salt suits and drenched in hydrogenated oils. That said if you're caught between a nut and a hard place, opting for any nut over a packet of crisps or sweets is still a smart move. You'll encounter an abundance of scientific terms in the world of nuts. Here's a quick decoder:

Phytochemicals: These are the plant's personal bodyguards, protecting seeds and nuts from various threats. Let's call them 'phytonutrients' for a friendlier vibe.

Phytosterols: Plant-based cholesterol lookalikes that, paradoxically, can help lower our body's cholesterol absorption.

Polyphenols: Antioxidant champions, combating diseases and feeding our friendly gut bacteria.

Flavonoids: Over 4,000 varieties of these super antioxidants add colour to our fruits and veggies and pack a healthful punch.

Lignans: Plant oestrogens that may have anti-cancerous and anti-inflammatory properties, showing promise in reducing cardiovascular disease risks.

The Excellent Nutty Eight

In the grand assembly of superfoods, a special commendation is reserved for the 'Excellent Nutty Eight'- a revved-up group of nuts heralded for their high fibre content, potent antioxidants, and wealth of minerals and vitamins.

Aim to encounter them in their most natural state when embarking on your nutty adventure. Venture beyond the glitz of the snack aisle and seek solace in the baking section, where nuts lie in their purest form- unsalted, unroasted, and free from the deceptive allure of artificial flavourings. They are often cheaper, as ingredients don't carry the same VAT as processed, packaged nuts. Besides providing fibre, here are some further benefits of these delicious eight nuts:

Almond: Packed with Vitamin E, a guardian of heart health.

Pistachio: Packed with potassium and fibre, championing heart health and digestive wellness.

Hazelnuts: A trove of healthy fats and folate, supporting brain health and cellular function.

Pecan: Abundant in antioxidants, waging war against free radicals.

Macadamia: Brimming with monounsaturated fats. It champions heart health and metabolic balance.

Brazil: A selenium powerhouse offering a shield against oxidative stress.

Walnut: A brain food extraordinaire, brimming with omega-3 fatty acids.

Cashews: Rich in magnesium and zinc, fostering bone strength and immune defence.

The endorsements for these nutty superstars extend beyond anecdotal praise. In June 2015, The Independent newspaper highlighted a study by epidemiologist Professor Piet van den Brandt at Maastricht University. The study's revelations were nothing short of remarkable, asserting that merely a handful of nuts each day could significantly diminish the risk of heart attacks, cancer, and diabetes. Such a small dietary change, yet the potential for a profound impact on health and longevity. Plus, whilst travelling, they offer a convenient way of putting *Fibre First*.

5. The 'Magnificent Seven' of the Seed World

Each tiny seed kernel is a dynamo of health, teeming with vitality. While it's crucial to be cautious of their potentially hazardous transformation into oils, seeds, in their pure form, stand tall in our superfood line-up. They boast an impressive array of fibre, antioxidants, minerals, and vitamins.

As you traverse the supermarket aisles, make a purposeful trip to the baking section. Here, seeds reveal their true essence, free from the clutches of oils and artificial flavourings that can mask their natural virtues. Embrace these seven seeds in their pristine state and let the symphony of their natural flavours and intrinsic benefits resonate through your diet.

Chia: Tiny yet mighty. These seeds are a nutrient powerhouse.

Flaxseed: Rich in omega-3 fatty acids and fibre, flaxseeds are a boon for heart and digestive health.

Hemp: Packed with complete protein and essential fatty acids, hemp seeds are a nutritional treasure.

Poppy: Beyond their decorative appeal, poppy seeds add a subtle nuttiness and a boost of minerals to any dish.

Pumpkin: These seeds are not just for Halloween; they're a year-round source of zinc, magnesium, and healthy fats.

Sesame: Tiny sesame seeds are big on flavour and health, offering a wealth of nutrients in each crunchy bite.

Sunflower: Cheerful sunflower seeds are a delight to the taste buds and a provider of essential fatty acids and vitamins.

These seeds offer a simple yet profound way to enrich your diet. They remind us that sometimes, the smallest things can have the most significant impact on our well-being. So, sprinkle, mix, or blend these fibrous seeds into your daily meals and revel in the healthful bounty they provide.

6. The Fab Four of the Berry World

The 'Fab Four' reigns supreme in the vibrant world of berries. While the health benefits of acai and goji berries, cherries, cranberries, and redcurrants are undeniable, four berries take the nutritional crown. Bursting with vitamins, minerals, and fibre, these berries are unique in their sugar composition, primarily comprising xylitol, sidestepping the pitfalls associated with fructose. Plus, as we've explored in our sugar discussions, xylitol is even a friend to your teeth.

Raspberries
Meet the cancer-fighting champions of the berry world. Raspberries are brimming with antioxidants, boasting a concentration ten times higher than that of tomatoes. Their mood-boosting and memory-retaining properties make them a must-have in any diet focused on longevity and vitality.

Blackberries
Reminiscent of childhood summers and foraging adventures, blackberries are not just a nostalgic treat but a nutritional marvel. One cup provides a third

of your daily fibre needs, half the recommended vitamin C intake, and many other vitamins and minerals. Their natural sweetness belies their low-calorie profile, making them a guilt-free indulgence with health benefits.

Blueberries
The humble blueberry is a delicious powerhouse, considered one of nature's most potent antioxidant-rich foods. A study in America revealed remarkable cognitive benefits for seniors who indulged in two and a half cups of blueberries daily over 12 weeks. The study's lead, Dr Robert Krikorian, shared, 'These findings support previous animal and preliminary human studies, underscoring the potential of blueberries to enhance memory and cognitive function in some elderly individuals.'[10] And the best part? Their antioxidant prowess remains unfazed by freezing, making them a year-round superfruit.

Strawberries
These quintessentially British delights are not just a treat for the palate but a boon for health. Contrary to popular belief, strawberries are not sugar-loaded, and as we discovered in our *Blood Sugar Trial*, they don't spike your blood glucose levels. Rich in vitamins (notably vitamin C) and minerals, they're an exemplary source of fruit antioxidants.

7. The Stable of Cruciferous Vegetables

The cruciferous family are often the unsung heroes of the vegetable kingdom and, per cup, offer between two to five grams of fibre. They are a culinary delight and a fortress of health, brimming with compounds that wage war against diseases. For decades, a diet rich in these vegetables has been a shield against cancer. The secret? Sulphur-containing compounds like sulforaphane impart a slightly bitter flavour but are valiant warriors fighting cancer cells.

But the prowess of cruciferous vegetables doesn't stop at cancer prevention. They are a signal of health, significantly reducing the risk of obesity, diabetes, and heart disease. Imagine a natural medicine that enhances longevity and provides radiant skin, lustrous hair, and fortified bones and nails. That's the magic of these nutrient-dense vegetables, offering a bounty of vitamins and minerals with minimal calorie investment.

In a world where convenience dictates dietary choices, the humble cauliflower emerges as a versatile hero. It's not just a vegetable; it's a culinary chameleon. In regions where traditional rice is a staple yet poses a challenge for those managing diabetes or weight, cauliflower offers a revolutionary alternative.

Chopped into fine grains and cooked, it mimics rice's texture and appearance, minus the carb overload. However, this ingenious solution has stirred a whirlwind in certain states of America, where, in a bid to protect rice farmers and the substantial taxes they contribute, 'cauliflower rice' has been barred from bearing the 'rice' title!

8. The Glucomannan Miracle: Nature's Carb-Free Filler

Enter the world of Glucomannan, the unassuming, fibrous, mighty hero from the depths of the Konjac plant. It is a wizard of water-soluble fibre with an extraordinary ability to expand 50 times within our stomach. When this fibre takes the culinary stage, it transforms into an illusionist, mimicking the look and feel of pasta or noodles while being a wizard of low carbs and calories.

Glucomannan products are gradually claiming their rightful place on UK supermarket shelves, and yes, yours truly has a brand too (see at page 955). These mystical pouches come cradled in water, ready to unleash their magic in your kitchen. Drain, rinse, and cook them just like you would with any pasta or noodle. Though they might be naturally flavour-neutral, they are avid learners, eagerly absorbing the zest of spices and oils you introduce them to. Whether it's a rich curry, a hearty soup, a robust Bolognese, or even jazzing up an English breakfast, glucomannan is your versatile sidekick. Imagine feasting on a plate that mirrors pasta or noodles in every way but leaves calories and carbs as mere spectators.

But here's where glucomannan's enchantment truly lies: its role as a natural weight-loss ally. Like a sponge in a vast ocean, it soaks up water, expanding gently in your stomach, creating a feeling of fullness and taming the beast of appetite. It's an unassuming champion for those on a quest to shed pounds naturally. But a word to the wise: while I'm singing praises for this fibrous marvel, remember, I might be a tad biased.

9. Spinach the Leafy Green Superhero

The verdant champion of the vegetable realm, a powerhouse brimming with antioxidants, minerals, and an array of vitamins. By simply incorporating two cups of spinach into your daily salad, you're enlisting a dynamic duo of antioxidants—lutein and zeaxanthin. These warriors stand guard over your vision and bolster your heart's defences, all while tipping the scale at a mere 15 calories. In those identical two cups, you'll find 1.5g of fibre. While this amount may not significantly slow sugar absorption into the bloodstream on its own, it can contribute to a nutritious, fibre-rich salad.

But spinach's prowess extends beyond mere ocular sharpness and cardiac strength. It's a veritable armoury stocked with potassium for optimal nerve function, zinc to boost your immune defence, and an array of other minerals ready for battle. Vitamins E, K, and B9 (folate) join the fray, each contributing its unique strengths to the symphony of your overall health.

The tale of Popeye and his spinach-fuelled escapades is a misadventure in scientific notation. Back in the 1870s, German chemist Erich von Wolf, while documenting the iron content in spinach, made a decimal point misstep, catapulting spinach to legendary status as an iron behemoth. This error suggested spinach was packed with ten times more iron than in reality, fuelling the myth of its miraculous strength-enhancing capabilities, further immortalised by Popeye's animated exploits.

Yet, the true essence of spinach lies not in its iron, which, while present, plays hard to get because of spinach's oxalate content. These oxalates link up with iron, hindering its absorption and debunking the myth of spinach as the ultimate source of iron. Instead, according to insights from the Karolinska Institute in Sweden, spinach's real superpower may lie in its rich supply of nitrates. These nitrates are the unsung heroes, boosting our cells' efficiency and endurance, especially during physical exertion.

The spinach story is peppered with flavonoids, those silent sentinels guarding against the onslaught of free radicals, ensuring our well-being remains unchallenged. Spinach is not merely a vegetable. It's a leafy emblem of health, a green superhero in the epic quest for vitality, ready to unleash its powers with every bite.

A note for the health-conscious crusader: with its enormous surface area, Spinach can often be a clandestine rendezvous for unwanted chemical guests. A simple rinse is no match for these stubborn foes; instead, a bath in a vinegar-water solution is your spinach's best detox. Better still, to avoid the shadowy spectre of pesticides, choose organic.

10. Tomatoes: The Lycopene Capital

These humble fruits (or vegetables, depending on whom you ask) are not just culinary staples; they are potent allies in our quest for health. Imagine thousands of phytonutrients, each with its unique role, converging in a single tomato. As research continues into the realm of these phytonutrients, especially in combating diseases and warding off cancer, incorporating tomatoes into our daily diet seems not just wise but essential.

Tomatoes are a sanctuary for lutein and zeaxanthin, a dynamic duo of nutrients celebrated for their myriad health benefits. But the show's real star is lycopene, a superhero phytonutrient that provides tomatoes with their rich red hue. Lycopene isn't just about adding colour; it's an antioxidant par excellence, a veritable shield against the barrage of toxins and pollutants we encounter in our modern lives.

Consider this: the humble tomato, with its lycopene-rich heart, is a detoxifying agent, a guardian of cellular health, and a champion in slowing the progression of certain cancers,[12] as suggested by researchers from the University of Portsmouth. It's not just about the body, either. Lycopene keeps our cognitive connections sparkling and our bones as sturdy as oak.

Fret not for those who aren't fans of the tomato's taste but yearn for lycopene's bountiful benefits. This miraculous phytonutrient is now available as a supplement, ensuring the tomato's gifts are within everyone's reach. So next time you see a tomato, remember, it's not just a fruit or a vegetable; it's a lycopene-packed powerhouse ready to supercharge your health.

11. Peppers-From Mild Marvels to Fiery Flames

There is a diverse universe of peppers, where the spectrum ranges from the mild-mannered bell to the fire-breathing chilli. Peppers are a culinary delight and offer a vibrant palette of health benefits. Whether you prefer a hot curry adventure or the colourful tranquillity of bell peppers, there's a pepper for every palate and preference. When choosing peppers, always lean towards organic to ensure you get the purest punch of goodness.

Mild to Sweet Peppers

Enter the bell peppers, or capsicum, a veritable vitamin C powerhouse. Picture this: a single yellow bell pepper packs the vitamin C punch of five oranges! The bell pepper family brings a carnival of colours and tastes to your plate, each colour variant boasting its unique nutritional profile. Green peppers are simply the unripe version of the red, their vitamin C content blossoming as they ripen. Beyond their vitamin C glory, bell peppers contribute significantly to our daily fibre intake and are an excellent source of vitamin B6, magnesium, and potassium.

Hot Peppers

For the thrill-seekers, the world of hot peppers offers a fiery escapade measured in Scoville heat units (SHU). But it's not just about the heat; these peppers are bursting with the phytonutrient capsaicin, the plant's natural defence mechanism and our metabolic booster. Capsaicin is not merely a spice; it's a marvel of nature. It's been shown to aid weight loss, alleviate chronic pain, and even possess cancer-fighting properties. Imagine harnessing the power of capsaicin to rev up your metabolism, turning every curry into a weight-loss ally.

12. Onions-The Understated Tonic of Health

Onions, the unsung heroes of the culinary world, are not just the backbone of countless recipes but also a treasure trove of health benefits. As cousins to garlic in the Liliaceae plant family, onions bring more to the table than just flavour. They are a rich source of polyphenols, notably tannins and flavonoids, making them a formidable shield against harmful bacteria and a promoter of good health.

Beyond their pungent aroma and distinctive taste, onions are celebrated for their potential to ward off diseases. They're thought to play a protective role against various cancers, diabetes, and even neurodegenerative disorders such as Alzheimer's and Parkinson's disease. With their natural antibiotic prowess, they support heart health, bolster bone strength, and mitigate the risks of arthritis and asthma.

An old wives' tale suggests draping a string of onions around your neck to clear congested sinuses. While it may not be a fashion statement you'd want to make today, incorporating onions into your diet is a time-tested way to combat colds and flu. And for those unexpected nosebleeds, the age-old remedy of holding an onion under your nostrils could surprisingly help stem the flow, thanks to its natural coagulating properties.

Onions owe their tear-inducing quality to the sulphur they absorb from the soil, which transforms into the amino acid sulfoxide upon slicing. This release is the plant's self-defence mechanism, a testament to the robust antioxidants they contain. Remember that much of their nutritional arsenal lies beneath the skin when peeling onions, so peel minimally. Onions are rich in two antioxidants, quercetin and anthocyanin, which are renowned for their health benefits.

But the wonders of onions don't stop at the kitchen door. Rubbing onion on your skin or placing it in a water bowl can deter mosquitoes, offering a natural alternative to chemical repellents. Regarding nutritional value, a cup of diced onion packs a punch, delivering a significant portion of your daily vitamin C, vitamin B6, manganese, folate, potassium, and vitamin B1 needs.

While onions are among the top 20 superfoods, if you have the time and patience, consider upgrading them to shallots; they are the 'gourmet choice' for adding a more subtle, sweet, yet rich flavour to your dishes.

13. Olives: The Mediterranean Marvel

In the sun-kissed landscapes of the Mediterranean, olives are not just a food item; they're a symbol of culture, health, and longevity. This small yet mighty fruit is a cornerstone of the Mediterranean diet, a lifestyle choice closely associated with reduced heart disease risk and a notable population of centenarians. The virtues of olives are not confined to their delectable flesh alone; their extracted oil is a golden tonic treasured worldwide.

While we've discussed the wonders of olive oil in another section, it's worth pausing to appreciate the humble olive in its whole form. Olives are a testament to the fact that good things often come in small packages. Olives are more than a culinary delight, packed with monounsaturated fats, antioxidants, and a constellation of vitamins and minerals.

14. Organic Meats and Poultry

The meat aisle is not just a section of the supermarket; it's a treasure trove of nutrition, especially when we opt for organic meats. Among the array of choices—bison, venison, goat—three stand out for their popularity and profound health benefits: beef, pork, and lamb.

To earn a spot on this list, meat should be organic or at least raised in its natural environment. This ensured the animals were nourished as nature intended, grazing freely and savouring their natural diet. This distinction is pivotal. While certain studies paint meat with a broad brush of health concerns, these often focus on factory-farmed varieties. In contrast, meat from animals that have lived and thrived in their natural habitat is altogether a different story.

Whether beef from the meadows, lamb from the hills, or pork from the pastures, these meats are bastions of protein and healthy fats. To those who decry all meat as a health hazard, let's set the record straight. Our ancestors didn't just forage for berries and roots; they were hunters, thriving on a diet rich in wild game. They instinctively knew the value hidden in every part of the animal, from muscle to organ, each morsel dense with life-sustaining nutrients.

In modern supermarkets, organ meats are often overlooked, their value unrecognised by a generation that has drifted from traditional cooking. Yet these organs are nutritional gold mines, inexplicably affordable due to their current unpopularity. Contrast this with high-end restaurants, where organ dishes are celebrated for their rich flavours and nutritional profile.

Let's evaluate the specifics, assuming you've opted for organic or naturally raised, pure meats:

Beef: Beyond being an exceptional source of protein, grass-fed beef is a reservoir of omega-3 and a hidden gem: conjugated linoleic acid (CLA). CLA's prowess in reducing tumours in various cancers is remarkable. It's a warrior against asthma, a shield against cardiovascular disease, and a guardian against osteoporosis. CLA supplements have entered the market for those not inclined towards meat, promising benefits like diabetes management and weight control through muscle mass retention.

Pork: Regarding pork, the organic label is your sign of quality. Beware of mass-produced pork, often raised in conditions far removed from the animal's natural habitat. Opting for organic is a win-win: kinder to the animal, better for our health, and more sustainable for the planet. Pork, adorned with an organic label, is a symphony of vitamins, minerals, and proteins, offering a balanced diet without the burden of carbs or excessive fats.

Lamb: Much like its counterpart beef, lamb is a powerhouse of protein and omega-3. It is also laden with a spectrum of minerals and B vitamins. The great news is that lamb is nearly always reared naturally in the British countryside, offering a lean, nutrient-rich option that supports local agriculture and your health. Its rich flavour and nutritional profile make it a superb choice for anyone looking to diversify their diet with high-quality, sustainable meats.

Let's now look at the meat we get from poultry. If it's not both organic and free-range, think twice before buying it—not just for our health but also for the sake of the birds and our planet. Only organic birds offer a totally clean source of protein and healthy fat.

In the UK, it is estimated that 46% of the average Brit's protein comes from chicken, and British farmers rear 1 billion broilers (chickens raised for meat) for food every year, contributing more than £4.6 billion to the UK economy.[11]

Here are a few details that you might find on labels. First, it's important to cut through all the nonsense. 'Natural', 'Farm-Fresh', 'Premium Chicken' and 'Country Style' are entirely meaningless and just marketing fowl play! They're prominently placed on the packaging to encourage us to pick up the produce and feel good about it.

Organic Poultry: In the UK, The Soil Association regulates this, limiting flock size to 1000 chickens. Every bird must have continuous and easy daytime access to outdoor pastures, and each bird should have a minimum of four square metres to roam freely. The pasture must be covered with suitable vegetation, and the bird must reach a minimum age of 81 days. The chicken must be fed organic foods, and antibiotics must not be used.

Free-range: Chickens must have outdoor access for at least half of their lives, and each chicken must have the equivalent of one square metre of land. The minimum slaughter age is 56 days.

Freedom Food: This welfare scheme run by the RSPCA applies to indoor, organic, or free-range chickens. It limits the number that can be raised in each space and details such things as how much straw they get, the size of their perch, etc.

Red Tractor: From what I understand, it seems to be nothing more than a paid-up membership for farmers to use the logo. Their website has very few rules and guidelines beyond what the EU requires. That said, it does mean that the food can be traced back to the original British farm.

15. Oily Fish-The Slippery Six

The ocean and rivers teem with thousands of edible fish, each a treasure trove of health benefits. But before you cast your line or pick up that fish fork, it's essential to consider where and how these fish were caught or raised. The spotlight here is on the 'Slippery Six,' a selection of fish known not just for their elusive nature but for their rich content of omega-3 oils. These fish are the aquatic equivalent of nature's multivitamins, but with a catch, the benefits we reap depend heavily on their habitat.

In the aquatic world of farmed vs. wild, the choice is clear. Farmed fish, often fed synthetic diets, lack the natural nutrients found in their wild counterparts. Remember, we are what our food eats; if that's a diet of artificial pellets, it's not something we want on our plates. So, let's dive into the positives of these slippery six, focusing on those caught in the wild, where the health benefits are as vast as the ocean itself.

Salmon: Crowned the king of British waters, salmon reigns supreme with its wealth of omega-3 fatty acids, making it a stalwart ally for heart health. Its tender, moist texture speaks volumes of its beneficial oil content, rendering every ounce of this wild-caught marvel a trove of nutrition. From its shimmering skin to the succulent flesh, each part of the salmon promises a comprehensive health boon, fostering cardiovascular wellness and cognitive function and offering a bulwark against various diseases. A single fillet embodies a holistic approach to health, making salmon an indispensable part of a balanced diet.

If the case for going organic with your entire diet still leaves you on the fence, then Felicity Lawrence's *Eat Your Heart Out* might tip the scales. Subtitled 'Why the food business is bad for the planet and your health', Lawrence delves into the underbelly of the food industry, from milk production to cattle and pig farming, revealing insights that are as enlightening as they are disturbing. What struck me most profoundly was her exposé on SalmoFanTM, a revelation that forever altered my perception of farmed fish. Lawrence describes the SalmoFan as akin to a collection of Dulux paint charts designed for salmon farmers to dictate the intensity of pink their salmon will boast based on the amount of food dye mixed into their feed. This eye-opening insight into the manipulation behind farmed fish's aesthetic allure is a stark reminder of the importance of choosing organic, naturally sourced foods for our health and the planet.

Trout: A milder cousin of salmon, trout offers a similar nutritional profile, rich in omega-3 and a host of other beneficial nutrients.

Mackerel & Tuna: These members of the Scombridae family are like the ocean's version of a nutrient-dense feast. Mackerel, with its distinct taste, and tuna, the versatile star of both cans and sushi, are loaded with omega-3 and a spectrum of other vital nutrients.

Sardines & Anchovies: These small but mighty fish are not just a treat for the taste buds but a boon for health. Sardines, with their wild-caught purity and anchovies, despite their divisive taste, are packed with omega-3 and a plethora of vitamins and minerals.

16. Garlic-The Pungent Dynamo of Health

In the grand league of superfoods, garlic stands out for its pungent aroma, distinct flavour and remarkable health benefits. It's a culinary staple that has earned its stripes in the annals of natural medicine across civilisations-from the ancient Egyptians and Babylonians to the Romans and Chinese. And it's no wonder Hippocrates, the father of Western medicine, famously declared, 'Let food be thy medicine, and medicine be thy food,' often prescribing garlic for various ailments.

At the heart of garlic's power is allicin, the compound responsible for its potent aroma and a host of medicinal properties. This natural warrior battles against unhealthy bacteria and fungi, acting as an all-natural antibiotic that has been revered for millennia.

But garlic's prowess doesn't stop at fighting infections. It's a nutritional treasure trove, rich in selenium and a suite of vitamins, including C, B1, B2, B3, B6, and folate. Its mineral content is just as impressive, boasting calcium, iron, manganese, phosphorus, potassium, magnesium, sodium, and zinc. This makes garlic a flavour enhancer and a formidable ally in maintaining overall health.

Examining the chart below, you'll start to grasp why garlic is hailed as a natural remedy, with just a single raw clove offering:

Fibre (g)	0.19	Manganese (mg)	0.15
Calcium (mg)	16.29	Selenium (mcg)	1.28
Iron (mg)	0.15	Lutein + zeaxanthin (mcg)	2.34
Magnesium (mg)	2.25	Thiamine (mg)	0.02
Phosphorus (mg)	13.77	Riboflavin (mg)	0.01
Potassium (mg)	36.09	Niacin (mg)	0.06
Sodium (mg)	1.53	Panothenic acid (mg)	0.05
Zinc (mg)	0.1	Vitamin B6 (mg)	0.11
Copper (mg)	0.03	Folate (mcg)	0.27
Vitamin K (mcg)	0.13	Folate, DFE (mcg)	0.27

Garlic's ability to lower blood pressure is well-documented, making it a heart-friendly choice. Recent studies also point to its antioxidant capacity, positioning it as a powerful tool in cancer prevention. For those battling acne, garlic offers a natural remedy that attacks the problem from within, cleansing the skin and promoting a clear complexion.

For the age-conscious, garlic is akin to a fountain of youth. It aids in preserving collagen, the essential protein that keeps our skin supple and wards off wrinkles and signs of ageing.

17. Fermented Foods: The Gut's Natural Allies

In our quest for gut health, we often stumble upon the realm of supplements promising a flourishing microbiome. Yet nature has its own masterful solution: fermented foods. This isn't about championing the fermentation process that turns grapes into wine, tempting as that may be. Instead, it's about embracing a more traditional and natural approach to nurturing our gut's friendly bacteria.

Fermented foods undergo lacto-fermentation, a transformative dance where, in the absence of oxygen, natural bacteria feast on the sugar and starch in the food, producing lactic acid. This process, named after the bacteria *Lactobacillus*, discovered during milk fermentation studies, is what gives fermented vegetables their tangy taste and remarkable health benefits.

But why invite lactic acid to the party in our gut? It's a versatile guest, aiding our immune system in fending off harmful bacteria, acting as a natural antibiotic, fortifying the gut lining, and keeping our vitamin and enzyme levels in harmony.

The tradition of fermenting foods isn't just a culinary art; it's a time-honoured method of preservation. In *Nourishing Traditions*, Sally Fallon praises fermented vegetables' virtues, highlighting their role in enhancing digestibility, boosting vitamin levels, and producing beneficial enzymes. It's a natural symphony that preserves food and amplifies its nutritional profile.

Probiotics, the heroes of fermented foods, are renowned for their myriad health benefits, from reducing Alzheimer's risk to managing blood pressure and alleviating digestive discomforts. The world of fermented foods is vast and varied, with each offering its unique blend of health perks:

Yoghurt: The result of fermenting milk lactose, yoghurt is a haven for friendly bacteria. Opt for grass-fed, organic varieties without added flavourings for the purest form of this probiotic powerhouse.

Kefir: A fermented milk drink that's a blend of milk and yoghurt, kefir is rich in vitamin B12, calcium, magnesium, vitamin K2, and an army of healthy bacteria. It's a soothing ally for those grappling with IBS or seeking a diverse probiotic profile.

Non-Pasteurised Cheese: Raw milk cheeses are a delight not just for the palate but also for the gut, brimming with naturally fermented goodness.

While they're a beneficial part of a balanced diet, don't overlook yoghurt or kefir, as cheese alone might not cover the full spectrum of beneficial bacteria.

Pickles: Organic pickles are a crunchy source of vitamins, minerals, antioxidants, and friendly bacteria. They're a simple yet effective way to add a probiotic punch to your meals.

Sauerkraut: A traditional food with a lineage stretching back over 2,000 years, sauerkraut is not only a probiotic treasure but also a rich source of vitamins C, K, and B and a multitude of minerals. It supports digestion, blood circulation, bone strength and fights inflammation. Its cousin, kimchi, offers a spicier, more seasoned take on fermented cabbage, adding a flavourful twist to the probiotic narrative.

18. Dark Chocolate: The Decadent Delight with a Health Twist

I'm not referring to the sugary realms of Cadbury™, Nestle, or even the whimsical wonders of Wonka. Let's draw a clear line between the genuine article and those sugary facades impersonating chocolate bars. Authentic chocolate, the epitome of indulgence, is born from the Cocoa bean, the prized progeny of Central and South American cocoa trees. These beans were once exalted as 'theobroma cacao', or 'food of the gods' by the Maya Indians, not for creating sweetened chocolate bars, but for a robust and tangy brew known as 'chocolatl'.

In the realm of home pantries, cacao powder is the unsung fibre hero, waiting to be transformed into homemade chocolate marvels. If cookery escapades aren't your forte, fret not! Venture into the world of store-bought dark chocolate bars but be discerning; aim for those boasting a cacao content north of 70%. Supermarkets are a treasure trove of choices, but remember, dark chocolate is an acquired taste. Initially, you might shy away from the boldness of 90% cacao bars, but given time, your palate might surprise you, evolving to savour these richer, darker delights.

But be aware that not all cacao is created equally. Enter the distinction between cacao and 'cocoa'. The difference primarily lies in how they're processed from the beans, which affects their nutritional content and flavour.

Cacao

Raw cacao refers to the Cacao beans that have been minimally processed, keeping them in a more natural state.

Cacao powder is made by cold-pressing unroasted Cacao beans, which removes the fat (cacao butter) but preserves the rich fibre and enzyme content and maximises the antioxidant properties.

Cacao nibs are Cacao beans chopped into smaller pieces. They offer a crunchy texture and a bitter, chocolatey flavour.

I consider Cacao a 'superfood' due to its richness in fibre (over 30% by weight), and high content of antioxidants, vitamins, and minerals, particularly magnesium and iron. It's less processed and closer to the natural state of the bean, making it richer in antioxidants.

Nutrient	Amount per 100g
Energy	228 kcal
Protein	19.6 g
Fat	13.7 g
Saturated fat	8.1 g
Carbohydrate	57.9 g
Sugars	1.75 g
Fibre	33.2 g
Calcium	128 mg
Iron	13.86 mg
Magnesium	499 mg
Phosphorus	734 mg
Sodium	1524 mg
Zinc	21 mg
Copper	6.81 mg
Manganese	3.788 mg
Selenium	3.385 µg
Caffeine	230 mg
Theobromine	2057 mg
Vitamin K	2.5 µg
Riboflavin (Vitamin B2)	0.241 mg
Niacin (Vitamin B3)	2.185 mg
Folate (Vitamin B9)	32 µg
Choline	88.8 mg

Don't let the carbohydrate content deter you. As we explored in chapter two during our investigation into food labelling, the carbohydrate figure encompasses fibre. When you subtract the fibre, cocoa boasts a ratio of fibre to sugar that tips the scales towards fibre—a rarity indeed. This means cocoa has a minimal impact on blood sugar levels, exhibiting a low glycaemic effect.

Cocoa

Cocoa powder is still made from the same beans but has been roasted at high temperatures and ground into a powder. The roasting process enhances the flavour, but can reduce the nutritional value. Cocoa is typically used in products like dairy milk chocolate bars and baking chocolate. It's sweeter and has a milder chocolate flavour compared to cacao.

In summary, cacao is the cocoa bean's fibrous, raw, less processed form, retaining more of its natural nutrients and antioxidants. Indulge guilt-free in dark chocolate as it unfurls its tapestry of ten health benefits:

- Its high fibre content helps create a beneficial microbiome
- Boosts insulin sensitivity, helping to control blood sugar levels
- Shields against the stealthy creep of type 2 diabetes
- Takes a stand against high blood pressure, keeping it in check
- Supports brain functions, sharpening memory like a well-oiled machine
- Dials down inflammation, keeping your body at peace
- Bolsters your cardiovascular system, ensuring it hums a healthy tune
- Restores flexibility to arteries, keeping them supple and youthful
- Prevents white blood cells from going rogue and sticking to blood vessel walls
- Triggers leptin, the internal memo that kindly reminds you, you're full. Yes, dark chocolate might be your unexpected ally in weight management
- Shields against free radicals, standing guard against certain cancers

So, there you have it, a chocolate lover's dream, a treat that tantalises the taste buds and bestows a bounty of health benefits.

19. Bone Broth: The Caveman's Cappuccino

Close your eyes and picture cavemen gathered around a crackling fire, nonchalantly gnawing on a bone as if it were the Palaeolithic equivalent of a TV dinner. And if that image doesn't tickle your fancy, envision a dog, man's eternal sidekick, blissfully lost in the ecstasy of a good bone chew. This isn't a scene from a prehistoric sitcom or an ode to canine culinary tastes—it's nature's way of hinting at the treasure trove of benefits nestled within bones.

Bones are veritable vaults of nutrients, vitamins, and minerals from chicken to cow. They're brimming with gelatine and marrow, nature's remedies for aching joints and creaky hinges. Brewing these bones into a hearty broth is like alchemy, transforming gelatine's larger protein molecules into the superstar amino acid, collagen. Dubbed 'Kolla' by the Greeks, meaning 'glue', collagen is indeed the body's adhesive, binding us together with youthful elasticity and vigour.

Age, however, is a cunning thief. It pilfers our body's collagen reserves, leaving us with joint pains and skin that's less 'spring chicken' and more 'wrinkled prune'. Enter bone broth, your fountain of youth, bubbling with collagen to replenish what time steals away. This broth isn't just a treat for your taste buds; it's a spa session for your skin and a chiropractic adjustment for your joints, all simmered into a single, steaming bowl.

But wait, there's more! Glycine, the unsung hero in this savoury tale, is the smallest amino acid involved in everything from skin health and digestion to muscle repair and hormone balance. Glycine's résumé is impressive, and while our bodies can craft this amino acid, they're about as efficient as a tortoise running a marathon. So, it's time to give your body a helping hand with a generous helping of bone broth.

Whether you're a DIY kitchen wizard brewing your own (by the way I have several broth recipes with loads of tips on my website) or a pragmatic soul reaching for a ready-made cube, ensure this ancient medicine finds its way into your modern menu. It's not just food; it's a ritual, a nod to our ancestors, and a toast to our health. Bone appétit!

20. Marvellous Mushrooms: The Mighty Fungi

Step aside, superheroes of the plant world, for the mushroom, the outlier of the fungus kingdom, is here to claim its rightful place in our Superfood Hall of Fame. With carbs so low they'd make a glucomannan blush, mushrooms have been the toast of the East for millennia, revered for their health-boosting properties and mystical allure.

These umami-packed marvels are not just gastronomic delights but nutritional powerhouses, teeming with protein, fibre, water-soluble vitamins B and C, calcium, vitamin D, selenium, and potassium. Mushrooms are the knights in shining armour for our immune system, fending off villains like cancer with their arsenal of beta-glucans. These noble compounds, found in the cell walls of the bacteria found in mushrooms, are so adept at halting cancerous cells that they've been transformed into pill form, standing guard for those battling cancer and diabetes.

And let's not forget linoleic acid, the unsung hero in mushrooms that holds the line against excess oestrogen, a known nemesis of post-menopausal breast health. But the magic of mushrooms doesn't stop at bodily defences. They're also brain food, casting spells on our cognitive functions to keep our minds sharp and agile. Remember that headline from The Mirror about mushrooms warding off dementia? That's not just journalistic jazz; it's the stuff of legend.

Now, a word to the wise: mushrooms are like sponges, soaking up the good, the bad, and the downright toxic from their surroundings. So, when it comes to picking your fungi (I mean from the supermarket shelf, not in the wild, as without sufficient knowledge, that could be lethal), think organic or nothing.

Honourable Mentions: The Nutrient-Rich Notables

While the luminaries of the superfood world have had their moment in the spotlight, let's not overlook the supporting cast, a diverse ensemble of nutrient-rich virtuosos that may not have made the top 20 but certainly deserve a standing ovation. These nutrient-rich virtuosos, like the tunes that linger in the background, compose my very own Top 40. Each ingredient boasts its own melody, harmonising effortlessly to create a symphony of wellness for our bodies. So, here's to celebrating the unsung chart climbers of the nutrient world, proving that healthful living is indeed a melody worth dancing to. From the depths of the ocean to the citrus groves, from the legume fields to the seaweed-strewn shores, these foods are a testament to nature's bounty:

Shellfish: The Tiny Titans of Nutrition

Observing nutrient density, shellfish are the undisputed champions of the sea. Whether it's the elegant oyster, the hearty mussel, or the unassuming clam, these oceanic treasures offer a wealth of health benefits packed into their shells. But let's not forget our crustaceous comrades, the shrimp and prawn, which, despite their diminutive size, deliver a nutritional punch that's nothing short of spectacular. And if we're talking about sea royalty, we can't ignore the likes of lobsters and tiger prawns, rich sources of selenium and B12, fit for a seafood feast!

Lemon and Lime: More Than Just a Gin's Best Friend

If your idea of lemon and lime is limited to garnishing your gin and tonic, it's time to give these zesty wonders the recognition they deserve. Beyond their sharp, bitter bite lies a vitamin and mineral treasure trove. In fact, their remarkable notability in the world of nutrition dates back centuries. In 1747, Scottish physician James Lind conducted what might be the first-ever clinical trial at sea, proving that a diet of oranges and lemons cured scurvy among sailors. This discovery led to the Royal Navy adding lime to sailors' drinks, earning them the nickname 'Limeys.' The secret behind this scurvy-busting magic? Vitamin C is found abundantly in lemons and limes. These citrus heroes are packed with antioxidants that ward off free radicals and a phytonutrient called limonin, which can halt inflammation and give common illnesses a run for their money. So don't limit them to cocktails—squeeze them into your daily routine!

Kiwi: The Small Wonder with a Big Impact

Don't underestimate the power of the humble kiwi. One small kiwi hosts two to three grams of fibre and your entire recommended daily intake of vitamin C, and it doesn't stop there. It's also a rich source of potassium, magnesium, and iron, all wrapped up in a sweet, low-sugar package. It boasts antioxidants and phytonutrients that support everything from eyesight (thanks to carotenoids) to youthful skin (by synthesising collagen) and even a good night's sleep (thanks to serotonin). And if you need another reason to love kiwis, say hello to lutein, a carotenoid vitamin that's like a superhero for your eyes, preventing age-related macular degeneration, cataracts, and more.

Celery: The Crunchy Cure-All

Celery is not just a vehicle for fibrous peanut butter or cheese. This crispy green superstar has been used as a natural remedy for centuries. A single medium stick of celery (about 40 grams) contains approximately 0.6 to 1.2 grams of dietary fibre. Packed with phytonutrients, celery can lower blood pressure, prevent heart disease, and fight inflammation. With its high-water content and many minerals, celery is your go-to for staying hydrated and replenishing essential electrolytes. Dr Josh Axe, the brains behind one of the most informative natural health websites, even credits celery with protecting the digestive tract from ulcers. Its unique ethanol extract can replenish gastric mucus, keeping your stomach lining in tip-top shape. So, whether you're munching on it raw or adding it to your favourite dishes, celery is your crunchy companion to health.

Celeriac: The Unsung Hero of the Root World

Celeriac, the Cinderella of the vegetable world, may not win any beauty contests at first glance, but what's beneath the surface counts. This knobbly, rough-looking root might not catch your eye on the vegetable aisle, but its unassuming appearance belies a treasure trove of culinary versatility and nutritional prowess.

Lingering in the background, often overshadowed by its starch-laden cousin, the potato, celeriac is my culinary ace. Consider the numbers: a cup of boiled celeriac cubes packs just 42 calories and a modest nine grams of carbohydrates (of which a quarter is our beneficial fibre), in stark contrast to its potato counterpart, which tips the scales with 134 calories and a hefty 31 g of carbohydrates for the same amount. This unassuming root is a virtuoso of versatility in the kitchen, effortlessly stepping into the shoes of potatoes yet leaving a much lighter footprint. Roasted with a fragrant mix of garlic and rosemary, it emerges from the oven transformed, its earthy tones complemented by the aromatic herbs. Mashed with a generous dollop of butter and a sprinkle of cheese, it becomes a luxurious, velvety treat that makes you question your loyalty to traditional mash. And let's not forget the thin, crispy chips, perfectly baked or air-fried to golden perfection- a testament to celeriac's surprising and delightful adaptability.

Celeriac is more than just a culinary substitute; it's a nutritional treasure chest. Beneath that rough exterior lies a heart rich in vitamins, minerals, fibre, and antioxidants. Low in calories yet high in satisfaction, celeriac is a dieter's dream, offering a depth of flavour and texture that belies its humble appearance.

In a world where appearances often deceive, celeriac is a testament to the beauty of substance over style. It's a reminder that the most extraordinary treasures are often found in the most unexpected places.

Artichoke: A Tough Nut to Crack

Meet the artichoke, nature's armoured vegetable. While most people enjoy the heart, don't overlook the leaves packed with antioxidants. Artichokes are nutritionally rich, boasting vitamins B12, K, C, manganese, magnesium, potassium, and more. These rugged globes are renowned for helping prevent conditions like diabetes, various cancers, and heart disease. They also moonlight as liver detoxifiers and digestive tract champions. Thanks to phytonutrients like quercetin, rutin, cynarin, and gallic acid, combined with their high fibre content, artichokes have been reported to alleviate IBS symptoms.

Peanuts: The Stealthy Titans of Nutrition

Let's crack the shell on this one: Peanuts may not have made the elite echelon of nuts, mainly because they're legumes, not nuts! But don't let their classification fool you. These ground dwellers pack a punch with 9% fibre, which might explain their modest 14 on the GI scale. They're almost as chill as a cucumber in the world of glycaemic indices!

Peanuts are like the unsung heroes in the world of fats, boasting monounsaturated fats that would make olives and their oleic acid companions proud. They're about 50% fat-but listen: it's the good kind.

Let's talk numbers: a hearty handful of these gems (we're talking roughly 40 peanuts or 30 g) is like a nutritional treasure chest. They offer copper, manganese, magnesium and many other essentials, from vitamin B3 to phosphorus. And antioxidants? Peanuts rub shoulders with berries in this arena, flaunting an impressive array, including the showstopper resveratrol, the heart's guardian and cancer's adversary, famously found in red wine. But let's not go nuts here-moderation is key. Despite their 50% fat, 30% protein, and rich fibre content, an overindulgence, especially in social settings (we've all been there), can lead to an energy ambush. Though packed with health, each peanut carries over four calories, each with as much power as a tic-tac. A single handful equals 152 calories, more than a pack of Walkers crisps!

Lentils: The Plant-Powered Protectors

Enter lentils, the paradox in the pulse world. In our quest to dodge excessive carbs, these little gems shine bright, securing their spot in the Top 40 for their plant-based protein prowess. Lentils are the quiet revolutionaries of the carb world, with their complex nature landing them at the lower end of the GI spectrum.

Packed with fibre (8 g in every 100 g), folate, and a mineral medley from iron to zinc, lentils are the unsung heroes in the plant kingdom. While my plate might be more carnivore-centric, for my vegetarian and vegan compatriots, lentils are like the Swiss Army knife of nutrition, adept at filling those dietary gaps.

Seaweed: The Ocean's Nutrient Nectar

Seaweed isn't just for sushi's embrace. This oceanic wonder, often overlooked, is a feast of calcium, folate, iodine, magnesium, and a symphony of vitamin Bs. If the only seaweed you've encountered is wrapped around rice, it's time to experiment. From soups to salads, seaweed is versatile, nutritious, and, above all else, delicious.

Research from the University of Newcastle upon Tyne highlights seaweed's fibre-rich profile, praising its ability to keep our digestive passages leisurely and our hunger at bay. It's the vegetable of the sea, and it's making a splash in the world of health.

Kale and Romaine Lettuce: Champions of the Leafy Greens

In the verdant kingdom of leafy vegetables, Romaine lettuce has emerged victorious, leaving its relative Iceberg in the shadows with its richer nutrient profile. Loaded with vitamin K, a crucial ally in fortifying our bones and defending against adversaries like osteoporosis and cancer. Equipped with lutein and zeaxanthin, Romaine transcends its role as a mere ingredient in salads, becoming a protector of our vision. Yet, standing tall above all in the garden of greens is the formidable kale. Check out my kale crisp recipe on our website for a taste of its glory.

The following chart is based on a 150 g serving, mirroring roughly two small cups of chopped lettuce—the perfect amount for crafting a salad in your kitchen.

Per 150g	Kale	Romaine	Iceberg
Calories	75	25	21
Vitamin K	1500%	198%	45%
Vitamin A	462%	261%	15%
Manganese	58%	12%	9%
Calcium	21%	5%	3%
Vitamin B6	21%	6%	3%
Copper	21%	3%	2%
Vitamin C	18%	3%	0%
Potassium	15%	8%	5%

The fibre content for Romaine lettuce, Iceberg lettuce, and kale per 150-gram serving is approximately as follows:

- Kale: Approximately 5.4 g
- Romaine Lettuce: About 3.2 g
- Iceberg Lettuce: Around 1.8 g

These values highlight the nutritional density of these leafy greens, with kale leading in fibre content, making it a robust choice to boost your dietary fibre intake. Romaine lettuce also offers a good amount of fibre, surpassing the more water-rich Iceberg lettuce in nutrient density.

Grapefruit: The Citrus Conundrum

Grapefruit, with its tangy twist, carries a legacy tinged with caution. Its excursion from being a kidney stone troublemaker to a potential guardian is a tale of evolving science and misunderstood virtues. Rich in citric acid, it's now hailed for its potential to combat kidney stones, shifting the urinary battlefield in our favour. But as with all fruits, eat it and don't drink it!

Beyond its role in renal health, grapefruit is a citrus sentinel, brimming with antioxidants, fibre, and vitamin C. Emerging reports whisper promises of its prowess in guarding against insulin resistance, positioning this bittersweet marvel not just as a breakfast staple but as a purveyor of health.

Pineapple: The Tropical Healer

Pineapple isn't just a holiday in fruit; it's a power-pack of health. Rich in vitamin C and manganese, its crowning glory is bromelain, a mix of enzymes with a reputation for battling inflammation and possibly even warding off tumour growth and cancer. It's adept at reducing swelling, providing a ray of hope for arthritis sufferers and a natural remedy for muscle injuries. Bromelain's prowess doesn't stop there; it's also a natural anticoagulant, potentially safeguarding against strokes and heart attacks.

But hold the fruit knife momentarily; pineapples carry a sugar load. However, they still tip the scales with fewer calories than apples or bananas. Fret not for those on a sugar watch or not fans of the tropical twist. The market is blossoming with bromelain supplements, making it easy to harness pineapple's benefits without the sugar spike.

Pomegranates: The Ruby Riches

Pomegranates have recently blossomed in my family's fruit repertoire, and it's clear why. These ruby gems are more than a pop of colour for your morning yoghurt or salad; they're a nutritional fortress. Pomegranates stand at the crossroads of seed and fruit, offering a dual dose of health benefits.

A medium-sized pomegranate (about 282 grams) contains approximately 11 grams of dietary fibre. Packed with vitamin C, vitamin K, and potassium, pomegranates are like the knights of the fruit world, combating cancer, inflammation, high blood pressure, oxidative stress, and hyperglycaemia. And let's not forget their reputation as an aphrodisiac, backed by studies linking pomegranate juice to lowered cortisol levels and a boost in testosterone for both men and women. Pomegranates are not just a fruit; they're a symbol of vitality.

Asparagus: The Love Spear

Asparagus isn't just a side dish; it's steeped in history as the ultimate aphrodisiac, celebrated in the Kama Sutra and Greek poetry. The French historically dined on it before weddings, banking on its reputed libido-boosting properties to ward off any matrimonial mishaps.

But my personal tale with asparagus is more about renal redemption than romance. Picture this: I emerge from the hospital, kidney stones lurking within me like unwanted tenants waiting for an eviction notice. But fear not, for my resourceful wife, armed with nothing but determination and a trusty Google search, concocted a plan involving copious amounts of mashed asparagus. I was sceptical, to say the least, but desperate times call for desperate measures, so I devoured plate after plate until I felt like I might sprout a green spear myself.

And lo and behold, the stones vanished into thin air within days! Yes, you heard that right. Asparagus, with its high potassium content, not only cleanses the kidneys and urinary tract but also possesses some mystical power to banish kidney stones faster than you can say 'operation postponed.' It's the kind of magic that makes you wonder if Hogwarts has a branch specialising in vegetable-based wizardry.

Beyond its kidney-conquering capabilities, asparagus is a nutrient fortress from tip to stem, packing around two grams of fibre per 100 g. It contains aspartic acid, which neutralises excess ammonia and reignites lost libido. Asparagus is truly the vegetable of love and health.

Cucumber: The Cool Crusader

Think cucumbers, and you might picture the quintessential spa day. Yet, these crisp, refreshing favourites go beyond mere eye relief to stand as unsung heroes in the quest for health. Packed with unique phytonutrients such as lariciresinol, secoisolariciresinol, and pinoresinol, cucumbers act as the immune system's ally, harmonising hormone levels and warding off cardiovascular diseases and various cancers.

Nestled within the Cucurbitaceae family, alongside relatives like squash, watermelon, and pumpkin; cucumbers proudly wear the fruit label. With a roster of over 100 varieties, the tour through cucumber's health wonders promises endless variety.

But the accolades don't stop there. Enter fisetin, a nutrient that not only sharpens the mind but also offers hope in the fight against Alzheimer's progression, as demonstrated in animal studies. Found also in strawberries, kiwis, grapes, certain vegetables, nuts, and even in a glass of wine, fisetin dazzles with its anti-inflammatory, antioxidant, and anti-cancer prowess.[13]

Beyond brain health, cucumbers have a knack for blood sugar regulation, playing a role in diabetes prevention and management. The research in the Journal of Complementary and Integrative Medicine reveals cucumber's prowess in maintaining steady blood sugar levels, showcasing its anti-diabetic capabilities.[14]

While predominantly made up of water, making their fibre content modest, cucumbers quietly deliver a spectrum of minerals and vitamins. Plus, for those pursuing youthfulness, the ascorbic and caffeic acids found in cucumbers offer a natural elixir against the march of time, smoothing away wrinkles and refreshing the skin. So, next time you reach for a cucumber, remember it's not just for show—it's a nutritional powerhouse cloaked in cool simplicity.

Courgette: The Versatile Virtuoso

Courgette, or zucchini as it is known in some parts of the world, is more than just a vegetable; it's a canvas of culinary creativity. This humble member of the squash family may appear unassuming, yet it harbours a treasure trove of culinary potential. Among its most celebrated feats is its capacity to morph into a superb substitute for traditional pasta, heralding a new era of wholesome dining.

The spiraliser, an affordable kitchen marvel under £20, unlocks the courgette's transformative power, turning it into delectable, twirl-worthy 'zoodles.' This ingenious conversion is more than a visual delight; it's a portal to a realm of nutritious indulgence.

Beyond the realm of zoodles, courgette shines brightly in its versatility. Whether sautéed to tender brilliance or incorporated into dishes for an added nutritional punch, it is a dietary powerhouse. Packed with fibre, it aids in promoting digestive wellbeing, while its rich assortment of vitamins and minerals, including vitamin C, potassium, and manganese, bolster overall health. The gifts of courgette extend further, offering antioxidant properties that combat oxidative stress and inflammation, contributing to heart health and potentially reducing the risk of chronic diseases. Its significant water content ensures it nourishes us without weighing us down.

Carrots: The Visionary Root

Carrots, the underground champions of twilight vision, are more than crunchy snacks. Laden with beta-carotene, they perform an enchanting metamorphosis within our bodies, converting into vitamin A and subsequently into rhodopsin in the retina, boosting our prowess to peer through the dusk. Yet, the virtues of carrots stretch far beyond the shadows. Beta-carotene, a vigilant guardian against various cancers, and vitamin A, a rejuvenator for our skin, hair, and nails, elevate the humble carrot to a treasure trove of well-being. A medium-sized carrot (weighing between 50 to 60 grams) provides about two grams of fibre, rooting us in health and guiding us towards a vibrant future.

While carrots might tip the scales with a higher sugar content than other vegetables, they wield anti-diabetic powers, as unveiled in a Food and Nutrition Sciences review. The study illuminated a fascinating correlation: lower levels of carotenoids—the pigments painting carrots in vibrant orange hues—were linked to elevated blood sugar and insulin levels, suggesting carotenoids as potential allies in diabetes management.[15] The soluble fibre in carrots emerges as a regulator, balancing blood sugar and insulin post-meal, and their placement on the lower end of the glycaemic index ensures a sustained release of energy, showcasing carrots as not just a feast for the eyes but a foundation for health.

Cheese: The Gourmet's Delight

Cheese, the crown jewel of the culinary world, is not just a food item; it's an experience. But let's be clear, we're not talking about those neon-hued factory creations. True cheese is an art form, preferably organic, from cows that haven't been turned into pharmaceutical repositories.

Now, about the lactose dilemma. Cheese lovers, rejoice! The fermentation fiesta that transforms milk into cheese is like a magic show for lactose, significantly reducing its sugar content. The ageing process is like a fine wine, giving healthy bacteria ample time to make lactose a mere memory. From Brie to Blue, Cheddar to Camembert, these cheese champions boast less than 4% carbs. Just tread lightly with cottage cheese; it's more carb-conscious. And a word of caution: Beware of the 'low-fat' brigade. It's often code for 'added sugar and strange sorcery.' Stick to the real deal, and your taste buds (and health) will thank you.

Coffee: The Brewed Awakening

Coffee, nature's own pesticide, is like the plant world's version of a superhero, warding off predators with its caffeine shield. For us, it's not a foe but a friend, igniting our central nervous system like a spark plug. I find it the perfect companion for weight training, transforming fat into fuel with the finesse of a biochemical alchemist.

But coffee's powers are not one-size-fits-all. While I can court sleep even after a coffee serenade, it's like a rude awakening for others, keeping the sandman at bay. If coffee's nocturnal notes are too lively for you, turn to herbal tea with ginger-it's like a lullaby in a cup.

A Finnish study found that those who indulge in three to five cups daily could be 65% less likely to tango with Alzheimer's.[16] Why? Coffee is like a pep rally for gut-friendly bacteria, giving them a 60% growth spurt. It's not just a brew; it's a guardian of mental prowess with a generous side of antioxidants.

Tea: The Tincture of Vitality

Tea, the ancient brew, has been celebrated for centuries as the potion of health, happiness, and wisdom, particularly cherished in Eastern traditions. Renowned for its vast array of benefits, tea is believed to be a formidable ally against ailments like cancer, heart disease, and diabetes. But let's steep a little deeper into the world of teas, dividing our exploration into green tea and its diverse brethren.

Green tea, derived from the leaves of Camellia sinensis, is a bounty of health advantages. Epigallocatechin gallate (EGCG) is at the forefront, a powerhouse driving metabolic activity and simultaneously silencing hunger pangs. Every sip offers a dual benefit: it enhances adrenaline production, fuelling a metabolic blaze while combating free radicals and offering protection against certain cancers and the common cold and flu.

Ah, the fascinating world of centenarians and their timeless relationship with tea. In Ikaria, nestled among the Greek islands, these wise elders embrace the local teas, crafting brews from wild oregano, sage, and rosemary. It's a testament to the power of local, organic infusions in their daily rituals—a reminder that tea isn't just a beverage; it's a lifestyle, a legacy, and perhaps the secret to a life well-lived.

But our journey doesn't end there. Picture yourself in Japan, where tea-making is elevated to an art form. Here, centenarians may enjoy delicate cups of matcha, the vibrant green tea powder whisked to perfection, or find solace in the comforting embrace of genmaicha, with its nutty undertones and toasted rice accents. Now, let's journey to the misty mountains of China, where tea has been cultivated for centuries. Among the centenarians of these ancient lands, you might discover a reverence for the subtle complexities of oolong tea, with its floral aromas and lingering aftertaste, or an appreciation for the earthy richness of Pu-erh tea, aged to perfection like fine wine.

Across cultures and continents, one thing remains constant: tea isn't just a beverage; it's often a way of life, a cornerstone of their daily rituals, and perhaps the secret ingredient to their remarkable longevity. Cheers to a life well-lived, one sip at a time!

Other Teas: The Flavourful Fleet

Who knew a casual supermarket quest with my daughter, Jessica, would unveil a tea treasury of 97 flavours? From the exotic whispers of ginger with cranberry to the soothing embrace of chamomile, the world of tea is a mosaic of flavours, each telling its own story, each a potential key to longevity and wellness, as evidenced by the tea rituals on the storied isles of Ikaria and Okinawa.

For someone who has flirted with alcoholic beverages a tad too much, I've found solace in the aromatic arms of flavoured teas. They're not just drinks; they're an exploration, a way to tame the 'alcohol monkey' (a nod to Steve Peters' *Chimp Paradox*). Sometimes, in a moment of alchemical inspiration, I'll even blend two different tea bags, crafting my own unique tea cocktail.

Having armed yourself with a pantheon of 40 natural wonders to elevate your culinary escapades, we now arrive at a pivotal interlude. Before we march further, let's bridge the chasm between pantry and plate with 10 transformative tips designed to weave these wholesome marvels into your daily feast seamlessly. This isn't just about turning your kitchen into a bastion of health; it's about seasoning your cooking prowess with a dash of rebellion against the siren songs of ultra-processed fare. Prepare not just to cook but to concoct magic, making your homemade flavours a resounding echo of authenticity that outshines the hollow allure of profit-driven fast foods.

Transforming Your Cooking: A Gateway To Healthy Habit Mastery

Venturing beyond the alluring grasp of processed foods, your kitchen is primed to become a haven of innovation and wholesome habits. Remember the deceptive allure of industrial food giants unveiled in chapter four? It's time to reclaim the narrative, transforming your culinary space into a sanctuary where the artistry of flavours and the pursuit of health converge harmoniously.

Before we travel into the heart of flavour exploration, let's consider your kitchen's transformation. It's not just about stocking up on ingredients; it's about forming enduring, healthy habits. Each spice jar, each bottle of oil, and every fresh herb is a stepping stone on this path. These aren't just ingredients; they're tools in your arsenal to combat the routine of unhealthy eating, guiding you gently towards a lifestyle where good choices become second nature.

Redefining Convenience

Benjamin Franklin once said, *'By failing to prepare, you are preparing to fail,'* a mantra perfectly suited for the quest back to health. Or, as my pal Paul Da Vinci puts it, *'Spontaneity Sucks,'* emphasising the chaos unprepared eating brings into our lives. Without meal planning, the lure of quick, easy, and often unhealthy food options becomes hard to resist, derailing our progress.

So, how do we combat this? Start by decluttering your kitchen of temptations. But here's the dilemma: nobody likes waste. Here's an idea: why not donate what you can to food banks? And remember, bread is a no-go for ducks—it's not their natural diet, so don't throw your last loaf at them. For everything else, why not host a ceremonial pantry purge? Light a bonfire (but do it cautiously, as half of what's in your cupboards might as well be rocket fuel given its chemical content) and share the spectacle on social media. It should be fun, a bit mad, but ultimately liberating.

Would our cave-dwelling ancestors recognise the stuff in your cupboards? If the answer's no, it's time for it to go. Imagine the purification of stomping on a box of cornflakes or turning sugary cereals into an unrecognisable mush. It's not just about cleaning out your pantry; it's about setting the stage for a healthier you.

I've dubbed this step 'Redefining Convenience.' Your brain loves the simple route, if junk food remains within arm's reach, it will be eaten. It's confirmed by my chats with countless folks and my own battles at home. Despite my transformation from a chubster to a trimmer me, the odd bag of chips or tub of ice cream still finds its way into our home, courtesy of my eternally slender wife who, mysteriously, hasn't read a page of any of my books. So, while I strive for pantry perfection, real life—and marriage—often complicates things.

But remember, any temptations left lurking in your kitchen will get consumed eventually. While some unhealthy cravings might fade away, others linger. The key is removing convenience and temptation as much as possible to stay on track with your health goals.

Top 10 Home Cooking Hacks

Now it's time to explore ten essential ingredients, each a key player in the symphony of your gastronomic creations. These ingredients aren't just about adding taste; they're about crafting a new narrative for your meals, where every flavour is an opportunity to nourish your body and your commitment to a healthier, more vibrant lifestyle.

Salt: The Bedrock of the Pantry
Salt isn't just a seasoning; it's a survival instinct bottled up! It's nature's way of ensuring we get what our body craves for survival. But be wary, as Steven Witherly points out in *Why Humans Love Junk Food*, packaged foods often transform this essential mineral into an overdose, making up about 1% of their weight. It's like the food industry has a gigantic salt shaker and is not afraid to use it! But, as you're now ditching processed foods, chances are you will need to add more salt at meal times.

Oils/Fats: Natural Goodness
Oils and fats are the Kardashians of the culinary world; they add richness and drama! Our brain is like a calorie detective, always on the lookout for

dense sources of energy. But remember, not all fats are created equal. Stick to A-listers: lard, butter, ghee, coconut oil, and extra virgin olive oil.

Vanilla: The Secret Whisper of Sweetness
Vanilla, with its floral, sweet embrace, is like a culinary hug. It's the secret ingredient in many dishes, often hiding in plain sight. But let's keep it real-ditch the artificial stuff and invest in a tiny bottle of pure vanilla extract. It's a precious and long-lasting diamond of your spice rack; a little goes a long way. Just like Steven Witherly's advice, 'When in doubt, almost any dish will benefit from either a dash of vanilla or a clove of garlic,' I must admit, I have taken that advice literally, and I promise you, it works. Virtually everything I create in my kitchen will contain just a dash of either of these two ingredients.

Garlic: The Bold and the Beautiful
Garlic is the scene-stealer of the home cooking world. When it steps into a dish, it doesn't just mingle; it takes centre stage with a bold and irresistible presence. This powerhouse creates a dance of flavours on your palate, offering a performance that ranges from a gentle warmth to a dynamic contrast that leaves a memorable impression. And it's not just a treat for the taste buds-garlic is like a health hero in disguise, armed with enough potency to ward off any unwanted vampires or the common cold! It's a trigeminal sensation, providing a natural zing without the shock of an electric stimulant. Its oreosensory magic teases the tongue with a delicate sizzle akin to the allure of black pepper and onions, turning each bite into an exciting culinary adventure.

Butter/Cream: The Dynamic Duo of Decadence
Butter and cream are the Batman and Robin of the kitchen; together, they combat blandness and rescue dishes in distress. They're not just purveyors of richness but culinary matchmakers, seamlessly blending other flavours into a blissful union of taste.

Why single out butter from other oils and fats, you ask? Well, because butter and cream boast a unique taste-bud tantaliser known as nucleotides. These little marvels activate the umami sensors on your tongue, adding an extra layer of depth to your dishes. This intriguing interplay is why you'll often encounter both oil and butter co-starring in the same recipe, even when you might initially think one would suffice.

Shallots: The Secret Weapon of Gourmet Kitchens
Shallots might seem like high-maintenance cousins of the humble onion, but they're culinary gold for those in the know. Top chefs swear by them,

and here's why: their flavour is simply unparalleled, turning any dish from mundane to magnificent. They might test your patience a bit more when peeling, but the flavour payoff is astronomical. Plus, they pack such a punch that you won't need many. A couple of shallots can elevate a dish like Pliny the Elder, elevating the art of sauce-making 2,000 years ago.

Egg Yolk: The Nutrient-Packed Emulsifier
Envision egg yolk as the ultimate kitchen MVP (most valuable player)- versatile, crucial, and teeming with essential nutrients. Dr Malcolm Kendrick hit the nail on the head when he praised eggs as the ultimate nourishment package. It's akin to nature's multivitamin, neatly wrapped in its tiny package. Adding egg yolk to your culinary creations is akin to blending health with indulgence- a harmonious balance of nutritional wealth and pure pleasure! Don't throw away those egg whites either; they have hundreds of uses, from thickening up a cocktail to making a low-carb mousse.

Cheese: The Flavourful Alchemist
Cheese isn't merely a flavour enhancer; it conducts a tantalising performance in terms of taste sensations. With its unmatched energy density and captivating contrast, cheese commands the spotlight, while its complex, flavour-rich compounds engage our senses in a dance of delight. Could it be that cheese's casomorphins hold the key to its irresistible allure?

Here's a cheesy tip: elevate your cooking creations by baking cheddar to a bubbling, golden perfection, draping your dishes in a cloak of deliciousness that turns the mundane into the extraordinary. Try pouring this molten masterpiece over a medley of vibrant vegetables for a truly unforgettable feast.

Black Pepper: The Key to Unlocking Full-Flavoured Feasts
Why does black pepper elevate virtually every dish to a food delight? It's more than a spice; it's a master key to unlocking the full potential of your palate. This unassuming condiment is a taste bud provocateur, gently nudging your senses awake and heightening your perception of every flavour note. As an irritant, black pepper does more than add a kick; it coaxes your taste buds to unfold, enhancing your ability to savour each ingredient to its fullest. Imagine your tongue as a canvas and black pepper as the brush that primes it to absorb the full spectrum of flavours. The real magic of black pepper lies in its ability to complement and intensify the following flavours, creating a harmonious blend that turns a simple meal into a symphony of taste.

Herbs and Spices: Nature's Aroma Wizards
Herbs and spices are not just ingredients; they're a bridge to centuries of

wisdom and healing. They were the ancient world's pharmacies, with legends like Hippocrates using them to heal and soothe. Today, they're our healthy living kitchen's heroes, adding flavour and a touch of nature's magic to every dish. Let herbs and spices be your trusted allies, transforming your meals from ordinary to extraordinary and turning your kitchen into a haven of health and happiness.

Whether you're growing them in your garden or sprinkling them from a jar, they're your secret ingredient to a vibrant, healthful life.

Revamp Your Kitchen

Remember the thrill of starting a new school term with a sparkling set of stationery? That pristine pencil sharpener, the ruler still untouched by teeth marks or graffiti—it wasn't just about the tools, but the promise of a fresh start. As you embark on this new chapter in your life, it's time to infuse that same enthusiasm into your kitchen.

Transforming your kitchen isn't just about sprucing it up; it's about setting the stage for a new chapter of health and happiness. Imagine equipping yourself not just with the basics but with the culinary equivalent of those school-day treasures. It's time to invest in the best knives your budget allows. While you didn't need them for slicing through a microwave dinner, for the tactile pleasure of prepping fresh veggies and meats like a pro, you certainly will.

It's not about spoiling yourself but investing in your health and joy. Those top-tier knives? They're not just tools; they're an invitation to fall in love with cooking at home. And don't stop there. Seek kitchen gadgets that delight in form and function—pieces that feel right in your hand and inspire you to create. Display your culinary tools proudly; let them remind you of your commitment to wellbeing; think spice racks, wooden knife blocks, stylish mixing bowls or a set of high-quality pans. And don't forget that essential playlist to set the mood—whether it's the Rocky soundtrack or a compilation of cheesy 80s ballads that get your cookery juices flowing.

Unlock your kitchen's full potential and transform into a cooking superstar with these must-have gadgets.

Here are 10 essentials that I can't live without:

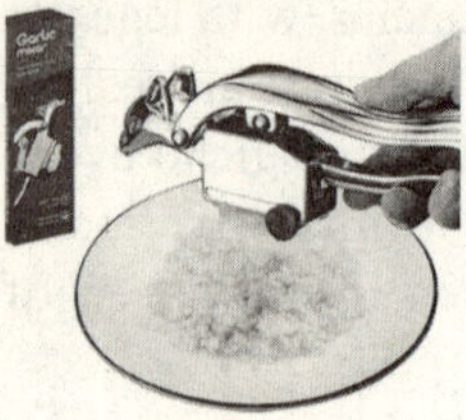

Garlic Crusher
Here is the one I use, its like the Rolls Royce of garlic crushers, it costs £9.99 on Amazon, but prices start from about £4.99.

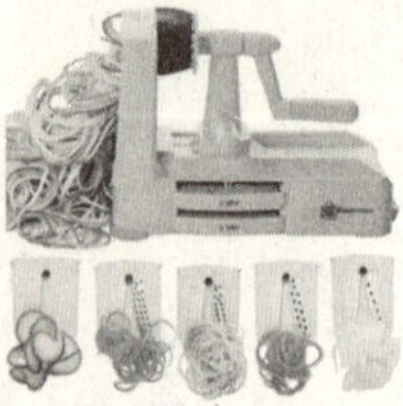

Spiralizer
This is how you make courgetti (spaghetti alternative) and jazz up your salads. If you are really investing in your health, then get one similar to the one I use, it cost around £29. I got mine from Amazon, but Argos do one too. Alternatively you could go for a hand held spiralizer and these cost around £9.

Mandoline Slicer
Firstly, NEVER buy one of these unless they come with either special gloves or some other method to protect your finger tips. I have twice seriously hurt my self with one of these and I don't want the same to happen to you. That said, they are awesome for slicing fruit and vegetables and will help you prepare meals like a professional chef. Prices range from about £20 to £30 and are available from Argos and Amazon.

Chopping Board
Get yourself a nice chopping board. I like this one on Amazon because it's made out of bamboo (very good for the planet). Prices from £10 to £30

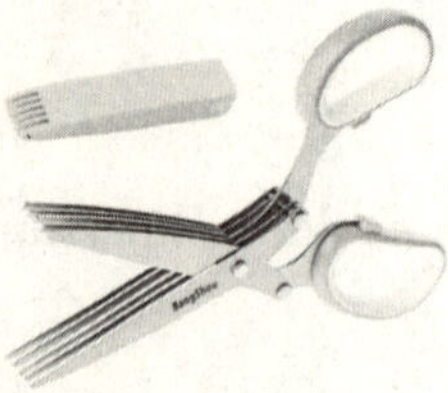

Herb Scissors
I use these quite a lot to quickly chop up herbs and also for spring onions etc. They cost around £7 on Amazon.

Burger Maker
Make your own burgers look awesome. Prices start from about £7.

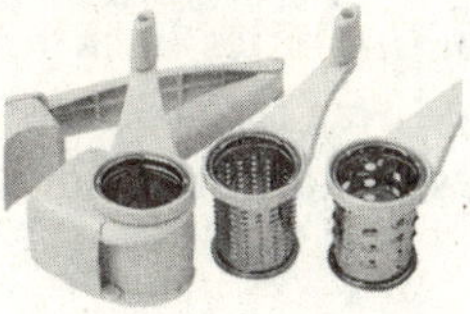

Cheese Grater
I don't like traditional cheese graters because I have cut my fingers too many times. You can buy these on the internet from about £9 to £12.

Blender
Owning a blender and a food processor is like having sous chefs in your kitchen, ready to assist with every culinary task. The blender smoothly blends ingredients for delicious smoothies, soups, and sauces while the food processor expertly chops, slices, and shreds with precision. Sometimes, they are available on the same device, streamlining meal prep and making creating nutritious and flavourful dishes easier.

Deep Fat Fryer
One of the things that surprises most people, is how, if you choose the right fat (I use dripping) and the right coatings, you can make super healthy foods in a deep fryer. Prices from about £20.

Slow Cooker
Consider getting yourself a slow cooker. Really great for preparing simple healthy meals. Prices from £30 to £100.

Supplementation: Bridging The Nutritional Gap

In the 1930s, a visionary dentist named Dr Price embarked on a global odyssey, not in search of the world's best toothpaste, but to uncover the dietary secrets of remote communities. From the icy realms of the Inuit to the vibrant cultures of the Māori, Dr Price's exploration revealed a startling contrast between the nutrient-rich diets of these communities and the comparatively lacklustre dinner plates back in the USA. His research extended to transporting traditional foods from these far-flung communities back to his laboratory in America for analysis. What he uncovered was remarkable: in comparison to the typical American dinner plate, these traditional diets boasted a vastly superior nutrient profile:

- They contained **seven times** the amount of calcium.
- The levels of magnesium and copper were **four** times higher, with some instances showing up to **twenty times** higher.
- Iron content was up to **fifty times** richer.
- Iodine levels were often **fifty times** greater.
- A notably higher concentration of vitamins C and B was consistently observed.
- There were also significantly higher concentrations of vitamins A, D, and K.

Dr Price's research illuminated the significant nutritional benefits of traditional diets compared to standard American meals, emphasising the crucial role of nutrient density in our diet. Considering this comparison was made 90 years ago, it leaves one to ponder what he would uncover in today's era of ultra-processed foods.

Did our primal ancestors pop supplements like we do morning toast? Certainly not. In an ideal world, our diets would be as diverse and nutrient-packed as theirs, free from the clutches of processed foods, refined sugars, and the less-than-stellar offerings of modern agriculture. They feasted on an assortment of plants, insects, and animals, their menus changing with the seasons, their soils untouched by chemicals, their air unspoiled by pollutants.

Fast forward to today, and it's clear that while evolution has been busy, it hasn't quite kept up with the pace of our environmental and dietary shifts. Our modern lives are a far cry from the nutrient utopias of our ancestors. Our soils, exhausted by overuse, no longer offer the nutrient buffet they once did, and the idea of munching on a diverse range of leaves and bugs isn't precisely a modern-day palate pleaser.

So, here we are, facing a fork in the road: to supplement or not to supplement? While the purists might baulk at the idea, the reality is that for many, a life sans supplements is akin to a garden without sunshine. Even at their organic best, our modern diets often fall short of meeting our nutritional needs. It's not about replacing food with pills but complementing our diets, filling in the gaps left by our less-than-perfect food chain.

My mantra? Eat a rainbow of organic, nutrient-dense foods, making your plate a canvas of natural abundance. Then, judiciously supplement to meet any dietary deficits. Think of supplements not as a crutch but as a bridge, a way to connect our modern lives with the nutritional wisdom of our primal past, ensuring that even in our fast-paced world, every cell in our body is humming a happy, healthy tune.

Here is what Patrick Holden, who was the CEO of the Soil Association for more than two decades, told me.

> *'Today, if you go to a supermarket and buy normal salad vegetables, I am talking about lettuces, tomatoes, cucumbers, peppers, and all the salad crops; none of them are grown in the soil anymore! They are all grown hydroponically (hydroponics is the science of growing plants without using soil) in this rockwool or equivalent. It's like a sort of nutrient-holding medium, and they are nourished with fertilisers in solution, which has replaced soil-grown vegetables. You can't buy soil-grown salads in the UK anymore unless you buy organic. It's even worse in America, where the conventional growing lobby has just changed the standards and made growing even organic vegetables hydroponically possible! There are bound to be long-term consequences for our health. Imagine if we had passed a law that if you were growing hydroponically, you had to label the vegetables. I think that would have quite an impact.'*

'Orthomolecular' Medicine

Dive into the realm of 'Orthomolecular' medicine, an underappreciated yet potentially game-changing approach to health. Conceived by Nobel Peace Prize laureate and biochemist Linus Pauling in 1968, this philosophy redirects our focus from drug reliance to the power of nutrition. It's a perspective mirrored in the words of orthomolecular proponent Dr Carl C. Pfeiffer, who astutely observed, 'For every drug that benefits a patient, there is a natural substance that can achieve the same effect.' This method isn't just about substituting pills with supplements; it's about realigning our health strategy to nature's rhythm, emphasising prevention over cure, and nurturing our bodies with the right blend of fibre, vitamins, and minerals. Orthomolecular medicine isn't merely a term; it's a pathway to a healthier existence championed by a Nobel laureate's visionary thinking.

Imagine a world where tiny but mighty elements are essential for the vibrant tapestry of life. This is the realm of vitamins and minerals. The term 'vitamin' springs from the Greek 'vita', meaning 'life'; these organic compounds, created by plants and animals, are vital for life. They are the essence of life, derived from the living. In contrast, minerals are the inorganic counterparts, naturally occurring in soil and water, silent yet foundational.

Vitamins and Minerals: The Micro Marvels of Nutrition

Look at your dinner plate, and you'll find it dominated by the heavy hitters: carbohydrates, fats, and proteins. These dietary titans form the bulk of our intake, turning into sugars, amino acids, and fatty acids post-digestion. But hold onto your folks. There's more to our food tale than these macro musketeers. Enter the realm of vitamins and minerals, the unsung heroes of our inner cosmos. Think of them as the secret fuel to our body's performance, akin to the finest additives ensuring your car's engine purrs like a contented cat. They're not mere extras in the nutritional script but pivotal players ensuring every cellular cog turns with precision.

The Vivacious Vitamins

In the bustling marketplace of life, vitamins are the organic artisans, crafting health in every living nook, from the humble broccoli to the mighty steak. Only a select few organic compounds make the grade, earning the coveted title of 'vitamin' when their absence throws our health off balance.

Thirteen essential vitamins await your acquaintance, a number echoing superstitions but harbouring no luck in deficiency. They split into two camps: fat-soluble and water-soluble. The fat-soluble quartet vitamins A, D, E, and K can be tucked away in our body's storage, somewhat like squirrels hoarding nuts for winter. Conversely, the water-soluble troupe, including all the B vitamins and Vitamin C, are the live-in-the-moment types, staying briefly and needing constant top-ups.

These vitamins and minerals don't fly solo; they're social butterflies, mingling and synergising. Calcium, for instance, leans on Vitamin D for a stellar performance in bone fortification. This intricate interplay underlines the sophisticated nutritional ballet happening within us.

The Mighty Minerals

Now, allow me to spotlight minerals, those steadfast supporting actors in our dietary drama. They hail from the earth and water, not born but borrowed, infusing our food with their inorganic essence. They're the underpinning of our well-being, the silent sentinels guarding everything from robust bones to the rhythmic beating of our hearts.

But here's a modern-day problem: Our mineral-rich world has thinned, and its once bountiful soil is now whispering tales of depletion. It's a cascading crisis: Soils bereft of minerals lead to nutrient-starved plants and animals, culminating in a human populace yearning for these foundational nutrients.

So, what's the grand finale in this nutritional narrative? Our modern plates, though filled, often echo the emptiness of our depleted soils. To echo the diverse diets of our ancestors, we must weave a tapestry of varied, organic foods enriched with the occasional supplement cameo. It's about recapturing the lost art of a truly nourishing diet, ensuring that every vitamin and mineral, no matter how small, plays its part in the magnificent symphony of life.

The Nutritional Landscape: A Glimpse into a Transforming Ecosystem
As we travel through the terrains of health and nutrition, it becomes increasingly clear that our world is undergoing profound changes. The landscapes that once nourished generations are not what they used to be, and our bodies are whispering (and sometimes shouting) the tales of these transformations. The shifts are undeniable, from the very soil that cradles our food to the intricate biological processes within us. Let's take a moment to explore these pivotal changes, unveiling the challenges and opportunities that lie within our modern nutritional ecosystem.

A Snapshot of Our Changing World

Soil Nutrient Decline: According to the U.S. Food and Drug Administration (FDA), our soil has seen an 81% plunge in nutrient richness over the last three decades. To put it into perspective, you'd need to consume five times the food you did 30 years ago to receive the same nutritional benefits. This staggering statistic paints a grim picture of the declining health of our once-fertile lands.

Crop Breeding vs. Nutrient Availability: Donald Davis's research at the University of Texas sheds light on a modern agricultural paradox. Our pursuit of higher crop yields, pest resistance, and adaptability to climate extremes has inadvertently led to a nutritional dilution. These super-sized crops may grow rapidly, but their nutrient content isn't keeping pace, raising questions about the true cost of our agricultural advancements.

Age and Nutrient Absorption: Aging gracefully isn't just about aesthetics; it's a nutritional challenge, too. Our bodies lose their knack for nutrient absorption as we age, a situation often exacerbated by medications that can strip away essential nutrients. Conditions like atrophic gastritis affect around 20% of the elderly and hinder the absorption of key nutrients such as vitamin B12 and magnesium, so it's clear that our nutritional needs evolve with time.

The Microbiome and Modern Living: As you have already read, the microbiome, the microscopic universe within us, is pivotal in disease prevention and overall wellness. Yet, our modern lifestyles, characterised by an overreliance on chemicals and an obsession with sterility, might be unsettling this delicate balance. Nurturing our gut biome through a balanced diet rich in vitamins, minerals, and omega-3 oils is more crucial than ever to safeguard our immune system.

Medication and Nutrient Absorption: Medications, while often lifesaving, can have unintended nutritional side effects, hindering the absorption of vital vitamins and minerals. Coupled with lifestyle factors like alcohol consumption, which notably affects the assimilation of B vitamins, it's evident that our health is at the intersection of various forces.

Exploring the World of Supplements: My Personal Perspective

Instead of cataloguing the many supplements available on the market within these pages, I'll share the specific ones I choose to take and the rationale behind my choices. For complete transparency, it's important to note that as the founder of Primal Living, a supplement company, my tour through the supplement landscape may be guided by a compass that occasionally points towards the shores of supplementation. While I strive for objectivity, it's important for you to note that a subtle breeze of bias may influence my insights.

The world of dietary supplements is as varied as the spices in a master chef's kitchen, each with its own flavour and purpose. It's not about a universal recipe; it's about finding the right blend for your unique nutritional needs.

For instance, basking in sun-drenched adventures and feasting on a sea of oily fish might keep your vitamin D levels jubilant. But if you're more of a shade seeker with a diet that sidesteps fish, a vitamin D supplement might be your ray of light, especially when the British sun plays its seasonal game of peek-a-boo.

Here's a peek behind the curtain of my personal supplement theatre—a carefully curated ensemble designed to patch any potential nutritional gaps seamlessly. My approach is simple: champion a diet rich in fibre and brimming with natural nutrients and then enlist supplements as a secondary insurance policy. It's akin to crafting a bespoke suit—what's tailored perfectly for one may not be a precise fit for another, yet it should resonate with the needs of many across the UK:

- Glucomannan
- Two Omega-3 soft gels
- One gram of magnesium bisglycinate
- A personalised multivitamin and multimineral
- Resveratrol alternated with turmeric
- Coenzyme Q10
- Probiotics
- 10g Collagen
- NAD
- 30 g of whey protein post-workout

As you read through the next few pages, see it as akin to leafing through a personalised nutritional diary aimed at optimising health and vitality. It's my daily routine to fill the nutritional voids that modern life and diet often leave behind.

Glucomannan: The Fibrous Companion

First on our list is glucomannan, a fibre that's become a staple in my dietary regimen, revered not just for its nutritional prowess but for its versatility. While I won't dwell on the basics (you're well-versed in the fibre narrative by now), it's worth noting how glucomannan weaves its way into my daily routine. This isn't just any fibre; it's a dietary chameleon, adapting to various forms and functions.

Glucomannan is my go-to, whether I'm navigating a day of fasting, adhering to a carnivore diet, or simply looking to maintain a balanced intake. I invite it into my diet in multiple guises: as a satiating fibre drink with Slimshotz, a convenient, swallowable capsule named Hunger Bulletz, or transformed into glucomannan noodles for a hearty, nutritious meal. Each variant offers a unique way to incorporate this fibrous ally into my diet, ensuring that, no matter the day's dietary theme, glucomannan is there to fill the gaps, providing a consistent, fibrous foundation (discover the details of these variants on page 955).

Omega-3 (Rich in DHA): The Brain and Joint Guardians

Meet Omega-3, the caped crusaders of the fatty acid world. Laden with DHA, these superheroes don't just soothe inflammation; they ignite the fireworks of cognition and grease the wheels of joint mobility. These fatty warriors are indispensable in a dietary landscape where the focus is on trimming the waistline and enriching our cerebral expanse. Each capsule of Omega-3 is akin to dispatching a cavalry of support, ensuring our brain health and joint function are in top-notch form, ready to conquer the challenges of daily life.

Magnesium Bisglycinate: The Night-Time Serenade

As night falls and the world quiets down, magnesium bisglycinate steps onto the stage, a lullaby encapsulated. This mineral, the unsung star of tranquillity, doesn't just pacify your nerves; it coordinates calmness, guiding you into restorative slumber. Amidst the daytime hustle of balancing blood sugar with fibre-rich meals, magnesium bisglycinate emerges as the night's guardian, ensuring our sleep is not just a pause but fully rejuvenating.

But Magnesium's role is not confined to the twilight hours. It's a pillar of wellness, a linchpin in over 300 bodily functions. From bolstering bones to banishing fatigue, its influence is vast. Yet, it's often missing in action in the modern dietary script. The culprit? A duo of environmental shifts and the transformative tale of modern food processing. The result is a nutritional paradox: to match the magnesium intake of yesteryears, our plates would have to be fivefold more bountiful.

A magnesium shortfall doesn't just whisper; it echoes through our health, manifesting in muscle twitches, mental fog, erratic heartbeats, and more. Coupled with the common vitamin D deficiency during the UK's winter months, the magnesium drought deepens, as vitamin D plays a pivotal role in magnesium's absorption.

In the realm of supplements, not all are forged equal. magnesium bisglycinate stands tall, with its bioavailability and gentle nature making it the preferred envoy of calmness. Beyond capsules, magnesium's versatility shines through topical applications and bath salts, offering solace to weary muscles, a boon to skin health, and a passport to improved sleep quality.

Multivitamin and Multimineral

Even with the most kale-packed, berry-bursting *Fibre First* diet, it's easy to overlook a nutrient or two. That's where a comprehensive multivitamin and multimineral supplement becomes invaluable. However, not all supplements are created equal. It's essential to choose wisely, as many multivitamins may contain diluted concentrations. Opt for quality over cost-cutting measures.

For instance, vitamin K. There are two varieties: K1 and K2. While the former is more affordable, it's also less effective. On the other hand, vitamin K2, albeit pricier, boasts significantly higher bioavailability, making it a superior choice for supplementation. Remember, investing in your health today can yield invaluable benefits tomorrow.

Resveratrol and Turmeric (Alternating)

Think of these as your internal age-defying, inflammation-fighting antioxidant warriors. Both help keep free radicals under control, perfectly complementing our quest to keep sugar spikes at bay. They both appear on the ORAC (Oxygen Radical Absorbance Capacity) scale, which we will discuss shortly. Why the dance of alternation, you ask? Simply put, the research spotlight keeps shifting from one to the other, praising their individual virtues. So, I juggle them in my routine, embracing diversity and betting on the best of both worlds.

CoEnzyme Q10: The Cellular Dynamo and Age-Defying Energiser

Envision Coenzyme Q10 as the master spark plug of your cells, igniting the engines of energy production. This remarkable molecule isn't just another cog in the cellular machine; it's the essence of vitality, transforming every morsel of nourishment into a surge of energy.

CoQ10's role in our bodies is multifaceted. Beyond its primary function as a cellular dynamo, it is a vigilant protector, shielding your cells from the ravages of free radicals, diminishing inflammation, and acting as a bulwark against chronic ailments like heart disease. This isn't merely an energy enhancer; it's your heart's clandestine confidant, a steadfast companion ensuring the robustness of every beat.

In Japan, a country revered for its meticulous approach to health, CoQ10 holds a place of honour. If you're prescribed a statin, it's standard practice to pair it with CoQ10, a testament to its esteemed role in supporting heart health and mitigating potential side effects. This practice underscores the global recognition of CoQ10's pivotal role in maintaining cardiovascular wellness.

As we age, our body's natural ability to produce CoQ10 gradually diminishes, making supplementation a wise choice for maintaining optimal levels. It's not just about replenishing what's lost; it's about rekindling the fiery furnace of our cells' mitochondria, the powerhouses of energy production. With CoQ10, you're not just supplementing; you're reigniting the youthful vigour of your cells, ensuring they produce energy with the efficiency and zest of their prime.

The Power of Probiotics

Having discussed the fascinating world of the microbiome earlier, we've uncovered the profound impact these microscopic residents have on our health. Now, let's spotlight the role of a probiotic, the keystone in maintaining this delicate internal ecosystem we've come to appreciate.

A potent probiotic acts as a pivotal guardian within the gut's environment, coordinating the beneficial bacteria to work in unison. These advantageous microbes do more than assist in digestion; they bolster our body's defence mechanisms and foster a harmonious immune system. In the complex interplay of gut flora, where equilibrium is essential, a premium probiotic guides the gut's inhabitants precisely and ensures a seamless integration of functions. Adopting probiotics into our routine is a strategic move towards enhancing our gut's durability to withstand the impacts of modern life's dietary shifts and environmental factors.

In the intricate tapestry of our gut's microbiome, probiotics are akin to a meticulously trained army poised to defend, balance, and nurture our internal landscape. But even the most elite troops require strategic support to ensure their successful deployment. Here are three crucial tips for enlisting a probiotic force that's not just formidable but also effective:

> **Survivability in the Gauntlet of the Stomach:** The passage to the intestines is a perilous pilgrimage akin to crossing a treacherous battlefield. The stomach's acidic environment is the first line of defence, where many probiotic strains meet their demise. To ensure your probiotic battalion reaches its destination, opt for strains known for their resilience in this hostile terrain. Some probiotics, like the

ones my company crafts, come equipped with patented shields such as BioTract™. This technology fortifies the probiotics, boosting their survival rate by up to 15 times, ensuring they traverse the acidic abyss unscathed and arrive where needed most.

Strength in Numbers: Just as an army's might is measured by its numbers, the potency of a probiotic is gauged by its bacterial count. Starting with a baseline of 3 billion CFUs (colony-forming units) ensures you're deploying a formidable force. These billions of micro-warriors stand ready to colonise your gut, forging a wall against imbalances and fortifying your health defences.

Diversity and Specialisation: An effective army isn't just about numbers; it's about each unit's unique skills. Similarly, in the realm of probiotics, diversity is key. Seek formulations that offer a spectrum of strains, each backed by contemporary research illuminating their specific benefits. This variety ensures a well-rounded approach to gut health, with different strains contributing their specialised functions, much like a well-coordinated platoon with varied expertise.

By adhering to these guidelines, you're not just choosing a probiotic but strategising a robust defence and nurturing system for your gut. It's about assembling an elite force, ready to march into the dynamic terrain of your microbiome and establish a bastion of balance and health.

Collagen (10g): The Structural Essence of Vitality

In the intricate workings of our dietary habits, a crucial thread often goes missing- collagen. This structural protein is not just an ingredient; it's the scaffolding of our bodies, integral for skin elasticity, joint flexibility, and overall resilience. Once, our ancestors naturally absorbed collagen by consuming animals whole, but modern diets overlook these collagen-rich parts. Introducing a collagen supplement is akin to welcoming back a long-lost friend, reviving the holistic nourishment of bygone days.

Collagen's significance is demonstrated by its ability to bypass the usual breakdown into amino acids, maintaining its form to meet our body's demands directly. Dr Malcolm Kendrick, in *The Clot Thickens*, aptly likens collagen to the steel bars in reinforced concrete-without it, our body's structure starts to falter, particularly our blood vessels.

It is the most abundant protein in our bodies, infusing every aspect, from our hair to our joints. As we age, our natural collagen production wanes, making supplementation not just a cosmetic choice but a fundamental one for maintaining our body's integrity.

Here are just a handful of collagen's myriad benefits:

- Enhances skin health by improving elasticity and hydration
- Alleviates joint pain and stiffness
- Bolsters muscle mass, especially when paired with resistance training
- Supports gut health by fortifying the intestinal lining
- Strengthens bones, reducing the risk of osteoporosis
- Minimises the appearance of cellulite
- Promotes healthy hair and nail growth
- Supports cardiovascular health, potentially reducing blood pressure
- Protects brain health, possibly slowing cognitive decline
- Aids in weight management by promoting satiety

I recommend 2.5 to 10 grams daily to reap these benefits. Collagen's impact on skin health is particularly noteworthy, promoting a firm, smooth complexion, reducing cellulite, and accelerating nail growth. It counteracts the loss of collagenous extracellular matrix, effectively rejuvenating the skin from within. In embracing collagen, we're not just addressing superficial needs. We're fortifying the very framework of our bodies, ensuring every fibre of our being is nurtured and supported. Collagen is more than a supplement; it's a cornerstone of our structural health, a tribute to our body's enduring strength and resilience.

When to take it? I recently attended a health conference where I had the opportunity to record an interview with the renowned fitness guru, Dr Ben Bocchicchio, author of 15 Minutes to Fitness. During our discussion, he highlighted groundbreaking research by Dr Keith Baar, sponsored by the University of California. This study revealed that consuming collagen, alongside vitamin C—a crucial cofactor for its metabolism, 20 to 40 minutes before exercise can enhance its absorption by up to fivefold.

NAD: The Essence of Cellular Vitality and Mental Clarity

NAD, or Nicotinamide Adenine Dinucleotide (more on this in the next chapter), isn't just a component of our cells; it's the expert coordinating the work of cellular vitality and mental acuity. The magic of NAD lies in its dual role. On the one hand, it's a sentinel overseeing the energy production within our mitochondria, the power plants of our cells. On the other, it's a protector, a molecule that ensures the continuity and efficiency of essential cellular functions.

Envisioned as the brain's rejuvenating tonic, NAD stands at the forefront of our quest for longevity and robust health. In Dr David Sinclair's groundbreaking book, Lifespan: Why We Age-and Why We Don't Have To, this coenzyme emerges as a pivotal player in the ageing and cellular narrative.

At its core, NAD is a fundamental molecule found in every living cell, instrumental in driving key biological processes. It's the linchpin in energy metabolism, ensuring that the transfer of electrons during oxidation-reduction unfolds with precision and efficiency. But NAD's role extends beyond mere energy production; it's integral to the optimal functioning of a multitude of enzymatic processes, casting it as a guardian of cellular integrity and functionality.

Whey Protein

Whey protein is more than just a post-workout replenisher; it's a vital ally for muscle recovery and overall health. Essential for those who exercise regularly, whey protein assists in repairing and rebuilding muscle tissues that are stressed during workouts. It's important to choose a whey protein that's as pure as possible. Opting for a natural, additive-free whey protein ensures you're fuelling your body with what it needs without the extra baggage that can impede your health and fitness goals. This mindful approach aligns perfectly with a lifestyle committed to minimising sugar spikes and maximising nutritional value.

And what's my method for taking them? In the same big glass of water as my morning fibre powder. Incorporating fibre with my protein routine slows its absorption and allows me to maximise the effect of each and every gram. This gradual process ensures a steady nutrient release and absorption, effectively averting any potential blood sugar spikes that an overload of protein may occasionally cause.

This regimen encapsulates my present personal strategy for dietary supplementation, which aims to sustain optimal health and, with luck, promote longevity. Let's wrap up this exploration with an in-depth look at the individual health benefits of each vitamin, mineral, and electrolyte, which will serve as a handy reference for nutritional wellness. But before I get going, here is a true story from Patrick Holford.

'In the early 80s, when I set up the Institute for Optimum Nutrition, one of my students was a schoolmaster headmaster of a secondary school in Wales, and we devised an experiment. We took 90 school kids and put a third on a high-strength vitamin and mineral supplement. We put a third onto a dummy pill that looked identical and a third onto nothing. And we measured their IQ.

Our proposition was that vitamins could affect your IQ. Now, back in the early 80s, that was an outrageous idea, and we thought we'd get slaughtered for it. So, we didn't actually run the study ourselves. We got a professor of psychology called Professor David Benton, University of Swansea, who thought we were nuts.

He thought that a simple vitamin pill could not change one's IQ. But he still ran the study, and it was very well-designed. We approached BBC Horizon, and they filmed it. They said that if it doesn't work, you'll be exposed as fraud or something like that.

At the end of the seven months when they cracked the code, we'd had an increase of 10 points on what's called the nonverbal IQ on the vitamins and three points on the placebo. So, a seven-point difference would get half of all children classified as Special Educational Needs back into the normal category. So it's a big effect. And it hit every major newspaper and every major TV news; I mean, the next day, literally every single vitamin supplement in shops sold out.'

Fat-Soluble Vitamins: A Deeper Insight

Vitamin A: Is key for sharp vision in dim light, supporting neurological functions, bolstering the immune system, and ensuring bone health. Rich sources include green veggies such as kale, spinach, broccoli, eggs, and carrots, which aid in night vision.

Vitamin D: Essential for calcium absorption in bones to prevent osteoporosis and enhance the immune system, helping the body combat cancer and Alzheimer's. Sun exposure aids in vitamin D synthesis, with oily fish, dairy, and eggs as beneficial dietary sources.

Vitamin E: Acts as a powerful antioxidant, aiding in the fight against free radicals, Alzheimer's, and hypertension. Sunflower Seeds, almonds, and hazelnuts are potent sources, with green vegetables like broccoli, spinach, and avocados as great alternatives.

Vitamin K: Plays a crucial role in maintaining bone health and ensuring proper blood clotting; it also offers protective effects against cancer and contributes to cardiovascular wellbeing.

> **Vitamin K1**, predominant in green leafy vegetables like kale, broccoli, cabbage, and spinach, is essential for the body's blood clotting mechanisms.
> **Vitamin K2**, found in dairy products and certain fermented foods, is pivotal for bone health and cardiovascular function. It's important to highlight that MK-7, a specific form of K2, is recognised as the natural and most bioavailable variant, offering the most significant health benefits.

Water-Soluble Vitamins: Maximising Health

Vitamin C: A formidable antioxidant, it lowers high blood pressure, wards off infections, and fights strokes and certain cancers. It's also key for skin health and combating colds and flu. Daily intake is necessary as the body cannot produce or store it. Top sources include blackcurrants, bell peppers, and kiwis.

The B Vitamin Ensemble: Each Note Matters

Vitamin B1 (Thiamine): Strengthens the immune system, enhances cognitive functions, and reduces stress. Thiamine supplementation is especially important for those who consume alcohol, as it hampers absorption. It can be found in vegetables, meats, fish, seeds, and nuts.

Vitamin B2 (Riboflavin): Works with other enzymes to extract nutrients from food, acting as an antioxidant. It prevents mouth and nose cracks, depression, and sore throats, with rich sources including meats, green vegetables, nuts, and seeds.

Vitamin B3 (Niacin): Supports a healthy cardiovascular system, balances cholesterol levels, aids cognitive functions, and prevents skin dryness. Prime sources are chicken, beef, and fish like tuna and salmon.

Vitamin B5 (Pantothenic Acid): Crucial for extracting nutrients from food and maintaining nervous system health. Found in a wide range of foods, including avocado, sunflower seeds, meats, and green vegetables.

Vitamin B6 (Pyridoxine): Involved in serotonin production and removing excess amino acids from the blood. Deficiency is common in those who drink alcohol excessively. Sources include carrots, spinach, meat, poultry, fish, and eggs.

Vitamin B7 (Biotin): The beauty vitamin for enhancing hair, nails, and skin. It acts as a coenzyme in metabolising macronutrients. Found in liver, eggs, salmon, nuts, cheese, and avocado.

Vitamin B9 (Folate): Critical for cell production and repair, supporting nerve and immune functions, and preventing cognitive decline. Rich in liver, spinach, asparagus, broccoli, and fruits like mango and oranges.

Vitamin B12 (Cobalamin): Essential for red blood cell formation, preventing anaemia, and supporting the nervous system. It helps control homocysteine levels (people with elevated homocysteine may have a higher risk for cardiovascular disease and Alzheimer's), impacting energy, mood, and digestion. It can be found in animal products like liver, fish, and dairy.

Vitamin Synopsis: A Harmonious Health Symphony

While there is no need to memorise the above details, note the recurrence of superfoods like liver, green veggies, avocados, nuts, and seeds across various vitamins. This pattern underscores the nutritional disparity between whole and processed options, highlighting the importance of fresh, minimally processed foods for optimal health.

Marvellous Minerals: The Unsung Heroes of Our Diet

Imagine playing a game of 20 questions, with 'animal, vegetable, or mineral' as your starting point. Spoiler alert: almost everything on your dinner plate will be categorised as the first two. Minerals, those elusive party crashers of the nutritional world, hitch a ride into our diet via water and soil, not inherently part of plants or animals.

The soil that once fed our ancestors was a mineral buffet, and their water was essentially nature's own marque of mineral water, straight from the earth's crust—a veritable treasure trove of nutritional wealth. Back then, plants were part veggie, part mineral superstars, soaking up earth's offerings through their roots and becoming mineral magnets. Then came the animals, feasting on these mineral-packed plants and joining the mineral club. In its infinite wisdom, nature figured since everyone's on a mineral diet, why not make these elements key players in our bodily functions? And so, over eras, minerals became as integral to our wellbeing as the latest episode is to a binge-watcher. But alas, like the final season of a beloved series, this mineral abundance has dwindled, thanks to our knack for playing fast and loose with soil health. Now, plants find the mineral cupboard bare, animals are missing out on their mineral munchies, and we humans, the end consumers, are left consuming a nutritious, sparse lunch.

Think of minerals as the dietary equivalent of a solid foundation. Just as you wouldn't build a house on quicksand, your diet needs a sturdy mineral base. These nutritional handymen are the behind-the-scenes workers constructing sturdy bones, crafting muscles, knitting together skin and hair, and keeping the metabolic machinery well-oiled.

And just as we categorise vitamins into water-soluble and fat-soluble teams, minerals split into two squads: the heavy lifters and the trace tricksters. Picture gemstones—nature's bling. They're mostly a mix of minerals, but without a dash of trace elements, they'd be as dazzling as a fogged-up window. These trace elements, nature's own seasoning, transform the colourless into the colourful, making rubies red and emeralds green. Similarly, our bodies need a hearty dose of some minerals (enter stage left, milligrams) and just a whisper of others (cue the micrograms) to truly sparkle.

Mineral Metrics: The Scale of Significance

To put the concept of mineral scale into perspective, imagine a wedding ring that weighs around four grams. For a comparison, consider the mineral chromium, which is recommended at about 30 micrograms daily. It would take you several lifetimes, accumulating day by day, to gather enough chromium to match the weight of that ring—a perfect illustration of the phrase, 'Good things come in small packages.' On the other hand, for minerals like calcium, the daily goal is around one gram, a much more significant amount.

As we study the diverse world of minerals, it's important to remember that minerals play a crucial role in safeguarding our health, although they might not grab the spotlight as vitamins often do. They're the unsung heroes, silently supporting our wellness and ensuring that we do more than get by; we flourish, thanks to these tiny yet mighty elements.

In the chart below, minerals are arranged starting from those required in the largest amounts. I've also included the U.S. recommended dietary allowances and, in brackets, the U.K.'s NHS guidelines. While there may be slight variations between the two, I advise you to err on the side of caution and aim for the higher recommendation whenever there's a discrepancy.

Mineral	Calcium	Phosphoros	Magnesium	Iron	Zinc
Magnesium =		(mg/d) thousandth of a gram			
RDA/AI/NHS	RDS (NHS)	RDS (NHS)	RDS (NHS)	RDS (NHS)	NHS Rec.
Males					
9-13	1300	1250	240	8	
14-18	1300	1250	410	11	
19-30	1000 (700)	700 (550)	400 (300)	8 (8.7)	9.5
31-50	1000 (700)	700 (550)	420 (300)	8 (8.7)	9.5
51-70	1000 (700)	700 (550)	420 (300)	8 (8.7)	9.5
70+	1200	700 (550)	420	8	
Females					
9-13	1300	1250	240	8	
14-18	1300	1250	360	15	7.0
19-30	1000 (700)	700 (550)	310 (270)	18 (14.8)	7.0
31-50	1000 (700)	700 (550)	320 (270)	18 (14.8)	7.0
51-70	1000 (700)	700 (550)	320 (270)	8 (8.7)	7.0
70+	1200	700 (550)	320	8	

Calcium: The Architect of Our Body's Framework

Imagine your body as a fortress. How strong are its walls? That's where calcium steps in, playing the pivotal role of architect and builder, ensuring our bones and teeth are as formidable as possible.

Our skeleton and pearly whites stockpile around three pounds (1.5kg) of calcium, highlighting the critical need to replenish our calcium reserves. Beyond its role in construction, calcium is the whisperer among nerve cells, facilitating seamless conversations throughout the body and the secret to keeping our muscles in a state of graceful flexibility. It's even on the front lines in the battle against certain cancers, with colon cancer being a notable adversary. Calcium emerges as a formidable fat-fighting ally for those trying to lose weight.

Peeking into the chart, you'll notice an emphasis on higher calcium intake during our youth, a time of rapid bone growth. And while milk might not be suitable for many adults, it's undeniably a calcium heavyweight, with a single pint delivering approximately 85% of the NHS's recommended daily intake. So, it turns out our mothers were onto something: milk is a calcium treasure trove, along with other dairy champions like yoghurt and cheese. But the dairy aisle isn't the only place to find calcium; leafy greens such as broccoli and cabbage are also contenders (though, spinach, you're sitting this round out), as are certain nuts and seeds, and small fish that bring their bones to the table, like sardines and pilchards.

Here's a list of 20 nutrient-packed foods abundant in calcium, along with their typical serving sizes:

- 30 g parmesan-300 mg
- 40 g edam-300 mg
- 30 g cheddar/hard cheese-200 mg
- 30 g halloumi-200 mg
- 80 g cottage cheese-100 mg
- 40 g Camembert-100 mg
- 200 ml pot of yoghurt-260 mg
- 50 g canned sardines-200 mg
- 105 g canned salmon-100 mg
- 90 g green or French beans-50 mg
- 95 g green or white cabbage-50 mg
- 110 g broccoli (steamed)-50 mg
- 40 g watercress-50 mg
- 400 g tinned tomatoes-50 mg
- 1 heaped tsp tahini (sesame paste)-100 mg
- 1 tablespoon of poppy seeds-125 mg
- 1 tbsp sesame seeds-100 mg
- 10 whole almonds-50 mg
- 9 whole Brazil nuts-50 mg
- 30 g scoop of whey protein-150 mg

However, calcium doesn't work in isolation; it needs the sunlight serenade of vitamin D for optimal absorption. So, while encouraging the consumption of calcium-rich drinks and foods is a step in the right direction, pairing it with outdoor adventures is crucial. Stay tuned, for I will shortly spotlight vitamin D and the sunny side of health.

Phosphorus: The Unsung Hero in the Shadows

Phosphorus might share the stage with calcium in the bone and dental department, but it also has a unique role as the body's internal messenger, transmitting crucial information cell-to-cell about our very blueprint—our DNA. And as much as we embrace the cycle of life and death at the cellular level, phosphorus ensures we remain, well, fundamentally us, by facilitating the seamless transition of cells. While the thought of transforming into someone entirely different due to a phosphorus deficit is a stretch, it underscores the mineral's importance in maintaining our essence. Phosphorus also acts as the great mediator, maintaining the delicate balance between acidity and alkalinity within our bodies.

Rich sources of phosphorus mirror those of calcium, painting the plates of those who indulge in red meat, dairy, fish, poultry, nuts, and seeds with its presence, making a deficiency in this mineral a rare occurrence. So, as you make dietary choices, remember these unsung heroes—calcium and phosphorus—not just for their structural roles but as vital players in the grand concerto of our health.

The Marvel of Magnesium

I've touched on this before, but it bears repeating: I take a magnesium supplement every day without fail. For good reason, magnesium is a cornerstone mineral vital for our well-being, playing a pivotal role in over three hundred biochemical reactions within our body. It's instrumental in regulating body temperature, detoxification processes, forming and maintaining healthy bones, controlling blood glucose levels, and managing blood pressure, among numerous other functions. A shortfall in this critical mineral can unleash a cascade of health issues, particularly as we age.

In her groundbreaking book, *The Magnesium Miracle*, Dr Carolyn Dean highlights 56 conditions linked to magnesium deficiency, ranging from acid reflux and Alzheimer's disease to depression, diabetes, heart disease, and more. Considering the remarkable benefits of magnesium, allow me to spotlight a selection of its healing effects as evidenced by recent studies:

Magnesium and Osteoporosis: Research consistently shows that combining calcium with magnesium enhances bone mineral density, making magnesium supplementation a proactive step for many women at risk of osteoporosis.[17]

Magnesium and Diabetes: Magnesium plays a crucial role in carbohydrate metabolism, aiding blood glucose control and serving as a beneficial supplement for diabetes management.[18]

Magnesium for Headaches and Migraines: Increasing magnesium intake has shown promise in being more effective than traditional tablets for those plagued by frequent headaches or migraines.[19]

Magnesium for Better Sleep: Taking magnesium before bedtime can significantly improve sleep quality, relieving those battling insomnia.[20]

Magnesium and Heart Health: Numerous studies have demonstrated magnesium's efficacy in reducing the risk of coronary heart disease.[21]

Understanding the multitude of benefits magnesium offers, it's worth examining the NHS's recommended daily intake of 300 mg for men and 270 mg for women. The requirements for magnesium are substantial, and, in my view, the recommended values are just the starting point—think of them as the nutritional equivalent of a minimum wage. Who wouldn't want to aim higher for their health?

Here are my top 20 picks for natural foods rich in magnesium. Given the challenge of obtaining sufficient magnesium from food alone, I'm a strong advocate for enhancing our diets with magnesium supplements:

- 28 g of pumpkin seed-168 mg
- 28 g of almonds-80 mg
- ½ cup spinach (boiled)-78 mg
- 28 g cashews-74 mg
- 28 g pumpkin seeds-74 mg
- 1 can of tuna-64 mg
- 40g peanuts-63 mg
- 1 avocado-58 mg
- ½ cup edamame-50 mg
- 28 g cocoa-50 mg
- 2 tbsp peanut butter-49 mg
- ½ cup kidney beans (canned)-35 mg
- 1 banana-32 mg
- 80 g salmon- 26 mg
- 80 g halibut-24 mg
- 1 chicken breast-22 mg
- 80 g beef-20 mg
- 1 pot plain Greek yoghurt-19 mg
- ½ cup broccoli-12 mg
- 1 medium-sized carrot 7 mg

Iron: The Oxygen Courier

Iron plays a crucial role in our health, acting as the essential oxygen carrier in our blood. This mineral works in tandem with two vital proteins, haemoglobin and myoglobin, ensuring oxygen is efficiently transported to every cell in our body.

Our diet has two types of iron: haem and non-haem iron. Haem iron, which our bodies absorb more efficiently, is found in animal products like meat, fish, and poultry. You can absorb up to 30% of the haem iron you consume, making it a potent source for boosting iron levels. On the flip side, according to recent research by the British Red Cross, non-haem iron, sourced from plant-based foods such as fruits, vegetables, and nuts, is absorbed at a significantly lower rate—between two and 10%.

Despite this difference in absorption rates, foods containing non-haem iron remain crucial for a balanced and nutritious diet. However, the efficiency of iron absorption can be enhanced. When you consume haem iron alongside foods rich in non-haem iron, your body absorbs the iron more completely. Additionally, incorporating foods high in vitamin C, such as tomatoes, citrus fruits, and peppers in various colours, can aid in absorbing non-haem iron, making it a strategic approach to maximising the benefits of iron in your diet.

I've opted not to provide an exhaustive list of iron-rich foods, as adhering to the nutritious diets outlined in this book and including a balanced intake of meat, nuts, seeds, eggs, and iron-packed leafy greens like watercress and curly kale should more than suffice in meeting your daily if not weekly iron needs.

Zinc: The Cellular Architect

Zinc is the master builder of new cells, hormones, and enzymes, playing a crucial role in the metabolism of carbohydrates, proteins, and fats. It's as if our bodies prefer absorbing zinc, especially from meat and shellfish, over plant-based sources. However, leafy greens and dairy products are commendable sources of this vital mineral. Incorporating a mix of these foods into your diet can help ensure you're getting enough zinc to support your body's myriad functions.

Voyaging on a Quest for Trace Minerals

Now, let's pivot our focus to the unsung heroes of our diet- the trace minerals. Though required in tiny amounts, their significance to our health is as colossal as their role in bestowing emeralds with their lush green hue and rubies with fiery red brilliance. Just as these gemstones wouldn't dazzle without their trace elements, our bodies wouldn't thrive without these microscopic marvels.

Mineral	**Manganese**	**Copper**	**Iodine**	**Selenium**	**Molybdenum**	**Chronium**
Magnesium =	(mg/d) thousandth of a gram	(mcg/d) millionth of a gram	(mcg/d) millionth of a gram	(mcg/d) millionth of a gram	(mcg/d) millionth of a gram	(mcg/d) millionth of a gram
RDA/AI/NHS	AI	RDA (NHS)	RDA (NHS)	RDA (NHS)	RDA	AI (NHS)
Males						
9-13	1.9	700	120	40	34	25
14-18	2.2	890	150	55	43	35
19-30	2.3	900 (1.2mg)	150 (140)	55 (75)	45	35 (25)
31-50	2.3	900 (1.2mg)	150 (140)	55 (75)	45	35 (25)
51-70	2.3	900 (1.2mg)	150 (140)	55 (75)	45	35 (25)
70+	2.3	900	150 (140)	55	45	35 (25)
Females						
9-13	1.6	700	120	40	34	21
14-18	1.6	890	150	55	43	24
19-30	1.8	900 (1.2mg)	150 (140)	55 (60)	45	25 (25)
31-50	1.8	900 (1.2mg)	150 (140)	55 (60)	45	25 (25)
51-70	1.8	900 (1.2mg)	150 (140)	55 (60)	45	25 (25)
70+	1.8	900	150 (140)	55	45	20

Manganese: The Tea-Loving Element

Manganese, a bit of a socialite in the mineral world, loves to mingle in our glands with a holiday home in our bones. Manganese helps the body form connective tissue, bones, and sex hormones. It plays a role in metabolism, calcium absorption, and blood sugar regulation. Fancy a cuppa? Tea isn't just for relaxation; it's also brimming with manganese, alongside its pals' nuts and certain green veggies like peas and runner beans. Next time you make a brew, remember you're sipping on a mineral cocktail!

Copper: The Blood Cell Architect

Copper is the unsung hero in the saga of blood cell production, moonlights as a bouncer, deciding when iron can join the haemoglobin party in our blood cells. It's also known to throw a mean punch at free radicals and stand guard against infections. Found in the VIP lounge of offal (the organ meats from cows, sheep, pigs, and chickens) and nuts, tea, coffee, dark chocolate, leafy greens, and shellfish. Considering we need just a hint of copper, sticking to a low-carb or ketogenic diet means you're likely already in the copper club—no ID required.

Iodine: The Thyroid's Best Friend

Iodine plays a lead role in thyroid hormone production. It is like the construction foreman for bone repair and a cheerleader for our nervous system. Its hangout spots include fish, shellfish, and seaweed. Once upon a time, it partied with vegetables, too, but the soil's invite got lost in the mail.

Selenium: The Cellular Bodyguard

Selenium, with a resume boasting cell and tissue protection, immune support, and a possible side gig in cancer prevention, is the protector we didn't know we needed. Brazil nuts are its secret lair, with cameos in meats, fish, and eggs. In the UK, don't expect to find this hero in vegetables—the soil's just not what it used to be.

Molybdenum: The Tongue-Twister Mineral

Molybdenum, or as it prefers during its undercover missions, 'molib-dunum,' is essential in the enzyme world for creation and activation. Its headquarters are located in the green metropolis of broccoli, spinach, cauliflower, and the nutty suburbs.

Chromium: The Insulin Whisperer

Chromium plays a crucial role in our energy economy, determining how much fuel we get from our meals. Its entourage includes meat, broccoli, nuts, seeds, and spices, making every meal a potential energy boost.

That almost concludes our vitamin and mineral adventure; remember, it's not just about eating your greens (and seeds and nuts)—it's about fortifying your body's inner workings, one trace element at a time. And who knew nutrition could be so entertaining? But we haven't quite finished yet.

Understanding the Essentials of Electrolytes

Electrolytes, named for their ability to carry electrical currents, are major players in regulating heartbeat, muscle contractions, and overall cellular function. The six core electrolytes—sodium, potassium, chloride, calcium, phosphorus, and magnesium—might be needed in small amounts, but their impact on our well-being is profound.

However, maintaining the right balance of electrolytes is crucial. Factors such as dehydration, illness, excessive exercise, or even a poor diet can disrupt this balance, leading to serious health issues. Dehydration and overhydration become more of a risk as we age due to decreased kidney efficiency, making it vital to monitor electrolyte levels to prevent a range of problems from muscle spasms and irregular heartbeats to confusion and more. We have already discussed magnesium, calcium and phosphorus, so let's touch on the additional trio.

Sodium, Chloride, and Potassium: A Balancing Act

Sodium and chloride, the components of table salt, often get a bad rap due to their abundance in processed foods. The NHS notes that the UK's average daily consumption is twice the recommended amount. However, as you follow the various natural food diets in this book, a slight increase in salt may be beneficial to ensure adequate electrolyte levels. The recommended daily intake is about 4 grams of salt, combining the needs for both sodium (1.6 grams) and chloride (2.5 grams).

Potassium

A pivotal electrolyte in our diet, essential for various bodily functions, with a daily recommendation of 3,500 milligrams (3.5 grams). It's abundantly available in a well-rounded diet, with prime sources of vegetables, nuts, seeds, and meats. However, despite the availability of potassium-rich foods, there's a global trend of consuming too much sodium and not enough potassium. The World Health Organisation advises a correct daily balance of less than two grams of sodium and at least 3.5 grams of potassium per person. Yet, according to recent findings published in the BMJ, a staggering 91% of people in the UK fell short of reaching this potassium intake goal.

Acknowledging this nutritional gap, I've compiled a detailed list of 20 foods high in potassium to help bridge the shortfall and promote a healthier balance:

1. 1 cup Swiss chard: 960 mg
2. 1 cup lentils: 730 mg
3. 1 cup of edamame: 670 mg
4. 1 cup of tomato juice: 580 mg
5. ½ cup black beans: 490 mg
6. 250 ml glass of coconut water: 460 mg
7. 10 small mushrooms: 410 mg
8. 1 medium tomato: 290 mg
9. 1 kiwi: 210 mg
10. 100 g spinach: 466 mg
11. 100 g watermelon: 112 mg
12. 1 pomegranate: 660 mg
13. 1 cup bok choy: 630 mg
14. ½ cup white beans: 600 mg
15. 1 cup of beetroot: 520 mg

16. 1 cup of Brussels sprouts: 500 mg
17. 1 cup broccoli: 460 mg
18. 1 medium banana: 420 mg
19. ½ cup kidney beans: 260 mg
20. ½ a cucumber: 220 mg

This list serves as a guide to increasing your potassium intake and a reminder of the diverse and delicious ways we can meet our nutritional needs while enjoying various foods. By consciously incorporating these potassium-rich foods into our diets, we can work towards achieving a healthier electrolyte balance, which is crucial for our overall health.

*****

Sunbathing: A Bright Idea Or A Burnout Blunder?

Ever pondered why folks living closer to the Arctic Circle could give Casper a run for his money in a paleness contest? It all boils down to one of health's most essential particles: vitamin D, with the sun as its most generous benefactor. As our ancestors ventured away from the equatorial VIP lounge, their skin tones adapted, turning paler to soak up every possible bit of vitamin D from the increasingly stingy sun. Ever the strategist, Mother Nature tossed cold-water oily fish into the mix as a dietary Plan B for those venturing into less sunny territories.

There's a nifty little life hack our bodies play when we enter sunlight. Our primal selves perk up, thinking, 'Ah, springs on the horizon! Time to hunt and gather more grub.' Sun-induced optimism gives our metabolism a hearty nudge, filling us with vim and vigour. On the flip side, hunkering indoors, we send out winter's-coming signals, dialling down our energy levels as our body braces for a food shortage. It's fascinating how a simple choice between indoors and outdoors can create a domino effect on our energy and overall health.

Regrettably, my dear mother has missed numerous family vacations under the sun, heeding her doctor's advice to shun sunlight. Despite a chorus of experts now singing a different tune about the sun's health benefits, convincing her remains an impossible task. It's ironic, considering the mounting evidence that dodging the sun might actually invite the ailments we're taught it causes.

Of course, turning into a human lobster is a no-go for anyone, but basking in a gentle glow? That's where the magic happens. Not only does it boost our spirits, but it also ramps up our vitamin D production—a critical player in our health line-up.

Did our cave-dwelling forebears hole up all day, fearing the sun? Hardly. They were out hustling for their next meal sans SPF 50. Our DNA demands sunlight exposure, mirroring our hunter-gatherer ancestors. The trick is to find that sweet spot of basking responsibly based on our skin type and seeking shade when we've hit our sun quota rather than shunning those golden rays entirely.

In a U-turn worthy of a daytime drama, a 2017 report by The Daily Telegraph flipped decades of sun avoidance advice on its head. Esteemed health organisations, including Cancer Research UK and the National Osteoporosis Society, advocated for a sensible sun exposure of about 10 minutes at midday during summer to kickstart vitamin D synthesis. With such a heavyweight line-up of health authorities backing this guidance, it's clear: a judicious dance under the midday sun might be the health tune-up we never knew we needed.

The Vitamin D Dilemma: How Much Do We Really Need?

Navigating the world of vitamin D requirements can feel like decoding an ancient script. According to Public Health England's 2016 guidelines, everyone over the age of one should aim for 10 micrograms or 400 International Units (IU) of vitamin D daily. This includes everyone from sun-seeking toddlers to pregnant and breastfeeding women, not forgetting those more prone to a vitamin D shortfall. But let's pause for a moment—what exactly is an IU? It's essentially a unit of measure for vitamins, akin to measuring sugar in teaspoons rather than grams. To put it in perspective, 1,000 IU equals 1 gram, meaning the recommended 400 IU is just shy of half a gram.

But here's where it gets sunny: how long does basking in glorious sunshine take to conjure up this half-gram of vitamin D magic? Surprisingly, just a brief 10-minute daily rendezvous with the sun, exposing as much skin as politely possible, can generate a whopping 1,000 IUs. Our vitamin D quota for two days is covered in just a few minutes. Fancy building a vitamin D stockpile? Extend your sun session a tad longer. Yet, here's the rub—overcooking it, so to speak, isn't wise. Limit sunbathing to 25-50% of your skin's pink-turning threshold to dodge the lobster look.

Boston scientists struck gold in 2002 with their discovery that modest sun exposure significantly slashes the risk of breast, colon, and prostate cancers. Fast-forward to 2016, and Swedish research threw a spotlight on a startling revelation: sun dodgers had a life expectancy eerily akin to smokers, cutting their time on this planet by up to 2.1 years compared to their sun-kissed counterparts. This underscores sunlight's pivotal role in vitamin D synthesis, a key player in calcium metabolism and, by extension, bone health.

There's a silver lining for those of us in the often so-gloomy UK. Thanks to vitamin D's fat-soluble nature, our bodies can hoard it for extended spells, ensuring we're not left in the dark during those sun-scarce months.

Sunlight and Aging: A Delicate Dance

As the pages of our lives turn, our body's ability to convert sunlight into vitamin D begins to wane, a fact my dear mother exemplifies. When she most needs the sun's healing embrace, she ventures outdoors clothed as if bracing for an Arctic expedition, not a gentle bask under the sun. The sun's gifts extend far beyond vitamin D. Its rays are a natural mood enhancer, a stress buster, and even a combatant against high blood pressure and acne.

A 2016 Mirror newspaper article boldly proclaimed the health benefits of sunbathing, declaring them a victor over the risks of skin cancer. This piece sheds light on how sunlight exposure triggers the release of nitric oxide in our blood vessels, lowering blood pressure and, in turn, reducing heart attack risks. Echoing this sentiment, Dr Malcolm Kendrick, in a conversation with me, highlighted nitric oxide's crucial role in maintaining our cardiovascular health, presenting sunshine as a heart's ally.

For those of us in the sun-starved UK, the question arises: how long can our bodies treasure the vitamin D gleaned from sunny holidays? Research published in Paediatric Nephrology (2010) unveils that our fat tissue can store vitamin D for up to two months. Interestingly, the study advises against immediate post-sun exposure showers with soap, as our skin needs time to complete the vitamin D synthesis process.

The Sunbed Debate: A Glimmer of Hope or a False Dawn?

Turning our gaze to sunbeds, could they be beneficial without natural sunlight? The answer lies in their ability to mimic the sun's UVA and UVB balance, with modern low-pressure lamps making them akin to a sunny day but without the beach. However, caution is advised—older models, which primarily emit UVA rays, offer little beyond aesthetic tanning benefits. It's the UVB rays we crave for vitamin D production.

Navigating the balance between embracing the sun's nourishing rays and safeguarding our health is a nuanced affair, especially as we age. The sun, much like anything in life, demands respect and moderation. Whether soaking in natural sunlight or seeking solace in sunbeds, the goal remains the same: to harness the myriad benefits of sunlight, from vitamin D to improved mood, without overstepping into the realm of risk. And before I forget, the concept of a 'base tan' via sunbed, a pre-holiday ritual for some, toes the line between preparation and peril. Melanin fortification offers a sliver of natural defence, but moderation is the mantra.

Dr Michael Holick's Sunny Insights

Dr Michael Holick's book, *The UV Advantage* is a treasure trove of enlightenment for those curious about the sun's holistic benefits. With the precision of an endocrinologist and the passion of a sun advocate, Holick dismantles the myth that all sun exposure is harmful. His take on sunscreen is particularly eye-opening: high SPF levels may be doing us more vitamin D-blocking harm than good. According to him, a brief, unprotected dalliance with the sun—say, 10 minutes—is enough to reap the benefits without courting danger. Holick also draws parallels between sunlight exposure and exercise for heart health—a perspective that casts the sun in an even more vital role. He even delves into the ancestral understanding of sunlight's virtues, suggesting that our cave-dwelling forebears were as keen on sun therapy as we are on Netflix binges.

Holick's musings touch a nerve in our contemporary narrative: when did the sun transition from a worshipped life force to a feared foe? The answer, tinged with cynicism, points to the lucrative industry built around sun protection and the emphasis on skin cancer risks. Yet, as American researcher Dr William Grant points out, the scales of health benefits versus risks tip overwhelmingly in favour of sensible sun exposure, with potential reductions in internal cancers vastly outweighing the number of skin cancer fatalities.

The Bennett's Sunshine Ritual

My family has a sun-soaked ritual that we cherish. We chase the warmth during school holidays, venturing to climes where the sun generously shares its vitamin D bounty. Each morning, we let the kids and even our smallest adventurer, eight-year-old Louie, immerse themselves in play and swim sessions sans sunscreen. They achieve a healthy, sun-kissed hue, finding their sweet spot of sun exposure without overdoing it.

This delicate dance with the sun is not about arbitrary limits but understanding our skin's conversation with the rays. After basking in just enough sunlight to trigger their natural vitamin D factory, they retreat to the shade, allowing their bodies to absorb nature's gift fully. Only then do we apply sunscreen, choosing organic formulas that align with our health ethos. And here's a tropical twist: When a mild SPF is all we need, coconut oil becomes our go-to sunblock. Yes, the superfood we advocate for in the kitchen doubles as nature's SPF 4 to 5.

Some might question the wisdom of letting our youngest frolic under the sun unprotected. However, this practice is far from reckless. It's a thoughtful approach grounded in understanding the vital role of sunlight in vitamin D synthesis. By embracing ample sunshine during the summer, we're banking on vitamin D, potentially stretching its benefits into the early winter months. Should we suspect a dip in our levels, a simple blood test can confirm our vitamin D status, guiding us towards dietary adjustments or supplements if necessary.

Vitamin D: Beyond the Sun's Embrace

For those still on the fence about the merits of basking in the sun, there's a trove of alternatives to ensure your vitamin D levels don't dwindle. The culinary route via eggs, oily fish, and a thoughtful selection of vitamin D supplements can bridge the gap, especially during the sun-scarce months. And get a hold of Jeff T Bowles's book, *The Vitamin D3 Miracle*. I am sure Jeff will if I haven't convinced you about its importance. One of my favourite quotes from his brilliantly written work is, 'Since the early 1980s when doctors started warning us about too much sun, obesity rates in adult humans and many other diseases (including asthma and autism) have skyrocketed!'

During late autumn and winter, everyone in Great Britain needs to rely on dietary sources of vitamin D. The NHS states, 'Since it is difficult for people to meet the 10-microgram recommendation from consuming foods naturally containing or fortified with vitamin D, people should consider taking a daily supplement containing 10 micrograms of vitamin D in autumn and winter.' What I find very encouraging about this article is that it is one of the first times I have seen the British government recommend the use of supplements. Let's hope this is a change of tide to prevention rather than cure.

Having uncovered the myriad benefits of vitamins and minerals, let's focus on the vibrant world of herbs. These natural powerhouses not only add zest and flavour to our meals, but are also imbued with health-boosting properties that can complement our daily wellness routines. Explore the green wonders of the herbal kingdom with me and discover how these aromatic treasures can enhance your health and vitality.

*****

Herbs And Spices Detailed

Herbs and spices have been used for centuries as medicines in cultures from Asia to the Native Americans, from Southern Europe to the Aztecs. While herbal practitioners did not know why or how herbs worked, they successfully identified the right herb for the right aliment through trial and error.

Over 2,000 years ago, Hippocrates offered bark from the willow tree and instructed sufferers to chew on it to reduce fevers and inflammation in his patients. In 1897, the German pharmaceutical company Bayer developed an aspirin-branded tablet from the same bark. In fact, most pioneering Western pharmaceutical companies created their initial pills by extracting nutrients from herbs. Even today, over 100 well-known pills, medicines and tablets still base their remedies on plant extracts. While aspirin no longer comes from willow bark (it's now synthetic), codeine and morphine are still made from opium poppy seeds.

What I love about using them in my cooking is that they add flavour to just about anything. And the flavour is really important. As we start living more healthily, there will undoubtedly be the odd occasion when we will miss our fast food or sugar-rich snacks. While it is okay now and again to fall off the wagon and have whatever we want (remember, I am not promoting a diet but a lifestyle change), ideally, the more times we can stay true to what we were designed to eat, the healthier we will ultimately be. I recommend you experiment with as many herbs and spices as you can get your hands on. Even better still, get out in the garden and grow your own. There is no more satisfying meal than one where you know the flavour was created in your own backyard.

Spreading the gospel of a natural lifestyle among family and friends becomes a delightful endeavour when we tantalise their taste buds with the vibrant palette of herbs and spices. It's not just about nourishing our bodies; it's about creating a sensory experience that makes healthy living irresistible.

And for those among us who rely a bit too heavily on over-the-counter remedies, fear not! As you read ahead, you'll arm yourself with the knowledge needed to gently nudge away from the medicine cabinet and towards the greener pastures of botanical healing. So let's close the door on pills and open up a world of wellness by planting the seeds of good health together.

Everything you have read so far in this book is backed by research, much of which is recent. However, as I sprinkle the knowledge of herbs and spices, the evidence I am about to share is supported not by modern-day clinical studies but by thousands of years of history. It is, therefore, up to you to interpret as you wish.

Tip: The stronger the aroma and the more pungent the taste, the denser their nutrients and curing properties.

Basil

An aromatic herb from the mint family, both the leaves and flowers are edible. There are over 30 varieties, but Holy Basil is the most common. Its scientific name is *Ocimum Sanctum L.* In India, Holy Basil is worshipped for its healing properties. It is a powerful antioxidant containing calcium, iron, magnesium, and omega-3 fatty acids. Basil also contains vitamin K, vitamin A and vitamin C.

Basil's health benefits come from its phytonutrients and essential oils. It is a powerful adaptogen that helps the body respond to stress and fight disease. The antioxidants in basil make it a natural anti-inflammatory and are believed to help the body fight cancer. Basil can also be used for natural pain relief and reduces fever. Its phytonutrients can also help relieve stress.

Bay Leaves

In medieval medicine, bay leaves were used to treat gastric diseases. Many herbs are titled bay leaves, but the real one comes from the laurel tree, first grown in the Mediterranean. This herb provides a rich source of vitamin A, B6 (pyridoxine), and vitamin C. Bay leaves contain iron, magnesium, zinc, copper, calcium and magnesium.

Bay leaves' antioxidants and antibacterial nutrients are said to cure fungus in toenails and other body parts. According to the international journal Nutrition and Cancer, bay leaves are believed to help fight colorectal cancer. They are also recognised for their ability to detoxify the body and slow down the ageing process.

Cacao

We have discussed this amazing fibrous ingredient in detail already. Just be sure to add a tub to your cupboard and find as many ways as possible to incorporate it into dishes and drinks.

Cinnamon

Prized and worshipped as a medicine for over 2,000 years. In Ancient Egypt, it was said to have been a gift from the kings. A spice ground from bark, cinnamon contains over 20 different phytonutrients, including beta-carotene and tannin. It provides a rich source of minerals, including calcium, copper, iron, manganese and zinc. It contains vitamin A, vitamin C and vitamins B1, B2 and B3. Add it to coffee and consider sprinkling it on yoghurt-based desserts.

In a recent study that compared 26 spices for their levels of antioxidant activity, cinnamon was the clear winner, even beating garlic and turmeric! It is said to help fight insulin resistance. As with many of the herbs in this list, cinnamon relieves both sickness and diarrhoea. When you have a toothache, try brushing your teeth with cinnamon powder. It is believed to help both prevent and cure colds and flu. Cinnamon thins the blood and can, therefore, be used to aid circulation.

Coriander

Also known as Chinese parsley or cilantro, it is a herb of the *Apiaceae* family. Both its leaves and seeds provide numerous health benefits. Coriander is full of phytonutrients and flavonoids and is a rich source of vitamin A, as well as smaller concentrations of vitamin C, E and K. Coriander contains linoleic, ascorbic, palmitic, oleic and stearic acids, all of which have many health benefits. Coriander provides a rich source of minerals, including iron, calcium, magnesium, and potassium. In addition, it contains many trace elements.

It is said to be good for our cardiovascular system and can aid in lowering blood pressure. Herbalists often recommend coriander to those with diabetes, and, in many parts of Europe, it is even believed to prevent the development of this disease. The essential oils found in coriander leaves contain antibacterial properties; therefore, it is often used as a natural fungicide. If you make a paste out of the seeds (known as a poultice), it can be applied externally to relieve soreness, painful joints, rheumatism and inflammation.

Fennel

The entire fennel plant is full of goodness, from the roots through the stem to the leaves and fruit. It is a source of minerals, including calcium, magnesium, manganese, and selenium. It also contains vitamins B1, B2, B3, C, and E. Toss it in a tray of roasted vegetables or lightly fry it in almost all Asian curries.

In Alchemy of Herbs, author Rosalee de la Forêt writes, 'Fennel is known for soothing muscle tension, digestive spasms and menstrual cramps.' It is often used in weight loss to suppress appetite. Great to chew on after a meal as it helps with digestion and leaves us with fresh breath.

Ginger

Ginger is like a trusty lifeboat in the stormy seas of sickness. Whether nibbling on a chunk or blending it into a berry smoothie, ginger is your go-to first mate. It's not just about soothing your stomach; ginger is a warrior against muscle soreness, a champion against pain, and a guardian against inflammation. It's rich in nutrients, from vitamin B6 to magnesium, making it a spice and a slice of health heaven.

Mint

A family of herbs whose members include peppermint and spearmint. Many phytonutrients are discovered in the flowers and leaves, including alpha-carotene, perillyl alcohol, eugenol, menthol and tannin. A source of minerals including calcium, iron, magnesium, manganese, selenium and zinc. Mint contains vitamins A, B1, B2, B3 and E.

It is reported to help reduce sickness and diarrhoea. In several research studies, mint has proven to help ease suffering caused by IBS. It is also believed to boost digestion, relieve asthma, strengthen the liver and fight off several types of cancer. Because mint contains menthol, it's great as a natural remedy for acne. Perfect for our teeth and breath, it stops bad bacteria from developing in our mouths and fights against oral infections.

Mustard Seeds

A member of the cruciferous family of vegetables, its phytonutrients include caffeic acid, ferulic acid and vanillic acid. Mustard seeds also contain allyl isothiocyanates, which in recent clinical trials have shown to help reduce DNA damage and may prove beneficial in preventing certain cancers. A significant source of potassium, iron, calcium, selenium, omega-3 and magnesium, they also contain vitamins B6 and C.

Health Benefits: In animal studies, mustard seed's phytonutrients have been found to protect against gastrointestinal cancer. It helps our digestive system function properly. When applied externally, it can reduce inflammation and pain in joints. It can also ease congestion in both the sinuses and lungs, as well as reduce arthritic pain. Its strong taste helps relieve the symptoms of colds and flu.

Nutmeg

From the tree of the same name, its seeds are an absolute favourite with herbalists and chefs alike. Nutmeg contains two essential oils, myristicin and malignant, which have been proven to reduce cognitive function degradation and benefit those suffering from Alzheimer's. Nutmeg also contains a compound similar to menthol, which is a natural pain reliever. It contains potassium, magnesium, iron and calcium.

Nutmeg relieves tension and anxiety, making it an excellent aphrodisiac. Its oily content is good for hypertension and can help relieve a whole host of digestive problems. Many people who struggle to get a good night's sleep put nutmeg into a glass of milk, as it helps to overcome insomnia; however, it takes around three to four hours to work. Nutmeg is said to help detoxify the body and revitalise our hair and skin.

Oregano

It contains thymol (also found in thyme and available separately as a supplement), one of the most potent antioxidants found in nature. It also contains carvacrol oil, which has antibacterial, antifungal, and antiparasitic benefits. It contains vitamins A, B6, C, E, and K, plus iron, magnesium, folate, calcium, manganese, and omega-3.

The list of medical benefits of oregano is so extensive that there are now many oregano oil supplements on the market. Claimed cures and benefits include improved joint and muscle flexibility, aid in treating respiratory problems, boost in immunity, ease digestion, reduced swelling and pain from arthritis, promoted bowel movements, and reduced symptoms of IBS. Wow, what a compelling list!

Parsley

The entire parsley plant is full of goodness, from its roots to its stem, leaves and fruit. Parsley hosts an impressive line-up of health benefits because of its antioxidant flavonoids and essential oils, especially myristicin and apiol (also known as the green oil of parsley). It is a source of minerals, including calcium, copper, iron, manganese, selenium and zinc. Parsley contains insoluble vitamins K, A, and E and soluble vitamins B1, B2, B3 and C.

Parsley is a natural diuretic, encouraging the kidneys to release water through urine. It prevents the build-up of kidney stones, and its vitamin K helps keep our hearts healthy. It helps the thyroid function normally and reduces the spread of cancer by preventing tumours from growing. Parsley can reduce or even cure acid reflux, bloating and constipation. Consumed regularly, it can reduce the symptoms of IBS. Chewing on parsley helps reduce smelly breath, which is helpful for the first few days of a ketogenic diet.

Rosemary

Its leaves contain phytonutrients, including beta-carotene, caffeic acid, luteolin, rosmarinic acid, and tannin. They are also a source of minerals, including calcium, iron, magnesium, manganese, phosphorus, potassium, and zinc. Rosemary also contains vitamins A, B1, B3, and C. Fresh rosemary is always more flavoursome than dried, but you can also freeze it to retain its flavour for another day.

Rosemary is believed to battle against free radicals and can help prevent various cancers. It is said to boost memory retention and other cognitive functions and is thought to help delay the onset of dementia. Rosemary detoxifies the liver, cleansing us from the inside out. It is also said to help prevent bad moods and reduce stress. Rosemary's antioxidant properties are said to aid vision and healthy skin.

Sage

Both the Greeks and Romans were said to have prized the various healing properties of sage. Its leaves contain phytonutrients, including beta-carotene, caffeic acid, ferulic acid, limonene, saponin and tannins. It is a source of minerals, including boron, calcium, iron, magnesium, manganese, phosphorus, potassium, selenium and zinc. Contains vitamins B1, B2, B3, B5 and C.

Antioxidants in sage are said to reverse the signs of ageing, such as wrinkles and fine lines. It's also said to be good for the hair. Researchers at the University of Vienna in Austria found that its micronutrients have strong anti-inflammatory properties. Sage is said to help treat depression and improve concentration. The essential oil in sage is believed to help to keep our brains in good working order.

Thyme

Related to oregano, thyme berries, leaves, and flowers contain phytonutrients, including carvacrol, thymol oil, ferulic acid, limonene, phytosterols and tannins. Minerals include iron, manganese, calcium, magnesium, copper, zinc, potassium and fibre. Thyme contains vitamins A, riboflavin, B6 and C. Said to be good for respiratory problems, including asthma and bronchitis. Thyme's natural antimicrobials make it a perfect herb for fixing sore throats. Its thymol oil kills fungi and is added to many antifungal creams and sanitisers brands. Thyme lowers blood pressure and can improve moods. It has been used for hundreds of years to treat bronchitis and the common cold.

Turmeric

Celebrated in the supplement section, turmeric is an inspiration for health and is known for its potent antioxidant properties. Ranking high on the ORAC scale, which measures antioxidant capacity, turmeric offers more than just colour and flavour to our meals. It embodies a rich source of health benefits, including anti-inflammatory effects and potential support in maintaining overall vitality.

Herbs and Fibre

Now, you didn't think I'd leave you hanging without diving into their fibre content, did you? Shame on you for doubting! Even though we often use herbs in tiny amounts, it's still worth paying homage to their fibrous prowess. After all, every little bit adds up when it comes to our daily intake of this essential nutrient. So let's grind these little treasures and discover the fibrous delights that they have to offer:

Herb	Amount per 100g	Herb	Amount per 100g
Cinnamon	53.10 g	Black pepper	25.30 g
Oregano	42.50 g	Turmeric	22.70 g
Coriander seeds	41.90 g	All spice	21.60 g
Sage	40.30 g	Dill seed	21.10 g
Fennel seed	39.80 g	Ground mace	20.20 g
Caraway seed	38.00 g	Poppy seeds	19.50 g
Chilli powder	34.80 g	Anise seed	14.60 g
Clove	33.90 g	Rosemary	14.10 g
Cardamom	28.00 g	Ground ginger	14.10

In wrapping up this segment, we should approach herbs and spices with a mix of curiosity and scepticism. The ubiquitous health claims surrounding these natural enhancers suggest a universal truth, much of which is not yet evidenced in science. But undoubtedly, incorporating a variety of organic, preferably home-grown, herbs into our diet is a simple and delicious way to step towards a healthier lifestyle. So, as I close this chapter, let's carry forward the wisdom that a sprinkle of nature's bounty can be a step towards achieving overall wellness.

Chapter 10

A Quest for Centenarian Status

Imagine the preceding chapters as the trusty compass that has guided you through the tempests of health and wellness, leading you safely into your vibrant 90s. Now, it's time to upgrade to a state-of-the-art GPS, steering you towards the elite league of centenarians and beyond.

This chapter promises to be a thrilling expedition, not just a stroll in the park. We're jumping both feet into the nitty-gritty, the fine print of longevity. Consider this chapter your telescope into the future, illuminating the path to reaching and thriving beyond the 100-year mark.

Redefining Longevity: A Different Perspective

Aiming for a ripe old age? Steady yourself as we set out on a quest to redefine longevity in a world filled with temptations like fake foods and the lure of technology. It's time to outsmart the corporate giants and reconnect with the timeless wisdom of nature and the humble farmer. Over recent decades, our trust has tilted towards science and innovation, but at what cost to our natural lifespan? Unfortunately, the Industrial Revolution, which we Brits initiated, was meant to liberate us, but in reality, we've become its captives. Our exceptional intelligence ensnares us, the very intelligence that distinguishes us from all other species. This intelligence leads us to invent an exercise bike to burn off the excess energy from our indulgence in processed foods. The same intelligence drives us to endure excessively long and stressful work hours, all to afford technological conveniences like TV remote controls and order online takeaway meals. As a result, we find ourselves heading to the gym on sunny days to cycle on indoor stationary bikes that lead nowhere! So much for happiness and freedom; everything seems topsy-turvy. Modern humanity has effectively smashed its own window only to turn around and sell itself a burglar alarm. Today, when we feel a pebble in a shoe, our first instinct is to reach for a painkiller.

My point? I am utterly convinced that embracing the *Fibre First* diet, abundant in real, wholesome food, coupled with an active outdoor lifestyle, bolstered by today's advanced healthcare services, and guided by scientific insights into cellular health, provides us with the arsenal needed not only to reach centenarian status but to flourish as supercentenarians.

Rewinding to the 1870s, adult men in England enjoyed a longer life expectancy than many do today[1], an astonishing revelation I shared earlier. However, historically, lifespans were notably brief. Our ancestors navigated a world brimming with peril, from the threat of lethal animals lurking in their living spaces to the harrowing one-in-three chance of not surviving birth. Then, there was the spectre of malnutrition, a dire consequence of food scarcity. And if you somehow dodged these obstacles, many diseases awaited alongside the unpredictable fury of volcanoes and tsunamis. But fast forward to the present, the landscape has dramatically transformed. We're now armed with early warning systems to sidestep natural disasters, while modern marvels like vaccines, robust healthcare, and antibiotics have relegated many infectious diseases to the footnotes of history. Unlike a century ago, when such diseases were the leading cause of death, today's threats have evolved. Accidents, including car crashes, while still present, are statistically rare. And the once-common plight of poor sanitation in modern cities is now a relic of the past. Our battle for longevity has shifted from surviving nature's whims to navigating a hazardous world of our own making.

To answer the question of 'How long could I live?' let me take you on an adventure around the remote corners of the world, from the mountainous terrains of Russia to the Andean valleys, where the tales of centenarians challenge our understanding of lifespans. Take, for instance, the story of Shirali Mislimov, a shepherd from Barzavu, Russia, reported by Soviet gerontologists and noted by CNN to have reached the ripe old age of 168![2] Cynicism aside, this claim stirs the imagination.

Then there's Dr David Davis, a gerontologist from University College London, who, between 1971 and 1973, investigated the long-living mysteries of the Vilcabamba valley in the Andes. His findings? Death certificates bearing witness to lives stretching up to 150 years, with one inhabitant thriving at 126 during his visit. Remarkably, these longevity achievers were untouched by the plagues of cancer, heart disease, diabetes, or hypertension that afflicted the 'modernised' world merely 50 miles away.

The same year, Dr Leaf from Harvard University ventured to Abkhazia, a secluded town in Georgian Russia. There, he encountered Khaf Lasuria, who had surpassed 130 years of age. Having retired just two years prior, she, at a century old, held the title of the village's swiftest tea leaf picker, a record verified by Dr Leaf himself. National Geographic's 1973 article on her captured her philosophy: 'Every day is a gift when you are over 100.' Her secret appeared to lie in ceaseless movement and labour.

Further evidence comes from another study by a Russian gerontologist who observed over 15,000 individuals aged 80 and above in Georgia. Astonishingly, most maintained active lifestyles, with regular mountain walks and ongoing work. A nine-year investigation into 123 centenarians in Abkhazia found none had cancer, with most enjoying robust neurological and psychological health.

These vignettes from across the globe offer a peek into the extraordinary potential of human longevity and a reflection on the profound impact of lifestyle choices. As we ponder 'how long could I live,' these stories serve as both inspiration and a call to action, urging us to re-evaluate our daily habits and the environments we choose to inhabit.

Before we evaluate the intricacies of health at the cellular level, let me share a couple of personal tales closer to heart. These stories, one featuring a beloved tennis coach and the other my father, serve as inspiring examples of enhancing health span. They'll provide you with a dose of motivation and practical insights into living a healthier, more vibrant life.

Jen's story

At my local tennis club, among a crew of exceptional coaches, stands Jen, the team's sole female member. More than just an outstanding tennis coach, Jen is an inspiration of kindness and humanity. My weekly lessons are booked for 8:30 a.m., but it's not uncommon for Gavin, my coach, to be stuck in traffic. Every time this happens, and it's not a rarity, Jen emerges from the clubhouse like a guardian of the courts. Should she find herself without a client, she'll leap into action with me, sharing her wisdom on the court without a second thought or any expectation of recompense. Her joy in aiding others is palpable and purely selfless.

Yet Jen's brilliance transcends her prowess on the tennis court (where she's a key player for the British team) and her compassionate nature. In her 80s, she navigates life and the tennis court with remarkable vivacity, shattering the age-old myth that passion or pursuit diminishes with age. Jen personifies the inspiring truth that deep engagement with our interests or hobbies can diminish the perceived effects of ageing. Her story serves as a poignant reminder that what often accelerates ageing isn't merely the passage of years but rather the absence of passion. Too many resign themselves to a sedentary existence, spending their days on the sofa with the television remote in hand, awaiting the delivery of their takeaway, living in the shadows of memories rather than pursuing goals for the future.

Jen's story is a testament to the ageless spirit of those who refuse to let the number of years define their capacity for enthusiasm, learning, and contribution. She is a luminous example that when you're genuinely invested in something that stirs your soul, you can 'almost forget to get old.' It's a lesson on the vitality of maintaining interests and hobbies as bulwarks against the premature ageing of body and spirit.

Embracing The Future At Every age

My dad is another sterling example of someone who views his life with an unwavering, forward-looking gaze. Despite his illness and the responsibility he shoulders as my mother's sole carer, which restricts him from engaging in sports, he remains tirelessly focused on the future. At the vibrant age of 83, he recently invested in a new leisure boat and now dedicates his days to designing and crafting new furniture for it. His past is dotted with a fascinating career and nights spent playing in jazz bands, each chapter brimming with intriguing and amusing stories. Yet, his anticipations for the future, the plans and dreams he looks forward to realising, dominate conversations.

This forward momentum resonates with my life choices. I was the founder and owner of the largest online jeweller in the UK and head of the biggest privately owned TV shopping company. However, entrenched in my office, I realised that more of my time was spent guarding our top spot, glaring down the mountain, weary of other companies climbing up and trying to steal our uninterrupted view of the horizon, than looking to the future. This realisation led me to hand over my company to the employees. Having scaled one peak, I was eager to seek new challenges and explore terrains unlike any I had conquered before, no matter how big or small. This constant pursuit of what lies ahead, I firmly believe, is a crucial ingredient for a healthy life. By setting our sights on goals far into the future, say 20 years ahead, we are less likely to fall into the trap of unhealthy eating habits or allow them to form the cornerstone of our dietary choices.

The Voyage To 100 And Beyond

We're on the brink of exploring uncharted territory, where the fountain of youth awaits discovery. This isn't simply a chapter; it's your invitation to pioneer the future of your health. Setting out on this quest isn't just about accumulating years but mastering the art of living well within those years. It's a challenge to the essence of mortality, transforming the inevitable march towards the end into a strategic game of longevity and vitality.

Consider the recent revelation that the seeds of atherosclerosis, a stealthy precursor to heart disease, are sown as early as childhood. This insight serves as a stark reminder: the spectre of ageing begins its work long before we're aware, silently laying the groundwork for future challenges. The antidote? A proactive embrace of perpetual youthfulness, not as a cosmetic aspiration but as a profound, life-affirming philosophy.

The common narrative might suggest that concerns about ageing are for the later chapters of life, yet the reality is far more urgent. The process begins subtly in our youth, with each decade introducing its own challenges, from the gradual decline of collagen in our 20s to the sneak attack of sarcopenia in our 40s and the nuanced dance with vitamin B12 absorption in our 60s.

But here's the silver lining: these biological shifts are not mere inevitabilities to be passively accepted. They are opportunities for intervention and active engagement with our health. The quest towards a century of life is punctuated with possibilities for action and strategies that can reshape our trajectory.

Congratulations on reaching this juncture. Turning these pages means you've already committed to navigating your health with intention and insight. The voyage to 100 and beyond starts with awareness, and you, dear friend, are well on your way.

Rewinding The Hands Of Time: A Pathway To Ageless Existence

Imagine a world where certain jellyfish possess the key to everlasting youth, effortlessly renewing themselves and toying with the concept of immortality. These aquatic marvels, untouched by time's relentless march, prompt a tantalising question: Why can't humans undergo a comparable rejuvenation, mirroring the tale of Benjamin Button?

As we stand on the precipice of groundbreaking scientific revelations, the concept of dramatically extending human life expectancy transitions from the realm of fantasy to a tangible future. Envision living to 100, not just as a number but as a vibrant testament to health, with a mind and body in peak condition, liberated from the chains of chronic illness and pharmaceutical dependence. This is not mere dreaming but a future within reach, inspired by the longevity of jellyfish and Greenland sharks' 3 to 5-century lives.

What if we could halt or reverse the subtle decay of our cellular integrity? Through a symphony of optimised nutrition, restorative sleep, purposeful physical activity, and a fortress against environmental toxins, we're not merely slowing the ageing process but architecting our fountain of youth. Our genetic blueprint for vitality doesn't evaporate; it awaits our rediscovery and activation.

This book has charted a course through the essentials: a diet abundant in natural fibres, the rejuvenating power of sleep, the critical role of stress reduction, and the undeniable benefits of regular exercise, all grounded in scientific evidence. Yet, to traverse the extra mile toward a century of robust health, we must delve into the 'information theory of ageing.' This concept hypothesises that the diminishment of our cellular repair mechanisms scripts the narrative of our ageing.

Picture a future where reversing our biological clock isn't just a fantasy but a tangible reality. Inspired by jellyfish's regenerative abilities and sharks' remarkable resilience, our cells undergo a transformation, regaining their youthful vigour and vitality. It's a pathway not for the faint-hearted but for the daring souls ready to seize it, equipped with a trio of strategic approaches:

Tackling Insulin Resistance: Throughout earlier chapters, I've emphasised the significant impact of insulin resistance on various health issues. Confronting this underlying menace is crucial for warding off diseases spanning from diabetes to Alzheimer's. It transcends mere dietary choices; it involves prioritising sleep, embracing physical activity, and nurturing an environment conducive to optimal health.

Elevating Nutritional Wisdom: The resounding chorus of research highlights the virtues of a diet abundant in essential nutrients. This narrative extends beyond food selection to encompass the strategic incorporation of fibre, Omega-3 fatty acids, CoQ10, glucomannan, and resveratrol. This journey entails nourishing our cells and sculpting a youthful internal locale that mirrors the vibrancy of our aspirations.

Avoiding Chemicals and Toxins: Adopting a real-food diet is already a significant step in the right direction. In the upcoming pages, we'll discuss the best practices for avoiding additional hazardous toxins.

As we set sail toward the horizon of a hundred years and beyond, each decision we make is a deliberate stitch in the fabric of longevity. This expedition is measured not in years alone but in the quality and vitality of those years. It's a celebration of life's persistence, a testament to the possibility that every day can be imbued with the essence of youth, every moment a step toward a legacy of enduring health and vitality.

Deciphering The Tonic Of Eternal Youth At The Cellular Level

We are now going on an exhilarating excursion into the heart of near immortality, where the 'information theory of ageing' serves as our guide. Imagine a world where the slow but inevitable wear and tear on our cellular repair systems, the essence of ageing, could be halted.

Our expedition takes us deep into the cellular cosmos, aiming to rejuvenate the fading essence of youth within our biological manuscripts. To chart this complex adventure, we'll expand upon the foundational biological principles that have underscored our exploration thus far, introducing a series of intriguing concepts that are vital in understanding the potential for cellular renewal:

Cellular Reprogramming: Imagine being able to coax your cells into shedding years, urging them back to a sprightly, youthful state, a cellular fountain of youth that makes even the most stubborn grandparents seem like vibrant teenagers.

Cellular Senescence: Picture cells morphing into the grouchy old-timers of the cellular world, stubbornly halting division and spreading inflammatory rumours. These 'zombie cells' are like the grumpy neighbours who've overstayed their welcome, born from drama like DNA damage or the cacophony of epigenomic noise.

Chromosomes and DNA: Your chromosomes are the meticulously packed suitcases of your cellular expedition. DNA is the master script, a molecular saga twisted in a double helix, robust yet vulnerable to the trials and tribulations of life's narrative.

Genes: The individual stories within your life's book, dictating the roles and responsibilities of every cell, crafting the unique narrative of you.

Feeling a twinge of nostalgia for biology class? Don't worry; I will keep it as light as possible:

Enzymes: These biochemical virtuosos within our bodies orchestrate reactions with the precision and artistry of a top-tier chef, all in mere nanoseconds.

Hormesis: This principle embodies resilience, serving as a cellular pep talk advocating for strength through adversity, where a dash of stress propels our cells into a state of repair and fortification. It exemplifies the principle that what doesn't kill you makes you stronger.

Epigenetics: These are the subtle notes and annotations atop your DNA script that guide your cellular machinery through the complex narrative of life without altering the core text.

Stem Cells: These are the ultimate cellular multitool, poised to morph into any cell type needed, embodying versatility and readiness for any challenge.

FOXO3 Gene: It serves as the custodian of longevity, a gene in the quest for cellular endurance and a lifespan that defies the conventional bounds of time.

Let's gaze beneath the ocean's surface to where 300-year-old sharks and immortal jellyfish roam, offering a glimpse into the boundless potential encoded within our genes. Our connection with these timeless creatures, particularly through the FOXO3 gene, unveils a universal symphony of life echoing across all living beings. Research on worms has unveiled the FOXO3 gene's astonishing ability to rewind the biological clock, a phenomenon not limited to the worm realm but crucial for our own cellular longevity. This gene narrates a tale spanning from the microscopic to the magnificent, underscoring the intricate genetic dance governing insulin regulation and longevity. It reflects the overarching theme of this book: the pursuit of a life brimming with vitality and longevity.

The lifestyle of worms during periods of scarcity, mirrored by human communities renowned for their longevity through practices like intermittent fasting, reveals a fundamental truth: a life shaped by resilience and moderation leads to enduring vitality. The FOXO3 gene epitomises our shared pursuit of longevity, bridging the gap between the humblest creatures and the most majestic entities. As Dr David Sinclair points out, under the microscope, life's fabric is interwoven with identical strands, swirling together in an eternal dance of survival and rejuvenation.

Our Epigenetic Landscape: Charting The Pathways Of Cellular Destiny

As we venture further into the molecular wilderness, I would like to pause and acknowledge Professor Conrad Waddington's visionary work. Back in 1957, at the University of Edinburgh, he pondered a profound puzzle: How does an embryo, a cluster of identical cells, transform into the myriad of specialised cells that compose the human body?

Waddington pioneered the 'epigenetic landscape,' a terrain that helps us navigate the complex interplay between our genes and their expression. (see his drawing on the next page). He envisioned the embryonic cell as a marble perched atop a mountain, ready to embark on a developmental excursion.

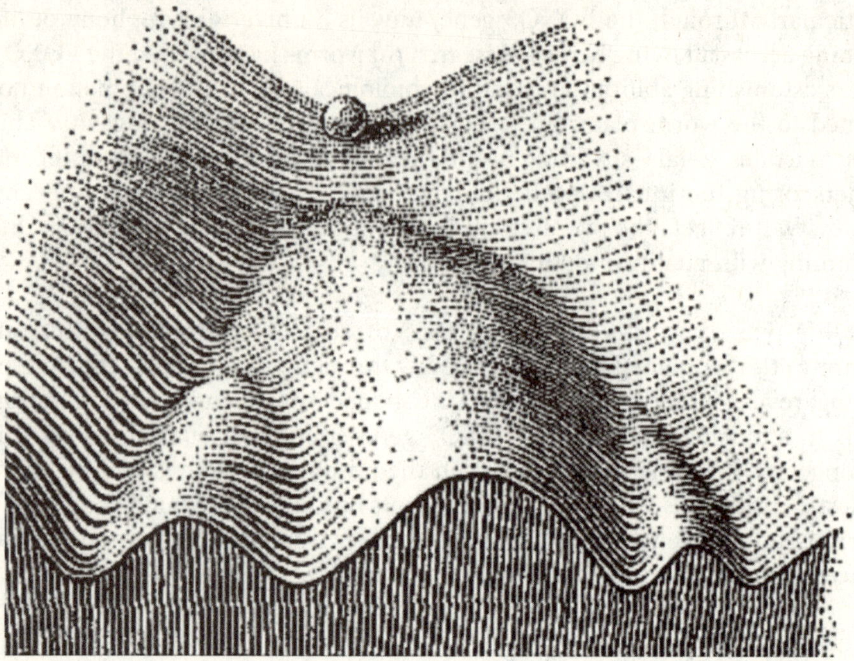

As the marble (cell) rolls down the mountain (developmental pathway), it settles into one of the many valleys (cell types), a process known as differentiation. The epigenome is the guide, subtly directing the marble's path. Yet, it's also subject to the relentless pull of gravity, ensuring that once at the valley floor, the marble (cell) remains anchored, preserving cellular stability.

But life's mountainsides aren't as steep as we'd like, and the gravitational pull is not as unyielding. Perhaps the valleys are more profound, the gravitational grip firmer for the shark and the immortal jellyfish. But for us humans, the terrain is less hilly. The marble can settle, evolve, and manifest into a thriving adult if all goes well.

Yet, the tranquillity of this valley is not immune to tremors. Each dietary and environmental disruption –excess sugar, unwelcome chemicals, or a surge in insulin- is akin to an earthquake, dislodging the marbles, compelling them to leap into new valleys, morphing them into what some term 'zombie cells.' As time passes, cells may lose their sense of self, leading us to the pivotal inquiry: 'How do we fortify these valleys, intensify the gravitational hold on our cells, and preserve the intended order for as long as humanly possible?'

Enter Dr David Gems, a biogerontologist who theorises that ageing is not an inevitable chapter of life but a treatable spectrum of conditions. Echoing his sentiment, Dr David Sinclair outlines a regimen for awakening our longevity genes: embrace fasting, engage in frequent exercise, and occasionally expose the body to cold. These seemingly simple practices are profound in their impact, nurturing our cellular resilience and stimulating our internal defence mechanisms.

Venturing into the very heart of our cells, we find organelles, the cellular equivalents of organs, each performing a crucial function. Among these, the mitochondria we discussed previously stand out as the powerhouses, the energy suppliers of the cell. If a cell were a bustling metropolis, the mitochondria would be the power plants, lighting up the streets and energising every corner. Caring for these cellular powerhouses is paramount. Nourishing them with healthy fats, particularly MCTs and coconut oil (specifically C8), is a crucial strategy. With their shorter chain length, these nutrients effortlessly penetrate the mitochondrial walls, ensuring a steady energy flow.

The mitochondria are the dynamic dynamos within each cell, demanding the right fuel to thrive. The number of these energy factories varies dramatically among different cells, from just a few in some to thousands in others, such as those in our heart muscles and brains. Among their myriad functions, one of the most critical is their role in signalling when a cell's time should come to an appropriate end. This cellular curtain call is vital for maintaining balance; when cells ignore this final bow and continue to proliferate, they set the stage for the formation of cancerous tumours.

As I emphasised in my first health book, *Primal Cure*, our dietary choices have profound implications for our mitochondria. Feeding these cellular engines with a diet laden with sugars and devoid of fibre, essential minerals, and vitamins is akin to fuelling a sophisticated jet with low-grade fuel. This nutritional oversight has far-reaching consequences. The health of our mitochondria is not just a cellular concern; it's a cornerstone of our overall wellbeing, influencing the narrative of our health and the quality of our lives.

Deciphering the Biological Symphony: Sirtuins, NAD, mTOR, and AMPK

Let me introduce a few more intriguing players to our biological ensemble, ensuring we correctly set the scene for health and longevity. Here's a handy cheat sheet before we begin this exciting yet unfamiliar terrain for most:

Sirtuins: Your DNA's personal fountain of youth. Nourish these genes with fasting and NAD to keep unwelcome genetic guests under wraps.

NAD: Premium fuel for your sirtuins. Do they have low NAD levels? Empower them with a menu featuring tuna, salmon, sardines, mushrooms, avocado, eggs, and green veggies like asparagus.

mTOR: The master architect of growth. Essential, yes, but it's all about balance. Avoid letting it run amok, as unchecked mTOR activity can stifle AMPK and halt autophagy.

AMPK: Think of this as your inflammation firefighting brigade. Crank it up with fasting, turmeric, fibre (notably glucomannan), and fish oil to keep your cells vibrant and shielded from disease.

Autophagy: Your body's internal 'clean-up crew.' Kickstart this self-repair mechanism with intermittent fasting and a ketogenic diet to keep your cellular neighbourhood spick and span

Now let us look at each one in a little more detail:

Sirtuins: The Cellular Lifeguards: Imagine sirtuins as the vigilant lifeguards of your DNA, diligently ensuring that most genes remain in their dormancy, safeguarding the integrity of your cells. These proteins are like the guardians at the gate, keeping everything orderly and serene. But when they're pulled away to deal with cellular mishaps, it's like having a lifeguard distracted by a beachside ice cream truck; chaos ensues, and ageing accelerates. When it comes to sirtuin-activating compounds (known as STACs), NAD is the VIP guest, activating all seven sirtuin genes, making it a veritable rockstar of cellular security.

NAD: Adding Life to Years: Scientists have uncovered that NAD (nicotinamide adenine dinucleotide – a source of vitamin B3) is not just a molecule; it's a central conductor of numerous biological events, from disease management to anti-ageing. And importantly, it is believed that NAD helps ensure that our cellular marbles stay in their rightful valleys, reinforcing the walls and amplifying the gravity of our genetic landscape. Sadly, without intervention, its levels in our body, especially in critical areas like the brain and muscles, wane with age, a fact that's as concerning as finding your coffee supply dwindling on a Monday morning. Recent research states, 'NAD influences many key cellular functions, including DNA repair, chromatin remodelling and cellular senescence.'[3] Foods that are believed to increase levels of NAD include avocado, green vegetables, peanuts, and fish; it is enhanced by fasting, exercise, and the ketogenic diet.

mTOR: The Delicate Dance of Growth and Repair: mTOR, which we discussed during our look-at exercise, is a champion for regulating cell growth and protein synthesis, akin to a foreman on a construction site. But here's the issue: while it's busy building, it puts cell repair and the self-cleansing process of autophagy on the back burner. It's a cellular juggling act we need to grow, but we also need to repair. Striking the right balance is key, and it turns out that both fasting and exercise play pivotal roles in this delicate dance. Consider mTOR as the switch that toggles between building and repair modes, requiring ample time in each mode to maintain a healthy balance.

AMPK: The Guardian of Youth and Vitality: Last, let's spotlight AMPK, the enzyme that's like a cellular distress signal, rallying the troops when inflammation strikes. It's been said that activating AMPK is like finding the secret to a longer, better life. It's an energy sensor, a creator of new mitochondria, and a stimulator of SIRT-1, the sirtuin that's all about DNA repair. But beware, overindulgence at the dinner table can put AMPK to sleep, while fasting, high-intensity exercise, and a fibre-rich diet (hello, glucomannan!)[4] can awaken this sleeping giant. It's about keeping our cellular engines revving and our biological clock ticking gracefully.

If this chapter seems misty, rest assured you're in good company. I have to revisit it often to sharpen my grasp on the intricacies of cellular ageing. The expedition to decode the secrets of cellular longevity is a united quest, with pioneers like Dr David Sinclair shedding light on the path via their research sanctuaries. Within this worldwide pursuit, a vast community of scientists, numbering in the thousands, are passionately investigating the enigmas of ageing. Dr Sinclair, among others, has distilled the essence of longevity into tangible, actionable steps: embrace regular fasting, focus on certain longevity nutrients, prioritise fibre intake, avoid insulin resistance, steer clear of toxins, commit to regular exercise, and occasionally jolt your body with a cold shock. Let me turn that into a 'Seven Key Longevity Actions', kind of a to-do list for longevity:

Seven Key Longevity Actions

1. Embrace regular fasting
2. Focus on certain longevity nutrients
3. Prioritise fibre intake
4. Avoid insulin resistance
5. Steer clear of toxins
6. Commit to regular exercise
7. Occasionally, jolt your body with a cold shock

Sinclair advocates for the transformative power of hormesis, a catalyst that breathes life into our epigenome, sparking our longevity genes into vibrant action. It's a nuanced ballet of cellular mechanisms-activating AMPK, tempering mTOR, fuelling up on NAD, and rallying the sirtuins-our cellular guardians. Together, they erect a formidable defence against the inexorable tide of time, not just prolonging our existence but infusing it with quality and vitality.

Imagine, if you will, the possibility of significantly decelerating the ageing process. It's not just a dream; it's a vision grounded in the reality that our genetic blueprint for youthfulness remains intact, quietly residing within us even as we age. What if we could turn back the hands of time on our cellular clock, preserving the essence of our cells, much like the immortal jellyfish, perpetually rejuvenating? Perhaps we won't achieve eternal life, but why not aspire to mirror the longevity of whales or sharks, with whom we share a profound genetic bond?

The quest unfurls: how do we coax our ageing cells to revisit their original blueprint, to rediscover the vibrancy of their youth? Imagine your cells as a cherished collection of Bob Dylan CDs or 'Back to the Future' DVDs- timeless classics that have weathered the years. Just as those discs, with their spiralling grooves, hold a universe of data, our cells encapsulate an astonishing wealth of information within their DNA, all compacted into a space tinier than a speck of cosmic dust. Over time, though, just like a beloved CD might gather scratches, our DNA can get shrouded in epigenetic noise, repeating the tunes of ageing.

To revive a treasured disc, you might opt for a state-of-the-art player or resort to the old-school trick of a gentle clean with soapy water. Each method has its charm, right? In the realm of cellular rejuvenation, 'buying a new player' equates to the cloning wizardry that brought us Dolly the Sheep- a leap in science, yet not quite the everyday solution for us mere mortals. Instead, picture 'cleaning your DVD' as our approach to scrubbing away the epigenetic noise cluttering our cellular records.

Remember, the secret melody of youth is encoded in your DNA, silently waiting to be played anew. With a nudge from our cellular guardians, the sirtuins, cells that have lost their rhythm, can be coaxed back into their harmonious grooves, much like restoring the clarity of a cherished DVD or nudging a marble back into its rightful valley.

Feeling overwhelmed by the biology whirlwind? Here's the gist, served with a side of simplicity:

Embrace the biological blueprint. Adopting a fibre-first approach, engaging in intermittent fasting, exploring ketogenic diets, and harnessing the power of autophagy aren't just contemporary health strategies; they're time-honoured practices deeply ingrained in our biology, offering a pathway to infuse your years with vitality and vigour.

Align with the cellular alliance. Nutritional champions like sardines and green veggies, the essential benefits of omega-3, and potent supplements such as glucomannan, NAD, turmeric, resveratrol, and vitamin B3 are not just parts of your dietary routine; they are critical players in nurturing the intricate web of life at the cellular level, each contributing to the collective wellbeing of your body's microcosm.

So, you now hold the keys to the complex kingdom of longevity, where each component is essential, and the pursuit of a life brimming with vitality is relentless. Yet, before we close this chapter, there's a critical aspect to consider: a contemporary challenge that has subtly infiltrated our existence over the past two centuries, aside from the sporadic encounters our ancestors had with the odd poisonous berry or the rare venomous bite.

Steer Clear Of Toxins

The European Environment Agency recently sounded the alarm, attributing a staggering '8% of deaths to chemicals'.[7] And this figure is only climbing, representing just a fraction of the chemicals whose effects are well understood. It's eye-opening to discover that researchers have detected 300 to 400 foreign chemicals in the average Western adult's body, scarily 237 in umbilical cords alone[5] - substances absent just half a century ago - with their impacts largely veiled in mystery. So, it's crucial to sidestep toxins in your diet, of which ultra-processed foods are a prime culprit. And remember, your skin isn't just your body's largest organ; it's a gateway. Chemicals can permeate it, bypassing the filtration of the liver and diving straight into your bloodstream.

You might wonder why toxins, given their potential to cause nearly 1 in 10 deaths, didn't make it to my *Tree of Afflictions* diagram. I pondered it, but due to the inability to link toxins directly to all the conditions on the tree, I opted for accuracy and left them out. Yet, with research accelerating in this area, I might add it to a future revision.

To underscore the lethal potential of toxins, let's recall two high-profile incidents: In 2006, ex-Russian spy Alexander Litvinenko met his demise in London, a victim of polonium-210 slipped into his tea. Then, in 2017, Kim Jong Nam, the estranged brother of North Korea's leader, was fatally attacked with the nerve agent VX at Kuala Lumpur Airport. Why spotlight these dramatic cases? To drive home the undeniable truth: toxins are lethal. And while our primal ancestors occasionally faced dangers like poisonous mushrooms or venomous creatures, today, we confront a barrage of modern toxins. These threats aren't limited to what we consume or apply to our skin; they also encompass what we breathe and even the electromagnetic fields we experience daily. The landscape of our lives has changed dramatically, and with it, there is a need to be ever-vigilant about the unseen dangers that lurk in our modern world.

Toxins in What We Eat and Drink:

While we've covered this topic previously, it's worth reiterating the importance of mindful consumption. Opting for unpackaged, organic produce is your best bet for minimising exposure to toxins. Our bodies are remarkably adept at handling the occasional minor toxic encounter, with our gut and liver working as diligent detoxifiers. Yet vigilance extends beyond just choosing what we eat. How we store and prepare our food is equally critical. Steer clear of plastic containers unless they're certified BPA-free, particularly when using a microwave. Be wary of Teflon-coated cookware showing signs of wear, as damaged surfaces may leach harmful chemicals. Aluminium cookware has come under scrutiny due to potential links to Alzheimer's, making food-grade stainless steel a safer and more durable option.

Toxins in What We Inhale:

The message is clear and non-negotiable: smoking is out. Be cautious even when navigating smoke-filled areas, whether it's the clusters of smokers outside buildings or the exhaust-laden air of congested streets. In urban jungles, towering buildings can trap pollutants, forming what's known as 'urban canyons.' Intriguing findings from the University of the West of England underscore the stark differences in pollution exposure based on proximity to traffic. Cyclists, mere meters away from vehicles, face significantly more pollutants than pedestrians. So, when navigating densely populated cities, remember that distance is your ally against pollution. Seeking quieter, less-travelled paths isn't just a respite for the mind; it's a strategic move for your health, keeping you safe from the invisible but palpable threat of air pollution.

Toxins in What We Apply to Our Skin:

In the interest of transparency, it's worth noting that I'm associated with Primal Living, a brand offering a range of natural skincare products. That said, my insights remain grounded in the principles laid out long before our product line was conceived.

Have you ever paused to ponder what goes into the shampoos and shower gels we generously slather on ourselves? Or the mysterious alchemy that makes antiperspirants so enduringly effective? What about the concoctions we trust enough to apply to our skin, our body's largest and most exposed organ? A Canadian initiative delved into the contents lurking in everyday cosmetic products in a quest for answers. Their findings paint a concerning picture in detail. Testing items from the handbags of six individuals, they found startling levels of harmful substances like nickel, lead, cadmium, and even arsenic in all tested products. We are not talking about cheap products either; most brands tested were regarded as the most luxurious[6]. Imagine the shock of Erin Charter, who discovered her most trusted, expensive product was the most laden with toxins. Her sentiment echoes a universal desire: transparency in labelling and stricter regulations to shield us from these hidden dangers.

While debates continue over what chemical exposure levels might be deemed 'safe,' it's a perplexing puzzle. How do we gauge the long-term impact of daily, low-dose exposure to substances we instinctively know should be avoided? Consider this: if we presented modern cosmetics to an isolated tribe, touting their benefits but confessing their toxic ingredients, would they abandon their natural, time-tested adornments for our lab-concocted potions? Highly unlikely.

Is applying products containing known toxins to our skin genuinely harmless, or spray them onto our hair and underarms? Reflecting on earlier chapters, we recall how our liver acts as a vigilant gatekeeper, screening what enters our bloodstream from our gut. But what we apply to our skin bypasses this critical checkpoint, gaining direct entry into our bloodstream. It's an unsettling thought: ingesting these products might be 'safer,' triggering our body's natural defence mechanisms, whereas applying them topically often allows them to infiltrate our system unchecked.

Here's a simple rule of thumb for choosing skincare products: if the ingredient list isn't something you'd comfortably ingest, think twice before letting it absorb into your skin.

Our bodies have evolved robust defences against potentially harmful ingestibles, a testament to our ancestors' varied diet and occasional run-ins with less-than-friendly flora. However, our exposure to synthetic chemicals through skincare is a relatively new phenomenon that our bodies haven't had time to adapt to. While immediate reactions, like rashes or swelling, are clear distress signals, the concern lies in the subtle, long-term effects of a lifetime's exposure to these low-dose toxins.

In the realm of immunity and thyroid health, there's a noticeable gender disparity, often linked to the higher volume of products women apply to their skin. Dr Izabella Wentz's *Hashimoto's Protocol* and articles like *'Why Your Makeup is More Harmful Than You Think'* from The Huffington Post drive home a crucial point: substances applied to the skin can bypass our body's natural filtration systems, leading to potential health risks.

A chilling BBC report highlighted the risks of skin creams containing paraffin, demonstrating how clothes soaked in such creams can become highly flammable—a stark reminder of the potential hazards lurking in seemingly benign products.

And it's not just about what you put on your skin; even your clothing choices matter. Choose natural fibres like organic cotton or bamboo over synthetic materials. Be particularly cautious of those containing PFAS (per and poly-fluoroalkyl substances), BPA, formaldehyde, and phthalates (known endocrine disruptors).

A recent eye-opening study by the Centers for Environmental Health (CEH) uncovered alarmingly high levels of BPA lurking in the sports bras and athletic shirts of major fast fashion brands. Shockingly, individuals could be exposed to a whopping 40 times the safe limit.[8]

While washing your clothes before the first wear can help eliminate some of the chemicals used in production, it's akin to trying to scrub pesticides off a vegetable – you can't thoroughly cleanse away all the toxins and synthetics from a piece of clothing with just a spin in the washing machine.

In summary, navigating the landscape of topical toxins requires vigilance, an understanding of potential risks, and a preference for products and materials that align with our body's natural harmony. Remember, our choices for our skin are not superficial; they resonate throughout our wellbeing.

Navigating the Invisible Threat: Electromagnetic Fields (EMF)

While electromagnetic fields (EMF) don't fit the traditional mould of toxins, their potential impact is too significant to overlook, especially in an era where our mobile phones feel like extensions of our hands. As a parent, the ambiguous assurances about the safety of low-frequency EMF exposure are more unsettling than comforting. The World Health Organisation's classification of the electromagnetic fields from mobile phones as 'possibly carcinogenic to humans' sends a shiver down the spine. It's a statement that resonates with caution, particularly when you consider the immense influence of telecommunication conglomerates. Will the complete truth emerge? Perhaps, but it may take decades.

The WHO advises that the intensity of EMF exposure diminishes significantly with distance from the device.[9] Texting, internet browsing, or using hands-free devices can drastically reduce exposure compared to pressing the phone against your ear. Limiting call duration and frequency and opting for areas with strong reception (minimising the phone's power output) are practical steps to mitigate risks.

My counsel? Embrace hands-free options or, better yet, minimise mobile phone use. However, it's not just about the phone. Our homes, particularly kitchens and bedrooms, are EMF hubs. While most likely safe for cooking, the microwave is best observed from a distance during operation. Other appliances like washing machines and blenders contribute to the EMF landscape, but much less. In the bedroom, consider embracing the simplicity of our ancestors by letting your hair air-dry naturally and limiting the use of hairdryers and other gadgets.

In our modern lives, where technology is ever-present, understanding and mitigating the potential risks of EMF exposure is crucial in safeguarding our welfare and aligning our contemporary lifestyle with a mindful and informed approach to health.

Dr Robert Lustig

'My colleague Chris Madsen at UC Berkley did a study showing that kids who charge their mobile in the room at night get 28 minutes less sleep than those who charge them outside the room. And what we all need to do is to stop using screens one hour before bedtime. No screens. Books are fine, but not screens, as they are detrimental to the production of serotonin. Technology damages the pre-frontal cortex, and you need it for creativity. The problem is, with digital media, we see everything

rather than imagine it, and therefore, kids get stupid. And it's been going on since TV, but it has revved up since the digital revolution.'

Author Patrick Holford
'About ten years ago, and this is a bit controversial, there was a survey that showed that left-handed people had more left-sided brain tumours and right-handed people had more right-sided brain tumours. We are talking about mobile phone use. And there is this rather aggressive brain cancer that is on the increase; it's gone up tenfold in the last twenty or so years, called glioblastoma. Two years ago, a big study in a top journal said that ten years of mobile phone use more than doubles your risk of glioblastoma. So, we have an association. Then, last year, a very good study took these glioblastoma cells and exposed them to the amount that would be normal in a mobile call. It found that the DNA was fragmented, and bad things happened. So, we have a mechanism. But we will never have proof because it takes ten years to develop. So, you would have to have two groups for ten years, all doing the same things, but one group using mobiles and one not. But we are in the age of technology, so we will not all stop, but it's better to use it on speaker away from your head and always try to get a good signal.'

The Power Of Antioxidants

Just as science unveiled that scurvy was a lack of vitamin C and that rickets were a lack of vitamin D, a whole area of recent science suggests that a lack of antioxidants in our diet is leading to many of today's chronic illnesses. A lack of dietary antioxidants may contribute to diseases such as Alzheimer's, cancer, and hypertension and may play a role in health issues as diverse as cataracts and infertility. I was deliberating whether to add this topic to the end of our discussion on superfoods and supplements; however, as we have just been discussing protecting ourselves at the cellular level, I thought it appropriate to place it here. Engaging in the antioxidant conversation is like stepping into a classic tale of defence against unseen chaos. Imagine your body as a bustling metropolis, and free radicals are the unruly elements, subtly disrupting the peace of cellular life. In this narrative, antioxidants are the quiet guardians, always on patrol to restore balance and fend off the molecular mischief caused by these radicals.

Our cellular defenders face a myriad of challenges, from digesting food to warding off viral invaders. Yet, among these adversaries, free radicals stand out. These atomic renegades emerge from the essential act of turning food into fuel, but they don't stop there. They sometimes pop up after a strenuous workout, a walk in polluted air, or a stressful day at the office, leaving a trail of oxidative stress in their wake.

Think of free radicals as the clandestine operatives in a spy thriller, stealthily stealing electrons from stable molecules, causing a cascade of cellular turmoil. This electron pilfering can fundamentally alter the 'victim's' structure or function, turning a once orderly molecule into a source of chaos. The impact of their actions can even extend to altering the sacred genetic codes within our DNA.

Enter antioxidants, the unsung heroes in our daily diet, equipped with the power to neutralise these disruptive forces. Consuming a diet rich in antioxidants is akin to fortifying your cellular city, with a vigilant defence force poised to protect against a spectrum of ailments from heart disease to the stealthy advance of certain cancers.

To assemble your antioxidant arsenal, look no further than the produce section. Broccoli, spinach, carrots, and dark chocolate are not merely staples of a healthy diet; they are your allies in the fight against oxidative stress. Joining them is a diverse brigade of herbs and spices, each armed with its own unique antioxidant capabilities. And for those with a penchant for culinary adventure, sprinkling spices in your cooking is not just for taste—it's a strategic move in bolstering your antioxidant defences.

Oxygen Radical Absorbance Capacity (ORAC)

Welcome to the world of Oxygen Radical Absorbance Capacity (ORAC), a term that sounds like it belongs in a sci-fi novel rather than your kitchen. But fear not; this concept is not about defending the galaxy but about protecting your body at the cellular level. Picture a league of extraordinary herbs, spices and vegetables, each with its unique power to absorb those pesky free radicals, akin to a natural medicine for your health.

In 2007, a group of intrepid scientists at the National Institute of Health and Aging assembled a database under the auspices of the US Department of Agriculture. Not just any database, but one that could measure the antioxidant capacity of different foods, ranking them by their ability to neutralise free radicals. Imagine a leaderboard where foods compete in an antioxidant championship, vying for the top spot in safeguarding your health.

But why aren't these foods more celebrated in the medical community? Well, it turns out that, much like your favourite comic book heroes, these foods can't be patented. And without the potential for huge profit, big pharmaceutical companies often overlook their benefits, leaving this crucial information out of the spotlight and medical journals. Yet, the connection between high-antioxidant foods and their rich content of vitamins and minerals is an open secret among those in the know, especially for anyone concerned about combating the likes of dementia, Alzheimer's, or Parkinson's, essentially any arch-villain of degenerative illness that thrives on free radicals.

The FDA suggests a daily intake of ORAC units between 3,000 to 5,000 μmol TE (that's micromole Trolox equivalent per gram for those who don't speak science), particularly when facing constant pro-oxidant factors.

The spotlight on the perils of free radicals, sparked by discoveries showcased in the National Library of Medicine, might steal the spotlight as this year's most groundbreaking health revelation[10] (though perhaps trailing slightly behind the revelation of embracing the *Fibre First* diet, naturally). So, when you're picking out your next meal, envision yourself gathering your very own League of Extraordinary Antioxidants. It's not just dinner; it's your arsenal against the nefarious forces of free radicals, poised to safeguard your health with every bite.

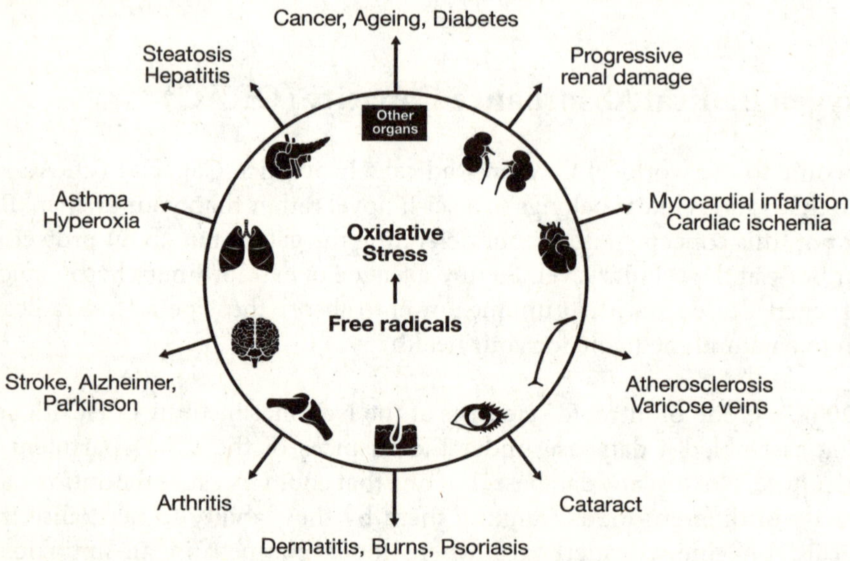

In the visual guide, chart 766, I've laid out exactly how much of each superfood you need to hit an ORAC score of 3,000. This isn't just a shopping list; it's your blueprint for building a fortress against oxidative stress, as the American FDA recommends. The catch? These measurements hinge on the assumption that your food comes from organic sources, untouched by the diminishing effects of modern agriculture. If you aim for what the FDA deems 'positive health effects,' consider drafting three or four antioxidant-rich allies on your team daily. However, moderation is key.

Enter the paradox of hormesis: it's the Goldilocks zone of stress, where just the right amount fortifies, and too much can backfire. In the fascinating equation, some stress, like the mild toxins found in plants, can bolster our resilience. This principle suggests that what doesn't challenge us essentially makes us stronger. Think of it as the body's boot camp, where a controlled dose of adversity toughens the troops.

This isn't about pushing your cellular defences to their breaking point but tuning them like a finely crafted instrument. While pinning down the exact threshold for 'too many' antioxidants remains challenging, aiming for the FDA's recommendation of up to 10,000 ORAC units may strike an appropriate balance. It appears enough to invigorate your body's defences without overstepping into the realm where benefits fade and risks begin to loom.

Turn page for ORAC chart ›

The ORAC Scale

	ORAC Score per 100g	Gram weight needed to achieve 3000 ORAC	Approximate serving size needed to achieve 3000 ORAC
Cinnamon	267,536	1	1 tsp
Oregano (dried)	200,129	1	1 tsp
Turmeric	159,277	2	1 tsp
Cocoa (dry powder)	80,933	4	1 or 2 tsp
Cumin seeds	76,800	4	1 or 2 tsp
Parsley (dried)	74,349	4	2 or 3 tsp
Basil (dried)	57,553	5	2 or 3 tsp
Dark Chocolate	49,926	6	2 or 3 squares
Curry Powder	48,504	6	3 or 4 tsp
Sage (fresh)	32,004	9	6 0r 7 tsp
Thyme (fresh)	27,426	11	8 or 9 tbs
Black Pepper	26,681	11	8 or 9 tbs
Goji Berries	25,300	12	Handful
Chilli Powder	23,636	13	10 or 11 tbs
Pecan Nuts	17,940	17	Handful
Paprika	17,919	17	15 tbs
Ginger	14,840	20	15 tbs
Walnuts	13,541	22	Handful
Cranberries	9,584	31	Handful
Hazelnuts	9,454	32	Big handful
Artichokes	9,416	32	1/4 of the vegetable
Pistachio Nuts	7,983	38	Big handful
Blueberries	6,552	46	1/2 cup
Blackberries	5,347	56	1/2 cup
Garlic	5,346	56	8 or 9 cloves
Coriander Leaves	5,141	58	Handful
Cabernet Suavignon	5,304	60	1/2 glass
Raspberries	4,882	61	1 cup
Almonds	4,454	67	2 handfulls
Granny Smith Apple with skin	3,898	77	1/2 apple
Red Wine	3,873	77	1/2 glass
Strawberries	3,577	84	1 cup
Peanut Butter Smooth	3,432	87	5th of a jar
Cherries	3,365	89	1/2 cup

The ORAC Scale

	ORAC Score per 100g	Gram weight needed to achieve 3000 ORAC	Approximate serving size needed to achieve 3000 ORAC
Peanuts	3,166	95	Handful
Cabbage (red)	3,145	95	1/2 cup
Broccoli	3,083	97	1 1/2 cups
Blueberry Juice	2,906	103	1 glass
Asparagus Raw	2,150	140	3
Pear	2,021	148	1
Cashew Nuts	1,948	154	3 handfulls
Avocado	1,922	156	1 half
Radish	1,736	173	1 cup
Red Onion	1,521	197	1
Spinach	1,515	198	6 cups
Red Grapes	1,260	238	40 grapes
Tea (brewed)	1,253	239	3 or 4 cups
Onion	1,220	246	1
Olive Oil (extra virgin)	1,150	261	1 cup
Oragne Bell Pepper	984	305	2

You might be wondering how to incorporate ORAC-rich foods into your meals, especially if you're following a ketogenic or carnivore diet. Fear not, for I have a straightforward trick up my sleeve. Sprinkle a teaspoon or two of cocoa powder into your morning coffee or toss a generous helping of herbs into glucomannan noodles. Mix in some butter or olive oil and pair it with your preferred meat or fish dish. Voilà! A delicious, antioxidant-packed meal that fits seamlessly into your dietary regime.

Chapter 11

Nurturing Wellness: From Actions to Habits

Congratulations! You've adventured through the depths of this book, exploring the vibrant tapestry of health and longevity. As we approach the final chapter, it's a moment to pause and applaud your dedication and curiosity. Your presence here is a testament to your commitment to understanding and actively crafting a healthier, more fulfilling life.

In this conclusive chapter, I'll translate the insights we've uncovered into tangible, actionable steps. We'll focus on half a dozen ideas and strategies that will help transform your newfound knowledge into a lived reality:

Life's Adventure & Goal Setting

As you've come this far, you're likely already planning or initiating changes, embracing the *Fibre First* diet, being mindful not to spike insulin, and rethinking lifestyle choices. But how do you ensure that these changes aren't just a fleeting trend but the foundation of a lifelong adventure? Surprisingly, the comedian Jimmy Carr provides an unexpected yet profound perspective in his book *Before and Laughter*. He muses about the life he aspires to lead two decades from now, recognising today's choices as the building blocks of tomorrow's reality. It's a perspective that gains weight and urgency as we progress through life's stages, transforming from a whimsical notion to a compelling strategy for intentional living.

Imagine your life twenty years from now. What picture comes to mind? This isn't about dreaming; it's about concrete envisioning. It's about seeing today as a vital step toward the vibrant, health-filled life you aim to lead two decades on. You are the architect of your future; every choice and every action today are a brushstroke on the canvas of your life. And now, as the captain of your ship and the navigational charts you have discovered in this book, the compass is in your hands. Where will you steer for the remainder of your lifetime? It's a role that demands courage, as it will often require you to swim against the tide of conventional (corporate-created) wisdom.

Venturing beyond comfort zones isn't just advisable; it's essential. You've already taken the first steps by engaging with the concepts in this book. Recognise that declining health isn't an inevitable descent but a challenge to be met and overcome. Remember, every day is a celebration of better health; every milestone is a testament to your commitment. You are the sculptor of your destiny. Teachers can guide, doctors can advise, and trainers can support, but ultimately, the journey is yours and yours alone.

Consider this book and my Health Results website resources as your trusted map. Our knowledge, like the sea, is broad but ever-changing. We continually update our charts, marking new hazards and chronicling courses to new discoveries.

Charting A Path To A Fulfilling Future: The POST Method - Purpose, Objectives, Strategy, Tactics

Setting out towards a fulfilling and vibrant future is akin to navigating an uncharted territory with a map of our own making. It requires a blend of vision, planning, and daily actions, all aimed at weaving the rich tapestry of a life well-lived. This pilgrimage can be distilled into a four-step blueprint, each a critical milestone in the quest for a life brimming with purpose, joy, and connection.

Purpose

Imagine going on an expedition without knowing your destination; you wouldn't do it, right? Purpose serves as your North Star, illuminating the path and providing a sense of direction. It's about defining the legacy you wish to leave and the impact you aspire to make on the world. Your purpose is the heartbeat of your existence, the underlying 'why' that fuels your future.

Objectives (Goals)

Setting out your objectives and long-term goals with your purpose in sight is akin to visualising the landscapes you'll explore and the experiences you'll cherish. It's picturing yourself twenty years from now, whether basking in the joy of playing with grandchildren, embarking on soul-stirring adventures, or engaging in hobbies that ignite your passion. Your goal is the vivid portrait of your future, painted with the strokes of your deepest desires and aspirations.

Strategy

No expedition succeeds without a compass. Your strategy is the pointer guiding you towards your objectives, ensuring every step taken is a step closer to the vision you've set for yourself. It may involve embracing a holistic lifestyle, prioritising healthy foods, quality sleep, regular exercise, and cultivating meaningful relationships. Your strategy is the framework within which your purpose starts to take shape, turning the abstract into the achievable.

Tactics

Every quest comprises small steps, each a victory in its own right. Tactics are these steps, the daily decisions and habits that gradually build the bridge to your envisioned future. They're the practical, actionable items on your to-do list: opting for fibre-rich foods, choosing stairs over elevators, winding down before bedtime, and creating habits that collectively propel you forward. Your tactics are the building blocks of your strategy, the tangible expressions of your commitment to your objectives and purpose.

Envisioning and executing this four-step blueprint isn't merely an exercise in goal-setting; it's an invitation to sculpt a life that resonates with purpose, joy, and fulfilment. As you ponder these steps, draw inspiration from the wise and the successful and the stories of those who've lived through the tapestry of time. Commit your plan to paper, infuse it with imagery that sparks joy, embed it in your memory, and share it with those you hold dear. Just as the Bhutanese reflect on the impermanence of life to appreciate each day, let your purpose and goals be a daily reminder of the path you've chosen to tread.

In life, your purpose is the person you want to be, your objectives are your goals visualised, your strategy is your roadmap, and your tactics are your footsteps in the sand. Together, they form the compass that guides you through the voyage of life, ensuring that each day is a step towards a future filled with purpose, happiness, and an enduring legacy.

Let me share with you my personal POST, which outlines my Purpose, Objectives, Strategies, and Tactics. This isn't just a blueprint for navigating life's complexities; it's a glimpse into who I am, what I stand for, and how I aspire to leave an imprint on the world. In revealing my POST, I invite you into a space of mutual understanding and connection. I hope to impart knowledge and inspire and kindle a flame of curiosity and determination within you. As we've traversed topics, theories, and personal anecdotes, I have aimed to build a bridge of trust and camaraderie between us.

My passage, like yours, is ongoing, a perpetual quest for growth, understanding, and impact. By sharing my POST, let it be a catalyst for your own reflection on purpose, objectives, and the strategies and tactics that will guide your path.

Purpose:

To help as many people as possible, especially my family, myself, friends, and others, maximise their potential health span while always loving life.

Objectives:

- I want to still be kite surfing in my 80s, focusing more on dreams than memories and ensuring my focus is still 20 years out.
- To go snowboarding on my 85th birthday.
- To play tennis in my 90s and with an attitude to learn something new each day.
- To celebrate my 100th birthday with a walk, a smile, and a laugh.

Strategy:

- Prioritise 20 years from now.
- Eat *Fibre First* and be in ketogenesis as much as possible.
- Prioritise exercise.
- Focus on family happiness.
- Be kind and inspiring to everyone.
- Keep learning.
- Be grateful for everything.

Tactics:

- Stay curious.
- Treat yourself like someone you are responsible for helping.
- Pursue what is meaningful, not what is convenient.
- Focus on happiness, not pleasure.
- When communicating, try to be more precise in my speech.

Today is the day to plant that tree, to lay the cornerstone of the life you envision two decades from now. The future is not just a distant dream; it's the reality you start building today. So, let's embark on this final chapter with the same curiosity, passion, and commitment that brought you this far. Here's to a life of health, vitality, and the richness of a life well-lived. When you're ready to craft your own POST, flip to page 995 and let your dreams take shape on paper.

Why Do I Talk About Objectives And Purpose, Not Goals?

While the allure of a long-term, 20-year vision is undeniable, navigating the path with care is crucial, especially when setting shorter, stepping-stone goals. Let's unravel this a bit: Many of us quickly chalk up resolutions at the dawn of a new year, setting our sights on what we hope to achieve. Yet, often, these resolutions fade into oblivion, leaving us wondering where we went astray. Yes, goal setting is instrumental in fostering accountability, fuelling motivation, and pushing the boundaries of procrastination. But what if the way we've been setting goals in the past has been misguided?

You might be intrigued to learn that goal-setting never took centre stage in my business ventures. Journalists often probe, asking about the targets I set to build the UK's number one fastest-growing company not once but twice (two companies I created won the Sunday Times fastest-growing UK company in

1996 and 2012). My response that I steer clear of rigid goals and, instead, craft systems, methodologies, and ideologies, often meets with disbelief. But here's the reason I do it the way I do:

Short to medium-sized goals, while measuring progress, can also be the source of undue stress. For some, stress is a catalyst; for others, it's a crippling force leading to further delays and detours. The art of setting realistic goals is a tightrope walk. Aim too high, and the unattainable summit can leave you feeling deflated, overshadowing the strides and growth you've experienced along the way. By fixating solely on the goal, we often overlook the journey, the lessons learned, and the incremental triumphs.

Achieving a goal can be euphoric, but it's often fleeting. Goals tether our happiness to brief, transient moments. The joy erupts at the finish line but can recede just as quickly. Goals paint life in stark contrasts-success or failure, joy or despair. They rarely account for the spectrum of experiences, emotions, and growth that happens in between.

So, as we venture through this final chapter, I encourage you to think beyond the confines of rigid goals. Instead, focus on creating systems and adopting philosophies that support continuous growth and learning. Shift your perspective from chasing fleeting moments of success to nurturing a sustainable life of progress and self-discovery.

What's the alternative to setting lofty, distant goals? Oliver Goldsmith poetically stated, 'Life is a journey that must be travelled no matter how bad the roads and accommodations.' Why aim solely for the destination when the pathway itself is where the true magic unfolds? I've spearheaded the fastest-growing companies in the UK, not by fixating on a finish line but by championing Continual Performance Improvements or, as all my team members know it, CPI.

The crux isn't hitting a specific number on the scale; it's about habits formed, the knowledge gained, and the skills honed. These are the treasures that endure, unlike the fleeting triumph of meeting a weight target, which can vanish with just one indulgent celebration. Instead of obsessing over losing 50 pounds, why not commit to always eating the *Fibre First* diet and a 30-minute workout thrice a week? Over a year, that's over four thousand minutes of movement, a testament to your dedication.

Ah, the perilous risks of goal setting: many embark with numeric targets as their compass, only to find themselves marooned in the desert of burnout, momentum a distant mirage. The secret? Swap that cumbersome treasure map of distant, grandiose goals for a series of manageable, bite-sized X marks the spot. Aim for short-term victories paired with a rolling 20-year vision that's more horizon than a mirage.

Beware of mid-term ambitions. They often lead to a sea of disillusionment where motivation drowns, and surrender waves its white flag. And should you reach that elusive goal, what then? Like a party where the music stops abruptly, you're left wondering, 'What's next?'

Let's take a leaf out of the British Cycling Team's playbook. In 2003, Dave Brailsford took the helm as their performance director. The team's track record was modest, with a solitary gold medal since 1908. Enter Brailsford's game-changing strategy: the philosophy of marginal gains. Imagine dissecting the art of cycling into its minutest components and enhancing each by a mere 1%. Cumulatively, these micro-improvements translate into monumental gains. Under Brailsford's guidance, the team embraced minute tweaks-even scrutinising massage gels for optimal muscle recovery. The outcome? A staggering haul of 178 world championships and 66 Olympic and Paralympic gold medals between 2007 and 2017. This wasn't just about clinching a one-off victory; it was about constructing a sustainable system of success, a continuous drive for excellence that didn't wane post-victory.

Reimagining Life's Adventure: From Vision To Victory

Embarking on the path of self-improvement and health revitalisation, it's crucial to sculpt your POST: Purpose, Objectives, Strategies, and Tactics. It's akin to setting sail on a grand voyage of transformation, with your compass calibrated to your deepest values and aspirations. Yet, the waters are not sailed in a one-size-fits-all vessel. Some of us thrive on the gentle currents of daily betterment, relishing each moment of the adventure without rigid milestones. Others, however, chart their course with precise coordinates, propelled by the thrill of pursuit and the satisfaction of reaching marked landmarks.

I'm incredibly sceptical of traditional goal setting, especially when it's prescribed as the universal remedy for weight loss or a health reboot. My stance isn't from a place of disdain but from a recognition of our unique compositions. We're a vibrant mosaic of perspectives and drives, each piece unique and coloured by individual experiences. For some, the glass isn't just half full—it's brimming with potential, sparkling under the sunlight of optimism. For others, the glass is half empty, marked by caution or shaped by past storms. It's a reminder that what fuels one person's adventure might not even get another's engine started. Recognising this tapestry of personalities enriches our understanding of one another and adds a dash of spice to the human experience.

Yet, let's not dismiss the power of our personal POST and a well-defined purpose and a meticulous plan to pursue it. Enter the art of 'chunking it down,' a method akin to the age-old question: 'How do you eat an elephant?' One bite at a time.

Chunk it Down

Let me transport you to the icy expanse of the North Pole for a tale that unfolds in April 2014. Picture a team of four adventurers embarking on a daring quest to traverse the final degree of Earth's frosty terrain on foot. Among us were my son-in-law Jake, a seasoned doctor and an experienced guide. As we ventured deeper into the stark white solitude, fate dealt us a challenging hand. Five days into our expedition, our companion, Dr Phillip, fell victim to frostbite, thrusting us into a harrowing predicament. In the frozen wilderness, we stayed inside our cramped two-man tents for the next 48 hours, surrounded by nothing but shades of white, anxiously awaiting rescue.

Nestled in my tent, with Alan Chambers, a seasoned polar explorer, as my freezing camping partner, we pondered over the daunting vastness that lay ahead. With tales of polar conquests, Alan shared a nugget of wisdom from a previous expedition. A few years back, he embarked on a groundbreaking exploration from Canada to the North Pole; he faced the monumental challenge of leading the first team to traverse this daunting route on foot. Nestled in the icy embrace of the Arctic, amidst the hush of endless nights and the rugged terrain that stretched before them, progress was painstakingly slow. For the initial ten days, the sun remained a mere memory, shrouded by the polar night, casting the expedition into a realm of perpetual twilight. His team's morale wavered as the harsh reality of their endeavour set in. The vast expanse of the map, unfurled within the confines of their tent, loomed over them as a daunting reminder of the distance yet to cover—a seemingly insurmountable task that weighed heavily on their spirits.

Then, Alan, with a spark of ingenuity, transformed their perspective. He meticulously divided the map into six vertical sections, and that night, he only showed them the one page they were traversing. This act of breaking the overwhelming goal into smaller, achievable milestones rekindled the team's resolve. By focusing solely on the segment at hand, without the burden of the entire route looming over them, each step forward felt like a tangible progression towards their goal.

Alan's strategy illuminated the power of perspective in overcoming adversity. By segmenting the trek, he eased the psychological strain on his team and instilled a renewed sense of purpose and momentum. Each section of the map became a new chapter in their epic narrative, a series of mini-victories that collectively paved the way to their historic achievement.

This tale of resilience and strategic ingenuity underscores the importance of adaptability and mental fortitude in the face of seemingly insurmountable challenges. Alan Chambers and his team's pioneering expedition to the North Pole is a testament to the human spirit's capacity to explore the vast, uncharted territories of the physical world and the landscapes of our determination. So, as we stand on the brink of our own personal quests, let us embrace the method of 'chunking it down.'

The Journey From A to Z

While I personally lean away from strictly numerical goals, as they tend to engage the prefrontal cortex rather than evoke emotional resonance, which isn't always conducive to driving meaningful change, I understand that some individuals thrive on setting specific targets. If you find motivation in goal-setting, allow me to introduce a fresh perspective that flips the traditional approach on its head, integrating the 'chunk it down' methodology.

Imagine it's the start of a new year, and you've set a lofty goal: shedding three stones by your birthday in March. While ambition fuels our dreams, realism shapes our achievements. Rather than sprinting towards an improbable finish line, consider the power of gradual, sustainable change. For those carrying an extra five or six stones, envisioning a four-stone weight loss over the year isn't just a fantasy; it's a tangible target within grasp. Indeed, one of the issues with goal-setting is that it often underestimates our potential by failing to recognise the breadth of our capabilities.

The adage, 'How do you climb a mountain? One step at a time' rings true here. Incredible feats are accomplished through a series of small, deliberate actions. Let's apply this wisdom: envision shedding four stones in a year. Start by marking your desired weight a year from now on your calendar; make it unmissable. Then, break it down: two stone lighter in six months, one in three months, and perhaps a modest half-stone in the first 45 days. Adjust your milestones to reflect realistic expectations, acknowledging that weight loss may speed up initially, then plateau as you draw closer to your goal.

This approach, 'chunking down' your grand aspiration into manageable pieces, transforms an overwhelming challenge into a series of achievable steps. It's about starting at Z—your ultimate goal—and meticulously planning your way back to A, focusing solely on the immediate next step. This method, just as Alan did when first conquering his route to the North Pole, makes your path more digestible (if you'll pardon the pun) and frames each small success as a significant victory.

What should your goal embody? It should be ambitious yet realistic, deeply personal, and reflective of what motivates you. Is it the allure of a slimmer physique or the more profound desire for health and vitality? Understanding your 'why' is crucial. If you're unsure, take time for introspection—meditate, reflect, and explore your innermost desires without outside influence. Once your purpose is clear, and if your support network radiates positivity, share your mission and seek their encouragement.

Remember, without a profound desire driving you, the temptation to hit snooze on the alarm or succumb to fast-food pressure from friends becomes all too easy. As Rich Roll, author of *Finding Ultra*, advises, prioritising your path to self-actualisation above all else is critical to overcoming obstacles and realising your dreams. His advice to break down goals into tangible, daily actions breeds confidence and transforms the seemingly impossible into an achievable reality. Every small victory is a step closer to your purpose and objectives, replacing doubt with certainty and apprehension with excitement.

In conclusion, setting your purpose and objectives is not just about envisioning an endpoint but also about understanding the journey's significance. It's a process of self-discovery and, most importantly, celebrating every small victory along the way. Embrace each step, and let your exploration redefine what you thought possible.

Habits vs Willpower

Let's shatter the myth that equates being overweight or in poor health with a lack of willpower. The truth is far more nuanced: willpower isn't the hero or the villain in this narrative; it's about recognising and reshaping our habits. Consider this: an alcoholic will traverse oceans for a drink, a smoker will scavenge for a cigarette, and a drug addict may resort to breaking into your home to fund their addiction. These actions aren't indicative of weak wills; they signify the formidable force of habit. And those who queued for hours outside McDonald's after the Covid lockdown weren't lacking in willpower; they were following deeply ingrained routines.

It's high time we stopped pointing fingers and labelling people as 'weak-willed' or lacking in self-discipline. The notion that obesity stems from a simple lack of self-control is not just infuriating; it's flawed. The secret to change lies in shifting our mindset towards food and habits rather than relying on willpower.

My philosophy is straightforward: It's not about enduring a life of relentless willpower or feeling deprived. Remember, back to my opening words at the beginning of this book, it's more about 'giving up, giving up'. It's about reprogramming the way we perceive and desire certain foods. Does it require immense willpower to drive on the correct side of the road? Absolutely not! It's a habit, ingrained and automatic. This approach isn't about feeling like you're missing out or battling constant hunger. It's about realignment and enjoyment, not discipline or deprivation.

The stark truth is that willpower is not the answer-it never was. Most individuals grappling with obesity are aware of the risks, yet knowledge alone isn't enough to break the cycle. The more we fixate on the foods we 'shouldn't' have, the more alluring they become, a classic case of the forbidden fruit syndrome. It's a vicious cycle: the more we dwell on our dietary restrictions, the more we feel deprived, and the more intense the guilt and frustration after succumbing to temptation.

Permanent weight loss and good health isn't a battle of wills; it's a matter of rewiring our brains. The oft-repeated advice to 'eat less and move more' is an oversimplification, a convenient narrative that shifts the blame onto individuals. It's a story that ignores the complexity of human behaviour and the power of habits.

So, let's set the record straight. Being overweight or out of shape isn't about lacking willpower; it's about being stuck in a system that doesn't support healthy habits. It's about needing a new approach, a fresh perspective that goes beyond the superficial 'eat less' mantra. It's time for a total reboot, a reprogramming of the outdated code in our brains to align with the world we live in today.

It's not the brute force of willpower that paves the way to healthier living;

it's understanding your 'why.' It's about defining the deeper reasons behind your food choices and aligning them with your identity and values. Once you establish your POST and grasp your 'why,' your 'will' follows naturally, driving you toward choices that resonate with who you are and aspire to be. Remember, it's not about summoning willpower; it's about embracing 'why power' and initiating a transformation of habits and self-discovery.

Life, Freedom, Happiness And The Avoidance Of Pain

As you stand on the precipice of a new approach to life, you must arm yourself with a powerful mantra that aligns with the transformation you've embarked upon. Aristotle's ancient wisdom posits that the essence of human endeavour is the pursuit of happiness and the evasion of pain. This principle, when woven together with the promises enshrined in the American Declaration of Independence—life, liberty, and the pursuit of happiness—creates a holistic vision that can serve as a guiding light. 'Life, freedom (I prefer freedom to liberty as it says better what it does on the tin), the pursuit of happiness, and the avoidance of pain' isn't just a mantra; it's a clarion call to action, an affirmation of your commitment to a life that is as fulfilling as it is free from unnecessary suffering. Let this be the foundation upon which you build your POST, a reminder of the ideals that drive your every decision and action.

Sadly, as portrayed in this book, our contemporary reality starkly differs from this idealised concept. ***Life*** expectancy, rather than stretching further, is beginning to shrink. The invisible shackles of food addiction, forged by profit-centric food corporations, compromise our ***freedom***. Amidst this, the radiant glow of genuine ***happiness*** dims, overshadowed by a nationwide struggle against depression. And what of the ***avoidance of pain***? Regrettably, as you have already discovered, nowadays, more adults are on medication that are not. This stark deviation from the cherished principles of Aristotle and the American Declaration of Independence is evident and troubling. In the current era, where the scales of priority tilt heavily towards corporate profit at the expense of individual health and happiness, these foundational pillars face distortion. This isn't for lack of desire for betterment but stems from a global narrative prioritising economic gains over human welfare.

Reflecting on the words of The Carpenter's classic song from the 70s, 'There's a kind of hush all over the world', it's as if a quiet has settled across the globe, signalling a collective resignation to these compromised ideals. One might wonder if these critical issues of life, freedom, and happiness are on the governmental radar, perhaps only to be conveniently hushed in the political dance for re-election.

To authentically embody our mantra-to revel in freedom, happiness, and a life brimming with vitality and extended pain-free years-we must cultivate new habits. But what constitutes a habit? Think back to your initial bike rides or your first driving lessons. Each step required meticulous attention, from igniting the engine to synchronising the clutch. Over time, these deliberate actions transformed into second nature. Initially, each decision requires conscious effort, but as you persist, these choices seamlessly become habits, as instinctive as breathing. So, as we embark on this final chapter, remember that the road to 'Freedom, happiness, infusing life with vitality, and extending our years with pain-free life' is intricately interwoven with habits. Let's commence this transformation, one deliberate step at a time.

The Pathway To New Habits

Back to Aristotle, he wisely stated, 'We are what we consistently do,' adding, 'Excellence, then, is not an act, but a habit.' This understanding lays the groundwork for the seven widely accepted phases of healthy habit formation:

Precontemplation: The denial phase, where change isn't on the horizon
Contemplation: Acknowledging the need for change and considering its benefits
Preparation: Equipping yourself with tools and resources for the adventure ahead
Act: Taking the plunge and initiating change
Maintenance: Reinforcing new habits and embracing the improved lifestyle
Relapse: The occasional slip-up, a momentary return to old ways
Recovery: View relapses as learning moments and bounce back stronger

It's crucial to remember that willpower and self-control are unsatisfying and unsustainable. Why? Because every habit, at its core, has a reward, a satisfying outcome that fulfils a craving. Trying to merely suppress a craving without addressing its root or replacing the habit with something equally satisfying is a recipe for frustration and, ultimately, failure.

Habits start as conscious decisions but eventually transition to subconscious actions, effortlessly integrated into our daily routines. Dr Brian Wansink (a professor of consumer behaviour) reveals that we make around 200 food-related decisions daily, with 90% happening subconsciously. They are, in essence, food habits.

In his transformative book *Atomic Habits*, James Clear explains the power of habit formation: it offloads tasks from the conscious to the subconscious mind, preserving our mental bandwidth for more critical tasks. This is the magic of habits. They reduce cognitive load, freeing up mental space for other essential aspects of life.

A habit has three stages: cue, action, and reward (CAR). Once the cue has been activated, even the anticipation of the reward is often enough to trigger a craving. If the reward doesn't materialise, the craving intensifies. Ingrained in our survival instincts, this mechanism ensures that we seek out what is beneficial or enjoyable. Creating new eating habits is about making conscious choices and forming new routines. As numerous studies suggest, the most effective way to do this is to have a plan. Understanding the reward — the perceived pleasure driving your eating habits — is crucial. By analysing your habits, you can transform your relationship with food.

Here's a fascinating tidbit: The uniformity of packed foods and fast-food chains isn't coincidental. They standardise their branding and architecture to serve as consistent cues to trigger eating habits. Their foods are engineered to deliver immediate, consistent rewards. This is the cue-action-reward loop in action, manipulated to keep you returning.

In conclusion, a habit begins with a cue that often triggers a craving, leading to an action that provides a reward. This reward becomes associated with the cue, completing the neurological feedback loop. Does that make sense? When replacing an action within this loop, ensure the replacement is enjoyable, easily accessible, and provides a comparable reward. Over time, cues often fade into the background, becoming automatic. Swiss psychiatrist and psychoanalyst Carl Jung wisely noted, 'Until you make the unconscious conscious, it will direct your life, and you will call it fate.'

Your Personal Habit Loop Charts

In the appendix, you'll discover a valuable resource: the Habit Loop Charts. These charts were meticulously crafted for participants of my 49-day online Health Reset course, designed to empower participants to better their habits. Let's explore how you can leverage these charts to gain insights into your current habits and pave the way for transformative change.

Analysing Your Current Habits

The first set of charts serves as a mirror to reflect on your existing habits. Picture this: whenever you indulge in something you now recognise as unhealthy and wish you hadn't, these charts become your compass. Here's how to use them effectively:

Identify the Cue: What triggered the consumption of the unhealthy item? Was it stress, time of day, boredom, or something else?
Document the Action: What did you eat or consume in response to the cue?
Analyse the Reward: What immediate gratification did you feel? Was it a momentary pleasure, a distraction from discomfort, or something else?
Evaluate the Result: Hours later, how did you feel physically, mentally, and emotionally? Did the action align with your long-term purpose?

Take your time with this analysis, immersing yourself in the details. Remember, every habit follows the same pattern: cue - action - reward.

Creating New Habits with Conscious Intent

Next, focus on the 'NEW Habit Loop Analysis' charts. Once you've become adept at documenting your old habits, these charts become your canvas for consciously shaping new food decisions. Here, you're recording how you feel and capturing the tangible results of your empowered choices.

Embrace the opportunity to infuse these charts with rich detail, vividly depicting your journey towards healthier habits. With each entry, you're not just documenting progress; you're sculpting a new way of living that aligns with your aspirations for vitality and wellbeing.

So, grab your pen and let the Habit Loop Charts become your trusted companions on the path to a healthier, more fulfilling life. Celebrate every step forward as you rewrite the script of your habits for a brighter tomorrow.

Navigating Habit Transformation: Insights from my Journey

Drawing from my experiences as a steadfast creature of habit with a somewhat addictive personality, where my thirties and forties were generously sprinkled with extra stones (the weight variety), I've traversed through a web of habits, encountering some remarkably resilient ones along the way. It's been an expedition of self-discovery, complete with detours and dead ends, leading me to a handful of enduring insights. So, consider me your somewhat roundabout guide in pursuing habit transformation. Here's to sidestepping the potholes I've stumbled into and streamlining your path to change with these seven nuggets of wisdom, each a stepping stone towards reshaping your daily rituals.

Embrace Authentic Desire: If the thought of a new habit makes you groan with an obligatory 'I Should' it's time to find an alternative replacement. A proper habit shouldn't seem like a tedious task.
Seek Joy, Not Austerity: You've missed the mark if your new habit feels like a self-imposed exile from joy. Actual habit change doesn't thrive on deprivation; it blossoms in the joy of new, positive experiences. Give up-giving up! Instead, foster a feeling of escaping something, not giving it up.
Cherish Instant Rewards: The promise of future benefits is fine, but the power of immediate gratification is undeniable. Make sure your new habits offer instant rewards, lighting up your day.
Genuine Rewards are Key: Don't try to fool yourself with faux rewards. Your brain's reward system is smarter than you think. It craves authenticity, not make-believe treats.
Outsmart Convenience: Your old habits love the easy path. Turn the tables by making these old patterns a logistical headache while paving a smooth road for your new, healthier habits.
Plan B is Your Best Friend: Life is unpredictable. Craft alternative routes and strategies for when your preferred path is blocked. A solid Plan B keeps you on track, no matter the detours life throws your way.
Follow Relapses with Recovery: Each time you succumb to an old habit, don't allow the disappointment to derail you. Recognise that relapses can happen and return to recovery mode quickly. See relapses as a learning experience, not a failure.

To truly break free from the chains of old habits, it's imperative to shift your self-perception. Your belief in your capacity for change is the most potent catalyst for transformation. Remember, your identity is a tapestry woven from the threads of your actions, many of which are habits. In *Atomic Habits*, James Clear eloquently captures this: 'True behaviour change is identity change.'

As we travel through life, perfection should never be the destination. Embrace the beautiful chaos of the passage, the 'perfect imperfections' that make life unique. A minor misstep isn't a derailment but part of the adventure. High achievers know this well: strive for excellence, not flawlessness. In the quest for perfection, remember the wise words from the iconic film Top Gun: seeking perfection is often a 'Highway to the Danger Zone.' Aim for high performance, understanding that the occasional slip is not a catastrophe but a stepping stone on your path to success.

As we bid adieu, remember that your future brims with potential, ready to be unlocked by the power of well-crafted habits. Step confidently into tomorrow, knowing that every choice and habit is a brick in the foundation of the vibrant, fulfilling life you're building.

Mastering The Art Of Convenient Healthy Living

In today's fast-paced world, convenience plays a pivotal role in shaping our dietary habits, impacting our health both positively and negatively. While it's easy to fall into the trap of discussing the downsides of our quest for quick and easy meals, let's shift our focus towards harnessing the power of convenience to enhance our wellness. The key to transforming our relationship with food lies not in a battle of willpower but in understanding and adapting our fuel sources.

Consider this: before reading this book, and possibly still today, your body operated as a sugar-fuelled entity. Accustomed to burning sugar for energy, your body naturally gravitated towards quick fixes, those snacks laden with sugar. The alluring pastry from Greggs, or the deceptive energy burst from a foot-long Subway sandwich. The allure of a pack of crisps or a fizzy drink for that instant sugar hit was or may still be hard to resist. But here's the thing. Just as cars signal when it's time to refuel with petrol, our bodies respond to their perceived needs based on available fuel sources.

However, the analogy doesn't end there. The convenience engineered by food companies, tempting as it is, aligns more with filling up on the wrong type of fuel rather than what truly nourishes us. Imagine if, instead of reaching for that quick carb fix, we could refuel with something that sustains us longer and supports our health—like pulling into a station not for petrol but for a boost of nutrient-rich broccoli or a satisfying mix of unsalted nuts.

This section is dedicated to reimagining convenience in the context of healthy living. It's about recognising that our 'fuel system' can indeed be upgraded from sugar dependency to one that thrives on wholesome, nourishing foods. As we turn the pages of this transformative adventure, embracing the *Fibre First* diet, you're on the brink of becoming what we affectionately term 'metabolically flexible'. Picture yourself as the ultimate hybrid vehicle—capable of efficiently running on either sugar or fat. It's akin to having the eco-friendly option to run on electric power, which is splendid for your chassis and Mother Earth. Yet, for sheer convenience, we've all been guilty of opting for the petrol option for more times than we'd care to admit!

Upon completing this book, your food choices will become deliberate acts of consciousness, not impulsive grabs driven by cravings. Despite this newfound enlightenment, your inner Gremlin, the one with a sweet tooth, may still whisper sugary nothings in your ear. But fear not! The reprogramming and neural rewiring you're undergoing ensures that your intellect and future inner wisdom steer you towards choices that bolster your freedom, health, and genuine joy rather than fleeting sugary highs.

Yet, as you take the reins of your dietary destiny, be warned: the titans of the processed food realm won't take kindly to losing a loyal subject. As our collective march towards dietary emancipation gains momentum, these corporate Goliaths will double down on their efforts to lure us back with the song of convenience.

But here's where the plot gets tastier! Once you're aware of the omnipresence of junk food, much like suddenly noticing a specific car model everywhere after a friend buys one, you'll see processed temptations at every turn. It's almost as if these fast-food empires are personally challenging you, lining up their most tempting offerings like soldiers at the gates of your dietary resolve. Yet, fear not, for I'm about to arm you with an arsenal of fibre-filled conveniences that make healthy eating not just easy but irresistibly enjoyable.

Imagine your kitchen stocked with quick, wholesome snacks that laugh in the face of processed temptations: crisp apple slices with almond butter, vibrant veggie sticks with hummus, or a handful of mixed nuts seasoned with your favourite spices. These are your quick fuel stops, your clean energy that powers you through the day without a hitch.

And for those moments when the Gremlin's whispers grow louder, you'll have an array of delicious, fibre-rich responses at your fingertips. These convenient, nutritious options are your culinary shield against the onslaught of empty calories.

As we forge ahead, transforming convenience from a pitfall into a pillar of our health journey, let's revel in the knowledge that every fibre-rich choice we make is a step towards metabolic flexibility, a victory for our health, and a defiant stand against the processed food empire. Let the revolution begin—one delicious, fibre-filled snack at a time!

The Two-Phase Playbook For Foodie Freedom

Living a healthier lifestyle doesn't mean we have to forsake the call of convenience—it's all about redefining it with a sprinkle of zest and a dash of real food. Let's face it: navigating the world of nutritious eating can often feel like trying to solve a Rubik's cube blindfolded. But fear not, for I have a two-phase strategy that's as satisfying as finding that last piece of chocolate in the box—without the guilt!

Phase One: The Convenience Crusade

In the initial stages of our journey, convenience is king. However, we're not talking about the kind of convenience that leaves you feeling like a contestant on a cooking show where everything goes wrong. Instead, we're crafting a convenience that's all about guilt-free, grab-and-go goodness. Picture this: you're as metabolically flexible as a yoga instructor, seamlessly switching between fuel sources without a hiccup. And while you may occasionally hear the call of the sugar siren, you're equipped with an arsenal of tasty, fibre-rich alternatives that are as easy to reach as the remote control.

During this phase, it's all about having your cake (metaphorically speaking) and eating it too. Healthy biscuits and home-roasted nuts become your new best friends, ready at a moment's notice.

Phase Two: Savouring the Sweet Taste of Victory

As you graduate to phase two, you'll find yourself in a serene state of metabolic flexibility—capable of going all day on a single meal without so much as a grumble from your stomach. Whether you're an OMAD (One Meal a Day) aficionado or a three-meals-a-day traditionalist, the choice is yours, and it's all about what tickles your taste buds while keeping you on the path to vitality.

This is where the magic happens: as you pass by fast food joints, you'll find yourself offering a smug smile rather than salivating, knowing their greasy grasp no longer holds sway over your dietary decisions. You've transformed into a culinary Houdini, escaping the chains of processed temptations with the ease of a seasoned escape artist.

But let's circle back to phase one for a moment, where the battle lines are drawn in the kitchen. It's here that we arm ourselves with convenient, healthful delights that don't just satisfy hunger but tantalise the taste buds. From spicing up store-bought nuts to crafting your own snack masterpieces from scratch, the goal is clear: make healthy eating so convenient and delightful that your Gremlin throws in the towel and joins you in a chorus of 'Kale yeah!'

So, from the land of convenience to the realm of conscious, joyful eating, let's embrace the adventure with a smile. After all, who knew that the road to health could be paved with homemade treats, culinary creativity, and the sweet victory of turning our backs on the fast-food fray? Here's to making healthy living not just convenient but utterly irresistible!

To kickstart your journey through phase one, here are 10 straightforward snacks that are both handy and healthful. And before you even venture into the kitchen, remember you can simply purchase nuts and seeds ready to go. Our free Health Results app provides detailed information on each, making following the *Fibre First* diet easy and enjoyable. We've touched on some of these in exploring 20 ideas designed to enhance your fibre intake. These snacks are not just about satisfying hunger; they're stepping stones to a lifestyle rich in nutrition and vitality:

Homemade flaxseed biscuits: High in fibre, omega 3, magnesium, iron, zinc and a great source of protein, these biscuits are super easy to make. I often batch cook on a Sunday; they stay fresh for 3 or 4 days. It's one of the most popular recipes on my app.

Energy balls: The no-bake, low-carb cousin of granola and protein bars. They're easy to make and combine several high-fibre ingredients like nuts or nut butter, seeds, and chia seeds.

Popcorn: I can't quite believe I'm saying this, but popcorn is one of the best snack options for weight loss (but not the cinema type) due to its high-fibre content. It's only beneficial when it's air-popped and lightly seasoned. Add spices, herbs, and seasonings to ramp up the flavour.

Kale Crisps: Transform your kale into a crispy delight by roasting it with a sprinkle of salt. Keep a watchful eye to prevent charred disappointments. In just 20 minutes, they turn into a snack you can't resist.

Herbed Nuts: Venture to the baking aisle for VAT-free, chemical-free nuts. Toss them in olive or coconut oil, sprinkle with salt, pepper, and your choice of herbs, and roast for a harmonious blend of flavours in just 20 minutes.

Carrot Fries: Cut carrots into thin strips, toss with olive oil and your much-loved spices, then roast until crispy. A veggie-packed twist on a fast-food favourite.

Edamame Delight: Steam edamame and sprinkle with sea salt. It's a protein-packed snack that's both fun to eat and good for you.

Berry Frozen Yogurt Bites: Mix berries into Greek yoghurt, spoon onto a tray, and freeze. These frosty bites are perfect for a hot day or when you need a creamy treat.

Spiced Pumpkin Seeds: At Halloween, don't throw out the seeds. Toss them in olive oil, garlic powder, and smoked paprika. Roast for a crunchy snack packed with minerals. Most other seeds are also great for convenient snacking.

Smoothies: They aren't just for breakfast; they make great snacks, too. You can easily add lots of high-fibre ingredients like berries, peanut butter, vegetables, greens and chia seeds. Prepare them in the morning before work or school and add them to a flask to keep cool

The Truth Behind Why Diets Fail: They Don't Replace The Reward

The fundamental flaw in traditional dieting lies not in its execution but in its premise. Diets falter, not because they lack structure or rigour, but because they fail to address the root cause of our dietary dilemmas. It's not a battle of the bulge we're fighting; it's a complex tangle of biological, hormonal, and neurological challenges. This isn't about counting calories or summoning willpower; it's about understanding the intricate dance of hormones within our bodies and the neural pathways that dictate our eating habits. The real battleground is in the mind, not the stomach; the hormones, not the calories, hold the key.

Diets often end in frustration and rebound weight gain because they cast us into a world of deprivation. And let's be honest: Who aspires to a lifetime of feeling deprived? True, sustainable weight loss and the joy of learning new, healthier food choices come from an entirely different approach. Success lies in discovering foods that not only nourish but also satisfy and reward us on a level that rivals the fleeting pleasures of our former indulgences.

True transformation and lasting change are only possible when these new habits not only meet but exceed the levels of satisfaction we previously derived from less healthy choices. This heightened sense of fulfilment is the cornerstone of lasting dietary change, cementing new learnings and guiding us towards a healthier, happier lifestyle.

Conscious vs Subconscious Decisions

Humans break the mould compared to other species thanks to our dual-core processing unit: the conscious and subconscious mind. The conscious mind gets all the limelight, and rightly so, as it's where we do our daytime thinking: solving puzzles, making plans, and getting irked when our coffee machine decides to join the dark side. It's where we proudly figure out that 2 plus 2 equals 4, set our lofty goals, and where we're supposed to be the captain of the ship, steering through the iceberg-laden waters of daily life.

Then there's the subconscious mind, the unsung hero that believes in fairy tales because, bless it, it doesn't know how to doubt. Picture it as the mind's wide-eyed child, absorbing everything from before we even enter the world. It's like a sponge, soaking up laughs, tears, and the melodrama of human expressions without a shred of cynicism. It's incredibly impressionable during our tender years, mainly because the human brain at this stage is more playdough than a fortress. This part of the mind is so sensitive that it can go from being delighted to throwing the mother of all tantrums in aisle five of the supermarket, all because it records everything unfiltered and stamps it as gospel truth. And voilà, just like that, your belief system is set up in childhood, ready to navigate the choppy seas of adulthood with a map drawn in crayon.

This part of the show doesn't get a season finale; it sticks around, quietly directing the drama behind the scenes. Most of us are blissfully unaware of its influence until we find ourselves on a therapist's couch, profoundly diving into why we do what we do. Have you ever found yourself wondering why certain feelings ambush you or why you act in ways that leave you scratching your head? Chances are, it's your subconscious pulling the strings, running the backstage of your life's theatre without involvement from your conscious.

Now, if you're pondering, 'Why on earth didn't I catch on to this sooner?', take comfort in knowing you're in good company. Most people don't know about the subconscious narratives scripting their lives. Crafted in the early years, your subconscious mind houses the master plan of your existence. But here's the issue: as you strut confidently into your teens and your conscious mind begins to flex its muscles, dreaming big dreams and setting high bars, it remains unwittingly tethered to the deep-seated beliefs that are now part of the subconscious furniture.

This explains the enigma of why, despite knowing better, you find yourself reaching for sweets, crisps, chocolate bars, or a glass of whiskey with the danger label flashing in neon. Your conscious mind is about achieving that sleek silhouette, gasping less on the stairs, and slipping into those skinny jeans you've been optimistically hoarding. Meanwhile, your subconscious has sprinkled these forbidden fruits with emotional fairy dust, embedding them so deeply into your belief system that resistance feels futile.

Unbeknownst to you, your subconscious is essentially having a meltdown, demanding ice cream with the intensity of a toddler in full meltdown mode. It cranks up the pressure, morphing from a whisper of 'I want' to the roar of 'I NEED,' amplifying its demands the more you try to stand your ground. And all the while, you're none the wiser to this inner conflict. Beginning to connect the dots on why healthy living feels like an uphill battle? It's not you; it's the silent screenplay written by your subconscious.

But here's the good news: Just as DNA serves as the blueprint for our genetic makeup, with the potential for modification through epigenetics—adding layers atop our genes—we can architect new narratives over our subconscious scripts. To outwit our conscious selves and rewrite the story, we must understand different brain areas' nuanced roles.

I'm about to hand you the keys to your subconscious, equipping you with the savvy to pause, ponder, and pivot from its hidden influences. Picture yourself as a mental ninja, armed with an arsenal of strategies to delve deep into your subconscious, tweaking those beliefs that have set up roadblocks on your path to the life you yearn for. I'm not suggesting a life devoid of ice cream—far from it. I guarantee, however, that every food choice from here on out will be a deliberate decision you make at the helm, not some autopilot setting dictated by your subconscious.

Imagine this: your conscious brain, honing its skills to detect the whispers of the subconscious, learning to pause its narratives, then taking charge. It's about cultivating a belief in the potential, believing in the not yet seen, and embracing faith in your ability to shape your reality. Awareness of your subconscious and mastering the art of interruption and management is your ticket to true liberation. Only then can you claim the freedom to steer your life toward your dreams.

Desire Better Health? Better Manage Your Gremlin

Setting out to tame your subconscious might echo a tale from a fanciful storybook. Yet, it is an essential chapter in the narrative of better health and fostering a harmonious relationship with food. Despite being armed to the teeth with nutritional insights, there dwells within you a sly character, which I dub your 'Gremlin', a playful homage to the hormone ghrelin. This little trickster, once stirred, can lead you on a wild chase of hunger pangs and cravings that seem almost insurmountable. If you are familiar with Prof. Steve Peters' *The Chimp Paradox*, you'll recognise some of the upcoming concepts.

Imagine your brain as a bustling metropolis, brimming with activity and pathways. These aren't mere roads but neural pathways that guide your decision-making from indulgent feasting at the metaphorical all-you-can-eat buffet to the thoughtful consideration found on mindful eating street. This city within your head isn't a monolith but a vibrant mix of diverse districts, each with its own character and purpose. In our journey through this cerebral cityscape, we focus on two principal districts: the dynamic, emotion-rich limbic area and the sophisticated, reflective prefrontal cortex, positioned in a prime location just behind your forehead.

Imagine your brain as an epic narrative, with the limbic system starring as the seasoned lead, a stalwart of aeons, piloting primal impulses such as hunger, emotions, and survival instincts. This innate guide, primed for the 'feast today for we might starve tomorrow' way of life, is indispensable; without it, our story would have concluded before it even began.

Then comes the prefrontal cortex, the brain's innovative force, a recent addition in evolutionary terms, which developed later because our ancient ancestors didn't require its complex functionalities. Initially, survival depended more on immediate reactions and less on intricate planning or social intricacies. This advanced region emerged as our lifestyles and societies became more complex, necessitating foresight, strategy, and enhanced social cooperation.

The prefrontal cortex focuses on the finesse of long-term strategising and social nuances. Picture it as the brain's penthouse suite, where future feasts are thoughtfully curated, and memories are archived for nostalgia and strategic deployment. This segment of the brain is akin to the latest tech gadget: sleek, formidable, and capable of marvels that its predecessors could hardly envisage. It's what distinguishes us from our fellow creatures, enabling us to ponder the cosmos, craft symphonies, and organise our diets via digital platforms.

The narrative of excess weight is thus a saga of internal conflict, with the old-school gambits of the primal brain often eclipsing the sophisticated tactics of the prefrontal cortex. Our limbic system is anchored in bygone days, persuaded that every meal could be our last, propelling us to indulge as though we're still foragers on the savannah rather than consumers navigating the grocery aisle.

The key to sustainable weight loss and a wholesome food relationship is mending the communication rift between these two cerebral domains. It's about elevating the dialogue from basic impulses to thoughtful discourse, ensuring the prefrontal cortex gains the upper hand, or more aptly, the leading neuron.

Keeping your prefrontal cortex in prime condition is akin to fine-tuning a high-performance machine. The correct nutrients, particularly healthy fats and oils, can supercharge it, while the wrong types, like those in processed and fast foods, can clog its operations, leaving the limbic system in charge and driving your dietary choices off the rails. Sidestepping ultra-processed foods, securing ample sleep, engaging in suitable exercise, and managing stress form the support team that keeps the prefrontal cortex in optimal shape. This allows it to make informed, healthful decisions and to assert control over the limbic system with a gentle yet firm grip.

The challenge lies in transitioning the brain's command centre from the limbic system to the prefrontal cortex, empowering us to traverse our world of plenty with intellect, not mere instinct. By doing so, we can turn the leaf on our primal past and pen a fresh chapter for our wellbeing, where the enlightened brain must take charge, guiding us through the grocery aisles and beyond with knowledge and consciousness.

The crux of our discussion is this: The primal brain secured our survival against ancient threats, yet in today's complex world, our human brain must be fully engaged to tackle modern challenges.

A quick recap before we move on: Your human brain organises your consciousness, thoughts and calculations. We've discovered that neurotransmitters, like dopamine and serotonin, regulate our pleasure and happiness. We've also learned that our actions are driven either consciously or subconsciously. Echoing Dr Brian Wansink, we face around 200 food-related decisions daily, with 90% made without conscious thought. Beyond neurotransmitters, we have discussed how the hardwiring of your limbic brain urges you to consume as much as possible, while a chorus of hormones also seeks to influence your choices.

Brain psychology is a hugely complex subject that no scientist has a complete handle on. And in some ways, it's a blessing that they don't; otherwise, the food and tech companies could own us completely! But while it is complex, what follows is going to really give you a solid understanding of what goes on in your brain and why you do the things you do. It will help you put the previous learning to use and set the foundation for seeking more happiness than pleasure. It will also help you break old habits and create new ones.

While there are many different areas of the brain, all with their own functions, we will concentrate on just three. These three areas make up the psychological mind and shape your food decisions. They are the frontal cortex and the limbic, which I have already mentioned, and one more, the parietal (pronounced *puh-rie-uh-tl*). We will borrow a couple of comparisons from the *Chimp Paradox* here:

- The frontal cortex, which we will call your 'Intelligent Brain', is the essence of who you are.
- Let's dub the limbic system 'the Gremlin.'
- Your parietal cortex, 'The Computer', completes the trio.

Your intelligent brain is rational and makes rational decisions but is slow to act. While he is mischievous and often gets things wrong, your Gremlin is super-fast. It has to be, as your Gremlin looks after fight, flight, and freeze. Without his speedy decisions, you wouldn't have run from the lion, fought off the bore, or froze in front of the deadly bear.

Today, your Gremlin is helpful at stopping you from stepping out in front of the bus and not much else. Have you ever thought about why first impressions count or why you judge a book by its cover? Because your limbic, your Gremlin had to go with first impressions to survive. Yes, first impressions really count for survival. Is that snake going to kill me, or am I going to kill it for dinner? Pretty important, hey, first impressions.

It's no good wondering, deliberating, and pondering to see if the lion wants to eat you or whether the snake is poisonous. It's a do-or-die decision. It's the do-or-die part of the brain, but only in the immediate scenario.

For this reason, motivation is an action of the Gremlin because it needs to be motivated to act immediately. I will explain later why I mention motivation and our Gremlin, it's an important point, but I want to seed the idea for now. Your Gremlin is not only super-fast to act but also very emotional. I want you to see your Gremlin as a pet. You are not responsible for the nature of your

Gremlin, but are you responsible for managing him? I promise this will all make more sense as we progress.

Your Gremlin, like a pet, is highly emotional. It doesn't think like your intelligent brain, and occasionally, that's a good thing. It might save your life one day, but sometimes, in fact, most of the time in the modern world, especially for food, your Gremlin is disastrous.

Let me give you a non-food example. In a store, you see a dress or a shirt, and your Gremlin emotionally falls in love with it; he really wants it. You try it on, and his emotions get stronger and stronger, and he loves how you look in it. His emotions begin to dream about the comments you will get from your friends. Then you look at the price tag, and gosh, it's five times more expensive than you expected. It's not actually from the 60% off rail you thought it was from. So now your Intelligent Brain kicks in and says, 'No, no – I can't afford it.' And let's say you can't – but then Gremlin says, 'But I want it!' And acts childlike and has tantrums when it doesn't get its own way. And you know what that's like, I am sure. If it's happened to you, it's an awful fight, right? What tends to happen? I bet you might give in. Let's leave that thought there and not see how it plays out just yet.

While the two facets of your brain, the Intellectual and the Gremlin, can sometimes coexist peacefully, they clash more often than not. Each believes it could steer your life solo. As our world becomes progressively safer, where accidents are less frequent and diseases less deadly, even in a post-COVID era, we might argue that we could manage without the Gremlin. Yet, life would undoubtedly lose much of its spice and excitement without this mischievous companion.

Back to pleasure vs happiness. Your Gremlin is always seeking pleasure. Without him/her, no sex. No human race. It was in your brain before you were born, but it is not you.

You are the Intelligent Brain. Let me repeat this because it is crucial. Your Gremlin developed before you were born, but it is not you. You are the Intelligent brain. This is part of the reason that I keep telling you that being overweight is not your fault; it's in part your Gremlin's fault, and it's your primal brain being so well developed. Those who are obese would have been awesome 30,000 years ago; you would probably have been head of a tribe and certainly would have lived longer than average.

As I just said, your limbic, your Gremlin, is like a pet. While you can't be held accountable for every one of its whims, how you handle it falls squarely on your shoulders. Imagine, if you will, having a large dog. It might overpower you physically, making it all the more crucial to understand and wisely manage. Mastering the art of Gremlin management is akin to uncovering one of life's great secrets to happiness, ensuring it neither turns on you nor unleashes havoc.

This means getting to grips with the nuances of your Gremlin's personality: recognising when it's trying to assert dominance, causing a ruckus, or making demands like a dog incessantly barking for attention. When this happens, it's time to engage your Intelligent Brain in a lively debate with your Gremlin, using logic and persuasive reasoning to keep it in check.

Now, within the psychological sector of the brain, essentially the arena where any mental or emotional processing occurs, there lies the third critical area: the parietal, which we have named 'The Computer'. This component functions much like its namesake, devoid of independent thought and reliant on programming by either the Gremlin or the Intelligent Brain. It is a vast data repository, its content gathered by either your Gremlin's impulsive directives or your Intelligent Brain's deliberate considerations.

The significance of The Computer lies in its ability to ease the cognitive load on your Gremlin and Intelligent Brain, automating processes and embedding habits, such as those subconscious food choices we often make without a second thought. The Computer fulfils a secondary function as an invaluable reference library, offering data support when the Gremlin and Intelligent Brain find themselves at loggerheads.

In our exploration of habits, the emphasis was placed on cues, actions, rewards, and your internal dialogue. This dialogue, in essence, is a negotiation between your Gremlin and your Intelligent Brain, highlighting the importance of recognising when your Gremlin attempts to override your thoughts.

Understanding who is currently steering your food choices is crucial. Acknowledging the presence of two distinct cognitive forces within you is vital, yet only one truly represents your conscious self.

Should you find yourself reaching for a biscuit without conscious thought, only to realise its presence as it touches your lips, it's likely that neither the Gremlin nor the Intelligent Brain was at the helm. Instead, The Computer acted on an old command from your Gremlin.

Professor Steve Peters says, *'You and your chimp [what we call Gremlin] think in very different ways. As we go about our day, receiving information from around us, they both receive the same input but interpret it differently'.* The Gremlin interprets it with feelings and impressions. Everything is based on emotional thinking. With emotional thinking, the Gremlin often fills in blanks or makes assumptions. It has hunches and, at times, feels paranoid. It has gut feelings, sometimes right, sometimes wrong. But because it also has to deal with *fight or flight*, it is always quick to react.

Your Gremlin often embodies the essence of unpredictability, irrational, unstable, and inconsistent. It operates not on the basis of hard facts but on its own perception of truth; proof is unnecessary. Such immediacy is crucial in a world where hesitation could mean the difference between survival and death. In contrast, your intelligent brain is the seeker of facts, always striving to uncover the truth. This quest, naturally, requires time; it deliberates and rationalises every decision, employing logical thought and often devising a strategic plan.

But what ensues when these two forces collide? As previously noted, the Gremlin possesses a more formidable force, often seizing the reins of your thoughts and actions. Recognising these moments of intrusion and implementing strategies to reclaim control is crucial, and that's precisely what we will look at now.

At times, you must engage in a stern dialogue, asserting, 'Gremlin, regardless of your feelings, we're proceeding with this plan,' or 'It matters not that you're disinclined to walk; we're doing it regardless, and any objections can be addressed post-event.'

Be wary of your Gremlin's child-like tantrums, the incessant 'I need it! I need it!' On these occasions, a firm stance is essential. Inform your Gremlin, 'You don't need it; it's mere want and not on the agenda. Instead, this is what's happening.' It's about conveying the message, 'You chase fleeting pleasure, but I seek lasting happiness. You crave the taste, but I yearn to see my abs.'

Navigating this tumultuous relationship requires a blend of firmness, strategy, and the occasional complicated conversation, steering you and your Gremlin towards a harmonious existence where happiness, not just immediate gratification, is the ultimate goal.

Beyond its pivotal role in fight, flight, freeze responses, procreation, and staving off starvation, it's clear the Gremlin often acts as a relentless bother in our modern existence. If we were to distil its essence into a single word, it would unequivocally be 'survival.' Yet, in today's world, the necessity of such a primitive force has drastically diminished.

Consider this: while deeply emotional, motivation is essentially a sandbox for the Gremlin. That's precisely why depending on motivation for weight loss often leads to disappointment; it stimulates those parts of the brain that we'd rather keep silent when faced with decisions about what to eat. Can you see how this aligns with your experience? This revelation underscores why motivation and willpower frequently fail to be reliable allies in weight loss endeavours.

The battle with your Gremlin is constant, ready to exploit any moment of vulnerability with an emotional jab, such as, 'See, that didn't work. I knew it wouldn't. Now, hand over that doughnut, you idiot.' And yes, in moments of frustration, Gremlins are known to indulge in a bit of colourful language.

Contrastingly, commitment stems from the Intelligent Brain. Here's a clever manoeuvre to outwit your Gremlin. Proclaim your intentions to others. Doing so increases your likelihood of following through, as it appeals to your Gremlin's aversion to embarrassment and deep-seated concern for others' perceptions. While it may resent the Intelligent Brain internally, it understands the importance of presenting a united front to the outside world.

Here's a critical insight that could revolutionise your approach to stress and its dietary temptations. When stress hits, thinking gets muddled because your Gremlin switches into survival mode, fight, flight, or freeze. I believe this is why I instinctively reach for a glass of wine to unwind, while others might crave sugar. The trick lies in recognising that this urge for a drink or sweet treat is your Gremlin's emotional plea. The solution? A moment of pause. Take a deep deliberate breath through your nose, not your mouth, to detach from the immediate stressor. Then, pivot to your alternative strategy, Plan B, cultivated from forming new habits, guiding you towards an automatic, healthier response.

Here's the strategy I propose:

Spot the Gremlin's Influence: Awareness and acknowledging when your Gremlin is pulling the strings will help strengthen your resolve and choices.

Quick Trigger Word: Since your Gremlin operates at lightning speed, arm yourself with a swift mental counter like '*fibre first*,' 'primal,' or even whimsical words such as 'banana,' 'balls,' or 'new me' to snap back control.

Pause and Breathe: Halt and breathe deeply to regain composure.

Switch to Plan B: Implement your backup plan - your new healthier habit.

Celebrate Your Triumph: Reward yourself with a smile, a laugh, or even a moment of smug satisfaction for overcoming the temptation.

To simplify it further, consider **AIM**, Awareness, Interrupt, and Manage. Then, FIRE! Awareness is the first step; by recognising the manipulations and tantrums of our subconscious Gremlin, we pave the way for transforming our relationship with food.

In my 49-Day Health Reset Course, a unique tool I offer subscribers in their welcome pack is three rubber wristbands. The advice is simple: wear them daily, and whenever you feel your Gremlin trying to take charge, give the band a gentle pull so it snaps against your wrist. This physical cue interrupts the Gremlin, carving out space for your Intelligent Brain to step in and steer the ship.

Turn page ›

Limbic	Pre Frontal Cortex
Your Gremlin	Your Intelligent Brain
Primitive Brain	Developed Brain
Survival focused. Fight, Flight or Freeze	Not survival focused. Calculates decisions
Quick to react	Takes time to process
Seeks pleasure & reward	Seeks happiness – purpose - meaning – self-fulfillment
Emotional	Rational – Your Jiminy Cricket
Black & white - harsh	Many shades, balanced judgement
Gut feel	Fact based
Instinct	Searches for truth - evidence
Child-like	Adult–like
Ego – alpha-male	Societal – Team player

Let's travel further into the fascinating world of our brain, a marvel of nature composed of billions of neurons. These nerve cells are not just any cells; they're social butterflies, engaging in constant chatter across an intricate network that spans the entirety of our brain. When these neurons form a clique based on similar functions, they're known as a nucleus, showcasing the brain's knack for teamwork.

Thanks to the wonders of PET scans, scientists can now play voyeurs to our brain's activities. By tracking blood flow, they observe how different brain regions throw a light show, glowing with activity when we gaze upon various foods or objects. It's as if our brain is hosting its own little party, reacting vividly to visual stimuli in real-time.

Within this neural soiree, three main pathways are critical in brain communication, each linking distinct brain regions that handle diverse tasks.

The first VIP pathway revolves around rewards and pleasure, primarily facilitated by the red-carpet travel of dopamine. Imagine dopamine as the brain's own telegram service, a neurotransmitter delivering messages of motivation, desire, and learning. This pathway teaches us the allure of shopping, the sweetness of sugar, the buzz from booze, and the thrill of sex.

When dopamine delivers its message, it triggers the release of another neurochemical, akin to the brain's version of morphine. Dr Robert Lustig eloquently describes these as endogenous opioid peptides (EOPs), natural painkillers that mimic the blissful effects of morphine and heroin, bathing our brain in waves of pleasure.

The second pathway is the scenic route to happiness and contentment, where serotonin gently meanders, carrying communiqués of wellbeing and satisfaction.

The third and final pathway navigates the stormy seas of stress and fear, marked by the flutter of cortisol, the stress hormone, through your Fight, Flight, or Freeze (FFF) response.

These pathways are the conductors of the brain's symphony, orchestrating a wide range of human emotions, particularly those tied to reward, pleasure, and happiness. Understanding these pathways illuminates the science of our brains and the art of our emotions, revealing the intricate ballet that influences our every feeling and decision.

Alright, the brain biology lesson is over. Let's pivot back to our cheeky Gremlin, and here's where things get a tad unconventional. We're about to adopt a bit of a dual-minded strategy with our Gremlin and Intelligent Brain. Now, I know comparing anything to schizophrenia, a genuinely challenging condition, can raise eyebrows. But hear me out: the battle against chronic illness and obesity is no less dire, so I'm borrowing this metaphor to drive home the point. Your Gremlin is hankering for that junk food fix, while your Intelligent Brain is staunchly saying no. The crux of the matter? Indecision. It turns out not even your Gremlin likes being bossed around.

When it's time to negotiate with your Gremlin, as Oonagh Duncan vividly illustrates in her book, *Healthy as F*ck*, she invites us to confront our internal doubletalk head-on. She introduces what she calls the 'anti-bullshit artillery,' with step two being the break-up speech. It's about crafting those decisive words you'll use to stand up to your Gremlin's nonsense the next time it tries to cosy up and derail you. Her advice? Be gentle yet unwaveringly firm. Much like breaking up with an ex, your language needs a clear, direct message from you to understand it's really over. Then, march forward with your new habit, regardless.

Our bodies are factories of chemicals, enzymes, hormones, and neurotransmitters, all rallying to satisfy the Gremlin's whims. Honesty with yourself is paramount. If you veer off course and indulge in a snack that's a step away from your purpose, don't weave tales to justify it. Instead, have a frank chat with your Gremlin, acknowledging the slip but making it clear it's a one-off concession.

Deceiving yourself not only muddies the waters between your Intelligent Brain and your Gremlin but also throws your internal 'Computer' into a state of disarray. Truthfulness, on the other hand, preserves your health and nurtures your burgeoning habits rather than letting them wither. The slippery slope of self-deception is perilously easy to slide down, becoming as habitual as the habits you're trying to replace.

Oonagh brilliantly highlights the seductive nature of self-deception, pointing out how it lulls us into the comfortable embrace of what's familiar, allowing us to dodge the discomfort that comes with growth. At the moment, it feels like the 'best damn idea,' but deep down, we know it's a mistake, much like the pang of regret after rekindling an old romance with an ex. This very act of self-deception keeps us stuck, anchored to old habits and patterns we're trying to escape. Oonaghs' three-step mantra: 1. Spot the Bullshit. 2. Deliver that kind but firm breakup speech. 3. Pursue your new habit, regardless. She brilliantly states, *'Unmask your bullshit and reveal it for the stinking saboteur it has always been,'* encouraging us to confront and overcome our self-harm tactics, pushing us beyond our comfort zones into the realm of true growth and change.

Be forewarned: there's a conspiracy afoot, with Mother Nature and the corporate world conspiring to put your Gremlin behind the wheel. In its raw wisdom, nature only recognises the primal instincts of fight or flight, acknowledging just your subconscious mind. Meanwhile, the corporate giants, particularly those in the food industry, craft their marketing calls directly for your Gremlin, bypassing your Intelligent Brain. They're not just targeting you; they're targeting the impulsive, unthinking part of you. Next time their advertisements flash before your eyes, why not give them the proverbial middle finger? Recognise their game. AIM, fire, and seize control. Refuse to let their cunning marketing coat your beautiful, slender self in layers that don't belong.

Closing thoughts – The truth is, if you've been struggling with your weight or health, it's likely because your Gremlin has been calling the shots for far too long. Deep down, amidst all those ice cream tubs and chocolate wrappers, you knew they weren't doing you any favours. But understanding why you couldn't stop is the game-changer. Now that you do, remember that perseverance is your new best friend. Yes, there will be times when the Gremlin scores a point. Don't beat yourself up. Instead, listen, learn, and aim to do better next time. It's all about understanding, outmanoeuvring (remember to AIM), and ultimately, coexisting with your Gremlin for a healthier, happier you

Unravelling The Complex Web Of Addiction

Why venture into the maze of addiction? Understanding it sheds light on why some things cling to us more tenaciously than others. Consider for a moment the routine act of driving on the left side of the road; it's a habit, learned, ingrained, and automatic. However, the narrative shifts dramatically when we peel back the layers to examine our dietary habits, especially considering the colossus food industry's offerings.

Despite big food corporations' persistent denial, a growing body of research unequivocally supports the addictive nature of certain foods. My charity, the Bennett Foundation, is funding pioneering research into food addiction and helping our good friend Dr Jen Unwin and her team organise one of the world's inaugural Food Addiction Conferences. This event has sparked significant interest within the health community, highlighting the urgency and relevance of this issue.

The evidence is compelling and, frankly, startling. Scientists at Princeton University, through their research, unveiled that sugar could hijack the brain's reward system more potently than some of the most addictive class A drugs. Further afield, a French study unveiled the truth that's hard to swallow. Sugar and sweeteners can outmatch the allure of intravenous cocaine in terms of reward.

These findings aren't just academic footnotes; they're blaring alarms signalling the need for a profound revaluation of how we perceive food and addiction. The implication is clear: if our daily choices are being influenced by factors as potent as drug addiction, then it's high time we address these issues with the seriousness they deserve. Let's explore ways to traverse this challenging landscape towards healthier, more conscious eating habits.

Decoding Food Addiction: Beyond The Misconceptions

Perhaps the most straightforward way to understand the perplexity of addiction is to define it as an act that gravitates towards the harmful, not the beneficial. Contrary to Robert Palmer's catchy tune, one cannot indeed be 'addicted to love.' Addiction, from my perspective, is an unwelcome guest in our lives. A behaviour we engage in far too often despite wishing we could stop or at least cut back. It's the deceptive promise of joy from something detrimental, impersonating happiness but sowing seeds of misery and ruin.

Alcoholics Anonymous frames addiction as an insatiable yearning for the very thing that exacerbates our suffering, leading to irrational behaviour and deepening isolation. This description resonates with my own previous battles against cigarettes. If you find yourself ensnared by food addiction, I'm here to assure you that these chains can be shattered.

It's crucial to distinguish habits from addictions. Unlike their more stubborn counterparts, habits can be altered with relative ease. Consider driving on the left side of the road; it's automatic and a habit. Yet, when driving abroad, this habit is swiftly adjusted. This adaptability underscores the difference between habit and addiction and sets the stage for our approach, which targets the subconscious level through a proven logical methodology.

The allure of addiction, whether to alcohol, cigarettes, or certain foods, is a driver for corporate profit, not public health. These vices share common ground, from their inception in seductive advertising to the false narrative that we're somehow incomplete without these products. This indoctrination leads us to believe in the fleeting happiness that these substances supposedly provide, filling an imagined void within us. Yet, the withdrawal, manifesting as irritability, hunger, and insecurity, reveals the true culprit: the items we believed were our salvation.

As we descend into dependence, the illusion of satisfaction from these addictive substances grows fainter, leaving us in a perpetual chase for a pleasure that's always just out of reach. The tragedy is that we've been conditioned to believe that escaping these addictions is a Herculean task and that striving for freedom only amplifies our sense of deprivation and misery. However, the truth lies in reprogramming our understanding and relationship with these substances, unveiling the path to genuine freedom and wellness.

Drawing wisdom from Alan Carr's transformative courses, which have freed countless individuals from the grips of cigarette and alcohol addiction, we delve into the nuanced dance of desire and relief that defines addiction. These courses illuminate the torturous cycle experienced by addicts, the incessant yearning for their next fix, whether it's a drink, a smoke or a chocolate bar, and the fleeting reprieve it offers from life's stresses.

But what makes these intervals of craving so excruciating? Consider the analogy of a barely noticeable itch. Initially, it's a minor nuisance, but once your attention homes in, the urge to scratch becomes overwhelming. The relief of scratching, though momentarily satisfying, doesn't stem from the pleasure of the action itself but from quelling the irritation. This scenario mirrors the addict's plight: genuine relief comes not from the substance consumed but from silencing the clamour of craving.

Imagine a burglar alarm droning on in the distance; its persistence fades into the backdrop of your consciousness until it abruptly ceases. The ensuing silence feels blissful, not because you were acutely aware of the noise but because its absence lifts a subtle burden you bore unconsciously. Similarly, indulging in junk food offers a semblance of pleasure not because the food itself is inherently gratifying but because it momentarily halts the discomfort of desire.

Now, picture that alarm not as a distant echo but as an incessant blare outside your window which is impossible to ignore. It invades every moment, making relaxation or focus unattainable until silence is restored. This relentless disturbance is akin to the mental craving for addictive substances, a force so potent that it overshadows all else until it's addressed. This analogy sheds light on the true nature of addiction: a cycle of seeking relief not from pursuing joy but from the urgency to extinguish an underlying discomfort. Healthy eaters continuously experience freedom from this cycle, enjoying a peace that comes not from indulgence but from the absence of craving itself.

Once a snacker decides they can satisfy their craving for a packet of crisps or a chocolate bar, they will be utterly miserable until they can munch. And the longer that misery lasts, the greater the relief and the illusion of happiness will be. I don't need to tell you that the misery of the bits between the meals is perfectly real. And in itself, so is the pleasure that alcoholics feel when they are allowed to satisfy the craving. The illusion is that junk food provides pleasure and satisfies the craving. Imagine not being allowed to remove a pair of tight shoes for an entire week and, at the same time, being expected to function normally at both work and play. Of course, you would experience a feeling of intense relief when you were finally allowed to remove those shoes. But suggesting that junk food provides genuine pleasure is equivalent to claiming that wearing tight shoes is relaxing.

No one would be stupid enough to deliberately wear tight shoes for a whole week to receive a few moments of pleasure after removing them. Far from satisfying the craving, junk food, with its chemical enhancements, is both the initial cause of it and the sole reason for its continuance. Do not confuse the end of misery, caused by a craving, with happiness. Being put to sleep for an operation certainly ends the pain, but it is not pleasure or happiness in itself.

The misery felt by abstaining always seems so long, but when you actually consume it, it's only the very first bite that is pleasurable. Just that one taste on the lips is a life on the hips. Because we are so miserable when we aren't allowed to eat what we want, we assume we must get some immense pleasure from it. It is an illusion created by nature for our survival. It's just that it's outdated and has been messed with by the food industry.

As we close on food addiction, let's anchor our resolve in a decisive shift in perspective, one that transforms our battle against addiction into a triumphant escape towards freedom. Just as I advise my friends battling nicotine's grip not to view quitting as a loss but as a liberating escape, I hope you, too, have begun to see the journey away from processed, fibre-stripped foods not as a deprivation but as an exhilarating break for freedom. The day will come when you won't pine for junk food; you won't grieve its absence. After all, who laments the downfall of a foe? Instead, you'll celebrate each day with the knowledge that you've outsmarted the snare laid by the behemoths of the food industry.

The most effective strategy to conquer addiction is to frame it as a liberation from the clutches of the few billionaires steering the goliath corporations behind our food supply. It's a reclamation of our autonomy, a rediscovery of the joy of making wholesome, nourishing food choices that feed our bodies and souls.

Processed food addiction doesn't end with simply avoiding what harms us; it's about enriching our lives with alternatives that offer genuine satisfaction and joy. Replace the fleeting highs of sugar rushes with the enduring contentment that comes from foods rich in fibre and nutrients that heal, energise, and rejuvenate.

As you step further away from the allure of addictive foods, remember you're not just breaking free from an unhealthy past; you're stepping into a future where food is a source of strength, vitality, and happiness. This is not merely a dietary change; it's a transformation that touches every aspect of your life, bringing clarity, health, and genuine pleasure back into your daily existence. Let this be your rallying cry: not just to escape the grip of addiction but to embrace a life of freedom, where every meal is a choice made in defiance of those who once sought to control your palate and, in turn, your health. Stand proud in your newfound liberty, savouring the richness of a life unencumbered by the chains of processed temptations. This is your victory, your journey back to the essence of nourishing not just your body but your spirit.

> **My good friend Dr Robert Lustig says:**
> *'Nature wired our brains for both contentment and motivation, two seemingly dichotomous states [I had to look up dichotomous, which means divided or divided into two states]. Everyone wants to believe they have free will – they have a choice over their own actions. Then why would anyone freely choose addiction or depression, with more choosing them every day? Addiction and depression are not choices people make willingly. Our environment has been engineered to make sure our choices are anything but free. It chronically nudges us towards reward and drives us away from happiness and contentment.'*

Always remember, it's happiness you are after, not just small moments of pleasure.

Tracking Progress And The Art Of Keeping A Diary

Welcome to the fascinating world of journaling, a strategy not just for the introspective poet or the diligent student but a powerhouse tool to underpin your path to health and wellness. A study highlighted in the American Journal of Preventive Medicine revealed that adults who kept food diaries while embarking on a healthier lifestyle shed an impressive average of 13 pounds over six months. The twist? The frequency of their diary entries was the magic wand; those who consistently journaled saw double the weight loss of their less diligent peers. The pen (or app) might be mightier than the dumbbell!

Now, before you groan at the thought of becoming a calorie-counting scribe, let me stop you right there. If you've been paying attention, you'll know that transforming your health isn't about obsessing over calories. It's about understanding your body's hormonal needs and forming sustainable habits. And yes, while mentioning a food diary might conjure up images of meticulous calorie counters, the goal here is motivation, not mathematics.

Enter the Health Result app journal, a modern twist on the classic diary. Imagine a space where jotting down your meals, emotions, and victories becomes less of a chore and more of a cheerleader. This digital companion doesn't just store your daily eats but becomes a visual high-five for every healthy choice you make. And for those moments when temptation lurks around the corner, a quick glance at your entries can be the shield against falling back into old habits.

Let's address the elephant in the room—the thought that this all sounds too 'homework-y.' I get it. The initial leap into diary-keeping can feel like a throwback to school days filled with assignments and deadlines. Yet, the individuals I've had the pleasure of coaching through this process often discover a surprising truth: the act of engaging with their journal propels them towards their goals at warp speed. It turns out the simple act of reflection can turbocharge you to better health.

This isn't about reverting to your school days; it's about unlocking a powerful tool in your health arsenal. The more you interact with your journal, the quicker and more profound your results will be. And who knows? You might find that turning down that slice of cake or glass of wine feels less like a sacrifice and more like a victory lap when filling in your journal. The road to a healthier you may be paved with your own insights and reflections. So, why download the free app? Because the only thing you have to lose is... well, perhaps a few pounds and some old habits.

Navigating The Health Results App: A Guide To Enhanced Well-being

Augment your path to optimal health with the Health Results App, your digital companion in the quest for a healthier lifestyle. This app, born from the collective wisdom of an Olympian, medical professionals, nutritionists, and culinary wizards, is your all-access pass to transforming your health. A simple design ensures you can dive into its features without feeling overwhelmed. Best of all, it's offered completely free, reflecting our commitment to making health accessible to everyone.

Here's a glimpse of what the Health Results App brings to your wellness toolkit:

Journaling with Purpose: At the heart of the app is a powerful and intuitive journal feature. It's designed to track your daily food intake and lifestyle choices as effortlessly as tapping your screen. This isn't just about logging what you eat; it's about understanding the patterns that shape your health.

Revitalising Your Workout Routine: Discover a diverse collection of exercise support featuring videos and tips for various workouts, from bodyweight basics to dumbbell drills and beyond. Our fitness gurus guide you through each movement, ensuring you harness every workout's full potential. Plus, with our progress tracking feature, you can celebrate every triumph along your fitness route.

Culinary Exploration at Your Fingertips: Feast your eyes on our Cooking Masterclass section, boasting over 700 meticulously curated recipes. Each dish comes alive with vibrant photos and step-by-step guides, making culinary excellence within your reach. Deciding on dinner is a breeze; with a simple click, you can populate your shopping list with all the necessary ingredients. Our comprehensive food database, possibly the largest globally, is your trusted companion on this flavourful voyage of nutrition and delight.

Gamified Motivation: Who says tracking health can't be fun? With a unique point-scoring system, the app turns your daily activities into a challenge. Each day, you accumulate points that reflect your effort. A monthly tally isn't just a number; it's a badge of honour showcasing your commitment to staying on course.

Discover Your HRM Score: A pivotal feature discussed earlier, the HRM Score is crucial for understanding your metabolic health. Refer to page 954 for details on acquiring your HRM360 home test device. Once you have your readings, input them into the app to unveil your metabolic score.

Getting Started

Start by familiarising yourself with the journal feature and setting aside a few minutes daily to reflect on your choices. Engage with the scoring system to encourage a competitive edge, challenging yourself to improve with each passing day. Remember, this app is more than a tool; it's a catalyst for change designed to empower you to reach your fullest health potential.

Search Health Results in the App Store or Play Store, or scan the QR code

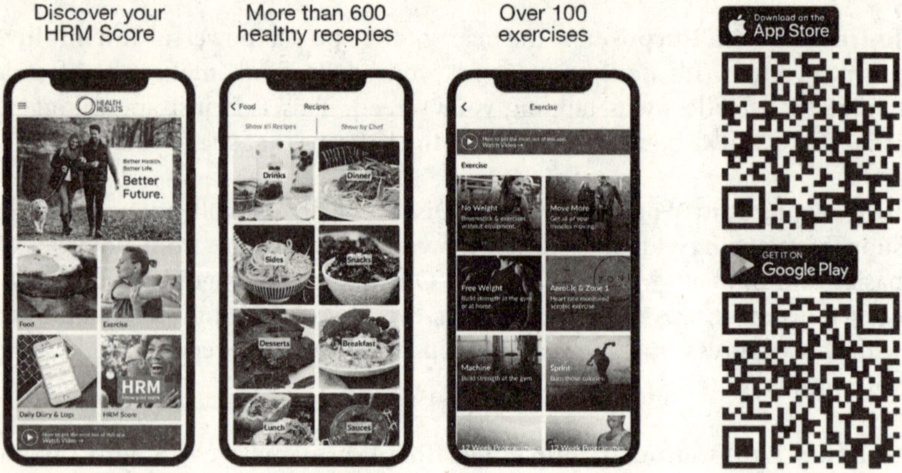

Believe In Your Ability To Become Healthier

Ralph Waldo Emerson famously said, *'The only person you are destined to become is the person you decide to be'.* As you begin your passage of transformation, tap into the mystical powers of the Law of Attraction, the philosophical gem that asserts our thoughts, be they dipped in sunshine or shadow, to sculpt the reality that surrounds us. This universal principle operates unfailingly, like gravity, indifferent to whether you're its biggest fan or staunchest cynic. It doesn't pause to check if you believe before exerting its influence, seamlessly weaving the fabric of our experiences based on the threads of our innermost thoughts.

If you are overweight, I want you to imagine that within you lies a slender figure, merely cloaked in a layer that doesn't truly belong to you. It is not you. Think of it as wearing a fat suit you gained by following the directives of your internal software and the corporate food giants that gave it a free upgrade. The task at hand isn't about reinventing who you are but shedding this unrequested attire to unveil the true essence of your being.

Yes, you heard right. You are inherently slender, a truth veiled by accumulated layers you're now set to dissolve, revealing the magnificent sculpture that lies beneath. It's time to rewrite the narrative, tune into the whispers of your inner self that affirm your slender nature, and cast aside the physical guise that no longer serves you. Remember, it's not about becoming someone new; it's about returning to the splendid form you've always been, merely obscured by temporary additions. As you regain control of your health, be guided by the Law of Attraction, and watch as the universe conspires to match the vibrancy of your newly polished belief in your health and vitality.

Belief is the cornerstone of transformation. Consider the bumblebee: by all scientific measures, with its plump body and diminutive wings, flight should be impossible. Yet, the bee buzzes blissfully unaware of these calculations, defying gravity with every flap. This is the power of belief, unshackled by the constraints of what's 'proven' or expected.

Now, picture yourself with a similar disregard for the so-called limits. Within you lies a slender, radiant being, temporarily obscured by an uninvited layer. This layer isn't an integral part of you but an addition, courtesy of nature's excesses and corporate agendas. Yet, with unwavering belief, you will bid it farewell. Yes, it requires faith, especially when the goal seems as improbable as a bumblebee's flight. But if your belief wavers, borrow mine. I have ample to share, and our combined faith will be unstoppable.

So, I ask you to hold tight to this belief. If doubting yourself is a hurdle, then stand on my conviction in you. Maintain the faith, for I assure you, the moment belief falters, the enchanting journey we're on together might miss its mark. Yet, by nurturing this belief and keeping faith in the face of the improbable, we invite the magic we seek into our lives. Let's keep the faith alive, for the magic awaiting you is too precious to let slip through your fingers.

See it as a linguistic challenge, where the words you choose become the compass directing you toward health and vitality. Transform your narrative from a chronicle of past defeats to a sense of future victories. Instead of lamenting, 'I always fail on diets,' let the mantra be, 'I used to encounter challenges on diets.' If restless nights were your old foes, narrate the tale as, 'In the past, sleep was elusive.'

Project your intentions into the future with unwavering certainty. Banish the tentative prospects of 'I am hoping to lose weight' for the assured declaration of 'I will shed the weight.' This shift in dialogue with yourself eliminates the shadows of doubt, paving a straight path toward your goals despite the road's inevitable undulations.

Speak to yourself with the kindest, most affirmative words. The transformation you seek begins with self-respect, and it begins this instant. Proclaim, 'I am actively changing my relationship with food,' and 'I am already navigating my health journey.' In moments when uncertainty creeps in, replace 'If I could lose a stone, I would feel great' with 'When I lose a stone, I will feel fantastic.' The word 'if' is the thief of certainty, breeding doubt that will derail progress.

To embody health, you must first cultivate it in your thoughts, for your thoughts are the architects of your emotions, which sculpt your actions. This is the essence of Cognitive Behaviour Therapy (CBT), the realisation that viewing yourself through a critical, negative lens fuels behaviours that veer from your goals. It's crucial to understand that while merely envisioning yourself as healthy or slender isn't a standalone solution, the spark ignites the actions leading to change.

The Power Of Why

Upon reaching the conclusion of this segment, I encourage you to delve deeper into the transformative power of discovering your 'why.' Your 'why' is the heartbeat of your journey, the driving force that propels you forward even when the path ahead seems daunting. It's the fuel that ignites your passion, guiding every decision and action you take towards a healthier, more fulfilling life.

Now, as you stand on the threshold of self-discovery, I invite you to turn to page 992 and embark on a soul-stirring journey within the section labelled 'If nothing changes, I am...' This profound exercise has proven to be a catalyst for transformation, touching the lives of many who have taken my 49-Day Health Reset Course.

Consider David's story, a testament to the profound impact of uncovering one's 'why.' With his blessing, I share his journey to illuminate the transformative potential that awaits you as you embark on this introspective voyage.

> *'I'm most likely to keep getting heavier and end up with diabetes like my dad, and probably I'll get Alzheimer's like my mum. I'll never be able to take my T-shirt off around the swimming pool on holiday because I will be too embarrassed, and I'm worried that I'm setting an awful example for my children. Likely, if nothing changes, these will continue to get worse, and eventually, I won't be able to drive my car without painkillers. And if nothing changes my chances of ending up on even more medication is most likely.'*

Grasp the intensity of David's revelation. Don't hasten this process; let your thoughts meander onto paper before crystallising them on page 992. It's crucial that these words resonate with your core and reflect your deepest, most candid thoughts.

Following this self-analysis, turn the page to 'Once I have regained my freedom, control of my health and happiness, I will be'... Here, let your imagination run wild. Envision the hues of your new skinny swimming shorts in vivid detail. Write with such fervour and specificity that your future self becomes palpable, your excitement nearly overwhelming. This visualisation isn't just an exercise; it's crafting your new identity.

Consider Barbra's contribution, which was shared with enthusiastic permission. Like David's, her narrative serves as a testament to the transformative power of confronting our current trajectory and vividly imagining our potential for renewal. This is more than an exercise; it's an invitation to redefine your existence, to connect indelibly with the vibrant, liberated version of yourself waiting just beyond the horizon of change.

Here is what Barbra wrote, and again, she was so keen for me to share it with you:

> *'I will be able to once again chase after my children in the park without feeling my lungs will explode. I am going to be able to fit into all my dresses I hid in the loft, without my bulges embarrassingly oozing out. I will look great at the school gate, be awesome in my blue bikini on the beach, and even have the confidence to return to my yoga class. And I am going to love my kitchen like never before. I know if I love my kitchen, it will return the love tenfold. But more than anything, I will enjoy looking forward to the future with optimism.'*

Isn't that lovely? I invite you to carve out a moment of tranquillity and to envision the sheer joy and boundless freedom awaiting you once you reclaim your health, happiness, and freedom. Immerse yourself in the art of visualisation. Add authentic detail, from the texture of the fabric to the way the sunlight catches its colour. Let your pen glide across the page, fuelled by an exhilarating rush of excitement, until your heart swells with the promise of what's to come. Forge a bond so intimate with this envisioned self that it feels inseparable from your essence. This vision you're crafting. It's not just a daydream; it's the blueprint of your transformed self.

Why is spending time to visualise and write down these thoughts so pivotal?

In the modern world, full of short-term pleasures, navigating to better health isn't for the faint of heart; it demands a super tanker's worth of desire fuelling your drive. Otherwise, you may find yourself faltering at the first hint of adversity. This quest requires more than a tepid wish; it calls for a monumental, unwavering craving for change. Your zeal must be at a rolling boil, ready to transform every obstacle into a stepping stone. Imagine your determination as a tenacious pit bull terrier, gripping its cherished bone, refusing to let go despite the challenges.

Grasping the 'why' behind your aspiration to embrace fitness, shed pounds, and rejuvenate your health is not just important; it's fundamentally foundational. Take to your journal pages and let them be a canvas for your deepest motivations. This isn't about cold, hard figures but the stirring emotions driving your transformation. Pour your heart out, and don't limit yourself to mere numerical goals; they lack the emotional charge that fuels change.

Dedicate time to reflect deeply on this. Initially, you might only unearth one or two reasons propelling you forward, but don't stop there. As days morph into weeks and new insights bubble to the surface, return to your journal pages. Add each newfound motivation, however big or small, to this growing tapestry of 'whys'. This evolving document isn't just a list; it's the emotional bedrock of your journey to a healthier, happier you.

I urge you not to leap into this exercise just yet. Reserve a special time for it, a moment when you can truly dedicate your focus and heart to it without haste. This step isn't merely another item on your to-do list; it's a pivotal chapter in the narrative of your health restoration. Approach it with the reverence and earnestness it deserves.

Develop A Personal Mantra

On page 994, you'll find I've started a segment for you. Why take such a liberty? Through my experiences as a health coach, I've observed a common thread among those I've guided: the inception of their transformation often echoes with remarkably similar sentiments. And I trust you'll find the words I've chosen not just fitting but imbued with a potent force.

My Health Mantra

I will push through short-term challenges and discomforts I may face while creating new habits and regain my health once and for all because...

Perhaps it's time to intertwine the mantra we've meticulously woven together in previous pages: ...it ushers in freedom and happiness, breathes vitality into my days, and promises more years to my life.

Keep this mantra concise, and you will be able to summon it with ease. It's your secret weapon, a talisman to wield against your Gremlin. Whenever a situation or someone tempts you away from your path, summon your mantra with the speed of thought. Let it be your reliable trustworthy anchor, a swift reminder of your POST, empowering you to stand firm in the face of temptation and continue on your path to wellness.

Transforming Self-Perception To Ignite New Habits

The first step in revolutionising old eating and lifestyle patterns is reshaping how you view yourself. Belief isn't just powerful; it's the catalyst for all change. Doubting your capacity for transformation sets you up for stagnation. This transcends mere habit change; it's about redefining your identity. The concept of identity-based habits might seem like a dive into technical jargon, yet it's the cornerstone of genuine and enduring behavioural change.

Atomic Habits, James Clear's groundbreaking book that has influenced millions, illuminates this beautifully: *'Most people don't even consider identity change when they set out to improve. They think I want to be skinny (outcome), and if I stick to this diet, then I'll be skinny (process).'* But true transformation beckons a deeper question: Who do I envision myself to be, and how do my habits reflect this identity?

It's not merely about avoiding chronic illness or adopting a diet; it's about seeing yourself as a person who embodies health and wellness, for whom healthy habits are as natural as breathing. This is where actual change begins—not just in what you do but in how you perceive yourself at your very core.

In the tapestry of self-improvement, many chart out goals and meticulously plan the steps to reach them, yet overlook the engine powering their journey, their beliefs. This oversight leaves them wrestling with an unchanged self-view, a relic identity that clandestinely undermines their aspirations for transformation. You see, our identities are not innate; they are sculpted through our actions, which are a mosaic of our habits, both the commendable and the less admirable. The person you are today, your very identity, is the culmination of past deeds, propelled by beliefs that were not birthed with you but were instead woven from your experiences.

Every action you repeat, every choice you make cements the association with that identity. Here's a lesser-known gem: the term 'identity' traces back to the Latin 'identidem' and 'essentitas,' translating to 'repeated being.' Thus, your identity unfurls through repetition. If you've ever been ensnared by smoking but broke free, you're no longer branded a smoker. This brings us to a pivotal shift in perspective, something I mentioned from the beginning: it's not about relinquishing something but liberating yourself from it. As I counsel my friends yearning to quit smoking, it's an escape, not a sacrifice—a mindset we should also embrace when renouncing junk food and the allure of processed temptations.

Define who you wish to become and lay down the stepping stones with small victories. These triumphs are not just achievements but affirm your evolving identity. This is how you start to weave the belief in your new self, stitch by stitch, into the fabric of your being. Decide who you wish to be, celebrate each minor success, and watch as the belief in your new identity flourishes.

Up To Now, You've Been Trapped

'Each dawn heralds the beginning of the rest of our journey,' echoes a sentiment often draped in cliché, yet its truth remains undiminished by familiarity. I urge you to shed the cloak of self-blame for past indulgences in junk food or a sedentary lifestyle. Recognise that you haven't been misusing food; instead, it has taken advantage of you. At this moment, no one, including yourself, should expect more from you than the strides you're currently making toward change. Our focus is on celebrating each success, big or small.

I invite you to embrace joy as your constant companion. This manuscript was crafted as a book of fun and light-heartedness, aiming to coax a smile or even laughter from you occasionally. Happiness isn't just an add-on; it's a crucial ingredient in the recipe for successful weight loss and health rejuvenation. Thus, harbouring guilt for being overweight is counterproductive. The fault doesn't lie with you. You've simply been responding according to your natural wiring, which we're now set to recalibrate for thriving in today's world.

Your mission is to outsmart this trap, reconfiguring your approach to nourishment and wellness. Rewrite your narrative, transforming from the unwitting prey to the triumphant escapee, armed with knowledge, humour, and a renewed zest for life. You're not the antagonist in your story; you're the protagonist caught in a meticulously laid snare, a collaboration between nature's cunning and corporate strategy, known as the processed food trap.

The Corporate Food Industry: A Venus Fly Trap Analogy

The corporate food industry cleverly ensnares us, much like the Venus fly trap ensnares its prey. A fascinating carnivorous plant, The Venus fly trap lures in flies with the promise of sweet nectar, only for them to discover a fatal trap.

Imagine the plant's interior, slick with nectar, irresistible to any fly. The sight of fallen comrades does little to deter the newcomers, who are convinced of their unique ability to partake without peril. They're lured by the illusion of a simple escape, seduced by the sugary reward promised at the plant's depths.

Owning a Venus fly trap (you can buy them in most garden centres) reveals its cunning design: tiny hairs pointing downwards, creating a one-way slide into its clutches. The nectar, akin to the junk food dangled by corporations, lies at the bottom, tempting the unsuspecting. The fly, emboldened by its perceived superiority, indulges, only to realise the gradual closing of the trap above too late. Overwhelmed by its greed, the fly finds itself too heavy to escape, its fate sealed by the indulgence it thought it could outsmart.

This natural mechanism mirrors the corporate food producers' strategy. The parallel with flies, whose lives span merely a week, accentuates the swift efficiency of such traps. Our entrapment in the processed food snare, however, unfolds more insidiously. The gradual weight gain eludes our daily notice, a slow creep rather than an overnight transformation. We don't transition from the physique of a professional athlete to that of a sumo wrestler in a single night. If we did, the shock might deter us from ever indulging again. Instead, the decline into lethargy and ill health is so gradual that we scarcely notice the change from one day to the next, leading us to accept our diminished state as the new normal.

This slow encroachment of ill health, masked by the day-to-day constancy of our reflection in the mirror, is the processed food industry's most deceptive trick. Like the fly in the trap, we're often unaware of our peril until escape becomes a feat greater than we're prepared to tackle.

Reframing Perspectives On Weight

The stigma surrounding obesity remains a deeply entrenched prejudice in today's society, often leading to discrimination against individuals based on their weight across many areas of their lives. Rather than serving as a catalyst for weight loss, this stigma has been shown by recent research to do the opposite. While I do not endorse the trend of featuring overweight individuals in advertising, fearing it may inadvertently glamorise a health condition with severe consequences, the intentions behind these efforts are understood to be well-meaning but misguided. That said, it is vital to recognise that facing weight stigma can drive individuals toward behaviours that further contribute to obesity, such as engaging in disordered eating patterns[1], showing resistance to dieting, and avoiding physical activity.

The outcomes of recent studies shed light on a troubling pattern: weight discrimination is not merely offensive but can cause marked increases in body weight and waist circumference. These findings underline the urgent necessity for broad-based interventions to challenge and eliminate weight stigma and discrimination, paving the way for a healthier, more accepting approach to managing weight.

A fantastic investigation from three London-based researchers, Sarah Jackson, Rebecca Beeken and Jane Wardle[1], looked into the effects of perceived weight discrimination. Their analysis drew upon data from thousands of individuals, both men and women aged 50 and above, participating in the English Longitudinal Study of Ageing. The investigation centred on experiences of weight discrimination reported during 2010-2011, juxtaposed against weight and waist circumference measurements taken in 2008-2009 and 2012-2013. The analytical framework employed ANCOVAs (analysis of covariance- a method for comparing data sets that consist of two variables) to explore the relationship between perceived weight discrimination and changes in weight and waist circumference, adjusting for baseline BMI, age, sex, and wealth.

Their findings were telling; perceived weight discrimination was linked with significant increases in weight (approximately 1.66 kg) and waist circumference (around 1.12 cm). There was a stark association with the likelihood of becoming obese over the study period, with those experiencing weight discrimination showing a markedly higher risk.

The evidence presented clearly shows that weight discrimination does not motivate weight loss. On the contrary, it is a catalyst for weight gain and the development of obesity. These findings underscore the urgent need for societal-level interventions aimed at eradicating weight stigma and discrimination. By addressing these issues head-on, we stand a better chance of reducing obesity rates and fostering a healthier population. Such interventions would not only alleviate the psychological burden on those experiencing discrimination but could also have a profound impact on public health by reversing the trend of increasing obesity.

Building on these insights, drawing parallels with other public health initiatives, such as national no-smoking days, is enlightening. Interestingly, these well-intentioned efforts often backfire, leading to increased cigarette consumption on those very days. This counterintuitive outcome stems from a fundamental human trait: a resistance to being dictated to, coupled with the stress of self-criticism. Smokers, feeling cornered and chastised, may turn to cigarettes with even greater eagerness, mistakenly believing it alleviates the stress compounded by the spotlight on their habit.

This phenomenon underscores a critical lesson for our approach to weight management. The moment we categorise ourselves as 'overweight' and dwell on that label, we risk falling into a similar trap of stress-induced counter-productivity. Instead, it's imperative to shift our perspective. Recognise that you are already on the path to your desired destination. You're not 'overweight'; you're a traveller on a transformative journey toward better health and happiness. Embrace where you are now as a positive stepping stone, not a point of shame. Celebrate your progress, maintain a positive outlook, and keep moving forward with joy and confidence. This mindset, free from the weight of self-reproach, paves the way for a more effective and fulfilling journey towards health and wellness.

Let's talk strategy, and yes, there's even room for a bit of fibre-fuelled humour in this transformation tale. From this moment forward, banish the word 'fat' from your vocabulary; it's about as helpful as a chocolate teapot. If a less-than-cheerful thought dares to cross your mind upon glimpsing your reflection, squash it like a bug! Instead, pep-talk yourself with affirmations like, 'You're packing your bags, extra pounds,' or, 'I'm on the victory lap to beating you.' Doubts and negativity are about as welcome as a soggy sandwich at a picnic. They don't define your future; they merely acknowledge the current scenery on your journey to a leaner, healthier you.

Now, I hear you thinking this sounds like wishing upon a star while munching on magic beans. 'Psychological mumbo jumbo,' you might say. And to that, I tip my hat and gently remind you: the path to shedding those pounds isn't paved with denial but with a hearty dose of psychology seasoned with positivity. After all, our battles with the bulge are often fought not at the dinner table but in the murky depths of our subconscious, where habits are formed and cravings take root.

You've laid down a solid foundation by turning the pages up to this point. Don't diminish your progress with thoughts of inadequacy. Embrace the mantra: 'I am what I believe.' No amount of sprinting can outrun a diet that's off-kilter, as Dr Aseem Malhotra famously quipped, 'You can't out-exercise your folk.' It's not about a shortage of willpower or motivation; it's about equipping you with the tools to rewire your brain for the modern assortment of life.

Our brains, those masterful survivalists, have been doing an outstanding job keeping us alive. But now, we're updating the software with positive affirmations and a generous serving of fibre because, let's face it, everything's better with fibre! It's about speaking life into your goals, using the present tense as if they're already unfolding. If self-talk feels foreign, start with, 'It might not be showing yet, but success is just around the corner.' It's a perfectly reasonable pep talk, right?

Banish any whispers of doubt. Forget about 'hoping' for willpower or weight loss; that's like waiting for a bus on a train track. As sure as fibre slows your sugar spike, stepping on the scales in the weeks ahead will reveal progress; that's a promise. Keep your thoughts and words anchored in the present and positive. 'I am embracing health.' 'I am a warrior of wellness.' 'I am absorbing wisdom.' 'Step by step, meal by meal, I'm crafting a healthier me.' 'I am actively rewiring my brain.' 'I am mindful of my eating.' 'I am reshaping my relationship with food.'

Remember, transformation is not just about shedding pounds; it's about cultivating a mindset where positivity reigns supreme.

In the Roaring Twenties, a French psychologist named Emile Coue pioneered a groundbreaking method known as optimistic auto-suggestion. His mantra, 'Every day, in every way, I'm getting better and better,' has transcended time, finding its place in the toolkits of modern psychologists and cognitive behaviour therapists globally. Coue's insight was simple yet profound: by repeating a positive phrase 20 times upon waking and again before slumber, we can coax our minds into embracing the future we yearn for.

This principle was strengthened by Alex Ikonn, the entrepreneur behind the *Five Minute Journal*. As we tackled the majestic Himalayas together, Alex championed the practice of penning down one's positive affirmations, reinforcing the timeless truth that the words we repeat to ourselves have the power to sculpt our reality, elevate our spirits, and propel us toward our goals with unwavering conviction.

Imagine your journal as a mirror reflecting your aspirations. Each morning as you greet the day, and each night as you bid it farewell, affirm to yourself: 'I am in control, and I will become leaner and fitter.' This declaration is only the beginning. In time, it might naturally evolve to something like, 'I am healthy, and I think about food before I eat it.' These statements, rooted in Coue's wisdom, are potent, present, and pinpoint precisely the transformation you seek.

Do not underestimate the force of positive affirmation; it's a technique championed by elite athletes and high achievers in all fields. I encourage you to embrace this practice for up to 10 minutes daily in the coming weeks. As these affirmations weave into the fabric of your being, you may find mere minutes a day suffice, and a year from now, a few repetitions will maintain the momentum of change. This practice isn't just about optimism; it's about forging new neural pathways, enhancing the dialogue between your conscious and subconscious mind, and moulding your reality from the inside out.

As we wrap up this section, let's solidify a crucial mindset: banish all traces of doubt from your internal dialogue and the words you share with the world. Cultivating positivity and happiness is not just an aspiration; it's a practice essential to unlocking your potential. This isn't mere speculation; in 2017, researchers in the USA found that feelings of shame and self-criticism could lead to increased hunger and weight gain. The journey ahead demands that you start appreciating and loving yourself today. Happiness isn't a destination but a path we choose to walk each day, and understanding that any past struggles with health or weight aren't your fault liberates you from the unfair burden. In its quest for survival, your brain doesn't differentiate between the jungle and the abundance of today's world, where food is just an app click away. Our mission is to chart a course beyond doubt and negativity, laying the foundation for a healthier, joy-filled life.

Indulge In Your Cake And Eat It Too!

Let's combine all the lessons from this chapter and bake a cake! Earlier, we discussed why governments seem to be tiptoeing around the elephant in the room, avoiding forcing food corporations to make significant changes to the claims on their packaging and the taxation of unhealthy foods (unless you're basking in Chile's culinary revolution).

But while we wait for government intervention to catch up with our cravings, let's chew on this: How can we help folks best exercise personal responsibility and spark a societal shift? I propose we must look at four key areas:

The Four Pillars to Support Personal Responsibility

Convenience
Affordability
Knowledge
Enjoyment

Luckily, the first letter of each pillar spells the word **CAKE**, making it readily memorable. Let's break them down and add a little detail.

Convenience:

Unfortunately, many individuals find themselves entrenched in a food swamp, surrounded by fast-food chains and even local grocery stores where real food seems like a mere afterthought. We must strive to provide more people with access to real food. Fortunately, in the UK, certain home delivery services offered by major supermarkets are stepping up to the plate. Additionally, services like Deliveroo now offer the convenience of delivering healthy foods right to your doorstep, even during unconventional hours.

Another convenient aspect includes teaching people about batch cooking and ensuring they always have healthier, high-fibre snacks readily available in case their Gremlin comes knocking at the door.

Affordable:

Ensuring that real, nutritious food remains affordable is paramount. Currently, it seems the government subsidises all the wrong things, but over time, we hope our farmers will receive more support, making real food more accessible and, through taxes, pushing the cost of fake food higher.

However, it's worth noting that once you have the knowledge, real food is often more affordable than you first realise. For instance, on my website, Health Results, chef Emma Porter and I have curated over 50 recipes under the ACE label—Affordable, Convenient, and Easy—each costing under £2 per meal. Let's keep working together to make nutritious eating beneficial for our bodies and wallets!

Knowledge:

Learning to improve your health requires uncovering the truth. With a barrage of advertisements promoting 'low-fat' and 'fat-free' coupled with a sea of corrupt research and misleading food labels, gaining accurate knowledge about health can be an uphill battle for many.

That's why spreading the truth about health is at the core of my mission. Through the words of this book, I aim to reach as many people as possible. As mentioned in the book's introduction, feel free to snap photos of any pages and share them with your loved ones. Let's empower ourselves with knowledge and pave the way for healthier choices together!

Enjoyment:

So, you've conquered the hurdles of convenience, affordability, and knowledge. But now comes the ultimate challenge: making the healthier choice, the more enjoyable one. Picture this: you're faced with two foods, one healthier than the other. How do you nudge yourself towards the better option? Not every time, because let's face it, that might be a stretch for some, but more often than not.

The key lies in making healthy eating as satisfying as indulging in junk food. It's about rewiring those taste buds, sticking two fingers up at food corporations, and discovering the joy in natural, wholesome ingredients. The more you revolt against what big food corporations do to your health, the more delicious real food becomes.

Drawing from my two decades of coaching TV presenters in the art of selling on my family's live shopping channels, we learned that buying something non-essential is a two-step process: emotional attachment followed by a rational conclusion. It's a dance we do with virtually every purchase. You must become emotionally attached to an item first, and before you part with your hard-earned cash, your prefrontal cortex will help you rationalise the decision.

Initially, I had planned to designate the fourth pillar of CAKE as 'emotion'. However, after years of health coaching and attempting to apply the same logic to food choices, I've found it doesn't yield optimal results. One of the challenges is the multitude of steps between consuming something unhealthy and experiencing adverse effects later on. Too many nodes of separation.

So, instead of making it solely an emotional decision, it's crucial to help people genuinely enjoy their new food choices. I have hundreds of free, delicious recipes on my website. However, grab a copy of my cookbook *Primal Gourmet* if you prefer a physical book.

Yet, even armed with all the knowledge and recipes in hand, many people, myself included, still occasionally gravitate towards the unhealthy, addictive, sugar-loaded, ultra-processed nonsense. And hey, that's okay every now and then. But when it becomes too frequent, it's time to reassess. While the adage 'you only live once' holds true, I've got to admit I genuinely enjoy healthier foods; the flavours are out of this world. But sometimes, the wires in the brain don't connect. It's a common conundrum that I'm currently funding Dr Kristina Curtis, Head of Behavioural Science at University College London (UCL) Centre for Behaviour Change Research, to explore further. Stay tuned on my website or sign up for my weekly newsletter; we might uncover the answer soon. And who knows, maybe it starts with an 'S', and then we can all have our CAKES. After all, having your cake and eating it is quite the treat!

A Heartfelt Congratulations

Arriving at the end of this book, take a moment to appreciate the steps you've taken towards a healthier, more vibrant you. Your dedication and curiosity have been the true driving force behind every page turned and every new habit formed. This book was merely a guide; your actions and choices have catalysed change.

By embracing the *Fibre First* diet and fine-tuning your lifestyle, you're not just living but thriving. The path to increased health span and lifespan is a road of many miles, and you've already taken the first, most crucial steps. Your commitment speaks volumes about your desire for a life lived to its fullest, not just in years but vitality and joy.

Thank you for allowing me to be a part of your adventure. It's been an honour and a privilege to walk this path with you. May the knowledge you've gained be the light that guides you, your family, and your friends towards a future where health is not just an aspiration but a daily, joyous reality. Remember, the best time to plant a tree was twenty years ago, but the second-best time is now. Here's to your health, happiness, and a beautifully lived life.

I would love to stay connected with you as you continue to flourish. Please visit my website, www.healthresults.com, and sign up for my newsletter to keep the conversation going. Your thoughts, experiences, and feedback are incredibly valuable to me and the entire community we're building together.

Spread the word, share your story, and create a health and vitality ripple effect. Use the hashtags #FibreFirst, #TheFibreDiet, #TreeOfAfflictions, #Fibrehydrates, and #HealthResults to connect with others and to inspire those who are just beginning.

Thank you, and here's to your continued health and happiness!

Fibre First Recipes

*****

Introduction

In the delicious extravaganza that awaits you in the following pages, you'll embark on a taste adventure crafted by the illustrious Chef Emma Porter and yours truly. Think of us as your culinary assistants, weaving magic with fibre-rich ingredients to create dishes that don't just tickle your taste buds but give them a full-on giggle fit. Whether you've pledged allegiance to the Human Diet, sworn fealty to the Low Carb regime, or you're a devout follower of the Ketogenic creed, we've got your plate covered. And if you've ever wondered whether deliciousness and a high-fibre diet can coexist, these recipes will make your taste buds sing operas of approval. Prepare your aprons and your appetite; you're about to discover that the path to dietary enlightenment is paved with more than just good intentions—it's sprinkled with delicious and a whole lot of fibre!

In addition, there are four more resources for you:

Page 440 is your go-to for 20 ingenious, fibre-rich food ideas guaranteed to delight your palate and your gut. If you're always on the move, check page 788 for 10 quick, fibre-filled snacks that easily slip into any bag.

Remember the Health Results website, which boasts over 700 healthy, low-carb, and keto-friendly recipes alongside enlightening instructional videos. For the ultimate convenience, the free Health Result app is your culinary companion, offering a vast recipe selection, a detailed food database, and a handy shopping list builder—all at the unbeatable price of free.

High Fibre Breakfasts

Ah, breakfast – the meal that's been on a publicity tour for almost a century, claiming to be 'the most important meal of the day.' Let's be honest: unless you're the boss of a cereal empire, that might not strictly be the case. But here's a twist: if you're in the mood for breakfast, suddenly, it skyrockets to the top of the importance charts! Choosing breakfast is like picking your character in a video game; choose wrong (hello, toast and sugary cereals), and you're on the express train to Carb City – a ride so wild, your health will be clinging on for dear life, reminiscing about the good old days of stable blood sugar levels. So, buckle up, ditch the juice, and embark on a high-fibre morning adventure that'll keep you off the dreaded carbocoaster!

Fish Flake Fibre Fry-Up

Servings: 4
Prep Time: 2 mins | Cooking Time: 5 mins | **Total Time: 7 mins**

Wave goodbye to the carb-heavy start of the day and hello to a sea of possibilities with our Fish Flake Fibre Fry-Up. This culinary delight is a voyage into the rich, nutritious waters of the ocean without the usual anchor of bread and cereals. Crafted in the galley of your kitchen within the span of a mere 7 minutes, this one-pan wonder is as versatile as the ocean is deep. Choose your vessel, be it the robust salmon flakes found in the supermarket, the humble canned tuna, or even the venerable English kipper, and set sail towards a breakfast or lunch that's both quick and laden with treasures of nutrition.

Ingredients:

- Konjac Tagliatelle (200g): The fibre wave upon which our ingredients surf.
- Fish (variable): Choose your swimmer: salmon flakes, canned tuna, or traditional kippers.
- 2 Eggs: The golden sunrise in our dish.
- Tomato: A burst of colour, freshness, and rich in Lycopene.
- Garlic (3 cloves): Nature's medicine.
- Salt & Pepper: To excite the tastebuds.
- Herbs (optional): To add antioxidants.

Method:

Begin by preparing your chosen fish, cooking it ahead if it hasn't already been, and set it aside as if docking it at the port.

Chop the garlic as finely as the sands on a beach and let it dance in a large frying pan with a drizzle of olive oil. As it begins to tan like a holidaymaker, introduce the eggs to the pan, stirring them into the scramble of a sunrise.

Weave in the konjac tagliatelle, finely chopped tomatoes, and prepped fish in this morning's dance. Stir the ensemble on the heat for 2 to 3 minutes, long enough to warm through without losing the sea's freshness.

Season with salt and pepper, casting them like a net to capture the full range of flavours.

Serve a portion to the young sailors at your table before stirring in a whirlpool of chilli for yourself if you desire that extra kick to navigate the day.

Bacon and Egg Fibre Fry-Up: A Morning Marvel

Servings: 3
Prep Time: 3 mins | Cooking Time: 5 mins | **Total Time: 8 mins**

Imagine finding a way to fuel your family's morning adventures with a burst of fibre, steering clear of the carb-laden bread and cereals that usually crowd the breakfast table. Here is a one-pan wonder that's the epitome of quick, easy, and brimming with goodness. Enter the 'Bacon and Egg Fibre Fry-Up, ' your new breakfast hero that's ready in a flash and packed with flavours that wake you up better than an alarm clock.

Ingredients:

- Konjac Spaghetti: The secret to our fibre boost.
- Bacon (6 rashers): For that irresistible smoky flavour.
- Garlic (2 cloves): A flavour kick that says 'good morning' in style.
- Eggs (2 tbsp): Full of nutrients.
- Tomatoes (2 large): A juicy burst of freshness.
- Olive Oil (a drizzle): For Mediterranean health.
- Salt & Pepper – To season the day ahead.

Method:

Start by dicing the bacon and garlic, then let them sizzle in a large frying pan with a drizzle of olive oil, crafting a base layer of flavour as comforting as a warm blanket.

As the bacon edges towards its perfectly cooked crescendo, welcome the eggs into the mix, stirring them into a scramble that's as fluffy as clouds at sunrise.

Introduce the konjac spaghetti, tomatoes, and any additional veggies you fancy to the pan, gently folding them into the mix for a warm, 2 to 3-minute embrace that ensures each ingredient is nicely coated.

Season with salt and pepper, and sprinkle in your chosen herbs or spices, turning a simple fry-up into a personalised morning anthem.

Nutty Blueberry Breakfast Slice: A Morning Delight

Servings: 2
Prep Time: 10 mins | Cooking Time: 3mins | **Total Time: 13 mins**

Welcome the dawn with a breakfast that combines the lightness of pancakes with the satisfying crunch of nuts and the natural sweetness of blueberries. This 'Nutty Blueberry Breakfast Slice' is a testament to breakfast innovation. It uses konjac flour to create a texture that's both tender and delightfully chewy, perfect for those who love a bit more bite in their morning meal.

Ingredients:

- Blueberries (150g): For bursts of sweetness and a pop of colour.
- Coconut Flour (1 or 2 tbsp): Add a hint of fibrous tropical flavour and thicken the batter.
- Large Eggs: The binding element that brings everything together.
- Water (1 tbsp): To achieve the perfect batter consistency.
- Coconut Oil (1 tsp): For frying and infusing the dish with a subtle sweetness.
- Konjac Flour: To give the breakfast slice its unique texture and body.

Method:

Begin by preheating your grill to 180°C, a preparatory step for the final flourish of cooking.

Combine coconut flour, large eggs, water, and konjac flour in a mixing bowl. Embrace the whisk and blend until you achieve a smooth, cohesive batter, setting the stage for your slice's base.

Warm the coconut oil in a non-stick pan over medium heat. Add 3/4 of your blueberries to the pan, letting them sizzle and soften for 2-3 minutes. Their juices will mingle with the oil to create a fragrant foundation.

Pour the batter over the softened blueberries gently to cover the fruit. Scatter the remaining blueberries atop the batter, dotting the surface with their vibrant hue.

Allow the underside to cook on medium-low heat for 4 to 5 minutes. Watch for the moment you can nimbly lift the edges, signalling it's time for the grand finale.

Transfer the pan under the preheated grill, letting the top firm up for 2 to 3 minutes until you're met with a breakfast slice that's golden and gratifying.

Our 'Nutty Blueberry Breakfast Slice' emerges as a glorious morning meal, light yet fulfilling. Each forkful offers a harmony of textures and tastes. It's a dish that speaks of lazy weekends and leisurely breakfasts, of taking a moment to savour the start of your day with something fibrously special.

The Full English

Servings: 1
Prep Time: 5 mins | Cooking Time: 10 mins | **Total Time: 15 mins**

Kickstart your day with a breakfast that doesn't just whisper 'good morning' but sings it, all in the span of 15 minutes! We're talking about the Full English one-pan wonder that's a symphony of historical flavours, textures, and colours, bringing the essence of a hearty morning feast straight from the pan to plate. And the cherry on top? It's a wallet-friendly marvel, costing about £1 per serving.

Unlock the full experience!
Scan the QR code to watch the video

Ingredients:

- Eggs (2 large): The morning's protein-packed stars.
- Bacon Rashers (2): For that irresistible, crispy delight.
- Sausages (2, chopped): A hearty addition, chopped for convenience.
- Plum Tomatoes (½ can): Adds a tangy sweetness to balance the savouriness.
- Spinach (a small handful): For a fresh, fibrous crunch.
- Butter (1 tsp): Because everything's better with butter.
- Konjac Noodles (optional): For a heightened fibre intake.

Method:

Start by dicing the bacon and garlic, then let them sizzle in a large frying pan Melt and Sizzle: Heat a frying pan over medium-high heat and let the butter dance until it melts. This is the stage for your breakfast ballet.

Meaty Performance: Toss in the bacon and the bite-sized sausage pieces. Let them fry to a chorus of sizzles, pushing them to one side like a seasoned choreographer when they start sporting those golden tan lines.

Tomato and Egg Ensemble: With the meats basking in their glory on one side, introduce the plum tomatoes to the pan, laying out the red carpet for the eggs. Crack the eggs gently, letting them fry until the whites set firm, like a perfect soft cloud.

Spinach Ovation: While the pan conducts its magic, lay a bed of fresh spinach on the plate, ready to embrace the warm ensemble.

Curtain Call: As everything closes in on perfection, add the optional noodles for the final minute or two and usher the contents of the pan onto the spinach bed with the grace of a breakfast maestro serving up the first (and now the most important) meal of the day.

Note: Chopping the sausages saves time and ensures every bite is infused with the flavours of your morning symphony.

Behold, a breakfast that's as delightful to eat as it is simple to prepare.

Zero Carb Cheese Waffles: The Chaffle Revolution

Servings: 2
Prep Time: 2 mins | Cooking Time: 5 mins | **Total Time: 7 mins**

Discover the buzz around 'chaffles' and cheese waffles that are taking the low-carb world by storm with a twist that elevates them to new heights of deliciousness. With a special ingredient for that sought-after bread-like consistency, these aren't just waffles but game-changers. Please note: You'll need a waffle maker to bring these delights to life.

Ingredients:

- Cheddar Cheese (50g grated): The show's star, offering richness and melt.
- Large Egg: The binder that brings cohesion to your mix.
- Greek Yoghurt (50g): Adds creaminess and a subtle tang.
- Fresh Chives (optional -1 tsp chopped): For a hint of freshness and colour.
- Konjac Fibre Flour or other fibre flour: The magic ingredient for that bread-like feel.

Method:

Begin your chaffle journey by warming up your waffle machine, which will prepare it to transform your batter into golden perfection.

In a mixing bowl, unite the grated cheese, egg, and yoghurt, stirring until they form a harmonious blend. This mixture promises the creamy, rich base of your waffles.

Gently fold in the konjac fibre flour, stirring to a thicker consistency. A word to the wise: resist the urge to add more than 6g of fibre flour to keep the balance just right.

Approach your preheated waffle maker with batter in hand, carefully depositing it into the iron. Close the lid with a sense of anticipation and allow the cooking magic to happen for about 5 minutes.

As the timer ticks down, prepare yourself for the unveiling. Once done, gently liberate your chaffle from its iron clasp and behold the beauty of your creation. Enjoy these Zero Carb Cheese Waffles fresh and hot from the maker. They're not just a meal; they're an experience. Whether you're looking to satisfy those bread cravings without the carbs or simply diving into the delightful world of chaffles, this recipe is your ticket to a taste sensation. Perfect for breakfast, as a snack, or even as an innovative sandwich base – our chaffle is here to revolutionise your low-carb lifestyle.

Zero Carb Pancakes: A Fluffy Delight

Servings: 12
Prep Time: 5 mins | Cooking Time: 5 mins | **Total Time: 10 mins**

Embark on a culinary adventure with these Zero Carb Pancakes, where simplicity meets versatility most deliciously. Made with konjac flour, these pancakes are quick to whip up and boast a delightful springiness and a light, fluffy texture that's sure to impress. Whether you're hungry for something savoury or sweet, this recipe is the perfect canvas for your culinary creativity. Berries, cinnamon, chocolate, or herbs and spices – the choice is yours!

Ingredients:

- Konjac Flour (5 to 6g): Our zero-carb, high-fibre pancakes base.
- Ground Almonds (20g): Adds a nutty flavour and helps with the structure.
- Large Eggs: For richness and fluffiness.
- Vanilla Essence (1 tsp): A splash of sweetness for those going the dessert route.
- Milk (155g): Brings everything together into a smooth batter.
- Coconut Oil (1 tsp): For cooking and imparting a slight tropical hint.

Method:

Dive into the creation process by whisking together the wet ingredients in a deep bowl. If you're veering towards a savoury version, skip the vanilla essence.

Sprinkle in the ground almonds, blending well before the grand introduction of konjac flour. Aim for no more than 6g to keep the batter from becoming too thick – you're going for a custard-like consistency that pours easily but holds together.

Heat a dash of coconut oil in a frying pan, waiting for it to melt into readiness. With anticipation, dollop 1-2 tablespoons of batter for each pancake, spreading lightly if needed.

Watch closely as the edges firm up and bubbles dare to break the surface; this is your cue to flip. Each side will cook swiftly, turning golden and puffing up to perfection.
Continue the process until your batter is transformed into a stack of warm, inviting pancakes.

Serve these versatile Zero Carb Pancakes straight from the pan, ready to be adorned with your chosen toppings. From a sprinkle of sweet cinnamon to a lavish spread of Fibrella or a savoury sprinkle of spices and herbs – these pancakes are your blank slate for a low-carb feast. Enjoy the freedom to indulge in a breakfast classic or a dessert treat without straying from your fibrous goals.

Blueberry Drop Pancakes: A Burst of Morning Joy

Servings: 1
Prep Time: 2 mins | Cooking Time: 10 mins | **Total Time: 12 mins**

Wake up to the delight of Blueberry Drop Pancakes, a recipe that turns the day's first meal into a fibre celebration. Simple, scrumptious, and wonderfully cost-effective, thanks to the use of frozen blueberries, these pancakes promise a burst of flavour in every bite. Whether you're brightening up your morning or packing a snack for later, these little drops of joy are sure to satisfy you.

Ingredients:

- Blueberries (50g): Frozen to keep things cool on the budget front.
- Eggs (2): The binding glory that holds it all together.
- Coconut Flour (2 tbsp): For a tender crumb and a hint of fibre sweetness.
- Cinnamon (½ tsp): A sprinkle of spice for that warm, comforting flavour.
- Butter: Just a dab for greasing the pan and making everything golden.
- Baking Powder (1 tsp): The lift that brings fluffiness to the feast.

Method:

Pan Prep: Start by melting a little butter in a non-stick frying pan, setting the stage for pancake magic.

Batter Up: In a mixing bowl, whisk together the eggs, coconut flour, and cinnamon until smooth. This is your canvas; those eggs and flour are about to turn into something beautiful.

Berry Mix-In: Fold half the blueberries into your batter, adding pops of colour and bursts of flavour.

Drop and Cook: Spoon your batter into the pan, forming small circles of potential. For those who appreciate perfection, silicone egg dividers can keep your pancakes distinct and dignified. Dot a few more blueberries on top for good measure.

Flip and Serve: Once the underside is golden and dreams are being made, flip them to cook through thoroughly. When they're firm and ready, plate up and dive in.

There you have it—Blueberry Drop Pancakes, each bite a mix of fluffy texture, sweet berries, and a hint of cinnamon. Perfect for a leisurely breakfast or a grab-and-go snack, these pancakes are versatile, delicious, and ready to keep you company throughout the day. Stored in an airtight container, they're good in the fridge for up to 48 hours or can be frozen for a future treat. Just remember to reheat until they're piping hot before serving. Here's to starting your day on a berry-delicious note!

Coconut 'No-Oats-Oat Meal'

Servings: 1
Prep Time: 5 mins | **Chill Time: Overnight**

Wake up to a bowl of Coconut 'No-Oats,' where the traditional oatmeal takes a backseat, allowing a rich, creamy, and utterly indulgent fibrous alternative to steal the morning spotlight. Crafted for those who yearn for the comforting embrace of oats without the carb-heavy commitment, this breakfast celebrates texture, flavour, and wholesomeness. Prepare it before you slumber and arise to a breakfast that's eagerly awaiting your spoon's dive. Adding homemade berry jams or other delectable toppings turns each bite into a moment of low-carb luxury.

Ingredients:

- Almond Milk (150ml): The liquid base that brings everything together.
- Desiccated Coconut (15g): Adds a tropical, fibrous twist.
- Ground Almonds (15g): For that nutty fibre depth and body.
- Chia Seeds (15g): Tiny seeds that pack a mighty fibre punch of texture and nutrients.
- Milled Nuts (15g): More nutty goodness for a satisfying crunch.
- Ground Cinnamon (a pinch): A sprinkle of spice to warm the soul.

Method:

Mix and Mingle: In a bowl, combine almond milk, desiccated coconut, ground almonds, chia seeds, nuts, and a pinch of ground cinnamon. Stir until well combined. It might look a bit too liquid at first glance, but trust the process.

Set and Forget: Once everything is thoroughly mixed, set your concoction aside. It's good to give it at least an hour to thicken, but letting it sit overnight is where the magic truly happens.

Morning Majesty: Come morning, unveil your creation and adorn it with a crown of your favourite toppings. Chopped nuts, a dollop of berry jam, or even a swirl of homemade Fibrella chocolate spread can elevate this dish to celestial heights.

Embrace the anticipation of breakfast with Coconut 'No-Oats,' a dish that promises a morning filled with excitement and satisfaction. This isn't just a meal; it's a ritual that begins the night before, culminating in a moment of pure, indulgent pleasure as the first rays of sun grace the sky. Good morning, indeed!

Crunchy Fibre Nut and Seed Mix

Servings: 15
Prep Time: 25 mins | Cooking Time: 35 mins | **Total Time: 60 mins**

Dive into the day with a bowlful of Crunchy Fibre Nut and Seed Mix, a breakfast marvel that satisfies your granola cravings without straying from your fibre-full, low-carb commitments. This blend is a symphony of nuts and seeds, lightly kissed with natural sweetness, all while dodging the refined sugars and grains that weigh down traditional granola. Perfect for a nutritious start or a midday snack, this mix is your ticket to a grain, gluten, and dairy-free delight.

Ingredients:

- Coconut Flakes (40g): For a tropical crunch.
- Almonds & Flaked Almonds (230g): The heart of your mix, bringing texture and nuttiness.
- Mixed Seeds (150g): A scatter of healthful variety.
- Pecans (150g): Buttery and rich, adding depth.
- NKD Syrup (4 tbsp): A high-fibre, low-carb alternative to honey; I buy mine from Amazon.
- Coconut Sugar (2 tbsp): For a caramel hint.
- Coconut Oil (3 tbsp): Bonds flavours and adds crispness.
- Chia Seeds (4 tbsp): For a pop of texture and nutrition.
- Cinnamon (1 1/2 tsp): A sprinkle of spice.
- Sea Salt (1/4 tsp): Elevates the flavours.

Method:

Warm-up Act: Preheat your oven to 160°C. In a celebration bowl, toss together all nuts and seeds, forming the base of your granola greatness.
Sweet Symphony: In a saucepan over medium heat, gently melt the NKD Syrup with coconut oil, blending their sweetness. Once liquid, drizzle this over your nutty-seedy ensemble, stirring well to coat every piece in glossy sweetness.

Spice and Salt Sprinkle: Infuse your mix with cinnamon and a whisper of sea salt to achieve the perfect sweet-salty balance.

Bake to Perfection: Line your baking tray with parchment paper, and introduce your granola mix to its surface. Spread it out for even baking. Bake for 20 minutes, give it a toss for luck, and then return it to the oven, cranking the heat up to 170°C for another golden 5 minutes.

Once golden and tempting, allow your granola to cool, transforming into that sought-after crunch. Store it in an air-tight container to keep it crisp and delicious. When the morning calls or snack time whispers, serve yourself a 50g crown of granola adorned with fresh berries and a splash of milk for a truly regal keto feast. Welcome to the new dawn of granola, where every bite is a crunch of joy, and every spoonful is a step towards wellness.

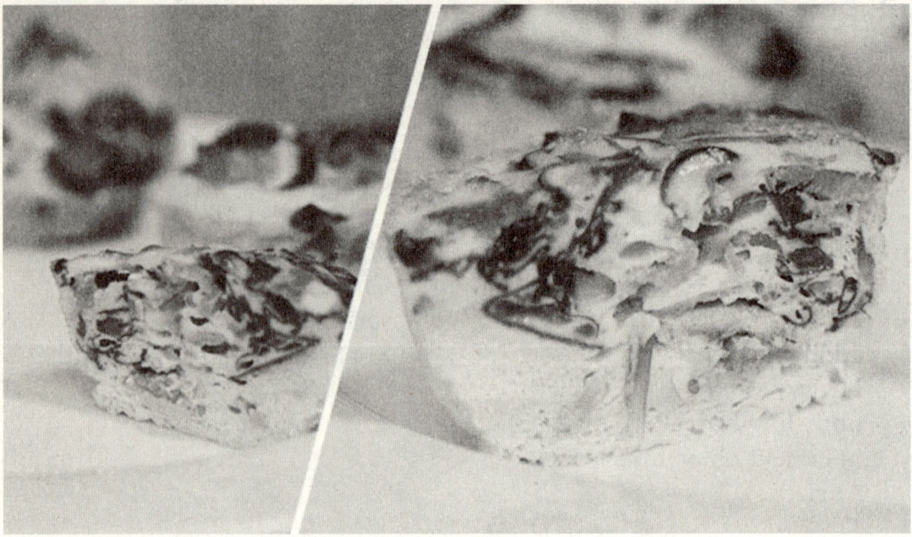

English Egg Muffins

Servings: 6
Prep Time: 3 mins | Cooking Time: 20 mins | **Total Time: 23 mins**

Welcome to a breakfast where convenience, nutrition, and tastiness hold hands in a delightful dance. Perfect for busy bees, prep-ahead aficionados, or anyone in between, these muffins are your ticket to a low-carb, nutrient-rich meal on the move. Whether you're craving a warm breakfast, a quick lunch, or a snappy snack, these muffins are ready to be your delicious companions, hot or cold, anytime, anywhere, all for under £1 per serving.

Unlock the full experience!
Scan the QR code to watch the video

Ingredients:

- Large Eggs (4): The golden base of your muffins.
- Spinach: A green twist of health in every bite.
- Mushrooms (130g, sliced): Earthy and rich, adding depth.
- Bacon (2 rashers, sliced into bite-sized pieces): Smoky flavour in every nibble.
- Seeds (handful): To add fibre and dynamic contrast.
- Butter (1 tbsp): For that perfect sauté.

Method:

Preheat to Perfection: Kick things off by warming your oven to 180°C. Prep your muffin tray with a swipe of grease to make sure nothing sticks.

Sauté Savvy: In a pan, let the mushrooms and bacon frolic with a dab of butter until they're perfectly tender and deliciously cooked.

Whisk Away: Crack those eggs into a bowl and whisk them into oblivion. Feel free to invite some black pepper to the party.

Mix Master: Toss the raw spinach into the bowl along with your sautéed stars, bacon, and mushrooms, and give them a good stir to mingle.

Muffin Magic: Spoon this mixture into your muffin moulds, filling each just shy of the top. Now, off they go into the oven for a 20-minute bake until they've risen to the occasion and set beautifully. Sprinkle some seeds on top for that oreosensory fibrous finish.

There you have it, English Egg Muffins that are as ready to take on the world as you are. Serve them fresh out of the oven or store them for an eat-and-run option throughout the week. Stash them in the fridge for up to 5 days. Bon appétit!

Almond and Coconut Porridge

Servings: 2
Prep Time: 7 mins | Cooking Time: 7 mins | **Total Time: 14 mins**

Dive into the day with a bowl of Almond and Coconut Porridge, the perfect keto alternative for those chilly mornings when only something warm and hearty will do. This recipe cleverly swaps traditional oats with a blend of ground almonds and desiccated coconut, ensuring each spoonful is low in carbs but high in satisfaction. While naturally sweetened by its ingredients, there's room to personalise with your preferred low-calorie sweetener, making your morning just right.

Ingredients:

- Ground Almonds (8 tbsp): The bulk of your fibre porridge is rich and nutty.
- Desiccated Coconut (5 tbsp): Adds texture and tropical notes.
- Macadamia Nuts (2 tbsp, very finely chopped): A buttery crunch.
- Almond Milk (2 cups): The liquid base is subtly sweet and nutty.
- Ground Flaxseed (1 tsp): A fibre boost to start the day strong.
- Coconut Oil (1 tbsp): For richness and smooth consistency.
- Cinnamon & Ginger (1 tsp each): Warm spices to wake the senses.
- Raspberries (1/4 cup): A burst of tart sweetness and colour.
- Salt (a pinch): To enhance all the flavours.

Method:

Nutty Foundation: In a saucepan, combine the ground almonds, desiccated coconut, flaxseed, and finely chopped macadamia nuts.

Soak and Soften: Lavish with a cup of almond milk, letting the mixture soak up the liquid for 5 tender minutes.

Spice and Melt: Sprinkle in the cinnamon, ginger, and a pinch of salt. Add the coconut oil and gently heat, stirring to blend the aromatic oil into the burgeoning porridge.

Simmer and Thicken: Pour in the remaining almond milk and elevate to a simmer. Stir for 4-5 minutes as the porridge thickens to perfection, whispering tales of warmth and nourishment.

Personalise: Taste and adjust. A sprinkle of sweetener? A splash more almond milk? Your bowl, your rules.

Garnish and Serve: Crown with fresh raspberries, adding a pop of colour and a burst of freshness to your morning masterpiece.

In just 14 minutes, transform simple ingredients into a bowl of Almond and Coconut Porridge that's as comforting as it is nutritious. Perfect for those on a keto journey or anyone looking for a low-carb start to their day, this porridge proves you don't need oats to achieve that classic breakfast experience. Here's to mornings filled with warmth, wellness, and a dash of delicious innovation.

High Fibre Sides & Starters

Welcome to the art gallery of Gastronomy, a vibrant exhibition of the *Fibre First* diet, where every dish is a masterpiece, and you're the artist. Picture this: a canvas of possibilities laid out before you, each recipe a chance to paint with the bold colours of fibre-rich foods. Like the snack ideas shared on page 788, these dishes are your palette for culinary creativity.

Imagine swapping a vegetable here and a seed there, making each creation uniquely yours. Today's masterpiece might feature a splash of chia; tomorrow's a stroke of pumpkin seeds.

So, take these recipes, along with the treasure map of high-fibre foods found on page 430, and set sail on a voyage of variety. Repetition is a banned ingredient, and the only rule is to remix, reinvent, and revitalise your meals. Let's turn the *Fibre First* diet into an ever-evolving gallery of gastronomic delight, where variety isn't just the spice of life—it's the very essence of it!

Crab and Noodle Mushrooms

Servings: 4
Prep Time: 5 mins | Cooking Time: 5 mins | **Total Time: 10 mins**

Unveil the elegance of simplicity with our 'Crab and Noodle Mushrooms,' a starter that promises a symphony of flavours in every bite. Whether you're graced with fresh crab or opt for the convenience of tinned, this dish will surely delight your guests with its rich, oceanic charm. Accompanied by the unique, salty, crispness of samphire and the earthy depth of mushrooms, this dish is a culinary exploration that's both refreshing and satisfying.

Ingredients:

- Crab (80g): Fresh or tinned, bringing the essence of the sea to your plate.
- Konjac Noodles (200g): The perfect low-carb base, ready to twirl around your fork.
- Samphire (1/2 cup): A briny green that adds crunch and zest.
- Coriander (a handful): For that fresh, aromatic finish.
- Mushrooms (4 large): Sautéed or grilled to add a rich, umami depth.
- Olive Oil (6 tbsp): For cooking, lending a silky texture and fruity notes.
- Coconut Aminos (2 tbsp): A soy sauce alternative, adding sweetness and umami.
- Fish Sauce (2 tbsp): To enhance the dish's savoury, salty dimension.
- Black Pepper (to taste): For a gentle, warming heat.

Method:

Start by warming olive oil in a frying pan or grill. Add the mushrooms and bathe them in the warmth until they begin to soften. Stir in the fish sauce and coconut aminos, letting the mushrooms absorb these rich flavours for 4 to 5 minutes.

Meanwhile, give your samphire a brief, 2-minute boil to tame its natural salinity without losing its crispy vitality.

Shift the mushrooms aside to a serving dish, preserving their juices in the pan. Drain the konjac noodles and introduce them to the pan, encouraging them to mingle with the residual flavours for a quick 2 minutes. Gently fold in the crab, allowing the heat to bring out its delicate taste. Then, add the samphire for a crunchy contrast.

Finish with a scattering of black pepper and a generous garnish of fresh coriander, adding a burst of colour and a hint of citrusy aroma.

Our 'Crab and Noodle Mushrooms' recipe is more than just a starter; it's an invitation to a flavour-filled, indulgent and mindful journey. As you lay this dish before your guests, you're not just serving a meal; you're offering an experience that's bound to linger on their palates long after the plates are cleared. Perfect for any occasion that calls for a touch of sophistication without the fuss.

Thai Drunken Beef Noodle Salad

Servings: 2
Prep Time: 20 mins | Cooking Time: 7 mins | **Total Time: 27 mins**

Cherish the flavours of Thailand with this Thai Drunken Beef Noodle Salad, known as Pad Kee Mao, in its homeland. This dish captures the essence of Thai cuisine with its spicy kick and refreshing ingredients. While we've dialled down the heat a tad, this salad remains a vibrant homage to its authentic roots.

Ingredients for the Thai dressing:

- Birds Eye Chilli (2 tsp, finely chopped): The fiery heart of the dressing.
- Garlic (2 cloves, grated): For a robust flavour foundation.
- Olive Oil (2 tsp): Smooths and carries the flavours.
- Coriander Stalks (finely chopped): Add a fresh, herby punch.
- Fish Sauce (4 tsp): Injects the umami soul of Thai cuisine.
- Lime Juice (3 tsp): A citrus spark to cut through the richness.
- 1 teaspoon of stevia, erythritol or xylitol. A hint of sweetness balances the heat.

Ingredients for the salad:

- Konjac Noodles (200g): A low-carb base without skimping on texture.
- Beef Rump (400g): The protein powerhouse, tender and flavourful.
- Bean Sprouts (a handful): Adds crunch and freshness.
- Cucumber (1/2, sliced): For an excellent, crisp contrast.
- Cherry Tomatoes (10, halved): Sweet, juicy bursts of flavour.
- Radish (2, sliced): Peppery and crisp.
- Red Onion (1/2, sliced): Sharpness and colour.
- Coriander Leaves (a handful): Bright and aromatic.
- Mint Leaves (a few): A cool, fresh twist.
- Spring Onion: A sharp, green accent.
- Sesame Seeds (1 tsp): For a nutty fibrous finish.
- Lime: Wedge for garnishing, bringing a zesty flourish.

Method:

1. Craft the dressing by blending chilli, garlic, olive oil, and coriander into a smooth paste. Quickly blitz in fish sauce, lime juice, and stevia, erythritol or xylitol. Set this flavour bomb aside.
2. Heat a frying pan or griddle, ready your steak with olive oil, salt, and pepper, then sear to perfection, aiming for medium-rare or to your liking. Let the steak rest, gathering its juices and flavours.
3. Drained noodles (briefly sauté them in a dry pan to lessen their moisture), cucumber, red onion, radish, bean sprouts, and tomatoes should be tossed in a large bowl. Half the Thai dressing should marry the components.
4. Thinly slice the rested beef, then gently fold it into the salad, drizzling the remainder of the dressing. Introduce coriander and mint leaves, stirring softly to distribute the flavours evenly.
5. Plate with artistic flair, garnishing with sesame seeds, spring onion, and a lime wedge to squeeze over.
6. Our 'Thai Drunken Beef Noodle Salad' celebrates contrasts: spicy yet refreshing, hearty yet light. Each bite is a journey through the streets of Thailand, bringing its vibrant culinary culture to your table. It's an ideal dish for those looking to indulge in the rich tapestry of flavours that Thai cuisine offers, all while keeping things light and health-conscious.

Portobello Mushroom Burger

Servings: 2
Prep Time: 15 mins | Cooking Time: 15 mins | **Total Time: 30 mins**

This isn't just any burger; it's a symphony of flavours and textures, with a melt-in-the-middle cheddar beef patty that promises a gourmet experience in every bite. Topped with golden, fibrous, toasted sesame seeds, this burger is a testament to simplicity, nutrition, and unabashed deliciousness - all while keeping your carb count admirably low.

Ingredients:

- Minced Beef (250g): The heart of your burger, ready for transformation.
- Portobello Mushrooms (2): Nature's buns provide a rich, meaty base.
- Medium Egg (1): The binding agent for your patty mixture.
- Ground Almonds (2 tsp): A fibrous breadcrumb alternative.
- Cheddar (20g): A cheesy surprise nestled within the beef.
- Lazy Garlic or Garlic Powder (1 tsp): Adds a punch of flavour.
- Low Salt Beef Stock Cube (1/3 cube): Deepens the umami.
- Smoked Paprika (1 tsp): For a hint of smokiness.
- Ground Cumin (1 tsp): Brings warmth and depth.
- Olive Oil (1 tbsp): For cooking and bringing everything together.
- Sesame Seeds (1 tbsp): Adds more fibre and a nutty crunch.
- Shallot (1, diced): A subtle sharpness complementing the beef.

Method for the portbello burger:

Prep the 'Buns': Trim and clean your Portobello mushrooms to resemble a burger bun. Sear them in a hot pan with olive oil until each side is perfectly browned. Sprinkle sesame seeds in the pan to toast to a golden hue.

Method for the beef burger:

Sauté for Flavour: Gently cook the shallot and garlic in olive oil until softened, setting the stage for your beef mixture.

Mix the Masterpiece: Combine the sautéed mixture with minced beef, adding the stock, smoked paprika, and ground almonds. Introduce the whisked egg bit by bit until the mix binds into a firm yet mouldable consistency.

Cheese Core: Encase chunks of cheddar within your patties for a cheesy core that promises a molten surprise.

Seal and Bake: Sear the patties in a pan before transferring them to the oven, allowing the inside to cook thoroughly while preserving the juicy, cheesy centre.

Building your burger:

Assemble with Artistry: Begin with a mushroom base, add your cheddar-stuffed beef patty, and cap it with another mushroom, sesame seed side up. This isn't just building a burger; it's crafting an experience.

This Portobello Mushroom Burger is more than a meal; it's a celebration of flavours, a testament to the joy of low-carb eating without sacrificing depth or delight. At under £2 per serving, it's a luxurious yet economical choice, perfect for any day of the week when the craving for something deeply satisfying yet wholesomely light strikes. Enjoy the melding of textures, the burst of cheesy goodness, and the earthy foundation only Portobello can provide.

Unlock the full experience!
Scan the QR code to watch the video

Tom Yum Thai Prawn Noodle Soup

Servings: 2
Prep Time: 8 mins | Cooking Time: 25 mins | **Total Time: 33 mins**

Tom Yum Prawn Noodle Soup encapsulates the essence of Thai cuisine with its harmonious blend of hot, sour, and aromatic flavours. This version offers a milder take on the traditionally fiery soup, making it accessible without sacrificing authenticity. Including Konjac noodles adds a fibre-rich twist to this classic soup, enhancing its health benefits while keeping it delightfully satisfying.

Tip: There are a lot of ingredients here; don't worry if you don't have one or two of them.

Ingredients:

- Prawns: The star of the soup, offering seafood sweetness.
- Konjac Noodles (200g): A low-carb, high-fibre alternative to traditional noodles.
- Chicken Stock (700ml): The flavourful base of the soup.
- Red Onion (1/2): Adds depth and sweetness.
- Thai Red Curry Paste (1 tbsp): The source of the soup's vibrant flavour and mild heat.
- Kaffir Lime Leaves: For that distinctively Thai citrus note.
- Lemon Grass (1 stick): Infuses the soup with its lemony essence.
- Ginger or Galangal (1.5cm cube): A spicy, aromatic kick is added.
- Button Mushrooms: For earthiness and texture.
- Fish Sauce (1 tbsp): Contributes a salty, umami depth.
- Lime Juice (3 tbsp): Brightens the soup with tanginess.
- Spinach (a handful): Adds colour and nutrition.
- Olive Oil (2 tbsp): For sautéing the onion.
- Stevia, erythritol or xylitol (1 tbsp): Balances the soup's flavours with sweetness.
- Fresh Chilli: To adjust the spice level to your taste.
- Baby Tomatoes: For a burst of juiciness and colour.

Method:

1. Briefly sauté the Konjac noodles in a dry pan to lessen its moisture, then set aside.
2. Heat olive oil in a large pan, sautéing the onion until soft. Stir in the Thai curry paste, letting the flavours meld for a minute before deglazing with a splash of chicken stock.
3. Add the remainder of the stock along with kaffir lime leaves, fish sauce, chilli, stevia, erythritol or xylitol, and lemon grass, thinly slicing the ginger or galangal into the mix. Simmer to infuse the broth with these aromatic components.
4. Introduce quartered mushrooms and baby tomatoes to the broth, continuing to simmer and blend the flavours.
5. Add the prawns, cooking until they turn a perfect pink. Stir in the spinach until just wilted.
6. Add the noodles and lime juice, adjusting the heat to ensure a gentle warmth suffuses through. Taste and fine-tune the seasoning with additional fish sauce for umami or stevia for a hint of sweetness, tailoring the soup to your palate.

Penne Alle Vongole: A Seafood Symphony

Servings: 2
Prep Time: 15 mins | Cooking Time: 8 mins | **Total Time: 23 mins**

Embark on a culinary journey to Venice with Penne Alle Vongole, a dish that marries the briny sweetness of clams with the hearty, satisfying texture of konjac penne. Once a humble peasant fare, this dish has ascended to the heights of gourmet cuisine, celebrated by food enthusiasts everywhere for its simple elegance and profound flavours.

Ingredients:

- Fresh Clams (500g, in shells): The oceanic stars of the dish.
- Konjac Penne (200g): A fibre-rich, low-carb alternative to traditional pasta.
- Cherry Tomatoes: For a burst of sweetness and colour.
- Garlic (2 cloves, chopped): Adds depth and aroma.
- White Wine (a splash): Enhances the sauce with its acidity (optional).
- Fresh Chilli (1/2): Introduces a subtle heat.
- Extra Virgin Olive Oil (3 tbsp): For cooking and finishing with a fruity richness.
- Parsley (a handful, chopped): Brings fresh, herbaceous notes.

Method:

1. Start by prepping the Konjac penne. Drain any water, then dry fry them over medium heat for up to a minute to reduce moisture, setting them aside to cool.
2. Carefully rinse the clams under cold water, weeding out any that refuse to close when lightly tapped, as these are best left out of the dish.
3. Halve the cherry tomatoes, readying them to add colour and juiciness to the sauce.
4. Warm the olive oil in a large pan, sizzling the garlic and chilli for a fleeting 20 to 30 seconds, just enough to release their fragrant oils.
5. Toss in the tomatoes, then the clams, bathing them in a splash of white wine for an optional but recommended depth of flavour. Season with salt and pepper, then watch as the mixture comes to a lively boil.
6. Cover the pan and let the clams steam open in their aromatic bath for 3-4 minutes. Unveil the pan to a treasure trove of opened clams, then introduce the penne, tossing everything with the chopped parsley for an even distribution of flavours.
7. Serve this marine melody in bowls, drizzling with a final flourish of olive oil to tie together the rich tapestry of tastes.
8. Penne Alle Vongole is a testament to the timeless appeal of Italian cooking, offering a plate where simplicity and sophistication converge. With its nod to modern dietary preferences, this rendition ensures that all can share the joy of indulging in Italian cuisine, regardless of dietary restrictions. Dive in and let each bite transport you to the Venetian canals, where food is an art form and every meal a celebration.

Thai Green Curry Noodle Soup

Servings: 4
Prep Time: 15 mins | Cooking Time: 30 mins | **Total Time: 45 mins**

A Thai Green Curry Noodle Soup that brings the aromatic and bold flavours of Thailand right to your table. This soup, rich with the complexity of homemade Thai green curry paste, is a testament to the art of Thai cooking, blending spicy, sweet, sour, and savoury elements in harmony. While making the paste from scratch adds a bit of time to your prep, the depth of flavour it brings to the soup is well worth the effort.

Ingredients:

- Chicken Breast: Tender and lean, ready to soak up the flavours.
- Konjac Noodles (200g): A low-carb, high-fibre alternative to traditional noodles.
- Thai Paste (2 tbsp): The soul of the dish, packed with herbs and spices.
- Shallot: Adds a subtle sweetness.
- Olive Oil (2 tbsp): For sautéing the base.
- Chicken Stock (600ml): The flavourful liquid foundation.
- Lemon Grass (1 stalk): Infuses the broth with a citrusy, herbal note.
- Broccoli Stem: Adds dynamic contrast and nutrients.
- Coconut Milk (1 can, full fat): Gives the soup a creamy texture.
- Fish Sauce (3 tbsp): Adds a salty depth.
- Stevia, erythritol or xylitol (1 tbsp): A touch of sweetness to balance the flavours.
- Lime (1/2): Adds a zesty brightness.
- Kaffir Lime Leaves: Aromatic leaves that impart a unique citrus flavour.
- Basil Leaves (1/2 cup): Offers a peppery, minty freshness.
- Bean Sprouts (a handful): Adds dynamic contrast and freshness.
- Chilli, Spring Onion: For garnish, adding heat and crunch.

Method:

1. Bring the chicken stock to a boil before lowering to a simmer. Add the lemon grass and kaffir lime leaves for a fragrant infusion.
2. Dice the chicken and broccoli, adding them to the simmering broth, allowing the chicken to cook through and the broccoli to tenderize slightly.
3. Stir in coconut milk, Stevia or erythritol or xylitol, fish sauce, and lime juice, blending these rich flavours into a harmonious soup base.
4. Taste the soup and adjust the seasoning with more chilli to dial up the desired heat.
5. Add the drained konjac noodles to the soup, warming them through and allowing them to absorb the flavours.
6. For a beautiful presentation, serve the soup garnished with spring onion, bean sprouts, chili, lime wedges, and Thai basil.
7. To make the Thai Paste: Combine green chilli, shallots, garlic, lemongrass, lime rind, coriander root, kaffir leaves, coriander seed, cumin seeds, fish sauce, olive oil, ginger, black pepper, and dried shrimp paste in a food processor. Blitz to create a vibrant green curry paste that can be used immediately or stored for future culinary creations.

Bang Bang Chicken

Servings: 2
Prep Time: 15 mins | Cooking Time: 20 mins | **Total Time: 35 mins**

Feast your taste buds on Bang Bang Chicken, a culinary composition that hits every note perfectly, from sweet melodies to salty beats. This dish is destined to be a family classic and is as simple to make as it is complex in flavour. Whether you're dividing it between two or savouring it across multiple meals, it promises satisfaction for under £2 per serving.

Unlock the full experience!
Scan the QR code to watch the video

Ingredients:

- Chicken Breast (250g): The canvas for our flavour masterpiece.
- Peanut Butter (100g): For that fibrous, creamy, nutty baseline.
- Light Soy Sauce (2 tbsp): Adds the perfect touch of salty harmony.
- Erythritol (2 tsp): Sweetens the deal without the sugar spike.
- Milk (3 tbsp): Blends everything into a smooth symphony.
- Handful of peanuts: Adding dynamic contrast and even more fibre

Method:

Boil to Perfection: Begin by gently boiling the chicken breast until fully cooked, about 15-20 minutes. A quick check at the halfway mark ensures no surprises in the encore.

Prepare the Stage: Once the chicken has received its standing ovation, drain and set aside the water, but keep the pan for the next act.

Fibre Breakdown: Place the chicken in its backstage dressing room (a.k.a. a sandwich bag or between greaseproof paper) and give it a good bash with a rolling pin. This tenderises the meat, making it ready for its solo.

Culinary Mix: Return the chicken to the pan over medium flame. Introduce the peanut butter, light soy sauce, erythritol, and milk to the mix. Stir well, combining all the elements into a dish that's ready to steal the show.

Serve Up the Applause: At the last moment, sprinkle on a handful of fibrous nuts for that true oreosensory sensation.

This Bang Bang Chicken recipe isn't just food; it's a performance, a testament to the power of simple ingredients coming together in perfect harmony. So, gather your audience, serve this sweet and salty sensation, and watch as it becomes a headlining act in your culinary repertoire.

Mini Smoked Fish Pie: A Gourmet Starter

Servings: 4
Prep Time: 10 mins | Cooking Time: 20 mins | **Total Time: 30 mins**

Elevate your starter game with our Mini Smoked Fish Pie, a recipe that combines the smoked depth of mackerel with the lightness of whiting; all brought together with a touch of finesse in presentation. Whether you aim to impress at a dinner party or treat yourself to a fine dining experience at home, this dish will surely be a hit, offering a balance of flavours and textures that celebrate the sea.

Ingredients:

- Whiting Fillets (2 or 3): Light and delicate, providing a subtle fish flavour.
- Smoked Mackerel Fillets (2 or 3): Rich and smoky, adding depth.
- Konjac Flour (2 tsp): To thicken the mixture without adding carbs.
- Eggs: Helps to bind the filling, adding richness.
- Garlic (4 cloves): Adds aromatic warmth.
- Wholegrain Mustard (3 tsp): For a tangy kick.
- Shallots: For a hint of sweetness.
- Chives (a handful): Add a mild oniony flavour for garnishing.
- Coriander (a handful): Adds a fresh, citrusy touch.
- Aubergine: Provides a velvety texture contrast.
- Olive Oil: For cooking, adds a fruity note.

Method:

Begin by grating the garlic and finely chopping the shallots. Sauté them in a pan with olive oil until golden, ensuring the garlic doesn't burn, to set a flavourful base.

Cut the fish into small, bite-sized pieces and add them to the pan. Gently cook until the fish is almost done, letting the flavours meld together.

Stir in the konjac flour, wholegrain mustard, and beaten eggs to the fish mixture. Continue to cook, stirring constantly to prevent the eggs from scrambling, until the mixture thickens and comes together, about 5 to 10 minutes.

Meanwhile, slice the aubergine thinly and fry in another pan with olive oil until each slice is beautifully caramelised.

Assemble the pies using a cookie cutter of your choice for shape and structure. Press the fish mixture firmly into the cutter, creating a compact layer. Top with a slice of fried aubergine, pressing gently to adhere.

Garnish each mini pie with chives or wild garlic grass for an elegant finish.

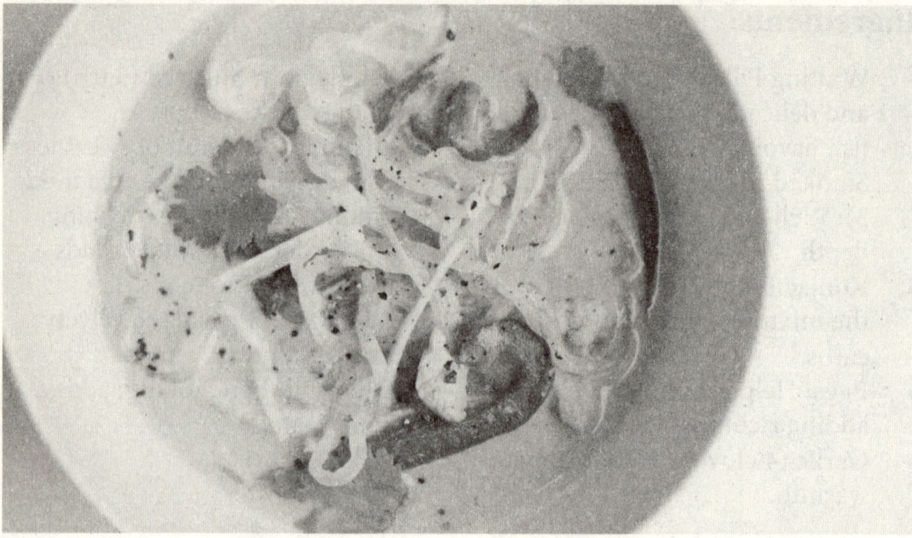

One Pot Indonesian Chicken Noodle Soup

Servings: 4
Prep Time: 10 mins | Cooking Time: 20 mins | **Total Time: 30 mins**

Delve into the rich flavours of Indonesia with this One Pot Indonesian Chicken Noodle Soup, a delightful rendition of the traditional 'Soto Ayam'. This version is tailored for those seeking a low-carb alternative, utilising konjac noodles to complement the vibrant, turmeric-infused chicken broth. Inspired by a memorable trip to Indonesia, this soup brings the essence of Indonesian cuisine to your kitchen, offering a comforting, flavourful meal that's as nourishing as it is satisfying.

Ingredients:

- Chicken (300g, diced): The protein-rich base of the soup.
- Red Pepper (1 medium, sliced): Adds sweetness and colour.
- Spring Onion (3, sliced): For a fresh, oniony crunch.
- Ginger (1 tsp, fresh): Brings warmth and spice.
- Garlic (3 cloves, crushed): Aromatic and flavourful.
- Lime Juice (1 tbsp): Cuts through the richness with acidity.
- Turmeric (2 tsp): Gives the broth its signature yellow hue and earthy taste.
- Tinned Coconut Milk (400ml): Lends creaminess and a subtle sweetness.
- Konjac Noodles (200g): Our carb-free noodle alternative.
- Sea Salt (to taste): Enhances the flavours.
- Coriander Leaves (a handful): Adds freshness and colour.
- Lime Wedges (1/2 a lime): Add a tangy zing for serving.
- Coconut Oil (1 tsp): For sautéing the vegetables and spices.
- Red Chilli (1/2, finely diced): Introduces a mild heat.
- Water (200ml): Adjusts the soup's consistency.

Method:

Sauté Veggies and Spices: Heat the coconut oil in a deep pan over medium heat. Sauté the spring onion and red pepper until slightly softened. Stir in the ginger and garlic, coating the veggies in fragrant oils.
Cook the Chicken: Add the diced chicken to the pan, cooking until the pieces are evenly white. If the mixture begins to stick, lower the heat.
Spice It Up: Sprinkle turmeric and diced chilli, thoroughly mixing to distribute the spices.
Simmer: Pour in the lime juice, coconut milk, and water, bringing everything to a boil before reducing it to a simmer. Allow the soup to thicken as it cooks for 10-15 minutes.
Add Noodles: Introduce the konjac noodles to the soup, ensuring they're well integrated and heated through.
Final Touches: Stir half the coriander leaves and season with sea salt according to your preference.
Serve Warm: Dish up the soup adorned with the remaining coriander and a lime wedge for an extra burst of flavour.

Tahini Fibrous Coleslaw

Servings: 2
Prep Time: 5 mins | Cooking Time: 5 mins | **Total Time: 10 mins**

Who said a gourmet side dish has to be complicated? Enjoy our 'no cook wonder Tahini Fibrous Coleslaw', where simplicity reigns supreme. Designed for the budget-conscious, convenience-loving, and culinary-simplistic among us, this recipe transforms the humble coleslaw into a nutrient-packed, flavour-bursting delight. Say goodbye to tedious chopping and lengthy prep times; with just a bag of stir-fry veggies, some pantry staples, and a whirl of a spoon, you're all set. And all for under £1 per serving!

Unlock the full experience!
Scan the QR code to watch the video

Ingredients:

- Mixed Stir Fry Vegetables (150g): The colourful base of your coleslaw.
- Mayonnaise (2 tbsp): For creaminess and tang.
- Mixed Seeds (2 tbsp): Adds crunch and a nutritional punch.
- Tahini (1 tsp): A sesame twist elevates the flavour profile.

Method:

Veggie Toss: Start with a vibrant toss of mixed stir-fry vegetables into your bowl.
Creamy Blend: Introduce the mayonnaise and tahini to the veggie ensemble. With a gentle stir, blend them together until each vegetable piece is lovingly coated in this creamy, sesame-kissed dressing.

Seed Symphony: To finish, sprinkle the mixed seeds over the top like a chef, adding the final touch to a masterpiece. Not only do they add a delightful crunch, but they also pack a fibrous punch.

In mere minutes, you've created a Tahini Fibrous Coleslaw that's as easy on the wallet as it is on the palate. Perfect as a side dish for a barbecue, a companion to your favourite high-fibre meal, or as a standalone snack, this coleslaw proves that great flavours don't require complex recipes or expensive ingredients. Just mix, sprinkle, and serve to see how delicious simplicity can be.

Thai Chicken Pie: A Fusion Delight

Servings: 4
Prep Time: 25 mins | Cooking Time: 30 mins | **Total Time: 55 mins**

Combining the heartiness of a traditional pie with the exotic flavours of Thai cuisine, this Thai Chicken Pie is a culinary masterpiece waiting to delight your taste buds. Perfect for those who cherish pies and Thai curries, this recipe is versatile enough to inspire variations such as Chicken Tikka or Balti pies. Dive into the rich, flavourful world of fusion cooking with this easy-to-follow recipe.

Ingredients for the pastry:

- Almond Flour (7 heaped tbsp): Provides a nutty, high-fibre base.
- Coconut Flour (4 heaped tbsp): Adds fibre and aids in thickening.
- Konjac Flour (2 heaped tsp): Enhances the fibre content while keeping carbs low.
- Baking Powder (1 tsp): Helps the pastry rise.
- Egg (1 large): Binds the ingredients.
- Olive Oil (3 tbsp): Adds moisture and richness.
- Salt (a pinch): Seasons the dough.
- Water (6 tbsp): Achieves the right dough consistency.
- Butter: To grease the pan, ensures a non-stick bake.

Ingredients for the curry filling:

- Chicken Breast (2 large): Boiled and diced, the protein star.
- Spring Onion, Red Onion, Red Bell Pepper: Fresh veggies for crunch and colour.
- Lemongrass (1 stick), Garlic (4 cloves), Ginger (2cm square): The aromatic trio that infuses the filling with authentic Thai flavours.
- Soft Cream Cheese (250g): Adds creaminess to the filling.
- Thai Curry Paste (2 tbsp): The heart of the dish, offering deep, complex flavours.
- Paprika Powder (1 tsp): Adds a mild, smoky heat.
- Salt and Pepper: Fine-tunes the seasoning.
- Eggs: Binds the filling, adding richness.

Method for the pastry:

Combine all pastry ingredients to form a dough. If it is too thick, adjust with a bit of water. Grease a 20cm round baking tray with butter and line it with greased parchment paper for easy dough handling and baking.

Roll out the dough, forming a base and sides in the prepped tray and a separate top on another piece of paper.

Bake the empty shell (but not the top) at 180°C for 15-20 minutes until just starting to golden

Method for the curry:

Boil the chicken, then sauté the chopped veggies, lemongrass, garlic, and ginger in olive oil. Stir in the curry paste and diced chicken, cooking briefly. Incorporate beaten eggs, soft cheese, konjac flour, and seasonings, cooking until the mixture thickens.

Assembly: Spoon the curry filling into the pre-baked pastry shell. Cover with the pastry top, sealing the edges. Bake for an additional 10 minutes or until golden.

Serving Suggestion: Garnish with fresh coriander and a sprinkle of chilli flakes for an extra kick.

Crab Linguine

Servings: 4
Prep Time: 10 mins | Cooking Time: 12 mins | **Total Time: 22 mins**

Enjoy a delectable world of seafood with this Crab Linguine recipe, where the natural sweetness of crab meat shines through in a simple yet sophisticated dish. This recipe uses konjac spaghetti as a low-carb, high-fibre alternative to traditional pasta. It is an excellent choice for adhering to the Fibre First diet without sacrificing flavour or satisfaction.

Ingredients:

- Crab Meat (160g): The star of the dish, offering delicate sweetness and luxurious texture.
- Konjac Spaghetti (200g): A perfect pasta substitute, rich in fibre and low in carbs.
- Garlic (4 cloves): Adds depth and aroma.
- Red Bell Pepper (1 or 2): Brings sweetness, vitamin C, and colour.
- Red Onion (1 or 2): For a mild, slightly sweet flavour.
- Spring Onion: Adds a crisp, oniony bite.
- White Wine (1 glass): Deglazes the pan and adds acidity.
- Lime Juice (2 tbsp): Provides a bright, citrusy tang.
- Coriander or Parsley (1 cup): For a fresh, herbal finish.
- Olive Oil (drizzle): To cook and bring flavours together.
- Black Pepper (to taste): For a bit of heat.
- Birds Eye Chilli (1, optional): For those who like spicy.
- Chilli Flakes (1 tsp, optional): Add more heat.
- Dried Onion Flakes (2 tsp, optional): For an extra oreosensory oniony crunch.

Method:

Sauté the Vegetables: Start by grating the garlic and finely chopping the onions, spring onions, and red bell peppers. If using, finely chop the Birds Eye chilli. Heat a drizzle of olive oil in a saucepan and sauté the prepared vegetables for about a minute.

Deglaze and Simmer: Pour in a glass of white wine, lime juice, and a sprinkle of black pepper. Let the mixture cook for an additional 5 minutes, allowing the alcohol to evaporate and the flavours to meld.

Cook the Spaghetti: Drain and rinse the konjac spaghetti, then add it to the saucepan. Toss and cook with the vegetable mixture for 2 to 3 minutes, ensuring the spaghetti is well coated in the sauce.

Add the Crab Meat: Gently fold in the crab meat, allowing it to warm through and absorb the flavours without breaking apart. Stir in the fresh herbs (coriander or parsley) during the last minute of cooking to preserve their vibrant colour and taste.

Dish up this exquisite Crab Linguine, garnishing with additional herbs, chilli flakes, and dried onion flakes if desired. Serve immediately, offering a dish that's as pleasing to the eye as it is to the palate.

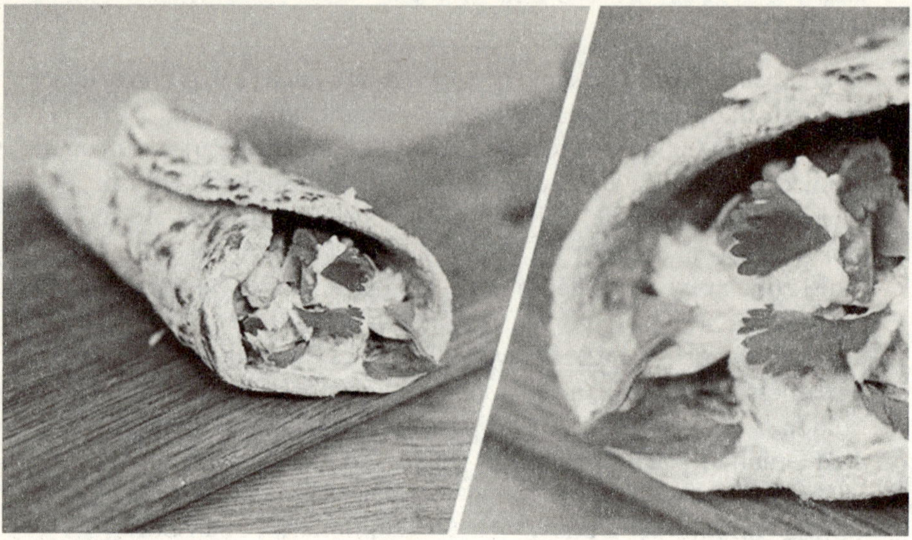

Fibrous Flatbread

Servings: 6
Prep Time: 6 mins | Cooking Time: 10 mins | **Total Time: 16 mins**

Introducing the Fibrous Flatbread, a culinary marvel about to change your mealtime game! Crafted from the humblest pantry staples and a dollop of Greek yogurt, this flatbread is your ticket to a low-carb, high-fibre feast. Say goodbye to sandwich monotony and hello to a versatile base ready to be adorned with your favourite toppings, all for under £1 per six servings.

Unlock the full experience!
Scan the QR code to watch the video

Ingredients:

- Coconut Flour (50g): For that fibrous foundation.
- Psyllium Husk Powder (15g): The magic ingredient for texture and fibre.
- Water (150g): To bring it all together.
- Sea Salt: Just a pinch for flavour.
- Greek Yogurt (50g): For creamy moisture.
- Olive Oil (15g): For richness and pliability.

Method:

Dry Mix Magic: In a bowl, combine coconut flour and psyllium husk powder. These two are about to become very good friends.

Wet Into Dry: Add a twist of sea salt, then pour in the olive oil and Greek yoghurt for a stir of epic proportions.

Dough Development: Gradually introduce the water, watching the psyllium husk work its absorbing wonders. Add just enough to form a manageable dough.

Shape and Roll: Divide your doughy treasure into six even balls. Between two sheets of baking parchment, roll them into the thin, flat discs of potential.

Pan Perfection: Heat a pan or wok to high heat. No oil is necessary, thanks to the dough's olive oil content.

Cooking Time: Gently lay your flatbread in the pan. After a couple of minutes, once the bottom side whispers of golden perfection, flip it to its other side for an equal tan.

Voilà! Your Fibrous Flatbread is ready to steal the spotlight, whether it's breakfast, lunch, or dinner you're thinking of. Perfect for wrapping, topping, or dipping, these flatbreads are best enjoyed fresh within 24 hours. But fear not, for the adventurers who plan ahead, the uncooked dough freezes beautifully for up to a month. Just thaw, roll, and pan-fry to transport yourself back to this moment of culinary creation. Let the flatbread fiesta commence!

Tangerine Tuna & Avocado Salad

Servings: 4
Prep Time: 15 mins | Cooking Time: 3 mins | **Total Time: 18 mins**

Dive into the vibrant world of seafood salads with this Tangerine Tuna & Avocado Salad, inspired by the classic duck à l'orange. This recipe combines the freshness of tuna, the creaminess of the avocado, and the sweet tanginess of tangerine in a symphony of flavours. Adding chia and flax seeds not only introduces a crunchy texture but also boosts the fibre content, making this dish a healthy yet indulgent choice for any meal.

Ingredients for the salad:

- Tuna Steaks (1 or 2): Fresh from the fishmonger, cut into 2.5 to 3cm chunks.
- Chia Seeds (1/2 cup): For dynamic contrast and fibre.
- Golden Flax Seeds (1/2 cup): Adds more fibre, texture and nutrients.
- Olive Oil: For searing the tuna.
- Soft Cheese (100g): Adds creaminess to the avocado mash.
- Red Onion, Bell Pepper: Fresh veggies for crunch and colour.
- Tangerine: For zest and segments.
- Tomato (1 large): Adds freshness.
- Rocket (2 cups): Peppery greens as the salad base.
- Black Pepper: To season the tuna.
- Lemon Juice (1 tbsp): Brightens the avocado mash.

Ingredients for the À la Orange Sauce:

- Tangerine: Zest and juice for the sauce base.
- Double Cream (3 tbsp): Adds richness.
- Stevia (1 tsp): Sweetens the sauce.
- Vanilla Extract (1/4 tsp): A hint of aromatic sweetness.
- Apple Cider Vinegar (1 tbsp): Adds a tangy note.
- Konjac Flour (1 tsp): To thicken the sauce, if needed.

Method:

À la Orange Sauce Preparation: Combine tangerine zest, juice, stevia, vanilla, double cream, and apple cider vinegar in a saucepan. Simmer on low, stirring occasionally. Thicken with konjac flour if needed.

Tuna Preparation: Mix chia and flax seeds in a dish with a sprinkle of black pepper. Coat tuna chunks in the seed mixture. Heat olive oil in a pan and sear the tuna for about 40 seconds on each side, aiming for a pink centre.

Avocado Mash: Mash avocados in a bowl and blend in soft cheese, finely diced red onion, and bell pepper. Season with lemon juice.

Assemble the Salad: Shape the avocado mash with a cookie cutter, placing it on a bed of rocket. Top with a tomato slice and tangerine segments.

Serve: Arrange the seared tuna around the avocado mash. Drizzle the à la orange sauce over the salad before serving.

Pad Thai Egg Noodles

Servings: 4
Prep Time: 20 mins | Cooking Time: 10 mins | **Total Time: 30 mins**

Unlock the secrets to a healthier version of the classic Pad Thai, a dish renowned for its perfect balance of sweet, sour, salty, and spicy flavours. You can enjoy this beloved Thai dish anytime without guilt by substituting rice noodles with konjac noodles and making a few other tweaks. This recipe promises an authentic taste that's nutritionally dense and bursting with flavour, proving that traditional favourites can be just as delightful in their low-carb incarnations.

Ingredients for the dish:

- Konjac Noodles (200g)
- Beansprouts (300g): Adds crunch and freshness.
- Prawns (300g): For a protein-rich seafood twist.
- Onion, Spring Onion: Provide aromatic base flavours.
- Eggs: These are used to create the traditional egg net.
- Coconut Oil: For frying, add a subtle coconut flavour.
- Chives (10g): For a mild oniony crunch.
- Garlic (4 cloves): For a punch of flavour.
- Coriander (a handful): Fresh and vibrant for garnish.
- Chopped Nuts (1 cup): Adds fibre, dynamic contrast and a nutty flavour.
- Lime (1 or 2): For acidity and brightness.
- Birds Eye Chilli (optional): For those who dare with extra heat.
- Chilli Flakes (1 tsp): Adds a spicy kick.

Ingredients for the sauce:

- Tamarind Puree (2 tbsp): Provides the signature tangy backbone.
- Xylitol (2 tsp): For a hint of sweetness.
- Fish Sauce (2 tbsp): Delivers umami and saltiness.
- Kecap Manis (2 tbsp): A sweet soy sauce alternative for depth and complexity.

Method:

Egg Net Preparation: Beat 2 eggs and slowly drizzle into a hot pan coated with coconut oil, creating a net-like pattern. Once cooked, set aside on kitchen paper.

Prep the Vegetables: Chop the onion, grate the garlic, and slice the spring onions.

Sauce Creation: Mix tamarind puree, xylitol, fish sauce, and kecap manis in a bowl.

Cooking the Dish: In a large pan, sauté garlic and onion in coconut oil. Add beansprouts, konjac noodles, spring onions, prawns, and the prepared sauce, tossing gently until the noodles are well coated.

Final Touches: Stir in chives and half of the chopped nuts, cooking briefly before removing from heat.

Serve: Dish out the Pad Thai, garnishing with the remaining nuts, lime wedges, a sprinkle of chilli flakes, fresh coriander, beansprouts, and the optional Birds Eye chilli. Squeeze lime juice over the dish to taste.

Prawn Tagliatelle

Servings: 4
Prep Time: 5 mins | Cooking Time: 15 mins | **Total Time: 20 mins**

Dive into the light and fibrous world of our Prawn Tagliatelle, where the richness of prawns meets the innovative low-carb konjac tagliatelle for a dish that promises indulgence and nutrition. This recipe offers a tangy and tasty twist to the traditional prawn linguine, perfect for those embracing a low-carb lifestyle without wanting to miss out on Italian classics.

Ingredients:

- Prawns (300g): Juicy and nutritious, the dish's star.
- Konjac Tagliatelle (400g): A fantastic, low-carb alternative.
- Cherry Tomatoes: Adds a burst of sweetness and colour.
- Shallots: For a subtle depth of flavour.
- Garlic (4 cloves): A must-have for its aromatic qualities.
- White Wine (1 glass): For deglazing and adding complexity.
- Lime Juice (3 tbsp): Brings a zesty, tangy kick.
- Coriander (1/2 cup): Fresh and vibrant for garnishing.
- Chilli Flakes: Add gentle heat to the dish.

Method:

Simmer Wine and Lime: Combine the white wine and lime juice in a saucepan, bringing the mixture to a simmer. This base will infuse the dish with a tangy depth.

Sauté Aromatics: Add finely chopped garlic and shallots to the pan, letting them soften and become fragrant in the tangy mixture.

Prepare Tomatoes: Halve the cherry tomatoes. For firmer tomatoes, add them towards the end of cooking. Add softer tomatoes early into the simmering sauce.

Cook Tagliatelle and Prawns: Stir in the konjac tagliatelle and prawns, cooking for about 2 minutes. The konjac noodles are quick to cook and absorb the sauce's flavours beautifully, while the prawns should be just turned pink and tender.

Garnish and Serve: Once everything is beautifully cooked, plate your prawn tagliatelle and garnish with freshly chopped coriander and a sprinkle of chilli flakes for an extra flavour kick.

Our Prawn Tagliatelle is not just a meal; it's a celebration of flavours and textures, making it a perfect option for a quick yet elegant lunch or dinner. Serve with a side of green salad or steamed vegetables for a complete, nutritious meal that keeps carbs in check while delivering on taste, fibre and satisfaction. Enjoy the ease and simplicity of this dish, proving that a low-carb lifestyle can still be rich, varied, and utterly delicious.

Mushrooms and Angel Hair Noodles: A Simple Symphony

Servings: 2
Prep Time: 15 mins | Cooking Time: 30 mins | **Total Time: 45 mins**

Dive into the culinary simplicity of a dish that pairs the sleek, zero-carb elegance of konjac noodles with the earthy charm of mushrooms. This delightful combination promises a meal that's as kind to your carb count as tantalising to your taste buds. Ideal for those on a weight loss journey, managing diabetes, or maintaining ketosis, this dish is a testament to the fact that simplicity can be sublime.

Unlock the full experience!
Scan the QR code to watch the video

Ingredients:

- 200g Konjac Noodles – The slender strands of guilt-free indulgence.
- 200g Mushrooms – Sliced thinly, these are the humble heroes of our dish.
- Fresh Herbs – A verdant flourish to match your culinary theme.
- 2 Knobs of Butter – The golden droplets that bring our ensemble to life.

Method:

Begin this culinary ballet by warming the butter in a frying pan until it whispers secrets of flavour to come. Watch as it melts, ready to envelop the other ingredients in its rich, comforting embrace.

Introduce the konjac noodles and mushrooms to the pan simultaneously, allowing them to mingle with the butter. This is where simplicity meets sophistication, as each ingredient begins to take on the warmth and richness of the butter.

Now, consider the theme of your main dish. Whether it whispers the exotic tales of India, carries the vibrant zests of China, or echoes the aromatic spices of Thailand, let this theme guide your choice of fresh herbs and spices. This is your moment to infuse the dish with personality and flair, turning the simple into the extraordinary.

As the noodles and mushrooms sizzle gently, toss them lovingly, ensuring they're coated with the golden sheen of butter and imbued with the flavours of your chosen herbs and spices.

There you have it – 'Mushrooms and Angel Hair Noodles,' a dish that proves that with just a few quality ingredients and a dash of creativity, you can create a side dish that's not only easy and quick but packed with flavour and nutrition. It's a culinary hug in a bowl, ready to complement any main dish while standing proudly on its own.

High Fibre Lunches & Mains

Several of the recipes featured in this collection use konjac noodles or spaghetti, a staple ingredient for those seeking a healthy, low-carb option. We're proud to introduce our own brand of Konjac products, which are made exclusively from glucomannan. The details can be found on page 955. Our konjac noodles stand out from the crowd for a few reasons. First and foremost, we commit to avoiding any chemical preservatives, ensuring our noodles have a fresher taste and don't require washing before use – a convenience we think you'll appreciate. While this means our noodles may not have the near-infinite shelf life of others, we reckon the trade-off for superior taste and quality is well worth it. Of course, we understand the importance of choice and encourage you to explore other brands as you see fit.

Garam Masala Beef & Noodles: Speedy Gourmet

Servings: 2
Prep Time: 1 mins | Cooking Time: 3 mins | **Total Time: 4 mins**

Imagine a dish that wraps up the aromatic essence of Garam Masala with the robustness of beef and the guilt-free pleasure of konjac spaghetti, all in less than the time it takes to check your email. our 'Garam Masala Beef & Noodles' are a culinary sprint to the finish line, proving that speedy cooking doesn't have to sacrifice depth of flavour or nutritional value.

Ingredients:

- 200g Konjac Spaghetti: A noodle that's all about health, no carbs attached.
- Steak: The centrepiece, ready to meld with exotic spices.
- 2 tbsp Garam Masala: A spice mix that's a ticket to the vibrant streets of India.
- 2 Knobs of Butter: For that silky, richly spiced sauce that coats every strand and steak piece.

Method:

Begin by warming the butter in a saucepan over medium heat, melting it into a golden foundation for our culinary adventure.

As the butter starts to sing, introduce the konjac spaghetti and the steak to the pan, welcoming them to a bath of warmth and flavour.

Sprinkle the Garam Masala evenly over the mix, stirring to ensure that the spices caress each piece of steak and every noodle, absorbing the rich, complex flavours.
Cook the mix to your preference, allowing the steak to reach your ideal point of doneness. Whether you prefer a blush of pink or a more thorough warmth, this dish is about crafting it your way.

For those who enjoy sliced steak, now's the moment to remove it from the heat and carve it into tender strips that can be easily mixed with the noodles, ensuring every forkful is a perfect blend of meat and masala.

Our 'Garam Masala Beef & Noodles' serves up a feast of flavours in a flash, embodying the essence of quick, health-conscious cooking without skimping on the culinary experience.

Tip: When buying, the supermarket home brands are often more pure, with just the spices and nothing added.

Gammon on Spaghetti: Effortless Elegance

Servings: 1
Prep Time: 1 mins | Cooking Time: 12 mins | **Total Time: 13 mins**

Indulge in the simplicity of a meal that boasts just four ingredients yet delivers a powerhouse of flavour. Our 'Gammon on Spaghetti' is a testament to the magic that happens when minimalism meets the keto-friendly marvel of konjac spaghetti, all seasoned to perfection with Moroccan spices or, in fact, any spices of your choosing. It is ideal for when time is of the essence, but the craving for something hearty and satisfying prevails.

Ingredients:

- 200g Gammon: A rich, savoury cut ready to take centre stage.
- 200g Konjac Spaghetti: The perfect low-carb base for our flavourful journey.
- Moroccan Spice Mix: Or a sprinkle of your favourite spice blend.
- 2 tbsp Butter: For that silky, sumptuous texture.
- Black Pepper (optional): Freshly ground, to taste, for a final kick.

Method:

Kick-off this culinary escapade by melting the butter in a pan over medium heat, setting the stage for a melding of flavours.

Lay the gammon in the glistening butter and let it cook gently for about 10 minutes. This is when the gammon transforms, browning and softening into a tender delight.

As the gammon nears perfection, introduce the konjac spaghetti to the pan, a nod to tradition with a modern, carb-conscious twist.
Sprinkle your chosen spices over the duo, followed by a generous grind of black pepper, stirring to ensure the spaghetti and gammon are evenly coated in the rich, aromatic blend.

Cook together for just a minute more, just long enough for the spaghetti to warm through and absorb the essence of the spices and the richness of the gammon.

There you have it: Our 'Gammon on Spaghetti,' a dish that's as quick and easy as it is deeply satisfying. With no prep time and a total cooking time of barely over ten minutes, it's the perfect solution for a nourishing, flavour-packed meal on those nights when simplicity is your culinary mantra. This dish proves that less indeed can be more, especially when creating delicious, high-fibre, keto-friendly meals.

Duck Breast with Orange Sauce

Servings: 4
Prep Time: 15 mins | Cooking Time: 10 mins | **Total Time: 25 mins**

Embrace the elegance of French cuisine with this Duck Breast with Orange Sauce recipe, a low-carb take on the classic 'duck à l'orange'. This dish combines the succulence of perfectly cooked duck with the vibrant tang of an orange sauce, minus the traditional sugar content. It's a recipe designed to impress, offering a sophisticated yet straightforward dining experience.

Ingredients for the duck:

- Duck Breasts: The star of the show, rendered perfectly to achieve crispy skin and tender meat.
- Dried Coriander (3 tsp) and dried Cumin (2 tsp): Spices that enhance the duck's flavour.
- Salt (1/2 tsp) and pepper (1/2 tsp): Basic seasonings that elevate the meat's taste.
- Olive Oil: Just a drizzle for cooking the duck to perfection.

Ingredients for the orange sauce:

- Orange Juice (from 1 or 2 oranges): This fresh and tangy juice forms the base of the sauce.
- Apple Cider Vinegar (2 tbsp): Adds a sharp depth.
- Butter (1 tbsp): Enriches the sauce, giving it a smooth texture.
- Orange Zest (from 1 orange): Brings bright citrus notes.
- Stevia (1 tsp): The natural sweetener alternative.
- Olive Oil (1 tbsp): Helps to emulsify the sauce.
- Konjac Flour (1 tsp): A thickening agent that boosts fibre content

Method:

Prepare the Duck: Mix salt, coriander, cumin, and pepper. Rub this blend on the flesh side of the duck breasts. Heat a drizzle of olive oil in a skillet until very hot. Place the duck skin-side down, cooking until the skin is crisp and golden, about 6 minutes. Spoon out excess fat as needed.

Achieve Perfect Doneness: After cooking skin-side down, flip the duck and cook to your preferred level of doneness. The ideal internal temperature is between 52°C to 55°C, or use the finger test for a firm yet springy feel. Slice the duck partially to check doneness, returning to the pan if necessary.

Enhance with Orange: Optionally, add orange slices to the pan while cooking the duck for added flavour and a decorative touch.

Create the Orange Sauce: Combine orange juice, vinegar, butter, orange zest, stevia, and olive oil in a saucepan. Bring to a boil, adjusting the consistency with konjac flour and water if needed.

Serve: Arrange the sliced duck on plates, accompanied by the fried orange slices and a generous drizzle of the orange sauce. Pair with parmesan broccoli for a complete meal.

This Duck Breast with Orange Sauce recipe is a testament to the beauty of gourmet cooking made simple and healthy. Combining juicy duck with the citrusy, tangy sauce creates a palate-pleasing dish that's as nutritious as delicious. Enjoy this culinary masterpiece as a special weekend dinner or to mark a celebratory occasion.

Lamb Shank in Red Wine Sauce: A Slow-Cooked Delight

Servings: 4
Prep Time: 15 min | Cooking Time: 360 mins | **Total Time: 375 mins**

Dive into the heart-warming comfort of Lamb Shank in Red Wine Sauce, a dish that epitomises slow-cooked perfection. This recipe marries the robust flavours of red wine with tender lamb, falling off the bone into a rich, antioxidant-packed sauce. Ideal for a leisurely weekend dinner, this one-pot wonder minimises kitchen clean-up without skimping on taste.

Ingredients:

- Lamb Shank (Approx: 800g): The centrepiece is rich and ready to become tender.
- Red Wine (1/2 to 1 bottle): Choose a good quality Pinot Noir for flavour and health benefits.
- Red Onion: Adds sweetness and depth.
- Thyme, Rosemary, Oregano: Herbs that infuse the meat with earthy, aromatic flavours.
- Garlic (5 or 6 cloves): For a robust foundation.
- Carrots (3 or 4) and celery (3 sticks): Two vegetables that contribute to the dishes complexity.
- Tomato (1 can), Tomato Puree (1 or 2 tsp): For acidity and thickness.
- Beef Stock (300ml, optional): Use if you need more liquid to cover the meat.
- Konjac Flour (1 or 2 tsp): A thickening agent that adds fibre.
- Salt & Pepper: Essential seasonings to enhance all the flavours.

Method:

Browning the Lamb: Start by searing the lamb shanks in a hot frying pan with olive oil until they're nicely browned. This crucial step locks in flavours and sets the stage for slow cooking.

Prepare the Vegetables: Chop the red onion, carrots, and celery into rough pieces. Mince the garlic for a more profound taste.

Layer and Pour: In a snug-fitting pot, place the seared lamb shanks on top of the vegetables. Pour the red wine over the meat, ensuring it's completely covered. Add beef stock if necessary.

Thicken the Sauce: Stir in tomato puree and konjac flour to the pot, mixing well to avoid clumps. This will help thicken the sauce during cooking.

Slow Cooking: Transfer the pot to an oven preheated to a low temperature (around 160°C) and cook for at least 3 hours. For those with more time, slow-cooking in a cooker on a low setting for up to 6 hours is ideal, making the meat incredibly tender.

Garnish and Serve: Once cooked, garnish with fresh thyme sprigs for an added touch of flavour and presentation

Thai Red Curry

Servings: 2
Prep Time: 5 min | Cooking Time: 15 mins | **Total Time: 18 mins**

Imagine being marooned on a desert island with just one dish for company. It's a no-brainer for me: I would take this Red Thai Curry, a treasure trove of flavours. It's a culinary SOS that delivers comfort, spice, and everything nice, costing less than £2 per serving. Dive into this fragrant escapade, ideally nestled on a bed of Konjac Angel Hair pasta or sidekick by courgetti or cauliflower rice.

Ingredients:

- Chicken Thighs (2, chopped): The hero of our island story, cheaper than breast and more flavoursome.
- Coconut Milk (½ can): Creamy fibrous base for our curry dreams.
- Fresh Coriander (2 tbsp): For that herby freshness.
- Spring Onions (2, sliced): A crispy, oniony touch.
- Lemongrass (1 stick, dried): The aromatic backbone.
- Lazy Garlic (1 tsp): Because on a desert island, no one likes peeling garlic.
- Lime Juice (a splash): For a zesty finale.
- Red Thai Curry Paste (2 tsp): The spice that starts the party.
- Optional: Konjac Angel Hair pasta, courgetti or cauliflower rice.

Method:

Sauté and Aromatise: Heat your wok with a splash of olive oil. Sizzle 1.5 spring onions and garlic until they soften, whispering secrets of flavours to come. Introduce the lemongrass, letting its aroma set the scene.

Spice It Up: Welcome the red Thai curry paste to the pan. Stir well, letting each ingredient get to know each other.

Chicken Tango: Add the chicken, tossing it in the spicy mix with a sprinkle of fresh coriander. Once it's dressed in white, pour in the coconut milk, stirring the pot of potential.

Simmer and Season: Let it bubble gently for 15 minutes. As the sauce thickens and the chicken cooks, add a splash of lime juice and adjust the seasoning.

Serve in Style: Lay down a bed of Konjac Angel Hair pasta or uncooked courgetti (or lightly sautéed, if you prefer), scoop the aromatic curry atop, and garnish with the remaining spring onion and coriander. A feast fit for a castaway king!

Low-Carb Spaghetti and Basil Meatballs

Servings: 4
Prep Time: 10 min | Cooking Time: 25 mins | **Total Time: 35 mins**

Indulge in the comforting embrace of basil meatballs nestled in a vibrant tomato sauce, served over low-carb spaghetti. This dish redefines comfort food for those navigating the realms of low-carb or keto diets, infusing fresh herbs and spices into homemade meatballs for a nourishing and satisfying meal.

Ingredients:

- Beef Mince: The foundation of our hearty meatballs.
- Parmesan Cheese: For a salty, umami kick within each meatball.
- Fresh Basil (2 tbsp, finely chopped): For a burst of herby freshness.
- Egg: The binder that keeps our meaty orbs intact.
- Sea Salt (1/2 tsp) & Black Pepper (1/2 tsp): Seasoning to taste, laying the flavour groundwork.
- Onion Granules (1/2 tbsp): For subtle sweetness and depth.
- Chilli Flakes (1 tsp): A hint of heat to spark the palate.
- Dried Basil (1 tbsp): Doubling down on the herb's aromatic charm.
- Chopped Tomatoes: The base of our luscious sauce.
- Olive Oil (3 tbsp): For frying and richness.
- Konjac Tagliatelle (2 packets): The guilt-free vehicle for our sauce and meatballs.
- Spinach (2 handfuls): A green, nutritious twist to the dish.

Method:

Combine beef mince, Parmesan cheese, egg, salt, pepper, onion granules, chilli flakes, dried, and fresh basil in a bowl. Dive in with wet hands to mix and form into succulent meatballs.
Warm olive oil in a pan over medium heat. Introduce meatballs to the pan, browning them to perfection on all sides.

Stir in the chopped tomatoes around the meatballs, letting the ensemble simmer for 15 minutes to marry the flavours, adding more salt and pepper to taste.

As the sauce thickens and bubbles, fold in the spinach, allowing it to wilt gently into the sauce, infusing it with a pop of colour and a dose of vitamins. Now add the konjac noodles or tagliatelle.

Our 'Low-Carb Spaghetti and Basil Meatballs' dish is a testament to the joy of adapting classic comforts to fit modern dietary preferences. Each bite delivers the familiar warmth of spaghetti and meatballs with a fresh twist that keeps your carbs in check and your taste buds delighted. Perfect for a cosy family dinner or impressing guests with your culinary prowess—all while sticking to your healthful eating goals.

Prawn Spaghetti with a Creamy White Sauce

Servings: 4
Prep Time: 20 min | Cooking Time: 30 mins | **Total Time: 50 mins**

Dive into a dish that marries the luxury of king prawns with spaghetti's comfort, all swathed in a sumptuous creamy white sauce. This culinary creation is a nod to classic indulgence, redesigned for those on high-fibre and keto diets. It's a testament to the possibility of enjoying rich, satisfying meals while adhering to a health-conscious lifestyle.

Ingredients:

- Extra Virgin Olive Oil: A drizzle for pan-kissed flavours.
- Butter (1 tsp): For that silky foundation.
- Garlic Clove (1 tbsp): Minced for aromatic fervour.
- Asparagus: Freshly snipped to add a tender crunch.
- King Prawns: Succulent treasures from the sea.
- Parsley: Freshly chopped for a verdant garnish.
- Konjac Noodles (1 or 2 packs): The low-carb hero of our dish.

Ingredients for the white sauce:

- Full-Fat Cream Milk (300ml): For a velvety smooth base.
- Cream Cheese: For richness and tang.
- Salt (1/2 tsp) & Black Pepper (1/4 tsp)
- Nutmeg (1 large pinch): A whisper of warmth and depth.

Method:

Warm a pan with a drizzle of olive oil and a teaspoon of butter over medium heat, letting the butter melt into an inviting pool. Stir in the minced garlic, sautéing just until fragrant, mindful to let it sing, not scorch.

Introduce the asparagus, letting it bask and turn in the garlicky butter for 5 minutes until it captures a bit of colour and tenderness.

Transfer the asparagus to a plate, making room for the next act. If needed, add a touch more oil, then welcome the king prawns, sautéing until they blush pink and confirm their readiness.

For the white sauce, combine cream milk, cream cheese, salt, pepper, and nutmeg in a non-stick saucepan over medium heat. Whisk and simmer, letting it bubble gently to a thickened glory.

Reunite konjac noodles with heat in a pan, stirring for 2-3 minutes to warm through. Return the prawns and asparagus to the fray, melding with the noodles.

Lavish the creamy sauce over your noodle mix, deciding on the sauce's generosity according to your preference for creaminess. With a final seasoning tweak, the dish comes together in harmony.

Serve the spaghetti, crowning each plate with a sprinkle of parsley for that final touch of fresh, herbal brightness.

Our 'Prawn Spaghetti with a Creamy White Sauce' is a shining example of how high-fibre, low-carb eating can still encapsulate the essence of gourmet dining. Each forkful promises indulgence, balanced with the nutritional virtues of a carefully curated diet. Enjoy this lush, comforting dish, secure in the knowledge that pleasure and health can indeed coexist beautifully on your plate.

Basil and King Prawn Tomato Spaghetti

Servings: 2
Prep Time: 10 min | Cooking Time: 5 mins | **Total Time: 15 mins**

Prepare to dazzle your taste buds and those of your dining companions with a dish that's bursting with flavour yet astonishingly quick to bring to the table. Our 'Basil and King Prawn Tomato Spaghetti' marries the succulence of king prawns with the robust tang of tomatoes and the aromatic delight of fresh basil, all entwined with konjac spaghetti's convenience and health benefits. A dream come true for anyone embracing a high-fibre, low-carb lifestyle or managing diabetes, this recipe reimagines pasta night as a quick, nutritious, and flavour-packed feast.

Ingredients:

- Konjac Spaghetti (200g): Our dish's low-carb, high-fibre backbone.
- Fresh Cooked King Prawns (150g): The show's star is tender and rich.
- Olive Oil (2 tbsp): For sautéing to perfection.
- Sun-dried Tomatoes (60g): Intensely flavoured jewels of the kitchen.
- Fresh Basil (2 tbsp, chopped): A burst of herby freshness.
- Tinned Tomatoes (200g): The base of our rich, tangy sauce.
- Whole Garlic Cloves (2, chopped or minced): For that essential aromatic kick.
- Apple Cider Vinegar (2 tbsp): A touch of acidity to brighten the flavours.
- Black Pepper (1/4 tsp): Just a hint for a spicy edge.
- Oregano (1/2 tsp): For that classic, herby depth.

Method:

Warm the olive oil in a pan over medium heat, setting the stage for a culinary creation that's both simple and sublime. Introduce the garlic and sun-dried tomatoes, letting them sizzle for 2 minutes until fragrant and slightly softened.

Stir in the apple cider vinegar, oregano, tinned tomatoes, and prawns, transforming the pan's contents into a simmering pot of potential. Watch as the sauce thickens, melding the flavours into something extraordinary.

Welcome the chopped fresh basil and black pepper into the mix, followed by the konjac spaghetti. Ensure the spaghetti is prepped according to pack instructions for the best result. Blend everything together, cooking for 2 minutes until the dish is thoroughly heated.

Serve this magnificent concoction steaming hot, with a choice of garnish, a sprinkle of Parmesan or a scattering of toasted nuts (high in fibre), each adding its own final flourish to the dish.

Our 'Basil and King Prawn Tomato Spaghetti' is a testament to the joy of cooking and eating well without spending hours in the kitchen. It's a perfect solution for a midweek dinner or a casual dining experience with friends, offering all the complexities of flavour and nutrition you desire with none of the fuss. This dish is a vibrant celebration of pasta, reinvented for a fibre-conscious era.

Tagliatelle Pistachio Pesto with Chicken

Servings: 2
Prep Time: 15 min | Cooking Time: 25 mins | **Total Time: 40 mins**

Prepare to dazzle your guests with a dish that marries the rustic charm of Italian cuisine with the innovative twist of Konjac pasta, all wrapped in the rich, nutty embrace of pistachio pesto. This Tagliatelle Pistachio Pesto with Chicken is not just a meal; it's a statement of culinary finesse, promising to turn an ordinary evening into a gourmet experience.

Ingredients for the pistachio pesto:

- Basil Leaves (3 cups): The verdant heart of the pesto.
- Pistachios (1/3 cup, shelled): Adds a unique, nutty depth.
- Parmesan (1/2 cup, grated): Lends a salty, umami richness.
- Garlic (2 cloves): For that essential aromatic kick.
- Lemon (1/2): Brightens the pesto with a hint of acidity.
- Extra Virgin Olive Oil (1/2 cup): For a luxurious texture.
- Salt (to taste): Balances and enhances all the flavours.

Ingredients for the pistachio pesto:

- Konjac Tagliatelle (400g): A low-carb, high-fibre alternative.
- Pistachio Pesto (4 tbsp): Brings the dish to life with its vibrant flavour.
- Chicken Breast: The protein-packed centrepiece.
- Cherry Tomatoes: Adds a pop of sweetness and colour.
- Salt & Pepper (to taste): The final seasoning touch.

Method for the pistachio pesto:

Combine basil, pistachios, Parmesan, and garlic in a food processor, pulsing to chop coarsely. Squeeze in lemon juice, then drizzle in olive oil while blending, creating a harmonious pesto. Season with salt, adjusting to your preference.

Method for the chicken tagliatelle:

Kickstart your culinary creation by preheating the oven to 180°C and readying it for the chicken's transformation.

Briefly sauté the Konjac Tagliatelle in a dry pan to lessen its moisture, then set aside in a sieve for that perfect al dente finish.

Sear the chicken breast, skin side down, in a hot pan with olive oil. Season as it sizzles to golden perfection, then flip and repeat. Transfer to the oven, letting it roast to juicy readiness.

As the chicken nears completion, toss the pesto with the tagliatelle and cherry tomatoes in a large bowl, ensuring each strand gleams with the pesto's nutty allure.

Slice or leave the chicken whole to nest atop your pesto-coated tagliatelle, ready to serve and impress.

Our 'Tagliatelle Pistachio Pesto with Chicken' is an ode to the joy of cooking with heart and eating with gusto. Each forkful is a journey through layers of texture and bursts of flavour, making it an unforgettable addition to your culinary repertoire. This dish doesn't just feed the body; it nourishes the soul.

Spaghetti Alla Puttanesca: A Low-Carb Italian Classic

Servings: 2
Prep Time: 8 min | Cooking Time: 20 mins | **Total Time: 28 mins**

Spaghetti Alla Puttanesca brings a bold, robust flavour to the table, a testament to its vibrant Neapolitan roots. Traditionally rich with the tang of tomatoes, the brininess of olives and capers, and a hint of garlic and anchovy, this dish has been reinvented here with Konjac spaghetti to satisfy those seeking a low-carb option without compromising on taste.

Ingredients:

- Konjac Spaghetti (400g): The low-carb backbone of our dish.
- Capers (30g): For bursts of tangy brine.
- Garlic (2 cloves, smashed): To infuse the oil with its aromatic flavour.
- Anchovies (2 fillets, chopped): Adding a salty, umami depth.
- Black Olives (50g): For a touch of Mediterranean bitterness.
- Chilli (1 tsp, chopped): Bring gentle heat to the dish.
- Spinach (a handful): For colour and a nutritious boost.
- Olive Oil (4 tbsp): The medium that carries and amplifies the flavours.
- Tomatoes (1 can, chopped): The acidic, sweet base of the sauce.

Method:

Begin by warming the olive oil in a large pan over medium heat. Introduce the smashed garlic, savouring the fragrance as it infuses the oil, cooking for 1 minute. Stir in the anchovies, letting them dissolve into the base, before adding the chopped tomatoes, olives, capers, and chilli. Allow the mixture to bubble to a boil, then simmer gently for 10 minutes, laying the foundation for a richly flavoured sauce. Toss in the spinach last, letting it gently wilt into the sauce, marrying its freshness with the robust flavours.

Next, prepare the konjac spaghetti by draining it and then frying it in a non-stick pan for 2-3 minutes. The aim is to dry out the noodles slightly, achieving a texture reminiscent of traditional pasta, ready to soak up the sauce.

Combine the spaghetti with the puttanesca sauce, generously coating each strand. Serve this marriage of flavours proudly. This dish pays homage to Italian culinary tradition while embracing modern dietary preferences.

This Spaghetti Alla Puttanesca celebrates Italian cuisine's bold flavours and the versatility of high-fibre, low-carb alternatives. Perfect for a keto-friendly meal that doesn't skimp on taste or satisfaction, it invites you to enjoy the richness of Italian cooking in a health-conscious and heartily delicious form.

Spaghetti Carbonara: A Fibre-Rich Twist on a Classic

Servings: 2
Prep Time: 6 min | Cooking Time: 12 mins | **Total Time: 18 mins**

Our good friend and chef Will Procter reinvented this creamy, comforting embrace of Spaghetti Carbonara to suit a fibre-rich diet without sacrificing the soul-satisfying flavours of this Italian classic. Utilising konjac spaghetti, this version brings a health-conscious approach to a beloved dish, ensuring you can indulge guilt-free.

Ingredients:

- Pancetta (4 slices): The crispy, salty spark of the dish.
- Eggs: The creamy binder for our carbonara sauce.
- Parmesan Cheese (40g): For that sharp, umami richness.
- Konjac Spaghetti (400g): A high-fibre, low-carb alternative to traditional pasta.
- Spinach (a handful): Adds colour and a nutritional punch.
- Garlic (2 cloves): For a subtle, aromatic depth.
- Full Fat Cream (4 tbsp): Ensures the sauce is indulgently smooth.
- Extra Virgin Olive Oil (4 tbsp): For sautéing and combining flavours.
- Black Pepper (to taste): Add spicy warmth to the dish.

Method:

Begin by separating the eggs and placing the yolks in a bowl. Grate the Parmesan cheese into the yolks, season with black pepper, and whisk. Set this creamy concoction aside for the magic moment.

Dice the pancetta, readying it for its crispy fate. Gently crush the garlic, infusing olive oil with its flavour in a pan over medium heat. Add the pancetta, frying until perfectly crisp.

Next, prepare the konjac spaghetti by draining and pan-frying to reduce moisture, ensuring a pasta-like texture that's ready to soak up the sauce.

Reintroduce the pancetta to the pan, and now add the spaghetti. Toss thoroughly, allowing the spaghetti strands to fully embrace the garlic and pancetta's rich flavours.

Stir in the cream, mixing well. Introduce the spinach, allowing it to wilt beautifully into the mix. Season with pepper, then gently pour the egg and Parmesan mixture.

Plate this masterpiece, garnishing with additional Parmesan and a twist of black pepper for that final touch.

This Spaghetti Carbonara version is a testament to culinary creativity, proving that even the most traditional dishes can be adapted for today's health-conscious connoisseurs. Enjoy the harmony of flavours and textures, from the crispy pancetta to the silky sauce, all wrapped around fibrous konjac spaghetti—a truly modern take on a classic comfort dish.

Creamy Spinach & Mushroom Spaghetti

Servings: 2
Prep Time: 2 min | Cooking Time: 8 mins | **Total Time: 10 mins**

Dive into the heart of Italian culinary tradition with a keto-friendly and fibre-rich twist. This Creamy Spinach & Mushroom Spaghetti swaps traditional pasta for konjac spaghetti, offering a delightful dish that's as nourishing as it is luxurious. Perfect for a cosy night in or a nutritious lunch, this recipe promises all the richness of Italian cuisine without the carb load.

Ingredients:

- Konjac Spaghetti (400g): A zero-carb, high-fibre alternative to traditional pasta.
- Chestnut Mushrooms (200g): Earthy and meaty, perfect for adding depth.
- Double Cream (100ml): For that rich, velvety sauce.
- Shallot: Adds a subtle sweetness to the dish.
- Parmesan Cheese (30g): For a silky texture.
- Mascarpone (1 tbsp): Enhances the creaminess of the sauce.
- Cracked Pepper & Salt (to taste): For seasoning perfection.
- Olive Oil (2 tbsp): The base for sautéing.
- Spinach (a handful): Brings colour, texture, and nutrition.
- Garlic (2 cloves): A must-have for that aromatic foundation.

Method:

Begin by finely chopping the shallot, slicing the mushrooms, and grating the garlic, setting the stage for a flavour-packed sauté.

Warm olive oil in a pan, gently sautéing the shallot until translucent and soft, laying the groundwork for the dish's aromatic profile.

Introduce the mushrooms to the pan, allowing them to brown and release moisture. Follow with the garlic, seasoning the mix with salt and cracked pepper, stirring until fragrant.

Gradually blend in the double cream and mascarpone, stirring to achieve a silky and glossy sauce. A dash of hot water can help unify the sauce, drawing out the full richness of the ingredients. Melt in the Parmesan, then dial down the heat to preserve the sauce's velvety texture.

Fold the spinach, letting it wilt and meld with the sauce, ensuring every leaf is coated in creamy goodness.

Prepare the konjac spaghetti by draining it and then lightly frying it to reduce any excess moisture, enhancing its pasta-like quality.

Combine the noodles with the sauce, ensuring they are thoroughly coated and warmed through. If the sauce thickens more than desired, stir in a teaspoon of hot water to adjust the consistency.

Serve this sumptuous Creamy Spinach & Mushroom Spaghetti garnished with extra Parmesan and a twist of cracked pepper, inviting you to enjoy a dish that's as satisfying and heart-warming as health-conscious. This recipe is a testament to the art of substitution, proving that dietary restrictions are no barrier to gourmet indulgence.

Pork Tenderloin & Mushroom Noodles

Servings: 4
Prep Time: 10 min | Cooking Time: 20 mins | **Total Time: 70 mins**

Introduce your friends to a dish that not only boasts fine dining aesthetics but also packs a punch in the fibre flavour department while keeping carbs at bay. This Pork Tenderloin & Mushroom Noodles recipe is a delight to prepare and devour, offering a sweet twist that will win over everyone in the family. Its one-pan wonder status means enjoying the feast without worrying about a mountain of dishes afterwards.

Ingredients:

- Pork Tenderloin (800g): Ready to take on the sweet and savoury marinade.
- NKD Syrup (4 tbsp): A high-fibre, low-carb alternative to honey; I buy mine from Amazon.
- Shiitake Mushrooms (120g): Adds an earthy depth and texture.
- Konjac Noodles (200g)
- Coriander (a bunch): For freshness and a pop of colour.
- Red Chilli Pepper: Adds a customisable kick of heat.
- Garlic (4 cloves): For a robust flavour foundation.
- Spring Onion: Brings a sharp, green crunch.
- Black Pepper (a sprinkle): For a bit of spice.
- Coconut Oil (1 tbsp): The medium for sautéing and combining flavours.

Method:

Begin by prepping your pork tenderloin. Slice into manageable pieces or score almost through to create a butterfly effect, stopping at chopstick height to keep the piece intact.

Not done this before? It's really simple. Place the loin between two chopsticks and cut until your knife hits the fork.

Warm coconut oil in a pan over medium heat. Sauté the garlic until fragrant, then drizzle the pan with NKD syrup before introducing the pork. Allow it to sear and caramelise, flipping once to ensure even browning.

As the pork takes on a golden hue, scatter in the spring onions, sliced shiitake mushrooms, and a handful of coriander, including the aromatic stalks. Embrace another splash of syrup to enhance the sweetness.

For those who enjoy a spicy note, add sliced red chilli into the pan or reserve it as a garnish for later, catering to all palates at your table.

After the pork and veggies are beautifully melded, stir in the konjac noodles to combine and warm through. This final twist ensures that each element is coated in the savoury-sweet sauce.

For those who dare, serve this culinary creation garnished with a crack of black pepper, fresh coriander leaves, and red chili slices.

Chicken & Coriander Noodles

Servings: 4
Prep Time: 10 min | Cooking Time: 25 mins | **Total Time: 35 mins**

A dish that champions both health and taste, combining tender chicken with the refreshing zing of coriander over a bed of konjac noodles. This Chicken & Coriander Noodles recipe is a culinary breeze to whip up, offering a meal that's not just satisfying to the palate but also kind to your wellness goals.

Ingredients:

- Chicken Breast: Sliced into thin strips for quick cooking and easy eating.
- Konjac Noodles (200g): A fantastic, fibre-rich pasta alternative.
- Coriander (a bunch): Fresh and vibrant, used in cooking and garnish.
- Red Onion: Adds a sweet, sharp bite to the dish.
- Garlic (6 cloves): For a rich, aromatic base.
- Coconut Milk (400g): Lends fibre creaminess and a subtle tropical flavour.
- Lemon: The juice brings brightness and acidity, balancing the dish.
- Red Chilli: For a touch of heat, adjust to your preference.
- Black Pepper (a sprinkle): For a bit of spice.
- Coconut Oil (1 tbsp): Ideal for frying with its high smoke point and added flavour.

Method:

Prepare the Chicken: You can boil the chicken strips for a softer texture or fry them for a golden finish. Boiling is recommended for a tender bite, especially for this dish's light, brothy style.

Prep Aromatics and Noodles: While the chicken cooks, prepare your garlic, coriander stalks, onion, and konjac noodles. Grating, chopping, and rinsing as needed sets the stage for a quick assembly later.

Sauté Aromatics: Heat the coconut oil in a large pan and fry the garlic to unlock its fragrance. Quickly follow with the onions and coriander stalks, stirring until they're softened and infused with flavour.

Simmer: Add half the can of coconut milk to the pan, squeezing in the lemon juice for an added zing. This creamy citrus base will allow your noodles and cooked chicken to mingle.

Combine: Add the konjac noodles and chicken to the pan, seasoning with black pepper. Stir to ensure each noodle strand is coated in the aromatic, creamy sauce.

Garnish and Serve: For those who appreciate a spicy kick, finish the dish with a generous scattering of fresh coriander leaves and, if desired, slices of red chilli.

Mexican Beef Pie: A Low Carb Delight

Servings: 4
Prep Time: 15 min | Cooking Time: 40 mins | **Total Time: 55 mins**

Elevate your pie game with this Mexican Beef Pie, a favourite in my home that beautifully marries the hearty flavours of Mexican cuisine with the innovative approach of low-carb baking. Mastering our special low-carb pastry, which leverages the binding power of soft cheese, eggs, and konjac flour, opens up a world of delicious, guilt-free pie options. This particular version boasts a filling rich in spices, tender beef, and fibrous black beans, all encased in a flavourful, tender crust.

Ingredients for the pastry:

- Almond Flour (7 heaped tbsp): For a fibre nutty, low-carb base.
- Coconut Flour (3 heaped tbsp): Adds texture and fibre.
- Konjac Flour (2 heaped tsp): Helps to bind the dough (and adds more fibre).
- Baking Powder (1 tsp): Ensures the pastry rises slightly.
- Egg: Binds the ingredients together.
- Olive Oil (3 tbsp): Adds moisture and richness.
- Salt (a pinch): Balances the flavours.
- Butter: To ease the pan, ensure nothing sticks.

Ingredients for Mexican filling:

- Minced Beef (500g): The protein-packed star of the filling.
- Konjac Flour (2 tsp): Thickens the filling without adding carbs.
- Spring Onion (6, sliced): Adds a fresh, crisp texture.
- Black Beans (1 can): For heartiness and fibre.
- Soft Cheese (250g): Creates a creamy, rich base for the filling.
- Red Onion: Brings sweetness and colour.
- Eggs: Helps set the filling.
- Chilli Powder (1 tsp), Cumin (2 tsp), and Oregano (2 tsp) are the spices that give the filling its Mexican flair.
- Red Bell Pepper (1, diced): Adds sweetness and a pop of colour.
- Garlic (4 cloves): The aromatic base of many great dishes.

Method for the pastry:

1. Combine all pastry ingredients to form a dough. If it is too thick, adjust with a bit of water.
2. Grease a 20cm round baking tray with butter and line it with greased parchment paper for easy dough handling and baking.
3. Roll out the dough, forming a base and sides in the prepped tray and a separate top on another piece of paper.
4. Bake the empty shell (but not the top) at 180°C for 15-20 minutes until just starting to golden.

Method for the filling:

1. Sauté garlic in olive oil, add onions and beef and cook until browned. Mix in spices for a deep flavour.
2. Whisk eggs and blend with soft cheese and konjac flour. Then, fold in beans, spring onions, and other filling ingredients, cooking together briefly.
3. Spoon the mixture into the pre-baked pastry shell, packing it down to avoid air gaps.
4. Cover with the pastry top, sealing the edges, and bake for another 15-20 minutes until the pie is golden and the filling is set.
5. Serve this Mexican Beef Pie as a stand-out addition to any meal. It combines Mexico's complex flavours and textures with the satisfaction of a traditional pie, all while keeping it low-carb and high-fibre. It's a testament to the versatility of low-carb cooking and the joy of sharing good food with family and friends.

Beef Bolognese with Konjac Tagliatelle: A Low-Carb Delight

Servings: 6
Prep Time: 15 min | Cooking Time: 60 mins | **Total Time: 75 mins**

Revel in the rich flavours of this Beef Bolognese with Konjac Tagliatelle, a dish that masterfully combines traditional Italian cooking with modern dietary needs. This recipe is low in carbs and high in protein, making it an ideal choice for those monitoring their blood sugar levels or following a grain and gluten-free diet. Including konjac tagliatelle ensures a satisfying fibre experience without the carb load, complementing the deeply flavourful bolognese sauce in every bite.

Ingredients:

- Beef Mince (500g): The heart of the bolognese, offering rich, meaty flavour.
- White Onion (1 large)
- Red Pepper (1 medium)
- Courgette (1 medium)
- Garlic (4 cloves, crushed): For aromatic depth.
- Olive Oil (2 tbsp): For sautéing the vegetables and meat.
- Coriander (1 tsp), Smoked Paprika (2 tsp), Italian Mixed Herbs (2 tsp): Spices that infuse the dish with complexity and warmth.
- Beef Stock Cube: Enhances the meaty flavour of the sauce.
- 90% Chocolate (4 squares, optional): Adds an unexpected depth and richness.
- Chopped Tomatoes (2 x 400ml tins): The tomato base of the sauce.
- Water (400ml): Adjust the sauce's consistency.
- Sea Salt: To season.
- Konjac Tagliatelle (400g): A low-carb pasta alternative that's surprisingly satisfying.
- Parmesan (a handful): Adds a nutty, salty finish.
- Butter (1 tbsp): Enriches the tagliatelle.

Method:

Sauté the Vegetables: In a large pan, heat olive oil over high heat and sauté the diced onion, red pepper, and grated courgette until soft.

Brown the Mince: Mix the beef mince with the vegetables until fully coated and browned. Stir in the spices and crumbled beef stock cube, cooking a few minutes more.

Simmer the Sauce: Incorporate the chopped tomatoes and water, bringing the mixture to a boil before reducing to a simmer. Let it cook for about 50 minutes, stirring occasionally to prevent sticking.

Enrich with Chocolate: Stir in the optional dark chocolate, melting it into the sauce for a luxurious fibrous richness and season to taste.

Prepare the Konjac Tagliatelle: In a separate pan, sauté the konjac tagliatelle with butter and a dash of olive oil for 3-4 minutes. Sprinkle in a handful of parmesan to coat the noodles evenly.

Serve: Plate the konjac tagliatelle topped with the hearty beef bolognese sauce. Accompany with steamed broccoli for a complete, nutrient-rich meal.

Teriyaki Turkey Balls with Konjac Noodles

Servings: 4
Prep Time: 10 min | Cooking Time: 20 mins | **Total Time: 30 mins**

Indulge in a fusion of flavours with our Teriyaki Turkey Balls served with konjac noodles. This dish promises the comforting warmth of homemade cooking while keeping your health goals in check. This recipe transforms simple ingredients into a satisfying and nutritious meal, perfect for you and me on our high-fibre, low-carb journey without sacrificing taste or texture.

Ingredients:

- Turkey Mince (500g): Lean and flavourful, forming the base of the meatballs.
- Ground Flax (4 tbsp): Adds fibre and helps bind the meatballs without traditional breadcrumbs.
- Garlic Puree (3 tbsp or 4 cloves, minced): Infuse the meatballs with aromatic depth.
- Olive Oil (1 tbsp): Frying the meatballs to golden perfection.
- Teriyaki Sauce (3 tbsp): Coats the meatballs in a sticky, sweet, savoury glaze.
- Sesame Seeds (3 tbsp): Adds a fibrous crunch and a nutty flavour.
- Pak Choi (1 large, cleaned and chopped): A green side that steams to tender crispness.
- Coriander (a handful, chopped): Provides freshness, antioxidants and colour.
- Konjac Noodles (200g): Our carb-free fibre noodles that love to absorb flavour.
- Spring Onion (3, chopped): Add a mild oniony bite.
- Chilli (1, finely chopped): For a customisable kick of heat.

Method:

Prepare the Turkey Balls: In a large bowl, combine turkey mince, ground flax, garlic, spring onions, and a pinch of sea salt. Massage and mix well, then shape into 16-20 meatballs.

Cook the Meatballs: Heat olive oil in a deep pan over medium-high heat. Fry the meatballs, turning regularly, until golden and cooked through - about 12 minutes.

Glaze: Add teriyaki sauce (ok, this is a little naughty) and sesame seeds to the pan, allowing the sauce to thicken and coat the meatballs evenly.

Incorporate Noodles: Stir in the konjac noodles and cook for an additional 3-4 minutes to integrate them with the flavours.

Steam Pak Choi: Meanwhile, steam the pak choi until tender. If you don't have a steamer, sauté with a bit of water and oil.

Serve: Mix the pak choi with the noodles and meatballs. Serve in bowls, garnishing with fresh chilli and chopped coriander for an extra burst of flavour.

Korean Venison Meatballs

Servings: 4
Prep Time: 15 min | Cooking Time: 15 mins | **Total Time: 30 mins**

Venture into the bold flavours of Korean cuisine with our Korean Venison Meatballs, an adventurous dish that combines the rich taste of venison with a spicy, profoundly flavourful sauce. Whether or not you've been to Korea, this recipe offers a taste of its authentic, spicy food culture, all from the comfort of your kitchen.

Ingredients for the meal:

- Venison (500g, minced): Lean and richly flavoured, perfect for meatballs.
- Halloumi Cheese (80g): Adds a salty, creamy surprise in the centre of each meatball.
- Red Onion, Bell Pepper, Broccoli, Spring Onion: A mix of vegetables for balance and nutrition.
- Olive Oil: For cooking the meatballs and vegetables.
- Salt & Pepper: To season the meat and veggies.

Ingredients for the sauce:

- Gochujang Paste (1 heaped tbsp): The heart of the sauce, offering heat and depth.
- Coconut Aminos (3 tbsp): A soy-free alternative that adds umami.
- Stevia (1 tsp): A hint of sweetness without the sugar.
- Garlic (4 cloves), Ginger (2.5cm square): Aromatic bases of many Korean dishes.
- Full Fat Soft Cheese (100g): Adds creaminess to the sauce.
- Rice Wine Vinegar (1 tsp): Balances the sauce with acidity.
- Konjac Flour (1 tsp): Thickens the sauce while adding fibre.
- Toasted Sesame Oil (optional 2 tsp): For a nutty finishing touch.

Method:

Sauce Preparation: Finely chop the ginger and crush the garlic. Combine with gochujang paste, rice wine vinegar, coconut aminos, soft cheese, stevia, and a splash of water in a saucepan. Simmer until the sauce thickens, adjusting with konjac flour as needed. Stir in toasted sesame oil for extra flavour if using.

Meatball Magic: Shape the minced venison into balls, embedding a piece of halloumi in each. Brown the meatballs in olive oil over medium heat until cooked through.

Vegetable Sauté: In a separate pan, sauté the bell pepper, spring onions, red onion, and broccoli in olive oil, seasoning with salt and pepper.

Serving Suggestion: Arrange the meatballs and vegetables on a plate, garnish with coriander and a sprinkle of black pepper.

This Korean Venison Meatball recipe is a testament to the versatility and global appeal of Korean flavours, seamlessly blending them with the gamey goodness of venison. Perfect for a hearty dinner or as a standout lunch, it's sure to impress with its bold tastes and satisfying textures. Enjoy a culinary journey to Korea through this spicy, delicious dish.

Tuna Silom Coconut Noodles

Servings: 4
Prep Time: 15 min | Cooking Time: 20 mins | **Total Time: 35 mins**

Drawing inspiration from the vibrant streets of Bangkok, this Tuna Silom Coconut Noodles recipe encapsulates the essence of Thai cuisine with a healthy twist. Replacing traditional noodles with konjac noodles enhances the dish's fibre content and makes it a perfect choice for those following a Fire First low-carb lifestyle. The result is a light, coconutty (absolutely a word in our book!), and authentic meal that's as nourishing and flavourful.

Ingredients:

- Tuna Steaks (4): Fresh and ready to be seared to perfection.
- Konjac Noodles (200g): Our low-carb, high-fibre alternative to regular noodles.
- Creamed Coconut (150g block): Offers a rich, fibrous, and creamy texture.
- Turmeric (2 tsp, freshly grated if possible): Adds antioxidants and a warm, earthy flavour.
- Ginger (1 tbsp, chopped): Brings a spicy, zesty kick.
- Garlic (4 cloves): For a robust aromatic base.
- Red Bell Pepper: Adds vitamin C, sweetness and crunch.
- Pak Choi (2 stalks): Brings a crisp, fresh element.
- Sweet Chilli Sauce (1 tbsp): For a hint of sweetness and heat.
- Lime: A squeeze adds a bright, citrusy finish.
- Black Pepper (a sprinkle): Enhances the overall flavour.
- Coconut Oil (for cooking): To cook the tuna and vegetables.

Method:

Prepare the Coconut Sauce: Slowly melt the creamed coconut in a pan with boiling water, stirring until you achieve a slightly fluid texture. Incorporate turmeric and sweet chilli sauce, adjusting the water as needed for the desired consistency.

Cook the Tuna: Heat a drizzle of coconut oil over medium-high heat in a separate pan. Sear the tuna steaks to your liking—just a couple of minutes per side for a pink centre.

Flash-fry the Veggies: Quickly sauté the red bell pepper, garlic, ginger, and pak choi just until they're tender-crisp.

Combine with Noodles: Add the konjac noodles to the coconut sauce, stirring constantly to ensure the noodles are thoroughly coated and infused with the sauce's flavours.

Assemble and Serve: Arrange the noodles on plates, topping with the seared tuna and sautéed vegetables. Finish with a sprinkle of black pepper and a generous squeeze of lime juice.

This Tuna Silom Coconut Noodles dish not only brings a taste of Thailand to your table but does so in a health-conscious and utterly satisfying way. Combining creamy coconut, tangy lime, and spicy ginger with the richness of tuna creates a culinary experience that's sure to impress.

Fibrous Pork Pie: A Healthy Twist on a Classic

Servings: 6
Prep Time: 15 min | Cooking Time: 40 mins | **Total Time: 4 mins**

Imagine a dish that wraps up the aromatic essence of Garam Masala with the robustness of beef and the guilt-free pleasure of konjac spaghetti, all in less than the time it takes to check your email. our 'Garam Masala Beef & Noodles' are a culinary sprint to the finish line, proving that speedy cooking doesn't have to sacrifice depth of flavour or nutritional value.

Ingredients for the pastry:

- Almond Flour (7 heaped tbsp): For a fibre nutty, low-carb base.
- Coconut Flour (3 heaped tbsp): Adds texture and fibre.
- Konjac Flour (2 heaped tsp): Helps to bind the dough (and adds more fibre).
- Baking Powder (1 tsp): Ensures the pastry rises slightly.
- Egg: Binds the ingredients together.
- Olive Oil (3 tbsp): Adds moisture and richness.
- Salt (a pinch): Balances the flavours.
- Butter: To ease the pan, ensure nothing sticks.

Ingredients for the filling:

- Pork Tenderloin (400g): Lean yet flavourful, diced for the filling.
- Spring Onion (150g), Garlic (4 cloves), Shallots: Aromatic vegetables that add depth.
- Red Chilli (1, finely sliced): Injects a spicy kick.
- Konjac Flour (2 tsp): Thickens the filling without adding carbs.
- Soft Cheese (250g): Contributes creaminess.
- Red Onion (1, optional): For sweetness and colour.
- Peas (1/2 cup): Adds texture and a hint of sweetness.
- Paprika Powder (1 tsp), Green Curry Paste (2 tbsp): Spices that bring warmth and complexity.
- Black Pepper & Salt: For seasoning to taste.

Method for the pastry:

1. Combine all pastry ingredients to form a dough. If it is too thick, adjust with a bit of water.
2. Grease a 20cm round baking tray with butter and line it with greased parchment paper for easy dough handling and baking.
3. Roll out the dough, forming a base and sides in the prepped tray and a separate top on another piece of paper.
4. Bake the empty shell (but not the top) at 180°C for 15-20 minutes until just starting to golden.

Method for the filling:

1. Sauté the pork, garlic, and shallots in olive oil until browned. Beat the eggs and incorporate them with the rest of the filling ingredients, cooking until the mixture thickens.
2. If the filling is too runny, add an extra egg and more konjac flour to achieve the right consistency. Let it cool before assembling.
3. Fill the pre-baked pastry with the pork mixture, topping it with the remaining pastry. Seal the edges with damp fingers and bake for an additional 10 minutes.

Serve this delightful Fibrous Pork Pie garnished with black pepper or chilli flakes, offering a meal that effortlessly merges indulgence with health. Perfect for those seeking to enjoy classic flavours without compromising their dietary goals, this dish is a testament to the versatility and joy of cooking. Enjoy the rich, savoury flavours and the textural contrast between the tender filling and the crisp pastry, making every bite a celebration.

Braised Venison and Swede Hotpot

Servings: 4
Prep Time: 15 min | Cooking Time: 120 mins | **Total Time: 135 mins**

Explore the rich flavours of the wild with this Braised Venison and Swede Hotpot, a dish that celebrates the robust and earthy notes of venison complemented by the sweet, nutty undertones of swede. This meal is not just a culinary journey into the adventurous but also a nod to the nutritional prowess of venison as a high-protein, low-fat alternative to traditional meats.

Ingredients:

- Venison Steaks (4): Rich in flavour and protein, the dish's star.
- Swede: Adds a sweet and earthy contrast.
- Celery (4 sticks): For a subtle, aromatic crunch.
- Garlic (4 cloves, diced): Infuse the dish with depth.
- Onion: A foundational flavour builder.
- Beef Stock (2 cubes): Enhances the meaty richness.
- Bay Leaf: Adds a layer of herbal complexity.
- Dried Thyme (1 tsp): Offers a slight, earthy lemon aroma.
- Olive Oil (a drizzle): For browning the venison.
- Konjac Flour (1 tbsp): Thickens the sauce without adding carbs.

Method:

Sear the Venison: Heat a drizzle of olive oil in a large pan and brown the venison steaks on both sides for a few minutes. If desired, deglaze the pan with a splash of red wine, adding the garlic to sauté until aromatic.

Prep the Swede: Dice the swede into small, triangle-shaped pieces for a unique presentation. Fry until slightly browned, adding a unique texture to the dish.

Make the Broth: Dissolve the beef stock cubes in 400ml of boiling water, stirring until fully integrated. Thicken the broth with konjac flour to create a rich, flavourful base.

Combine and Cook: Transfer the venison, swede, celery, onion, bay leaf, and thyme into an oven-safe dish or slow cooker. Pour the thickened broth over the ingredients, ensuring everything is well combined.

Oven Method: Cook at 180°C for about 1.5 hours until the venison is tender and the flavours meld beautifully.

Slow Cooker Method: Cook for 2.5 hours or more on a low setting for an even deeper melding of flavours.

Alternative Swede Preparation: For a different texture and presentation, cook the swede separately on a baking tray, seasoned with olive oil and herbs to serve alongside the hotpot.

Serve this Braised Venison and Swede Hotpot to celebrate rustic flavours and comforting warmth. Whether enjoyed as a lavish dinner or a nourishing lunch, this dish promises satisfaction with every bite.

Chicken Penne Pasta

Servings: 4
Prep Time: 10 min | Cooking Time: 75 mins | **Total Time: 85 mins**

Discover a guilt-free way to indulge in the classic comfort of penne pasta with our Chicken Penne Pasta recipe, featuring a low-carb, high-fibre alternative to traditional pasta. This Italian-inspired dish captivates with its robust flavours and satisfying texture, proving that healthy eating doesn't have to compromise on taste or comfort. Perfect for family dinners or a nourishing meal any time of the day, it's a dish that will delight children and adults alike.

Ingredients:

- Chicken Breasts: Tender and lean, perfect for shredding.
- Tomatoes (can): For a rich and hearty sauce base.
- Cherry Tomatoes: Adds a burst of sweetness.
- Mini Bell Peppers: Brings colour and a slight crunch.
- Konjac Penne (400g): Our high-fibre, zero-carb pasta alternative.
- Olive Oil: For cooking and flavour.
- Oregano (2 tsp): Adds an authentic Italian herbaceous note.
- Chilli Flakes (1 tsp): For a hint of heat.
- Basil or Coriander: Fresh herbs for garnishing.
- Shallots: Mild and slightly sweet; they enhance the sauce.
- Garlic (4 cloves): Essential for any Italian sauce.
- Parmesan (40g, grated): Add an Italian finish for serving

Method:

Cook the Chicken: Boil the chicken breasts for about an hour until tender and easy to shred.

Prepare the Sauce: Combine olive oil, whole tomatoes (preferably plum tomatoes for less water content), garlic, and shallots in a saucepan. Bring to a simmer, allowing the flavours to meld together.

Shred the Chicken: Once cooked, use a rolling pin or a fork to shred the chicken into bite-sized pieces.

Combine Ingredients: Add the shredded chicken, penne, whole cherry tomatoes, and sliced mini bell peppers to the sauce. Cook for an additional 5 minutes until the pasta is tender and the vegetables are just cooked.

Dish this hearty pasta with a generous sprinkle of grated Parmesan, a pinch of chilli flakes, and fresh basil or coriander leaves for a burst of flavour.

Tips: For a thicker, more decadent sauce, opt for whole plum tomatoes over chopped tinned tomatoes. The Konjac penne will absorb the sauce's flavours as it cooks, making it deliciously cohesive.

This Chicken Penne Pasta reinvents a classic, making it accessible for those on a high-fibre, low-carb diet without losing the essence of Italian cuisine. Serve it as a family meal or a satisfying lunch that energises you without the carbocoaster crash.

Pork Ramen

Servings: 4
Prep Time: 10 min | Cooking Time: 20 mins | **Total Time: 30 mins**

Relish in the warmth and comfort of this Pork Ramen, a dish inspired by the beloved flavours of Wagamama's but tailored for optimal nutrition. Featuring konjac noodles as a low-carb, high-fibre alternative, this ramen ensures you can indulge in your noodle cravings while sticking to your dietary goals. It's a perfect blend of taste, texture, and health, making it a hit for kids and adults.

Ingredients:

- Pork Loin (500g): The protein star is carefully sliced and prepared.
- Shallots: Adds a subtle sweetness to the broth.
- Konjac Noodles (400g): A guilt-free, low-carb noodle alternative.
- Carrots (1 cup, julienned): Adds colour and slight sweetness.
- Garlic (3 cloves, grated): Essential for depth and aroma.
- Ginger (2cm cubed, finely sliced): A spicy, warm note is added.
- Bok Choi: For a crunch and a dose of greens.
- Egg: Soft-boiled, adding nutrients, richness and texture.
- Sesame Oil (1 tbsp): For that unmistakable Asian flavour note.
- Salt & Pepper: To season the dish to perfection.
- Vegetable Stock (2 cubes): Forms the flavourful broth base.

Method:

Prepare the Pork: Slice the pork loin into quarters, then score each piece without cutting all the way through. To do this, place the loin between two chopsticks and cut until your knife hits the fork. Once sliced, sear in olive oil until browned.

Build the Broth: Add a splash of boiled water to the pan with the pork, dissolving the vegetable stock cubes. Bring to a boil, then simmer on medium heat.

Simmer with Flavours: Incorporate carrots, sesame oil, garlic, and ginger into the broth, letting the pork absorb these rich flavours over 10 minutes.

Add Greens and Noodles: Introduce bok choi and konjac noodles to the mix, cooking for an additional 5 minutes. Ensure the bok choi stays vibrant and the noodles become tender.

Egg Addition: Separately, soft-boil an egg. While it's not strictly one-pot, this step can be skipped for a more straightforward preparation, though it adds a lovely richness and texture to the dish.

Serve this Pork Ramen hot, garnished with a halved soft-boiled egg, a sprinkle of sesame seeds, and a few drops of sesame oil for an extra layer of flavour. It's a fulfilling meal that satisfies the soul without compromising health, making it a delightful option for any day of the week. Enjoy the complex flavours and wholesome ingredients that make this dish a Japanese classic with a fibrous twist.

Moroccan Tuna Penne: A Quick Culinary Escape

Servings: 2
Prep Time: 1 min | Cooking Time: 3 mins | **Total Time: 4 mins**

Dive into a dish with just four ingredients and bring the vibrant flavours of Morocco to your table in less time than it takes to brew a cup of tea. The 'Moroccan Tuna Penne' is a one-pan wonder that combines the richness of tuna with the lightness of konjac penne, all wrapped in the warm embrace of Moroccan spices. With minimal clean-up and a cooking time that's as brief as a commercial break, this dish is a testament to the magic of quick, healthy, and flavourful cooking.

Ingredients:

- Tuna Steak: The ocean's pride, ready to be infused with spices.
- 200g Konjac Penne: The guilt-free pasta alternative that's all pleasure, no carbs.
- Moroccan Spice Mix: A treasure trove of flavours transporting you to bustling markets and sun-drenched streets. Just be sure to check the label to make sure nothing is added other than spice.
- 3 Knobs of Butter: The silky base that carries the spices and coats the penne.

Method:

Ignite your stove to a high flame, letting the butter melt in the saucepan until it sings of readiness, becoming a golden pool of flavour.

Prepare the tuna to your liking, either diced for quick cooking or left whole for a steak-like experience, then introduce it to the pan alongside the konjac penne.

Shower the duo with your Moroccan spice mix, whether a homemade concoction or a trusted store-bought blend. This is where the dish starts to come alive with colour and aroma.

With a chef's flourish, keep turning the ingredients with a big spoon, ensuring every piece of tuna and penne gets a kiss of spices and butter. Cook to your preference, whether you yearn for blushingly pink tuna in the centre or are thoroughly embraced by heat.

Our 'Moroccan Tuna Penne' is more than just a meal; it's a quick escape to the heart of Moroccan cuisine, a dish that proves fast food can be both luxurious and nourishing. Garnish with fresh herbs if you have them, adding a final touch of greenery that's like a nod to the oases of Morocco.

Top Tip: home brand spice mixes tend to have fewer fillers, chemicals and sugar added than the famous brands.

Prawns, Scallops, and Thai Noodles: A Flash in the Pan

Servings: 3
Prep Time: 1 min | Cooking Time: 4 mins | **Total Time: 5 mins**

Embark on a whirlwind culinary adventure with a dish that teleports you to the heart of Thailand in less time than it takes to choose a movie on a Friday night. This 'Prawns, Scallops, and Thai Noodles' concoction marries the ocean's bounty with the ease and simplicity of one-pan cooking, delivering a meal that's as effortlessly exquisite as it is brimming with healthful delights.

Ingredients:

- 150g King Prawns: Sea jewels, ready to dazzle your palate.
- 180g Mini Scallops: Tiny treasures bursting with sweet, maritime flavours.
- 200g Konjac Noodles: The perfect, carb-conscious companion to our seafood stars.
- 3 Knobs of Butter: For that rich, melt-in-your-mouth foundation.
- Thai Spices Mix: Choose a mix with nothing added but spices.
- A handful of Coriander: The final, fresh flourish that sings Thailand.

Method:

Ignite the flame of culinary creativity by melting the butter in your pan, transforming it into a liquid canvas ready for the masterpiece to come.

Introduce the prawns and scallops to the pan, showering them with your chosen Thai spices or mix. This is where the magic begins – as they sizzle and cook, they take on Thailand's rich, aromatic essence.

As the seafood whispers tales of the ocean, weave in the konjac noodles, stirring with the enthusiasm of a street-food maestro, ensuring every strand dances through the butter and spices.

Serve this vibrant concoction in bowls, each garnished with a sprinkle of coriander. This final touch is like the last brush stroke on a painting, adding a burst of freshness that elevates the dish to a work of art.

In mere minutes, you've crafted a dish that's a testament to the wonders of quick, healthy cooking without compromising flavour or sophistication. 'Prawns, Scallops, and Thai Noodles' is not just a meal; it's a celebration of minimal clean-up and maximal enjoyment, a true culinary coup. It's perfect for those nights when time is of the essence, but the craving for something utterly delicious is even more pressing.

High Fibre Desserts & Puddings

Often, the first tragic casualty in the battle of the bulge, the misunderstood pariah of the dieting world. But hold onto your spoons, forks, and whatever utensil you prefer for indulgence. In the realm of the *Fibre First* diet, desserts aren't just allowed; they're practically knighted and given a seat at the round table. Yes, you heard right: it's time to have your cake, eat it too, and then some, all in the name of fibre!

Welcome to a world where flaxseed biscuits flirt shamelessly with cheese. Coconut ice cream isn't a summertime fling but a lifelong love affair, and cocoa and peanut butter come together in a delicious and saintly, fibrous embrace. Welcome to the dessert revolution, where every sweet bite is a fibre-fuelled joyride.

Chocolate Gateau Cups: A Sweet Spectacle

Servings: 6
Prep Time: 10 mins | Cooking Time: 7 mins | **Total Time: 17 mins**

Behold the Chocolate Gateau Cups, ready to dazzle any table with minimal effort and maximum flair. A dessert that's as delightful to make as it is to devour, proving that gourmet doesn't mean hours in the kitchen. Enjoy the layers of joy, bite after blissful bite!

Ingredients:

For the Sponge:
- 60g ground brown linseed (high in fibre)
- 1 tsp baking powder
- A few teaspoons of either stevia, erythritol or xylitol
- 2 Large eggs
- 2 tbsp cocoa powder
- A splash of milk

For the Raspberry Jam:
- 150g raspberries
- 1/2 tsp Konjac flour (optional)
- 2 tsp powdered sweetener

For the Chocolate Cream:
- 100g dark chocolate
- 200ml double cream

Method:

Sponge Creation: Whip up the sponge mix by blending linseed, sweetener, cocoa, baking powder, eggs, and milk into a smooth batter. Spread on a silicone mat or greased paper, bake at a preheated oven for 6-7 mins. Once firm, let it cool off the heat.

Raspberry Jam Alchemy: Simmer raspberries with a dash of water until they sizzle. Mash, sweeten and reduce to a thick, jammy consistency. For extra thickness, whisk in Konjac flour. Set aside to cool.

Chocolate Cream Indulgence: Melt dark chocolate, then whip cold cream to thickness. Fold in the chocolate for a lush cream.

Assembling the masterpiece:

Layer up in small jars or any elegant vessel of choice. Start with the crumbled sponge, add a layer of raspberry jam, followed by a generous dollop of chocolate cream. Repeat with a sponge circle, more jam, and cream, finishing with a crown of chocolate cream.

Final Flourish: Garnish with blueberries, freeze-dried raspberries, and a hint of greenery for that eye-catching finish.

Caramelised Strawberry and Coconut Primal Ice Cream

Servings: 15
Prep Time: 10 mins | Freezing Time: 120 mins | **Total Time: 130 mins**

Indulge in the ultimate treat with Caramelised Strawberry and Coconut Primal Ice Cream, where every scoop is a blend of creamy delight and caramelised sweetness. This recipe elevates the ice cream experience with a secret ingredient and a dash of culinary magic, making it as close to traditional ice cream in texture as it gets—without straying from the path of health. Here's to satisfying your sweet tooth in the most indulgent yet nourishing way!

Ingredients:

- Strawberries (2 punnets): The show's star, ready for caramelisation.
- Full-fat Coconut Milk (2x400g cans): The creamy fibrous base that dreams are made of.
- NKD Syrup (1 tbsp): A high-fibre, low-carb alternative to honey.
- Coconut Oil (1 tsp): For cooking the strawberries to perfection.
- Chia Seeds (1/4 cup): The secret to that irresistible creaminess.
- Fresh Strawberries (1/2 cup, extra): For delightful berry bursts in every bite.
- Cinnamon (1 tsp): A sprinkle of spice to elevate the flavour.

Method:

Caramelise to Perfection: Melt coconut oil over medium heat in a pan. Add strawberries, drizzle with NKD Syrup, and sprinkle with cinnamon. Caramelise them until they're beautifully golden and fragrant, about 5 minutes.

Blend the Base: Transfer the caramelised strawberries to a food processor, pour in the coconut milk, and add chia seeds. Blend until you achieve a smooth, velvety consistency.
Berry Chunks: Chop the extra fresh strawberries into bite-sized pieces. Stir these chunks into the ice cream mixture by hand, distributing them evenly for little surprises in every spoonful.

Freeze and Serve: Pour the mixture into a loaf tin or suitable container and freeze until set, about 1-2 hours. For the best experience, allow the ice cream to defrost slightly until it reaches a creamy, soft-serve texture before diving in.

Caramelised Strawberry and Coconut Primal Ice Cream isn't just a dessert; it's an experience—a luxurious, health-conscious escape into sweetness that leaves you feeling satisfied, not guilty. Patience is key: let it soften slightly for that perfect creamy texture. Here's to a primal treat that will become a cherished indulgence!

Peanut Butter Fibre Fudge Dessert

Servings: 8
Prep Time: 5 mins | Cooking Time: 60 mins | **Total Time: 65 mins**

Introducing the ultimate fudge experience, where simplicity meets sublime taste and texture. Our 'Peanut Butter Fibre Fudge' is a revelation for those on a low-carb journey, delivering a treat that's not only decadent but also rich in fibre. Easy to make and irresistibly delicious, it's the perfect way to satisfy your sweet tooth without straying from your health goals.

Ingredients:

- Smooth Peanut Butter (120g): For that creamy, nutty base we all crave.
- Ghee (50g): Adds richness and a silky texture to the fudge.
- Konjac Flour (5 to 6g): The secret ingredient for adding fibre without compromising taste.
- Powdered Sweetener (5 to 18g, depending on what sweetener you choose).
- Vanilla Paste or Essence (1/4 tsp): A hint of vanilla to elevate the flavours.

Method:

Begin by placing a small pan over medium heat. Spoon in the peanut butter and ghee, letting them mingle and melt together into a luscious mixture. Await the gentle bubbles of a low simmer, a sign that things are heating up.

Infuse this nutty blend with the vanilla and powdered sweetener, stirring until everything is beautifully combined and the sweetener has dissolved into the mix.

Fold in the konjac flour off the heat, ensuring it's thoroughly mixed in. This step transforms the mixture into a fibre-rich fudge base, ready to take on a solid form.

Pour the fudgy goodness directly into a silicone mould. At this stage, feel free to stir in any extras you fancy—be it chocolate chips for double decadence or nuts for an extra crunch.

The fridge becomes your ally as you let the fudge cool and solidify into its final, tempting form. Patience is key; let it chill until firm. Once set, release your creation from its mould and cut it into bite-sized pieces, ready to be enjoyed.

Our 'Peanut Butter Fibre Fudge' is more than just a treat; it's a testament to the joy of indulging in something fibrous without any dietary compromise. Perfect for sharing or keeping all to yourself, this fudge is a delightful way to end a meal or to enjoy as a snack.

Dive into the world of guilt-free pleasure, where every bite celebrates flavour and fibre.

Blueberry Buttery Cookies

Servings: 8
Prep Time: 5 mins | Cooking Time: 10 mins | **Total Time: 15 mins**

Introducing a twist on the classic oatmeal cookie that's bound to become your new favourite treat. These 'Blueberry Buttery Cookies' swap out traditional raisins for the tangy sweetness of freeze-dried blueberries, creating a high-fibre, low-carb snack. Soft with a delightful golden edge, each cookie is a treat for your taste buds and a fibre-rich boon to your diet, thanks to the flaxseeds, almonds and Konjac flour.

Ingredients:

- Ghee (40g): For that irresistible buttery taste.
- Large Egg: Binds the ingredients.
- Freeze Dried Blueberries (15g): For bursts of tangy sweetness and antioxidants.
- Ground Brown Flax (50g): Adds texture, nuttiness, and fibre.
- Ground Almonds (65g): The low-carb, high-fibre, gluten-free alternative.
- 4 teaspoons of stevia, erythritol or xylitol: Sweetens without the sugar.
- Konjac Flour: Provides binding and an extra fibre boost.
- Vanilla Extract (1 tsp): A dash of aromatic sweetness.
- Sea Salt (a pinch): Enhances all the flavours.

Method:

Kickstart your baking adventure by preheating the oven to 180°C, setting the stage for cookie magic.

Dive into a deep mixing bowl, where ghee meets blueberries, sweeteners, flax, konjac flour, a hint of sea salt, and ground almonds. Stir these treasures together, creating the foundation of your dough.

Welcome vanilla and a large egg into the mix, blending until a thick, cohesive dough forms. Patience is key; let the mixture sit momentarily to allow the konjac flour to absorb any excess moisture, making the dough easier to handle.

Embrace the dough with a spoon, scooping portions to arrange on a greaseproof baking sheet. Gently press each scoop into a cookie shape, ready for the oven's warmth.
Bake for about 10 minutes or until the cookies have a golden edge and are firming up to perfection.

Serve our 'Blueberry Buttery Cookies' as a wholesome snack, a delightful dessert, or a companion to your afternoon tea. Each cookie is a testament to the joy of baking with health-conscious ingredients, offering a low-carb, fibre-rich treat that doesn't skimp on flavour. Perfect for sharing or savouring solo, these cookies are a heart-warming reminder that indulgence and wellbeing can indeed go hand in hand.

Blueberry and Coconut Slices

Servings: 12
Prep Time: 5 mins | Cooking Time: 10 mins | **Total Time: 15 mins**

Embrace the morning rush, snack time, or dessert cravings with these Blueberry and Coconut Slices – a recipe that defies the usual carb-laden confections. Perfect for when you're dashing out the door, packing a treat for the little ones, or seeking a sweet finish to your meal with a dollop of clotted cream. Utilising arrowroot powder for a springy, spongey texture, these slices astonish with their lightness and low-carb content, all while being grain, gluten, and nut-free. Feel free to adapt the batter to your heart's savoury or sweet whims.

Ingredients:

- Coconut Flour (40g): For a tender fibrous experience.
- Arrowroot Powder (15g): For that perfect sliceable texture.
- Baking Powder (1 tsp): The lift that brings it all together.
- Blueberries (80g): Bursts of juicy sweetness.
- Vanilla Powder (1/4 tsp): A whisper of exotic flavour.
- Eggs (2 large): The binding magic.
- Greek Yogurt (100g): For creaminess and tang.
- Milk (150ml): To unite the mix into smooth harmony.

Method:

Dry Mix Magic: Begin by sifting together coconut flour, arrowroot powder, and baking powder in a bowl—your dry ingredient ensemble is awaiting its cue.

Wet the Good Bit: Add eggs, Greek yoghurt, and milk to the mix, beating them into a smooth and enticing batter.

Berry Drop: Tease in a handful of blueberries, letting them dive into the batter, eager for their oven transformation.

Prepare to Bake: Pour the batter onto a lined baking tray, creating a canvas for your culinary art. Scatter the remaining blueberries across the top like jewels.

Bake to Perfection: Slide into a preheated oven at 180°C and bake for a golden 10 minutes until the slice stands firm and proud.
Cool and Slice: Once baked, transfer to a wire rack to cool, then slice into generous pieces, ready for devouring.

These Blueberry and Coconut Slices are more than a treat; they're a testament to the joy of baking with health in mind. Stored in a sealed container, they're your loyal companions for up to 3 days at room temperature or 5 in the fridge, ready to be savoured slowly. You can also freeze them for a future moment of indulgence. Here's to snacking, breakfasting, and desserting without compromise!

Your Pathway to Wellness: Equipment, Supplements and Courses, for a Healthier You

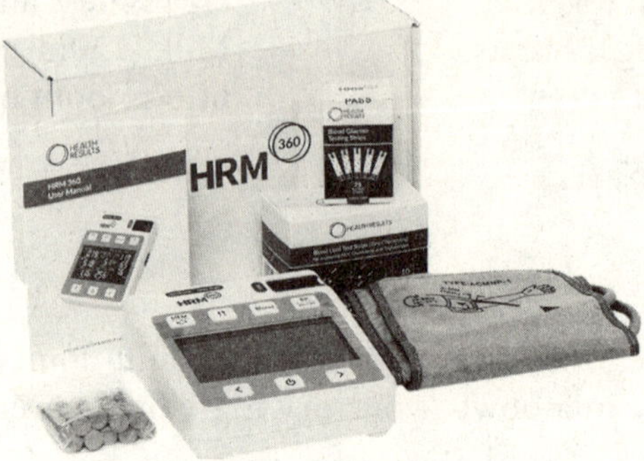

The HRM360 Health Guardian

Empowering vibrant health, one household at a time.

The must-have companion for your health transformation, introducing the HRM360 Health Monitor – the guardian of internal health for every home! Experience the ultimate convenience of measuring blood lipids, blood glucose, and blood pressure, all with a single device. With the HRM360, understanding and managing your inner health has never been easier. In just 5 minutes, complete your assessment and seamlessly input your results into the Health Results App. Witness as it instantly calculates your current health profile, empowering you to utilise tailored programs on our website for subtle adjustments to your diet and lifestyle.

Scan the QR code and use code **FIBREFIRST** to get a 10% discount on your first purchase

or visit www.healthresults.com/products/hrm360

HUNGER
BULLETZ
BY SLIMSHOTZ
Primal Living
WEIGHT LOSS CAPSULES

Charities

BENNETT FOUNDATION

The Bennett Foundation

> *'We focus our efforts and funding on health education, backing organisations with the potential to deliver disproportionately high impacts.'*

Our mission is anchored in health education. We channel our efforts and funding towards organisations that can bring about significant change. The Bennett Foundation takes pride in covering all operational costs, ensuring that every donation received directly benefits the charitable partners we champion. From research to the creation of this book, our family has transparently borne every expense.

Here are the charities we currently support:

Public Health Collaboration (PHC)

We are the principal funder of the Public Health Collaboration. We help support the charity's running costs and provide our time and guidance. The PHC has more than 200 Health Ambassadors, who, amongst other things, keep GP surgeries up to date with the latest research in health, nutrition and lifestyle. We hold an annual conference, to keep the medical profession up to date with the latest research. We consider ourselves as the much-needed preventative arm of the NHS.

The Lifestyle Club (TLC)

We funded the creation of the The Lifestyle Club (a new arm of the PHC charity), which through primarily GP surgeries, enrolls individuals suffering with Obesity, Pre-Diabetes or Diabetes type 2 onto a 12-week program, to reverse their condition.

Real Food Rebelion Project

Real Food Rebellion (a PHC project) is a school-based project focused on improving the health and wellbeing of children and adolescents and their future life chances. The project aims to plant seeds of change that will grow and transform the lives of children, their parents, and future generations to come. Knowledge is power, and we will provide the key that unlocks and clarifies the perplexing food environment we live in. This, in turn, will lead to improved long-term health outcomes and lessen the future burden on the NHS.

Food Addiction

Liberate forms an integral part of the PHC, offering a treasure trove of evidence-based learning materials, guidance, and support designed to assist individuals in comprehending and conquering food addiction. Its mission extends to fostering awareness about the addictive nature of certain foods, particularly ultra-processed sugary ones

Public Health Collaboration
Charity Number: 1171887 | www.phcuk.org

Ace Africa

Our support enables ACE Africa to conduct various health education programs in rural Kenya and Tanzania. While disease, lack of hygiene and minimal resources are clearly problems in much of rural East Africa, the bigger problem is lack of awareness of these issues and the simple steps that could be taken to minimise exposure to risk. Our Community Health and Wellbeing programme exists to provide people with the knowledge and the training they need to make better decisions regarding their health and to work proactively to prevent the spread of diseases such as HIV and AIDS.

Charity Number: 111283 | www.ace-africa.org

Big Change

We support BIG CHANGE, a charity that is trying to transform education and learning in the UK. We want to see a world where all young people are set up to thrive in life, not just in exams. We begin with a simple question, what is the purpose of education?

Charity Number: 1145224 | www.big-change.org

The Colourful Life Foundation India

This charity was born out of a company that the Bennett family founded in Jaipur. Over the years we have helped build/renovate 15 schools, which today educate more than 4,500 children. We provide ongoing support for these schools, focusing our resources on health education for the children.

Food For The Brain

Their mission is to create a future where the importance of nutrition in optimising mental wellbeing and brain health as a means of prevention and treatment is understood by all and implemented by many.

Charity Number: 1116438 | Company Number: 5885305
www.foodforthebrain.org

Collaboration for Kids

CFK is an ambitious, scientific, evidence-based project of voluntary collaboration between parents, carers, children of all ages, educational and healthcare professionals, researchers, academics and more.

Their goal is to make children and families aware of the dangers of ultra-processed foods inspiring them to choose real and natural foods, the way nature intended, to improve the health and well-being in children. CFK helps people embrace foods that build and maintain healthy bodies and brains, encouraging them to turn away from ultra-processed 'filler' foods that do not supply the nutrients needed to thrive.

Charity Number: 1207031
www.reachvolunteering.org.uk/org/collaboration-kids

References

Forward

[1] Report by the British Nutrition Foundation (2021) British Nutrition Foundation survey reveals 62% of Britons have altered their diet to get. An online survey by YouGov.

*****

Introduction

[1] Mokdad AH, Ballestros K, Echko M, Glenn S, Olsen HE, Mullany E, Lee A, Khan AR, Ahmadi A, Ferrari AJ, Kasaeian A, Werdecker A, Carter A, Zipkin B, et al. (2018 April 10) The State of US Health, 1990-2016: Burden of Diseases, Injuries, and Risk Factors Among US States doi: 10.1001/jama.2018.0158

[2] Stephen Jones (2017 March 30) Article in Mirror Newspaper. In 1967 the average man weighed 11st 8lb, in 2017 Mr Average is 13 stone 3 lbs

[3] Report by the British Nutrition Foundation (2021) British Nutrition Foundation survey reveals 62% of Britons have altered their diet to get. An online survey by YouGov.

[4] Heald AH, Stedman M, Davies M, Livingston M, Alshames R, Lunt M, et al. Estimating life years lost to diabetes: outcomes from analysis of National Diabetes Audit and Office of National Statistics data. Cardiovascular Endocrinology & Metabolism. 2020;9(4):183-5.

[5] Outcomes from analysis of National Diabetes Audit and Office of National Statistics data 2020/2021

*****

Chapter 1

[1] Paul Clayton, Judith Rowbotham (2009 March 6) How the Mid-Victorians Worked, Ate and Died doi: 10.3390/ijerph6031235

[2] Janet M. Wojcicki and Melvin B. Heyman (2012 September) Reducing Childhood Obesity by Eliminating 100% Fruit Juice. doi: 10.2105/AJPH.2012.300719

[3] Ruhl, C.E., Everhart, J.E. (2015). Fatty liver indices in the multi-ethnic United States National Health and Nutrition Examination Survey. doi: 10.1111/apt.13012.

*****

Chapter 2

[1] Alpana P. Shukla, Radu G. Iliescu, Catherine E. Thomas, and Louis J. Aronne (2015 June 11) Food Order Has a Significant Impact on Postprandial Glucose and Insulin Levels doi: 10.2337/dc15-0429

[2] Nishino, K., Sakurai, M., Takeshita, Y., Takamura, T. (2018). Consuming Carbohydrates after Meat or Vegetables Lowers Postprandial Excursions of Glucose and Insulin in Nondiabetic Subjects. doi: 10.3177/jnsv.64.316.

[3] Christiani Jeyakumar Henry, Bhupinder Kaur and Rina Yu Chin (2020 February 19) Chrononutrition in the management of diabetes doi: 10.1038/s41387-020-0109-6

[4] IQVIA Institute for Human Data Science – (2019 January 29) The Global use of medicine in 2019 outlook to 2023 - Global spending on medicines reached $1.2 trillion in 2018 and is set to and is set to exceed $1.5 trillion by 2023

[5] https://www.statista.com/statistics/301914/ (2022) Leading brands of 'Breakfast Cereals (Including Porridge/Oats)' in Great Britain (GB) 2022, by number of consumers

[6] Nicole M. Wedick, Elizabeth J. Mayer-Davis, Deborah L. Wingard, Cheryl L. Addy, Elizabeth Barrett-Connor (2001 June) American Journal of Epidemiology - Insulin Resistance Precedes Weight Loss in Adults without Diabetes: The Rancho Bernardo Study doi.org/10.1093/aje/153.12.1199

[7] Carlotta De Filippo, Duccio Cavalieri, Monica Di Paola, Matteo Ramazzotti, Jean Baptiste Poullet, Sebastien Massart et al. (2010 August 02) Impact of diet in shaping gut microbiota revealed by a comparative study in children from Europe and rural Africa doi: 10.1073/pnas.1005963107

[8] Birketvedt, G.S., Shimshi, M., Erling, T., & Florholmen, J. (2005). Experiences with three different fibre supplements in weight reduction. Med Sci Monit, 11(1), PI5-8. Retrieved from https://pubmed.ncbi.nlm.nih.gov/15614200/

[9] Walsh, D.E., Yaghoubian, V., & Behforooz, A. (1984). Effect of glucomannan on obese patients: a clinical study. International Journal of Obesity, 8(4), 289-293. Retrieved from https://pubmed.ncbi.nlm.nih.gov/6096282/

[10] Doris Vandeputte, Gwen Falony, Sara Vieira-Silva, Jun Wang, Manuela Sailer, Stephan Theis, Kristin Verbeke, and Jeroen Raes (2017 February 17) Prebiotic inulin-type fructans induce specific changes in the human gut microbiota doi: 10.1136/gutjnl-2016-313271

[11] Leach, J.D., & Sobolik, K.D. (2010, June). High dietary intake of prebiotic inulin-type fructans in the prehistoric Chihuahuan Desert. Br J Nutr, 103(11), 1558-1561. https://doi.org/10.1017/S0007114510000966

[12] Collado Yurrita, L., San Mauro Martín, I., Ciudad-Cabañas, M.J., Calle-Purón, M.E., & Hernández Cabria, M. (2014). Effectiveness of inulin intake on indicators of chronic constipation; a meta-analysis of controlled randomised clinical trials. Nutr Hosp, 30(2), 244-252. doi.org/10.3305/nh.2014.30.2.7565

[13] [14] Nicola D. Guess, Anne Dornhorst, Nick Oliver, Jimmy D. Bell, E. Louise Thomas, and Gary S. Frost (2015 October 24) A randomised controlled trial: the effect of inulin on weight management and ectopic fat in subjects with prediabetes doi:10.1186/s12986-015-0033-2

[15] Bahram Pourghassem Gargari, Parvin Dehghan, Akbar Aliasgharzadeh, and Mohammad Asghari Jafar-abadi (2013 April 16) Effects of High-Performance Inulin Supplementation on Glycaemic Control and Antioxidant Status in Women with Type 2 Diabetes doi: 10.4093/dmj.2013.37.2.140

[16] Nicola D. Guess, Anne Dornhorst, Nick Oliver, Jimmy D. Bell, E. Louise Thomas, and Gary S. Frost (2015 October 24) A randomised controlled trial: the effect of inulin on weight management and ectopic fat in subjects with prediabetes doi: 10.1186/s12986-015-0033-2

[17] Susan S Lang (2006 December 22) 'Mindless autopilot' drives people to dramatically underestimate how many daily food decisions they make, Cornell study finds.

[18] Hallen-Adams, H.E., & Suhr, M.J. (2017). Fungi in the healthy human gastrointestinal tract. Virulence, 8(3), 352-358 doi: 10.1080/21505594.2016.1247140

[19] van Doorn, H.R. (2014). Emerging infectious diseases. Medicine, 42(1), 60. https://www.sciencedirect.com/science/article/pii/S1357303913003010

[20] World Health Organisation (2023 January 18) -https://www.who.int/news-room/fact-sheets/detail/soil-transmitted-helminth-infections

[21] Yeong Rhee, Ardith Brunt (2011 May 09) Flaxseed supplementation improved insulin resistance in obese glucose intolerant people: a randomised crossover design doi: 10.1186/1475-2891-10-44

[22] Ruben Meerman, Andrew J Brown (2014 December) When somebody loses weight, where does the fat go? doi: https://doi.org/10.1136/bmj.g7257

[23] Nettleton, J.A. et al. (2009). Diet soda intake and risk of incident metabolic syndrome and type 2 diabetes in the Multi-Ethnic Study of Atherosclerosis (MESA). Diabetes Care, 32(4), 688-94.

[24] Daniells, S. (2006, November 9). Prebiotic effects of Konjac get control trial boost. NutraIngredients. https://www.nutraingredients.com/Article/2006/11/09/Prebiotic-effects-of-konjac-get-control-trial-boost

[25] Mia Rozenbaum (2020 November 18) Understanding Animal Research UK - Study in mice shows that allergies can be passed on to offspring

[26] https://www.allergyuk.org/about-allergy/statistics-and-figures/

*****

Chapter 3

[1] Shari S Bassuk, Nader Rifai, Paul M Ridker (2004 August 29) High-sensitivity C-reactive protein: clinical importance doi.org/10.1016/j.cpcardiol.2004.03.004

[2] John P Bantle, Susan K Raatz, William Thomas, Angeliki Georgopoulos (2000 November) Effects of dietary fructose on plasma lipids in healthy subjects https://doi.org/10.1093/ajcn/72.5.1128

[3] Lewsley, J. (2022, October 28) -https://www.livescience.com/52802-what-is-a-calorie.html

[4] Liljeberg H, Bjorck I. Delayed gastric emptying rate may explain improved glycaemia in healthy subjects to a starchy meal with added vinegar. European journal of clinical nutrition 1998;52:368-71.

[5] H Liljeberg, I Björck (1998 May) Delayed gastric emptying rate may explain improved glycaemia in healthy subjects to a starchy meal with added vinegar doi:

10.1038/sj.ejcn.1600572

[6] https://scottishwildlifetrust.org.uk Blog: Did you know in the UK 35 million plastic bottles are discarded everyday?

[7] Frederick S vom Saal, Laura N Vandenberg (2020 September 23) Update on the Health Effects of Bisphenol A: Overwhelming Evidence of Harm doi: 10.1210/endocr/bqaa171

[8] Christian Løvold Storhaug, Svein Kjetil Fosse, Lars T Fadnes (2017 July 06) Country, regional, and global estimates for lactose malabsorption in adults: a systematic review and meta-analysis https://doi.org/10.1016/S2468-1253(17)30154-1

[9] Cardiff Times. (2015, June 25). Channel 4's new Superfoods show explores Xylitol: Finland's secret to healthier teeth. And it's already available right here in the UK. Cardiff Times. Retrieved from https://www.cardiff-times.co.uk/channel-4s-new-superfoods-show-explores-xylitol-finlands-secret-to-healthier-teeth-and-its-already-available-right-here-in-the-uk/

*****

Chapter 4

[1] Report by the British Nutrition Foundation (2021) British Nutrition Foundation survey reveals 62% of Britons have altered their diet to get. An online survey by YouGov.

[2] (Published 2024 January 9) Gov.uk website https://www.ethnicity-facts-figures.service.gov.uk/health/diet-and-exercise/physical-activity/latest/#main-facts-and-figures article on physical activity

[3] Agnes Ayton, Ali Ibrahim (2020 July 01) The Western diet: a blind spot of eating disorder research? -a narrative review and recommendations for treatment and research doi: 10.1093/nutrit/nuz089

[4] World Health Organisation, UNICEF (2022 February 23) How the marketing of formula milk influences our decisions on infant feeding. https://www.who.int/teams/maternal-newborn-child-adolescent-health-and-ageing/formula-milk-industry

[5] Hugues Chevassus, Eric Renard, Gyslaine Bertrand, Isabelle Mourand, Raymond Puech, Nathalie Molinier, Joël Bockaert, Pierre Petit, Jacques Bringer (2002 June) Effects of oral monosodium (l)-glutamate on insulin secretion and glucose tolerance in healthy volunteers doi: 10.1046/j.1365-2125.2002.01596.x

[6] J W Olney (1969 May 9) Brain lesions, obesity, and other disturbances in mice treated with monosodium glutamate doi: 10.1126/science.164.3880.719

[7] Rhona Shennan writing in the Edinburgh Evening News (2022 February 08) Where does vanilla flavouring come from? Beaver castoreum explained - and why it's used in cakes and icing.

[8] Article on the UK Flour Millers website, last read on 14th March 2024, titled: How Much Bread Does the UK Eat?

[9] Annalise Mantz (2020 March 09) Staggering Statistic: How Old Is That Apple? https://thrivemarket.com/blog/

[10] (2018 April 10) The State of US Health, 1990-2016 Burden of Diseases, Injuries, and Risk Factors Among US States JAMA. 2018;319(14):1444-1472. doi:10.1001/jama.2018.0158

[11] Gwen Ridler (2018 July 25) article on. www.foodmanufacture.co.uk, titled UK seventh highest consumer of soft drinks.

[12] NHS Website - https://www.nhs.uk/live-well/eat-well/food-types/how-does-sugar-in-our-diet-affect-our-health

[13] (2024 January 17) Aspartame and Cancer Risk article on cancer.org website

[14] Stephen D Anton, Corby K Martin, Hongmei Han, Sandra Coulon, William T Cefalu, Paula Geiselman, Donald A Williamson (2010 August) Effects of stevia, aspartame, and sucrose on food intake, satiety, and postprandial glucose and insulin levels doi: 10.1016/j.appet.2010.03.009

[15] U.S Department of Health and Human Services – National Toxicology Program -15th Report on Carcinogens

[16] Research published on NHS website - National Child Measurement Programme, England 2020/21 School Year https://digital.nhs.uk/data-and-information/publications/statistical/national-child-measurement-programme/2020-21-school-year

[17] Genevieve Timmins, Ryan O'Hare (2021 June 14) Urgent action needed to reduce harm of ultra-processed foods to British children – Imperial College London

[18] Royal College of Paediatrics and Child Health (2020 March) Healthy weight. Obesity rates in young children are showing no sign of improvement. Overweight children have increased chance of developing other health conditions, including heart disease, high blood pressure and diabetes.

[19] Gary Pilnick (2024 February) CNBC interview: Guardian News. Kellogg's CEO says cereal for dinner is 'on trend now': https://www.youtube.com/watch?v=GjKhyl3DzDo

*****

Chapter 5

[1] Artemis Simopoulos (2011 October) Evolutionary Aspects of Diet: The Omega-6/Omega-3 Ratio and the Brain doi:10.1007/s12035-010-8162-0

[2] study led by the MRC London Institute of Medical Sciences (2020 March 19) Sugar leads to early death, but not due to obesity https://www.eurekalert.org/news-releases/621703

[3] Miki Kakutani-Hatayama, Manabu Kadoya, Hirokazu Okazaki, Masafumi Kurajoh, Takuhito Shoji, Hidenori Koyama, Zenta Tsutsumi, Yuji Moriwaki et al. (2017 August) Nonpharmacological Management of Gout and Hyperuricemia: Hints for Better Lifestyle doi: 10.1177/1559827615601973

[4] Zgaga, L., Theodoratou, E., Kyle, J., Farrington, S.M., Agakov, F., Tenesa, A., Walker, M., McNeill, G., Wright, A.F., Rudan, I., Dunlop, M.G., Campbell, H. (2012). The association of dietary intake of purine-rich vegetables, sugar-sweetened beverages and dairy with plasma urate, in a cross-sectional study. PLoS One, 7(6), e38123. doi: 10.1371/journal.pone.0038123.

[5] Pei-En Chen, Chia-Yu Liu, Wu-Hsiung Chien, Ching-Wen Chien, Tao-Hsin Tung (2019 December 04) Effectiveness of Cherries in Reducing Uric Acid and Gout: A Systematic Review doi: 10.1155/2019/9896757

[6] Rongrong Li, Kang Yu, Chunwei Li (2018) Dietary factors and risk of gout and hyperuricemia: a meta-analysis and systematic review https://apjcn.nhri.org.tw/server/APJCN/27/6/1344.pdf

[7] Ben Salem, C., Slim, R., Fathallah, N., Hmouda, H. (2017). Drug-induced hyperuricaemia and gout. Rheumatology (Oxford), 56(5), 679-688. doi: 10.1093/rheumatology/kew293.

[8] Paulus, H.E., Coutts, A., Calabro, J.J., Klinenberg, J.R Clinical significance of hyperuricemia in routinely screened hospitalised men. JAMA, 211(2), 277-281.

[9] Kidney Care UK website facts page. https://kidneycareuk.org/kidney-disease-information/about-kidney-health/facts-about-kidneys

[10] Doo Yong Park, Yeon Soo Kim, Seung Ho Ryu, Yu Sun Jin (2019 August 13)

he association between sedentary behavior, physical activity and hyperuricemia doi: 10.2147/VHRM.S200278

[11] Zhuang Guo, Jiachao Zhang, Zhanli Wang, Kay Ying Ang, Shi Huang, Qiangchuan Hou, Xiaoquan Su et al. (2016 February 08) Intestinal Microbiota Distinguish Gout Patients from Healthy Humans doi: 10.1038/srep20602

[12] Ming-Chang Chiang, Tsung-Yu Tsai, Chieh-Ju Wang (2023 March 28) The Potential Benefits of Quercetin for Brain Health: A Review of Anti-Inflammatory and Neuroprotective Mechanisms - Int. J. Mol. Sci. 2023, 24(7), 6328; https://doi.org/10.3390/ijms24076328

[13] Yuanlu Shi, Gary Williamson (2016 January 20) Quercetin lowers plasma uric acid in pre-hyperuricaemic males: a randomised, double-blinded, placebo-controlled, cross-over trial doi: 10.1017/S0007114515005310.

[14] Hyon K. Choi, Xiang Gao, PhD, Gary Curhan (2010 March 09) Vitamin C Intake and the Risk of Gout in Men – A Prospective Study doi: 10.1001/archinternmed.2008.606

[15] Joseph Pizzorno (2014 April 13) Mitochondria—Fundamental to Life and Health – National Library of Medicine Integr Med (Encinitas) v.13(2); PMC4684129

[16] J Physiol (2016 March 01) Mitochondrial function at extreme high altitude doi: 10.1113/JP270079

[17] Martin Picard, Bruce S McEwen, Elissa S Epel, Carmen Sandi (2018 April) An energetic view of stress: Focus on mitochondria doi.org/10.1016/j.yfrne.2018.01.001

*****

Chapter 6

[1] Peter Densen (2011) Challenges and Opportunities Facing Medical Education Trans Am Clin Climatol Assoc. 2011; 122: 48–58. https://www.ncbi.nlm.nih.gov/pmc/articles/PMC3116346/

[2] Ruth J. F. Loos, Giles S. H (2021 September 23) The genetics of obesity: from discovery to biology doi: 10.1038/s41576-021-00414-z

[3] Peter Arner (2018 July 10) Fat Tissue Growth and Development in Humans doi: 10.1159/000486491

[4] Meghan O'Hearn , Brianna N Lauren, John B Wong, David D Kim, Dariush

Mozaffarian (2022 July 12) Trends and Disparities in Cardiometabolic Health Among U.S. Adults, 1999-2018 doi: 10.1016/j.jacc.2022.04.046

[5] Ben Bikman (2020) Why We Get Sick. Insulin and Puberty P47.

[8] Heald AH, Stedman M, Davies M, Livingston M, Alshames R, Lunt M, et al. Estimating life years lost to diabetes: outcomes from analysis of National Diabetes Audit and Office of National Statistics data. Cardiovascular Endocrinology & Metabolism. 2020;9(4):183-5.

[9] Outcomes from analysis of National Diabetes Audit and Office of National Statistics data 2020/2021

[10] Sky News (2020 February 27) Diabetes: More than 9,000 amputations a year in England caused by the disease

[11] Basilio Pintaudi, Giacoma Di Vieste, Matteo Bonomo (2016 October 11) The Effectiveness of Myo-Inositol and D-Chiro Inositol Treatment in Type 2 Diabetes doi: 10.1155/2016/9132052

[12] Reza Tabrizi, Vahidreza Ostadmohammadi, Kamran B. Lankarani, Payam Peymani et al. (2018 May 24) The effects of inositol supplementation on lipid profiles among patients with metabolic diseases: a systematic review and meta-analysis of randomized controlled trials doi: 10.1186/s12944-018-0779-4

[13] Vittorio Unfer, Fabio Facchinetti, Beatrice Orrù, Barbara Giordani, John Nestler (2017 September 20) Myo-inositol effects in women with PCOS: a meta-analysis of randomized controlled trials doi: 10.1530/EC-17-0243

[14] Soana K Motuhifonua, Luling, Jane Alsweiler, Tineke J Crawford, Caroline A Crowther (2023 February 15) Antenatal dietary supplementation with myo-inositol for preventing gestational diabetes doi: 10.1002/14651858.CD011507.pub3

[15] Joseph Levine, Mirtha Gonsalves, Izak Babur, Shaul Stier, Avner Elizur, Ora Kofman, R. H. Belmaker (1993 February) Inositol 6 g daily may be effective in depression but not in schizophrenia https://doi.org/10.1002/hup.470080109

[16] Vitrag N Tejani, Sukhmeet S Dhillon, Nanush Damarlapally, Nia Uswanti Binti Usman, Tanusha Winson, Prithvi Basu Roy, Binay K Panjiyarcorresponding (2023 September 15) The Relationship Between Dietary Fiber Intake and Blood Pressure Worldwide: A Systematic Review doi: 10.7759/cureus.46116

[17] Chuang, H.L., Chiu, C.C., Lo, C. et al. (2022). Circulating gut microbiota-related metabolites influence endothelium plaque lesion formation in ApoE knockout rats. PLoS One. https://journals.plos.org/plosone/article?id=10.1371/journal.pone.0264934

[18] Libby, P. (2021). The changing landscape of atherosclerosis. Nature, 592(7855), 524-533. doi: 10.1038/s41586-021-03392-8.

[19] Luo, T., Guo, Z., Liu, D. et al. (2022). Deficiency of PSRC1 accelerates atherosclerosis by increasing TMAO production via manipulating gut microbiota and flavin monooxygenase 3. Gut Microbes, 14(1), 2077602. doi: 10.1080/19490976.2022.2077602

[20] chwedhelm, E., von Lucadou, M., Peine, S., Lezius, S., Thomalla, G., Böger, R., Gerloff, C., Choe, C.U. (2021). Trimethyllysine, vascular risk factors and outcome in acute ischemic stroke. Amino Acids, 53(4), 555-561. doi: 10.1007/s00726-021-02969-x.

[21] https://www.nhs.uk/conditions/cancer/#:~:text=1%20in%202%20people%20will,lung%20cancer

[22] https://www.macmillan.org.uk/about-us/what-we-do/research/cancer-statistics-fact-sheet

[23] -https://www.who.int/activities/preventing-cancer

[24] https://www.cancerresearchuk.org/health-professional/cancer-statistics-for-the-uk

[25] https://www.cancerresearchuk.org/about-cancer/causes-of-cancer/obesity-weight-and-cancer

[26] (2023 August) https://ash.org.uk/resources/view/smoking-and-cancer

[27] Papa, V., Pezzino, V., Costantino, A., Belfiore, A., Giuffrida, D., Frittitta, L., Vannelli, G.B., Brand, R., Goldfine, I.D., Vigneri, R. (1990). Elevated insulin receptor content in human breast cancer. Journal of Clinical Investigation, 86(5), 1503-1510. Doi: 10.1172/JCI114868.

[28] (2023 January) https://www.yorkshirecancerresearch.org.uk/insights/hpv-explained#:~:text=Around%204%20in%205%20men,some%20point%20in%20their%20lives.

[29] Jared Meacham, Zia Sherrell (2023 September 6) Which foods can cause cancer? - https://www.medicalnewstoday.com/articles/cancer-causing-foods

[30] Sood, N., Baker, W.L., & Coleman, C.I. (2008). Effect of glucomannan on plasma lipid and glucose concentrations, body weight, and blood pressure:

systematic review and meta-analysis. Am J Clin Nutr, 88(4), 1167-1175. https://doi.org/10.1093/ajcn/88.4.1167

[31] Jun-yi Li, Fei Sun, Hai-feng Zhou, Jia Yang, Cong Huang, and Heng Fan (2019 August 23) A Systematic Review Exploring the Anticancer Activity and Mechanisms of Glucomannan doi: 10.3389/fphar.2019.00930

[32] Gonçalves, P., & Martel, F. (2013). Butyrate and colorectal cancer: the role of butyrate transport. Curr Drug Metab, 14(9), 994-1008. doi.org/10.2174/1389200211314090006

[33] Pool-Zobel, B.L. (2005, April). Inulin-type fructans and reduction in colon cancer risk: review of experimental and human data. British Journal of Nutrition, 93(Suppl 1), S73-90. https://doi.org/10.1079/BJN20041349

[34] Emília Hijová, Viktória Szabadosova, Jana Štofilová, Gabriela Hrčková (2013 December 19) Chemopreventive and metabolic effects of inulin on colon cancer development doi: 10.4142/jvs.2013.14.4.387

[35] (2024 February 14) Cancer Research UK online article - How does obesity cause cancer? https://www.cancerresearchuk.org/about-cancer/causes-of-cancer/bodyweight-and-cancer/how-does-obesity-cause-cancer

[36] https://www.nhsinform.scot/illnesses-and-conditions/stomach-liver-and-gastrointestinal-tract/non-alcoholic-fatty-liver-disease-nafld/

[37] Stanhope, K.L., Schwarz, J.M., Keim, N.L., Griffen, S.C., Bremer, A.A., Graham, J.L., Hatcher, B., Cox, C.L., Dyachenko, A., Zhang, W., McGahan, J.P., Seibert, A., Krauss, R.M., Chiu, S., Schaefer, E.J et al. (2009). Consuming fructose-sweetened, not glucose-sweetened, beverages increase visceral adiposity and lipids and decreases insulin sensitivity in overweight/obese humans. doi: 10.1172/JCI37385.

[38] Yuan, J., Chen, C., Cui, J., Lu, J., Yan, C., Wei, X., Zhao, X., Li, N., Li, S., Xue, G., Cheng, W., Li, B., Li, H., Lin, W., Tian, et al. (2019). Fatty Liver Disease Caused by High-Alcohol-Producing Klebsiella pneumoniae. doi: 10.1016/j.cmet.2019.08.018.

[39] Mala Dharmalingam and P. Ganavi Yamasandhi (2018 June) Nonalcoholic Fatty Liver Disease and Type 2 Diabetes Mellitus - doi: 10.4103/ijem.IJEM_585_17

[40] Fiona Kirkham-Wilson, Elaine Dennison, Hampshire Hospitals NHS Foundation Trust, MRC Lifecourse Epidemiology Centre Southampton. Epidemiology of Osteoporotic Fracture: an overview. Online article on the Royal Osteoporosis Society website. https://theros.org.uk/healthcare-professionals/

clinical-quality-hub/epidemiology-of-osteoporotic-fracture-an-overview

[41] Tanya J W McDonald , Mackenzie C Cervenka (2019 November 22) Lessons learned from recent clinical trials of ketogenic diet therapies in adults doi: 10.1097/MCO.0000000000000596

[42] Adam Rogers (2017 May 11) Article on www.Wired.com Star Neuroscientist Tom Insel Leaves the Google-Spawned Verily

[43] Albert Danan, Eric C. Westman, Laura R. Saslow, Georgia Ede (2020 July 06) The Ketogenic Diet for Refractory Mental Illness: A Retrospective Analysis of 31 Inpatients https://doi.org/10.3389/fpsyt.2022.951376

[44] Ronald C Kessler, Patricia Berglund, Olga Demler, Robert Jin, Kathleen R Merikangas, Ellen E Walters (2005 June) Lifetime prevalence and age-of-onset distributions of DSM-IV disorders in the National Comorbidity Survey Replication doi: 10.1001/archpsyc.62.6.593

[45] Matthew P. Pase, Jayandra J. Himali, Paul F. Jacques, Charles DeCarli, Claudia L. Satizabal, Hugo Aparicio, Ramachandran S. Vasan, Alexa S. Beiser, Sudha Seshadria (2017 March 6) Sugary beverage intake and preclinical Alzheimer's disease in the community doi: 10.1016/j.jalz.2017.01.024

[46] Prof Gill Livingston, Jonathan Huntley, Andrew Sommerlad, David Ames, Clive Ballard, Sube Banerjee et al. (2020 July 30) Dementia prevention, intervention, and care: 2020 report of the Lancet Commission doi.org/10.1016/S0140-6736(20)30367-6

[47] Food for the Brain Foundation, Patrick Holford (2024 March) Raised Homocysteine Predicts over 100 Diseases

[48] Guts Charity UK (2024 March 170 https://gutscharity.org.uk/

[49] Andre Kleinridders,W eikang Cai, Laura Cappellucci, Armen Ghazarian, William R. Collins, Sara G. Vienberg, Emmanuel N. Pothos, Ronald Kahna (2015 March 17) Insulin resistance in brain alters dopamine turnover and causes behavioural disorders doi: 10.1073/pnas.1500877112

[50] Bruce Goldman (2021 September 22) Insulin resistance doubles risk of major depressive disorder, Stanford study finds. Stanford Medicine News Center

[51] Knüppel, A., Shipley, M.J., Llewellyn, C.H., Brunner, E.J. (2017). Sugar intake from sweet food and beverages, common mental disorder and depression: prospective findings from the Whitehall II study. doi: 10.1038/s41598-017-05649-7

[52] Yang, Y., Zhou, B., Zhang, S., Si, L., & Liu, X. (2023). Prebiotics for depression: how does the gut microbiota play a role? Frontiers in Nutrition. doi.org/10.3389/fnut.2023.1206468

[53] Quentin Leyrolle, Renata Cserjesi, Maria D.G.H. Mulders, Giorgia Zamariola, Sophie Hiel, Marco A. Gianfrancesco, Daphné Portheault, Camille Amadieu et al. (2021 January 28) Prebiotic effect on mood in obese patients is determined by the initial gut microbiota composition: A randomised, controlled trial https://doi.org/10.1016/j.bbi.2021.01.014

[54] Elizabeth G Neal, Hannah Chaffe, Ruby H Schwartz, Margaret S Lawson, Nicole Edwards, Geogianna Fitzsimmons, Andrea Whitney et al. The ketogenic diet for the treatment of childhood epilepsy: a randomised controlled trial doi: 10.1016/S1474-4422(08)70092-9

[55] Martin-McGill KJ, Bresnahan R, Levy RG, Cooper PN (2020 June 24) Ketogenic diets for drug-resistant epilepsy www.cochrane.org

[56] McDonald, T.J.W., & Cervenka, M.C. (2018). Ketogenic Diets for Adult Neurological Disorders. Neurotherapeutics, 15(4), 1018–1031. doi:10.1007/s13311-018-0666-8

[57] Lozovsky, D., Saller, C.F., & Kopin, I.J. (1981). Dopamine receptor binding is increased in diabetic rats. Science, 214(4524), 1031-1033. doi: 10.1126/science.6458088.

[58] Fernando Caravaggio, Carol Borlido, Margaret Hahn , Zhe Feng, Gagan Fervaha, Philip Gerretsen, Shinichiro Nakajima, Eric Plitman, Jun Ku Chung , Yusuke Iwata et al. (2015 February 25). Reduced insulin sensitivity is related to less endogenous dopamine at D2/3 receptors in the ventral striatum of healthy nonobese humans. doi: 10.1093/ijnp/pyv014

[59] Iciar Aviles-Olmos, Patricia Limousin, Andrew Lees, Thomas Foltynie (2012 February 17) Parkinson's disease, insulin resistance and novel agents of neuroprotection doi: 10.1093/brain/aws009

[60] (2024 January 18) Article Keto for Parkinson's https://charliefoundation.org/am-i-a-candidate/keto-for-parkinsons/

[61] Caleb W Grote, Douglas E Wright (2016 December 23) A Role for Insulin in Diabetic Neuropathy doi: 10.3389/fnins.2016.00581

[62] Rebecca C Burch, Dawn C Buse , Richard B Lipton (2019 August 27) Migraine: Epidemiology, Burden, and Comorbidity doi: 10.1016/j.ncl.2019.06.001

[63] Mario Fernando Prieto Peres, Luiz Paulo Queiroz, Pedro Sampaio

Rocha-Filho et al. (2019 August 01) Migraine: a major debilitating chronic non-communicable disease in Brazil, evidence from two national surveys doi: 10.1186/s10194-019-1036-6

[64] Starbucks website (2024 March) - https://www.starbucks.com/menu/product/424/iced/nutrition

[65] M. Ashraf Ganie, Sanjay Kalara (2011 December) Polycystic ovary syndrome – A metabolic malady, the mother of all lifestyle disorders in women – Can Indian health budget tackle it in future? doi: 10.4103/2230-8210.85571

[66] (2020 January 6) Why are ED rates sky rocketing in men? https://austinurologyinstitute.com/

[67] (2024 March 16) Polycystic Ovary Syndrome (PCOS) Guidehttps://ivi.uk

[68] John C. Marshall, Andrea Dunaif (2012) Should all women with PCOS be treated for insulin resistance? doi.org/10.1016/j.fertnstert.2011.11.036

[69] Nestler, J.E., Jakubowicz, D.J., de Vargas, A.F., Brik, C., Quintero, N., Medina, F. (1998). Insulin stimulates testosterone biosynthesis by human thecal cells from women with polycystic ovary syndrome by activating its own receptor and using inositolglycan mediators as the signal transduction system. Journal of Clinical Endocrinology and Metabolism, 83(6), 2001-2005. doi: 10.1210/jcem.83.6.4886

[70] Article on the website of the American Diabetes Association. Low testosterone is a common condition that often goes undiagnosed because its symptoms are similar to other conditions. https://diabetes.org/health-wellness/sexual-health/low-testosterone

[71] Turky H Almigba (2019 March 21) Erectile dysfunction in men with type two diabetes: Is it associated with poor glycaemic control? doi: 10.22374/jomh.v15i1.104

[72] D Simon, P Preziosi, E Barrett-Connor, M Roger, M Saint-Paul, K Nahoul, L Papoz (1992 February) Interrelation between plasma testosterone and plasma insulin in healthy adult men: the Telecom Study doi: 10.1007/BF00402551

[73] (2024 January 11) article https://www.centreformenshealth.co.uk/mens-health-services/testosterone-replacement-therapy

[74] Karim Sultan Haider, Ahmad Haider, Farid Saad , Gheorghe Doros, Markolf Hanefeld , Sandeep Dhindsa et al. (2020 June 19) Remission of type 2 diabetes following long-term treatment with injectable testosterone undecanoate in patients with hypogonadism and type 2 diabetes: 11-year data from a real-world registry study. doi.org/10.1111/dom.14122

[75] Nishant Verma, Vandana Jain, Shweta Birla, Richa Jain, Arundhati Sharma (2012) Growth and hormonal profile from birth to adolescence of a girl with aromatase deficiency doi: 10.1515/jpem-2012-0152

[76] (2022 October 12) What You Eat Could Contribute to Your Menstrual Cramps https://www.menopause.org/docs/default-source/press-release/diet-and-menstrual-pain-release.pdf

[77] Haruki Usuda, Takayuki Okamoto, Koichiro Wada (2021 July 16) Leaky Gut: Effect of Dietary Fiber and Fats on Microbiome and Intestinal Barrier doi: 10.3390/ijms22147613

[78] Wiwat Chancharoenthana, Supitcha Kamolratanakul , Marcus J Schultz , Asada Leelahavanichkul (2023 April 26) The leaky gut and the gut microbiome in sepsis - targets in research and treatment doi: 10.1042/CS20220777

[79] Chang-Fu Kuo, Matthew J Grainge, Christian Mallen, Weiya Zhang, Michael Doherty (2014 January 15) Rising burden of gout in the UK but continuing suboptimal management: a nationwide population study doi: 10.1136/annrheumdis-2013-204463

[80] Lavinsky, L., Oliveira, M.W., Bassanesi, H.J.C., D'Avila, C., Lavinsky, M. (2004). Hyperinsulinemia and tinnitus: a historical cohort. International Tinnitus Journal, 10(1), 24-30

[81] Nicole Bregenzer, Alexander Hartmann, Ulrike Strauch, Jürgen Schölmerich, Tilo Andus, L Cornelius Bollheimer (2006 January 12) Increased insulin resistance and beta cell activity in patients with Crohn's disease doi: 10.1097/01.mib.0000195975.97673.f5

[82] Elena V Tchetina, Galina A Markova, Eugeniya P Sharapova (2020 May 21) Insulin Resistance in Osteoarthritis: Similar Mechanisms to Type 2 Diabetes Mellitus doi: 10.1155/2020/4143802

[83] Diego Montiel-Rojas, Andreas Nilsson, Aurelia Santoro, Claudio Franceschi, Alberto Bazzocchi, Giuseppe Battista, Lisette C. P. G. M. de Groot, Edith J. M. Feskens, Agnes Berendsen, Barbara Pietruszka, Olga Januszko, Susan Fairweather-Tait, Amy Jennings, Claudio Nicoletti, Fawzi Kadi (2020 April 13) Dietary Fibre May Mitigate Sarcopenia Risk: Findings from the NU-AGE Cohort of Older European Adults doi: 10.3390/nu12041075

[84] Mohit Nagpal, Dipankar De, Sanjeev Hand, et al. (2016 April) Insulin Resistance and Metabolic Syndrome in Young Men With Acne JAMA Dermatol. 2016;152(4):399-404. doi:10.1001/jamadermatol.2015.4499

[85] (2024 March 03)-https://www.allergycliniclondon.co.uk/why-are-allergies-on-the-rise-in-the-uk/#:~:text=In%20the%20UK%2C%20the%20number,of%20these%20people%20are%20children.

[86] (2024 March 03)-https://www.imperial.ac.uk/news/185058/fish-probiotic-supplements-pregnancy-reduce-allergy/

[87] (2024 March 08) https://www.food.gov.uk/research/food-hypersensitivity#:~:text=What%20is%20the%20impact%20of,and%20600%2C000%20with%20Coeliac%20Disease.

[88] (2024 March 07)-https://www.kentcht.nhs.uk/leaflet/gentle-low-fodmap-diet/#:~:text=A%20low%20FODMAP%20diet%20is,be%20suitable%20for%20some%20individuals.

*****

Chapter 7

[1] Charlotte Walker (2021 December 13) Waist of money: UK adults spend £20,000 on weight loss tactics over a lifetime - https://www.benenden.co.uk

[2] https://fdc.nal.usda.gov/fdc-app.html#/food-details/171706/nutrients

[3] Nicola M McKeown, George C Fahey, Jr, Joanne Slavin, Jan-Willem van der Kamp (2022 July 20) Fibre intake for optimal health: how can healthcare professionals support people to reach dietary recommendations? doi: 10.1136/bmj-2020-054370

[4] M L Hartman, J D Veldhuis, M L Johnson, M M Lee, K G Alberti, E Samojlik, M O Thorner (1992 April) Augmented growth hormone (GH) secretory burst frequency and amplitude mediate enhanced GH secretion during a two-day fast in normal men doi: 10.1210/jcem.74.4.1548337.

[5] Belinda S Lennerz , Jacob T Mey , Owen H Henn, David S Ludwig (2021 November 02) Behavioral Characteristics and Self-Reported Health Status among 2029 Adults Consuming a "Carnivore Diet". doi: 10.1093/cdn/nzab133

*****

Chapter 8

[1] Orfeu M. Buxton, Milena Pavlova, Emily W. Reid, Wei Wang, Donald C. Simonson, Gail K. Adler (2010 June 28) Sleep Restriction for 1 Week Reduces Insulin Sensitivity in Healthy Men doi: 10.2337/db09-0699

[2] Karine Spiegel, Kristen Knutson, Rachel Leproult, Esra Tasali, andEve Van Cauter (2005 November 01) Sleep loss: a novel risk factor for insulin resistance and Type 2 diabetes doi.org/10.1152/japplphysiol.00660.2005

[3] Written by Annabel Rackham (2023 August 9) BBC News online - Fitness: Fewer than 5,000 steps a day enough to boost health – study, quoting Prof Maciej Banach, from Lodz university.

[4] https://www.nytimes.com/2009/11/08/health/research/08morris.html

[5] Ploug T, Galbo H, Richter EA. (1984, December). Increased muscle glucose uptake during contractions: no need for insulin. Am J Physiol. 247(6 Pt 1):E726-31. https://doi.org/10.1152/ajpendo.1984.247.6.E726

[6] Kevin R. Short, Janet L. Vittone, Maureen L. Bigelo, David N. Proctor, Robert A. Rizza, Jill M. Coenen-Schimke, K. Sreekumaran Nair (2003 August 01) Impact of Aerobic Exercise Training on Age-Related Changes in Insulin Sensitivity and Muscle Oxidative Capacity https://doi.org/10.2337/diabetes.52.8.1888

[7] A Tremblay, J A Simoneau, C Bouchard (1994 July) Impact of exercise intensity on body fatness and skeletal muscle metabolism doi: 10.1016/0026-0495(94)90259-3

[8] Araújo, C.G., de Lima, A.C.G., Nóbrega, A.C.L., & de Oliveira, P.B. (2022). Successful 10-second one-legged stance performance predicts survival in middle-aged and older individuals. British Journal of Sports Medicine, 56(17), 975-980.

[9] https://www.ageuk.org.uk/hull/our-services/falls-prevention-eb335360-6621-ee11-a81c-6045bd94e88e/#:~:text=Why%20do%20older%20people%20fall,over%20the%20age%20of%2075.

[10] (2024 January 03) https://www.renalandurologynews.com/home/conference-highlights/american-urological- association-annual-meeting/aua-2016-annual-meeting

[11] Jeffrey Lee-Heidenreich, David Lee-Heidenreich, Jonathan Myers (2017 January 26) Differences in life expectancy between Olympic high jumpers, discus throwers, marathon and 100 meter runners - BMC Sports Science, Medicine and Rehabilitation volume 9, Article number: 3

[12] Ladislav Kováč (2010 January 11) The 20 W sleep-walkers doi: 10.1038/embor.2009.266

[13] Siobhan Chan of the British Heart Foundation (2020 February 03) Statins:

10 facts you might not know -https://www.bhf.org.uk/for-professionals/healthcare-professionals/blog

[14] Constantine E. Kosmas, Shanna Rodriguez Polanco, Maria D. Bousvarou, Evangelia J. Papakonstantinou, Edilberto Peña Genao, Eliscer Guzman, Christina E. Kostara5 (2023 March 01) The Triglyceride/High-Density Lipoprotein Cholesterol (TG/HDL-C) Ratio as a Risk Marker for Metabolic Syndrome and Cardiovascular Disease doi: 10.3390/diagnostics13050929

[15] Nikolic, Dragana et al. "Lipoprotein subfractions in metabolic syndrome and obesity: clinical significance and therapeutic approaches." Nutrients.

[16] Boizel, R, Benhamou, P.Y, Lardy, B, Laporte, F, Foulon, T, Halimi, S. (2000, November). Ratio of triglycerides to HDL cholesterol is an indicator of LDL particle size in patients with type 2 diabetes and normal HDL cholesterol levels. Diabetes Care, 23(11), 1679–1685. doi.org/10.2337/diacare.23.11.1679

[17] British Heart Foundation https://www.bhf.org.uk/informationsupport/conditions/familial-hypercholesterolaemia

[18] Elke A. Trautwein, Sue McKay (2020 September 01) The Role of Specific Components of a Plant-Based Diet in the Management of Dyslipidaemia and the Impact on Cardiovascular Risk doi: 10.3390/nu12092671

[19] Makridakis S, Kirkham R, Wakefield A, Papadaki M, Kirkham J, Long L - Forecasting, uncertainty and risk; perspectives on clinical decision-making in preventive and curative medicine https://ideas.repec.org/a/eee/intfor/v35y2019i2p659-666.html

[20] Crescent B. Martin, Craig M. Hales, Qiuping Gu, Cynthia L. Ogden (2019 May) National Center for Health Statistics: Prescription Drug Use in the United States, 2015–2016 www.cdc.gov

[21] Betteridge DJ, Carmena R. The diabetogenic action of statins-mechanisms and clinical implications. Nat Rev Endocrinol. 2016;12(2):99-110.

[22] Hirst JA, Farmer AJ, Feakins BG, Aronson JK, Stevens RJ. Quantifying the effects of diuretics and β-adrenoceptor blockers on glycaemic control in diabetes mellitus-a systematic review and meta-analysis. Br J Clin Pharmacol. 2015;79(5):733-43.

[23] Suissa S, Kezouh A, Ernst P. Inhaled Corticosteroids and the Risks of Diabetes Onset and Progression. The American Journal of Medicine. 2010;123(11):1001-6.

[24] Greabu M, Badoiu SC, Stanescu S, II, Miricescu D, Totan AR, Badoiu

SE, et al. Drugs Interfering with Insulin Resistance and Their Influence on the Associated Hypermetabolic State in Severe Burns: A Narrative Review. Int J Mol Sci. 2021;22(18).

[25] Daniel Levitin (2015 September) How to stay calm when you know you'll be stressed. TED Talk London.

[26] Zarrinpar, A., Chaix, A., Xu, Z.Z. et al. (2018). Antibiotic-induced microbiome depletion alters metabolic homeostasis by affecting gut signalling and colonic metabolism https://pubmed.ncbi.nlm.nih.gov/30030441/

*****

Chapter 9

[1] B Barkeling, N A King, E Näslund, J E Blundell (2007 March 31) Characterisation of obese individuals who claim to detect no relationship between their eating pattern and sensations of hunger or fullness. doi: 10.1038/sj.ijo.0803449

[2] Koutatsu Maruyama, Shinichi Sato, Tetsuya Ohira, Kenji Maeda, Hiroyuki Noda, Yoshimi Kubota et al. (2008 October) The joint impact on being overweight of self-reported behaviours of eating quickly and eating until full: cross-sectional survey doi: 10.1136/bmj.a2002.

[3] Elizabeth Hopper (2020 July 03) Greater Good Magazine published by Berkeley University of California - How Volunteering Can Help Your Mental Health

[4] Rei Otsuka, Koji Tamakoshi, Hiroshi Yatsuya, Keiko Wada, Kunihiro Matsushita, Pei OuYang, Yo Hotta et al. (2007 August 03) Eating fast leads to insulin resistance: findings in middle-aged Japanese men and women doi: 10.1016/j.ypmed.2007.07.031

[5] Oxford Academic website, published by The Journal of Clinical Endocrinology & Metabolism - https://academic.oup.com/jcem/pages/About

[6] Julianne Holt-Lunstad , Timothy B Smith , Mark Baker, Tyler Harris, David Stephenson (2015 March 10) Loneliness and social isolation as risk factors for mortality: a meta-analytic review doi: 10.1177/1745691614568352

[7] UK National Institute for Health and Care Research (2016 February 16) Lowering blood pressure reduces the risk of heart disease, stroke and death doi: 10.3310/signal-000201

[8] Orava, J. et al. (2011). Different metabolic responses of human brown adipose tissue to activation by cold and insulin. Cell Metabolism, 14(2), p. 272

[9] K Alexander Iwen, Jenny Backhaus, Melanie Cassens, Maren Waltl, Oana C Hedesan, Martin Merkel, Joerg Heeren et al. (2017 November 01) Cold-Induced Brown Adipose Tissue Activity Alters Plasma Fatty Acids and Improves Glucose Metabolism in Men doi: 10.1210/jc.2017-01250

[10] Robert Krikorian, Marcelle D Shidler, Tiffany A Nash, Wilhelmina Kalt, Melinda R Vinqvist-Tymchuk, Barbara Shukitt-Hale, James A Joseph (2010 April 14) Blueberry supplementation improves memory in older adults doi: 10.1021/jf9029332

[11] (2024 January 15) Countryside Online - All you need to know about the British poultry meat sector https://www.countrysideonline.co.uk/articles

[12] Erica N. Story, Rachel E. Kopec, Steven J. Schwartz, G. Keith Harris (2013 December 04) An Update on the Health Effects of Tomato Lycopene doi: 10.1146/annurev.food.102308.124120

[13] Harish C Pal, Ross L Pearlman, Farrukh Afaq (2016) Fisetin and Its Role in Chronic Diseases doi: 10.1007/978-3-319-41334-1_10

[14] Anayatullah Khan , Anuradha Mishra, Syed Misbahul Hasan , Afreen Usmani , Mohd Ubaid , Naimuddin Khan and Mohd Saidurrahman (2021 May 27) Biological and medicinal application of Cucumis sativus Linn. – review of current status with future possibilities doi.org/10.1515/jcim-2020-0240

[15] João Carlos da Silva Dias Instituto Superior de Agronomia, University of Lisbon, Lisboa, Portugal (2014 December) Nutritional and Health Benefits of Carrots and Their Seed Extracts doi: 10.4236/fns.2014.522227

[16] Ana de Barros (2014 December 04) Life Long Consumption of 3-5 Cups of Coffee Lowers Alzheimer's Risk by 20 Percent https://alzheimersnewstoday.com/news

[17] Mariangela Rondanelli, Milena Anna Faliva, Alice Tartara, Clara Gasparri, Simone Perna, Vittoria Infantino, Antonella Riva et al. (2021 May 06) An update on magnesium and bone health doi: 10.1007/s10534-021-00305-0

[18] Mario Barbagallo, Ligia J Dominguez (2015 August 25) Magnesium and type 2 diabetes doi: 10.4239/wjd.v6.i10.1152

[19] Lisa A. Yablon, Alexander Mauskop (2011) Magnesium in the Central Nervous System -https://www.ncbi.nlm.nih.gov/books/NBK507271

[20] Behnood Abbasi, Masud Kimiagar, Khosro Sadeghniiat, Minoo M. Shirazi,

Mehdi Hedayati, Bahram Rashidkhani (2012 December 17) The effect of magnesium supplementation on primary insomnia in elderly: A double-blind placebo-controlled clinical trial PMCID: PMC3703169

[21] Nuria Rosique-Esteban, Marta Guasch-Ferré, Pablo Hernández-Alonso,Jordi Salas-Salvadó (2018 February 1) Dietary Magnesium and Cardiovascular Disease: A Review with Emphasis in Epidemiological Studies doi: 10.3390/nu10020168

*****

Chapter 10

[1] Paul Clayton, Judith Rowbotham (2009 March 6) How the Mid-Victorians Worked, Ate and Died doi: 10.3390/ijerph6031235

[2] Kamilla Rzayeva, CNN (2019 December 10) Article published on CNN website - Azerbaijan's secret to long life? Mountain air

[3] Anthony J. Covarrubias, Rosalba Perrone, Alessia Grozio, Eric Verdin (2020 December 22) NAD+ metabolism and its roles in cellular processes during ageing doi: 10.1038/s41580-020-00313-

[4] Qian Li, Haixia Chen, Min Zhang, Tao Wu, Rui Liua (2019) Altered short chain fatty acid profiles induced by dietary fiber intervention regulate AMPK levels and intestinal homeostasis – Article in the journal Food & Function, Published by Royal Society of Chemistry

[5] Environmental Working Group (2005 July 14) A benchmark investigation of industrial chemicals, pollutants and pesticides in umbilical cord blood

[6] (2024 March 07) kicking out toxic chemicals https://environmentaldefence.ca/campaign/toxics/

[7] (2023 September 14) European Environment Agency-https://www.eea.europa.eu/en/topics/in-depth/chemicals

[8] Parija Kavilanz reporting on CNN (2023 May 18) A growing number of sports bras, shirts and leggings brands found with high levels of toxic chemical, watchdog warns

[9] World Health Organisation (2016 August 04) https://www.who.int/news-room/questions-and-answers/item/radiation-electromagnetic-fields

[10] Lavinia Lorena Pruteanu, David Stanley Bailey, Andrei Cristian Grădinaru, Lorentz Jäntschi (2023 April 02) The Biochemistry and Effectiveness of Antioxidants in Food, Fruits, and Marine Algae doi: 10.3390/antiox12040860

*****

Chapter 11

[1] Sarah E. Jackson, Rebecca J. Beeken, Jane Wardle (2014 September 11) Perceived weight discrimination and changes in weight, waist circumference, and weight status https://doi.org/10.1002/oby.20891

Index

F

G

H

I

J

K

L

M

N

The Power of Why

If nothing changes, then I am

The benefits

Once I have regained my freedom, control of my health and happiness, I will be...

My Mantra

Craft your own Mantra to help keep your on track.

I will push through short term challenges and discomforts that I may face while creating my new habits and lose my weight once and for all because...

Craft your own POST, and let your dreams take shape on paper.

Purpose

Objectives

Strategy

Tactics

Habit Loop Analysis

Trigger / Cue

How hungry I felt (1 to 10): ________ Time ____________

Where am I? ______________________________

What have I just been doing? ______________________________

What am I feeling? ______________________________

Write down, your feelings:

How do you feel as soon as you decide to eat it?

____

____

How did you feel as soon as you saw it?

____

____

1 CUE

How do I feel just after eating it?

____

____

How I felt hours after or the morning after eating it?

____

____

RESULT/ MONITOR 4

2

ACTION

What was the habit?

____

____

____

____

____

REWARD
PERCEIVED PLEASURE

3

How I feel as soon as I tasted it?

____

____

____

____

____

Habit Loop Analysis

Trigger / Cue

How hungry I felt (1 to 10): ________ Time ____________

Where am I? ____

What have I just been doing? ______________________________

What am I feeling? ____

Write down, your feelings:

How do you feel as soon as you decide to eat it?

____

____

How did you feel as soon as you saw it?

____

____

How do I feel just after eating it?

____

____

How I felt hours after or the morning after eating it?

____

____

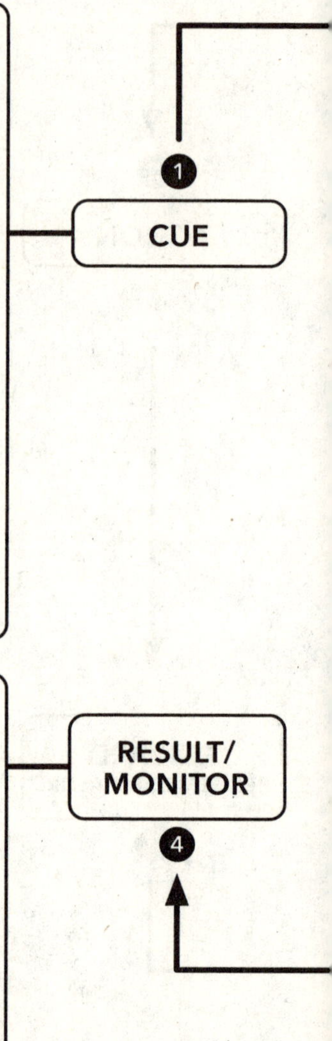

2

ACTION

What was the habit?

____

____

____

____

____

REWARD
PERCEIVED PLEASURE

3

How I feel as soon as I tasted it?

____

____

____

____

____

Habit Loop Analysis

Trigger / Cue

How hungry I felt (1 to 10): ________ Time ____________

Where am I? ____

What have I just been doing? ____________________________

What am I feeling? ______________________________________

Write down, your feelings:

How do you feel as soon as you decide to eat it?

____

____

How did you feel as soon as you saw it?

____

____

How do I feel just after eating it?

____

____

How I felt hours after or the morning after eating it?

____

____

2

ACTION

What was the habit?

____

____

____

____

____

REWARD
PERCEIVED PLEASURE

3

How I feel as soon as I tasted it?

____

____

____

____

____

New Habit Loop Analysis

1 CUE

Trigger / Cue

How hungry I felt (1 to 10): ________ Time ________

Where am I? ________________________

What am I feeling? ________________________

What have I just done? ________________________

Write any 3 to 5 words

________ ________

________ ________

____

2 ACTION

What was the habit/temptation?

____

____

____

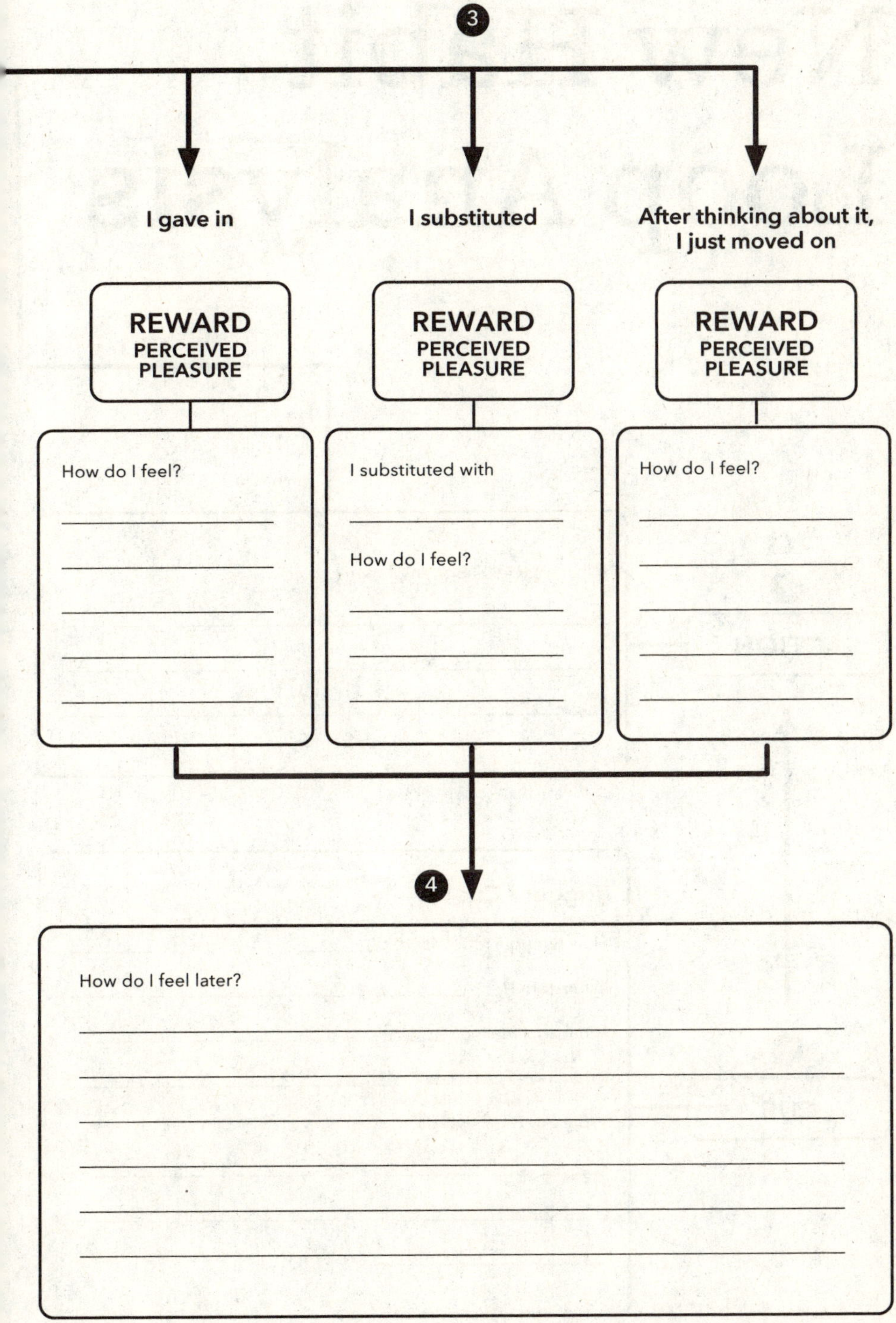
3
I gave in
I substituted
After thinking about it, I just moved on
REWARD
PERCEIVED PLEASURE
REWARD
PERCEIVED PLEASURE
REWARD
PERCEIVED PLEASURE
How do I feel?
I substituted with
How do I feel?
How do I feel?
4
How do I feel later?

New Habit Loop Analysis

2

ACTION

What was the habit/temptation?

____

____

____

1

CUE

Trigger / Cue

How hungry I felt (1 to 10): ________ Time __________

Where am I? ______________________________

What am I feeling? __________________________

What have I just done? ________________________

Write any 3 to 5 words

__________________ __________________

__________________ __________________

____

3

I gave in

REWARD
PERCEIVED PLEASURE

How do I feel?

I substituted

REWARD
PERCEIVED PLEASURE

I substituted with

How do I feel?

After thinking about it, I just moved on

REWARD
PERCEIVED PLEASURE

How do I feel?

4

How do I feel later?

New Habit Loop Analysis

2

ACTION

What was the habit/temptation?

____

____

____

1

CUE

Trigger / Cue

How hungry I felt (1 to 10): ________ Time ________

Where am I? ______________________________

What am I feeling? ______________________________

What have I just done? ______________________________

Write any 3 to 5 words

______________ ______________

______________ ______________

____

3

I gave in

REWARD
PERCEIVED PLEASURE

How do I feel?

I substituted

REWARD
PERCEIVED PLEASURE

I substituted with

How do I feel?

After thinking about it, I just moved on

REWARD
PERCEIVED PLEASURE

How do I feel?

4

How do I feel later?